# THE
# NEW BOOK
## OF
# KNOWLEDGE

# THE NEW BOOK OF KNOWLEDGE

Scholastic Library Publishing, Inc.
Danbury, Connecticut

VOLUME 15

P

P, the 16th letter in the English alphabet, was the 17th letter in the ancient Hebrew and Phoenician alphabets and the 16th letter in the classical Greek alphabet. The Hebrews and Phoenicians called it *pe* (pronounced "pay"). The Greeks called it *pi* (pronounced like the word "pea").

Many language scholars believe that the Phoenician letter *pe* represented a mouth and that the word *pe* meant "mouth." The letter *pe* looked like this: ⌐

The Greeks based their alphabet on the Phoenician alphabet. The letter *pi* looked like this at first: Γ Later this form developed into the classical Greek letter *pi:* Π (pronounced "pie").

Before the Greek letter reached its final form, the Romans learned the earlier Greek form from the Etruscans (another ancient people, who lived in Italy). The Romans used the letter for the same sound as the Greeks, but they changed its form slightly to the P used in the English language today.

In English the sound of P is most often that of the words *pill* or *pen.* When P is followed by H, it is usually pronounced like F, as in the word *phonograph.* Before N and some other letters, P at the beginning of a word is silent. Many of the words in which P is silent, such as *psalm* and *pneumatic,* come from the Greek.

In chemistry, P is the symbol for the element phosphorus. In music, P stands for piano, which is an instruction to play in a soft or quiet manner.

The letter P is also found in many abbreviations. P.T.A. stands for Parent-Teacher Association, and p. stands for page. P.S. is written at the end of a letter when something left out of the letter is added. The initials come from the Latin *postscriptum,* which means "written afterward."

The Latin *post,* meaning "after," is also used in the abbreviation P.M., or *post meridiem,* which stands for "afternoon."

Reviewed by MARIO PEI
Author, *The Story of Language*

See also ALPHABET.

## SOME WAYS TO REPRESENT P:

The **manuscript** or printed forms of the letter (left) are highly readable. The **cursive** letters (right) are formed from slanted flowing strokes joining one letter to the next.

The **Manual Alphabet** (left) enables a deaf person to communicate by forming letters with the fingers of one hand. **Braille** (right) is a system by which a blind person can use fingertips to "read" raised dots that stand for letters.

The **International Code of Signals** is a special group of flags used to send and receive messages at sea. Each letter is represented by a different flag.

**International Morse Code** is used to send messages by radio signals. Each letter is expressed as a combination of dots (•) and dashes (––).

*Left:* White sandy beaches, clear blue waters, and towering palms are typical of the coral islands of the Pacific. This is one of the numerous islands of Micronesia. *Above:* Kayangel, part of Palau in the western Carolines, shows the distinctive shape of an atoll, with coral formations enclosing a lagoon.

# PACIFIC OCEAN AND ISLANDS

The Pacific is the largest and deepest of the world's oceans. With an area of some 70,000,000 square miles (180,000,000 square kilometers), including neighboring seas, the Pacific has nearly half of the earth's ocean surface and makes up more than one third of its total surface. It is more than twice the size of the Atlantic Ocean, the world's second largest body of water. Because of its enormous area, the Pacific Ocean is often considered the earth's principal physical feature.

The Pacific was given its name, which means "peaceful," by the Portuguese navigator Ferdinand Magellan. Magellan, who sailed across the Pacific in the 1520's, found its waters especially calm. But he may have been luckier than he realized. The Pacific, although it can be peaceful, is also subject to destructive typhoons, or storms similar to hurricanes.

**Boundaries, Extent, and Depth.** The Pacific extends from the Arctic Ocean on the north to Antarctica on the south, a distance of more than 9,000 miles (14,480 kilometers). The coastlines of North and South America make up its eastern boundary. The western boundary is more difficult to define, because of the numerous islands and seas found there, but it is broadly formed by the mainland of Asia, Indonesia, and Australia. The Pacific measures about 11,000 miles (17,700 kilometers) from east to west along the equator, which divides it into the North Pacific and South Pacific oceans.

The Pacific and Indian oceans are linked by the Strait of Malacca (between Malaysia and Indonesia). They also join south of Australia. The Bering Strait connects the Pacific with the Arctic Ocean, and at Cape Horn (at the southern tip of South America), the Pacific merges with the Atlantic Ocean.

The Pacific has an average depth of about 14,000 feet (about 4,270 meters). The Earth's greatest known depth, the Mariana Trench, is located there, near the island of Guam. It plunges 36,198 feet (11,033 meters)—or more than 7 miles—below the ocean surface.

Pacific islanders often employ fine carvings in their art. This intricate shield is from the Solomon Islands.

**Islands: Continental and Oceanic.** The Pacific has an enormous number of islands, estimated at about 25,000, most of which are found in the southern ocean and particularly in its western reaches. Although they vary in size, most are relatively small in area. The islands fall into two main but very different groups—continental and oceanic.

The continental islands rise from the continental shelves, the underwater areas surrounding most continents. These islands are really partially submerged mountain chains. They belong to the long chain of mountains and volcanoes that border the Pacific Basin.

Two processes helped to form the Pacific's oceanic islands—volcanism and subsidence. In volcanism, lava (hot, melted rock) is extruded, or poured out, from the earth's interior and then cools. An island forms if enough lava is extruded to produce a mass rising above the ocean surface. Hawaii is the largest of the Pacific islands formed by volcanism.

In subsidence, the great weight of the volcanic mass forces the crust of the ocean basin to sink, or subside. The older an island is, the more it will have sunk and, therefore, the lower it appears in the water.

In 1993 oceanographers mapping the ocean floor discovered more than 1,000 volcanoes in an area of the South Pacific. It was considered to be the largest known concentration of active volcanoes on earth.

**Coral Reefs, Islands, Atolls.** As a volcanic island subsides, colonies of small organisms called corals, living just below the surface of the water, sometimes attach themselves to it.

In time the volcanic material may disappear beneath the ocean. But the corals go on building upward, forming reefs. If sand, formed by breakup of the coral rock, collects on top of the rock, a low sandy island results. If this sandy island is shaped like a ring, it is called an atoll. The water enclosed by an atoll is a lagoon. In some cases masses of coral rock have been lifted above the surface by upward movement of the earth's crust. Many islands of the Tonga group were formed in this way.

**Oceania: Land of the Pacific.** The islands of the Pacific are often called Oceania. Australia and the islands and island groups in the shallow waters off the Asian mainland (such as the Philippines and Japan) are generally not considered part of Oceania. New Zealand is sometimes included.

The islands of Oceania are divided into three main groups—Polynesia ("many islands"), Melanesia ("black islands"), and Micronesia ("small islands").

Polynesia, the largest division, is made up of a large triangle of islands in the central and southeastern Pacific. It includes French Polynesia; the Hawaiian Islands; Tonga; Tuvalu; American Samoa and Samoa; part of Kiri-

*Below:* Fiery lava pours from Hawaii's Kilauea volcano. Many of the Pacific islands were created by volcanic action. *Right:* A ceremonial mask from Vanuatu depicts the body of a man and the head of a woman.

Yap islanders prepare copra, or dried coconut meat. Most of the low coral islands have little fertile soil, and copra is usually the main cash crop.

Melanesia, in the southwestern Pacific, includes Papua (the Indonesian half of the large island of New Guinea); New Caledonia; and the nations of Papua New Guinea, Vanuatu, the Solomon Islands, and Fiji. The larger Melanesian islands are mountainous, and many of them are densely forested.

The many small islands in northwestern Oceania are known as Micronesia. This region includes Nauru, Wake Island, part of Kiribati, the Marshall Islands, the Carolines (including the Federated States of Micronesia), and the Marianas. Most of the islands of Micronesia are low-lying coral atolls.

**Peoples of the Pacific.** The peoples of Oceania are often divided into three ethnic groups that parallel the geographic division of the islands. This is not strictly correct, as only the Polynesians form a distinct ethnic group. Melanesians and Micronesians include peoples of many different origins. Other groups include Americans, Japanese, and Chinese on the Hawaiian Islands and people of East Indian descent, who make up about half the population of Fiji. Native Fijians are a mixture of Melanesian and Polynesian ethnic groups.

Polynesians share the same basic language and have common physical and cultural characteristics. Before Europeans came to Oceania, Polynesians occupied almost all the

bati; Easter, Midway, and Niue islands; and the Tokelau, Cook, Pitcairn, and Wallis and Futuna island groups. The Maori, who are the original inhabitants of the islands of New Zealand, are also Polynesian. Many of the Polynesian islands are the tops of submerged mountains. Others are atolls or coral islands.

Open-pit mines produce copper for export on Bougainville, one of the islands making up Papua New Guinea—the largest of the Pacific island nations.

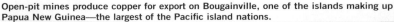

## What is the Great Barrier Reef?

The Great Barrier Reef is the world's longest coral formation. Situated in the Coral Sea, it stretches for some 1,250 miles (over 2,000 kilometers) between New Guinea and the northeastern coast of Australia. The great reef is actually a series of reefs and coral islands, extending between 10 and 100 miles (15 and 160 kilometers) off the Australian mainland. Over many millions of years, the hundreds of different types of corals have built up "gardens" of unusual and beautiful shapes in varied colors. These attract a wide variety of marine life, including brightly colored fish, sea birds, green turtles, and giant clams and other mollusks. The Great Barrier Reef is an Australian national park and an especially popular tourist attraction.

islands of the South Pacific, as well as Hawaii and New Zealand.

Most Melanesians live on New Guinea and nearby islands. Although generally dark-skinned, they differ in appearance, language, and customs. Many of them, especially in the remote, mountainous areas of New Guinea, had little contact with the outside world until fairly recent times. The Micronesians live mainly on the small islands scattered over a vast area of the northwestern Pacific. They, too, have different languages, customs, and physical characteristics.

Most islanders live in villages or small towns. There are few large cities, except on Hawaii and New Zealand.

**Climate.** Most of the islands of Oceania lie within the tropics, and the climate here is uniformly warm. Temperatures along the equator vary only from about 70 to 81°F (21 to 27°C) throughout the year. By contrast, in the far northern and southern waters, temperatures fall to less than 14°F (−10°C). The amount of rainfall varies considerably, with most of the islands having distinct wet and dry seasons. The most destructive typhoons occur in the western and southwestern Pacific.

**Economic Activity.** Agriculture remains the region's most important economic activity. Most Pacific islanders practice subsistence farming, growing food for their own use. On the low coral islands, which have little fertile soil and receive relatively light rainfall, copra (dried coconut meat) is the only cash crop. On the higher volcanic islands, which usually have more rainfall and better soil, such crops as pineapples, sugarcane, cacao, and bananas are grown for export. The surrounding waters teem with fish.

There is little industry, aside from the processing of copra and other agricultural products, although tourism is a major source of income on some of the Pacific islands. Mineral resources are limited. New Caledonia has important nickel deposits, and copper is found on Bougainville. New Guinea has oil and gold, and tiny Nauru is rich in phosphate rock, used in making fertilizer.

**Early History.** The first migration of peoples to the Pacific islands probably originated from Southeast Asia tens of thousands of years ago, when the largest islands were linked by a land bridge. Later, seafarers ventured farther out on the uncharted waters of the Pacific.

**The Europeans and Americans.** The first European known to have seen the Pacific was the Spanish explorer and adventurer Vasco Núñez de Balboa. After crossing the Isthmus of Panama in 1513, Balboa sighted the great ocean, which he called the South Sea. Magellan, a few years later, gave the ocean its present name during his attempt to sail around the world. Although Magellan himself was killed, his crew completed the epic voyage. Other Spanish and Portuguese navigators explored the islands in the 1500's and 1600's. The greatest of the Pacific explorers, the British captain James Cook, discovered Hawaii and mapped much of Oceania during the late 1760's and 1770's. American and British whaling ships also began to call at the islands. Europeans and

The art of the Marquesas Islands includes this stern-looking figure, carved from bone.

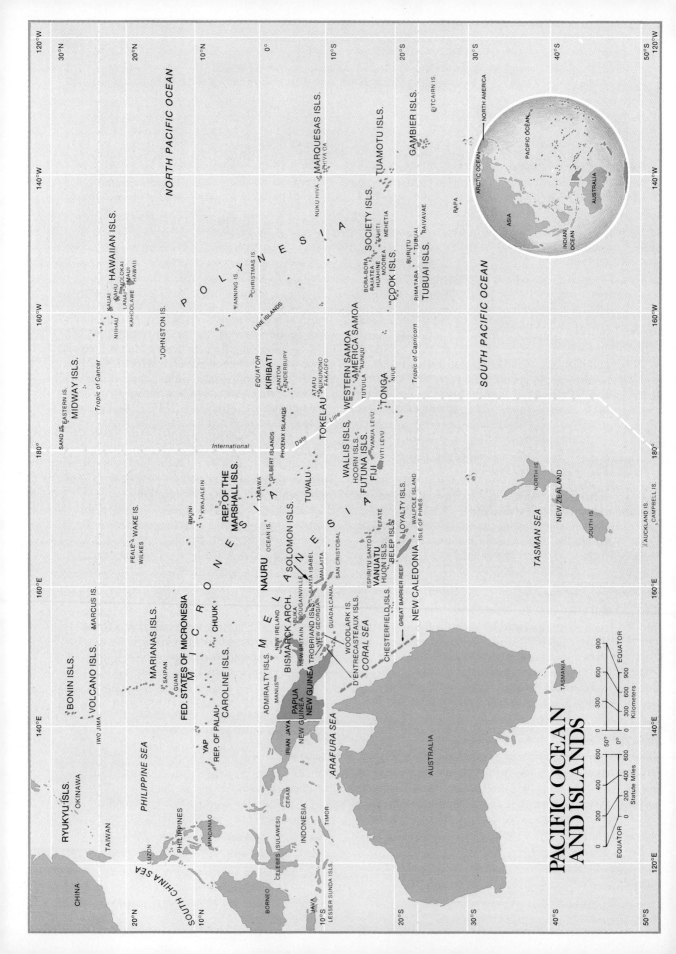

# PACIFIC OCEAN AND ISLANDS

*Left:* The British navigator Captain James Cook landed at Tana, in the New Hebrides (now Vanuatu), in 1774. Tragically, Cook was killed in Hawaii, in 1779, after a misunderstanding with the islanders. *Below:* U.S. Marines under Japanese attack wade ashore on Saipan (in the Marianas) in 1944, during World War II. The Pacific was a major theater of operations in the war.

Americans settled here as planters and traders, and missionaries soon followed. A few of the islands became important as naval bases or as coaling stations in the days when ships were fueled by coal. By the end of the 1800's, Britain, France, Germany, and the United States all had established themselves as colonial powers in the Pacific.

See the biographies of Balboa, Cook, and Magellan in the appropriate volumes.

**Two World Wars and After.** Germany lost its Pacific colonies after its defeat, in 1918, in World War I. Japan received the German colonies in the Marianas, the Carolines, and the Marshalls under a mandate from the

League of Nations. During World War II, many of the islands were battlegrounds in the Pacific war (1941–45). Its defeat in the war forced Japan to give up the islands, which then became a United Nations trust territory, administered by the United States.

Since the 1960's, several Pacific islands have gained independence. Hawaii became a state of the United States in 1959. The islands of the U.S. Trust Territory of the Pacific became independent in 1986 and 1994, in free association with the United States.

WARD BARRETT
University of Minnesota
Author, *Mission in the Marianas*

See also CORALS; ISLANDS; OCEANOGRAPHY; OCEANS AND SEAS OF THE WORLD.

Brief descriptions of some of the Pacific islands and island groups follow.

## INDEPENDENT NATIONS OF OCEANIA

| COUNTRY | CAPITAL | AREA[1] | |
| --- | --- | --- | --- |
| | | (sq mi) | (km²) |
| **Fiji** | Suva | 7,056 | 18,274 |
| **Kiribati** | Tarawa | 281 | 728 |
| **Marshall Islands, Rep. of**[2] | Majuro | 70 | 181 |
| **Micronesia, Fed. States of**[2] | Palikir | 271 | 702 |
| **Nauru** | No formal capital | 8 | 21 |
| **New Zealand**[3] | Wellington | 103,736 | 268,676 |
| **Palau, Rep. of**[2] | Koror | 192 | 497 |
| **Papua New Guinea** | Port Moresby | 178,260 | 461,691 |
| **Samoa** | Apia | 1,097 | 2,842 |
| **Solomon Islands** | Honiara | 10,983 | 28,446 |
| **Tonga** | Nuku'alofa | 270 | 699 |
| **Tuvalu** | Funafuti | 10 | 26 |
| **Vanuatu** | Port-Vila | 5,700 | 14,763 |

[1] Land area.
[2] In free association with the United States, which is responsible for their defense.
[3] New Zealand is sometimes included in Oceania.

These children of the Cook Islands are Polynesians, one of the three main Pacific peoples. This native Fijian is a mixture of Polynesian and Melanesian groups.

## PACIFIC ISLANDS AND ISLAND GROUPS

The following is an overview of many of the islands and island groups of Oceania. Cross-references to other articles are noted where appropriate. Areas given are land areas, with measurements in square miles (sq mi) and square kilometers (km²).

**Admiralty Islands (Papua New Guinea)** are part of the Bismarck Archipelago. (An archipelago is a chain of islands.) They are located in the southwestern Pacific and are volcanic in origin. Manus is the largest of the Admiralty group. Area: about 800 sq mi (2,072 km²).

**American Samoa (U.S.A.)** consists of seven islands in the eastern part of the Samoa group. The western part forms the independent country of Samoa. American Samoa is a U.S. territory. It has local self-government under an elected governor and legislature. Area: 75 sq mi (195 km²). See also TERRITORIAL EXPANSION OF THE UNITED STATES (American Samoa); and UNITED STATES (Outlying Areas of the United States).

**Belau, Republic of.** See entry **Palau**.

**Bismarck Archipelago (Papua New Guinea)** consists of New Britain, New Ireland, the Admiralty Islands, and other islands, making up part of Papua New Guinea. Most of the larger islands are volcanic. Area: 19,200 sq mi (49,730 km²).

**Bonin Islands (Japan)** are a group of small volcanic islands in the western Pacific. Area: 40 sq mi (104 km²).

**Borneo,** the world's third largest island, is shared by the nations of Indonesia, Malaysia, and Brunei. See BORNEO.

**Bougainville (Papua New Guinea)** is the largest island of the Solomon Islands chain. It has one of the world's largest copper mines. Area: 3,880 sq mi (10,049 km²).

**Buka (Papua New Guinea)** is one of the Solomon Islands. Area: 190 sq mi (492 km²).

**Caroline Islands** number nearly 1,000 coral and volcanic islands, spread over a vast area of the western Pacific but with a total land area of only about 450 sq mi (1,165 km²). At the end of World War II, they became part of the U.S. Trust Territory of the Pacific. They include the Republic of Palau and the Federated States of Micronesia.

**Christmas Island (Kiribati),** one of the Line Islands of the central Pacific, is the largest island of Kiribati. Area: 60 sq mi (155 km²).

**Chuuk** (formerly called **Truk),** in the Carolines, is the main island of Chuuk state in the Federated States of Micronesia. Area: 39 sq mi (100 km²).

**Cook Islands (New Zealand)** are a group of 15 small islands in the South Pacific. The largest is Rarotonga. The islands are internally self-governing. Area: 93 sq mi (240 km²).

**Easter Island (Chile).** See ISLANDS.

**Ellice Islands.** See TUVALU.

**Fiji.** See FIJI.

**French Polynesia** includes Clipperton Island, and the Society, Marquesas, Gambier, Tuamotu, and Austral islands. A French overseas territory, its people are citizens of France. The capital is Papeete, on the island of Tahiti. Extending over a large area of the Pacific, the islands have a land area of about 1,550 sq mi (4,000 km²).

**Gilbert Islands (Kiribati)** are a group of coral atolls in the central Pacific. See KIRIBATI.

**Guadalcanal (Solomon Islands)** is the largest island of the nation of Solomon Islands. It was the site of one of the decisive battles of the Pacific in World War II. Area: 2,500 sq mi (6,500 km²).

**Guam (U.S.A.)** is the largest and most populous of the Marianas Islands, in the west central Pacific. It was ceded by Spain to the United States in 1898. See UNITED STATES (Outlying Areas).

**Hawaiian Islands (U.S.A.).** See HAWAII.

**Iwo Jima** (see **Volcano Islands**).

**Kiribati.** See KIRIBATI.

**Kosrae** is the largest island of Kosrae state in the Federated States of Micronesia. Area: 42 sq mi (110 km²).

**Line Islands (Kiribati)** are a group of small coral islands in the central Pacific. Area: 222 sq mi (576 km²).

**Marianas, Northern, Commonwealth of the, (U.S.A.)** includes all the islands of the Marianas chain except Guam. The islands are internally self-governing. Saipan, the largest island, and Tinian were the scene of fierce fighting in the Pacific war. See UNITED STATES (Outlying Areas).

**Marquesas Islands (France)** are the northernmost islands of French Polynesia. They consist of twelve volcanic islands. Area: 492 sq mi (1,274 km²).

**Marshall Islands, Republic of.** See MARSHALL ISLANDS.

**Micronesia** includes more than 2,000 islands scattered over a vast area in the northwestern Pacific Ocean. See MICRONESIA, FEDERATED STATES OF.

**Midway (U.S.A.)** consists of a coral atoll and two islets, lying in the north central Pacific. The islands are a naval base, as well as a national wildlife preserve. The U.S. victory at the Battle of Midway (1942) was a turning point in World War II. Area: 2 sq mi (5 km²).

**Nauru.** See NAURU.

**New Britain (Papua New Guinea)** is the largest island of the Bismarck Archipelago. Rabaul is its largest town and chief port. The island is mountainous, with several active volcanoes. Area: 14,570 sq mi (37,736 km²).

**New Caledonia (France)** is a large island in the southwest Pacific, with several smaller island dependencies. An overseas territory of France, its people are French citizens. The capital is Noumea. Nickel is the chief export. Area: 7,243 sq mi (18,760 km²).

**New Guinea,** the world's second largest island, is divided between Indonesia and Papua New Guinea. See NEW GUINEA; PAPUA NEW GUINEA.

**New Hebrides** is the former name of the nation of **Vanuatu**. See VANUATU.

The boys are Melanesians from Papua New Guinea. The man with the sea turtle is from Chuuk and is a Micronesian, the third of the major Pacific peoples.

The people of Tahiti are mostly of Polynesian ancestry.

**New Ireland (Papua New Guinea)** is the second largest of the islands of the Bismarck Archipelago. Area: 3,700 sq mi (9,600 km²).

**New Zealand** is sometimes considered part of Oceania. See NEW ZEALAND.

**Niue (New Zealand)** is an island in the South Pacific Ocean. Its people have internal self-government and are New Zealand citizens. Area: 100 sq mi (259 km²).

**Northern Marianas.** (See **Marianas, Northern.**)

**Okinawa (Japan)**, in the western Pacific, is the largest of the Ryukyu Islands chain. It was the site of the last major battle between U.S. and Japanese forces in World War II. Area: 454 sq mi (1,176 km²).

**Palau** includes numerous small islands in the western Carolines. The last of the U.S. trust territories of the Pacific, it gained independence, in free association with the United States, in 1994. See PALAU.

**Papua New Guinea** includes the eastern half of New Guinea, the Bismarck Archipelago, the northern Solomon Islands, and other islands. See PAPUA NEW GUINEA.

**Pitcairn Island (U.K.)** is a British dependency in the South Pacific. Area: 2 sq mi (5 km²).

**Pohnpei** (formerly Ponape) is the largest island of Pohnpei state in the Federated States of Micronesia and home to its capital, Palikir. Area: 129 sq mi (334 km²).

**Samoa**, an island group in the South Pacific, is divided, politically, into American Samoa and the nation of Samoa (formerly Western Samoa). See WESTERN SAMOA.

**Society Islands (France)** are a chain of 14 islands in French Polynesia. They are an overseas territory of France. Area: 650 sq mi (1,660 km²).

**Solomon Islands** are an archipelago in the southwestern Pacific. The northernmost islands, including Bougainville, Buka, and smaller islands, are part of Papua New Guinea. The remainder, including Guadalcanal and other islands, make up the nation of Solomon Islands. Total area: 15,130 sq mi (39,190 km²). See SOLOMON ISLANDS.

**Tahiti (France)**, the largest of the Society Islands, is the chief island of French Polynesia. Its scenic beauty and tropical climate make it a byword for the ideal South Pacific island. The French artist Paul Gauguin painted some of his greatest works here in the 1890's. Area: 402 sq mi (1,042 km²).

**Tokelau (New Zealand)** is a small island group in the central Pacific. Area: 4 sq mi (10 km²).

**Tonga.** See TONGA.

**Truk.** (See **Chuuk.**)

**Tuamotu Islands (France)** are a chain of about 75 atolls spread over a large area of the South Pacific. Politically, it is part of French Polynesia. Area: 300 sq mi (775 km²).

**Tuvalu.** See TUVALU.

**Vanuatu.** See VANUATU.

**Volcano Islands (Japan)** are three small islands southeast of the Bonin Islands. Iwo Jima, the largest island, was the site of a major battle between U.S. and Japanese troops in World War II. Area: 11 sq mi (28 km²).

**Wake Island (U.S.A.)** consists mainly of a coral atoll in the central Pacific. See UNITED STATES (Outlying Areas).

**Wallis and Futuna Islands (France)** are two groups of islands in the southwestern Pacific west of Samoa. Area: 106 sq mi (274 km²).

**Yap** is an island group and one of the Federated States of Micronesia. The island of Yap is the largest of Yap state's four islands. Area of Yap state: 85 square miles (220 km²).

A woman of Vanuatu displays face markings of the Cargo cult, a religious movement founded in Melanesia.

# PADDLE TENNIS

Paddle tennis was invented in 1898 by two boys, Frank and Charles Beal. They were permitted by their father, a professor at Albion College in Michigan, to watch the college students play tennis. But because of the high cost of tennis rackets and balls, the boys' father did not allow them to play.

However, the Beals were not to be denied. In their backyard Frank and his brother halved the dimensions of a tennis court and laid out a playing area 11.9 meters (39 feet) by 5.5 meters (18 feet). They set up a net of chicken wire and made paddles from pieces of maplewood 2.5 centimeters (1 inch) thick. At first they used "seconds"—inexpensive, imperfect tennis balls. Then the boys found that inflated 5-cent rubber balls were just as satisfactory.

The Beal brothers decided to call the game "paddle tennis." They kept all the rules of tennis, changing only the racket, the ball, and the court size. Soon they had an audience. Students and neighbors watched them from a raised sidewalk above the playing field. The game was later introduced in New York City and immediately became popular with children. The ball was easier to control with the paddle than with a tennis racket, the basic skills were easy to learn, the game required little space, and it was inexpensive to play.

In 1923, the American (now the United States) Paddle Tennis Association was formed. It standardized the sizes of the court, net, paddle, and ball and arranged for the equipment to be manufactured. The National Recreation Association helped introduce paddle tennis to municipal playgrounds.

Paddle tennis reached its height of popularity during the 1920's and 1930's. Then, interest in the sport declined. This was due mainly to the players' improvement in the overhead serve and the rush to the net. The game became one of constant slamming—that is, hitting hard, fast shots that are impossible to return. There were hardly any rallies.

Interest in paddle tennis was revived in 1959 when new rules, equipment, and court size were instituted.

▶ **PLAYING THE GAME**

The ball used today is a deadened tennis ball. The tennis ball is punctured, usually with a safety pin, so that it will not bounce so high. The net is 79 centimeters (31 inches) high and is pulled taut across the court. The paddle may be solid or perforated and not more than 44.5 centimeters (17½ inches) long and 21.6 centimeters (8½ inches) wide. The court is 15.2 meters (50 feet) long by 6.1 meters (20 feet) wide. It is the same size for singles and for doubles. The area is divided into four service courts. Each is 6.7 meters (22 feet) long by 3 meters (10 feet) wide. The surface may be asphalt, cement, clay, composition, or any other material used for tennis courts.

Paddle tennis is played in basically the same way as lawn tennis. But there are certain differences. Children under 14 years of age are permitted two overhand serves, as in lawn tennis, but only one underhand service is allowed for adults (players 14 years and older). To serve, the player stands behind the baseline, which is the end line of the paddle tennis court. The server may bounce, drop, or throw the ball into the air and then strike it with the paddle at a point not higher than the top of the net. A player must continue with one method of serving throughout the set.

To prevent slamming a return of a serve, there is a "one-bounce" rule that applies only to adult singles. The served ball must hit the ground once before the receiving player may return it. Then the server must let the returned ball bounce once before hitting it.

Tennis champion Althea Gibson's career started with the paddle tennis she played on the street in front of her home in Harlem, in New York City. Sidney Wood, Bill Talbert, Bobby Riggs, Jack Kramer, Pancho Gonzales, and other tennis champions became expert at paddle tennis and did much to increase its popularity.

Paddle tennis is still a great game for children, and the rule changes of 1959 have made it a popular sport for adults. Thousands of courts have been built in the United States, and participation in the sport is increasing. There is a National Open Men's Doubles Championship, held annually in New York City, in which players from throughout the United States play this exciting, fast-moving sport for prize money.

MURRAY GELLER
President, U.S. Paddle Tennis Association

See also TENNIS.

# PAGEANTS

A pageant is a special kind of play in which large numbers of people take part. Usually it takes place outdoors before an audience, and its purpose is generally to celebrate some great event.

▶ RELIGIOUS PAGEANTS

During the Middle Ages pageants were usually held for religious reasons. Since this was a time when very few people could read or write, other means had to be found to teach religion. One way was the morality play, in which characters named Pride, Greed, Honesty, or Laziness represented human traits. The struggle in life between good and evil could be shown by the characters on stage, with good winning out over wickedness.

Another type of religious pageant is the Passion play, which tells the Passion (suffering and death) of Jesus. The people of Oberammergau, Germany, threatened by a terrible plague, made God a promise: if their town was spared, they would honor Him forever with a pageant every 10 years. And they have done so since 1634.

▶ HISTORICAL PAGEANTS

A historical pageant tells the story of a well-known event. At Roanoke Island, North Carolina, a pageant called *The Lost Colony* is held every year. It commemorates the ill-fated Virginia colony that left no survivors. The colony was founded on Roanoke Island by Sir Walter Raleigh in 1584, more than 20 years before the Jamestown colony was established.

A pageant held each year in Interlaken, Switzerland, is performed in the woods outside the town and retells the story of the legendary hero William Tell. More than 600 years ago, Tell was supposed to have refused to salute the cap of the Austrian imperial governor. The cap had been put in the marketplace by order of the governor, as a symbol of Austrian authority. For his disobedience Tell was ordered to shoot an apple from his son's head. Using a bow and arrow, Tell succeeded. Later on, he shot the governor, helping to free Switzerland from Austrian rule. Thus Tell became a symbol of national independence and freedom.

JAMES W. HOERGER
Great Neck Public Schools

# PAINE, THOMAS (1737–1809)

A citizen of three countries and a champion of two great revolutions, Tom Paine has come down in history as a man with two sharply contrasting reputations. The most widely read author of his day, he aroused both admiration and hate. To many he was an unselfish idealist fighting for the cause of universal freedom. To others he was an immoral atheist and a vicious radical. In his own day Paine was admired by such men as Benjamin Franklin, Thomas Jefferson, and George Washington. He was attacked by such individuals as John Adams and the French revolutionary leader Robespierre.

Later writers have reflected some of these conflicting opinions. To one 19th-century historian Paine was "of all the human kind . . . the filthiest and the nastiest." To Theodore Roosevelt he was "a dirty little atheist." But to others Paine was "the greatest pamphleteer that the English race has produced, and one of its great idealists"; and "one of the noblest of our humanitarians."

The truth lies more with Paine's admirers than with his attackers. He was neither little nor an atheist. Quite the contrary. Paine was in many ways a great man and a passionate believer. But he was a troubled man, possibly as a result of a poor and humble background, and somewhat wayward in his personal behavior. Nevertheless, he was a courageous fighter for democracy as he saw it and a brilliant writer whose words can still arouse warm response. Paine's chief weakness was an inability to conform or to compromise. In addition, he had a compulsion to speak the truth bluntly, as he understood it. This helps to explain the hatred many felt toward him.

### Early Years

Paine was born on January 29, 1737, at Thetford, England, the son of a poor corset maker. His father was a Quaker, but Paine never became a Quaker himself. He explained later that when, at the age of 8, he heard a sermon on the Redemption, he was repelled by the cruelty of Christianity. At the age of 13 Paine was apprenticed to a corset maker. He left home 6 years later and spent the next 17 years in various English towns, holding odd jobs. His two brief marriages ended in failure. He was depressed by a life of ugliness and monotony, relieved only by his avid reading.

By a stroke of luck, Paine met Benjamin Franklin in London. Franklin, impressed by the "ingenious, worthy young man," gave him letters of introduction to Americans. Paine emigrated to America, arriving in Philadelphia in 1774. He had never published a word before. But soon he was caught up in the political excitement of the time, especially the question of American independence from Great Britain. "It was the cause of America," he said, "that made me an author."

### Common Sense

In 1776 Paine published a 2-shilling, 47-page pamphlet called *Common Sense*. The pamphlet became a sensational success and one of the most influential publications in history. It was read by nearly everybody.

*Common Sense* was a fighting book. It sparkled with unforgettable phrases. Those who favored reconciliation with Great Britain were described as "Interested men, who are not to be trusted, weak men who cannot see, prejudiced men who will not see." To those who said that America had flourished under British rule, Paine answered: "We may as well assert that because a child has thrived upon milk, that it is never to have meat."

The basic conclusion of *Common Sense* was a call for independence from Great Britain. "Everything that is right or reasonable," Paine wrote, "pleads for separation. The blood of the slain, the weeping voice of nature cries, 'TIS TIME TO PART.'" Such flaming words worked, in the words of George Washington, "a powerful change . . . in the minds of men." There is no doubt that *Common Sense* influenced the Declaration of Independence.

Paine joined Washington's army and was with it during the New Jersey retreat in the winter of 1776. "Writing at every place we stopped at," he composed No. 1 of *The Crisis* papers. It began with the stirring words "These are the times that try men's souls." The last of *The Crisis* papers came out in 1783. By then Paine could justly say: "The times that tried men's souls are over." The American Revolution was won.

In 1777 Congress appointed Paine secretary of its committee on foreign affairs in reward for his services. He resigned in 1779 and was made clerk of the Pennsylvania Assembly. In 1781 he was a member of an American diplomatic mission to France. From 1783 to 1787 he lived in Bordentown, New Jersey, and New York City, working on the invention of an iron bridge.

### The French Revolution

In 1787 Paine went to France and then to England. After the outbreak of the French Revolution in 1789, he traveled between London and Paris, acting as a defender of the new revolutionary cause. In 1791 Paine published his *Rights of Man*. Outlawed in England because of his book, Paine fled to France. There he became an honorary French citizen and a member of the revolutionary Convention. In the struggle between the Jacobin and Girondist parties Paine was arrested and spent nearly a year in jail. He was released in November, 1794.

While in prison, he had begun his famous book *The Age of Reason*. The book brought widespread hostility upon him for its rejection of orthodox religion. In the first chapter Paine stated his beliefs: "I believe in one God, and no more; and I hope for happiness beyond this life. I believe in the equality of man; and I believe that religious duties consist in doing justice, loving mercy, and endeavoring to make our fellow creatures happy."

Paine returned to the United States in 1802. There he spent the last 7 years of his life, socially rejected and suffering from poverty and ill health. He died on June 8, 1809, and was buried in New Rochelle, New York. In 1819 his bones were removed to England.

Time is softening the undeserved hostility to Paine. He deserves to be remembered as a man whose motto was, "My country is the world, and my religion is to do good."

SAUL K. PADOVER
Author, *The Genius of America*

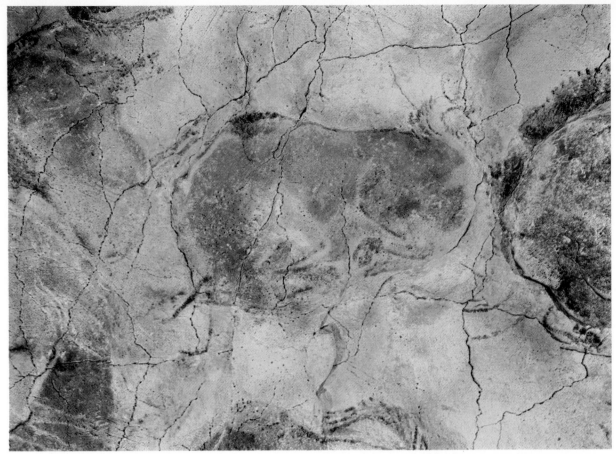
*Wounded Bison.* Cave painting, Altamira, Spain (15000 B.C.).

# PAINTING

The history of painting is a never-ending chain that began with the very first pictures ever made. Each style grows out of the styles that came before it. Every great artist adds to the accomplishments of earlier painters and influences later painters.

We can enjoy a painting for its beauty alone. Its lines, forms, colors, and composition (arrangement of parts) may appeal to our senses and linger in our memories. But enjoyment of art increases as we learn when and why and how it was created.

A painting always describes something. It may describe the artist's impression of a scene or person. It also describes the artist's feelings about the art of painting itself. Suppose, for example, the artist paints a picture of the birth of Venus, the Roman goddess of love—a subject that has been used many times. The viewer may not learn anything new about the subject from the more recent version that could not have been learned from the older one. Why, then, do painters bother to depict the same scene again? The answer is that they want to tell us something new about the way the scene can be painted. In a way, the artist is saying, "I have painted the birth of Venus as no other artist before me has painted it." The artist not only depicts the birth of Venus but also makes a statement about the art of painting itself.

Many factors have influenced the history of painting. Geography, religion, national characteristics, historic events, the development of new materials—all help to shape the artist's vision. Throughout history, painting has mirrored the changing world and our ideas about it. In turn, artists have provided some of the best records of the development of civilization, sometimes revealing more than the written word.

## ▶ PREHISTORIC PAINTING

Cave dwellers were the earliest artists. Colored drawings of animals, dating from about 30,000 to 10,000 B.C., have been found on the walls of caves in southern France and in Spain. Many of these drawings are amazingly well preserved because the caves were sealed up for many centuries. Early people drew the wild animals that they saw all around them. Very crude human figures, drawn in lifelike positions, have been found in Africa and eastern Spain.

The cave artists filled the cave walls with drawings in rich, bright colors. Some of the most beautiful paintings are in the Cave of Altamira, in Spain. One detail shows a wounded bison, no longer able to stand— probably the victim of a hunter. It is painted in reddish brown and outlined simply but skillfully in black. The pigments used by cave painters were earth **ochers** (iron oxides varying in color from light yellow to deep orange) and **manganese** (a metallic element). These were crushed into a fine powder, mixed with grease (perhaps animal fat), and put on with some sort of brush. Sometimes the pigments were used in sticks, like crayons. The grease mixed with the powdered pigments made the paint fluid and the pigment particles stick together. The cave dwellers must have made brushes out of animal hairs or plants, and sharp tools out of flint for drawing and scratching lines.

As far back as 30,000 years ago, people had invented the basic tools and materials for painting. Techniques and materials were refined and improved in the centuries following. But the discoveries of the cave dweller remain basic to painting.

▶ **EGYPTIAN AND MESOPOTAMIAN PAINTING (3400–332 B.C.)**

One of the first civilizations was developed in Egypt. From the written records and the art left by the Egyptians, much about their way of living is known. They believed that the body must be preserved so that the soul may live on after death. The great pyramids were elaborate tombs for rich and powerful Egyptian rulers. Much Egyptian art was created for the pyramids and tombs of kings and other important people. To make absolutely sure that the soul would continue to exist, artists made images of the dead person in stone. They also recorded scenes from the person's life in wall paintings in the burial chambers.

Egyptian techniques of painting remained the same for centuries. In one method watercolor paint was put on mud-plaster or limestone walls. In another process outlines were cut into stone walls, and the designs were painted with watercolor washes. A material called gum arabic probably was used to make the paint stick to a surface. Fortunately, the dry climate of the region and the sealed tombs have prevented some of these watercolor paintings from being destroyed by the dampness. A number of hunting scenes from the walls of tombs in Thebes of about 1450 B.C. are well preserved. They show hunters stalking birds or spearing fish of many varieties. These varieties can still be identified today because they were so accurately and carefully painted.

The Mesopotamian civilization, which lasted from 3200 to 332 B.C., was located in the valley between the Tigris and Euphrates rivers in the Near East. The Mesopotamians built mostly with clay. Because clay is softened by rain, their buildings have crumbled away to dust, destroying any wall paintings there may have been. What has been preserved are the decorated **ceramics** (painted and fired pottery) and colorful mosaics. Although mosaics should not be considered painting, they frequently influenced the forms of painting.

▶ **THE AEGEAN CIVILIZATION (3000–1100 B.C.)**

The third great early culture was the Aegean civilization, on the islands off the shores of Greece and in the peninsula of Asia Minor. The Aegeans lived around the same time as the ancient Egyptians and the Mesopotamians.

In 1900 archeologists began to excavate the palace of King Minos at Knossos on the island of Crete. The excavations turned up works of art painted around 1500 B.C. in an unusually free and graceful style for that time. Evidently the Cretans were a lighthearted, nature-loving people. Among their favorite themes in art were sea life, animals, flowers, athletic games, and processionals. At Knossos and other Aegean palaces, paintings were made on wet plaster walls with paints made of mineral substances, sand, and earth ochers. The paint soaked into the wet plaster and became a permanent part of the wall. This kind of painting was later called

Roman wall painting (50 B.C.) at the Villa of the Mysteries near Pompeii.

Justinian and His Court (A.D. 550?), a Byzantine mosaic. Church of San Vitale, Ravenna.

**fresco**, an Italian word meaning "fresh" or "new." The Cretans liked bright yellow, red, blue, and green.

## ▶GREEK AND ROMAN CLASSICAL PAINTING (1100 B.C.–A.D. 400)

The ancient Greeks decorated their temples and palaces with mural (wall) paintings. We can tell from ancient literary sources and from Roman copies of Greek art that the Greeks painted small pictures and made mosaics. The names of the Greek master painters and something of their lives and works are also known, although very little Greek painting has survived the effects of time and wars. The Greeks did not paint much in tombs, so their works were not protected.

Painted vases are about all that remains of Greek painting. Pottery making was a large industry in Greece, especially in Athens. Containers were in great demand for exports, such as oil and honey, and for household purposes. The earliest style of vase painting was known as the **geometric style** (1100–700 B.C.). Vases were decorated with bands of geometric shapes and human figures in a brown glaze on light-colored clay. By the 6th century, vase painters were using the **black-figured style**, in which human figures were

painted in black on the natural red clay. The details were cut into the clay with a sharp instrument. This allowed the red beneath to show through.

The **red-figured style** eventually replaced the black. It is just the opposite; the figures are red and the background black. The advantage of this style was that the painter could use a brush to make the outlines. A brush gives a freer line than the metal tool used in black-figured vases.

Roman mural paintings were found chiefly in the villas (country homes) of Pompeii and Herculaneum. In A.D. 79 these two cities were completely buried by an eruption of the volcano Vesuvius. Archeologists who have excavated the area have been able to learn much about ancient Roman life from these cities. Almost every house and villa in Pompeii had paintings on its walls. Roman painters carefully prepared the wall surface by applying a mixture of marble dust and plaster. They put the mixture on in layers and polished it to a marblelike finish. Many of the pictures are copies of 4th-century B.C. Greek paintings. The graceful poses of the figures painted on the walls of the Villa of the Mysteries in Pompeii inspired artists of the 18th century when the city was excavated.

The Greeks and Romans also painted portraits. A small number of them, mostly mummy portraits done in the Greek style by Egyptian artists, have survived around Alexandria, in northern Egypt. Founded in the 4th century B.C. by Alexander the Great of Greece, Alexandria became a leading center of Greek and Roman culture. Mummy portraits were painted in the encaustic technique on wood and were fitted into mummy cases after the death of the person portrayed. Encaustic paintings, done in paint mixed with melted beeswax, last for a very long time. Indeed, the mummy portraits still look fresh, though they were done as long ago as the 2nd century B.C.

### ▶ EARLY CHRISTIAN AND BYZANTINE PAINTING (A.D. 300–1300)

The Roman Empire began to decline in the 4th century A.D. At the same time Christianity gained strength. In A.D. 313 the Roman Emperor Constantine gave the religion official recognition and became a Christian himself.

The rise of Christianity greatly affected the arts. Artists were commissioned to decorate the walls of churches with frescoes and mosaics. They made panel paintings in the church chapel and illustrated and decorated the books of the Church. Under the authority of the Church, artists had to communicate the teachings of Christianity as clearly as possible.

Early Christians and Byzantine artists continued the technique of **mosaic** that they had learned from the Greeks. Small, flat pieces of colored glass or stone were set into wet cement or plaster. Sometimes other hard materials, such as bits of baked clay or shells, were used. In Italian mosaics the colors are especially deep and full. The Italian artists made the background with pieces of gilded glass. They set the human figures in rich colors against the glittering gold. The general effect is flat and decorative, not realistic.

The mosaics of Byzantine artists often were less realistic and more decorative than those of the early Christians. "Byzantine" is the name given to a style of art that developed around the ancient city of Byzantium (now Istanbul, Turkey). The mosaic technique perfectly suited the Byzantine taste for splendidly decorated churches. The famous mosaics of Theodora and Justinian, made about A.D. 547, show the taste for rich display. The jewelry on the figures glitters, and the brilliantly colored court dresses are set against a shining gold background. Byzantine artists also used gold liberally in fresco and panel paintings. Gold and other precious materials were used throughout the Middle Ages to set spiritual subjects apart from the everyday world.

### ▶ MEDIEVAL PAINTING (500–1400)

The first part of the Middle Ages, from about the 6th to the 11th centuries A.D., is commonly called the Dark Ages. In this time of unrest, art was kept alive mainly in the monasteries. In the 5th century A.D. barbarian tribes from northern and central Europe roamed over the continent. For hundreds of years they dominated Western Europe. These people produced an art that has a strong emphasis on pattern. They were especially fond of designs of intertwining dragons and birds.

The best of Celtic and Saxon art is found in manuscripts of the 7th and 8th centuries. Book illumination and miniature painting, practiced since late Roman times, increased in the Middle Ages. **Illumination** is decoration of the text, the capital letters, and the margins. Gold, silver, and bright colors were used. A **miniature** is a small picture, often a portrait. Originally the term was used to describe the decorative block around the initial letters in a manuscript.

Charlemagne, who was crowned emperor of the Holy Roman Empire in the early 9th century, tried to revive the classical art of the late Roman and early Christian periods. During his reign painters of miniatures imitated classical art, but they also conveyed personal feelings about their subjects.

Very little wall painting survives from the Middle Ages. There were several great series of frescoes painted in churches built during the Romanesque period (11th–13th centuries), but most of them have disappeared. Churches of the Gothic period (12th–16th centuries) did not have enough wall space for mural paintings. Book illustration was the main job of the Gothic painter.

Among the finest illustrated manuscripts were the books of hours—collections of calendars, devotional prayers, and psalms. A page from an Italian manuscript shows elaborately decorated initials and a finely detailed marginal scene of Saint George slaying the dragon. The colors are brilliant and jewel-like, as in stained glass, and gold shimmers over the page. Exquisitely delicate leaf and flower designs border the text. Artists probably used magnifying glasses to do such intricate work.

## ▶ ITALY: CIMABUE AND GIOTTO

Italian painters at the close of the 13th century were still working in the Byzantine style. Human figures were made to appear flat and decorative. Faces rarely had any expression. Bodies were weightless and seemed to float rather than stand firmly on the ground. In Florence the painter Cimabue (1240?–1302?) tried to modernize some of the old Byzantine methods. The angels in his *Madonna Enthroned* are more active than is usual in paintings of that time. Their gestures and faces show a little more human feeling. Cimabue added a new sense of monumentality, or largeness, to his paintings. However, he continued to follow many Byzantine tradi-

tions, such as the gold background and patternlike arrangement of objects and figures.

It was the great Florentine painter Giotto (1267?–1337) who actually broke with the Byzantine tradition. His fresco series in the Arena Chapel in Padua leaves Byzantine art far behind. In these scenes from the lives of Mary and Christ, there is genuine emotion, tension, and naturalism. All the qualities of human warmth and sympathy are present. The people do not seem at all unreal or heavenly. Giotto shaded the contours of the figures, and he put deep shadows into the folds of their clothing to give a sense of roundness and solidity.

For his smaller panels Giotto used pure **egg tempera**, a medium that was perfected by the 14th-century Florentines. The clearness and brightness of his colors must have greatly affected people accustomed to the darker colors of Byzantine panels. Tempera paintings give the impression that soft daylight is falling over the scene. They have an almost flat appearance in contrast to the glossiness of oil paintings. Egg tempera remained the chief painting medium until oil almost completely replaced it in the 16th century.

## ▶ LATE MEDIEVAL PAINTING NORTH OF THE ALPS

Early in the 15th century, painters in northern Europe were working in a style quite different from Italian painting. Northern artists achieved realism by adding countless details to their pictures. Every hair was delicately outlined, and each detail of drapery or floor pattern was faithfully set down. The invention of oil painting made it easier to paint details.

The Flemish artist Jan van Eyck (1370?–1441) contributed to the development of oil painting. When tempera is used, the colors have to be put on separately. They cannot shade into one another very well because the paint dries quickly. With oil, which dries slowly, an artist can achieve more intricate effects. *The Moneylender and His Wife* by Quentin Massys (1466?–1530) was done in the Flemish oil technique. All details, and even the mirror reflection, are clear and precise. The color is strong and has a hard, enamel-like surface. The wood panel on which the painting was done was prepared in much the same way that Giotto prepared his panels for

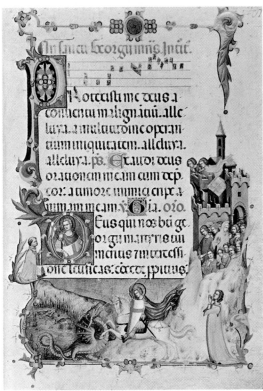

A page from a medieval illuminated
manuscript. Vatican Library, Rome.

*The Moneylender and His Wife (1514)*
by Quentin Massys. Louvre, Paris.

*The Descent from the Cross (1306?)*, by Giotto. Arena Chapel, Padua.

Detail from *The Tribute Money* (1425?), a fresco by Masaccio. Church of Santa Maria del Carmine, Florence.

tempera. Van Eyck built up the painting in layers of thin color, called **glazes.** Tempera was probably used in the original underpainting and for highlights.

### ▶ITALIAN RENAISSANCE PAINTING

At the same time that van Eyck was working in the North, the Italians were moving into a golden age of art and literature. This period is called the Renaissance, which means rebirth, or revival. Italian artists were inspired by the sculpture of the ancient Greeks and Romans. The Italians wanted to revive the spirit of classical art, which glorifies human independence and nobility. Renaissance artists continued to paint religious subjects. But they emphasized the earthly life and accomplishments of human beings.

### Florence

Giotto's accomplishments in the early 14th century laid the foundation of the Renaissance. Fifteenth-century Italian artists continued the movement. Masaccio (1401–28) was one of the leaders of the first generation of Renaissance artists. He lived in Florence, the wealthy merchant city where Renaissance art began. By the time of his death in his late twenties, he had revolutionized painting. In his famous fresco *The Tribute Money* he puts solid sculptural figures into a landscape that seems to go far back into the distance. Masaccio may have learned perspective from the Florentine architect and sculptor Brunelleschi (1377?–1446).

The fresco technique was very popular during the Renaissance. It was particularly suitable for large mural paintings because the colors dry perfectly flat. The picture can be viewed from any angle without glare or reflections. Frescoes are also available. Usually the artists had several assistants to help them. Work was completed by sections because it had to be finished while the plaster was still wet.

Masaccio's full three-dimensional style was typical of the new progressive trend of the 15th century. The style of Fra Angelico (1400?–1455) represents the more traditional approach used by a number of early Renaissance painters. He was less concerned with perspective and more interested in decorative pattern. His *Coronation of the Virgin* is an example of tempera painting at its most beautiful. The gay, intense colors are set against a gold background and accented with touches of gold. The picture looks like a greatly enlarged miniature painting. The long, narrow figures have little in common with Masaccio's. The composition is organized in sweeping lines of movement circling about the central figures of Christ and Mary.

Another Florentine who worked in the traditional style was Sandro Botticelli (1444?–1510). Flowing, rhythmic lines link the sections of Botticelli's *Primavera*. The figure of Spring, carried by the West Wind, sweeps in from the right. The Three Graces dance in a circle, the fluttering folds of their dresses and graceful movements of their arms expressing the rhythms of the dance.

The famous artist Leonardo da Vinci (1452–1519) studied painting in Florence. He is known for his scientific studies and inventions, as well as for his paintings. Very few of his pictures have survived, partly because he often experimented with different ways of making and applying paint, rather than using tried and true methods. The *Last Supper* (painted between 1495 and 1498) was done in oil, but unfortunately Leonardo painted it on a damp wall, which caused the paint to crack. Even in its poor condition the painting has the power to stir emotions in all who see it.

One of the distinguishing characteristics of Leonardo's style was his method of painting lights and darks. The Italians called his half-dark lighting *sfumato,* which means smoky, or misty. The figures in the *Madonna of the Rocks* are veiled in a sfumato atmosphere. Their forms and features are softly shaded. Leonardo achieved these effects by using very fine gradations of light and dark tones.

### Rome

The climax of Renaissance painting came in the 16th century. At the same time, the center of art and culture shifted from Florence to Rome. Under Pope Sixtus IV and his successor, Julius II, the city of Rome was gloriously decorated by Renaissance artists. Some of the most ambitious projects of the period were begun during the papacy of Julius II. Julius commissioned the great sculptor and painter Michelangelo (1475–1564) to paint the ceiling of the Sistine Chapel and to carve sculpture for the Pope's tomb. Julius also invited the painter Raphael (1483–1520) to help with the decoration of the Vatican. With assistants, Raphael frescoed four rooms of the Pope's apartments in the Vatican Palace.

Michelangelo, a Florentine by birth, developed a monumental style of painting. The figures in his painting are so solid and three-dimensional that they look like sculpture. The Sistine ceiling, which took Michelangelo 4 years to complete, is composed of hundreds of human figures from the Old Testament. To paint this tremendous fresco Michelangelo had to lie on his back on scaffolding. The brooding face of Jeremiah among the prophets that surround the ceiling is thought by some people to be his self-portrait.

Raphael came to Florence from Urbino as a very young man. In Florence he absorbed the ideas of Leonardo and Michelangelo. By the time Raphael went to Rome to work in the Vatican, his style had become one of great beauty. He is especially beloved for his beautiful paintings of the Madonna and Child. These have been reproduced by the thousands and can be seen everywhere. His *Madonna del Granduca* is successful because of its complete simplicity. Timeless in its peacefulness and purity, it is just as appealing to us as it was to the Italians of Raphael's time.

### Venice

Venice was the chief northern Italian city of the Renaissance. It was visited by artists from Flanders and other regions who knew of Flemish experiments with oil paint. This stimulated an early use of the oil technique in the Italian city. The Venetians also painted on tightly stretched canvas, rather than on the wooden panels commonly used in Florence.

Giovanni Bellini (1430?–1516) was the greatest Venetian painter of the 15th century. He was also one of the first Italian painters to

*Madonna of the Rocks* (1485?), by Leonardo da Vinci. Louvre, Paris.

Above: *View of Toledo* (1604–14?), by El Greco. Metropolitan Museum of Art, New York. Below left: *Madonna with Saints and Members of the Pesaro Family* (1528), by Titian. Church of the Frari, Venice. Below right: *Prince Phillip Prosper of Spain* (1660), by Diego Velázquez. Kunsthistorisches Museum, Vienna.

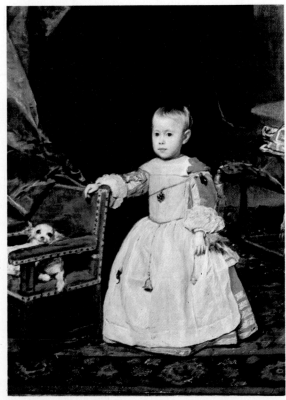

use oil on canvas. Giorgione (1478?–1511) and Titian (1488?–1576), who is the most famous of all Venetian painters, were students in Bellini's workshop.

A master of the oil technique, Titian painted huge canvases in warm, rich colors. In his mature paintings he sacrificed details to the sweeping effect of the whole painting, as in the *Pesaro Madonna*. He used large brushes to make broad strokes. His colors are especially rich because he patiently built up glazes of contrasting colors. Usually the glazes were put on over a brown tempera ground, which gave the painting a unified tone.

Another great 16th-century Venetian painter was Tintoretto (1518–94). Unlike Titian, he usually worked directly on the canvas without making preliminary sketches or underpaintings. He often distorted his forms (twisted them out of shape) for the sake of the composition and drama of the scene. His technique, which includes broad brushstrokes and dramatic contrasts of light and dark, seems very modern.

The painter Kyriakos Theotokopoulos (1541–1614) was known as El Greco ("the Greek"). Born on the island of Crete, which was occupied by the Venetian army, El Greco was trained by Italian artists. As a young adult he went to Venice to study. The combined influence of Byzantine art—which he saw all around him in Crete—and of Italian Renaissance art made El Greco's work outstanding.

In his paintings he distorted natural forms and used even stranger, more unearthly colors than Tintoretto, whom he admired. Later El Greco moved to Spain, where the grimness of Spanish art influenced his work. In his dramatic *View of Toledo* a storm rages above the deathlike stillness of the city. Cold blues, greens, and blue-whites cast a chill over the landscape.

## ▶ THE RENAISSANCE IN FLANDERS AND GERMANY

The golden age of painting in Flanders (now part of Belgium and northern France) was the 15th century, the time of van Eyck. In the 16th century many Flemish artists had taken up the discoveries of Italian Renaissance painters. Some Flemings, however, continued the Flemish tradition of realism. They painted **genre**—scenes from everyday life, which were often charming and sometimes fantastic. Hieronymus Bosch (1450?–1516), who preceded the genre painters, had an unusually vivid imagination. He invented all sorts of weird, grotesque creatures for *The Temptation of St. Anthony*. Pieter Brueghel the Elder (1525?–69) also worked in the Flemish tradition but added perspective and other Renaissance characteristics to his genre scenes.

Albrecht Dürer (1471–1528), Hans Holbein the Younger (1497?–1543), and Lucas Cranach the Elder (1472–1553) were the three most important German painters of the 16th century. They did much to soften the grim realism of earlier German painting. Dürer made at least one visit to Italy, where he was impressed with the paintings of Giovanni Bellini and other northern Italians. From this experience he brought to German painting a knowledge of perspective, a feeling for color and light, and a new understanding of composition. Holbein absorbed even more of the Italian achievements. His sensitive drawing and ability to select only the most important details made him a master portrait painter.

## ▶ BAROQUE PAINTING

The 17th century is generally known as the baroque period in art. In Italy the painters Caravaggio (1571–1610) and Annibale Carracci (1560–1609) represented two contrasting viewpoints. Caravaggio (whose real name was Michelangelo Merisi) always painted directly from life. One of his main concerns was to copy nature as faithfully as possible without glorifying it in any way. Carracci, on the other hand, followed the Renaissance ideal of beauty. He studied ancient sculpture and the works of Michelangelo, Raphael, and Titian. Caravaggio's style was admired by many painters, especially by the Spaniards Ribera and the young Velázquez. Carracci's painting inspired Nicolas Poussin (1594–1665), a major French painter of the 17th century.

### Spain

Diego Velázquez (1599–1660), court painter to King Philip IV of Spain, was one of the greatest of all Spanish painters. An admirer of Titian's work, he was a master in the use of rich, harmonious color. No artist could better create the illusion of rich fabrics or human skin. The portrait of little Prince Phillip Prosper shows this skill to great advantage. His remarkable brushwork was much admired by the 19th-century French impressionists.

### Flanders

The paintings of the Flemish artist Peter Paul Rubens (1577–1640) are representative of the full-blown baroque style. They are bursting with energy, color, and light. Rubens broke with the Flemish tradition of painting small, detailed pictures. His were huge canvases filled with human figures. He was given many more commissions for large pictures than he could possibly handle. Therefore he often painted only a small, colored sketch. Then his assistants transferred the sketch to a large canvas and completed the painting under Rubens' supervision.

### Holland

The accomplishments of the Dutch painter Rembrandt (1606–69) are among the most outstanding in history. He had a remarkable gift for capturing human emotions. Like Titian, he worked long at building up a painting in many layers. Earth colors—yellow ocher, brown, and brown-red—were his favorites. His paintings are basically dark in tone and have many very dark areas. The rich values of these dark areas, created with many layers of color, make his technique unusual. Important sections of his paintings are dramatically illuminated by brilliant light.

Jan Vermeer (1632–75) was one of a group of Dutch artists who painted the humble scenes of daily life. He was a master at painting textures of every kind—satin, Persian rugs, bread crusts, metal. The overall impression of a Vermeer interior is that of a sunny, cheerful room filled with cherished household objects.

### ▶ 18TH-CENTURY PAINTING

In the 18th century, Venice produced several fine painters. The most famous was Giovanni Battista Tiepolo (1696–1770). He decorated the interiors of palaces and other buildings with tremendous, colorful frescoes representing scenes of wealth and pageantry

Francesco Guardi (1712–93) and Antonio Canaletto (1697–1768) painted scenic views, many of them recalling the past glories of Venice. Guardi was very skillful with a brush. With a few patches of color he could conjure up the idea of a tiny figure in a boat.

### France: The Rococo Style

In France a taste for pastel colors and intricate decoration brought about the development of the rococo style in the early 18th century. Jean Antoine Watteau (1684–1721), a court painter to King Louis XV, and, later, François Boucher (1703–70) and Jean Honoré Fragonard (1732–1806), were associated with the rococo trend. Watteau painted visions of a dream life in which all is gaiety. There are picnics in the park or woodland parties where gallant gentlemen and elegant ladies amuse themselves.

Other 18th-century painters portrayed scenes of ordinary, middle-class life. Like the Dutch Vermeer, Jean Baptiste Simeon Chardin (1699–1779) valued simple domestic scenes and still-life arrangements. His colors are sober and calm compared to Watteau's.

### England

In the 18th century the English, for the first time, developed a distinct school of painting. It consisted mainly of portrait painters who were influenced by Venetian Renaissance artists. Sir Joshua Reynolds (1723–92) and Thomas Gainsborough (1727–88) are the best-known. Reynolds, who had traveled in Italy, was devoted to reviving the Renaissance ideals of painting. His portraits, although charming and touching, are not particularly interesting in color or texture. Gainsborough, on the other hand, had a talent for brilliant brushwork. The surfaces of his paintings glow with shining color.

### ▶ 19TH-CENTURY PAINTING

The 19th century is sometimes regarded as the period during which modern art began to take shape. One important reason for the so-called revolution in the arts at this time was the invention of the camera, which forced artists to re-examine the purpose of painting.

A more important development resulted partly from the widespread use of manufactured paints. Before the 19th century, most

*The Polish Rider* (1655?), an oil painting by Rembrandt van Rijn. The Frick Collection, New York.

*Marie de' Medici, Queen of France, Landing in Marseilles* (1622–23), by Peter Paul Rubens. Pinakothek, Munich.

*Embarkation for Cythera* (1717), by Antoine Watteau. Louvre, Paris.

Above: *The Snow Storm* (1842), by J. M. W. Turner. National Gallery, London.
Below: *Madame Julie Récamier* (1800), by Jacques Louis David. Louvre, Paris.

artists or their assistants made their own paints by grinding pigment. Early commercial paints were inferior to handmade paints. Artists late in the 19th century found that the dark blues and browns of earlier paintings were turning black or gray within a few years. They began to use pure colors again. These artists used pure colors in order to preserve their work and sometimes because they were trying to capture the effects of sunlight in outdoor scenes more accurately.

### England

Although France was the great center of art in the 1800's, the English landscapists John Constable (1776–1837) and Joseph Mallord William Turner (1775–1851) made valuable contributions to 19th-century painting. Both were interested in painting light and air, two aspects of nature that 19th-century artists explored fully. Constable used a method known as **divisionism**, or broken color. He put contrasting colors side by side in thick, short strokes or dots over a basic background color. He often used a palette knife to apply the color thickly. *The Hay Wain* made him famous when it was shown in Paris in 1824. It is a simple rural scene of a hay wagon (wain) crossing a river. Clouds drift over meadows dappled with patches of sunlight. Turner's paintings are more dramatic than Constable's. He painted the majestic sights of nature—storms, seascapes, glowing sunsets, high mountains. Often a golden haze partially conceals the objects in his pictures, making them appear to float in unlimited space.

### Spain: Goya

Francisco Goya (1746–1828) was the first great Spanish painter to appear since the 17th century. As the favorite painter of the Spanish court, he made many portraits of the royal family. The royal personages are outfitted in elegant clothes and fine jewels, but in some of their faces all that is reflected is vanity and greed. Besides portraits, Goya painted dramatic scenes such as *The Third of May, 1808.* This picture shows the execution of a group of Spanish rebels by French soldiers. Bold contrasts of light and dark, and somber colors pierced by splashes of red, bring out the grim horror of the spectacle.

### France

The period of Napoleon's reign and the French Revolution saw the rise of two opposing tendencies in French art—**classicism** and **romanticism**. Jacques Louis David

*Self Portrait* (1815), by Francisco Goya. San Fernando Academy, Madrid.

*Orphan Girl at the Cemetery* (1823), by Eugène Delacroix. Louvre, Paris.

Above: *Field of Yellow Corn* (1889), by Vincent van Gogh. National Gallery, London. Below: *Kitchen Table* (1888–90), by Paul Cézanne. Louvre, Paris.

(1748–1825) and Jean Auguste Dominique Ingres (1780–1867) were inspired by ancient Greek and Roman art and the Renaissance. They emphasized drawing and used color mainly to aid in creating solid forms. As the favorite artist of the revolutionary government, David often painted historical events of the period. In his portraits, such as that of Madame Récamier, he aimed at achieving classical simplicity.

Théodore Géricault (1791–1824) and the romanticist Eugène Delacroix (1798–1863) revolted against David's style. For Delacroix, color was the most important element in painting, and he had no patience for imitating classical statues. Instead, he admired Rubens and the Venetians. He chose colorful, exotic themes for his pictures, which sparkle with light and are full of movement.

The Barbizon painters were also part of the general romantic movement that lasted from about 1820 to 1850. They worked near the village of Barbizon on the edge of the Fontainebleau forest. They sketched out-of-doors and completed the paintings in their studios.

Other artists experimented with everyday, ordinary subject matter. The landscapes of Jean Baptiste Camille Corot (1796–1875) reflect his love of nature, and his figure studies show a kind of balanced calm. Gustave Courbet (1819–77) called himself a realist because he painted the world as he saw it—even its harsh, unpleasant side. He limited his palette to just a few somber colors, which he sometimes put on with a palette knife. Édouard Manet (1832–83) also took his subject matter from the world around him. People were shocked by his colorful contrasts and unusual techniques. The surfaces of his pictures often have a flat, patternlike texture of brushstrokes. Manet's techniques and methods of recording the effects of light on form influenced younger painters, especially the impressionists.

Working in the 1870's and 1880's, the group of artists known as the **impressionists** wanted to paint nature exactly as it was. They went much further than Constable, Turner, and Manet in studying the effects of light on color. Some of them worked out scientific theories of color. Claude Monet (1840–1926) often painted the same view at different times of day to show how its ap-

pearance changed under different conditions of light. Whatever the subject matter, his scenes are made up of hundreds of tiny brushstrokes laid side by side, often in contrasting colors. From a distance the strokes blend to give the impression of solid forms. Pierre Auguste Renoir (1841–1919) used the impressionist techniques to capture the festivity of Parisian life. In his *Dance at the Moulin de la Galette* people in vividly colored clothes mingle and dance gaily. Renoir painted the entire picture with small, even brushstrokes. The dots and dashes of paint create a texture on the surface of the painting that lends it a special kind of unity. The crowds of people seem to dissolve in sunlight and shimmering color.

## ▶ 20TH-CENTURY PAINTING

A number of artists soon became dissatisfied with impressionism. Artists such as Paul Cézanne (1839–1906) felt that impressionism did not describe the solidity of forms in nature. Cézanne liked to paint still lifes because they allowed him to concentrate on the shapes of fruits or other objects and their arrangements. Objects in his still lifes look solid because he reduced their forms to simple geometric shapes. His technique of placing patches of paint and short brushstrokes of rich color side by side shows that he learned much from the impressionists.

Vincent van Gogh (1853–90) and Paul Gauguin (1848–1903) reacted against the realism of the impressionists. Unlike the impressionists, who said that they were viewing nature objectively, Van Gogh cared little for accurate drawing. He frequently distorted objects in order to express his ideas more imaginatively. He used the impressionist device of putting contrasting colors next to each other. Sometimes he squeezed paint from the tubes right onto the canvas in thick ribbons, as in *Field of Yellow Corn*.

Gauguin did not care for the spotty color of the impressionists. He applied color smoothly in large flat areas, which he separated from one another by lines or dark edges. The colorful civilizations of the tropics provided much of his subject matter.

Cézanne's method of building up arrangements in space with simple geometric forms was further developed by Pablo Picasso

(1881–1973), Georges Braque (1882–1963), and others. Their style became known as **cubism**. The cubists painted objects as if they could be seen from several angles at once, or as if they had been taken apart and reassembled on a flat canvas. Often the objects barely resemble anything in nature. Sometimes the cubists cut out shapes from cloth, cardboard, wallpaper, or other materials and pasted them on the canvas to make a **collage**. Textures were also varied by adding sand or other substances to the paint. Since Manet, the trend has been to put less emphasis on subject and more emphasis on composition and technique.

▶ PAINTING IN THE UNITED STATES

American painting before the 20th century had mainly consisted of portraits and landscapes based on European styles. Many American artists, such as James Abbott McNeill Whistler (1834–1903) and John Singer Sargent (1856–1925), lived abroad and were influenced by European art. There was, however, an important group of American genre painters, the best of whom were Winslow Homer (1836–1910) and Thomas Eakins (1844–1916).

In the 1890's a group of young painters known as The Eight, led by Robert Henri (1865–1929), tried to create an art that was distinctly American. John Sloan (1871–1951) and George W. Bellows (1882–1925) painted life in the alleys, backyards, harbors, and slums. Members of The Eight helped organize the 1913 Armory Show of New York City. This exhibition, held in an armory, brought together modern art from the United States and Europe. At this show Americans saw the daring art of the cubists and other modern Europeans for the first time.

By the beginning of World War I, United States artists were aware of everything that was going on in modern European painting. But they did not make use of the new ideas until years later. Many painters in the 1930's were

## THE ARTIST'S PAINTS

**ACRYLIC**—Also called plastic paint or acrylic-resin paint. Depending on how the painter handles it, acrylic paint may be as transparent as watercolor or as thick and pasty as some oil paints. It will stick to almost any surface. It will not yellow, and it is not affected by heat and humidity. All these qualities make it one of the most popular paints today.

**DISTEMPER**—Pigment and glue. This somewhat impermanent kind of paint is used in schools a great deal, for it is cheap and dries quickly.

**EGG TEMPERA**—Pigment ground into egg yolks and thinned with water. Tempera dries almost immediately. It is usually applied with short strokes of a soft, small brush. Most tempera paintings are done on wooden boards that have been prepared with several coats of gesso—white chalk mixed with glue. Tempera is transparent and is often applied in several layers.

**ENCAUSTIC**—Pigment and wax. In this ancient technique the color and vehicle are heated and applied, while still hot and liquid, to a wall or other surface.

**FRESCO**—Painting done with watercolors on moist plaster walls or ceiling.

**GOUACHE**—Opaque (it cannot be seen through) watercolor. Gouache (pronounced "gwash") is applied like watercolor, but white may be used to lighten colors.

**OIL PAINT**—Pigment ground into oil. For centuries after its invention, probably in the 15th century, oil painting dominated all other techniques until the development of acrylics. It dries slowly. It can be wiped off or painted over. It can be applied thickly or thinly. It can be transparent or opaque. The most common oil used for mixing is linseed oil, but for various effects, varnish, turpentine, beeswax, and other kinds of oils can be added. Until commercially made oil paints became available, the artist had to grind powdered pigment on a marble slab while adding oil little by little.

Oil paintings can be made on wood prepared in the same way as tempera boards. More frequently, however, stretched canvas is used. Most canvas is made of linen, which is available in a great variety of weights and weaves. Cotton sailcloth is much cheaper and less permanent, but it is also widely used. The canvas is tacked to a frame called a stretcher. Then it is coated with glue made from the hide of a rabbit or some other animal. This shrinks and sizes the canvas, which means that air can no longer pass through the spaces between the strands of linen. Then the tightly stretched canvas is primed with gesso, or white lead, a pasty paint that must be spread with a knife. Priming and sizing protects the canvas from rotting. Ideally, the oil paint should remain on top of the surface. It should be absorbed only slightly by the primer. The sizing prevents oil from touching the fabric itself.

Oil paint is applied with a variety of brushes, most of which are stiff and long-bristled. It can also be applied with a flexible knife (spatula) or even squeezed directly onto the surface from the tube.

**PASTELS**—Powdered pigment mixed with just enough glue to hold it together in ball or stick form. Working with pastels is as close as the artist can come to working with pure pigment. The stick or ball is stroked against a roughly textured piece of paper (some artists even use sandpaper). Since the vehicle is not liquid and cannot be absorbed, pastel paintings must be sprayed with varnish or lacquer (fixative) to prevent the pigment from coming off the paper.

**PIGMENT**—The material from which colors are made. Today some pigments can be chemically produced in laboratories. But all early paints were made from natural pigments found in such minerals as cobalt, cadmium, and lead.

**VEHICLE, or MEDIUM**—The substance with which pigment is mixed to make paint. The vehicle is usually liquid.

**WATERCOLOR**—Pigment ground into water. Regular water-color paints are transparent (you can see through them). Watercolors are usually applied to textured paper with a soft-bristle brush, such as sable hair. Since there is no such thing as white transparent paint, the artist must leave the white area of the paper unpainted. To lighten the colors, he adds more water.

Green Still Life (1914), by Pablo Picasso. Museum of Modern Art, New York.

Double Metamorphosis II (1964), by Vaacov Agam. Marlborough-Gerson Gallery, New York.

Green Coca-Cola Bottles (1962), by Andy Warhol. Whitney Museum of American Art, New York City.

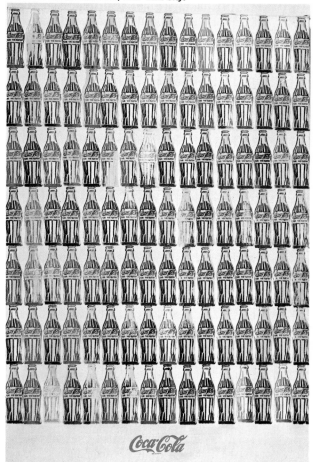

regional artists like Grant Wood (1891–1942), who painted realistic scenes of life in the Middle West.

After World War II, the United States became the world center of painting. Arshile Gorky (1904–48) and Jackson Pollock (1912–56) were among the leaders who helped to create a new style called **action painting** or **abstract expressionism**. Instead of trying to represent specific objects, they were interested mainly in color, design, rhythm, and new ways of applying paint. Pollock experimented with flinging and dripping color on his canvases from sticks dipped into buckets of paint. Such a bold technique is just one example of the 20th-century artist's search for originality and freedom of expression.

Early in the 1960's a group of artists in the United States reacted against abstract expressionism. These artists went to the other extreme. In trying to produce an art that expresses the spirit of today, they began to paint realistic pictures of everyday things. Their subjects included dart boards, light bulbs, comic strips, and street signs. The innovators in this movement included Robert Rauschenberg (1925–   ) and Jasper Johns (1930–   ). Roy Lichtenstein (1923–97), Claes Oldenburg (1929–   ), and Andy Warhol (1930?–87) were some of its leaders. Sometimes called "pop" (for popular) art, it represented a phase through which art passed. To many people, however, pop art presented an invitation to take a good look at the objects all around them. The design on a soup can or a bottle of cola might never have been noticed otherwise. Abstract expressionism opened people's minds; pop art opened their eyes.

In the mid-1960's, other types of art emerged. "Op," or optical art, was one. In op art, the tricks our eyesight can play become part of the artist's style. In Vaacov Agam's *Double Metamorphosis II,* the specially arranged patterns of line and color seem almost to vibrate.

Some abstract artists, such as Frank Stella (1936– ) and Ellsworth Kelly (1923– ), sometimes shape the canvas itself into circles, triangles, and other forms. Using bright colors, they often apply paint in hard-edged geometric shapes that conform to the shape of the canvas. So, it may be difficult to distinguish between painting and sculpture today, but we appreciate purity of color and relationships of shapes.

SARAH BRADFORD LANDAU
Department of Fine Arts
New York University

See also BAROQUE ART AND ARCHITECTURE; COLOR; DESIGN; MODERN ART; PREHISTORIC ART; RENAISSANCE ART AND ARCHITECTURE; names of individual artists, as REMBRANDT; and art of individual countries, as ITALY, ART AND ARCHITECTURE OF.

# PAINTS AND PIGMENTS

High on the supports of a bridge a man brushes a shiny protective surface over a heavy metal beam. In a nursery school a child brushes streaks of color across a sheet of paper. Both the man and the child are painting. The man is using paint for one of its two main purposes: protection. The child is using paint for the other main purpose: decoration.

Paint can change the appearance of a surface by giving it a different gloss or texture. A coat of paint may cover a surface with a film only a few thousandths of an inch thick. Yet the protection and decoration it gives last for many years.

Paints usually are made up of a **pigment**, a **vehicle**, and a **thinner**.

The pigment of a paint gives the paint color and the ability to hide a surface. It also gives hardness and bulk. The texture and quantity of the pigment determine the gloss of a paint. Rough pigments or large quantities of pigment make dull paints. Finely ground pigments make glossy paints. White lead, iron oxide (rust), and carbon black (soot) are some examples of pigments.

The vehicle is the part of the paint that carries the pigment particles and holds the entire film to the surface. Vegetable oils and natural or synthetic resins are often used for paint vehicles. (Natural resins are gummy liquids that come from trees and other plants. Synthetic resins are completely man-made.)

The thinner usually evaporates after the paint is applied. Its job is to make the paint flow freely. The thinner does not affect the quality of the dry paint. Sometimes water is used as a thinner, and sometimes mineral spirit (a liquid made from petroleum) or turpentine is used.

## ▶TYPES OF PAINTS

What kind of paint is best for a particular use? This depends upon many different things: the type of surface to be painted, the weather it will be exposed to, the wear it will receive, and the length of time the paint is expected to last. There are several hundred different types of paints available. The chief types are listed here.

### Paints for Exterior Use

The commonest paint is exterior paint, or **outside house paint**. It is usually made with linseed oil, although other oils may be used. It is applied to the sides of wooden houses. These paints keep their color and appearance for long periods of time in spite of rain and sunlight. They are able to take the swelling and shrinking of wood.

Some house paints use **alkyd resins** (types of liquid plastics) or **latexes** (synthetic rubber materials) as vehicles. They may allow water vapor to pass through them fairly easily. This is very important in house paints—if water builds up in the wood under the paint, the paint will blister.

Exterior latex paints are especially useful for painting masonry because they can be put on before the masonry is completely dry. Also, latex paints are alkali-resistant. This is

Paints are exposed outdoors to test the effects of all kinds of weather.

important because nearly all masonry, such as concrete, brick, stone, or stucco, is either alkaline itself or is put together with an alkaline mortar.

Steps, decks, and similar surfaces are usually treated with floor and deck enamels made for taking a lot of wear. **Enamels** are glossy (shiny) paints that flow out into a hard, smooth coat when they are applied.

Metal exposed to dampness is usually given a coat of **anticorrosive primer**—a first coat of a paint that prevents rusting. On top of this are painted one or more coats of an exterior enamel. Because metal expands and contracts with changes of temperature, paints for metal must be flexible.

### Interior House Paints

The walls of rooms are usually painted with **flat paints**. Flat paints are dull paints. Instead of being shiny, they diffuse, or spread out, light that shines on them. Either alkyd or latex paints are used. The alkyd is more washable and hides the wall surface better. The latex paint is easier to apply and gives brighter and stronger colors.

Bathrooms, kitchens, and trimming around doors and windows all need to be covered with a paint that will take a lot of wear and can easily be washed. For them a **gloss** or **semigloss enamel** is generally used. Enamels with a gloss are very shiny. Semigloss paints have a dull shine.

**Floor enamels** are made to wear well despite a lot of rubbing and walking. They also dry rapidly, so that the floor can be used soon after it is painted.

### Chemical Coatings

Paints that give special protective coatings are called chemical coatings. These coatings are used for manufactured articles, such as automobiles and refrigerators. The paints, applied while the articles are on a production line, dry rapidly. Even textiles and paper are often coated with this kind of paint.

### Paints for Use in Industries

The walls, floors, and machines in industrial plants often require special paints. Chemical plants, for instance, need paints with very high resistance to acids or other chemicals. Usually the proper paint for an industrial job cannot be chosen until all the jobs that the paint must do are known.

### Marine Finishes

A surface that is always underwater requires a very special paint. Not only do boats stay in either fresh or salt water a good part of the time, but they are likely to have barnacles, algae, and other plants and animals growing on them. Special **antifouling paints** are used to discourage this growth. Many antifouling paints have copper in them for a poison.

A boat may need to be painted with three different marine paints. One will be an antifouling paint for the bottom. Another will be for the area that is sometimes underwater and sometimes exposed. The third will be for the deck that is exposed to salt air and strong sunlight. Making marine paints is such a difficult job that many paint companies make nothing else.

### Special Paints

There are hundreds of paints for special uses. The **highway paints** used for the center lines on highways, for example, are made for this one purpose and would be almost useless for anything else. Highways paints must dry rapidly so that their drying does not delay traffic. They must stay colorful and be easy to see in both daylight and dark. They must resist being worn out by tires, chains, salt, snow, rain, and sun. They must be suitable for either concrete or asphalt. All in all, this is a long set of requirements for a paint.

To slow down the spread of fire, **fire-retardant paints** are used. No paint can make a piece of wood fireproof. Paint film is only a few thousandths of an inch thick. But fire-retardant paint can slow down the spread of fire and in this way save both lives and property.

Another interesting special paint is **luminous paint**. Luminous paints may be either **fluorescent** or **phosphorescent**. Fluorescent paints glow brightly when they are exposed to ultraviolet light rays. These paints are used in signs, on instrument dials, and on parts of airplanes for extra safety in the dark. Phosphorescent paints glow for several hours after being exposed to sunlight. They are used for exit signs and other emergency guides. Unfortunately, few of them are bright enough to do more than point the way to safety.

### ▶ WAYS TO APPLY PAINT

The way paint is applied depends on the type of surface being painted and the thickness of the paint being used. Paints are usually applied by brush, roller, or spray. There are a number of other methods, like roll coating and dipping, but these are used only for factory-applied finishes.

**Painting by Brush.** The usual method of applying paint is by brush. Paintbrushes come in dozens of sizes and shapes, each with its special use. When furniture is painted, it is usually by brush.

**Painting by Roller.** When large flat areas, such as walls and ceilings, are to be coated, rollers are fast and do the job well. Special rollers are made for corners and other difficult places.

**Spraying Paint.** Spraying is often used for paints that dry too rapidly to be put on by brush or roller. Spraying is fast and gives a smooth surface with no brush marks. Spraying is often used in factories to paint cars, refrigerators, and other large items. When it is difficult to protect the surfaces that should not be painted, spray cannot be used. In homes spray paint is most useful for carved or wicker pieces where the surface cannot easily be given an even coat by brush. But it is difficult to use spray paints where there is poor ventilation or where the painting quarters are small.

FRANCIS SCOFIELD
National Paint and Coatings Association

See also PAINTING.

# PAKISTAN

Pakistan, a country of South Asia, is a young nation in an ancient land. The region that is now Pakistan has a history going back thousands of years, to the Indus Valley civilization, the remains of which can still be seen. But the present-day nation of Pakistan was first established in 1947. It was created from areas of the British Indian empire that had a majority Muslim population.

When Pakistan won its independence, it consisted of two parts, West Pakistan and East Pakistan, which were separated by about 1,000 miles (1,600 kilometers) of territory belonging to India. In 1971, following a civil war and war between Pakistan and India, East Pakistan broke away from Pakistan and declared its independence as the nation of Bangladesh.

The faces of Pakistan reflect the country's four main ethnic groups: A Sindhi girl (*left*); an elderly Baluchi (*below*); a Punjabi wearing the traditional Jinnah cap (*below left*); and a young Pashtun rug seller (*bottom*).

## ▶ THE PEOPLE

**Ethnic Groups.** The Pakistanis are the descendants of the varied peoples who arrived in the land, either as conquerors or settlers, over the course of its long history. There are four main ethnic groups, who traditionally have inhabited the regions that now form the country's four provinces.

The largest group is the Punjabis, who make up nearly 60 percent of the population and live chiefly in the plains of the Punjab. The second largest, the Sindhis, occupy the southern province of Sind. The Pashtuns, who are related to a people of neighboring Afghanistan, are found mainly in the mountainous North-West Frontier Province. The Baluchi consist of numerous nomadic tribes who inhabit Baluchistan, the largest but most desolate of the four provinces, in the southwest.

**Language and Religion.** Pakistan's languages are as diverse as its people. The official language is Urdu, which is similar to the Hindi of northern India but includes words from Arabic and Persian and is written in a modified Arabic script. It is used as a primary language, however, only by a small minority of the people. Most Pakistanis speak their regional languages, chiefly Punjabi, Sindhi, Pashto, and Baluchi. English, a reminder of

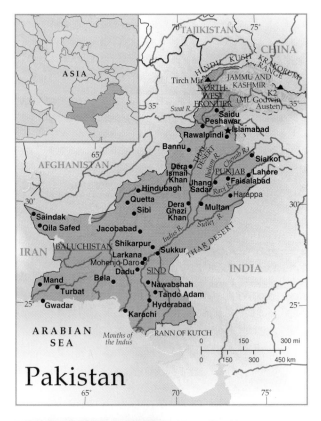

Pakistan

the centuries of British rule, is also used widely and has semiofficial status.

Nearly all Pakistanis are Muslims. The great majority belong to the Sunni branch of Islam, although there are numerous other sects.

**Education.** Primary education, for children between the ages of 5 and 10, is free but not compulsory by law. There are shortages of teachers and educational facilities, and only about half of the primary-age students actually attend school. Secondary school begins at age 10 and lasts for four or five years, depending on the course of study. Pakistan has more than 20 universities. The largest is the University of Peshawar. About 36 percent of the adult population is literate (that is, able to read and write).

▶ **WAY OF LIFE**

**The Village.** Although young Pakistanis are increasingly attracted to the growing cities, chiefly because of job opportunities, more than 70 percent of the people still live in rural areas, in villages of varying sizes.

Pakistani villages are built close together, usually around a well or irrigation canal. Almost every village has its mosque (the Muslim house of worship), from whose minaret, or tower, the faithful are called to prayer five times a day. Villagers grow most of their own

Villages like this one are home to the majority of Pakistanis. Houses are usually square in shape with flat roofs. Bread, baked in a clay oven, is a staple food.

food in the nearby fields, while other needs are supplied by local blacksmiths, potters, carpenters, barbers, and tailors.

Homes are made of local materials, such as mud, stone, or reed thatch. A typical house is square, with a flat mud roof covered by a layer of thatch and supported by wooden beams. Most homes have a veranda, or front porch, where guests are received. Sleeping rooms usually have cots of fiber woven on wooden frames. The main room is part living room and part kitchen, traditionally with a clay fireplace in the corner where meals are cooked. A farmer's house will have an outside enclosure, where cattle, farm implements, and grain are kept.

**Foods.** Bread, supplemented by vegetables and meat, is the staple food, while tea is the most commonly drunk beverage. Pilaf, or rice cooked with meat and broth, is traditionally served on ceremonial occasions. More sophisticated dishes include kebabs, or broiled meat usually cut into squares. Pakistani meat dishes consist mostly of lamb or beef. Chicken is also used. Pork is not eaten, however, because it is forbidden by Muslim religious law. A wide variety of spices are used in preparing foods.

**Dress.** Traditional dress for men in rural areas usually consists of the *pugri*, a long strip of cloth wound around the head as a turban, the *shalwar*, or baggy trousers, and a long shirt worn outside the trousers. More formal dress may include a fur hat known as a Jinnah cap (after the leader of Pakistan's independence movement, Mohammed Ali Jinnah), a long jacket called a *sherwani*, and *churidars*, or tight-fitting trousers.

Pakistani women traditionally wear the *shalwar*, together with a shirtlike garment called a *kurta* and a long scarf called a *dupatta*. Both men and women in the cities may also wear Western-style clothing.

**Holidays and Festivals.** Many holidays and festivals are religious in nature. Ramadan, the ninth month of the Muslim year, is a period of fasting and prayer. It is followed by Id-al-Fitr, a festival that breaks the fast. Id-al-Adha is a feast celebrating Abraham's offering of his son as a sacrifice to God. Those Muslims who can afford it buy a sheep to sacrifice at this time. Secular holidays include Independence Day, August 14th, and Pakistan Day, March 23rd.

▶ **THE LAND**

Pakistan shares borders with four other countries: Iran on the southwest, Afghanistan on the west and northwest, China on the northeast, and India on the east and southeast. The northeastern boundary includes the disputed territory of Jammu and Kashmir, claimed by both India and Pakistan, part of which is under Pakistani control.

**Land Regions.** Eastern Pakistan is made up largely of the great plains of the Punjab and Sind, which are drained by the Indus River and its tributaries. The Punjab and, to a lesser extent, Sind are the most heavily populated regions and, where irrigated, provide most of the country's fertile farmland. Baluchistan in the southwest is a vast, barren plateau. There are two desert areas, the Thar in the southeast and the Thal farther north. Most of the rest of Pakistan consists of rugged hills or mountains that culminate, in the far north, in the lofty, snowcapped ranges of the Hindu Kush and the Himalayas.

**Climate.** Pakistan's climate varies, depending on the season and elevation. Summers are generally quite hot, with temperatures of

---

## FACTS and figures

**ISLAMIC REPUBLIC OF PAKISTAN** is the official name of the country.

**LOCATION:** South Asia.

**AREA:** 310,402 sq mi (803,941 km$^2$).

**POPULATION:** 159,200,000 (estimate).

**CAPITAL:** Islamabad.

**LARGEST CITY:** Karachi.

**MAJOR LANGUAGES:** Urdu (official), Punjabi, Sindhi, Pashto, Baluchi, English.

**MAJOR RELIGIOUS GROUP:** Muslim.

**GOVERNMENT:** Republic. **Head of state**—president. **Head of government**—prime minister. **Legislature**—Majlis-e-Shoora (parliament), consisting of the National Assembly and Senate.

**CHIEF PRODUCTS: Agricultural**—wheat, cotton, rice, corn, millet, sugarcane, citrus fruits, livestock. **Manufactured**—cotton textiles and clothing, processed foods, chemicals, fertilizers, refined petroleum and petroleum products, machinery, iron and steel. **Mineral**—petroleum, natural gas, coal, limestone, gypsum, chromite.

**MONETARY UNIT:** Rupee (1 rupee = 100 paisa).

The lofty peaks of the Hindu Kush form part of Pakistan's northwestern border. Terraced farming is practiced in the mountain foothills to utilize all available land.

land is still forested, most of the valuable timber coming from the foothills of the Himalayas. There is a variety of wild animal life, including tigers, bears, and snow leopards, but many of these species are now endangered.

▶ THE ECONOMY

**Agriculture.** Agriculture has traditionally been the mainstay of the economy, although only about one-fifth of the land is under cultivation. Agriculture employs about half of Pakistan's workforce and provides about one-quarter of the national income. Most farms are relatively small. Their size is limited by the government, which has sought to distribute some of the larger holdings among landless peasants. The government has also encouraged farm mechanization, expanded irrigation, and the use of improved seeds in order to obtain larger crop yields.

Wheat is the basic food crop. Cotton is the main commercial crop. Rice, corn, millet, sugarcane, citrus fruits, and vegetables are also grown, with rice being an important export. Land unsuited to farming is used to graze livestock, including cattle, goats, sheep, and camels.

**Manufacturing.** The country's industry has increased greatly in recent decades, to where it now engages about one-fifth of the labor force and provides more than one-quarter of income. The chief industries are the manufacture of cotton textiles and clothing, along

120°F (49°C) not uncommon in the lower elevations, although the mountainous areas are much cooler. Winters are often cool and dry. Rainfall is limited, with most of it coming during the summer monsoon. The eastern plains receive only from 10 to 35 inches (250 to 900 millimeters) of rain a year and the northern mountains slightly more.

**Natural Resources.** Pakistan's most important mineral resources are petroleum and natural gas. It also has deposits of coal, limestone, gypsum, and chromite (chromium ore). The richest soils are in the eastern plains, but because of the arid climate, cultivation is dependent on irrigation from the Indus and its tributaries. Less than 5 percent of Pakistan's

A farmer in the North-West Frontier Province examines the remains of a sugarcane harvest. Sugarcane is one of the country's main crops.

This striking mosque, or Muslim house of worship, typifies the modern architecture of Islamabad, Pakistan's capital since 1967.

with the processing of foods and other agricultural products. Heavy industry includes the production of chemicals, fertilizers, refined petroleum and petroleum products, machinery, and iron and steel.

**Mining and Fishing.** Pakistan obtains close to half of its energy needs from its own deposits of natural gas (found chiefly in Baluchistan) and petroleum. It also exports some of its petroleum and petroleum products.

The country's long coastline on the Arabian Sea has made fishing an important economic activity. Shrimp, salmon, mullet, and mackerel are all caught in offshore waters. Some seafood is intended for domestic consumption, while the rest, shrimp in particular, is exported.

**Transportation and Trade.** Railroads linking the larger cities carry much of Pakistan's passenger and freight traffic. The national airline, Pakistan International Airlines (PIA), flies to cities within Pakistan and to countries abroad. Buses and trucks operate along Pakistan's network of highways and roads, but there are few private automobiles.

Pakistan has generally suffered from an unfavorable balance of trade, importing more than it exports. The United States is the chief market for its exports.

▶ **MAJOR CITIES**

While the great majority of the people still live in rural areas, Pakistan has a number of large cities. Several have populations of 1 million or more, and others are rapidly approaching that figure.

**Karachi**, Pakistan's largest city and former capital, is situated on the Arabian Sea. It is the country's chief port and the center of its commerce and industry. See the separate article on Karachi in Volume J-K.

**Islamabad**, Pakistan's capital since 1967, is a modern city that was designed to be the country's administrative center. It is situated in northern Pakistan, in the Himalayan foothills. **Lahore**, the second largest city and the capital of the province of Punjab, has many historical monuments, including the fort of the Emperor Akbar, the Badshahi Mosque, and the Shalimar Gardens. **Faisalabad** (formerly called Lyallpur), the third largest city, is an industrial and transportation hub. **Rawalpindi**, another major city of the Punjab and situated just a few miles south of Islamabad, served as Pakistan's interim capital until Islamabad was completed. **Hyderabad** is a principal city of the province of Sind. **Multan** is one of Pakistan's oldest cities and one of the first centers of Muslim culture in the region. **Peshawar**, capital of the North-West Frontier Province, lies

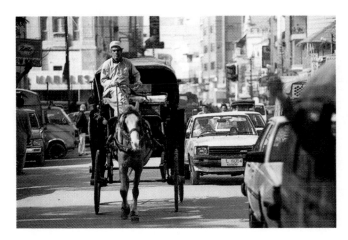

By contrast, Karachi, Pakistan's largest city, is a bustling metropolis where the old and the new exist side by side.

near the famous Khyber Pass leading into Afghanistan. **Quetta** is the capital and largest city of Baluchistan.

## ▶ GOVERNMENT

In 1999, General Pervez Musharraf, commander in chief of the army, seized power and ousted Pakistan's elected government. In 2000, Pakistan's Supreme Court validated the coup and gave Musharraf executive and legislative authority for three years from the time of the 1999 takeover. Musharraf was sworn in as president in 2001, and a revised constitution was restored in 2002.

The president serves as head of state, and a prime minister serves as head of government. The legislature, called the Majlis-e-Shoora (parliament) is made up of two houses, the Senate and the National Assembly. Senators, who serve 4-year terms, are indirectly elected by provincial legislatures. Members of the National Assembly, who also serve 4-year terms, are elected by popular vote.

## ▶ HISTORY

The early history of the region dates back to the Indus Valley civilization, which flourished more than 4,000 years ago. Its progress is still evident in the ruins of its chief cities, Mohenjo-Daro and Harappa. The two cities were first un-

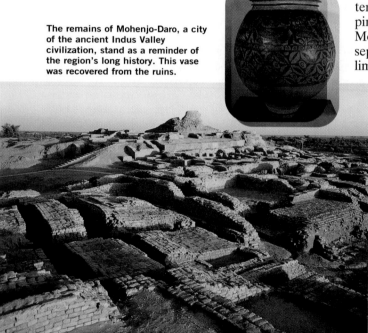

The remains of Mohenjo-Daro, a city of the ancient Indus Valley civilization, stand as a reminder of the region's long history. This vase was recovered from the ruins.

earthed in the 1900's, revealing a civilization that has been compared to those of ancient Egypt and Mesopotamia. See ANCIENT CIVILIZATIONS (Asia: Harappan Civilization) in Volume A.

In about 1500 B.C., a people known as Aryans, whose language was the ancestor of the Indo-European languages of India and Pakistan, entered the region from the north. In the centuries that followed, numerous other invaders—Persians, Greeks, Turks, Arabs, and Mongols among them—arrived in the land, leaving their mark on what would become the Pakistani people. At different times, various kingdoms and empires ruled over parts of what is now India and Pakistan.

**From Islam to British Rule.** Islam was introduced by Arab conquerors, who established themselves in Sind, in the south, in the A.D. 700's. By the early 900's, the north had also come under Muslim rule.

The last great native empire, that of the Moguls, lasted until the 1700's, when the empire came under the control of the British East India Company. In the 1850's the British government took over the Indian empire. Indian nationalism first manifested itself in the 1800's and grew into demands for complete independence from Britain in the 1900's.

**Independence.** After World War II ended in 1945, Britain announced its intention to withdraw from its Indian empire. Muslims under the leadership of Mohammed Ali Jinnah demanded a separate state of their own. The Muslims, fearful of Hindu domination under a united India, wanted their own nation with their own culture, language, and traditions.

Independence and the partition of the Indian subcontinent in 1947 saw a vast exchange of populations, as Muslims moved from their homes in India into Pakistan and Hindus living in Pakistan migrated to India. This large-scale movement of peoples created a host of problems for the new nation. Later, Muslim and Hindu religious riots further hindered the government's attempt to maintain order and improve living conditions in both East and West Pakistan. Also, tensions between

Mohammed Ali Jinnah (far right), the father of Pakistan's independence and its first governor-general, is seen in 1947 with Britain's Lord Mountbatten (center) and India's Jawaharlal Nehru (far left).

Pakistan and India over the state of Jammu and Kashmir ultimately brought about a series of wars. This political instability led to a military takeover by General Mohammed Ayub Khan in 1958. But by 1969, the people were rioting for a return to direct elections, and Ayub Khan was forced to resign. He was succeeded by General Agha Mohammed Yahya Khan.

**Civil War.** Although they shared a common religion, Islam, East and West Pakistanis were dissimilar in many ways, notably in language and ethnic origin. The country began to break up in 1970, with the elections for the National Assembly. Most of the seats allotted to East Pakistan were won by the Awami League, which favored local self-government. When the government postponed the opening of the National Assembly, strikes broke out in East Pakistan. Troops were sent to put down what the government believed was a separatist movement, and a civil war ensued.

In 1971, India joined the war on the side of East Pakistan and quickly defeated the West Pakistani forces. East Pakistan then declared itself the independent nation of Bangladesh. Yahya Khan resigned and was replaced by Zulfikar Ali Bhutto, who became prime minister in 1973. But continuing political turmoil and the breakdown of law and order led to a military coup in 1977 headed by General Mohammed Zia ul-Haq. Bhutto, convicted of involvement in the murder of a political opponent, was executed in 1979.

**Recent History.** In 1988, Bhutto's daughter, Benazir, succeeded Zia as prime minister, but she was removed from office in 1990 on charges of corruption. Her Pakistan People's Party was later defeated by the Islamic Democratic Alliance, led by Nawaz Sharif. In 1993, Bhutto and her party were returned to power, but she was again dismissed in 1996. Sharif returned as prime minister in 1997. Soon after, the president's right to dismiss elected governments was eliminated.

In 1998, Pakistan conducted nuclear tests. Regional tensions mounted in 1999 when the army, led by General Pervez Musharraf, ousted the elected government and seized power. He dissolved parliament, suspended the constitution, and in 2001 declared himself president as well as head of the army.

Pakistan was greatly affected when the United States declared war on terrorism, aiming its first strikes against terrorists in neighboring Afghanistan. Despite anti-American demonstrations, Musharraf strongly supported the United States' efforts to bring the terrorists to justice while Pakistan absorbed huge numbers of Afghan refugees. Meanwhile, tensions with India grew over the disputed region of Kashmir, and militant attacks raised the possibility of another war until India initiated peace talks in 2003.

In a national referendum in 2002, Musharraf was granted a 5-year term as president. He redrafted Pakistan's constitution, which greatly expanded his powers at the expense of parliament. That October, the first free and fair parliamentary elections since the 1999 coup were held.

In 2004, parliament passed a bill allowing Musharraf to keep his post as army chief, despite an earlier promise he had made to opponents that he would step down. Supporters claimed the move would strengthen the country's ability to fight terrorism.

On October 8, 2005, a violent earthquake struck the Pakistani-controlled region of Kashmir. More than 74,000 Pakistanis were killed and tens of thousands were injured.

Reviewed by KHALID BIN SAYEED
Author, *Politics in Pakistan*

See also BANGLADESH; BHUTTO, BENAZIR; BHUTTO, ZULFIKAR ALI; INDIA (History); JINNAH, MOHAMMED ALI; KASHMIR.

# PALAU

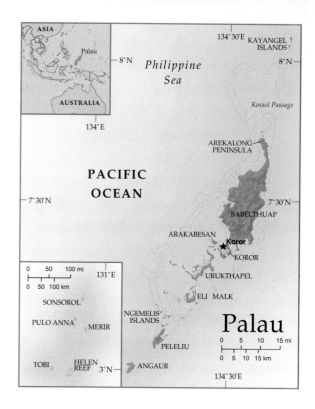

The Republic of Palau is an island nation situated in the northwestern Pacific Ocean. It consists of more than 200 islands and islets making up the western end of the Caroline Islands chain. Most of the islands are small, and only about eight of the larger ones are permanently inhabited. Palau was the last of the territories administered by the United States as part of the United Nations Trust Territory of the Pacific Islands. In 1994 it gained independence in free association with the United States.

**The People.** Palau has a population of about 16,000. The Palauans are chiefly Micronesians. Physically, they are generally of medium height, brown-skinned, with wavy or curly hair. Filipinos make up the largest ethnic minority. The official languages are Palauan and English. Most Palauans are Christians, primarily Roman Catholics.

**The Land and Climate.** Palau has a land area of about 192 square miles (497 square kilometers). Most of the islands are coral, while others are of volcanic origin. Nearly all the islands lie within an extensive barrier reef. Babelthuap, the largest and highest of the volcanic islands, makes up about three-quarters of Palau's total land area. The most populous island is Koror, which has about two-thirds of the country's people and is the site of the interim capital, Koror.

The climate is warm and humid. Monthly temperatures average about 80°F (27°C). Rainfall is heavy, with Koror receiving about 150 inches (3,800 millimeters) a year.

**The Economy.** The Palauans have traditionally relied on subsistence agriculture and fishing for their livelihood. The country's deposits of phosphates, its only mineral resource, have been exhausted. At present the government is the largest employer and depends on financial aid from the United States. Money sent home by Palauans living and working abroad is another important source of income. Hopes for the future rest on increasing tourism and the leasing of Palau's fishing grounds to other countries.

**History and Government.** The first Europeans to visit Palau were the Spanish, who arrived in the 1500's. The islands remained a possession of Spain until 1899, when they were sold to Germany. At the outbreak of World War I in 1914, they were occupied by Japan, which governed them after the war under a mandate from the League of Nations. The islands fell to the United States in 1944, during World War II. In 1947, Palau was made a U.S. trust territory by the United Nations. Negotiations for Palauan independence were complicated by a non-nuclear clause in its constitution, adopted in 1980. The United States' offer of a Compact of Free Association, which would allow nuclear materials to enter the country, was finally approved by Palauans in 1993. Independence took effect in 1994. Under the Compact, the United States provides financial aid to Palau and is responsible for its defense.

The government consists of a president and legislature, the National Congress, which is made up of the Senate and House of Delegates. The president and Congress are elected for 4-year terms.

WARD BARRETT
University of Minnesota

# PALESTINE

Palestine is a historic region in southwestern Asia. It is situated at the eastern end of the Mediterranean Sea and forms part of the larger region known as the Middle East. Strategically located at a crossroads between East and West and near where Africa and Asia meet, Palestine has been the site of countless invasions and movements of peoples. It is, moreover, the land of the Bible and is considered holy by three major religions—Judaism, Christianity, and Islam. Few regions of such relatively small size have been so bitterly fought over through the centuries.

The word "Palestine" comes from "Philistine," the name for one of its early peoples. The Roman province in this region was known as Syria Palestina. Palestine's boundaries have varied widely over its long history. Although it once extended over a wider area, it is generally thought of today as the geographical region extending from the Sinai Peninsula on the south to Lebanon and Syria on the north and from the Mediterranean Sea on the west to the Jordan River and the Dead Sea on the east.

The article that follows provides a brief historical overview of Palestine.

## ▶ THE HEBREWS AND JUDAISM

Palestine has been inhabited since prehistoric times. In about 2000 B.C., the Hebrews, a nomadic people then living in Mesopotamia (modern Iraq), began their migration to the land of Canaan, as Palestine was then known. The twelve Hebrew tribes were united under their first king, Saul, to form the kingdom of Israel, and they eventually controlled most of the region. In about 1000 B.C., Saul's successor, David, made the city of Jerusalem his capital. Israel reached the height of its power under King Solomon, son of David, but after his death in 922 B.C., it was divided into two rival kingdoms—Israel in the north and Judah in the south. (The term "Jew," which

**Ancient Palestine**

originally applied only to a Hebrew of Judah, eventually came to be used in referring to any Hebrew.)

Weakened by internal quarrels, the two kingdoms fell prey to stronger neighbors. In the 700's B.C., Israel was conquered by the Assyrians and its people were dispersed. Judah survived until the 500's B.C., when it fell to the Babylonians and many of its inhabitants were forced into exile. The Babylonians were succeeded by the Persians, under whom the Jews were allowed to return, and the Persians by the Greek and Macedonian armies of Alexander the Great. After Alexander's death in 323 B.C., his followers founded kingdoms in Egypt and Syria, which ruled Palestine in turn. Attempts by the Seleucid rulers of Syria to introduce Greek religious practices into the region in 167 B.C. provoked the Jews to revolt. After a long struggle led by Judah Maccabee and his brothers, they re-established an independent Jewish kingdom, which lasted until 63 B.C.

## ▶ ROME AND CHRISTIANITY

From 63 B.C. to about A.D. 630, Palestine was part of first the Roman and then the Byzantine empires. During the reign of Herod the Great, who ruled Judea (the Roman name for Judah) as a Roman protectorate, Jesus was born in the town of Bethlehem. It marked the humble beginning of what would become Christianity and eventually spread throughout the Roman world.

Roman rule over Palestine led to repeated Jewish revolts. The first, from 66 to 73, resulted in the destruction of the Temple in Jerusalem, the center of Jewish worship, along with much of the city itself. A second revolt broke out in 115 and a third in 132. The last, led by Simon Bar Cocheba (or Bar Kokhba), while at first successful, was eventually put down with great harshness. An independent Jewish nation would not appear again in the region for more than 1,800 years.

### ▶ THE ARABS AND ISLAM

Shortly after 630, a powerful new force erupted out of the deserts of the Arabian Peninsula. The Arabs, united under the banner of Islam, the religion of the Muslims, swiftly conquered Palestine, along with most of the rest of the Middle East. Jews and Christians continued to live in Palestine, but Muslim Arabs became the dominant people of the region. Since Islam shared some of its traditions with the two earlier religions and Muslims believed that their prophet, Mohammed, had ascended to heaven from Jerusalem, Palestine became a holy land for them as well.

For most of the centuries that followed, Palestine remained under the rule of one or another Muslim dynasty. The exception was a period during the 1100's, when European Crusaders ruled Jerusalem and other small states in the region.

Palestine was the birthplace of three great religions—Judaism, Christianity, and Islam. An elderly Jew (*above*) prays at the Western Wall, the remnant of the ancient Temple in Jerusalem and Judaism's most sacred site. A cross is borne by a clergyman of the Greek Orthodox Church (*left*), one of the region's Christian denominations. Muslim women (*below left*) gather before Jerusalem's Dome of the Rock, an Islamic holy place.

In the 1500's, Palestine became part of the empire of the Ottoman Turks and remained so until the 1900's.

### ▶ ZIONISM AND ARAB NATIONALISM

In the late 1800's and early 1900's, two nationalist movements—both involving Palestine—began to develop. The first was Zionism, which sought to re-establish a Jewish homeland in the region. From the 1880's on, considerable numbers of Jews from Europe settled in Palestine. A separate Arab nationalist movement, begun not long after, had as its aim independence from Ottoman rule. Arab nationalism was not focused specifically on Palestine, as Zionism was, but considered it part of the larger Arab community.

To this was added the role played by Britain, which sought the aid of both Arabs and Jews during World War I. In 1917, British forces occupied Palestine. That same year the British government issued the Balfour Declaration (named for Arthur J. Balfour, then the British foreign secretary). It pledged support for a Jewish homeland in Palestine while acknowledging the rights of its non-Jewish population. Arab leaders also claimed that Britain had promised to make Palestine part of an independent Arab state. These competing aspirations and claims set the stage for the clash between Jews and Arabs over the region that continues to the present day.

### ▶ THE BRITISH MANDATE

After World War I ended in 1918, the Ottoman Empire was broken apart, its core becoming the republic of Turkey. Palestine itself was placed under British administration in 1922 as a mandate of the League of Nations, the forerunner of the United Nations. The mandate also included land east of the Jordan River, where Britain established the state of Transjordan (now Jordan) in 1923.

Arab opposition to Zionist aims led to violent incidents in the 1920's. These grew worse during the 1930's, as increasing numbers of Jews, fleeing Nazi persecution in Europe, arrived in Palestine. Britain was increasingly hard-pressed to contain what had become an Arab rebellion. In 1939, just before the outbreak of World War II, the British government proposed the creation, within ten years, of an independent Palestine, composed of both Arabs and Jews but maintaining an Arab majority. Jewish immigration was to be limited and would end entirely within five years, unless approved by the Arabs. Both sides rejected the plan.

The murder of millions of European Jews by Nazi Germany during World War II intensified Zionist efforts to win a Palestinian homeland. After the war's end in 1945, the Jewish population swelled with the arrival of concentration camp survivors. Because of the immigration restrictions imposed by Britain, many of these refugees were smuggled into Palestine by Jewish underground groups, some of which used guerrilla warfare, sabotage, and terrorist tactics against the British forces.

### ▶ PARTITION

In 1947 the British, unable to find a solution acceptable to both sides, turned the issue of Palestine over to the United Nations, which voted to partition the region into separate Jewish and Arab states. Jerusalem was to be an international city, administered by the United Nations. The Jews of Palestine and Zionists elsewhere generally accepted this decision. Palestinian Arabs and Arab nationalists almost universally opposed it.

As the British prepared to depart, the new Jewish state of Israel was proclaimed on May 14, 1948. It was invaded almost immediately by armies of neighboring Arab countries, beginning the first Arab-Israeli war. When the war ended in 1949, Israel had not only

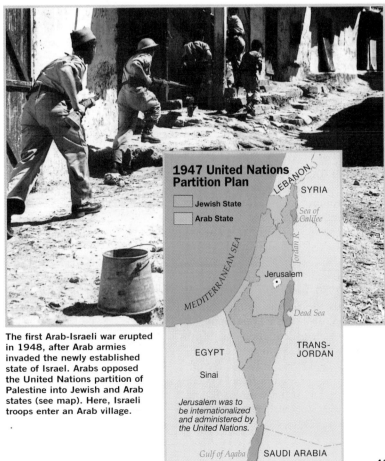

The first Arab-Israeli war erupted in 1948, after Arab armies invaded the newly established state of Israel. Arabs opposed the United Nations partition of Palestine into Jewish and Arab states (see map). Here, Israeli troops enter an Arab village.

**1947 United Nations Partition Plan**

Jewish State

Arab State

LEBANON
SYRIA
Sea of Galilee
Jordan R.
MEDITERRANEAN SEA
Jerusalem
Dead Sea
EGYPT
TRANS-JORDAN
Sinai

*Jerusalem was to be internationalized and administered by the United Nations.*

Gulf of Aqaba    SAUDI ARABIA

## THE WEST BANK AND THE GAZA STRIP

The West Bank and the Gaza Strip are parts of the territory allotted to the Arabs by the United Nations when, in 1947, it partitioned Palestine into separate Arab and Jewish states.

The West Bank takes its name from its location on the western side of the Jordan River. It has an area of about 2,263 square miles (5,860 square kilometers) and a mostly Arab population of about 2.3 million. It produces citrus fruits, vegetables, olives, and beef and dairy cattle.

Historically, the region included ancient Samaria and Judea (Judah), and it has many sites of religious interest to Jews, Christians, and Muslims. Towns include Hebron, Nablus, Jericho, and Bethlehem. The region was occupied by Transjordan (now Jordan) during the 1948–49 Arab-Israeli war, and in the 1967 war it came under Israeli control. In 1996, West Bank Palestinians gained a degree of self-rule. But when conflicts again erupted, Israel began to reoccupy some of the Arab-ruled areas.

The Gaza Strip is a small, narrow territory, situated on the Mediterranean coast, north of the Sinai Peninsula. It has an area of about 147 square miles (380 square kilometers) and a population of nearly 2 million, about two-thirds Arab and one-third Israeli. Gaza is the main city. The region fell to Egypt during the 1948–49 war and was occupied by Israel in the 1967 war. It has been governed since 1996 by the Palestinian National Authority (PNA).

---

successfully defended itself but had won additional territory as well. During the fighting, Transjordan occupied the West Bank, the region west of the Jordan River (subsequently changing its name to Jordan), and Egypt took over the Gaza Strip. Both were areas that had been allotted to a Palestinian Arab state. The war left Jerusalem divided between Israel and Jordan. Large numbers of Palestinian Arabs fled from Israeli to Arab territory, particularly the West Bank and the Gaza Strip.

▶ **EFFORTS TOWARD PEACE**

The question of a Palestinian Arab state has remained one of the main causes of hostility between Israel and the Arab countries. Three more Arab-Israeli wars followed—in 1956, 1967, and 1973. During the 1967 war, Israel gained control of the West Bank, all of Jerusalem, the Gaza Strip, and the Sinai peninsula of Egypt, as well as Syria's Golan Heights. Israel's occupation of the West Bank and the Gaza Strip brought large numbers of Palestinian Arabs under its control. Israel returned the Sinai following a peace treaty with Egypt concluded in 1979. The treaty also discussed, in general terms, the possibility of a Palestinian Arab state in the West Bank and Gaza, but there was no agreement on how the state would be set up and governed.

Palestinian Arab nationalism, meanwhile, found expression in militant guerrilla organizations. Most were included in an overall body, the Palestine Liberation Organization (PLO), headed by Yasir Arafat. The PLO was eventually accepted by Arab countries as the "sole legitimate representative of the Palestinian people" and was granted observer status by the United Nations. Although the diverse groups had different aims, most shared the goal of replacing Israel with a predominantly Arab state.

Israeli opinion on the Palestinian question has been mixed. Some Israelis have been willing to trade

**Palestine Today**

☐ Administered by the Palestinian Authority
☐ Occupied by Israel

LEBANON
Damascus
SYRIA
Sea of Galilee
GOLAN HEIGHTS
Haifa
MEDITERRANEAN SEA
Jordan R.
WEST BANK
Tel Aviv-Jaffa
Jericho
Amman
Jerusalem
Gaza
GAZA STRIP
Dead Sea
EGYPT
JORDAN
Sinai

*Under the 1993 and 1995 accords, the Palestinian Authority has increasing self-rule in the West Bank.*

Gulf of Aqaba
SAUDI ARABIA

Yasir Arafat (left), chairman of the Palestine Liberation Organization (PLO), and Israeli prime minister Yitzhak Rabin signed historic accords in 1993 and 1995.

West Bank city of Jericho. In 1996 the Arabs elected a self-ruling Palestinian National Authority (PNA), headed by Arafat. But when the 2000 deadline for a final accord was not met, Arab extremists renewed attacks on Israel.

In 2003 the United States proposed a "road map" for peace, calling for Palestinian statehood by 2005. But renewed violence ended negotiations.

Arafat died on November 11, 2004. Mahmoud Abbas succeeded him as chairman of the PLO, and his election as president of the PNA in 2005 led to a new era of peace talks with Israel. In 2005, Israel withdrew all its settlers from Gaza and some from the West Bank. Palestine also took control over the border crossings from Gaza into Egypt and Israel.

JAMES JANKOWSKI
Coauthor, *The Middle East:
A Social Geography*

See also ARABS; ARAFAT, YASIR; ISRAEL; JERUSALEM; ZIONISM.

territory for peace; others have opposed a Palestinian Arab state, fearing that it would mean the elimination of Israel.

In 1987, Arabs in the Gaza Strip launched an uprising against Israeli occupation that soon spread to the West Bank. In 1993, Israel and the PLO signed a historic agreement giving Arabs self-rule in the Gaza Strip and the

---

## PALESTRINA, GIOVANNI PIERLUIGI DA (1525?–1594)

Giovanni Pierluigi, called Palestrina after the Italian town where he was born, was a great composer of Roman Catholic church music. He was born about 1525 and began his musical training in the choir of the local cathedral. He later became a choirboy at the Church of Santa Maria Maggiore in Rome.

In 1544, Palestrina was appointed organist and choirmaster at the cathedral in his hometown. In 1551, when the bishop there became Pope Julius III, he made the composer choir director of the Julian Chapel at St. Peter's Basilica. Several years later, Palestrina dedicated his first book of masses to Pope Julius. In appreciation, Julius made him a member of the papal choir, which sang in the Sistine Chapel. But in 1555 the new pope, Paul IV, declared that married men could no longer sing in the choir. Because Palestrina had married in 1547, he was dismissed.

During the next 16 years, Palestrina held several posts in Rome and published many masses and motets—sacred choral compositions based on Latin texts. In 1571 he resumed his post as choirmaster of the Julian

Chapel. Pope Gregory XIII gave him the title Master of Music at the Vatican Basilica.

All of Palestrina's music was written to be sung without instrumental accompaniment. One of his best-known works is the mass *Missa Papae Marcelli*, published in 1567.

In 1580, Palestrina's wife and several other family members died during a severe outbreak of disease. Upset by these tragedies, Palestrina thought of becoming a priest. But in 1581 he married a wealthy widow, enabling him to publish many compositions. His works include more than 100 masses, some 375 motets, and about 150 madrigals. (Madrigals are musical compositions for several voices, based on non-religious texts.)

Palestrina remained at St. Peter's until his death on February 2, 1594. He was buried in a side chapel of the old basilica. The inscription on his casket reads, "Prince of Music."

Reviewed by JON GILLOCK
The Juilliard School

**PALLADIO, ANDREA.** See RENAISSANCE (Profiles).

**PALMER, ARNOLD.** See GOLF (Great Players).

# PANAMA

Panama is a small nation of Central America. It occupies the narrowest part of Central America (known as the Isthmus of Panama), where it joins South America. The isthmus narrowly separates the Caribbean Sea, an arm of the Atlantic Ocean, from the Pacific Ocean.

Panama's shape and geographical location have played an important role in its history. For its earliest inhabitants, American Indians, Panama was a land bridge between North and South America. To Spanish colonists, who first arrived in the region in the 1500's, it was a short overland route between the Atlantic and Pacific oceans. The construction of the Panama Canal, linking the two oceans, in the early 1900's, greatly enhanced Panama's importance. (An article on the Panama Canal follows this article.)

## ▶THE PEOPLE

As a people, the Panamanians have been strongly affected by living in a country that is a crossroads of the world. Their character and culture, however, have been formed by a variety of influences.

**Origins.** Panamanians are descended from three main ethnic groups: American Indians, Europeans, and black Africans. Only a small minority of Indians remain. Most live in isolated regions—the Guaymí in the northwestern mountains, the Kuna (or Cuna) on the coastal islands of the northeast, and the Chocó in the rain forests of Darién.

Many of the Spaniards who settled in Panama intermarried with the Indians. Their mixed-race descendants (*mestizos*) now make up the country's largest ethnic group. Blacks originally were imported from Africa as slaves. Later, other blacks came from the West Indies to work on the Panama Canal. The building of the canal also brought smaller numbers of people from other European countries, from North America, and from the Middle East, India, and China. Racial harmony is the rule, although antagonisms exist.

**Language and Religion.** All Panamanians speak Spanish, the official language. English is also used widely, particularly by people of West Indian and North American origin. Panama has the largest share of English-speaking inhabitants in Latin America. Indians speak their native languages among themselves, but learn Spanish to deal with outsiders or when seeking work away from their own regions.

Roman Catholicism, brought by the Spaniards, is the religion of most of the people. Many other faiths, however, are practiced freely. Panamanians of West Indian origin are largely Protestant. Most Indians prefer to follow their traditional religions. There also are small Hindu, Buddhist, and Jewish communities. Religious freedom is guaranteed under the Panamanian constitution.

**Education.** Panamanians take pride in their school system. The government devotes a considerable part of its budget to education. As a result, the literacy rate (the number of people able to read and write) is about 90 percent. The University of Panama, founded in 1935, enrolls students from all over the country. Many Panamanians also study at universities abroad.

**Way of Life.** The Panamanian way of life is a mixture of several cultures. The centuries-old Spanish tradition prevails in language, architecture, family life, food, and in many

The Panama Railroad (*above*) crosses the narrow but rugged Isthmus of Panama. Much of the land is covered with dense rain forests. Indians, like this Kuna girl (*left*), were Panama's earliest inhabitants. *Mestizos*, or people of mixed Indian and European ancestry, such as these sidewalk vendors (*opposite page*), are the largest ethnic group.

leisure activities. As in other Latin American countries, the holidays of Carnival and Christmas dominate the calendar, and each town celebrates its saint's day in the Spanish manner. The traditional dress worn during these festivals comes from Spain, as does the music, particularly the *tamborito* ("little drum"), the national dance. It is performed by couples accompanied by drummers and a hand clapping audience. A relatively few Panamanians, often well-to-do, proudly trace their ancestry back to Spain.

Many other cultural influences can also be seen in Panamanian daily life. Baseball, introduced by Americans, draws as many fans as soccer. The large American community also contributed french fries, rock music, and mini-skirts. The West Indies brought the calypso music of the African-American and Caribbean culture. The Indians gave Panama many of its handicrafts and certain foods, including plan-

tains (a kind of banana) and potatoes. Other immigrant groups brought elements of their own way of life, adding great variety to the country's life-style and outlook.

## ▶ THE LAND

Panama is shaped roughly like the letter "S" laid on its side. It is bordered on the north by the Caribbean Sea, on the east by the South American nation of Colombia, on the south by the Pacific Ocean, and on the west by the Central American country of Costa Rica.

**Overview.** Mountain ranges form a backbone stretching nearly the entire length of the country. The highest point is Barú, an inactive volcano near the Costa Rican border, which rises to 11,401 feet (3,476 meters). At its narrowest point, just east of the canal, the isthmus measures only some 32 miles (51 kilometers) across. Its mountains divide Panama into distinctive Caribbean and Pacific regions. The plains and valleys have moderately fertile soil. Less than one quarter of the land, however, is suitable for farming.

**Climate and Vegetation.** Panama has a tropical climate, with generally warm, humid days and cool nights. Temperatures vary little throughout the year, averaging about 81° F (26° C) on the coasts, but less in the mountains. Rainfall is considerable but seasonal. It falls heaviest on the Caribbean coast, which

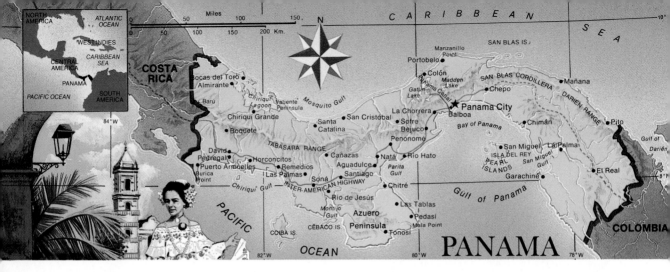

receives about 128 inches (3,250 millimeters) a year. The Pacific coastal region receives about half that amount.

Jungle and tropical rain forests cover much of Panama. The Caribbean area and Darién, the eastern region of Panama, are the most densely forested. They are sparsely inhabited, mainly by Indians. Parts of the Pacific region consist of savanna, or thinly wooded grassland. This was the chief area of settlement by the Spanish.

**Natural Resources.** Panama has large deposits of copper and smaller amounts of coal, manganese, zinc, gold, and silver, although its mineral resources are still largely undeveloped. The forests of Darién have been a source of mahogany and other hardwoods, and the surrounding waters abound in fish and other seafood. By far, however, the country's most important natural resource is its narrow shape, which favored the building of the Panama Canal.

▶ **ECONOMY**

Panama's largest economic enterprise is the Panama Canal. Fees received for the use of the canal help to offset Panama's trade deficit.

**Agriculture.** About one quarter of the work force is engaged in farming. The majority of Panamanian farms are small. Farmers grow such basic food crops as rice, corn, beans, and potatoes for their own use and for sale in nearby towns or in cities. The main commercial crops—bananas, sugarcane, and coffee—are grown on plantations. Bananas are the country's chief export. Panama is self-sufficient in some foods, but it must import others. Cattle are raised in the southwest.

**Fishing and Forestry.** Fishing plays an important role in the economy. Exports of shrimp, in particular, are a leading source of income. Much of the shrimp is now harvested in saltwater "farms."

Some logging is carried out in the Darién region. But the government has temporarily limited the felling of trees to allow the regrowth of valuable hardwoods.

**Manufacturing and Services.** Panama is too small a country to support large-scale industries. Its major industry is oil refining and the processing of petroleum products. Processed foods, construction materials, clothing, and shoes are other manufactured products.

## FACTS and figures

**REPUBLIC OF PANAMA** (República de Panamá) is the official name of the country.

**LOCATION:** Central America.

**AREA:** 29,761 sq mi (77,082 km²).

**POPULATION:** 2,800,000 (estimate).

**CAPITAL AND LARGEST CITY:** Panama City.

**MAJOR LANGUAGES:** Spanish (official), English.

**MAJOR RELIGION:** Roman Catholic.

**GOVERNMENT:** Republic. **Head of state and government**—president. **Legislature**—Legislative Assembly.

**CHIEF PRODUCTS: Agriculture**—rice, sugarcane, bananas, corn, beans, coffee, cattle and other livestock. **Manufactured**—Refined petroleum and petroleum products, processed foods (including refined sugar, fish and shrimp), clothing, shoes, construction materials. **Mineral**—copper, gold, silver, manganese.

**MONETARY UNIT:** Balboa (1 balboa = 100 centésimos).

The Colón Free Zone is one of the world's largest free-trade areas. Here, raw materials and partly finished goods can be imported and transformed into finished products for export without payment of duties (taxes).

Important service industries include banking, inexpensive ship registry, and other commercial activities. The Panama Canal, as one of the world's great engineering feats, also attracts tourists.

**Transportation.** Two main highways link Panama's cities. The Inter-American Highway runs from Costa Rica to Panama City and on to Chepo, where it has stopped due to the difficulty and cost of construction in the dense Darién rain forests. The Trans-Isthmian Highway runs parallel to the canal and links Panama City and Colón. The two cities are also joined by a railroad. Tocumen airport near Panama City is a center of air transportation between the Caribbean and South America.

▶ **MAJOR CITIES**

Panama City is the commercial and cultural heart of the country as well as its capital and largest city. It is situated on the Bay of Panama, near the Pacific end of the Panama Canal. The population of the city proper is more than 400,000, with a much larger number of people living in its metropolitan area. Virtually all of the nation's business is conducted here. The city's architecture varies from Spanish colonial, in the old district, to modern high-rise in the newer areas.

The modern section of Panama City, Panama's capital and largest city, juts out into the Bay of Panama on the Pacific Ocean. The original city, or Old Panama, was founded by the Spanish in 1519. The present city dates from 1673. A statue of the Spanish explorer Vasco Núñez de Balboa stands in Panama City, overlooking the Pacific. Balboa crossed the Isthmus of Panama in 1513 and was the first European to see the Pacific Ocean.

The original city, or Old Panama, was founded by the Spanish in 1519, and soon became an important port. It was destroyed by pirates in 1671, and the present city was established, a few miles away, in 1673.

Colón, the second largest city, lies at the Caribbean end of the canal. It was founded in 1851 as the northern station of the Panama Railroad. Colón's docks and warehouses serve ships using the Panama Canal. The city grew in importance after a free-trade zone was established here in 1948.

Panama's provincial cities, such as David, Santiago, Penonomé, and La Chorrera, are quiet and attractive places rarely visited by tourists. They are situated in a part of the country that Panamanians call the interior.

## GOVERNMENT

Panama is a republic. Its government is based on a 1972 constitution, amended in 1983. The president, who is head of state and government, is elected (together with two vice presidents) for a 5-year term. The law-making body is the Legislative Assembly, which is also elected for five years. The judiciary (court system) is headed by the Supreme Court, whose nine members are appointed by the president. At various times in Panama's history, the military has exercised considerable power in the government.

## HISTORY

**Colonial Era.** The Indians who inhabited the region put up little resistance to the Spanish when they arrived in the isthmus in 1501. After Vasco Núñez de Balboa crossed Panama and reached the Pacific Ocean in 1513, ports were established on both coasts. (See the article on Balboa in Volume B.)

Panama enjoyed a golden age in the 1600's, as silver from Peru was transported across the isthmus for shipment to Spain. Panama declined in importance in the 1700's, and after 1740 it was governed as part of the Spanish colony of New Granada (which included modern Colombia).

**Union with Colombia.** When the wars of independence broke out in Latin America in the 1800's, Panama at first remained loyal to Spain. After Colombia won independence in 1821, however, Panama joined the Colombian union. For the next 82 years, Panama was Colombia's most troublesome province. Several times Panama broke away from Colombia. Each time it was brought back by military force.

In the 1880's a French company tried to build a canal across Panama. It failed, but in the 1890's interest grew in the United States for the construction of such a canal.

**Independence and a Canal.** Colombia at first encouraged purchase of the canal rights by the United States. But in 1903 it rejected the U.S. terms of a canal treaty as inadequate. At this point, on November 3, 1903, Panama declared its independence. U.S. president Theodore Roosevelt sent warships to the area to prevent Colombia from suppressing the revolt. Soon after, the United States and Panama signed the Hay-Bunau-Varilla Treaty of 1903. Under its terms, the United States guaranteed Panama's independence in return for rights to build a canal. In 1904, Panama adopted its first constitution. Construction of the canal was begun that same year. The waterway was opened in 1914.

**Modern History.** Much of Panama's later history revolved around the struggle to gain more benefits for Panamanians from the canal. These years often were marked by political instability. One president, Arnulfo Arias, who first won office in 1940, was elected to the presidency several times. Each time he was deposed by the military. Arias was removed from office for the last time in 1968 by General Omar Torrijos, head of the National Guard, the Panamanian armed forces. Under Torrijos, Panama and the United States signed new canal treaties in 1977, under which ownership of the canal passed to Panama at the end of 1999.

Torrijos died in 1981. In 1983, General Manuel Antonio Noriega became commander of the armed forces, giving him control over the government. Although several civilian presidents were elected, real power rested with Noriega. The United States cooperated with him at first but later used diplomatic and, finally, military means to oust him. Captured by U.S. troops in 1989, he was taken to the United States and tried for drug trafficking.

U.S. troops deposed Panama's military ruler, General Manuel Noriega, in 1990. Many Panamanians welcomed Noriega's overthrow.

Meanwhile, a new government was sworn in, headed by Guillermo Endara, whose earlier election had been nullified by Noriega. In 1994, Endara was succeeded as president by Ernesto Pérez Balladares. In the 1999 election, Balladares was defeated by Mireya Moscoso, the widow of former president Arias and Panama's first woman president. In 2004, Martin Torrijos, son of the former dictator, was elected president.

MICHAEL L. CONNIFF
University of New Mexico

## PANAMA CANAL

The Panama Canal is a waterway built across the Isthmus of Panama in Central America, connecting the Atlantic and Pacific oceans. Before the canal was opened in 1914, ships traveling between the two oceans had to make a long voyage around the southern tip of South America. The canal shortened the interocean journey by more than 7,000 miles (11,200 kilometers). Upon its completion, the canal was hailed as one of the world's engineering marvels.

The Panama Canal was built by the United States under a treaty signed with the Republic of Panama in 1903. Under the treaty, the United States operated the canal with little participation by Panama. New treaties were signed by the two countries in 1977. They provided for Panamanian cooperation in running the canal until its ownership was transferred to Panama at the end of 1999.

**Description.** The Panama Canal has a length of 51 miles (82 kilometers). It extends from the Caribbean Sea, a part of the Atlantic Ocean, on the northwest to the Pacific Ocean on the southeast. The canal follows an irregular path, taking advantage of natural features of the land.

Ships cross the canal through a system of locks. These are large open chambers, made of concrete, with a gate at each end. Each lock is 1,000 feet (305 meters) long and 110 feet (33 meters) wide. Their function is to raise and lower ships from one level of the canal to another. Ships are raised by flooding locks with water, and lowered by emptying them. The locks are built in pairs, so that ships can pass in both directions.

**Route.** A ship entering the canal on the Atlantic side crosses Limón Bay, near the town of Cristóbal and the city of Colón, and passes into a channel. It is then raised by locks 85 feet (26 meters) to the surface of Gatun Lake, a vast lake created by the

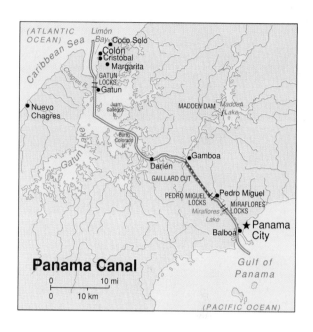

Panama Canal

damming of the Chagres River. In addition to Gatun, another artificial lake, Miraflores, forms part of the canal.

The ship follows the old Chagres River valley until it is about halfway across the canal. It then enters another channel, the Gaillard Cut, which takes it through the Continental Divide, the highest mountains on the canal route. Finally, the ship is lowered, by the Pedro Miguel and Miraflores locks, to the level of the Pacific Ocean. The town of Balboa marks the Pacific terminus of the canal. The crossing takes about eight hours.

**Economic Importance.** By reducing the cost of interocean shipping, the canal has long played a vital role in world commerce. On average, some 12,000 ships pass through the canal each year. The United States uses the canal more than any other country. Under the 1977 treaties, Panama received about $50 to $60 million a year for use of the canal. Its economy also benefited from wages paid to Panamanians employed by the canal.

Ships cross the canal through locks, which raise and lower them from one level to another. The locks are in pairs, so that ships can pass in both directions.

The first important step toward the goal of creating a canal came in 1855, with the completion of the Panama Railroad. The railroad made it easier to cross the narrow but rugged isthmus.

In 1881 a French company headed by Ferdinand de Lesseps attempted to build a canal across Panama. De Lesseps, who earlier had built the Suez Canal, sought to construct a similar sea-level canal at Panama. He did not foresee the difficulty and cost that this would involve, and in 1889 De Lesseps' company went bankrupt.

(See the article on De Lesseps in Volume L, and the article on the Suez Canal in Volume S.)

**U.S. Interest.** The French failure renewed the interest of the United States in building a canal across Central America. Two sites were considered—Nicaragua and Panama. The Panama site eventually was chosen, and in 1902 the U.S. Congress approved purchase of the French canal rights. As Panama was then a part of Colombia, the United States negotiated a treaty with the Colombian government. The Hay-Herrán Treaty was signed in 1903, but it was rejected by the Colombian legislature as unfavorable to Colombia.

**Panamanian Independence.** Soon after Colombia's rejection of the treaty, Panama declared its independence on November 3, 1903. The independence movement was supported

Although the Panama Canal is still an important waterway, it can no longer handle the largest ships now in use. The United States and Panama have studied ways to improve service. Panama already has an oil pipeline, the Trans-Panamanian pipeline, which bypasses the canal altogether. This has reduced the need for oil tankers to use the canal. Other possible changes include a third set of locks and a new sea-level canal, which would make locks unnecessary. Any new canal project would need the approval of both countries.

**The Dream of a Canal.** The dream of building a canal across Panama dates from 1513, when the Spanish explorer Vasco Núñez de Balboa crossed the region from the Atlantic Ocean to the Pacific Ocean. The first European to see the Pacific, Balboa also discovered that only a narrow neck of land—the Isthmus of Panama—separated the two oceans.

by U.S. president Theodore Roosevelt, who dispatched warships to Panamanian waters to prevent the landing of Colombian troops and soon recognized the new nation. Two weeks later, the United States and Panama signed the Hay-Bunau-Varilla Treaty.

**The 1903 Treaty.** The 1903 treaty permitted the United States to build a canal in Panama. It also gave the United States complete authority over a 10-mile (16-kilometer)-wide strip of land across the isthmus, on which to build, operate, and defend the canal. The government of this territory, known as the Canal Zone, was headed by a governor appointed by the U.S. president. The United States also maintained military bases in the zone. The rights of the United States to the Canal Zone were to last "in perpetuity"—that is, forever.

In return, Panama received $10 million and a yearly rental fee of $250,000, beginning in 1913. This amount was increased two times. The United States also guaranteed Panama's independence.

**Building the Canal.** The canal took ten years to build and required the excavation of more than 232 million cubic yards (177 million cubic meters) of soil and rock. An average of 35,000 workers, the great majority of them blacks from the West Indies, labored on its construction.

Three men played especially important roles in the successful outcome. President Roosevelt guided the canal project. Colonel George W. Goethals, a U.S. Army engineer, supervised construction from 1907 to the canal's completion. Colonel William C. Gorgas, an Army doctor, introduced health measures that greatly reduced cases of malaria and yellow fever, which had been one of the major causes of the failure of the French canal project.

The Panama Canal was opened to commercial traffic on August 14, 1914. It had cost some $380 million to build.

**U.S.-Panamanian Relations.** Although Panama's leaders had agreed to the 1903 canal treaty, most Panamanians never really accepted it. They increasingly came to resent U.S. control over what they considered Panamanian territory. Panama won some changes in the treaty, but these did not satisfy Panamanian hopes.

Panamanian discontent reached a climax in 1964, with the outbreak of riots in the Canal Zone and in several Panamanian cities. The outburst, which left dozens dead, convinced the two governments that a new basis for operating the canal had to be found. After years of negotiations, the United States and Panama concluded two new treaties in 1977. They went into effect in 1979.

**The 1977 Treaties.** The first treaty abolished the Canal Zone and gave most of the territory back to Panama. The remaining territory—necessary for the operation and defense of the canal—was called the Panama Canal Area. The United States had primary responsibility for the canal until December 31, 1999, when the canal passed to Panamanian control, and the remaining U.S. military bases were closed. The treaty also calls for a study by both countries of the possibility of a new sea-level canal. The second treaty guarantees the permanent neutrality of the canal.

**Administration of the Canal.** Until the treaty expired, the canal was operated by the Panama Canal Commission, a U.S. government agency. The commission was supervised by a board of directors made up of five Americans and four Panamanians. In 1990 a Panamanian became administrator, the chief operating official of the canal. Today almost all of the canal's employees are Panamanians. An enormous expansion program was launched to increase the canal's ship-handling capacity by 20 percent.

Michael L. Conniff
University of New Mexico
Author, *Black Labor on a White Canal: Panama—1904–1981*

See also PANAMA.

A political cartoon of 1903 depicts President Theodore Roosevelt digging the Panama Canal himself, after Colombia had rejected the terms of a treaty.

# PANDAS

Pandas are extremely rare animals native to central and eastern Asia. There are two animals called pandas—the giant panda and the red, or lesser, panda. They were once considered members of the same family, but today the giant panda is classified as a member of the bear family (Ursidae). The red panda is usually classified as a member of the raccoon family (Procyonidae), but some scientists believe it should be grouped in its own separate family (Ailuridae).

## ▶ GIANT PANDAS

Giant pandas start life at the surprisingly small weight of 4 ounces (104 grams). This tiny infant grows into an adult weighing between 180 and 270 pounds (80 and 120 kilograms). Adult giant pandas have a bear-like body, coarse black and white fur, small black ears, and large black eye patches that give them their unique appeal.

Giant pandas in the wild are found only in central China. They are protected in forest reserves, but the growing human population, a decrease in their food supply, and illegal hunting threatens their existence. Only about 1,500 pandas live in the wild.

**Diet.** Giant pandas spend most of their time roaming the forest feeding on bamboo. Bamboo is the giant pandas' main food, although they sometimes eat other kinds of plants. Pandas have dietary needs that are very similar to animals that regularly eat meat, so they must eat great quantities of bamboo to obtain the nourishment they need.

To help them eat such tough, fibrous food, pandas have extremely powerful jaws and large, flattened molars designed for crushing. They also have an unusually shaped wrist bone that sticks out like a small thumb. This bone helps pandas hold stalks of bamboo.

**Reproduction.** The giant panda is a solitary animal, but once a year, between March and May, males and females come together for the breeding season. They find each other in the thick forest by leaving scent markings on trees, bushes, logs, or other objects. Pandas communicate with each other using bleats, chirps, honks, moans, and growls.

**Pandas in Captivity.** In 1936 the first giant panda was exhibited in a zoo outside China.

Hunting and the destruction of its habitat has made the giant panda, which inhabits the bamboo forests of eastern China, one of the rarest animals on Earth.

Today there are more than a dozen pandas in zoos in other countries. In the United States, giant pandas can be seen in Washington, D.C., Atlanta, and San Diego. Pandas in captivity are often given double names, following the Chinese custom, to indicate affection. Scientists study the zoo pandas in hopes of learning how to save pandas still in the wild from extinction.

## ▶ RED PANDAS

The red panda lives in the bamboo forests of China, Tibet, Myanmar, and Nepal. The average adult weighs only 9 to 13 pounds (4 to 6 kilograms). The body and tail are covered with long, rust-brown fur. The tail has cream-colored bands on it.

Red pandas spend much of their time in trees. They come down to feed on bamboo, grasses, roots, and fruit. Occasionally red pandas will eat meat. Like giant pandas, red pandas are generally solitary animals. During the breeding season male and female pairs travel together. The young remain dependent on their mothers for up to a year.

LISA M. STEVENS
Panda Collection Manager
National Zoological Park

**PANDORA.** See GREEK MYTHOLOGY (Profiles).

# PAPER

The paper on which these words are printed is made of millions of tiny fibers. The fibers are cellulose, a substance from the cell walls of plants. The average length of cellulose fibers is about 1/20 inch (1.3 millimeters). The fibers have been mixed in water and treated with chemicals, matted into a sheet, and dried to form paper.

Paper is one of the most important products ever invented. Widespread use of a written language would not have been possible without some affordable and practical material to write on. The invention of paper meant that more people could be educated because more books could be printed and distributed. Industry could grow because all the plans, blueprints, records, and formulas it uses could be written down and saved. Together with the printing press, paper provided a very important way to communicate knowledge.

Paper is important for other reasons. Paper and paperboard are made into cartons, wrappers, and containers for hundreds of products. Everything from washing machines to candy comes wrapped in paper or in paper cartons. Paper is made into many useful objects, such as plates, cups, and towels. New types of paper have been developed for use as clothes, bedsheets, and pillowcases.

The word "paper" comes from the word "papyrus." Papyrus was not really paper. It was a writing material made, originally by the ancient Egyptians, from the fibers of the papyrus plant. Papyrus was too brittle to be bound into books, so it was glued together in long strips and carefully rolled up on wooden or ivory rods.

▶ HOW PAPER IS MADE

All paper is made in basically the same way. A mixture of cellulose fibers, water, and chemicals is placed on a fine-meshed screen that lets the water drain off. As the fibers dry, they mat together to form a sheet. The sheet is removed from the screen, dried, and pressed smooth to form paper.

Heavy rolls of newsprint are unloaded from a delivery truck in London. Newsprint, used for newspapers, is one of many different types of paper.

Until about 150 years ago, all paper was made by hand. Today, paper is made by machine. Some of the large papermaking machines can produce more than 2 million pounds (900,000 kilograms) of paper in a single day.

## Materials

The cellulose used in paper today comes from wood waste, fiber from recycled paper, and trees.

Fiber to make pulp comes directly or indirectly from the forest. Fast-growing species of trees, such as softwoods and some hardwoods, are grown on tree plantations specifically for use as wood pulp. After being cut, these logs are hauled to the pulp mill by truck or railroad, and the plantation is replanted with the next crop of trees. Sometimes logs are taken to the nearest river and floated down to the mill. In other cases, wood fiber comes from a sawmill in the form of bark, shavings, and other wood waste left over from the manufacture of lumber, plywood, and similar products. This way, virtually no part of a harvested tree is wasted.

Recycled paper, such as used boxes, computer paper, and old newspapers and magazines, comes from commercial and retail outlets, household curbside collection programs, and paper converting facilities.

Pulp, a material from which paper is made, comes from wood and recycled paper.
*Above:* At a paper plant in Maine, logs are lifted from a truck and placed on a huge pile.
*Above right:* A towering wall of wastepaper waits to be recycled.

Paper mills are built near water, because papermaking requires a large supply of water. The water must be pure, because any impurities will show up in the finished product. Paper mills have their own equipment for purifying water, and they use the same water over and over to keep consumption down.

### Converting the Wood into Pulp

The first step is to prepare the wood for papermaking. Wood arrives at the mill in the form of pulpwood, chips, and sawdust. Pulping is done either by grinding up the pulpwood or by cooking the chips and sawdust with chemicals. Some pulping methods use both grinding and cooking.

The wood is ground up by being pressed against a large, rapidly turning grindstone. Water is sprayed over the wood and grindstone to cool the stone and carry away the pulp. Wood is ground into pulp when the paper does not have to be very strong or durable. One of the largest users of groundwood is newsprint, the paper on which newspapers are printed.

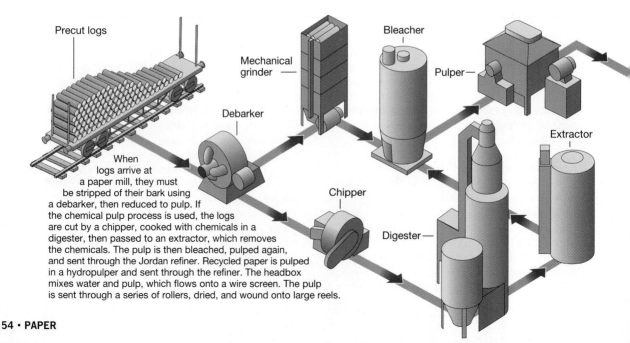

Precut logs

Mechanical grinder

Bleacher

Pulper

Debarker

Extractor

When logs arrive at a paper mill, they must be stripped of their bark using a debarker, then reduced to pulp. If the chemical pulp process is used, the logs are cut by a chipper, cooked with chemicals in a digester, then passed to an extractor, which removes the chemicals. The pulp is then bleached, pulped again, and sent through the Jordan refiner. Recycled paper is pulped in a hydropulper and sent through the refiner. The headbox mixes water and pulp, which flows onto a wire screen. The pulp is sent through a series of rollers, dried, and wound onto large reels.

Chipper

Digester

For chemical processes, the wood must be in the form of chips. The wood chips are cooked with several different chemicals to turn them into pulp. The sulfate process is the major chemical pulping method.

Other pulping processes include the semichemical process and the sulfite process. In the semichemical process, the wood is ground up as well as being cooked with chemicals. This pulp is most often used for making corrugated paperboard. The sulfite process results in nearly pure cellulose fibers, which are used to make high-quality paper for expensive stationery, maps, and photographs.

Another way of making pulp is by exploding the wood. Chips of wood are put under high pressure in a closed vessel. Then the pressure is suddenly released, causing an explosion. Pulp made in this way goes into the paper used in building construction.

Recycling wastepaper is another important way of making pulp. For more information, see the Wonder Question on page 57.

### Preparing the Pulp

Wood pulp is screened and washed to clean out impurities and chemicals. If the pulp is to be bleached, the bleaching is done right after the cleaning. Bleaching removes impurities from paper. It also makes the paper whiter.

After cleaning and bleaching, the pulp is beaten in a large mixing machine and mixed with water. The beating frays the fibers, which helps them mat together. Starch, clay, or other materials may be added to improve the surface of the paper for printing and writing. To make "wet-strength" paper, which is used for such things as paper towels, special additives are added to the pulp.

After wood is chipped into pieces, it is poured into a machine that will cook the wood along with different chemicals to make pulp.

The pulp then goes into a machine called a Jordan refiner, where the fibers are trimmed evenly. At this stage the pulp consists of 99 percent water and 1 percent fiber. It is now ready to go into the papermaking machine.

### Sheet Formation

Most of the paper produced in the United States is made on Fourdrinier machines. The machine has a tank called a headbox, in which pulp and water are mixed. The pulp

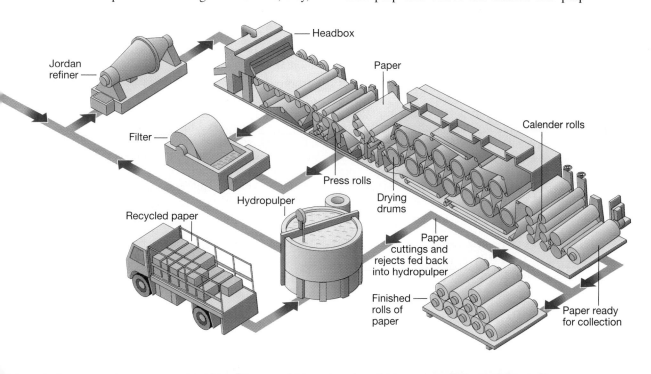

A layer of pulp moves along a Fourdrinier machine. Water drains out of the pulp and down through a wire screen. Suction pumps remove more water.

flows onto a wire screen that moves along like a conveyor belt. Water drains out of the pulp and down through the screen. Suction pumps underneath help remove more water. The screen vibrates to make the fibers interlock and mat together.

The wet mat passes under a metal roller, called a dandy roll, that presses it down into a smoother sheet. The dandy roll may contain a design that will be pressed into the sheet of fibers. This is the watermark, which can be seen when the paper is held to the light.

At the end of the trip on the screen, the sheet passes over a suction roller called a couch roll. By this time the pulp consists of about 80 percent water.

The sheet goes through a series of pressing rolls, which squeeze out water and make the paper dense and smooth. Until this point, the paper has been in the "wet end" of the machine. It now passes into the machine's "dry end," traveling through a series of heated drums called dryers. At this time, coatings can be applied to make the paper slick and shiny.

To give the paper a smooth, hard surface, it is threaded through a series of rollers called calenders. Then it is wound onto large reels and taken off the machine.

Another type of papermaking machine, the cylinder machine, is generally used for making paperboard and heavy building paper. In a cylinder machine, the pulp and water are mixed in a vat. A revolving wire-mesh cylinder turns in the vat. The cylinder picks up cellulose fibers and deposits them on a moving belt. The sheet is carried to rollers that press and dry it in the same way as the rollers of a Fourdrinier machine.

Cylinder machines can produce paper that is made of more than one layer of pulp. The surface of a sheet of paper may be made of expensive pulp, while the body of the paper is made of cheaper pulp. The different pulps can be mixed in different vats and laid onto one another and rolled into a single sheet.

Paper comes off the machines in large rolls. It is trimmed to take off the rough edges and cut to the desired width. Some kinds of paper, such as printing and writing paper, are cut into sheets. Paper used for printing newspapers and magazines and for wrapping is rewound onto rolls.

▶ TYPES OF PAPER PRODUCTS

There are many different types of paper. Each type is made to best serve a special purpose. **Newsprint**, the paper used for newspapers, does not have to be very durable. Therefore it is made of groundwood pulp. Other types of **groundwood papers** are used for directories and similar publications.

Paper for books and magazines must be of better quality. This **book paper** is also used for commercial printing. Magazines are usually printed on coated book paper.

The highest-quality paper, a type of fine paper, is made mostly from cotton fibers obtained from rags. Fine papers are also made from chemical pulp. They are used for bank checks, expensive stationery, photographic papers, and papers for computers.

**Coarse papers** are heavy-duty papers. They are used for grocery bags, brown and colored wrapping paper, and paper sacks such as those for cement and flour. Brown paper envelopes, gummed paper, and coin wrappers are also made of coarse paper.

**Absorbent papers**, a type of specialty paper, are made in such a way that they can absorb a certain amount of liquid or purify air without falling apart. They are used chiefly for blotters and filter papers.

Facial tissues, toilet paper, paper towels and napkins, and the soft paper used for wrapping gifts, fruits, and vegetables are made of **tissue paper**.

**Paperboard** is one of the most-used types of paper. An important variety of paperboard is called **containerboard**. It is made into boxes and containers. Corrugated containerboard is made by passing the paper through rollers that have ridges and grooves. This gives the board a wavy contour. Corrugated board is often covered on each side with smooth paperboard. This sandwich construction makes the paperboard very sturdy. It is used for making heavy shipping containers.

**Boxboard** is another type of paperboard. It is made into boxes to hold cereals, soap powder, toothpaste, and many other products. Sometimes a coating is applied to the surface to make it easier to print graphics.

Other special types of paperboard are used for milk and ice cream cartons, frozen-food packages, shoeboxes, candy boxes, and paper plates. Some of these paperboards are coated with wax or plastic to keep substances from seeping through. The material known as **cardboard**, used as a backing for writing tablets and picture frames, is a special type of paperboard. It should not be confused, as it often is, with containerboard.

Very thick paperboard is used for the bindings of books and as linings between the inner and outer soles of shoes. This paperboard is called **wet machine board**. It is too thick to go through drying rollers and must be taken from the papermaking machine while still wet and dried in an oven.

▶ **HISTORY**

Before paper was invented, people used a great variety of writing materials. Records were scratched and written on stone, wood, metal, ivory, wax tablets, leaves, papyrus, animal skins, and tree bark.

In the ancient Mediterranean world, the chief writing material was papyrus. It was made originally in Egypt, and eventually its use spread to Greece and Rome.

In the later Roman Empire and in the Middle Ages, writing was done mostly on parchment and vellum, made from animal skins. These materials were expensive and scarce. Paper was the first practical, inexpensive, and plentiful writing material.

Paper was first made about 2,000 years ago, when the first sheets of paper were produced in China. The materials used were pulp made from the bark of a mulberry tree and fibers from cloth and hemp. These were

## WONDER QUESTION

### How is paper recycled?

To obtain recycled fiber from wastepaper, one and sometimes two operations are needed.

Hydropulping involves mixing the recycled paper with water to form a slurry, or a mixture containing paper, water, and chemicals. The action that takes place is like that of a kitchen blender. Afterward, screens and cleaners are used to remove non-fibrous contaminants, such as tape, glue, metal, and plastic.

Following hydropulping, some pulp goes through a second process called de-inking. There are two types of de-inking processes, washing and flotation. The washing system uses strong countercurrent washers that literally wash ink from the pulp. In the flotation process, air is injected into the pulp, and ink and other non-fibrous particles collide with the air bubbles and become attached to them. The inky "foam" is then skimmed off the top.

mixed with water, spread on a piece of cloth, and allowed to dry to form a sheet of paper.

The knowledge of papermaking spread from China to Arabia and Europe by the 1100's. Papermaking in Europe may have been introduced by the Muslims who conquered Spain. In the 1200's, paper mills were set up in Italy. These were soon followed by mills in Germany, France, and the Netherlands. Papermaking started in England late in the 1400's. In 1690, the first paper mill in the United States was built by William Rittenhouse (1644–1708) and William Bradford (1663–1752) in Philadelphia.

Until about the mid-1800's, linen and cotton rags were almost the only source of papermaking fibers. Although early Chinese papermakers used both wood pulp and cloth fibers for their paper, later papermakers did not seem to realize that wood pulp could also be made into paper.

Early in the 1700's, the French naturalist René Antoine de Réaumur (1683–1757) pointed out that wood pulp might also be used for making paper. Réaumur had noticed that wasps build paper nests out of wood pulp by chewing off pieces of old timbers and logs and moistening them with saliva.

It was not until the middle of the 1800's, however, that wood pulp was used for papermaking on a large scale. A less expensive raw material was needed, because at about the same time, a papermaking machine was developed that could rapidly produce large quantities of paper. Until this time, all paper had been made by hand.

A machine for making paper in an endless sheet had been patented by Nicholas Louis Robert (1761–1828), a Frenchman, in 1798. The machine was later developed in England by two brothers, Henry (1766–1854) and Sealy (?–1847) Fourdrinier. At this time the machine did not have drying rollers. The paper had to be taken from the machine wet and hung up in lofts to dry. But the machine still could turn out as much paper as six hand-operated paper mills.

The first machine-made paper in the United States was made in 1817, not on a Fourdrinier, but on a cylinder machine. The first Fourdrinier machine in the United States was put into operation in 1827.

With abundant raw material and a machine for making paper, paper production increased greatly in the 1800's. In the United States between 1810 and 1840, paper production increased by about 10 times. It has been steadily increasing ever since. In 1810, 3,300 tons (3,000 metric tons) of paper were made in the United States. Today, more than 91 million tons (83 million metric tons) of paper are used each year in the United States.

The demand for paper has steadily increased with the spread of education and the growth of industry. To keep up with the demand, Fourdrinier machines have been improved to produce paper much faster. In the 1860's, a machine could turn out about 100 feet (30 meters) of paper a minute. Today's Fourdriniers can produce about 5,000 feet (1,500 meters) of paper a minute.

More paper than ever will be made and used in the future. One of the challenges in satisfying the growing demand for paper is to provide an adequate supply of cellulose fiber, the main raw material for making pulp. The world's forests are enormous, but they must serve many purposes, and not all are suitable for growing trees to harvest. In addition to wood pulp, forests supply the lumber used in building homes and making furniture.

Another challenge is finding new supplies of recycled paper, as more and more new paper is made wholly or partially with recycled fiber.

The paper industry has an interest in the use and care of forests. Along with other industries that use wood, it sponsors a tree-farming program designed to replant trees that were harvested. It also sponsors research to lead to faster-growing trees and to more efficient use of trees.

Methods have been developed to make pulp from almost every kind of tree and from the leftovers of lumber and plywood mills. More than one-fourth of the wood used for making paper comes from such leftovers. The industry helps conserve its resources by recycling paper to make new paper. More than one-third of the fiber used in making paper and paperboard comes from recycled paper.

Paper will continue to be one of the basic materials in our lives. In new forms and with new uses, paper may become even more important than ever before.

Reviewed by VIRGIL K. HORTON, JR.
American Forest and Paper Association

See also WOOD AND WOOD PRODUCTS.

# PAPERBACK BOOKS

No development in book publication since the invention of movable type in the 1400's has brought about greater changes than the introduction of paperback books. Books bound with paper covers appeared in large numbers after 1945. In the years that followed, the publication of paperback books became a major industry all over the world. Paperbacks are now sold in bookstores, stationery stores, drugstores, airports, and supermarkets.

In a bookstore, a youngster tries to select from the many titles that are available in paperback.

### ▶ HISTORY

The ancestor of today's paperback was the chapbook. Chapbooks, small illustrated books or pamphlets, were sold from the 1500's to the 1700's by peddlers known as chapmen. Throughout the 1600's and 1700's, chapbooks were quite popular in England and the North American colonies. The contents of chapbooks covered a wide range of subjects. Some were almanacs; some narrated sensational tales. Many contained songs and ballads or stories for children. Produced to be sold quickly and inexpensively, they were of poor quality and design.

The day of the fine-quality paperback was a long way off. Although publishers were constantly seeking ways to provide good low-cost books for larger audiences, this advance depended on many factors. Paper that was made by machine rather than by hand had to be introduced, as well as mechanical typesetting machines and fast cylinder presses. It was not until the 1800's that most of these changes came about.

In the late 1800's, a new kind of paperback, the dime novel, gained popularity. As its name implies, this paperback often sold for 10 cents. These books were usually poorly written adventure tales. In spite of their great success, dime novels did little to advance the cause of the superior paperback.

During the late 1800's and early 1900's, several attempts were made to persuade the reading public to buy paperbound books. The movement had notable success in Europe, particularly with the Tauchnitz series published in Germany and with Penguin books in England. Travelers learned the advantages of buying the books at railway stations, reading them on their journey, and then discarding them if they wished to do so. However, most early attempts to interest people in buying paperbacks failed, since most readers considered them to be inferior.

After World War II (1939–45), publishers began to experiment with paperbacks on a large scale. Lists of titles were enlarged, and distribution methods were improved. The public was made aware of the many advantages, other than price, of buying books of this kind.

### ▶ PAPERBACK BOOKS TODAY

One of the earliest manufacturers of paperback books in the United States was Pocket Books. Other publishers, encouraged by their success, began to produce paperbacks. When paperbound books first appeared, most titles sold for as little as 25 cents. Today, although increases in paper and production costs have caused prices to rise, paperbacks continue to sell for less than hardcovers.

Readers have come to appreciate the many great advantages of paperbacks. Aside from their price, paperbacks are light in weight, can be carried easily, and take up less shelf space at home.

At one time, owning books was a privilege for only a few people who could afford to spend large sums of money on their collections. Today, thanks to good-quality paperbacks, the enjoyment of building a personal library is within the reach of countless numbers of people.

LAVINIA DOBLER
Head Librarian, Scholastic Book Services

Papier-mâché masks are fun to make. After you decorate them, they can be worn again and again.

# PAPIER-MÂCHÉ

Papier-mâché is a French term that means "chewed paper." Although this art had been practiced for centuries in Asia, the term was first applied to a process used in Paris in the 1700's. Old posters were ripped from walls, converted into pulp, and mixed with size—a gummy preparation made by combining glue or paste with resin and drying oil. When the papier-mâché hardened, it was lacquered and decorated. Papier-mâché was used to make boxes, trays, decorative pieces, and statuettes.

Today young and old alike enjoy making different objects out of papier-mâché. The material is fast to work with and easy to handle, and the finished product is lightweight.

### ▶ HOW TO MAKE PAPIER-MÂCHÉ

Before you begin, lay down newspapers where you plan to work and wear a smock to protect your clothing.

You can use various types of paper to make papier-mâché, but you will find that old newspaper is the best because it tears easily and absorbs water and paste quickly. Its torn edges blend into one another and give a smooth overall surface.

Tear several sheets into small pieces. For larger projects, it is quicker to use strips of newspaper.

Different mixtures can be used for your papier-mâché paste. One is made of glue and water. (This is used in the project on the opposite page.) You can also use a simple flour and water recipe. Pour 1 cup of cold water into a bowl. Add about 1 cup of flour to the water and stir until there are no lumps. Your mixture should be a thin paste. You can also use wallpaper paste (an excellent adhesive sold in hardware stores), which comes as a powder. Put 2 cups of cold water into a bowl. Slowly stir in enough powder to form a smooth paste.

Papier-mâché can be pasted onto balloons or bowls, which are used as molds. You can also cover cardboard boxes. When your object is completely dry, you can paint and decorate it any way you wish.

You can make masks, puppets, bracelets, pencil holders, and even musical instruments. Because papier-mâché is a strong material, objects made with it can be expected to last a long time.

CATHERINE ROBERTS
Author, *Real Book of Real Crafts*

## How to Make a Papier-Mâché Piggy Bank

To make this piggy bank, you will need a balloon, masking tape, scissors, paint, a paintbrush, and an egg carton. First, blow up the balloon and tie a knot in it. Then, since papier-mâché tends to be very messy, put newspapers down where you are going to work, and wear an old shirt or smock to protect your clothing. Now you are ready to make your papier-mâché mixture. Start by diluting $1/2$ cup of nontoxic white glue with $1/2$ cup of cold water. Stir well. If you need to make more, just add equal parts of water and glue. Tear some newspaper into small pieces.

Cover the balloon with water or petroleum jelly. Then cover the balloon with four or five layers of papier-mâché, leaving a small hole where the balloon is knotted. Put the balloon in a warm place so that it will dry.

Once the papier-mâché layers are completely dry, hold the balloon by the knot, pop it, and remove it. To make the pig's feet and snout, cut up an egg carton. Using masking tape, attach the egg carton pieces as shown.

Cut triangles from the egg carton. These will be the pig's ears. Attach them with masking tape. Use papier-mâché to cover the ears, snout, and feet.

To make the tail, spread glue on a piece of newspaper and fold it into a thin strip. Curl it around a pencil so that it will have a coil shape. Attach it to the balloon with papier-mâché.

Apply a coat of paint, using any colors that you like. When it has dried, apply another coat. Give your pig a face.

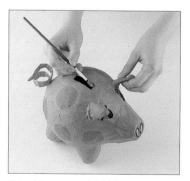

Cut out the money slot. Make sure to make it wide enough so you can get your money out. Apply any finishing details you like, and let your piggy bank dry.

# PAPUA NEW GUINEA

Papua New Guinea lies in the southwest Pacific Ocean just north of Australia. It is a country made up of part of one very large island plus many smaller islands and island groups. The largest land area is the eastern half of the island of New Guinea (the western half belongs to Indonesia). To the east are New Britain, New Ireland, the Admiralty Islands, and other islands of the Bismarck Archipelago; Bougainville and Buka in the Solomons; Woodlark, and the Trobriand, D'Entrecasteaux, and Louisiade island groups. Formerly administered by Australia, Papua New Guinea became independent in 1975.

### ▶ THE PEOPLE

The people of Papua New Guinea generally show the physical characteristics of the Melanesians of the Pacific—short to medium height, brown to black skin, broad noses, and curly or frizzy hair. In fact, the word "papua," which comes from the Malay language, has been translated as "frizzy hair." Most of the people live in villages, which are often small and sometimes isolated from each other by the mountainous terrain. Most vil-

lagers are farmers, growing just enough food for their own needs. In recent years some of the people have migrated from the rural areas to the cities, especially to Port Moresby, the capital, and Lae, the second largest city.

Tribal and family relationships are important in everyday life. Families remain together, so that one house may shelter several brothers, their wives, their children, and their grandchildren. A typical village house is built on stilts to protect it against flooding in rainy weather. The ordinary houses show little decoration. But ceremonial buildings display painting and sculpture related to religious beliefs.

About half the people of Papua New Guinea belong to Christian churches. But in the isolated villages change comes slowly, and traditional religion holds sway. Ancestor and spirit worship is common and the people believe that their ancestors watch over them.

Papua New Guinea lacks a single common language. There are an estimated 750 different languages spoken, some by thousands of people, others by only a single village. However, Melanesian Pidgin, an altered and simplified form of English with some words from other languages, is widely understood. English is spoken by educated people and serves as the language of commerce and government.

### ▶ THE LAND

Papua New Guinea is 461,691 square kilometers, or 178,260 square miles, in area.

**Port Moresby is the capital, the chief port, and the largest city of Papua New Guinea.**

**PAPUA NEW GUINEA** is the official name of the country.

**LOCATION:** Southwest Pacific Ocean north of Australia.

**AREA:** 461,691 km² (178,260 sq mi).

**POPULATION:** 4,400,000 (estimate).

**CAPITAL AND LARGEST CITY:** Port Moresby.

**MAJOR LANGUAGES:** English and Melanesian Pidgin.

**MAJOR RELIGIOUS GROUPS:** Christian and traditional religions.

**GOVERNMENT:** Parliamentary democracy. **Head of state**—British monarch represented by a governor-general. **Head of government**—prime minister. **Legislature**—House of Assembly.

**CHIEF PRODUCTS: Agricultural**—copra, coffee, tea, cacao, rubber, yams, corn, beans, bananas. **Manufactured**—coconut and timber products. **Mineral**—copper, gold, silver, manganese.

**MONETARY UNIT:** 1 kina = 100 toea.

# PAPUA NEW GUINEA

Towering mountain ranges, deep valleys, great swamps, swiftly flowing rivers, and vast forests make up the varied landscape of the mainland. Mountains in the Owen Stanley Range in the southeast rise to a height of over 3,900 meters, or over 13,000 feet. The highest point is Mount Victoria, at 4,073 meters (13,363 feet). The chief rivers are the Fly, Kikori, and Purari in the south and the Sepik in the north. Many of the smaller islands are also mountainous, some of the peaks being active volcanoes. The climate is tropical, though temperatures vary with elevation. Rainfall is abundant.

## ▶ THE ECONOMY

Agriculture and mining are basic to the country's economic life. The most important mineral is copper. The country's largest copper mine, on Bougainville island, was closed indefinitely in 1989 due to violence by separatist rebels there. Other valuable minerals include gold, silver, and manganese. The chief commercial crops are coffee, tea, copra (dried coconut meat), rubber, and cacao. Major industries center around wood and wood products. Fishing is important in the coastal areas.

## ▶ HISTORY AND GOVERNMENT

In the late 1800's the Germans set up trading settlements on the northeast coast of New Guinea, and the British established a protectorate over the southeast. In 1906, Australia took over British New Guinea and governed it as the Territory of Papua. At the start of World War I, Australian troops occupied the German-held area in the northeast, and later administered it as the Territory of New Guinea under a mandate from the League of Nations.

During World War II much of the region was occupied by the Japanese and saw some of the heaviest fighting of the Pacific war. After the war the Territory of New Guinea became a United Nations trust territory, again administered by Australia.

In 1973 Papua New Guinea achieved self-government, and on September 16, 1975, it won full independence. The country has a parliamentary form of government with a prime minister and a single-chamber legislature, the House of Assembly. It is a member of the Commonwealth of Nations.

Tragedy struck in July 1998 when a tidal wave caused by an earthquake washed away numerous villages on the nation's northwest coast, killing an estimated 3,000 people.

CHARLES PAUL MAY
Author, *Oceania: Polynesia, Melanesia, Micronesia*

See also NEW GUINEA.

A rectangular canopy parachute gives a much softer and more accurate landing than a round parachute.

# PARACHUTES

If you throw a package out of an airplane, it falls rapidly toward the ground and lands with a crash that probably breaks everything in it. But if you attach a parachute to the package, it falls slowly and lands gently.

A parachute is an umbrella- or wing-shaped device. Its shape creates resistance to the air, which, in turn, slows the descent of a package or body so it falls to the ground safely.

As early as the 1100's, the Chinese amused themselves by jumping from high places with rigid umbrella-like structures. Some 300 years later the Italian artist and inventor Leonardo da Vinci designed a pyramid-shaped parachute. The first successful parachute jumps were made in the late 1700's from a tower and, later, from a balloon. The first jump from an airplane was made in 1912.

During the first and second world wars, parachutes were used to drop supplies and troops behind enemy lines and to drop flares for nighttime reconnaissance. It was not until after World War II that sport parachuting developed. Today, many people enjoy this sport. The military continues to use parachutes to deliver troops, foods, vehicles, and other loads. Parachutes are used as landing brakes on jet airplanes that land on aircraft carriers and for recovering instruments from missiles.

A parachute has five basic parts. The pilot chute is a small canopy used to pull out the larger canopy. The main canopy is most commonly made of nylon. Round canopies used in sport jumping vary in diameter from 6.7 to 9.8 meters (22 to 32 feet). Those used for cargo may be as much as 30 meters (100 feet) across. Suspension lines run from the canopy to the harness. The harness is a series of straps that fit around and support the person's body. Attached to the harness is the ripcord. When pulled, it causes the main canopy to inflate. The container, or pack, holds everything except the harness.

There are three ways of opening the parachute. It may be opened by hand, by pulling the ripcord. It may be opened automatically by a line, called the static line, that is hooked to the aircraft. This is used by military jumpers and beginning sport jumpers. The canopy may also be opened at a pre-set altitude by an automatic opening device.

In typical sport jumps, parachutists usually wear protective jumpsuits, helmets, gloves, and goggles. Besides the main parachute, jumpers always wear reserve parachutes for protection in case something goes wrong.

An airplane carries jumpers up into the sky. The higher they go, the longer they have for free-fall—the period before opening the main canopy. When the plane reaches the desired altitude, the jumpers leave the plane.

Free-fall feels more like flying than falling. Jumpers can reach speeds of more than 300 kilometers (187 miles) an hour during this period. They feel the air pressure against the body and learn to use this pressure to perform loops and rolls. Experienced jumpers may leave the aircraft together and, by maneuvering their bodies, join up to form a wide variety of formations.

Jumpers carry altimeters, which tell how high they are. At 760 meters (2,500 feet), they end their free-fall by pulling the ripcord. People who are jumping together must move apart before opening their parachutes.

The open canopy greatly slows the jumpers' speed. By pulling on steering lines that they hold in their hands, jumpers can control the forward speed and direction of the parachute. Experienced jumpers can steer precisely to a landing spot no larger than 10 centimeters (4 inches) in diameter.

ALAN T. KING
United States Parachute Association

A fife and drum band is an important part of many parades.

# PARADES

There have been parades for almost as long as there have been crowds of people to enjoy them. Paintings on ancient Egyptian tombs and monuments show the pharaohs and their priests in many processions.

Roman victory parades were grand affairs. The procession, called the triumph, celebrated the return to Rome of a victorious general and his army. Flowers were scattered and incense was burned as the troops marched from the Campus Martius (a large grassy field where many military events took place) to the Capitol, where there was a temple dedicated to Jupiter. Behind the dignitaries paraded men carrying the spoils of war, important captives, priests with incense burners, and the general with his army.

## ▶ MILITARY AND PATRIOTIC PARADES

Today many parades are held for patriotic purposes and take place on national holidays. In the United States, soldiers and sailors parade on Memorial Day, Armed Forces Day, and Veterans' Day. In Canada, Dominion Day is marked with parades.

In many European countries parades are held to celebrate independence.

In France on Bastille Day, July 14, there are military parades down the Champs Élysées. In Moscow, military units, students, and workers march each year in Red Square to celebrate the October Revolution of 1917.

In the United States there are parades held by people of various national origins. March 17 is a great day for the Irish in New York. On that day thousands of real and would-be Irish march down Fifth Avenue in the St. Patrick's Day parade. Italian Americans feel that Columbus Day is their holiday, and they have a similar parade on that day.

JAMES W. HOERGER
Great Neck (New York) Public Schools

# PARAGUAY

Paraguay is a small landlocked country in the heart of South America, bordered by Brazil, Argentina, and Bolivia. It is also one of the smallest countries in South America, with an area slightly smaller than the U.S. state of California.

The country is divided into two very different areas. The Oriental Region, in the east, contains rich agricultural lands and forests. The western two-thirds, known as the Gran Chaco, is a desolate plain covered with scrub forests and grasslands.

## ▶ PEOPLE

Most Paraguayans are mestizo (of mixed European and Indian origin) and live in the Oriental Region. About 2 percent of the population is made up of indigenous (native) peoples, most of whom live in the Gran Chaco region. The Guaraní Indians, who originally inhabited the Oriental Region, have mainly been absorbed into the mestizo population.

Historically, Paraguay has attracted many immigrants, most notably from Germany, Brazil, and Korea. Some immigrants have formed separate colonies. The most prosperous has been that of the Mennonites (members of a Protestant sect). Since they first arrived in 1926 and bought land in the Gran Chaco region, they have established successful farming communities and followed their own customs, language (mainly German), and religion.

**Language.** Paraguay is one of the few countries in the world with two official languages, Spanish and Guaraní, and most of the people are bilingual (able to speak two languages). But in the countryside many people speak only Guaraní, while in Asunción, the capital, some people speak only Spanish.

**Religion.** Approximately 90 percent of the people are Roman Catholic. However, there has been no official state religion in Paraguay since 1992, and freedom of worship is guaranteed by law.

*Clockwise from above:* Paraguayan children in traditional dress dance at a festival. A gaucho (South American cowboy) performs at a local celebration. During the rainy season, portions of the Gran Chaco become marshy, particularly near the Paraguay River.

**Education.** Education is free and required by law until the age of 16. About 92 percent of Paraguayans age 15 and over can read and write. The country's one public university, the National University, is located in Asunción. There are 15 private universities, the largest of which is the Catholic University, also located in the capital.

**Way of Life.** Slightly fewer than half the people of Paraguay earn their living from the land. Some work on the large agricultural estates where most of the export crops are grown, or harvest timber and other forest products. A smaller number are gauchos (cowboys), who herd cattle. But most of the rural people live on small farms, where they grow food for their own use and keep livestock. In recent decades, an increasing number of people have moved from rural areas to the larger cities, attracted by the hope of work, education, and a better life.

Many dishes are made with meat and corn or other vegetables. The staple food of the country is cassava, a starchy root. Cassava is also dried and ground into flour. The most popular drink in Paraguay is *tereré*, which is made by adding iced water to ground yerba maté leaves, flavored with lemon or leaves and roots. If hot water is added to the yerba maté leaves, the drink is called maté.

Popular pastimes include playing soccer and basketball, and singing to the accompaniment of guitars and the beautiful Paraguayan harp. Traditional Paraguayan music is renowned throughout South America. The most popular traditional dance is the Paraguayan polka. Another famous dance features women who skillfully perform while balancing up to eight bottles on their heads.

Paraguay is also well known for its handicrafts. These include colorful hammocks and blankets, intricate silverwork called filigree, and beautiful embroidery known as *ñandutí*.

There are many religious festivals, the most popular of which is held each December 8 in honor of the Little Virgin of Caacupé. People walk all or part of the 34 miles (54 kilometers) from Asunción to Caacupé as a way of thanking the Virgin for favors or blessings.

▸ **LAND**

Paraguay has no seacoast, but the great Paraná-Paraguay river system provides a water route to the Atlantic Ocean, some

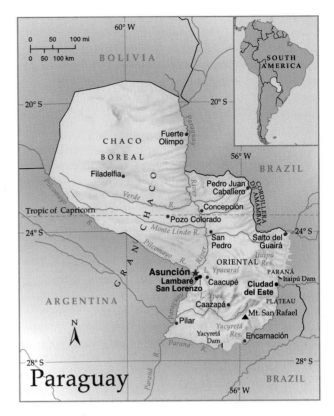

1,000 miles (1,600 kilometers) away. The Paraguay River divides the country into two parts—the Oriental Region in the east and the larger Gran Chaco in the west.

The Oriental Region is split into two sections by a high ridge of hills. The country's highest point, Mount San Rafael, is located in these hills and is about 2,763 feet (842 meters) above sea level. East of the hills lies the Paraná Plateau, once heavily forested but now the center of cotton and soybean production. To the west lie fertile grasslands. Coconut palms and jacaranda trees grow in this part of the country, which also contains Lake Ypacaraí and Lake Ypoá.

The Gran Chaco is a vast plain covered by dense, infertile scrub forests, palm trees, and marshes. It is inhabited by just 2 percent of the population. In the rainy season, it contains many slow-moving rivers, streams, and lakes, but in the dry season much of it becomes parched wasteland.

The Paraguay River is filled with floating islands in the wet summer season. These little islands, called *camalotes*, are torn from the riverbanks by the heavy rains and drift downstream with the current.

**Climate.** Paraguay's climate is generally subtropical, with humid conditions in the east and dry tropical savanna conditions in the west. Except for parts of the Gran Chaco, it rains year-round. The rainy season—October to April—is also the hottest season, and the north wind can bring oppressive heat. The winter—June to August—is short and temperatures rarely go below 50°F (10°C).

**Natural Resources.** Eastern Paraguay has fertile soils and valuable forests. But widespread cattle farming, crop production, and illegal logging have led to significant deforestation. This in turn has affected the environment, from wildlife to rainfall and the climate.

The country contains a wide variety of animals, mainly in the forests of eastern Paraguay. Parrots, hummingbirds, and flamingos, as well as Paraguayan alligators (known as *yacaré*), jaguars, tapirs, and monkeys can all be found. The beautiful *lapacho* tree, with its colorful blossoms, and the sweet-scented passionflower are distinctive plants.

▶ **ECONOMY**

Paraguay's economy has traditionally been based on agriculture and forestry. A lack of good communications systems and basic ser-

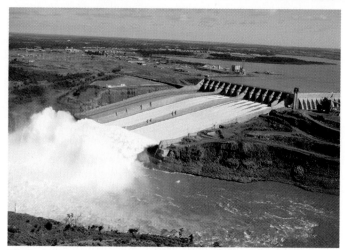

The huge Itaipú Dam crosses the Paraná River between Paraguay and Brazil. The dam has helped make Paraguay one of the world's largest producers of hydroelectric power.

vices has limited development in most parts of the country, and it remains less developed than Brazil and Argentina.

In recent decades, however, Paraguay has developed two huge hydroelectric dams along the Paraná River—the Itaipú Dam with Brazil and the Yacyretá Dam with Argentina. As a result, Paraguay has become one of the world's largest producers of hydroelectric power, most of which is exported.

Despite Paraguay's beauty, the tourist industry is underdeveloped. The banking industry has suffered a number of crises since 1997, resulting in the closure of some of the biggest banks. Not included in official economic statistics are thousands of unregistered small businesses, ranging from street vendors to the illegal cocaine trade.

**Agriculture.** The leading agricultural exports include soybeans, cotton, and meat, but Paraguay also produces wheat, sugarcane, corn, tobacco, and fruit. Most rural families operate on a subsistence basis—producing a variety of crops for their own use—but also produce one or more cash crops. The Mennonite communities in the Gran Chaco are well known for their dairy products.

Much of the world's petitgrain extract (a fragrant oil used in perfumes) comes from the citrus trees in Paraguay's forests. Other forest products include timber and quebracho extract (a tannin used to cure leather).

**Manufacturing.** Manufacturing is limited to the processing of local raw materials, such as cotton, timber, hides, and oils.

## FACTS and figures

**REPUBLIC OF PARAGUAY** (República del Paraguay) is the official name of the country.

**LOCATION:** Central South America.

**AREA:** 153,398 sq mi (397,300 km²).

**POPULATION:** 6,000,000 (estimate).

**CAPITAL AND LARGEST CITY:** Asunción.

**MAJOR LANGUAGES:** Spanish and Guaraní (both official).

**MAJOR RELIGIOUS GROUP:** Christian (Roman Catholic).

**GOVERNMENT:** Republic. **Head of state and government**—president. **Legislature**—Chamber of Representatives, Chamber of Senators. **International co-operation**—United Nations, Organization of American States (OAS), Mercosur.

**CHIEF PRODUCTS: Agricultural**—cotton, sugar, soybeans, corn, wheat, tobacco, cassava, fruits, beef, dairy products. **Manufactured**—meat products, vegetable oils, sugar refining, flour milling, leather goods, textiles, cement, timber, quebracho extract, petitgrain oil. **Mineral**—limestone, small quantities of gold and silver.

**MONETARY UNIT:** 1 guaraní (G) = 100 centimos.

**Asunción**, on the Paraguay River, is the country's capital, principal port, and largest city. Founded in 1537, Asunción served briefly as the hub of the Spanish empire in southern South America. Today it is the center of Paraguay's political, economic, and cultural life. The city's population is approximately 500,000; Greater Asunción, which includes the city and its suburbs, is home to about 1.5 million people.

Asunción contains many beautiful colonial style homes and buildings, a national theater, and a government palace built to resemble the Louvre in Paris. A construction boom since the 1980's has resulted in high-rise buildings and shopping malls outside the city center.

**Ciudad del Este** is the country's second largest city, with a population of 500,000. Founded in 1957, it is the capital of Alto Paraná, one of Paraguay's 17 departments, or states. Until 1989 it was known as Puerto Presidente Strossner. Situated on the banks of the Paraná River bordering Brazil, it was originally designed as a beautiful garden city.

**Concepción** is a small but historic city located on the Paraguay River. Until the 1940's it was the second largest city in the country, but it has since declined in importance, partly due to its isolated location. With a population of approximately 50,000, it remains a pretty, tranquil colonial town.

▶ **GOVERNMENT**

Paraguay's government is based on the constitution of 1992. The president, who is head of both state and government, is elected for a term of five years. Congress consists of the Chamber of Representatives (80 seats) and the Chamber of Senators (45 seats). Both are elected every five years. Since 1992, Paraguay has also developed an independent supreme court and a system of democratic municipal and departmental government.

▶ **HISTORY**

At the time of the Spanish conquest, Paraguay was inhabited by

three main indigenous groups. The Guacurús and the Payaguás lived in the Gran Chaco, and the Guaraní lived in the east. The groups in the Gran Chaco were nomadic hunters, but the Guaraní were farmers and settled in villages.

Asunción, the capital of the Río de la Plata province for more than a century, was a starting place for colonization. Jesuit missionaries came to Paraguay in 1587 and organized the Guaraní into self-sufficient communities (*reducciones*) under Jesuit control. The Guaraní were taught Christianity, learned various trades, and grew crops—safe from the threat of the Portuguese slave trade in Brazil. By the mid-1700's, the Jesuits had become very successful commercially, inspiring jealousy in both the Spanish settlers and the Spanish monarchy. In 1767, the Spanish king drove the Jesuits from Latin America, and the *reducciones* fell into decline.

**Independence, Dictators, and Wars.** When Argentina revolted against Spanish rule in 1810, Paraguay refused to form a federation with Argentina, fearing it would be swallowed up by its larger neighbor. Instead, it declared its own independence in 1811. José Rodríguez Francia, a leader in Paraguay's independence movement, was elected dictator for life. Francia promoted agricultural and industrial development and economic self-sufficiency. These policies were continued after his death in 1840 by Carlos Antonio López, whose rule is known as a period of rapid economic and technological development. However, his son, Francisco Solano López, led Paraguay into the War of the Triple Alliance (1865–70) against Brazil, Argentina, and Uruguay. As a result, Paraguay lost more than half its population and over a quarter of its territory.

An aerial view of Asunción, Paraguay's capital and largest city. Asunción's location on the Paraguay River led to its development as the country's main port and trade outlet.

The country had just recovered from this tragedy when it went to war again (1932–35) over the Gran Chaco, which was claimed by both Paraguay and Bolivia. Paraguay won, but the Chaco War left more than 90,000 people dead and the country bankrupt. The next 20 years saw continued political instability, including a savage civil war in 1947.

**Modern Governments.** In 1954, General Alfredo Stroessner took control of the government in a military coup. His dictatorship gave Paraguay political stability and some economic growth but at the cost of political freedom and individual rights. Stroessner was elected to an eighth term in 1988, but in 1989 he was removed from power in a coup led by General Andrés Rodríguez. Rodríguez was elected president and remained in office until 1993, during which time he began to reestablish democratic rights and institutions. In 1991, Paraguay signed the Treaty of Asunción with Brazil, Argentina, and Uruguay to form Mercosur, a regional free trade agreement, and in 1992 an elected constituent assembly approved a new democratic constitution.

In 1993, Juan Carlos Wasmosy of the Colorado Party was elected president. He was succeeded in 1998 by Raúl Cubas Grau, also of the Colorado Party.

In March 1999, Paraguay's vice president, Luís María Argaña, was assassinated. Although there was no proof, many people blamed President Cubas, who was already facing impeachment hearings on charges of abuse of power. Cubas resigned from office and was granted political asylum in Brazil. Senate leader Luis González Macchi of the Colorado Party was appointed to fill out his term.

But Macchi's popularity quickly declined, and his government was widely criticized for its inability to clean up corruption, reverse economic decline, and address the country's widespread poverty. He narrowly escaped impeachment in 2003. Ever hopeful of reform, the Paraguayans then elected Colorado Party candidate Nicanor Duarte Frutos president.

Reviewed by Dr. PETER LAMBERT
Senior Lecturer, Spanish and
Latin American Studies
University of Bath

**PARAMECIUM.** See PROTOZOANS.

# PARENT-TEACHER ASSOCIATIONS

A parent-teacher association is an organization that involves parents directly in the activities of their children's school. The idea behind such involvement is that children learn and develop best when the home and the school work closely together. Often school administrators and high school students are members, as well as parents and teachers.

Usually the association in each school decides what it wishes to do to provide better opportunities for children and youth. For instance, the association may buy equipment or books for the school, or it may sponsor health programs that provide medical and dental care. But some activities may extend beyond the school system to benefit the entire community. Programs that seek to obtain better housing and well-run juvenile courts are examples. Parent-teacher associations may support scholarship funds for training teachers and draw up guidelines for teenage groups in the community. They may form committees to study ways of improving television, radio, and movies for children or to study such subjects as family life and child development.

There are parents' groups in schools throughout the world. They are known by different names in different countries. In Britain and the United States, the school groups are called parent-teacher associations, or PTA's. Japan also uses this name. In Canada, local groups are called home and school associations or parent-teacher associations. In Denmark, committees of parents, known as parents' advisory councils, are appointed by town councils. They meet with teachers and administrators.

▶ **THE NATIONAL CONGRESS OF PARENTS AND TEACHERS (UNITED STATES)**

Most parent-teacher associations in the United States are connected with the National Congress of Parents and Teachers, also known as the National PTA. It has more than 6.5 million members and 26,000 local units, made up of PTA's from each state, the District of Columbia, the U.S. Virgin Islands, and U.S. schools abroad (the latter are served by the European Congress of American Parents, Teachers, and Students). Many parents of parochial-school pupils belong to separate organizations called home-school associations. Private, or independent, schools generally have their own associations, such as parents' leagues.

The National PTA—called at first the National Congress of Mothers—was founded on February 17, 1897, in Washington, D.C., by Alice McLellan Birney and Phoebe Apperson Hearst, mothers of schoolchildren. Their purpose was to help children by teaching parents about child development. The mothers gradually became interested in schools and held their meetings there. Men and teachers joined the organization, and in 1924 the current name was adopted. In 1970 the National Congress of Colored Parents and Teachers—which existed in those states having segregated schools—and the National Congress of Parents and Teachers were united into one organization. Local units of the National PTA are called parent-teacher or parent-teacher-student associations.

In the early days, PTA's often raised money for needed school supplies and equipment. PTA's still raise funds for such purposes, but they are equally active in other areas. The activities sponsored by the National PTA are guided by these objectives:

To promote the welfare of children and youth in home, school, community, and place of worship.
To raise the standards of home life.
To secure adequate laws for the protection of children and youth.
To bring into closer relation the home and the school, that parents and teachers may cooperate intelligently in the education of children and youth.
To develop between educators and the general public such united efforts as will secure for all children and youth the highest advantages in physical, mental, social, and spiritual education.

One of the National PTA's first important projects was to encourage the formation of kindergartens in public schools. The National PTA has planned programs in such areas as health education and urban education, and it has helped provide volunteer workers in juvenile courts. Through a special office in Washington, D.C., it actively supports federal legislation that will benefit public education. It encourages local PTA's to influence school policies by working with school administrators and boards of education.

The work of the National PTA is carried out largely by three commissions and certain special committees. There are commissions on education, health and welfare, and individual development. The National PTA publishes a number of pamphlets, a legislative newsletter, and a periodical, *Our Children*. Headquarters are at 330 North Wabash Avenue, Suite 2100, Chicago, Illinois 60611.

▶ **CANADIAN HOME AND SCHOOL AND PARENT-TEACHER FEDERATION**

In Canada, local parents' groups belong to a national association called the Canadian Home and School Federation. The national association is organized into ten provincial federations.

The first parents' group in Canada was formed in Baddeck, Nova Scotia, in 1895. Its founder was Mabel Hubbard Bell, the wife of the inventor Alexander Graham Bell. Other groups formed independently and became organized into provincial federations. The national organization was formed in 1927.

The objectives of the Canadian Home and School Federation are very similar to those of parent-teacher groups elsewhere. They include raising the standards of home life; obtaining the best for each child, according to the child's physical, mental, social, and spiritual needs; fostering high ideals of citizenship; and promoting goodwill and peace.

Activities of the national federation have included studies of smoking habits among Canadian schoolchildren and of broadcasting aimed at children. Many of the national group's activities deal with needs expressed at local association meetings. Examples include the national group's support of vocational courses in high schools, preschool education programs, school lunch programs, and the elimination of commercial advertising directed at children. The headquarters are at Fisher Park School, 250 Holland Avenue, Room 216, Ottawa, Ontario, K1Y 0Y6.

Reviewed by the National PTA (U.S.)

# PARIS

Paris is the capital and largest city of France. It is often called the City of Light, not just because of its brightly illuminated boulevards and awe-inspiring monuments but because it has long been one of the intellectual capitals of western civilization—a center of enlightenment. Many people consider it the most beautiful city in the world. Few capital cities form the heart of a country as completely as does Paris. It is not only the seat of government but the administrative, industrial, transportation, scientific, and artistic center of France. It is also one of the world's primary tourist destinations.

The River Seine flows through Paris, dividing it into two distinct parts: the respectable and fashionable Right Bank to the north and the trendier, more bohemian Left Bank to the south. The Seine also encircles two famous islands, the Île de la Cité—the original heart of the city—and the nearby Île St. Louis. By taking a pleasure cruise along the river in one of many water buses called *bateaux-mouches*, sightseers can glimpse dozens of historic landmarks and the charming stalls of the *bouquinistes* (secondhand booksellers) along the banks.

On a walk through the old sections of the city, at nearly every step one will find an exquisitely carved door, a colorful sign outside a quaint shop, or an ancient courtyard to admire. This is also true of a walk down the Rue Saint-Honoré, where every shopwindow is itself a work of art. Souvenir shops, bookshops, and famous tearooms line the covered arcades of the Rue de Rivoli. Collectors strolling along the Rue Bonaparte will enjoy browsing in the antique stores filled with ancient clocks, porcelain miniatures, and old books bound in leather and gold. And everywhere are indoor and outdoor cafés, where people can relax, have a drink or a light meal, and watch the passersby.

Paris has long been a center of international gatherings. Several world institutions, including the United Nations Educational, Scientific, and Cultural Organization (UNESCO) and the Organization for Economic Cooperation and Development (OECD), are headquartered there. Many important international peace treaties have been signed in or near the city, including those ending the Seven Years' War (1763), the American Revolutionary War (1783), the Napoleonic Wars

(1815), the Crimean War (1856), the Spanish-American War (1898), World War I (1919), the Vietnam War (1973), and most recently the war in Bosnia (1995).

## LAND

Paris lies in the lowlands of the Paris Basin in north central France, a little more than 100 miles (160 kilometers) southeast of the English Channel. The city itself covers an area of just 41 square miles (105 square kilometers). Its highest point, Montmartre, rises 420 feet (128 meters) above sea level.

## PEOPLE

The Paris metropolitan area has a population of about 10 million people, a number that increases every year. About 2 million live in the city proper.

### Education and Libraries

Paris contains 13 branches of the University of Paris. About 15 percent of the students come from foreign countries. The Sorbonne, the oldest and most famous branch, was founded about

1257. It is situated in the heart of the Latin Quarter, so-called because the students in medieval times spoke in Latin. Other notable academic institutions include the École des Beaux-Arts (School of Fine Arts), the Collège de France, the American University of Paris, and several engineering and technical colleges.

The Bibliothèque Nationale (National Library), was begun in the late 1400's as a royal collection of manuscripts. By law, every book published in France since 1537 has become part of the collection. In 1996, the printed volumes were moved to new facilities called the Bibliothèque Nationale de France, which houses more than 12 million volumes. The original library still contains one of the world's most priceless collections of original manuscripts, engravings, photographs, and maps.

### Museums and the Arts

Few cities can compete with Paris as a center of arts

*Clockwise from left:* The soaring Eiffel Tower is the most celebrated modern landmark in Paris. Patrons relax at the Café de Flore in the Latin Quarter. The River Seine flows around the Île de la Cité, where Paris was first settled about 2,300 years ago.

and culture. It features more than 170 museums and monuments, many of them world-famous. Perhaps the most impressive is the Louvre, the national art museum of France. This immense structure, once a royal palace, houses the world's most celebrated collections of paintings and sculpture, including Leonardo Da Vinci's most famous painting, *Mona Lisa* (known in France as *La Joconde*), and the ancient Greek statue *Venus de Milo*.

Other important art museums in Paris include the Musée d'Orsay, a restored railway station that now houses mostly the works of French impressionists; the Pompidou Center (also known as the Beaubourg), a center for modern art; the National Museum of the Middle Ages (formerly the Cluny Museum), featuring one of the world's finest collections of medieval artifacts; the Picasso Museum, with the world's largest collection of works by the great modern artist; the Rodin Museum, dedicated to the works of France's most famous sculptor; and the Orangerie Museum, featuring the famous water lily series of paintings by Claude Monet. Other types of museums include the Cinema

The Musée d'Orsay, a national museum that is housed in a restored railway station, is best known for its collection of French painting and sculpture.

Museum, containing one of the world's largest archives of motion pictures; the Carnavalet Museum, devoted to the history of Paris until the French Revolution; and the Army Museum, depicting the history of French warfare, from the Stone Age through World War II.

Paris is also a world-renowned center for the performing arts. Concerts, operas, and ballets are staged at various locations by the national Paris Opera. The Comédie-Française has performed classic French theater for more than 300 years. Paris is also the center of the internationally acclaimed French film industry.

**Parks**

Paris is filled with exquisite parks and gardens that serve as quiet places of retreat from the commotion of the city. The city's largest park, the Bois de Boulogne, has a spectacular rose garden and an open-air theater. The gardens at the Jardin des Tuileries are famous for their ornamental ponds. The Parc Monceau and the Jardin du Luxembourg are distinguished by their beautiful statuary and playgrounds. The Jardin des Plantes, a

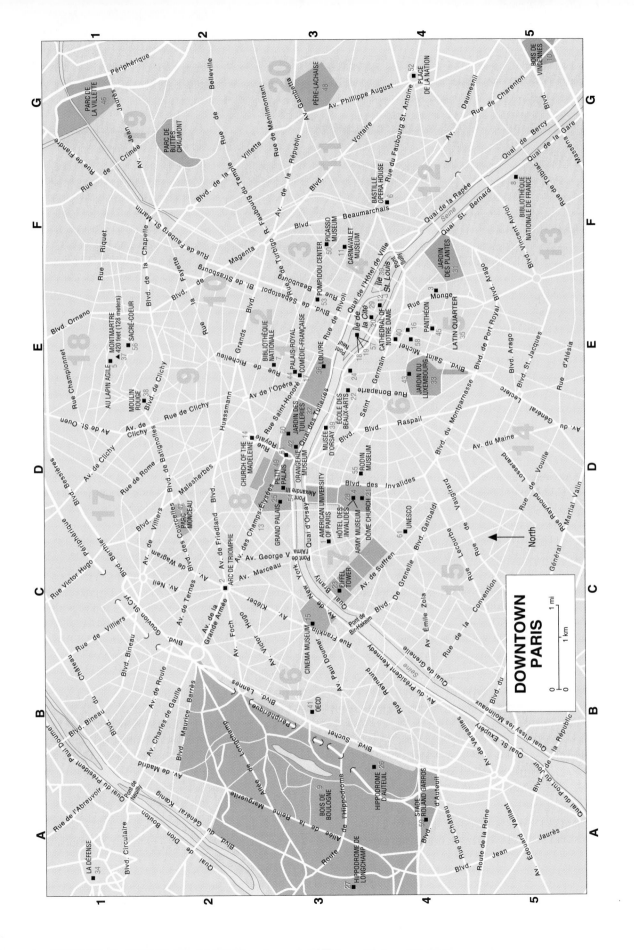

# DOWNTOWN PARIS

Arc de Triomphe

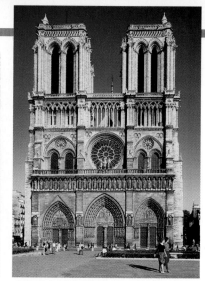

Cathedral of Notre Dame

**Arc de Triomphe**, one of the world's most recognized landmarks, towers over the Place Charles de Gaulle (formerly Place de l'Étoile) at the western end of the **Champs-Élysées**, the city's most famous boulevard. The arch was commissioned in 1806 by Napoleon I to welcome his troops home from the Napoleonic Wars, although construction was not completed until 1836. Many of the arch's magnificent stone carvings celebrate French military victories. At its center lies the Tomb of the Unknown Soldier, commemorating the soldiers killed in World War I whose remains were never identified.

**Cathedral of Notre Dame**, a masterpiece of the early Gothic style of architecture, is the most visited attraction in Paris. Situated in the heart of the city on the Île

de la Cité, the building was begun in 1163 on the site of a Roman temple. The cathedral has been at the center of many great events in French history, including the coronation of Napoleon I as emperor in 1804. It was also the setting of Victor Hugo's famous novel *The Hunchback of Notre Dame*.

**Château de Versailles**, situated in the Paris suburb of Versailles, was commissioned by King Louis XIV to showcase his immense power and riches. Completed in 1682, it remained the center of court life until the French Revolution. The building was designed by the architects Louis Le Vau and Jules Hardouin-Mansart. Charles Le Brun designed the interior spaces, including the spectacular Hall of Mirrors. The surrounding formal gardens were planned by André Le Nôtre.

**Conciergerie**, originally built as a fortress, later became a royal prison. It earned an infamous reputation during the Revolution, when it served as a detention center for prisoners awaiting execution, among them Queen Marie-Antoinette.

**Eiffel Tower**, the city's most celebrated modern landmark, is a 1,063-foot (324-meter) iron structure built for the 1889 Universal Exposition (World's Fair). It was the world's tallest building until 1931, when the Empire State Building was completed in New York City. From the top, one can see all of Paris and the hills surrounding the city. For more information, see the biography of Alexandre-Gustave Eiffel in Volume E.

**Hôtel des Invalides**, with its graceful colonnaded facade, was built by King Louis XIV in the 1670's as a home for

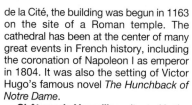

botanical garden, houses plants and flowers from all over the world. The Parc de la Villette features a museum of science and industry, a theater, and a music center. The lovely Bois de Vincennes, once a royal hunting ground, contains a zoo.

Two amusement theme parks—Disneyland Paris and Parc Astérix, named for France's most beloved cartoon character—are located just outside the city.

### Sports

The Bois de Boulogne is home to two prominent horse racecourses, the Hippodrome de Longchamp and the Hippodrome d'Auteuil. It is also the site of the Stade Roland Garros, where the annual international French Open tennis tournament is

played. Every July, the Tour de France, the world's most famous bicycle race, ends with great fanfare on the Champs-Élysées boulevard. Paris has twice hosted the Summer Olympic Games (in 1900 and 1924) and the World Cup soccer championship games (in 1938 and 1998).

### ▶ ECONOMY

Paris is the most vital economic center in France. The headquarters of most of the nation's largest corporations are located there.

### Services

France's most important service industries are centered in Paris. These include national and municipal government operations as well as the principal college-level public educa-

Montmartre

ca called **Sacré-Coeur** (Sacred Heart). Montmartre has long been a renowned and unconventional community for artists and writers. It is home to the legendary Au Lapin Agile nightclub and the Moulin Rouge dance hall.

**Panthéon**, dominating the hill of Sainte-Geneviève in the Latin Quarter, was originally built by King Louis XV as a church. But during the Revolution it was converted into a memorial tomb for French luminaries. Among those buried there are the philosophers Voltaire and Jean-Jacques Rousseau, writers Victor Hugo and Émile Zola, and scientists Pierre and Marie Curie.

**Père-Lachaise** is one of the world's most famous cemeteries. An enduring tourist attraction, this enormous and beautifully landscaped park contains the gravesites of hundreds of famous people, including the writers Jean de La Fontaine, Molière, Honoré de Balzac, Oscar Wilde, Marcel Proust, and Gertrude Stein; actors Sarah Bernhardt, Yves Montand, and Simone Signoret; singers Édith Piaf and Maria Callas; composers Georges Bizet and Frédéric Chopin; artists Honoré Daumier, Eugène Delacroix, Jean Auguste Dominique Ingres, Jean-Baptiste Corot, Camille Pissarro, and Georges Seurat;

French presidents Adolphe Thiers and Félix Faure; Paris city planner Georges Haussmann; the modern dance pioneer Isadora Duncan; and the rock music legend Jim Morrison.

**Roman Ruins** dating back nearly 2,000 years can still be seen in Paris. Major sites include the Crypte Archéologique, 393 feet (120 meters) beneath the square of Notre Dame on the Île de la Cité, and two sites on the Left Bank—the Arènes de Lutèce amphitheater and the Thermes de Cluny (thermal baths) at the National Museum of the Middle Ages.

**Sainte-Chapelle**, known for its soaring stained-glass windows, was built in 1248 by King Louis IX (St. Louis) as a sanctuary for Christ's Crown of Thorns, one of the most sacred of Christian relics.

Stained-Glass Windows, Sainte-Chapelle

wounded and homeless veterans of French wars. A church beneath its gilded dome houses the tomb of Napoleon I and other notable French military heroes. Among them is Marshal Foch, the last commander in chief of the Allied forces in France during World War I.

**Louvre** is perhaps the world's most famous art museum. Originally built about 1200 as a fortress, it was later converted into a royal palace and occupied as such until the Court moved to Versailles in 1682. In 1793, during the Revolution, the building was transformed into the Musée de la République (Museum of the Republic). For more information on the history of the building and its art collection, see the article LOUVRE in Volume L.

**Montmartre**, the highest point in Paris, is crowned by an enormous basili-

---

tional facilities. It is also the center of French finance and the headquarters of BNP Paribas, one of the world's largest banks. But tourist-related industries by far make up the largest segment of the city's economy and employ the most people.

## Manufacturing

About one-quarter of all French manufacturing is centered in Paris. Automobiles, machine tools, electric and electronic goods, chemicals, and processed foods are produced mainly in the suburbs. Famous luxury items—such as perfumes, jewelry, fine leather goods, and haute-couture (high-fashion) clothing, are made in or near Paris. Familiar Parisian designer names include Chanel, Givenchy, and Christian Dior.

## Transportation

City planners have developed a complex network of mass-transit systems designed to ease traffic on Paris' famously crowded streets. The subway system, which opened in 1900, is known as the Métropolitain (or simply the Métro). Subway cars, covering about 125 miles (200 kilometers) of railway track, make regular stops at more than 300 stations. Since 1969, an additional railway system—the Réseau Express Régional (or RER)—has provided supplemental high-speed rail service in and around the city. As the heart of the national railway network, Paris also has six major train stations providing both national and international rail service.

Surrounding the city is a ring road called the Périphérique. Commuters can park at highway exits and take the Métro into the city. Taxis and buses also provide transportation. The *bateaux-mouches* are primarily used by tourists.

Paris has two major international airports, Orly and Charles de Gaulle. A third airport, Le Bourget—the airfield where pioneer aviator Charles Lindbergh landed his plane the *Spirit of St. Louis* in 1927—is now home to an aerospace museum and the Paris Air Show, held every other year.

### Communication

Most French television and radio stations broadcast from Paris. The city is also the core of the nation's printing and publishing industries. Several world-renowned daily newspapers are printed there, including *France-Soir*, *Le Monde*, and the English-language *International Herald Tribune* as well as the popular entertainment magazine *Paris Match*.

### ▶ GOVERNMENT

Paris is one of 96 departments that make up the national government of France. In addition it is the center of the Île-de-France, one of the country's 22 official regions. Paris itself is divided into 20 numbered districts called arrondissements. Each arrondissement has its own mayor and city council members, all elected to 6-year terms. The Council of Paris—made up of a select number of members from each arrondissement—elects a mayor of Paris to represent the entire city.

Unlike other French cities, Paris does not have its own municipal police force and is secured by national government forces.

### ▶ HISTORY

Archaeological studies indicate that the Île de la Cité was settled as early as 300 B.C. by a Celtic tribe of fishermen known as the Parisii. They built a small village on the island as a refuge against invaders. In 52 B.C., the Romans—during their campaign to conquer Gaul (present-day France)—seized the island, where they built a city called Lutetia (meaning "marshy place").

The Romans ruled Gaul for more than 500 years until they were defeated in 486 by Clovis, the Germanic king of the Franks, at the Battle of Soissons in northern France. Clovis established the first Christian kingdom in France. Lutetia, by then known as Paris, be-

came his capital in 508. Some sections of Paris are still known by the names given to the many churches and monasteries built by the early Christians, such as Sainte-Geneviève, Saint-Germain-des-Prés, and Saint-Germain l'Auxerrois.

The first royal palaces were built on the Île de la Cité, where the Courts of Justice stand today. About 1200, the Louvre was begun on the Right Bank. At first it served as a fortress but was later converted into the royal residence and seat of government. Additional palaces and mansions were built during the first half of the 1600's. Among these were the Palais du Luxembourg (now the home of the French Senate), the Palais-Cardinal (today's Palais-Royal), and the Palais-Mazarin (now the Institut de France and seat of L'Académie Française, or French Academy).

In 1648, early in the reign of King Louis XIV, an uprising called the *Fronde* caused serious riots in Paris. As a result, the king later decided to leave Paris and build a palace in Versailles, 10 miles (16 kilometers) to the southwest. The court moved in 1682, and from that time on, one spoke of the Court and the Town as two separate worlds. Paris, however, remained the focal point of intellectual life. By the 1700's it had become a center of the Enlightenment, where philosophers, artists, political analysts, and other thinkers gathered to exchange ideas. (See the article on the Enlightenment in Volume E.)

In 1789, the French Revolution began in Paris when its citizens stormed the Bastille, the royal prison, and burned it to the ground. Later came a period called the Reign of Terror. Prisons were filled with the enemies of the Revolution, and thousands—including King Louis XVI—were executed. (See the article on the French Revolution in Volume F.)

The revolution ended in 1799 when the great general Napoleon Bonaparte seized power. Declaring himself emperor in 1804, Napoleon centralized the government under his authority, established order, and launched a war of European conquest. Napoleon commissioned many of Paris' greatest landmarks, including the Arc de Triomphe, the Church of the Madeleine, and the Rue de Rivoli. (See the biography of Napoleon I in Volume N.)

After Napoleon I was defeated in battle at Waterloo and sent into exile in 1815, King Louis XVIII, brother of the executed king,

*Left:* Ancient Roman artifacts are displayed at the Thermes de Cluny and elsewhere throughout Paris. *Below:* The ultra-modern Bastille Opera House, completed in 1989, was built near the site where the historic royal prison once stood.

was given the throne. In 1830 the Parisians overthrew Louis's brother and successor, Charles X, and called to the throne his cousin Louis Philippe, the head of the Orléans branch of the royal family.

During the European revolutions of 1848, Louis Philippe was expelled by the people. He was succeeded by Louis Napoleon (later emperor Napoleon III), nephew of Napoleon I.

Paris soon became a city devoted to big business and real estate development. During the Second Empire (1852–70), Napoleon III hired Baron Georges Eugène Haussmann, a government administrator and town planner, to rid Paris of its decaying and disease-ridden slums. Haussmann built large avenues and boulevards and new residential quarters. The city was extended west, toward the Champs-Élysées, a trend that continued under the government of the Third Republic (1871–1940). (See the biography of Napoleon III in Volume N.)

World's fairs held in Paris in 1878, 1889, and 1900 inspired the building of several of today's now-familiar landmarks, including the Eiffel Tower, the Grand Palais and the Petit Palais, and the elaborate Pont Alexandre III, one of the many bridges that cross the Seine.

Three wars endangered the freedom and even the existence of Paris. In 1870, during the Franco-Prussian War, the city was bombarded by the Prussians. When the French government surrendered, a popular uprising established a revolutionary city government, the Commune of Paris, which was quickly suppressed. (See the article on the Franco-Prussian War in Volume F.) In 1914, during World War I, Paris was saved from a German invasion by an Allied victory at the Marne. Then in 1940, during World War II, the French declared Paris an "open city" to prevent its destruction by German bombs. Paris was then occupied by the Germans, and the French government relocated south to the city of Vichy.

When Paris was finally liberated by Allied forces in 1944, General Charles de Gaulle, leader of the Free French movement, led triumphant troops down the Champs-Élysées. (See the articles on World War I and World War II in Volume WXYZ.) Thereafter, Paris remained calm until 1968, when workers' strikes and student demonstrations sparked a brief revolutionary movement.

Several postwar architectural renovations have altered parts of the Parisian landscape. Ultra-modern facilities include the building complex known as La Défense, the Pompidou Center, the Bastille Opera House, and the soaring glass pyramid that serves as the visitors' center at the Louvre.

Reviewed by KEITH BAKER
Director, France-Stanford Center for
Interdisciplinary Studies, Stanford University

**PARKER, BONNIE.**   See OUTLAWS (Profiles).

**PARKER, CHARLIE.**   See KANSAS (Famous People).

**PARKER, ELY S.**   See INDIANS, AMERICAN (Profiles).

## PARKS, ROSA (1913–2005)

On December 1, 1955, in Montgomery, Alabama, a black seamstress named Rosa Parks was on her way home from work when she was arrested. Her crime was refusing to give up her seat on a public bus to a white man, as was then required by law. Parks later said, "My resisting being mistreated on the bus did not begin with that particular arrest." In fact, she and many other blacks had often protested the humiliation of being treated like second-class citizens. But "that particular arrest" sparked a citywide bus boycott by African Americans that lasted 381 days. The boycott, led by a young Dr. Martin Luther King, Jr., marked the birth of the modern

civil rights movement. The attention it received increased national awareness of racial segregation and discrimination. Since that time, Parks has been known as the mother of the civil rights movement.

She was born Rosa Louise McCauley on February 4, 1913, in Tuskegee, Alabama. At age 19, she married Raymond Parks, a barber. Rosa was the first woman to join the Montgomery chapter of the National Association for the Advancement of Colored People (NAACP). She worked there as chapter secretary and adviser to the youth council. She also helped blacks register to vote.

After her arrest in 1955, Parks could no longer find work in Montgomery. She and her husband moved north and eventually settled in Detroit, Michigan. She continued working as a seamstress until 1965, when she joined the staff of Democratic U.S. congressman John Conyers, Jr. She retired in 1988.

Rosa Parks received many awards in her lifetime, including the Spingarn Medal (1979), the Presidential Medal of Freedom (1996), and the Congressional Gold Medal (1999). Her memoir, *Rosa Parks: My Story*, was published in 1992. She died in Detroit on October 24, 2005, at the age of 92. She was the first woman to lie in honor in the Capitol rotunda.

Reviewed by WILLIAM E. SHAPIRO
Consultant, children's encyclopedias

See also CIVIL RIGHTS MOVEMENT; JIM CROW LAWS.

## PARKS AND PLAYGROUNDS

Parks and playgrounds are areas of land set aside for public enjoyment. Parks may range in size from small plots of land to many square miles of forests and lakes. Playgrounds are small areas, usually created for children. Amusement parks, which combine entertainment and technology, are a modern invention.

One of the earliest known parks was the Hanging Gardens of Babylon, built about 600 B.C. It was considered one of the seven wonders of the ancient world. The forerunners of our modern playgrounds were the outdoor gymnasiums of ancient Greece, where young men trained for the Olympic Games, first held in 776 B.C.

▶ PARKS

Before the 1700's, parks were developed by the wealthy for their private use. Some of these were landscaped "hunting parks" stocked with game animals. Others were spacious formal gardens that surrounded palaces and villas and blended nature and art. These gardens featured great lawns, ornamental trees, and shrubbery clipped into decorative shapes (topiary) or sheared to form dense arches over paths. Statuary, reflecting pools, elaborate fountains and water cascades, and outdoor stages for concerts and theatrical productions were commonplace.

In England and France, garden design was formal. Many private parks contained a maze (an intricate series of paths enclosed by high hedges) designed so that once someone was inside, it was difficult to find the way out.

Private parks were rarely opened to the public. But social changes such as those brought about by the French Revolution (1789–99) opened many private estates to public use. Rising property taxes and inheritance taxes often forced owners of large estates to turn them over to the community. Some parks were given to the public by generous owners.

Former market squares and military drill grounds in large cities became public parks after they had outlived their original

The Sissinghurst Gardens, in Kent, England, are a fine example of formal garden parks, with magnificent scenery and great rolling lawns.

uses. Village greens, or commons, were widespread in Europe and were duplicated by settlers in the colonies.

Early in the 1800's in England, a totally new idea of park design developed. Regent's Park in London, created by an act of Parliament in 1812, was planned to be informal in design. Its landscaping was a reflection of nature. A lake was made for boating. Trees flanked large grassy meadows where people took part in the popular games of the day.

This park set a pattern for people's parks everywhere, though many older parks kept their formal appearance.

**Urban Parks.** The creation of public parks in urban areas was influenced by the rapid increase in city populations. Meadows and forests were cleared to build new homes and factories, and open land for recreation disappeared. Riverbanks and bays were spoiled for recreational use by piers and docks. The waters became polluted with industrial waste and refuse. In many cities, cemeteries were the only open spaces left where working people could spend their few hours of leisure time.

On Manhattan Island, in New York City, the lack of open space was most acute. The need for a public park was recognized early in the 1800's. Influential and public-spirited citizens returning from European capitals urged the creation of a large public park similar to those in London, Paris, and Berlin.

It was not until 1853 that public demand for such a park brought about the acquisition of the land for Central Park. The design for the park, drawn up by Frederick Law Olmsted and Calvert Vaux in 1857, kept the natural features of the land and was a milestone in park development. It included three play-

*Left:* During the winter months, ice-skating is a popular activity at New York City's Central Park. This urban park has been in existence since the mid-1800's. *Below:* In crowded cities, parks are especially valued as places for outdoor recreation.

Few experiences are as thrilling as a ride on a roller coaster, a major draw at most amusement parks.

grounds for children—a completely new concept in park planning.

**Regional and National Parks.** Regional, state, and national parks and forests preserve natural scenery and wildlife for present and future generations. Larger parks, with recreational resources that city parks cannot provide, such as shorelines and wildlife preserves, have become more and more important. To preserve these extensive lands from commercial development, large sections have been acquired by national governments for future park systems. For more information, see the articles NATIONAL PARK SYSTEM and NATIONAL FOREST SYSTEM in Volume N and those on individual national parks.

**Amusement and Theme Parks.** Amusement parks, sometimes called theme parks, specialize in rides, games, and entertainment. Unlike public parks, these parks are owned by private businesses or individuals. Amusement and theme parks charge admission, and they usually also charge for all goods and services inside the park.

The oldest amusement park still operating is Bakken Amusement Park, in Copenhagen, Denmark. It was started more than 400 years ago. But Copenhagen has a more famous park—Tivoli Gardens, located right in the middle of the city. This park combines rides and games with theaters, concert halls, restaurants, and beautiful gardens.

The first amusement parks in the United States were built by streetcar companies in the mid-1850's. There were no automobiles then, and only wealthy people owned carriages. If average-income people wanted to go somewhere, they had to walk or ride the streetcars. The streetcars were crowded six days a week, but no one rode them on Sundays. So streetcar owners decided to build places for people to go on Sundays. They built parks at the ends of streetcar lines, equipping them with swings, slides, pony rides, merry-go-rounds, picnic areas, and places to dance. Soon many people rode to these parks to have fun on Sundays.

Some early parks are still operating. Cedar Point, near Sandusky, Ohio, began in 1870 when Great Lakes steamboats stopped there to let passengers swim and picnic. In 1888 a dance pavilion was added, and in 1894 a roller coaster was built. Coney Island, on the Atlantic Ocean near New York City, New York, began with a sandy beach that was popular with vacationers. The Switchback Railway ride made its debut in 1884, thrilling everyone with its speed of over 6 miles (9.5 kilometers) an hour. Hersheypark, in Hershey, Pennsylvania, had its beginnings in 1907. Milton S. Hershey, the chocolate manufacturer who founded the town, built the park for factory workers and their families. A roller coaster was added in 1927.

When Walter and Cordelia Knott moved to Buena Park, California, in 1920, they began to grow boysenberries. Then they set up a roadside stand to sell the jams and jellies made from the berries. Soon they were serving chicken dinners to visitors in their home. By 1940, so many people were coming for dinner that long waiting lines formed. The Knotts built a replica of a ghost town to entertain the people. Today Knott's Berry Farm is a full-fledged amusement park that entertains millions of people.

Safety was not always a consideration in the early amusement parks. Rides sometimes collapsed, and fires were a frequent occurrence at some parks. Others were flooded out by spring rains.

Every year, millions of people visit theme parks. Walt Disney's are among the best known, including Animal Kingdom in Lake Buena Vista, Florida.

During the Great Depression of the 1930's, many parks were forced to close because people had little money to spend on entertainment. From 1939 to 1945, the world was involved in World War II, and there was little time for fun. Even after the war was over, many amusement parks had to struggle to stay open.

Then, in 1954, Walt Disney announced plans to build a 180-acre (72-hectare) park in Anaheim, California. A year later, Disneyland opened. This was the first theme park, in which rides, restaurants, shows, costumes, and other attractions were all related to a central idea. Disneyland was composed of five theme areas—Fantasyland, Tomorrowland, Frontierland, Adventureland, and Main Street U.S.A. Three more theme areas were later added: Critter Country, New Orleans Square, and Mickey's Toontown.

Other theme parks followed. Kings Island, near Cincinnati, Ohio, uses cartoon charac-ters as a theme. The Old South is the theme of Carowinds, in Charlotte, North Carolina. Parks that feature animal preserves, such as Busch Gardens in Florida, are also thought of as theme parks. The Six Flags Theme Parks focus on the history of U.S. settlers who came from other countries.

A second Disney theme park, Walt Disney World, opened near Orlando, Florida, in 1971. Today Walt Disney World is an enormous entertainment complex. It includes the EPCOT (Experimental Prototype Community of Tomorrow) Center, which features different displays of the latest technology. It opened in 1982. Disney-MGM Studios, opened in 1989, features film studios open to the public so that visitors can see how movies are made. Disney's Animal Kingdom, located in Lake Buena Vista, Florida, opened in 1998. A popular activity is going "on safari" and seeing wild animals roaming free.

Other Disneyland parks opened near Tokyo, Japan, in 1983, and near Paris, France, in 1992.

Today, in many countries of the world, amusement parks offer entertainment. All the major parks have at least one roller coaster and one carousel, along with rides that carry out the theme of the park. There is much greater concern for safety today than there was in the early days.

Live music and computer-animated shows are always park favorites. Midways, or "main streets," are lined with games of chance, gift shops, and restaurants. At some parks, animal preserves and white-water rides provide excitement. There is something for everyone at today's amusement parks.

## ▶ PLAYGROUNDS

Playgrounds designed as recreational areas for children are a modern development. Playgrounds provide a wide variety of play and exercise equipment, courts for active games, numerous types of sports fields, and rooms for indoor recreation.

Playground equipment is designed to satisfy the natural desire of children to climb, swing, jump, balance, and slide.

Some countries have pioneered in creating "junk" playgrounds, where children may play on obsolete locomotives, boats, trucks, and airplanes. Highly imaginative sculptured forms for play and exercise are installed in some playgrounds. Others use natural materials such as cross sections of big trees in various lengths, which are placed to form climbing and balancing equipment.

The greatest benefit of playgrounds is that they provide a safe place for children to play. When the woods and fields were turned into

A playground provides a wide variety of activities for children. Playing with a group of friends on the swings is always a favorite.

Playground equipment is designed to be colorful and fun as well as safe. Children develop strength and improve their coordination as they climb, swing, jump, balance, and slide.

cities, children had to play on the city streets. First, horse-drawn, and later, motor, vehicles were a constant danger. Dirt in the streets was a health hazard.

Playground programs under the guidance of recreational leaders offer a great variety of activities for all age groups. These programs are planned to help children progress from games requiring only simple skills to those that demand greater coordination, speed, strength, and endurance.

The first consideration in designing a playground is to make sure it will serve the community's immediate and future needs. When planning playgrounds, communities must consider the recreational needs of young children. Swings, small slides, and simple exercise apparatus are required. Larger exercise equipment, ball fields, and basketball, volleyball, handball, and paddle-tennis courts are needed for older children.

Safety equipment must be provided. The play areas of young children should be set apart from those of older boys and girls so that small children will not be injured. Backstops for baseball and softball fields and fences for tennis courts are necessary to protect spectators. Benches should be provided for parents supervising children.

VIENO RAUTIO
Department of Parks, City of New York

ELIZABETH VAN STEENWYK
Author, *Behind the Scenes at the Amusement Park*

# PARLIAMENTARY PROCEDURE

Parliamentary procedure is the method by which meetings are run in a fair and orderly manner. The British Parliament, the Congress of the United States, and other lawmaking bodies follow strict parliamentary procedure. In simpler form the rules are used by business and professional groups, church and school organizations, student councils, and social clubs. A basic principle of parliamentary procedure is to make certain of majority rule and minority rights.

Parliamentary procedure is known also as parliamentary law and, especially in the United States, as rules of order. *Robert's Rules of Order,* a book about parliamentary procedure, was published in 1876. It is still the book used by most organizations in the United States.

## History

Most historians agree that the lawmaking bodies of ancient Greece and Rome must have used certain rules of order. But parliamentary procedure as it is known today was developed in the British Parliament.

The English settlers in the American colonies brought with them the basic rules of parliamentary procedure. They used the rules in colonial assemblies and later in state legislatures. Strict parliamentary procedure was followed in the formation of the first two-house Congress of the United States in 1789. During his term as vice president under John Adams, Thomas Jefferson drafted *A Manual of Parliamentary Practice,* which is still used in the Senate and the House of Representatives of the United States.

## How an Organization is Set Up

When people meet to form a new organization, one of the first things they do is choose a temporary chairperson. A temporary secretary is then elected to keep the minutes (official records) of the meetings. Next, a temporary committee is formed to help the temporary chairperson draw up a constitution and a set of bylaws. The constitution describes the general structure, purpose, and principles of the organization. The **bylaws** state how the purpose and principles will be carried out. They describe qualifications for membership, procedure for selection of members, and the amount of dues each member must pay. The bylaws also explain how officers will be elected and what their duties will be. And they state how permanent (standing) committees will be formed and what their functions will be.

## Officers

After the members have voted to accept the constitution and the bylaws, the officers of the organization are elected. Most officers are elected to serve for a specific period of time. An organization usually elects a chairperson or president, a vice president, a secretary, and a treasurer. Some groups also elect a sergeant at arms.

The president (or chairperson) heads the organization. The president occupies the place of authority at meetings and supervises the work of committees and other officers. The vice president helps the president and takes over when the president is absent. The secretary keeps the minutes and reads them aloud at the next meeting. The secretary's other duties include taking care of all correspondence and committee reports, making announcements, and notifying members of changes in schedule. The treasurer takes care of the organization's finances and prepares the financial reports and annual budget. The sergeant at arms keeps order during meetings.

How does an organization choose its officers? First, a member nominates another member. Usually after two or more people have been nominated, the voting takes place. The person receiving the majority vote is the elected officer. A majority vote is a vote of at least one more than half of all present.

Most organizations require that a quorum be present at elections and at meetings where important decisions are to be made. A **quorum** is a majority of the total membership (or a greater or lesser fraction if specified in the bylaws).

## How Meetings Are Held

In parliamentary procedure, the president (or presiding officer) calls the meeting to order by rapping on a hard surface with a gavel and announcing, ''The meeting will please come to order.'' The gavel, a small wooden hammer, is also rapped to quiet disturbances.

The secretary then calls the roll. The list of members present is included in the minutes to be read at the next meeting. The **minutes** are a record of everything that happens at a meeting. Following the roll call, the secretary reads the minutes of the previous meeting. The president asks if anyone would like to correct or add to the minutes. If so, members vote on each correction and addition. If not, the minutes are accepted as read.

The meeting then proceeds according to the agenda. An **agenda** is the list of items to be taken care of at a meeting.

As a rule, committee reports are first on the agenda of regular meetings. (Special meetings can be called for a particular purpose.) The chairperson of each committee gives the report. Members may ask questions, make suggestions, or approve the reports, or they may refer the report back to committee.

Unfinished business left over from earlier meetings is then given attention. If action must be taken, members vote on a decision. If action can be postponed, the matter may be **tabled** (set aside) for consideration at a later meeting or it may be given to a committee.

New business is then introduced. Before a member may introduce a new subject, he or she must stand up and be **recognized**— given permission to speak—by the president. After being recognized, the speaker **has the floor.** The speaker may discuss only one subject at a time, and no interruptions are allowed. If, however, the speaker changes the subject or speaks too long, a member may rise and claim that the speaker is **out of order.** If the president agrees, the speaker must either stop talking and sit down or return to the original subject. If members become disorderly, the president raps the gavel and calls for order. If members do not obey the call for order, they may be put out of the meeting by the sergeant at arms.

### Motions

Often a member asks to be recognized in order to make a motion. A **motion** is a plan or suggestion that must either be approved or rejected by the other members. After one member makes a motion, it must be seconded by another member. If seconded, it must be approved or rejected. The motion is stated by the **chair** (the presiding officer). The group then debates (discusses) the motion. Debate continues until all members who wish to speak have had an opportunity to do so. All speakers for and against the motion must first be recognized by the presiding officer.

One of the ways to end debate is to make a specific motion to close the debate. If such a motion is made, seconded, and approved by a majority vote, the motion under discussion must then be put to a vote. All those who approve the motion say ''Aye''; all those against the motion say ''No.'' If the vote is very close, the presiding officer may call for a show of hands or a rising vote. With a rising vote, members stand up to indicate their vote. The presiding officer can vote to break a tie vote or vote to make a tie. A tie defeats a motion. If the majority of members present vote to accept the motion, it is approved. If the majority vote to reject the motion, it is dismissed.

Every motion must be taken care of in some way before the organization gives its attention to any other item.

After all action has been taken and matters needing further consideration have been tabled or otherwise disposed of, the business ends. A member moves that the meeting be closed, and another member seconds the motion. A vote is then taken; if a majority vote for adjournment, the presiding officer announces that the meeting is over.

### Committees

Certain jobs are often handled better and more efficiently by small groups, or committees, than by the whole membership of an organization.

Permanent, or standing, committees are set up after the election of officers. Depending on the bylaws of the organization, standing committees may be either appointed by the president or elected by the membership.

Temporary, or special, committees (ad hoc committees) are formed whenever necessary to work on a particular job. For example, a special committee may be selected to organize an exhibit, to plan a picnic, or to draft a new constitution or set of bylaws. Special committees break up when their job is done. The president of the organization usually selects one member of the committee to be its chairperson. In some cases the committee members may elect a chairperson.

Reviewed by GEORGE R. HOUSTON
Former Assistant Librarian
Supreme Court of the United States

# PARLIAMENTS

Many countries throughout the world are governed by legislative bodies called parliaments. These are broadly patterned on the government of Britain. Unwritten customs and traditions are an essential part of the British constitution. For this reason the parliamentary system is more difficult to understand than a system based on a written constitution like that of the United States.

## ▶HISTORY OF PARLIAMENTS

Originally the word "parliament" meant a "talk" in which the ruler discussed business with a group of advisers. The oldest parliament in existence is Iceland's Althing, which first met in A.D. 930. In the Middle Ages several European countries had parliaments. The Cortes, or assembly of states, developed in Spain. The Netherlands formed the States General of the Republics of the United Provinces.

During the late 1200's, elected bodies representing all the people began to meet in England to decide how the king should raise money. These early parliaments were not much like the British Parliament of today. But they marked the first time that a representative assembly became part of the English system of government.

The cabinet, the important ruling group within a parliament, developed and became strong because of several historical accidents. Early rulers of England had advisers called the Privy Council. But as government became more complicated, the rulers began to meet fairly regularly with only a few of the more important councillors. This small council was called the cabinet. As the role of the cabinet grew more important, it became an unwritten rule that all the members of the cabinet should sit in parliament to explain and defend government policies.

Modern parliamentary government by cabinets began in Britain in the 18th century. At that time the German-born king George I, who ruled Britain from 1714 to 1727, stopped attending cabinet meetings because he did not understand English. Left alone to make decisions, the cabinet gradually took over all the work and many of the powers of the king. Because they reported their decisions to the king as a group rather than as individuals, all cabinet members had to agree on those decisions. This agreement has become known as cabinet solidarity. Today any cabinet member who disagrees with a decision is expected to resign. Since the cabinet members had to cooperate, the ruler usually chose persons who shared the same political ideas. This led to the development of the modern system of political parties.

During the course of the growth of the parliamentary system in Britain, the House of Commons and the House of Lords were frequently involved in bitter power struggles. The House of Commons often showed its strength through the "power of the purse." Whenever British rulers or, later, cabinets wanted money, the House of Commons—by refusing to approve new taxes—could force rulers to change their policies or their councillors. Today this means that a cabinet must have the support of a majority of the House of Commons. Otherwise, it gets no money, and none of its policies will be approved. Over the centuries the House of Commons has become more powerful and the House of Lords has become less powerful in conducting the business of Parliament.

## ▶HOW A PARLIAMENT WORKS

A parliament has three parts—a chief of state, an upper chamber, and a lower chamber. In Britain the chief of state is the king or queen; the upper chamber is the House of Lords (nobles who inherit their right to a seat and others appointed for life); and the lower chamber is the House of Commons (democratically elected representatives). In other countries these names, and the means of appointing or electing, may differ. The head of state may be an elected president. The upper chamber may be called the senate or some other name. In Canada, for instance, the two houses are called the Senate and the House of Commons. But the part each plays in parliament is roughly the same. The lower house passes laws; the upper house examines these laws and, if necessary, revises them; and the head of state then approves the laws to make them official.

The power of the cabinet in parliamentary government is always present. The king or head of state reigns, but the prime minister and

Queen Elizabeth II presides at the opening session of the British Parliament.

In the British parliamentary system, Parliament is all-powerful. The cabinet—the executive branch of government that shapes government policies—sits in Parliament and must answer to it. Parliament is the nation's chief legislative body. It not only makes new laws but also has the power to revise or repeal existing laws and to determine whether or not a law is constitutional.

Parts of Canada's Constitution Act of 1982 broke with British parliamentary tradition. The Constitution Act gave the Supreme Court of Canada, rather than Parliament, the power to interpret the constitution and the right to declare a law unconstitutional. It also made a bill of rights and freedoms a part of the written constitution.

The congressional system of the United States is not, strictly speaking, a parliamentary system. Presidents of the United States are both heads of state and heads of government. They appoint cabinet members and remove those members if they wish. Cabinet members do not sit in Congress, and the government can be changed only by the presidential elections held every four years. But the U.S. system grew out of the parliamentary system practiced in the American colonies at the time of the Revolutionary War.

▶THE INTER-PARLIAMENTARY UNION

In 1889, representatives of the parliaments of nine countries met in Paris. As a result of this meeting the Inter-Parliamentary Union was established. This union is an organization of countries having some form of parliamentary government. Its purpose is to unite the governments of these countries and to promote international peace and harmony.

Parliaments of countries all over the world send delegates to meetings of the union. Many of the countries represented, such as the United States, do not have parliaments in the strictest sense. But all of them have governments in which there is some form of general election. The union meets at least once a year. Its official headquarters are located in Geneva, Switzerland.

JOHN S. MOIR
University of Toronto

See also LEGISLATURES.

the cabinet actually rule as long as a majority of the elected representatives support them. This means that the cabinet is "responsible to" parliament.

In a parliamentary system, governments can be defeated by a vote in parliament. However, a change of government usually comes at a general election. General elections must be held after a fixed number of years. But they can be held earlier if the party in power fails to get its policies approved. When an election is held, the voters can reject the government by electing more members from the opposition side. Or they can return the same government to power by electing more of its supporters. If the opposition party wins more than half the seats in the lower house, the head of state asks the leader of the majority party to serve as prime (first) minister and to choose a cabinet.

**PAROCHIAL SCHOOLS.** See EDUCATION; PREPARATORY SCHOOLS.

# PARROTS

When you hear the word "parrot," you probably think of a colorful bird with a hooked beak that lives in a cage, kept as a pet. Parrots are fascinating as pets, but they are even more intriguing in the wild. More than 330 different species of parrots make up the order, or group, of birds known as Psittaciformes. Cockatoos, macaws, budgerigars, lorikeets, lovebirds, conures, and cockatiels are only some of the different types.

Most parrots are forest birds, dwelling in the Southern Hemisphere—in South America, Australia, sub-Saharan Africa, and Indonesia. Parrots are also found in the forests of India, Asia, and Central America. Some parrots have adapted to life in other habitats besides the forest. In Australia, New Zealand, and on other nearby islands, parrots live in the grasslands, in snowy mountains, and on rocky, seaside cliffs. Only a handful of species are native to the Northern Hemisphere.

Whether it is the nectar-collecting lory (*left inset*), the cockatoo with its crest of feathers, or the brightly colored macaw (*right inset*), a parrot can be recognized by its curved beak, large head, and reversed toes (two pointing forward, two pointing backward).

## ▶ THE CHARACTERISTICS OF PARROTS

Many, but not all, of the different parrot species have brightly colored feathers. Some parrots, including the few ground-dwelling or nocturnal species, have feathers that are dull, dark colors, which help conceal the birds in their environment. The bright plumage of many parrots also serves as camouflage. High up in flowering tropical trees, under the blazing sun, multicolored birds are not at all easy to spot.

Although parrots of different species have widely different colors, all parrots have the same kind of hooked beak. A parrot's beak is very strong and sharp, enabling the bird to crack and crush a variety of very tough seeds. Some of the larger parrots, such as macaws and cockatoos, have such powerful beaks, they can cut through fence wire. A parrot's beak is also extremely flexible, so the bird can use it as a third foot. It climbs across a web of high branches or up a tree trunk, clenching a branch or bark in its beak to steady itself while bringing one foot and then the other foot forward.

Parrots also have perfect feet for these jungle acrobatics. Most birds have four toes, three pointing forward and one pointing backward; parrots have two toes facing forward and two facing backward. This gives the bird a sure grip as it moves to the very tips of branches and feasts on fruits and flowers few other birds can reach.

Finally, unlike other birds, parrots use their beaks and claws together to manipulate food and other objects with ease. Just as people can be right- or left-handed, parrots can be right- or left-footed. Way up in the treetops, a parrot might hang upside down by one foot, bring a seed to its mouth with the other foot, and crack the seed with its beak. By such dizzying feats, the parrot gained its nickname: monkey of the bird world.

### ▶ THE LIFE OF PARROTS

Parrots are social birds. Parrots that inhabit the forests tend to stick together in family groups. Those that inhabit more open areas tend to form huge flocks, sometimes made up of thousands of birds.

A parakeet's green color (*left*), the most common color of a parrot, keeps it well hidden as it perches on a tree branch. Parrots, such as these macaws dotting a cliff (*above*), tend to gather in large, noisy flocks.

Most parrots nest in hollowed-out tree branches or trunks and mate for life. Small parrots lay up to eight eggs; large parrots lay one or two eggs. Usually the female broods the eggs, that is, she sits on them to protect them and keep them warm. Brooding may go on for a month or longer. During this time, the male usually brings food to the female, who stays on the nest.

When the young hatch, they are small, naked, blind, and completely helpless. They are fed food that their parents have partially digested. However, the female budgerigar, a parrot native to central Australia, feeds its young milk that it makes in its esophagus.

Young parrots remain in the nest for a long time, compared with most birds. Most cannot fly for at least a month; young macaws cannot fly until the end of their third month. Once they learn to fly, young parrots practice swooping and swerving through the forest and climbing through the uppermost branches of the trees. Most parrots stay with their parents for at least a few months after they have learned to fly. They leave their parents to join with flocks made up of other young parrots. The young parrots stay with their flock one to three years, until they have matured. Then they seek out a mate and start their own family.

### ▶ PARROTS AND THEIR ENVIRONMENT

Wild parrots face two major threats: They are popular as pets, so many people try to capture them for sale to pet dealers, and they live in forested areas, which are being cut down at alarming rates.

Because of these threats, more than one-fifth of all parrot species in the world are endangered. Some parrot species have such small populations that, despite strong efforts to save the birds, they are likely to become extinct. For instance, the imperial amazon—a parrot native to the Caribbean island of Dominica—has a population of less than 50.

With breeding programs carried out by zoos and other institutions that work to conserve different types of animals, some parrot species may be rescued from the brink of extinction. Efforts to save the rain forests and other parrot habitats are equally essential for the survival of many species. Just as important, the laws against capturing, selling, or buying endangered species must be enforced. Many types of parrots are bred in captivity for sale as pets. To help save the parrots, only these captive-bred birds should be brought into homes. Most wild parrots breed slowly; they will not survive if people continue capturing them to sell as pets.

ELIZABETH KAPLAN
Series Coauthor, *Ask Isaac Asimov*

See also BIRDS; BIRDS AS PETS.

**PARTHIANS.** See PERSIA, ANCIENT.

# PARTIES

Everyone loves a party. It's fun to go to a party at a friend's house, and it can be even more fun to give one at your own house. Your fun can actually begin beforehand as you think of ideas to make your party a success. The key to a successful party is planning and preparing ahead of time.

There are many occasions throughout the year for giving a party. Birthdays, Halloween, Christmas, St. Valentine's Day, St. Patrick's Day, Easter, and patriotic holidays are some of those times. Do not feel that you must wait for a special day to justify having a party. Sometimes people have parties just because they want to, and that is fine, too.

### ▶PLANNING THE PARTY

Before you begin the plans for your party, you must have one very important thing and that is permission from your family. It might not be possible for you to have a birthday party every year. Some years you might just have one special friend come over for dinner (your favorite dinner, of course) and birthday cake.

If this is your lucky year and it is all right for you to have a party, the first step is to sit down with an older member of your family and make plans. Decide, first, whom you would like to have at your party. The number of guests that you are able to invite will depend a great deal on the size of your house or apartment. Remember that overcrowding a party can take away from everyone's fun. Your age and the age of the children attending your party is another thing to consider when trying to decide how many guests to invite. A good rule to follow seems to be to invite as many guests as you are years old—for example, eight children at your eighth birthday.

If your home is simply too small to accommodate all of the children you were hoping to invite, your family might consider letting you have a party at a nearby restaurant. Many restaurants offer birthday party packages that include everything from the invitations to the hats and food at a very reasonable price. You might also consider taking a small group of friends to a special children's movie or to a bowling alley, a rollerskating rink, or a miniature golf course. A beach or a local park or playground are other possible places for a party.

Next you will need to pick out a theme for your party. Perhaps this could come from some special interest or hobby that you have, such as trains, cowboys, Indians, pirates, outer space, the circus, or dolls from many lands. The chart at the end of the article shows you how a theme can be carried out in all phases of your party.

You might prefer to choose a color scheme instead of a theme. You could choose two colors that you think go well together and use them for everything from the invitations to the favors and decorations.

### ▶INVITATIONS

The invitations can carry out your theme or color scheme. You can make very simple ones by cutting colored construction paper to fit into a standard-size envelope and writing your party information on the cut paper with a crayon or marker. If you are using one of the party themes suggested on the chart in this article, you might want to follow the suggestion given for making special invitations to go along with that theme.

Whatever kind of invitation you decide to use, you must be sure to include on each one

all of the information your friends will need to attend the party. You should include the day, date, and the time the party begins and ends. You should also include your name and your address or the address of the place where the party is going to be. It is also a good idea to put the letters *RSVP* on your invitation with your phone number next to the letters. The letters stand for the French words *Répondez s'il vous plaît,* which means "Please reply." It is helpful to the planning of your party for you to know ahead of time who is able to come and who is not. If you have any special information your guests might need to know such as "wear play clothes"—if it is a picnic —this should be written on your invitation, too.

The invitations need to be in the mail or hand-delivered a week to ten days before your party. It is not a good idea to take your invitations to school to hand out. It is likely that those children you were not able to invite will notice that invitations were handed out to others and feel hurt because they have been left out.

### ▶ DECORATIONS AND FAVORS

Decorations for the house and table, favors (small gifts for each guest), and prizes all add to the fun of a party. Crepe paper streamers hung from the ceiling to the corners make any room look festive. Crepe paper needs to be hung with tape, so be sure it won't harm the paint or wallpaper in that room. Balloons also add to the cheerful atmosphere of a party. Blow them up an hour or so before your guests are scheduled to arrive and stick them to the walls of the room by first rubbing each one on your clothes. You might also want to tie several balloons together to hang from the ceiling in the middle of the room.

For your party table, paper cups and plates and a paper tablecloth in the theme or color scheme of your party look pretty and save work. You can also purchase plain paper plates and cups and decorate them yourself using stickers or markers. If the theme of your party is one mentioned on the party chart included with this article, you might want to try the special suggestions given under the "table setting" column of the party chart. A bedsheet makes an excellent tablecloth. Today's sheets are so bright and colorful that the pattern you need to set off your table might be found right in your linen closet.

The list of possible party favors is almost endless. Small cars, dolls and stuffed animals, stickers, marbles, and pipe bubbles are all popular favors. Find out how much your family would like to spend for favors, then go to the store with them to find something you would like to give your friends within the budget. You might also want to shop for some prizes to award to those children who win games. You need not have prizes for all your games, but it does add to the excitement.

If you are planning to hand out favors or game prizes, it would be helpful to your guests to provide each one with a lunch bag with his or her name on it.

### ▶ GAMES

Next you will need to plan the kinds of activities with which to entertain your guests once they arrive. It is a good idea to have more games planned than you think you will need. Your friends may tire of some of the games sooner than you expected, so be prepared with other games to play to keep your party going. Do not be upset if there is one boy or girl who does not wish to join in any of the games. Make an effort to include everyone, but do not try to force anyone to play. All the guests should feel comfortable and enjoy the party in their own way.

It is not unusual to feel a bit shy as your first guests start to arrive. It is helpful to have an older member of your family at the door with you to help you greet your guests and make them feel welcome. If you have access to an instant-photo camera, you might want to take a picture of each guest as he or she arrives. Everyone will crowd around eagerly to see the results. Another way to get your party off to a good start is by pinning the name of a famous person to the back of each guest as each one arrives. The only way they can discover who they are is by asking the other

guests questions. This is a great way to get your friends talking to each other quickly.

When you are planning your list of games, try to alternate active games with quieter games so that your guests are not worn out before the party is over. You might start your party off with a lively game such as "musical chairs," then go to a word game where everyone will need to sit down and think about their answers. A good word game would be to ask your guests to see how many words they can make using only the letters of your first and last name. Give them about ten minutes to work on it, then award a prize to the person who has made the most words.

Another good resting game is to show your guests a tray with 20 objects on it for one minute. When the tray is taken away, ask your friends to write down as many of the objects as they can remember. The winner of the game is the person who is able to recall the most objects from the tray.

*Charades, Simon Says, Pin the Tail on the Donkey, Bingo,* hunts, relay races, and guessing games are all popular party activities. Many of these can be made to fit into the theme of your special party with just a little extra thought and work on your part. If you are having a Halloween party, you could play "Pin the Nose on the Witch" instead of "Pin the Tail on the Donkey." For a picnic party, you could play "Pin the Handle on the Picnic Basket." If you are having a hunt for candy, pennies, or small prizes, you could call that hunt something that fits in with your party theme. For example, if you were having a pirate party, it could be a "treasure hunt"; or if you were having a circus party, it could be a "peanut hunt."

As you grow older, you will probably become interested in playing records and dancing at your parties. If you decide to include this in your list of activities, a Cinderella dance might be fun. Have all of the boys leave the room and have each girl remove one of her shoes and place it in the middle of the floor. When the boys come back, each boy must quickly grab a shoe from the pile and find his Cinderella, who is his partner for that dance.

▶REFRESHMENTS

After all of the fun and excitement of the games, your guests are sure to be hungry. Ice cream and cake are traditional party foods, especially if you are having a birthday party. But there are lots of other party foods to serve along with them if you would like to put some extra time and effort into the refreshments.

If you are thinking of serving lunch or dinner before having cake and ice cream, it is again time to go back to your party theme and see if you can make the food a part of your theme. Pizza, sandwiches, hamburgers, hot dogs, pasta, cut-up raw vegetables or fresh fruit, and "munchies"—such as potato chips or popcorn—are all favorite party foods. If you are having a picnic, hamburgers and hot dogs on an outdoor grill would be perfect. For a Valentine's Day party, you might want to serve heart-shaped sandwiches filled with strawberry jelly. At Halloween time you could have individual pizzas with a jack-o'-lantern face, made of cheese, on each pizza.

Think about the kinds of foods you enjoy and would like to serve your friends at your party, then try to think of ways to make that food fit into the theme of your party. The extra thought and time you put into this will be well rewarded by the response from your guests. If you decide to serve ice cream and cake only, you can still be creative. Be sure that the cake in some way carries out the theme of your party if you have one. Or, as a special treat for your guests, you could set up a "make your own sundae" table with bowls of ice cream, different sauces, nuts, sprinkles, and fruit.

Time always goes by quickly at a party. Before you know it, you will be saying goodbye to your guests and thanking them for coming. Your party will be over except for the pleasure of remembering it.

Reviewed by KATHY ROSS
Director, Kenwood Nursery School

See also HALLOWEEN.

On the following pages is a party chart. It will give you lots of party ideas as well as show you how to carry out a party theme.

## Valentine's Day

**Heart Whale**

Put all the hearts inside the whale.

Date   Time   Name   Add.

Glue this side. →

Come to my party!   Phone

Leave ↗ top open.   Folded heart.   Heart tail.

**Heart Mouse**

Heart head.

Folded heart for body.

Glue heart on end of flat lollypop and slip into folded hearts so stick forms mouse's tail.

**Candy Heart Hunt**

**Beautiful Valentine Contest** - Give each guest materials to create a valentine. Ask an adult to judge. After the party, take valentines to a hospital or retirement home to be distributed.

## Teddy Bear Picnic

**Circles Bear**

Write party information on the bear's tummy. Tell each guest to "Bring a Bear."

**Bag Bear Puppet**
Use a brown lunch bag.

Fill with prizes and candy. Staple shut.

**Pom-Pom Bear Pin**
Tie large pom-pom in center. Use tiny pom-poms for ears, nose, and paws. Add black felt eyes and glue a tiny pin to back.

**Bear Judging** – Judge the fattest, oldest, best dressed, etc. Make ribbons to pin on each bear.
1ST
**Musical Bears** – Sit guests in a circle. All but one have a bear. Each time music starts, pass bears to left. When music stops, guest with no bear is "out."

## Easter

**Chick-in-an-Egg**
Decorate 2 egg halves and glue together around edges to form pocket. Write party information on back.

Use large sheet of construction paper.

Front of hat. Cut along each of four dotted lines.

Staple point 1 to point 2 on each side, tucking points A and B under front of hat. Add yarn ties.

• Easter Egg Hunt.
• Guess how many jelly beans in a jar.
• **Bunny Hop Relay** – Each person on a team must hop to a line and back with a basket of jelly beans. Racer must pick up any spilled ones before continuing.
?

## Snow Party

**Snowman Mobiles**
Glue paper circles (6) to front and back of string. Decorate snowman's front. Write party information on back.

**Felt Ear Warmers** – Glue felt circles onto a ribbon. Add felt face or design.
**Snowman Pins** – Glue 3 cotton balls on a strip of felt. Add felt or paper details and a fabric-strip scarf. Glue safety pin to back.

• Make angels in the snow. Add faces and details with squeeze bottles full of colored water.
• See who can throw the most snowballs into a carton from a distance. Indoors, use styrofoam "snow balls."
• **Mitten race** – Mix guests' mittens in a carton. Guests must race to carton, find and put on their own mittens, and race back.

## Space Party

**Orbiting Invitation**
Color a paper plate to look like the world. Write party information on the world in black marker.

Use paper fasteners to attach a paper rocket to one end of a cardboard strip and to attach the other end to the back of the plate.

**Space Helmet**

Cut away part of plastic jug. Turn over and cover with foil.

**Space-Robot Finger Puppet**
Glue half an egg shell on cardboard tube. Cover with tinfoil. Glue on nuts and bolts for face.

• Hang a decorated cardboard carton about a foot above guest's head. Have them make paper airplanes and fly them into the carton.
• Each guest must try to spoon as many cotton ball "clouds" as possible from one tray to another while blindfolded. 1 minute time limit.

## Halloween

**Pop-up Ghost**
Cut long, sealed envelope in half.

Cut hole here.

Write party information on ghost stapled to a straw. Push and pull on straw to pop ghost in and out.

① **Ghostly Candy Cups** - ① Draw a ghost on a white styrofoam cup. ② Cut away just the top part of cup around the ghost.
**Ghostly Lollypops** - Tie a tissue around a lollypop. Draw a ghostly face on it.

**Pumpkin Decorating Contest** - Use permanent markers to draw with. **Drop the Clothes Pin in the Pumpkin** - Use a real pumpkin.

**Pumpkin Roll** – Draw a pumpkin on the front of a box. Cut a hole for the mouth. See who can roll in the most tennis balls.

**Table Settings**

- White or lace tablecloth.
- Large red paper heart placemats
- Cut rings from a cardboard tube and glue a red heart to each one, for napkin rings.
- Put valentine stickers on plain styrofoam cups and plates.

**Food**

- Strawberry Sundaes.
- Heart-shaped red jello.
- Red jelly sandwiches cut with a heart-shaped cookie cutter.
- Drop red sour balls into each section of a filled ice tray. Freeze. Use in red punch.

**Cake**

**Hearts and Flowers Cupcakes**

Straws with paper hearts and flowers glued on one end. Chocolate frosting. For flower pots, bake cakes in ice cream cones.

---

Staple round teddy bear ears to paper plates and have each guest draw a bear face on the plate while waiting to be served. Fill a basket with teddy bears for a centerpiece.

- Pack each guest's lunch in a box or basket lined with a napkin.
- Let each guest toast a marshmallow and squeeze it between 2 graham crackers with half of a chocolate bar.

The cake is chocolate, of course.
Bake 2 round layers.
Make cupcake ears and paws.
Use chocolate icing and a candy face (try Necco wafers).

---

**Bunny Plates**

Staple small white plate to large one. Add face, paper ears, and cotton tail.

**Basket Cups**

Glue pipe cleaner to white cup. Use ice with jelly beans frozen in center.

**Marshmallow Bunnies**

Use large and miniature marshmallows held together with toothpicks. Use scissors to cut ears from large marshmallow.

**Boiled Egg Chicks**

Use half of a hard-boiled egg with whole yolk. Make face with cloves or peppercorns.

2 round layers.

Frost white. Use candy for face and bow tie.

Cut on dotted line.

---

- Let each guest cut a snowflake placemat from a large sheet of paper.
- Staple a paper hat to each plate. Leave a crayon at each place so guests may design snowman faces.

**Marshmallow Snowman**

Join with tooth pick. Add clove face. Float in hot chocolate.

**Ice Cream Snowman**

Flat-bottom cone hat. Vanilla ice cream (1 or 2 scoops) with M & M face.

Round layers – 2.

White icing – sprinkle with coconut, if desired. Add candy details. Cut hat and scarf from "fruit leather" (fruit roll-ups).

---

- Paint or cover cardboard paper-towel tubes with foil. Glue on paper cones and fins. Wrap silverware in napkins and slide into rockets. Write guest's name on tube.
- Make placemats by covering shirt cardboards with foil. Glue on paper stars.

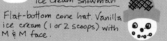

- Space creature sandwiches. Cut funny faces out of dark bread so filling shows through.
- Drink like real space people do – serve punch in a twist-tied bag with straw.
- Rocket salad – stand half a banana in a pineapple slice. Place on a bed of shredded carrot.

**Spaceship Cake**

Wrap photo of you in plastic wrap. Put in spaceship "window."

Rectangular cake.

---

Staple a green paper stem to the top of each orange paper plate. Carve out a large pumpkin for the center of the table – for a punch bowl.

**Ice Cream Cone Witch**

- Cone
- Cookie
- Ice Cream

Use candy for the face.

**Jack-O'-Lantern Pizzas**

Use English muffins with pizza sauce. Cut stem and face from cheese.

**Jack-O'-Lantern Cake**

Make an orange layer cake with orange frosting. Use licorice whips to outline features. Use candy corn teeth and jelly bean eyes.

# PARTS OF SPEECH

The term "parts of speech" refers to the classification of words according to their common uses in sentences. Traditionally, words have been classified into eight parts of speech: noun, pronoun, verb, adjective, adverb, preposition, conjunction, and interjection. Sometimes a ninth part, the article, is added.

Many modern grammarians distinguish between four basic parts of speech, called **form classes** (nouns and pronouns, verbs, adjectives, and adverbs), and **function words.** Function words fall into groups such as prepositions (of, by, for, with, over, after, at, in, among, toward), various kinds of conjunctions (and, but, for, either . . . or, yet, still, when, while, as, since, because), and interjections (well, ouch! oh! hey!).

Usually a word cannot be classified until it is used in a sentence. Many words may be two parts of speech: A *whistle* shrilled (noun). Can you *whistle* the national anthem (verb)? Some words may be several parts of speech: I *long* for a glimpse of the ocean (verb). She worked *long* into the night (adverb). Vacations are never *long* enough (adjective). That's the *long* and the short of it (noun).

## ▶THE FOUR CLASSES

A sentence is built up from words in the four basic classes.

### Noun

A noun is a word that refers to one or more persons, places, objects, or ideas. *Guitar, spinach, downtown, galaxy, infant,* and *soccer* are nouns. Most nouns indicate one or more than one by changing their form: *laser, lasers; werewolf, werewolves; child, children; peach, peaches.* A few nouns do not change their form to show number: *a sheep, a flock of sheep; an elk, a gang of elk; one fish, a school of fish* (*fishes* is sometimes used).

Nouns are usually classified as common or proper. Proper nouns are the names of particular persons and places: *Fred, Pac-Man, Uncle Sam, Oklahoma City, Nicaragua.* Proper nouns are always capitalized. All nouns that are not proper nouns are common nouns: *frog, celery, telephone, truth, beauty.* Common nouns are not capitalized.

In the list above it is easy to see that *truth* and *beauty* are different kinds of nouns from *frog, celery,* and *telephone.* The last three things you can see and touch. *Truth* and *beauty* name qualities or ideas. Such nouns are called abstract nouns. Nouns that refer to objects that can be touched are called concrete nouns. Some nouns may be either concrete or abstract, depending on the way they are used. The word "will" is concrete in this sentence: They found the old miser's will in his desk. But it is abstract in this sentence: Where there's a will, there's a way.

**Pronoun.** A word used in place of a noun is called a pronoun. Many languages have developed pronouns in order to avoid repeating a noun. For example, "Pooh was sitting in his house one day, counting his pots of honey" is easier to read than "Pooh was sitting in Pooh's house one day, counting Pooh's pots of honey." When a pronoun is used in a sentence, it must agree in number, person, and gender with the noun it is replacing: Jennifer's violin was in *its* case on *her* desk. Mark took the socks back to the store, saying *they* didn't fit *him.* May I present *my* uncle to you and *your* aunt?

The case of a pronoun depends on its use in a sentence: *I* stayed home all day (subjective case, because "I" is the subject of "stayed"). Then Mom took my sister and *me* to a movie (objective case, because "me" is the object of "took"). I think I caught *my* cold walking there in the snow (possessive case, because "my" shows who possesses "cold").

Personal pronouns have many forms. Pronouns in the first person (I, my, mine, me; we, our, ours, us) indicate the speaker. Pronouns in the second person (you, your, yours) indicate the person spoken to. Pronouns in the third person (he, his, him; she, hers, her; it, its; they, their, theirs, them) indicate the person or thing spoken about. Older forms, such as *thou, thy, thine, thee,* and *ye,* survive in prayers and religious literature but are seldom used otherwise.

Demonstrative pronouns point out a particular person or thing: *This* is mine; *that* is yours. *These* look good enough to eat; *those* over there are even better.

Interrogative pronouns (who, whom, which, and why) ask questions. *Who* said that? *What* do you mean? To *whom* do you think you are speaking? *Which* dog did you say bit you?

The indefinite pronoun "it" is used in certain set expressions. For instance, we say, "It is raining." We do not say, "Rain is." In other expressions "it" postpones the subject to give it greater emphasis: "I could tell *it* was going to be a terrible, horrible, no-good, very bad day."

A relative pronoun joins an adjective clause or a noun clause to an independent clause. The most common relative pronouns are who, whose, whom, what, that, and which: That is the girl *who* ate my pizza. I wonder *whose* alligator that is. She disliked the boy *whom* you thought charming. Eat *what* you like from the buffet. The poodle *that* ran away was wearing her bracelet. Your nose isn't as nice as mine, *which* is perfect. Compound relative pronouns are made by adding *ever* to who, whom, what, or which: Do *whatever* you want with it. He will interview *whomever* you suggest to fill the position.

## Verb

A verb is a word that expresses an action or a state of existence. In English grammar a sentence contains a subject (noun or pronoun) and a verb: Julia *cooks*. I *eat*. Charles *washes up*. Dinner *is* over.

Verbs may be identified by their forms. All verbs that are not special auxiliaries (such as *be, can, may, shall, will, ought, must*) add *s* to the present-tense form to make the third person singular: He *creeps*. The grass *rustles*. The deer *looks up*. The camera *clicks*. The other forms show whether the verb is regular or irregular.

Regular verbs add *d, ed,* or *t* to the present-tense form to make the past tense and the past participle. These three forms—the present tense, the past tense, and the past participle—are the principal parts of a verb. Here are the principal parts of some regular verbs:

| Present | Past | Past Participle |
|---------|------|-----------------|
| smile | smiled | smiled |
| gaze | gazed | gazed |
| blush | blushed | blushed |
| sleep | slept | slept |

In most cases, irregular verbs form the past tense and past participle by a change of vowel. Some irregular verbs have only one form for all three parts.

| Present | Past | Past Participle |
|---------|------|-----------------|
| sing | sang | sung |
| set | set | set |
| sit | sat | sat |
| ride | rode | ridden |
| buy | bought | bought |
| lie | lay | lain |

The verbs *go, do,* and *say* are also common irregular verbs. Some verbs that are usually regular may have an alternative irregular form: *prove, proved, proved* (or *proven*); *dive, dived* (or *dove*), *dived*.

When a verb expresses an action that is performed by the subject upon an object, the verb is called a transitive verb: Tom *grabbed* his hat. Sally *hailed* a taxi. When the verb expresses an action performed by the subject without an object or when it indicates a state of existence, it is called an intransitive verb: Johnny *jumped*. Spot *sits* in the street. The grass *grew* shoulder-high. Many verbs may be either transitive or intransitive: Sue *ate* elegantly (intransitive). Peter *ate* a pie (transitive).

## Adjective

An adjective is a word, phrase, or clause that describes a noun or limits it in its meaning in some way. These are single-word adjectives: a *mighty* oak, a *funny* story, twelve *brave* men, only *one* slice each. If the adjective follows a linking verb (a form of "be") that joins the subject to the predicate, it is called a predicate adjective: The oak was *tall* and *mighty*. That's *funny!* They were *brave* to do that. These are adjectival phrases: The tree *on the hill* was struck by lightning. The people *at the party* had a good time. *Standing in the corner,* Sally watched what was happening. These are adjectival clauses: The man *who is climbing the flagpole* is my uncle. The package *that came this morning* is hidden under your desk.

Single-word adjectives usually come before the noun. Phrase and clause adjectives generally follow.

## Adverb

An adverb is a word, phrase, or clause that modifies or qualifies the meaning of a verb. It sometimes modifies an adjective or another adverb. Many adverbs are formed by adding *ly* to an adjective, as in *curious, curiously*.

These are single-word adverbs modifying

verbs: I gazed *happily* around me. *Soon* the ball would begin. Pierre *eagerly* drank his champagne. These are adverbial phrases: The house stood *in the shadow of a volcano.* He borrowed a calculator *to balance his checkbook.* The rabbit was *in a hurry.* These are adverbial clauses: *When I reached the finish line,* the tortoise was already there. Alexander fell *because he could not balance himself on his skateboard.* The impatient audience left *before the play had even begun.*

These adverbs modify adjectives: This plum is *too* ripe. The breeze from the lagoon was *refreshingly* cool. These adverbs modify other adverbs: Please walk a *little* faster. The cat's grin vanished *quite* slowly. She was not *too* favorably impressed.

Some adverbs have two forms: *slow, slowly; quick, quickly; loud, loudly; soft, softly.* In modern English the short form is generally used in commands and exclamations, while the longer form is preferred for statements and questions: Drive *slow!* Susan cycled *slowly* down the street. Come *quick! Quickly* he explained his plan of escape. Not so *loud!* He had to speak *loudly* to be heard over the noise of the demonstrators. The wind whistled *softly* in the trees.

▶**FUNCTION WORDS**

All the words that do not fit into the four basic classes are called function words, because their meaning comes from their use, or function, in a sentence. Prepositions, conjunctions, and interjections are function words.

**Prepositions**

Prepositions are words that come before a noun or pronoun and connect it to the rest of a sentence. The preposition, the noun, and the modifiers of the noun form a prepositional phrase. Prepositional phrases usually modify nouns or verbs. English has many prepositions. Some of the most common are *about, above, across, after, along, among, at, before, behind, beside, between, down, for, from, in, like, near, of, off, on, out, over, since, to, under, up,* and *with.*

These prepositional phrases modify nouns: The price *of each cassette* is clearly marked. The cat *behind you* is about to pounce. The tall blond man *with one black shoe* is here. These prepositional phrases modify verbs: But this letter is addressed *to me!* They divided the watermelon *into small pieces.* It all came out right *in the end.*

Prepositions are sometimes used in pairs or groups: His feet emerged *from under* the car. He ran *up along* the ridge and disappeared.

**Conjunctions**

Conjunctions are words that join together elements of a sentence, such as words, phrases, or clauses. When the elements joined together are of equal rank, the conjunction is called a co-ordinating conjunction. When one element is joined to another that is not of equal grammatical rank, the conjunction is called a subordinating conjunction.

*And, but, yet, for, or, nor,* and *so* are co-ordinating conjunctions: Snow *and* sleet fell all day *and* all night. I swam hard, *but* I could make no progress against it. Throw Paul that raincoat, *or* he will get wet, too. He won't wear it, *for* it is the wrong color. Jennifer had just washed her hair, *so* she didn't go out.

When co-ordinating conjunctions are used in pairs, they are called correlative conjunctions: *Either* we all contribute, *or* no one gets to go. *Neither* Jerry *nor* his brother would agree to that.

*When, while, as, since,* and *because* are examples of subordinating conjunctions. They connect a modifying clause to an independent clause: *Since* you came first, you may have the biggest piece of pie. You may go *when* you have finished it. Wait here *while* I put on my boots. The team began to smile *as* the crowd began to cheer. Geraldine picked Walter *because* he is tall and dances well.

**Interjections**

Interjections are exclamations that are used alone or inserted into a sentence. The word "interjection" means "something thrown in or into." Interjections generally express an emotion. *Hey! Ouch! Gosh! Oh my fur and whiskers!* are exclamations of this kind.

Interjections are sometimes filler words used to start sentences: *Well,* what next? *Now then,* let me get this straight. *Oh,* I don't care! These occur very frequently in speech, but they are usually omitted in writing. *Aha!* and *alas* are sometimes found in literature.

ROBERT C. POOLEY
Author, *Teaching English Grammar*

See also GRAMMAR.

**PASCAL'S TRIANGLE.** See NUMBER PATTERNS.

# PASSOVER

Passover is the Jewish feast of freedom. It celebrates the Jews' deliverance from bondage in Egypt, described in the Bible as having happened about 3,000 years ago. It begins in late March or April (the Hebrew month of *Nisan*), about the same time as Easter, and lasts for eight days (seven days in Israel). It is a happy time, marked by synagogue services and a feast called the Seder.

At a Passover Seder, Jewish people read the *Haggadah*, which tells of the Jews' escape from slavery. The foods served are symbolic of the story.

### ▶ THE STORY OF PASSOVER

In ancient times Egypt was one of the mightiest nations in the world. It conquered smaller nations and made their people slaves. Among these people were the Hebrews, or Jews.

Pharaoh, the Egyptian king, forced the Hebrews to work putting up buildings. They had to pull heavy stones across the hot desert sands. They had little food. Even worse, they had no freedom. They dreamed of escaping from Egypt to find a land of their own.

They found a great leader in Moses. The Bible, in the Book of Exodus, tells us that Moses was a Hebrew baby whom Pharaoh's daughter found floating in the Nile River in a basket. Moses grew up surrounded by luxury in Pharaoh's court. But he gave up all his riches to lead the Hebrews.

The Bible tells that Moses was commanded by God to lead the Hebrews out of slavery into the land of Canaan (today known as Israel), which God had promised to the descendants of Abraham. Repeatedly, Moses asked Pharaoh to free the Hebrews. Each time that Pharaoh refused, a plague fell upon the Egyptians. After the tenth plague, in which the firstborn in every Egyptian household died, Pharaoh agreed to let the Hebrews go. Pharaoh then changed his mind and ran after them. When they came to the Red Sea, a miracle happened. Moses raised his staff over the water, and it parted so that the Hebrews could escape. He lifted his staff again, and the sea closed up and drowned Pharaoh's army. The Hebrews wandered for 40 years before they found their promised land. Moses died and never reached it at all.

The Hebrew flight from Egypt, called the Exodus, was the first known movement in the name of freedom. The Pilgrims, who came to America to escape oppression in England, compared their flight to the Exodus. In the American South, black slaves sang about the Exodus as they dreamed of winning freedom.

### ▶ THE OBSERVANCE OF PASSOVER TODAY

Jews everywhere gather every year to retell the Passover story. They eat **matzo**, the crisp, flat cracker that commemorates the unleavened dough the Hebrews took with them in haste from Egypt. This is the same kind of bread that Jesus broke with his disciples at the Last Supper, which was a Passover feast.

Passover is celebrated by worship services in the synagogue and gala feasts, or Seders, at home for family and guests. The Seder is held on the first two nights of the holiday (in Israel, only on the first night).

The most important part of the Seder ceremony is the reading of the *Haggadah*, a book that tells the story of Passover. All read the story as if they themselves had been slaves in Egypt and had been freed by God. Prayers are said, and songs of thanksgiving are sung.

Children take part in the songs and reading. To the youngest goes the honor of asking the ceremonial four questions. The answers to these give the meaning of the Passover feast. A ceremonial Seder plate contains foods symbolic of Passover and of the ancient Jewish past. On the plate are a shank bone of lamb, an egg, bitter herbs, *charoset* (chopped apples, nuts, and wine), and parsley. The shank bone of lamb is a reminder of the time in the spring when Hebrew farmers sacrificed young lambs at the Temple in Jerusalem to celebrate the first harvest. The egg is the symbol of the renewal of life in the spring. The bitter herbs (usually horseradish) signify the bitterness of slavery in Egypt. The *charoset* stands for the mortar the Jews had to mix when they built buildings for Pharaoh in Egypt. The parsley dipped in salt water marks both the salty tears of bondage and the green shoots of hope.

The matzo eaten during the eight days of Passover stands for the "bread of affliction" the Hebrew slaves had to eat in Egypt. It also stands for the unleavened dough the Hebrews brought with them from Egypt.

The Passover ceremony includes the drinking of four cups of wine. Another cup of wine is set aside for the prophet Elijah. According to Jewish tradition, Elijah will appear on a Passover night to announce the Messiah and bring peace to the world. At a certain point in the ceremony, the door is opened to let the Prophet's spirit come in.

TOBY KARL KURZBAND
Coauthor, *The Story of the Jewish Way of Life*
Reviewed by LAWRENCE GROSSMAN
Coeditor, *The American Jewish Year Book*
See also MOSES.

## PASSPORTS AND VISAS

A passport is an official government document identifying a traveler as a citizen of the country that issued it. It also requests other governments to allow the bearer to travel freely.

With a few exceptions, all U.S. citizens need passports to leave or enter the United States and to enter most foreign countries. U.S. citizens do not need passports for travel to Mexico and Canada. But these countries may require proof of citizenship.

The United States government issues three types of passports. The diplomatic passport is for persons traveling on diplomatic missions for the government. The official passport is for persons traveling on official government business. The regular passport is for all other travelers.

A U.S. passport is valid for ten years from the date of issue. After that time, a new passport must be obtained. Passports are issued in the United States by the Passport Office of the Department of State. They are obtained through passport agencies in 13 major cities and through certain courts, many post offices, and some libraries. Previous passport holders may usually obtain a new passport by mail. While abroad, a U.S. citizen may obtain a new passport from a U.S. embassy or consulate. Canadian citizens obtain passports through the Department of Foreign Affairs and International Trade in Ottawa.

A visa is an approval placed on the passport by a foreign government. "Visa" comes from the Latin word that means "to see." The visa indicates that the bearer has been granted permission to visit the country. The U.S. government issues several types of visas. The immigrant visa is for persons who intend to live and work permanently in the United States. The nonimmigrant visa is for foreigners who wish to visit the United States temporarily for a specific purpose. Visa fees vary among countries. Many are free. If a government does not wish a person to enter its country, it can refuse to grant a visa. Some governments require exit permits for residents leaving the country.

The United States requires visitors from most other countries to have both a passport (issued by their own country) and a visa (issued by the U.S. Foreign Service) to enter the United States. All persons wishing to immigrate permanently to the United States must obtain immigrant visas from consular officers of the U.S. Foreign Service.

Reviewed by EMIL W. KONTAK
Passport Office, U.S. Department of State
See also ALIENS; FOREIGN SERVICE; IMMIGRATION.

**PASTE.** See GLUE AND OTHER ADHESIVES.

Pasteur helped prove that diseases are caused by harmful micro-organisms, or germs. His process for killing micro-organisms in food is now called pasteurization.

## PASTEUR, LOUIS (1822–1895)

Louis Pasteur was a French chemist and microbiologist (someone who studies microscopic organisms) who contributed some of the most important ideas to modern science. He was one of the first people to discover that many diseases are caused by micro-organisms, or germs. The word "pasteurize," usually used in reference to milk, comes from his name.

Louis was born on December 27, 1822, at Dôle, Jura, in eastern France. His father was a tanner. The family moved to Arbois when Louis was very young, and it was there that he grew up. One of his favorite hobbies as a boy was painting portraits.

In the fall of 1838, when he was 16 years old, Louis went to Paris to attend school. Homesickness drove him back to Arbois. The following year, Louis went to the college at Besançon, about 40 kilometers (25 miles) from Arbois. When he graduated in 1840, he became a teacher there.

### Pasteur's Introduction to Chemistry

In 1842, Pasteur took the entrance examinations for the École Normale in Paris. This was a famous school established by Napoleon to train teachers for all of France. Pasteur passed the exams but decided his scores were not good enough. He studied and took the tests again a year later. He then entered the École Normale as the fourth-ranking student in his class.

Pasteur was fortunate in having excellent teachers, including three famous chemists of that time. All three chemists recognized that Pasteur had great ability in chemistry. From these men he learned of the latest discoveries in chemistry and the problems of greatest interest to chemists. One of these problems was that of the structure of crystals. While a student at the École Normale, Pasteur began research on crystal structure and other chemical problems.

In exchange for his education at the famous École Normale, Pasteur was required to serve as a schoolteacher for at least ten years. The leading French chemists were upset by this. They wanted Pasteur assigned to a research job, where they knew he held great promise. They pressured government officials. And as a result, Pasteur became a professor at the University of Strasbourg in 1848.

The next year he married Marie Laurent, the daughter of the rector, or head, of the university. They had five children (four girls and one boy). Only the boy and one of the girls survived early childhood.

At Strasbourg, Pasteur continued the research he had begun in Paris. Many of the crystals he studied were produced by the growth of mold and the spoiling of milk. This brought Pasteur to study the chemistry of living things. It was his introduction to **biochemistry**, the branch of science that deals with the chemical makeup and processes of living things.

### Pasteur Helps the French Wine Industry

In 1854, Pasteur was appointed professor of chemistry and dean of science at the University of Lille. One important industry of the region was the production of alcohol from beet sugar. The beet sugar was fermented to produce alcohol. The producers of alcohol in Lille asked Pasteur to study fermentation, so that their product could be improved.

The producers of wine in eastern France learned of Pasteur's work on fermentation. Wine is produced by the fermentation of sugar in grapes. The wine producers were having serious trouble. The wine was turning sour instead of remaining sweet. The wine producers called upon Pasteur to investigate the source of the trouble.

At that time, most scientists thought that wine soured by itself because of some unknown action that took place in the wine. Pasteur doubted that wine could sour all by itself.

He went to eastern France and set up a laboratory there. After many experiments, he thought he had the answer to the problem. In 1857 he made a statement that was new to the world of science. He said that there were tiny micro-organisms (microscopic living things), floating in the air, that could cause chemical changes. When certain kinds of these micro-organisms got into wine, they caused the wine to sour. He said that some kinds of micro-organisms also caused milk to sour. Other kinds caused fermentation to take place.

Pasteur next showed that if the wine was heated to a certain temperature (about 57°C, or 135°F) and then cooled rapidly, many of the harmful micro-organisms were killed. This process, which is now called pasteurization in honor of Pasteur, kept the wine from spoiling.

### Experiments with Milk

To show that micro-organisms from the air caused milk to spoil, Pasteur did another experiment. He heated some milk to kill many of the harmful micro-organisms in it. That is, he pasteurized the milk. Pasteur then showed that the milk soon spoiled when it was exposed to the air, because new micro-organisms were able to get into the milk. When he sealed pasteurized milk in a sterilized container, no new micro-organisms could get into the milk and it did not spoil so quickly.

In the 1850's many scientists thought that living things (such as micro-organisms) could arise from nonliving things. This idea was known as the **theory of spontaneous generation.** Pasteur's experiments helped prove this to be false. He believed that living things could only grow from other living things. A living micro-organism did not come from wine or milk. It appeared only when another micro-organism like itself reproduced.

### The Germ Theory of Disease

Pasteur's reputation for solving practical problems spread rapidly. In 1865 the French Government asked him to study diseases of silkworms. By this time, Pasteur had come to think that diseases were caused by harmful micro-organisms called germs. This theory is called the germ theory of disease. Pasteur succeeded in finding the germs of two different silkworm diseases. He also found a way to prevent the spread of the diseases to healthy silkworms.

In 1877, Pasteur began an investigation of the disease called anthrax. This disease is found mainly in cattle and sheep. The animals that caught anthrax almost always died.

Pasteur found that he could inject healthy cows or sheep with weakened anthrax germs. That is, he **vaccinated** them against anthrax. The animals then did not get the disease.

But many scientists questioned Pasteur's results. To convince them, Pasteur conducted a public experiment with a herd of 50 sheep. He vaccinated half the herd against anthrax. A few days later he injected all the sheep with strong, live anthrax germs. He put the vaccinated sheep in one fenced-in field and the nonvaccinated sheep in another. Two days later the vaccinated sheep were healthy, but the others had all died of anthrax. Thus, Pasteur showed that vaccination against anthrax was effective.

Pasteur then developed other ways of making disease germs weak. He injected healthy persons with a small dose of weakened germs. These persons then became **immune** to the disease—they could not become sick from it.

Pasteur's most famous work in giving immunity to disease was with rabies. This disease is transmitted by the bite of a dog or other animal that carries the rabies virus. In 1885 he treated two boys who had been bitten by infected dogs and prevented the boys from getting rabies.

Pasteur's successful treatment for the prevention of rabies drew worldwide attention. People from all over the world contributed money for the establishment of a research institute in honor of Pasteur. This institute, located in Paris, was called the Pasteur Institute. Here Pasteur continued his research. Important research is still done there today.

Honors from many countries and scientific societies were showered upon Pasteur. Despite a stroke that partially paralyzed him, Pasteur continued his work for many years. He died in Villeneuve l'Éstang on September 28, 1895.

DUANE H. D. ROLLER
University of Oklahoma

# PATENTS

Hundreds of years ago, English kings gave to some of their subjects papers known as **letters patent**. These papers gave to the person who received them some special privilege or favor. This might be the right to own a large tract of land or to explore a new territory. Or it might be the right to make and sell some product or article. In modern times the word **patent** has come to have a special meaning. It means the rights given by a government to a person who invented something. This includes the right to make and sell the invention or discovery or to profit from it by allowing another person or company to sell or use it.

The writers of the Constitution of the United States wanted to protect the rights of inventors. Article I, Section 8, says: "The Congress shall have Power…to promote the progress of Science and useful Arts, by securing for limited Times to…inventors the exclusive Right to their…Discoveries."

In 1790 the U.S. Congress passed the first patent law, and a Patent Office was set up soon afterward. The law provided that the inventor or discoverer has the right to own a patent for 17 years. After the 17-year period, anyone may use the patent without payment to, or permission from, the inventor.

The first U.S. federal patent was issued to Samuel Hopkins of Vermont for the "… making of Pot ash and Pearl ash by a new Apparatus, and Process." Since then, more than 5 million patents have been granted in the United States. In 1975 the Patent Office was renamed the Patent and Trademark Office. It is an agency of the U.S. Department of Commerce, and its offices are located in Arlington, Virginia.

The British Patent Office in its present form was created in 1883. British patent law is contained in the Patents Act of 1949. It gives an inventor the right to a patent for 16 years. After that the inventor may apply to have it extended for another five to ten years.

Most other countries have their own patent laws. Some countries recognize inventors' achievements by awarding them certificates. Such papers do not give them ownership of their inventions. In some countries the invention must be produced within a certain period after the patent is granted. Otherwise the owner loses the right to the patent.

Many countries have signed international patent treaties that protect the rights of patent owners in countries other than the one granting the patent. An agreement called the Patent Co-operation Treaty took effect in 1978. It made it easier for inventors to obtain protection in several countries.

**Some Famous Patents.** The patent granted in 1906 to the Wright brothers for their flying machine formed the basis of today's aircraft industry. The patented inventions of Samuel Morse and Alexander Graham Bell were the beginnings of the electronic communications industry. Edward H. Land's invention of a camera that could take, develop, and print pictures established a new field of photography. Thomas A. Edison, one of the most prolific inventors in history, obtained more than 1,000 patents.

**How to Obtain a Patent.** To be eligible for a patent, an invention must meet four legal requirements. The inventor must describe it in writing in enough detail for a person skilled in the art of technology to make and use it. The invention must be new. It must be useful. And it must be what is called "unobvious." An unobvious invention is one that is sufficiently different from earlier inventions that it does not appear obvious to a person of ordinary skill in that field.

When a patent application is submitted, it is assigned to an examiner. The examiner searches the files to be sure that the invention is new and unobvious. If the invention meets the four legal requirements, a patent is issued, and the inventor's rights come into effect. If the request for a patent is rejected, the inventor can attempt to convince the patent examiner that the invention should receive a patent. Or the inventor may alter the invention so that it meets the legal requirements. Inventors may file applications directly, but most inventors hire patent attorneys to obtain their patents for them. Patent law is a highly specialized field.

DONALD W. BANNER
U.S. Commissioner of Patents and Trademarks

See also INVENTIONS.

**PATERSON.** See NEW JERSEY (Cities).

**PATERSON, KATHERINE.** See CHILDREN'S LITERATURE (Profiles).

**PATERSON, WILLIAM.** See NEW JERSEY (Famous People).

## PATRICK, SAINT (389?–461?)

Saint Patrick is the most famous Irish saint. He was born in the late A.D. 300's, probably in Britain. His father, a Christian, was an official of the Roman Empire. When Patrick was about 16, he was captured by slave traders and taken to Ireland to be a shepherd.

Patrick led a life of hardship among the non-Christian Irish. One night he heard a voice telling him to return to his native land. He journeyed to the sea and in time made his way back to his people. Later, in another vision, he was told to return to Ireland as a missionary.

It is believed that Patrick studied for the priesthood in France and was made a bishop. He returned to Ireland around 430 with a group of missionary priests. For almost 30 years, Patrick worked among the Irish, establishing churches and baptizing thousands. He is also credited with founding a church and monastery at Armagh. Patrick resigned as bishop of Armagh in the late 450's and went to Saul in the north of Ireland, where it is believed he died in 461.

Many legends have grown up about Saint Patrick. One tells how he drove all the snakes of Ireland into the sea. Another relates how he explained the Trinity—the union of three persons in one God—by showing the people a shamrock, which has three leaves that grow from one stem. The shamrock became a national symbol of Ireland.

Saint Patrick's feast day is March 17.

KATHLEEN MCGOWAN
*Catholic Youth Encyclopedia*

## PATTON, GEORGE S. (1885–1945)

Outspoken, hot-headed, and strong-willed, General George S. Patton was one of the most controversial of the Allied commanders of World War II. Known as Old Blood and Guts, Patton was an inspired leader on the field of battle but lacked the diplomatic skills that would have made him one of the top-level commanders of the war.

Born in San Gabriel, California, on November 11, 1885, George Smith Patton, Jr., was descended from a long line of Virginia military officers. Upon graduation from the U.S. Military Academy at West Point in 1909, he was commissioned a second lieutenant in the cavalry. He served as an aide-de-camp to General John J. Pershing in Mexico (1916–17) and was the first man to lead a tank brigade in World War I, participating in the Saint-Mihiel and Meuse-Argonne offensives (1918).

When the United States entered World War II on December 8, 1941, Patton was a temporary major general and the commander of the Second Armored Division. In November 1942 he led the Western Task Force in the invasion of Morocco, in North Africa. He later took command of the Second Corps in Tunisia, and in July 1943 he was given command of the U.S. Seventh Army for the invasion of Sicily. After the Sicilian Campaign, Patton slapped two soldiers while visiting a hospital, believing the men were faking illness to avoid further combat. Patton, compelled to make a public apology, was called back to Britain in temporary disgrace.

On June 6, 1944, Patton led the Third Army in the invasion of Normandy, and in August he was promoted to major general. Advancing his troops through northern France, he assisted the Allied counterattack at the Battle of the Bulge, forcing the Germans to retreat from Bastogne. Patton later advanced across the Rhine River and relentlessly made his way through enemy territory.

When Germany collapsed in May 1945, Patton was made a full general and placed in charge of occupational forces in the American zone. But another controversial incident forced his removal to the inactive command of the Fifteenth Army. On December 9, 1945, Patton was severely injured in a car crash near Mannheim, Germany. He died on December 21 and was buried in Luxembourg.

Reviewed by JOHN KEEGAN
Author, *Who's Who in the Second World War*

# PAUL, ALICE (1885–1977)

Alice Paul was a major figure during the final stages of the women's suffrage (right to vote) campaign and the author of the Equal Rights Amendment.

Born on January 11, 1885, in Moorestown, New Jersey, Paul was highly educated for a woman of her time. She earned a bachelor of arts degree (1905) from Swarthmore College; a masters (1907) and a doctoral degree (Ph.D.) (1912) from the University of Pennsylvania; and several law degrees, including one from Washington College of Law (1922).

While studying in England between 1907 and 1910, Paul took part in a number of militant demonstrations organized by Emmaline Pankhurst. She was arrested and imprisoned three times. In 1912, back in the States, Paul joined the National American Woman Suffrage Association (NAWSA) but quickly concluded that political speeches without militant action would not win the vote. Paul left NAWSA in 1913 and cofounded what became the National Woman's Party (NWP).

On January 10, 1917, under Paul's leadership, the NWP began picketing the White House. That year, 500 women were arrested and 168, including Paul, were convicted of blocking a sidewalk. The women received sentences of up to seven months. In protest, Paul went on a hunger strike. She was force-fed and briefly transferred to a psychiatric hospital. A court of appeals later ruled that all the suffragists had been "illegally arrested, illegally convicted, and illegally imprisoned."

On August 26, 1920, the 19th Amendment to the U.S. Constitution was adopted, at last granting women the vote. Alice Paul drafted the Equal Rights Amendment in 1923 and campaigned tirelessly on its behalf until her death on July 9, 1977.

KATHRYN CULLEN-DUPONT
Author, *The Encyclopedia of Women's History in America*

See also WOMEN'S RIGHTS MOVEMENT.

# PAUL, SAINT

Saint Paul was born at Tarsus in Asia Minor near the time of the birth of Jesus Christ. He was a Roman citizen as well as a Jew and was raised as a member of the strict sect called the Pharisees. His Jewish name was Saul, but outside the Jewish community, he was called Paul.

Paul became a leader in the persecution of the Christians. But on his way to Damascus to take action against the Christian community there, an event took place that changed the course of Christianity. The New Testament tells us that as Paul neared the city, a bright light blinded him. He heard a voice, which identified itself as Jesus, that commanded him to end his persecutions of the Christians. Paul was then taken to Damascus, where Ananias, a Christian, baptized him and his sight returned.

Paul spent the rest of his life establishing churches and spreading Jesus' teachings, often enduring abuse or imprisonment. Important to Paul's work were the epistles, or letters, that he wrote to various Christian communities. Known as the Pauline letters, they appear in the New Testament and teach much about the early Christian Church.

During Paul's last trip to Jerusalem, he was set upon by a mob accusing him of bringing non-Jews into the Temple. To protect him from the mob, the Romans arrested and later released him. It is believed he again took up his mission but was returned to Rome during the reign of Nero and executed about A.D. 67.

The Roman Catholic Church celebrates the feast of Saint Paul on June 29. It also honors his conversion with a feast day on January 25.

KATHLEEN MCGOWAN
*Catholic Youth Encyclopedia*

## PAUL VI, POPE (1897–1978)

Giovanni Battista Montini was born in Concesio in northern Italy on September 26, 1897. Montini was educated by the Jesuits at the seminary in Brescia. After ordination to the priesthood on May 29, 1920, he was sent to the Gregorian University in Rome for higher studies. A brilliant scholar, he also studied literature at the University of Rome.

In 1922, Montini entered the Academy of Noble Ecclesiastics, the training school for papal diplomats. While still a student, he was assigned to the nunciature, or papal embassy, of Poland. Poor health cut short this service, and he was recalled to Rome. In 1924, he entered the Vatican Secretariat of State.

From 1924 to 1933, Montini served as chaplain of the Federation of Italian Catholic University Students. In the growing struggle between church and state, Mussolini, the Fascist dictator, finally banned the federation. In 1937, Pope Pius XI made Montini Substitute Secretary of State of the Vatican.

Montini was appointed Archbishop of Milan in 1954. Four years later he became the first cardinal created by Pope John XXIII.

In 1963, after the death of Pope John, Montini was elected pope. He chose the name Paul and reconvened the Second Vatican Council, begun by Pope John, continuing the reform of the church and the efforts toward Christian unity. Pope Paul worked for world peace. In 1968 he issued an encyclical, "Humanae Vitae" ("Of Human Life"), maintaining the church's ban on artificial birth control.

Pope Paul was called the Pilgrim Pope because of his travels in many lands. He died at the Vatican on August 6, 1978.

Msgr. FLORENCE D. COHALAN
Cathedral College

## PAULING, LINUS (1901–1994)

The American chemist Linus Carl Pauling was the only person to receive two unshared Nobel Prizes. Pauling's many other honors included the international Lenin Peace Prize (1972). His book *The Nature of the Chemical Bond* (1939) is considered a landmark of 20th-century science.

Pauling, who was born in Portland, Oregon, on February 26, 1901, had a searching and independent mind. He earned a bachelor's degree in chemical engineering from the Oregon Agricultural College. Pauling then attended the California Institute of Technology, earning a Ph.D. in physical chemistry in 1925. After studying in Europe for two years, Pauling returned to the California Institute of Technology to teach, becoming a full professor in 1931. He had a long and successful career there but left in 1963 to join the Center for the Study of Democratic Institutions in Santa Barbara, California. In 1969 Pauling joined Stanford University's faculty and helped to establish the Linus Pauling Institute of Science and Medicine.

His early work, for which Pauling received a Nobel Prize for chemistry in 1954, dealt with the structure of molecules. Through his studies, he was able to determine the physical properties of certain carbon compounds. It was also during the 1950's that Pauling became so concerned about nuclear bomb testing that he rallied other scientists to sign a petition against it. The petition, with more than 11,000 signatures, was presented to the United Nations. He also wrote *No More War!*, in which he presented his case against nuclear weapons. For this work he was awarded the Nobel Peace Prize in 1962.

Pauling's later work, which proved to be controversial, included the study of vitamin C and its role in preventing colds and cancer. He wrote *Vitamin C and the Common Cold* (1970) and coauthored *Vitamin C and Cancer* (1979). He died on August 19, 1994.

THOMAS H. METOS
Arizona State University

## PAVLOV, IVAN (1849–1936)

Ivan Petrovich Pavlov was a famous Russian biologist. His studies of digestion in dogs led to new understandings about behavior in animals as well as in people. In 1904, he was awarded the Nobel Prize in physiology or medicine for his work.

Ivan was born on September 14, 1849, in the town of Ryazan, Russia. His father was a country priest in the Russian Orthodox Church. Because of ill health, Ivan did not enter school until he was 11. He attended a local seminary after finishing high school, but he was not enthusiastic about religious studies.

In 1870, Ivan entered the University of St. Petersburg. One of his teachers persuaded him to enter the field of physiology, which is the study of how the parts of living organisms function. He graduated in 1875 and went on to earn a degree in medicine from the Military Medical Academy in St. Petersburg. While still a student, Pavlov had already begun important research. His work focused on how the nervous system regulates blood circulation and digestion.

After studying in Germany for several years, Pavlov returned to St. Petersburg to study and teach. In 1895, he was appointed professor of physiology at the Military Medical Academy. While there, he also directed the Institute of Experimental Medicine, where he improved the standards of treatment and care for laboratory research animals.

Pavlov continued to be curious about digestion and how it was regulated by nerve impulses. He investigated the production of digestive juices, such as saliva, as a way to measure digestive processes. His best-known discovery concerned the flow of saliva in dogs. Pavlov was able to show that certain influences unrelated to food could start the flow of saliva.

In his now-famous experiments, Pavlov rang a bell every time one of his research dogs was fed. As the dog ate, saliva flowed in its mouth. After repeating this feeding routine many times, Pavlov then rang the bell without showing the dog any food. Even though no food was given to the dog, saliva still flowed from the dog's mouth. This happened each time the bell rang. Pavlov called this response, which was triggered by an external signal, a **conditioned reflex**. He believed it to be the basis for many kinds of animal behavior.

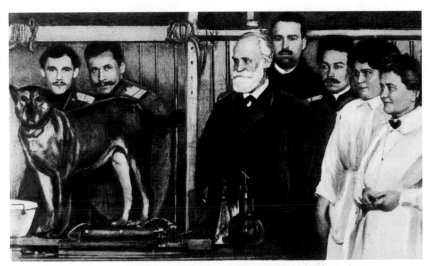

Before students of the Military Medical Academy, Ivan Pavlov (in center) demonstrates his famous experiment showing the conditioned reflex in a dog.

Pavlov later extended his theories to human psychology, stating that learned behavior is made up of many conditioned reflexes. He used these theories to develop treatments for mental illness, which he believed is caused by a breakdown in the brain's ability to process nerve impulses properly. He advocated quiet surroundings, hospitalization, and rest for people with mental illness.

Pavlov's work remains important because he showed that behavior—in both animals and humans—can be studied by examining small components of the behavior. He also showed that physiology can be used to understand problems of the mind. These ideas formed an important part of modern psychiatry. Pavlov died on February 27, 1936.

DUANE H. D. ROLLER
University of Oklahoma

See also LEARNING; PSYCHOLOGY.

A farmer in Belize works with a Peace Corps volunteer. Volunteers are trained in such fields as agriculture and health care and pass on their knowledge to their hosts.

## PEACE CORPS

The Peace Corps is an organization of volunteers, sponsored by the United States Government. Its goal is to promote world peace, friendship, and understanding. To achieve this goal, members of the Peace Corps go to interested countries to help them meet their needs for trained workers.

President John F. Kennedy established the Peace Corps by executive order in March of 1961. Since 1971 it has been a part of ACTION, the U.S. Government agency for volunteer activities at home and abroad.

Peace Corps volunteers must be United States citizens and must be at least 18 years old. Many are over 60. In the early days most volunteers were teachers who staffed classrooms around the world. Today volunteers are also asked to help a country improve its health care, food production, or water supply, especially in rural areas.

Some volunteers come to the Peace Corps already trained in such fields as nursing, forestry, and agriculture. But most volunteers are trained by the Peace Corps. Host countries explain what they need, and volunteers are trained to do a specific job.

No matter what their jobs, all volunteers are still involved in teaching, although they are no longer mainly in classrooms. Their aim is to work themselves out of a job by training local people to take their place.

Volunteers for the Peace Corps are selected on merit. Candidates must first fill out a questionnaire. Those who have the needed skills are invited to train for a project in a certain country. They may accept or refuse the invitation, state a preference for another country, or ask to be invited for another project at a later date.

Volunteers must be dedicated to their jobs —whether they are teaching in a school, helping to improve local farming methods, working in a hospital, or surveying for mineral resources. They must be prepared to work hard, and they must always show understanding. Peace Corps members are a kind of ambassador for their country.

Training of Peace Corps volunteers is held at colleges and universities in the United States and at other sites. Extensive training within the host country gives trainees experience in the culture in which they will work. They spend 60 or more hours a week in study of the language, history, geography, economy, and customs of the host country.

The term of service is about 24 months, not including the training period. Volunteers are given allowances that cover clothing and living costs. When they leave the Peace Corps, they receive a payment for each month of satisfactory service, including the training period. All necessary transportation between a member's home, training station, and overseas post is provided.

Today Peace Corps volunteers serve in many countries in Africa, Asia, and Latin America. The number in each country varies widely. The success of the Peace Corps program can be measured by the fact that most countries where members are at work ask that more be sent.

For many members, service in the Peace Corps is a great adventure. This sense of adventure is heightened by the Peace Corps ideal of service to people in other nations of the world. Returning members have gained new understanding of the people, language, beliefs, and traditions of another country.

CAROLYN R. PAYTON
Former Director, Peace Corps

# PEACE MOVEMENTS

For as long as there have been wars, people have sought ways to keep peace. Those who oppose violence as a means of settling disputes are known as pacifists. Most of the world's great religions preach the wickedness of war and hold forth the vision of achieving peace and harmony among people. The belief in nonviolence and nonresistance is characteristic of such Asian religions as Buddhism, Taoism, and Hinduism. There is also a strong element of pacifism in Christianity, especially among such sects as the Quakers (Society of Friends), Moravians, and Mennonites. Members of these sects oppose all forms of militarism.

▶ **THE FORMATION OF PEACE SOCIETIES**

The first significant, organized peace movements emerged in the early 1800's. In 1815, three peace societies were formed in the United States—in New York, Massachusetts, and Ohio. Noah Worcester, founder of the Massachusetts society, wrote a book entitled *A Solemn Review of the Custom of War* (1814). He was one of the first to urge cooperation among peace societies. In 1828, William Ladd, another pioneer of the peace movement, united the groups under the name American Peace Society.

Between 1843 and 1851, five international peace conferences were sponsored by societies in various Western countries. In 1848 a Universal Peace Congress was held in Brussels, Belgium, to bring about "the entire abolishment of war." It supported the suggestion made by an American abolitionist and humanitarian, Elihu Burritt, that a congress of nations prepare a code of international law. At a similar congress in Paris in 1849, the famous French novelist Victor Hugo urged the formation of a United States of Europe. After the fifth congress took place in London in 1851, efforts toward peace were abandoned due to the outbreaks of three major wars—the Crimean War (1853–56), the United States Civil War (1861–65), and the Franco-Prussian War (1870–71).

When peace efforts were revived in the 1870's, they became more practical and effective than earlier movements had been. A vast peace congress in Paris in 1878 endorsed three basic goals: for nations to settle disputes through peaceful discussions; to disarm; and to develop a code of international law. The Paris congress also proposed an international federation of peace societies. Most of these societies took part in the Universal Peace Congress in 1889 and in similar congresses held almost every year thereafter. By 1900, more than 400 peace societies were in existence.

In the late 1960's and early 1970's, American citizens opposed to the war in Vietnam demonstrated to stop U.S. bombings in Southeast Asia.

In 1899 and 1907, two major peace conferences were held in The Hague in the Netherlands. They attracted the world's attention to the problems of disarmament and arbitration and to the principles of international law. Although no agreements were reached on arms limitations, the conferences established a code of conduct for the treatment of civilians during wartime.

▶ **PEACE EFFORTS IN THE EARLY 1900'S**

Many prominent Americans were active in the early days of peace movements. Andrew Carnegie, the famous industrialist and philanthropist, built the Carnegie Peace Palace at The Hague, which now houses the International Court of Justice. The Hague Academy of International Law, the Peace Palace, and the Carnegie Endowment for International Peace were all founded in 1910. They are living memorials to Andrew Carnegie's lifelong interest in world peace.

Two other outstanding American peace workers were Jane Addams, president (1915–29) of the Women's International League for Peace and Freedom, and Nicholas Murray Butler, president (1925–45) of the Carnegie Endowment for International Peace. Addams and Butler were joint winners of the Nobel Peace Prize in 1931.

President Woodrow Wilson was one of the greatest champions of world peace. In his quest to "make the world safe for democracy," he devised a plan for a League of Nations that was incorporated into peace treaties that ended World War I (1914–18). The League of Nations was the forerunner of today's United Nations.

In the period between the two world wars (1918–39), many of the peace movements supported the League of Nations and were associated with the International Federation of League of Nations Societies. Notable among them was the Kellogg-Briand Peace Pact, which condemned war as a solution to international problems. Sponsored by the French foreign minister Aristide Briand and U.S. secretary of state Frank B. Kellogg, the plan was signed by 15 nations in 1928. By 1934, an additional 49 nations had signed the pact.

## WONDER QUESTION

### What is a conscientious objector?

Pacifists who refuse to take up arms against an enemy are called conscientious objectors. Some may agree to join the armed forces, but only to perform jobs that do not require engaging in actual combat.

At one time, American law protected only those conscientious objectors who refused to fight due to their religious beliefs. For example, Quakers in colonial America were exempt from joining their local militias. It was not until 1970, during the Vietnam War, that the U.S. Supreme Court expanded protection to those who objected to war on moral and ethical grounds.

Perhaps the most famous conscientious objector of the Vietnam era was heavyweight boxing champion Muhammad Ali. In 1967 he was convicted and stripped of his title for refusing to enter the U.S. Army. But in 1971, the U.S. Supreme Court overturned the conviction, ruling that Ali had been drafted improperly.

▶ **WORLD WAR II AND THE NUCLEAR AGE**

Despite the efforts of the world's peace societies, World War II broke out in 1939. The horrors and devastation of this six-year struggle only increased the urgency to find peaceful ways to settle international disputes. When the war ended in 1945, the United Nations was established to promote a lasting peace. Its central purpose is "to maintain international peace and security."

Two of the most notable pacifists of the postwar era used nonviolent methods to combat oppression. Mohandas Gandhi, the leader of the nationalist movement in India, encouraged nonviolent resistance and civil disobedience to gain India's independence from Great Britain, achieved in 1947. In the 1950's and 1960's, Dr. Martin Luther King, Jr., a Baptist minister from Georgia, used similar tactics to energize the civil rights movement in the United States. King won the Nobel Peace Prize in 1964 for leading a nonviolent protest against discrimination.

In the 1960's, opponents of the Vietnam War formed many new peace groups, in the United States and elsewhere. Antiwar demonstrators marched in parades and protested against the war and the role the United States played in it. Peace groups also ran candidates for public office and issued statements explaining their antiwar stand.

Since the 1970's a movement against nuclear weapons and nuclear power has grown, especially in Europe and the United States. The antinuclear movement is supported by a wide variety of religious and nonreligious groups and organizations. The movement also has the sympathy, and occasionally the formal support, of political parties. In Germany a political party known as the Greens, formed in 1979, has made opposition to nuclear weapons a central feature of its platform.

Peace movements exist in all parts of the world. Some are limited in their aims. Others have almost unlimited goals, such as general and complete disarmament, world government, or the complete abolition of war. All have given new dimensions to the search for peace in the nuclear age.

NORMAN D. PALMER
The University of Pennsylvania

See also DISARMAMENT; INTERNATIONAL LAW; INTERNATIONAL RELATIONS; LEAGUE OF NATIONS; UNITED NATIONS.

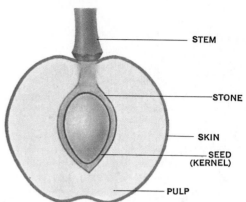

**CROSS SECTION OF A PEACH**

STEM

STONE

SKIN

SEED
(KERNEL)

PULP

# PEACH, PLUM, AND CHERRY

Peaches, plums, and cherries are similar types of fruit. They have a thin outer skin, a soft juicy pulp, and a single seed in the center. The seed is covered with such a hard shell that these fruits are known as **stone fruits.** Stone fruits are also called **drupes.** Other drupes are apricots and nectarines.

### ▶ PEACH

The peach was first grown in China thousands of years ago. It came to Europe by way of Persia (Iran) and was known for many years as the Persian apple. The Romans planted peaches in the sunny and mild parts of their empire. When the Spanish explorers set out for the New World, they, too, took the seeds of many plants, including peaches, with them. Peaches soon grew wild over the southern part of what is now the United States.

Peaches are grouped as **freestone** or **clingstone.** Freestone peaches have a pit that separates easily from the flesh. The pit in clingstone peaches is firmly attached.

Commercial peaches are carefully selected varieties that are bred from two groups—the so-called Persian peaches from Europe and other peaches brought from China. The Elberta peach, for example, is a cross between a Persian peach and a Chinese cling peach. Today more than 100 varieties of peaches—differing in season of ripening and color of skin and flesh—are grown commercially.

The United States is among the top producers of peaches, along with China, Italy, Spain, and Greece. Peach trees also thrive in Asia and Europe, as well as in parts of Canada, South Africa, Australia, and South America.

**Nectarines.** Nectarines are fuzzless, or smooth-skinned, peaches. They have been in existence as long as the ordinary peach, but they have never been as widely grown.

**Apricots.** Apricots look like fuzzless small peaches but have a slightly tart taste. In most temperate areas, apricots bloom so early that the blossoms are usually killed by frost. In warm, humid climates, the fruit cracks and decays. The warm, dry areas bordering on the Mediterranean Sea are well suited for apricots. California, where the climate also is warm and dry, is the center for apricot production in

Apricots are a stone fruit, like peaches, plums, and cherries. They look like small, smooth peaches.

These colorful Stanley prune plums are ready to be harvested. They will be dried and used as prunes.

the United States. Apricots are eaten fresh, canned, or dried, or they are made into juice, jams, and preserves.

### ▶PLUM
There are three basic groups of plums—European, Japanese, and American.

European plums first grew in western Asia. Today eastern and central Europe are very important plum-producing areas. European plums were taken to North America by English and French colonists. The prune plum, which is meaty and suitable for drying, has done especially well in California. Today the United States is the largest producer of prunes.

Japanese plums actually had their beginning in China. They came to Japan at an unknown date. They were introduced to the United States about 1870. Luther Burbank helped to popularize them, and now they are extensively grown, mainly in California. The flesh is generally soft and juicy.

American plums have little commercial value today, but they were an important source of food in early America. Commonly called beach plums, American plums are very hardy and can be grown in colder climates than the Japanese and European varieties. They make very good jams and jellies.

### ▶CHERRY
The cherry trees most commonly grown today originated in Europe and western Asia. There are two main groups of cherries, sweet and sour (or tart). Sour cherries are mainly canned or frozen for later use in pies, preserves, and juice. Sweet cherries are eaten fresh, or they are canned or made into maraschino cherries. Maraschino cherries are colored bright red and are used as a decoration in drinks and desserts.

Cherries thrive in cool, temperate regions. But since they do not keep well, not many are exported fresh. In the United States, sour cherries are grown mostly near the Great Lakes. Most sweet cherries are grown in California, Oregon, and Washington.

### ▶GROWING STONE FRUITS
Stone fruits are not grown straight from seed because the fruit of a tree grown from seed may be very different from the fruit of the parent tree. Instead the trees are budded onto a rootstock. A rootstock is usually a seedling of a variety of peach, plum, or cherry.

Stone-fruit trees grow best in a crumbly, fairly rich soil. Fruitgrowers cultivate the ground in spring and early summer, but they stop as the crop is beginning to ripen. In the fall a cover crop, such as rye or buckwheat, may be planted, or weeds are allowed to grow to keep the soil around the trees from eroding. The cover crops or weeds are turned under in the spring to enrich the soil. Fertilizing with nitrogen, and in some areas with potassium, also helps the trees.

Peach trees are more heavily pruned than other fruit trees. Because the color of the fruit improves with the amount of light that reaches it, young peach trees are usually pruned into the shape of a vase or a bowl. Young plum and cherry trees are trimmed to three to five branches on one main trunk. The trees must also be kept at a good picking height. Some varieties, such as Japanese plums, put out such a large crop of fruit that they must be as heavily pruned as peach trees.

Fruit trees are attacked by many insects, fungi, and viruses. New varieties of fruit trees, resistant to certain diseases, are being developed by plant geneticists. Various sprays have also been developed to combat insects and fungus diseases. Trees may be sprayed up to five or six times during the growing season.

Montmorency sour cherries are pulled from their stems and boxed for shipment to a cannery. Cherries that will be sold fresh are picked with their stems on.

### ▶ BLOOMING AND FRUIT BEARING

To bloom normally in the spring, peach, plum, and cherry trees need a period of a few weeks to several months of fairly cold temperatures in winter. The cold weather stops the growth of the trees and allows them to rest. But too severe a winter damages the fruit buds on the trees. Since peach trees bloom very early, they also are in danger from spring frosts. The hardiest stone fruits are the sour cherry and the American plum.

Most varieties of peach, sour cherry, and apricot trees are self-fruitful. This means that their blossoms can be fertilized by pollen from trees of the same variety.

The leading variety of sour cherry, the **Montmorency**, is self-fruitful, but sweet cherries are not. But if the fruitgrower plants the proper varieties of sweet cherry trees together, pollen is carried by honeybees and other insects from trees of one variety to another. Many varieties of plum trees can be fertilized only by pollen from certain other varieties of plum trees.

In some areas, peach trees may pass good producing condition in 10 years, but they may last 20 years or more in other sections. Plum trees and cherry trees last longer. Sour cherries generally do not give a good crop after 25 years, nor do sweet cherries after 30 years.

### ▶ HARVESTING

Peaches become ripe from June to October, depending on their variety and location. Peaches are picked at different stages of ripeness, depending on how far they have to be shipped and whether they will be sold as fresh fruit or sent to canneries. Peaches soften rapidly at warm temperatures, but they can be held in storage about a month if they are kept a little above freezing temperatures.

Peaches are covered with a light fuzz. Those that are sent to fresh markets are passed through a brush machine that removes most of the fuzz from the fruit.

Plums ripen from June through October and are usually harvested several times as they ripen. Plums for canning can be picked all at one time. Prune plums are gathered in two ways: Some fall naturally from the trees; the others must be shaken off. Mechanical shakers are widely used for prune plums. Plums can be kept fresh for three to four weeks if they are stored at temperatures just above freezing.

Cherries are picked from June to August. The picker must wait until the cherries are fully ripe to get them at their best. But birds can often damage the crop. Rainy weather is also a threat because the rain soaks into the ripe cherries, and they crack open. Cherries are picked with their stems on when they are to be sold fresh. Cherries for canning are "pulled" (the stems are left on the tree).

To prevent sour cherries from spoiling, they are often hauled to processing plants in trucks equipped with tanks of cold water. The water washes the cherries and prevents crushing. Sweet cherries can be left in cold storage for about three weeks.

### ▶ PROCESSING

Nearly half the peaches grown in the United States are canned. Plum, cherry, and apricot canning is a smaller part of the fruit-canning business. Stone fruits can also be dried or frozen fresh. Poorer grades of fruit are used to make jams, jellies, and pie fillings.

Reviewed by RODNEY W. DOW
State University of New York Agricultural and
Technical College at Farmingdale

See also AGRICULTURE; FOOD PRESERVATION; FRUITGROWING.

**PEALE, NORMAN VINCENT.** See OHIO (Famous People).

# PEALE FAMILY

Peale is the name of a distinguished family of American painters who flourished in the 1700's and 1800's.

**Charles Willson Peale** (1741–1827), born in Queen Anne's County, Maryland, was a leading portrait painter. He taught himself to paint as a young man, after learning saddle making, clock repair, and several other trades. In 1766 he went to London to study with the American painter Benjamin West. During the Revolutionary War, Peale fought with the Philadelphia militia. Resuming his painting career after the war, he painted portraits of famous Americans of his day, notably George Washington. In 1782 he opened a portrait gallery next to his home.

Peale had many scientific interests, including archaeology, engineering, and taxidermy, and he patented several inventions. In 1786 he established a natural history museum, the first of its kind in the nation. He also helped found the Pennsylvania Academy of the Fine Arts (1805) and the Society of Artists (1810), which were among the first professional organizations in the United States to promote the development of the arts.

Peale had 17 children, some of whom were named for famous artists. He instructed them in painting, and several became artists in their own right. **Raphaelle Peale** (1774–1825) was a painter of still lifes—arrangements of fruits and flowers—which he depicted with a high degree of realism. But his masterpiece is a painting called *After the Bath* (1823), which showcases his ability to create a convincing illusion of reality. **Rembrandt Peale** (1778–1860) specialized in portraits of famous Americans, especially idealized images of George Washington. **Rubens Peale** (1784–1865) painted nature subjects and opened a museum in New York City. **Titian Ramsay Peale** (1799–1885) was a naturalist and scientific illustrator.

Charles Willson's brother **James Peale** (1749–1831) was also a painter. He was known particularly for his miniatures and still lifes. Three of James's daughters achieved success as painters. **Anna Claypoole Peale** (1791–1878) was a noted miniaturist; **Margaretta Angelica Peale** (1795–1882) painted still lifes; and **Sarah Miriam Peale** (1800–85) specialized in portraits of famous people.

Reviewed by KENNETH HALTMAN
New Britain Museum of American Art

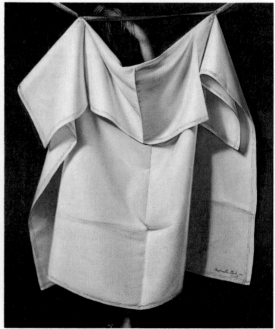

*Left:* In *The Artist in His Museum*, Charles Willson Peale painted himself at the entrance to his natural history museum. *Below: After the Bath* is considered the masterpiece of Charles Willson's son Raphaelle.

# PEANUTS AND PEANUT PRODUCTS

The peanut is one of the important foods discovered in the New World. It has a pod that contains two or more nutlike seeds. In the United States the word "peanut" is used for these seeds and their pod. The same pods and seeds are called groundnuts in Britain because the pods develop underground. Both names suggest that the peanut is really a nut, which it is not. The peanut produces underground pods from above-ground flowers, making it a very unusual plant.

Peanuts can be used for many different products. George Washington Carver, who rose from slavery to become a great agricultural chemist, found many new uses for peanuts. He used them to make substitutes for milk, butter, cheese, coffee, and flour. He also used them to make nonfood products, such as ink, dye, soap, and insulation.

▶ THE HISTORY OF PEANUTS

Peanuts probably originated in Bolivia or Brazil. Even now many varieties of wild peanuts grow in central South America. Cultivated peanuts, *Arachis hypogaea*, have been grown in both North America and South America for thousands of years.

Early in the 1500's, Portuguese traders carried peanuts to several places in Africa. The plants spread so quickly that a hundred years later they were as plentiful as native African plants. Portuguese and Spanish traders probably carried the plants to the East Indies and from there, it is believed, on to India and China.

Today India and China together grow about half the peanuts in the world. The plants are still grown in much of Africa and in Myanmar, Indonesia, and Brazil. Argentina and the United States also grow large quantities of peanuts.

▶ WHAT IS THE PLANT LIKE?

There are different varieties of peanut plants, but all of them have an erect central stem that grows from 8 to 36 inches (20 to 90 centimeters) tall. There are three main types. Spanish varieties have a bunchy plant. Virginia varieties have many branches. Runner varieties have branches that stretch out into a mat that is about 3 feet (1 meter) or more in diameter.

The peanut plant has flowers that look like yellow buttercups. They last only for a day. They develop during the night and open at sunup. The flowers are almost always self-pollinated, usually even before the blossoms open. During the afternoon the flowers wither. By midnight the process of fertilization is complete.

After a few days the fertilized part of the flower starts to grow toward the ground. It grows down 2 to 4 inches (5 to 10 centimeters) into the soil. In the soil, the peg, or stem, begins to enlarge at the end and form a pod with seeds. In about 65 days the seeds in the pod are fully grown.

**SOME USES OF PEANUTS**

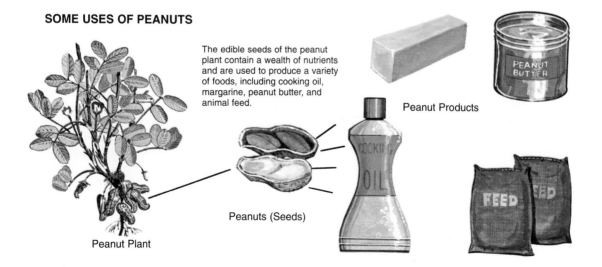

The edible seeds of the peanut plant contain a wealth of nutrients and are used to produce a variety of foods, including cooking oil, margarine, peanut butter, and animal feed.

Peanut Products

Peanuts (Seeds)

Peanut Plant

Different varieties produce different sizes of peanuts. Runner peanuts are the largest, averaging about 700 seeds per pound (1,500 per kilogram). Virginia peanuts are smaller, and Spanish peanuts the smallest of all.

▶ **GROWING AND HARVESTING PEANUTS**

Peanut plants need hot weather and plenty of moisture during the time they are blooming and forming pods. After this stage the plant does not need so much warmth and moisture for good growth. If it is rainy during the time just before harvest, the pegs weaken. Some of the peanuts break off and are left in the ground during harvest.

If the soil in which a peanut is planted is warm and moist, the roots grow rapidly. By the time leaves appear above ground, the roots may be more than 14 inches (35 centimeters) long. By the time the pods are fully grown and ready to harvest, the roots may reach a depth of 3 to 5 feet (1 to 1.5 meters). The deep roots enable the plant to reach moisture far down in the soil during a dry spell and also help it use nutrients that are deep in the soil. A well-drained, loose sandy-loam soil is best for peanut crops.

Before the seeds are sown, the soil is plowed and harrowed into a smooth seedbed. The seeds are shelled and are treated with a fungicide. They are planted soon after a rain so that they will sprout immediately.

In harvesting peanuts, a mechanical digger lifts the plants and shakes the soil off. It inverts them in long rows, where they dry for two days or more. Then the pods are threshed from the vines by harvesters.

When they are properly dried, peanuts contain only 7 to 10 percent moisture. They may then be stored for months if kept dry or longer in cold storage. Much of a year's crop is shelled and processed by spring.

▶ **PEANUTS AS FOOD**

Peanuts are among the most nutritious of all vegetable foods. Because about half the seed is oil, it has a very high energy value. There is more protein in peanuts than in the same weight of steak or ham. Peanuts have little starch and are rich in the vitamin B complex. Peanuts are eaten in many different ways—as salted peanuts, peanut candy, peanut butter in sandwiches, or peanut oil in fried foods.

When salted peanuts are being prepared, they usually are blanched. This is done by heat or water treatments, which loosen the skins, and blowers, which remove them. Then the nuts are roasted in oil and salted, or they may be dry-roasted (roasted without oil).

The peanuts used to make peanut butter are dry-roasted, blanched, and then ground very fine. Sometimes small amounts of other foods—such as salt, honey, vegetable oils, or yeast—are added to make the peanut butter tastier, easier to spread, and more nutritious.

Not everyone can eat peanut products. For a small percentage of the population, even the smallest trace of peanuts in food can trigger a potentially life-threatening allergic reaction. This may involve severe difficulty in breathing, among other symptoms. People with such an allergy must avoid all products containing any peanuts or peanut oil. To help prevent allergic individuals from being exposed to peanuts, some schools have established peanut-free tables in the lunchroom, and some airlines offer peanut-free flights.

A large part of the world production of peanuts is used to make peanut oil. Peanut oil is much like olive oil. In Europe it is used to make margarine. In North America it is used as a salad and cooking oil. It is an excellent oil for frying because it can become very hot without spattering.

Peanuts are also used in feed for animals. Peanut meal adds protein to the diet of livestock, and hogs and cattle eat the vines.

ROBERT C. LEFFEL
United States Department of Agriculture

See also NUTS.

---

**See For Yourself**

### How to Make Your Own Peanut Butter

If you have a food grinder or an electric blender, you can easily make peanut butter. You need dry-roasted peanuts and peanut or vegetable oil.

Grind about 1/4 cup of the peanuts at a time. Grind until the mixture is like a paste. Add a teaspoon or less of oil to make it smoother. You may also wish to add a dash of salt. Mix thoroughly.

Store the peanut butter in a tightly covered container, and keep it in the refrigerator. Because your peanut butter has no chemical additives, it will separate on standing. Stir it before using.

# PEAR

The pear is native to Asia and nearby Europe. Stone Age people discovered and ate the juicy fruit of the pear tree. As civilization developed, pear trees were improved by selecting and planting the best of the wild trees.

The Romans gave us the name for the group of fruits to which pears belong. The Roman word for fruits was *poma*, and **pome fruits** is the name now applied to apples, pears, and quinces. These fruits all have a thin outer skin, a fleshy pulp, and a core that has five parts in which the seeds are borne.

During the 1700's fruitgrowers in Europe, especially in Belgium and France, tried to improve the quality of pears by crossing different varieties. A Belgian priest, Nicolas Hardenpont (1705–74), developed the first of the pears having soft, juicy pulp that are now called butter pears. He and other pear breeders created many high-quality varieties. Some of these varieties are still grown.

The colonists brought European pears to America, and at first they did well. About the time of the Revolution, however, the trees began to die. The disease that killed them, called fire blight, was later found to be caused by bacteria that live in the bark. Although all high-quality European pears can be attacked by fire blight, the disease is less severe on the Pacific coast. For this reason 90 percent of

the pears in the United States are grown in California, Oregon, and Washington.

Pears brought from eastern Asia were found to resist the fire blight disease. They were so hard and gritty, however, that they were called sand pears. Some of the sand pears and European pears growing nearby crossed naturally. Several of these crosses proved resistant to the blight and were also of better quality than the sand pears. The variety called Bosc is one of these. It is the most widely grown pear east of the Rocky Mountains. But it is very poor in quality compared to European varieties. Recently some high-quality varieties that resist fire blight have been developed by scientific breeding.

Fire blight has spread to Europe, but so far it has not been a serious problem there. The pear is an even more important crop in Western Europe than in North America.

All countries in the temperate zones, both north and south of the equator, produce pears. Commercially grown pears are not produced directly from seed because the fruit on trees grown from seed is usually poor. Instead, buds or shoots from the desired variety are grafted onto a young tree grown from seed. The new tree grown in this way will produce fruit like that of the parent.

Insects attack pears, and in rainy areas, fungus diseases must be controlled. The trees are sprayed several times a year to control these pests and diseases.

For the best quality, pears must be picked while still hard and still green in color. If they are to be kept for a long time, they are placed in cold storage immediately at a temperature set at freezing. If they are to be used soon, they are held at 65 to 70°F (18 to 21°C). At this temperature, they become ready for eating in one to two weeks.

The Bartlett variety, called Williams in Europe, is the most important in the United States and other pear-growing countries. It is used fresh or canned. Some pears are dried. In Europe, pears are also used for making perry, a fermented pear juice.

Reviewed by RODNEY W. DOW
State University of New York
Agricultural and Technical College
at Farmingdale

See also FRUITGROWING.

**BARTLETT PEAR**

CROSS SECTION

A Japanese bay (*above*) is the site of an unusual kind of farm. Cages of oysters hang from rafts floating in the calm waters. Within the captive oysters, precious gems are forming. At harvest time, the oysters are gathered, and lustrous pearls (*shown in inset*) are plucked from the oysters.

## PEARLS

The pearl is one of the most popular of all precious gems. It is the only one created by a living creature. Its softly shining beauty has made the word "pearl" mean almost the same thing to us as "beauty" and "great worth."

Pearls are made by certain kinds of oysters, clams, and mussels. All these animals are called **mollusks**, from a Latin word meaning "soft," because they have soft bodies inside their hard shells. The pearl is actually composed of the material with which a mollusk coats an irritating particle that it cannot get rid of. This irritant may be a piece of broken shell, a parasite that has bored through the shell, or even a tiny grain of sand. The material the mollusk keeps layering onto the piece to keep it from being an irritation is **nacre**, or **mother-of-pearl**. As many layers of mother-of-pearl are built up, a pearl is made.

### What Makes a Pearl Valuable?

Natural pearls are found rarely, and large natural pearls even more rarely. The largest known natural pearl is one such rare find. Found in the shell of a giant clam and named the *Pearl of Lao-tze*, it weighs 14.06 pounds (6.38 kilograms)!

Only a few of the pearls found are considered valuable. A valuable pearl has a beautiful shimmering luster, which jewelers call the pearl's **orient**. The luster comes from below the surface of the gem. It is caused by light that is reflected and refracted (broken up) by the different layers of the pearl. Pearls that come from saltwater mollusks are the most sought after since they have a high degree of luster. Color, texture, and shape also determine a pearl's value.

Color is influenced by the type of oyster, the salt content of the water, the depth at which the oyster lives, and the temperature of the water. Pearls are usually white, cream, pink or rose, blue-gray, or black. White is generally the most popular color. Black pearls are especially treasured for their rarity.

The **round pearl** has the most desirable shape. It develops in the soft parts of the mollusk. A solid pearl in any irregular shape is called a **baroque pearl**. When a pearl becomes attached to the inside of the shell, it becomes a **button pearl**, rounded on one side and flat on the other. Sometimes a mollusk covers an injured spot on its shell with extra nacre, and then a **blister pearl** forms.

### ▶NATURAL PEARLS

Not every pearl formed is valuable. Only those mollusks whose shells are coated on the inside with iridescent mother-of-pearl produce precious pearls. The most beautiful and costly pearls are almost all found in species of the *Pinctada*, a pearl oyster that lives in tropical seas. The pearls in edible clams and oysters are usually of poor quality and valueless.

**Saltwater Pearls.** Many of the finest natural pearls come from the Persian Gulf, especially the area off the coast of the island country Bahrain. In ancient times, Bahrain had a thriving pearling industry. However, Bahrain's economic activity now centers around the oil industry. Beautiful white and silvery pearls are found off the west coast of Sri Lanka. The pearl beds of Sri Lanka have been a source of pearls for more than 2,000 years, making them the oldest pearl fisheries. Fine black pearls are found off the west coast of Mexico and the United States. Natural saltwater pearls are also found near Australia and some islands of the South Pacific and of the Caribbean.

**Freshwater Pearls.** Pearls are also found in the mollusks inhabiting rivers and lakes of North and South America, Europe, and Asia. At one time, pearl-bearing mollusks were abundant in the rivers of the upper Mississippi Valley. But overfishing caused the population to fall so sharply that it was almost eliminated. Freshwater pearls from the Mississippi Valley are now rarely found.

### ▶CULTURED PEARLS

Hundreds of years ago the Chinese discovered that objects would be covered with mother-of-pearl if they were placed inside the shells of clams and oysters. After experimentation

To produce a cultured pearl, the shell of a young oyster is opened, and a small bead made of mother-of-pearl is inserted (*above*).

Oysters with beads implanted are carefully tended in submerged cages (*above*). One to three years later, the oysters are gathered and the pearls nestled safely within (*below*) are harvested.

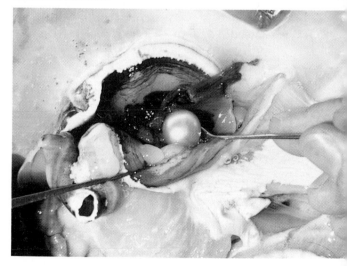

**How are artificial pearls made?**

Artificial, or simulated, pearls do not come from oysters at all. Instead they are manufactured from glass or plastic beads, which are covered with a nacrelike film. The film is made from fish scales. Artificial pearls may also be made by coating the inside of hollow glass beads with the nacre film.

that started in the late 1800's, some Japanese researchers learned how to treat oysters to produce "cultured" pearls at a fairly low cost. Cultured-pearl production is now a large industry in Japan.

To produce a cultured pearl, a smooth, round bead of mother-of-pearl is skillfully set into the living tissue of a pearl oyster. Then the oyster is returned to the water. The cultured pearls produced are less expensive than natural ones, but only an expert can tell the difference between them.

Most oysters used for making cultured pearls are gathered in special netting lowered from rafts. Others are gathered by divers. Once gathered, the oysters are taken to pearl "farms," where they are cleaned and graded according to age, size, and health. This sorting eliminates unsuitable oysters. The shells of suitable oysters are then cleaned of any sea growth and parasites. When the oysters open their shells, skilled workers cut into the **mantle** (the fleshy, glandular area) and insert the bead of mother-of-pearl covered with a bit of living tissue from another oyster. The treated oysters are then placed in cages suspended from rafts and anchored in sheltered water. Later the oysters are transferred to permanent rafts where they are protected against disease and natural enemies.

One to three years after treatment, the oysters are removed from the rafts, and their pearls are removed. The pearls are sorted according to shape, color, size, and luster. Only a very few are of truly fine quality. The pearls are then sent to manufacturers to be drilled and strung or set into pieces of jewelry. Pearls are selected carefully for each use. The pearls for necklaces, for example, must be of similar color and value and of the same size or of gradually increasing size.

MORTON R. SARETT
Jewelry Industry Council

See also GEMS; JEWELRY.

---

## PEARSON, LESTER B. (1897–1972)

Lester Bowles Pearson served as prime minister of Canada from 1963 until 1968. He was born in Toronto on April 23, 1897. After serving in the Canadian Army and Royal Flying Corps in World War I, he attended Oxford University and the University of Toronto, where he later taught history (1924–28).

Pearson became a career diplomat in 1928. He was appointed ambassador to the United States in 1945 and represented Canada at the United Nations Charter Conference. In 1948, Pearson entered the Canadian Parliament as secretary of state for external affairs. In this post he signed the North Atlantic Treaty Organization (NATO) agreement for Canada.

In 1957, Pearson was awarded the Nobel Peace Prize for his work in creating the United Nations Emergency Force. This kept peace between Israel and Egypt from 1956 to 1967 following a conflict over the Suez Canal.

As leader of the Liberal Party (1958–68), Pearson stressed the need for programs to end unemployment and boost Canada's economy. He also promoted better relations with the United States. In 1963 a crisis arose over the United States and Canada's joint defense policy, and a general election was held. The Liberals won enough seats to defeat the Conservatives under John G. Diefenbaker, and Pearson became prime minister.

Despite his weak position in Parliament and the threat to Canadian unity from separatists in the province of Quebec, Pearson's ministry was noteworthy for the establishment of the Canada Pension Plan, which became effective in 1966, and for the adoption of the Canadian flag in 1965.

On April 20, 1968, Pearson retired as prime minister and was succeeded by Pierre E. Trudeau. Pearson died at his home in Rockcliffe, Canada on December 27, 1972.

JOHN S. MOIR
University of Toronto

# PEARY, ROBERT E. (1856–1920)

Robert Edwin Peary is credited with leading the first successful expedition to the North Pole. Born on May 6, 1856, in Cresson, Pennsylvania, Peary was raised in Maine, where he spent much of his spare time hiking, collecting rocks and plants, writing poetry, and keeping a diary. He was an outstanding student and athlete, and in 1877 he graduated from Bowdoin College with top honors in civil engineering. In 1881 Peary became an engineer for the United States Navy in Washington, D.C.

One day in 1885, Peary found an old pamphlet written by a Swedish explorer, describing his journeys in Greenland. The pamphlet lured Peary to the Far North. In 1886 he explored Greenland's inland ice cap for several months. From 1891 to 1892 he again explored Greenland, this time with his young wife, Josephine. He went to Greenland five times in all. During each expedition, he made scientific findings about tides, polar seas, winds, temperatures, ice floes, plant and animal life, and the native people, the Inuit. He risked his life to cross northeastern Greenland—a distance of 1,200 miles (1,930 kilometers)—by dogsled. By charting the distance, he proved that Greenland was a huge island, not a continent as many had thought.

In the late 1890's Peary vowed that he would be the first man to visit the North Pole. His trips to the Arctic had taught him much about exploring on ice. He had his crew dress in light but warm clothes. He trained them to set up advance camps, carry few supplies, travel in small parties, hunt for food, and move quickly.

Peary first tried to reach the North Pole between 1898 and 1902 but failed. Early in this expedition his feet were so badly frostbitten that eight of his toes had to be amputated. Yet nothing could stop him. Once, while he was temporarily stranded in a deserted hut during a blizzard and in terrible pain, he wrote these words on a wall: *Inveniam viam aut faciam*— Latin for "I shall find a way or make one."

Peary headed for the North Pole again between 1905 and 1906 but failed once more to reach it. In 1908 he set out on his third polar expedition, sailing from New York City to Ellesmere Island in Canada. He built a base camp at Cape Columbia, about 450 miles (725 kilometers) from the North Pole.

Robert E. Peary once said, "The fame of Columbus will be equaled only by the man who stands at the top of the world—the discoverer of the North Pole." Seeking that place in history for himself, Peary conquered the North Pole on April 6, 1909.

In March 1909, he and his crew left by sledge for the Pole. For nearly a month they battled freezing cold, violent winds, and sudden openings in the ice. Many of his colleagues were sent back to the base camp, now 300 miles (480 kilometers) away.

By early April, only Peary, his aide and companion, Matthew Henson (1866–1955), and four Inuit guides remained. The small band pushed forward another 133 miles (214 kilometers). On April 6, 1909, they made their final march and reached the Pole. Peary unwound the American flag he had worn under the furs around his waist and planted it at the Pole. The flag had been hand-sewn by his wife. Later he announced his discovery to the world with this cable message: "Stars and Stripes nailed to the Pole—Peary."

Five days before Peary cabled his message, explorer Frederick A. Cook announced that he had reached the Pole in 1908. His claim was generally dismissed, but for decades it clouded Peary's accomplishment. Nevertheless, Peary returned home to praise and honors. A U.S. warship was named after him, and Congress promoted him to rear admiral. The world's most northerly land area, in northern Greenland, was named Peary Land.

Peary died on February 20, 1920, and was buried with military honors in Arlington National Cemetery in Arlington, Virginia. In 1989 the National Geographic Society sponsored a study of his famous expedition. After extensive research, investigators concluded that Peary had come within at least 5 miles (8 kilometers) of the North Pole.

TONY SIMON
Author, *North Pole:
The Story of Robert E. Peary*

## PEEL, SIR ROBERT (1788–1850)

Sir Robert Peel served three terms as prime minister of Great Britain and is considered the founder of that country's Conservative Party. He was born near Bury, England, on February 5, 1788. In 1809, at the age of 21, Peel entered Parliament as a member of the Tory Party. As chief secretary for Ireland (1812–18), he opposed seating Roman Catholics in Parliament. He later served as home secretary (1822–27) and as a leader in the House of Commons (1828–30).

In 1829, Peel modified his earlier views on the Catholics and sponsored the Catholic Emancipation Act, which removed many of the political and civil restrictions on Catholics in Britain and Ireland. He also reorganized the London police force with the Metropolitan Police Act. London's police have since been known as "Bobbies" in his honor.

During Peel's brief first term as prime minister (1834–35), he formed the Conservative Party in opposition to the Whigs and their Reform Act of 1832, which had extended the vote to 50 percent more people. During Peel's second (1841–45) and third (1845–46) terms, he reimposed an income tax, abolished import taxes on food and raw materials, and passed the Bank Charter Act (1844), which established many of Britain's most enduring financial policies.

After the potato famine struck Ireland in 1845, Peel pushed to repeal the Corn Laws, which had kept farm prices high due to tariffs on imported grain. This controversial action split the Conservative Party. Peel lost many of his supporters and was forced from office. He died on July 2, 1850, from injuries sustained after falling from his horse.

GEORGE CAREY
Georgetown University

---

## PEI, I. M. (1917–    )

The Chinese-American architect Ieoh Ming Pei was born on April 26, 1917, in Guangzhou (Canton), China. He moved to the United States in 1935 to study architecture at the Massachusetts Institute of Technology (MIT) and at Harvard University. Pei became an American citizen in 1954. A year later he opened his own architectural firm in New York City.

Pei's buildings are noted for their bold geometric shapes and functional design. They also reflect his interest in designing small-scale units of space that work together as a whole. He succeeded in this approach with the design of the Everson Museum of Art (1968) in Syracuse, New York. A later example is the East Wing of the National Gallery of Art in Washington, D.C., completed in 1978. This structure was designed in the shape of two connecting triangles to conform to an awkward building site. Pei's firm also designed the immense Jacob K. Javits Convention Center in New York City, which opened in 1986.

One of Pei's most challenging commissions came in 1984, when President François Mitterand of France selected him to expand the Louvre Museum in Paris. Pei's plan included the construction of a glass pyramid 65 feet (20 meters) tall in the center of the old Louvre courtyard. This pyramid would serve as the new main entrance to the museum. Critics throughout France opposed the plan. Yet when the project was completed in 1989, it was found to be thoroughly functional and to lend unity to the entire architectural setting.

Pei's other works include the John F. Kennedy Library (1979) in Dorchester, Massachusetts, the Fragrant Hill Hotel (1983) in Peking, and the 70-story Bank of China headquarters (1989) in Hong Kong.

HOWARD E. WOODEN
Director Emeritus
The Wichita Art
Museum

The architect I. M. Pei sits in front of the giant glass pyramid he designed to serve as the new entrance to the Louvre, the national art museum of France.

PEKING.  See Beijing.

# PELÉ (1940–   )

As a boy, Edson Arantes do Nascimento shined shoes and ran errands. But on days when his father played soccer, Edson forgot about earning money to help his family. He watched his father play and dreamed of being a player himself. Later, he became—in the opinion of many people—the greatest soccer player in the world.

Pelé, as Edson was nicknamed, was born on October 23, 1940, in Três Corações, Brazil. He left school after the fourth grade and was apprenticed to a shoemaker. But he continued to think of playing soccer.

When Pelé was 15, his coach took him to São Paulo to join a professional team. But the team there turned him down. Not discouraged, the coach took him to another team, in Santos. Pelé made a poor showing, but the Santos coach decided to accept him for the second team. In his first game, Pelé scored four goals. He soon moved to the first team and became a sports hero to all Brazil. He could kick with either foot, "head" the ball with accuracy, and put a curve on it as well.

In 1958, Pelé helped the Brazilian national team win the World Cup. He was already a legend in world play. Not surprisingly, he became a target for other players, and he began to lose some of his enthusiasm for the game. But before he stopped playing in international games in 1971, he led Brazilian teams to three World Cup, two World Club, and five South American championships.

Pelé in action.

Pelé continued to play for Santos until 1974. Partly because of him, people in the United States became enthusiastic about soccer. Pelé came out of retirement in 1975 to join the New York Cosmos. In 1977, he led them to the North American Soccer League title. He then retired from the game.

Reviewed by Richard B. Rottkov
United States Soccer Federation

# PELICANS

"A wonderful bird is the pelican!" says the old rhyme. "Its bill will hold more than its belly can." And indeed, the bill of a pelican is remarkable. Attached to its bottom half is a large skin pouch. People sometimes think pelicans store food in their pouches, but they do not use the pouches in this way. Pelicans live on fish. When they catch fish, they use the pouch like a dip net. They scoop up the fish, let the water drain out, and then swallow the fish.

Pelicans are large water birds. Some kinds may be as long as 6 feet (180 centimeters) and have a wingspread of up to 10 feet (3 meters). Although they are large, they are good swimmers and graceful flyers. They form a family all of their own, with some six to eight species. Most are white or grayish, sometimes with pink tints or darker wing tips. One of the American species is brown or blackish gray. A variety of this species, the Eastern brown pelican, is the state bird

Pelicans are sociable birds. They band together in colonies to feed and build their nests.

the fish reach the shallower water near the shore, the pelicans scoop them up easily.

The American brown pelican has a fishing method unlike that of other pelicans. It flies above the water, then dives or spirals down, plunges under the water to seize a fish, and bobs back to the surface.

Pelicans build simple nests, always near water and sometimes floating on it. They lay one to four eggs and sit on them for four or five weeks. The young hatch naked and blind but are soon covered with down. They feed on predigested fish, which they take from the parents' pouches. The young leave the nest for good after about four months. But they do not get their adult plumage (feathers) for a couple of years and do not breed until a year or two later.

Pelicans are long-lived birds. They may live for over 30 years. The adults have few natural enemies. But they are easily disturbed when nesting and may then abandon their eggs or chicks. Many animals prey on young pelicans. And pelicans share two problems with many other birds and animals. Their habitats (the places where they live and breed, which for pelicans are wetlands) are being destroyed by human beings as they clear land for building projects and for agriculture. And pelicans are being poisoned by pesticides (weed- and insect-killing chemicals) in the environment.

▶PELICANS IN ART AND LEGEND

People once believed that if food was scarce, a mother pelican would stab her own breast with her beak and feed her young with the blood. At breeding time, some pelicans have a reddish spot on their breasts. Perhaps this spot helped give rise to the legend. Because of the legend, in the Middle Ages the pelican was considered a symbol of Christ, who, according to Christian belief, shed his blood for humankind. Pictures or carvings of "a pelican in her piety" (as depictions of this legendary behavior were called) are sometimes found in Christian churches. Following this tradition, a pelican "in the act of tearing its breast to feed its young" appears on the seal and flag of the state of Louisiana.

Reviewed by JOHN BULL
American Museum of Natural History

See also BIRDS.

of Louisiana. A few other families of water birds—such as the tropic birds, gannets, and cormorants—are like pelicans in certain ways. Together, they make up the bird order Pelecaniformes, meaning "pelican-shaped."

▶WHERE AND HOW PELICANS LIVE

Pelicans are found in lakes, swamps, lagoons, and coastal waters of all the continents except Antarctica. The American species range the farthest north. Those that live in cooler climates migrate to warmer areas in winter. In Europe, pelicans are now found only in the areas around the Black and Caspian seas and in the Balkans. The Danube delta is a favorite breeding ground.

The kinds of fish that pelicans eat are not eaten by people or caught for sport. And the droppings, called guano, of pelicans are used as fertilizer.

Pelicans are sociable birds. They feed and nest in large groups. Some species even engage in cooperative fishing. They form lines or semicircles and swim toward the shore, driving the fish before them. When

# PELOPONNESIAN WAR

The Peloponnesian War was one of the most important conflicts of ancient Greece, lasting, in its various phases, from 431 to 404 B.C. At a time when Greece was composed of many independent city-states, the war involved two of the most powerful, Athens and Sparta, and their allies. Much of what we know about the war has come down to us from the account written by the historian Thucydides, an Athenian, who took part in it.

**Background.** When the Persians invaded Greece in 480–479 B.C., during the conflict known as the Persian Wars, the Greek city-states had been defended by an alliance of Athenians and Spartans. Athens' superb fleet and Sparta's disciplined infantry had combined to drive off the invaders.

However, this wartime alliance soon disintegrated. The Athenians had used their navy to build a strong defensive league of island and coastal city-states against further Persian attack. Eventually they converted the league into an Athenian empire. The Spartans, suspicious of Athenian expansion, withdrew into their mountainous homeland in the Peloponnesus, the southern part of Greece, from which the war takes its name. There they strengthened their own alliances against threats from Athens.

**Outbreak of War.** Hostility between Athens and the city-state of Corinth, an ally of Sparta, finally led to the outbreak of war in 431 B.C. It was clear from the start that the Athenian navy would dominate the seas, while the Spartan army was virtually invincible on land. Therefore, as long as Athens, protected by its strong walls, retained access to the sea and avoided battle with the superior Spartan troops, it was safe.

This was the strategy adopted by Pericles, the Athenian leader, and it worked well. The Spartans regularly invaded Attica, the region around Athens. But the city itself held firm, in spite of a plague that struck in 430 B.C. and killed many of the inhabitants, including Pericles. After years of sporadic fighting, a truce—the Peace of Nicias—was signed in 421 B.C.

**Sicilian Expedition.** Although the Spartans were prepared to honor the peace, in 415 B.C. the Athenians launched a naval expedition against Syracuse, a city-state on the island of

## GREECE IN THE PELOPONNESIAN WAR

Sparta and Allies    Athens and Allies

Sicily and a colony of Corinth. The Athenians also interfered in the affairs of some of Sparta's neighboring cities. The result was a resumption of the war. The undertaking of the Sicilian expedition, urged by the Athenian Alcibiades, ended in disaster. Nevertheless, the Athenian navy remained strong and the maritime empire it guarded provided continuing support for Athens. The Spartans realized that they would have to develop their own fleet in order to defeat the Athenians.

**Fall of Athens.** At just this moment, the Persians, who had never forgiven the Athenians for their role in the earlier Persian defeat, decided to intervene on the side of Sparta. They supplied money to construct and maintain a Spartan fleet. Although they were an inland people who lacked a seafaring tradition, the Spartans turned out to be excellent sailors. In a series of naval engagements in 406 and 405 B.C., they defeated the Athenian fleet that had protected the ships carrying grain to Athens from overseas Greek colonies. With its food supply cut off, Athens was starved into submission in 404 B.C. The defeat marked the end of the Golden Age of Athens and left Sparta as the leading Greek power.

EUGENE N. BORZA
The Pennsylvania State University
Author, *In the Shadow of Olympus*

See also PERICLES.

**PENCILS.** See PENS AND PENCILS.

A penguin travels over snow and ice by tobogganing.

# PENGUINS

Penguins are birds, but they are unlike other birds in several ways. Their wings are flippers, and they cannot fly in the air. Penguins do, however, "fly" in the water, at speeds up to 30 miles (48 kilometers) an hour. While swimming, they can dive with a thrust of their flippers and travel 30 feet (9 meters) underwater before surfacing. They surface with such force that they may soar into the air, like porpoises. Some can leap out of the water onto a ledge 7 feet (2 meters) above the surface.

On land, penguins use their flippers for fighting and for balancing as they walk. Penguins waddle slowly along, standing up straight like a person. When traveling over snow and ice, they may flop on their bellies and "row" with their feet. They also use their flippers when in a great hurry. This way of traveling is called tobogganing.

Penguins differ from most other birds in that their feathers cover the body completely. Penguin feathers are so small they look like scales. They are tightly packed together and form a dense covering that sheds water and helps keep the birds warm.

Penguins spend most of their lives in water. They come on land to mate and to produce their young. Penguins are very social birds; tens of thousands live together in breeding grounds called **rookeries**.

There are 17 known species, or kinds; all live in the Southern Hemisphere. Though many people think of the Antarctic as the home of the penguins, only seven species nest there. The others breed on islands outside the Antarctic Circle and on the shores of South Africa, Australia, and New Zealand, as well as on the coasts of South America and on the Galápagos Islands of the Pacific.

▶**MEMBERS OF THE PENGUIN FAMILY**

All 17 penguin species have white fronts and black or blue-gray backs. This coloring probably helps hide them from their main enemy in the sea—the leopard seal. To an enemy swimming below a penguin, the pale front may blend with the sky. From above, the dark back may blend with the sea.

The most obvious differences among species are in the colors and patterns around the face and across the chest. The macaroni and the rockhopper penguins have bright yellow feathers above their eyes. The emperor penguin is the most beautiful of all, with its purple bill and a golden sheen to its breast.

The coloring and markings of the chicks vary, too. The gray emperor penguin chick looks as if it were wearing a pair of big, black spectacles.

The emperor is the biggest member of the penguin family. It stands 4 feet (1.2 meters) tall and weighs about 60 pounds (27 kilograms). The Adelie penguin is one of the smaller species. It stands about 1½ feet (0.5 meter) tall when fully grown and weighs about 12 pounds (5 kilograms).

The Adelie penguin is one of the kinds that live in the Antarctic. It is the penguin that has been studied the most and is a good example of how the other species live.

## The Adelie Penguin

During the Antarctic winter, February to October, the Adelies live at sea, hunting small shrimplike animals called krill. In October, which is early spring in the Antarctic, the Adelies pop out of the sea and start a long trek to their rookeries, or breeding grounds. The penguins may have to walk and slide, scramble and toboggan 60 miles (96.5 kilometers) across the sea ice to reach the rocky Antarctic coast. They arrive at their rookeries, singly or in groups, about the middle of October. Usually the males arrive first and go directly to their nests of the previous year. The nests are made of stones. The males seem to find the right nest even when it is covered by a foot or two of snow.

The male Adelie performs what is called the ecstatic display. The male stretches his neck, lifts his bill toward the sky, and slowly waves his flippers back and forth. He lets forth a raucous "caw." Like the songs of other birds, this call serves to warn other males to keep away from the nest territory. At the same time it attracts females to the nest.

When the female approaches the nest, the two birds face each other. They wave their heads and necks and make sounds to each other. This is called a mutual display.

The pair has to make a nest before the eggs are laid. One bird stays on the nest and guards it. The other goes back and forth, collecting stones from the outskirts of the colony or from unguarded colony piles. If a pair of penguins is so foolish as to leave the nest unguarded, the stones rapidly disappear. All the other penguins are also collecting stones. Penguins carry stones in their beaks. Both male and female collect stones and guard the nest in turn. The stones are dropped around the partner on the nest, who arranges them into a neat pile.

**The Laying and Hatching of Eggs.** In mid-November, about three weeks after arrival at the rookery, the female Adelie lays two bluish-white eggs. Then she leaves for the sea to feed. About two weeks later, the female returns to the nest. The penguins greet each other with very noisy and excited mutual displays. There is much of this display before the

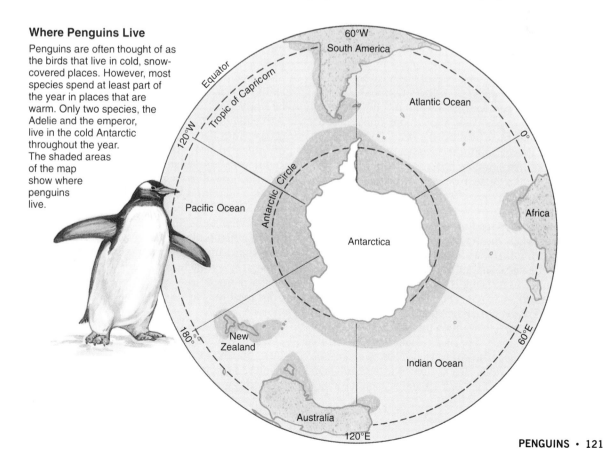

**Where Penguins Live**

Penguins are often thought of as the birds that live in cold, snow-covered places. However, most species spend at least part of the year in places that are warm. Only two species, the Adelie and the emperor, live in the cold Antarctic throughout the year. The shaded areas of the map show where penguins live.

**Male and female penguins greet each other.**

1½ pounds (0.7 kilograms) of food in one meal. While it is growing, the chick is fed about every two days.

When the chicks are about 4 weeks old, they leave the nest. By now their down is thick enough to protect them against the cold. Usually the parents manage to raise one chick to full growth. Sometimes harsh weather kills the eggs or chicks.

When the chicks are 4 or 5 weeks old, both parents are feeding at sea most of the time. They come back only for very short periods to feed their young. Left to themselves, the chicks gather together into large groups, called crèches, of 100 or 200 birds. This seems to protect them from the gull-like skua, which attacks and eats sick or starving chicks that become separated from the group. The crèche formation keeps the chicks warm, too.

Parents recognize their own chicks among the hundreds of others in the crèche, and feed only their own chicks. At 9 weeks the Adelie chicks are as big as their parents. They have shed their soft down for a coat of feathers. A young bird now looks like the parents, except that it has a white throat. In another year, the young Adelie sheds these feathers and gets adult feathers, including the black throat feathers. An Adelie changes its feathers every year. Sometimes Adelies molt on land, but most often they do so away from land, on floating pack ice.

The adult penguins desert their fully grown chicks. The chicks wander down to the beaches until large groups have gathered. After much excitement and noise, the birds plunge into the water in little groups. Adults do not give swimming lessons, and the first swimming movements of the chicks are clumsy bobbings up and down. Some of the young penguins are hurt or killed by leopard seals, which lurk in the water waiting to catch plump young penguins.

The remaining penguins head for the pack ice where the adults spend the winter. The young remain there for their first two or three years. They do not appear again at the rookeries until they are 3 or 4 years old.

### The Emperor Penguins

The emperor penguin, unlike all other species, breeds during the dark and stormy polar winter. The emperors return in March to their breeding grounds on sea ice close to the Ant-

female changes place with the male. The male gets up stiffly. He looks thin and weary. He has fasted for about six weeks! A male Adelie starts off weighing about 13 pounds (6 kilograms), and at the end of the fast he weighs about 8 pounds (4 kilograms); he has lost about 40 percent of his weight.

The male collects a few more stones for the nest and then goes to the sea. The open sea may be right up to the coast by this time, because the summer is fast advancing. In two weeks the male Adelie has regained a good amount of the lost weight, and he again takes over the nest from the female. She now leaves for another feeding trip. By remarkable timing, when the female comes back to the nest with a full stomach, her chicks are coming out of the eggs and are ready for their first meal. It has taken the eggs 35 days to hatch.

**Adelie Young.** The fluffy down-covered chicks are closely guarded by their parents. One parent sits right on top of them while they are still small. The parents take turns guarding and going off to feed. They feed on small sea animals, which are partly digested and later forced up to the beak. A chick can eat about

Female penguin feeds her chicks.

Penguin chicks gather together for protection.

arctic shore. The birds pair off much as the Adelies do, except that they make no nest. In May the female lays one egg, which weighs about a pound. She gives the egg to her mate and goes off to sea to break her fast. The male keeps the egg warm until it hatches about 64 days later. He tucks the egg on top of his feet, between his legs. There it is kept warm by a flap on his belly. He can shuffle short distances without dropping the egg.

During all the time that he is incubating the egg, the male lives in continuous cold and darkness. During the gales and snowstorms of the Antarctic winter, the temperature may drop as low as $-70°F$ ($-57°C$). To protect themselves from the cold during this time, the males huddle close together.

The females return a few days before or after the egg is hatched. When the female returns, the male leaves for the sea. He has gone without food for three months. He feeds for several weeks before returning to the nest.

At birth the chick weighs about 11 ounces (312 grams) and is covered with gray down. Its parents take turns guarding it and keeping it warm beneath their bellies. When the chicks

A young emperor penguin, investigating the world, peers between the legs of its mother.

King penguins incubate eggs for about 54 days.

Strawlike plumes decorate head of the macaroni penguin.

are about half grown, they huddle together, like the Adelie chicks. In spite of this huddling, many chicks freeze in blizzards.

By early January the sea ice breaks up and spreads out into the oceans. The emperors go off with the ice. Their chicks are fully grown and ready for life in the sea.

### The King and Macaroni Penguins

The king penguin nests on the islands off Antarctica. It lays one egg and raises a huge chick that eventually weighs about 30 pounds (14 kilograms). The parents take care of their chick for almost a year. Then when the chick is fully grown, the adults go off to the sea to grow fat again.

The king penguins lay their eggs between the beginning of summer and the beginning of winter. The parents incubate an egg for about 54 days. On this schedule a pair of kings can raise no more than two chicks in three years.

The macaroni penguin also breeds in the outlying Antarctic islands. It lays one big egg and one little one. The little one does not develop into a chick. This strange arrangement remains a puzzle for naturalists.

### ▶PENGUINS IN CAPTIVITY

In the protection of zoos, king penguins have raised their young. The penguins in Edinburgh Zoo, Scotland, have done so most successfully. The African penguin adjusts well to captivity in the right surroundings.

However, it is difficult to keep captive penguins healthy. Penguins need a large fish supply. A male Humboldt penguin weighing about 9 pounds (4 kilograms) eats up to 3 pounds (1.4 kilograms) of fish every day. When he is about to molt, he will eat twice this amount. A penguin has to be taught to take a dead fish from someone's hand, or to eat it when the fish is thrown into the water. At first food may have to be forced into the penguin's mouth, so that the bird keeps a good weight while it learns this new way of feeding.

When penguins lose a lot of weight, they are almost certain to catch a lung disease that is usually fatal. This disease is caused by a fungus that grows in the lungs and in the airsacs that lead from the lungs. However, the disease can sometimes be cured.

Today most penguin rookeries are protected from too much interference by humans. Scientists of many different nations are working together to preserve the Antarctic penguins. To ensure the safety of penguins, some nations have made their penguin breeding grounds legally protected bird sanctuaries.

BRENDA SLADEN
WILLIAM J. L. SLADEN
The Johns Hopkins University

**PENMANSHIP.** See HANDWRITING.

# PENN, WILLIAM (1644–1718)

William Penn was the founder of the colony of Pennsylvania in America. He is also important in English history. And the world remembers him because he worked for human liberty and co-operation among nations long before these ideas became popular.

Penn was born in London, England, on October 14, 1644. His father, also named William Penn, was an admiral on the side of the Parliamentary forces during the English Civil War (1642–46). But later he became involved in a dispute with Oliver Cromwell, the head of the government. Admiral Penn switched his allegiance to the exiled king, Charles II, and took his family to Ireland. There young William Penn continued the education he had begun in England. In 1660, when Charles II was restored as king, Penn was 16 and ready to enter Oxford University.

William Penn belonged to the ruling class. But he did not remain sympathetic to its ideals. Instead, he turned away from the pomp and worldliness of England at that time to the ideas of the Quakers. This was a new and radical religious group that had been founded in England in the 1650's by George Fox (1642–91). Penn was in Ireland in 1667 when he made the final decision to become a Quaker.

Penn lived at a time when religious toleration was almost unknown. As a member of the Quakers, a small and despised sect, he was persecuted and imprisoned. Penn worked for religious toleration and political liberty in England. He wrote and spoke out in defense of the fundamental rights of the people. He insisted that they have proper elected representation in the government.

In 1681, Penn obtained a charter from Charles II as founder of a new colony in North America. The King had owed Admiral Penn £16,000. When he granted the colony to William Penn in payment of the debt, Charles insisted that it be named Pennsylvania in honor of the naval hero. Penn recruited settlers, wrote a constitution for the colony, and prepared for the voyage to the New World. He arrived in Delaware Bay on the ship *Welcome* in late October, 1682.

Penn granted the colonists a great deal of self-government and guaranteed religious toleration to all. He signed treaties with the Indians and watched Pennsylvania's rapid economic growth with satisfaction. Penn was head of the colony in three different capacities. As governor, he was its political leader. As proprietor, he was landlord of all the inhabitants. In addition, he was the spiritual leader of the Quakers, who made up the vast majority of the colony's population.

Penn spent two years in Pennsylvania before returning to England. During his second and last visit, between 1699 and 1701, he granted the colony the Charter of Privileges of 1701. This remained the constitution of Pennsylvania until 1776. He also drew up a plan for uniting the English colonies under one government. But unification did not become a reality until after the Revolutionary War.

In the 1690's, Penn wrote his famous *Essay Towards the Present and Future Peace of Europe*. In it he proposed the establishment of a European parliament to settle international disputes. The League of Nations and the United Nations owe much to Penn's proposals. Penn published more than 150 works during his lifetime. His two other most famous works are *No Cross, No Crown* and *Some Fruits of Solitude*.

In 1672, Penn married Gulielma Springett, who was also a Quaker. They had eight children, but only two lived to maturity. After his first wife died in 1694, Penn married Hannah Callowhill, the daughter of a wealthy merchant. She accompanied Penn to America in 1699 and gave birth to a son called John the American. Seven other children were born, but only four of the eight survived.

William Penn suffered many setbacks and disappointments during his lifetime. A friend and a supporter of King James II, he was arrested several times after a revolution forced James into exile in 1688. He even lost control of Pennsylvania for two years. Because he placed too much trust in his business adviser, Penn had financial difficulties and spent a long period in debtors' prison.

Penn died on July 30, 1718. He was buried on the grounds of Jordans Meetinghouse, northwest of London.

EDWIN B. BRONNER
Author, *William Penn's Holy Experiment*
See also PENNSYLVANIA; QUAKERS.

# PENNSYLVANIA

*In 1681, England's King Charles II granted one of his subjects, William Penn, a large region in America west of the Delaware River. The new colony, named in honor of Penn's father, was called Pennsylvania, the Latin phrase for "Penn's Woods." William Penn established the colony as a "Holy Experiment," a safe haven for the Society of Friends, a religious sect whose members are more commonly known as Quakers. Pennsylvania thus became known as the Quaker State. Today it is known as the Keystone State because of its important central location within the original 13 colonies.*

State flag

The Commonwealth of Pennsylvania, located in the northeastern United States, is a Middle Atlantic state with access to the Atlantic Ocean through Delaware Bay. Its pastoral landscape rises out of a low level coastal plain in the east, to rolling hills and farmlands in its central region, to the Allegheny Mountains and Plateau in the west.

Pennsylvania's largest city, Philadelphia, is the fifth largest city in the nation. Since colonial days, it has served as the state's eastern hub of finance, manufacturing, and culture. Pennsylvania's western hub, Pittsburgh, was once the steel-making capital of the world. Approximately half of all Pennsylvanians live in or around Philadelphia and Pittsburgh. Harrisburg is the state capital.

Once an industrial giant, Pennsylvania now has a service-driven economy. In some communities, school and medical centers have replaced iron and steel mills as the largest employers. However, Pennsylvania is still a leader in manufacturing, energy production, and mining. It is the only state still producing anthracite (hard coal) and is a leading supplier of electricity to the northeast. Pennsylvania is the nation's leading producer of mushrooms, plantation-grown Christmas trees, and hardwood lumber.

Every year millions of tourists visit Pennsylvania to enjoy its spectacular scenery, cultural attractions, and interesting historic sites. Most important among them are Independence Hall in Philadelphia, where the Declaration of Independence (1776) and the Constitution of the United States (1787) were signed; Valley Forge, where General George Washington and the Continental Army passed the cruel winter of 1777–78 during the Revolutionary War; and Gettysburg, the site of the most important battle (1863) of the Civil War.

Pennsylvanians have always played an important role in the nation's history. In addition to the industrialists who made their fortunes there, the state has brought forth an impressive array of world-renowned artists, writers, singers, composers, actors, entertainers, dancers, athletes, scientists, explorers, and statesmen.

## ▶ LAND

Pennsylvania is roughly rectangular in shape. It features a picturesque assortment of plains, wide and narrow valleys, hills and low mountains, rivers, lakes, and streams.

### Land Regions

Pennsylvania spreads across four major land regions—the Coastal Plain, the Piedmont, the Appalachian Highlands, and the Great Lakes Plain.

**The Coastal Plain** covers the extreme southeastern corner of the state, where the city of Philadelphia is located. The portion of this region that lies within Pennsylvania's borders is a low-lying level, narrow strip of sand and gravel along the Delaware River.

*Opposite page, clockwise from left:* Philadelphia is Pennsylvania's largest city. Its name comes from the Greek phrase meaning City of Brotherly Love. The Liberty Bell, in Philadelphia, is a cherished symbol of the nation's struggle for independence. Amish children walk to school in Lancaster County.

State flower:
Mountain laurel

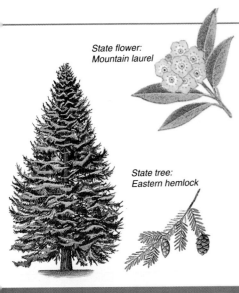

State tree:
Eastern hemlock

# FACTS AND FIGURES

**Location:** Northeastern United States; bordered on the north by Lake Erie and New York, on the east by New York and New Jersey, on the south by Delaware, Maryland, and West Virginia, and on the west by West Virginia and Ohio.

**Area:** 46,058 sq mi (119,291 km²); rank, 33rd.

**Population:** 12,281,054 (2000 census); rank, 6th.

**Elevation:** *Highest*—3,213 ft (980 m) at Mount Davis; *lowest*—sea level, along the Delaware River.

**Capital:** Harrisburg.

**Statehood:** December 12, 1787; 2nd state.

**State Motto:** *Virtue, liberty, and independence*.

**State Song:** "Pennsylvania."

**Nickname:** Keystone State; Quaker State.

**Abbreviations:** PA; Penn.

State bird:
Ruffed grouse

*Left:* Raystown Lake in central Pennsylvania is just one of the hundreds of beautiful recreational spots that attract vacationers to the state. *Below:* The fertile soils of the Piedmont and the Ridge and Valley regions support farms that raise crops and livestock.

**The Piedmont** consists of gradually rising hills that extend inland for about 100 miles (160 kilometers). This region contains some of the nation's most fertile farmland.

**The Appalachian Highlands** can be divided into four distinct sections. The **New England Upland**, also called the Reading Prong, is a small mountain range between Easton and Reading. The **Blue Ridge**, which Pennsylvanians call South Mountain, is the northernmost extension of the Blue Ridge Mountains. In the center of the state lies the **Ridge and Valley Region**. Its southeastern rim is a wide lowland known as the Great Valley, where well-kept farms from Chambersburg to Allentown raise much of Pennsylvania's crops and livestock. To the north and west of the Great Valley are wooded ridges, rising as high as 1,200 feet (370 meters). These ridges rise like accordion folds above wide and level valleys. The **Allegheny Plateau**, the northern portion of the Appalachian Plateau, covers almost all of northern and western Pennsylvania. It is a vast region of rolling highlands and deep ravines. Streams have chiseled cliffs and gorges out of soft sandstone and shale, making farming difficult. The Allegheny Mountains form the eastern border of this region and contain the state's highest point, Mount Davis, which rises 3,213 feet (980 meters) near the Maryland border.

**The Great Lakes Plain** covers a small strip of land in Pennsylvania's northwestern corner. Here the land levels out into a fertile plain as it slopes toward Lake Erie. The level land and moderate climate make this area suitable for agriculture.

### Rivers and Lakes

Pennsylvania has three important river systems that drain 95 percent of the state—the Delaware, the Susquehanna, and the Ohio.

The Delaware River forms Pennsylvania's eastern border and flows south into Delaware Bay and the Atlantic Ocean. Its most important tributaries are the Schuylkill and Lehigh rivers. The Susquehanna River flows south through the center of the state and empties into Chesapeake Bay. Its main tributaries are the West Branch and Juniata rivers. The Delaware and the Susquehanna systems drain the eastern part of the state. The Ohio River is formed at Pittsburgh at the junction of the Allegheny River from the north and the Monongahela River from the south. These three rivers drain all of western Pennsylvania.

Pennsylvania has about 4,400 streams and about 300 lakes, both natural and artificial.

Lake Conneaut, in the northwest, is the largest natural lake lying entirely within the state. Lake Wallenpaupack, in the northeast, is the state's largest artificial lake. However, several of the lakes formed by dams on rivers are much larger. These include Pymatuning Reservoir on the Ohio border and the Allegheny Reservoir on the New York border. In addition to its many lakes and streams, the Pocono Mountain region is also graced with beautiful waterfalls.

### Climate

Temperatures in Pennsylvania vary according to location and elevation. The average temperature in January ranges from 22° to 32°F (−6° to 0°C). In July the average temperature ranges from 66° to 76°F (19° to 24°C). Annual rainfall averages 41 inches (1,041 millimeters) across the state. Snowfall varies greatly, from 20 inches (51 centimeters) per year in the southeast to 90 inches (229 centimeters) in the north.

Southern Pennsylvania has the longest growing season, lasting about 200 days. The northern counties, except for the Great Lakes Plain, have the coldest weather and a growing season that lasts only about 130 days.

### Plant and Animal Life

Forests once covered more than 95 percent of Pennsylvania but now cover only 60 percent due to clearing for farms and towns. The most plentiful varieties of trees include maple, beech, and hemlock in the north; ash, birch, cherry, hickory, locust, maple, oak, pine, poplar, sycamore, tulip, and black walnut in the south; and pine in the mountains. Flowering shrubs, including mountain laurel (the state flower), azaleas, and rhododendron abound. Common wildflowers are violets, honeysuckle, and black-eyed Susans.

Many kinds of mammals, birds, and fish thrive in Pennsylvania. Deer are abundant, even in some populated areas. Black bears can still be found in the mountains of the north and west. Smaller mammals, such as fox, beaver, otter, mink, raccoon, opossum, woodchuck, skunk, squirrel, and rabbit, survive in large numbers, as do wild turkeys, geese, ruffed

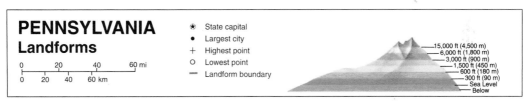

# PENNSYLVANIA
## Landforms

* State capital
* Largest city
+ Highest point
o Lowest point
— Landform boundary

0  20  40  60 mi
0  20  40  60 km

15,000 ft (4,500 m)
6,000 ft (1,800 m)
3,000 ft (900 m)
1,500 ft (450 m)
600 ft (180 m)
300 ft (90 m)
Sea Level
Below

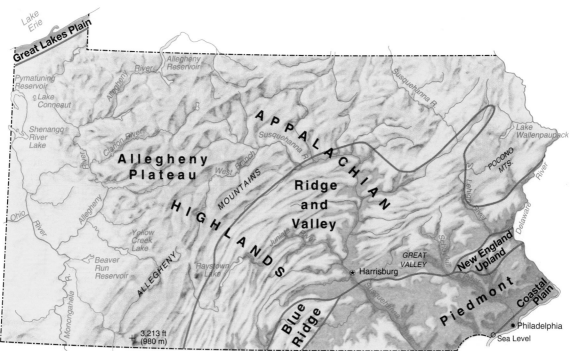

*Left:* Summer festivals and parades are common along Philadelphia's main boulevards. *Above:* Field hockey is one of Pennsylvania's most popular collegiate sports.

grouse, quail, pheasant, and songbirds. The rivers, streams, and lakes contain a bounty of fish, including trout, pike, pickerel, bass, white carp, and catfish.

### Natural Resources

The rich soil of Pennsylvania's Piedmont region, Great Valley, and Great Lakes Plain is one of the state's great natural assets. Coal is the most plentiful mineral. About 75 billion tons of bituminous (soft) coal, mostly in the southwest, and 23 billion tons of anthracite (hard coal), in the northeast, are yet available. Iron ore exists in the southern half of the state along with small quantities of copper, lead, zinc, nickel, and chromite. Petroleum and natural gas lie beneath the surface in the northwestern and western parts of the state.

### ▶ PEOPLE

Pennsylvania is the sixth most populous of the fifty states. About 85 percent of its residents are of European ancestry. Approximately one-third of this group are Pennsylvania Dutch, who are not Dutch at all, but German. (*Deutsch,* the German word for

"German," long ago was mistaken for "Dutch.") Other ancestries include English, Welsh, French, Dutch, Irish, Scotch-Irish, and peoples from southern and eastern Europe, particularly Italians and Slavs. About 10 percent of Pennsylvanians are African American. The remaining 5 percent include Asian and Native Americans and others. Of the total population, 3 percent claim Hispanic heritage.

### Education

Before public elementary and secondary schools were widely established, religious and ethnic groups provided education for their own members. Some of these schools still exist, most notably the William Penn Charter School, founded in 1689 by Quakers in Philadelphia. Since 1834 the state has provided public education; attendance is mandatory for those between the ages of 8 and 16.

Among the fifty states, Pennsylvania has one of the highest numbers of institutions for higher learning, both state-supported and private. The largest is the Pennsylvania State University, with campuses at University Park and more than twenty other locations. It is state-related, as are Temple University in Philadelphia and the University of Pittsburgh. Pennsylvania is also known for its many professional schools in medicine, law, and business.

The state's oldest private university is the University of Pennsylvania in Philadelphia.

Founded in the 1740's as a school for the poor, today it is the southernmost of the Ivy League schools. Among the dozens of private colleges and universities are Swarthmore in Swarthmore, Bryn Mawr in Bryn Mawr, Haverford in Haverford, Dickinson in Carlisle, Franklin and Marshall in Lancaster, Carnegie-Mellon in Pittsburgh, Villanova in Villanova, Lehigh in Bethlehem, Bucknell in Lewisburg, and Gettysburg College in Gettysburg.

### Libraries, Museums, and the Arts

In 1731, Benjamin Franklin founded the Library Company of Philadelphia, the first circulating library in the United States. Today it is recognized for its outstanding collection of rare books. More than 500 public libraries are found throughout the state, as well as dozens of college and university libraries.

Pennsylvania has produced an impressive array of first-rate artists, many from the state's two major cultural centers, Philadelphia and Pittsburgh. Philadelphia boasts the Pennsylvania Academy of the Fine Arts, the Rodin Museum, the Philadelphia Museum of Art, and the Barnes Foundation collection in the suburb of Merion. Several Pittsburgh museums also contain priceless and varied collections, including the Carnegie and the Frick Museum. Other distinguished museums include Philadelphia's Academy of Natural Sciences, the oldest such institution in the country, and the Franklin Institute, which houses a science museum and a planetarium.

Pennsylvania is well established in the performing arts. Philadelphia and Pittsburgh have distinguished symphony orchestras; the Philadelphia Orchestra has made more classical music recordings than any other American orchestra. Philadelphia and Pittsburgh also support ballet and opera companies and numerous theater groups. Community drama groups are active throughout the state.

Philadelphia's Independence Hall is one of the nation's most important historic landmarks. The Declaration of Independence (1776) and the Constitution of the United States (1787) both were signed there.

Some of the nation's most outstanding architecture is located in Pennsylvania. Philadelphia's State House, now known as Independence Hall, is one of the finest examples of colonial architecture. Another of the state's most acclaimed buildings is a house called Fallingwater. Designed by Frank Lloyd Wright, it was built in the 1930's over a waterfall at Bear Run, near Pittsburgh.

### Sports

Pennsylvanians are tremendous sports enthusiasts. South Williamsport hosts the annual Little League World Series. Collegiate highlights include the football rivalry of Penn State and Pittsburgh, the rowing regattas on the

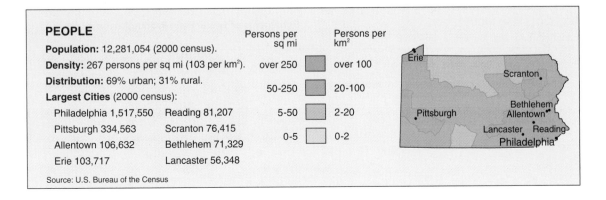

**PEOPLE**

**Population:** 12,281,054 (2000 census).

**Density:** 267 persons per sq mi (103 per km²).

**Distribution:** 69% urban; 31% rural.

**Largest Cities** (2000 census):

| | | Persons per sq mi | | Persons per km² | |
|---|---|---|---|---|---|
| | | over 250 | | over 100 | |
| | | 50-250 | | 20-100 | |
| Philadelphia 1,517,550 | Reading 81,207 | 5-50 | | 2-20 | |
| Pittsburgh 334,563 | Scranton 76,415 | 0-5 | | 0-2 | |
| Allentown 106,632 | Bethlehem 71,329 | | | | |
| Erie 103,717 | Lancaster 56,348 | | | | |

Source: U.S. Bureau of the Census

From spring through late autumn, roadside stands display the bounty of Pennsylvania farms. Homemade jams, jellies, and baked goods are commonly sold along with the fresh produce.

Schuylkill River, and the Penn Relays, a major annual track meet sponsored by the University of Pennsylvania. Basketball, wrestling, and field hockey also are popular.

Pennsylvania has a full range of professional sports teams—the Philadelphia Eagles and the Pittsburgh Steelers of the National Football League; the Philadelphia 76ers of the National Basketball Association; the Philadelphia Flyers and the Pittsburgh Penguins of the National Hockey League; and the Philadelphia Phillies and the Pittsburgh Pirates of baseball's National League.

## ▶ ECONOMY

Over the past several decades, Pennsylvania's economy has changed. Traditional heavy "smokestack" industries have declined while the service industries have grown. Transportation, communication, and utilities are also important income producers.

### Services

Service-oriented businesses are the fastest-growing in Pennsylvania. They currently employ about 76 percent of the state's entire workforce. Services provided in areas such as business, law, medicine, tourism, and recreation as well as community and social services generate the most income, followed by financial services (banking, insurance, and real estate); wholesale and retail trade (the buying and selling of industrial and personal goods); transportation, communication, and utilities; and government services.

### Manufacturing

Pennsylvania, once an industrial giant, remains one of the nation's leading manufacturing centers. Nineteen percent of the workforce is employed in the production of such items as primary and fabricated metals, processed foods, heavy machinery, machine tools, electrical machinery, transportation equipment, and paper and printed materials.

### Agriculture

Farms cover more than 9 million acres (3.6 million hectares) in Pennsylvania, mostly in the southeast. Agriculture in the state is varied. Livestock, milk, eggs, and poultry are the state's most profitable agricultural products.

Pennsylvania leads the nation in the production of hardwood lumber and plantation-grown Christmas trees. It also leads the other states in mushrooms. Other principal products are corn, hay, apples, pears, and greenhouse plants. However, despite these many farm and forestry products, agriculture contributes only a small amount to the state's overall income.

### Mining and Construction

Pennsylvania's coal mining industry was once one of the most important in North America. In 1917–18, its peak production

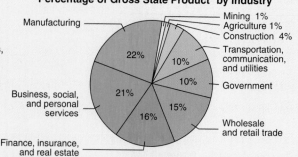

**PRODUCTS AND INDUSTRIES**

**Manufacturing:** Primary metals, fabricated metal products, food processing, nonelectrical machinery.

**Agriculture:** Cattle, hogs, sheep, dairy products, eggs, poultry, turkeys, corn, hay, Christmas trees, apples, pears, greenhouse and nursery products, wheat, soybeans, rye, oats, barley, tobacco, mushrooms, potatoes, tomatoes.

**Minerals:** Bituminous (soft) coal and anthracite (hard coal), natural gas, petroleum, iron, limestone, sand and gravel.

**Services:** Wholesale and retail trade; finance, insurance, and real estate; business, social, and personal services; transportation, communication, and utilities; government.

*Gross state product is the total value of goods and services produced in a year.

**Percentage of Gross State Product* by Industry**

Manufacturing — 22%
Mining 1%
Agriculture 1%
Construction 4%
Transportation, communication, and utilities — 10%
Government — 10%
Wholesale and retail trade — 15%
Finance, insurance, and real estate — 16%
Business, social, and personal services — 21%

Source: U.S. Bureau of Economic Analysis

Pennsylvania is one of the nation's leading producers of energy. *Right:* Three Mile Island, on the Susquehanna River near Harrisburg, is one of two nuclear power plants now operating within the state. *Below:* For many decades, Pennsylvania was the nation's leading producer of steel. Today it ranks third behind Indiana and Ohio.

supplies 20 percent of the nation's natural gas. Dams on the Ohio and Susquehanna rivers provide hydroelectric power.

The nation's first atomic energy plant was built in Pennsylvania. Today nuclear energy is produced at Three Mile Island on the Susquehanna River and at Limerick on the Schuylkill River. All of these utilities contribute significantly to the state's income.

### Transportation

Pennsylvania's waterways and port cities play a significant role in transportation. Philadelphia, on the Delaware River, is the state's busiest and the nation's fourth largest port. It receives more international freighters than any other port in the nation. Pittsburgh, at the head of the Ohio-Mississippi River route, is the nation's largest inland port. In addition to these is the port at Erie on the Great Lakes. Increasing amounts of freight have moved through since the St. Lawrence Seaway was opened to oceangoing vessels in 1959.

A number of interstate highways cross the state, including the Pennsylvania Turnpike, the nation's first superhighway. The state's 115,000 miles (185,000 kilometers) of highways make up the fourth largest state network in the nation. Pennsylvania's 44 railroads run on about 6,000 miles (9,700 kilometers) of track and carry one sixth of the nation's rail tonnage. Passenger travel and freight shipment by air are mostly done through the Philadelphia International and Greater Pittsburgh International airports. Smaller commercial airports service several other cities.

year, the state produced 270 million tons. The industry declined dramatically through the century, and production reached only 65 million tons in 1991. Nevertheless, the state remains the nation's only producer of anthracite (hard coal) and among the top producers of bituminous (soft) coal. Pennsylvania also produces more stone and stone products than any other state; its limestone is used in the manufacture of agricultural lime, cement, and building stone. Today mining contributes a relatively small portion to the state's economy overall. However, the state's construction industry is a very profitable enterprise, especially in and around Philadelphia.

### Energy

Pennsylvania is the nation's third largest producer of electricity; western Pennsylvania

# Places of Interest

Fallingwater, near Bear Run

Longwood Gardens, near Philadelphia

The Carnegie Museum of Natural History, in Pittsburgh

Gettysburg National Military Park, in Gettysburg

**Delaware Water Gap National Recreation Area**, shared with New Jersey, preserves a scenic gorge carved by the Delaware River. It provides a gateway to the Pocono Mountains, a popular winter and summer resort area.

**Fallingwater**, near Bear Run outside of Pittsburgh, is a spectacular home built over a natural stream and waterfall. Completed in 1936, it is considered a masterpiece of architect Frank Lloyd Wright.

**Flagship *Niagara***, docked at Erie, is a reconstruction of the warship commanded by Oliver Hazard Perry during the War of 1812. He later became known as the Hero of the Battle of Lake Erie. (For more information, see the article PERRY, OLIVER HAZARD, in Volume P.)

**Fort Necessity National Battlefield**, in Farmington, marks the site of the opening battle of the French and Indian War (July 3, 1754). A 22-year-old George Washington, commanding the British colonial troops, was defeated there by the French.

**Gettysburg National Military Park**, in Gettysburg, commemorates the site of the Civil War's most decisive battle (July 1–3, 1863). Hundreds of monuments, erected in honor of both Union and Confederate forces, decorate the battlefield. The park features a visitors' center containing a museum and an electric map

that expertly explains the Union and Confederate troop movements over the course of the three-day battle. Tourists may also visit the National Cemetery where President Abraham Lincoln delivered the Gettysburg Address.

**Hershey**, near Harrisburg, is the site of the world's largest chocolate manufacturing plant, founded in 1903 by Milton S. Hershey. A visitors' tour through "Chocolate World" describes how chocolate is made. Nearby Hersheypark features rides, games, shows, and a zoo.

**Little League International Headquarters**, in Williamsport, is the home of all United States and foreign leagues as well as the Little League International Museum. Little League Baseball was founded in Williamsport in 1939.

**Longwood Gardens**, in suburban Philadelphia, is an internationally recognized horticultural site. Its beautiful formal gardens, greenhouses, decorative fountains, and seasonal exhibits cover several hundred acres.

**Pennsylvania Dutch Country** is a region that generally encompasses Lancaster and York counties in the southeastern part of the state. Of particular interest is its quaint population of Amish and Mennonites, members of small Protestant religious sects, who maintain their time-honored traditions by

rejecting modern ways. They are known for their plain dress, horse-drawn carriages, and beautifully kept farms.

**Philadelphia** is home to dozens of fine museums, performing arts centers, and important historical sites. Among the most frequently visited are Independence Hall, Carpenters' Hall, the Liberty Bell, Elfreth's Alley, and the U.S. Mint. For a detailed description of attractions, see the article PHILADELPHIA in this volume.

**Pine Creek Gorge**, near Wellsboro, is known as the Grand Canyon of Pennsylvania. The Pine Creek runs along the bottom of the gorge, which is more than 1,000 feet (300 meters) deep.

**Pittsburgh**, western Pennsylvania's cultural hub, features the Carnegie, a vast complex of museums. For a detailed description of attractions, see the article PITTSBURGH in this volume.

**Valley Forge National Historical Park**, in Valley Forge, preserves the site where General George Washington and his army camped during the winter of 1777–78.

**State Recreation Areas**. Pennsylvania has more than 100 state parks in addition to numerous scenic trails, state campgrounds, and picnic areas. To obtain more information, write to the Bureau of State Parks, P.O. Box 8551, Harrisburg, Pennsylvania 17105.

## Communication

Pennsylvania has extensive communications systems that broadcast over more than 350 radio and 35 television stations. Pittsburgh's KDKA, the nation's first commercial radio station, began broadcasting in 1920. Radio and television have become increasingly important news sources as the number of newspapers printed in the state has declined. Among the state's major daily newspapers today are the Philadelphia *Inquirer*, the *Philadelphia Daily News*, the *Pittsburgh Post-Gazette*, and the *Allentown Morning Call*.

## ▶ CITIES

Pennsylvania has six cities with more than 75,000 residents. Harrisburg, the capital, is relatively small, with only about 49,000 residents. The largest cities are in the southeastern and southwestern corners of the state and are located on major waterways.

**Harrisburg**, located in south-central Pennsylvania, has been the state capital since 1812. It grew up in the early 1700's as a trading post and ferry station on the lower Susquehanna River. Today state government is the city's primary economic activity.

**Philadelphia**, Pennsylvania's largest city, is located on the Delaware River at the mouth of the Schuylkill River. Founded by William Penn in 1682, the city has always been a busy port. Today it is the financial, medical, educational, and cultural center of the state. An article on Philadelphia appears in this volume.

**Pittsburgh**, the state's second largest city, was founded as a fort in 1754 at the head of the Ohio River. It was named for William Pitt the Elder, a prime minister (1766–68) of England. No longer the "Smoky City" it was in the heyday of the steel industry, today Pittsburgh is the nation's leading inland port and the hub of business, culture, medicine, and education in southwestern Pennsylvania. An article on Pittsburgh appears in this volume.

**Allentown**, on the Lehigh River in eastern Pennsylvania, was founded in 1762. Along with its neighboring cities of Bethlehem and Easton, Allentown is important for its manufacturing industries and as a processing and shipping center for agricultural products. Six colleges are located within the tri-city area.

**Erie**, the state's fourth largest city, is located on Lake Erie in the northwest. Its port lies at the westernmost end of the St. Lawrence Seaway, which connects it to the Atlantic Ocean. Founded in 1795, Erie today is an important transportation, commercial, and industrial city. It was named for the Erie Indians who once lived in the area.

**Scranton** is located on the Lackawanna River in northeastern Pennsylvania. Together with the city of Wilkes-Barre, to the south, it is the center of one of the largest anthracite regions in the world. Although the coal industry has declined, Scranton remains an important manufacturing center. The United Mine Workers of America, a large labor union, was organized here in 1897.

The mighty city of Pittsburgh grew up at the site of Fort Duquesne, later Fort Pitt. Today it is the nation's leading inland port and a major center of culture and industry.

The state capitol in Harrisburg was completed in 1913. The main building contains floor-to-ceiling murals with scenes of Pennsylvania's history.

## ▶ GOVERNMENT

Pennsylvania is one of four states known officially as commonwealths. (The other three are Virginia, Massachusetts, and Kentucky.) Pennsylvania has had several constitutions. The present one was adopted in 1873, although it was revised extensively in 1968.

The governor, the head of the executive branch, serves a 4-year term and may be re-elected once. Other executive officers include the lieutenant governor, who presides over the state senate; an auditor general and an attorney general; and various commissioners, board members, and department heads.

The legislature, known as the General Assembly, consists of the Senate and the House of Representatives, whose members vote to pass the laws of the state. Pennsylvania's

### GOVERNMENT

**State Government**
Governor: 4-year term
State senators: 50; 4-year terms
State representatives: 203;
  2-year terms
Number of counties: 67

**Federal Government**
U.S. senators: 2
U.S. representatives: 19
Number of electoral votes: 21

For the name of the current governor, see STATE GOVERNMENTS in Volume S. For the names of current U.S. senators and representatives, see UNITED STATES, CONGRESS OF THE in Volume U-V.

## INDEX TO PENNSYLVANIA MAP

• County Seat   Counties in parentheses   ★ State Capital

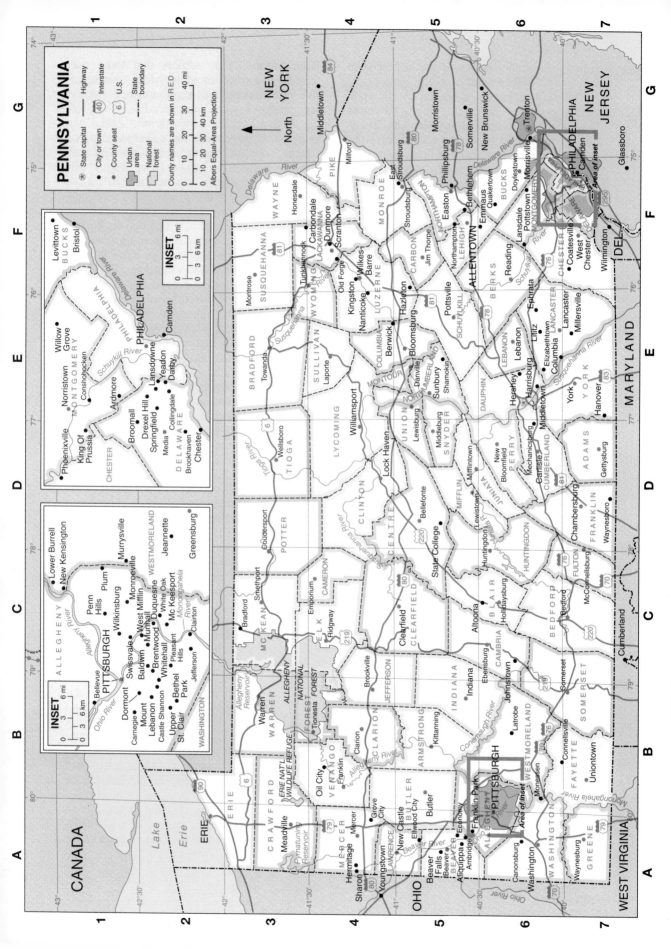

General Assembly is one of the largest state legislatures in the country.

The judicial branch is headed by the state Supreme Court. This court judges the most important cases and administers the lower courts, including the superior court and the commonwealth court. Each of these courts has justices who are elected to 10-year terms and may be re-elected. There are sixty judicial districts, each with a court of common pleas. At the local level, community courts, justices of the peace, aldermen, and magistrates preside over the less important cases.

## ▶HISTORY

Archaeologists believe that the first Pennsylvanians were prehistoric hunters and gatherers, who settled the region about 12,000 years ago. It is estimated that their Native American descendants numbered about 15,000 when Europeans first came to Pennsylvania in the early 1600's. They belonged to a variety of tribes that included the Delaware (also called Lenni-Lenape or Lenape), Susquehannock, Shawnee, Monongahela, Erie, and Iroquois Seneca.

### European Exploration and Settlement

Records show that Dutch explorers sailed up the Delaware River in 1614. French explorer Etienne Brulé traveled up the Susquehanna River the following year. Swedish fur traders moved into Delaware Bay in 1638. They established the first permanent European settlement in Pennsylvania, on Tinicum Island near Philadelphia in 1643. Johan Printz acted as governor of this colony that they called New Sweden.

In 1655 the Swedes were conquered by Dutch forces, who in turn were routed by the English in 1664. The English came to Pennsylvania by way of New Jersey and established themselves in the Delaware Valley.

This decorative Pennsylvania Dutch sign says "Welcome."

### William Penn's Colony

In 1681, England's King Charles II granted a tract of land to William Penn, an English Quaker, in payment of a debt owed to Penn's father, Admiral Sir William Penn. Describing his colony as a "Holy Experiment," William Penn promised his settlers that there they would have freedom of worship, representative government, and economic opportunity. His promises were incorporated in the colony's first written constitution, called the Frame of Government. Penn also made peace treaties with the Native Americans and purchased settlement rights from them. His Charter of Privileges, granted in 1701, gave additional rights to the colonists.

The colony prospered almost from the very beginning. Large numbers of English, Welsh, Scotch-Irish, and German-speaking colonists of various religions, as well as a few African slaves, settled there. They cultivated the fertile soil, growing crops for food and for trade. Flour, bread, and biscuits were sent to the West Indies, although most of the colony's goods went to England. Iron ore and iron products, such as kettles, stoves, and plows, were widely produced. In Philadelphia and other towns, craftspeople made hats, furniture, silver and pewter utensils, and rifles. The Conestoga covered wagon originated in Lancaster County about 1725.

Peaceful development continued until 1754, when the French and Indian War began with a clash of French and British colonial forces near the French Fort Duquesne. In an attempt to gain full control of the Ohio Valley, the British sent two armies into Pennsylvania, one in 1755 and another in 1758, which forced the French to withdraw. When the Treaty of Paris concluded the war in 1763, the British took control over the North American continent.

### The Revolutionary War and Statehood

After the French and Indian War ended, the British became more strict with their colonial policies. Resisting British authority, the American colonists established the First Continental Congress in Philadelphia in 1774. During the Revolutionary War that ensued, the Second Continental Congress met in Philadelphia and on July 4, 1776, issued the Declaration of Independence.

Philadelphia was by then the largest city in the colonies. It became the seat of the American government and the leading supplier of the

The Constitutional Convention took place in Philadelphia in 1787. George Washington (standing on platform) presided over 55 delegates from twelve states (Rhode Island declined to participate). The document they created was the Constitution of the United States. It was signed by 39 delegates on September 17, 1787, and ratified by a majority of states the following year. Since that time it has served as the framework of the United States government.

Continental Army. In 1777 the battles of Brandywine and Germantown were fought near Philadelphia, and during the harsh winter of 1777–78, General George Washington and his army made camp at Valley Forge on the banks of the Schuylkill River.

After declaring their independence, the American colonists developed their own system of government. The Second Continental Congress, while meeting in York in 1777, created the nation's first written constitution, the Articles of Confederation. This was replaced by the present Constitution of the United States, which was drawn up in Philadelphia in 1787. Benjamin Franklin, Robert Morris, and Gouverneur Morris were among the eight delegates who signed for Pennsylvania. Pennsylvania was the second state (after Delaware) to ratify the new Constitution on December 12, 1787, and for a short time (1790–1800), Philadelphia served as the nation's capital.

Pennsylvanians made numerous efforts to ensure democracy in their state. They formed America's first antislavery society (1775), and the Pennsylvania legislature was the first to move toward abolishing slavery. During the 1800's Lucretia Mott, Sarah and Angelina Grimké, Thaddeus Stevens, and many others based in Pennsylvania tried to persuade southern slave owners to free their slaves. Those slaves who escaped to Pennsylvania by way of the Underground Railroad often received help, especially from Quakers and free African-Americans, such as James Forten and William Still.

### The Civil War (1861–65)

Largely because of the states' disagreement over slavery, the Civil War broke out in 1861. Over the next four years, Pennsylvania sent nearly 400,000 troops to fight for the Union. Its factories produced uniforms and weapons, and its railroads transported troops and supplies to the battlefronts. About 80 percent of all the pig iron used by the Union Army during the war came from Pennsylvania.

From July 1 through July 3, 1863, the war's most important battle was fought at Gettysburg, not far from the Maryland border. Union forces, led by Pennsylvania's own General George Gordon Meade, defeated the Confederates and for the first time turned the war to the Union's favor. On November 19, 1863, while visiting the town to dedicate a cemetery to the thousands of soldiers who lost their lives there, President Abraham Lincoln delivered his famous Gettysburg Address, which many consider to be the most stirring speech ever written. (The article GETTYSBURG ADDRESS appears in Volume G.)

### Prosperity and a New Century

By the turn of the century, Pennsylvania was the nation's leading producer of steel and coal and was among the largest producers of oil and lumber. Small businesses combined to form vast corporations and trusts, controlled by some of the world's most powerful industrialists. Among them were Andrew Carnegie, who came to dominate the steel industry, and his partner, Henry Clay Frick, who controlled

# Famous People

**Richard Allen** (1760–1831), born a slave in Philadelphia, founded and was first bishop of the African Methodist Episcopal (A.M.E.) Church. In 1787, following a racial incident at St. George's Methodist Church in Philadelphia, Allen organized the Free African Society to provide spiritual guidance to a black congregation in a nondiscriminatory environment. In 1799 he was ordained a deacon of the Methodist Church. In 1816 he founded the A.M.E., a national organization of black congregations. It is the oldest continuous organization of African Americans in the United States.

**Andrew Carnegie** (1835–1919), born in Dunfermline, Scotland, made a fortune developing the Pennsylvania steel industry. After he sold his Carnegie Steel Company to J. P. Morgan in 1901, he devoted himself to helping people and causes. He donated more than $350 million in support of museums, libraries, universities, and the international peace movement. A biography of Andrew Carnegie appears in Volume C.

**Benjamin Franklin** (1706–90) was born in Boston but spent much of his life in Pennsylvania. Considered one of the most remarkable people in all of history, Franklin was an accomplished scientist,

Andrew Carnegie

inventor, printer, writer, diplomat, civic leader, and statesman. In 1752 he performed the famous kite experiment, proving that lightning is electricity. A biography of Benjamin Franklin appears in Volume F.

**Martha Graham** (1894–1991), born in Allegheny, was a major force in the evolution of modern dance. A brilliant dancer and choreographer, she pioneered extremely bold body movements to express a full range of human emotions. Her themes ranged from literary figures in ancient Greece to rituals of Native Americans. Among her most memorable works

are *El Penitente* (1940), *Appalachian Spring* (1944), *Clytemnestra* (1958), and *Rite of Spring* (1984).

**Andrew William Mellon** (1855–1937), born in Pittsburgh, amassed a fortune in his family's banking business. He used his wealth to promote oil, steel, and other industries in the Pittsburgh area. The financier served as U.S. secretary of the treasury (1921–32) and later served as ambassador to Great Britain (1932–33). In 1937, Mellon donated his art collection, worth approximately $35 million, to the people of the United States. He also donated $15 million to build the National Gallery of Art in Washington, D.C., which now houses the collection.

**William Penn** (1644–1718), born in London, England, was a prominent English Quaker and reformer who founded the colony of Pennsylvania and the city of Philadelphia. A biography of William Penn appears in this volume.

**Fred Rogers** (1928–2003), born in Latrobe, was a children's entertainer and educator known as Mister Rogers. He was the host and creator of the television show *Mister Rogers' Neighborhood*, which aired for more than 30 years. The show's popularity was attributed to Rogers' gentle personality and the com-

much of the coal and coke production. John D. Rockefeller dominated the state's oil business, and the Pennsylvania Railroad, led by J. Edgar Thompson and Thomas C. Scott, became the nation's leading freight carrier.

## Labor Conflicts

While businesses grew enormously rich and powerful, most miners and laborers lived and worked in wretched conditions. To fight more effectively for higher wages, shorter hours, and safer working conditions, the workers joined together and formed some of the nation's first labor unions. Among the most notable founded in Pennsylvania were the Noble Order of the Knights of Labor (1869), the American Federation of Labor (1886), and the reorganized Congress of Industrial Organizations (1938).

**Pennsylvania was the first oil-producing state. Edwin L. Drake (in top hat), a retired railroad conductor, drilled the nation's first oil well, near Titusville, in 1859.**

forting way he spoke to children about a wide variety of topics. Rogers won numerous television awards, including an Emmy Award for Lifetime Achievement (1997) and the Presidential Medal of Freedom (2002).

**John Hoyer Updike** (1932–  ), born in Shillington, is a renowned author of American fiction. His carefully crafted novels and short stories are concerned mainly with small-town, middle-class American life. In novels such as *Rabbit Is Rich* (1981), which won the 1982 Pulitzer Prize for fiction, the characters lead worldly lives but search for spiritual fulfillment. Updike's other works include *Rabbit Run* (1960), *Rabbit Redux* (1971), and *The Witches of Eastwick* (1984). In 1991 he won a second Pulitzer Prize for *Rabbit at Rest* (1990).

**August Wilson** (1945–2005), born in Pittsburgh, was a prize-winning playwright. His cycle of plays, each set in a different decade of the 20th century and often in his hometown, examines the issue of black identity through the generations. His first theatrical breakthrough was *Ma Rainey's Black Bottom* (1984). He won his first Pulitzer Prize for drama in 1987 with *Fences* (1985); a second was awarded in 1990 for *The Piano Lesson* (1987).

Martha Graham

Consult the Index to find more information in *The New Book of Knowledge* about the following people who were either born in Pennsylvania or are otherwise associated with the state:

ALCOTT, Louisa May
ALEXANDER, Lloyd
ANDERSON, Marian
ANDERSON, Maxwell
BARRYMORE Family
BLUFORD, Guion
BLY, Nellie
BOONE, Daniel
BUCHANAN, James
CALDER, Alexander
CARSON, Rachel
CASSATT, Mary
CHAMBERLAIN, Wilt
CHAMBERS, Whittaker
DALLAS, George Mifflin
DEPREIST, James
EAKINS, Thomas

FORTEN, James
FOSTER, Stephen
FULTON, Robert
GARRETT, Thomas
GRANGE, Harold ("Red")
HORNE, Marilyn
JACKSON, Reggie
LEMIEUX, Mario
LIPINSKI, Tara
MARSHALL, George C.
MCCLELLAN, George B.
MEAD, Margaret
MEADE, George Gordon
MERRIAM, Eve
MONTANA, Joe
ORMANDY, Eugene
PAINE, Thomas

PALMER, Arnold
PEALE Family
PEARY, Robert E.
PINKNEY, Jerry
PRIESTLEY, Joseph
ROSS, Betsy
RUSTIN, Bayard
STEIN, Gertrude
STEVENS, Thaddeus
STEWART, James
STILL, William
TARBELL, Ida
WARHOL, Andy
WATERS, Ethel
WILLIAMS, Daniel Hale
WYETH Family

Workers often came into violent conflict with industrial leaders. Irish immigrant coal miners, who called themselves the Molly Maguires, terrorized Pennsylvania mine owners in the 1870's. Major conflicts included the Great Railroad Strike of 1877 and the Homestead steel strike in 1892. However, for half a century corporate giants were able to prevent the passage of most labor-reform laws due to their powerful influence over state politics.

### Industrial Decline

By the 1920's, Pennsylvania's economy was beginning to decline, despite the boost that World War I had provided to its industries. Then came the Great Depression of the 1930's, when many industries, businesses, and banks failed. American participation (1941–45) in World War II restored prosperity to Pennsylvania's heavy industries due to the country's need for war supplies. But after the war, coal, steel, and textile production fell, and the railroad industries also declined. Between 1950 and 1962, Pennsylvania had the second highest percentage of jobless workers in the nation.

### Recent Trends

Pennsylvania continues to face serious challenges, including unemployment and overcrowding in its cities. However, the state still ranks high in steel production, and statewide economic conditions have slowly improved due to the growth of other industries, particularly tourism. New technology has created jobs in the fields of telecommunications, biotechnology, and computer research and development. Nuclear power is also a strong industry, despite a disaster at the Three Mile Island plant near Harrisburg in 1979. Also expanding is the number of jobs in business, education, and health care services. In spite of its struggles, Pennsylvania has consistently remained one of the largest income-producing states in the nation.

JOHN B. FRANTZ
The Pennsylvania State University
See also PHILADELPHIA; PITTSBURGH.

# PENS AND PENCILS

Pens and pencils, like many other simple tools we use, have a great effect on our lives. Ideas that are written down for people to read can have great power. In the words of an old proverb,

*"The pen is mightier than the sword."*

## ▶PENS

A pen is a writing tool that uses ink. The first such tool was a swamp reed that had a writing end that was slightly frayed, like a brush. The swamp-reed pen was used about 2,000 years before the time of Christ. This reed pen was first used with ink to write on a sheet of **papyrus** (a paper-thin sheet of pressed papyrus plant) and later used on **parchment** (thin-scraped animal skin).

Quills were first made into pens early in the 600's. A **quill** is the hollow, hard part of a large feather, usually from a goose. The word "pen" comes from the Latin word *penna*, meaning "feather." Quill pens were usually used for writing on parchment. As a writer used a quill pen, he or she had to sharpen it several times. The little knife used for this was known as a **penknife**, a term still used today for a small knife.

Steel **pen nibs** (points) came into general use early in the 1800's. Since steel pens did not need sharpening, they were more efficient than quill pens. But like quill pens, they still needed to be dipped in ink after every few words were written.

## Fountain Pens

The first practical fountain pen was manufactured in the United States in 1884. Like all fountain pens since, it had four basic parts: a

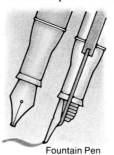

Fountain Pen

barrel to hold ink, a point for writing, a feed bar that supplied ink to the point, and a cap to protect the point and keep the ink from drying up when the pen was not in use. To fill the pen, the user had to unscrew the point and drop ink into the barrel with an eyedropper. This was a messy chore, but fountain pens held enough ink for a great deal of writing, so they did not need to be filled often.

Between the late 1800's and 1950, most pens were filled by the use of a lever on the side of the barrel. The lever squeezed a rubber ink sac inside the barrel. When the lever was released, the rubber sac expanded and sucked up ink. Some pens used a plunger instead of a lever.

Later two other methods of filling a fountain pen became common. In one an **ink cartridge** (a small plastic container of ink) is put into the ink barrel. In the other method the pen is filled with many tiny tubes, or channels. When the pen is set into ink, the channels suck up ink by capillary action, much as a sponge soaks up water. There is nothing to put into the barrel and nothing to squeeze.

## Ballpoint Pens

A ballpoint pen has as its point a small rotating metal ball that continually inks itself as it turns. The ball is set into a tiny socket. In the center of the socket is a hole that feeds ink

Ballpoint Pen

to the socket from a long tube inside the pen. Small hairlike grooves run from the center hole almost to the edge of the socket. The grooves help to spread the ink over the inside of the socket. As the ball spins, it picks up a thin layer of ink and transfers it to the paper as a line.

The first practical ballpoint pen was made in South America in 1943 by a journalist and printer named Laszlo Biro. His first model had a roller instead of a ball at the tip. But this model could only write straight lines, and handwriting is full of curves. So Biro replaced the roller with a ball, which can revolve freely in any direction and therefore make the curves of handwriting.

Early ballpoint pens had ordinary ball bearings as writing tips. The small, smooth balls tended to skip over the paper instead of rolling. In 1957 a ball made of finely powdered metal was developed. The tiny particles of the metal powder fuse together when the ball is shaped under great pressure and heat. The powdered-metal ball has about 50,000 tiny ridges on its surface. The ridges grip the paper much as the tread of an automobile tire grips the road. They keep the ball from skipping and skidding. This type of ball or a synthetic jewel ball is now used in most ballpoint pens.

The ink used in ballpoint pens is different from the ink used in fountain pens. The free-flowing fountain-pen ink would run out of a ballpoint pen. Therefore, a thick, more flow-resistant ink is used.

A ballpoint pen looks simpler than a fountain pen, but it is very difficult to manufacture. Exceedingly fine work is needed to place a ball in a tiny socket so that it will spin freely yet not fall out. Ballpoint pen manufacturers work with measurements as precise as those used in spacecraft.

### Soft-Tip and Rolling-Ball Pens

Since 1950 two other types of pens have been introduced. Soft-tip pens have a tip made

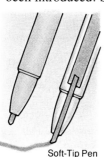

Soft-Tip Pen

of felt or soft, absorbent plastic that is fed a free-flowing ink from a reservoir. Rolling-ball pens combine the tip of a ballpoint pen with the free-flowing ink of a soft-tip pen for smooth writing. The flow of ink between the reservoir and the tip is controlled by a wick that can only hold a certain amount of ink at a time.

**Special-Purpose Pens.** Some pens are designed for specific purposes. Technical pens come with changeable tips of different sizes. Artists use these pens to achieve special effects in their work.

ALFRED P. DIOTTE
The Parker Pen Company

## ▶PENCILS

The simple pencil we use today developed gradually over a long period of time. A pencil is a writing stick made of a slender rod of **graphite** (a soft, black, lustrous form of carbon) and clay surrounded by a wooden case. But it did not take this form until late in the 1600's.

Probably the first pencils—sticks of metallic lead that drew faint lines—were those used by the Greeks and Romans around the beginning of the Christian Era. Such lead pencils were still being used in the 1800's.

The use of graphite in pencils dates back to 1564. There is a story that at that time a hurricane roared across the British Isles. Wind uprooted a great tree near Borrowdale, England, and a strange black substance was turned up. A farmer discovered that the black stuff made marks that would not wash off. He and other farmers began to use it to mark sheep. The material was graphite.

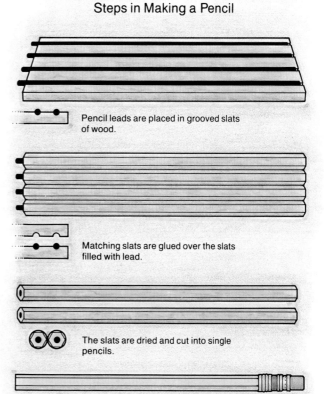

## Steps in Making a Pencil

Pencil leads are placed in grooved slats of wood.

Matching slats are glued over the slats filled with lead.

The slats are dried and cut into single pencils.

Sometimes an eraser is added to the finished pencil.

Scientists who examined the graphite called it *plumbago*—Latin for a kind of lead ore. The name "lead" has stuck to this day.

The Borrowdale graphite was so solid that it could be cut into lengths to be peddled in London streets as writing sticks. At first the sticks were used without any covering. Then they were wrapped in string to keep the user's fingers from getting dirty. Metal cases were also used. Around 1686 a way of putting the graphite between strips of wood was discovered, and the pencil took its present form.

Although the Borrowdale graphite was mined very carefully, it began to run out near the end of the 1700's. About the same time, a French chemist, Jacques Conté, discovered that graphite could be mixed with other substances and still make marks. He mixed powdered graphite with powdered clay and water. Once this material was baked, it wrote as smoothly as Borrowdale graphite.

Around 1839 a German named Johann Lothar von Faber (1817–96) developed the idea of forcing graphite paste through a die, or mold. This made pencil leads all the same thickness. Von Faber also developed machinery to cut and groove the wood that surrounds a pencil.

Pencils are made in different degrees of hardness, which are usually identified by the numbers 1, 2, or 3. Variations in hardness depend on the use of different proportions of clay and graphite; the more clay a pencil has, the harder it is. A number 1 pencil is very soft and makes a heavy black mark with little pressure. A number 2 is an ordinary (medium-soft) writing pencil. A number 3 is a hard pencil, good for making light, fine lines.

**Mechanical Pencils.** A mechanical pencil has a metal or plastic body with a long, thin holder inside, into which one or more sticks of lead are set. There are two methods of bringing the lead out. In one, the lead is moved forward by turning the top of the pencil. In the other, a button on the pencil's cap or side is pressed to push the lead forward.

**Special-Purpose Pencils.** Pencils are made in a large variety of colors and in many types of leads. Colored pencils, often used by editors, are made with dyes in place of graphite. Grease or wax pencils are used to make marks on glass, plastic, and film. Charcoal pencils are used by artists.

For certain jobs, pencils may be specially shaped or colored. For example, a carpenter's pencil has a flat shape, so that it will not roll when set down. The outside is bright red, so that it will show up quickly in wood shavings.

ARTHUR VAN DER KAR
Venus Pen and Pencil Corporation

---

**PEORIA.** See ILLINOIS (Cities).
**PEPPER.** See HERBS AND SPICES.

# PERCENTAGE

A percent is one-hundredth of something. The "something" can be almost anything—a sum of money, a group of people, or the number of games in a baseball season. Percentages are widely used in schools, businesses, sports, government, and many other fields.

The word "percent" comes from the Latin *per centum* and the Italian *per cento*, meaning "for each hundred" or "out of each hundred." Italian merchants in the 1400's were the first to use a symbol for percentage. When they computed how much waste or spoilage had occurred in shipping, they abbreviated *per cento* to *p c°*. Later this became *c°*, still later $\frac{o}{o}$, and finally the symbol we use today: %.

▶ **UNDERSTANDING PERCENT**

The total amount of something is always 100%. If a bag contains 25 golf balls, 100% of the total is 25 golf balls. If you answer all the questions on a test correctly, your score will be 100%, whether there are 15 or 150 questions on the test. If a candidate in an election wins 65% of the vote, 65 out of every 100 people voted for that candidate.

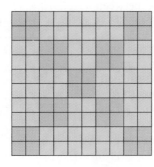

There are 100 squares in this blue and green grid. What percent of them are blue? Since 36 out of the 100 squares are blue, 36% of the squares are blue.

If everyone voted for the candidate, he or she would win 100% of the vote—100 out of every 100 votes.

## PERCENTS, FRACTIONS, AND DECIMALS

Since percents are hundredths of something, they can be written in the form of a common fraction or a decimal fraction. To write a percent as a common fraction, drop the percent sign and add a denominator of 100. You can then reduce the fraction.

$$75\% = \frac{75}{100} = \frac{3}{4}$$
$$20\% = \frac{20}{100} = \frac{1}{5}$$

To write a percent as a decimal, change the percent to a common fraction. Then change the common fraction to a decimal.

$$25\% = \frac{25}{100} = 0.25$$
$$80\% = \frac{80}{100} = 0.8$$

To change a decimal fraction to a percent, you simply move the decimal point two places to the right and add the symbol for percent. Thus 0.05 becomes 5%. To change a common fraction to a percent, first change it to a decimal fraction. To do this, divide the numerator by the denominator, then change the decimal to a percent.

$$\frac{2}{5} = 2 \div 5 = 0.4 = 40\%$$

## PERCENTAGE PROBLEMS

Since percents can be written as common fractions or as decimal fractions, percentage problems are solved in the same way as fraction or decimal problems.

**Finding a Percentage of a Number.** If a salesclerk receives a 15% commission on the price of goods sold, how much is the commission on a sale of $34? First change the percent to its equivalent decimal: 15% = 0.15. Then multiply the price of the item sold by the decimal fraction: 0.15 x $34 = $5.10. The commission is $5.10 on a sale of $34.

Usually you do not have to write this type of problem down on paper or use a calculator. You can often compute the answer in your head. For example, if you are making a $10 purchase for which there is a 10% discount, you can think of the percentage as a common fraction. Thus 10% is the same as $\frac{1}{10}$, and $\frac{1}{10}$ of $10 is $1. For every $10, the dis-

count is $1. If the price is $20, the discount is $2, and the purchase costs only $18.

In some situations you can also use estimation to determine the amount by rounding it off to the nearest ten. If the purchase price is $27, you would think $27 is close to $30, so the discount will be almost $3. The purchase will then cost $27 – $3, or about $24.

**Finding What Percent One Number Is of Another.** Suppose there are 15 questions on your science test. If you answer 12 correctly, what should your grade be if it is expressed as a percentage? To find out, first write your test score as the fraction $\frac{12}{15}$. Divide the numerator by the denominator to change the fraction to a decimal. Then change the decimal to a percentage.

$$\frac{12}{15} = 12 \div 15 = 0.8 = 80\%$$

You should receive a grade of 80% on the test.

**Finding a Number When the Percent Is Known.** Imagine that a baseball team wins 56% of its games. You know that the team won 14 games. How many games did the team play? The question "14 is 56% of what

$$\begin{array}{r} 25\phantom{.00} \\ 0.56\,{\overline{\smash{\big)}\,14.00\phantom{0}}} \\ \underline{112\phantom{00}} \\ 280\phantom{0} \\ \underline{280\phantom{0}} \end{array}$$

number?" can be written 14 = 0.56 x ? To find the answer, divide 14 by 0.56.

Since 14 is 56% of 25, the team played 25 games.

## USES OF PERCENTS

There are many common uses of percents. You are probably most familiar with percents as grades—the percent of the correct answers on your test scores. Some test scores, however, are expressed as **percentile** scores. A percentile is a value based on a scale of 100. If you receive a percentile rank of 80 on a test, it means that you scored as well as or better than 80% of the people who took the test. It does not mean that you got 80% of the questions correct.

**Making Comparisons.** The standings of sports leagues or teams are often expressed as the percent of games won out of the total games played. Even though this is called a

there are laws regulating whether a discount or the sales tax is calculated first on a purchase? Why does it make a difference?

Suppose you want to buy a $25 shirt that is on sale for 20% off the original price. There is also a 5% sales tax. Does computing the sales tax before or after you take your 20% discount make any difference in the total amount you pay? Does it make any difference in how much money the store earns or the state gets in taxes?

If you take the 20% off first, you are actually paying 80% of $25, or $20. The sales tax is 5% of $20, or $1. Your total bill is $21. The store gets $20 for the purchase and the state gets $1 in taxes.

If you compute the tax first, 5% of $25 is $1.25. The total price becomes $26.25. The result of the discount of 20% on $26.25 is $21. You still pay $21, but since the state gets $1.25 in taxes, the store gets only $19.75 for the purchase of the shirt. State laws often

specify that stores need only collect sales tax on the money they actually receive. As a result, they can

compute the discount before the tax and keep more of the amount you pay for a product.

percent, it is actually written as a decimal to the thousandths place. Percents make it easy to compare one team or one player against another, even though both may not have played the same number of games. Percents are used for comparisons in other fields, too.

**In Business.** Stores and other businesses use percents to show price discounts and to state the commissions earned by salespeople. Profits, or the income left after subtracting the costs of doing business, are also usually expressed as a percent of total income. Packaged foods are labeled to show the percent of vitamins and minerals they contain. Clothing labels list what percent of different fibers make up the fabric.

**Interest.** Banks charge interest on money they lend, and they pay interest on money that is deposited in the bank. The interest on a loan is sometimes figured as a percentage of the total amount of the loan. Interest on savings deposits is also a percentage, and it is usually compounded. This means that the bank calculates interest on the total amount of money in an account, including previous interest payments. Credit card companies also charge interest on balances left unpaid at the end of a month.

**Taxes.** Taxes are often figured as percentages. For example, the sales tax on an item is usually a percentage of the item's selling price, and income taxes are usually a percentage of a person's earnings.

**Inflation.** The rate of inflation—how much prices rise over a certain time—is shown in percents. If something that cost $1 one year costs $1.25 the following year, it costs 25% more, and the rate of inflation is 25%. The new price is 125% (100% + 25%) of the old price.

**Probability.** Percents are also widely used to express probability, the chance that something will happen. A weather forecaster may tell you that there is a 40% chance of rain today. Experience has shown the forecaster that on 40 out of every 100 days with weather conditions like those shaping that day's weather, it rains.

There are many other situations in which percents are used. Knowing about them will be useful often.

JESSICA DAVIDSON
Author, *Using the Cuisenaire Rods*
Reviewed and updated by ERICA DAKIN VOOLICH
Solomon Schechter Day School

See also INTEREST.

# PERCUSSION INSTRUMENTS

Almost anything that gives off a sound when struck can be used in music as a percussion instrument. The word "percussion" comes from a Latin word meaning "to beat." When primitive people danced, they stamped on the ground with their feet. The thudding sound they made became a rhythm. Planks laid across a hollow pit in the earth made a more satisfactory sound because the air in the pit resonated. Hollow trees struck with the hands had even greater resonance. Before long, drums were invented.

## How Drums Are Made and Played

Drums are found all over the world. They are hollowed out from solid wood or built up from thin strips. Pottery or metal bowls and empty gasoline cans are turned into drums.

Drums are usually made by stretching a membrane across one end or both ends of an open cylinder. The membrane is usually thin parchment (skin or vellum). The drum is sounded by making this membrane vibrate. The vibrations, passing through the air, reach our ears as sound.

Vibrations are set up in the drum by striking the membrane. It may be struck with the fin-gers, the flat of the hand, a drumstick, or a pair of drumsticks.

Very delicate tappings may be made with the fingers. As the fingers move from the edge of the membrane toward the center, the sound grows stronger and more resonant. If the flat of the hand is used, there is more of a dull boom. Asian drummers are especially clever at making contrasts in the sound.

Drumsticks, too, can be used in different ways: sometimes lightly, sometimes violently; sometimes near the edge of the membrane, sometimes near the center. When the stick is light and hard, the sound is dry. A heavier stick will make a more booming sound, especially when it is covered at the end with a soft material, such as felt. A wire brush is often used by jazz drummers to make a swishing sound.

Sometimes the drummer chooses to strike the rim of the drum or another part of the cylinder. This, too, makes the drum vibrate. But it gives off a much harsher sound than striking the membrane.

In Asian orchestras, the chief drummer may squat on the ground with the drums set out in a half circle, so that they can all be reached with equal ease. Using only fingers and the flat of the hand, the drummer plays on the

Two street musicians at an outdoor concert in New York City play percussion instruments: drums, cymbals, and a xylophone.

drums like a virtuoso pianist. The sounds vary from very soft to rather loud. A good drummer does not use any great violence but makes a sort of shading and tone coloring. And each drum in turn gives a note of different pitch.

Many drums can give a distinct note that is perfectly in tune. The drum is tuned by altering the tightness of the membrane. The tighter the membrane, the higher the note. Little drums sound higher than big drums when the tightness is the same.

Not all drums can give a distinct note. There are big drums that sound powerful but have no distinct note of their own. There are smaller drums that clatter excitingly but, again, give no special note. The big drums are bass drums. The smaller ones may be tenor drums or side drums. Side drums have a special feature: The end that is not struck has cords stretched lightly across it. These rattle when the drum is played. The cords are called snares, so this kind of drum is called a snare drum.

In the symphony orchestra, bass drums and side drums are not so common as kettledrums, or timpani as they are sometimes called. The kettledrum has a deep, bowl-shaped body that looks like half of a huge eggshell. The top is covered by a large parchment of the finest quality. The shape of the kettledrum affects its tone. The rounded bottom reflects back sound as evenly as possible. Since kettledrums are made of brightly polished metal—usually brass or copper—they stand out in the orchestra.

The kettledrum gives a beautifully distinct note. It can be tuned exactly. The kettledrummer turns thumbscrews or operates a pedal mechanism to tighten or slacken the parchment until the note is tuned exactly right. The note of a drum may have to be changed in the middle of a piece. A skilled drummer does this quickly and carefully.

Like the Asian drummer, the kettledrummer sets the drums out in a half-circle. But the kettledrums are larger, and there are usually only three to five of them. They are played with two drumsticks.

The heads of the sticks are covered with felt. The drummer has a choice of sticks, some covered with thick, soft felt and some with thin, hard felt. By using different sticks and by playing sometimes near the edge and sometimes near the center, the drummer can vary the sound.

For a soft sound, the sticks hardly need to be lifted. For a loud sound, they are raised high. A special technique is the roll. Instead of separate sounds, we hear a continuous sound. When soft, it is like a murmuring wind. But when it is louder, it is like the roar of a waterfall. The roll is done by rapidly striking two sticks close to the parchment. Because the sticks strike so rapidly, the sound has no time to die away between strokes.

### Drums in the Orchestra

Drums are often very important in Asian orchestras. Sometimes there are no other instruments at all. Sometimes there are other percussion instruments like bowls, bars, and clappers. An orchestra of drums and percussion instruments makes powerful music. The sound can be both subtle and exciting.

In Western symphony orchestras the drums are rarely as important. But they add a range of sounds all their own, from the deep bass drum and the snarling side drum to the mellow kettledrums. The kettledrums are the aristocrats of the percussion section. Their clear notes are so finely outlined that they are occasionally given solo passages to play.

The drums also set the rhythm. Music is full of varying rhythms. The drums and other percussion instruments mark these rhythms with the utmost sharpness. Rhythm is especially prominent in dance music.

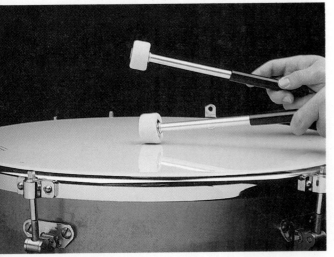

**A kettledrum is played with two padded drumsticks.**

## Other Percussion Instruments

In the 1700's, Europeans became fascinated with the marching bands of the Turkish Army. These bands used an assortment of instruments that made clashing sounds. One instrument was the Turkish crescent. This was a tall stick mounted with metal plates. It was played simply by shaking it in rhythm with the music. This instrument and other Turkish noisemakers became very fashionable.

Two Turkish instruments, the cymbals and the triangle, became permanent members of the Western orchestra. The cymbals are a pair of brass plates. They come in all sizes, but in the orchestra they are usually large and resonant. The player can jingle them together softly or clash them loudly. A jazz percussion player usually has them set on a stand, so that they can be played with a foot pedal. The player's hands are then free for the drums and other percussion instruments.

The triangle is simply a bent rod of steel. One corner of it is left open so that the rod can vibrate freely, giving a ringing sound. The triangle is played with another rod of steel. It can be struck powerfully, or it can be made to give a continuous trill by rattling the rod in one corner of the triangle.

One instrument is half drum and half cymbals. This is the tambourine. It is about the size of a dinner plate, and the frame is only about 3 inches (7 centimeters) deep. Parchment covers one end, and the other end is left open. Pairs of tiny cymbals are set around the outside. The players can strike the parchment with the hand or rub it with the fingers to produce a throbbing sound. Or they can shake the tambourine at rhythmic intervals. Whatever they do, the cymbals jingle together.

Castanets are a pair of wooden clappers, held in one hand. They have a dry, brittle sound when clapped together in rhythm with the music. Dancers in Spain use castanets.

Bells of all sizes have been used in the orchestra. But since large bells take up much room and are very expensive, the sound of bells is usually produced on long, hollow tubes of steel. A row of tubes of different lengths is mounted on a frame, making it easy to play different notes.

Another bell-like instrument is the glockenspiel. (The word is German for "bell play.") It is a row of metal bars played with hammers held like drumsticks. An instrument very much like the glockenspiel is the celesta. It has a keyboard for working the hammers. The sound of these two instruments is light and ringing. The xylophone (from the Greek words meaning "wood sound") has bars made of wood instead of metal. The playing sticks are hard, and the tone crisp and hollow. The xylophone is usually used for a special effect.

Strange instruments sometimes find their way into the percussion section. Gongs are close relatives of cymbals, but they are played with soft, heavy drumsticks. Anvils are heard in the "Anvil Chorus" of Verdi's *Il Trovatore*, and in Wagner's opera *Das Rheingold* to create the sound of dwarfs hammering away at their work. In one famous passage of Schoenberg's *Gurre-Lieder*, heavy iron chains have to be lifted and dropped. The effect of the passage is meant to be exceedingly gloomy, and that is how it sounds.

It is no wonder that orchestral players sometimes call the percussion section the kitchen of the orchestra.

ROBERT DONINGTON
Author, *The Instruments of Music*

See also DRUM.

A Turkish crescent, also called a "Jingling Johnnie," is topped by a crescent and an ornament shaped like a Chinese hat, from which another crescent, bells, jingles, and two horsehair tails are suspended.

**PÉREZ DE CUÉLLAR, JAVIER.** See UNITED NATIONS (Profiles).

# PERFUMES

Perfume is a delightful fragrance. It may come from a woodland after rain, an apple tree in bloom, a freshly cut orange, or a liquid in a pretty bottle.

The fragrances of natural materials are caused by oils within them. These oils are used to make perfumes in either a liquid or a solid form. The liquid perfumes are those usually found in bottles, aerosol sprays, and bath oils. Liquid perfumes are also used to add a pleasant scent to soap, hand cream, and other toilet preparations. Perfume sticks, incense, and perfumed candles are examples of perfume in solid form.

Usually we think of perfumes as flowery or fruit-scented substances used to make a person or a room smell pleasant. But it is also possible to make scents that smell like popcorn, new cars, or a seashore.

## ▶ HISTORY OF PERFUME

The use of perfumes goes far back in time. Some of the first perfumes were fragrant woods and spices that were burned as incense in religious ceremonies. In fact, the word "perfume" comes from the Latin *per* ("through") and *fumus* ("smoke"). Later it was discovered that some perfumes helped to prevent decay. People came to believe that scent had magical properties. For these reasons perfumes were used in treating the sick and embalming the dead.

The people of ancient Egypt used fragrant oils and ointments when bathing. Cleopatra is famous for her use of perfumes. She is said to have perfumed not only herself but also the sails of her boat. Flower perfumes were first used in Greece. Both the Greeks and the Romans used perfumes very freely. At that time people probably made their fragrances by dipping flowers and herbs into hot oils or wines. Or they may have spread petals out on trays of fat until the fat absorbed the odor of the petals. The Persians learned to boil off and collect the fragrance of petals.

After 1500 the habit of wearing perfumes became especially fashionable in Europe. Men and women hung from their waists ornamental pomanders (a mixture of fragrant dried leaves, blossoms, and other substances enclosed in a perforated bag or box). Wealthy households contained a room called a still, where the family's perfumes were made. Italy and France began to grow flowers especially for perfumes.

## ▶ WHAT GOES INTO A PERFUME?

The materials with which perfumes are made come from all over the world—rich spices from Asian lands, rare blossoms from jungles, musk from the musk deer that roam the Himalayan mountains of Tibet. As many as 300 different materials may be used to make one perfume. Three types of materials are used—fragrant essential oils, fixatives, and synthetic aromatic chemicals.

The fragrant essential oils once were available only from natural materials, such as flowers, leaves, fruits, roots, and seeds. These oils are still used. But chemists now can make identical or very similar oils in laboratories. Today most perfumes contain a combination of natural and synthetic oils.

The natural oils provide a large number of different odors. Some of the most familiar ones are listed in the chart. Others that are also used are clove, heliotrope, lilac, bay, eucalyptus, wintergreen, angelica, orris, bergamot, and lime. Synthetic perfume oils have been created that smell like lemon verbena, hyacinth, rose, gardenia, orange blossom, hawthorn, and wintergreen.

Most perfumes contain fixatives that keep the fragrance from evaporating quickly. The fixatives do not spoil the odor of the perfume

## WONDER QUESTION

### What are toilet water and cologne?

Cologne is a perfumed liquid that is used in or after a bath and for a skin freshener. It is largely alcohol. Traditionally, cologne has been based on the fragrance of citrus, and this fragrance has distinguished cologne from toilet water. But few companies today make toilet water and cologne in the traditional way. Now the words "cologne" and "toilet water" refer to different concentrations of perfume oils. Toilet water is usually the stronger of the two. Both are intended to be splashed freely over the body or sprayed in the hair. Because they contain a great deal of alcohol, toilet water and cologne are much less expensive than perfume. Because they are more diluted, their fragrance does not last nearly so long as the fragrance of perfume.

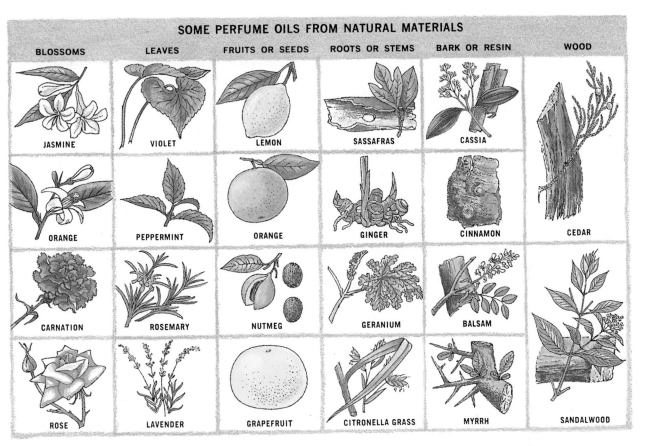

## SOME PERFUME OILS FROM NATURAL MATERIALS

| BLOSSOMS | LEAVES | FRUITS OR SEEDS | ROOTS OR STEMS | BARK OR RESIN | WOOD |
|----------|--------|-----------------|----------------|---------------|------|
| JASMINE | VIOLET | LEMON | SASSAFRAS | CASSIA | |
| ORANGE | PEPPERMINT | ORANGE | GINGER | CINNAMON | CEDAR |
| CARNATION | ROSEMARY | NUTMEG | GERANIUM | BALSAM | |
| ROSE | LAVENDER | GRAPEFRUIT | CITRONELLA GRASS | MYRRH | SANDALWOOD |

even though they may be, themselves, unpleasant. Some fixatives have a pleasant odor that can be blended with that of the essential oils. The most valuable fixative is **ambergris**—a waxy material that is formed in the stomachs of sperm whales and is found floating on oceans. Other valuable fixatives are animal products that come from the scent glands of the civet cat, the male musk deer, and the beaver. Only a very small amount of fixative is needed in a perfume.

### ▶ HOW ARE PERFUMES MADE?

The first step in making perfume is to obtain the essential fragrance oils. This is done in many different ways. The oils may be dissolved out of flowers and leaves by solvents such as alcohol. Another method is to squeeze the oils out by pressure from heavy rollers. In some cases the petals are placed in great tanks that are heated gently. As the petals become hot, the vapors from them rise. As they cool, the vapors are collected on overhead trays.

In still other cases, flat trays are covered with thin layers of pork or beef fat, and the petals are spread over them. The fat absorbs the fragrance from the petals. The old petals are picked off, and new ones are put on until the fat is saturated with the perfume oils. Petals may also be soaked in hot, melted fats. The fragrant fat that is made by these two methods is called a **pomade**. It is usually further treated to remove the perfume oils.

Perfumers are specialists who blend raw materials to create fragrances. They must have an especially sensitive sense of smell. An expert perfumer can recognize the odors of a thousand perfume ingredients and knows how they will interact with one another.

The raw materials for a perfume and its method of manufacture are often well-kept trade secrets. Typically, the raw materials are dissolved in pure grain alcohol and are aged in darkness for perhaps a year until a smooth perfume is formed. The mixture is chilled to freeze out unwanted solids, and then it is filtered. The final perfume is sparkling clear.

RICHARD K. LEHNE
Contributor, *Cosmetics: Science and Technology*

See also COSMETICS.

# PERICLES (495?–429 B.C.)

Pericles, the greatest statesman of ancient Athens, was born about 495 B.C. Though of a noble family, he was always on the side of the common people. When he entered politics, the government of Athens was still partly controlled by the Areopagus, a permanent council of former magistrates. In 461 Pericles and his friends took away most of its power. From then on Athens was governed by an assembly of all male citizens. Pericles usually led it, partly because he was known to be honest and patriotic and partly because he was a powerful speaker. He created an overseas empire by planting Athenian colonies on the coasts of the Aegean Sea, along the Dardanelles, and even in southern Italy. Also, he took over control of a Greek league. He used the league's treasury to strengthen the Athenian fleet and erect public buildings, including the magnificent temple called the Parthenon, which still stands in Athens.

Pericles was an able general and a highly intelligent man, but his life ended sadly. Jealous of the growing power of Athens, the Greek states of the Peloponnesus (the southern peninsula), headed by Sparta, declared war on the Athenians (the Peloponnesian Wars). Through its navy Athens controlled the sea. Refugees fleeing from the Spartan invasion packed miserably into the city, and a terrible epidemic broke out. Pericles was blamed for the invasion and the epidemic and was publicly disgraced. He died soon afterward in 429.

None of Pericles' speeches have been preserved. But the historian Thucydides (455?–400?) describes a memorial service for the Athenians killed in the first year's fighting and reports a speech made at it by Pericles. It is full of the noble spirit of patriotism that inspired him, and it is one of the finest statements of the ideals of democracy.

GILBERT HIGHET
Columbia University

---

**PERIODICALS.** See MAGAZINES; NEWSPAPERS.

**PERIODIC TABLE.** See CHEMISTRY; ELEMENTS, CHEMICAL.

**PERIODONTAL DISEASE.** See DISEASES (Descriptions of Some Diseases).

**PEROT, H. ROSS.** See TEXAS (Famous People).

# PERRY, MATTHEW C. (1794–1858)

Matthew C. Perry, like his brother Oliver Hazard Perry, was a famous American naval commander. Matthew Perry, however, gained fame not in battle but through diplomacy.

Matthew Calbraith Perry was born in Newport, Rhode Island, on April 10, 1794. He entered the navy as a midshipman when he was 14, serving first under his brother. In 1814 he married Jane Slidell. They had ten children.

In 1820, Perry went to Africa to help American blacks establish themselves in Liberia. He fought pirates in the West Indies and visited Turkey and Greece. In 1830, commanding the *Concord*, he brought the new American minister to Russia, John Randolph, to St. Petersburg. Czar Nicholas I urged Perry to join the Russian Navy, but he refused.

From 1833 to 1843, Perry made his home in New York City, where he pioneered in the construction of steam vessels and the development of naval weapons. He also helped found the United States Naval Academy. In 1843 he returned to Africa in command of a squadron to protect American settlements in Liberia and eliminate slave trading. During the Mexican War (1846–48), Perry took part in the capture of Veracruz.

Perry's greatest task was to persuade the Japanese rulers to open diplomatic and trade relations with the United States. In July 1853, he arrived in Tokyo Bay—previously closed to foreigners—carrying a letter from President Millard Fillmore to the Japanese emperor. The Japanese, reluctant at first, were impressed by Perry's determination and his naval force. The Treaty of Kanagawa, signed in March 1854, gave the United States trading rights in two ports and ended Japan's isolation from the Western world.

Perry spent most of his remaining years writing a book on his expedition to Japan. He died in New York City on March 4, 1858.

JOHN D. HAYES
Rear Admiral, United States Navy (Ret.)

## PERRY, OLIVER HAZARD (1785–1819)

Oliver Hazard Perry gained his place in American history by his victory over the British on Lake Erie in the War of 1812.

Perry was born in South Kingston, Rhode Island, on August 20, 1785. At the age of 14 he was appointed a midshipman. His father was a captain in the Navy, and young Perry first served aboard his father's ship, the *General Greene*, in the West Indies and then took part in the Tripolitan War (1801–05). In 1811 he married Elizabeth Champlin Mason, who bore him five children.

Early in the War of 1812, Perry, then a lieutenant, was given command of the American squadron on Lake Erie. Perry had ten vessels. However, he could not get his largest ships, the *Lawrence* and the *Niagara*, across the sandbar at Presque Isle without first removing their heavy guns. This could not be done while the British squadron blockaded the harbor. Unwisely, the British commander abandoned the blockade for several days. This gave Perry his chance.

On September 10, 1813, Perry met the British in battle. Perry's battle flag on the *Lawrence* was inscribed with the motto "Don't give up the ship." These had been the dying words of Captain James Lawrence, whose ship the *Chesapeake* had been defeated by the British some months earlier.

After two hours of fighting, the *Lawrence* was almost a wreck, and Perry transferred to the *Niagara*. The enemy had also suffered heavily, and when Perry brought the undamaged *Niagara* into action, the British ships were forced to surrender. "We have met the enemy and they are ours," wrote Perry to General William Henry Harrison. Perry then ferried Harrison's soldiers across Lake Erie, where they defeated the British at the Battle of the Thames.

Perry survived his victory by only six years. In 1819, while on a naval diplomatic mission to Venezuela, he fell ill with yellow fever. The hero of the Battle of Lake Erie died on board ship on August 23, 1819.

JOHN D. HAYES
Rear Admiral, United States Navy (Ret.)

---

**PERSEPHONE.** See GREEK MYTHOLOGY (Profiles).

**PERSEUS.** See GREEK MYTHOLOGY.

## PERSHING, JOHN J. (1860–1948)

John Joseph Pershing, commander of the American Expeditionary Forces (A.E.F.) in World War I, was born on September 13, 1860, near Laclede, Missouri. He attended the teacher-training school at Kirksville and later entered the U.S. Military Academy at West Point, New York. He graduated as president of his class in 1886.

Pershing began his active service as a cavalry officer, fighting in campaigns against American Indians. He then taught military science and mathematics at the University of Nebraska while earning a law degree. In 1897 he returned to West Point as an instructor.

Pershing served in the Spanish-American War (1898). The following year he was sent to the Philippines to subdue the Moro tribes, who had rebelled against the new American government of those islands. By hard fighting and wise diplomacy, Pershing persuaded the Moros to make peace. In 1906, President Theodore Roosevelt promoted him from captain to brigadier general.

Pershing married Helen Warren in 1905. He then returned to the Philippines for eight years as military governor. In 1916, Pershing was ordered to capture the Mexican bandit and revolutionary Pancho Villa, who had raided U.S. border towns. Though unable to catch Villa, he scattered the bandit forces.

In 1917, when the United States entered World War I, Pershing was given command of the A.E.F. At his insistence, the 2 million men of the A.E.F. fought in Europe as an independent unit instead of simply filling in the ranks of the Allied armies. They played an important role in defeating Germany.

In 1919, Pershing was made general of the armies—a rank previously conferred only on George Washington. Pershing retired in 1924. His book *My Experiences in the World War* won the Pulitzer Prize for history in 1932. He died on July 15, 1948.

Reviewed by STUART ROCHESTER
Historian, U.S. Department of Defense

**PERSIA.** See PERSIA, ANCIENT.

The walls of Persepolis, one of the two capitals of the Achaemenid Empire, were adorned with relief sculptures. The guards are Persians (in fluted hats) and Medes (in round hats).

## PERSIA, ANCIENT

In the ancient Middle East, centered in what is now Iran, the Persians created a universal empire, which was made up of varied peoples and was a model for the later Roman Empire. At its height, in the 500's B.C., the Persian Achaemenid Empire stretched from the Indus River (now in Pakistan) to the Mediterranean Sea and northern Africa, encompassing much of what was then the known world. The empire was distinguished by its code of laws, roads and postal system, new methods of government administration, and for its tolerance of many religions. The Achaemenid Empire lasted for some 220 years and was succeeded in the region by later empires, both Persian and non-Persian, that ruled for nearly a thousand years more.

**Origins.** The Persians were one tribe of a group of peoples who called themselves Aryans and who migrated to the Iranian plateau from the north sometime about 1000 B.C. A related tribe, the Medes, settled to their north. At some unknown time during the Persians' migration, a prophet, Zoroaster, appeared among the eastern tribes. He preached a new faith, called Zoroastrianism or Mazdaism, after its god, Ahura Mazda, which became the religion of Persian kings and later of the em-

pire itself. This religion still exists but now mainly in India. (See the article on Zoroastrianism in Volume W-X-Y-Z).

In the 600's B.C., the Medes united and formed their own state. Allying themselves with the Babylonians, they overthrew the empire of the Assyrians. The Median Empire that resulted lasted until about 549 B.C., when Cyrus, leader of the Persians, defeated Astyages, the last ruler of the Medes, and inherited their empire.

**The Achaemenid Empire.** Cyrus, known as the Great, was the founder of the Achaemenid Empire. He extended his domain, conquering the kingdom of Lydia (in what is now Turkey) and absorbing the Babylonian lands. His reign was noted for its mildness toward subject peoples, including the Jews, whom he freed from Babylonian captivity and allowed to return to their homeland. Cyrus was preparing for an invasion of Egypt, when, in 530 B.C., he was killed fighting in Central Asia. He was succeeded by his son Cambyses II, who conquered Egypt but died in an accident in 522 B.C. After a period of turmoil and revolt, Darius I, who belonged to another branch of the Achaemenid dynasty, became ruler.

**Organization of the Empire.** The empire was divided into satrapies, or provinces, ruled by satraps, or governors, appointed by the king.

The army was organized into units of tens, hundreds, and thousands, and a military intelligence service was developed. A postal system was established, which much impressed the Greek historian Herodotus, who wrote that "neither snow nor rain nor heat nor darkness stays these couriers from their appointed rounds." (This description was to be adopted as part of the motto of the U.S. postal service.)

The policy of tolerance for all religions, begun by Cyrus, was continued. A system of laws was established for the entire empire, although local laws and customs were retained. A network of roads (the Royal Road) connected the far-flung parts of the empire. The imperial bureaucracy, or government administration, used a single language, Aramaic (a Semitic tongue then in common use), everywhere in the empire, and it became the model for later governments of the region.

**Taxes, Trade, and Arts.** Taxes and trade were mostly in goods, such as grain, cattle, and precious stones and metals, rather than money, until 490 B.C., when gold and silver coins were introduced. Their use was important both for the growth of trade and for the financial stability of the empire. Taxation was based mainly on land but was also imposed on caravans of merchants traveling from area to area. There were also fees on ships using harbors and many other taxes. Military service was often rewarded with grants of land, and the empire gradually came to depend on foreign mercenaries, or professional soldiers.

Achaemenid art and architecture was influenced by Egyptian, Assyrian, and other styles. Workers from all over the empire were brought to build the royal palaces at Susa and Persepolis, whose imposing columns and beautifully carved relief sculptures still stand amid their ruins. The Achaemenids, in turn, strongly influenced the art and architecture of India and Central Asia.

**Decline of the Empire.** The revolt of Greek city-states in Ionia (western Turkey) had prompted an unsuccessful expedition by Darius I against Greece in 490 B.C. Other revolts after his death detached lands from the empire for periods of time, but the empire survived in spite of weak rulers. Darius I's successor, his son Xerxes I, launched a full-scale invasion of Greece in 480 B.C., but it, too, was repulsed.

**Alexander and His Successors.** In 334 B.C., Alexander III of Macedon (or Macedonia), the Great, invaded the empire. His defeat of Darius III in 331 B.C. at the Battle of Gaugamela and the burning of Persepolis marked the end of the Achaemenid dynasty and the rise of a new, Greek empire.

Alexander's early death, in 323 B.C., led to years of fighting between his generals, until one of them, Seleucus, established his rule over Alexander's old empire, minus Greece and Egypt, in about 301 B.C. Greek became the official language, but Aramaic remained in use in government administration. In less than a century, however, the Seleucid rulers lost control over the eastern part of the empire, although Hellenic, or Greek, culture remained very strong there. The first to break away from the Seleucids were the Greeks of Bactria (in present-day Afghanistan). They were followed, in about 247 B.C. by the Parthians.

Alexander the Great of Macedon invaded the Persian lands in 334 B.C. His defeat of King Darius III at the Battle of Gaugamela (331) and the burning of Persepolis marked the end of the Achaemenid dynasty, or ruling family, and the rise to power of a Macedonian-Greek empire. The Greeks were succeeded, in turn, by the empire of the Parthians.

This formidable-looking bronze figure depicts a Parthian prince. An Iranian people, like the Achaemenids, the Parthians ruled Persia for nearly 500 years.

**The Parthians.** Like the Persians, the Parthians were an Iranian people and Zoroastrians. But although they followed Achaemenid traditions, the early Parthian rulers were patrons of Greek culture. They used the Greek language on their coins and in their government, which became a union of many local rulers rather than a centralized empire. By the A.D. 100's, however, local culture and the Parthian language had replaced Greek in the Parthian domains.

For more than 300 years, the Parthians were formidable enemies of the Romans. Expert horsemen and archers, they had employed hit-and-run cavalry tactics to destroy a Roman army at the Battle of Carrhae in 53 B.C. Thereafter, Rome's rule ended at the Parthians' western borders, although warfare continued between them. In spite of this, trade and commerce flourished in the Parthian subject kingdoms, most of which were located in Mesopotamia (modern Iraq).

Confronted in the west by the Romans, in the east the Parthians faced nomadic invaders from Central Asia, among them the Kushans, who established a wealthy kingdom in the eastern part of the Iranian plateau. This was to be a historical pattern for the Persians—situated between a strong settled state to their west and nomadic conquerors to their east. A lack of unity among the Parthian rulers led to their decline and to the rise of a new dynasty, that of the Sassanians.

**The Sassanians.** The first great ruler of the Sassanians (or Sasanians) was Ardashir I, who defeated his Parthian overlord, Artabanus, in about A.D. 224, and within a few years had conquered the Parthian lands. His rise to power in the historical homeland of the Persians, Persis (the present Fars province of Iran), parallels that of Cyrus the Great. The Sassanians claimed descent from the Achaemenids, even though they knew about the earlier empire only from legends. They adopted the title of *shahinshah* ("king of kings") for their rulers and re-established a centralized empire, with Zoroastrianism as its official religion.

Ardashir had begun a campaign against the Romans in Mesopotamia. War with Rome continued under his son and successor, Shapur I, who captured the emperor Valerian in battle in A.D. 259. Many of the Roman prisoners were settled in Persia, where they became the nucleus of a Christian community in the empire. The Sassanians fought the Romans many times, and the borders between the two great empires were constantly changing. The eastern part of the empire was also threatened by new invasions from the east.

**Persian Society.** Persian society under the Sassanians was strictly organized into a system of four castes, or classes. At the top were the warriors, or nobility. Below them were the priests; and below the priests were the scribes, or clerks. The fourth and lowest caste was that of the common people, the peasant farmers and workers. This organization of society was the heritage of the ancient Aryan social divisions. Castes later disappeared in Persia but long remained in India, where a related Aryan people had invaded and settled.

---

**SOME NOTABLE PERSIAN RULERS**
**(and their reign dates)**

**Achaemenids**
Cyrus the Great (549–530 B.C.)
Darius I (522–486 B.C.)
Xerxes I (486–465 B.C.)
Artaxerxes III (359–338 B.C.)
Darius III (336–330 B.C.)
**Parthians**
Arsaces I (247 B.C.–?)
Mithradates I (171–138 B.C.)
Artabanus V (A.D. 213–224)
**Sassanians**
Ardashir I (A.D. 224–239)
Shapur I (A.D. 239–272)
Shapur II (A.D. 309–379)
Chosroes I (A.D. 531–579)
Yazdegird III (A.D. 632–651)

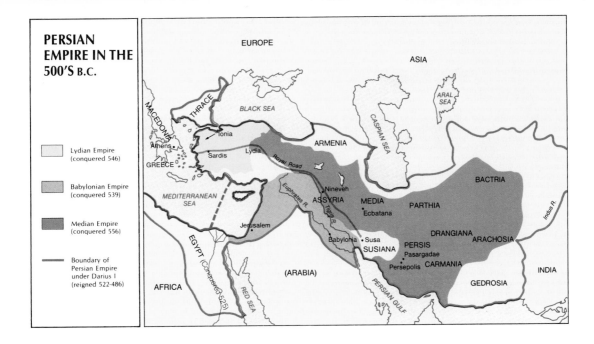

**PERSIAN EMPIRE IN THE 500'S** B.C.

Lydian Empire (conquered 546)

Babylonian Empire (conquered 539)

Median Empire (conquered 556)

Boundary of Persian Empire under Darius I (reigned 522-486)

**Art and Commerce.** The Sassanians followed the style of their time by building in brick, which was more flexible than stone. As a result, intricate decoration became a hallmark of Sassanian architecture, which also included domed roofs. Late Sassanian art was dominated by stylized flowers and geometric designs, while representation of human and animal forms, typical of the Achaemenids, almost vanished. This style continued into the Islamic period, which followed the Sassanians.

During the A.D. 500's, the Sassanians increased their trade with India, exchanging Persian textiles and carpets for Indian spices. The "Silk Road" to China also became more important as the demand for luxury goods increased. Hostilities with their neighbors made commerce profitable only in the most expensive goods.

**Expansion and Decline.** During the long reign of Shapur II, from 309 to 379, the borders of the empire were expanded in the east and west. Under Kavad I, who reigned from 488 to 531, a social and religious revolt led by a priest, Mazdak, threatened the stability of the Sassanian state. The revolt was crushed by Chosroes (or Khosrow) I, who ruled from 531 to 579. Under his reign many reforms of government and society were made and the power of the nobility was checked.

Meanwhile, wars continued with the Byzantine Empire, successor to the Romans, in the west, while the east was overrun by new invaders, the Turks. The constant hostility and fighting between the Byzantines and Sassanians eventually so weakened both empires that they fell prey to a new threat from the south—the Arabs. Infused with the new religion of Islam, the Arabs defeated the Sassanians at the final battle, at Nihavend, in 642. The last Sassanian ruler, Yazdegird III, died in 651. Persia became part of a wider Islamic Empire, and, culturally, one of its most important parts.

RICHARD N. FRYE
Harvard University
Author, *The Heritage of Persia*

See also ALEXANDER THE GREAT; ANCIENT CIVILIZATIONS; BABYLONIA; GREECE, ANCIENT; IRAN; ISLAMIC ART AND ARCHITECTURE; MESOPOTAMIA.

A decorated plate and vessel made of silver and gold are part of the Sassanian artistic heritage.

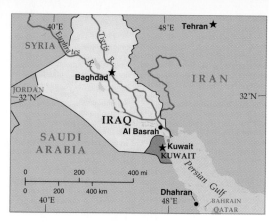

Allied tanks, part of an international coalition of forces led by the United States, liberated Kuwait from Iraqi occupation in the 1991 Persian Gulf War.

# PERSIAN GULF WAR

The Persian Gulf War was a brief but decisive conflict that took place from January to March of 1991. It was fought between Iraq on one side and a large coalition, or alliance, of nations on the other. The anti-Iraqi forces were led and directed by the United States, which provided by far the largest number of troops, aircraft, ships, and arms. The cause of the war was the invasion and occupation by Iraq of Kuwait, its small but wealthy neighbor. The conflict took its name from the location of the two countries on the northwestern shore of the Persian Gulf.

**Background.** Iraq had often been ambitious and aggressive in its relations with neighboring states. An unprovoked attack against Iran in 1980 led to a costly eight-year war. Iraq had made threats against Kuwait on a number of occasions—in 1961, 1973, and in the 1980's. Iraq's claim was that Kuwait should properly be a part of Iraq. This argument was weak, however, since Kuwait has been ruled by the Sabah family since the 1750's, when it was nominally a part of the Ottoman (Turkish) Empire. Iraq, by contrast, had never existed before the 1920's. When the Ottoman Empire, defeated in World War I, broke up, Iraq was created by Britain out of three of its former administrative divisions. Oil, discovered just before the outbreak of World War II, made Kuwait very rich and a tempting prize.

**Invasion and Crisis.** In the spring of 1990, Iraq's leader, Saddam Hussein, began voicing various grievances against Kuwait, mostly connected with the overproduction and price of oil, which threatened Iraq's own oil-based economy. On August 2, 1990, the day after walking out on negotiations, Iraq invaded and quickly overran Kuwait.

Six months of crisis and intense diplomatic activity followed. To counter a possible Iraqi advance southward into oil-rich Saudi Arabia, U.S. forces were dispatched to the region under Operation Desert Shield. International reaction against Iraq's aggression was strong and included most Arab countries. Skillful diplomacy by the United States made possible the passing of resolutions by the United Nations Security Council that condemned Iraq, imposed economic sanctions against it, and finally authorized the use of force. When Iraq ignored the United Nations deadline of January 15, 1991, for withdrawal, the war, code-named Operation Desert Storm, began.

**Course of the War.** The Allied forces were commanded by U.S. General H. Norman Schwarzkopf. The first phase of the war, from January 16 to February 22, consisted entirely of air bombardment of Iraqi military facilities. While destructive, this did not produce any willingness by Iraq to withdraw. In fact, on January 17, Iraq began launching long-range Scud missiles against Israel. The second phase, which began on February 25, was a large-scale ground offensive against Iraqi troops. Dramatically successful, it resulted in the complete liberation of Kuwait by February 27. Hostilities were formally ended on March 2, 1991.

ARTHUR CAMPBELL TURNER
University of California, Riverside
Author, *Ideology and Power in the Middle East*
See also KUWAIT.

**PERSIAN WARS.** See GREECE, ANCIENT.

# PERU

Peru, the third largest country in South America (after Brazil and Argentina), is located on the western coast of the continent. Much of the country lies in the towering, snowcapped Andes, the great mountain range that runs the length of South America.

Peru was once the center of the vast Indian Inca Empire. Conquered by the Spanish in the 1500's, it was a source of great wealth for Spain, which ruled it as part of its own South American colonial empire for almost 300 years.

**Peru, known for its rugged beauty, was once the center of the Inca Empire. Much of the country lies in the central part of the Andes, the world's second largest mountain range. Most Peruvians are descendants of the Incas and other Indian people or are mestizos, persons of mixed Indian and Spanish ancestry.**

## ▶ PEOPLE

Most Peruvians are either descendants of the Incas and other Indian people or are mestizos, persons of mixed Indian and Spanish ancestry. About 10 to 15 percent are of pure Spanish origin. The rest of the population includes descendants of black African slaves who intermarried with Peruvians, and immigrants from China, Japan, Italy, Germany, Britain, and other European and Latin American countries.

The whites and some mestizos live mostly in the coastal cities. Other mestizos live in the highland towns, where they work as storekeepers, teachers, government officials, and technicians.

**Peru**

Spanish, though they may speak Indian languages as well. Most of the people are Roman Catholic, although evangelical Protestantism is increasingly important.

**Education.** Education is free and compulsory for all Peruvian children between the ages of 7 and 16. Almost all towns and villages have primary schools, but high schools and colleges are found mainly in the large cities. The National University of San Marcos in Lima, the capital, is one of the oldest universities in the Americas.

**Housing.** Housing varies according to region. In the cities, some families live in colonial-style mansions with balconies and ornate iron window grilles. But most people live in apartment buildings and row houses. Increasing numbers of people live in squatter settlements around the cities, which include both temporary and permanent dwellings.

In the highlands, houses and buildings are typically made of adobe (sun-dried mud bricks) and have red tile roofs. Houses in the towns are often coated with white plaster. Housing in the Amazon Basin region ranges from brick and mortar buildings in the cities to thatched-roof open shelters in the rural jungle areas.

**Food and Drink.** Peru's cuisine reflects a blend of influences. Traditional foods in the cities include soups, spicy chicken and fish

Many of the Indians also inhabit the highlands. Those who live in the towns often work for the mestizos as servants and laborers. Most learn Spanish and adopt mestizo ways. They are usually called *cholos*.

Other Indians—about 50 different tribes—live in small villages in the Amazon region, which includes the eastern slopes of the Andes and the interior lowland. There they farm, hunt, and catch fish. The Indian peoples of this region have lived in this way for thousands of years. However, the government has tried to develop the area by building airports and roads, which has brought the Indians into contact with other Peruvians. As a result, their ways of life have changed, causing economic and social problems for many.

**Language and Religion.** Spanish and Quechua are the country's official languages. Some people also speak Aymará, another Indian language. Mestizos generally speak

## FACTS and figures

**REPUBLIC OF PERU** (República del Perú) is the official name of the country.

**LOCATION:** Western coast of South America.

**AREA:** 496,222 sq mi (1,285,216 km²).

**POPULATION:** 23,000,000 (estimate).

**CAPITAL AND LARGEST CITY:** Lima.

**MAJOR LANGUAGE:** Spanish and Quechua (both official).

**MAJOR RELIGIOUS GROUP:** Roman Catholic.

**GOVERNMENT:** Republic. **Head of state and government**—president. **Legislature**—single-chamber Congress.

**CHIEF PRODUCTS: Agricultural**—cotton, sugarcane, potatoes, rice, wheat, corn, beans, barley, coca, coffee, livestock, fruits, vegetables. **Manufactured**—paper, textiles, steel, leather goods, processed foods, rubber, petroleum products. **Mineral**—copper, lead, zinc, silver, iron ore, gold, vanadium.

**MONETARY UNIT:** Nuevo sol (new sol; 1 nuevo sol = 100 céntimos).

About 30 percent of Peru's population lives in Lima, its capital and largest city. Lima and other Peruvian cities have grown rapidly in recent years.

dishes, and caramel custard. Among the more popular restaurants are the *chifas*, which serve Chinese-Peruvian style food. In the highlands, the staple food is the potato, which is native to Peru. It is typically served with cheese sauce and local spices.

**Sports and Recreation.** Many people enjoy Peru's beaches along the Pacific Ocean during the summer. Boys often play soccer (called *futbol*), and girls play volleyball (called *voli*). Peru's professional soccer teams and the national women's volleyball team are well known. Horse racing and bull fights are popular, as are golf, tennis, polo, and mountain climbing.

▶ **LAND**

Peru spans the central part of the rugged Andes, which are second only to the Himalayas in altitude. Geological faults, or deep fractures in the layers of rock, run the entire length of the Andean mountain range. These faults have produced many devastating earthquakes. Because the Andean slopes are very unstable, there are also many landslides. Building and maintaining highways is therefore difficult and costly.

**Land Regions.** Peru is bordered by Ecuador, Colombia, Brazil, Bolivia, and Chile and has about 930 miles (1,500 kilometers) of coastline along the Pacific Ocean. It has many ecological and climatic zones, each with its own special plant and animal life. The country has three natural regions: the Pacific coastal area, the Andean highlands, and the Amazon Basin.

The Pacific coastal area is a long, narrow strip of land between the Pacific Ocean and the western slopes of the Andes. This area may have rain only once or twice in ten years. But rivers flowing down from the Andes have deposited fertile soil that has been intensively irrigated for 7,000 years. Most of Peru's large cities and the huge farms where crops are grown for export are in the coastal valleys.

The Andean highlands consist of the lower slopes of the Andes. They have little irrigated land and tend to be sparsely populated. Most highlanders live in a zone that begins at 8,000 feet (2,440 meters) above sea level and extends to 11,500 feet (3,500 meters). This is an area of beautiful valleys suitable for farming.

The region just above this area is rugged and also sparsely populated, except around Lake Titicaca. The Aymará and Quechua peoples who live along its shore sail the lake in reed boats, called *balsas*, to fish.

Between 13,000 and 15,700 feet (3,960 and 4,785 meters) is a region of vast grassy plains, the altiplano. This region is used extensively for grazing cattle and sheep and has few permanent residents. It has freezing temperatures and some light snows in the winter and heavy, unpredictable rains in the summer. Above these plains rise great mountain peaks that are permanently covered with snow and glaciers. Among these peaks is Huascarán, Peru's highest point, which has an elevation of 22,205 feet (6,768 meters).

The lower eastern slopes of the Andes, called the Montaña, and densely forested interior plains form part of the Amazon Basin. This region covers more than half the area of Peru but is sparsely populated. Few roads cross the Andes to link the Montaña with the coast. Many small groups of Indians live along the lakes and rivers throughout the jungle.

**Rivers and Lakes.** Peru's chief rivers are all tributaries of the Amazon. The largest are the Marañón, the Ucayali, and the Huallaga,

forests of this region contain many kinds of valuable trees. The Amazon jungles are also home to a wide variety of plant and animal life. In addition, Peru is rich in minerals. Oil is found in Piura and in the Amazon jungle near the border with Ecuador.

The Peru, or Humboldt, Current surges north from Antarctica and creates one of the world's richest fishing grounds off Peru's coast.

### ▶ ECONOMY

Although Peru's economy greatly declined in the 1980's, it is now one of the fastest growing in Latin America. This has been due in part to strong foreign investment, brought about by the Camisea natural gas pipeline project, gold investments, and abundant cheap labor. However, unemployment is

*Above:* Potatoes, which are native to Peru, are among the crops grown by Indians in the Andean highlands. *Right:* Peru's coastal waters include one of the world's richest fishing grounds.

which flow north and east before joining to form the Amazon. Rivers are the roads and highways of the Amazon Basin.

Lake Titicaca in Peru's southeast corner, on the border with Bolivia, is the largest lake in South America.

**Climate.** Along the Pacific coast the climate is hot and dry in the north and cool and humid farther south. During the cool winters (June to September), the sun rarely shines, and there are heavy fogs and mists. In the Amazon, the climate is hot and humid, and rainfall is heavy throughout the year. In the highlands, the climate is temperate. Rains fall only in the summer, which lasts from December through March.

**Natural Resources.** Water is a precious commodity in the highlands and along the coast. Special irrigation councils control its use for agriculture in many areas, but there are still frequent conflicts between users. In the highlands the Mantaro, Santa, and Urubamba rivers are sources of hydroelectric power for the entire country. The dense

widespread and many Peruvians are still very poor. One of the government's main challenges is finding a way to distribute the country's wealth and resources more equally.

**Services.** Services account for about 65 percent of Peru's economy. Of these, wholesale and retail trade are the most significant.

Tourism is also important. Many tourists are drawn to Peru by its splendid scenery, fascinating pre-Columbian ruins, and interesting peoples. The major attractions are the former Inca capital of Cuzco and the nearby "lost city" of the Incas, Machu Picchu.

**Manufacturing.** Manufacturing accounts for about 25 percent of the economy. Chief export industries are metal refining and smelting and the processing of agricultural and fish products. Other industries include the processing of petroleum products and cement, steel, textile, and clothing production.

**Agriculture.** Traditionally a few wealthy families owned most of the land, including the cotton, sugarcane, and rice plantations on the coast and the grazing lands in the highlands that produced agricultural exports. Today, as the result of government reforms, Indian and mestizo farmers operate many former estates as cooperatives. But the amounts of cotton, sugar, and rice—Peru's major export crops—have decreased.

The Indians of the highlands also grow a variety of crops for their own use, such as potatoes, corn, and plantains, and raise livestock. The native Andean llamas, which belong to the camel family, are used for meat and as beasts of burden in southern Peru. A related animal, the alpaca, is also bred at high altitudes. The Indians spin and weave its wool, as well as sheep's wool, into beautiful ponchos and other clothing.

Llamas, which belong to the camel family, are used in some parts of Peru as beasts of burden.

Many attempts have been made to expand the irrigated areas along the coast. The fertility of the soil in the coastal valleys makes such projects attractive but costly. The government has also tried to open the Amazon jungle for farming and logging. But enormous costs and many environmental problems continue to delay the work.

Peru is also one of the world's largest producers of coca. Although the hardworking Indian farmers have chewed coca leaves for thousands of years (a practice believed to have various health benefits), most of the coca produced now is used to make cocaine. The government has therefore made many efforts to eliminate this crop.

**Mining.** Mining has long been an important part of the Peruvian economy. A variety of metallic minerals are extracted, including copper, silver, and gold. Oil, natural gas, iron ore, coal, phosphate, and potash are also mined.

▶ **MAJOR CITIES**

All cities in Peru have grown rapidly in recent years. Mestizos and *cholos* have moved to the coastal cities from the small highland towns in search of a better life.

**Lima**, the capital, is the most important city in Peru. It is the country's industrial, commercial, artistic, and literary center and offers the greatest opportunities for employment. Greater Lima is the home of almost 30 percent of all Peru's people and has a population of about 7.6 million. An article on Lima appears in Volume L.

**Callao**, near Lima, is the country's leading port. It has a naval school and submarine base. Other important cities include **Trujillo** in the north, known for its historic ruins and beautiful colonial architecture; **Arequipa**, the commercial center of southern Peru; and **Iquitos** in the Amazon Basin. Because it is located in such a dense jungle area, Iquitos can be reached only by river or air.

▶ **CULTURAL HERITAGE**

**Music and Dance.** The music and dance of Peru reflect its ethnic diversity, particularly the mingling of Indian and Spanish traditions. Lively songs and dances called *huaynos*, which are based on ancient Indian music, are very popular. These are often performed by *conjuntos*, or native bands. In the highlands, musicians perform on traditional drums, rattles, flutes, and panpipes, as well as instruments introduced by the Spanish, such as guitars, horns, and mandolins. Music and dance are also an important part of Peru's many festivals.

**Art and Literature.** Peru's rich artistic heritage also reflects combined Indian and Spanish traditions. Mestizo art is particularly common and is represented in architecture, sculpture, ceramics, metalwork, and textiles.

Peruvian literature in the 1800's and early 1900's included a number of novelists and poets. Among the most notable were novelist Ciro Alegría and poet César Vallejo. Since World War II (1939–45), several Peruvian

Men in traditional dress perform during a festival celebrating the Inca winter solstice. Festivals are held throughout the year in Peru to mark important events.

writers have become internationally known. These include Mario Vargas Llosa, Alfredo Bryce Echenique, and Alonso Cueto.

## ▶ GOVERNMENT

Peru is a constitutional republic. The president, who is elected for a 5-year term, is both chief of state and head of the government. The government's executive branch also includes two vice presidents and a council of ministers appointed by the president. Under a constitution approved in 1993, the bicameral (two-house) Congress was replaced by a single-chamber legislature. It has 120 members who are elected by popular vote for 5-year terms.

## ▶ HISTORY

The first people came to what is now Peru at least 12,000 years ago. The oldest known city in the Western Hemisphere is located at Caral, an archaeological site north of Lima.

**Pre-Columbian Peru.** People in the Andes learned to domesticate plants and animals by 5500 B.C. They also discovered how to weave the cotton and wool textiles for which Peru is now famous. By about 3800 B.C., people in Peru had begun to irrigate their crops. A large political and religious cult called Chavín emerged in the highlands around 1500 B.C. and lasted for hundreds of years. The Moche people irrigated large areas around modern

Trujillo about 500 B.C. They also built enormous temples. And they made beautiful pottery and gold and silver objects, which are highly prized by museums today. The Huari and Tiahuanaco empires controlled much of highland Peru and Bolivia by about A.D. 500. These states lasted for about 500 years.

In the 1200's the Quechua-speaking Inca tribe of Cuzco began its conquest of the region. Beginning in 1438 the armies of the Inca emperor Pachacuti and his son Topa Inca Yupanqui conquered much of the Andean area. Eventually the Inca Empire became one of the largest in the world. It stretched from Colombia to central Chile and ruled about 16 million people.

The Incas were famous for their efficient government. They were skilled engineers who built cities, roads, forts, irrigation systems, religious centers, and large suspension bridges to span the Andean chasms. The vast Sacsahuamán fortress, the Coricancha (Sun Temple), and other Inca buildings made of large, beautifully carved stones can still be seen in Cuzco, the Inca capital.

A smallpox epidemic swept the Inca Empire in 1524. It killed millions of people, including the emperor. This led to a government crisis and civil war. The empire was thus disorganized when a small group of Spaniards led by Francisco Pizarro arrived in Peru. Pizarro captured the Inca leader Atahualpa in 1532. Atahualpa was executed in 1533. Later that year the Spanish reached Cuzco, and the largest native American Indian nation came to an end. (For more information, see the article INCAS in Volume I.)

**Colonial Peru.** After the Spanish conquest, the Inca Empire became the Viceroyalty of El Peru, owned by the kings of Spain. Lima, founded by Pizarro in 1535, became the first important Spanish outpost in South America.

During the 289 years of colonial rule, Peruvian society and culture were greatly changed. Spanish became the official language and Catholicism the state religion. Land ownership fell into the hands of a few powerful families. The Indians were afflicted by European diseases and harsh working conditions, and many of them died. There were several Indian rebellions. The most famous was that of Tupac Amaru II, in 1780.

**The Peruvian Republic.** International forces commanded by José de San Martín, of Argentina, declared Peru's independence from Spain in Lima on July 28, 1821. And the Venezuelan general Antonio José de Sucre led rebel troops to victory over the Spanish forces in Ayacucho in 1824. Mestizos and Peruvians of Spanish descent then took charge of the new government and the economy. One unstable regime followed another as military *caudillos* (strong leaders) fought for control. General Ramón Castilla freed the slaves in 1854.

Peru's first civilian president, Manuel Pardo, involved Peru in Bolivia's quarrel with Chile over valuable nitrate deposits in the Atacama Desert. The War of the Pacific (1879–83) ended with the occupation of Peru by Chile. Peru lost substantial portions of its territory to Chile and was left bankrupt.

The economy improved in the late 1800's and early 1900's, under Nicolás de Piérola and Augusto Leguía. The latter also helped re-establish Indian community rights over ancient lands. But his dictatorship provoked rebellion. A new political party, the American Popular Revolutionary Alliance (APRA), was formed in 1924. Its leader, Víctor Raúl Haya de la Torre, played a major role in Peruvian politics until his death in 1979.

Continued demands for modernization and social justice led to the election of Fernando Belaúnde Terry as president of Peru in 1963. Belaúnde began some reforms but was overthrown by the military in 1968.

Peru's military rulers carried out wide-ranging economic and social reforms. The system that bound workers to landowners was abolished, as was tenant farming. New taxes were imposed and Indian communities were reorganized. The government also nationalized many industries. But these reforms did not promote prosperity; instead they increased inflation and brought social unrest.

**Recent History.** Public demand forced Peru's military leaders to accept a new con-

Machu Picchu, high in the Andes, is one of the world's most famous archaeological sites. Historians believe it was built by the Incas in the 1400's.

stitution based on civilian rule. Belaúnde again served as president (1980–85), followed by Alan García Pérez (1985–90). In 1990, Alberto Fujimori won election. Faced with huge economic problems and a spreading Communist guerrilla movement called Shining Path, Fujimori temporarily suspended the constitution in 1992 and ruled with the aid of the army. A new constitution in 1993 paved the way for his re-election in 1995 and 2000. But in November 2000, Fujimori resigned amid charges of federal fraud and went into exile in Japan. Valentin Paniagua served as interim president until 2001, when the opposition leader, Alejandro Toledo, was elected. The following year, to shift power away from the central government, regional presidents were elected to govern each of the country's 24 administrative departments and one province.

Since taking office, Toledo has encountered considerable opposition. He and his family, as well as his advisers, have been involved in a number of scandals.

Meanwhile, Peru's economy continues to improve, despite widespread unemployment. In 2004, discussions were held to create a free trade agreement with the United States.

HENRY DIETZ
University of Texas

**PÉTAIN, HENRI PHILIPPE.** See WORLD WAR II (Profiles: Axis Powers).

# PETER, SAINT

The Roman Catholic Church honors Saint Peter, the Prince of the Apostles, as the first pope. According to the New Testament, he was born in Bethsaida. His original name was Simon, and he was the son of John and the brother of Saint Andrew the Apostle. Matthew's gospel tells how Jesus named Peter. "You are Peter," Jesus said, "and on this rock I will build my church...." The name Peter comes from the Greek *petra*, whose meaning is "rock."

Before he became an Apostle, Peter was a fisherman and lived with his wife in the city of Capernaum. Jesus promised to make Peter and his brother Andrew fishers of men, which meant that, like Jesus, they would try to save men's souls. The two brothers answered Jesus' call to follow him. Peter became the leader of the Apostles and witnessed Jesus' most important miracles.

The New Testament tells how Peter declared his undying love for Jesus at the Last Supper. But Jesus predicted that before the following day Peter would deny him three times. Later that evening Jesus allowed himself to be arrested. Peter fled with the other Apostles and then went to the house where Jesus had been taken. Under questioning, Peter three times denied knowing Jesus. Thus the prophecy was fulfilled.

The New Testament records Peter's great sorrow and repentance for denying Christ. After Jesus' death, Peter's authority as leader of the Apostles continued, and he made many important decisions.

Peter's later life is somewhat obscure. He is known to have visited Antioch and may have made a trip to Corinth. An early and widely believed tradition tells us that Peter made his way to Rome. There he is said to have been crucified during the reign of the emperor Nero, about A.D. 64.

The Catholic Church celebrates two feast days in honor of Saint Peter—his martyrdom on June 29 and the Feast of the Chair of Saint Peter on February 22.

KATHLEEN MCGOWAN
Catholic Youth Encyclopedia

# PETER I (THE GREAT) (1672–1725)

The Russian czar Peter I, commonly known as Peter the Great, introduced radical reforms that transformed a weak and provincial Russia into a great European power. He was born in Moscow on May 30, 1672, the son of Czar Alexis I. At the age of 10 he was named joint czar with his half-brother Ivan, but Ivan's sister Sophia governed for a time as regent. When Ivan died in 1696, Peter became sole ruler.

Peter had legendary qualities. He was keenly intelligent, curious, and energetic. At 6½ feet (200 centimeters), he was remarkably tall and had great physical strength. When he was 17, he embarked on a trip through Europe, where he absorbed the ideals of the new Age of Enlightenment. Forced to return to Russia to put down a revolt, Peter quickly made changes to transform his country. He decreed that Russians adopt western European styles of dress and culture. He established a regular army, strengthened the navy, and encouraged industry. He introduced reforms in government and promoted education among the nobility. Symbolically, he moved his capital from Moscow westward and built a new city—St. Petersburg—to serve as a "window to the west." But Peter could also be cruel and tyrannical. He persecuted clergy members who resisted changes in church traditions. He raised funds by excessively taxing the peasants. And he had his son and heir, Alexis, killed for opposing him.

Peter's victory over Sweden in the Great Northern War (1700–21) greatly enlarged Russian territory and gained a strategically important outlet to the Baltic Sea. In 1721 Peter was given the title of emperor. He died in St. Petersburg on January 28, 1725, and was succeeded by his wife, Catherine I.

Reviewed by ROBERT K. MASSIE
Author, *Peter the Great: His Life and World*

**PETERKIN, JULIA MOOD.** See SOUTH CAROLINA (Famous People).

**PETER PAN.** See BARRIE, SIR JAMES MATTHEW.

**PETERSON, ESTHER E.** See UTAH (Famous People).

**PETRARCH, FRANCESCO.** See RENAISSANCE (Profiles).

# PETROLEUM AND PETROLEUM REFINING

After you have been awakened by the ringing of your plastic alarm clock, you put on clothes made of synthetic fibers. At breakfast, you drink milk that comes from a container coated with wax and you eat an orange that was wrapped in a plastic package. You then ride to school on a bicycle with synthetic rubber tires or in a gasoline-powered car. Although it is still early in the day, petroleum already has played a big part in your life.

Petroleum, or crude oil, is one of the world's most important natural resources. Plastics, synthetic fibers, and many chemicals are produced from petroleum. It is also used to make lubricants and waxes. However, its most important use is as a fuel for heating, for generating electricity, and especially for powering vehicles.

The word "petroleum" comes from the Latin words *petra*, meaning "rock," and *oleum*, meaning "oil." The word is appropriate since petroleum is found in rock formations under the ground. The petroleum found in different areas can vary in appearance, from a thin, clear liquid to a black substance as thick as molasses. It can range in color from reddish to greenish yellow to brown or black. It can also vary in density and in chemical composition. These various characteristics affect the refining process by which petroleum is turned into valuable products, such as gasoline.

▶ **THE ORIGIN OF PETROLEUM**

Petroleum is a fossil fuel that was formed over millions of years by the accumulation and compression of organic, or plant and animal, material. Many of today's land areas were under water millions of years ago. The living things in the water stored the sun's energy in their bodies. When these plants and animals died, their remains sank to the bottom and were covered by sediments, which are tiny particles of rock and mineral. As plant and animal remains settled under layers of sediment, chemicals and bacteria began to break them down. Meanwhile, new sediments continued to accumulate, burying older sediments to great depths. Heat and pressure slowly changed these deep sediments into layers of sandstone, limestone, and other

A derrick on an offshore platform drills for oil in deep reservoirs under the Gulf of Mexico, one of the most important oil exploration areas in the world.

types of sedimentary rock. The tremendous temperatures and pressures also changed the organic materials into petroleum.

Some of the layers of sedimentary rock contained many tiny holes, or pores, which made the rock porous. Over time, oil seeped into the porous rocks and was held there just as water is held in a sponge. These porous rocks are known as reservoir rocks because they contain reservoirs of oil. The oil is trapped in the reservoirs by surrounding layers of clay, salt, or other nonporous materials.

While oil was being formed, the Earth's crust was shifting. Over millions of years, great movements changed the location of old ocean floors and the oil beneath them. Some ocean floors were pushed deeper beneath the sea. Others were raised above the ocean surface and became land areas. Continents gradually changed in size, shape, and appearance. As a result of these changes, oil-bearing layers of rock are now found in various areas, including some that are inland and far from present ocean shorelines. Other oil deposits lie offshore on the continental shelf—the relatively shallow, gently sloping ocean bottom lying between the shorelines and the deeper areas of the oceans.

### ▶ EARLY USES AND EXPLORATIONS

Even in ancient times, petroleum and tar seeped to the Earth's surface at certain places. These seepages, known as oil springs, were easy to locate. People used the oil and tar as medicine, as waterproofing for baskets, and as caulking for ships. They also burned oil in lamps and torches. For the most part, however, petroleum was a curiosity. The richest oil deposits lay deep underground, and there were few clues to their existence on the Earth's surface. The real history of the oil industry began during the 1800's when better lamp fuels were needed to light factories created by the Industrial Revolution.

In the early 1800's, people who were drilling for brine, or salt water, often struck oil, much to their disgust. Such wells were abandoned because at that time there was no demand for the sticky, smelly substance they called "rock oil." Then, in the mid-1800's, George Bissell, a New York lawyer, sent a sample of crude oil to Benjamin Silliman, a chemist at Yale University. Silliman analyzed the substance and reported that petroleum could yield many useful products, including lamp oils, lubricating oils, and wax. Silliman's report, published in 1855, was a milestone in the history of petroleum because it convinced people that profitable businesses could be developed with oil.

In 1857, Bissell and his partner, Jonathan Eveleth, hired Edwin Drake, a retired railroad conductor, to take charge of oil properties they owned near Titusville, Pennsylvania. Drake began to bore a hole near the site of a well-known oil spring there. On August 28, 1859, "Uncle Billy" Smith, a veteran well digger working at the site, saw a dark fluid down in the hole. It turned out to be oil. News of the oil well spread rapidly, and people raced to the area to buy or lease land where oil might be found. The world's first oil rush had begun.

### ▶ LOCATING OIL DEPOSITS

Since the 1800's, scientists have learned much about searching for oil, and technological advancements have made the search easier. The chances of finding oil are now better than ever because new ways to locate oil deposits and new methods of drilling into those deposits have been developed. Scientists first gather information about potential oil deposits. While all oil deposits occur in sedimentary rock, not all sedimentary rock contains oil; only certain sedimentary rock formations offer good conditions for oil accumulation. These types of formations, called **traps**, have an arrangement of rock layers that holds the oil in a limited space and prevents it from further movement (Figure 1).

The most common traps are anticlines, fault traps, and stratigraphic traps. An **anticline** is an arch or dome formed by an upward fold in rock layers. A **fault trap** is a formation caused by a shearing movement in the rock layers, resulting in a porous layer being cut off by a nonporous layer. A **stratigraphic trap** is a rock formation in which porous layers are pinched between nonporous layers. Traps also occur near **salt domes**, which are gigantic underground columns of rock salt forced up from deeply buried salt beds by the weight of overlying rocks. Since oil cannot pass through salt, it is often trapped near rock salt domes.

Aerial photographs are commonly used to speed the search for oil. Taken from airplanes

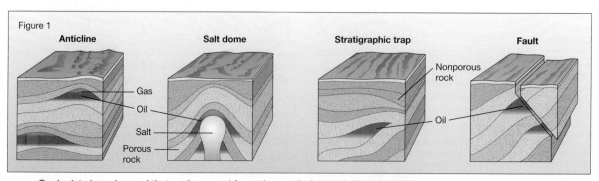

Figure 1

Anticline    Salt dome    Stratigraphic trap    Fault

Gas
Oil
Salt
Porous rock

Nonporous rock

Oil

Geologists have learned that underground formations called traps indicate possible oil accumulation. In each case, porous rock is surrounded by layers of nonporous rock.

in the past, aerial photographs now usually are taken by Earth-orbiting satellites. After examining the photographs, surveyors and geologists make detailed surface maps and collect rocks and fossils in land areas that look promising. By studying fossils, scientists can estimate the age of rocks. They compare this data to what they know about the geologic periods in which oil was formed and add this evidence to data already collected.

Geologists also gather clues to underground rock layers and oil traps by using three basic measuring instruments. The **seismograph**, which measures vibrations of the Earth, is the most widely used device. Geoscientists—scientists who study the Earth—explode dynamite just below the surface or use special trucks that "thump" the surface with heavy weights to create small artificial earthquakes. Large air guns are shot toward the bottom of the ocean to produce a similar effect on the ocean floor. The shock waves from these "earthquakes" move through the Earth and bounce back from the different rock layers. The waves are received by devices called geophones. As each geophone receives the reflected shock waves, it relays an electric current to the seismograph. By collecting a number of such seismic records, scientists are able to map the depth and position of underground rock layers and, possibly, oil traps within them.

The **magnetometer** measures differences in the Earth's magnetism. This information discloses the character of the rock surface on which the layered rocks rest. Fortunately, large magnetic surveys can be made quickly over a wide area by trailing the magnetometer from an airplane.

The **gravity meter** measures differences in gravitational pull in different places on the Earth's surface. Heavy, dense rocks have a greater gravitational pull than lighter, less dense rocks. Thus a salt dome will register a weaker gravitational pull than surrounding sedimentary rocks. Rocks near the surface have a greater pull than the same kinds of rocks at greater depths. Different gravity measurements give further clues to the nature and depth of rock beneath the surface.

Computers have revolutionized the search for oil by making it easier for scientists to process complex seismic data and other information. Computers have also helped them

An oil worker checks the dials of a giant wheel on an oil well's Christmas tree, a collection of steel valves and gauges used to divert crude oil coming out of the ground into a storage tank.

develop more-sophisticated testing techniques. In the past, scientists could create only two-dimensional maps using seismic surveys. With computers, they can create highly detailed three-dimensional maps, improving their ability to locate oil successfully.

After data is gathered and analyzed, scientists can pinpoint places where oil is likely to be found, but only the drilling process can actually locate oil. If the evidence indicates that a site is promising, a decision may be made to drill a "wildcat," or exploratory, well.

▶ DRILLING FOR OIL

When you think about oil drilling, you may picture a tall steel structure—an oil derrick—with black oil gushing out the top. Gushers are a thing of the past. Modern drilling techniques generally prevent oil from "gushing" from a well, thus improving production and protecting the environment around the well.

Today's oil derricks have also been adapted to particular jobs and locations. Some are as tall as a 20-story building. Others are small enough to be attached to trucks that bring them to drilling sites. Some oil derricks are placed on large platforms and barges and used for drilling offshore on the continental shelf.

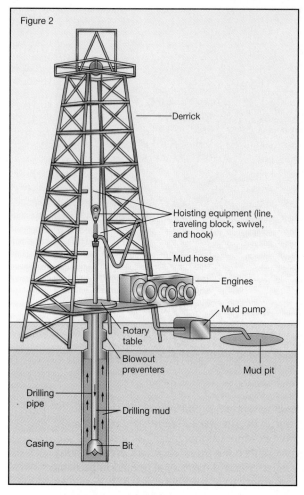

Figure 2

Derrick

Hoisting equipment (line, traveling block, swivel, and hook)

Mud hose

Engines

Mud pump

Rotary table

Blowout preventers

Mud pit

Drilling pipe

Drilling mud

Casing

Bit

A rotary rig uses a rotating bit to cut and crush rock as it drills a hole in the ground.

There are two methods of drilling for oil: cable-tool and rotary. Cable-tool drilling is an older method. In this type of drilling, a heavy, button- or chisel-shaped bit on a cable is raised and then dropped suddenly. When it strikes the ground, the heavy bit literally punches its way through dirt and rock. From time to time, the bit is pulled out of the hole, and the crushed rock is removed. It is used now primarily for drilling shallow wells.

Most modern drilling is done by the rotary method (Figure 2). Rotary drilling utilizes a rapidly turning bit that bores into the Earth. Different bits are used, depending on the type of rock. Most bits have small carbon steel buttons with artificial diamonds on them. Others have three rotating cones. Attached to the drill bit is drilling pipe in 30-foot (9-meter) sections called joints.

In the middle of the derrick is the **rotary table**, a round, flat, steel turntable turned by a powerful motor. This rotates the drilling pipe. When the pipe turns, the bit attached to it cuts into the Earth. As the drill chews its way down, more pipe is attached. Joint after joint is added, and the combined length and weight of the sections make the heavy steel pipe behave like a thin, flexible rod. It takes skill to control the pipe and keep the hole going straight down. The workers who handle this equipment are known as roughnecks.

During "mud-rotary" drilling, a special mixture of water, clay, and chemicals that is called **drilling mud** is pumped down inside the pipe. The mud flows through holes in the bit, cooling and lubricating it. The mud then comes back to the surface between the drill hole and the pipe, carrying chips of broken rock with it. As the hole deepens, the crew adds **casing**, a steel pipe large enough to let the drilling pipe pass through it. After drilling with the first string of casing in place, a second string of casing may be slipped inside the first one. Each string of casing, sometimes several hundred feet long, must be a little smaller than the previous one.

Instead of using drilling mud, some rotary drilling rigs rely on high-pressure air to cool, lubricate, and bring cuttings to the surface. The bit in such an "air-rotary" unit turns and vibrates vertically like a jackhammer. Like cable-tool drilling, this method is most useful for drilling shallow holes less than 3,000 feet (1,000 meters) deep.

Horizontal drilling has become popular for reaching certain oil formations. In this method, drillers steer the drill bit into an oil-bearing formation so that it enters horizontally. This bores a larger hole in the formation, allowing oil to drain more easily than in a vertical well. The use of horizontal drilling also helps recover oil from some difficult-to-reach oil reservoirs.

Along the seacoast, drillers may use a technique called **whipstocking**, or directional drilling, in which workers bend a hole in a wide curve from shore to under the seafloor by changing the angle of the bit at intervals. This allows them to reach offshore oil fields from land.

New technology has allowed drillers to overcome a number of challenges in their work in offshore oil fields. For instance, drilling platforms at sea can now drill for oil in water over 1/2 mile (0.8 kilometer) deep, and they will soon be able to drill in water over 1 mile (1.6 kilometers) deep. These oil rigs are floating platforms anchored to the seafloor on huge cables. Some offshore platforms also have undersea pipeline systems that link them to other offshore wells. Oil from the various wells is sent to one undersea collection point and is then pumped through a pipeline to shore.

Cutting through rock dulls the drill bits, making it necessary to replace them frequently. Rotary bits generally need to be replaced about every 1,850 to 3,600 feet (564 to 1,097 meters). Very hard rock, however, may require new bits as often as every 5 feet (1.5 meters).

After a well has been drilled to a desired depth, engineers evaluate whether there is evidence of enough petroleum to make the well worthwhile to complete. Many times, though, despite promising signs that led to the decision to drill, the hole is dry.

▶ PRODUCING OIL

The most exciting part of oil drilling is bringing in the well, or preparing it to produce oil. The bit and drilling pipe are pulled out of the hole. Casing is run to the bottom of the well and filled with chemical mud. A specialized gun is lowered into the hole to shoot holes through the casing into oil deposits in order to open passages through which oil may flow. Generally, however, nothing happens because the heavy column of mud acts like a liquid cork, preventing entry of oil into the drill hole.

The derrick is then removed and a collection of steel valves and gauges, called a **Christmas tree**, is lowered into place and bolted to the top of the casing. Water is pumped in to thin the heavier mud, which is then pushed out of the hole by natural pressures. When crude oil without water or mud appears, another valve on the Christmas tree is turned, diverting the oil to a pipe connected to a storage tank. Natural gas and brine usually are produced along with crude oil when the well is brought in and are separated from the oil before it leaves the oil field for processing.

In the best wells, oil will flow upward from the oil reservoir as a result of underground pressure. However, as a well ages, this pressure lessens and a pumping mechanism must be installed to produce artificial lift in order to get the oil to the surface.

In the past, oil was allowed to flow at its natural rate or was pumped at the maximum rate possible. Today oil producers try to produce as much oil as they can over the longest period of time. To do this, they hold down production from a well when it begins operating. This helps slow the reduction in natural pressure and generally results in greater long-term production. It was once thought that drilling more wells in an area would increase oil production. Now it is known that drilling fewer wells produces better results. Most modern oil fields have one well for every 40 acres (16 hectares) or more.

Experts estimate that there is between 1.4 and 2 trillion barrels (a barrel is 42 gallons, or 159 liters) of recoverable oil in the world. Recoverable oil is oil that can be brought to the surface economically. Additional oil deposits may exist, but they await discovery or the technology needed to reduce the costs of production. Until recently, only about 30 percent of the oil in a reservoir was recoverable, but new methods now capture more oil from known reservoirs.

When natural production is no longer economical, other methods may be used. One such method involves drilling special wells called service wells into an oil reservoir and injecting natural gas. The pressure of the gas forces more oil into the producing wells. In another method known as water flooding, large quantities of water are injected into the oil reservoir. The water displaces the oil and pushes it toward the producing well. A third method is to inject steam into the reservoir, which causes the heavy oil to flow more freely. Another technique, called fire flooding, injects air into the rock, making it possible to ignite some of the heavy oil. This leaves the remaining oil thin enough for water flooding. Although expensive now, these methods may become more affordable in the future.

In the United States, the largest oil and gas companies not only search for and produce oil, they also transport and refine oil and market petroleum products. Many other companies are also involved in the American oil industry. These independents concentrate on only one segment of the industry, such as oil exploration and production. In most of the rest of the world, large companies, often government owned, control the oil industry. In countries where governments have established their own oil companies, such as in Saudi Arabia, Mexico, and Venezuela, foreign companies are often not allowed to operate.

## ▶ REFINING PETROLEUM

Crude oil is made into useful products through a process called **refining**. A modern oil refinery is a large maze of tanks, spheres, and towers connected by as much as 300 miles (500 kilometers) of pipe. After crude oil is brought to the refinery by truck, tanker, or pipeline, it is changed into other products by a process that involves heating, cooling, chemicals, and pressure.

Petroleum is a mixture of hundreds of different chemicals called hydrocarbons—combinations of hydrogen and carbon atoms—and various impurities. Some hydrocarbons consist of only two or three carbon atoms, while others have thousands strung together in long chains. The hydrogen atoms are arranged in various patterns around these carbon atoms. The more carbon atoms in a hydrocarbon molecule, the thicker and heavier the hydrocarbon. Gasoline consists of a mixture of lighter hydrocarbons. Slightly heavier hydrocarbons make up kerosene and distillate fuel oil. Asphalt, which is often used for paving streets, is composed of very heavy hydrocarbons.

Different hydrocarbons boil at different temperatures, making it possible to separate hydrocarbons by a process called **fractional distillation** (Figure 3). This process involves several steps. First, pipes carry crude oil into a furnace, where it is heated to about 800°F (425°C). The heat causes most of the hydrocarbons in the oil to change into hot vapors. These vapors then pass into a cooling tower, called a fractionating tower, that is hotter at the base than at the top. The tower is divided into a series of trays arranged one above the other. The various hydrocarbon vapors change back into liquids at different temperatures, with each collecting on a separate tray in the tower. The liquids are then drawn off through pipes for further processing.

Although the original crude oil mixture is now separated, further refining is required to obtain different petroleum products. During the distillation process, for example, only 20 percent of each barrel of oil can be made into gasoline. To create more gasoline, the natural proportions of the hydrocarbons in crude oil must be changed. This is done by using **catalysts**, special chemicals that increase the speed of chemical reactions. Together with heat and pressure, catalysts are able to make one kind of hydrocarbon change into another. For example, in a process called **catalytic cracking**, one type of catalyst helps split large hydrocarbons into smaller ones. In a process called **polymerization**, other catalysts transform smaller hydrocarbons into larger ones. It is estimated that more than 500,000 different materials can be made from crude oil. What is actually made, however, depends on what consumers want.

## ▶ TRANSPORTING PETROLEUM PRODUCTS

A vast transportation system exists to transport crude oil to refineries and refined petroleum products to customers. In the United States, for example, about 200,000 miles (322,000 kilometers) of pipelines carry petroleum to refineries and refined products to distribution centers around the country. Most pipelines are underground. One exception is the Alaskan pipeline, an 800-mile (1,288-kilometer) pipeline that carries petroleum from oil fields in northern Alaska to the port of Valdez in southern Alaska. The Alaskan pipeline is above ground in order to prevent damage to the **permafrost**, which is a layer of permanently frozen ground that is found in far northern areas near the Arctic Circle.

Pipelines are the most important means of transporting oil in the United States. One reason for their importance is that they often carry oil long distances. Some oil is also transported by tankers or barges along the coast or up rivers. Trucks transport all the gasoline within the country, but they transport it only for short distances, usually between a distribution center and local gasoline stations.

## ▶ HOW PETROLEUM IS USED

In industrialized societies such as the United States and Canada, there is a great demand for petroleum products. While most often used to produce fuel, petroleum is also used to make lubricants and greases, asphalt and waxes, and various petrochemicals.

Figure 3

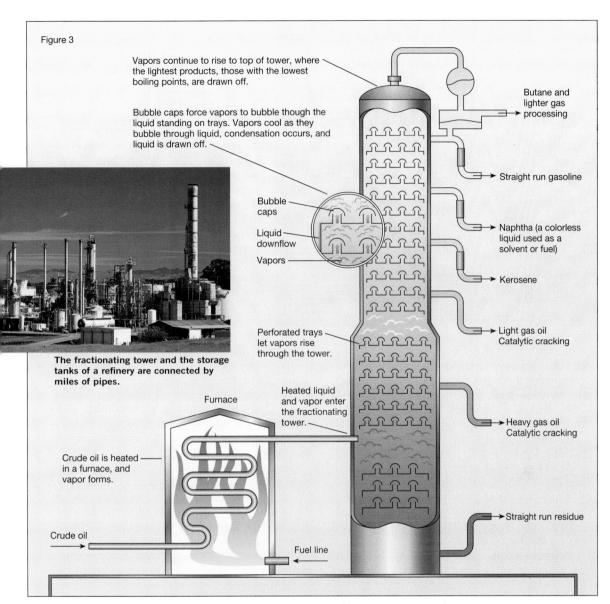

Vapors continue to rise to top of tower, where the lightest products, those with the lowest boiling points, are drawn off.

Bubble caps force vapors to bubble though the liquid standing on trays. Vapors cool as they bubble through liquid, condensation occurs, and liquid is drawn off.

Butane and lighter gas processing

Straight run gasoline

Bubble caps

Liquid downflow

Vapors

Naphtha (a colorless liquid used as a solvent or fuel)

Kerosene

Light gas oil Catalytic cracking

**The fractionating tower and the storage tanks of a refinery are connected by miles of pipes.**

Perforated trays let vapors rise through the tower.

Heavy gas oil Catalytic cracking

Furnace

Heated liquid and vapor enter the fractionating tower.

Crude oil is heated in a furnace, and vapor forms.

Straight run residue

Crude oil

Fuel line

At an oil refinery, crude oil is heated in a furnace, and the resulting vapors are turned back into different liquids at different temperatures in the fractionating tower.

The major fuels derived from petroleum are gasoline, diesel fuels, fuel oils, jet fuels, kerosene, and liquefied petroleum gas, also called bottled gas. The most important of these are transportation fuels used to power cars, trucks, buses, planes, ships, trains, and farm machines. Petroleum-based fuels are also burned for heating, for running industrial machinery, and for generating electricity.

Automobiles use the largest share of the petroleum consumed for transportation. Some kinds of vehicles, such as jet planes and supertankers, consume tremendous quantities of these fuels. A jumbo-sized jet plane, for example, may burn as much as 3,500 gallons (13,248 liters) of fuel during each hour of flight. A supertanker may consume 25,000 gallons (94,625 liters) of fuel oil for each day of operation. On a long voyage, a single ship might consume over 1 million gallons (3.8 million liters) of fuel.

Many different kinds of lubricants and greases are made from petroleum. Some of these products are used for lubricating delicate watch and machine parts. Others are used as lubricants for locomotives and giant

At a modern refinery, crude oil is changed into many useful products by processes that involve heating, cooling, the use of chemicals, and pressure.

electric generators. Different lubricants and greases often are formulated to withstand different types of climates.

Asphalt is a dark, solid or semisolid substance that turns to liquid when heated. Its major use is as a paving material for roads, parking lots, and airport runways. It is also used in the manufacture of roofing materials and in automobile undercoatings.

Waxes obtained from petroleum are used primarily to waterproof packaging, such as milk cartons. Some petroleum-derived waxes are used in making candles.

**Petrochemicals** are chemicals obtained from petroleum or natural gas that can serve as raw materials to make other products. For example, when the petrochemicals benzene and ethylene are reacted together, they produce styrene, a material used to make synthetic rubber, plastic, and latex paint. Although only a small percentage of petroleum ends up as petrochemicals, these chemicals are used to make thousands of different products, including plastics, synthetic rubber, synthetic fibers, paints, and fertilizers.

▶ **PETROLEUM PRODUCERS AND CONSUMERS**

Petroleum is produced in many areas of the world. Yet about half of all this oil must be shipped from where it is produced to where it is needed. As a result, most countries around the world are either oil exporters or oil importers.

The United States uses more oil than any other country, more than 25 percent of the world's total consumption. The nation once consumed an even greater share of the world's oil, but in recent years, petroleum use has grown more slowly in the United States and in other industrialized nations than it has in developing countries around the world.

The United States was one of the first producers of oil, and its oil production grew steadily until 1970. At that time, the nation produced about 20 percent of the world's oil. Since 1970, however, oil production in the United States has fallen. The country remains one of the top oil producers in the world, but because it consumes more than it produces, it must import oil from other countries. Many industrialized nations must also import oil. Japan, for instance, imports almost all the oil it consumes, as do many countries in Europe.

Much of the world's oil is found in undeveloped areas of nonindustrialized countries. Among these are a number of countries in the Middle East, where about 65 percent of the world's known oil reserves are located. These nations produce much more oil than they consume. As a result, they have become major exporters of oil. In 1960 a group of oil exporters formed the Organization of Petroleum Exporting Countries (OPEC). Its members include Algeria, Indonesia, Iran, Iraq, Kuwait, Libya, Nigeria, Qatar, Saudi Arabia, the United Arab Emirates, and Venezuela. Since the early 1980's, OPEC has controlled the price and supply of much of the oil used around the world.

▶ **PETROLEUM FOR TODAY AND TOMORROW**

There is only so much petroleum in the Earth. Once the supply is used up, there will be no more. Several times in the past, people have thought that the supply of oil was about to run out. To everyone's surprise, new oil reserves were discovered and scientists found ways to recover more oil from old oil fields. Such developments have led to increased supplies of oil and better prospects for finding more.

Another important development has been the discovery of new ways to obtain liquid fuels that could substitute for petroleum. These methods include getting liquid fuels from oil shales and tar sands. **Oil shale** is a slatelike rock containing organic matter called kerogen. When oil shale is crushed and heated to about 900°F (480°C), the kerogen changes to a thick liquid, from which crude oil can be extracted. **Tar sands** are sandstones that contain a thick hydrocarbon residue called bitumen. Treating the sands with steam or hot water releases the bitumen. When hydrogen is added to the bitumen, crude oil is produced.

Venezuela has large deposits of bitumen in its Orinoco region and has looked for ways to exploit this vast resource for decades. Recently, Venezuela has begun processing the bitumen into a special heavy fuel oil mixed with water. Known as **Orimulsion**, this fuel is burned in power plants to produce electricity.

Despite Venezuela's success in producing Orimulsion, few attempts to exploit oil shales and tar sands have been able to compete with conventional oil supplies. Until oil prices rise substantially and remain high, the potential of these resources will be limited.

▶ PETROLEUM AND POLLUTION

The quality of our environment is a major concern in today's world. Many efforts are being made to prevent damage to the environment by petroleum and its refined prod-ucts. Some causes of pollution that were common decades ago have been eliminated. In the early days of the petroleum industry, for example, oil wells often had "blowouts," which were sudden and uncontrollable escapes of gas and oil from wells caused by high pressures within the underground oil reservoirs. This no longer happens. Instead, special devices that prevent blowouts save oil from being wasted and prevent the pollution of surrounding areas.

During recent decades, environmental rules and practices have helped prevent pollution in two ways: by controlling how oil is produced, refined, transported, and stored; and by controlling the quality of the refined product that is burned as a fuel.

Environmental rules also dictate how to prevent pollution from an oil well after it is no longer producing and how far apart oil wells should be. The disposal of by-products of drilling, including drilling mud and brine, are also carefully controlled.

Oil refineries once produced great amounts of air and water pollution. However, now they must obey many regulations that prevent or greatly reduce the output of pollutants during the refining process. For example, before water used in refining can be returned to waterways, it must be purified and cooled.

Serious environmental problems can result if oil is spilled into the sea by oil tankers. Oil spills can injure or kill fish, marine animals, and aquatic birds. They can also foul beaches and damage microscopic organisms living in

A tanker takes on some of the unspilled oil from the *Exxon Valdez*, which ran aground in Alaska's Prince William Sound in 1989. The oil spill that resulted was the largest ever to occur in U.S. waters.

Oil pollution is a serious problem. Onshore workers use hoses to clean up oil and other debris from an oil spill (*left*). Medical workers treat a duck that was injured during an oil spill at a refinery in Fidalgo Bay, Washington (*below*).

tidal basins. Such damage can be overcome in time, but the speed of recovery depends on various factors, including the type of oil spilled, the depth of the water, and the action of the waves. Oil spills can affect not only the environment, but also industries, such as fishing and tourism, that depend on the sea.

Rules to prevent pollution from oil spills have become stricter since a tanker spilled 11 million gallons, or 258,000 barrels, of oil into Alaska's Prince William Sound in 1989. Companies must now pay heavy penalties for spills or careless practices that can lead to spills. Shipowners must replace existing tankers with ships that have double hulls. If a hole is poked in the outer hull by running aground or by hitting an obstacle, the inner hull helps prevent oil from leaking out. Since these rules have gone into effect, pollution from oil spills has declined in the United States.

Because burning petroleum products can also cause pollution, the quality of fuels is also controlled. For example, environmental rules require gasoline to evaporate more slowly in the summer to prevent smog and other forms of air pollution. In some areas, gasoline must contain more oxygen in winter in order to prevent carbon monoxide pollution. Beginning in the mid-1970's, pollution-preventing devices that run only on unleaded gasoline were installed on many cars in the United States. Since then, new knowledge about the dangers of lead have resulted in the banning of leaded gasoline. In 1995 some

regions of the United States also began using a new kind of low-pollution fuel known as reformulated gasoline.

Other petroleum products must also meet stricter environmental standards. Many rules, for example, limit the amount of sulfur that petroleum products can contain. To produce low-sulfur products, refiners must use more expensive low-sulfur crude oils that are low in natural sulfur, or they must remove the sulfur with special processes. Sometimes they must do both. These strict environmental rules allow people to continue using petroleum products and protect the environment at the same time. Other less-polluting fuels may become widely available in the future. For now, such fuels would be too expensive to compete effectively with petroleum.

CHERYL J. TRENCH
Executive Vice President
Petroleum Industry Research Foundation, Inc.
SCOTT ESPENSHADE
Independent Petroleum Association of America

See also DISTILLATION; ENERGY SUPPLY; FUELS; GASOLINE; KEROSENE; ORGANIZATION OF PETROLEUM EXPORTING COUNTRIES (OPEC).

## PETS

If a creature is four-footed or two-footed, or if it flies, swims, crawls, or hops, you can be sure that someone at some time has made a pet of it. Interesting pets from all over the world have won places in the homes and hearts of people who keep animals for pleasure.

Of all the animals, the domestic cat and dog continue to hold the preferred places around the family hearth. The dog is still the favorite animal out-of-doors.

### ▶MAMMALS AS PETS

Mammals are animals that have backbones and nourish their young with milk. They include domestic and wild animals. Among the small domestic mammals are dogs, cats, rabbits, guinea pigs, mice, and hamsters.

There are over 100 breeds of dogs from which to choose. Your choice of a dog should depend upon whether you live in the city or in the country. If you live in the city, you will be wise to have one of the smaller breeds, such as a pug, cocker spaniel, or Pekingese or a small mixed breed if you do not wish to buy a purebred dog. If you live in the country, you may enjoy one of the hounds, a sporting dog, a terrier, or maybe one of the working dogs, such as a Newfoundland or a boxer. These dogs require considerable exercise, which they can have easily in the country.

Most dogs are easy to feed and to train. They are naturally meat eaters but will thrive on good-quality prepared dog foods, which can be bought in any market.

All dogs should be inoculated against distemper, hepatitis, leptospirosis, and parvovirus when they are puppies. They should receive boosters every year.

There are many kinds of domestic cats, and most of them are easy to care for. Feeding has been simplified by commercial cat foods. Consider the several breeds—long-haired and short-haired—and pick the one that appeals most to you. But remember that long-haired cats, such as the Persian, must be combed frequently. All cats should be inoculated against cat distemper.

Rabbits breed readily in cages and eat a simple diet of hay, greens, and rabbit pellets, which are small bits of compressed food, ob-

Above: Puppies of almost any breed are firm favorites with children. Below: Short-haired Siamese cats are very popular pets.

A green Amazon parrot. Parrots and parakeets, if properly trained, can often repeat phrases that they hear.

flower seeds, apples, and carrots. Both hamsters and gerbils reproduce very rapidly.

Mice, in their great variety of colors, make particularly interesting pets. There are many sizes, and some are fat and some are thin. These pets should be kept in a cage and should have an exercise wheel. They breed rapidly and tame easily. If you decide to have mice as pets, clean the cage frequently, or the odor will be very unpleasant. Feed your mice hamster food and let them drink from a tube attached to a bottle.

▶ FEATHERED PETS

If you are thinking of a bird as a pet, you will find an interesting variety from which to choose. Domestic bird pets are parakeets, canaries, pigeons, finches, chickens, parrots, mynas, ducks, and geese.

Chickens, ducks, and geese are often tamed, but bantam chickens are those usually kept for pets. They range from tiny to larger varieties, and there are long-legged, short-legged, bare-legged, and feather-legged breeds.

Pigeons are fun to own if you have the space. They are raised outdoors in lofts or pigeon houses. There are dozens of fancy varieties with differing features. These varieties include tipplers, which fly high in kits, or schools, for hours at a time; tumblers, which fly up and do somersaults in the air; parlor tumblers, which somersault close to the ground; and racing homers, which return home from distances as great as 1,600 kilometers (1,000 miles) and are used in sport.

Parakeets are little birds that talk, if properly trained. They are simple to care for and can be permitted freedom of the house. They eat a standard seed diet, which is available even in grocery stores, and they enjoy some greens, too. Many thousands are bred for sale and for show, and new varieties in size and color are being produced.

Like parakeets, parrots make entertaining pets because of their ability to mimic human speech. But parrots need much more care and attention than parakeets do. A parrot's living quarters must be larger, and its seed diet must be supplemented with protein foods, fruits, and greens.

It should be pointed out that pigeons, parakeets, and parrots can pass on to people a

tainable at pet stores. Since they stand cold weather well, they can be kept outdoors. Rabbits can be housebroken and make fine indoor pets. Their soft fur makes them particularly endearing.

Guinea pigs (cavies) are fascinating creatures, although some people object to the sharp, loud whistling sound that they make. They come in many colors, with short, wiry or very long hair, depending upon the breed. The young of the guinea pig look quite mature directly after birth. They nurse, but they also eat adult food almost immediately. In the wintertime guinea pigs need some artificial heat. Thousands of guinea pigs are bred and exhibited for prizes at pet shows. If you don't mind their whistling, you can have great enjoyment from raising guinea pigs.

Hamsters and gerbils are also popular pets. Hamsters can be fed prepared food, some raw vegetables, nuts, and grains. Gerbils originated in the dry, sandy regions of Africa and southwestern Asia. They need water. But because of their desert background, they need relatively little. Their diet may include sun-

serious disease. This disease, called psittacosis, or ornithosis, is an infection like pneumonia. Anyone who handles sick birds or cleans their cages is in danger of catching it. Sometimes an infected bird will not appear to be very sick. For this reason a bird with any sign of illness should be checked immediately by a veterinarian. The bird should be cared for by the veterinarian until it is well. People who catch the disease are treated with antibiotics.

Canaries are pleasant pets, and many of the males are lovely songbirds. The females are not singers. There are many breeds and colors. Some are yellow, some green, some shaded with red. Canaries are easy to keep. They, too, eat seeds and greens. Cages can be bought at pet stores.

Myna birds, which are natives of India, make interesting pets. The hill myna is the most satisfactory. With patient training they can become wonderful talkers. Some have considerable vocabularies, and some whistle tunes. Their favorite diet is fruit, but they also eat meat, insects, eggs, and bread.

### ▶WATER PETS

Among the many fish of the world, only four kinds are domestic pets. These four are goldfish, Roman eel, carp, and paradise fish. The goldfish bred under domestic conditions has been greatly changed into many forms by selection. All the other fish kept in aquariums (glass tanks) are natural wild species but are adaptable and easily tamed. Fish fall into two classifications—warm-water and cold-water species. This fact should guide the choice and treatment of fish.

Goldfish are carp that are not always gold. Some are silver, some black, some mixtures of colors. They are best kept in water with a temperature of about 15°C (60°F). If there is enough aeration, they will live in ponds that freeze over in winter. They eat aquarium plants, as well as worms, daphnia (water fleas), chopped beef, and liver.

Of all aquarium fish the tiny guppy is the most popular. The guppy comes in a great variety of colors and shapes. Guppies bear live young instead of producing eggs.

You can net some wild fish and make pets of them. Baby bullheads, minnows, and several other species will live in captivity if you

Fish kept as pets range from ordinary goldfish to tropical fish in brilliant colors.

simulate (copy) their natural habitat. The food and the temperature of the water must be the same as in nature.

Turtles, especially box turtles, can be kept in backyards. They will thrive on worms, slugs, and other garden pests. They learn to know their owner and will come for food, which may be bread, meat, angleworms, or mealworms. They will drink from a pan sunk in the ground and filled with water. If a male and a female are kept, the female will lay eggs from which baby turtles will hatch.

### ▶HOW TO CARE FOR PETS

A pet is not a plaything but a living creature that depends on its owner for its very life. There are different requirements for the care of various kinds of pets. Here is a list of general suggestions that can be applied to the care of almost any pet:

**(1)** It should have fresh water every day, always within easy reach.

**(2)** The pet must have regular feeding times but must never be overfed. It must be housed in clean living quarters.

**(3)** Above all, each pet owner should learn how to take care of the pet's special needs and to handle it gently.

LEON F. WHITNEY
Author, *Complete Book of Home Pet Care*

See also BIRDS AS PETS; CATS; CATS, WILD; DOGS; FISH AS PETS; GUINEA PIGS, HAMSTERS, AND GERBILS.

**PEWTER.** See TIN.

**PHENYLKETONURIA (PKU).** See DISEASES (Descriptions of Some Diseases).

# PHILADELPHIA

In 1682, the Englishman William Penn founded a city on the Delaware River in southeastern Pennsylvania where he and his fellow Quakers could practice their religion freely. Penn named the place Philadelphia, meaning "brotherly love" in Greek. This "greene countrie towne," as he called it, became one of the world's most influential cities.

Philadelphia was settled 75 years after Jamestown, Virginia, and 62 years after Plymouth, Massachusetts. But it was in Philadelphia that the United States was truly born. The historic sites encompassed in Independence National Historical Park alone include Independence Hall, where the Declaration of Independence was signed, the Constitution was written, and the Liberty Bell first rang out; Congress Hall, in Independence Square, where Congress met when Philadelphia was the nation's capital (1790–1800); Carpenters' Hall, where the first Continental Congress met; Christ Church and Burial Ground, where Benjamin Franklin is buried; and Library Hall of the American Philosophical Society. Nearby are the Betsy Ross House, where the first American flag may have been made, and Elfreth's Alley, one of the oldest streets in the United States. Philadelphia was also the site of the first American hospital, the first American medical college, the first women's medical college, the first paper mill, the first bank, the first daily newspaper, and the first U.S. mint.

## The City Today

Philadelphia originally covered about 2 square miles (5 square kilometers). Today it is a great metropolis covering about 135 square miles (350 square kilometers). With approxi-

mately 1.5 million residents, Philadelphia is the nation's fifth most populous city. More than 6 million people live in the greater metropolitan area, which includes parts of New Jersey and Delaware.

Industries in Philadelphia produce electrical machinery, chemicals, pharmaceuticals, medical instruments, and transportation equipment. Other important enterprises include printing and publishing, food processing and distribution, health services, telecommunications, and business, legal, and financial services. The Philadelphia Naval Shipyard, once the city's largest employer, closed in 1995. It is now the site of the Philadelphia Naval Business Center.

Philadelphia is also a major port city, located on the Delaware River, which connects to the Atlantic Ocean. The port of Philadelphia and Camden is one of the largest, busiest, and best-equipped ports in the United States.

Philadelphia's skyline features both modern skyscrapers and historic buildings.

City Hall, crowned with a statue of William Penn, rises behind Swann Fountain in the heart of Philadelphia, one of the most historically significant cities in the United States.

The city's downtown area features several large shopping malls, including the Gallery and the shops at Liberty Place; the Avenue of the Arts, lined with theaters, music clubs, and restaurants; and Society Hill, the largest concentration of restored residences from the 1700's in the United States.

The city is the home of fine cultural institutions. The Philadelphia Orchestra is internationally famous. The Pennsylvania Academy of the Fine Arts, the nation's oldest art institution, has exhibits of painting, sculpture, and graphic arts. The Philadelphia Museum of Art and the Rodin Museum are among the finest art museums in the world. The Franklin Institute Science Museum and Planetarium is one of the leading museums of its kind. The American Philosophical Society, which was founded by Benjamin Franklin in 1743, is the oldest learned society in the United States. The Academy of Natural Sciences, the first natural history museum in the United States, has nature exhibits, live-animal shows, and a children's museum.

Philadelphia is also a center of education. The University of Pennsylvania and Temple University are among its many well-known institutions. The city is also an important medical center, known for many excellent hospitals and schools of medicine, dentistry, pharmacy, and veterinary medicine.

Amateur sporting events in Philadelphia include the Penn Relays, a track-and-field meet sponsored by the University of Pennsylvania. The city is also home to several professional sports teams: The Philadelphia Phillies of baseball's National League and the Philadelphia Eagles of the National Football League play in Veterans Stadium. The Phila-

*Above:* Elfreth's Alley, opened in 1703, is one of the oldest streets in the United States. Many of Philadelphia's older neighborhoods are lined with narrow lanes filled with beautifully preserved houses.

*Left:* The Liberty Bell, a treasured symbol of American independence, is located in Independence National Historical Park, Philadelphia's most popular tourist site.

delphia Flyers of the National Hockey League and the Philadelphia 76ers of the National Basketball Association play in First Union Center. For general recreation, Fairmount Park, one of the world's largest city parks, offers golf courses, trails for riding and hiking, and winter ice-skating areas. It also contains the Philadelphia Zoo, the oldest zoo in the country. The Schuylkill River, which runs through the park, is favored for crew races and other recreational activities.

Reviewed by JOAN WELSCH
Greater Philadelphia Chamber of Commerce

# PHILIP

Philip is the English translation of a Greek name that means "lover of horses." Many European kings have reigned (r.) under this name. The French rulers were called Philippe. The Spanish were known as Felipe.

### ▶ KING OF MACEDONIA

**Philip II** (382–336 B.C.) (r. 357–336 B.C.), the father of Alexander the Great, laid the foundation for his son's later success in conquering much of the known civilized world. Philip united Macedonia, strengthened his army, and defeated his neighbors before intervening in central Greece and defeating the Athenians at Chaeronea in 338 B.C.

### ▶ KINGS OF SPAIN

**Philip II** (1527–98) (r. 1556–98), the only son of Holy Roman Emperor Charles V, ruled the Spanish Empire at the height of its power and influence. An eager supporter of the Catholic Counter Reformation, Philip battled Muslims in the Mediterranean and Protestants in northern Europe. He lost power in the Netherlands after the Dutch provinces revolted in 1566. Later he intervened against the Protestant Huguenots in the French Wars of Religion. In 1588 he unsuccessfully opposed the Protestant Queen Elizabeth I of England, whose navy defeated Philip's famed Armada. But within Spain he strengthened royal authority and kept the peace. In 1565, Spain settled the Philippines, which was named for him. He was succeeded by his son, Philip III.

An illuminated manuscript from the Middle Ages shows the future King Edward II of England paying his respects to King Philip IV of France.

**Philip V** (1683–1746) (r. 1700–24; 1724–46), the first Spanish king of the Bourbon dynasty, was a grandson of the French King Louis XIV. In 1700, Philip inherited the Spanish throne from his great-uncle, the childless King Charles II. Fearing the combined forces of France and Spain, several other European countries waged the War of the Spanish Succession (1701–14) to limit the growing power of the Bourbon family. When the war ended, Spain lost all of its territorial possessions in Europe. In 1724, Philip gave up his throne to his son Louis, who died soon after. Philip then reoccupied the throne. He was succeeded by another son, Ferdinand VI.

### ▶ KINGS OF FRANCE

**Philip II** (1165–1223) (r. 1180–1223), son of Louis VII, was known as Philip Augustus. During his reign, he greatly expanded French territory at England's expense and turned France into one of the strongest states in Europe. After taking part in the Third Crusade (1190–92) with King Richard I of England, Philip attacked Richard's French territories of Aquitaine and Normandy and later those of Richard's successor, King John, whose forces were driven from Normandy, Maine, Anjou, Touraine, and Poitou. Philip consolidated his success by defeating John's ally, Holy Roman Emperor Otto IV, at Bouvines in 1214. Philip was succeeded by his son, Louis VIII.

**Philip IV** (1268–1314) (r. 1285–1314), known as Philip the Fair, succeeded his father, Philip III. Disputes over taxation of the clergy led Philip to challenge the power of Pope Boniface VIII. In 1303, after winning wars against England and Flanders, Philip had Boniface arrested and then installed a French archbishop as Pope Clement V in the French city of Avignon. Philip then proceeded to persecute the Knights Templar, a religious and military order, probably to gain access to their vast wealth and landholdings. Philip was succeeded by his son, Louis X.

JEREMY BLACK
University of Exeter

**PHILIP, KING (METACOMET).** See MASSACHUSETTS (Settlement and Colonial Days).

**PHILIP, PRINCE.** See ENGLAND, HISTORY OF (The Monarchy in Recent Times).

# PHILIPPINES

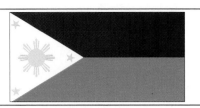

The Philippines is an island nation situated off the southeastern coast of Asia. It encompasses about 7,100 islands that extend approximately 1,100 miles (1,800 kilometers) along the western edge of the Pacific Ocean. Most of the Philippine islands are small and uninhabited. The vast majority of the people live on the eleven largest islands, two of which—Luzon and Mindanao—contain more than two-thirds of the country's land area.

Located at a crossroads between East and West, the Philippines has been influenced by both Asian and Western cultures. An Asian land, it was acquired in the early 1500's by Spain, which brought European traditions and the Christian religion to the islands. After Spain's defeat in the Spanish-American War in 1898, the Philippines was ceded to the United States, which governed it for 48 years. The people of the Philippines gained their independence on July 4, 1946.

## ▶ PEOPLE

Most people of the Philippines are Malayo-Polynesian and are closely related to the people of Malaysia and Indonesia. In appearance, they are usu-

ally of medium height, with brown skin and straight black hair. Their ancestors migrated to the Philippines by boat in ancient times. Chinese make up a small minority of Filipinos. Some Spaniards and Americans also live in the Philippines.

The Philippines has one of the highest rates of population growth in Asia. About half the people live on Luzon, the largest island. About 70 percent live in rural areas, though in recent years many people have moved to the cities, especially to the large metropolitan area of Manila, the capital, on Luzon.

**Language.** The ancestors of the Filipinos settled in different parts of the islands and were often isolated from each other by the sea and mountains. As a result, many differ-

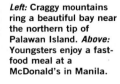

*Left:* **Craggy mountains ring a beautiful bay near the northern tip of Palawan Island.** *Above:* **Youngsters enjoy a fast-food meal at a McDonald's in Manila.**

# Philippines

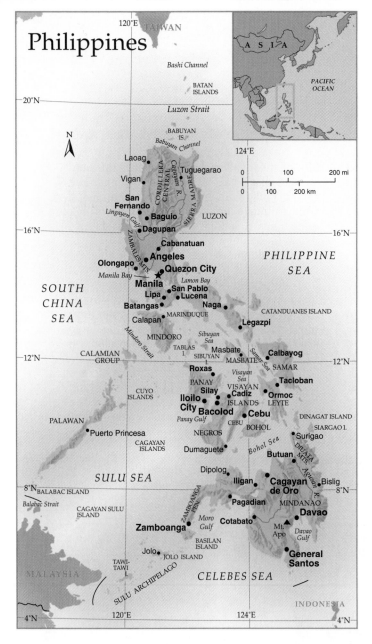

**Religion.** The Philippines is the only country in Asia with a predominantly Christian population. The development of Christianity resulted from Spanish rule of the islands. More than 80 percent of Filipinos are Roman Catholics; 9 percent are Protestants. There are also a small number of Buddhists. Other non-Roman Catholic religions include the Philippine Independent Church (*Aglipayan*), founded in 1902, and the *Iglesia ni Kristo* (Church of Christ), founded in 1914.

Filipinos living in the southernmost islands had been converted to Islam (the religion of the Muslims) centuries before the arrival of the Spaniards. Today Muslim Filipinos, sometimes called *Moros* by the Christians, make up about 5 percent of the population. Most live in southern Mindanao and the Sulu Archipelago. Freedom of religion and separation of church and state are guaranteed to all by the Philippine constitution.

**Education.** The Philippines has one of the highest reported literacy rates in Asia. About 95 percent of the people are able to read and write. Public education consists of four years of primary school, two years of intermediate school, and four years of high school. Public school attendance is compulsory through the first four grades. Pilipino is a required language of instruction in primary schools. English is also taught and spoken widely.

The oldest university is the University of Santo Tomás, founded in 1611, in Manila. Other universities in Manila include the University of the Philippines, Ateneo de Manila University, and De La Salle University. Silliman University is located in Negros Oriental, and San Carlos University in Cebu. The Asian Institute of Management in Makati is known for graduate studies in business.

**Way of Life.** There are marked economic and lifestyle differences between persons leading cosmopolitan lives and those living in a more rural or traditional manner.

In big cities, such as Manila, many Filipinos appear to live much like people in the United States. They speak English and Pilipino and

ent languages developed. More than 80 languages are spoken in the Philippines. Many rural Filipinos are fluent only in their local language.

In order to create a common language, the government adopted Pilipino as a national language. Pilipino is based on Tagalog, one of the major Philippine languages, although other Philippine languages are evident. In conversation, Pilipino may be freely mixed with English. Both Pilipino and English are official languages.

dress in Western-style clothing. They attend good schools and live in modern houses. Children often become Girl Scouts and Boy Scouts. Basketball is the most popular sport.

Most Filipinos live in small towns (*poblaciones*) or villages (*barrios* or *barangay*). Their houses are often built on bamboo stilts, with nipa and bamboo walls and roofs thatched with nipa palm leaves. Many houses lack electricity and running water. People often earn their living by fishing, farming, and casual labor. There are often five or more children in a family.

▶ **LAND**

The Philippines is located in the western Pacific Ocean, northeast of Borneo and south of Taiwan. The nation's land area is about the same as that of the state of Arizona.

There are three main island groups in the Philippines. The Luzon group in the north contains the islands of Luzon and Mindoro. The central group contains Palawan Island in the west and the Visayan Islands (including Bohol, Cebu, Leyte, Masbate, Negros, Panay, and the Samar islands) in the east. The Mindanao group in the south is composed of Mindanao and the Sulu Archipelago, which extends southwest toward Borneo.

Luzon is the largest island. Northern Luzon has high mountains. Central Luzon is a wide plain, where rice and sugarcane are grown. The island also has many active volcanoes. Mount Pinatubo, in central Luzon, erupted in 1991, causing extensive damage. Mount Mayon, in the southeast, last erupted in 2000.

The second largest island is Mindanao. Mount Apo, the highest peak in the Philippines, is located there. Mindanao has some good ports, such as Zamboanga and Davao.

Corn is grown on many islands in the Visayan group. On Negros, which is known as the sugar bowl of the Philippines, there are vast sugarcane fields in the western plains.

**Rivers.** The Cagayan River in northeastern Luzon is the longest river in the Philippines. The Pampanga and Agno rivers on Luzon and the Agusan and Pulangi (Rio Grande) rivers on Mindanao are important as sources of waterpower. However, these rivers are too short or turbulent for commercial navigation.

**Climate.** The annual rainfall of the Philippines averages more than 80 inches (2,030 millimeters). Typhoons (called *bagyos* in Pilipino) happen most commonly between July and November. Their strong winds and heavy rains often cause great damage. Earthquakes also occur. Annual temperatures average 75 to 85°F (24 to 29°C).

**Natural Resources.** Most soils in the Philippines are tropical and not very fertile. The richest soils are in the central plain and Cagayan River valley of Luzon and in parts of Mindanao. Heavy rainfall and improper use of the land has caused serious erosion.

As late as 1980, forests covered half the Philippines. But because of illegal commercial exploitation and slash-and-burn agriculture, it is estimated that only about one-third of the country is now forested. Types of vegetation reflect elevation and climate. Nipa palm and mangrove swamps are found in the coastal region. In the lowland areas are tropical rain forests. Many trees found there are of commercial value.

Rare orchids and tropical plants are plentiful in the rain forests. Other areas of the Philippines produce flowers and plants of exquisite beauty. The national flower is the sweet-smelling *sampaguita*, reminiscent of the honeysuckle in the United States.

---

## FACTS and figures

**REPUBLIC OF THE PHILIPPINES** (Republika ng Pilipinas) is the official name of the country.

**LOCATION:** Southeast Asia.

**AREA:** 115,600 sq mi (299,404 km²).

**POPULATION:** 79,000,000 (estimate).

**CAPITAL AND LARGEST CITY:** Manila.

**MAJOR LANGUAGES:** Pilipino (national language), English.

**MAJOR RELIGIOUS GROUPS:** Christian, Muslim.

**GOVERNMENT:** Republic. **Head of state and government**—president. **Legislature**—Congress (consisting of the Senate and the House of Representatives).

**CHIEF PRODUCTS: Agricultural**—rice, corn, coconut products, sugarcane, bananas, tobacco, peanuts, livestock. **Manufactured**—processed food, textiles, pharmaceuticals, chemicals, wood products, assembled automobiles, electronics equipment, glass, rubber and steel products. **Mineral**—chromite (chromium ore), nickel, copper, manganese, iron ore, silver, gold.

**MONETARY UNIT:** Peso (1 peso = 100 centavos).

A rice farmer uses a water buffalo to pull his plow. Rice, the most important food crop in the Philippines, is grown on Luzon and other islands.

Many wild animals—such as the civet, mongoose, Malayan badger, porcupine, wild tamarau (small buffalo), and long-tailed monkey—live in the Philippines. There are about 1,000 varieties of birds, including brightly colored parrots. Lizards abound in the country. Over 2,000 species of fish inhabit Philippine waters, but this resource is threatened by overfishing and the destruction of the coral reef ecosystem.

## ▶ ECONOMY

The Philippines is mainly an agricultural nation, although it is developing other industries. About 40 percent of the labor force is engaged in agriculture or related industries.

**Services.** Service industries employ almost 18 percent of the Philippine labor force. Much service work is closely associated with agriculture, the export trade, and domestic services, such as gardening and housekeeping.

**Manufacturing.** Manufacturing is dominated by the processing of agricultural products, although Filipinos are now producing more consumer goods, such as clothing. Light industry, such as food processing, is also expanding. Industry is concentrated in the area around Manila and is growing in Cebu City. A large industrial complex has been built in Mindanao. Less than 10 percent of the labor force is engaged in manufacturing.

**Agriculture.** Rice, the most important food crop, is grown on many islands. Corn is also important, especially in the Visayas. Copra (dried coconut meat), sugarcane, and abaca are the chief cash crops. Copra is produced mainly in southern Luzon, Mindanao, and the Visayas. Abaca, or Manila hemp, a fiber used to make ropes, is raised in southeastern Luzon and southern Mindanao. Tobacco, bananas, sweet potatoes, and peanuts are also grown.

Livestock raising is also important to the economy. Cattle, hogs, goats, sheep, chickens, ducks, and turkeys are raised. Carabao (water buffalo) are used to pull plows.

**Trade.** The Philippines is a major exporter of skilled labor to the United States, the Middle East, and Europe. Money sent home from Filipinos working abroad is a significant source of foreign exchange earnings and an important contributor to many native Filipino household incomes.

Leading exports include electronic products and components and apparel. The chief trading partners of the Philippines are the United States, Japan, the European Union, and Singapore.

**Transportation.** In a nation of islands, water transportation is very important. Numerous inter-island shipping lines operate out of Manila to hundreds of Philippine ports. Many Filipinos use small homemade boats to travel from one part of an island to another or to nearby islands.

Roads are often unpaved and are difficult to use during the monsoons. Buses and trucks are the most common vehicles for travel on the islands. Railroad traffic is insignificant. The main islands of the country are connected by domestic air service. International airports are located in Manila and Cebu.

**Communication.** The Philippines is in the process of developing a modern communication system. There are more than 260 radio stations and 31 television stations. Internet service providers are found in Manila and Cebu City.

## ▶ MAJOR CITIES

**Manila** is the capital, largest city, leading port, and most important commercial and industrial center of the Philippines. Located on Luzon, it was founded by the Spanish in 1571. The greater metropolitan area, called Metro-Manila, was created as a government entity in 1975. After 1986, most local government authority was returned to the constituent cities and towns. The metropolitan population exceeds 4 million. For more information, see the article MANILA in Volume M.

**Quezon City**, the second largest city in the Philippines, is located near Manila. It served as the nation's capital from 1948 to 1976.

**Cebu City** is the leading port of the Visayan Islands and an important regional trading center. Founded by the Spanish in 1565, it is the oldest city in the Philippines.

## ▶ CULTURAL HERITAGE

Filipinos are an artistic people. Filipino music includes ancient melodies played on bamboo flutes or on century-old bronze gongs. Westernized Filipino music ranges from classical to rock. Many lively songs and dances, accompanied by guitars, reflect a Spanish influence. The Philippine *kundiman* (or art song) possesses great melodic and lyric beauty.

The University of Santo Tomás in Manila is the oldest university in the Philippines. Founded in 1611, it is run by Dominican friars.

Factory workers assemble parts to produce television sets. Electronic products are among the leading exports of the Philippines.

Paintings and sculpture by Filipino artists often use styles that uniquely blend Asian and Western influences. Filipino artistic talent is also seen in delicately woven fabrics that combine silk and pineapple fibers or in baskets of intricate design woven from rattan.

Novels and short stories by such Filipino authors as José Rizal, N. V. M. González, and Benvenido Santos have been translated into many languages. Nick Joaquin, Carlos P. Romulo, and Salvador Lopez achieved international reputations as writers in English.

## ▶ GOVERNMENT

Under the 1987 constitution, the president is both head of state and government and is elected for a 6-year term. The president is assisted by a cabinet of ministers. A bicameral legislature consists of a 24-member senate and 221-member house of representatives. A supreme court, consisting of a chief justice and 14 associate justices, are appointed by the president.

Local governments—72 provinces, 61 chartered cities, and numerous municipalities—have popularly elected local officials but are subject to national government control.

Several southern provinces with large Islamic populations are designated autonomous provinces or regions and have been granted special privileges.

## ▶ HISTORY

The first people to live in the Philippines probably migrated there from Southeast Asia as early as 50,000 years ago. In 1521, the explorer Ferdinand Magellan claimed the islands for Spain, which were later named for the future king, Philip II. The first Spanish settlement was established in Cebu in 1565.

**The Philippines and Spain.** The Philippines was a colony of Spain for more than 300 years. The Spanish brought some benefits of European civilization, but Filipinos were denied freedom, economic opportunity, and many other civil rights. This persecution led to a full-scale revolt against Spain.

On May 1, 1898, a week after the Spanish-American War began, a U.S. fleet under the command of Commodore George Dewey steamed into Manila Bay and defeated the Spanish. (See the biography of Dewey in Volume D.) Four months later the United States, aided by Filipino general Emilio Aguinaldo, forced the Spanish to surrender.

**The Philippines and the United States.** Under the Treaty of Paris (1898), the United States gained sovereignty over the Philippines, but Aguinaldo called for immediate independence. Soon, armed conflict erupted between American and Filipino military forces. Aguinaldo was captured in 1901. Most Filipino forces surrendered the following year, but some military action continued until 1913. The Americans then ruled the Philippines as a colony, while Filipinos prepared for eventual self-government.

In 1935, the Philippine Commonwealth was declared, and Manuel Quezon became its first president. The Commonwealth was to administer the Philippines for ten years in transition to Philippine independence, but World War II delayed this.

The Japanese attacked the Philippine Islands on December 8, 1941, and in May 1942, Filipino and U.S. troops surrendered. Quezon and members of his cabinet escaped, and a government-in-exile was established in Washington, D.C. The Japanese eventually surrendered the Philippines, and the war in the Pacific ended on September 2, 1945.

**Independence.** On July 4, 1946, the Philippines was granted independence, and Manuel A. Roxas became the first president. In 1948,

Ferdinand Marcos, president of the Philippines (1965–86), was accused of corruption and forced into exile.

Elpidio Quirino succeeded to the presidency. He soon faced a growing rebellion by guerrillas, which was put down by the army under Secretary of Defense Ramón Magsaysay with American support. Magsaysay became president in 1953. He was followed in office by Carlos P. Garcia in 1957, Diosdado Macapagal in 1961, and Ferdinand E. Marcos in 1965.

**The Marcos Years.** Progress was made during Marcos' first term, and he was re-elected in 1969. But civil unrest and economic problems marked his second term, and in 1972 Marcos declared martial law. It lasted until 1981. By then, Marcos' health was declining and corruption had become rampant.

Opposition to Marcos became widespread after the assassination of a political opponent, Benigno S. Aquino, in 1983. Marcos appeared to lose the 1986 presidential election to Corazon Aquino, Benigno's widow, but he refused to step down. The loss of popular and military support and pressure from the United States forced Marcos into exile in Hawaii, where he later died. Corazon Aquino became president. (See the biography of Aquino in Volume A.)

**Recent Events.** In 1992, Fidel V. Ramos, a former general, succeeded Aquino. Ramos restored some degree of economic and political stability. He was succeeded in 1998 by Joseph Estrada, a popular movie actor and a former mayor. Charged with corruption, Estrada was impeached and removed from office in 2001. He was replaced by his vice president, Gloria Macapagal-Arroyo. A failed coup attempt by the military in 2003 led to a temporary "state of rebellion," which allowed police to make arrests without warrants.

In 2004, Macapagal-Arroyo was elected president in her own right. Shortly after, in response to threats made by Iraqi insurgents, she withdrew Filipino troops from the U.S.-led coalition of forces in the Iraq War. In 2005, Arroyo was accused of rigging the previous year's election. She faced impeachment, but the legislature cleared her of all charges.

ARTHUR R. WILLIAMS
University of Missouri at Kansas City

# PHILOSOPHY

Philosophy, science, art, and religion are the four major achievements of the human mind. Like science, philosophy calls for careful reasoning and exact language. Like art, it expresses one's feeling about life. Like religion, it offers a vision of the universe and humanity's place in it. There is no sharp difference between philosophy and the other three branches of culture. The writings of great artists, scientists, and religious leaders have often been classified as philosophy.

At one time all fields of study were accepted as parts of philosophy. Religion and science were particularly important in every philosophic system. But with the rapid advance of knowledge the sciences and the humanities separated from philosophy. They developed their own ways of investigation and their own vocabularies. Philosophers now tend to concentrate on general ideas common to various fields.

Philosophy can be understood in either a popular way or a technical way. In the popular sense any set of deeply held beliefs about human beings, nature, society, and God is called a philosophy. Everyone who has wondered about the meaning of life and found an answer that is satisfying has a philosophy. In its more technical sense philosophy means a highly disciplined and rational method of criticizing fundamental beliefs to make them more clear and reliable. This method was first developed by the ancient Greeks in the 6th century B.C. Thales, Anaximander, Anaximenes, Pythagoras, and other learned people began to speculate about the underlying causes of natural phenomena like birth and death, rainfall and drought, the perfectly regular motions of the planets, the reach of fire toward the sky, and the fall of heavy objects toward the earth.

## ▶ANALYTICAL METHOD

The ancient Greeks formed the word "philosophy" from *philos* ("lover") and *sophia* ("wisdom"). A philospher to them was a person who was devoted to the pursuit of knowledge for its own sake without regard for its practical uses. The kind of knowledge that interested Thales and other philosophers of the 6th century B.C. was knowledge of nature and its laws. Socrates (470?–399 B.C.) turned attention away from nature toward human beings and society. His motto was "Know thyself." He placed knowledge of right conduct above natural science as deserving of the name wisdom. Socrates was the first to use the analytical method of reasoning. This method searches for clear definitions of central ideas like virtue, justice, and knowledge. It explores the reasons for beliefs so common that people tend to accept them without question, such as the belief that physical objects are more real than ideas or that pleasure, wealth, and power are the best things in life.

Socrates challenged his fellow Athenians to justify their assumptions and usually showed that their reasons were unsound. His refusal to accept established principles without question disturbed many people. Some of his enemies accused him of corrupting the youth and introducing new gods to Athens. In 399 B.C. Socrates was sentenced to death. He accepted his punishment philosophically—calmly and without complaint. He reassured his friends that death should not be feared, since the soul is immortal. Socrates' teaching inspired his disciple Plato (427?–347 B.C.) to write his dialogues, the first masterpieces of philosophical writing to come from the Western world. Their influence on Western civilization has been second only to that of the Bible.

## ▶SYNTHETIC METHOD

Plato founded a school known as the Academy. Its most gifted pupil was Aristotle (384–322 B.C.). Aristotle combined a concern for pre-Socratic speculations about nature with the Socratic concern for social and moral problems. He continued the task begun by Plato of organizing all the fields of human knowledge into a unified view of nature and humankind. This is called synthetic philosophy. Aristotle set down in a clear and systematic form the general principles of most of the sciences and humanities. He established logic, metaphysics (the study of the nature of reality), and art criticism as fields of rational study.

The synthetic method of philosophizing developed by Plato and Aristotle is better known to the public than the analytical method of Socrates. Philosophers who have excelled at building new world views have deeply influenced the beliefs and attitudes of later generations. The great synthetic philoso-

**700** B.C.     **500** B.C.     **300** B.C.     **100** B.C.     A.D. **100**     **300**     **700**

Left: Plato and Aristotle (standing beneath the arch). Below: Saint Augustine.

**Old Testament Prophets**
**Zoroaster** (7th century B.C.)
**Thales** (640–546 B.C.)
**Anaximander** (611?–547? B.C.)
**Lao-tzu** (604?–531 B.C.)
**Pythagoras** (582?–500? B.C.)
**Gautama Buddha** (563?–483? B.C.)
**Confucius** (551–479 B.C.)
**Socrates** (470?–399 B.C.)
**Plato** (427?–347 B.C.)
**Diogenes the Cynic** (412?–323 B.C.)
**Aristotle** (384–322 B.C.)
**Chuang Tzu** (365?–290 B.C.)
**Zeno of Citium** (4th–3rd century B.C.)
**Epicurus** (341?–270 B.C.)

**The Early Christians**

**Saint Augustine** (354–430)

**The Early Muslims**

phers, or system builders—Plato, Aristotle, Saint Augustine (354–430), Saint Thomas Aquinas (1225?–74), René Descartes (1596–1650), Thomas Hobbes (1588–1679), Baruch Spinoza (1632–77), Immanuel Kant (1724–1804, and G. W. F. Hegel (1770–1831)—created new ways of thinking that have guided people ever since. The most remarkable achievement of a philosopher is to develop a new system of ideas that can be used to fit together pieces of knowledge in different fields in order to form a single picture of nature.

Plato believed that ideas were more real than things. He developed a vision of two worlds—a world of unchanging ideas and a world of changing physical objects. Aristotle did not believe in a separate world of ideas. He provided a vision of nature as a single system of things that can be classified by genus and species. He said that each natural object contains its destiny within it, as an acorn contains a tendency to grow into an oak tree. Saint Augustine fashioned a view of life as a stage on which creatures of God act out a drama of good and evil. Aquinas combined the thought of Augustine and Aristotle. His philosophy

later became the official doctrine of the Roman Catholic Church.

Hobbes and Spinoza developed a mechanistic vision of the world in which all events are governed by strict mathematical laws. They said that with sufficient scientific knowledge events would be as predictable as clockwork. Descartes set God and the human mind apart from the world machine and created the view known as Cartesian dualism. Kant deepened the division between mind and matter by separating moral laws from laws of science. But he drew mind back into nature by claiming that the mind organizes natural events into a logical structure the way pudding is given form by the container into which it is poured. Hegel worked out a vision of the world produced by the evolution of mind through many stages, the highest of which are nature, society, and philosophy.

900   1100   1300   1500   1700   1900   2000

Above: René Descartes.
Left: Jean Jacques Rousseau.
Below: Jean-Paul Sartre.

Shankara (788?–820)

Avicenna (980–1037)

Averroës (1126–1198)

Moses Maimonides (1135–1204)

Saint Thomas Aquinas (1225?–1274)

Niccolò Machiavelli (1469–1527)

Thomas Hobbes (1588–1679)

René Descartes (1596–1650)

Baruch Spinoza (1632–1677)

John Locke (1632–1704)

G. W. von Leibniz (1646–1716)

Jean Jacques Rousseau (1712–1778)

Immanuel Kant (1724–1804)

G. W. F. Hegel (1770–1831)

John Stuart Mill (1806–1873)

Søren Kierkegaard (1813–1855)

Karl Marx (1818–1883)

William James (1842–1910)

Friedrich Nietzsche (1844–1900)

Bertrand Russell (1872–1970)

Martin Buber (1878–1965)

Paul Tillich (1886–1965)

Jean-Paul Sartre (1905–1980)

Albert Camus (1913–1960)

## ▶BRANCHES OF PHILOSOPHY

The synthetic type of philosophy that organizes knowledge into a single picture of the world has become more difficult to carry out as human knowledge has grown in scope and detail. It is hardly possible today for one person to master all the fields of specialized knowledge. Philosophers now set themselves more limited goals. They connect psychology with biology in explaining the relation between the mind and the body. Or they relate science to religion in order to try to explain how the world began and how life grew out of inanimate matter. Philosophy today is analyti-

Information about the philosophers listed on this chart may be found in this encyclopedia. Use the index as a guide for finding this information.

cal in the Socratic style, rather than synthetic in the Aristotelian manner.

The advance of philosophical understanding has made it necessary to divide philosophy itself into smaller areas according to the type of problems investigated.

**Ethics** is the study of the standards for judging whether things are good or bad, and the analysis of terms like justice, virtue, morality, and responsibility.

**Epistemology** deals with the problems of defining knowledge, truth, logic, and perception. It investigates the ways in which knowledge is acquired.

**Metaphysics** deals with the nature of reality: What is real, and what only appears to be real? One branch of metaphysics, called ontology, searches for the standards by which we can judge the reality of different types of things, such as material objects, mental states, numbers, and relations. Cosmology, another branch of metaphysics, interprets the findings of physics and astronomy, attempting to decide whether the world was created by God or evolved by chance and whether the world is finite or infinite in space and time.

**Aesthetics** is concerned with the definition of art and beauty, and with discovering general standards of art criticism.

In addition to these wide areas of philosophical study, each field of scholarship faces philosophical problems in defining its subject matter and methods of procedure. Thus, for example, we have the philosophy of physics, the philosophy of religion, the philosophy of history, and the philosophy of law.

In brief, philosophy is disciplined thinking about basic principles and common beliefs. Whenever a person is not satisfied with specific answers and tries to understand how all his or her information fits together and what it adds up to, that person is philosophizing.

RAZIEL A. ABELSON
New York University

---

# PHOENIX

Phoenix, the capital of Arizona and the state's largest city, is the sixth most populous city in the United States. More than 1 million people live within the city limits. More than 3 million live in the greater metropolitan area. Surrounded by low mountain ranges, Phoenix covers 450 square miles (1,166 square kilometers) of flat desert terrain in the Salt River valley.

Known for its clear, dry air and sunny weather, Phoenix is a popular resort area and retirement center. Throughout most of the year, the temperature averages 72°F (22°C), except in the summer, when it can soar above 100°F (38°C). Precipitation averages a mere 8 inches (203 millimeters) annually and comes mostly from rainstorms that can occur in July and August. Consequently, most of the city's special events take place during the winter tourist season. Among the most notable are the Phoenix Open Golf Tournament, the Jaycees Rodeo of Rodeos, the Fiesta Bowl football game and parade, the Desert Botanical Garden Cactus Show, the Arizona Boat Show, and the Chandler Ostrich Festival.

Phoenix is a major center of commerce, industry, and agriculture in the southwestern

United States. Important economic activities include tourism, telecommunications, mining, and high technology. Chemicals, electronics, aircraft, textiles, and leather goods are significant manufactures. Lettuce, melons, cotton, citrus fruits, and other agricultural produce are processed and packaged locally.

### Places of Interest
Phoenix offers a wide variety of interesting places to visit. The Heard Museum features collections of primitive and Indian artifacts, including a significant collection of Hopi Indian Kachina dolls donated by former U.S. senator Barry Goldwater, a native of Phoenix. The museum also sponsors an In-

dian Arts and Crafts Fair every spring. The Phoenix Art Museum features Western American, Asian, and modern art exhibits. The Arizona Mineral Museum contains outstanding rock specimens. The Hall of Flame Museum displays antique fire-fighting equipment dating as far back as 1725. The Pioneer Outdoor Living History Museum re-creates an early historical settlement. The Pueblo Grande Museum features ancient relics of the Hohokam Indians. Heritage and Science Park includes the Phoenix Museum of History and the new Arizona Science Center. The old State Capitol, constructed of native stone, includes a museum of Arizona historical memorabilia. The Phoenix Zoo and the Desert Botanical Garden are located in Papago Park.

Local institutions of higher learning include Grand Canyon College, the DeVry Institute of Technology, and the American Graduate School of International Management, known as the Thunderbird School. Arizona State University is located nearby in Tempe.

### History

From about 300 B.C. to A.D. 1450, Phoenix was inhabited by the Hohokam Indians, who are believed to be the ancestors of today's O'Odham tribes. It is known that the Hohokam built an impressive system of irrigation ditches to water their crops. However, by the time the first Spanish explorers arrived in 1539, the Hohokam had disappeared from the area. For the next 300 years, the entire region was controlled by Spain and later Mexico. The United States acquired the land in 1848, following the Mexican War.

The first American pioneers came to Phoenix in 1865 to establish a hay camp to feed the horses at Camp McDowell, a nearby army outpost. In 1867 a soldier-prospector, Jack Swilling, and an Englishman, Darrell Duppa, began to rebuild the ancient irrigation canals used by the Hohokam. Duppa named the site Phoenix after the legendary sun-bird that rose from its own ashes. He hoped that a city would rise from the ruins of the old Indian settlement.

The town grew as a commercial center and was incorporated as a city in 1881. Phoenix became the capital of the Arizona Territory in 1889, two years after the town was linked to the Southern Pacific Railroad.

In 1911 the U.S. Reclamation Bureau built the Theodore Roosevelt Dam on the Salt River east of Phoenix. The dam controlled floods, produced electricity, and provided water for agriculture. The following year,

Phoenix, the capital of Arizona and the state's most populous city, is a major center of commerce in the southwestern United States.

when Arizona became a state, Phoenix became the state capital.

In 1941, during World War II, the U.S. armed forces took advantage of Phoenix's year-round warm climate for aviation and desert-warfare training. When the war ended in 1945, many military personnel returned to settle in the Phoenix area.

In the 1950's the city's population boomed due to the rising use of air conditioning. However, its continued growth was largely dependent on the availability of water. The Central Arizona Water Project, completed in 1985, now supplies the city with water from the Colorado River, 190 miles (306 kilometers) away. Phoenix has grown ever since.

Reviewed by the Phoenix Chamber
of Commerce

# PHONICS

Phonics is the study of relationships between written letters and speech sounds. These relationships can be used to help figure out the pronunciations of written words. Phonics is a part of reading instruction in schools throughout the world.

In the teaching of phonics, a big problem is that in many cases a single letter can represent different sounds. For example, the letter *a* stands for different sounds in the words *ate, cat,* and *about.* Even with this problem, however, phonics is a useful way of helping pupils figure out words on their own.

Before pupils learn to read, they are prepared for phonics instruction. They learn to hear differences in the pronunciation of sounds. They learn the letters of the alphabet and how to tell one letter from another. They learn to listen for likenesses and differences in the pronunciation of words.

Then formal phonics instruction starts. The exact order of instruction varies. Usually the letters that are always pronounced the same are presented first. These include consonants such as *b, d, f, k, l, m, n, r,* and *t.* Then the letters that can stand for a variety of sounds are taught. These include the vowels and some consonants, such as *c, g,* and *w.* Finally, combinations of letters and the sounds they represent are taught—*ch, sh,* and *th,* for example.

Much attention is given to learning the letter-sound relationships in the early grades. In the later grades, pupils learn how to divide words into syllables, how to pronounce the syllables, and how to blend the sounds together to form the words. They also learn how to stress, or accent, the proper syllable.

Since phonics was first introduced as a part of reading instruction, its popularity has risen and fallen many times. Today teachers recognize the importance of phonics, and it is taught in schools throughout the world. But teachers know that reading involves more than just using phonics. Phonics is taught as one of a number of ways to help readers understand what they read.

NICHOLAS DiOBILDA
Glassboro State College (New Jersey)

# PHONOGRAPH

Thomas A. Edison, who invented the first practical phonograph, was a bit deaf. He found he could not trust his ears to tell him how much sound was coming out of the telephone receiver. But he noticed that a small disc inside the receiver vibrated as the person on the other end of the line spoke. Edison thought to attach a tiny needle to the center of the disc. The force of the needle on his finger told him the amount of sound—loud or soft—that was being sent out.

A few months later a second discovery showed Edison something else about sound. This time he was working on a device to improve the telegraph. He was running a paper tape covered with Morse code dots and dashes through an instrument at high speed. Each time the dots and dashes passed over the end of a steel spring, Edison heard strange soft sounds that were very much like the sound of people talking. Edison had found out that a human voice could make a needle move. Why, he wondered, couldn't that same needle prick the pattern of the sound waves on paper tape?

The inventor lost no time in rigging up an experiment. A disc with a needle in it was set vibrating by the human voice, while paper coated with paraffin was moved under the needle at a fairly high speed. The needle pricked the paper just as Edison thought it would. But the gadget needed work before it could store up any kind of sound that was recognizable.

The first thing Edison did was to replace the paraffin paper with a metal cylinder. Edison wrapped tinfoil around the cylinder and attached two disc-and-needle units. One was to speak into. The other was for sound to come out of.

When the "in" disc vibrated, Edison hoped the needle would make little indentations in the tinfoil as the cylinder turned. When the "out" needle traveled over these same marks, its disc should vibrate, too, re-creating the sound. It was a memorable day in 1877 when Edison put on the first cylinder, leaned close to the in disc, and shouted, "Mary had a little lamb." He then set the out needle in the same groove and turned the crank of the cylinder.

Back came his voice. He admitted later, "I was never so taken aback in my life."

There was a great deal of excitement over this spectacular device. Edison manufactured about 500 sets, which he sent around the country to be displayed to curious audiences. People were glad to pay admission to hear the machine play back "Yankee Doodle" and other songs. Some of the machines made as much as $1,800 in a single week.

An important development occurred when Emile Berliner put the first phonograph record on the market in 1895. His record was made of zinc coated with wax. A needle vibrating to the sound of a voice scratched a pattern in the wax. The record was then dipped into acid, which ate into the zinc where the needle had cut through the wax. Berliner proudly announced that he had etched the human voice.

In 1901, Berliner and a former watch-maker, Eldridge Johnson, created the Victor Talking Machine Company. Berliner had found an effective way to stamp out hundreds of records from one master. Up to this time, singers had to sing the same song over and over again because only a few copies could be made of each recording. But with Berliner's new stamping method, great singers were eager to record their voices. The marches of the famous United States Marine Band, directed by John Philip Sousa, were also very popular.

Singers made most of the first records because the voice was easier to record than a musical instrument. It was difficult for a large group of musicians in an orchestra to get close enough to the recording horn to be heard properly. And a single record side, turning at the standard speed of 78 rotations a minute, could hold only 4½ minutes of music. Symphonies, of course, were much longer.

Victor was the most successful company in the competition to make good records as fast as possible. A famous Victor trademark showed Nipper, a white fox terrier, listening to "His Master's Voice" coming out of the brass horn of a phonograph.

By 1925, electric microphones began to replace the old brass recording horn. The microphone changed the sound vibrations of the voice or musical instrument into electrical energy. This energy, in turn, was used to drive

Nipper listening to "His Master's Voice" was the symbol of the Victor Talking Machine Company, an early manufacturer of phonographs.

the recording needle, or cutter, as it cut grooves into the wax of the master disc. One sensitive microphone could pick up with fair accuracy a whole roomful of sounds.

In 1948 came the long-playing microgroove record. The record was made of smooth vinyl plastic, which was very quiet in playback. It turned at 33⅓ rotations a minute. Twenty-five minutes or more of music could be heard on each side. New equipment—sensitive needles, wide-range speakers, powerful amplifiers—made records sound even better. This equipment was known as high-fidelity, or hi-fi, because it produced such accurate, clear sound.

A new dimension was added to high fidelity in 1957, when it was found that two separate tracks could be cut into the groove of a record. The two tracks were then played back through separate speakers. This system, which produced stereophonic sound, created a broad spread of sound very much like the live sound heard in a concert hall.

Today, compact disc (CD) players have all but replaced the phonograph. Introduced in the 1980's, these players reproduce recorded music very accurately by bouncing a laser beam off tiny pits in a CD's mirrored plastic surface. Although the sound quality from CD's is generally much better than that from phonographs, many people still enjoy listening to their old records, some of which have become prized collector's items.

SHIRLEY FLEMING
*High Fidelity* magazine

See also EDISON, THOMAS ALVA; HIGH-FIDELITY SYSTEMS.

# PHOTOELECTRICITY

Have you ever noticed how streetlights go on by themselves at dusk? Or how the doors of some buildings open by themselves as you approach? Devices that turn lights on and off and open and close doors operate as the result of a phenomenon called the **photoelectric effect**, or **photoelectricity**. Electronic components that take advantage of this effect are called **photoelectric cells**.

## ▶ HOW PHOTOELECTRICITY WORKS

Light is a form of energy. When light, in the form of visible light, infrared rays, or ultraviolet rays, strikes certain chemical substances, it interacts with the atoms in the material. If the light energy is strong enough, it causes the electrons in the atoms to break free and either escape from the substance into the surrounding space or move to another substance touching it. This flow of electrons—in fact, any flow of electrons—is called an **electric current**.

Photoelectricity takes two basic forms: the photovoltaic effect and the photoconductive effect. In the **photovoltaic effect**, an electric current is generated and flows between two different substances when light falls upon them. In the **photoconductive effect**, the ability of a material to conduct electricity is changed as light falls upon it. The photoelectric devices that utilize these effects are known specifically as photovoltaic cells and photoconductive cells.

### Photovoltaic Cell

A photovoltaic cell generates electricity by itself when light shines on it. Silicon is one substance often used to produce the electric current in a photovoltaic cell, which is made up of two thin wafers, or slabs, of silicon to which impurities have been added. These impurities might include such substances as boron, arsenic, selenium, platinum, or copper oxide. One wafer in the cell is mixed with an impurity that easily gives up its electrons; the other is mixed with an impurity that attracts electrons. The resulting materials are known as **semiconductors** because they are able to conduct an electrical current under certain conditions. A junction is formed along the boundary where the two semiconductor wafers meet. It is called the p-n junction.

Thousands of photovoltaic cells connected together within solar panels (*above*) are at the heart of large solar energy systems that can produce electricity for remote communities. A small floating lighthouse (*right*) also has solar panels that produce electrical energy in daylight. That energy is then stored in a battery used to keep its lights on after dark.

When light strikes the p-n junction at the heart of a photovoltaic cell, the atoms in one semiconductor wafer release some of their electrons, and the atoms in the other wafer attract electrons. This causes a shortage of electrons in one wafer and an excess of electrons in the other. If a wire or some type of electric circuit or device is connected between the two wafers, electrons will move from one wafer to the other in an attempt to restore the atoms to equilibrium, or a state of balance. This movement of electrons is an electric current.

---

### Did you know that...

the photovoltaic effect was discovered in 1839 by French physicist Antoine-César Becquerel? Thirty-four years later, in 1873, English scientist Willoughby Smith became the first person to observe the photoconductive effect. The first practical application of these effects occurred around 1895, when German physicists Julius Elster and Hans Geitel invented the photoelectric cell. But it was not until the early 1900's that the photoelectric effect was fully understood and played an important role in Albert Einstein's and Max Planck's development of quantum theory. Photoelectric cells were not produced commercially, however, until the 1950's.

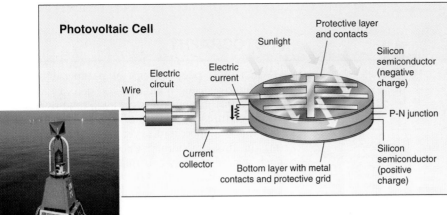

**Photovoltaic Cell**

Sunlight

Protective layer and contacts

Silicon semiconductor (negative charge)

Electric circuit

Electric current

Wire

P-N junction

Current collector

Bottom layer with metal contacts and protective grid

Silicon semiconductor (positive charge)

When sunlight strikes the p-n junction inside a photovoltaic cell, it causes electrons in the atoms of the cell's two semiconductor layers to move between them, creating an excess of electrons in one layer (treated to attract electrons) and a shortage in the other (treated to give up electrons). When a wire, electric circuit, or other device connects the layers, the motion of the electrons, called an electric current, continues in an attempt to restore the atoms in each layer to a state of balance. This current can be collected and used as a power source to operate many different and useful objects.

A photovoltaic cell will produce electricity as long as light continues to strike it. If the light becomes brighter or the light energy greater, the photovoltaic cell will generate more electrical current up to a certain maximum. This maximum, known as the **saturation current**, depends on the surface area of the p-n junction and the types of semiconductors used in the photovoltaic cell.

### Photoconductive Cell

A photoconductive cell does not generate electricity by itself when light shines on it. Instead, it strengthens an electric current that is already flowing. A photoconductive cell is similar in structure to a photovoltaic cell, except that it is connected to a battery or some other power source. It is this power source that generates the electrical current.

A **photodiode**, one of the most common types of photoconductive cells, is a semiconductor device that is a good conductor of electricity in one direction, but not as good a conductor in the other direction. This difference in conductivity is caused by the behavior of the atoms at and near the p-n junction of the cell.

A photodiode is connected to a power source so that the electrical current flows in the same direction in which the diode conducts poorly. This is called **reverse bias**. When a photodiode is reverse biased, very little current flows in the circuit when no light is striking the p-n junction. When light strikes the junction, the photodiode conducts the electric current much better, allowing it to increase dramatically. The brighter the light, the better the photodiode conducts electricity up to a certain maximum.

Another type of photoconductive cell, a **phototransistor**, is similar to a photodiode. It allows an electrical current to be amplified as well as switched on or off. The ability of a phototransistor to conduct electricity also depends on the level of light striking the cell.

A third type of photoconductive cell is the **phototube**, which consists of a metal plate coated with a light-sensitive chemical and a metal rod placed near it. These two parts are enclosed in an airtight glass tube and connected to a battery outside the tube. When light strikes the metal plate, electrons are pushed out into the surrounding space. The electrons are then attracted to the metal rod. The flow of electrons from the plate to the rod constitutes an electric current. The amount of the electric current depends on the amount of light that strikes the phototube. Today, phototubes have largely been replaced by photodiodes for many applications.

▶ **USES OF PHOTOELECTRICITY**

Photoelectric cells are used in many ways. Solar panels made up of many photovoltaic cells connected together can be used to catch light from the sun and generate electricity for homes and buildings on Earth as well as for satellites in space. Photoelectric cells can act as switches to turn many devices on or off. For example, they are used to set off burglar alarms, to operate bar-code readers in stores, and to activate the exposure meters of cameras. These and many other uses of photoelectricity help make our lives easier and more productive.

STANLEY GIBILISCO

Editor, *Illustrated Dictionary of Electronics*

See also ELECTRONICS; FIBER OPTICS; LIGHT; MATERIALS SCIENCE; SOLAR ENERGY; TRANSISTORS, DIODES, AND INTEGRATED CIRCUITS.

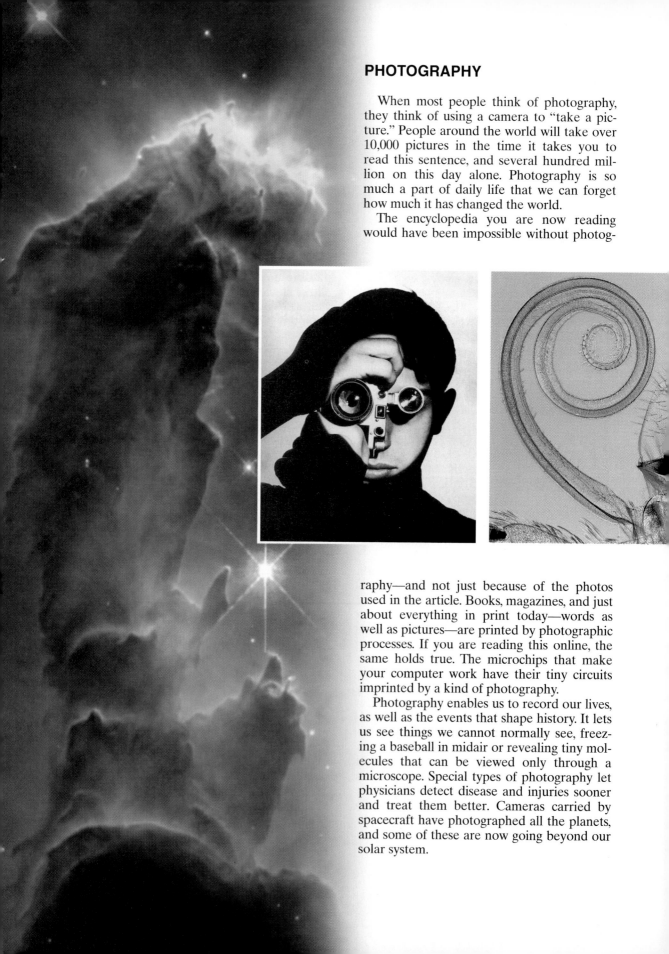

# PHOTOGRAPHY

When most people think of photography, they think of using a camera to "take a picture." People around the world will take over 10,000 pictures in the time it takes you to read this sentence, and several hundred million on this day alone. Photography is so much a part of daily life that we can forget how much it has changed the world.

The encyclopedia you are now reading would have been impossible without photography—and not just because of the photos used in the article. Books, magazines, and just about everything in print today—words as well as pictures—are printed by photographic processes. If you are reading this online, the same holds true. The microchips that make your computer work have their tiny circuits imprinted by a kind of photography.

Photography enables us to record our lives, as well as the events that shape history. It lets us see things we cannot normally see, freezing a baseball in midair or revealing tiny molecules that can be viewed only through a microscope. Special types of photography let physicians detect disease and injuries sooner and treat them better. Cameras carried by spacecraft have photographed all the planets, and some of these are now going beyond our solar system.

Skilled and imaginative photographers have made photography an art form. The beautiful pictures they take increase our appreciation and understanding of the world. Photographs documenting social problems and human suffering have moved people to take action and governments to change laws.

Today photography can be done almost in real time—people using digital cameras can see their pictures about as fast as they can take them. News photographers can instantly transmit photos from the scene of breaking

film or a digital imager, though, the cameras are otherwise very similar.

When you take a picture, light reflected from your subject enters the camera through the lens, which focuses it on the film or on the digital imager. If you use film, the light rays form a latent (not visible) image of the subject on the film. The film has now been **exposed**, but to make the latent image visible, the film must be **developed**, or treated with chemicals. In digital recording, the focused light strikes a grid of tiny picture elements, or

Ever since the first photograph was taken more than 150 years ago, photography has changed the way we see the world. *From far left:* Photographs taken by the Hubble Space Telescope provide glimpses of the universe, such as these star-forming towers of gas in the Eagle Nebula. This picture of a photojournalist is famous for its artful composition. Photomicrography combines a camera with a microscope to take pictures of objects—such as this butterfly proboscis—too small to be seen with the naked eye. Digital photographs can be enhanced using light painting and other techniques. Stop-motion photography is especially useful for sports photography.

news. A person sitting at a home computer can send a digital image halfway around the world in seconds.

### ▶ HOW PHOTOGRAPHS ARE MADE

The word "photography" comes from two Greek words meaning "writing" and "light," and photography is much like making a painting or drawing with light. To take a photograph, you need only three things: light, a camera, and a recording medium. For the first 150 years of photography, the recording medium was film—transparent plastic coated with crystals of a light-sensitive silver compound. In more and more cameras today, the recording medium is an electronic sensor or "imager" that converts the light that strikes it into digital information that can be stored in computer memory. Whether a camera uses

pixels. Each pixel records the brightness and color of the light that strikes it. Circuits in the camera then process the information into a bundle of organized information (an **image file**) that can later be read by a computer and reassembled into a picture.

### ▶ PHOTOGRAPHIC EQUIPMENT

The camera and the recording medium are the basic tools of photography. Other important equipment includes interchangeable lenses, lights, flash units, and filters.

#### The Camera

All cameras, whether simple or complex, have five basic parts—the body, lens, shutter, film holder (in a digital camera, this is the imager), and viewfinder. More complex cameras may have special features as well.

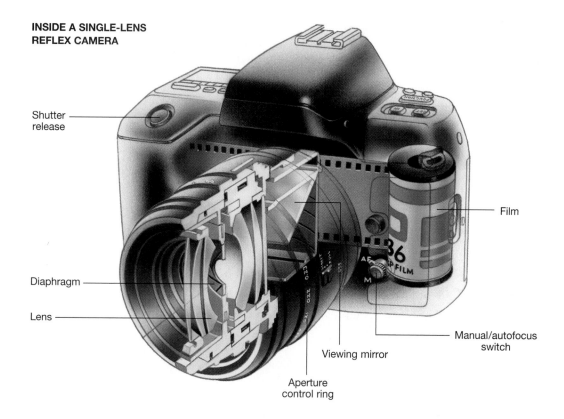

Shutter release

Diaphragm

Lens

Viewing mirror

Aperture control ring

Film

Manual/autofocus switch

The **body** of a camera is a lightproof framework, or box. It keeps out all light except what passes through the lens.

The **lens**—one or more pieces of glass or plastic with curved surfaces—is somewhat like a small magnifying glass. The lens concentrates the light entering the camera to make a sharp image of the photographed object on the film. All lenses must be **focused** so that the subject is as clear as possible.

The simplest cameras have a **fixed-focus** lens. This means the focus was set at one distance when the camera was made and cannot be changed. They are set to focus on objects beyond about 5 feet (1.5 meters).

With a more complex camera, the focus can be changed. Cameras that let you do this yourself—usually by turning a ring on the lens—are called **manual-focus** cameras. Those that change the focus automatically are called **autofocus** cameras. Some cameras are a combination of both.

The **shutter** is a mechanical device behind the lens that opens and closes to admit light. The photographer operates the shutter by pressing the shutter release, a button on the camera. In many cameras you can change the shutter speed. In dim light, a slower speed is preferable. This keeps the shutter open longer so that more light enters the camera. In bright sunlight, the shutter can be set at a faster speed, since there is plenty of light to produce an image on the film. A fast shutter speed lets you take pictures of subjects without blurring, even if they are moving.

When you press the shutter release on some digital cameras, the camera turns the

**Profiles: *A Dozen Great Photographers***

There are many photographers who, over the past 150 years, have raised photography to an art form. The following pages feature twelve of them. If you are interested in seeing the works of more great photographers, there are countless books and Web sites available, and many museums have photo collections.

digital imager on and off. This works much like the shutter on a film camera. Some digital cameras use mechanical shutters, however.

Very simple cameras have only one shutter speed. More complex and expensive cameras have many shutter speeds, ranging from 30 seconds to 1/8,000 of a second or even faster. Some cameras also have a setting that keeps the shutter open for long exposures.

Most cameras also have a diaphragm, which is used to make the **aperture**, or lens opening, larger or smaller to admit more or less light. Apertures are measured in f-numbers. The lower f-numbers, such as f/1.4 and f/2, are wide openings. These transmit more light to the film. The higher f-numbers, such as f/11 and f/16, are small lens openings. They transmit less light to the film.

The diaphragm also controls a photograph's depth of field. This is the amount of space in front of and behind the subject that is in focus. Higher f-stops increase the depth of field, and lower f-stops decrease it.

Film cameras include **film holders** to keep the film flat so that the image can be accurately focused. With small cameras, the film holder is built into the back of the camera. You load the film into the holder and close the camera. After taking a photograph, you advance the film so that the next blank spot on the roll (called a frame) is in place for the next picture. Most popular film cameras use cartridges of film that produce from 12 to 36 pictures and have frame counters to keep track of exposed pictures.

In digital cameras, the imager takes the place of the film holder. You do not have to load or advance film. But you will still have to store and keep track of the pictures you have taken, just as with a film camera. When you take a digital picture, the camera must move the image file to another place in the camera so you can take another picture. Some cameras have built-in memory, but that limits the number of pictures you can take—if you use all the memory, you have to either download the pictures to a computer or erase some of them. So most digital cameras instead store images on a memory card, which uses the same kind of memory chips a computer uses. These are about the size of postage stamps and are inserted into a side of the camera. The camera will indicate how many photos are stored on the card and how many more photos you can take before the card is filled up.

Every camera has a **viewfinder**—usually a small plastic or glass window—that shows the scene you are focusing on. Viewfinders in better cameras may also include lenses or reflecting prisms to provide a more accurate view of the picture being taken.

## GREAT PHOTOGRAPHERS

### A Pioneer of the Art:
## Julia Margaret Cameron
(1815–79)

When Julia Margaret Cameron was 48 years old, her two daughters gave her a camera. That may not sound unusual, but the year was 1863, when few people knew how to take photos. Cameron, born in Calcutta, India, learned the difficult wet plate process then used to make photographs and went on to become one of the greatest portrait photographers. Even today, photographers admire her dramatic use of lighting, which was considered ahead of its time, and her use of selective focus—a way of making only part of a picture sharp.

Julia Margaret Cameron, self-portrait.

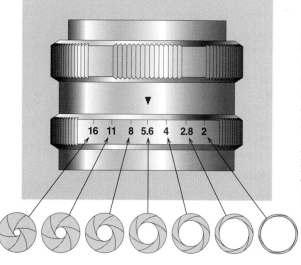

The aperture, or lens opening, is measured in f-numbers. The lower the f-number, the larger the aperture. Larger apertures transmit more light to the film.

All but the simplest cameras include electronic circuits that measure the amount of light coming from the subject. In many cameras the proper exposure settings are shown in the viewfinder as the user adjusts the shutter speed and f-stop. This is called manual exposure setting. Some cameras set the exposure automatically, which is called auto-exposure.

**Film Cameras.** Film cameras range from tiny pocket-sized units to very large cameras used primarily in professional studios.

The simplest cameras are called **one-time-use cameras**, or OTUC's. Also known as disposable cameras, these are the small cardboard and plastic cameras that are taken back to a store to get developed. An OTUC has a fixed-focus lens and a single exposure setting. You can get OTUC's with or without built-in flash. Some are designed for specific uses, such as taking black-and-white or underwater photography.

The **point-and-shoot** camera is more complex but is very popular because of its ease of use. It has an autofocus lens and different shutter speeds and lens openings that are set automatically, although some allow the user to make small changes in the exposure. This camera has a built-in flash that will fire when needed, unless it is turned off. It automatically loads the film, advances it to the next frame, and rewinds it when you finish the roll. Because you cannot change the lens, many

point-and-shoot cameras have zoom lenses, which let you change the view from wide-angle to telephoto. Most point-and-shoot cameras use 35mm film, but some types use Advanced Photo System (APS) film, which comes in a small cartridge that is easier to load.

**Instant cameras** produce a fully developed print shortly after the picture is snapped. This is possible because the film includes the developing chemicals. After an image is exposed, the film comes in contact with the developers and is automatically processed. Instant cameras are less popular now that digital cameras allow pictures to be viewed right away.

Cameras that can be focused and use different lens openings and shutter speeds are called **adjustable** cameras. Most of these measure the light and indicate the correct lens opening and shutter speed or set them automatically. Today the most widely used adjustable camera is the single-lens reflex.

The **single-lens reflex** (SLR) is the most popular type of camera for serious photography, whether for film or digital capture. In the SLR camera, a mirror behind the lens reflects the image upward through a prism and onto a viewing screen. You can then see your picture and focus it. When you shoot the picture, the mirror automatically swings up out of the light path. The image strikes the film or imager as the shutter opens, and the exposure is made.

Most SLR's now use both autoexposure and autofocus, but better models also allow you to focus manually and make your own exposure settings. Many use interchangeable lenses, have built-in electronic flash, and take pictures on 35mm (millimeter) film.

Some SLR's use a type of roll film known as 120/220. This is larger than 35mm film, and the photos taken with it can show finer detail. These cameras are usually larger than 35mm SLR's, so they are often used with tripods. (A tripod is a three-legged stand that holds the camera steady and prevents blurring of the image.)

**View cameras** are another type of adjustable camera. They are most common in professional studios, but they are also used outdoors for photographing landscapes and architecture. They are much larger than SLR's and use individual sheets of film (usually 4 by 5 inches, but sometimes larger). They are used mostly by photographers who make pictures of products for advertising or other types of photography that require precise control of the image.

Many roll-film SLR's, as well as view cameras, have interchangeable film backs that can be switched with digital backs. This way, a photographer can shoot both film and digital versions of a subject.

**Digital Cameras.** Most digital cameras for amateurs are the point-and-shoot type. They focus automatically, set the lens opening and shutter speed automatically, and fire the flash when needed. Digital cameras have various other kinds of adjustments, but a digital point-and-shoot can set these automatically, too.

A digital point-and-shoot camera usually has an LCD monitor screen, which is like a small computer screen on the back of the camera. You can compose a picture using this screen—for this reason some digital cameras have no viewfinder—as well as view pictures you have already taken. Digital point-and-shoot cameras use memory cards to store pic-

tures. The most popular are the Compact Flash (CF) and the Secure Digital (SD) types. Because digital pictures are electronic files, memory cards are not measured in frames but in megabytes, as in computer memory (1 megabyte equals about 1 million bytes). Memory cards come in sizes from 8 megabytes to 1 gigabyte (1 gigabyte equals 1,000 megabytes), and even larger ones are becoming available.

Most digital cameras for professional use are based on 35mm SLR's. These cameras use interchangeable lenses and allow a wide range of adjustments. They can take pictures that are sharper and clearer than digital point-and-shoot cameras and can often take pictures in a fast burst—several in less than a second. Digital SLR's are now widely used by news and nature photographers, among many others.

A new type of digital camera, the Electronic Viewfinder (EVF), works much like a SLR. However, the viewfinder eyepiece is really a tiny monitor. This eliminates the need for expensive and complex optical parts such as the mirror and prism.

## GREAT PHOTOGRAPHERS

### Photography for Art's Sake:
# Alfred Stieglitz
(1864–1946)

If Alfred Stieglitz had never taken a single photograph, he would still be one of the most important figures in photography. He founded the magazine *Camera Work*, which was one of the first dedicated to photography, and had a gallery called 291 that showed photographs as art—something that had never been done before. But Stieglitz, born in Hoboken, N.J., was also a superb photographer. His 1907 picture called *The Steerage*, of European immigrants aboard a ship, is considered one of the greatest photographs ever taken. He was married to the artist Georgia O'Keeffe, who is the subject of many of his photographs.

*The Steerage*, taken in 1907 by Alfred Stieglitz, shows immigrants on the lower decks of an ocean liner.

### Recording Media

**Film.** There are three main types of photographic film for general use: Black-and-white negative film for black-and-white photographs (usually prints), color negative film for color prints, and color reversal film (usually called color slide film) for color slides or transparencies.

All film has a plastic base thinly coated with crystals of a silver-bromide compound. The crystals are mixed in a transparent gelatin called an emulsion. Black-and-white film usually has just one layer of emulsion. Color film has three (or more) layers. Each is sensitive to, or records, one of the three primary colors of light—blue, green, and red.

When choosing general-use film, three factors must be considered—speed, graininess, and contrast. Film speed refers to a film's sensitivity to light, which can vary. Graininess is the degree of visibility of the silver crystals, or grains, in the photographic image. Graininess is especially noticeable when a photograph is enlarged. Contrast is the degree of difference between the light and dark areas of the subject. Generally, the faster the film, the grainier the photograph will be and the less contrast it will have. Photographs with too much contrast or too much grain lack fine detail.

Film speed is measured on a scale called the ISO film-speed index (for International Organization for Standards). Each film is given an ISO number that indicates its speed. Fast films have high numbers, and slow films have low numbers. The faster the film is, the more sensitive it is to light. Films for general purposes range from ISO 25 to ISO 3200. Films between ISO 200 and ISO 400 are the most commonly used all-purpose and outdoor films, but there are slower and faster special-purpose films.

## RECORDING MEDIA: FILM AND DIGITAL

In film photography, the light entering the camera forms a latent image of the subject on the film. This image becomes visible after the film is developed. In digital photography, the light entering the camera strikes a grid containing many tiny picture elements (pixels). Each pixel records the brightness and color of the light that strikes it. The camera then turns this information into an image file that can be read by a computer and reassembled into a picture.

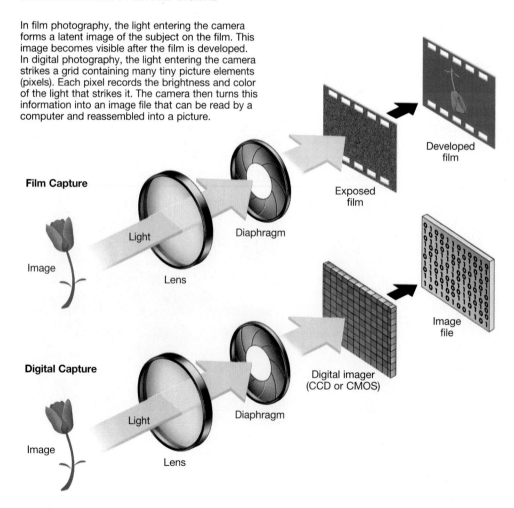

Film Capture
Image
Light
Lens
Diaphragm
Exposed film
Developed film

Digital Capture
Image
Light
Lens
Diaphragm
Digital imager (CCD or CMOS)
Image file

Most digital cameras include LCD monitor screens, which are like tiny computer screens. These are used to compose pictures or to view those already taken.

**Digital Imagers.** Digital cameras do not use film but a digital imager—either a charge-coupled device (CCD) or a complementary metal-oxide semiconductor (CMOS). Both devices have a chip containing millions of tiny receptors (pixels) that record the color and intensity of the light falling on them. The more pixels an imager contains, the sharper and finer grained the resulting picture will be. (That is, it has a higher resolution.) Digital camera imagers are rated by the maximum number of pixels they can use. If a camera can take a picture made up of 1,600 by 1,200 pixels, for example, that means it has a resolution of 1,920,000 pixels (just multiply 1,600 by 1,200). This would be called a 1.9 megapixel camera. A 2,560 by 1,920 imager works out to 4,915,200 pixels, or about 4.9 megapixels.

A digital camera can take pictures at different quality levels, not just the highest available. For instance, a typical 3.2 megapixel camera can take pictures at the full 3.2 megapixels or at 2 megapixels, 1 megapixel, or at 640 by 480 pixels. What resolution should you use? A simple rule is to divide the resolution measurements by 200. This will tell you how big a print you can make, in inches, with full photographic quality. For example, if you take a picture at 1,600 by 1,200 pixels, you should be able to make an inkjet print of about 8 by 6 inches that looks as good as one you took with film. (Going a little bigger might give prints some grain and duller colors.) If you are just making a picture to e-mail, 640 by 480 is fine.

## GREAT PHOTOGRAPHERS

### New Art in the Jazz Age:
## Man Ray
(1890–1976)

Emmanuel Radnitsky was born in Philadelphia, Pennsylvania, and became known as Man Ray, a member of the avant-garde in Paris during the 1920's and 1930's ("avant-garde" refers to artists who are experimenting with new forms). Man Ray produced a type of shadow photograph, without a camera, by placing various objects on photo printing paper and exposing it to light. He also used many ideas from modern art movements in his photography, films, paintings, and sculpture.

**Man Ray retouches a fashion photograph.**

Wide-Angle Lens

Using different lenses, photographers can change focus and picture composition. *Left:* A wide-angle lens shows a large area and gives a sense of depth. *Below:* A normal lens shows a scene the way the eye sees it. *Below left:* A telephoto lens focuses on a particular part of the scene and enlarges it. *Bottom:* A macro lens allows close focusing to show tiny details.

Telephoto Lens

Normal Lens

Macro Lens

Another setting on digital cameras is compression. This is a method of squeezing the information in a digital file so it takes up less memory. When the computer opens the picture, it uncompresses it, but some information may be lost. For the very best pictures, you should use as little compression as possible. But if you only want to e-mail pictures or make small prints, you can use more compression.

## Lenses

For SLR and view cameras, additional lenses are important accessories. These can be used to create images of different sizes and to take pictures of subjects that are far away or very close up.

Lenses come in a number of different focal lengths: normal, short, and long. With 35mm cameras, a normal-length lens—about 50mm—shows what the eye sees when looking at a scene.

Lenses with very short focal lengths are called wide-angle lenses. They take in a very large area but produce a small image of any object in a scene. One of the most interesting wide-angle lenses is the fish-eye lens. An 8mm fish-eye has a 180-degree angle (half circle) of view.

Telephoto lenses—those with long focal lengths—show less of the scene from a given spot. But they focus on a particular part of the scene and enlarge it, the way binoculars or telescopes do. Telephoto lenses are usually used for wildlife and sports photos.

Lenses with focal lengths that can be changed are called zoom lenses. You can get zoom lenses that stay in the telephoto range, such as 70-200mm, or zooms that stay in the wide-angle range, such as 17-28mm. The most popular zooms let you range from wide-angle to telephoto.

Lenses designed to focus very close up are called macro lenses. With these, you can photograph tiny details and small objects. You can also use simple, inexpensive lenses attached to the front of your normal or zoom lens to allow close focusing. These are called close-up lenses.

### Lighting, Flashes, and Filters

How can you tell whether the light is bright enough to take a picture? You use an **exposure meter**. This measures the light and provides the proper exposure settings for the type of film you are using. Most cameras have exposure meters built into them. You can also buy a separate, handheld meter.

With an **electronic flash**, you can take pictures even when the other light is not bright enough. Most point-and-shoot cameras, and many OTUC's, have flash units built in. These automatically provide the correct exposure for subjects up to about 20 feet (6 meters) away.

Better cameras such as SLR's can use bigger add-on flash units. These are more powerful and provide more light. Some photographers use several flash units at once for a picture. They may also use continuous lighting (called hot lights), which are like powerful lightbulbs.

**Filters** are transparent pieces of glass or plastic that are placed over the lens. They change the light that hits the film. When used with black-and-white film, they change the tones of gray. When used with color film, they usually change the actual colors. In some cases, filters improve the light reaching the camera. For example, a polarizing filter gets rid of reflections, so that pictures can be taken through windows. Polarizers can also make a blue sky darker without altering

## GREAT PHOTOGRAPHERS

### Reverence for the Natural World:
# Eliot Porter
(1901–90)

Eliot Porter was one of the first great nature photographers to use color, and he remains one of the most influential of all time. Born in Winnetka, Illinois, he earned an M.D. from Harvard Medical School in 1929 and spent the next decade teaching science at Harvard and Radcliffe. Porter began taking photographs in his spare time, then quit teaching to become a full-time photographer. He soon became known for his unique style: pictures of plants and animals that focused on rich textures and fine detail, as well as the subject's surroundings. Like Ansel Adams, Porter was also an activist for wilderness preservation.

**Fall leaves and pine needles, photographed by Eliot Porter in 1956, form a study in contrast and texture. Porter was a nature photographer for more than 40 years.**

Using continuous lighting (hot lights) and a light meter, a photographer and his assistant photograph a vase of flowers in a studio.

other colors. Other filters are used for special effects, such as mist or soft focus.

▶ STORING IMAGES AND MAKING PRINTS

When you finish a roll of film, the next step is developing and printing. If you take the film to the photofinishing counter in the supermarket or drugstore, it is usually sent to a large processing lab, especially if it is black-and-white or slide film. However, some places (minilabs) process color negative film at their own on-site labs, often within an hour.

Photofinishers can also make digital files from your negatives or slides and put them on a CD. This lets you view the images on a

## SPECIAL USES OF PHOTOGRAPHY

With special cameras, films, and other equipment, photography has been adapted to many uses in science and industry.

**Aerial photography** is photography from the air. Aerial photos are useful to mapmakers and surveyors. Archaeologists also use them to locate the boundary lines of ancient fields and long-forgotten cities.

**Astrophotography** is the photography of objects in space—such as the stars and planets—through a telescope. The space age saw the launching of telescopes aboard exploratory spacecraft. The Hubble Space Telescope, launched in 1990, gathers its images with a digital camera.

**Diagnostic imaging** is widely used in medicine and science. It includes X-ray photography, which uses invisible electromagnetic waves that can pass through objects that visible light cannot penetrate. X rays are used to indicate where bones are broken and to examine internal organs. They are also used in industry to test and inspect materials and parts. Since the introduction of digital photography, many other types of medical imaging have been developed. These include computerized axial tomography (or CAT scan) and magnetic resonance imaging (MRI). A CAT scan consists of a series of X rays that are interpreted by a computer and shown as cross-sectional slices of the body. An MRI provides a detailed picture of internal tissue and organs via digitally recorded electromagnetic impulses sent through the

body. There is now even a digital camera inside a pill that transmits pictures of a person's intestinal tract to an external digital recorder. (See the articles IMAGING, DIAGNOSTIC and X RAYS.)

**Holography** is three-dimensional photography. To create a hologram, part of a laser beam is directed at a subject, and is then reflected to a sensitized photographic plate. The other part of the beam is focused directly on the photographic plate. Together, the two parts of the beam record all the information needed to reproduce a three-dimensional image. Holography may be most familiar as the process used to make 3-D pictures on credit cards.

**Infrared photography** uses special film that is sensitive to infrared radiation. Infrared rays, which are invisible, have a longer wavelength than visible light, and can

Night-Vision Photograph of U.S. Army Training Range

computer or television screen, then e-mail them, post them on your Web site, or use them for greeting cards, school reports, and other printed material. Photofinishers can also send these pictures to a Web site where your family and friends can view them.

If you take pictures with a digital camera, you can download them to a computer and see them almost immediately. To download, you can use a cable supplied with most cameras that connects the camera to the computer; a dock (a little cradle that holds the camera); or a card reader. The card reader is like a small disk drive that can read your camera's memory card. After downloading, you can look at the pictures on the screen and e-mail them.

If you want prints or enlargements of your digital pictures, you can bring your memory card to a photofinisher or you can make them yourself. Fairly inexpensive color inkjet printers can make very good color prints and enlargements.

Using software for desktop publishing, you can put your photos into greeting cards, calendars, and announcements. You may also want to enhance these photos with image-editing software. This process is often called the digital darkroom. (For more information, see the feature accompanying this article.)

penetrate haze that scatters the waves of visible light. For this reason, infrared photographs are often much clearer than ordinary photographs. Infrared photography combined with aerial photography can provide detailed information on the type of vegetation growing below. Infrared photography is also used in medicine to inspect damage to veins and healing beneath scabs.

**Night-vision photography** is a special form of digital photography. A very weak image taken at night or in a dark area is amplified by electronic circuitry so more detail can be seen. This type of photography is used in surveillance, police work, and military operations.

**Photomicrography** combines a camera with a microscope to take pictures of things too small to be seen with the naked eye. These pictures, called photomicrographs, are very useful to scientists and engineers. They enable them to study the cells of living tissue, or the crystal structure of a piece of metal, or parts of ancient plants discovered in a thin slice of coal.

**Satellite photography** is photography from satellites. This is used for mapping, weather forecasting, and military intelligence. Military specialists study these images to learn about airfields, missile bases, and other military installations.

**Spectrography** combines a camera with a spectroscope, an instrument that breaks up light into its different wavelengths. Using spectrography, scientists can analyze the light emitted by the stars and the sun. Spectrographs of the planets reveal which gases are present in their atmospheres. Spectrographs can be used to analyze materials such as metal alloys.

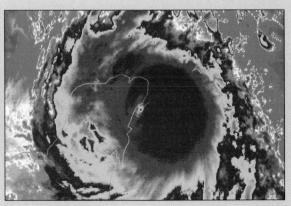

Satellite Image of Hurricane

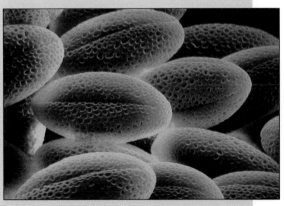

Photomicrograph of Pollen

## An American Classic:
# Ansel Adams
(1902–84)

Ask nearly any American to name a famous photographer and the answer is likely to be Ansel Adams. Adams, born in San Francisco, California, was noted for his stunning black-and-white landscapes of the American West (especially the national parks), as well as his work for environmental protection of these areas. While his pictures are considered fairly traditional, they also show the influence of modern art, such as the use of abstraction (reducing a picture to basic forms). He was also a scientific thinker, and devised the Zone System, a method for exposing and developing film to get the best tonal range (areas from very light to very dark) in photos.

**Ansel Adams' spectacular images of the American West are familiar to millions. This famous photo of the Snake River was taken in 1942 at Grand Teton National Park in Wyoming.**

▶ **CAREERS IN PHOTOGRAPHY**

At one time, most professional photographers were either self-taught or learned the trade as apprentices. Today, studying photography at a college or university is the best way to learn the profession. Those who just want to learn some of the basics—or perhaps concentrate on a specific topic in photography—can take individual courses in many colleges, universities, and some high schools. Taking one or two of these courses can also be a good way to decide if you want to pursue photography as a career.

Competition is strong for jobs in this field. Most professional photographers specialize in one or two kinds of pictures, such as advertising work, weddings and portraits, medical photography, nature photography, photomicrography, or photojournalism.

Stock photographers provide pictures to agencies, called stock agencies, which provide pictures to magazines and advertisers on a fee basis. The photographer usually shares a percentage of the fee. Stock photographers often specialize in specific areas.

▶ **HISTORY OF PHOTOGRAPHY**

A forerunner of the camera, the **camera obscura**, was invented hundreds of years before photography. It was actually a dark room with a tiny hole in one wall. Light came through the hole, producing an image on the opposite wall of the subject outside the hole.

For about 500 years, the camera obscura was used primarily for watching solar eclipses. Then artists and mapmakers realized it could be useful to them. As a result, portable versions were developed.

In time, the camera obscura was reduced to a small box much like a modern camera. A lens was placed in the hole where the light entered to help concentrate the light rays. There was also a diaphragm to control the amount of light coming in. The back of the box was a translucent screen. (Something translucent lets light pass through, but we cannot see detail through it.) A sheet of paper could be placed over the screen and the image traced on the paper. Artists such as Jan Vermeer used the camera obscura to make more realistic paintings.

In 1727, a German doctor, Johann Schulze, made the discovery that finally led to film. Schulze found that sunlight would blacken chalk that had been treated with a solution of silver nitrate. Modern photography is based on Schulze's discovery that light affects certain silver compounds.

The first successful photograph was made by a French inventor, Joseph Nicéphore Niepce, in 1826. He succeeded in capturing an image that did not immediately fade when light struck it. He placed the exposed metal plate (coated with an asphalt compound) in a solution that brought out the picture. The solution also washed away all the compound that had not yet been exposed to light. In other words, he fixed the picture. In 1829, Niepce became a partner of Louis Daguerre, a French theatrical designer. Before they had finished improving a developing process, Niepce died. Daguerre continued work on the process. In 1839, he revealed what became the first widely successful system of photography. His pictures were called daguerreotypes. Each was unique. There was no negative, and no prints could be made.

At about the same time, in England, William Henry Fox Talbot invented the first practical process that produced a negative from which prints could be made. This process, called calotype, began with a negative image on paper. It was then printed on another sensitized piece of paper to make a positive print.

Paper negatives had a drawback, however. The natural grain of the paper made the details of the picture somewhat unclear. To avoid this, people began experimenting with glass plates. Unfortunately, photographic chemicals would not stay on the glass. In 1847, Abel Niepce de Saint-Victor, the nephew of Joseph Niepce, tried something new. He coated a glass plate with albumen (the white of an egg). This sticky coating held the chemical fast.

In 1851, Frederick Scott Archer, an English chemist, introduced the wet collodion process. This process uses a syrupy, transparent liquid called collodion to hold the silver compounds on glass. The response of collodion plates to light was much faster than in other processes. But the photographer still had to coat the glass plate

This grainy view from an upstairs window is the world's first successful photograph. It was taken in 1826 by French inventor Joseph Nicéphore Niepce.

## GREAT PHOTOGRAPHERS

### The Photojournalist:
# Margaret Bourke-White
(1904–71)

Margaret Bourke-White, a pioneer in photojournalism, documented many important events.

Margaret Bourke-White, born in New York City, was a pioneer in photojournalism. The first photographer for *Fortune* magazine and a staff photographer for *Life* magazine, she was also the first Western photojournalist allowed into the Soviet Union. Bourke-White documented the crushing poverty of rural America during the Great Depression of the 1930's in her book *You Have Seen Their Faces*. During World War II she became one of the first female photojournalists allowed in combat zones and one of the first to photograph the Nazi death camps.

## TAKING GOOD PHOTOGRAPHS

Photography is a favorite pastime because nearly everyone knows how to take a picture. But following some simple rules can greatly improve your photographs.

The most important thing to remember is that no camera can "take" a picture. Only you can. And you can take excellent pictures with the simplest equipment. The key to good photographs is *seeing*.

### Using Simple Cameras

One of the easiest ways to learn the basics of photography is to use a disposable one-time-use camera, or OTUC. Since an OTUC has no settings to figure out, you can concentrate completely on composing your picture. Choose an OTUC with a built-in flash.

Taking outdoor pictures on bright days is a good starting point. Look through the viewfinder and see what happens to the picture in the frame if you aim the camera a little differently. Move closer to or farther from your subject. (Do not get too close or the picture will not be sharp.) Try crouching down to take a picture looking up. Or stand on a chair to take a picture looking down. The idea is to frame a picture, not just aim the camera. When you see a picture you want to take, hold the camera steady and press the shutter button. To take another picture, advance the film to bring another frame into position.

### Using Point-and-Shoot Cameras (Film or Digital)

Point-and-shoot cameras let you take pictures in more kinds of light than an OTUC and at many different distances. Autofocus point-and-shoot cameras let you shoot close to your subject—a couple of feet or less. Move close enough so that you see your subject from the waist or shoulders up. Try closing in on just the face. If your point-and-shoot has a zoom lens, you can get a closer view of your subject without actually moving closer. Try framing and taking pictures at different zoom settings.

Most point-and-shoot cameras let you choose different flash modes. The "flash on" or "fill flash" setting makes the flash fire in any picture you take. This is a good setting to use outdoors when there are shadows covering people's faces. The "flash off" setting will keep the flash from firing, whether it is light or dark, and keep the shutter open longer. This works well when you are shooting a sunset or a distant scene that is dim. For this you must hold the camera very steady, so try resting it on something.

### Light

Always consider your light source when taking pictures. Light from different directions—from above, below, behind, in front of, or to the side of the subject—produces entirely different shadow effects.

Light from behind, no flash          Light from behind, fill flash

Outside, the sun is your light source. The direction of the sun—and the shadows it makes—changes throughout the day. This can completely change the look of a scene.

Direct sunlight should be avoided for pictures of people, as it can make harsh shadows on your subject's face. You can lessen these by turning your camera's flash on, or by facing the subject away from the light. Do not let a cloudy, overcast day keep you from taking pictures. The soft, even light on such days is excellent for portraits and close-ups of flowers and other subjects.

### Focusing

To produce a sharp image, the camera must be properly focused. With OTUC's, the focus cannot be changed, so you will need to take the picture from the correct distance, usually at least 5 feet (1.5 meters) from the subject.

With an autofocus point-and-shoot camera, you will see a small set of brackets or a circle in the middle of the frame when you look through the viewfinder. This shows where the camera will focus. When you press very lightly on the shutter, the camera tries to focus on whatever is in that focusing point. Once the camera focuses, a small lamp next to the viewfinder will light up steadily. If the camera has trouble focusing, the small lamp will blink. Move back a bit, or aim the focusing point at a sharp detail, and try again.

You need not leave your subject in the middle of the frame. A point-and-shoot will let you lock the focus, then re-aim the camera so that your subject is off to the side. You should keep gentle but steady pressure on the shutter button to do this. (Try practicing with an empty camera.)

Most SLR's have both autofocus and manual-focus modes. In manual-focus, you turn a ring on the lens while looking through the viewfinder, until the subject looks sharp.

Aperture of f/2 decreases depth of field

Aperture of f/22 increases depth of field

### Exposure

Exposure is the amount of light that falls on the film or the imager. If the light is too weak, the picture will be underexposed and there will be no detail in the shadows. If the light is too strong, it will be overexposed and there will be no detail in the bright parts.

A simple camera, such as an OTUC, will have only one exposure setting. For this reason OTUC's are always loaded with film that has good exposure latitude. That is, it still results in fairly good prints even if the film has not been properly exposed.

Point-and-shoot and adjustable cameras have many shutter speeds and lens openings, so you can take pictures under many lighting conditions. (Many SLR's also have an autoexposure setting.) With film cameras, try using fast film, like ISO 800 or 1600 color-negative film, to take pictures indoors without flash. With digital cameras, you can increase the setting for "ISO equivalent" and try the same thing.

### Composition

Composition refers to the arrangement of the elements in a picture. The simplest pictures are often the best. They present one main subject, with no clutter in the background. As a rule, it is better not to have a person or other subject exactly in the center of a picture. The subject should be slightly away from the center, and other objects in the picture should guide the eye toward the subject. Avoid a cluttered background if possible. If you are using an adjustable camera, you can open the lens wide (that is, use a lower f-stop, such as f/1.4, f/2, f/2.8) to decrease the depth of field and blur out the background.

In a close-up shot, the subject will fill most of the picture, and less of the background will be seen. If you are taking pictures of lakes, parks, or other scenic spots, put people in the foreground. Doing so increases the feeling of depth and size in the picture.

Many subjects can be photographed either horizontally or vertically. Before pressing the shutter button, hold the camera in both positions. See which position provides a better picture.

Try to have each picture tell a story. A good way to do this is to show the subject doing something. For example, if you are taking a picture of a small child, show the child playing with a toy. When you take pictures, ask your subjects not to look at you. These pictures look more natural than posed pictures and are called candid photos.

## The Decisive Moment:
# Henri Cartier-Bresson
### (1908–2004)

**Like many photographs by Henri Cartier-Bresson, this image captures a pivotal moment in a sequence of events, as well as the relationship between subject and environment.**

At first glance, a photograph by Henri Cartier-Bresson might look like a snapshot. But if you keep looking, you will see how perfectly he captured an expression or a gesture that reveals something about the subject. Cartier-Bresson called the timing required for this "the decisive moment," and his work has been a tremendous influence on photojournalists right up to today. Born in Chanteloup, France, Cartier-Bresson began his photographic career in 1930. Over a period of several decades, he took photographs in many locales, including China, India, Spain, Cuba, the United States, Canada, and Japan. He was also a pioneer in available-light photography (photos taken without flash or studio light).

and load it into the camera. Then the plate had to be exposed, and the image developed, before the collodion dried. By the 1870's, gelatin-based dry emulsion began to replace the wet collodion plates.

### Advances

In the 1880's, two developments changed photography. First, flexible, roll-up film was introduced by George Eastman, founder of the Eastman Kodak Company in Rochester, New York. A few years later, Eastman brought out a hand-held roll-film camera. This camera was easy to carry and use. Eastman's company even processed the film, so amateur photographers no longer had to do their own developing. This marked the beginning of photography's popularity as a hobby.

Along with its increasing popularity, photography began to be recognized as an art. Some photographers of the early 1900's experimented with new printing techniques to make their photographs look more like paintings. Later photographers produced abstract compositions through various darkroom techniques and multiple exposures. Others continued to use the shapes and textures of the natural world to create beautiful photographs.

In the 1920's and 1930's, more technical advances affected amateur and professional photographers alike. In 1924, the Leica camera was introduced in Germany. This miniature 35mm camera came with a wide range of accessories and attachments. The Leica gave photographers new flexibility, allowing them to take sharp, detailed pictures under many conditions. It was the forerunner of today's 35mm cameras. The range of photography was further extended with the development of convenient flash equipment in the late 1920's and early 1930's.

Many photographers used this new flexibility to dramatize social issues, such as poverty, with moving candid shots. This became known as documentary photography. Other photographers concentrated on recording news events. With advances in printing, newspapers and magazines were demanding more and more photographs for illustration.

Meanwhile, color photography had been developing since the early 1900's. In 1935, Kodachrome slide film was introduced. It became the first popular, affordable color film and is still used today. Early in the 1940's color-negative film appeared. This captured images on a negative, and so it could be readily printed on color printing paper. Color-negative film quickly became the most popular type of film in the world and remains so today.

Instant film, which develops within seconds, appeared in 1947. It was invented by the American scientist Edwin H. Land for use in his Polaroid Land Camera.

One of the most important developments in photography was the electronic flash, invented in the 1930's by Dr. Harold Edgerton of the Massachusetts Institute of Technology (MIT). This consisted of a burst of electricity shot through a tube to create a short but brilliant light. Unlike the single-use flash bulbs that had come before, a flash could be fired many times. It could also be made one-millionth of a second or shorter. This enabled photographers to freeze motion.

## GREAT PHOTOGRAPHERS

Portraits from the Dark Side:
# Diane Arbus (1923–71)

Diane Arbus, born in New York City, took photographs that many consider disturbing. She began her career as a fashion photographer, working closely with her husband, but soon began taking documentary photographs of people in their homes, in stores, or on the street. She often photographed people who were physically different—midgets and giants for example—but even her portraits of "ordinary" people make them appear strange. Part of this was due to her technique. Arbus photographed people at odd angles, usually with direct flash, so that they were harshly lit. Her techniques, considered radical at the time, influenced many later photographers.

Diane Arbus photographing a man and his dogs. Arbus often photographed people she met on the street.

## THE DIGITAL DARKROOM

At one time, all photographs were processed with chemicals in a darkroom. Today this process is becoming obsolete, and the computer is the new "darkroom."

There are four basic steps to producing photos in the digital darkroom: capture, downloading, image editing, and printing.

**Capture** means getting an electronic **image file** that your computer can read. If you use a digital camera to take a picture, you already have one. To convert a negative, a slide, or a print to an image file, you will need to scan it with a scanner (or have it scanned at a photo lab). A scanner is basically a digital camera that takes a picture of a picture. A flatbed scanner has a glass plate like a photocopier's. You place the print face down on the glass plate, close the cover, and start the scan. To scan a negative or slide, you will need a film scanner, which has a special holder for film.

Once you have a digital file of your picture, the next step is **downloading** it, or getting it into your computer. If you have your own scanner, the scanner software has already done this. If you are transferring the image from a digital camera into your computer, you can use a cable, a dock, or a card reader. (For more information, see Storing Images and Making Prints in the main article.)

The process of modifying your picture is called **image editing**. This is done with image-editing software. This software is often included when you purchase a digital camera, printer, or scanner.

Image-editing programs let you modify your photos in many ways. You can lighten and darken them (entirely or in specific areas), adjust the contrast (for more or less), adjust the color, sharpen fuzzy images, and eliminate red-eye, which sometimes appears when people are photographed with flash. You can also use the program's cropping

A girl adds whimsical details to a digital image of herself. With image-editing software, photos can be modified in countless ways.

From the 1950's on, many of the advances in photography were for systems that automated various camera adjustments. In recent years remarkable improvements have been made in film, especially high-speed color-negative films.

### History of Electronic Photography

Discoveries about electricity and magnetism in the early 1800's led to the invention of the electric telegraph. Inventors soon began seeking ways to transmit pictures over telegraph wires by electrical signals and to record them as electronic impulses, without the use of film or chemicals. The first facsimile (fax) machine was patented in 1843. By the end of the 1800's, facsimile machines that could send pictures were being developed, and in 1920 a photograph was transmitted across the Atlantic via the underwater telegraph cable. This was one of the first digital transmissions of photography. From then on, the development of electronic photography was closely tied to the development of television and the technology that could send images via electromagnetic waves.

By the late 1950's the United States and the former Soviet Union were engaged in a space race. The U.S. government now became a major force in designing electronic cameras that could transmit images from manned and unmanned spacecraft. Some of these were used for spying. In 1964 the world saw the first electronic photos of Mars, taken by the *Mariner 6* and *Mariner 7* spacecraft. Five years later, people around the globe marveled at the first pictures taken on the moon's surface, made by an RCA television camera attached to a leg of the *Apollo 11* lunar lander.

tool to cut off unwanted portions of your picture and enlarge the rest. Before making any changes, however, you should make a separate copy of the original image so you can go back to it if needed.

Some image-editing programs let you make a picture look like stained glass, liquid, or metal or distort things or faces. (Just make sure your friends have a good sense of humor before you do this to pictures of them!)

Many people use image-editing programs to fix old photos that are faded and damaged. This is done by scanning the original photo, then using various tools to restore tone and color. One of these tools, called a clone tool, can cover up rips and tears. It does this by "memorizing" the tone and texture of an undamaged part of the picture, then lets you "paint" over the damaged areas.

Once you have made changes to your picture, it is time to print it. Inexpensive color inkjet printers can make very good color prints if you use photo paper. This paper is available in different surface textures and shows far more color and detail than regular printer paper. It is also important to use the printer profiles that come with the image-editing software. This lets you tailor the printing to a specific printer (which you can select from a list), which results in better prints.

## Social Commentary Through the Lens:
# Robert Frank
(1924– )

When Robert Frank set out in the mid-1950's to photograph America, he was not intending to take postcard images. Instead, he photographed on the streets and in diners, post offices, stores, and bus stations, taking unposed pictures of ordinary people. These photographs, published in the book *The Americans*, show a country that is lonely, disconnected, and divided by race and class. Many people have criticized the book, saying that it deliberately shows the United States in a bad light. But the book is a powerful document for many, influencing a generation of "street shooter" photographers. Frank was born in Zurich, Switzerland.

**Robert Frank, photographed in his studio.**

## Spokesman for Humanity:
# Sebastião Salgado
(1944– )

Many people consider Sebastião Salgado one of the greatest living photographers. Born in Aimores, Minas Gerais, Brazil, Salgado has dedicated himself to photographing the poor and displaced peoples of the world, such as families forced to flee their homelands. A good example is the series of portraits called *The Children*, pictures of small children who have been left homeless by war or poverty. Proceeds from his exhibitions often go to help refugee organizations.

**A visitor to a London gallery views photos by Sebastião Salgado. Salgado is one of the world's leading contemporary photographers.**

## The Colors of Nature:
# Frans Lanting
(1951– )

Frans Lanting is one of the most respected contemporary nature photographers. Born in Rotterdam, the Netherlands, Lanting is known for thoroughly researching his subjects before photographing them. He has often worked for *National Geographic* magazine on unusual assignments, such as searching for the last white rhinos in central Africa. His photos emphasize the need to preserve complete ecosystems, not just single species. Lanting's work, which includes seldom-seen aspects of nature, has encouraged governments to be more protective of endangered areas.

**Two albatross groom each other during a courting ritual. Photographer Frans Lanting took this photo on the sub-Antarctic island of South Georgia.**

Just a few months later, two men, Willard Boyle and George Smith, began work on a device that would revolutionize photography. This was the charge-coupled device (CCD), which could record images electronically. Within a few years, the first working CCD camera was made. By the late 1970's, CCD cameras were being made for industrial uses and were quickly adapted for astronomy and space exploration.

In the early 1980's, the Sony Corporation of Japan introduced a consumer electronic camera, the Mavica (for *m*agnetic *vi*deo camera). It recorded images on two-inch floppy disks and played them back on a television set or video monitor. Other electronic cameras soon followed, and news organizations began to use electronic cameras. Although these cameras recorded without film or chemicals, they were not digital cameras: They stored visual information as analog signals rather than as binary code.

Fully digital cameras began to appear in the early 1980's. In 1990, Kodak unveiled the DCS-100, a digital camera housed in a modified Nikon SLR body. This was the first digital camera designed as a full professional system. It was very expensive and had to be attached to an external hard drive, but the race was on. Within a few years, professional digital cameras became self-contained, with much greater resolving power (pixel count). Digital backs were also devised for existing professional cameras and for studio view cameras. A less expensive alternative to the CCD, the complementary metal-oxide semiconductor (CMOS), emerged in the 1990's.

In the late 1990's digital point-and-shoot cameras exploded in popularity. People liked seeing their pictures right away and having the ability to e-mail them. By the early 2000's digital cameras had greatly improved—their image quality was equal to or better than that of film. Digital cameras soon began to outsell film cameras in the United States.

Digital cameras are now being combined with other electronic devices, such as cell phones, laptop computers, and digital organizers. Cameras themselves are becoming more connected—several manufacturers already make cameras that can store e-mail addresses so you can send photos faster. We can expect more wireless transmission of photographs, as well as a camera that can transmit high-quality photos directly, without any other attachments.

As the cost of digital cameras continues to drop, more people will be able to afford them. And more picture "fixes" such as red-eye removal will likely become automated within the camera. All these factors will make it even easier to take good photos. But no piece of equipment can replace the value of a sensitive photographic eye.

DAN RICHARDS
*Popular Photography and Imaging*

See also LENSES; LIGHT.

# PHOTOSYNTHESIS

Green plants can make their own food. They take water from the soil and carbon dioxide from the air to make sugar. In doing so the plants give off oxygen. This process is called photosynthesis.

The energy for this process comes from sunlight. If plants are kept in the dark, photosynthesis stops. That is the reason for the name of the process. "Photosynthesis" comes from two Greek words meaning "putting together with light."

When a plant has formed sugar, using the energy of sunlight, it then can form starch and all the other complicated food substances it needs for life. For this reason we say that plant life is made possible by using energy from the sun.

Photosynthesis occurs only in the plant kingdom. But animal life as well as plant life depends on the sun. Animals cannot use the sun's energy directly. Since they cannot make their own food, animals must get food from plants or from other animals that eat plants.

Animals that just eat plants are called herbivorous (plant-eating) animals. Carnivorous (flesh-eating) animals do not eat plants. Instead they eat other animals. Usually they eat herbivorous animals, which get their energy from the plants they eat. And the plants, of course, produce food by photosynthesis. In the long run, then, nearly all life depends on the sun.

When chlorophyll breaks down, a leaf loses its green color and its ability to carry on photosynthesis. This happens in the fall as many leaves change color and die.

### ▶HOW DO PLANTS GET ENERGY FROM SUNLIGHT?

Plants can make use of the sun's energy if their leaves possess a green chemical substance called **chlorophyll.** Chlorophyll particles are contained in **chloroplasts,** which are small disk-shaped bodies located in many plant cells.

Plant leaves and often plant stems are green because of their chlorophyll content. The word "chlorophyll" comes from Greek words meaning "green leaf." Chloroplast means "green shape."

The leaves of some plants may have a dark reddish color. They contain colored substances that hide the green chlorophyll. But since the leaves do have chlorophyll, they still carry on photosynthesis.

Unlike the green plants, mushrooms have no chlorophyll. They cannot obtain energy from sunlight. They obtain it from dead and decaying plants.

When chlorophyll absorbs sunlight, it gains energy through a series of chemical reactions. That energy is used to carry out other chemical changes needed to make food.

A single particle of chlorophyll absorbs and passes on many bits of energy from sunlight. It provides energy for much chemical change, while remaining basically unchanged itself. Chemists call any substance that behaves in this way a **catalyst.** It helps a chemical process along, but it is not part of the chemical change that takes place.

### ▶HOW DO PLANTS USE THE SUN'S ENERGY?

Chlorophyll, using the energy of sunlight, chemically changes water molecules in the plant. (Water is absorbed by the plant from the soil.) The chemical change is the splitting apart of water molecules.

Water molecules consist of atoms of hydrogen and oxygen bound tightly together. A lot of energy must be added to water before its molecules split apart. Sunlight supplies this energy. The water molecules are split apart, and hydrogen and oxygen are formed.

Once this happens, some of the hydrogen and oxygen atoms recombine into water. The energy given off when this happens is used to form a certain compound called **adenosine triphosphate.** This is a long name even for chemists, and it is usually abbreviated **ATP.** Molecules of ATP are stored in the plant until they are needed as a source of energy. Then the ATP is broken down in another chemical process and the energy used.

Not all the hydrogen and oxygen formed by the splitting of water molecules recombines. The rest is used for other purposes, which will be explained later.

### Carbon Dioxide Traps

The carbon dioxide used by plants is absorbed from the air. The carbon dioxide molecules, once absorbed, are held fast by certain sugarlike molecules that are already present in plant cells. These sugarlike molecules are often called carbon dioxide traps.

Water, carbon dioxide, and sunlight combine during photosynthesis to produce food. A by-product of this process is oxygen, which is released into the air.

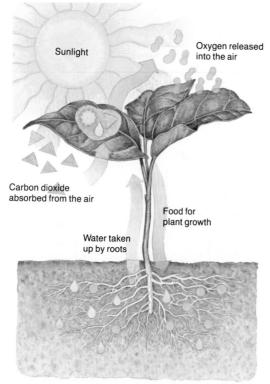

Sunlight

Oxygen released into the air

Carbon dioxide absorbed from the air

Food for plant growth

Water taken up by roots

Six trapped carbon dioxide molecules are used in forming one molecule of glucose. Glucose is an important sugar present in all living things. It is always present, for instance, in the blood of animals with spinal columns, including human beings.

The molecules of glucose can be put together to form large molecules of starch or even larger molecules of cellulose (the main substance of wood). Moreover, the plants absorb certain minerals from the soil. If these are added to the glucose molecules, complicated molecules of protein can be formed.

Carbon dioxide molecules cannot be built up into glucose without help. Hydrogen and energy must be added. The hydrogen comes from the water molecules that split and did not recombine. The energy comes from ATP. When hydrogen and energy are added to the carbon dioxide, glucose is formed.

You may wonder how photosynthesis can work if the carbon dioxide traps must be present in the plant tissues to begin with. How did those sugarlike molecules come to be there in the first place?

Most green plants produce new plants through spores or seeds. When a spore or seed is fully formed, it contains a supply of starch or other foodstuff. If you cut open a bean seed, for example, you will see the light-colored food supply beneath the seed's coat.

As the seed develops, it breaks down the food for energy. The seed uses that energy to build up compounds such as chlorophyll and carbon dioxide traps. A green shoot appears aboveground, and by the time the young plant has used up the original food supply, photosynthesis can take over.

These magnified plant cells contain the small, round chloroplasts where chlorophyll is found. The photosynthesis process, shown at left, takes place here.

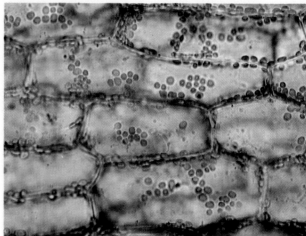

Energy
from sunlight

Carbon dioxide

Oxygen and Food

Photosynthesis
in plants

Water

## ▶ WHAT HAPPENS TO THE LEFTOVER OXYGEN?

Let us return to those water molecules that split up into hydrogen and oxygen and did not recombine into water. The hydrogen was used up. It combined with carbon dioxide, forming glucose. But what happened to the oxygen?

The plant uses only a part of it. The rest of it escapes into the air. That is another reason that photosynthesis is important. It supplies us with oxygen.

In order to get energy, animals combine the food they eat with the oxygen they inhale. In this process, water and carbon dioxide are formed. Animals then give off these unused compounds. You might think that after many, many years of animal life, all the oxygen in the atmosphere would have been used up and carbon dioxide would exist in its place.

Because of green plants, this has not happened. During photosynthesis, green plants combine carbon dioxide and water to form food and oxygen again.

Plants and animals working together keep the atmosphere in balance. There is enough oxygen for animal life and enough carbon dioxide for plant life. What is more, as plant food is eaten up by animals, more plant food is formed by plants through photosynthesis.

## ▶ HOW CAN PLANTS PRODUCE MORE FOOD?

As the world's population increases, new sources of food must be found. People are farming more efficiently by using better fertilizers and quick-growing varieties of plants with high food value. There is better control of insect pests. Researchers also are learning to make more use of food from the sea.

However, there will always be a limit to the total amount of food available. The amount of food depends on how efficiently the energy of sunlight can be turned into food by the chlorophyll of plants. Perhaps researchers will have to search for plants that make better use of sunlight than the plants now used for food.

For instance, there are microscopic one-celled seaweeds called **algae**. Unlike plants they have no roots, wood, flowers, fruit, or other parts that lack chlorophyll. Their entire structure can work at photosynthesis. For this reason and others, algae are more efficient at changing sunlight into food. Perhaps, scientists will learn how to grow algae and make tasty and nourishing food from them. Then the Earth's food supply would be vastly increased. (Even now, people in Asia and other parts of the world eat seaweed, a form of algae.)

Algae may be essential for space travel. If a spaceship is to go from Earth to Mars, for instance, it will have to spend many months in space. Astronauts will find it difficult to store enough food and oxygen on board ship for such a long journey. Instead, supplies of algae may be taken. Algae grow quickly under sun-lamps. And algae would keep the air fresh by restoring the oxygen astronauts use up in breathing.

ISAAC ASIMOV
Boston University School of Medicine

See also ALGAE; CELLS; FLOWERS; LEAVES; LIFE; PLANTS.

Swimming is one of the many sports included in physical education programs. Students may receive instruction in competitive swimming and in water safety and lifesaving.

## PHYSICAL EDUCATION

Physical fitness has always been one of the major goals of physical education. At one time the normal demands of everyday living provided enough exercise to keep people physically fit. Today machines do more and more of the work that our muscles used to do. As a result the body development of many modern people is far below what it should be. Most schools all over the world today stress the development of physical fitness. Students are helped to improve strength, balance, agility, posture, endurance, speed, and accuracy.

It is true that physical fitness depends greatly on exercise, but nutrition, sleep, rest, and good health habits are also important. Physical education programs in schools, therefore, emphasize the learning of good health habits as well as provide opportunities for physical activities.

Many physical education programs also include leisure-time activities or sports. Games such as tennis and bowling give people the opportunity to play a game regardless of age.

In North American schools, physical education activities may include the following.

### Individual Sports

| | |
|---|---|
| Badminton | Racquetball |
| Bowling | Skating |
| Boxing | Swimming |
| Golf | Table tennis |
| Gymnastics | Tennis |
| Handball | Track and field |
| Jogging | Wrestling |

### Team Sports
Baseball
Basketball
Football
Hockey (ice and field)
Soccer
Volleyball

### Rhythmical Activities
Calisthenics
Dance
Gymnastics
Marching

**Elementary School Programs.** Most elementary school programs include rhythms, dancing, exercises, and instruction in simple game and athletic skills. The programs help children develop their bodies and learn the basic concepts of good conduct and fair play.

**Secondary School Programs.** These programs include dance, calisthenics, tumbling, apparatus work, and team sports. Body growth is very rapid during the junior and senior high school years. Therefore, activities that promote balanced development are offered at this time. Current programs emphasize instruction in skills needed for team sports and encourage the development of teamwork, leadership, and a sense of responsibility.

**College Programs.** These programs continue the development of general athletic ability, as well as skills in various sports. In addition, fitness programs are receiving emphasis in colleges today. Many college programs include intramural and interscholastic competition in team and individual sports. Special programs are also available for students interested in professional physical education—who seek careers as trainers, teachers, coaches, and so on.

# HISTORY OF PHYSICAL EDUCATION

Physical education goes back to the first parents who taught their children to jump, throw, wrestle, climb, and swim. Early people needed these skills for survival.

The people of the ancient world needed soldiers who could fight well and who were able to take care of themselves on long marches. Young boys in ancient countries were trained in such skills as running, jumping, riding, and javelin throwing. The Spartans of southern Greece considered physical education important for both boys and girls. Boys were trained in running, wrestling, throwing weights, and other skills that would make strong, rugged soldiers. Physical education for the girls of Sparta included gymnastics, dancing, swimming, discus throwing, running, and wrestling. The same activities were developed in Athens, but body development, beauty, grace, and sportsmanship were stressed.

The Romans also stressed activities related to military training and added gladiatorial (fighting) contests, ball games, chariot races, and exercises with dumbbells.

For about 1,000 years after the decline of the Roman Empire in the 5th century A.D., there was little or no interest in formal physical education.

During the 15th and 16th centuries, there were important changes in general education and physical education. Vittorino da Feltre of Italy believed that physical training and mental training should be combined. He established a school in Mantua in 1423 in which special teachers taught dancing, riding, fencing, swimming, wrestling, jumping, running, archery, hunting, and fishing. In addition, students were taught academic subjects. Some other educators during this period emphasized the place of exercise and physical activity in the general curriculum.

Between 1750 and 1850, the countries of Europe developed somewhat distinctive styles of physical education. In Germany, Johann Basedow established a school in 1774 in which physical education was given a place in the daily program. He introduced high jumping, long jumping, and the use of such equipment as hoops and seesaws. Physical education in Germany was furthered in the early 1800's by Guts Muths, who wrote several books about gymnastics and games, and Friedrich Jahn, who established a formal sys-

Gymnastics has been an important part of physical education since the early 1800's. The sport helps students develop strength, agility, flexibility, and balance.

tem of gymnastics that involved exercises on such apparatus as the horizontal bar, vaulting horse, and parallel bars. Adolph Spiess (1810–58) used Jahn's methods and introduced physical education to schools in Germany.

During the same period, Per Henrik Ling was changing physical education in Sweden. His system of gymnastics included simple exercises that required little or no apparatus and were designed to promote body development.

In Denmark, under the leadership of Franz Nachtegall (1777–1847), the physical education program emphasized movements that would increase flexibility and grace.

The French in this period developed physical education by following the programs of other countries and selecting those activities they thought best.

Czarist Russia gave little thought to physical education, and it was given no importance until the development of the socialist state, after 1918.

In Britain the emphasis was on games and sports until the 1850's, when gymnastic exercises were added to school programs.

In the United States, gymnastics dominated the early physical education programs. But in the second half of the 19th century, intercollegiate sports started becoming popular—especially rowing, baseball, track and field, and football. The emphasis on team sports grew in the 20th century, but present trends in physical education also stress personal fitness.

LAWRENCE S. FINKEL
Chester Township, New Jersey, Public Schools

# PHYSICAL FITNESS

The body is an amazing thing; the more you ask of it, the more it can do. If you are sedentary (inactive) most of the time, your body may quickly become tired when you ask it to be active. But if you are active several times each day or week, your body will get used to the exertion and it will become easier to do. Children who want to play active games with their friends should exercise regularly so they have the energy to play as long as they want.

Many young people choose to be physically active because it helps them look and feel their best. Activity burns more calories than sitting still, so it is important for maintaining a healthy weight. Exercise also strengthens the muscles and bones, keeping the body well-conditioned and capable of doing daily tasks easily.

Physical activity also helps people stay healthy. Exercise strengthens the immune system, enabling the body to fight off illness. Participating in daily exercise also helps people sleep better. Active students rarely complain about being tired. They wake rested and have the energy to work hard and have fun each day.

Physical fitness is a balance of many areas including strength, cardiovascular fitness, and flexibility. This article will teach you how to use these activities to achieve your fitness goals.

## ▶ STRENGTH

Strength is the amount of force muscles can exert. People used to think only boys had to be strong, but that is not true. All people who want to be active and healthy must be strong. Strength training keeps your bones sturdy, boosts your metabolism, and tones your muscles. People who are strong can do chores and activities more easily and may learn sport skills more quickly.

Being strong does not necessarily mean having big muscles. Muscle size is determined somewhat by your genes—very few people will look like action heroes as they get stronger. Age also helps determine muscle size. Children of elementary-school age will become stronger by doing strengthening exercises, but their muscles probably will not grow noticeably bigger. A rise in certain hor-

Physical activity can be done in the winter or the summer, alone or as part of a team. Soccer and snowboarding are just two of the many activities you can do as part of a physical fitness plan.

mones during adolescence will lead to increased muscle size in males who do strength training. Females can become stronger and increase muscle development, but most will not develop extremely large muscles at any age because their balance of hormones differs from that of males.

### Making Muscles Stronger

To strengthen your muscles, you must make them work harder than usual. Lifting weights in a gym is not the only way to develop strength. You can build strength just by helping at home doing chores that involve lifting and carrying, such as bringing grocery bags from the car to the kitchen.

To increase strength, try moving a slightly heavier object than normal. This could be a heavier weight or a heavier grocery bag. After a while it will be easy to move this heavier object. Anytime an object becomes easy for you to move, you must increase the weight again if you want to continue to get stronger. Remember, it takes time to become strong. Increase weights gradually to avoid injury or discouragement.

Exercises such as push-ups and sit-ups will also build strength. When performing these exercises, the weight you move is that of your own body. Although you cannot increase your own weight, you can continue to build strength by increasing the number of sit-ups or push-ups that you do.

Strengthening exercises must be specific. Lifting weights with your arms will not make your leg muscles stronger. If you want stronger legs, you must do leg exercises. For the best fitness, it is a good idea to work on strengthening all your muscles by doing a variety of exercises. Suggestions for strength-building exercises can be found in the chart on this page.

### ▶ CARDIOVASCULAR OR AEROBIC FITNESS

The lungs supply oxygen to the blood, and the heart pumps the blood through the blood vessels to the muscles. **Cardiovascular fitness** is the body's ability to bring oxygen to the muscles for an extended period of time. The more oxygen you can bring to your muscles, the longer you will be able to exercise without becoming tired. Cardiovascular fitness is also called **aerobic** fitness.

Perhaps you have done aerobic activities, such as biking or running, that make you breathe faster and harder. You breathe harder because your body is trying to take

| Examples of Strengthening Exercises | |
|---|---|
| **Exercise** | **Muscles Strengthened** |
| Push-Ups | Arm, back, and chest muscles |
| Pull-Ups | Arm, back, and chest muscles |
| Two-Leg Squat (stand and bend your knees to a 90-degree angle) | Leg muscles |
| Sit-Ups | Abdominal muscles |
| Tip-Toes (move up to your toes and hold; repeat) | Ankle and calf muscles |
| Tennis Ball Squeeze | Grip strength and forearm muscles |

more oxygen from the air and deliver it to your muscles. The more work you do, the more oxygen you need. Regular physical activity makes the heart, lungs, and muscles become stronger and more efficient.

### Counting Your Pulse

Every time your heart beats, it pushes blood through your blood vessels. You can feel the small wave, or **pulse**, of blood with your fingertips. The best place to feel your pulse is near your wrist. Place your index and middle fingers at the base of your thumb on the inside of your wrist. (Ask a parent or teacher to help you if you cannot find your pulse.) To determine your heart rate, count your pulse for six seconds and place a zero at the end of the number you counted. For example, if you counted nine pulses (or heartbeats) in six seconds, your heart rate would be 90 beats per minute. Compare your heart rate when you are at rest with your heart rate during or just after aerobic exercise. Your heart rate during or after aerobic exercise should be much faster.

### Improving Your Aerobic Fitness

To maintain good health, everyone should try to be active for 30 minutes at least five days a week. But if you want to improve your aerobic fitness, you need to exercise hard enough to raise your heart rate into the **target heart rate zone** on at least three of those days. The target heart rate zone is the level at which the heart and lungs become stronger most quickly. When athletes train to perform better in a race, they try to keep their heart rate in the target heart rate zone for as long as possible.

A well-balanced physical fitness program includes exercises to strengthen the muscles. Push-ups are a good example of a strengthening activity.

## Examples of Flexibility Exercises

| Exercise | Motion |
|---|---|
| Bend and Twist | Starting position: Stand with your arms crossed, hands on opposite shoulders, knees slightly bent, and feet shoulder width apart. Movement: Bend forward at the waist (count 1). Twist the trunk and touch the right elbow to the left knee (count 2). Twist in the opposite direction and touch your left elbow to your right knee (count 3). Return to the starting position (count 4). |
| Sitting Stretch | Starting position: Sit on the floor with one leg extended forward and the other bent at the knee with the foot close to the other knee. Movement: Gradually bend forward, taking three counts to bend fully. Try to touch the toes of the extended leg with the fingertips of both hands. Return to sitting position on the fourth count. Repeat with the other leg extended. |
| Lower Leg Stretch | Starting position: Stand facing a wall with your feet about shoulder width apart. Place the palms of your hands on the wall at eye level. Movement: Slowly walk away from the wall, keeping the body straight, until a stretch is felt in the lower portion of the calf. The feet should remain flat on the floor during the stretch. |
| Achilles Tendon Stretch | Starting position: Stand facing a wall with your forearms on it. Place your forehead on the back of your hands. Back 2 to 3 feet away from the wall, then move one leg closer to the wall. Movement: Bend the leg closest to the wall until the stretch is felt in the Achilles tendon area. Both feet should remain flat on the floor as the leg closer to the wall is bent. Repeat with the other leg. |
| Standing Hip Bend | Starting position: Stand with your knees slightly bent, one hand on your hip and the other arm overhead. Movement: Bend to the side with your hand on your hip. The arm overhead should point and move in the direction of the stretch with a slight bend at the elbow. Reverse and stretch to the opposite side. |

You can determine if your activity level is strenuous enough to improve your aerobic fitness by taking your pulse following the procedure described earlier. If the number is between 125 and 170 beats per minute, your heart rate is in the target heart rate zone. Try to keep your heart rate in the target heart rate zone for at least 15 minutes. Gradually increase the amount of time you maintain your heart rate in the target heart rate zone until you can do it for 30 minutes each time you exercise.

### What Type of Activities Are Best for Aerobic Fitness?

Any activity that makes your heart beat faster and that you enjoy is a good choice for aerobic fitness. If you enjoy jumping rope or bicycling, that is the activity you should do. It is not necessary to do the same thing every day. In fact, two days of basketball, three days of swimming, and two days of bicycling can be more fun than jogging every day.

### ▶ FLEXIBILITY

Joints are points in your body that allow you to move. Your body has many joints, including the shoulders, elbows, wrists, hips, knees, and ankles. A joint that is healthy and moves easily can move throughout its **full range of motion**. If all your joints move well, you have good flexibility.

### Why Is Flexibility Important?

Your muscles and ligaments are important for joint health. Stretching activities are designed to keep joints healthy by stretching the muscles and ligaments. Flexibility slowly decreases as people age. By regularly doing stretching activities, you can help maintain the full range of motion at each joint.

If you watch some of your favorite athletes warm up, you will find that they all do stretching activities before playing. Stretching helps athletes avoid injuries because it moves blood to the muscles and prepares them for strenuous activity. Stretching after exercise moves blood throughout the body and reduces the amount of muscle soreness felt the next day.

Stretching can also help you feel relaxed. If you are tired or worried, try doing flexibility activities and deep breathing together. You may feel better and will keep your joints healthy at the same time.

### Flexibility Exercises

Flexibility exercises should be performed with slow, controlled movements. You should move slowly into position until the muscle being stretched starts to hurt slightly. Hold this position for 10 to 20 seconds and then relax. This is called **static** stretching. Examples of good stretching exercises can be found in the chart on this page.

## GETTING STARTED

Now that you know about the different types of physical activity, you may have questions about getting started. People who have not been very active in the past should begin slowly. Do not try to exercise too much at once. If you are normally active, you may want to try some new exercises.

### What Should You Wear?

The proper clothing will make exercise easier and more enjoyable. A good pair of shoes provides support to the feet during exercise. Athletic shoes do not have to be expensive, but they should fit well and be comfortable. Make sure shoes are tightly laced, and wear socks to help prevent blisters and improve the fit, if necessary.

You should choose clothing that is suited to the type of activity and the temperature. If you are exercising in warm weather, wear lightweight and light-colored clothing and a cap or hat to shade your head from the sun. If you are active in the cold, try wearing several layers of clothing instead of a heavy coat. This may keep you warmer and allow you to move more freely. If it is raining outside or you will be playing in the snow, wear clothing that is water-resistant—once your clothes get wet, it is difficult to stay warm.

It is important to wear protective equipment for certain activities. For example, you should always wear a helmet when bicycling. Pads, mouth guards, or protective eyewear might be necessary when participating in other activities.

### Soreness, Aches, and Pain

You may feel muscle soreness for a few days after trying a new activity. This may mean the activity you did was too strenuous or involved muscles you do not use often. Muscle soreness is normal and will usually go away in a few days. Soreness is different from pain. If you ever feel pain in a muscle or joint, you should tell an adult.

Sometimes you may develop an ache on the side of your upper abdomen during activity. Nobody knows exactly what causes a side-ache. Stretching the side that is hurting, taking deep breaths, or putting pressure on the ache with your hand may help. At other times, you might have to rest for a few minutes until the ache goes away.

Flexibility can be maintained by regularly doing stretching activities. Many martial arts, such as karate, require good flexibility.

## SELECTING AN ACTIVITY

There are many factors to consider when selecting a new physical activity. The most important is picking something you enjoy and will want to do often.

Everyone needs activities that help them maintain or improve their strength, aerobic fitness, and flexibility. You may wish to select an activity from an area in which you think you need improvement. For example, if you are flexible and able to run long distances but are not very strong, you could choose some activities that increase strength. If you are strong but need more aerobic fitness, try walking, jogging, biking, or dancing.

Different activities require different skills. Your school years are an excellent time to develop athletic skills. Some skills will improve with practice while others may always be difficult for you. Some people are better at certain activities than others, but do not let that discourage you. If you enjoy an activity, feel free to do it.

You may need to try several activities before you find the ones that are right for you. For example, you may find you enjoy activities you can do alone, such as running or biking. Or you may prefer to participate in team activities that are coached. Some people enjoy competition, while others prefer activities that do not have the pressure of winning or losing. Whatever activities you choose, becoming physically fit will make you healthier for life.

ROBERT P. PANGRAZI
Arizona State University

See also HEALTH; NUTRITION.

# PHYSICS

Physics is the study of matter and energy. Matter is the basic substance of which everything consists; energy is what makes matter move and change. By studying matter and energy, physicists try to understand the universe. Thus physics is the science behind such things as gravity, motion, magnetism, electricity, atomic energy, and black holes.

Unlike biologists, who study living things, physicists investigate nonliving things, from the smallest and simplest atoms up to vast and complex galaxies. Chemists and geologists also study nonliving matter, such as water, rocks, and plastics. But physicists study the basic elements of matter before they join together to form compound things like rocks or trees. Physicists want to know what forces hold atoms together, how gases change to liquids, why metals conduct electricity, and how stars and galaxies evolve.

The science of physics can be loosely divided into two traditional categories: classical physics and modern physics. Within each category are various branches of study.

Physicists study images of the collisions of highly charged subatomic particles sent racing through a bubble chamber by particle accelerators to help them analyze certain theories about the creation of the universe. One such theory, the Big Bang theory, begins with the explosion of a minute particle of matter.

## ▶ CLASSICAL PHYSICS

Classical physics deals with several fields of study that were quite well developed before the 1900's. These branches include mechanics, heat, sound, light, and electromagnetism.

### Mechanics

The science of **mechanics** is concerned with the effects of forces on bodies at rest or in motion. These effects are described by mathematical equations called **laws of motion**, which were introduced in 1687 by the English scientist Isaac Newton to explain why the planets orbit the sun. Newton demonstrated that a gravitational force of attraction acting between the sun and a planet causes the planet to move around the sun in an elliptical path.

Newton was able to apply his laws to the motion of all bodies, not just planets. According to Newton's laws, when no force acts on an object, it moves uniformly, that is, along a straight line at a constant speed. This is called the **law of inertia**. But planets and most bodies do not move uniformly. Newton discovered that their motion is changed or accelerated by pushes or pulls, which he called **forces**. For example, the motion of a baseball traveling through the air is determined by forces exerted on the ball by the air and gravity. An iron nail slides across a table toward a magnet because of the attractive force of magnetism. When a gas is heated, forces resulting from its molecules colliding with one another cause the gas to expand.

Everything from the activity of the electrons in an atom (electrons are tiny particles of matter that travel around the nucleus of an atom) to the rotation of a galaxy can be understood using Newton's laws of motion. The explanation of an object's motion in terms of the forces acting on it is the central idea in Newton's science of mechanics, which remained the foundation of physics until the 1900's.

## Heat

Closely related to motion is the idea of energy, which describes the activity of objects and their ability to do work. Since objects often generate heat as they do work, there is also a relationship between energy and heat. In fact, heat is a form of energy. For example, chemical energy stored in a battery supplies electrical energy to run a motor, which does mechanical work such as pulling or lifting. This transformation of energy may also produce heat, but no energy is created or destroyed in the process. The transformation of one form of energy into another without loss or gain is called the **conservation of energy**. It is one of the fundamental laws of science.

The idea that heat is a form of energy is essential to understanding how engines operate, why your hands heat up when you rub them together, how an atomic bomb works, and how the universe has evolved. The science of heat, which is known as **thermodynamics**, is the study of all energy transformations in matter. It is another fundamental branch of physics.

## Sound

All sounds result from the motion produced when the molecules making up a substance are made to vibrate, or move back and forth, very rapidly. Sound is caused by the vibrating motion of molecules in a medium such as air, water, or a solid such as wood. Sound travels as waves, which are vibrating disturbances that move through air or any other medium like ripples traveling on a lake. Since sound is caused by motion, the science of mechanics, with its laws of motion, explains how sound is generated and then travels through matter to reach our ears. The study of sound and its effects on objects is known as **acoustics**.

## Light

The study of light, how it is produced and how it behaves, is known as **optics**. In the 1600's and 1700's, many scientists thought that light consisted of tiny particles given off

A rainbow is formed by the reflection of sunlight off millions of raindrops. Each raindrop acts like a tiny prism, splitting the light into an array of colors called a spectrum. Sometimes a secondary rainbow, with the color sequence reversed, is produced when the sun's rays are reflected twice off each drop.

by shining objects. Then experiments in the 1800's indicated that light was a wave. In 1865 James Clerk Maxwell, a Scottish physicist, proved mathematically that light was a wave traveling in an electromagnetic field—a force in space that is both electrical and magnetic. The process in which energy is emitted, or given off, is called radiation. Light is only one form of electromagnetic radiation. Other forms include radar and X rays.

The wave theory of light helps explain how light moves through different materials and how it is reflected by some materials and refracted, or bent, when it passes from one material to another. It also explains many optical effects, such as the appearance of narrow light and dark bands at the edge of a shadow,

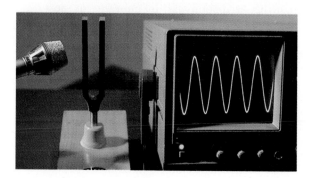

An oscilloscope can convert sound waves, which cannot be seen ordinarily, into electric signals and display them as wave patterns on its phosphorescent screen. Patterns formed by a vibrating tuning fork, shown here, are one example.

or the rainbow that appears on an oil slick on a wet street. The colors of light that can be seen when a beam of sunlight passes through a prism can also be understood in terms of light waves. Light waves of different frequencies (a frequency is the number of times per second that a wave vibrates) are associated with different colors, just as the different frequencies of a sound wave are associated with different pitches of sounds.

The wave theory does not, however, explain how light is emitted or absorbed. Nor does it answer the question of how a light wave can travel through empty space, as it does from the sun to the Earth. Even without knowing the exact nature of light, in the 1800's scientists were able to investigate how light rays are deflected by a mirror or a lens to form an image of an object. These studies led to the invention of many important optical instruments, such as the telescope, the microscope, and the camera.

### Electromagnetism

The study of electricity and magnetism and the relationship between these two forces is called **electromagnetism**. The effects of electrical and magnetic forces have been observed and used since ancient times. But it was not until the 1800's that the close relationship between electricity and magnetism was discovered and the laws of electromagnetism were stated. At that time, Michael Faraday, an English chemist and physicist, and Hans Christian Oersted, a Danish physicist, demonstrated the connection and introduced the idea of electric and magnetic fields. Oersted showed that when an electric current is passed through a wire, a magnetic field forms around the wire. This is the principle of the electromagnet. Faraday found that when he moved a loop of wire through a magnetic field, an electric current was produced in the wire. This is the principle behind generators and transformers.

James Clerk Maxwell summarized and combined all of the known effects of electricity and magnetism into a few mathematical equations. These equations demonstrated the unity of electric and magnetic fields as two aspects of the same force, which he called electromagnetism. His calculations also led

An electromagnet turned on by an electric current attracts iron, steel, and certain other metals and is commonly used in scrap yards and recycling centers to separate these metals from other materials.

him to the idea that the electromagnetic force moved through space in waves at the speed of light (186,000 miles per second), proving that light must be a form of electromagnetic radiation.

By the late 1800's, Isaac Newton's science of mechanics, together with James Maxwell's work on electromagnetism, could explain the motion of atoms, planets, and projectiles (objects that are propelled forward, like an arrow shot from a bow). Newton's and Maxwell's work also explained the basic principles behind what was then known about optical, acoustic, electric, and magnetic phenomena. Some problems concerning light and radiation remained, but at that time, it seemed that there was not much left to do in physics. At the turn of the century, however, scientists began to observe phenomena that could not be explained by classical physics, and modern physics was born.

### ▶ MODERN PHYSICS

Modern physics is concerned with the basic structure and behavior of matter and energy on a very large or very small scale—from distant stars and galaxies to the tiniest particles of matter. Three of the main areas of study in modern physics are relativity, quantum theory, and cosmology.

### Relativity

James Clerk Maxwell's theory of electromagnetic radiation predicted that light will always travel at the same speed regardless of the motion of the source or the observer. At first this prediction was unbelievable to most scientists because the measured speed of all objects, from trains to planets, depends on their relative motion—their motion in relation to the observer. Then, experiments performed between 1880 and 1920 proved that the speed of light is not relative, just as Maxwell predicted.

**Special Theory of Relativity.** In 1905, the German scientist Albert Einstein published a paper that assumed the truth of Maxwell's prediction and explored its consequences. Einstein formulated a special theory of relativity, which revolutionized physics. According to this theory, space and time are relative—the measurement of space and time depends on relative motion, or the observer's frame of reference—but the speed of light is not. He further stated that when an object travels at a high speed relative to an observer, the length of the object shrinks in the direction of travel, the mass of the object increases, and the object's clock appears slow to the observer. Although these effects seem impossible, they have all been verified by experiments. We are not aware of them because they are noticeable only if you travel at high speeds approaching the speed of light.

The special theory also examined mass and energy, proposing that mass and energy are equivalent (stated by Einstein's famous formula $E = mc^2$, in which $E$ represents energy, $m$ represents mass, and $c$ stands for the speed of light). Because they are equivalent, under certain circumstances they can change from one form to the other. Discovering how to produce such changes subsequently led to the development of the atomic bomb and many uses of nuclear energy.

**General Theory of Relativity.** In 1915, Einstein published a paper describing what he called the general theory of relativity, which revolutionized ideas about gravity. According to this theory, not only are space and time different for moving observers, but also they are warped or curved, like the surface of a sphere or an hourglass. According to Einstein, matter curves or distorts space, and it is this distortion that causes objects near one another to "gravitate" toward one another. With these ideas, Einstein was able to describe planetary motion more accurately than Isaac Newton had.

## Quantum Theory

If the discovery of the motion of light sparked the relativity revolution in physics, then theories about the emission and absorption of light started the quantum revolution. One of the things Maxwell's theory of light could not explain was the absorption of light waves that occurs in the **photoelectric effect**, in which electrons are emitted from certain metals when ultraviolet light falls on their surfaces, producing a current of electricity.

Albert Einstein and Max Planck, another German scientist, explained the emission and absorption of light by introducing the quantum hypothesis. **Quantization** means there is a grainy, or discontinuous, structure to matter and energy. According to this idea, atoms can vibrate only at certain quantized, or discrete (separate and distinct), frequencies. Also, energy such as light is emitted and absorbed only in tiny, discrete amounts. These discrete amounts of energy act like particles of matter rather than waves and help to explain the photoelectric effect.

**Quantum Theory and Atoms.** Danish scientist Niels Bohr applied the quantum idea to atoms. Bohr modified the picture of an atom as a tiny solar system with electrons moving in orbits around a nucleus. He assumed that the radius of each orbit and the energies of the electrons in an atom could have only certain quantized values. He then proved that when an atom is stimulated by electricity or heat, electrons may change their orbits, producing energy that leaves the atom in the form of photons of light. The atomic spectrum, or spread of color, of that light consists of separate, distinct lines of specific colors. Atomic spectra are discrete, not continuous, or unbroken, like the spectrum of sunlight. Only the quantized atom could explain this. This was one of the early applications of the theory of quantization.

The idea that electrons and light can act like either waves or particles depending on the circumstances demonstrated the dual nature of matter and energy that characterized the quantum hypothesis. These discoveries relating to the quantization of light, electrons, and atoms subsequently led to a new **quantum theory of matter and motion**, discovered by the European scientists Erwin Schrödinger and Werner Heisenberg.

The ideas of Newton were unable to explain the nature and behavior of atoms or the molecules they form. The quantum theory was refined by the American physicist Richard Feynman and others to explain the forms of matter and radiation and their behavior. Its explanations of electrical conductivity have led to the development of semiconductors, transistors, and microchips, and its use in optics has led to the development of lasers and fiber optics.

**Atoms and Subatomic Particles.** Quantum theory has enabled scientists to make discoveries about atomic forces. This work was pioneered by the German-American scientist Maria Goeppert-Mayer, among others. They have found that the nucleus of an atom is made of positively charged protons and uncharged neutrons. These are all held together by a **strong nuclear force**, which overpowers the electrical force of repulsion among the protons. This powerful force is responsible for the hydrogen bomb. Another atomic force, the **weak nuclear force**, is responsible for a form of radioactivity called beta decay, which causes atoms in certain elements to break down or disintegrate.

Within this Hubble Space Telescope image of a small region of the Orion constellation is an area where new stars have formed (*inset*). The gas and dust orbiting these stars could be protoplanetary disks that may someday evolve into planets. By studying such images, cosmologists hope to learn more about the evolution of the universe.

Quantum physics also has led to the discovery of a whole new world of subatomic particles. These particles, known as elementary particles, are thought to be the most basic components of the universe. Scientists now know that protons, neutrons, and many strange particles associated with the strong nuclear force are made of simpler particles called **quarks**. Another group of particles, the **leptons**, are governed by the weak nuclear force. The explanation of matter in terms of quarks and leptons and their interactions is

called the **standard model**, which is used to investigate how matter, stars, and galaxies originally formed.

Physicists hope someday to find an explanation of all particles and their interactions that is even simpler than the standard model. They think the four basic forces of nature—gravity, electromagnetism, the strong nuclear force, and the weak nuclear force—may be different versions of one unified force that split apart as the universe evolved.

## Cosmology

A third area of modern physics is cosmology, the study of the structure and evolution of the universe. The universe that scientists can observe today is far more vast than had ever been imagined. The stars visible in the night sky are just a fraction of the hundreds of billions of stars in our Milky Way galaxy, and the universe contains about a trillion other galaxies. Furthermore, the universe is not static, or unchanging, as scientists in the past assumed, but is thought to be expanding in all directions because of a cataclysmic explosion—the Big Bang—that scientists think occurred between 10 and 15 billion years ago.

This is the view of contemporary cosmology: a universe that began with the explosion of an infinitesimally small, compact "particle" of matter, energy, space, and time, and has been expanding ever since.

Cosmologists are unsure of the universe's ultimate fate. Will the universe continue to expand forever? Or will the expansion someday reach a maximum, and will the universe then collapse in a "big crunch"? Most cosmologists today think that the answer may lie between these two extremes—that the universe will expand forever, but at an ever-decreasing rate. Proving this will depend on future discoveries in physics. If these discoveries force physicists to change their ideas, it will not be the first time.

ROGER S. JONES
Associate Professor of Physics
University of Minnesota
Author, *Physics for the Rest of Us*

# PHYSICS, HISTORY OF

Physics is an old science. Its roots reach back about 2,600 years to when the Greek philosopher and mathematician Pythagoras discovered the mathematical rules of musical harmony. He found that the strings of a lyre, an ancient harp, were in tune when their lengths followed the ratios of simple whole numbers, such as 1:2 or 2:3. This discovery, that simple numerical ratios could explain the beauty of musical harmony, led Pythagoras to believe that the cosmos, or universe, was also governed by simple mathematical rules or natural laws that were themselves orderly and harmonious. This belief in the mathematical order of the cosmos has remained the guiding principle of physics to the present day.

## ▶ THE ANCIENT GREEKS

The Greek philosopher Plato expanded on the ideas of Pythagoras. Plato saw great order and harmony in the celestial realm of the stars and planets. The stars followed circles around the Earth in their nightly motions, thus demonstrating heavenly order to the Greeks who considered the circle to be the perfect geometrical form. Yet there were some objects in the sky—the sun, the moon, and the planets—that did not follow this orderly rule of circular motion. They lagged a little behind the stars every night; and now and then, the planets would even reverse direction and move ahead of the stars, only to return later to their normal motion. This reverse motion, called retrograde motion, disturbed Plato and his student Aristotle, who sought to find the perfect harmony of circular motion in the skies.

For 500 years after Aristotle, Greek astronomers tried to explain the apparent irregular motion of the planets in terms of perfect circular paths. The astronomer Ptolemy devised a complex system in which the planets moved on circles within circles, and this became the standard description of the motion of the planets for the next thousand years. Yet, as astronomical observations improved, it became clear that Ptolemy's system was not accurate.

## ▶ THE MODERN ERA OF PHYSICS

In 1543, *On the Revolutions of the Heavenly Spheres* by the Polish astronomer Nicolaus Copernicus was published in Europe.

Isaac Newton, known for his laws of gravity and motion, also made contributions to the science of optics. In a famous experiment, he guided sunlight through a glass prism, proving that ordinary white light is made up of many colors.

This book altered the course of history because it described a fundamental change Copernicus made in the celestial system devised by Aristotle and Ptolemy. In his book, Copernicus described a **heliocentric system** in which the sun (*helios* in Greek) rather than the Earth was at the center of the cosmos. According to Copernicus, the planets all revolve around the sun, and as the Earth moves around the sun, it passes and is passed by the other planets. This explained the reverse, or retrograde, motion of the planets as seen from the Earth. Copernicus, however, still assumed that the planets moved in circular orbits. As a result, his new heliocentric system still did not provide a completely accurate description of planetary motion.

In the early 1600's, the German astronomer Johannes Kepler spent many years studying the latest and most accurate data on planetary motion. Kepler realized that the orbit of the planet Mars could not possibly be a circle but, instead, was an oval curve called an ellipse. Based on this insight, Kepler devised three simple mathematical laws that ac-

Johannes Kepler spent many years formulating his three laws of planetary motion. Kepler also made important discoveries in optics and designed and built a new type of telescope.

curately described the orbits, orbital speeds, and times of revolution of all the planets. The stage was now set for the era of modern physics.

While Kepler was developing his laws of planetary motion, Galileo Galilei, an Italian astronomer, physicist, and mathematician, and René Descartes, a French philosopher and mathematician, had been studying motion in general. They realized that any material body free from other influences or forces has a natural tendency to move uniformly— that is, to move along a straight line at a constant speed. This **law of inertia** became the foundation of the laws of motion developed by the English scientist Isaac Newton.

Why do the planets move in elliptical orbits around the sun if their natural tendency, according to the law of inertia, is to move uniformly along straight lines? Newton realized that there must be a force of attraction acting between the sun and a planet that deflects the planet from its uniform path and bends it into a curved ellipse. Newton called this force of attraction the **force of gravity**. With this explanation for planetary motion, Newton devised a new method to explain motion in general. According to Newton, any material body departs from uniform motion if a force acts on it. In the case of the planets, their elliptical paths were caused by the universal force of gravity. But there is always some force—a push or pull, friction or air resistance, electrical attraction or repulsion— that causes the nonuniform motion of material bodies. Thus Newton's ideas became the basis for the science of **mechanics**, the study of the motion of objects as a result of forces acting on them. Mechanics became the basis of all of physics.

▶ **INVESTIGATION OF MATTER AND ENERGY**

As scientists began to understand the laws of motion, efforts were made to understand the nature and behavior of matter. The ancient Greeks were divided in their ideas about matter. Leucippus and Democritus believed that matter was "grainy," that it was made up of tiny indivisible particles called *atomos*. Aristotle, on the other hand, thought that matter was "smooth," or continuous. Aristotle's idea dominated scientific thinking about matter until the Renaissance.

In the 1500's and 1600's, new techniques of science were developed that involved careful observation and measurement and controlled experimentation. At that time, the Irish physicist Robert Boyle, the English chemist John Dalton, and the Italian scientist Amedeo Avogadro carefully weighed materials before and after they underwent a chemical reaction, and they observed how gases behaved when heated, cooled, and put under pressure. As a result of their separate studies, these scientists concluded that matter must be composed of tiny indivisible units, which we now call atoms.

Boyle discovered that as a gas is heated, its atoms move faster and faster, causing an increase in the temperature and pressure of the gas. This explanation of the behavior of a gas in terms of the motion of its atoms is known as the **kinetic theory of gases**. It was a remarkable new application of Isaac Newton's science of mechanics—this time applied to tiny atoms rather than to immense planets.

Included within kinetic theory was the idea that heat is a form of energy. Earlier, it had been thought that heat was a fluid contained within matter, and when matter was heated or burned, this fluid was released. But American scientist Benjamin Thompson and English physicist James Prescott Joule demonstrated in experiments that heat is

**The Electromagnetic Spectrum**

| $10^{24}$ | $10^{22}$ | $10^{20}$ | $10^{18}$ | $10^{16}$ | $10^{14}$ | $10^{12}$ |

Gamma rays  X rays  Ultraviolet  Visible light  Infrared

The electromagnetic spectrum includes all forms of electromagnetic radiation. Although they all travel through space as waves at the speed of light, each has its own frequency. Wave frequency values are shown here in hertz (cycles per second).

one of several forms of energy. Other forms of energy include electrical, chemical, and nuclear energy and the kinetic energy of motion. Through experimentation it was later demonstrated that these different forms of energy can be transformed into one another, but they can never be created or destroyed. This principle is known as the **conservation of energy**. It has been a cornerstone of physical science ever since it was stated clearly by the German physicist Hermann von Helmholtz in 1847.

The notion of atoms also reinforced evolving ideas about electricity and magnetism. The ancient Greeks were aware of the electrical and magnetic properties of certain materials, and early civilizations used magnetic compasses for navigation. Very little about these phenomena was understood, however, until the 1600's and 1700's. At that time, several people including English scientist Stephen Gray, American scientist and inventor Benjamin Franklin, French engineer and physicist Charles Augustin de Coulomb, and Italian physicist and chemist Allessandro Volta explored the basic properties and laws of electrical phenomena. They discovered that there are two kinds of electricity, or electrical charge—positive and negative. Both kinds exert attractive and repulsive forces. It was also found that metals are conductors of electricity—that is, they allow electrical charge to pass freely through them—while other nonmetallic minerals are insulators that block the flow of electric charge. These discoveries could be understood by assuming that electric charge was a property of the atoms contained in all matter. Chemical reactions also could be explained on the basis of the electrical attractions between atoms, which result in the formation of molecules.

▶ **THE 1800'S**

During the 1800's, ideas and theories about atoms were gradually improved and refined in an effort to explain the structure and behavior of matter. During this period, the mystery of light, which scientists had not yet explained, was also further clarified.

In ancient Greece, Pythagoras had thought that light consisted of particles emitted by shining objects. Aristotle believed that light was not a substance but a quality or action traveling through a medium. The Greeks also were able to apply some simple laws of light to their use of mirrors and lenses, which were very crude at that time.

In the 1600's, Isaac Newton demonstrated that when white light passes through a glass prism, it is separated into different colors to form a spectrum. Newton thought that this dispersion of light, as well as the transmission of light, could be explained by assuming that light consisted of particles. Other scientists, such as Dutch physicist Christiaan Huygens, believed that light was a wave similar to water waves on a lake or sound waves in the air. But Newton's great authority and prestige influenced many to accept his particle theory of light.

In the 1800's, scientific thinking began to turn against the particle theory of light. English physicist Thomas Young investigated the interference of light, in which two light beams cancel each other to produce darkness. Young explained this phenomena by assuming that light consists of waves rather than particles. Augustin Fresnel, a French physicist, also developed a wave theory of light to explain many optical phenomena.

Finally, in 1865, Scottish physicist James Clerk Maxwell developed his comprehensive theory of electromagnetism, proving that light was a wave. As Newton had done with mechanics and gravity 200 years earlier, Maxwell provided a unified explanation of all known electric and magnetic phenomena. But Maxwell went much further. He predicted the existence of electromagnetic waves traveling through space. Most remarkable of all was his discovery that these waves travel at the speed of light, thus demonstrating convincingly that light was a wave. In fact, light is only one of various electromagnetic waves. Others include radio, television, microwaves, radar, infrared, ultraviolet, X rays, and gamma rays. In 1886, German physicist Heinrich Hertz was able to demonstrate the existence

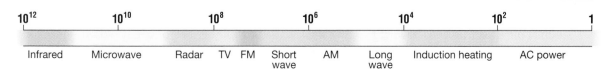

| $10^{12}$ | | $10^{10}$ | | $10^{8}$ | | | $10^{6}$ | | $10^{4}$ | | $10^{2}$ | | 1 |
|---|---|---|---|---|---|---|---|---|---|---|---|---|---|
| Infrared | | Microwave | | Radar | TV | FM | Short wave | AM | Long wave | Induction heating | | AC power | |

Biographies of the following physicists and scientists who played important roles in the history of physics are included elsewhere in *The New Book of Knowledge*: Antoine Henri Becquerel, Niels Bohr, Robert Boyle, Marie and Pierre Curie, Albert Einstein, Michael Faraday, Enrico Fermi, Galileo Galilei, Robert Goddard, Robert Hooke, Robert Milliken, Isaac Newton, Ernest Rutherford, and Benjamin Thompson.

Richard P. Feynman

**Richard P. Feynman** (1918–88), born in New York City, received the Nobel Prize in 1965 for work leading to the development of the theory of quantum elec-

Maria Goeppert-Mayer

trodynamics, the fundamental theory of electromagnetic radiation. He introduced Feynman diagrams — symbolic graphics that greatly simplify our understanding of the complicated interactions between charged particles and the electromagnetic field. During World War II,

Feynman worked on the Manhattan Project, which developed the atomic bomb. A great teacher, Feynman was very popular with his students, and his introductory physics textbook has become a classic. Feynman also helped discover that a frozen gasket was responsible for the tragic disaster of the space shuttle *Challenger*.

**Maria Goeppert-Mayer** (1906–72) was born in Kattowitz, Germany (now Katowice, Poland), and migrated to America in 1930. After arriving in America, her husband, Joseph Mayer, was hired as a professor of chemistry at Johns Hopkins University. The university did not offer her a position, however, since she was a woman. Nevertheless, Goeppert-Mayer did research in nuclear physics while raising a family. In 1940, she became an associate professor without pay at the University of Chicago. Goeppert-Mayer developed a theory of nuclear structure in terms of shells, or levels, occupied by the neutrons and protons in the atomic

---

of Maxwell's electromagnetic waves, making possible the electronics and telecommunication of the 20th century.

In the late 1800's, it seemed as though there was nothing new to be learned in physics and that no new discoveries would be made. Newton's science of mechanics, together with the new theories of heat and energy, explained the motion of atoms as well as of planets. The atomic theory of matter described the behavior of gases, and the electrical properties of atoms explained chemical reactions. Maxwell's theory of electromagnetism explained not only electricity and magnetism but also light. What was there left to do? It was time for engineers and technicians to work out marvelous applications based on what was known.

Nothing, however, could have been further from the truth. Toward the end of the 1800's, several significant discoveries occurred that challenged what physicists already knew. In 1887, Hertz would discover the photoelectric effect. In 1895, German physicist William Röntgen would detect X rays, and in 1897, J. J. Thomson, an English physicist, would discover electrons. Polish chemist Marie Curie would isolate radium in 1898. In 1900, German physicist Max Planck would apply a new

concept, called quantization, to explain radiation, and in 1905, another German physicist, Albert Einstein, would propose a new particle theory of light and would also introduce the theory of relativity. Physics was on a new threshold.

### ▶ PHYSICS IN THE 1900'S

During the first three decades of the 1900's, the physics of Newton, which had dominated the study of physics for more than 200 years, was upset by two revolutionary ideas—relativity and quantum theory—and by new thinking in the field of cosmology.

#### Relativity

In 1905 Einstein published a paper on the **special theory of relativity** in which he developed completely new ideas about space and time. He proposed that space and time are relative—that their measurement depends on the observer's frame of reference. Ten years later, he introduced his **general theory of relativity**, which enlarged his original theory to include gravity. In this second theory, Einstein demonstrated that space and time were warped and bent as well as relative. He replaced Newton's idea of a gravitational field with the idea of curved space to explain

nucleus. She was able to explain the great stability of certain nuclei, which had a specific "magic number" of both neutrons and protons. Goeppert-Mayer received the Nobel Prize in 1963 for her work.

**James Clerk Maxwell** (1831–79), born in Edinburgh, Scotland, showed great mathematical talent at an early age. After graduating from Cambridge University, he studied the rings of Saturn and showed that they could not be solid, but must consist of countless small bodies called planetoids forming a belt around the planet. Maxwell developed the kinetic theory of gases, which explained changes in the temperature and pressure of a gas by applying statistical methods to the motion of the gas molecules. During the 1860's, while at King's College in London, Maxwell developed the equations that completely summarized all electromagnetic phenomena and predicted the existence of electromagnetic waves traveling at the speed of light. Maxwell

James Clerk Maxwell

thus demonstrated the electromagnetic nature of light.

**Max Planck** (1858–1947) was born in Kiel, Germany. Although thoroughly trained in the classical physics of Isaac Newton and other early physicists, Planck went on to revolutionize the field with his quantum theory of

Max Planck

radiation. Planck and other scientists wondered why an iron poker changes in color from red to yellow to white when it is heated in a fire. Earlier theories could not explain the spectrum, or color, of this light radiation. By assuming that energy could be absorbed and emitted only in quantized, or discrete (separate and distinct) amounts, Planck was able to derive the correct spectrum. In the process, he initiated the quantum era in physics. Planck's quantization became the basis for Albert Einstein's idea of photons to explain the photoelectric effect and for Niels Bohr's atomic model. Planck won the Nobel Prize in 1918 for his contribution to quantum theory.

---

the curved motion of the planets. Furthermore, his idea of relativity correctly predicted other astronomical effects that could not be explained by Newton's theory of gravity.

### Quantum Theory

As the idea of relativity was developing, a new theory of matter was evolving as well. This new theory became known as the **quantum theory of matter**.

In 1900, German physicist Max Planck developed a new concept to explain radiation called quantization. Einstein then proposed that radiant energy such as light is released in small bursts, which were later called **quanta**, and not in a smooth, or continuous, stream as was previously thought. Einstein applied the idea of quantization to light in order to explain the **photoelectric effect**, in which electrons are released from the surface of a metal that is illuminated by ultraviolet light. Einstein assumed that light was quantized into tiny discrete (separate and distinct) bundles of energy or particles called **photons**. This

idea reopened the debate over whether light was a wave or a particle. We now know that light exhibits both characteristics—sometimes acting like waves, sometimes like particles.

Danish physicist Niels Bohr applied quantum ideas to the atom in 1913. When atoms

The theories of Nobel Laureates Albert Einstein and Niels Bohr contributed to the revolutionary thinking in physics that led to new paths of investigation and discovery at the beginning of the 1900's.

## *Profiles*

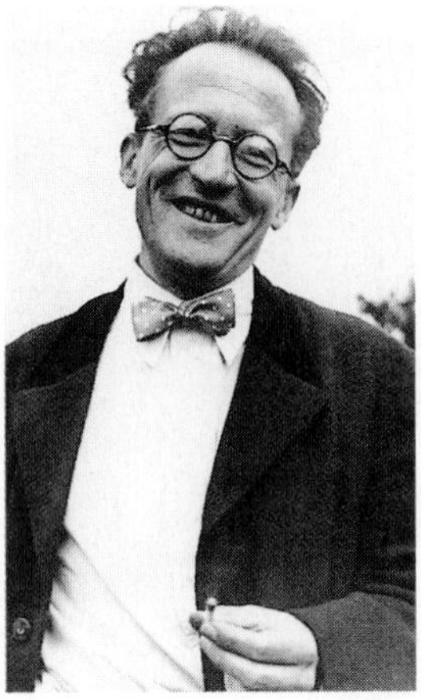

Erwin Schrödinger

**Erwin Schrödinger** (1887–1961), born in Vienna, Austria, was one of the creators of the fully developed mathematical quantum theory. In 1926, Schrödinger applied the idea of electron waves, first developed by French physicist Louis-Victor de Broglie, to Niels Bohr's model of the hydrogen atom. He developed a wave equation that treats electrons in the atom like standing wave patterns rather than orbiting particles. The standing electron waves can resonate only at certain quantized frequencies or energies, like the waves on a guitar string. Schrödinger thus was able to explain the quantized nature of the atom and of atomic spectra naturally, without requiring an arbitrary quantum hypothesis. Schrödinger was awarded the Nobel Prize in 1933 for his work in wave mechanics.

**Sir Joseph John Thomson** (1856–1940), born in Cheetham, England, is regarded as one of the pioneers of atomic physics. In 1884, Thomson became head of the illustrious Cavendish laboratory at Cambridge University, where he trained a whole generation of physicists in applying the new quantum ideas to matter and radiation. Thomson was the first scientist to identify the electron as a tiny charged particle circling the nucleus of the atom. By identifying a basic component of the atom, Thomson inaugurated a revolution in physics and opened the field of subatomic physics. He also helped to develop Maxwell's mathematical theory of electricity and magnetism and did pioneering work on the electrical conductivity of gases. In 1906, Thomson received the Nobel Prize for his work with electrons. Seven of his assistants went on to receive Nobel Prizes of their own.

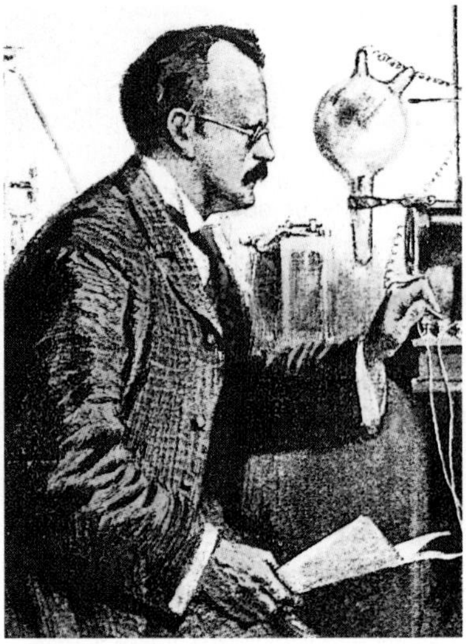

Sir Joseph John Thomson

are stimulated by electrical energy or heat, they emit spectra of light called atomic spectra. But an atomic spectrum is not a continuous band of colors like the spectrum of white light. Instead, atomic spectra consist of distinct color lines. Bohr explained this by assuming that electrons in the atom could have only certain specific quantized energies. When an excited electron drops from a high energy state into a lower one, the difference in energy is emitted in the form of a photon of light. Since the energies of each electron state have quantized, or separate and distinct, values, the energy differences are also quantized, and so are the frequencies of the light which determine their colors. Thus only certain specific color lines appear in the atomic spectra.

In 1923, French physicist Louis-Victor de Broglie argued that if light could sometimes act like a particle, then perhaps an electron could sometimes act like a wave. When this conjecture was verified, it became apparent that the concept of quantization was essential to any theory of matter and motion. A new mathematical theory known as quantum mechanics was developed by the work of several physicists, including Austrians Erwin Schrödinger and Wolfgang Pauli, Germans Werner Heisenberg and Max Born, and Englishman Paul Dirac. Quantum mechanics,

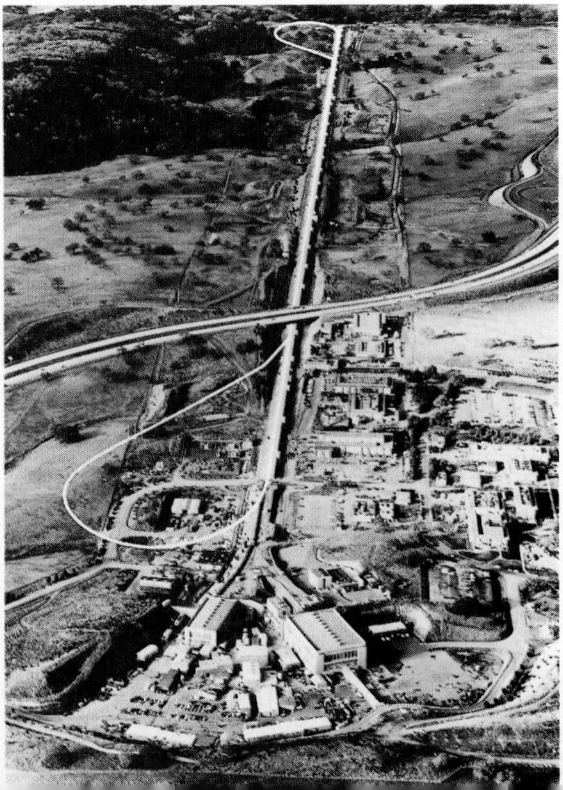

**In the Linear Accelerator at Stanford University, high-energy electrons streak along a 2-mile-long tube at close to the speed of light, then collide with other elementary particles. Physicists study the effects of these collisions to learn more about the structure of matter.**

which replaced classical mechanics, has since remained the principle theory of matter and motion and has led to many remarkable discoveries such as the laser and the microchip.

## Elementary Particle Physics and Cosmology

In 1932, British physicist James Chadwick discovered the neutron, a particle in the nucleus of an atom. This discovery was an important step in the study of elementary particle physics, which explores the components of the atomic nucleus. Probing nuclei and their subparticles at ever-higher energies in particle accelerators has been one of the main areas of physics research in the 1900's. This high-energy research has resulted in the development of what is called the **standard model**, an explanation of atomic and subatomic particles and their interactions. According to the standard model, elementary particles known as **quarks** and **leptons** are assumed to be the simplest and most basic components of all other atomic and nuclear particles. The standard model has given rise to new theories of unification, in which physicists attempt to combine the four basic forces of nature—gravity, electromagnetism, the strong nuclear force, and the weak nuclear force—into one unified force.

Research in elementary particle physics is closely tied to the latest theories in cosmology, the study of the origin, structure, and evolution of the universe. In the 1920's, American astronomer Edwin Hubble and others discovered that the universe was expanding. They determined that there were galaxies far beyond our Milky Way galaxy and that these other galaxies were moving away from the Milky Way at great speeds.

If the universe is growing larger, then it must have been smaller in the past. This idea led to the **big bang theory**, which assumes that the universe originated in a great cosmic explosion some 10 or 15 billion years ago. Originally proposed by American physicist George Gamow in the 1940's, the big bang theory has since been refined and strengthened by astronomical observations.

As the universe expands, it is also cooling. The cooling of the expanding universe is a crucial concept for understanding how matter

The movements of spiral galaxies such as these beyond the constellation Fornax have led astrophysicists to conclude that there is more mass in the universe than has been seen. Sometimes called "missing mass" or "dark matter," it may represent most of the total mass in the universe.

and energy evolved and ultimately produced the stars and galaxies. In the earliest instants after the big bang, the cosmos was so hot and active that only the most exotic forms of matter could exist. This was presumably the era of quarks and the unified force. As the universe cooled, the individual forces of nature and the more familiar particles of matter separated out and began to interact, ultimately forming galaxies and stars. Today some physicists think that we may be getting close to a "theory of everything" that will explain all the forces of nature and everything about matter and energy. Whether this represents another "end" of physics or a new beginning is for scientists of the 21st century to decide.

ROGER S. JONES
Associate Professor of Physics
University of Minnesota
Author, *Physics for the Rest of Us*

See also ATOMS; ENERGY; FORCES; MATTER; MOTION; PHYSICS; RADIATION; RELATIVITY; STARS; UNIVERSE.

**PHYSIOLOGY.** See BODY, HUMAN.

**PI.** See GEOMETRY.

# PIANO

The piano is a keyboard instrument with strings. Sound is produced when the keys are pressed down, causing felt-covered hammers to strike the strings. "Piano" is short for "pianoforte," which comes from the Italian words *piano* ("soft") and *forte* ("loud"). The piano's wide range of sounds, from very soft to very loud, is one of its main features.

## ▶ CONSTRUCTION

The main parts of the piano are the keyboard, action, strings, frame, soundboard, and pedals. All are attached to a strong wooden case.

The piano keyboard consists of 88 keys—fifty-two white and thirty-six black. They are made of wood. The white keys used to be covered with ivory and the black keys with ebony. Today, however, plastic is typically used instead. The keys are arranged in series of twelve tones that repeat up the keyboard, from lower versions on the left to higher versions on the right.

The tone of any stringed keyboard instrument is determined by its **action**, the mechanism that makes the strings vibrate. Strings are made to vibrate by being plucked or struck. The piano has a hammer action. The hammers are attached to the keys by levers. When a key is pressed down, its hammer jumps up and strikes a string. If the pianist presses gently, the sound is soft; if the pianist presses harder, the sound is loud. The string must vibrate to produce sound, but the vibrations must also be stopped so that the sounds will not build up and become blurred. Dampers are pieces of soft felt that descend onto the string when the key is released, stopping the vibrations of the string and stopping the sound.

Piano strings are made of steel and copper wire. Most of the tones of the piano are produced by three strings tuned to the same pitch. Middle-to-lower-range tones have two strings, and a few of the very lowest have only one. Pitch is determined mainly by the length and thickness of the strings—in general, the shorter and thinner the string, the higher the tone produced.

The strings are stretched tightly over the frame, which is made of iron or steel in order to withstand the enormous pulling force of the strings. The soundboard, a thin sheet of wood set into the frame, picks up vibrations from the strings and amplifies the sound.

Most modern pianos have three pedals. The pedal on the right is the one most often used. It is known as the sustaining pedal, because as long as it is held down all the notes played will continue to sound; it is also called the damper pedal, because it lifts all the dampers off the strings together.

The pedal on the left is called the soft pedal. When it is pressed down, the keyboard and hammers move to one side so that only one string (or sometimes two) is struck by each hammer. This makes the sound softer. *Una corda*, meaning "one string," is an

This overhead view of a Steinway grand piano (with its cover removed) reveals a piano's main parts: the metal frame, wooden soundboard, and steel and copper strings.

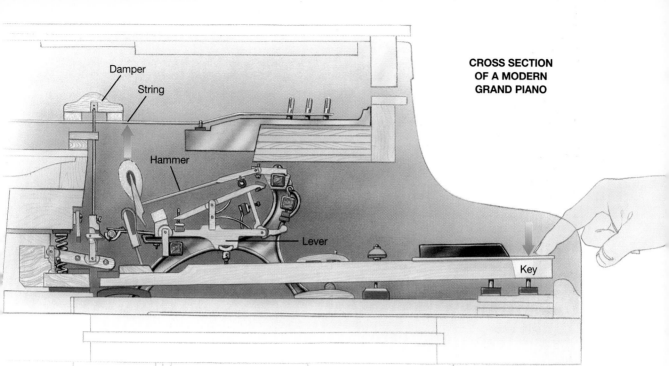

**CROSS SECTION OF A MODERN GRAND PIANO**

Labels: Damper, String, Hammer, Lever, Key

Italian term used in piano music to indicate the soft pedal.

The third pedal, called the sostenuto pedal, is rarely used. It is located in the middle, between the sustaining and soft pedals, and allows the player to sustain only certain notes. It is used for special effects, such as sustaining bass notes while other notes are played.

### ▶ TYPES OF PIANOS

The two basic types of piano are the upright and the grand. Upright pianos, so named because their strings and soundboard are vertical, come in various styles and are smaller than grand pianos. For this reason they are more practical for home use. The 9-foot concert grand is used almost exclusively in concert halls. Smaller grand pianos, such as the baby grand, are often found in homes.

### ▶ HISTORY

In the 1600's and most of the 1700's, the most popular keyboard instruments were the harpsichord and the clavichord. A harpsichord is a stringed keyboard instrument whose strings are plucked by quills or leather points. The clavichord is smaller, with a much quieter sound, and its strings are struck by pieces of metal called tangents. The earliest known piano was built about 1700 by Bartolomeo Cristofori, a maker of harpsichords for Prince Ferdinand de' Medici in Florence, Italy. In place of the tangents and plucking quills, Cristofori put small hammers that struck the strings from below. He called the new instrument a harpsichord with *piano e forte*. Its advantage over the harpsichord was that the player could control the loudness of each note. The harder a key was struck, the harder the hammer hit the string and the louder the sound. The advantage over the clavichord was its bigger sound and greater range. Even so, the first pianos had a rather weak sound. To produce a louder, richer sound, the strings were gradually made thicker, giving the string greater strength to take the stroke of the hammer.

About 1730, Gottfried Silberman built the first German pianos. In 1747, Johann Sebastian Bach played a Silberman piano at the palace of Frederick the Great and praised the instrument. Johann Andreas Stein was the first great piano maker in Vienna. Wolfgang Amadeus Mozart played a Stein piano in 1777.

The earliest pianos looked like the larger harpsichords. The first known upright piano was made by Christian Friederici, a pupil of Silberman's, in Gera, a city in Saxony. The frames of early pianos were usually made of wood. As the strings became thicker, their pulling force became too great for the wooden frames. After about 1788 the frames were reinforced with bars of iron or steel. Metal was used very cautiously in piano building until

In an upright piano, the strings and soundboard are placed vertically. Upright pianos are more practical for home use.

The earliest known piano was built in 1709 by Bartolomeo Cristofori in Florence, Italy.

Although small and lightweight, digital keyboards can reproduce the full sounds of a grand piano.

1827, when metal frames were adopted by John Broadwood in England.

In 1855, Steinway and Sons of New York City and Hamburg, Germany, produced a grand piano that became the model for the best piano makers. Other great piano makers of the 1800's and 1900's include Blüthner and Bechstein in Germany, Bösendorfer in Vienna, and Pleyel and Gaveau in Paris.

In the early 1900's, the player piano became popular. It worked mechanically, somewhat like a music box, using a pre-punched paper roll to cause the notes to play.

Today's digital keyboards and pianos reproduce the sounds of a grand piano yet are smaller, lightweight, and do not require tuning. Weighted action mimics the feel of an actual piano, and digitally sampled rhythms and instrument "voices" can be accessed. Other features include built-in songbooks and the ability to connect to a computer. (For more information, see ELECTRONIC MUSIC in Volume E.)

### ▶ PIANO VIRTUOSOS

During the 1830's and 1840's, piano virtuosos (skilled artists) dazzled concertgoers across Europe. Franz Liszt was one of the first to be idolized. During the 1850's the virtuosos began to show more concern for the substance of the music than for the simple display of technical ability. Clara Schumann, the wife of composer Robert Schumann, led the way. Anton Rubinstein, Hans von Bülow, and Ferrucio Busoni soon followed.

Great pianists of the 1900's included Sergei Rachmaninoff, Josef Hofmann, Artur Schnabel, Ignaz Friedman, Arthur Rubinstein, Dame Myra Hess, Walter Gieseking, Rudolf Serkin, Vladimir Horowitz, Sviatoslav Richter, Emil Gilels, and Vladimir Sofronitski.

### ▶ COMPOSERS FOR THE PIANO

The first great composer for the piano was Wolfgang Amadeus Mozart. Since Mozart's time, the most important composers for the piano have been Ludwig van Beethoven, Franz Schubert, Frédéric Chopin, Franz Liszt, Clara Schumann, Robert Schumann, and Johannes Brahms. In the 1900's, outstanding composers for the piano included Aleksandr Nikolayevich Scriabin, Sergei Rachmaninoff, Sergei Prokofiev, Maurice Ravel, Béla Bartók, Charles Ives, and Samuel Barber.

Reviewed by ARTHUR GREENE
University of Michigan

See also KEYBOARD INSTRUMENTS; biographies of individual musicians.

# PICASSO, PABLO (1881–1973)

Pablo Ruiz y Picasso—the most famous artist of the 20th century—was born on October 25, 1881, in Málaga, Spain. When Pablo was very young, his family moved to Barcelona. At an early age Picasso showed great talent. He especially liked to paint pictures of the city life around him. In 1896 he entered the School of Fine Arts, where his father was a professor.

Around the turn of the century, Paris was the world center of art and literature. Picasso visited the city in 1900 and fell under the spell of the artistic atmosphere. He returned a year later, and he settled on the Left Bank in 1904. He was very poor, but his studio became a meeting place for many artists, writers, and composers.

In Paris, Picasso still painted scenes of the day-to-day life of poor people in his neighborhood. He was also fascinated by circus life and painted a series of circus pictures. Early in the century his works were painted in varieties of gray-blues. The figures were long, thin, and sad. These paintings belong to what is called Picasso's blue period.

Like many other young artists in Paris at that time, Picasso was influenced by the work of Paul Cézanne. Cézanne had tried to show

Picasso's cubist *Three Musicians* (1921). Can you see the fourth head? It is imposed on the central figure.

the geometric forms that he saw in nature. Picasso and his friend the painter Georges Braque attempted to portray the many different geometric planes of an object all at once. For example, they might paint a full face with one eye and with the nose in profile (a side view). This style became known as **cubism** because in the paintings objects were composed of geometric forms such as cubes and cones. Picasso and Braque were also among the first to make **collages** by pasting various scraps of materials onto flat surfaces.

In 1917, Picasso went to Rome to design scenery and costumes for the Russian Ballet's production of *Parade*. He married Olga Koklova, one of the ballerinas, and they had a son, Paulo. Picasso did not care for the social world in which he found himself. But Olga enjoyed it. He became unhappy, and the distorted, sad figures in his paintings of this period reflect his unhappiness.

Civil war broke out in Spain in 1936. The following year, the ancient city of Guernica was destroyed by bombs. Picasso was enraged at this inhuman act. All his bitterness was released in his brilliant mural *Guernica*. Picasso worked at such a furious pace that the mural was completed within a few weeks and was shown at the Paris Exhibition in 1937.

*Child with a Dove* (1901) belongs to Picasso's blue period. During this time, his works were painted in gray-blues.

The mural shows the terrified people of the town, their mouths open wide in screams. Images from bullfighting are used to symbolize the brutality of war. While some artists might have painted the scene in bloody reds and other vivid colors, Picasso painted *Guernica* entirely in black, white, and shades of gray.

During World War II, Picasso lived in Paris, which was at that time under Nazi occupation. Because the Nazis did not approve of modern art, Picasso had to hide his paintings in a secret vault in the Bank of France. His work during this period included a play, *Desire Caught by the Tail* (1941).

After the war Picasso moved to a huge house in the south of France. There he continued to experiment with painting as well as sculpture, printmaking, ceramics, and collage. In 1958 he painted a large mural for a United Nations building in Paris. His marriage to Jacqueline Roque, a Frenchwoman,

took place in 1961. In 1962, he was awarded the Lenin peace prize.

Picasso's moods were known to change as often as his styles. He was thoughtful and distant at times, but he also displayed a fine sense of humor. His art was extremely valuable even in his own lifetime because of the great variety of his styles. He used elements from the work of Toulouse-Lautrec, the ancient Greeks, El Greco, and African sculptors. The large number of his fine works during any one period would have satisfied another artist. But Picasso never stopped experimenting. His great imagination and outstanding skill earned for him the name El Maestro ("the master") of modern art.

Picasso died at his home in southern France on April 8, 1973, at the age of 91.

Reviewed by ARIANE RUSKIN BATTERBERRY
Author, *The Pantheon Story of Art for Young People*

## PICCARD, AUGUSTE (1884–1962)

Auguste Piccard was a Swiss scientist, inventor, and explorer. He is famous for his work in exploring both the high atmosphere and the ocean depths.

Piccard was born in Basel, Switzerland, on January 28, 1884. He attended the Swiss Institute of Technology in Zurich, where he obtained a degree in mechanical engineering and a doctorate in natural science.

In 1913 Piccard made a balloon trip with his twin brother, Jean, who later became a famous aeronautical engineer. For 16 hours they drifted across Germany and France, taking measurements of the atmosphere.

Piccard married Marianne Denis, and they had five children. In 1922 he became a professor at the University of Brussels, Belgium.

One of Piccard's early inventions was an airtight aluminum cabin, called a gondola, that was attached to a balloon. On May 27, 1931, Piccard ascended to a height of nearly 10 miles (more than 15 kilometers), into that part of the atmosphere called the stratosphere. Piccard had made 28 balloon flights into the stratosphere by 1937. He then began to concentrate on inventing a vehicle that would take him to great depths in the ocean.

Piccard designed an underwater ship called a bathyscaphe ("deep ship") in 1946. Seven years later, he and his son, Jacques, also a deep-sea explorer, descended in a bathyscaphe to a depth of 2 miles (3 kilometers) beneath the sea's surface. In 1960 Jacques Piccard and Lieutenant Don Walsh of the U.S. Navy descended nearly 7 miles (11 kilometers) under the surface of the Pacific Ocean in the bathyscaphe *Trieste*. This set a world record as the greatest depth reached in a deep-sea diving machine.

Auguste Piccard ascended higher into the air and descended deeper into the sea than any person before him. His studies of cosmic rays and electricity in the atmosphere helped in the planning of spaceflights in later years. His bathyscaphe made deep-sea exploration and research possible.

Piccard remained an active inventor until his death at the age of 78. He died in Lausanne, Switzerland, on March 24, 1962.

DUANE H. D. ROLLER
University of Oklahoma

**PICKFORD, MARY.** See MOTION PICTURES (Profiles: Movie Stars).

**PICNICS.** See OUTDOOR COOKING AND PICNICS.

# FRANKLIN PIERCE (1804-1869)

## 14th President of the United States

### FACTS ABOUT PIERCE

Birthplace: Hillsborough County, New Hampshire
Religion: Episcopalian
College Attended: Bowdoin College, Brunswick, Maine
Occupation: Lawyer
Married: Jane Means Appleton
Children: Franklin (died soon after birth), Frank Robert, Benjamin
Political Party: Democratic
Offices Held Before Becoming President: U.S. congressman, U.S. senator
President Who Preceded Him: Millard Fillmore
Age on Becoming President: 48
Years in the Presidency: 1853–1857
Vice President: William R. D. King (died 1853)
President Who Succeeded Him: James Buchanan
Age at Death: 64
Burial Place: Old North Cemetery, Concord, New Hampshire

### DURING PIERCE'S PRESIDENCY

The Gadsden Purchase, negotiated with Mexico (1853), gave the United States additional territory in what is now Arizona and New Mexico. *Below:* Commodore Matthew C. Perry's second expedition to Japan resulted in the Treaty of Kanagawa (1854), which helped open Japan to Western trade. Congress enacted the Kansas-Nebraska Act (1854). *Above:* The Republican Party was founded (1854); its first presidential candidate (1856) was John C. Frémont. *Left:* The Bessemer process for converting iron into steel was patented in England by Henry Bessemer (1856).

---

**PIERCE, FRANKLIN.** When Franklin Pierce became president in 1853, he was, at age 48, the youngest chief executive the United States had yet had. Before achieving the presidency, Pierce had been a congressman and senator, a successful lawyer, and a general in the Mexican War. Although chosen as a compromise candidate by a divided Democratic Party, he had gone on to win election easily. As president he was faced with personal tragedy and a crisis over slavery that brought on a civil war in Kansas and gave the territory the name "bleeding Kansas."

### ▶ EARLY YEARS

Pierce was born in Hillsborough County, New Hampshire, on November 23, 1804, one of the eight children of Benjamin and Anna Kendrick Pierce. Benjamin Pierce was a rough frontier farmer who had served during the Revolutionary War, become a general of the state militia, and twice won election as governor of New Hampshire.

Pierce attended school at Hillsborough Center and later went to Hancock Academy. In 1820 he entered Bowdoin College in Brunswick, Maine. There he began a lifelong friendship with one of his classmates, Nathaniel Hawthorne, who would later become a famous author. Pierce's carefree and irresponsible attitude toward his studies soon carried him to the bottom of his class, although he was popular with the other students. After applying himself more diligently, however, he graduated near the top of his class in 1824. He then studied law and in 1827 was admitted to the bar.

### ▶ POLITICS AND MARRIAGE

Pierce took an active part in state politics, and in 1829 he was elected to the New Hampshire legislature. In 1833 he was elected to the U.S. House of Representatives, where he remained for four years loyally supporting the policies of President Andrew Jackson. In 1837 he won election to the U.S. Senate, becoming its youngest member.

In 1834, Pierce married Jane Means Appleton, daughter of a former president of Bowdoin College. The Appletons, an aristocratic New England family, did not approve of the young Democrat from the backcountry. Mrs. Pierce found life in Washington, D.C., so distasteful that her husband agreed to abandon his political career. He resigned his Senate seat in 1842 and returned to Concord, New Hampshire, to practice law.

The early years of the Pierces' marriage were saddened by the loss of two of their three sons. Franklin, the first child, lived only a few days after his birth. The second son, Frank Robert, died at the age of 4. Only the youngest child, Benjamin, born in 1841, was still left to them.

Jane Means Appleton married Franklin Pierce in 1834 and had three sons. One died in infancy, a second at age 4. Bennie, shown here, died in a train accident at age 12.

▶ MEXICAN WAR SERVICE

When the Mexican War broke out in 1846, Pierce enlisted as a private in the Concord Light Infantry. He was soon appointed a colonel and then a brigadier general of volunteers. In June 1847, he arrived in Mexico and led his 2,500 troops inland. At the battle of Churubusco, Pierce suffered a painful leg injury when his horse reared and fell. The next day, while again advancing into battle, he wrenched the injured leg so sharply that he fainted from the pain and was unable to take an active part in the fighting. In later years his political enemies twisted the facts about this incident and charged that he had been cowardly under fire. Pierce remained in the field until the capture of Mexico City, in September 1847, and then returned to his law practice in Concord.

▶ PRESIDENTIAL CANDIDATE

In the years that followed, Pierce's friendliness, kindness, and concern for people gained him increasing political popularity. His growing law practice brought him wealth, and his military career, though rather frustrating to him because of his accident on the battlefield, had made him a local hero.

Thus in 1851 many New England Democrats turned to Pierce as a presidential prospect. Few expected that he could be nominated. But some thought that he might have a chance if the Democratic convention came to a deadlock between the better-known candidates—Lewis Cass of Ohio, William L. Marcy of New York, Stephen A. Douglas of Illinois, and James Buchanan of Pennsylvania. When such a deadlock did arise, Pierce's friends introduced his name, and the delegates nominated him on the 49th ballot. William R. King of Alabama became Pierce's vice-presidential running mate.

▶ ELECTION OF 1852

In the campaign of 1852, Pierce ran against his former army commander, General Winfield Scott, the Whig Party candidate. Pierce promised, if elected, to respect the rights of the states and to conduct a vigorous foreign policy. His ease in meeting people was especially helpful during the campaign. He had the knack of remembering the name and face of nearly everyone he met. But his desire to please led him to make promises he could not always fulfill. Pierce won election handily, carrying all but four states. He received 254 electoral votes to Scott's 42 and won over 300,000 more popular votes.

### IMPORTANT DATES IN THE LIFE OF FRANKLIN PIERCE

| | |
|---|---|
| **1804** | Born in Hillsborough County, New Hampshire, November 23. |
| **1824** | Graduated from Bowdoin College. |
| **1827** | Admitted to the bar; began practicing law. |
| **1829** | Elected to the New Hampshire state legislature. |
| **1834** | Married Jane Means Appleton. |
| **1833–37** | Served in the U.S. House of Representatives. |
| **1837–42** | Served in the U.S. Senate. |
| **1847** | Saw action as a brigadier general of volunteers in the Mexican War. |
| **1853–57** | Served as 14th president of the United States. |
| **1869** | Died in Concord, New Hampshire, October 8. |

**Family Tragedy.** In January 1853, less than two months before his inauguration, the Pierces' remaining child, Benjamin, was killed in a train accident during a family trip. Mrs. Pierce, overcome with grief, came to believe that her son's life had been the price of her husband's victory. She would live in seclusion in the White House throughout Pierce's years in office, refusing to take part in public appearances. Pierce had to bear his wife's bitter accusations, as well as his own sorrow, at the very moment when he most needed strength and confidence.

**Cabinet.** Pierce invited into his cabinet a cross section of Democratic leaders, most without much experience. The only prominent members were William L. Marcy, as secretary of state, and Jefferson Davis, as secretary of war. (See the article on Jefferson Davis in Volume D.) The various members held different political views, and people predicted that the cabinet would soon break up. But it proved to be the first in U.S. history to remain unchanged throughout an entire 4-year presidential term. Vice President King, however, died soon after being sworn in.

**Domestic Issues: Kansas.** Pierce's term was marked by a bitter controversy over the expansion of slavery in the western lands. His hopes to quiet this debate received a setback when the Kansas-Nebraska bill was introduced in January 1854. The bill proposed to create two new territories, Kansas and Nebraska, and to allow settlers there to decide whether or not to allow slavery.

Pierce disliked the measure, but he promised to support it in return for Senate support of his political appointments and foreign policy. A furious debate over the bill raged in Congress. The prospect of slavery in Kansas split the Democrats into Northern and Southern wings, destroyed the Whigs, and gave birth to the Republican Party. When the

In the Mexican War, Pierce suffered a painful leg injury when his horse fell at the battle of Churubusco.

bill became law later in 1854, supporters and opponents of slavery rushed to Kansas, where a bloody struggle for control of the territory went on throughout Pierce's administration. See the article on the Kansas-Nebraska Act in Volume J-K.

**Foreign Affairs.** In 1853, Pierce acquired from Mexico the region known as the Gadsden Purchase, which included parts of present-day Arizona and New Mexico. Pierce also hoped to acquire Cuba from Spain and instructed his ministers in Europe to draft a plan for obtaining the island. Their proposal, called the Ostend Manifesto after the city in Belgium where they met, recommended purchasing Cuba but hinted that if Spain refused to sell, the United States might in certain cases be justified in seizing it. A garbled version of the proposal was leaked to the press and caused an uproar that damaged the administration. Pierce later tried to acquire Hawaii and Alaska, also without success.

The most far-reaching diplomatic event of Pierce's term was the opening of Japan to Western trade. The Treaty of Kanagawa, signed in 1854, allowed U.S. ships to stop at two Japanese ports. Treaties between Japan and other Western nations soon followed.

▶ **LATER YEARS**

Pierce hoped to win renomination for the presidency in 1856. But largely because of the difficulties in Kansas, the Democrats instead chose James Buchanan, who succeeded to the presidency in 1857. After leaving the White House, the Pierces toured Europe and eventually returned to Concord. Jane Pierce died in 1863. Franklin Pierce spent his last years virtually alone, dying in Concord on October 8, 1869.

PHILIP S. KLEIN
Coauthor, *A History of the United States*

**PIERRE.** See SOUTH DAKOTA (Cities).

**PIGMENTS.** See PAINTS AND PIGMENTS.

A sow with baby pigs.

## PIGS

A pig has a snout for a nose. Its eyes are small, and its tail is a little corkscrew. Its voice is either a grunt or a squeal. It has a thick body and short, rather thin legs. There are four toes on each foot. But only the longer, middle two are used in walking.

The pig has only a few thin bristles on its skin, instead of a thick coat of hair. It likes to wallow in mud. This keeps flies off and helps it to stay cool.

The pig's snout is long and tapered. It ends in a flat, leathery disk. The pig pushes the disk of its nose along the ground like a little plow, to dig up roots.

People have been raising pigs for as long as 5,000 years, but many kinds of pigs also live in the wild. The farm pig is raised in many countries for pork, ham, bacon, sausage, and lard. The male farm pig is called a **boar,** and the female a **sow**. In North America pigs are kept in pens or special houses and are fed corn, other grains, and specially prepared feed. They do not often need their plowing nose. The nose comes from their ancestors of millions of years ago. The ancestors of pigs had to root out tough plants that grew in swamps and along rivers. These ancestors were animals like the wild pigs of today that are called **wild boars**.

A pig eats almost anything. It eats roots and weeds, grass and grasshoppers, snails, mice, and lizards. It will also eat meat and bones, although pigs seldom kill for food.

Pigs belong to the **swine family**. They are also called **hogs**. Wild pigs also belong to the swine family. Some wild pigs are the wild boar, the warthog, the forest hog, the river hog, and the babirusa. The nearest relatives of the swine family are the peccaries and hippopotamuses.

Wild pigs are quite different from tame pigs. The wild boar of Europe and Asia is fast and fierce. When it is cornered, the wild boar is dangerous. It defends itself with long tusks that curve up from both the upper and lower jaws. The wild boar was once fairly common and was often hunted. Now it has disappeared in many areas. But it can still be found in various forested regions of Europe and Asia.

Some wild boars live in North America. They were brought in from other countries and turned loose for hunting. They live wild in the Great Smoky Mountains of Tennessee and North Carolina.

There are three kinds of African wild hogs. The giant forest hog lives in the forests. The bushpig, or river hog, lives in the jungle, too, but around water. It has long, pointed ears that end in tufts of hair.

The African warthog lives on the open plains of Africa along with antelopes and zebras. It has a mane of coarse hair, but the rest of its body is nearly naked. It has a gristly growth, or wart, the size of a golf ball, under each eye. Tusks grow out of its upper jaw, like the horns growing out of a cow's head. The warthog is often seen in zoos. It and other members of the pig family may live 15 years or so in captivity.

The babirusa of the East Indies is another unusual-looking wild pig. The male babirusa's upper tusks grow out of the snout and sweep backward in a curve. The babirusa is a good swimmer.

The only piglike animals native to the Americas are the peccaries. But peccaries are not true pigs. They are placed in a separate family.

Reviewed by ROBERT M. MCCLUNG
Author, science books for children

See also HOOFED MAMMALS.

**PILGRIMS.** See THIRTEEN AMERICAN COLONIES; MAYFLOWER; PLYMOUTH COLONY.

**PINCKNEY FAMILY.** See SOUTH CAROLINA (Famous People).

# PINEAPPLE

The pineapple is one of the best-known and most delicious fruits of the tropics. It has a strong aroma and a flavor that is both tart and sweet. The pineapple has the scientific name *Ananas comosus*. It was given the common name "pineapple" because it looks much like a large pinecone.

The pineapple originated in South America and was probably spread by early traders to Central America and the West Indies. Columbus found natives on the island of Guadeloupe eating pineapples during his second voyage to America. He and other explorers carried the plants to other areas of the world. The pineapple is now grown widely in tropical zones, mainly in Asia, Latin America, Africa, and Hawaii.

**Pineapple Plant and Cross Section of Fruit**

**The Plant.** The pineapple plant has a short stem and shallow roots. The stiff and slender leaves are specially adapted for holding moisture through long periods of dry weather. In some varieties, the leaves have sharp spines along the edges. A fully grown pineapple plant is about 3 feet (1 meter) tall.

Pineapple plants produce fruit one to two years after planting. The central stem grows

from a small shoot into a flower spike topped by a crown of leaves. The flowers are blue-violet in color. The fruit develops in one piece from the flower spike, but it is made up of 100 or more smaller fruits called fruitlets.

Each stalk bears one pineapple. While this fruit is developing, the plant produces new shoots called suckers from the stem near or beneath the soil. Each sucker will grow into a full-size plant and will bear a fruit the following year. This second crop is called a ratoon crop. New plants are started by planting suckers, crowns of older plants, or shoots called slips that grow from the fruit stalks.

Pineapples vary greatly in size, shape, and color. Their fruits may weigh from 2 to 15 pounds (1 to 7 kilograms). The most common colors are yellow and orange, but some varieties show some green and red. The fibrous flesh, which may be whitish or golden yellow, remains firm after ripening and canning.

**Harvesting.** Ripe pineapples are removed from the plants by breaking or cutting the stem just below the fruit. Harvesting is done by workers who pick the pineapples and place them on conveyor belts. The belts move the fruit to trucks, which haul the produce from the fields. The pineapples are then packaged whole or taken to canning factories.

Every part of a pineapple is used in the canning process. The flesh is canned in slices or cubes or in crushed form. The juice also is canned. The shells and other trimmings are shredded, pressed, and dried to make pineapple bran to feed livestock. Other by-products are sugar, alcohol, and vinegar.

Pineapple, canned or fresh, is a source of vitamins A and C. It is a good source of potassium and is rich in sugar. Fresh pineapple is often considered an aid to digestion.

The fruit may be served by itself, or it may be used in pies, ice cream, puddings, sauces, and salads. It may also be served with meats.

F. W. LIU
Cornell University

**PING-PONG.** See TABLE TENNIS.

**PINKERTON, ALLAN.** See CHICAGO (Famous People).

**PINKNEY, JERRY.** See CHILDREN'S LITERATURE (Profiles).

**PINOCHET UGARTE, AUGUSTO.** See CHILE (History).

**PINWORMS.** See DISEASES (Descriptions of Some Diseases).

# PIONEER LIFE

Pioneer life has a special meaning in America. In less than 300 years, civilization spread across a vast continental wilderness. From the first landings in Virginia and Massachusetts in the early 1600's, American settlers kept pushing westward behind an ever moving frontier. Into wild country went hunters, trappers, fur traders, miners, frontier soldiers, surveyors, and pioneer farmers. The farmers tamed the land and made it productive. Every part of America had its pioneers.

A pioneer family in the mid-1800's posed in front of the covered wagon that had brought them to Johnson County, Kansas.

## ▶ KINDS OF PIONEERS

The pioneers were as varied as human nature. Some were adventurous and independent. Some were irresponsible and lazy, like the Indiana squatter who moved eight times without ever clearing timber or fencing a field. "To move," he said, "all I have to do is put out the fire and call the dog." But most of the pioneers were determined and industrious people. Silas Garber, for example, settled in a sod-roofed dugout on a prairie creek bank in 1871. Four years later he had succeeded in becoming the governor of Nebraska.

Most pioneers were willing to face toil and hardship for the sake of opportunity. They meant to carve homes out of the wilderness. Yankee farmers went west from the stony fields of New England, and Southern families went west from the crowded lands of Virginia and the Carolinas. Still other pioneers were immigrants newly arrived from Europe. English, Scotch, Welsh, and German pioneers went into the Ohio Valley. Scandinavian colonists settled mainly in the upper Mississippi Valley and on the Great Plains beyond the Missouri River.

## ▶ REASONS FOR THE WESTWARD MOVEMENT

All of the pioneers hoped to find something better over the western horizon. New England families, tired of farming rocky valleys, were attracted to broad and fertile lands beyond the Appalachian Mountains. Southern farmers, suffering from bad luck or bad management, sought a new life in the West. To European immigrants the American frontier offered political freedom and economic opportunity. In the West, you could own your own land and work for your own future. For many people the West meant new opportunities.

In the Great Migration, which began after the War of 1812, multitudes of people went to the American interior. The population was growing in the eastern states. Families were large, and only one child could inherit the family home. The rest went to the growing cities or to the frontier. During hard seasons,

when crops failed or when farm prices fell, many headed for a new beginning in the West.

Many went almost empty-handed to the frontier. They traveled light and arrived with only an ax and a rifle. Others carried heirlooms and farming tools. Some took seed corn and orchard shoots, cattle, hogs, and poultry. But how does one prepare for sickness and danger, for accident and misfortune? Some settlers failed and returned to the East. Those who stayed and survived turned a wilderness into a civilization.

### ▶ BUILDING A CABIN IN THE CLEARING

On every new frontier the pioneers made homes for themselves, using what the wild land provided. In the great forests of the Ohio and Mississippi valleys the land provided timber. Here the pioneers' essential tool was the ax. The ax would clear the forest for the plow. But its first task was to shape a pioneer shelter.

When a family of settlers arrived at the spot where they planned to make their home, they began chopping saplings and trimming poles to build a lean-to. Between two forked trees they laid a crosspole. With the help of oxen or horses they rolled up a log, which was banked with dirt to form a low back wall. Then they laid poles, slanted upward, from the back log to the crosspole. The sloping roof was covered with bark and branches. The ends of the lean-to were walled with shorter poles and pickets. This was the pioneers' "half-faced camp." It always faced south, away from wind and rain. In front of the open side they dug a fire

After finding a location for a homestead, the pioneers' first task was to clear a field for a vegetable garden. They used the felled trees to build a temporary shelter.

pit. Logs smoldered there day and night, giving warmth and protection.

This served as a temporary home while the pioneer family prepared ground for their first crop. A real clearing took months of work, but a "deadening" could be done quickly. A few ax cuts were made in the tree trunks so that sap could not flow up to the branches. Soon the leaves withered, allowing sunlight to reach the damp soil. Seed corn was dropped into ax cuts in the ground. The crop from that crude planting provided food for the first winter.

Before winter came, the pioneer family hoped to have a small clearing and a snug

cabin. The forest was the settlers' enemy—it had to be destroyed to create their fields. At the same time, it was their friend—it gave them logs for their cabin, fuel for their fire, rails for their fences, wheels for their wagon, and a frame for their plow.

Notched logs formed the cabin walls. A ridgepole at the peak supported lighter roof poles, and a bark thatching made the roof complete. Logs, split into flat-faced planks called puncheons, were used to make the cabin floor. Two openings, a window and a door, were sawed out with patient labor. Typically the first doorway covering was an old quilt weighted with a log; later a board door would be hung on leather hinges. The first window covering was greased paper, which turned away wind and water and admitted a

for cooking, light, and warmth. Outside, the ax thudded and the smoke of brushfires hazed the air. Slowly the field was widened; a few new acres were cultivated every year. The cabin in the clearing was the pioneer homestead. When it gave way to a frame house, with a traveled road going past, the pioneer life had ended.

### ▶ TRAVELING ON THE OVERLAND TRAILS

In the 1840's and 1850's hundreds of thousands of pioneers made the long trek west to new frontiers in Oregon and California. For months they lived in covered wagons. These adventurers traveled in caravans, with 30 or more wagons rocking westward on the overland trails. On fine days a wagon train could cover 20 miles (32 kilometers); when the

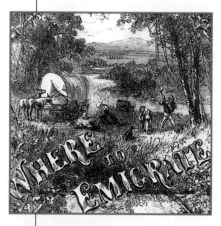

Attractive advertisements showing beautiful land and happy settlers encouraged hundreds of thousands of people to move west.

### OREGON FEVER

Based on the enthusiastic reports of people who had been (or perhaps claimed to have been) to Oregon, thousands of men uprooted their families and made the overland journey across the continent. This excerpt from a young pioneer's diary describes the kinds of exaggerated stories that were told to entice people to go west.

One Saturday morning father said that he was going…to hear Mr. Burnett talk about Oregon…. Mr. Burnett hauled a box out on to the sidewalk, took his stand upon it, and began to tell us about the land flowing with milk and honey on the shores of the Pacific…. He told of the great crops of wheat which it was possible to raise in Oregon, and pictured in glowing terms the richness of the soil and the attractions of the climate, and then with a little twinkle in his eye he said "and they do say, gentlemen, they do say, that out in Oregon the pigs are running about under the great acorn trees, round and fat, and already cooked, with knives and forks sticking in them so that you can cut off a slice whenever you are hungry." …Father was so moved by what he heard…that he decided to join the company that was going west to Oregon…. Father…was the first to sign his name ….

dim light. Pioneers used any paper they had. One settler greased his wedding certificate with bear fat and put it in his window frame.

Opposite the cabin doorway was the yawning chimney mouth. Clay from the creek bank, mixed with dried grass, was formed into clumsy bricks, which hardened in the sun. Laid against the cabin wall, the bricks formed a "cat and clay" chimney with a broad opening. The fire that smoldered there gave heat

rains brought mud, they would be satisfied to cover half that distance.

When a caravan was large, it was divided into two groups. Behind the line of wagons came the "cow column"—milk cows and spare oxen driven by men and boys on horseback. At night the wagons drew into a circle and the oxen were turned loose to graze. Men took turns at guard duty under the western stars.

On Sundays, unless a wagon train was behind schedule, the pioneers would stop to rest, play, and catch up on necessary chores.

At first daylight the guards went around the circle shouting "Arise! Arise!" Cows were milked while breakfast sizzled on the fire. The oxen were yoked and the wagons pulled into line. As the long bullwhips cracked, another day's travel began.

At noon the captain called a halt on a prairie ridge or beside a creek bank. While lunch was laid out, children ran over the prairie, gathering buffalo "chips" for the evening fire. (Buffalo dung was the travelers' main source of fuel.) After an hour's rest the march started again. The sun beat down, and heat waves shimmered on the horizon. When the shadows lengthened behind them, the captain began looking for a camping place. Supper was a restful meal. Children ran from one campfire to another. Men talked about the next day's travel, and women talked about the homes they would have at the end of the journey. After a fiddler played a few tunes, the people went to bed, some in the wagons, others on the ground. When the fires died down, the night wind brought the haunting call of coyotes.

Sunday was commonly a day of rest. However, even on Sundays the women washed clothes and baked bread, and the men repaired harnesses and greased the wagon wheels. While dinner was cooking, the whole company gathered in the shade of the circled wagons as the captain read a chapter from the Bible. Most often they turned to the Book of Exodus, which told of people wandering in the wilderness, seeking a promised land.

▶ SETTLING ON THE GREAT PLAINS

On the Great Plains, which were settled soon after the Civil War (1861–65), the pioneers built their first dwellings with the deeply rooted grass. Here farmers plowed up building material

On the plains, where fuel was scarce, pioneers collected buffalo "chips" (dung) to feed the evening fires.

Most pioneer homes on the plains were crude shelters made from whatever materials were available. A family in Oklahoma used sod, cloth, and bits of wood to build their dwelling (*left*). A family in Kansas dug their shelter straight into a hillside (*below*).

while breaking their first fields. With a spade they cut the furrows into 3-foot (1-meter) lengths. These they piled up like bricks, leaving openings for a door and window. Roof poles came from willow thickets along the infrequent prairie creeks. When a layer of sod covered the crisscrossed poles, the house was completed. It was cool in summer, warm in winter, windproof, and fireproof. But it did not keep out water. Spring rains seeped through the sod roof long after the sky had cleared. Sometimes a pioneer would have to hold an umbrella over the fire to cook a meal.

Outside the sod shanty a settler chopped into the broken ground and dropped seed corn into each cut. A year of wind and weather would soften the field for cultivation. But the first crop was sod corn, growing in the matted grass roots. On the prairie lay buf-falo bones left by hide hunters. Pioneer settlers hauled wagon loads of bones to the nearest railroad town, trading them for a wooden door, a glass-paned window, or some joints of stovepipe. The bones were ground up for fertilizer.

Near the first sod hut other pioneers marked their claims with a "straddlebug"—three boards nailed in a flimsy pyramid. New "soddies" appeared on the prairie, with new breakings beside them. These small fields, almost lost in the blowing grasslands, were the beginning of a changed country. In a few

Sturdy cooking pots and ladles were staples of the pioneer kitchen, along with herbs prized for their medicinal value. Essential tools included (*opposite page, from left to right*): a carpenter's adze, a boring auger, a striking maul, a hitting beetle, a barking spud, a scythe, and various axes.

years roads were graded along the section lines, settlements sprang up at the township corners, and wheat and corn grew where the buffalo grass had been.

## ▶ WAY OF LIFE

Whatever their surroundings, the pioneers had to depend on themselves and on the land. Self-reliance was a frontier requirement. Game provided food and leather clothing. New settlers gathered wild fruits, nuts, and berries. For salt they boiled the water of saline springs. Maple sugar was made by tapping maple trees in early spring and boiling the sap until it thickened into a tasty sweetening. Substitutes for tea and coffee were provided by boiling sassafras root and brewing parched corn and barley. With an ax and adze for cutting tools, the pioneers made beds, tables, benches, and stools. They split logs into rails to make the zigzag fence that enclosed their clearings.

Pioneer women learned to supply their own household goods. Gourds served as pails and dippers. Wood ash was sifted to make soap. Tallow (sheep and cattle fat) was molded into candles. Every cabin had two spinning wheels—a big wheel for wool and a smaller wheel for flax. With their own home-woven "linsey-woolsey," a coarse cloth of mixed linen and wool, pioneer women made their family's clothing. Clothes were also made from animal skins, which the pioneers tanned into leather.

Winter was a hard season on the frontier. In bitter weather the family huddled around the fire. When there was no leather, some people went barefoot and suffered frostbite.

On wash day, women would gather outdoors to do their weekly laundry.

Food was scanty and monotonous. For months there were no fresh fruits or vegetables. In early spring, women looked eagerly for the first wild mustard and dandelion plants, which they could boil into a dish of "greens."

As long as they had their health and strength, people could stand hardship. But every family had frequent bouts of illness. The most common frontier ailment was chills and fever. Young and old suffered from "the shakes," shuddering with cold and then breaking into a drenching sweat. This disease came at the end of summer and lasted until frost. Since it was most common in marshy districts, the settlers thought it came from breathing damp air. Actually it was malaria, carried by mosquitoes. When swamps were drained, there were fewer mosquitoes and the number of malaria cases declined.

For medicines the pioneers had to provide for themselves. Women soon learned the use of herbs for healing. They used boneset for fever, pennyroyal to purify the blood, horehound for coughs, and ginseng for tonic. Syrups and salves were made from cherry root, horseradish, and witch hazel. Wild mustard, poplar root, and red sumac root went into teas, poultices, and powders. The standard cure for a chest cold was to rub the chest with goose grease and apply a mustard plaster.

Some frontier remedies were based more on superstition than science. Among these were potions of walnut bark "peeled upward," boiled nettles, and "nanny tea," made from sheep dung.

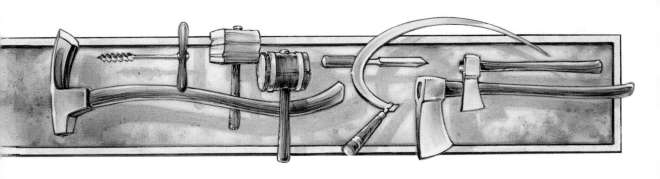

Pioneer families tended to be large. Most cabins had a cradle, hollowed from a poplar or cottonwood log, and the cradle was rarely empty. Children were helpful in new lands. Girls soon learned important household tasks—gardening, cooking, spinning, weaving, mending, sewing, making soap and candles. Boys worked in the woods and fields with their fathers. They learned to fell timber, to clear out brush, to split rails and build fences. A rail fence would keep hogs and sheep out of the corn, but deer could leap that barrier. It was the children's job to chase deer out of the fields and to keep squirrels from devouring the growing crop. Children pounded dried corn to make cornmeal. When gristmills came into the neighborhood, it was typically a boy's chore to ride to the millstream with

Pioneer children had many responsibilities on the frontier. Chores included (*clockwise from above*) mending clothes, chopping wood for fires, baking bread, hoeing fields, and fetching water.

a bag of grain behind his saddle and return with a dusty bag of meal.

Although pioneer families were extremely resourceful and nearly self-sufficient, neighbors were highly valued on the frontier. When fires went out, one could borrow a pan of glowing coals from the nearest cabin. Neighbors from miles around helped newcomers with logrolling, house-raising, and barn-raising. Entire communities joined in hunts for wolves, foxes, squirrels, and rabbits.

These common tasks, shared by pioneer neighbors, also provided amusement on the frontier. A house-raising was also a picnic, with women spreading a dinner on the grass while children swung from grapevines and the men laid up the roof poles on a new cabin. Neighbors gathered for "husking bees," competing to see who was the fastest at stripping the husks from ears of corn. The cornstalks were kept for fodder, while the husked corn was stored in a crib. Pioneer women held "quilting bees," exchanging family news while they sewed patchwork together. One amusement that did not involve household tasks was the barn dance. With a local fiddler playing such tunes as "Skip-to-my-Lou" and "Way Down in the Pawpaw Patch," men, women, and children joined in square and circle dances by lantern light on a rough barn floor.

### Schools and Churches

To pioneer people, "book l'arnin'" was less important than learning to use an ax and a plow, a loom and a spinning wheel. But as settlements grew, parents wanted their children to know the three R's—reading, 'riting, and 'rithmetic. In crude log schoolhouses, shelves fastened to the wall served for desks and the students sat on three-legged stools. They used charcoal to write on hand-smoothed writing boards. Later came slates and slate pencils. A slate, wiped clean after each lesson, could be used for years.

A teacher (known as a schoolmaster or schoolmistress) sat in the front of the schoolroom at a rough plank table. In the corner the teacher kept a bundle of hickory switches to whip unruly boys. Teachers "boarded round," a week at a time, in the homes of pioneer families. Often they slept in cabin lofts. They were paid according to the number of

Frontier schools were usually small. Children of all ages shared a classroom and a teacher (*above*). Most students in the 1800's learned from the McGuffey Readers (*left*). In addition to reading, writing, and arithmetic, these early textbooks stressed religious faith, thrift, courage, and obedience.

children they taught. All grades sat in the same room. About twenty students made a typical school, and a teacher's common salary was between $1 and $2 a term for each student. In wooded regions children walked as far as 5 miles (8 kilometers) on forest trails to the schoolhouse. On the prairie frontier they often went to school on horseback. They ate their lunch in the schoolyard in good weather and around the stove on winter days.

In frontier schools all over America, the most common textbooks were the McGuffey Readers. Their pages were full of references to rural and pioneer America. In McGuffey's primer the first lesson was "A is for ax." After *ax* came *box, cat, dog*—all familiar things. The

Preachers on horseback came to newly settled communities to deliver sermons and perform religious rites and ceremonies.

readings described children at work and play in barnyards, fields, and forests. These schoolbooks brought learning close to pioneer life.

Before the first churches were built, religion was carried to the frontier by the circuit rider, a preacher on horseback. The circuit rider visited pioneer families in their own cabins. He carried a Bible and a hymnbook in his saddlebag. He preached at crossroad settlements, standing on a stump or a wagon bed. He read from the Bible, prayed, and "lined out" hymns, reading one line at a time, which the people sang after him. In remote cabins he performed baptisms and marriages. He prayed over the graves of the dead.

As settlements grew, communities organized congregations and built churches at the crossroads. The church became a social as well as a religious center. It was a place of community socials and suppers, of Christmas enter-tainments, of Sunday school parties and neighborhood gatherings. The frontier church provided the first strong social bond in new communities.

### Government and Law

The first political organization on the frontier was the territorial government, with officials appointed by the president of the United States. Statehood could be sought when a region had a large enough population; 60,000 was the original requirement. With statehood the pioneers elected their own legislators and sent representatives to the U.S. Congress.

But pioneers went into new lands ahead of the law. Therefore, in its first years every frontier had its own unwritten laws, which were enforced by common consent. Some of the unwritten rules were remembered from older regions. Others evolved on the frontier to meet frontier needs. It was generally agreed that a stray horse became the property of the first man who could catch it. Horse thieves, the worst of criminals, deserved to die. Anyone involved in a quarrel had a right to defend himself. Killing another man in self-defense was not regarded as a crime. However, it was considered criminal to shoot an unarmed man or to strike anyone in the back.

In western communities bands of self-appointed vigilantes enforced their own ideas of justice. At its worst this action became mob violence. At its best it was a temporary assertion of community judgment. Though it was a necessity on the frontier, this lawless judg-

With new towns springing up overnight, lawyers, land agents, and other businessmen set up temporary shop outdoors.

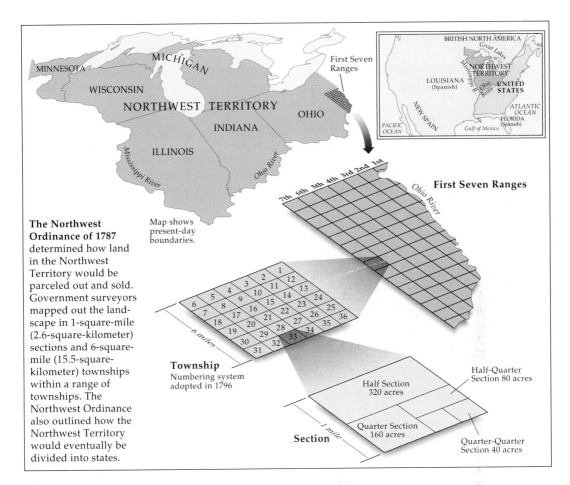

**The Northwest Ordinance of 1787** determined how land in the Northwest Territory would be parceled out and sold. Government surveyors mapped out the landscape in 1-square-mile (2.6-square-kilometer) sections and 6-square-mile (15.5-square-kilometer) townships within a range of townships. The Northwest Ordinance also outlined how the Northwest Territory would eventually be divided into states.

Map shows present-day boundaries.

MINNESOTA • MICHIGAN • WISCONSIN • NORTHWEST TERRITORY • INDIANA • OHIO • ILLINOIS • Mississippi River • Ohio River

First Seven Ranges

7th 6th 5th 4th 3rd 2nd 1st

**First Seven Ranges**

Ohio River

**Township**
Numbering system adopted in 1796

6 miles

1  2  12  13
3  11  14  24
4  10  15  23  25
5  9  16  22  26  36
6  8  17  21  27  35
7  18  20  28  34
19  29  33
30  31  32

**Section**

1 mile

Half Section 320 acres

Half-Quarter Section 80 acres

Quarter Section 160 acres

Quarter-Quarter Section 40 acres

Inset map: BRITISH NORTH AMERICA • Great Lakes • NORTHWEST TERRITORY • LOUISIANA (Spanish) • UNITED STATES • Mississippi R. • Ohio R. • NEW SPAIN • PACIFIC OCEAN • ATLANTIC OCEAN • FLORIDA (Spanish) • Gulf of Mexico

**After the Civil War,** railroad companies distributed thousands of posters encouraging easterners to take the train and move west. *Left:* The Hannibal and St. Joseph Railroad advertised land available in Missouri. *Below right:* The Chicago, Milwaukee, & St. Paul Railway hoped to bring farmers to Three Forks Country, Montana.

ment had to give way to a legal system. In the process some vigilantes became officers of the law. Still, the pioneer districts had no trained officials. In west Texas, one weathered justice of the peace was called Old Necessity because he knew no law. On his bench he kept a mail-order catalog, which he always consulted before making a judgment. Once, considering a man charged with a misdemeanor, he put on his spectacles, flipped open the catalog, looked at it a moment, and announced, "I fine you $4.88." When the man jumped up to protest, a friend yanked him back. "Sit down," he said. "You're lucky he opened it at 'pants' instead of at 'pianos.'"

**Roads**

In the interior of America, the first roads were rivers. The great rivers, notably the Ohio and the Mississippi, became frontier highways, carrying the population and the produce of the new West. The tributary streams were only slightly less important. Settlers paddled and poled up the side rivers, finding their way into a trackless land. On flatboats they took corn, wheat, pork, lard, and apples to market. Settlers and town builders alike chose sites on running waterways.

In a land run in 1893, homesteaders eager to enter a newly opened section of Oklahoma Territory gathered on Kansas' southern border and awaited the government's permission to cross over.

Through the forest the pioneers cut primitive roads called traces. Boone's Trace was a pioneer path in Kentucky. The historic Natchez Trace led north from Natchez, Mississippi, to Nashville, Tennessee. Zane's Trace ran through the Ohio woods; it began and ended at landings on the Ohio River.

The first improved highway—straight, wide, and smooth—was the National Road, begun at Cumberland, Maryland, in 1815. It eventually ran through the frontier capitals of Columbus (Ohio), Indianapolis (Indiana), and Vandalia (Illinois). Multitudes of pioneer settlers traveled the National Road, as later emigrants to the far West traveled the overland trails to Oregon and California. Canals between the Great Lakes and the Ohio and Mississippi rivers hastened the settlement of the Midwest.

### ▶ LAND LAWS

After the Revolutionary War (1775–83), the United States acquired a spacious domain extending beyond the original 13 colonies to the Mississippi River. The Louisiana Purchase in 1803 extended it farther, to the Rocky Mountains. And the annexation of Oregon and California carried it to the Pacific Coast by 1850. The western regions were sparsely occupied by Indians. A piece at a time, by treaty and purchase, the tribes ceded vast lands to the United States. So the public domain was offered to settlers, at first by purchase and finally as free homesteads.

Before land could be sold and legally settled, it had to be surveyed. Government surveyors mapped it into 1-square-mile (2.6-square-kilometer) sections and 6-square-mile (15.5-square-kilometer) townships. By this system any tract of land could be precisely located and its boundaries determined. With chain and compass the surveyors went into wild country. They left a numbered post at each mile and a marked cone of dirt at the township corners.

After it was surveyed, the land was open to sale and settlement. The first federal land law offered a minimum tract of 640 acres (256 hectares) at $2 an acre, half the price to be paid to the government within 30 days and the remainder within a year. Many settlers did not have that much money. They became known as squatters—people who lived on the public land without legal ownership.

In a series of reforms the land laws were made more democratic. The Harrison Land Act of 1800 allowed sales of 320 acres (128 hectares) at $2 an acre and allowed four years to pay. In 1820 the revised law offered 80-acre (32-hectare) tracts at $1.25 an acre.

This enabled a pioneer with $100 to buy a small farm. At last, in 1862, President Abraham Lincoln signed the Homestead Act, which offered land free to any adult who would live on it and improve it. People then sang a popular song: "Uncle Sam is rich enough to give us all a farm." The Homestead Act helped to fill up the Great Plains frontier. (For more information, see the article PUBLIC LANDS in this volume.)

On a stump-studded street in a raw new town stood the government land office, with survey maps on the wall and a big open ledger on a table. Steubenville, Marietta, Chillicothe, and Cincinnati had the first land offices in the Northwest Territory. As new districts were surveyed, land offices were opened at Zanesville, Vincennes, Shawneetown, and Kaskaskia. By 1820 they were extended to Detroit and St. Louis. In all these places a familiar scene was repeated. While a woman and her children waited outside in a wagon, a pioneer settler studied the survey maps in the land office. At last he counted out his advance payment and signed his name or made his mark in the ledger. He got a certificate that he could exchange for a deed of ownership when payment was completed. Then the wagon creaked on to the township and section numbered on his claim. So another pioneer family found their land.

### ▶ THE CLOSING OF THE FRONTIER

In 1889 central Oklahoma was opened to homesteaders. Thousands of people, on horseback, in wagons, and on foot, raced into the area to mark out homesteads. In this dramatic land rush, settlement came to the last large tract of public domain. In 1890 the U.S. Census Director declared, "There can hardly be said to be a frontier line." After more than 200 years the moving frontier had come to an end. Vast stretches of wilderness remained in the western mountains and deserts. Much of it would become national forestland. But an era of American history had closed, an era shaped by the hope, the hardship, and the toil and accomplishment of pioneer people.

Today the United States still has some remote and primitive areas, where resourceful, self-reliant people can go beyond the reach of civilization. Alaska is sometimes called the Last Frontier. With large areas of uninhabited land it attracts pioneer people as the American interior did in the 1800's.

### ▶ PIONEERING AND THE AMERICAN CHARACTER

From Virginia to Alaska, life on the frontier produced many common traits in pioneers. Among them were independence, resourcefulness, individualism, and belief in

In 1895, a group of Dutch emigrants posed in front of a picture of the ship that would bring them all to America. By the late 1800's, most of America's new pioneers were emigrants from European countries.

the future. Men especially were free and equal on the frontier, and democracy was strengthened by the pioneer experience. New lands stimulated initiative, energy, and determination.

But today, with no land left to discover and little left to explore, modern pioneers must look to other frontiers to break new ground. They must look to the oceans or the solar system—or even to the realms of social justice, education, public health and medicine, religion, or the arts. From finding water on the moon to discovering cures for cancer, the opportunities for the modern pioneer are endless.

WALTER HAVIGHURST
Author, *First Book of Pioneers*

See also OVERLAND TRAILS; TERRITORIAL EXPANSION OF THE UNITED STATES; WESTWARD MOVEMENT.

# PIRATES

Few characters in literature are more romantic or colorful than roaring, swaggering pirates, whose adventures have been popular with generations of readers. Many authors, among them Robert Louis Stevenson, Sir Walter Scott, and James Fenimore Cooper, have written exciting tales about pirates sailing under the skull-and-crossbones flag, searching for buried treasure, and making their prisoners walk the plank. James M. Barrie created the comic, cowardly Captain Hook in *Peter Pan*, and Gilbert and Sullivan poked fun at sea robbers in their operetta *The Pirates of Penzance*.

Although many of the familiar tales are exaggerated and fanciful (there is no proof, for example, that anyone was ever forced to walk the plank), real pirates did roam the seas for thousands of years. Until as recently as the 1800's, peaceful sailing ships were often at the mercy of ruthless pirates who captured crews and stole precious cargoes. Now considered a crime in all countries, piracy was once accepted as a common hazard of sea travel.

A pirate's flag was called a Jolly Roger, a term derived from an old English nickname for the Devil. Each pirate had his own design. This one may have belonged to Black Bart.

## ▶ HISTORY

The real story of piracy, or robbery on the high seas, is as old as the history of seafaring.

**Pirates of the Ancient World.** The ancient Phoenicians, Greeks, and Romans who sailed the Aegean and Mediterranean seas often ran the risk of having their cargoes stolen. Pirates became so powerful in the ancient world that they established their own seacoast settlements, from which they attacked trading vessels.

In 78 B.C., while crossing the Aegean Sea to Greece, the young Julius Caesar was captured by a band of pirates and held until ransom was paid. Attacks by pirate ships became so frequent that the Romans sent a naval expedition under Pompey the Great to force them from the Mediterranean area. Although the Roman Navy succeeded in conquering a large settlement at Cilicia in Asia Minor (67 B.C.), piracy was not completely wiped out,

---

## Profiles

The life stories of many pirates have been told and retold so many times that it is often difficult to distinguish between fact and fiction.

**Black Bart (Bartholomew Roberts)** (1682?–1722), born in Wales, is known as the most gentlemanly of pirates. He supposedly was so proper that he forbade all swearing, drinking, and gambling aboard his ship. He was extremely democratic with his crew and showed every mercy toward his victims. It is said that he plundered more than 400 ships in his lifetime. He was killed in a battle with a British warship off the coast of Africa.

**Blackbeard (Edward Teach)** (?–1718), born in Bristol, England, was nicknamed

Blackbeard

Anne Bonny and Mary Read

for the long black beard he sometimes wore braided. A privateer for the British in the West Indies during the War of the Spanish Succession (1701–14), Blackbeard later turned to piracy, plundering areas of the Caribbean and along the coasts of North Carolina and Virginia. Protected by the governor of North Carolina, with whom he shared his spoils, Blackbeard was finally killed in an attack by

ships sent against him by the governor of Virginia. In 1997, Blackbeard's most famous pirate ship, *Queen Anne's Revenge*, was discovered off Beaufort, North Carolina.

**Anne Bonny** (1697?–1720?) and **Mary Read** (?–1720) were history's most famous women pirates. Anne was born in Ireland but was raised on a plantation in

The pirates of the Caribbean in the 1600's and 1700's were known as buccaneers. They were known to plunder any ship that came within their grasp.

and sea robbers were soon roaming the waters once again. Many centuries later, as shipping in northern waters increased, Viking pirates began attacking ships in the Baltic Sea and English Channel.

**The Barbary Corsairs.** Beginning in the 1300's, bands of ruthless seafaring criminals known as corsairs established settlements along the North African coast. The lands they inhabited (parts of present-day Morocco, Algeria, Tunisia, and Libya) were known as the Barbary States. For hundreds of years Barbary corsairs attacked European, and later American, trading vessels. Cargoes were looted and crews were held for ransom or sold into slavery. In order to safeguard their shipping, many nations paid tribute, or protection money, to the corsair rulers in return for safe passage.

**Privateers.** By the 1500's, it had become common practice for the rulers of one nation to give privately owned vessels the right to carry arms and attack the ships of enemy nations. These armed vessels, as well as their commanders and crew, were called privateers. And privateering, a kind of legalized piracy, became a respected occupation. Some of the most famous privateers were the English "sea

the Carolinas. Disinherited by her wealthy father when she eloped with James Bonny, she settled on New Providence Island in the Bahamas, a haven for Caribbean pirates. She soon left Bonny for the pirate "Calico Jack" Rackham and joined the crew aboard his ship *Revenge*. Later Anne became fast friends with Mary Read, an Englishwoman who wore men's clothes and had once been a soldier in the English Army. Mary joined Rackham's crew and participated in several raids before they were all captured and convicted of piracy. Calico Jack was hanged, but Anne and Mary were spared by "pleading their bellies," or claiming to be pregnant. Mary became ill and died in prison. It is not known what happened to Anne.

**Captain William Kidd** (1645?–1701), born in Greenock, Scotland, is perhaps the most recognized name in the history of piracy. Many cruel exploits have been

A FULL

# ACCOUNT

OF THE

# ACTIONS

Of the late Famous

# PYRATE,

Capt. KIDD.

With the Proceedings against Him, and a Vindication of the Right Honourable *Richard* Earl of *Bellomont*, Lord *Colomy*, late Governor of *New-England*, and other Honourable Perfons, from the Unjuft Reflections caft upon tehm.

*By a Perfon of Quality.*

DUBLIN:
Re-printed for *Matthew Gunn*, Bookfeller in *Efex-Stret*, 1701.

A biography of Captain Kidd (1701)

attributed to him, and for years the mention of his name struck terror in the hearts of honest sea captains. A biography of Captain Kidd appears in Volume J-K.

**Jean Laffite**, or **Lafitte** (1780?–1826?), born in France, plundered ships and

Sir Henry Morgan

smuggled the stolen goods into New Orleans, where he sold them for profit. During the war of 1812, this pirate-turned-patriot offered his aid to U.S general Andrew Jackson and was largely responsible for winning the Battle of New Orleans. A biography of Laffite appears in Volume L.

**Sir Henry Morgan** (1635?–1688), born in Wales, was one of the cruelest and most notorious of all the English buccaneers. With the unofficial support of the English government, Morgan preyed on Spanish shipping and colonies in the Caribbean. His greatest conquest was the sacking of Panama City (1671)—Spain's largest colony in Central America—and the seizure of its stores of gold and jewels. Tales of Morgan's exploits captured the English people's imagination, and he became a romantic hero during his lifetime. Knighted by King Charles II, Morgan was eventually made lieutenant governor of Jamaica.

## BURIED TREASURE

According to legends, pirates often buried their stolen gold, silver, and jewels in secret hiding places. Captain William Kidd buried treasure on Gardiners Island, near Long Island, New York. When Kidd was jailed, this booty was recovered by the British and sent to London. Blackbeard supposedly buried vast amounts of gold and silver near Ocracoke Inlet, North Carolina.

Many expeditions have searched on Cocos Island, off the coast of Costa Rica, for the "Lost Loot of Lima" (Peru). Reportedly buried by the pirate Benito Bonito of the Bloody Sword, this treasure is estimated to be worth more than $65 million.

One of the most enduring pirate treasure mysteries concerns the fabled "Money Pit" on Oak Island, off the coast of Nova Scotia. Ever since a farm boy discovered a shaft there in 1795, treasure hunters have searched the island in vain. Other treasures are also said to be buried all along the Gulf Coast, from Florida to Texas.

**Captain Kidd buried treasure on Gardiners Island off the coast of New York. It was recovered following his arrest in 1699.**

dogs" Sir Francis Drake, Sir John Hawkins, and Sir Walter Raleigh.

**Pirates of the Caribbean.** Protected seas, with many islands and irregular coastlines, offered excellent hideouts for pirates. The Caribbean Sea and the Spanish Main (the northeastern coast of South America) offered just such advantages. Soon after the first settlements in the New World began to flourish, pirates began their plundering.

The pirates of the Spanish Main came to be known as **buccaneers**, from the *boucan*, or wooden grill, on which they cured their meat. From well-concealed hiding places on the islands of the West Indies, buccaneers attacked not only the Spanish galleons that traveled between Spain and her colonies, but also the colonies themselves. For more than 200 years buccaneers captured cargoes of jewels, gold, and silver and plundered island cities and the coastal settlements of South America.

As the hazards to shipping and colonies increased, many efforts were made to clear the seas of pirates. In 1718 an important pirate stronghold on New Providence Island in the Bahamas was destroyed by British warships called men-of-war. Pirate leaders were offered pardons if they would surrender their ships and give up their attacks. It was not until about the middle of the 1800's, however, that the combined efforts of the navies of the United States and several European countries succeeded in ridding the Mediterranean and Caribbean seas of pirates.

## ▶ PIRATE LIFE

From old diaries, letters, ships' logs, and memoirs, a great deal has been learned about the way pirates lived. Most of the people who became pirates were cruel and lawless. The capture of treasure was their chief aim, and human life was cheap. But there were laws of the sea, both written and unwritten, that even the most ruthless pirates observed.

Most pirate crews worked together and shared captured booty. Pirates usually displayed great loyalty to one another and always took good care of sick and wounded shipmates. Many crews practiced a strict democracy, whereby captains were elected by a majority vote and shares of treasure were agreed on in writing before a voyage.

Considering that the crews on merchant ships had no say in their daily routines, were paid very little, and suffered greatly from the hardships of life at sea, it is not difficult to imagine why so many seafarers chose a life of piracy.

Reviewed by HAMILTON COCHRAN
Author, *Pirates of the Spanish Main*

# PITT, WILLIAM, EARL OF CHATHAM (1708–1778)

William Pitt, Earl of Chatham, was a great British statesman. His leadership in a war with France enabled Britain to win control of Canada and opened up the Ohio Valley to settlement by American colonists.

Born in London on November 15, 1708, Pitt was educated at Oxford University and then spent four years in the Army. In 1735 he was elected to Parliament. An eloquent speaker, he aroused the hostility of King George II by attacking government policies. The King so disliked Pitt that he refused to appoint him to office, in spite of his ability. It was not until 1746 that the King was persuaded to make Pitt paymaster general.

When the French and Indian War broke out in 1754, Pitt became increasingly critical of the way the government was handling the war. George II was furious and dismissed Pitt. By 1756 the war in America had spread to Europe as the Seven Years' War. Things went so badly for Britain that the King was forced to take Pitt back into the government, where he directed the war against France. Pitt was so successful that the French were defeated in Canada and Europe and driven from their territory in the Ohio Valley. Fort Duquesne, which had been captured from the French, was renamed Pittsburgh in his honor. In 1760, George III came to the throne. The King and Pitt disagreed on how the war should be fought, so Pitt resigned the following year.

Much of the latter part of Pitt's life was spent in opposition to the policies of George III and his ministers. In 1766 he was made Earl of Chatham and became prime minister. But he suffered a severe nervous breakdown and resigned in 1768. For the rest of his life Pitt championed the cause of the American colonists in their struggle against the British Government. He died on May 11, 1778.

DOROTHY MARSHALL
Author, *Eighteenth Century England*

# PITT, WILLIAM, THE YOUNGER (1759–1806)

William Pitt the Younger, the second son of William Pitt, Earl of Chatham, was born in Hayes, in Kent, England, on May 28, 1759. Though sickly as a boy, he was determined to follow his famous father's example—to enter Parliament and become prime minister. After graduating from Cambridge University, Pitt studied law and in 1781 was elected to Parliament. His abilities, especially as a brilliant speaker in parliamentary debates, were soon recognized. When he was only 23 he became chancellor of the exchequer, the minister in charge of finance. In 1783, at the age of 24, he was asked by King George III to become prime minister. Pitt's opponents laughed at the idea of so young a man becoming prime minister. They thought he would last only a short time. They were wrong. Except for the period between 1801 and 1804, Pitt was prime minister until his death in 1806.

Pitt held what were then very modern ideas. He realized that the way the government collected taxes and raised loans was old-fashioned. Pitt succeeded in carrying out a number of financial reforms that increased Britain's commercial prosperity. He also united the separate Irish and British parliaments in 1801. This Act of Union created the United Kingdom of Great Britain and Ireland. Pitt also wished to pass a Catholic emancipation act, to end discrimination against Catholics. But George III was so strongly opposed to the measure that Pitt resigned in 1801.

Since 1793, Britain had been almost continuously at war with France. When Pitt returned as prime minister in 1804, Europe had long been dominated by the French under Napoleon. Pitt allied Britain with France's enemies, providing them with money to equip their armies. But they were no match for Napoleon, who crushed the British alliances. However, the British fleet ruled the seas, and Pitt used it to blockade French ports, seize French colonies, and protect Britain against invasion.

Pitt did not live to see the end of the war with France. He died on January 23, 1806. A lonely man, Pitt never married and had only a few close friends. His life was devoted almost entirely to politics. He is remembered today as one of Britain's great prime ministers.

DOROTHY MARSHALL
Author, *Eighteenth Century England*

# PITTSBURGH

Pittsburgh is the second largest city in Pennsylvania. Located in the southwestern part of the state, it is strategically situated at the point where two rivers, the Monongahela and the Allegheny, flow together to form the headwaters of a third river, the mighty Ohio. The jut of land that lies where the three rivers converge is aptly called the Point.

Pittsburgh's landscape of hills and valleys covers approximately 55 square miles (142 square kilometers), and the city's abundant waterways are spanned by more than 700 bridges, more than are found in any other city in the world except Venice, Italy. Pittsburgh's climate is temperate, averaging 30°F (–1°C) in midwinter and 72°F (22°C) in the summer. Normal annual rainfall is about 36 inches (914 millimeters); annual snowfall is about 43 inches (109 centimeters).

Approximately 335,000 live within the city, but more than 2 million people live in its greater metropolitan area, which covers parts of four counties, making Pittsburgh among the 25 largest metropolitan areas in the United States. The city has more than 100 neighborhoods, many of which are traditionally associated with a particular ethnic group or nationality.

## Education and Communications

Education is one of Pittsburgh's largest industries. More than 100,000 students attend 31 regional colleges and universities. Chief among these is the University of Pittsburgh, which is also the city's single largest employer. One of its special points of interest is its Cathedral of Learning, the world's second tallest classroom building. Other notable institutions include Carnegie Mellon University, Duquesne University, Robert Morris College, Chatham College, and Carlow College.

Pittsburgh is served by one major newspaper, the *Pittsburgh Post-Gazette*, six local television stations, and more than forty local radio stations.

## Culture and Recreation

Pittsburgh's largest museum complex is called the Carnegie, named for the steel baron Andrew Carnegie (1835–1919), one of Pittsburgh's greatest benefactors. The complex boasts the world-class Carnegie Museum of Art; the Carnegie Museum of Natural History, which displays one of the best dinosaur collections in the country; the Carnegie Science Center, containing an actual submarine; the Carnegie Music Hall; and the Library of Pittsburgh. Other notable local museums include the Frick Art Museum, the Fort Pitt Museum, the Stephen Foster Memorial, and the Pittsburgh Children's Museum.

Major arts groups in the city include the Pittsburgh Symphony Orchestra, the Pittsburgh Ballet Theatre, the Pittsburgh Opera, Pittsburgh Public Theater, and the City Theatre Company. Also, the emerging Cultural

Pittsburgh, Pennsylvania, is located at the junction of three rivers—the Allegheny (top), the Monongahela (right), and the Ohio (left). At the fork lies a triangular plot of land called the Point. Traditionally regarded as a major steelmaking center, today Pittsburgh is also renowned for its cultural and educational institutions and its advanced technology industries.

District downtown features two spectacularly renovated halls for the performing arts, the Benedum Center and Heinz Hall.

Despite its smoky reputation, Pittsburgh, with an extensive parks system, is actually one of the greenest cities in the United States. Major city parks include Schenley, Frick, Highland, and Mellon. In addition, one of the country's oldest and grandest amusement parks—Kennywood Park—lies just east of the city.

Pittsburgh has been called the City of Champions due to the achievements of its professional sports teams—the Pittsburgh Pirates of baseball's National League, the Pittsburgh Steelers of the National Football League, and the Pittsburgh Penguins of the National Hockey League. The Steelers play at Heinz Field, the Pirates play at PNC Park, and the Penguins play at the Mellon Arena, which is known as the Igloo because of its domed shape.

### History

Because of its easy river access from three directions, Pittsburgh was a strategic trading site for the Shawnee, Delaware, and Iroquois Indians who originally inhabited the area. Later the land became an important military site for French and British colonists, who competed for control of the territory. The British built the first fort there in 1754 and called it Fort Prince George. It was destroyed four months later by the French, who replaced it with Fort Duquesne. In 1758, the British destroyed Fort Duquesne and built the last fort to stand at this site—Fort Pitt, named after then prime minister William Pitt.

Because many travelers heading west on the Ohio River started their long journey from Fort Pitt, a town quickly grew up near the fort. The town was officially incorporated as Pittsburgh in 1816. The land around the city was rich in natural resources—especially coal and iron—and Pittsburgh quickly grew into a center of industry. By the mid-1800's, Pittsburgh's economy was booming. Glassmaking and ironworks became its principal industries, and by the latter part of the century, its factories were producing half of the world's glass and iron and two-thirds of the nation's steel. Pittsburgh became a magnet for immigrants from many countries, who came to labor in the mills.

During the first half of the 1900's, Pittsburgh's industrial growth continued to skyrocket, and when the United States took part in World War II (1941–45), Pittsburgh factories supplied the steel for America's war machines. The city became known worldwide as the Iron City and Steeltown. But there was a negative side to this explosive growth—pollution. Pittsburgh also came to be known by such nicknames as Hell with the Lid Off and the Smoky City. So thick was the soot in the air, businessmen had to change their white shirts at midday, and at times the smoke was so dense, street lights had to be turned on during the day so people could see.

In the late 1940's, Mayor David Lawrence joined forces with many of the city's business and civic leaders, including financier Richard King Mellon, and launched one of the country's first urban renewal projects. Called Renaissance I, the project encompassed flood control, air pollution control, and highway development. Several new buildings were erected in a once-blighted downtown area. Another urban renewal project, Renaissance II, was begun in the 1970's.

However, Pittsburgh faced a new challenge—the collapse of America's steel industry. One after another, the area's steel mills were shut down, and by 1983, unemployment had reached almost 15 percent. Nevertheless, Pittsburgh bounced back. By supporting the development of advanced technology, medical research, and its educational resources, the city reduced its unemployment to 5 percent by 1990.

Pittsburgh was once rated "the most livable city in the nation." Today it continues to boast a low crime rate, low housing costs, and a top-rated public education system.

BRUCE VANWYNGARDEN
Contributing editor, *Pittsburgh Magazine*

**PITUITARY GLAND.** See GLANDS (Endocrine Glands).

## PIUS XII, POPE (1876–1958)

Eugenio Pacelli, the future Pope Pius XII, was born in Rome, Italy, on March 2, 1876. A distinguished diplomat and expert on both church and civil law, he led the Roman Catholic Church during World War II and in the difficult years that followed the war.

Young Pacelli decided to become a priest while in his teens. He was educated at the Capranica seminary and Gregorian University in Rome. He later received doctoral degrees in theology, philosophy, and canon (church) and civil law. He was ordained a priest in 1899.

Pacelli's scholarly achievements brought him to the attention of the church government at the Vatican, and in 1901 he began a long and brilliant career in the papal secretariat of state. He taught law and served on diplomatic missions abroad. In 1917 he was made an archbishop and sent as nuncio, or papal ambassador, to Germany. Pacelli served there until 1929, when he was elevated to the rank of cardinal. The following year he was appointed papal secretary of state. In this post he represented Pope Pius XI and trav-eled to many countries on church matters. He visited the United States in 1936.

Pacelli was elected pope after the death of Pius XI in 1939, six months before the outbreak of World War II. As the "Pope of Peace," Pius XII worked tirelessly to try to prevent the war. When war came, he sought to lessen its spread. Through his efforts, many Jews were saved from death. Later, critics of Pius claimed that more lives might have been saved if he had spoken out more strongly against Nazi Germany. But many believe that if he had done so it would have led to even greater persecution of the Jews.

Pius strongly opposed the spread of Communism in the years after the war. But he was deeply concerned about social justice and supported the rights of workers.

Pius wrote many encyclicals, or letters to bishops on subjects concerning the church. He made Holy Communion more easily available to the people by encouraging evening Mass.

Pius XII died on October 9, 1958. He was succeeded by Pope John XXIII.

Reviewed by THADDEUS HORGAN, S.A.
Director, Graymoor Christian Unity Center

---

## PIZARRO, FRANCISCO (1475?–1541)

Francisco Pizarro, the conqueror of the Inca Empire of Peru, was born about 1475 in Trujillo, Spain. In 1502, seeking fame and fortune, he sailed for the recently discovered new world of America.

Pizarro served with the explorer Vasco Balboa in 1513. They were the first Europeans to cross the narrow strip of land in Central America known as Panama and reach the Pacific Ocean. Pizarro settled in Panama, where he heard of a wealthy land to the south—Peru, the heart of the Inca Empire. He formed a partnership with Diego de Almagro and Hernando de Luque to try to find this rich land. Their first attempt ended in failure. In 1526, Pizarro set out again. After much hardship, he reached Tumbres, a town rich in gold and silver. With this evidence of the wealth of the Incas, Pizarro received permission to conquer Peru.

Pizarro began with only about 180 men, a few cannons, and some horses. But the Incas had been weakened by civil war. At Cajamarca he trapped the much larger force of the Inca ruler, Atahualpa, took him prisoner, and demanded a huge ransom for him. But after it was paid, Pizarro had him killed.

In 1533, Pizarro entered Cuzco, the Inca capital, completing, in effect, the conquest of Peru. In 1535 he founded the city of Lima, now the capital of Peru. His partner Luque had died. But Almagro, feeling cheated of his share of the gold and power, gathered his own army and in 1538 marched against Pizarro. Almagro was defeated in battle and killed. His followers waited for a chance to gain revenge, and on June 26, 1541, they assassinated Pizarro in his palace in Lima.

SANFORD G. BEDERMAN
Georgia State College

**PLAINS INDIANS.** See INDIANS, AMERICAN (On the Prairies and Plains).

**PLANCK, MAX.** See LIGHT (The Quantum Theory); PHYSICS, HISTORY OF (Profiles).

Visitors to planetariums can attend exciting shows where dazzling views of objects and events in space are projected onto the domed ceilings of theaters.

# PLANETARIUMS AND SPACE MUSEUMS

Planetariums are wonderful places to learn about astronomy and space. In them you can go to shows on different topics in astronomy and see realistic images of stars, planets, galaxies, and other objects in space projected onto the domed ceiling of a theater. Planetariums are often part of science parks or museums that specialize in science or space-related topics. Planetariums may also be part of astronomical observatories, libraries, and universities.

### ▶EARLY PLANETARIUMS

The word "planetarium" was originally used to refer to a small model of the planets or the solar system. The first such model planetarium was designed in 1682 by the Dutch astronomer Christiaan Huygens (1629–95). Over the next 150 years, many other model planetariums were built. In early planetariums, models of the solar system usually consisted of a series of balls that represented the sun and the planets. These balls were attached to rods that were connected to gears. When a handle was turned, the gears would move the rods so that the "planets" circled the "sun." A small model like

this, called an **orrery**, demonstrated the motions of the solar system.

The first planetarium that people could walk into was built in 1654 in Germany. It was a hollow copper ball more than 11 feet (3 meters) in diameter and it weighed more than 3 tons. Painted on the outside of the ball was a map of the Earth, and the stars and constellations were painted on the inside. To the ten people who could sit inside on benches set on a platform, the painted stars seemed to rise and set in the sky as the globe was rotated.

Several similar planetariums were built in Germany shortly after this one was completed. Then, nearly 100 years later, one was built in Cambridge, England. In the United States, a globe planetarium was built at the Chicago Academy of Sciences and opened in 1913.

The first modern planetarium, which used a dome and a projector to display objects in space, was built in Germany in 1924. Today, modern planetariums can be found throughout the world. Some of the well-known planetariums in the United States are the Hayden Planetarium in New York, the Adler Planetarium in Chicago, and the Griffith Planetarium in Los Angeles.

This orrery—a small model of the sun and planets—was made in England around 1800.

## ▶MODERN PLANETARIUMS

Today's modern planetariums are much different from the early model planetariums. Most are built in rather large buildings and include planetarium theaters where people can attend shows about space and related topics. In addition to these shows, many planetariums also offer lectures and educational programs, live or recorded music concerts, and even live theatrical performances.

### The Planetarium Theater

Not all planetarium theaters look alike. While almost all the theaters are round, some are less than 15 feet (4.6 meters) in diameter and can seat only a few dozen people. Others are 75 feet (23 meters) or more in diameter with room for hundreds of people. Some theaters have flat floors with all seats facing the middle of the room. In others, the seats may all face one side of the room. Still other planetarium theaters have tilted floors. Despite such differences, a common feature of all planetarium theaters is a domed ceiling.

### The Planetarium Dome

The domed ceiling in a planetarium acts as a projection screen similar to those in movie theaters. Unlike the screen in a movie theater, however, the domed ceiling of a planetarium is usually made of sheets of thin metal with millions of tiny holes. These holes help reduce the weight of the dome and let air circulate through. The whole ceiling may be coated with a vinyl-like material, or it may be painted white or light gray, which allows it to reflect images like a movie screen.

In most planetariums, large speakers are located behind the metal sheets of the dome. This makes it seem as though the words, music, and sound effects for the planetarium shows come from the dome. Sounds may even

The mechanical star projector (*below* and *right*) is a key instrument in planetarium shows. It can show how the night sky would look from anywhere on Earth and project how the stars would change position in the sky over hundreds or thousands of years.

appear to move around the theater as the projected images move across the dome.

### Star Projectors

One of the most common and spectacular images projected on the planetarium dome is a clear night sky with thousands of stars. A special "star projector," usually located at the center of the planetarium theater, is able to show the sky as seen from anywhere on the Earth at any hour of the day or night. It can also show the sky as it would appear for any date within several thousand years of the present. The two most typical types of star projectors are mechanical star projectors and digital video star projectors.

**Mechanical Star Projectors.** The most common type of star projector is the mechanical star projector. Some of these projectors are shaped like large dumbbells with one or two spheres on each end. Others have single large spheres. Within a sphere is a powerful lamp and glass or metal plates with pinpoint openings. As the light from the lamp passes through these tiny openings, it is focused onto the planetarium dome by lenses that are on the surface of the sphere. These projections of light create an artificial sky with images of the stars. The process is similar to what happens in an ordinary slide projector when light shines through a slide to project an image on a screen.

Gears and motors on the star projector allow it to be turned in different directions, which makes the images of the stars move. Sometimes the stars move across the artificial sky of the planetarium dome as they do in the real sky at night. This type of motion, called **diurnal motion**, imitates the motion of the stars as seen from the Earth as it rotates on its axis. The planetarium theater, however, is like a time machine. Its star projector can make this happen in only seconds rather than the hours it would take in the real night sky. The star projector can also change the latitude from which the sky is observed. This type of motion allows the audience to see the sky as it appears from anywhere on Earth. The projector can also show how the sky changes as the Earth revolves around the sun or slowly wobbles on its axis. This latter motion, called **precession**, shows how the North Star would slowly change over the course of thousands of years.

Attached to the star projector, or located nearby, are other projectors used to display images of the sun, the moon, and the five planets that can be seen in the sky by the naked

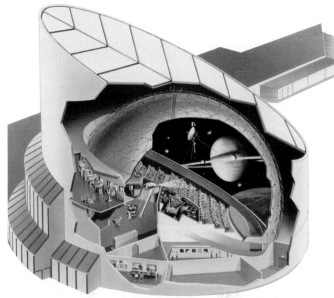

This diagram of a planetarium with a tilted floor shows the location of the projectors and computers and the spectacular view the audience has of the objects projected on the domed ceiling of the theater.

eye—Mercury, Venus, Mars, Jupiter, and Saturn. These projectors can be timed so that the stars, planets, sun, and moon move through the sky in harmony with each other. Changes in position that might take months or years in the real sky can be demonstrated in only seconds in the planetarium sky. Other projection devices are also used. They can create such things as the outlines of constellations and the faint glow of the Milky Way galaxy.

**Digital Video Star Projectors.** Mechanical star projectors date back to the 1920's, but the digital video star projector is a more recent

The orbits of the planets are displayed by a digital video star projector, which can also send audiences to distant stars.

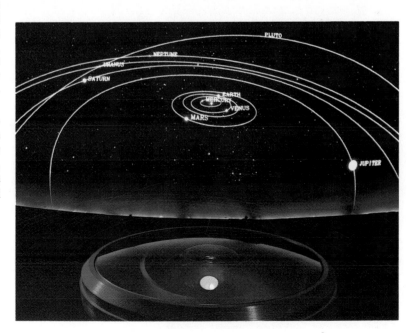

development. This projector is a special kind of television set connected to a powerful computer. The computer stores information about the planets and stars and their positions in space. It can then generate images of these objects on a circular television screen about 9 inches (23 centimeters) in diameter located at the center of the planetarium theater. A special lens then projects these images onto the planetarium dome.

While the mechanical star projector can only show the sky from on or near the Earth's surface, the digital video star projector can take an audience on imaginary flights to the stars. It can also move the audience forward or backward millions of years to show how the positions of the stars and the shapes of constellations change over time. The projector's computer can also create and project images of the sun, the moon, space stations, and spacecraft, and it can present information about these objects.

### Other Projectors

In the modern planetarium theater, the star projector is only one of dozens, or even hundreds, of computer-controlled projection devices. These projectors use slides, film, videotape, optical laser disks, and other media to create a wide variety of objects or scenes on the planetarium dome. Among the images they can create are moving clouds, shooting stars, rotating planets, galaxies, black holes, and landscapes of the surface of the moon or of planets in our solar system. With such images, the audience can experience trips to other planets or to the far corners of the universe, and they can see and learn about the latest discoveries in astronomy and space science. Some planetariums have devices in each seat that let audience members control the computers operating these projectors. In this way, audiences can decide for themselves what they wish to see and learn.

### Laser Systems

Many modern planetariums have powerful laser systems that can create colorful patterns or moving pictures or words in the planetarium sky. These images are generated by computer and can be used to help illustrate a wide variety of planetarium shows. They can also be used in combination with music during live or recorded concerts in the planetarium theater. Sometimes special machines that create a fine mist are used to generate an artificial fog inside the theater. As lasers pass through this fog they create colorful beams or patterns of light that move in the air above the heads of the audience. Recently, special glasses have been developed that give people the illusion of seeing these three-dimensional laser images move in mid-air without the use of the fog-generating machines.

This museum display of the solar system (*left*) is made up of scale models of the planets. Each model rotates on its axis as dots of light show its orbit. A designer (*above*) completes a scale model of the Hubble Space Telescope that will be used in a planetarium show.

## ▶CREATING A PLANETARIUM SHOW

The shows seen in planetarium theaters are often created by people whose work is similar to making movies for theaters or television.

A planetarium show is created in several stages. After a subject is chosen, someone must research the information about it that is to be used in the show to be sure it is correct and up to date. When all of the information is gathered and checked, a script is written. This script is usually written by an astronomer and it contains all the words the audience will hear during the show. It also indicates what the audience will see on the planetarium dome as the words are being spoken.

While working on a script, the scriptwriter must work with others who create the visual images that will appear on the dome. These visual images are created by artists using paints and brushes or perhaps computers. Sometimes an artist will also build models of spacecraft because they often look more realistic than paintings. When the paintings and models are finished, they are recorded on film, videotape, or optical laser disks for projection onto the planetarium dome during the show. Computer images may also be stored on film, videotape, or laser disks.

Creating special effects for a planetarium show requires the help of skilled technicians who build special projectors that can project moving images, such as planets or spacecraft, across the planetarium dome. Motion is sometimes created by moving a piece of film or a slide within a projector. Sometimes images from projectors are reflected from moving mirrors, which causes the images to move in the artificial sky of the dome.

After the script for a planetarium show is finished, it is read by one or more narrators and recorded on tape. Music and sound effects to generate excitement and build suspense are recorded on tape as well. The music and sound effects must work well with the script and images, and they must be just the right length to accompany the different parts of the show.

Finally, the planetarium show is put together. All slides, film, videotape, laser disks, and other visual materials are placed in projectors or other playback devices. This may require dozens or even hundreds of different projectors, all being turned on and off at various times during the program. Controlling all these projectors and timing their action with

Visitors to the National Air and Space Museum in Washington, D.C., can see full-scale models of the many kinds of spacecraft used to explore outer space.

narration and music can be very complicated. To do it manually would be almost impossible. Today, however, it is possible to control and time everything with a computer, and a special computer program is written for each planetarium show.

## ▶SPACE MUSEUMS

Many planetariums are part of science-technology centers or space museums that feature exciting exhibits on space and space-related topics. A well-known space museum is the National Air and Space Museum at the Smithsonian Institution in Washington, D.C.

The National Air and Space Museum is a particularly exciting place to visit. Its exhibits show how far people have progressed in the areas of flight and space exploration. These exhibits trace the development of flight from early hot air balloons to the first airplanes to more advanced aircraft and different types of spacecraft. Among the exhibits is a large col-

In the *Challenger* shuttle area of the Space Center in Iowa, you can experience some of the activities astronauts have in flight. Here students are using a computer to send messages to mission control.

lection of spacecraft replicas, including various weather and communication satellites, the *Mariner 10* and *Voyager* spacecraft sent to study other planets, the *Mercury* space capsule that carried the first American astronauts into space, and the *Apollo* lunar lander. There is even a replica of the Skylab Space Station that visitors to the museum can walk through. With its planetarium theater and hundreds of exhibits, slide shows, movies, replicas, and actual aircraft, the National Air and Space Museum provides a comprehensive look at space and space exploration.

**Types of Exhibits.** Space museums typically have a variety of exhibits. Many of these exhibits are interactive. This means that visitors can touch or manipulate (operate) parts of the exhibit. In some interactive exhibits, computers that can store large amounts of information and images are used to help explain the exhibit or to answer visitors' questions.

Museum exhibits often include real meteorites and models of planets, stars, and galaxies. They help visitors understand what these objects are made of and how they relate to each other in terms of size and distance. Other exhibits may include astronomical instruments and dioramas (three-dimensional scenes) of different objects or activities with explanations of how they work. Some space museums even have small observatories with working telescopes. When fitted with special filters, these telescopes can be used to look at the sun during the day and see explosive storms on its surface or huge glowing clouds of hot gas stretching far out into space. At night, the tele-scopes allow visitors to see the moon, planets, galaxies, nebulae, and stars. Images from such telescopes can also be projected onto television monitors or movie screens located elsewhere in the museum.

**Other Activities.** Many space museums, as well as planetariums, also have classrooms where people can take courses in astronomy or related subjects. They may also have lecture halls where experts speak about different topics related to space and astronomy. Some museums have libraries or research facilities where people can get information about topics in which they are interested. Many offer educational programs for students of all ages.

At some space museums, including the Houston Museum of Science and Natural History, and Discovery Place in Charlotte, North Carolina, young people can go on simulated missions to a space station or to the planet Mars. Working in teams, they learn what it is like to perform tasks similar to those done by astronauts. They also learn what it is like to be the engineers and scientists on the Earth who work with astronauts to solve problems that arise during space missions.

Space museums and planetariums are fascinating places. With their many shows, exhibits, and programs, they allow everyone who visits them to learn about and experience some of the wonders of space.

WILLIAM A. GUTSCH, JR.
Chairman, American Museum–
Hayden Planetarium

See also SPACE AGENCIES AND CENTERS; SPACE RESEARCH AND TECHNOLOGY.

# PLANETS

In ancient times, sky watchers observed that there were five special points of light in the night sky. All the other points of light always kept their same positions relative to one another. These were the stars, and the constellations they formed remained the same year after year, lifetime after lifetime. The five points of light were different because, from week to week and month to month, they slowly moved among the stars as if they had special powers. The ancient Greeks called these points of light the *plane´tai*, a word that means "wandering stars," and named them after their gods: Hermes, Aphrodite, Ares, Zeus, and Chronos.

Today we know that these points of light, which we call planets, wander slowly in the sky because they are other "worlds" in our solar system that are traveling at different speeds around our sun. Instead of using the names of the Greek gods, we call these planets by the names of the equivalent Roman gods: Mercury, Venus, Mars, Jupiter, and Saturn.

A planet is very different from a star. A star is a huge ball of fiery gases that gives off light. A planet shines by reflected light. The planets in our solar system travel around our star, the sun, in paths called **orbits**.

Our own Earth is one of these planets. If you could observe Earth from outer space, you would see that it too

seems always to be moving among the stars. Like the other planets, Earth gives off no light of its own. When a planet shines brightly in the night sky, it is reflecting the sun's light.

In addition to the five planets known since ancient times, three more—Uranus, Neptune, and Pluto—have been discovered since the invention of the telescope. Counting Earth, there are nine known planets in our solar system. Some of the planets have one or more satellites, or moons, that revolve around them. Earth's moon is one of these satellites. The planets with their satellites, and all of the asteroids and comets that orbit the sun, make up our solar system. Much of what we now know about the planets in our solar system has come from space probes. These probes, laden with sophisticated instruments, have orbited, flown by, or even landed on many of these planets and transmitted valuable information back to astronomers on Earth.

In this article, you will travel outward from the sun and visit the planets one at a time. Your first stop is Mercury.

Gas giants, such as Jupiter (*above*), have thick atmospheres surrounding oceans of liquefied gas. Other planets in our solar system, such as Mercury (*left*), have solid surfaces of rock and metal.

## ▶ MERCURY

Mercury is the closest planet to the sun. Its average distance from the sun is about 35.9 million miles (57.8 million kilometers). The orbits of all the planets are ellipses, or flattened circles, but Mercury's orbit is particularly flattened. As a result, at various points in its orbit Mercury can be as close as 29 million miles (46.7 million kilometers) from the sun or as far away as about 44 million miles (70.8 million kilometers). It takes 88 Earth days for Mercury to complete one trip around the sun. In other words, one Earth year of 365 days is longer than four Mercury years. Mercury rotates on its axis once every 59 Earth days, and its diameter is 3,032 miles (4,880 kilometers).

Mercury appears tiny and almost without features, even when observed with powerful telescopes. Little was known about this planet until *Mariner 10* flew past it in 1973 and sent back hundreds of images, showing thousands of craters, long cliffs called scarps, and a giant impact basin about 800 miles (1,288 kilometers) across.

An extremely thin veil of helium gas has been detected around Mercury. These atoms, which are actually given off by the sun, flow around the planet as it orbits the sun. In addition to this veil, a very thin atmosphere of oxygen, sodium, and hydrogen gases, which probably escape from Mercury's surface, has also been detected. The magnetic field that surrounds Mercury is much weaker than the Earth's magnetic field. Its gravitational pull is also much weaker than that of the Earth.

Because Mercury is so close to the sun, temperatures can reach about 800°F (427°C) during the day. However, Mercury's thin atmosphere retains little of this heat, so during its long nights the temperature can plunge to –280°F (–171°C). Mercury has no known satellites. For more information, see the article MERCURY in Volume M.

## ▶ VENUS

Your next stop is Venus. This planet travels around the sun in a nearly circular orbit, at an average distance of about 67.2 million miles (108.2 million kilometers). Venus takes 224.7 Earth days to make one trip around the sun. It is nearly the same size as the Earth, and its diameter is 7,519 miles (12,100 kilometers). Its gravitational pull is almost the same as that of the Earth.

Venus comes closer to the Earth than any other planet—it is only about 26 million miles (41.9 million kilometers) away. Even so, we can see virtually no details in a telescope because Venus is completely covered by thick clouds. These clouds reflect the sun's light, and at times Venus is the brightest object in the sky except for the sun and the moon.

Venus' atmosphere, composed mostly of carbon dioxide, creates a surface pressure that is about 90 times greater than the pressure at the Earth's surface. The carbon dioxide traps the sun's heat, driving the surface temperature of Venus to more than 800°F (427°C). Venus has no magnetic field and, like Mercury, has no known satellites.

sun

Uranus

Venus

Earth

Mercury

Mars

Pluto

Neptune

Saturn

Jupiter

**THE SOLAR SYSTEM**

The nine planets of our solar system revolve around the sun in elliptical orbits. Although each planet is shown at about the correct size in relation to the others and the sun, the planets' distances from the sun and each other are not to scale. These distances are so great, it would be impossible to show them to scale in one illustration. To get an idea of the immense distances of the planets from the sun and each other, see the feature How to Make a Solar System Model in the article SOLAR SYSTEM in Volume S. In addition, the planetary rings shown are simple representations of the real rings, which are much more intricate.

By using radar to penetrate the clouds of Venus, scientists have learned that while Venus' clouds can circle the planet in as little time as four Earth days, its surface spins very slowly, completing one rotation in 243 Earth days. Another discovery was that Venus rotates from east to west like Uranus and Pluto. All the other planets rotate from west to east.

Radar waves bounced off Venus from Earth as well as from spacecraft have allowed scientists to map the surface of this planet in great detail. Such maps show that about 60 percent of its surface is covered by flat, gently rolling plains and a few craters. Two large areas, the size of small continents on Earth, consist of mountainous terrain. Radar maps suggest that, unlike Earth, Venus is made of only one continental plate. There is nothing that resembles the Earth's mid-ocean ridges or similar features. For more information, see the article VENUS in Volume UV.

## ▶EARTH

Beyond the orbit of Venus is Earth. The Earth's orbit is almost as circular as that of Venus. The Earth travels around the sun at an average distance of 93 million miles (150 mil-

### WONDER QUESTION

**Would you weigh the same if you lived on a planet other than Earth?**

Each planet in our solar system has its own unique physical properties, such as size, mass, and gravity. When the gravitational pull on a planet is weaker than that of Earth, you would weigh less than you do on Earth. If the gravitational pull is stronger, you would weigh more. If you weigh 100 pounds on Earth, you would weigh 39 pounds on Mercury, 91 pounds on Venus, 38 pounds on Mars, 260 pounds on Jupiter, 110 pounds on Saturn, 88 pounds on Uranus, 114 pounds on Neptune, and only 5 pounds on Pluto!

## LOOK AT THE PLANETS

### Observing Mercury and Venus

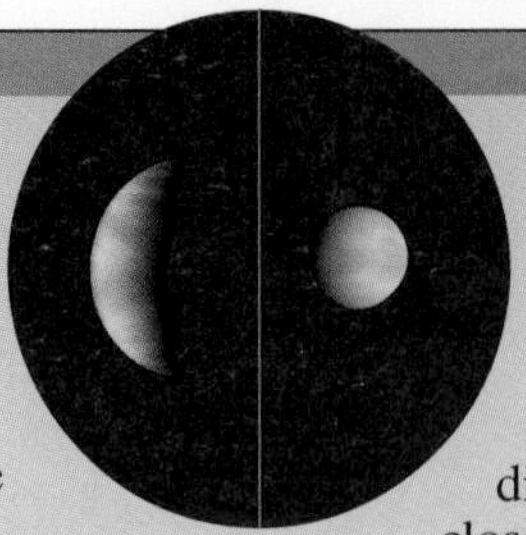

Venus and Mercury are closer to the sun than the Earth is, so we see them go through phases like those of the moon. You can observe these phases with a telescope.

When either planet is almost directly between the Earth and the sun, it is difficult to see. This is because the sunlit side of the planet is facing away from us, and the planet lies close to the sun in our sky. Over a period of days, as Mercury or Venus moves from this position, we are gradually able to see more and more of its sunlit side. During these times, a thin crescent of Venus or Mercury can be seen in a telescope. As the planet gradually moves around the sun, the crescent fills in. The planet also appears to be growing smaller during this time because its distance from the Earth is increasing. When the planet goes around the far side of the sun, it looks quite round and small.

Like the moon, Venus goes through phases. When it is close to the Earth, it appears as a large crescent (*far left*). As it moves away, it becomes smaller but appears fuller (*left*).

During such times it is also difficult to see because it is very close to the sun in the sky and the sun's glare blocks our view. Finally, as the planet again swings close to the Earth, it again appears to grow larger, but we see less and less of its sunlit face.

Because of this motion, Mercury and Venus alternately appear to the right or left of the sun in our sky. When they are to the left of the sun, they set after sunset and are visible for a while in the western sky during early evening. When they lie to the right of the sun, they rise shortly before sunrise and can be seen in the eastern sky a little before dawn. That is why the names "Morning Star" and "Evening Star" have been used for both planets, although they are not stars at all.

---

lion kilometers). It completes one orbit around the sun in 365.25 days, and it takes 23 hours and 56 minutes for the Earth to rotate on its axis.

The Earth is a ball of rock and metal. Its diameter is 7,923 miles (12,751 kilometers) at the equator. Surrounding the Earth, like a great blanket of gases, is an atmosphere made up mainly of nitrogen and oxygen. As seen from space, however, the Earth's atmosphere appears very thin. If the Earth were the size of an apple, its atmosphere would be thinner than the apple's skin.

Unlike Mercury and Venus, the Earth has a satellite—the moon. It orbits the Earth at an average distance of 240,000 miles (386,400 kilometers). Because the moon rotates on its axis in the same period of time as it revolves around the Earth, it always keeps the same face toward the Earth. The moon is 2,160 miles (3,478 kilometers) in diameter, which is more than one-fourth the diameter of the Earth. For more information, see EARTH in Volume E and MOON in Volume M.

### ▶ MARS

Your next stop is Mars, a planet that shines in the sky with a reddish color and is sometimes called the Red Planet. The orbit of Mars is more oval-shaped than that of the Earth, so the distance between Mars and the sun may be as little as 128.4 million miles (206.7 million kilometers) or as much as 154.8 million miles (249.2 million kilometers). The average distance between Mars and the sun is about 142 million miles (228 million kilometers). It takes Mars 687 Earth days to travel once around the sun, and it rotates once on its axis in 24 hours and 37 minutes.

Mars is a small, rocky world that is very dry. Its diameter is 4,200 miles (6,760 kilometers), only a little more than half that of Earth, and its gravitational pull is weaker.

Mars has two small satellites. Phobos, the larger one, measures about 16 miles (26 kilometers) in its longest dimension, and it circles its planet at a distance of 2,462 miles (3,964 kilometers). Phobos completes its orbit in about 7½ hours, which is less time than it

This image of the surface of Mars was taken by one of two robotic rovers that landed on the planet in 2004. New evidence suggests that water once flowed on this rocky world.

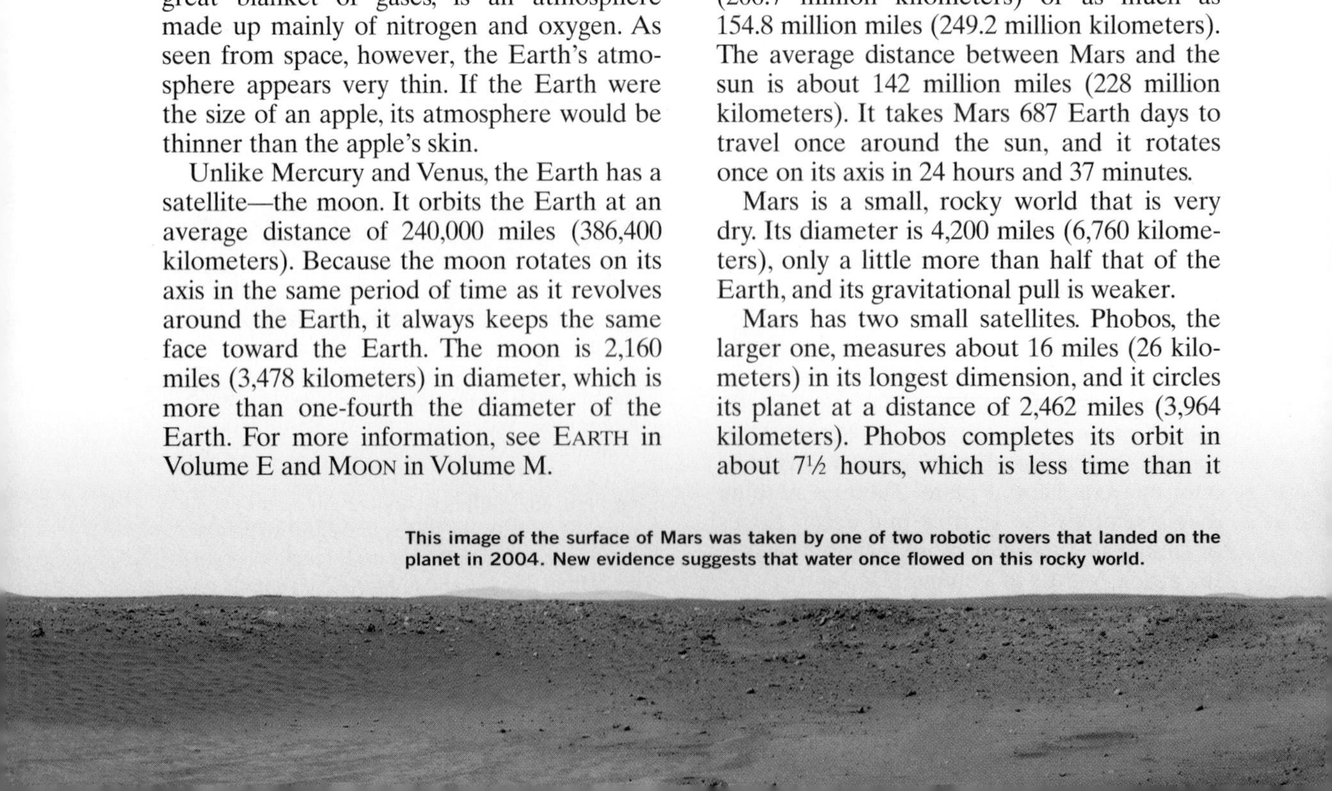

takes Mars to turn once on its axis. Therefore, to a visitor on Mars, Phobos would seem to rise in the west and set in the east. Deimos is smaller than Phobos, measuring about 10 miles (16 kilometers) long. It circles Mars at a distance of 14,700 miles (23,600 kilometers).

Early space probes provided a great deal of information about Mars. They learned that Mars has no magnetic field and that there is very little atmosphere surrounding it. The atmospheric pressure on its surface is $\frac{1}{600}$ of the atmospheric pressure on the Earth's surface. Its thin atmosphere is made up almost entirely of carbon dioxide. Temperatures at the planet's equator may occasionally reach 60°F (16°C), but nighttime polar temperatures can plunge to nearly –202°F (–130°C).

The surface of Mars has a variety of features, including craters, giant extinct volcanoes, and a canyon system almost as long as the width of the United States. In 2004, the robotic rovers *Opportunity* and *Spirit* touched down on the surface of Mars. They revealed many details about the planet's geology and topography, and they found signs that liquid water once flowed on the planet— enough to have possibly supported life. For more information, see the article MARS in Volume M.

▶ JUExpiter ⬛⬛⬛⬛

▶ JUPITER

After passing through a belt of asteroids beyond the orbit of Mars, the next stop on your planetary journey is Jupiter, which is more than five times farther from the sun than Earth. The planet travels around the sun at an average distance of 483 million miles (778 million kilometers), taking 11.9 Earth years to complete one orbit.

Jupiter, the largest planet, is one of the four gas giants in our solar system. Its diameter is 89,000 miles (143,000 kilometers)— more than eleven times greater than that of Earth. It takes less than ten hours to rotate once on its axis.

What appears to be Jupiter's surface is really the top of a thick, cloudy atmosphere. Nearly 90 percent of it is hydrogen, and most of the remaining 10 percent is helium. There are also very small amounts of methane, ammonia, and some other substances that give Jupiter's clouds their beautiful colors.

Instruments aboard the *Pioneer* and *Voyager* space probes, which flew by the planet in the 1970's, confirmed that at the top of Jupiter's atmosphere it is very cold, about –186°F (–121°C). Deeper down in the clouds, however, temperatures climb to thousands of degrees. The tremendous heat rising through the atmosphere combines with Jupiter's rapid rotation to produce large and violent weather systems. Cloud belts on Jupiter are driven by powerful winds that move at speeds of up to 350 miles (560 kilometers) per hour. The most amazing feature in Jupiter's clouds is an enormous orange-red area known as the Great Red Spot, which is more than twice the size of our planet.

Deep below the clouds there is no solid surface. Instead, astronomers think there is probably a planet-wide ocean that consists mostly of hydrogen compressed under such great pressure that it forms a liquid with metallic properties. At the center of Jupiter there is probably a core, consisting of iron and silicates. The molten metallic materials in the core create a strong magnetic field that extends far out into space. At the top of Jupiter's clouds, this magnetic field is about 14 times stronger than that of the Earth. Jupiter's gravitational pull is about two and one-half times stronger than the Earth's.

Jupiter has 63 known satellites. The largest, Ganymede, is 3,270 miles (5,270 kilometers) in diameter. Callisto is slightly smaller, with a diameter of 3,000 miles (4,800 kilometers). Each of these satellites has an icy surface covered with craters. Another satellite, Europa, which is 1,900 miles (3,100 kilometers) across, is also covered with a layer of ice. Io has a diameter of about 2,200 miles (3,500 kilometers), and its surface is covered with volcanoes and lava flows. There are 59 more known satellites, ranging from less than a mile to more than a hundred miles in diameter. Before the *Voyager* probes, little was known about Jupiter's satellites because they appear only as dots when seen through even the largest telescopes. The later *Galileo* probe found indications of liquid salt water beneath

| THE PLANETS | MERCURY | VENUS | EARTH | MARS | JUPITER | SATURN | URANUS | NEPTUNE | PLUTO |
|---|---|---|---|---|---|---|---|---|---|
| **Average Distance from Sun** (in millions of miles) | 35.9 | 67.2 | 93 | 142 | 483 | 885.5 | 1,800 | 2,800 | 3,700 |
| (in millions of kilometers) | 57.8 | 108.2 | 150 | 228 | 778 | 1,400 | 2,900 | 4,500 | 5,900 |
| **Length of Year** (in Earth days and years) | 88.0d | 224.7d | 365.25d | 687.0d | 11.9y | 29.5y | 84.0y | 165y | 247.7y |
| **Period of Rotation** (in Earth minutes, hours, and days) | 59d | 243d | 23h 56m | 24h 37m | 9h 55m | 10h 40m | 17h | 16h 5m | 6d 9h |
| **Diameter at Equator** (in miles) | 3,032 | 7,519 | 7,923 | 4,200 | 89,000 | 74,500 | 32,000 | 30,800 | 1,400 |
| (in kilometers) | 4,880 | 12,100 | 12,751 | 6,760 | 143,000 | 120,000 | 51,500 | 49,600 | 2,253 |
| **Number of Known Satellites** | 0 | 0 | 1 | 2 | 63 | 47 | 27 | 13 | 1 |

the ice of Europa, Ganymede, and Callisto. *Voyager 1* also discovered a thin, delicate ring of fine particles circling Jupiter. For more information, see the article JUPITER in Volume JK.

## ▶ SATURN

The next stop on your journey is Saturn, another gas giant. It orbits the sun at an average distance of 885.5 million miles (1.4 billion kilometers) and takes nearly 29.5 Earth years to make one trip around the sun.

Saturn, which is not quite as large as Jupiter, has a diameter of 74,500 miles (120,000 kilometers). Like Jupiter, Saturn rotates very quickly; it takes 10 hours and 40 minutes for it to turn once on its axis.

Saturn has a very deep atmosphere, which is made up mainly of hydrogen and helium, with some methane and ammonia. At the top of its atmosphere, the temperature is about –300°F (–185°C). This low temperature causes ammonia in the outer atmosphere to freeze, forming high-altitude haze. This gives Saturn a softer appearance than Jupiter. There are also spots similar to Jupiter's Great Red Spot in Saturn's atmosphere, but they are smaller. The largest is about the size of Earth.

The largest of Saturn's 47 known satellites is Titan. The diameter of Titan is 3,200 miles (5,150 kilometers). This is the only satellite in the solar system that has a thick atmosphere, and the pressure at its surface is about one and a half times greater than at the surface of the Earth. This atmosphere consists mostly of nitrogen.

Saturn is one of the most beautiful objects in the sky because of the rings that circle the planet at its equator. The entire ring system is more than 170,000 miles (274,000 kilometers) in diameter, but it is less than 1 mile (1.6 kilometers) thick. The rings may have formed at the same time as the solar system, or they may be the remains of a nearby satellite that was broken up by Saturn's gravitational pull, which is almost the same as that of the Earth. For more information, see the article SATURN in Volume S.

## ▶ URANUS

Leaving Saturn and traveling even farther from the sun, you come to the planet Uranus. Uranus is 32,000 miles (51,500 kilometers) in diameter. It orbits the sun at an average distance of 1.8 billion miles (2.9 billion kilometers), and it takes about 84 Earth years to complete one orbit. Uranus rotates once on its axis in an east-to-west direction in approximately 17 hours—the rate at which both its

Saturn's rings (shown here in a false-color image) are a spectacular sight. The material forming them includes ice and silicate minerals.

magnetic field, which is anchored in the planet's interior, and its interior rotate. Uranus' magnetic field is only about two-thirds as strong as that of the Earth.

The blue-green color of Uranus is caused by methane in its thick atmosphere. The temperature at the tops of its clouds is –355°F (–215°C). Scientists think that beneath the atmosphere is a vast ocean of water, methane, ammonia, and other elements surrounding a core consisting mostly of molten rock and metal. At the tops of Uranus' clouds, the gravitational pull is somewhat weaker than that of the Earth. A system of thin, very dark rings encircles the planet.

Most of the planets in our solar system spin in a more or less straight up-and-down position as they orbit the sun, although some are tilted a little more than others. If the solar system could be placed on a gigantic table, the planets would look like spinning tops as they moved around the sun. Uranus, however, tilts at the extreme angle of 97.8 degrees. You could almost say the planet lies on its side as it orbits the sun. This means that the north and south polar regions of Uranus experience alternate periods of day and night

(and summer and winter), each of which is up to 42 Earth years long. If Uranus were much closer to the sun, this could result in very extreme seasons. Because of the planet's distance from the sun and the odd wind patterns in its atmosphere, Uranus has rather even global temperatures, and the north and south polar regions are actually a little warmer than the regions around its equator.

Uranus has 27 known satellites. The largest is Titania, with a diameter of about 1,000 miles (1,600 kilometers). The smaller satellites range in size from about 12 to 96 miles (20 to 155 kilometers) in diameter. For more information, see the article URANUS in Volume UV.

## ▶ NEPTUNE

Traveling even farther away from the sun, you come to Neptune. This planet was discovered in 1846 when astronomers observed that the movement of the planet Uranus appeared to be influenced by the gravity of an unknown planet.

Neptune's average distance from the sun is about 2.8 billion miles (4.5 billion kilometers), and it takes nearly 165 Earth years to

Even a small portable telescope can reveal dark bands of clouds in Jupiter's atmosphere, as well as some of the planet's four large satellites.

## LOOK AT THE PLANETS

### Observing Mars and the Outer Planets

Mars, Jupiter, Saturn, and sometimes Uranus are visible to the naked eye, but Neptune and Pluto are too far away to be seen without a telescope. Because all of these planets are located outside Earth's orbit, they do not go through the moon-like phases that Mercury and Venus do.

Mars is easily recognizable through a telescope by its reddish color, and sometimes its white polar caps can be seen. The first things you may notice when looking at Jupiter through a small telescope are some of its four large moons, discovered by the Italian scientist Galileo in 1610. These moons—Io, Europa, Callisto, and Ganymede—appear as bright dots spread out in a line on either side of the planet. Observations on consecutive nights reveal the changing positions of the satellites as they orbit the giant planet. A small telescope will also reveal the many bands of

pastel clouds that cover the planet, and if the conditions are right, the Great Red Spot may be visible.

Saturn's bands of clouds are paler and more difficult to see without a powerful telescope, but the planet's most striking feature is its system of rings. As Saturn orbits the sun, the rings are visible from different angles because of the planet's tilted axis. Sometimes only the edges of the rings face the Earth, and they almost disappear from sight because they are so thin. Saturn's largest moon, Titan, can sometimes be seen.

Uranus and Neptune only appear as points of light through a small telescope, and none of their moons are visible. And even with a highly powerful telescope, Pluto is little more than a small, fuzzy disk of light.

complete one orbit. Its diameter is 30,800 miles (49,600 kilometers).

Like Jupiter, Saturn, and Uranus, Neptune is a gas giant with a thick atmosphere. This atmosphere, which is mostly hydrogen and helium along with traces of methane gas, is wrapped around an ocean of water, methane, and ammonia. The temperature at the ocean's surface may be 4500°F (2500°C), while the temperature in Neptune's upper atmosphere is about –355°F (–215°C).

At the time of the *Voyager 2* exploration in 1989, Neptune's upper atmosphere included the Great Dark Spot, an immense dark blue cloud formation. There were also several smaller dark spots and an unusual white cloud, which moved at a speed different from the speeds of the rest of Neptune's cloud cover. By the time the Hubble Space Telescope was pointed at the planet in the 1990's, the Great Dark Spot had disappeared, replaced by similar features that seem to come and go every couple of years.

Neptune's magnetic field rotates once in about 17 hours. The rate of rotation of the features visible in its atmosphere varies greatly and depends on the latitude of the features.

A system of thin rings encircles Neptune, and the planet has 13 known satellites. Triton, its largest, has a thin atmosphere, consisting mostly of nitrogen gas. For more information, see the article NEPTUNE in Volume N.

## WONDER QUESTION

### Do planets exist beyond our solar system?

In 1991, the first planets outside our solar system—**extrasolar planets**—were discovered orbiting a distant neutron star. Since then, hundreds of extrasolar planets have been found.

An extrasolar planet cannot be seen directly because the star it orbits emits far more light than the planet reflects. This glare tends to hide the planet from our view. But there are several ways to detect such a planet. A large planet like Jupiter can be discovered by studying the movement of the star it orbits. The planet's gravity tugs on the star, causing it to wobble slightly back and forth as the planet circles it. In another method, astronomers search for a star that brightens temporarily as the gravity of a planet passing in front of it acts as a lens and bends the star's light, an effect called **microlensing**. Similarly, the temporary dimming of a star may indicate a planet passing between the star and Earth, an event called a **stellar transit**.

Among the extrasolar planets found so far, studies have revealed a magnetic field around one and the presence of oxygen and carbon in the atmosphere of another. Astronomers have also found a star with more than one planet.

The search for extrasolar planets continues. The Kepler space telescope is scheduled for launch in 2007 and will search for Earth-size planets orbiting stars similar to the sun. It will use a photometer to measure any changes in a star's brightness due to the transits of planets. The Terrestrial Planet Finder observatory, scheduled for launch in 2012, will also search for extrasolar planets as well as study planet formation around young stars.

## ▶ PLUTO

You complete your planetary trip at Pluto, the smallest planet in our solar system. Pluto was discovered in 1930 after astronomers observed that Uranus and Neptune were being pulled a little bit away from their expected orbits, which indicated that there must be another planet beyond Neptune.

Pluto has a diameter of about 1,400 miles (2,253 kilometers), and its average distance from the sun is 3.7 billion miles (5.9 billion kilometers). Its trip around the sun takes 247.7 Earth years, and it takes 6 Earth days and 9 hours for Pluto to rotate once on its axis. Like Venus and Uranus, Pluto rotates from east to west. Its orbit is a long ellipse, bringing it as close to the sun as 2.8 billion miles (4.4 billion kilometers) and as far away as 4.6 billion miles (7.4 billion kilometers). At times, its orbit brings Pluto closer to the sun than Neptune ever gets.

Temperatures on Pluto probably never rise above –382°F (–230°C). Pluto consists of a mix of rocky materials and ice, and it has a thin atmosphere of methane gas. Its gravitational pull is very weak. Charon, Pluto's one known satellite, is about 746 miles (1,200 kilometers) across and orbits relatively close to the planet. For more information, see the article PLUTO in Volume P.

WILLIAM A. GUTSCH, JR.
President, The Challenger Center for Space
Science Education

See also ASTRONOMY; COMETS, METEORITES, AND ASTEROIDS; SATELLITES; SATELLITES, ARTIFICIAL; SOLAR SYSTEM; SPACE PROBES.

# PLANKTON

Life all over the world depends on the billions upon billions of tiny living things that drift like a pale mist in the waters of the world. This drifting mass of organisms is called plankton. Plankton is the cornerstone of the ocean's food chain and the major supplier of the Earth's oxygen.

Plankton is made up of many kinds of organisms, most of them so small they can only be seen with a microscope. All of these organisms are very different from one another. But in one respect they are all alike—they share a drifting way of life. In fact, the term "plankton" comes from a Greek word for "wandering" or "drifting."

Although a wide variety of organisms make up plankton, scientists generally separate it into two groups: phytoplankton and zooplankton. Phytoplankton includes single-celled plants and plantlike organisms, such as algae. Zooplankton includes minute protozoans and sea animals. Some organisms, such as diatoms, always remain plankton. Others, such as fish and lobsters, are plankton only while they are in the egg or larva stages of their development.

Plankton is not found at all depths in water. While phytoplankton gathers in the sunlit surface waters less than 500 feet (153 meters) deep, zooplankton avoids the light. It spends the daytime gathered in the darkness of deep water, hundreds to thousands of feet down. At dusk, the dense swarm of zooplankton comes to the surface to graze on the rich phytoplankton food source. Before daybreak it descends, sinking back to the depths beyond the sunlight.

## ▶ PHYTOPLANKTON

The smallest, and most plentiful, plankton organisms now known are microscopic phytoplankton called diatoms and dinoflagellates. These small algae, especially diatoms, exist in huge numbers. Just 1 gallon of seawater can contain between 1 million and 2 million diatoms.

The name "diatom"comes from Greek words meaning "cut through, " for a diatom looks as though it has been cut in two and then fitted back together again. It has a glasslike shell with one half overlapping the other. Diatoms come in a marvelous variety of shapes, such as stars, needles, and pillboxes, and with intricate markings.

The dinoflagellates are equally small, but they have no shells. Most dinoflagellates move by lashing the water with two thread-like whips called flagella. The name "dinofla-

## Some Common Kinds of Plankton

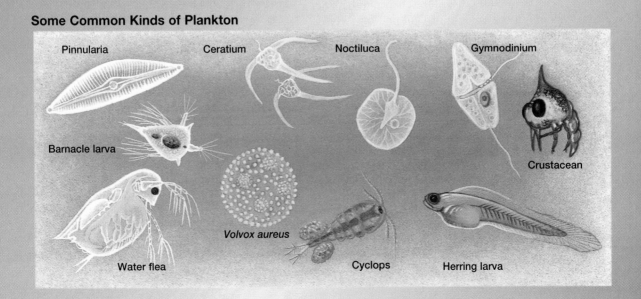

Pinnularia  Ceratium  Noctiluca  Gymnodinium

Barnacle larva

Crustacean

Volvox aureus

Water flea  Cyclops  Herring larva

the largest animal on Earth depends on some of the smallest living things for its survival? The blue whale, which can weigh up to 209 tons (190 metric tons), eats almost nothing but tiny shrimplike crustaceans called krill, some of which are only $3/10$ inch (8 millimeters) in length. Krill are part of the zooplankton inhabiting the world's oceans. They can be found from the surface to depths of about 6,500 feet (2,000 meters).

Blue whales, along with fin, humpback, and other whales, uses a special structure to feed on the krill. Instead of teeth, the blue whale has fringed plates called baleen, that hang from its upper jaw. The baleen have brushlike fibers on the inside edges.

When the whale takes in seawater, the fibers trap the krill inside the whale's mouth and filter out all the water. Whales that feed using this method are often referred to as baleen whales.

Sometimes whales have to strain thousands of tons of seawater to get enough krill. But there are species of krill that live in huge swarms, covering an area of 450 square feet (42 square meters) or more. Most often the whales feed on these concentrated masses, sometimes consuming 5,000 pounds (2,300 kilograms) at one feeding!

gellate" comes from Greek words meaning "whirling whips."

In one way, dinoflagellates, diatoms, and other algae are like green plants that grow on land—they contain the green pigment called chlorophyll. Through the action of chlorophyll, in the presence of sunlight, these organisms combine water and carbon dioxide to make their own food in a process called photosynthesis.

Diatoms and dinoflagellates are found in both fresh and salt waters. Their numbers depend on the amount of light and on the supplies of raw materials available. In some places the light and raw materials remain almost the same throughout the year, while in other parts of the world there are seasonal changes. During the North Atlantic winter, for example, diatoms grow and multiply slowly. Days are short, and there is little light for food production. However, spring brings longer days. Raw materials that have washed in from the land and welled up from the water's bottom during the winter are plentiful. During this time, diatoms may double their numbers every 24 hours. Such rapid growth is called a bloom. A bloom may make water look yellow, green, red, or brown, depending on what creature is blooming.

▶ **ZOOPLANKTON**

Drifting with and feeding on the phytoplankton are the countless small animals that make up zooplankton. These animals provide food for larger animals, which may in turn become food for people.

Among the smallest and most numerous organisms found in zooplankton are the pear-shaped crustaceans called copepods. The name "copepod" comes from Greek words meaning "oar feet." A copepod swims by jerky, oarlike movements of its tiny limbs. The largest copepod is less than $1/2$ inch (1.3 centimeters) long. Most are very much smaller. Yet copepods are an important food of many fish.

Crustaceans of many kinds spend the early stages of their lives as part of the drifting plankton mass. Saltwater varieties include shrimps, krill, crabs, lobsters, and barnacles, and freshwater, fairy shrimp and water fleas. The larvae of these crustaceans are tiny or even microscopic. They usually do not look very much like their parents. They are too small and weak to move off on their own.

This is true also of the young mollusks, such as snails, clams, and mussels, that are found in both fresh and salt waters. When they are fully grown, their drifting lifestyles end, and they take up life on the water's bottom. Plankton may also include the eggs and larvae of many kinds of fish. They swim off on their own when they reach adulthood. They may feed on plankton, but they are no longer part of the drifting mass of life.

In freshwater, animal plankton often includes developing insects. Mayflies, dragonflies, mosquitoes, water beetles, and many other insects lay their eggs in water. When the larvae hatch out, they live and feed on other plankton.

Rotifers, or wheelworms, are also commonly found in freshwater plankton. If the ponds they live in dry up, rotifers and their eggs may be blown about by winds for months. When at last they land in water—whether lake or puddle—they start growing and feeding again.

In saltwater plankton, small, finned arrowworms dart about, capturing diatoms and larvae in bristling "jaws." Because its body is as clear as glass, this animal is sometimes called a glassworm. If you put one under a microscope, you would probably see some small plankton organisms passing down the worm's digestive tube.

Other saltwater plankton includes young starfishes, sea urchins, sea cucumbers, comb jellies, and jellyfishes. When fully grown, all but the comb jellies and jellyfishes leave their plankton nursery to live and feed on the ocean bottom.

Sea squirts belong to a group of animals known as tunicates because of the tough, clear tunic (cloak) of flesh that covers the bodies of these animals. Their larvae look like tiny frog tadpoles and drift about as plankton. The larvae swim by bending their tails from side to side. Their bodies, which are clear enough to see through, are stiffened by a sort of spine, called a notochord. The notochord disappears as the animals develops. This saltwater group includes a number of organisms, such as salps and pyrosomes, that remain plankton all their lives.

▶ THE IMPORTANCE OF PLANKTON

Directly or indirectly, every living thing owes its existence to plankton. More than a billion years ago, plankton first started putting oxygen into the atmosphere, making life possible for land plants and animals, including people. All the living things in the

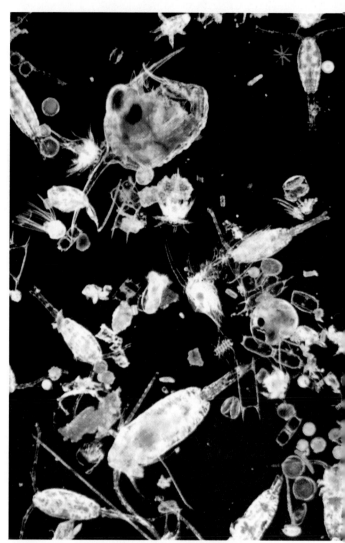

As the foundation of almost all the major food chains, the tiny organisms making up plankton support huge populations of creatures in oceans and large lakes.

oceans, seas, and other bodies of water depend on plankton for food as well as oxygen. The flow of food energy begins with phytoplankton, which are eaten by zooplankton, which are eaten by small fish, which are in turn eaten by larger fish, and so on. If we change the waters of the world, we risk destroying the plankton. This is dangerous because the health of our waters, and of our planet, depends on plankton.

Reviewed by N. J. BERRILL
McGill University

See also ALGAE; CRUSTACEANS; MICROBIOLOGY; OCEAN; OCEANOGRAPHY.

An attack by pine beetles, which feed on the bark of trees and on the wood inside, has left injured and dying trees throughout this Montana forest.

## PLANT PESTS

People depend on plants for many reasons. They provide food, wood, fibers for clothing, even oxygen for us to breathe. We grow plants for these and many more useful products as well as for the beauty of a world filled with trees, flowers and other greenery. Living things that eat or damage the plants we grow are called pests.

Throughout human history, crop failures due to pests have caused tremendous suffering. In 1845, the potato crop in Ireland was suddenly destroyed by a fungus disease. One day the potatoes looked fine; a few days later, the leaves had turned black and the potatoes were rotten! The disease destroyed most of the potato crop in Ireland for the next several years, causing the Potato Famine of 1847. It is estimated that in only a few years, as many

as 2 million people died of starvation in Ireland because of this one plant disease. Several million more people fled to the United States to escape the famine.

The appearance of vast destructive swarms of locusts, a type of grasshopper, are described in the Bible and still happen today. The locusts gather together in huge groups and fly hundreds of miles seeking food. A single locust swarm may contain millions of insects and darken the sky as it flies over! When the locusts land, they rapidly eat everything, stripping the area of all crops, tree leaves, and grass.

Dramatic pest disasters such as the Irish potato famine and locust plagues are unusual. Most of the time pests exist in smaller numbers, causing damage to crops and plants, but not total destruction. People also create pest problems, such as when they grow large fields of the same crop, providing pests with huge food supplies, or when they transport crops with hidden pests from one area to another. Plants may also be damaged by air pollution and toxic wastes produced by people.

### ▶THE ENEMIES OF PLANTS

There are many kinds of plant pests. Insects, mites, birds, and animals sometimes eat crops before people can harvest them. Plant diseases can cause crops to suddenly die, or make the crop rot before it can reach market.

### Imported Pests

In its native land, a pest has many enemies, such as parasites (a living thing that feeds and grows on another living thing), predators, and diseases, that keep its numbers small. However, in places where none of the pest's usual enemies exist, a pest problem can develop quickly.

The Japanese beetle is a shiny green and gold insect. It lays its eggs in grassy areas, and the young, called grubs, eat grass roots for a year until they emerge as adults in mid-summer. The adult Japanese beetle eats a wide variety of plants, including many cultivated plants. In Japan, this insect is not a pest because there are many other insects that eat the beetle. There are also many diseases that kill most of the grubs. In the United States, however, the Japanese beetle became a serious pest. The grubs damaged lawns, and the adult beetles ate just about everything in the garden!

The number of beetles in many areas was astounding. Now this beetle is controlled with a combination of chemical sprays and a disease called milky spore. The milky spore disease, which is grown in laboratories, is made into a powder and sprinkled on lawns, killing most of the grubs without harming the grass.

The gypsy moth was brought into the United States by a scientist who wanted to use it to produce a hardy silkworm. In Europe, its native land, the gypsy moth is not a serious pest. Unfortunately, it escaped from the laboratory and established itself in the forests of Massachusetts. The gypsy moth caterpillars eat the leaves of most trees. In the absence of the European parasites, diseases, and predators that kill the gypsy moth, its population exploded in the United States. Without control measures, the caterpillars are capable of eating the leaves off of every tree in the forest—making it look like winter in June! The gypsy moth is spreading slowly southward along the East Coast of the United States. Over time, parasites will appear and diseases will develop that affect the gypsy moth in the United States. But left to nature, this process could take hundreds of years. Scientists are therefore developing diseases, parasites, and other enemies to control the gypsy moth.

Many other exotic pests have caused large amounts of damage. The chestnut blight, a fungus disease, has killed the American chestnut tree throughout its entire natural range. Another fungus disease, Dutch elm disease, has killed many elm trees. The Mediterranean fruit fly, or Med fly, became a major pest after its arrival in California. The bacterial disease citrus canker caused similar problems in Florida when it was found in some nurseries.

While holding its plant prey in a dense tangle of vines, the parasitic dodder feeds off the plant's tissues.

## Weeds

Farmers are always working to protect their crops from all kinds of enemies. They probably spend the largest share of their time and energy controlling weeds—any plant that is growing where it is not wanted. Weeds compete with the plant crop for water, sunlight,

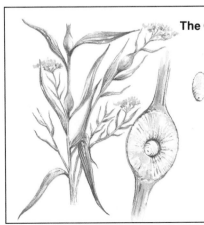

### The Gallmaker and Its Home

The swollen twisted stalks of the goldenrod are signs that a gallmaker, such as a fruit fly from the group *Eurósta*, is at work.

The gall is a safe home for the tiny worm-like larva. As the larva grows into an adult, the gall is a ready and plentiful source of food.

You can study a gallmaker by collecting and examining the plant galls. Put the galls you have collected into a jar. Place a fine screen on the top and wait to see what comes out of the gall.

and soil nutrients. In addition, some weeds actually harm the crop. The witchweed is a parasitic plant that grows next to the crop plant. The witchweed attaches its roots to the crop roots, taking the food that the crop plant is making for itself. In fields with witchweed, the crop ends up stunted (smaller than normal). Dodder is another common parasitic plant. It looks like yellow or orange spaghetti. It twines around the stems of the crop, and sends plant shoots, or suckers, into the stem to take water and food from the crop.

The boll weevil is the most destructive insect to attack cotton, feeding on its tender shoots and blossom buds.

### Insects and Mites

Insect pests come in many shapes and sizes. Caterpillars, beetles, beetle grubs, grasshoppers, and locusts are all **chewing** pests. They damage the plant as they bite off and eat pieces of leaves, fruits, or roots.

You can tell that a chewing insect is at work when you see the holes made in leaves and fruit. Some chewing insects are hidden from sight. They bore into the stems and twigs of the plant. Once inside, the insects feed on the plant. The plant, or part of the plant, wilts as the insect tunnels through it.

Other chewing insects dig into the soil to get at the plant roots. The adult corn rootworm is a beetle that eats corn leaves and lays its eggs in the soil. When the grubs hatch from the eggs, they eat the corn roots. Because of

the damage to the roots, the plants wilt and are smaller than normal; sometimes they even fall over when the wind blows.

Aphids, thrips, mealybugs, leafhoppers, scale insects, spider mites and many others are called **sucking** pests. Their mouths are specially formed for piercing plants and sucking the juices. When sucking pests feed on plants, they often stunt the plant's growth. The leaves of the plant curl and twist and develop blotches of yellow or brown.

Some pests live in close co-operation within the plant. The pest causes the plant to grow an elaborate swelling called a gall. **Gall** pests do this by making chemicals similar to the plant's own growth hormones. These chemicals cause the plant to form the gall. Then the gall-producing insect or mite lives and feeds inside the gall. Tiny wasps cause lots of different galls on the leaves and twigs of oak trees.

### Diseases

Plants get diseases just as people do. Diseases can stop plants from growing or make them grow in unnatural ways. Often diseases will kill plants. Plant diseases are caused by organisms so small they can only be seen with a microscope.

Viruses, viroids, fungi, bacteria, and microscopic worms called nematodes can all cause plant diseases. But organisms that cause plant diseases do not ever cause human or animal diseases. They are specialized to attack only plants and usually only certain plants.

When a wheat plant has a disease called wheat stem rust, you can see rusty-colored spots and streaks on the stems. If you rub the spots, a very fine red-brown powder comes off. The powder is made up of the microscopic spores of the wheat stem rust fungus. These tiny spores are easily carried long distances on wind currents to unaffected areas. Entire fields of wheat can be infected with wheat stem rust; if the disease is severe enough, no grain will be produced.

When plants are infected with powdery mildew fungus, white moldy spots suddenly appear on the leaves and stems of the plants. The white spots are made up of fungal strands and tiny chains of spores. Plant leaves curl and eventually die when attacked by powdery mildew. If the leaves die, they can't make the food needed to produce the crop. Powdery mildews are serious pests of grain crops, such

Corn smut, a fungus disease producing sooty black masses, gradually destroys infected corn plants.

caused by a fungus. Tiny insects called elm bark beetles carry the fungus from sick trees to healthy trees. When this beetle emerges as an adult from under the bark, it carries many of the fungus spores on its body. The newly emerged adult beetles fly to healthy elms to feed on the sap. When the beetle chews a small hole in the elm twigs in order to feed, it puts the spores of the Dutch elm disease fungus into the tree. Within a few weeks the fungus will grow in the tree's feeding network. Parts of the tree will wilt as the system becomes clogged and is no longer able to spread nourishment throughout the tree.

Sucking pests such as aphids can transfer plant diseases. If an aphid feeds on a plant with a virus disease and then flies to a healthy plant, it can carry the virus to the healthy plant. Vegetable plants are often infected with virus diseases originally found in weeds. The aphids feed on the virus-infected weeds, then fly into the crop and transfer the disease to the crop. Cucumber and squash plants produce very odd looking lumpy fruit if they are infected with a virus.

▶CONTROLLING PLANT PESTS

Over the long history of agriculture many methods and strategies have been developed to protect crops from pests. It is necessary to understand the pests so that methods can be developed to keep them from increasing in number—to the point where they damage the crop. When pests are few in number, they are usually not a problem. In fact, a few pests are needed so the population of a pest's enemies, which help control the pest, can be maintained. The basic rules of pest control are: Grow a plant that is not susceptible to pests or diseases; grow the plant when or where the pests are not present; and if the pest appears, destroy it.

Many of the basic practices used in agriculture play a role in controlling pests and diseases. Farmers plan to use seeds from the best plants for future crops. Often the best plants are those with pest resistance. Deep plowing buries weeds and any pests or diseases remaining from the previous crop. Burning the field before planting has long been used to destroy weeds and pests. Simply cutting the weeds on a regular basis is also a form of pest control.

The farmer can grow a mixture of many varieties of the crop, so even if a pest or dis-

as wheat, and of many vegetables and fruits. They also can be found on trees and flowers and even on grass. Like the rust spores, these mildew spores are easily carried on wind currents to infect new plants.

Some bacteria, fungi, and nematodes grow inside the plant, clogging it up so water and nutrients can't flow from the roots to the leaves. When this happens the plant wilts, the leaves may turn yellow, and the entire plant may die. Trees, flowers, vegetables and other crops can all have wilt diseases.

In other cases, a plant may wilt because its roots become diseased. Many nematodes and fungi also damage plant roots. Plants invaded by the root-knot nematode have lumpy knotted-looking roots. The tiny nematodes live inside the roots. Like the gall insects and mites, the root-knot nematode is able to make the plant produce these root-knot homes. When a plant has a lot of nematodes living in the roots, it may not have enough food left to grow normally after feeding all of the hungry nematodes.

Sometimes insect pests will carry a fungus, virus, bacterium, or nematode from a sick plant and put it into a healthy plant. The Dutch elm disease is a wilt disease of elm trees

Agricultural methods to control pests include (*left*) burning fields, then deep plowing the burnt stubble to bury any remaining weeds and pests, and (*above*) spraying pesticides to coat plants with a thin layer of chemical protection.

ease destroys some varieties, some will survive. Growing a different crop each year, a process called **crop rotation**, helps control pest populations. The pests and diseases do not build up in the field as they might if the same crop were grown year after year.

Using the natural enemies of pests is called **biological control**. The milky spore disease, which was used to fight the Japanese beetle, was discovered by scientists of the United States Department of Agriculture. It has been used successfully for more than forty years to control Japanese beetles. While the Japanese beetle was considered a pest, another beetle, called a lady beetle, or ladybug, was used as a biological control of a pest. More than one hundred years ago, ladybugs were imported into California to control a serious new pest of citrus plants, the cottony cushion scale insect. Within a few years, the ladybugs had spread throughout the entire state and had nearly eliminated the cottony cushion scale insect as a pest. Even today we think of the red and black ladybug as our friend.

Insects and plant diseases can also be used as control agents for weeds. One of the first examples of using an insect to control a weed was the case of the prickly pear cactus in Australia. In the late 1800's, the cactus was introduced to Australia, where it thrived and grew into dense, impenetrable thickets covering millions of acres of land. A variety of insects and mites that feed only on the cactus were introduced to Australia to control the cactus. Scientists are very careful to test a potential weed-control insect or mite to make sure it does not like to eat any crop plants.

**Chemical controls**, or pesticides, are relatively new in the long history of agriculture. The use of pesticides allows us to produce more food than ever before on less land. You can tell which insect or disease a pesticide is used to control by the pesticide's name. The first part refers to the pest, and the last part, "cide," is from the Latin word for "killer." **Insecticides** kill insects; **miticides** kill mites; **herbicides** kill plants (the word "herb" is from the Latin word herba for "plant"); a **fungicide** kills fungi. Like any rule, however, this one also has an exception: Chemicals used to kill bacteria are usually called **antibiotics**, not bacteriacides.

Pesticides work in a variety of ways. Some pesticides poison the pest and stop basic life processes, such as the ability to breathe. Other pesticides stop the pest from growing normally. Insecticides that are similar to an insect's natural hormones cause the insect to grow abnormally. The insect may never grow into an adult, so it would never reproduce. There are also herbicides similar to plant hormones that cause the weed to grow in a twisted, abnormal way that prevents the plant from producing seeds.

Some pesticides must be applied before the pest attacks the plant. Other pesticides, called systemics, are absorbed into the plant where they remain active inside the plant's system. Systemic insecticides are especially useful for the control of sucking insects. Some systemic fungicides can be applied to the leaves of the plant, and move into the roots where they control root rots. Other systemic fungicides are able to stop the growth of the fungus after it has invaded the plant.

A wide variety of herbicides exist to control weeds. Often several kinds of herbicides are used throughout the growing season of a crop. Some kill any plant they contact; other herbicides only kill certain kinds of plants. Many herbicides are applied to the soil before the weeds even begin to grow. As soon as the weeds start to grow, the poison takes effect and kills them.

Pesticides have been a tremendous benefit to people. Pesticides are used to perform some of the work that in the past was performed by the crop growers; so with the use of pesticides, fewer people are needed to cultivate the same amount of land. Chemical fungicides allow the farmer to grow fruit free of any spots and rot. Fruit and vegetables can be shipped long distances to cities without spoiling. The skillful use of pesticides can prevent the terrible disasters and crop failures that in the past have caused such great human suffering.

After any pesticide has been used in the same place over a long period of time, the pest may become resistant to the pesticide— that is, the insect is no longer harmed by the pesticide. Resistance develops because the pest population is composed of many individuals with slightly different survival abilities. Within every pest population there are a few individuals that can tolerate a particular pesticide. When most of the pests that cannot tolerate the pesticide are killed, only the few tolerant individuals are left to reproduce, thus creating a population of resistant pests. Insects and mites were the first pests noticed to develop pesticide resistance. Now weeds and fungi are also known to have resistance to specific chemical pesticides. Great care must be taken to use pesticides wisely to avoid creating pesticide-resistant pests. Different kinds of pesticides should be used in rotation rather than always using the same pesticide many years in a row.

Most pesticides will also harm people if large enough amounts are eaten, inhaled, or gotten on the skin. Pesticides can also kill the enemies of the pests, allowing the pest population to continue growing and creating a greater pest problem. This is why there is so much interest in combining a variety of pest control strategies for pest control.

▶ **FUTURE TECHNOLOGY**

The control of plant pests remains a difficult task requiring clever solutions to old and new pest problems. The search for better plants continues. Equally important is the preservation of populations of insects that may include important potential pest- or weed-control agents.

It is now possible to add specific traits to plants using **biotechnology**. In agricultural biotechnology, a new product is created by transferring genetic material. For example, certain bacteria have a gene that directs the production of a toxin called Bt. The Bt toxin is poisonous to the corn borer caterpillar. Scientists have inserted the bacterial Bt gene into corn plants to create new strains that are resistant to insect pests. When the corn borer eats a corn plant that produces Bt, it gets sick and dies from the poison. The toxin is not dangerous to people, however.

Experts estimate that weeds, pests, and plant diseases may destroy or damage as much as one third of the world's food. The number of people in the world increases every year, but the amount of land stays the same. It is important to understand pests and how to control them in order to allow our crops to make the most food possible.

Many other ideas for new forms of pest control are being developed. New ideas and a better understanding of how pests harm plants and how plants defend themselves can all be used in the future to improve agriculture for all of the people in the world.

ETHEL M. DUTKY
Director, Plant Diagnostic Laboratory
University of Maryland

See also BACTERIA; FUNGI; INSECTS; VECTORS OF DISEASE.

## PLANTS

Without plants, nearly all life on earth would cease. Directly or indirectly, most living things depend on plants for food. But more than that, we depend on plants for the very air we breathe. As plants perform their necessary life processes, they produce oxygen as a by-product. Human beings and other land animals breathe the oxygen in the atmosphere; fish and other water life breathe the oxygen that is dissolved in water. So it is the abundance and diversity of plants that determine how much animal life, including human life, can survive on earth.

It is difficult to imagine a landscape that does not have some kind of plant, whether it is a kind of tree, shrub, flower, or grass. Plants inhabit some part of every continent. They are found over most of the earth, wherever there is soil—unless it is too dry, too cold, or too hot. They are also found in the sea and in freshwater lakes, rivers, and ponds.

Each green plant, whether it is a delicate meadow flower bursting with colorful blooms or a massive tree towering high above the forest floor, possesses an amazing ability that sets it apart from every other type of living thing—it can capture the light energy of the sun and convert it to chemical energy. There is not another kind of organism that is able to do this. This unique ability has made green plants the essential link that transfers the sun's energy to all other organisms. Without green plants, we simply could not survive.

Scientists estimate that there are more than 300,000 species, or kinds, of plants. The greatest number of different kinds of plants can be found in the humid tropics. In fact, there are so many different kinds of plants in the tropics that have not yet been identified that scientists can only estimate how many species of plants inhabit the earth. Regrettably, many plant species will become extinct before they have even been seen. The fewest different plant species are found in the cold and barren areas of the Arctic and Antarctic.

People and other animals are able to capture the energy that is trapped and stored by plants. Some people receive the energy when they eat plants. Others receive the energy when they eat plant-eating animals. The string of events that occurs when energy is transferred as a herbivore (plant eater) eats a plant and in turn is eaten by a carnivore (meat eater) is called a food chain.

The sizes of plants range from the microscopic flowering duckweed, which is only about ³⁄₁₂₅ inch (0.61 millimeter) long and weighs ¹⁄₁₅ ounce (2 milligrams), to the giant sequoia tree of California, which can grow to over 270 feet (82 meters) tall and weigh 6,167 tons (5,594 metric tons).

There is an amazing variety in the size and appearance of plants; however, there are basic characteristics that all plants share: Plants are made up of many cells. Each cell is surrounded by a solid cell wall made of the substance **cellulose**. Each plant cell has a **nucleus**, or "control center." Each cell also has organlike structures called **plastids**, where many of the biochemical reactions of energy use and energy storage occur. Most plants make their own food during the process of **photosynthesis**. Plants also produce **embryos**—young plants that develop from an egg, or **ovum**. Plants are nonmotile; that is, they do not move about like animals do.

### ▶PLANTS AND THE CYCLE OF NATURE

All things on earth are linked, one to another, in the cycle of nature. Within the cycle there are complex relationships between living things and the elements in their environments. As the cycle progresses, many different processes work to create, exchange, and recycle the earth's chemicals.

Each living thing and element fulfills a role or function that helps keep the cycle intact. Plants are an essential part of the cycle. Plants could not survive without the energy they receive from the sun, the original source of all energy. Without the food and oxygen that plants supply, we could not live. The plants, with all their life-giving materials, return to the earth as waste matter when animals, including human beings, die. The waste matter provides food for other living organisms that break down, or decompose, the material. As the material is broken down, the chemicals are released and return to the air, water, and soil where they are once again available to growing plants. Humans and other living things use the plants as food, and the cycle continues.

This article presents an overview of the living things we call plants. The discussion focuses on the importance of plants; their evolution, diversity, and classification; their life cycle, including plant characteristics and processes; and in the final pages, the distribution of plants throughout the world and the impact of human activity on that plant life.

*The New Book of Knowledge* also contains many articles that provide in-depth material on plants. BIOMES; DESERTS; PRAIRIES; and RAIN FOREST examine plant communities. Information on plant features, traits, and destruction is supplied in articles such as LEAVES; PHOTOSYNTHESIS; and PLANT PESTS. Plant groups are covered in several articles, including GRASSES and TREES. Additional projects and activities can be found in GARDENS AND GARDENING; HOUSEPLANTS; and TERRARIUMS.

a plant was responsible for causing the famous mutiny aboard the British ship H.M.S. *Bounty*? In 1787, William Bligh was commissioned to sail the *Bounty* to Tahiti and pick up a cargo of breadfruit trees. From the Pacific island, Bligh was to sail to Jamaica. The journey to the Atlantic island would be long and difficult. Food and water became scarce. The crew's discontent reached a peak when they were denied water so that their dwindling store of fresh water could be used to keep the plants alive. Led by Second Lieutenant Fletcher Christian, they seized the *Bounty* on April 28, 1789. Captain Bligh and 18 crew members were set adrift in a small boat.

## ▶ PLANTS AND SOCIETY

Plants are a familiar part of the environment. We use plants every day, in every field of life to fulfill the need for foods, products, and raw materials.

Rather than rely just on plants that are native to one country or area, human settlers have carried plants with them from place to place whenever they have wandered. Early writings document plant travelers in the time of the ancient Romans and Greeks. Plant journeys also are revealed by comparing domesticated plants—plants that have been adapted so that they are useful to human beings—with their wild relatives.

Food plants were the first plant travelers. At first, plant material was carried by travelers as food to eat on their journeys. Later, travelers carried plants and seeds around the world in an attempt to extend the range of specific plants.

A sometimes unnoticed, but very important, function of plants is the role they play in soil renewal and conservation. The roots of plants secrete small amounts of organic acids that help break down mineral particles, adding nutrients to the soil. Matter from decaying plants also adds to the soil's nutrient stores. Soil is held in place by plant roots, thus slowing down the natural processes of wind and water erosion. Plants are also a source of recreation and enjoyment. The natural beauty of plants growing in parks and gardens provides enjoyment to all who view them. People grow many thousands of species and varieties of ornamental plants just because they are pleasing to look at.

Plants contribute to the celebrations, rituals, and artistic expressions of many cultures. Pollen from plants is used in an Apache Sunrise Ceremony (*above*), while a garden surrounding a Portuguese church (*right*) offers visitors a beautiful and tranquil setting for reflection.

## Food from Plants

A surprisingly small number of plant families supply most of the plant food used by people. Foodstuffs from the grass, legume (pea), potato, rose, citrus, crucifer (brassica), and palm families dominate the worldwide menu. Within the major plant families, only about 20 plant species supply 90 percent of the world's food.

Human beings have used every part of the plant as food. We eat seeds, fruits, leaves, stems, roots, even the flowers of some plants.

The seeds of grasses are the most important food source for much of the world's population. Wheat, rice, and corn supply the seeds that are most often used for food. Rice is the main food for the most people, especially in Asia. Wheat, which is the cereal produced in the greatest abundance, is used as a main food by slightly fewer people than rice is. Corn, or maize, is the main food in Latin America and parts of Africa. Barley, oats, sorghum, and millet also supply important seeds.

Although the fruit of the legume family is sometimes eaten, it is the seeds that are most often consumed. Beans, peas, lentils, and chickpeas are all legume seeds. The soybean, another important legume seed, is the most valuable crop in the United States.

Foods from the roots of plants are staples for much of the world, especially in areas where grasses do not grow well, such as tropical regions. Important root crops include yams, sweet potatoes, and cassavas. Carrots, parsnips, turnips, and beets also are important root foods in cooler climates.

**An incredible array of plants have been used as food, beverages, and flavorings. As many as 10,000 species have been recorded as having been tried, and certainly, many more have been tried but not documented. Modern crops, such as cranberries (*right*), pineapples (*below*), and wheat (*below right*), evolved as plants were selected based on those that were hardy, provided the most useful food, and could supply seeds for future crops.**

The fruit of a plant contains its seeds. Apples, pears, melons, peaches, plums, and oranges are all fruits. So are tomatoes, peppers, cucumbers, squashes, and nuts. Many fruits have been part of some peoples' diets for a long time. Dates, coconuts, olives, figs, and pineapples are all mentioned in writings and pictured in art from ancient times.

The stems, flowers, and leaves of a variety of plants are used as food. Edible stems include the potato, which is an enlarged portion of an underground stem, and celery and asparagus, which are stems that grow above the ground. The flowers of cauliflower and broccoli are regularly eaten, while the flowers of artichokes are eaten as a delicacy. The leaves of many different plants are eaten as food. While the leaves of plants such as brussels sprouts, spinach, and cabbage are the only part of the plant that is used as food, the leaves as well as other parts of turnips and beets are used as food. Although it is easy to recognize that it is the leaves of the spinach, cabbage, and lettuce plants that are being eaten, it is not so easy to recognize that it is the tightly wrapped, fleshly leaves of the garlic and onion plants that are eaten.

### Medicines from Plants

Thousands of medicinal compounds have been found in plants, many of commercial importance. The pain relievers morphine and codeine come from the opium poppy; quinine, the most effective agent against malaria, comes from the cinchona tree; digitalis, which comes from foxglove, is used to treat heart disease; and reserpine, which comes from rauwolfia, is used to treat high blood pressure.

In ancient and medieval times, almost all medicines came from plants. Plants were used to ease pain, heal wounds, and cure fever. Today some areas of the world still rely on plant medicines to meet the medical needs of the population. People who are often called healers practice traditional, folk, or herbal medicine, using plants as their main source of medicine. It is estimated that at least 25,000 plants are used by traditional practitioners.

Although the making of medicines now depends less on plants and more on antibiotics made by fungi and on synthetic chemicals made from petroleum, there is a renewed interest in exploring the potential of plants. Many synthetic medicines are patterned on the

Chinese herbalists are among the traditional practitioners who have developed a great botanical knowledge of local plants, their uses and properties.

substances found in plants, so the development of medicines still depends on a supply of newly discovered plant compounds. One recent example is a substance called taxol. Taxol, which is taken from yew trees, is being tested for use in treating stubborn tumors.

There is a renewed interest in exploring the potential of plant species in tropical areas where up to this time only 1 percent of the plants have been examined for use as medicines. Scientists believe that one out of ten plant species may contain compounds with ingredients that are active against cancer.

### Did you know that . . .

the most widely used pain reliever, aspirin, was named after Spiraea, a genus of flowering shrubs in the rose family? For thousands of years, soothing teas were brewed from the flowers of the meadowsweet plant (*right*), one of the spiraeas. The plant contained salicin—a naturally occurring pain reliever. When aspirin was developed, its activity was based on the properties of salicin.

## Raw Materials from Plants

Plants supply many of the raw materials that are used to provide people with fuel, shelter, and clothing. In the same manner as food products, raw materials can come from the leaves, stems, fruits, or roots of plants. Sometimes a material, such as coal, is formed from the entire plant. Other materials, such as cotton cloth and cooking oils, come from just one part of a plant.

Coal is a product of plants that died hundreds of millions of years ago. As the dead plants accumulated, they became compressed into coal. Peat, another fuel, is the product of plant remains that accumulate in a type of wetland called bogs in cold regions.

We depend heavily on plants for our shelter. Trees provide wood to make lumber for homes. Wood is also used in making many small and more specialized products, such as furniture, tool handles, and musical instruments. Whatever the product, the characteristics of its wood need to be matched to its use. For instance, soft balsa wood is used to make airplane models that can fly because it is lightweight and easy to shape.

Wood fibers are used to make paper, an indispensable tool of civilization. Fibrous stems are split into long, thin pieces to make baskets, matting, and wicker furniture. Plants with soft fibers, such as cotton, are used to make thread that is then woven into cloth. The fabric linen is made from long stem fibers of the flax plant. The coarse fibers of jute stems are useful for items such as carpet backing and cloth sacks. Other fibers are used to make nets, sailcloth, brushes, and as filler for mattresses and furniture.

Substances that are taken from plants are made into many different products. We cook with oils extracted from plants. Oils are also processed to produce cosmetics, fine lubricants, perfumes, and plastics. Animal hides are softened and preserved with tannins, chemical substances obtained from bark. Other chemical compounds are used as thickeners and gelling agents for food products, for making medicine tablets, and for stiffening fine papers and textiles.

Because plants are a part of the everyday landscape, it is easy to forget how much we depend on them for a wealth of goods. Raw materials from plants were used to produce these giant rolls of paper (*above*), the sturdy frames for these buildings in a housing development (*left*), and the peat being gathered from a bog in Ireland (*far left*).

Using plants, Gregor Johann Mendel (*above left*) discovered the basic principles of heredity. Mendel, who was an Austrian monk, began his breeding experiments in a monastery garden. There he used garden peas to examine characteristics such as plant height and seed color. His findings, published in 1866, laid the foundation for the science of genetics. The research work that Barbara McClintock (*above right*) conducted with corn plants led to a new understanding of how genes, the units of heredity, behave. She described how some genes can change their positions on the chromosomes and so change the traits that are inherited.

## ▶THE PLANT KINGDOM

Scientists who study organisms name them and classify them into groups according to the natural similarities they share. Along with aiding in the identification of an organism, the name and classification help reveal how the organism has evolved and its relationship to other living things.

Before the invention of the microscope, scientists classified organisms based on characteristics that were easily observed. It was generally accepted that there were two kinds of organisms: plants and animals. Plants were green and did not move about; animals moved about, ate food, and had complex behavior. When microscopic organisms were first described, they were classified as either plant or animal. But there are many organisms that do not fit neatly in either of these two large groups, called kingdoms.

Since the 1950's, biologists have divided all living organisms into five kingdoms. Plants make up one kingdom. Animals make up another. Certain one-celled organisms, some of which have characteristics of both plants and animals, belong to yet another kingdom called Protista.

Bacteria and fungi each have their own kingdoms, too. Living things in the same kingdom share more characteristics than living things in different kingdoms.

### The First Plants

The evolution of plants began more than 3.5 billion years ago with the earliest forms of life. Scientists believe the first organisms were bacteria known as cyanobacteria (formerly called blue-green algae). The ability to produce energy through photosynthesis probably developed in these simple water-dwelling organisms. However, it was not until about 1 billion years ago that ancient organisms developed into life-forms that released oxygen into the atmosphere during photosynthesis. This was first accomplished by green algae. Once there was oxygen in the atmosphere, life on land became a possibility.

The way living things are classified changes as botanists, the scientists who study plants, and other biologists learn more about them. When all living things were considered to be part of either the animal kingdom or plant kingdom, then organisms such as mushrooms (*left*) were considered to be plants, as were bacteria and algae.

Millions of years passed before there was enough oxygen in the atmosphere to support life out of water. The first organisms to move to land were freshwater green algae. They acquired the ability to survive in the newly oxygenated atmosphere and began to populate the earth's land surfaces about 600 million years ago. Many varieties of green algae developed. These early plant ancestors, with their simple, sticklike bodies, bear little resemblance to the plants we see today.

The first land plants, which appeared more than 400 million years ago, probably evolved from the land-dwelling green algae. The early land plants did not have complex structures or life cycles. They were multicelled organisms without roots, leaves, and flowers. Even though these early plants were primitive, they spread over the earth's surface and carpeted the ancient continents.

As plants evolved, they became more complex. Plants with numerous stems and branches developed, followed by plants with leaves and roots and then, about 300 million years ago, plants with seeds. Finally, more than 200 million years ago, the most important plant group appeared: flowering plants.

One way to trace the evolution of plants is to compare the features of existing plants to determine their relationships with each other. Another is to examine plant fossils. Fossils are the remains of organisms that have been preserved in rock. There are problems in identifying plants from fossils. Usually only a part of a plant is discovered, and it is difficult to match up a fossil leaf with a fossil stem of the same species.

Plant fossils have been found all over the world. A great array of extinct plants has been identified from the fossils that have been discovered. Scientists use fossils not only to identify the kinds of plants and the

Ancient magnolia leaves, preserved for 18 milion years in an Idaho bog, were found to have DNA that was identical to present-day magnolias (*above*).

length of their existences, but also to study ancient environments. In comparing fossils, paleobotanists (the botanists who study plant fossils) have found that many fossil remains are the same as existing plant species. The California redwood, which today grows only along the fog-bound coast of northern California, is a good example. Fossils of redwoods have been found throughout areas of North America that have a moderate climate. The redwood fossils were an indication to scientists that in ancient times there must have been widespread cool, moist habitats like that of the present-day northern California coast.

The newest tool in the study of the evolution of plants is the comparison of plant genes, the basic hereditary units that carry the characteristics of a plant from one generation to the next. Researchers attempt to recover a chemical substance called **DNA** (*d*eoxyribo*n*ucleic *a*cid) from plant genes. The DNA of different plants is then studied to determine if there are any similarities that could be used to show the relationship between the plants or the evolution of one kind of plant to another.

## How Plant Communities Change

Plant communities change in an orderly process called **plant succession**. Over a period of time, mineral and organic matter accumulate and soil becomes deeper and richer, creating a more favorable environment for additional life-forms. With each stage, the population of living things—plants and animals—changes as each generation adapts to the new environment. Soon one kind of plant community is replaced with another kind. The example below is the transformation of an abandoned field to a forest. The bare landscape of a field gradually fills with grasses and weeds. As more time passes, shrubs begin to dot the grassy habitat. Finally, trees start to emerge among the shrubs until the predominant plants are large trees—the field has gradually evolved into a forest. Natural events, such as volcanic eruptions and erosion, can interrupt or even reverse the process of plant succession. Human-produced events, such as agriculture and settlement development, can also disrupt the process.

**Abandoned field**

**Grasses (1 to 10 years)**

**Grasses and shrubs (10 to 25 years)**

Botanists have used fossil evidence and DNA analysis to learn about the origins of flowering plants. The oldest known flowering plant is *Archaefructus lianingensis*. Fossil evidence indicates that *Archaefructus* lived about 140 million years ago and had pod-shaped fruits, a defining trait of flowering plants. Genetic studies conducted in the 1990's suggest that Amborella is the most primitive living flowering plant. Amborella is a small shrub with creamy white flowers and red fruit that is found only on New Caledonia, an island in the South Pacific.

### ▶ KINDS OF PLANTS

When scientists classify the many different species of plants, they separate them into groups, depending on the characteristics the plants share. Major groups, called divisions, include plants that share one or more characteristics. Plants within each division are separated into groups called classes according to certain differences between the plants. The classes are further divided into orders, the orders into families, the families into genera, and the genera into species.

With each subdivision, the relationship between the plants becomes stronger, and the members of the group share more characteristics of appearance, body structure, and development. With the final separation into species, the plants share so many of the same basic characteristics that they look almost alike.

Along with scientific classification, plants can be separated in another way. Plants can be put into two basic groups: vascular and nonvascular plants. Vascular plants are those plants that have specialized tissues to transport materials from one part of the plant to another. Tissue composed of **xylem** conducts water throughout the plant, and tissue composed of **phloem** conducts food. Seed plants, ferns, whisk ferns, horsetails, and club mosses are the main types of vascular plants. Nonvascular plants are those plants that do not have specialized tissues to transport materials. Bryophytes, which include liverworts, hornworts, and mosses, are nonvascular plants.

**Vascular Plants.** **Seed plants** are vascular plants that, along with their specialized tissues, have an additional unique structure—the seed. Seed plants are separated into two groups: **gymnosperms**, plants with naked seeds, and **angiosperms**, plants with seeds enclosed in fruit. The principal gymnosperms are the conifers, trees that bear seeds on a female cone; the male cones produce pollen. Conifers are very important ecologically, forming the dominant vegetation in cold, moist regions. The cycads, a minor group of gymnosperms, bear one male or female cone at the top of the stem, surrounded by leaves. They are often mistaken for palms. Another unique gymnosperm is the ginkgo, or maidenhair tree, which bears naked seeds but no cones.

**Vascular plants** share one basic characteristic: They all have specialized tissues for transporting materials from one part of the plant to another. The large group includes ancient plants, such as the whisk ferns, horsetails, and club mosses, that lack roots and leaves or possess simple, primitive structures. It also includes those that are the most complex and evolved, that is, flowering plants.

**Emerging forest**
**(25 to 100 years)**

**Mature forest**
**(More than 100 years)**

The angiosperms, or flowering plants, are the most successful group of plants if the amount of landscape they cover and the number of species are measured. They can be divided into groups based on the number of leaves, called **cotyledons**, contained within their seeds. **Monocotyledons** (monocots) have one seed leaf, or cotyledon; **dicotyledons** (dicots) have two cotyledons.

**Ferns** are the oldest living vascular plants. Like the seed plants, ferns have true leaves, stems, and roots. All species of fern have two distinct reproductive forms. With each reproduction cycle the form alternates, so that one generation is the product of wind-borne spores, and the next generation is the product of a sperm and an egg. Ferns are usually found on the forest floor.

**Whisk ferns**, **horsetails**, and **club mosses** represent the primitive plant groups that are sometimes referred to as fern allies. They are among the first plants to have grown on land. Some, such as the whisk ferns, lack roots and leaves. Horsetails have hollow jointed stems with a rough-textured outer covering. The presence of the mineral silica, which is deposited in the walls of the stems' outer cells, makes the stems very coarse. Club mosses have true stems but primitive needlelike or scalelike leaves and no true roots.

**Nonvascular Plants.** The **bryophytes** are a division of ancient and rather simple plants. The plant groups that make up the bryophytes are the mosses, liverworts, and hornworts. None of them have true leaves, stems, or roots, as vascular plants have, but they do have structures that resemble them externally.

The bryophytes are fairly small plants that grow close to the ground. They are distributed all over the world. Although most bryophytes are found growing in moist, shaded areas, some of the mosses do live in deserts.

**Nonvascular plants** are small, multicellular plants with a simple system for transporting water and food through plant cells. Members of this ancient plant group, called bryophytes, include mosses, liverworts, and hornworts. Although bryophytes have structures that are stemlike and leaflike, they do not have true roots, stems, or leaves.

▶**PARTS OF A PLANT**

All plants, whether vascular or nonvascular, flowering or nonflowering, are made up of cells. Within the plant, groups of cells form tissues that perform specific functions, including transporting substances, respiration, and photosynthesis. The number of different tissues that make up a plant depends on the kind of plant. Not all plants have the same amount or kinds of tissues.

Plants also vary in their structures. Because there are many more flowering plants than any other kind, the flowering plant can be considered the typical plant. The basic parts, or organs, of such a typical plant include the roots, stems, leaves, and flowers. The roots, stems, and leaves of a plant are the vegetative organs, which function in photosynthesis and provide support for the plant. The flowers, along with the seeds and fruits, of a plant are the reproductive organs, which provide new young plants.

## WONDER QUESTION

### How big can a plant grow?

Plants are some of the smallest and the largest living things on earth. The duckweed (*below*) is less than an inch in length and under an ounce in weight, while a giant sequoia tree named General Sherman (*right*) stands almost 275 feet (84 meters) tall and is estimated to weigh 2,756 tons (2,500 metric tons).

## Roots

Roots are underground organs that support and anchor the aboveground parts of the plant, absorb water and dissolved minerals from the soil, and store food. They grow down into the soil, often branching again and again, sometimes forming miles of roots and penetrating deep into the earth. A single winter rye plant was shown to have produced an amazing 387 miles (623 kilometers) of roots, while the roots of a wild fig tree in South Africa were reported to have penetrated an estimated 400 feet (122 meters) deep into the soil.

There are three major types of roots. Some plants have only one kind of root system; however, many have a combination of the different types of roots. Dicots have a **taproot**, or primary root, extending from the bottom of the stem into the soil. Smaller lateral, or secondary, roots extend from the sides of the taproot. The taproot, which is a storage root, can be quite large and fleshy. The cells of the taproot are filled with starch grains, the plant's food reserve during a cold or dry season. Carrots, beets, and manioc are taproots widely used by humans for food.

Monocots have **fibrous** roots. Although a taproot first emerges from the seed, it dies and is replaced by a group of smaller roots extending from the bottom of the stem. The fibrous root system grows close to the soil's surface, collecting moisture before it sinks deep into the ground. Plants such as grasses and rushes have fibrous roots.

Some plants, such as ivies and mature corn plants, have **adventitious** roots. These roots grow from the side of a stem or leaf rather than as part of the main root system. Adventitious roots help to anchor a plant and keep it

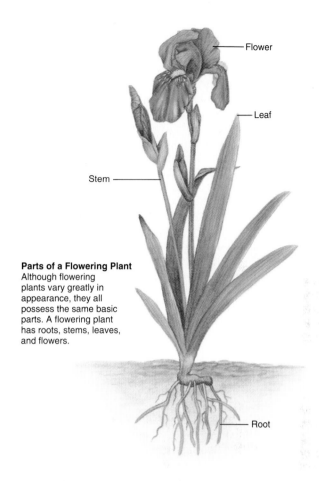

**Parts of a Flowering Plant**
Although flowering plants vary greatly in appearance, they all possess the same basic parts. A flowering plant has roots, stems, leaves, and flowers.

from being moved by the wind. In the mature corn plant, a ring of adventitious roots called prop roots extends from the stem to just above the soil to anchor the plant. In ivies, adventitious roots extend along the trailing stem to help stabilize the ivy as it climbs.

In addition to the primary and secondary roots, there are many tiny root hairs near the

**Types of Roots**
The roots of a plant anchor and support the plant, absorb water and nutrients from the soil, and store food. The major types of roots are taproots, fibrous roots, and adventitious roots. A plant's root system may be made up of just one kind of root or a combination of different kinds of roots.

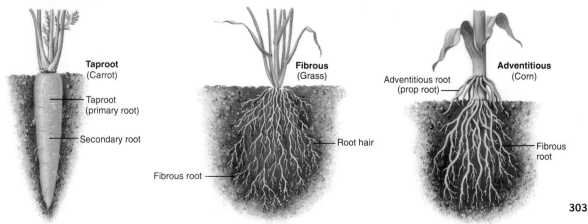

tip of each root. These are distinct from the other kinds of roots. Root hairs are specialized for absorbing water and dissolved minerals. They greatly increase the exposed surface of the root system, which in turn increases the plant's ability to absorb moisture and nutrients. Root hairs live for only a few days and "mine" water and minerals from a small zone of soil near the tip of the root. As the root grows in length, new root hairs appear nearer the tip.

At the very tip of each root is a root cap, a specialized structure of slimy cells that protects the newly produced root cells. The cells of the root cap secrete a lubricant that eases the way for the root and prevents the root from being worn away as it pushes down through the soil. The cells, which are constantly damaged and scraped off as they come into contact with soil particles, are rapidly replaced.

## Stems

The stem has a variety of functions: It supports the plant, houses a transport system, and provides storage for food. In some plants the stem is also the main location of photosynthesis, and the leaves are either very small or modified for some other function. There are also modified stems that perform special functions. Some modified stems store water or other plant materials, aid in the spread of new plants, or protect the plant from pests.

The leaves of a plant are attached to the stem at a **node**. The part of the stem between two nodes is called the **internode**. Just above each leaf, in the angle formed by the leaf and the stem, is a **lateral bud**. This bud, which is usually dormant, can grow into a branch, leaf, or flower.

The stem is usually the strongest part of a plant. Its strength comes from a material called lignin that is deposited in the stem's cell walls. Plants are either **woody** or **herbaceous** depending on the amount of lignin in the plant. If a stem is relatively soft and green, as in a tulip, the plant is herbaceous; if the stem is strong and hard, as in an oak tree, the plant is woody.

Whether a plant is herbaceous or woody, the stem's most important job is to support the plant. The stem holds the leaves and flowers up in the air so that they are in the best position to receive the sunlight that the plant needs to perform life-sustaining functions.

The transport system within the stem is made up of the tissues xylem and phloem, which conduct water, minerals, and other nutrients to various parts of the plant. The conducting cells of xylem tissue carry water and dissolved minerals upward from the roots of a plant. In the spring, these cells also carry dissolved food materials that have been stored in the roots during the winter. This is why sugar maples are tapped for their sweet sap in the spring. The cells of phloem tissue move material both up and down through the stem of the plant. Dissolved foods are transported from the leaves to the roots and stem for storage or to the growing parts of the plant for immediate use.

In some plants, photosynthesis takes place in the stem rather than in the leaves. Such plants, which include the asparagus and the cactus, have leaves that are either very small or that are modified for some other function. The stems of asparagus are branched so much

**Types of Stems**
The stem of a plant supports the plant, houses a transport system, acts as a food storehouse, and sometimes is a center for photosynthesis. Stems are either woody or herbaceous.

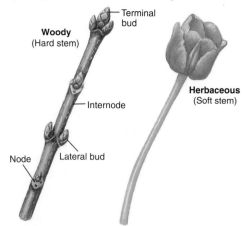

that they resemble feathers, but the leaves are small. The cactus has a large leafless stem, the site of photosynthesis as well as water storage. The needlelike spines covering the cactus take the place of leaves.

**Modified Stems.**  There are several kinds of modified stems. Some modified stems contain only stem tissue; others contain stem tissue and tissues from other parts of the plant. Each kind of modified stem has its own special function. **Rhizomes, tubers, corms,** and **bulbs**

are underground stems that are thickened for storage. The rhizome stores food and often serves as the main stem of a plant, so only the leaves protrude from the soil. Gingerroot, which is often used in cooking, is a rhizome. Most ferns growing in moderate climates have rhizomes as their main stem. So do some common ornamental flowering plants, such as the iris. Tubers are thickened underground stems, but not the main stem. The most common example of a food-storing tuber is the potato.

Corms and bulbs are storage structures that contain a dormant shoot, which when active will produce the stem and leaves. Corms are mostly stem tissue, while bulbs have very little stem tissue. They are mostly leaf tissue. The gladiolus forms a corm. Onions, garlic, and tulips form bulbs.

**Tendrils** can be a modification of a stem. The grape plant produces tendrils. The tendrils extend out from the plant to twist around and clasp another plant or an object for support.

Many herbaceous plants have modified stem structures called **stolons**, or runners. These thin green horizontal stems grow along the ground. When a stolon reaches a location that is suitable for growth, it may send out roots and produce leaves. Strawberries, grasses, and many weeds have stolons and spread in this way.

The sharp **thorns** and **spines** of some plants, such as roses, are protective structures that arise from stem tissue. These modified stems can help protect a plant from being eaten by insects and other animals.

### Leaves

Leaves produce food, in the form of sugar, for the plant. They are able to do this through the process of photosynthesis. Any green part of a plant has the ability to carry on photosynthesis; however, leaves are the primary site of food production. During photosynthesis, light energy from the sun is captured by **chloro-**

**Types of Leaves**
The leaves of a plant are responsible for producing most of a plant's food. A leaf's size, appearance, and arrangement vary according to the kind of plant. However, most kinds of leaves have two basic parts: a blade and a petiole. Some leaves also have stipules.

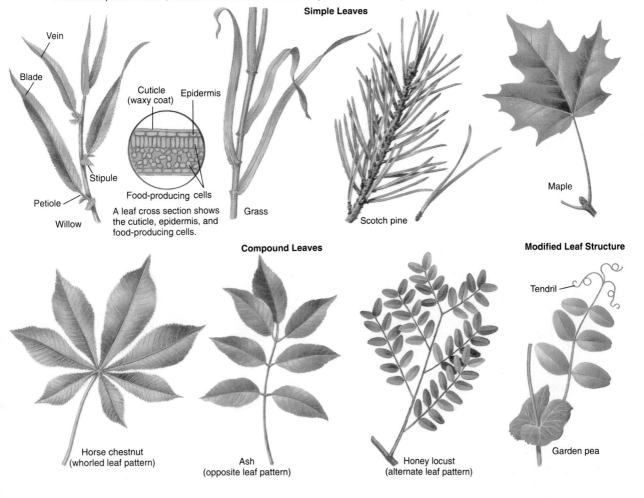

**Simple Leaves**

Vein

Blade

Cuticle (waxy coat)

Epidermis

Stipule

Petiole

Food-producing cells

Willow

A leaf cross section shows the cuticle, epidermis, and food-producing cells.

Grass

Scotch pine

Maple

**Compound Leaves**

**Modified Leaf Structure**

Tendril

Horse chestnut (whorled leaf pattern)

Ash (opposite leaf pattern)

Honey locust (alternate leaf pattern)

Garden pea

**Why do leaves change color in the autumn?**

The leaves of deciduous trees contain groups of different colored pigments. During most of the year, there is more chlorophyll, or green pigment, within leaf cells. Environmental changes, such as decreasing day length, trigger changes in the plant, including a decrease in the chlorophyll. As the chlorophyll diminishes, other pigments are exposed and a riot of color results.

**phyll**, the green substance in leaves, and turned into chemical energy that powers the plant's life processes.

A thin, tough layer of cells, the **epidermis**, covers the outside of a leaf. The epidermis secretes a thin waxy film, or **cuticle**, on the surface of the leaf, protecting the inside from injury and from losing moisture. Along with epidermal cells, a leaf has special cells called **guard cells** that control the flow of gases through the leaf. Two guard cells work as a pair, each changing shape to open or close the tiny pore, or **stoma**, between them. Carbon dioxide enters through the **stomata** (plural of stoma), and oxygen and water vapor exit.

There is great variety in the size and appearance of leaves. Generally they grow in a broad, flat shape that exposes the largest amount of their surface area to the sun's rays. But plants also produce leaves that are small and spinelike, needlelike, or scalelike. In addition, modified structures such as tendrils may form from leaf tissue.

Most kinds of leaves have two main parts: the **blade**, which is the flat part of the leaf, and the **petiole**, which is the thin stalk that grows from the node on the stem to the blade. Some kinds of leaves also have **stipules**, tiny leaflike structures that grow at the base of the petiole. A leaf that has only one blade is called a simple leaf; a leaf that has two or more blades is called a compound leaf.

Leaves grow along the stem in a particular arrangement. They may grow in an alternate pattern, with one leaf at each node; in an opposite pattern, with two leaves growing from opposite sides of the same node; or in a whorled pattern, with three or more leaves growing from one node.

### Flowers

Flowers vary widely in size, shape, and color. Each kind of plant grows a characteristic number of flowers. Some plants have only one flower, while others have many flowers grouped in clusters. A typical flower is made up of four kinds of organs at the end of a stem. At the base of the flower are the small, leaflike **sepals**. The sepals form an overlapping cover for the unopened flower bud. As the **petals** grow, these protective structures are pushed

**Types of Flowers**
Flowers contain a plant's reproductive organs. A flower with both male and female organs is called a perfect flower; a flower that has only male or female parts is called an imperfect flower.

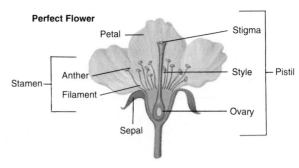

Perfect Flower — Petal, Stigma, Stamen, Anther, Filament, Style, Pistil, Sepal, Ovary

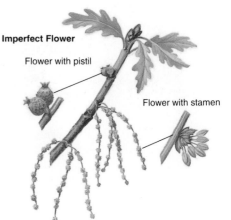

Imperfect Flower — Flower with pistil, Flower with stamen

apart. The petals are usually the largest and most brightly colored part of the plant and serve to attract insects, birds, and other animal pollinators to the flower.

The petals surround the reproductive organs of the flower. The male organs are the **stamens**. A stamen is made up of a long, stalklike **filament** that ends in an enlarged part called the **anther**. The anther produces the pollen grains that develop sperm, the male sex cells. The bottle-shaped **pistil**, the female reproductive organ, is made up of three parts: The flattened top is called the **stigma**, the slender neck is the **style**, and the large base is the **ovary**. The ovary contains one or more **ovules**. Each ovule contains an **egg cell**, which is the female sex cell. Stalks attach the ovules to the inside wall of the ovary.

A flower that contains both male and female parts is said to be a perfect flower. Other flowers, however, may have stamens or pistils, but not both. Such flowers are said to be imperfect flowers. The male and female flowers may be on separate plants, as they are in willows, cottonwoods, and holly. Or the two kinds of flowers may be present on the same plant, as in walnuts, oaks, and corn.

### Fruits and Seeds

When a pollen grain unites with an ovule, the ovule develops into a seed. Each seed is like a very small package of plant life. It contains a tiny new plant and food to nourish it. The seed's main parts include an embryo, food storage tissue, and a seed coat. The embryo contains the basic parts from which the new plant will develop. It is protected by the seed coat, or outer skin. The seed grows using food from food storage tissues, such as the **endosperm** in flowering plants.

As the seed develops, the ovary develops into a fruit around the seeds. The fruit may be fleshy and moist like that of melons, grapes, and pears, or hard and dry like that of nuts and bean pods. The fruit protects the seeds.

## WONDER QUESTION

### Which plant has the biggest seed?

The largest single seed in the plant kingdom is produced by a tall palm tree called the coco de mer or the double coconut tree. The tree grows only in the Seychelles in the Indian Ocean. It is there that one can find the two-lobed seed, which looks like two coconuts joined together, that can be 20 inches (50 centimeters) long and weigh up to 40 pounds (18 kilograms).

**Types of Seeds**
A seed contains the new plant and the food to nourish it. The two main types of seeds are naked (uncovered) and enclosed (enclosed by an ovary).

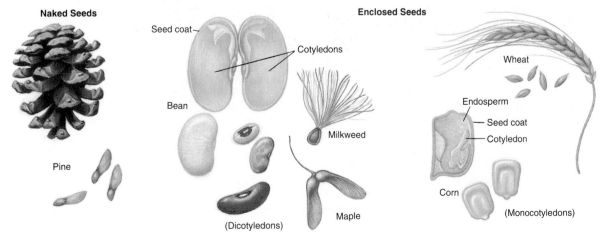

Naked Seeds

Seed coat
Cotyledons
Bean
Pine
Milkweed
Maple
(Dicotyledons)

Enclosed Seeds

Wheat
Endosperm
Seed coat
Cotyledon
Corn
(Monocotyledons)

## ►A NEW PLANT IS BORN

Plants produce new plants by sexual reproduction or asexual reproduction. In sexual reproduction, a male sex cell (sperm) and a female sex cell (egg) join to produce a seed that develops into a new plant, or seedling. In asexual reproduction, a new plant forms from some part of the old plant.

Butterflies and other animal pollinators are lured to their task by a flower's distinctive color combinations, bold markings, or rich fragrance.

### Sexual Reproduction

For seeds to be produced, two things must occur. Pollen must reach the stigmas. Then it must reach and unite with the ovules. Pollination is the first step; the second is called fertilization. When sexual reproduction is complete, the result is a new, individual plant that has some combination of characteristics from both the male and female parents.

**Pollination.** Pollination consists of a pollen grain landing on the stigma at the top of the pistil. There are two types of pollination: **self-pollination** and **cross-pollination**.

Some plants are able to pollinate themselves, in the process called self-pollination. No help is needed from any outside source. For example, in a perfect flower, which contains both male and female parts, the flower's pollen often spills onto the stigma of the same flower. This can happen before the flower even opens.

Most plants rely on cross-pollination, the process in which pollen from one flower lands on the stigma of another flower of the same species. Cross-pollination occurs in many ways. Pollen may be deposited by an insect or other animal as it searches for food. As it forages for pollen or the sweet nectar it eats, the insect rubs the anthers and dumps pollen on itself. This pollen is then spread to the stigma of the next flower it visits. Most flowers are pollinated by flying insects, such as bees, wasps, butterflies, and moths. A few flowers are pollinated by birds, such as hummingbirds, and ants and other small animals.

Flowers and their animal pollinators are adapted to each other. Adaptations in the color, shape, and smell of flowers make them attractive to the insects and other animals and also put pollen within their reach. Bees collect pollen from plants that produce great amounts of it. The bees' ability to see specific colors—white, yellow, and blue—enables them to find the flowers that produce the greatest amounts of pollen. Color also aids the moths that fly at night. Many night-blooming flowers are white, a color that makes them more easily visible in the dark.

Butterflies and moths have long tongues that allow them to gather nectar from flowers with long, tubular shapes. Flowers pollinated by flies often give off an odor like that of decaying meat, a smell that is attractive to flies that lay their eggs on rotting animal flesh.

Pollen is also scattered by the wind. Many trees and grasses are adapted to this method of pollination. The flowers do not have showy petals, sweet nectar, or pleasing aromas to attract animal pollinators. Instead, the flowers produce amazingly large amounts of pollen and vast numbers of female flowers. There may be so much pollen that the area around the plant looks as if it is coated with a yellow dust. Many wind-pollinated trees tend to have flowers of one sex, either on the same plant or on different plants.

A shower of light, dry pollen grains is produced by yew tree flowers. Air currents carry the pollen to other yew flowers, sometimes over great distances.

## Sexual Reproduction in a Flowering Plant

After a pollen grain reaches the stigma of a pistil (1), it sprouts, sending a slender pollen tube down to the ovule (2). The sperm nuclei travel down the pollen tube to the ovule (3). One nucleus unites with an egg cell to form the embryo (4); another unites with the polar nuclei to form the endosperm (5). The seed develops from the fertilized egg (6). Once the seed falls to the ground, it germinates in the soil and a seedling emerges (7).

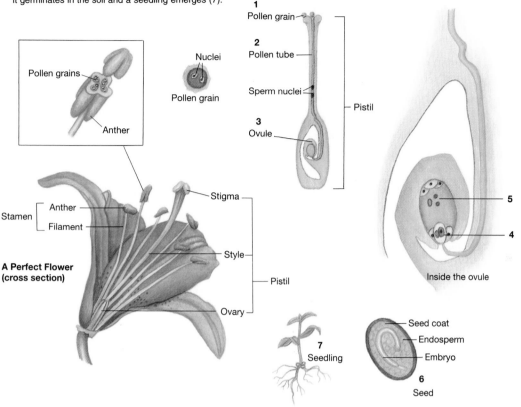

## Sexual Reproduction in a Conifer

Pollen grains from the male cone are carried by the wind to the female cone (1). The pollen grains attach to the cone scale and enter the pollen chamber (2). A pollen tube grows from the pollen grain into the ovule. Sperm travels through the tube to the egg cell. Fertilization occurs when a sperm cell and an egg cell unite (3). The fertilized egg develops into a seed containing an embryo and an endosperm (4). Once the cone matures, it opens and the wind scatters the winged seeds (5). The fallen seeds germinate, and a new plant begins to grow (6).

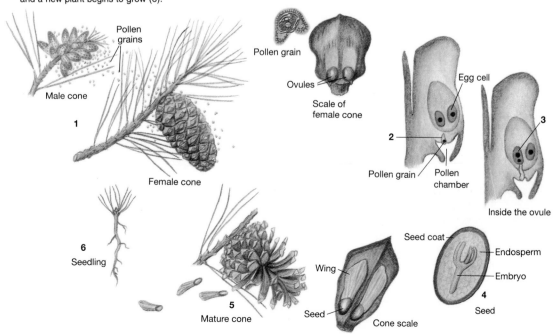

For cross-pollination to take place in corn plants, rows of male plants (with pollen-laden tassels at the top) are alternated with rows of female plants.

**Fertilization.**   After pollen lands or is deposited on the stigma, it must reach the ovule if a seed is to form. The pollen grain sprouts and soon sends a slender pollen tube down through the style into the ovary. The pollen tube enters an ovule and deposits sperm into the egg cell. With the joining of the egg nucleus and the sperm nucleus, the ovule is fertilized. Part of the ovule becomes food for the new plant, and part becomes the new plant itself.

A plant may have one, several, or even hundreds of ovules to be fertilized. Pollen tubes grow down to each one. In some flowers, it takes a long time for the pollen tube to grow down to the ovule. In witch hazel, for instance, it may take up to seven months. In others, such as barley, it takes about an hour.

Both the male and female sex nuclei contain genes, the basic units of heredity. The genes determine the characteristics of a plant. During fertilization, a new plant receives genes from each parent plant, making it a unique plant with a set of characteristics different from that of each parent plant.

## Asexual Reproduction

In addition to sexual reproduction, most plants are capable of asexual reproduction—that is, reproducing without seeds. When new, independent plants grow away from the rest of the plant or from a part that is physically separated from the rest of the plant, it is called asexual, or vegetative, reproduction.

Most of the non-cereal food plants you eat are grown from roots, stems, or leaves—not seeds. When gardeners and fruit tree growers use asexual re-

production to produce new plants, it is called **propagation**. The advantage of asexual reproduction is that the new plant is genetically identical to the parent plant, which means that the new plant will have all the same characteristics as the parent plant.

Even one single plant cell can be used to grow a new plant. In a process called **micropropagation**, plants are produced by placing plant cells in prepared nutrients, or cultures. Micropropagation is an efficient, inexpensive way to produce many plants at one time.

**Vegetative Reproduction**
Many plants can reproduce by vegetative reproduction. Strawberry stems, or stolons, take root and, when they are separated from the parent plant, grow into new plants.

Stolon

# ▶THE LIFE CYCLE OF A PLANT

All flowering plants go through similar stages as they grow and develop. During its life, a plant will germinate, flower, scatter its seed, and die. The life span of a plant varies with each different kind of plant. Life spans can range from months to years to centuries!

Plants that grow, produce seeds, and die all in one growing season are called **annuals**. Some plants live two or three years but usually do not flower until the second year of growth. These plants are called **biennials**. **Perennials** are plants that produce flowers and seeds year after year for many years.

## Growth and Development

Plants, unlike animals, tend to grow throughout their lives. As they grow, they develop new cells and increase in size. Growth also gives plants the ability to change their environment. By growing, plants can obtain a place or position that puts them closer to light, food, and substances such as water.

**Germination.** Seeds **germinate**, or sprout, at different times depending on the species of plant. Some seeds sprout as soon as they fall from the plant. Seeds enclosed in fleshy fruits, such as apples and tomatoes, do not sprout until they have been removed from the fruit. This is because the fruit contains substances that prevent sprouting. The seeds of certain desert plants do not sprout until heavy rains fall. Most seeds need a resting period before they will sprout. The seed can remain in this inactive, or dormant, state for several weeks, months, or even years.

When the proper amounts of water, oxygen, and warmth are

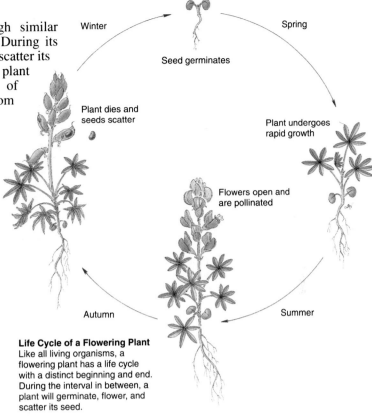

Winter

Spring

Seed germinates

Plant dies and seeds scatter

Plant undergoes rapid growth

Flowers open and are pollinated

Autumn

Summer

**Life Cycle of a Flowering Plant**
Like all living organisms, a flowering plant has a life cycle with a distinct beginning and end. During the interval in between, a plant will germinate, flower, and scatter its seed.

**Germination of a Seed**
A seed is in an inactive state (1) before it begins to germinate. When conditions are favorable, the seed starts to germinate. The embryo uses stored food to grow. The root emerges from the seed first (2), followed by the shoot with its cotyledons, or seed leaves (3). For the first few days, the plant lives on stored food. As its growth continues, leaves begin to develop (4). Once the plant has a few green leaves (5), it can begin the process of photosynthesis.

available, the seed begins to germinate. The dry dormant seed quickly swells as it soaks up moisture from the ground. Inside the seed, the embryo uses water, oxygen, and the food stored in the endosperm or the cotyledons (special seed leaves) to fuel its growth processes. As it absorbs water, the seed swells and its coat softens. Soon the seed coat breaks open and the root emerges from the seed. The root grows downward into the soil, anchoring the seedling. The root system, which will supply water and minerals to the growing plant, develops from this first root.

The shoot emerges next with its one or two cotyledons. For the first few days, as the shoot grows toward the surface, the new plant lives on stored food. Once it reaches the surface, the plant's first green leaves appear. With the appearance of green leaves, the plant is able to manufacture its own food through the process of photosynthesis.

**Patterns of Growth.** Once germination is complete, the plant grows quickly. Roots and stems grow in length near their tips only. The new growth takes place in three distinct zones, or areas, one behind the other. At the tip there is a zone of intense cell division. Just behind it is a zone of newly divided cells. Within this second zone, the cells expand to their final size by absorbing water. If there is not enough water, growth cannot occur. In the third zone, cells mature into the cell types that make up the different tissues of the plant.

The growth rings of a woody stem can be used to calculate a tree's age. They can also reveal when events, such as drought or injury, have altered a tree's growth.

**Plant Hormones**

Plant hormones, which were first discovered in the 1920's, travel throughout a plant and coordinate its activities. Sometimes only one hormone is responsible for regulating an activity, but usually it is the interaction of several hormones that guides a process. Below are the known plant hormones and the roles they play in a plant's growth and development.

**Abscisic acid** is most abundant during stress responses to factors such as dryness. It sets in motion activities that prevent water loss and guard against wilting and other injury.

**Auxins** affect many changes in plants, including the elongation of young stem and root cells, leaf fall, and the development of fruit.

**Cytokinins**, which are present and working in seeds, are the major hormones affecting the process of cell division. They are also involved in the development of new buds and stems.

**Ethylene** triggers the many changes that occur during fruit ripening. It is also a stress hormone that activates the plant's response to stress or injury.

**Gibberellins** are a group of growth hormones that are especially involved in stem growth, the production of flowers, and the digestion of stored food in germinating seeds.

In plants that also grow in thickness, such as trees, growth takes place in the **cambium** cells. The cambium cells form new layers of growth between the bark and wood. These layers form the rings that are visible when a cross section of a tree trunk is exposed.

Plant growth is finely controlled through the use of **hormones**. Hormones are chemical substances that act as messengers traveling throughout the plant, coordinating activities between cells. Depending on what tissue they enter, plant hormones trigger different patterns of growth or development. Hormones, which are present in very tiny amounts, generally are made in one tissue and transported to another tissue, where they perform their work.

Early in the life cycle of a plant, all the growth is vegetative; that is, the plant produces leaf, stem, and root tissue. Unlike animals, plants can keep growing as long as environmental conditions are favorable. Their growth is only limited by the nature of each kind of plant and by conditions around it. A plant that is tree-sized in one place may be only a shrub someplace else where growing conditions are less favorable.

Vegetative growth stops when reproductive growth begins. Age or an environmental condition can trigger the start of reproductive growth. Then, instead of making leaves, stems, and roots, the plant makes flowers. Following pollination and fertilization, the flower withers and reproductive growth includes the production and growth of the fruit and seeds.

**Spreading Seeds.** The last phase of a plant's life cycle—the scattering of its fruit or seeds—ensures that new plants will develop. Many plants have developed special adaptations to spread their seeds. Small, light seeds are often dispersed by the wind. The dry seeds of tobacco plants are as small as dust particles. They are swept into the air and carried by the wind over thousands of miles. Other larger, heavier seeds have special structures that allow them to be carried by the wind, too. Milkweed and dandelion seeds have small, silky parachutes. Maple seeds have a sturdy, flat wing that propels them short distances.

Some seeds are carried by water. The coconut is a large seed surrounded by a fibrous husk with a hard outer shell. The outer shell traps air inside, so that the entire fruit floats. Safe within its shell, the seed can float in the ocean for hundreds of miles.

Birds and other animals also help spread plant seeds. When they eat sweet fleshy fruits, the seeds pass through their digestive tracts unharmed. Those that land in suitable places sprout and grow. Some seeds have hooks or

A seed is more likely to germinate successfully if it does not have to compete with the parent plant for nutrients. Seeds can be carried to suitable new locations in several ways, including by animals (*above*) or air currents (*right*).

barbs that can catch onto an animal's fur. The hooked seeds of both the beggar's tick and the cocklebur can cling to an animal for several days and over many miles.

Once the seeds have been scattered about, they will remain dormant until conditions are right for germination. Then, the seeds will come alive, setting the cycle in motion again.

### Plant Processes

Throughout the phases of its life, a plant must obtain and transport food, move water, and perform photosynthesis and respiration.

**Obtaining and Transporting Food.** Plants cannot live, grow, and reproduce unless they have all they need of certain nutrients. The substances needed by plants are taken from the air, water, soil, and other living organisms.

Plants get carbon and oxygen from the air, hydrogen from water, and the other necessary nutrients, which include substances such as nitrogen, phosphorous, iron, and magnesium, from the water in soil.

Many plants live in a symbiotic association with fungi in or around their roots. This means that both the plant and the fungi benefit from their association with each other. These fungi are called mycorrhizal fungi. The fungi get their food, mainly sugar, from the plant. In turn, the fungi absorb minerals from the soil and pass them on to the plant. Plants grown without their normal mycorrhizal fungi will grow slowly.

## How Plants Move

Plants are affected by their environment. In fact, plants perform a variety of movements in response to environmental stimuli. These movements are called tropisms. Try the experiments below and see how plants move in response to light (phototropism), gravity (geotropism), and touch (thigmotropism).

Put a plant near a light source, such as a window, noting the positions of the stem and leaves. After the plant has been in the same place for several days, you will be able to see how the stem bends toward the light and the leaves turn to face the light.

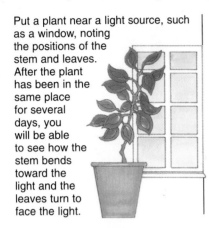

Plant two seeds in the same pot of dirt, but place one seed in the pot upside down. When the new plants start growing, you will see that in response to gravity the shoots from both plants reach up out of the soil and their roots grow downward.

Place a ruler or short pole in the soil near a climbing plant, such as a garden pea or an ivy. When the plant grows and touches the anchored object, you will see the tendrils wrap tightly around it.

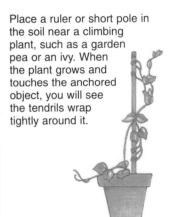

There are a small number of colorless plants that cannot perform photosynthesis and must absorb their food from organic matter in the soil like fungi do. A common example in the woodlands of the eastern United States is the Indian pipe.

There are several special methods that some plants use to obtain nitrogen, needed for making proteins and nucleic acids. Nitrogen in the air is abundant, but it is unavailable directly to plants. However, some bacteria can use nitrogen from the air, in the process of nitrogen fixation. Plants in several families, but especially the pea family, have little lumps on their roots called nodules that are full of these bacteria. The bacteria are fed carbohydrates by the plant and in turn secrete ammonia, a useful form of nitrogen, for the plant.

Another way in which some plants, called carnivores, obtain nitrogen is by eating animals. Pitcher plants have pitcher-shaped leaves that trap insects. Hairs pointing downward grow inside the pitcher and prevent the insects from crawling out. They are digested by digestive juices in a pool at the bottom of the pitcher. Other carnivorous plants trap insects by quickly closing a leaf, as in the Venus's-flytrap, or by trapping the insect in a sticky secretion, as in the sundew.

Parasitic plants live on other plants and get their food from them. Mistletoe is a common example, growing on the trunks and branches of trees. It is green and therefore can perform photosynthesis to make some of its food, but it gets most food from its host.

Food is transported through phloem tissue from wherever the food becomes available to wherever it is needed. Food travels either up or down by way of the **sieve tubes**. In a seedling, food is transported from the seed to the growing shoot tip and root tip. In a young plant, it is transported from the leaves to the growing points. In a mature plant, it is transported from leaves to a storage area, either fruit, seed, bulb, or root.

**Water Movement.** Water moves constantly from the soil through the plant and into the air. It moves through the cells of the plant by **osmosis**—the movement of water through cell membranes. The direction in which the water moves depends on the concentration of substances inside and outside the cell. Water moves through the membrane to the area with

The ghostly looking Indian pipe, which cannot make its own food, gets its nourishment from dead and decaying matter. Plants that survive in this manner—by absorbing nutrients from the breakdown products of once-living organisms—are called saprophytes.

the highest concentration of certain particles or molecules.

Water travels through the system of hollow tubes making up the xylem tissue. The tubes, which run the length of the plant, allow water to move in an upward direction through the plant. The energy for most water movement is supplied by sunlight.

**Turgor** movements are the fairly rapid movements of various parts of the plant that occur because of the rapid gain or loss of water in certain cells. Water is gained or lost because the concentration of potassium salts in the cell changes and, because of osmosis, so does the amount of water. The movement of the plant does not involve growth. Some examples are the opening and closing of stomata, the folding of leaves at night, the rapid closing of leaves of the sensitive plant when they are touched, the rapid twisting around of some tendrils, and the closing of the Venus's-flytrap leaf when it is touched. The movements can be performed over and over, as long as the in-and-out flow of water occurs.

Many plants can move some of their parts in response to touch or other stimuli. One of the most familiar examples is the sensitive plant (*above*), a tropical shrub. The fernlike leaves of the plant quickly fold together (*below*) if the plant is touched or shaken.

**Photosynthesis.** During photosynthesis, light energy is converted into chemical energy by the plant. In plants, this process takes place in special organs of the cell called **chloroplasts**. Within the chloroplast, chlorophyll converts the light energy to a chemical energy called **ATP** (*a*denosine *tri*phosphate) and stores it until it is needed.

ATP is the high-energy compound all cells use to drive chemical reactions within the cell. When the trapped energy is freed, one of the reactions it powers combines carbon dioxide from the air and water and minerals from the soil to produce the plant's food. In addition to the food substances produced during photosynthesis, oxygen is produced as a by-product. The oxygen is released into the environment surrounding the plant.

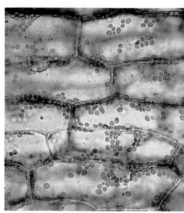

Chloroplasts are the pigment-containing structures that give plants their green color. The number of chloroplasts in a plant cell varies; there may be as many as 300 or as few as 1.

The plant also makes compounds to transport and store energy. The most common form of transported energy is sucrose, or table sugar. The most common form of stored energy is starch. Both of these can be converted to the simple sugar glucose, which can then be used in respiration.

**Respiration.** The function of respiration is the same as photosynthesis: to provide usable energy to the cell in the form of ATP. Respiration occurs in cell organs known as **mitochondria** (plural of **mitochondrion**).

During aerobic respiration, food molecules are broken down and combined with oxygen to form carbon dioxide and water. Another form of respiration takes place without using oxygen. Called anaerobic respiration, this process occurs when plants are unable to get enough or any oxygen, such as plants that are flooded with water or plants that have roots buried in mud. It yields a much smaller amount of ATP for the cell than does aerobic respiration. While it also produces carbon dioxide, it yields ethanol as its by-product.

## Plant Defenses

Plants have many enemies. They are eaten by large animals, such as cattle and deer, and by small animals, such as rabbits and raccoons. And they are eaten by still smaller animals, such as insects, snails, and worms. They are attacked by diseases and destroyed by frost, fire, and high winds.

Some plants ward off attacks by releasing poisons. However, they keep these weapons in reserve until predators actually start munching.

Plants, however, have defenses against these environmental extremes, diseases, and insects and other animals that feed on them. Their weapons include poisons, bad-tasting juices, unpleasant odors, thorns and burrs, deep roots, and thick seed coverings. Many defense mechanisms protect the plant against several threats.

**Structural Defenses.** Barbs, burrs, spines, and thorns are structures that protect many plants. They are not poisonous, but they can injure an animal's eyes and mouth or pierce its skin. Blackberries, many kinds of roses, honey locusts, cacti, cockleburs, and other plants have these prickly defenses.

Other plant structures also protect against extreme environmental conditions. Many desert plants have very thick stems and small leaves. Most cacti have no leaves at all. Since plants lose water as it evaporates through their leaves, small leaves help desert plants hold water. Water is stored in their thick stems.

The thick bark of many trees forms a good barrier against cold, as well as disease and insect invasion. The bark of the huge sequoias of California is sometimes more than a foot thick. Such thick bark also helps trees resist the heat of forest fires.

Many mountain plants, such as evergreens, must be able to survive the cold temperatures that would kill most other plants. They have gradually become suited to the cold climate of the high regions in which they grow. By growing close to the ground, some small mountain plants are able to find shelter and protection among rocks.

**Poisons and Other Chemicals.** Many plants contain poisonous substances that can and do kill. Poisons are one of the most effective plant defenses. A small piece of water hemlock root, for example, contains enough poison to kill a cow. The leaves of the death camas, which is part of the lily family, often kill cattle in the western United States. People have been poisoned by eating the bulbs of this plant.

Mountain laurel is a shrub that grows in parts of the eastern United States. The poison in its tough leaves can make sheep and other grazing animals sick. Soon these animals learn to leave the plant alone.

Many familiar plants contain poisons. These include lily of the valley, larkspur, foxglove, English ivy, and dumbcane. The nightshade family, to which tomatoes and white potatoes belong, has many poisonous members, including henbane, belladonna, mandrake, and jimsonweed.

The effects of some plant poisons from oils or saps can be felt by just touching some plants. When any part of the poison oak, poison ivy, or poison sumac plant is touched,

Plants have evolved an arsenal of strategies to defend themselves. For example, the thick stem of a cactus (*below left*) protects it from water loss, while poisons in the deadly nightshade (*below right*) protect it from being eaten by animals.

blisters, rashes, and other skin irritations can result. Similar problems are caused by members of the spurge family and the leaves and stems of lady's slippers.

Some plants are protected by nonpoisonous chemical substances that can injure or even kill the animal that dares to eat them. One example is the taro plant. The leaves and other parts of the taro contain sharp, slender crystals. When a leaf is chewed, these crystals pierce the lining of the animal's mouth, causing great pain. Although it is a dangerous plant, humans use the taro root for food. When the root is thoroughly cooked, the crystals are destroyed.

**Protective Relationships.** Special relationships exist between some plants and animals that provide benefits to both groups. This helpful, or protective, kind of relationship is called **mutualism**. The acacia plant has this most unusual defense. This tall, branching shrub is armed with heavy, hollow spines. It is not these spines, however, that protect the shrub. It is the stinging ants that live inside the spines. Sweet nectar is produced near the bases of the spines. The ants feed on this nectar and also on fruitlike bodies that grow at the tips of the leaves. In return for food and shelter, the ants patrol all parts of the shrub, driving off any leaf-eating insects.

▶ **SAVING OUR PLANTS**

Earth's original vegetation has been greatly altered where people have settled. Much of the temperate forests worldwide have been cut down and the land converted into farmland or second-growth forests. Original grasslands have been largely converted to cropland. Even semidesert grassland has been converted to scrub shrubland by overgrazing of cattle, sheep, or goats. Cropland has far fewer plant species—sometimes it only has one!—than the vegetation it replaces. Also, human intervention has greatly increased soil erosion by wind and water, resulting in less fertile land and, at times, gullies and eroded land. Significant areas of tropical rain forest are destroyed when all the plants are burned to make way for agriculture. The cleared land can only be farmed for a few years before soil fertility is severely depleted. In many poor countries, the forests have been harvested for firewood, leaving bare, eroded hillsides that are completely unproductive.

Each hour, close to 6,000 acres (2,428 hectares) of tropical forest are destroyed. Thousands of plant species vanish as forests fall to land developers.

Human activity and population growth are making many plant (and animal) species extinct, especially in the humid tropics. The long-term danger is that humans will destroy so many plant species that we will depend on only a few to supply our needs. These few would be vulnerable to plant diseases or insects. The most famous example of this was the potato famine in Ireland in the 1800's, when a fungal disease, called late blight, killed the entire potato crop. The potato was the main food for the population. Without the potato crop, many people starved and many more left the country.

There are various conservation organizations that are actively saving endangered plants. For instance, the Nature Conservancy buys land in threatened habitats for conservation purposes. Originally, land was bought only in the United States, but now it is also bought in other countries. The Wilderness Society is active in trying to save unique federal lands as wilderness areas. Saving a habitat with sufficient undisturbed land ensures the survival of all of the plants and animals in it. This method is much more efficient than trying to save one species at a time with heroic efforts. In the end these methods will succeed only if we learn to value the wealth of our green inheritance.

NEAL M. BARNETT
Department of Botany
University of Maryland

A description of plants and the biomes they occupy is presented on the following pages.

## PLANT DISTRIBUTION

Plants have successfully adapted to almost all of the earth's environments. Only the driest deserts, deepest oceans, coldest polar regions, and highest mountains are without some kind of plant life. The plants, animals, and other organisms that live and grow together in the same environment form a **community**.

Each community has its own specific kinds of plants and animals. When a community of living things covers a large area of the earth's surface, it is called a **biome**. Along with its own unique life-forms, each biome has distinctive conditions and physical factors, such as climate, type of soil, and amount of moisture.

The yellow poppy displays the great adaptability of plants. It thrives despite the harsh conditions of its tundra home, among them cold temperatures, scarce water, and frozen soil.

Climate is the major characteristic that scientists use to divide the earth's land surfaces into biomes. Important biomes include grasslands, deserts, chaparral, deciduous forests, coniferous forests, tundra, and tropical rain forests. There are also aquatic biomes in rivers, lakes, ponds, and oceans. Because similar communities occur in different parts of the world, there are similar biomes throughout the world. For example, grasslands exist in North America as well as in Asia and Africa. The map below identifies the major biomes of the world. The chart on the following page identifies some of the plants that are commonly found in the world's major biomes.

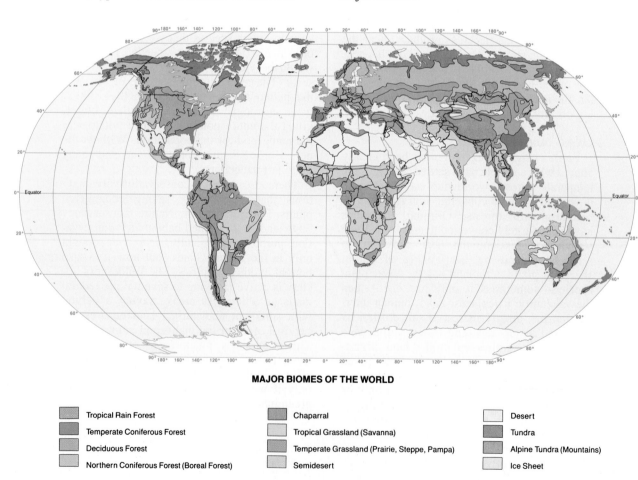

**MAJOR BIOMES OF THE WORLD**

- Tropical Rain Forest
- Temperate Coniferous Forest
- Deciduous Forest
- Northern Coniferous Forest (Boreal Forest)
- Chaparral
- Tropical Grassland (Savanna)
- Temperate Grassland (Prairie, Steppe, Pampa)
- Semidesert
- Desert
- Tundra
- Alpine Tundra (Mountains)
- Ice Sheet

# PLANTS AND THEIR BIOMES

## Plants of the Forest

### Deciduous Forest

Black cherry
Black locust
Blue violet
Deerberry
Dutchman's-breeches
Great laurel
Green ash
Harebell
Hickory
Indian pipe
Jack-in-the-pulpit
Lady fern
Pincushion moss
Primrose
Quaking aspen
Red maple
Royal fern

Shortleaf pine
Spicebush
Starflower
Teaberry
Tree club moss
Tulip tree
White oak
Wood anemone

Hawthorn

### Coniferous Forest

Balsam fir
Black spruce
Bloodroot
Bracken fern
Elderberry
Fireweed
Goldthread
Harebell
Horsetail
Mountain maple
Nodding trillium
Quaking aspen
Red baneberry
Red pine
Sheep laurel
Sphagnum moss

Starflower
Tamarack
White pine
Wood sorrel

Pink lady's slipper

### Rain Forest

Antarctic beech
Brazilwoods
Broadleaf evergreens
Bromeliads
Cassia
Epiphytes
Eucalyptus
Lianas
Mangosteen
Orchids
Redwood
Sapodilla
Shell seed
Sitka spruce
Strangler fig

## Plants of the Grassland

### Temperate Grassland (including prairies, steppes, pampas)

Bluestems
Bromegrass
Buffalo grass
Chokecherry
Crazyweed
Death camas
Evening primrose
Feather grass
Fescue
Foxtail barley
Green ash
Hackberry

Indian grass
Ironweed
Mexican hat
Milkweed
Needle-and-thread
Needle grass
Prairie acacia
Prairie alfalfa
Purple prairie clover
Smooth sumac
Snow-on-the-mountain

Solidago
Sunflower
Switchgrass
Timothy
Wild tulips
Wormwood

Indian paintbrush

### Tropical Grassland (including savannas)

Acacias
Baobab
Bermuda grass
Bluestem
Candelabra tree
Dropseed
Elephant grass
Spurges
Palms
Red oat grass
Umbrella thorn
Whistling thorn

## Plants of the Tundra (including alpine tundra)

Alpine bearberry
Bear grass
Bog bilberry
Bristlecone pine
Cotton grass
Dwarf clover
Englemann spruce
Fairy primrose
Fescue
Fireweed
Forget-me-not
Glacier lily
Goldenbush
King's crown
Moss campion
Mountain avens
Mountain heath
Mountain sorrel
Saxifrage
Sedges
Sheep laurel
White phlox
Willow

## Plants of the Desert

Agaves
Artemisia
Barrel cactus
Brittle bush
Creosote bush
Desert holly
Desert marigold
Desert paintbrush
Desert peach
Devil's claw
Giant wild rye
Gold poppy
Indian blanket
Indian rice grass
Joshua tree
Jumping cholla
Mesquite
Needle grass
Ocotillo
Organ pipe cactus
Paloverde
Prickly pear cactus
Pygmy cedar

Saguaro
Seep willow
Spurges
Tamarisk
Yuccas

Sagebrush

## Plants of the Chaparral

Black sage
Buckthorn
California buckwheat
Chamiso shrub
Coyote brush
Deerweed
Heath
Manzanita
Mountain lilac
Mountain mahogany
Oak
Prickly pear cactus
Scrub oak
Sugarbush
Sumac
White sage

Each biome has characteristic plants that are adapted to the environment of that particular biome. A desert biome (*above*) has succulent plants—plants with fleshy tissues that conserve water—and tough small-leafed shrubs. After an infrequent rain, many desert annuals will germinate, mature, flower, set seed, and die, all in a few days. The plants in an aquatic biome (*below*) are either floating plants or plants that root at the water's edge or in the shallow portions of the body of water. In the high altitudes of mountain tundra (*left*), the summers are short. The small, compact plants have to flower and produce seeds quickly before winter comes around again.

Forest biomes are dominated by trees, but they also include shrubs, vines, and herbs. The pine, spruce, and fir trees found within a coniferous forest (*above left*) keep it green throughout the year. The leaves of trees in a deciduous forest (*above*) turn colors and are shed every autumn. Woody shrubs and succulents cover the rocky landscape of a dry chaparral (*below*). A mixture of shrubs, colorful wildflowers, and grasses of various heights populate the grassland biome (*below left*).

# PLASTICS

Plastics have been around for only the past hundred years or so. But it is difficult to imagine what our lives today would be like without them. Plastics are used to make everything from toys and clothing fabrics to car bodies and bullet-resistant jackets. Plastics can be flexible or rigid, colored or transparent. Almost any property can be given to plastics, making them a nearly ideal material.

Plastics are very versatile. They are used in many sporting goods, such as this woman's helmet, goggles, clothes, and gloves—even her bicycle's handlebar grips (*left*).

Plastics can be used to make the bodies of some vehicles, such as this car developed by Chrysler (*below*). The plastic material can come from recycled soda bottles.

A compact disc (*below left*) has thousands of tiny pits, made in a single step by plastic molding. The patterns of pits can be used to store recorded music.

▶ **ADVANTAGES OF PLASTICS**

There are thousands of types of plastics now available, and more plastics are being developed all the time. This gives product manufacturers a wide variety to choose from. Each of these plastics has different properties. But they all share common advantages over more conventional materials, such as metal, wood, glass, and ceramics.

Most conventional materials can be used in only a limited number of ways. Plastics, on the other hand, are extremely versatile, meaning they can be used in many more ways. Versatility is the most important advantage of plastics.

Plastics can be molded, or formed, into extremely complex shapes. It is this moldability that allows manufacturers to minimize the number of parts and steps needed to make a product. For example, compact discs (CD's) have a plastic layer that stores recorded music in the form of complex patterns of tiny pits. Even though there are thousands of these pits in every CD, they can be made in a single step using plastic molding.

Plastics can be transparent, translucent (partially transparent), or opaque (light-blocking). Transparent plastics are used for things such as eyeglass lenses and aircraft canopies. All plastics can be colored by adding pigments when the plastics are in a melted state. Unlike metals, which must be painted after being fashioned into products, plastics can be colored and then molded directly into products, such as the housings for telephones. There is no paint to chip, and surface scratches are less obvious because the color is spread throughout the material.

Plastics are relatively lightweight and can therefore be used to make products that are easy to handle and transport. Solid plastics are a little heavier than wood but much lighter than glass or steel. Some plastics have a density just below that of water and will float. This low density of plastics is particularly important for manufacturing automobile parts, since lighter vehicles tend to use less fuel. Low weight is also important for portable appliances such as laptop computers and for sporting goods such as football and hockey helmets. Plastics can also be "foamed," or filled with a gas, to produce very lightweight materials.

Plastics can have many other advantages over conventional materials. Plastics do not rust, like steel, or rot, like wood. They can be made resistant to certain chemicals, too. Plastics are good electrical insulators and are therefore used in many electronic components. Plastics can also insulate against heat, making them useful cooking utensils. And they can be made slippery and smooth, producing little friction in moving parts.

building blocks—the monomers—that react together to form the chains. A third factor is the arrangement of those chains in relation to one another. And the final factor is the plastic's additives—other ingredients that are added to the material. Plastics can be tailor-made for a specific use by altering any of these factors.

### Length of Molecules

Polymer chains range in length from hundreds to many thousands of links long. Plastics with longer chains tend to be stronger. The longer the chains, the more the materi-

**STRUCTURE OF A PLASTIC MOLECULE**

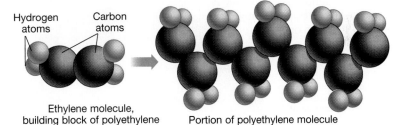

Ethylene molecule, building block of polyethylene

Portion of polyethylene molecule

**Plastics are made of molecules called polymers, which are chains of smaller molecules linked together. The polyethylene molecule is made from the monomer ethylene.**

▶ CHEMISTRY OF PLASTICS

The word "plastic" describes a type of material that can be shaped. The term comes from the Greek word *plastikos*, meaning "fit for molding." For example, we say that clay and wax are plastic, meaning that they can be molded easily. Usually, however, the word "plastics" refers only to synthetic materials.

Plastics consist of **polymers**—long molecules made of smaller molecules linked together in chains. The links are formed during the reaction of materials called **monomers**, from which polymers are made. The term "polymer" comes from the Greek words *poly*, meaning "many," and *meros*, meaning "part." Similarly, "monomer" means "one part." Wood and cotton are actually types of a naturally occurring polymer called cellulose, but they are not considered plastics because they do not soften or melt when heated and are therefore not moldable.

There are four important factors that make plastics different from one another. One is the length of the plastic's polymer chains. Another factor is the chemical structure of the

al's molecules are tangled together. This helps keep the material from deforming under stress. On the other hand, plastics with shorter chains tend to flow better, which is important when molding plastic parts. These conflicting factors must be balanced.

### Structure of Links

The chemical structure of the monomer building blocks determines both the stiffness of the chains and the strength of the forces holding the chains together. Polymers commonly consist of a "backbone" composed of atoms of carbon and hydrogen in various arrangements. Many polymers include other atoms—such as oxygen, nitrogen, sulfur, chlorine, and fluorine—in their structure.

Chemists identify a plastic by the structure of the monomers that make up its polymer chains. The technical name of a plastic is given in the following manner: poly(*chain link name*). The term in the parentheses usually identifies the monomer. For example, poly(ethylene) is produced by chemically combining a large number of ethylene gas molecules to produce a polymer chain. Poly(ethylene), which is written "polyethylene" in everyday language, is used in a wide variety of products, from supermarket grocery bags to milk bottles.

Many other types of plastics are simply made from different monomers. Propylene is the building block of polypropylene, a lightweight plastic used to make lunch boxes, for example. Styrene is the building block of polystyrene, which is the plastic material used to make Styrofoam products. The list goes on and on. Each of these plastics is chemically different, with its own unique properties. Plastic material names are often abbreviated, using "P" for "poly," and the first letter of the link name. For example, polyethylene is also known as PE, polypropylene as PP, and so on.

Plastic products can be made from raw plastic materials or from recycled plastics, such as these chips from ground-up milk containers. The chips can be melted and molded into new products.

### Arrangement of Chains

Plastics are classified according to their morphology, or the way their polymer chains arrange themselves. The morphology can be amorphous, with a random arrangement of chains. It can be crystalline, with chains arranged in a more ordered fashion. Or it can be semi-crystalline, meaning that it is partly amorphous and partly crystalline.

Plastics are also classified according to how they respond to heat during manufacturing. **Thermoplastics** do not undergo any type of chemical reaction when molded. They simply soften when heated and turn back into a solid, with a new shape, when cooled. Thermoplastics include certain transparent plastics, such as those used in car taillights, and durable plastics, such as polyvinyl chloride, or PVC—a tough material used for such things as floor coverings and house sidings.

**Thermosetting plastics**, on the other hand, do undergo a chemical reaction when they are made. Also called thermosets, these plastics soften when first heated but turn back into a solid when heated further, just as a soft egg becomes hard after boiling. Once a thermosetting plastic has been formed into a desired shape, its polymer chains link together to form a netlike arrangement. This netlike linking, or cross-linking, keeps thermosets from softening and melting when they are heated again. Epoxy adhesives are an example of a thermosetting plastic.

### Additives

All plastics are actually combinations of both a base polymer and other materials that have been added to enhance certain properties of the base polymer or to give it new properties. These additives are usually added to the plastic when the raw plastic material is produced, but they are sometimes added just before the plastic is melted and formed into a final product. Common additives include plasticizers (which reduce stiffness), fillers (which increase stiffness), pigments, fragrances, and even anti-static agents (which reduce the "cling" caused by static electricity).

These additives can also be used in combination. For example, a plastic milk bottle is commonly produced from unpigmented, translucent polyethylene. The polyethylene contains few additives, but may contain a chemical called an antioxidant (to prevent the plastic from degrading during manufacturing). However, recent studies have shown that many of the vitamins in milk are degraded when the translucent polyethylene container is exposed to the sun's ultraviolet rays, even for short periods of time. As a result, several milk companies have started packaging their milk in pigmented polyethylene bottles. A pigment additive causes the plastic to become opaque and prevents the milk from being exposed to the vitamin-degrading rays.

### ▶ MAKING PRODUCTS FROM PLASTICS

Plastic products begin their life as raw plastic materials, which are shipped from suppliers to manufacturers by truck or railroad. The

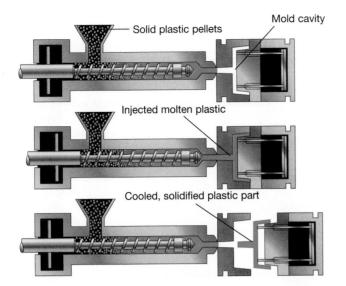

Solid plastic pellets

Mold cavity

Injected molten plastic

Cooled, solidified plastic part

## INJECTION MOLDING PROCESS

**Plastic pellets are fed into an injection molding machine, which melts them and injects the molten (liquid) plastic into a mold. The cool mold solidifies the part, which is pushed out.**

machines include a mold, which determines the shape of the plastic part. The machine melts the plastic pellets and injects the melted plastic into the mold, which is kept cool so that the melted plastic will become solid. The mold is in two pieces, enabling the part to be pushed out after it solidifies. Molds for very large parts, such as car door panels, have only one cavity, while molds for small parts, such as bottle caps, may have more than 50 cavities (so that many parts can be produced at once). The process is highly automated. Molded parts are often removed from the mold using robots. The entire process may take 5 seconds to 60 seconds depending on the size and thickness of the part.

There are many other plastics manufacturing processes.

The **extrusion process** is used to form continuous shapes called profiles, such as drinking straws or house siding. The melted plastic is continuously forced through a shaping tool called a die and is cooled in water into the desired profile. The cooled profiles can be cut to any length or can be wound up on large rolls. This process is also used to produce strong, durable, and lightweight plastic textile fibers, such as nylon.

plastic materials are usually shipped in the form of a powder or small pellets for ease of handling. In the case of thermoplastics, solid plastic pellets are first melted into a liquid, then formed into the desired shape, and finally cooled to solidify into the end product. There are a number of different manufacturing processes that are used to make thermoplastic products, but all of the processes involve these three fundamental steps.

**Injection molding** is the most common plastics manufacturing process. This process is used to make products ranging from CD's to automobile door panels. Injection molding

**Extrusion is a process used to make continuous shapes, such as piping (below). The shapes are produced by a die, through which melted plastic is forced. When the plastic cools, it can be cut to any desired length. By contrast, injection molding produces fixed shapes, such as these pails (right).**

**Thermoforming** is another plastics manufacturing process. Unlike injection molding or extrusion, which begin with plastic pellets, thermoforming begins with a plastic sheet. The plastic sheet is heated to the point where it softens but does not fully melt and is placed over an open mold cavity. The softened sheet is then pressurized. The pressure causes it to stretch and take the shape of the mold cavity. The formed sheet cools and is trimmed to produce the finished part. This process is used to manufacture items that range from disposable plastic drinking cups to aircraft canopies.

Disposable plastic drinking cups can be made by thermoforming—a process in which heated plastic sheets are pressurized and molded.

**Blow molding** is a modified extrusion process. It is used to make hollow parts such as plastic bottles or automobile fuel tanks. The blow molding process begins with the production of a hollow tube of plastic (made by an extrusion or injection-molding process). This hollow tube is heated (to soften it) and is inserted into a larger mold cavity. Once in place, the inside of the hollow tube is pressurized with compressed air, causing the tube to expand and take the shape of the mold cavity. After cooling, the part is ejected from the blow molding machine.

**Rotational molding** is another process used to make hollow items, such as the shells of kayaks. The process begins by placing plastic powder into a thin-walled aluminum mold. The mold is then closed and rotated in a hot oven. The heat causes the plastic powder to melt and coat the inside surfaces of the mold as it rotates. After melting is complete, the mold is cooled. Once the part is cool, the rotating action stops and the part is ejected from the mold.

▶ **PLASTICS AND THE ENVIRONMENT**

Like all materials, plastics can affect our environment in both positive and negative ways. In order to determine exactly how plastics affect the environment, we must consider their total life cycle—from when they are first made to when they are thrown away.

Most plastics are made from petroleum products, such as oil or natural gas. However, only about 1 percent of the oil and natural gas consumed in the United States is used to produce plastics. This is much less than the amount of petroleum products we use to fuel our cars and heat our homes. Plastics can actually save more energy than is consumed in manufacturing them. For example, plastic insulation used in buildings, homes, and refrigerators will save far more energy than that consumed to make the insulation. Using plastic parts in an automobile, boat, or airplane will almost always result in better fuel efficiency, since plastics are very lightweight materials. In this respect, plastics can be thought of as environmentally friendly.

However, like other materials, plastics can pose an environmental problem when they are ultimately discarded. Once a plastic product is no longer usable, it must be disposed of in some manner. The product can be buried in a landfill, burned in an incinerator, treated to recover some of its chemicals for further use, or recycled into other products.

Old plastic products that are **landfilled**, or taken to the dump, do not pose any particular problem to landfill sites. Plastics do take up landfill space, which is getting more expensive. But they are not considered hazardous materials that could poison land or water. Once buried, most plastics are inert and will not degrade, or break down.

This lack of degradability can be a problem, particularly when plastic parts or packages are improperly disposed of as litter. Plastic litter along the sides of roads, fields, and elsewhere is not only an eyesore. It can also pose a problem for some wildlife, which can get entangled in plastic fishing lines and can holders, for instance. It is for these reasons that many plastic packaging products are produced from **degradable plastics**. For example, some specially formulated plastics can be made to break down into harmless substances when exposed long enough to the sun's ultraviolet rays. Certain naturally occurring microorganisms can also safely break down some plastics, which are called biodegradable.

**Incineration** is another process that is used to dispose of discarded plastics. Most plastics will burn under certain conditions. In an incinerator, waste is burned and energy is recovered in the form of steam, which can in turn generate electricity. However, incineration also produces by-products such as gases and ash, which must also be properly cleaned or safely disposed of somehow. A number of other incineration-like processes can also be used to treat plastic waste. In processes such as pyrolysis, plastics are heated and degraded in a controlled environment in order to produce oil-like fluids that can be used for fuel.

An increasingly popular way to handle plastic waste is not to dispose of it, but rather to **recycle** it for making other products. Technically, any thermoplastic can be recycled since thermoplastics can be ground back into chips or powder and remolded (unlike thermosetting plastics, which cannot be remelted once they solidify). For example, plastic milk bottles, soft drink bottles, and other containers are commonly recycled.

Most plastic containers have a label that consists of a number surrounded by arrows. The label indicates what type of plastic the container is made from. A plastic milk bottle has the number 2 molded into the base of the container to indicate that it is made of polyethylene, a recyclable thermoplastic. Recycled chips from used milk bottles are not remolded into new milk bottles, since material that came into contact with the old plastic might contaminate the milk. However, these bottle chips are used to make other products, such as plastic lumber. Plastic lumber is widely used for outdoor applications such as playground structures because it will not splinter, degrade, or rot, and it has a good ap-

*Left:* The plastic bottles and other containers in the box this boy is carrying will be picked up by a truck and taken to a plastics recycling center. *Above:* At the recycling center, a worker sorts through the bottles and containers, which will be ground up and turned into useful products that can be recycled again.

pearance. After many years, the recycled plastic lumber itself will become waste, and it too can then be recycled.

▶ **HISTORY OF PLASTICS**

Shortly after the Civil War, the high cost of ivory led people who made billiard balls and other items from ivory to search for a substitute. A New York billiard ball company offered a $10,000 prize to anyone who could invent such a substitute. John Wesley Hyatt, a printer and inventor in Albany, New York, heard about the prize and began experimenting. In 1869, Hyatt discovered a way to transform cellulose from cotton or wood pulp into a useful, moldable material. He treated the cellulose with nitric acid to produce a chemical called nitrocellulose. Then he added camphor, a liquid from the bark of the camphor tree, which made the nitrocellulose easy to mold. Hyatt called his creation Celluloid. It quickly became an important material—not only as a good ivory substitute for billiard balls. Combs, buttons, false teeth, and photographic film were a few of the other products made from this plastic. (Celluloid has since been replaced by other plastics, since it could burn too easily.)

As years passed, people began making more plastics by modifying natural polymers, such as cellulose and rubber. However, only a few plastics could be produced this way.

Then in 1909, the Belgian-American chemist Leo Hendrik Baekeland developed the first totally synthetic, or artificial, plastic.

This worker is checking a manufacturing plant's large steel rollers, which wind strands of nylon—a synthetic polymer used to make fabrics for clothing, carpeting, and other products.

Unlike Celluloid, this plastic was not a modified natural polymer. Instead, it was formed by chemically combining phenol (from coal tar) with formaldehyde (from wood alcohol) to produce phenol-formaldehyde. Baekeland's discovery was an accident—he was actually trying to invent a substitute for shellac. Instead, he produced a dark syrup that would harden when heated. This new, thermosetting plastic had many valuable properties. It was not dissolved by ordinary solvents, it could be molded into any shape, it did not conduct electricity, and it was inexpensive. One of its early uses was in making insulators for wireless radios. Baekeland named the new material Bakelite, after himself.

After the introduction of Bakelite, the plastics industry grew steadily. Other plastics were also discovered by accident. But most plastics were developed to meet some specific need for which there was not suitable material available. This was particularly true during World War II, when scientists searched for ways to produce synthetic substitutes for rubber and other raw materials that were in short supply.

In later years, a number of so-called **engineering plastics** were developed, in part to meet the demanding needs of the space program. Engineering plastics are highly resistant to impact and heat—two desirable properties for materials designed to withstand the harsh environment of outer space. An example is polycarbonate, which is used in making unbreakable windows.

By 1979, the industry had grown so much that the volume of plastics produced and used in the United States exceeded that of steel for the first time (19 million tons that year). The plastics industry continues to grow as newer materials are developed and as new uses for existing materials are found.

Today, many of the plastics we have are finding new applications, especially in the area of packaging. For example, polyethylene terephthalate, more commonly known as PET, is a transparent, shatterproof, and lightweight material that is replacing glass bottles and metal cans for soft drinks and many other food products. After they are used, PET containers (identified by the number 1 molded into the bottom) can be recycled into fibers for clothing.

▶ **FUTURE OF PLASTICS**

One of the latest plastics manufacturing technologies is called **stereolithography**. The technology allows engineers and scientists to make plastic parts without using any mold. These plastic parts are particularly useful during the early stages of the development of a new product. They serve as prototype parts that engineers can test before the final product is made. Stereolithography is an automated process that starts with a computer

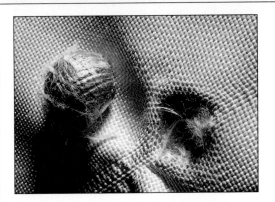

some plastics are stronger than steel? In 1964, Stephanie Kwolek, a scientist working for the DuPont chemical company, discovered a plastic fiber that could make automobile tires puncture-proof. The fiber, called Kevlar, is stronger and stiffer than many metals but very lightweight. When combined in layers of fabric, Kevlar can also make clothing bullet-resistant. Such "body armor" is now routinely used by police officers to protect themselves from gunfire. Kevlar is also used in the sails of some racing sailboats and to strengthen sports equipment such as skis, helmets, racquets, and hockey sticks. And Kevlar is used to make superstrong ropes such as those that secured the airbags in the landing equipment of the *Mars Pathfinder*.

*Above left:* When fired from a gun, this bullet left an indentation in a piece of Kevlar but did not puncture the superstrong material.

*Above:* Besides bullet-resistant vests, Kevlar is used to make many other products that need to be strong and lightweight, such as sails.

model of a part. The model is then made into the actual part layer by layer, each of which can be thinner than a single human hair. These layers are formed by a narrow laser beam shining over the surface of a vat containing a liquid thermosetting plastic. A computer directs the laser to the right locations within the vat according to the shape of the part being produced. The laser causes the plastic molecules to form networks of links and solidify.

Other new plastic materials are finding important uses in medicine. For example, plastic hip or knee joints can be implanted into patients whose own joints have become too brittle or stiff. Degradable plastics are another promising material. They can be used to make internal stitches that safely degrade inside a patient's body once a surgical wound has healed. Scientists are also working on plastics that may one day be used for making artificial muscles, skin, and other tissues.

Televisions, computers, and other electronic devices may soon benefit from new plastic technologies, too. Engineers are developing polymers that can store electrical charges. The polymers have already been used to make all-plastic batteries that are much lighter than conventional batteries and that can be molded into any shape. Other new polymers can convert electrical currents into different colors of light. The polymers could be used to make much thinner computer and television screens that use very little electricity.

The future applications for plastics—with their endless variety and versatility—are limited only by our imaginations.

ROBERT A. MALLOY
Professor, Plastics Engineering Department
University of Massachusetts at Lowell

See also NYLON AND OTHER SYNTHETIC FIBERS.

**PLATH, SYLVIA.** See MASSACHUSETTS (Famous People).

Plato, from a painting by Raphael.

## PLATO (427?–347 B.C.)

Plato, one of the greatest Greek philosophers, was born in Athens about 427 B.C. and died there in 347. He belonged to a rich and noble family. In his youth he met the philosopher Socrates, who molded his whole life. Plato admired Socrates for his strong character and was fascinated by his brilliant ideas.

In 399 B.C. Socrates was accused of not believing in the gods of Athens and of corrupting young men's minds. He was found guilty and put to death. Plato's friends urged him to enter politics, but he despised the Athenians who had condemned Socrates. He left home and stayed abroad for 12 years. All through his life he took no part in the political struggles of Athens.

Plato was determined to keep the teaching of Socrates alive. He himself had a quick and fertile mind. He returned to Athens and opened a school. It was called the Academy because it was in a grove sacred to the hero Academus. This was the first university in the world. It remained active for nearly 1,000 years. Plato and his friends taught science, law, and philosophical thinking to carefully picked students. His most famous pupil was Aristotle, who worked in the Academy for 20 years.

Plato wrote at least 25 books, some quite short, others long and complicated. These are truly wonderful works, for Plato has a clear and graceful style, and the ideas he discusses are most important. One strange thing about them is that they do not read like ordinary books. They are conversations. As we read them we hear Socrates talking with his friends, his pupils, and even his enemies. In each conversation a problem is raised, and then the talkers, usually guided by Socrates, try to find a solution on which all can agree.

Another strange thing is that Plato himself never appears or speaks. In many hundreds of pages his name is mentioned only twice. His brothers, his kinsmen, and his friends come in, but never Plato. Plato wanted his readers to know that the thoughts worked out in the books were originally the thoughts of Socrates, even if Plato wrote them down and carried them further.

The chief thoughts in the books are these: (1) There are two worlds—this world, in which everything keeps changing, nothing is perfect, and truth is almost impossible to reach; and another world where everything is perfect and permanent, and truth can be found. Our world is a poor copy of the other world. (2) Our bodies belong to this world and die. Our souls come from the other world, return to it, and never die. (3) We understand important truths, such as the laws of mathematics, because our souls bring knowledge of them from the other world. (4) Many important truths cannot be written down because books cannot explain them fully. They can be grasped only by a few men or women engaged in free discussion. (5) Virtue is knowledge. If you know what is good, you naturally do it. Therefore no one does wrong willingly. But most people do not know the truth, so they act stupidly and wrongly. (6) Democratic government is disorderly, inefficient, and corrupt because most people do not know what is best for them. They will vote for anyone who flatters them and promises them they can have everything they want. The only safe and sensible type of government is government by a few trained thinkers—a king who is a philosopher, with wise advisers, or a group of tightly disciplined philosophers.

The most important of Plato's books are *The Defense of Socrates,* Plato's version of the speeches Socrates made at his trial (this is the only book not set out as a conversation); *Phaedo,* the last discussion of Socrates with his friends in the condemned cell; *The Republic,* a dialogue about the meaning of justice and a plan for the ideal government; *Gorgias,* a keen argument about truth and lies in politics; and *Phaedrus* and *The Symposium,* talks on the meaning of love as an ideal that can bring our souls closer to perfection.

GILBERT HIGHET
Formerly, Columbia University

# PLATYPUS AND SPINY ANTEATERS

The platypus and the spiny anteaters live in Australia and a few nearby islands. They are among the most unusual animals in the world. The platypus has webbed feet and a flat, leathery bill somewhat like a duck's bill. A spiny anteater, or echidna, has long claws, a tube-like snout, and a covering of short, stiff spines like that of a hedgehog or porcupine.

The platypus and spiny anteaters are mammals—the females produce milk and nurse their young. But one of the strangest things about them is that they lay eggs, as birds and most reptiles do. They are the only mammals in the world that do this. Like birds and reptiles, they have only one body opening, which serves both for the elimination of all body wastes and for laying eggs. For this reason, platypuses and spiny anteaters are known by the group name **monotreme,** which means "single hole, or opening."

**The platypus has a long, skin-covered bill and heavily webbed feet.**

### ▶ THE DISCOVERY OF MONOTREMES

Australia has always been noted for its unusual animal life. Kangaroos and many other marsupials, or pouched mammals, live there. They were known before the platypus and spiny anteater were discovered. One of the first reports about a spiny anteater was written in 1792.

The platypus was first recorded in 1797, when colonists saw it in the Hawkesbury River in eastern Australia. They called the odd little creature a water mole. When the first platypus skin was sent to England, scientists thought it was a joke—that parts of different animals had been sewn together.

When scientists studied later specimens, they found that the platypus was not a joke. But just what was it? It had fur, and it was soon shown to have milk glands. It had to be a mammal. Yet it had a bill. And it was said to lay eggs—which seemed unbelievable. Finally, in 1884, two scientists, working separately, proved that the platypus and spiny anteater are mammals that lay eggs. They observed these animals and their eggs in the wild and reported what they had seen.

### ▶ THE PLATYPUS, OR DUCKBILL

The platypus lives in eastern Australia and Tasmania. It always lives near streams, lakes, or ponds, and it gathers its food in the water. The male measures as much as 60 centimeters (2 feet) in length and may weigh about 2 kilograms (4½ pounds). The female is smaller. Both sexes have thick coats of soft, dark brown fur. Platypuses were once widely hunted for their fur. Today, hunting these animals is against the law.

All four feet of the platypus are webbed. The webs of the front feet extend some distance beyond the claws. These outer portions are folded under when the platypus walks about on land. The tail is broad and rather thick. The adult male has sharp spurs on his hind legs. The spurs are connected to poison glands and can give painful wounds to an attacker.

The broad, flattened bill is covered with soft, flexible skin. In this skin are sensitive nerves that help the animal locate food. Adult platypuses have no teeth. Hard ridges on their bills help to crush and grind up their food.

Platypuses live in burrows that they dig in the banks of streams. They sleep in their burrows during the day but come out at dusk to hunt for food. Their appetites are enormous. Swimming along stream bottoms, they nuzzle through the mud and pebbles, gobbling worms, insects, crayfish, and other small freshwater animals.

### Baby Platypuses

The platypus breeds during September and October. Those are spring months in the Southern Hemisphere. At this time the female prepares a breeding burrow, which may vary in length from 5 to 18 meters (15 to 60 feet). In this burrow she prepares a special nesting chamber and lines it with leaves and grass. After she has mated, the female goes into her burrow and plugs it up with earth. Then she retires to her nest and lays her eggs—usually two but sometimes one or three. The eggs are almost round and are about 2 centimeters (³/₄ inch) in diameter. They are white and have wrinkled, leathery shells. The mother platypus curls around the eggs and incubates them for about ten days. Then the babies hatch.

Newborn platypuses are blind, naked, helpless, and little more than 2.5 centimeters (1 inch) long. They nurse by drinking milk that oozes from pores on the underside of the mother's body and dribbles onto her fur. The young platypuses develop quite slowly. They finally leave the nest when they are about 17 weeks old.

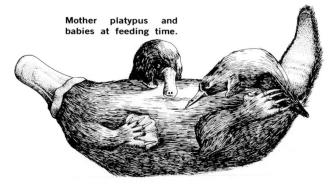

**Mother platypus and babies at feeding time.**

### ▶THE SPINY ANTEATER, OR ECHIDNA

The platypus is equipped for a life in the water. The spiny anteaters are equipped for digging and for gathering ants and other insects as their principal food. Spiny anteaters live in the same areas as the platypus and in New Guinea as well. They usually inhabit open woodlands or rocky areas.

A spiny anteater is perhaps even more unusual looking than a platypus. The stout body is covered with hair and also with a great many short, thick spines on the back and sides. The short, powerful legs have long,

**The spiny anteater, or echidna.**

curved claws for digging. The snout is long and narrow—shaped somewhat like a tube. The sticky, wormlike tongue can be thrust out like the tongue of any anteater.

During the day, the spiny anteater sleeps in a cavity under roots or rocks or perhaps in a hollow log. At dusk it goes out to search under stones and in the ground for ants, termites, and other insects. These are picked up with the long tongue. During times when there is insufficient food, spiny anteaters may become inactive or dormant (asleep). They are not true hibernators, however.

At breeding time, the female develops a pouch on her underside. The pouch opens to the rear. Almost always, she lays just one egg into the pouch. It is not certain exactly how the egg gets there. But the female probably curls her body so that the egg is laid directly into the pouch. She carries the egg until it hatches. The baby lives in the pouch until it becomes too big for the mother's comfort. Then the mother leaves it in the burrow or some other hiding place.

If it is threatened, a spiny anteater may roll itself into a ball or dig straight down, feet first, into the ground. Only its sharp spines can then be seen or felt by its enemies.

There are several different species of spiny anteaters. The largest is native to New Guinea. It may measure 75 centimeters (30 inches) in length.

ROBERT M. McCLUNG
Author, science books for children

See also ANTEATERS; MAMMALS.

When young children play, they may use everyday objects in creative ways, practice physical skills, or try out adult roles.

# PLAY

Play is a concept that is easier to describe than to define. When you observe kittens or puppies rolling about on the floor, nipping at their mates without really hurting them and making movements as if to fight or flee, you know you are watching animals at play. In a similar way, when your best friend pretends to punch you or calls you a funny name, you recognize these actions as play. But what exactly is play? What are its defining features?

It might come as a surprise to learn that play has been the subject of serious study, leading to important insights about human nature and animal behavior. The Dutch historian Johan Huizinga, in a book published in 1938, was the first to discuss the significance of play. Huizinga wrote that players create a "magical circle," a special place in which almost anything can happen or be imagined to happen.

## ▶ CHARACTERISTICS OF PLAY

Play, in its broadest sense, is the exercise of body and brain to create new and interesting arrangements of familiar things. This might involve wordplay and other forms of verbal communication. Or it might involve the use of objects, such as marbles or balls. Nearly all play calls for movement of the body.

Play allows people and animals to try out imaginary or temporary situations, to test themselves and their playmates, and to explore new possibilities. In doing so, players acquire and sharpen many physical, mental, and social skills. But the real motive for playing is the pleasure it brings.

## ▶ KINDS OF PLAY

There are many ways of playing. Play can be loud and exuberant, or it can be rather quiet. Some play emphasizes physical skills such as running and jumping; other play, such as riddling, exercises the mind. Play can be solitary, but it is more likely to be social. If we look at our own lives, it is easy to recognize two main varieties of play.

One common type of play is pretend play, or make-believe play, in which the players create an imaginary world. In the very first year of life, babies learn to play with simple objects. They may pretend these objects are other things—for example, a block of wood may become a car. The play of young children often involves mimicking adult activities. Setting up a pretend schoolhouse, hospital, or grocery store allows a preschooler to try out adult roles. As children get older, their pretend play becomes more elaborate, often drawing on ideas from television shows, movies, and books. Scholars be-

Sports are a form of organized play in which players compete according to accepted rules. This kind of play teaches important physical, mental, and social skills.

fierceness of their postures and actions as they wrestled and tumbled with one another. Yet somehow the monkeys all knew they were only playing, not fighting. How did the monkeys understand this distinction and communicate it to one another? Bateson theorized that the exaggerated style of the fighting signaled playful intentions. In human behavior, this same feature can be seen in the playful insults often exchanged by teenagers. Statements such as "Your mother wears army boots" are so outlandish that they could never be mistaken for real insults.

Much research has focused on how play helps people and animals acquire important knowledge and skills. The attacking and avoiding movements practiced by lion cubs and other young felines, as well as the chasing

lieve that pretend play is an important way for children to explore roles they will later assume in real life. Pretend play tends to be cooperative rather than competitive. It usually has no fixed rules, but takes shape in the course of playing.

A very different kind of play occurs when people organize themselves into teams and compete according to rules accepted by all the players. Here the playing becomes a game, and the object is to play well and win. The rules of the game may be official and widely known, as in sports such as soccer, basketball, and tennis. Or they may be unofficial, as in games invented and played by children in a particular neighborhood. Playing competitive games helps children develop mental and physical skills, teaches them to work together as members of a team, and helps them understand the importance of rules and fair play.

▶ THEORIES OF PLAY

Scholars have developed a number of theories about play. Some of the most interesting research has been done with animals such as monkeys and dogs, although many of these findings relate to human play as well. In all, these theories of play have contributed greatly to our understanding of who we are and how we behave.

One of the most exciting theories involves the notion of play fighting. A British anthropologist, Gregory Bateson, observed young monkeys at play and was impressed with the

Young animals, such as these lion cubs, often engage in playful fighting and wrestling. The rough-and-tumble play teaches them important survival skills.

games played by wolf pups, contribute to their ability to survive as adults. We have seen how skills developed in the play of human children help prepare them for roles they will perform as adult members of their communities.

Some scholars have expressed concern over the demanding schedules followed by many modern children, particularly those who live in industrialized countries. They remind parents and educators that periods of unstructured play with peers are essential to a child's development.

JOHN H. MCDOWELL
Folklore Institute
Indiana University

**PLAYGROUNDS.** See PARKS AND PLAYGROUNDS.

# PLAYS

A play is a story that is performed in front of an audience. Putting on a play is a way to have fun and entertain others at the same time. A successful play takes a great deal of preparation and cooperation, from the first production meeting to the final bow. It is hard work, but many performers and artists consider theater the most rewarding art form.

With the lines of their play memorized, four young actors are in costume and ready for an audience.

## ▶ CHOOSING A PLAY

The first step is choosing the play you want to perform. You need to consider a number of things.

How many roles or parts should the play have? Do you need parts for just a few people or a whole class?

What kind of play is best suited for your performers: musical, comedy, or drama? What type of play will your audience enjoy? A talky, sophisticated play may be a poor choice for a young audience. Be sure to choose a play that everyone can understand and enjoy.

How much money do you have for your production? Elaborate scenery and costumes can be expensive, even if you make them yourselves. What kind of scenery and costumes will be needed?

Where will you perform your play? Consider the size of the stage you will be working on. A huge cast cannot be squeezed onto a small stage. Do not choose a play with problem scenery, lighting, or special effects. Keep it simple.

Are there royalties involved with your script? (A royalty is the money an author gets when his or her play is performed. Every printed play states whether you have to pay royalties on it or not.)

## ▶ KINDS OF PLAYS

There are many kinds of plays to choose from. If you want to stage a drama, make sure the audience understands the main idea. If you choose a comedy, be sure that the humor is right for the age of your audience. If you want to put on a musical, be sure that you have performers who can sing and dance as well as act. You may also need to add to your staff a musical director, who will work with the actors on learning their songs; a choreographer, who will stage all the dancing in the show; and musicians who will play during the performances.

Other kinds of plays include story theater and revues. In story theater, a narrator tells the story while others act it out. Revues combine songs, scenes, or skits from various sources into one production. To stage a revue, first choose a theme, such as a holiday, then select stories and music about that holiday to put in your revue.

You may choose to write your own script. This way, you can be sure that all of your needs are met, and you will not have to pay royalties. You can also adapt a story into a play. Some stories require that royalties be paid for adaptations, but many do not, such as fairy tales by the Brothers Grimm and Hans Christian Andersen.

If you are looking for plays that are already written or for stories to adapt, your library is a good source. If you are having trouble deciding on a few different scripts, have a play reading. This is a way to test out the scripts and see which one you would most like to perform. Gather a group of friends together, and give them each a copy of the script. Assign roles and read the play out loud. Afterward, get everyone's reactions. Hearing the plays will give you a clearer idea of how they should be performed.

## ▶ ORGANIZING A PLAY

As with any large project, it is best to divide the work up among different people when you want to put on a play. Along with

### How to Play the Blocking Game

This game will help everyone learn stage directions.

Write each of the following stage directions on separate sheets of paper, fold them, and put them in a hat or bowl:

| | |
|---|---|
| Upstage left | Downstage center |
| Center stage left | Upstage right |
| Downstage left | Center stage right |
| Upstage center | Downstage right |
| Center stage | |

The director pulls a stage direction out of the hat or bowl and says, "Everyone cross …" and reads the direction out loud. In theater, the word "cross" means "walk." The director may make the direction even more specific by saying, "Everyone wearing green cross" or "Everyone who ate cereal for breakfast cross" and reading the next stage direction.

| Upstage right | Upstage center | Upstage left |
|---|---|---|
| Center stage right | Center stage | Center stage left |
| Downstage right | Downstage center | Downstage left |

Audience

---

the actors, many other people are involved in staging a play, including the director, producer, stage manager, and designers.

**The Actors.** Performing with their bodies and voices, actors bring the play's written words to life. Actors are responsible for conveying the play's message to the audience. In addition to solid memorization skills, an actor should have a strong, expressive voice and good body control.

**The Director.** The director is in charge of the production. He or she casts the play (chooses who will play what part) and decides on a concept for the play. For example,

the director may decide to set a classic play in modern times. He or she works closely with the designers to see that the sets, costumes, lighting, sound, makeup, and properties, or props—any items that are carried on stage by an actor—all work well together. The director blocks the play (tells the actors where to go on stage) and helps the actors say their lines.

**The Producer.** The producer is in charge of the business side of putting on a play, such as selling tickets and managing the budget. He or she will want to make sure that expenses do not exceed the income or ticket sales for the production.

**The Stage Manager.** The stage manager is the director's chief assistant. He or she organizes the rehearsals, makes sure that everyone knows the schedule, and sees that the rehearsal space is set up. The stage manager writes down where the actors will be on stage, and during performances, he or she "calls" the show. This means telling the crew when to adjust the lights, change the set, and make sound effects.

**The Designers.** Designers are the visual artists at work in a play. Different designers are in charge of specific areas. For example, set designers create the backdrop or scenery. Other designers include costume designers, lighting designers, sound designers, makeup designers, and properties designers (one who creates the props in a play).

### How to Play Hot Seat

This is a good exercise to do when actors are having trouble staying in character. Three or more people can play this game.

Have an actor make an entrance in character and sit in a chair in the middle of the stage. Everyone else asks him or her questions. The actor must answer in character. The others can ask anything they want, and the actor must make up an answer, even if he or she really does not know. For example, the others may ask what his or her favorite color is. Even if this is not mentioned in the play, the actor should imagine what the character's favorite color might be. There are no wrong answers in this game, but the actor must stay in character the entire time.

### PRODUCTION MEETINGS AND CASTING

Once you have the staff for your play, have a production meeting. At these meetings, the director, producer, stage manager, and designers get together to make sure all of their jobs will work well together. Continue to have production meetings throughout the rehearsal process.

The next step is to cast the play. The director holds auditions to see who would be best for each role. At auditions, the director may have an actor read from a script or perform a monologue (a scene in which an actor speaks to himself or herself, to the audience, or to another character in a play). After the first auditions, the director may arrange callbacks, that is, second auditions, to be sure that the right people are cast in the right parts.

### SCENERY AND LIGHTING

Scenery may be real furniture, painted backdrops, flats (a flat piece of scenery, such as a window painted on a large canvas), trees, or any other large items that help show the audience where the scene takes place. In theater, the scenery does not have to be realistic. People in the audience can use their imaginations, so that only a suggestion of the location may be needed.

Lighting can help set the mood of the play or show the audience what time of day it is. If the play is a comedy, you may want bright, colorful lighting. If a scene takes place outside in the evening, the lighting may be dim or perhaps dark blue. You can use lamps to create stage lighting and a flashlight to be a spotlight in your play.

Stage lighting is always electrical. Never use an open flame, such as a candle or a lantern, on the stage. Only the assigned person should touch the electrical equipment.

### COSTUMES AND MAKEUP

Costumes and makeup will tell the audience a lot about the characters and the play. Costumes may suggest the time period of the play. They can tell you what a character does for a living, or whether the character is rich or poor. Here, too, members of the audience use their imaginations, so only a suggestion of the costume may be needed. Makeup can let the audience know how old a character is. It can also be used to turn actors into animals, clowns, and anything else you can imagine.

## WONDER QUESTION

### Where did the terms "downstage" and "upstage" come from?

In earlier times, the front of the stage was slanted down so that the audience could see the action in back more easily. Because it was sloped down, the front of the stage was called downstage and the higher, rear portion of the stage was called upstage.

### REHEARSALS AND OPENING NIGHT

A play needs a lot of rehearsing. Many directors begin rehearsals with warm-ups, during which actors may practice tongue twisters to warm up their tongues and voices and perform stretches to warm up their bodies.

At the first rehearsal, called a read through, the actors read the script aloud to hear how it sounds and to begin getting ideas for the story and the characters.

Next come blocking rehearsals, when the director arranges the movement of the actors. In order for the director to communicate the blocking to the actors, everyone should know the terms for stage directions: Upstage is farthest from the audience; downstage is closest to the audience. Stage left is the actors' left,

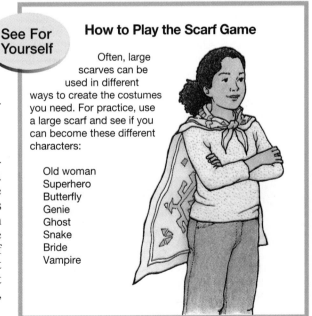

**See For Yourself**

### How to Play the Scarf Game

Often, large scarves can be used in different ways to create the costumes you need. For practice, use a large scarf and see if you can become these different characters:

Old woman
Superhero
Butterfly
Genie
Ghost
Snake
Bride
Vampire

## How to Use Makeup

For older characters, use a dark base and a makeup pencil to draw in the lines of your face. For animals, find a picture of the animal, and copy the colors and shapes onto your face with makeup pencils and brushes. It is best to draw out your makeup plan on a picture of a blank face before you actually draw it on your face.

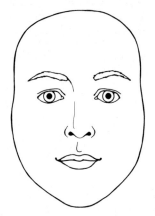 

not the audience's; stage right is the actors' right. Center stage is in the middle.

In blocking the play, the director should make sure that the audience can always see everyone on stage and that no actor has his or her back to the audience.

By the time the entire play has been blocked, the actors should have their lines and cues memorized. A cue is the line or action that happens just before a particular actor's line. It is important for actors to memorize their cues, so they know when to say their lines. Once the play has been memorized, run-throughs take place—rehearsals of individual scenes or the entire play.

While running the play, it is important that the actors always stay "in character." The way they move, walk, talk, and act should stay true to whatever character they are playing.

Tech week is the last week before the opening performance. It is the time when all the play's elements come together. A stage crew may be needed at this time. They can be the running crew, who change the set between scenes; the prop master, who is in charge of properties; or the light and sound-board operators, who run the lights and sound during performances. During tech week, dress rehearsals are held, at which the actors rehearse in full costume. The set should be completed, and all the other design elements should be ready. The director watches these rehearsals and gives notes, or advice, on how to improve the show after each run.

Once everything has come together, you are ready for an audience. If you are well rehearsed and organized, there is no need to be nervous. Just have fun, and your audience will, too. Enjoy your performance, and take a bow!

JEANNE BENDICK
Coauthor, *How to Have a Show*
Reviewed and revised by LISA BANY-WINTERS
Author, *On Stage: Theater Games and Activities for Kids*

See also DRAMA; THEATER.

**PLEDGE OF ALLEGIANCE.** See FLAGS (Saluting the Flag).

**PLUM.** See PEACH, PLUM, AND CHERRY.

### Did you know that...

it is all right to "cheat" when you are acting? In theater, a director may tell the actors to "cheat out." That means the actors should face the audience, even if they are talking to someone behind them.

# PLUMBING

When you fill a glass with water from the faucet in your kitchen sink, do you wonder how water reaches the faucet? If you pour the water down the drain, do you wonder where it goes? One system of pipes inside the walls of the building brings water to the faucet, and another system of pipes carries away waste. These pipes are the plumbing of the building.

The source of water that comes from your faucet is an underground well or a lake, reservoir, or river that may be far from your home. The water is brought to the people who use it in huge concrete pipes that are something like underground rivers. Such pipes are called **aqueducts.** If you live in a rural area, water may be pumped from a small well on your property directly into your home.

From the aqueducts water enters large metal pipes called **water mains.** Water mains are buried beneath city and suburban streets. From the mains, water is carried by smaller metal or plastic pipes into each building along the main.

Water that goes down the drain in your sink is carried away by a system of pipes called **drains.** The drains join a larger pipe called a **sewer** located under the building. The sewer runs out to the street where it joins a still larger pipe, a **sewer main,** buried beneath the street. The sewer main carries wastes to a sewer treatment plant. In rural areas, the sewer pipe empties into an underground **septic tank** where the wastes are broken down by bacteria.

**Fixtures** are also a part of the plumbing system. They are connected to both water and drain pipes. Sinks are fixtures. Other fixtures are drinking fountains, bathtubs, toilets, water heaters, and washing machines.

**Fittings** are small parts used to connect pipes together, to turn corners, and to attach pipes to fixtures. There are many hundreds of kinds of fittings, each for a particular size of pipe and a particular use.

Water that goes to a kitchen faucet or to any other fixture is under constant pressure—enough pressure to force the water up through the pipes in tall buildings. In order to let water out of the pipes when it is needed, **valves** are

The plumbing system in a two-story house is made up of pipes to supply fresh water and drains to carry away waste. Vents prevent unhealthy fumes from entering the house.

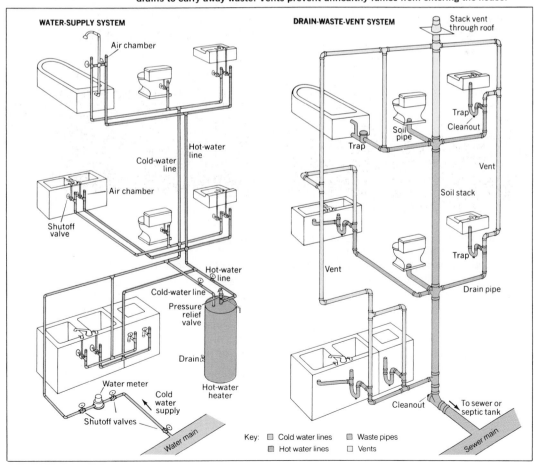

WATER-SUPPLY SYSTEM

- Air chamber
- Hot-water line
- Cold-water line
- Air chamber
- Shutoff valve
- Hot-water line
- Cold-water line
- Pressure relief valve
- Drain
- Water meter
- Cold water supply
- Hot-water heater
- Shutoff valves
- Water main

DRAIN-WASTE-VENT SYSTEM

- Stack vent through roof
- Trap
- Cleanout
- Soil pipe
- Trap
- Vent
- Soil stack
- Trap
- Vent
- Drain pipe
- Cleanout
- To sewer or septic tank
- Sewer main

Key: ☐ Cold water lines  ▨ Waste pipes
☐ Hot water lines  ☐ Vents

placed in the pipes. Valves control the flow of water in plumbing systems. The most familiar valves are those found at sinks, bathtubs, and fire hydrants. Larger valves control the flow of water in water mains and in the piping systems of large buidings.

Someone in your family should know about the valve that turns off all the water in your house or apartment. If a pipe inside the wall breaks or the toilet runs over, someone must turn off the water supply until the repairs can be made.

In the sewer system, there are no valves because there is no pressure in the pipes. Drains and sewers work by gravity. Water flows to a lower level because of its weight.

Sewers contain unpleasant fumes, so **stack pipes,** which are open at the top, run up through the roof to vent the drain pipes and to keep pressure from growing inside the system.

To keep unpleasant sewer fumes from entering your house, **traps** are used in each drain. A trap is an S-shaped pipe that stays filled with water, even when water is not running from the faucet. If you look under a sink you will see the trap just below the place where the drain pipe connects to the sink.

### Plumbers

While plumbing is the term for all the pipes, fittings, and fixtures in a building, it also refers to the work of installing and repairing the pipes and fixtures connected to them. The men and women who do this work are called plumbers.

Plumbers do two main kinds of work, installing and repairing. If you have a broken pipe or a leaking water heater, you need a plumber right away. If your sink is worn out or the faucet is beyond fixing, a plumber will install a new one.

Plumbers also work in construction. They know how to cut and join pipes so there are no leaks. They know how to work with steel, iron, copper, plastic, and glass pipes. They must be able to read engineers' drawings so they can install pipes and valves properly in new buildings. Plumbers also install gas pipes and heating and air conditioning pipes where they are needed.

Plumbers learn their trade in two ways. They serve an **apprenticeship** under a master plumber, and they also complete a technical training program offered by a trade school or a plumbers' union. A plumber who has completed this training is called a **journeyman** plumber.

Extra training is needed for plumbers who work on the special plumbing systems in ships, hospitals, refineries, and power plants. Another special plumbing field is pipe welding. Pipe welders join pipes and fittings by using gas or electric welding techniques.

### History of Plumbing

For thousands of years people have controlled the flow of water in order to grow crops or to save water in wet seasons so they would have it during drought. But the simple channels dug in the ground or the mud dams built to reserve water cannot be called plumbing systems.

The first plumbing system that we know of in a building was in the palace of King Minos of Crete. It was built about 4,000 years ago, and much of it remains today. Water was carried in clay ducts in the walls of the palace to the places where it was used. There was even a bathroom with running water. A sewer carried away unused water and wastes.

By Roman times, a thousand or more years ago, above-ground stone aqueducts moved water for many miles to bring it to populated areas. The water was piped into cities in buried clay pipes.

The Romans also used metal pipes, which they made by hammering a thin sheet of lead around a wooden rod. (The Latin word for lead is *plumbum,* which is where the words plumbing and plumber originated.) The Romans devised ways to keep the metal pipe from leaking by folding the edges together and hammering them flat. The person making the pipe had to mark the pipe with a special mark, because pipes were taxed by the Roman Government. From the marks we know that some of the pipe makers were women.

For centuries, most small pipes in home plumbing systems were made of lead like those in ancient Rome. In the 1960's and 1970's, scientists determined that by drinking water from lead pipes, people could absorb enough lead into their bodies to suffer from lead poisoning. Today, most small pipes in home plumbing systems are made of copper, iron, or plastic.

JAMES R. SKELLY
Co-author, *Pipes and Plumbing Systems*

# PLUTO

Cold, dark, and icy—these words describe the planet Pluto, a tiny world orbiting the sun at the distant outer edge of the solar system. At an average distance of about 3.7 billion miles (5.9 billion kilometers) from the sun, the planet receives 1,000 times less light and heat from the sun than does Earth. In addition to being the outermost planet, Pluto is also the smallest planet in the solar system—so small that some astronomers think Pluto should not even be called a planet.

Yellow arrows mark the spot of light identified by Clyde Tombaugh as a planet. When he compared these two photographs of the same area of the sky, he found the one spot that had changed position among the stars. It was later named Pluto.

## The Discovery of Pluto

Because Pluto is so far away, it remained undiscovered by astronomers until 1930. Long before its discovery, however, astronomers suspected that there was another planet beyond Neptune. They had noticed that Neptune deviated slightly from the orbit predicted for it. After taking into account the gravitational pulls from all the known planets, they concluded that this orbital deviation was caused by the gravitational pull of an unknown planet.

An astronomer named Percival Lowell was particularly fascinated by the idea that there might be another planet in the solar system. In the early 1900's he made extensive studies of the skies, hoping to learn where this "planet X" was hiding. Lowell even built an observatory in Arizona where for many years astronomers searched for planet X.

Astronomers looked for planet X by taking photographs of the sky at intervals several nights apart. Since the positions of the stars appear fixed in the sky but planets change position among them, astronomers compared photographs taken at different times, searching for a tiny dot of light that had changed position. This would be the mystery planet.

When Lowell grew too old to continue his work, the astronomers at his observatory continued the search. In 1929 they hired Clyde Tombaugh, a young amateur astronomer, to take photographs and to study them. A skilled observer, Tombaugh discovered planet X within a year of starting his search. As astronomers learned more about this planet, they named it Pluto after the god of the underworld, a mythical place of cold and darkness —a fitting name for such a dim and distant world.

## A Strange and Unusual Planet

Astronomers were astonished by some of the characteristics of this newly discovered planet. Because Pluto was so dim, astronomers determined that it was smaller than Lowell had predicted. They were also very surprised by the planet's peculiar orbit. During Pluto's 247.7-year trip around the sun, its distance from the sun varies from about 2.8 billion miles (4.4 billion kilometers) to as far away as 4.6 billion miles (7.4 billion kilometers). Although all the planets travel in elliptical (oval-shaped) orbits, Pluto's orbit is more elliptical than that of any other planet. At its **aphelion**, the point in orbit at which a planet is farthest from the sun, Pluto is the ninth planet, orbiting far beyond Neptune. But at its

---

## WONDER QUESTION

### Is Pluto really a planet?

Ever since the discovery of Pluto, astronomers have wondered whether it is really a planet. Pluto's small mass, its unusual orbit, and its tilted orbital plane make it very different from any other planet. Even some of the satellites, or moons, of the other planets are more massive than Pluto.

Some astronomers think that Pluto resembles an asteroid more than a planet. The largest known asteroid, Ceres, has a diameter that is almost half that of Pluto, and Ceres has nearly one eighth of Pluto's mass. Like Pluto, many asteroids also have orbits that are elliptical and tilted. Most astronomers, however, still choose to classify Pluto as a planet, even though it is not a typical one. Whatever it is, Pluto is certainly a unique member of the solar system.

## The Composition of Pluto

Crust (methane frost)

Mantle (ices)

Core

### Pluto

| | |
|---|---|
| **Position in the solar system** | Ninth planet from the sun |
| **Distance from the sun** (average) | 3,700,000,000 miles (5,900,000,000 kilometers) |
| **Revolution around the sun** | 247.7 Earth years |
| **Diameter** (compared to Earth's) | Less than $\frac{1}{5}$ or 0.20 times, the Earth's diameter |
| **Diameter** | 1,400 miles (2,253 kilometers) |
| **Mass** (compared to Earth's) | About $\frac{1}{406}$, or 0.0025 times, the Earth's mass |
| **Mass** | 14.7 quintillion tons |
| **Density** | 2.065 grams per cubic centimeter |
| **Rotation on its axis** | 6 Earth days 9 hours 18 minutes |
| **Tilt of rotational axis** | 98° |
| **Natural satellites known** | 1 |
| **Rings known** | None |
| **Surface** | Unknown, but assumed to be frozen methane |
| **Atmosphere** | Methane |
| **Temperature** (at surface) | −382°F (−230°C) |
| **Symbol** | ♇ |
| **In mythology** | Pluto, Roman god of the underworld |

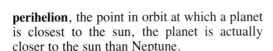

**perihelion**, the point in orbit at which a planet is closest to the sun, the planet is actually closer to the sun than Neptune.

Another strange characteristic of the planet is its orbital plane—the tilt of its orbit in relation to the orbits of other planets. While the orbital planes of the other planets are tilted only slightly from each other, Pluto's is tilted at a 17 degree angle.

Since Pluto was too far away for even the largest telescope to reveal any of its details, astronomers did not learn much about Pluto for many years. A few astronomers measured the planet's position and brightness from time to time and learned that it takes the small planet a little more than six days to rotate once on its axis. This fact was determined by observing the small variations in Pluto's brightness that are visible from Earth. Most astronomers, however, ignored Pluto until new discoveries about it were made in the late 1970's.

### The Discovery of Charon

In 1978, while measuring Pluto's position in a photograph, an astronomer named James Christy noticed an unusual bump on one side of the planet's image. He looked at other photographs and soon realized that the bump went around Pluto every six days, which is the same amount of time that Pluto takes to rotate on its axis. James Christy had discovered Pluto's only known satellite. He named it Charon after the ferryman of the underworld in Greek mythology. A few weeks after discovering Charon, Christy realized that Pluto and its satellite would each soon undergo a series of eclipses of one another. For astronomers this became a tremendous opportunity. By measuring how much the light given off by Pluto and Charon decreased during these eclipses and timing when the eclipses began and ended, they could determine the size and surface features of both the planet and its satellite. While these events occurred during the years 1987 through 1990, astronomers discovered most of what they now know about Pluto and Charon.

### New Findings About Pluto and Charon

Astronomers have discovered that Charon is a large moon in relation to Pluto. Its diameter of 746 miles (1,200 kilometers) is more than half the diameter of Pluto. Also, Charon is only 12,200 miles (19,640 kilometers) away

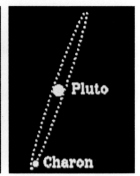

The diagram (*far right*) illustrates Pluto's moon Charon orbiting the planet. The photographs show that an image of the two taken by an Earth-based telescope (*right*) is not as clear as one taken outside the Earth's atmosphere by the Hubble Space Telescope (*middle*), which can see them as two distinct objects.

Pluto

Charon

from Pluto. No other satellite in the solar system is as large in relation to its planet or as close in distance to its planet.

Pluto is brighter than Charon and has bright regions at both its north and south poles. Fifty percent of the light that strikes the planet from the sun is reflected back into space, and the planet's surface has large bright and dark spots. Charon is a bit darker than Pluto; its surface reflects only about 40 percent of the light that strikes it.

Recent studies have determined that Pluto consists of a mix of rocky materials and ice and has a thin atmosphere of methane gas. Pluto may have only a part-time atmosphere, however. In 1989, Pluto was at its closest point to the sun and warm enough so that the methane on the planet was in a gaseous state. However, as Pluto moves farther away from the sun it will become colder. By the year 2020, Pluto will be so cold that all the methane in its atmosphere will freeze and form a layer of methane ice on the planet's surface. During its 247.7-year orbit around the sun, Pluto may have an atmosphere for only about 60 years.

### The Origin of Pluto

When astronomers compared the orbital periods of Neptune and Pluto (the time it takes the planets to travel around the sun), they noticed something odd. Neptune travels once around the sun in 165 Earth years. Pluto travels once around the sun in 247.7 Earth years. What is odd about this is that three orbital periods of Neptune are very nearly equal to two orbital periods of Pluto. Astronomers say that these planets are locked in **orbital resonance**, which means that the orbital period of one planet is almost an exact fraction of that of another planet of larger mass. In this case, their orbital resonance is 3:2, or 3 to 2.

Orbital resonance results in a series of gravitational pulls by the larger planet on the smaller one. This means that if Pluto slows down a bit, Neptune's gravity causes it to speed up again. If Pluto speeds up, Neptune's gravity causes it to slow down. The result of the orbital resonance of Pluto and Neptune is that the two planets will never collide.

Orbital resonance may also help explain what Pluto is and why it exists. Astronomers think that Pluto may be the sole survivor of

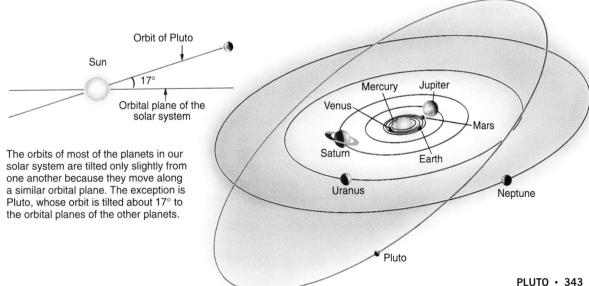

The orbits of most of the planets in our solar system are tilted only slightly from one another because they move along a similar orbital plane. The exception is Pluto, whose orbit is tilted about 17° to the orbital planes of the other planets.

Orbit of Pluto
Sun
17°
Orbital plane of the solar system

Mercury Jupiter
Venus
Mars
Saturn
Earth
Uranus
Neptune
Pluto

the time early in the history of the solar system when the planets were forming. When the sun condensed from a large cloud of interstellar gas, the matter that was left over formed a thin disk circling the sun. Solid materials formed as tiny grains of rock and ice in this disk stuck together in larger and larger clumps. Over the course of millions of years, these growing clumps of matter became the planets.

Astronomers think that during this period of planet formation, thousands of icy bodies about the size and shape of Pluto formed in space beyond Jupiter and Saturn. As these mini-planets orbited the sun, they collided with one another and formed the planets Uranus and Neptune. Eventually every Pluto-like body, except Pluto itself, had disappeared.

Why did Pluto never collide with Neptune even though its orbit takes it close to the larger planet? The answer may lie in the 3:2 orbital resonance between the two planets. Even though their orbits cross, Neptune and Pluto never move through the intersection at the same time. Therefore, Pluto was the one body out of thousands that escaped the larger planet's gravitational pull.

### Learning More About Pluto

Astronomers are anxious to learn much more about Pluto. If they are correct in their assumption that Uranus and Neptune formed from thousands of Pluto-like bodies, then Pluto may help reveal more about the nature of the early solar system. It will take a robotic spacecraft about ten years to travel through the solar system from the Earth to Pluto. Scientists are hopeful that a mission can be developed and launched in time to reach Pluto before 2020. After that time, Pluto's orbit will take the planet away from the sun and its surface will begin to freeze, making observations more difficult.

RICHARD BERRY
Author, *Discover the Stars*

See also PLANETS; SOLAR SYSTEM.

---

# PLYMOUTH COLONY

The colony of Plymouth in Massachusetts was founded in 1620 by a group of English settlers, who were known as Pilgrims because they traveled to the New World. It was the second permanent colony in the New World to be settled by the English (the first was Jamestown, Virginia, founded in 1607). About one third of Plymouth's original settlers were Puritans, who came to the New World in search of religious freedom. But most of the Pilgrims who journeyed to the New World were simply hoping to find a better life than they had known in England.

### The Puritans

The Puritans' search for religious freedom began in England in the 1500's. King Henry VIII (1491–1547) and later his daughter, Queen Elizabeth I (1533–1603), had tried to force all of the English people to practice Protestantism according to the ways of the newly formed Church of England. However, some of the English objected to the rituals of the new church, believing they too closely resembled the Roman Catholic form of worship. Because these objectors wanted to "purify" the church, they became known as Puritans. Some eventually broke away from the church. They were called Separatists.

King James I (1566–1625) made it a crime for anyone to hold privately organized religious services. Books and pamphlets that contained Separatist beliefs were seized. Many Separatist leaders were thrown in jail or condemned to death.

To escape this persecution, Separatists began to flee from England. About 100 of them settled in a small university town called Leyden in the Netherlands in 1609. Here they could worship as they pleased, but they found it difficult to earn a good living. They also worried that their children would forget their English heritage. As time passed, they longed to return to the English way of life.

Because they could not safely worship as they pleased in England, the Leyden Separatists decided to go instead to the English lands in North America. After long efforts their representatives persuaded the English government to let them settle there. Expecting that the King would soon fix his seal on their charter, the representatives set about raising

The Pilgrims who settled Plymouth Colony came to the New World in search of a better life. Many were Puritans, who sought religious freedom from the Church of England.

money for the venture. A group of about 70 Merchant Adventurers formed a joint-stock company for this purpose. It was decided that the Separatists would settle on land granted to the Second (Plymouth) Virginia Company and earn their living by fishing.

In July, 1620, a small group of about 46 men, women, and children sailed for England aboard the leaky little *Speedwell*. There they were joined by another group of about the same size. Its members had been recruited by the venture's merchant backers, and most of them belonged to the Church of England. The Separatists called themselves Saints. The others they called Strangers. A third group included 5 artisans (people with special work skills) and 18 servants, most of whom had pledged to work for their masters in return for their passage. Three of the best-remembered Pilgrims—Captain Myles Standish (1584?–1656), John Alden (1599?–1687), and Priscilla Mullins—were not Saints, but Strangers. When the *Speedwell* proved to be unseaworthy, the Saints and Strangers all crowded aboard the larger *Mayflower* in the port of Plymouth.

According to the Old Style calendar, the *Mayflower* set sail for Plymouth on September 6, 1620 (which would be September 16 by the calendar we now use).

### The Founding of Plymouth

After 65 long days at sea, the *Mayflower* dropped anchor on November 11 (or November 21) in the sheltered harbor of what is now Provincetown at the tip of Cape Cod, Massachusetts. Because they were far away from an established system of law and order and had begun to argue among themselves, the Pilgrim leaders decided they must create a governing authority. The drew up an agreement called the Mayflower Compact, which became the first agreement for self-government signed in America. This document was signed by the 41 men aboard the *Mayflower*, who pledged to obey its laws. After the signing, John Carver (1576?–1621) was chosen to be the colony's first governor.

---

**THE MAYFLOWER COMPACT**

In ye name of God Amen. We whose names are underwriten, the loyall subjects of our dread soveraigne Lord King James, by ye grace of God, of great Britaine, franc, & Ireland king, defender of ye faith, &c. Haveing undertaken, for ye glorie of God, and advancements of ye Christian faith and honour of our king & countrie, a voyage to plant ye first Colonie in ye Northerne parts of Virginia [land granted to the Virginia Company]. Doe by these presents solemnly & mutualy in ye presence of God, and one of another, covenant, & combine our selves togeather into a civill body politick; for our better ordering, & preservation & furtherance of ye ends aforesaid; and by vertue hereof to enacte, constitute, and frame such just & equall Lawes, ordinances, Acts, constitutions, & offices, from time to time, as shall be thought most meete & convenient for ye generall good of ye Colonie: Unto which we promise all due submission and obedience. In witnes wherof we have hereunder subscribed our names at Cap-Codd ye · 11 · of November, in ye year of ye raigne of our soveraigne Lord King James of England, france, and Ireland ye eighteenth, and of Scotland the fiftie fourth. Ano: Dom · 1620 ·

---

The Colony of
**New Plymouth**
*commonly known as 'The Plymouth Plantation'*
**1620 - 1691**
*with Adjacent Settlements*

Plymouth Colony was established by the Pilgrims, who sailed to the New World on the *Mayflower* in 1620. Although Plymouth lacked a royal charter, it maintained separate status as a colony until 1691. At that time it was taken over by the larger and more prosperous Massachusetts Bay Colony and became part of the royal province of Massachusetts.

After exploring the coast along Massachusetts Bay, the Pilgrims on December 11 (December 21) chose Plymouth as the site of their colony. Plymouth had been named by Captain John Smith on his trip to New England in 1614. According to legend the Pilgrims stepped ashore onto a large boulder, the famous Plymouth Rock. Cannons were dragged to the top of a nearby hill and set in place for protection. The first building to rise was the Common House. Then rough huts began to go up. Soon, however, sickness struck the Pilgrims. By the end of their first winter half the group were dead.

Toward the end of winter an Indian brave suddenly appeared among them. To their amazement he greeted them in English. His name was Samoset, and he had been in contact with English traders on the coast of Maine several years before. From him the Pilgrims learned that they had nothing to fear from the Indians of the region, as most of them had died in a smallpox epidemic a few years before. Later Samoset brought his friend Squanto (?–1622), who had once been captured and sold as a slave to Spain, but had later escaped to England and returned to America in 1619. Squanto became a trusted friend of the Pilgrims, acting as their guide and interpreter for the rest of his life.

Through Samoset, the Pilgrims had also met Massasoit (?–1661), chief of the Wampanoag Indians of what is now eastern Massachusetts. The Englishmen and the Indian chief made a peace treaty that remained in force for many years. Under this treaty Plymouth Colony prospered. Its population grew with new arrivals from England.

**Life in Plymouth Colony**

At first the colony had only a single street. On either side stood low wooden houses with small gardens in back. Larger homes were built in the neighboring countryside when each settler was granted land there in 1627. From the beginning, however, one building was more important than any of the others. This was the meetinghouse. On Sunday mornings the whole colony gathered there for religious services. They remained, sitting on hard wooden benches, all morning. After going home for midday dinner, they came back to spend the rest of the day praying, singing hymns, and listening to sermons that went on for hours.

The Indians taught the colonists how to plant maize (corn) in rows and how to use fish traps to catch herring for fertilizer. Corn and other vegetables as well as berries, wildfowl, game, and fish soon gave an ample and varied diet. To celebrate the first bountiful harvest, in 1621, the Pilgrims held a thanksgiving feast and invited their Indian friends.

To fulfill their contract with the London merchants, the Pilgrims had to contribute their labor for seven years in return for funds and supplies. They were not allowed to work for their own gain. Everything had to go into a common store, from which food and other necessities were drawn. Sometimes the London backers were slow in sending supplies, and the colonists did not have enough food to go around. The main source of the colony's wealth was beaver furs received in trade with the Indians in exchange for cheap trinkets. In 1627, profits from the beaver trade enabled the colony to buy out its London backers and to get their permission to continue trade with the Indians. The colonists built trading posts in the Connecticut Valley to the west and along the Kennebec and Penobscot rivers to the north, in what is now Maine.

**Religion and Government.** Religion remained the driving force in the affairs of Plymouth. Although the Pilgrims were victims of religious persecution themselves, they often were intolerant toward members of other persecuted religious groups. Thus, the Quakers, who had fled to the New World for the same reasons as the Pilgrims, were driven out of Plymouth Colony.

Although the governors of the colony were not ministers, they were devout churchgoers and frequently were called on for advice in church matters. The governors were elected, but only certain members of the community (called freemen) had the right to vote. The most notable governor was William Bradford, who headed the colony for 30 of the years between 1621 and 1656. Bradford was also Plymouth's leading historian. In his history, *Of Plymouth Plantation,* he wrote a long account of its founding and early years.

With the aid of his council the governor issued laws ruling the lives of the colonists. These laws were strict but not severe by the standards of the time. Only seven crimes, including witchcraft, were punishable by death. In England, on the other hand, hundreds of petty crimes could send a man to the gallows. In the entire history of Plymouth Colony only two men were hanged for their crimes. Lesser offenders usually had to pay fines. Sometimes, however, judges sentenced an offender to the stocks in order to make a public example of him. He would have to sit or stand for hours in the town square—his ankles, his wrists, and sometimes his neck locked in a wooden frame. The stocks were uncomfortable enough, but the stares and jeers of the passersby must have been even harder to bear for some offenders.

## Later Years

As time went on, other English settlements sprang up along the shore of Massachusetts Bay. One, Mount Wollaston, proved a troublesome neighbor. In 1628 its leader, Thomas Morton (?–1647?), renamed the settlement Merry Mount. He gave jolly parties for white men and Indians at which generous amounts of liquor were drunk. The Pilgrims were angered as much by Morton's success at trade with the Indians as by his high living. They sent after him a small group of armed men commanded by Captain Myles Standish. Morton was arrested and sent back to England.

The Pilgrims' most important neighbor was the Puritan colony of Massachusetts Bay, in the area of Boston and Salem. Many Puritans came there from England during the 1630's, and the colony grew rapidly. Thereafter, it overshadowed the colony at Plymouth more and more. Neither King James nor his successors ever fixed the royal seal to Plymouth Colony's charter. As a result, the Pilgrims' right to their land was never clearly established. In 1691, Massachusetts Bay Colony was granted a royal charter that included much of the area it had asked for, including Plymouth. Seventy-two years after the Pilgrims first stepped ashore, the Old Colony, as it had come to be called, was no more.

The Pilgrims proved beyond doubt that ordinary English people could support and govern themselves in the New World. Governor Bradford wrote, ". . . as one small candle may light a thousand, so the light here kindled hath shone unto many, yea, in some sort, to our whole nation."

Today the Pilgrim village has been rebuilt at Plymouth, Massachusetts, under its original name, Plimoth Plantation. In addition to seeing Plymouth Rock, visitors may go aboard *Mayflower II* (a replica of the original ship), and tour the First House, 1627 House, Fort Meetinghouse, Pilgrim Hall, and Burial Hill.

MARY LEE SETTLE
Author, *O Beulah Land*

See also COLONIAL LIFE IN AMERICA; MAYFLOWER; REFORMATION; THANKSGIVING DAY; THIRTEEN AMERICAN COLONIES.

**PNEUMATIC DEVICES.** See HYDRAULIC AND PNEUMATIC SYSTEMS.

**PNEUMONIA.** See DISEASES.

**POCAHONTAS.** See INDIANS, AMERICAN (Profiles); SMITH, JOHN.

## POE, EDGAR ALLAN (1809–1849)

Edgar Allan Poe, who became one of America's most famous poets and short-story writers, was born in Boston, Massachusetts, on January 19, 1809. His parents were actors. Edgar's father deserted his family, and his mother died in 1811. John and Frances Allan of Richmond, Virginia, took Edgar into their home.

Edgar received his early schooling in Richmond. In 1815 he went to England with the Allans and attended boarding schools there before returning to Richmond in 1820. In 1826 he entered the University of Virginia. He w's an honors student, but gambling debts forced him to drop out in less than a year.

Penniless, Poe enlisted in the army. He was discharged in 1829 so that he could enter West Point Military Academy. His first volume of poetry, *Tamerlane and Other Poems*, had been published in 1827. Two years later, *Al Aaraaf, Tamerlane, and Minor Poems* was issued. Unable to persuade John Allan to agree to his resignation from West Point so that he could pursue a literary career, Poe deliberately neglected his duties and was dismissed in 1831.

Poe married his cousin, Virginia Clemm, in 1836. He worked as an editor and critic for the *Southern Literary Messenger* in Richmond, and increased the magazine's circulation from 500 to 3,500. He later worked for magazines in Philadelphia and New York City.

Poe's contribution to the development of the modern short story was significant. His tales are filled with strange events, but Poe insisted that they were expressions of reality. He believed that a story should work toward a single effect. Among his best-known stories are *The Fall of the House of Usher*, *The Gold Bug*, *The Masque of the Red Death*, and *The Black Cat*. In *The Purloined Letter* and *Murders in the Rue Morgue*, Poe invented the detective story. The character of the brilliant Auguste Dupin, who solved mysteries by his intellectual genius, was a model for later fictional detectives.

Poe's last volume of poetry, *The Raven and Other Poems*, appeared in 1845. He continued to write, but in 1847 his wife's death from tuberculosis was a severe blow. The cause of his own death, on October 7, 1849, is unknown.

Reviewed by ERWIN HESTER
East Carolina University

---

In "Eldorado," Poe is saying that hope and something to strive for prevent despair.

### ELDORADO

Gayly bedight,
A gallant knight,
In sunshine and in shadow,
Had journeyed long,
Singing a song,
In search of Eldorado.

But he grew old,
This knight so bold,
And o'er his heart a shadow
Fell as he found
No spot of ground
That looked like Eldorado.

And, as his strength
Failed him at length,
He met a pilgrim shadow:
"Shadow," said he,
"Where can it be,
This land of Eldorado?"

"Over the Mountains
Of the Moon,
Down the Valley of the Shadow,
Ride, boldly ride,"
The shade replied,
"If you seek for Eldorado!"

*I wandered lonely as a cloud*
*That floats on high o'er vales and hills,*
*When all at once I saw a crowd,*
*A host, of golden daffodils;*
*Beside the lake, beneath the trees,*
*Fluttering and dancing in the breeze.*

William Wordsworth

## POETRY

Poetry is difficult to define. The children's poet David McCord once said poetry was "deeply felt, deeply moving language, written or spoken in a special form." That definition will serve us well. However, it is more helpful to understand what poetry does.

Rather than try to define poetry, many poets have offered their opinions of what poetry should be and how it should affect the reader. The British poet A. E. Housman recited poetry while he was shaving, and if he was so taken by the words that he stopped shaving, he felt he had found a real poem. American poet Emily Dickinson offered one of the most famous tests of a poem: "If I read a book and it makes my whole body so cold no fire ever can warm me, I know that is poetry. If I feel physically as if the top of my head were taken off, I know that is poetry." Perhaps the Welsh poet Dylan Thomas offered the best advice when he wrote: "If you want a definition of poetry, say, 'Poetry is what makes me laugh or cry or yawn, what makes my toenails twinkle, what makes me want to do this or that or nothing,' and let it go at that."

Poetry helps us stop in the midst of a busy day and notice the things around us—a flower, sunlight on autumn leaves, the sound of gently flowing water, or even the pattern of broken windows in an abandoned warehouse. Poetry also helps us discover our feelings about these and many other things.

Noticing things around us or the feelings inside us does not make a poem. That takes a lot of work. But noticing is often the first step in creating a poem. The poet will often record his or her observations in a journal or notebook. Then, slowly and thoughtfully, the poet will begin to craft a poem. The poetic process is often long and difficult, but the rewards can be very satisfying.

### ▶ A UNIQUE LITERARY FORM

The most obvious difference between poetry and other forms of literature is the way it appears on the page. As you look at this article, you can see how the lines of print run from one edge of the column to the other. New paragraphs are indented, but each column is practically a solid block of words. Poetry, on the other hand, is written in lines that can be of various lengths. In fact, some poems may have only a word or two in each line.

The poet chooses the best words to write his or her poem. As a result, the language of the poem is compact and economical. It is also rich—laced with comparisons and details that make a scene or a feeling come alive for the reader.

### ▶ ELEMENTS OF POETRY

Just as a painter uses paints, brushes, and canvas to create a picture, a poet has tools for writing a poem. Among these tools are sound, rhythm and meter, and figurative language.

Emily Dickinson

### Sound

Sound is very important in poetry. Because poetry is meant to be read aloud, the poet frequently chooses words for the way they sound. There are several devices poets use to achieve just the right sound for their poems.

**Alliteration, Assonance, and Onomatopoeia.** Alliteration is the repetition of the same first letter or sound in a group of words, such as in *P*eter *P*an or *t*erribly *t*ired. Assonance is the repetition of the vowel sounds within words, such as in h*i*gh f*i*ve. Onomatopoeia refers to words that sound like what they describe, such as "roar" or "buzz."

**Rhyme.** Rhyme is the device most often associated with poetry. It is the repetition of sounds at the end of words, usually at the ends of lines. For example, in the opening stanza (a group of lines of poetry, usually similar in length and pattern) of "Paul Revere's Ride" by American poet Henry Wadsworth Longfellow, notice how the first two lines and the fifth line end with the same sound:

Listen, my children, and you shall hear
Of the midnight ride of Paul Revere,
On the eighteenth of April, in Seventy-five
Hardly a man is now alive
Who remembers that famous day and year.

Of course, not all poems are written in five-line stanzas with rhymes like those Longfellow used. In fact, there are many ways that rhyme can be used in a poem. If you read a rhyming poem carefully, you will be able to hear which end-words rhyme, or in other words, its rhyme scheme. To indicate the rhyme scheme of a poem or stanza, a series of lowercase letters is used. For example, the rhyme scheme of the Longfellow stanza you just read is *aabba* because lines one, two, and five have the same end sound. Lines three and four rhyme, but their sound is different from the other rhyming lines. (Note that the letters merely show which lines end with rhymes. The letters do not indicate the sound of these rhymes.)

Not all poetry rhymes, however. In fact, much poetry written after 1900 has no rhyme scheme at all. Such non-rhyming poetry is called **free verse** because it is free of the rhyme and steady rhythm of earlier poetry. Emily Dickinson and Walt Whitman were among the first American poets to use free verse.

### Rhythm and Meter

Rhythm is one of the most distinctive features in rhyming poems. The rhythmic sound pattern in lines of poetry is made up of units called **feet**. The feet are determined by the stressed and unstressed syllables in a word or

William Shakespeare

feet), hexameter (six feet), heptameter (seven feet), and octameter (eight feet).

Regardless of what kinds of lines a poet writes, he or she can combine them into stanzas. The stanza from Longfellow's "Paul Revere's Ride" has five lines in it, but a stanza can have as few or as many lines as the poet wishes. Some common stanza lengths are the couplet (two lines), tercet (three lines), quatrain (four lines), quintet (five lines), sestet (six lines), septet (seven lines), and the octave (eight lines).

### Figurative Language

Figurative language is another tool used by good poets, and it provides greater meaning to the words by creating images in the reader's mind. Three types of figurative language commonly used in poetry are metaphor, simile, and personification. All three are comparisons, but each has something unique about it.

**Metaphor.** A metaphor is a direct comparison of dissimilar things in a way that shows some sort of equality between them. In Shakespeare's *Romeo and Juliet*, for example, Romeo uses a metaphor when he sees Juliet on her balcony and compares her to the sun:

phrase. Stressed syllables, indicated with an accent mark (´), have more emphasis on them when spoken or read than do unstressed syllables, which are indicated with a symbol called a breve (˘). For example, in the word "pattern," the first syllable is stressed and the second is unstressed (páttĕrn).

Each foot has a name, depending on how many syllables it contains and where the stress falls in that foot. Here are the four basic kinds of feet in poetry:

| Name | Syllables/Stresses | Example |
|------|--------------------|---------|
| iamb | ˘ ´ | ŭntíl, prĕpáre |
| trochee | ´ ˘ | súmmĕr, fíre |
| anapest | ˘ ˘ ´ | rĕĭmbúrse, sŭpĕrséde |
| dactyl | ´ ˘ ˘ | íntrŏvĕrt, házărdŏus |

The number of feet in a line determines its **meter**, which is the measurement, or description, of its rhythm pattern. For example, if a line has five feet of any kind in it, that line is called pentameter. If those five feet are iambs, the line is called iambic pentameter, the type of line frequently found in Shakespeare's verse. The other kinds of lines are the monometer (one foot), dimeter (two feet), trimeter (three feet), tetrameter (four feet), hexameter (six feet), heptameter (seven feet), and octameter (eight feet).

But soft! What light through yonder window
  breaks?
It is the east, and Juliet is the sun!

**Simile.** A simile is a comparison that uses the words "like" or "as." For example, note the simile in this line from a poem by Scottish poet Robert Burns: "O, my luve is like a red, red rose." And English poet William Wordsworth used a simile when he wrote: "I wandered lonely as a cloud."

**Personification.** Personification is a comparison that gives human qualities to objects, animals, or ideas. Note the personification in this line by Philip Sidney: "With how sad steps, O Moon, thou climb'st the skies."

Pablo Neruda

### ▶ KINDS OF POETRY

Many kinds of poetry have emerged throughout history, from the spiritual poems of early humans to the sonnets of William Shakespeare and the free verse of America in the 1900's. Each type of poetry arose in a time and place when poets felt an urge to create a new form for saying the things they needed to say.

### Lyric Poems

Most poems are lyric poems. They express a poet's observations, feelings, and personal experiences. Three kinds of lyric poems are odes, sonnets, and elegies.

**Odes.** An ode is a poem that celebrates or praises a subject using stately or noble language. The Greeks are often given credit for inventing the ode and, in fact, the word "ode" comes from the Greek word meaning "to sing." Classic odes followed a specific form and were written about subjects such as solitude or a decorative urn. You can get an idea of what a classic ode sounds like in this opening stanza from "Ode to the West Wind," by English poet Percy Bysshe Shelley:

> O, wild West Wind, thou breath of Autumn's being,
> Thou, from whose unseen presence the leaves dead
> Are driven, like ghosts from an enchanter fleeing.

Modern poets have written odes in more everyday language to more everyday subjects. For instance, Chile's Pablo Neruda wrote odes to his socks, his suit, and even a tomato.

**Sonnets.** The sonnet first appeared in Italian poetry early in the 1200's. Since then, it has been a favorite form of many poets, from Dante and William Shakespeare to such modern American poets as Robert Frost and Edna St. Vincent Millay. The sonnet is a 14-line poem written in iambic pentameter and normally divided into two sections: an octave (the first eight lines) and a sestet (the last six lines). A sonnet generally follows one of two rhyme schemes: *abba cddc efgefg* for an Italian sonnet, or *abab cdcd efef gg* for a Shakespearean sonnet. The poet will frequently present a situation in the octave of the poem, then meditate on the situation or write a response to it in the sestet.

Here is Shakespeare's famous Sonnet 18, in which he states that the person to whom the poem is addressed will live forever in its lines:

> Shall I compare thee to a summer's day?
> Thou art more lovely and more temperate:
> Rough winds do not shake the darling buds of May,
> And summer's lease hath all too short a date:
> Sometime too hot the eye of heaven shines
> And often is his gold complexion dimmed;
> And every fair from fair sometime declines,
> By chance or nature's changing course untrimmed;
> But thy eternal summer shall not fade,
> Nor lose possession of that fair thou ow'st;
> Nor shall Death brag thou wand'rest in his shade,
> When in eternal lines to time thou grow'st:
>   So long as men can breathe or eyes can see,
>   So long lives this, and this gives life to thee.

**Elegies.** Originally, an elegy was a poem that mourned the death of a friend or a public figure. But over time the elegy has come to be a poem about the loss of anything, including a person, a way of life, or even a building. In "Elegy Written in a Country Churchyard," written in 1750, the British poet Thomas Gray ponders the notion of death itself. Walt Whitman wrote "When Lilacs Last in the Dooryard Bloom'd" shortly after the end of the Civil War (1865). It is a free verse poem that mourns the death of Abraham Lincoln. Here are the first two stanzas:

When lilacs last in the dooryard bloom'd
And the great star early droop'd in the western
  sky in the night,
I mourn'd, and yet shall mourn with ever-
  returning spring.

Ever-returning spring, trinity sure to me you
  bring,
Lilac blooming perennial and drooping star in
  the west,
And thought of him I loved.

## Narrative Poems

Although most poems are lyric, the narrative, or story, poem is another kind of poetry that is also quite popular. Two types of narrative poems are the ballad and the epic.

**Ballads.** The ballad had its origin in the oral traditions of wandering minstrels who sang songs of daring deeds, love, and death long before the songs were written down and collected. Ballads are usually written in quatrains, with lines of three or four iambic feet, and with a rhyme scheme of *abac*. Sometimes the final line is repeated, making a five-line stanza. The ballad has a strong story and may close with a summary stanza. In many countries, the ballad was one of the first forms of literature. The United States has a rich heritage of ballads. One of the most popular American ballads is "John Henry." Here is the opening stanza:

John Henry was a little baby,
Sitting on his mama's knee,
Said, "The Big Bend Tunnel on the C & O Road
Is gonna be the death of me,
Yeah, gonna be the death of me."

Other popular ballads include "The Shooting of Dan Mc-Grew" (1907) by Canadian poet Robert W. Service and "Gunga Din" (1890) by British poet Rudyard Kipling.

Homer

**Epics.** The epic is a very long story poem usually about the adventures of a hero. Ancient epics were originally oral poems that were passed on from one generation to another. Some historians see the epic as an extension of the ode form. The epic is usually written in a series of books, or cantos. Many early epics were written in dactylic hexameter. The hero of an epic is often descended from a god and must perform many superhuman feats over the course of the tale. The adventures and virtues of an epic hero were often meant to inspire the audience. Among the most important epic poems are the *Aeneid* (29 B.C.?–19 B.C.) by the Roman poet Vergil, the *Iliad* and the *Odyssey* (both in the 700's B.C.) by the Greek poet Homer, and *Paradise Lost* (1667) by the English poet John Milton.

## Light Verse

Light verse is humorous, witty poetry that usually rhymes and has a bouncy rhythm. A popular form of light verse is the **limerick**. A limerick is made up of five lines, with lines 3 and 4 shorter than the others. Lines 1, 2, and 5 contain three iambic feet, or three stressed syllables, while the short lines have only two stressed syllables. The rhyme scheme of a limerick is *aabba*. Although it is unclear if British writer Edward Lear really invented the limerick, he was certainly responsible for its lasting popularity (he was even called the "Poet Laureate of the Limerick"). Here is one of Lear's limericks:

There was an Old Lady whose folly
Induced her to sit in a holly;
Whereupon, by a thorn
Her dress being torn,
She quickly became melancholy.

## How to Write Poetry

Writing a good poem takes hard work and practice. These suggestions will help you get started.

### Before You Begin

- Keep a journal in which you regularly write about what you see, hear, and feel.
- Read all kinds of poetry, especially the kind you would like to write.
- Collect words: Keep a place in your journal for words you come across that have an appealing sound or interesting meaning.

### Getting Started

- Choose a poem that you like—rhyming or free verse—and use it as a model for your poem. Do not worry about imitating other writers' styles; as you write more, you will develop your own.
- If you choose to try a poem on your own, you might start with a free verse poem so you can focus on what you want to say without the distraction of trying to create rhyme and regular rhythm.
- Use material from your journal—your thoughts and feelings—for your poem. Always write about what is important to you.

### Writing and Revising Your Poem

- Try to create images that will help the reader experience what you experienced. One way to do that is to include details that appeal to the senses: sight, sound, smell, taste, and touch.
- Make your poem come alive by using vivid and original metaphors and similes.
- Always look for the right word for each line of your poem. A thesaurus might help.
- Spend time revising your poem. The first draft will not be the best poem you can write. Ask a friend to read your poem and tell you what he or she thinks of it.
- Read your poem aloud as you work on it. The sound of poetry is a very important part of a successful poem.

▶ **THE DEVELOPMENT OF POETRY**

No one is sure exactly when or how poetry began. However, over the years, scholars and researchers have uncovered evidence of its origins.

Poetry probably began long before humans recorded history. Primitive people danced before they had the language to sing, but perhaps they punctuated their dances with grunts and cries. Over time, such dances, which often readied men for the hunt or the battle, became more elaborate. Gradually, language became a more important part of the dance, and a leader of the dance emerged: a poet, or bard.

Ancient peoples all had some type of early poetry. This poetry took many forms, and much of it was connected to religious ceremonies. Many Egyptian poems were chants that sang the praises of heroes and gods. Magic charms were also a very early form of poetry. Many of these ancient poems were meant to be sung—some were worksongs and lullabies. Because of this, they often contain a refrain or phrase that is repeated throughout the poem.

Some scholars consider parts of the Old Testament, the oldest section of the Bible, to be the most important examples of poetry from the ancient world. Other notable poetic works from this time include the Sumerian *Epic of Gilgamesh* (2000? B.C.) and Homer's the *Iliad* and the *Odyssey*.

As the centuries passed, poetry spread around the globe and many cultures produced their own poetic masterpieces. India gave us the sacred Hindu texts called the *Upanishads* (1500–500 B.C.) and the *Bhagavad Gita* (100's B.C.). Epic poems came from Rome (Ovid's *The Metamorphoses*, A.D. 8), the Anglo-Saxons (*Beowulf*, 700?), and France (*The Song of Roland*, 1100).

In addition to specific poems, cultures have produced their own unique poetic forms. From Japan comes the *haiku* and the *tanka*. Korea produced the *hyannga*. From Afghanistan we received the *ghazal*, and the *villanelle* came from France. Native Americans gave us many chants, and African Americans gave us the blues poem.

Poetry has truly become a world art, spanning borders and centuries. Poetry books are being published like never before. Public readings in book stores, coffeehouses, and libraries are thriving. Children are writing poetry in class and on their own. These readers and writers of poetry have discovered the riches that poetry holds for them.

PAUL B. JANECZKO
Poet and Anthologist

See also FIGURES OF SPEECH; NONSENSE RHYMES; NURSERY RHYMES; ODES.

# POISONS

Poisons are substances that can cause injury, illness, or death when they contact or enter the human body. Depending on the poison, this can happen if the poison is swallowed, inhaled, injected into or under the skin, or splashed on the skin or eyes. Some poisons cause damage only to the body area they touch. Others can enter the bloodstream, then cause harm to the nervous system (including the brain), heart, kidneys, or other body organs.

About half of all poisonings involve children under the age of 6. Such children cannot read labels. They cannot tell the difference between pills and candy, or between something good to drink and household cleaning items. Because young children learn by imitation, they will try to take medicine if they see someone else taking it. Older children are sometimes poisoned by taking the wrong medicine or by mixing cleaning products that make a poisonous gas.

High-school students and adults may be exposed to poisons at work. Or they may abuse drugs, take the wrong medicine, ignore labels on cleaning products, or attempt suicide with medicines or chemicals. Older people who take a variety of medicines may mix them up or take the wrong dosages. Most deaths from poisoning are among teenagers and adults who abuse drugs or commit suicide with drugs or chemicals.

▶ TYPES OF POISONS

More than 90 percent of poison exposures happen in the home. Some of the most dangerous poisons are described below.

**Caustic Products.** Many household products, including drain openers, oven cleaners, rust removers, and toilet-bowl cleaners, contain strong chemicals such as lye or concentrated acids. Known as caustic products, they cause burns as soon as they come in contact with the skin or eyes.

**Hydrocarbons.** Among the many hydrocarbons used in the home are furniture polish, lamp oil, baby oil, kerosene, gasoline, motor oil, turpentine, lighter fluid, and paint thinner. Hydrocarbons are usually oily liquids. When swallowed, they can easily go down the wrong way into the lungs. There they can cause pneumonia, a serious and sometimes fatal lung infection. Many hydrocarbons, including butane and certain products in spray cans, cause sudden death if they are inhaled deliberately.

**Pesticides.** Products used to kill mold and mildew; insects; rats, mice, and other pests; and weeds are called pesticides. Many pesticides are harmful if swallowed. Others can be harmful if they are inhaled or contact the skin. Depending on the type of product, pesticides can harm the lungs or nervous system. Others can cause bleeding because they prevent the blood from clotting.

**Antifreeze.** Used in car and boat engines, antifreeze is usually a chemical called ethylene glycol. When swallowed, it can damage the kidneys and nervous system.

**Windshield Washer Solution.** Used to clean windshields, windshield washer solution is usually a chemical called methanol or methyl alcohol. When swallowed, it can cause permanent blindness and damage to the nervous system.

**Carbon Monoxide.** A colorless, odorless, tasteless gas, carbon monoxide is formed when car, truck, boat, or lawn mower engines are running. It is also formed when wood,

## FIRST AID FOR POISONING

If someone may have been poisoned, the following simple steps can be life saving:
- If the victim is unconscious, not breathing, or having seizures, call 911 or the local emergency ambulance number immediately.
- For a poison on the skin or in the eyes, rinse the area with plenty of running water for 15 to 20 minutes. Then call the poison center at 1-800-222-1222 for further advice.
- For a poison that has been inhaled, get the victim to fresh air. If the person is not breathing, perform artificial respiration if trained to do so. Then telephone the poison center.
- If a household product or chemical was swallowed, give the victim about half a glass of water or milk. Then call the poison center.
- If a medicine was swallowed, call the poison center immediately.
- If the poison was injected—for example, a drug injection or a snake or spider bite—telephone the poison center at once.

coal, kerosene, gasoline, or other materials burn. If carbon monoxide is inhaled into the lungs, it prevents cells in the bloodstream from carrying oxygen to body organs. Victims first experience headache and nausea. They can have seizures, go into a coma, and die quickly.

**Lead.** Until about 1970, lead was commonly used in household paint and water pipes, and so it is often found in older homes. Lead is especially dangerous to young children because it damages their developing nervous systems. It can cause brain and hearing damage, stomach problems, and behavior problems. Young children who live in old homes can be poisoned if they eat paint chips, chew on windowsills, play in areas where lead particles are present in dust, or even drink the water. Local health departments can help families learn if there is lead in or around their homes.

**Medicines.** Despite the beneficial effects of medicines, many drugs can be dangerous when taken the wrong way or by a person for whom they were not intended. This is especially true if young children take medicine that has not been prescribed for them or take too much. Because of their small body size and developing body organs, children cannot process medicines the way adults can.

## ▶ POISON PREVENTION

Young children are especially at risk of poisoning because it is normal for them to explore their surroundings. Youngsters imitate adults, and they also tend to put everything they can reach into their mouths. To prevent poisonings in young children, the following steps should be taken:

- Medicine and household products should be stored in child-resistant packaging. Products that can be especially dangerous to children are required by law to have special packaging. Such packaging must be used at all times.
- Medicines and household products should be kept where children cannot see or reach them.
- Adults should not take medicine in the presence of children.

Other poison prevention steps apply to everyone:

- Follow the directions and guidelines regarding prescription and over-the-counter drugs.
- Store household products in their original containers and retain the original packaging labels.
- Use the proper cleaning product, paint, or pesticide for a particular job and do not mix different products.
- Store poisons in a special place, away from food and medicines.

## ▶ POISON CENTERS

Very few poisons have specific antidotes, or drugs that directly reverse the cause of symptoms. However, with correct treatment, most victims of poisoning will survive. Poison centers are the best source of information about preventing and treating all kinds of poisoning. Such poison centers are located throughout the United States and provide help to the public, 24 hours a day, seven days a week. Poison centers also distribute information on poison prevention and teach health care professionals how to recognize and treat poisonings.

You can contact the poison center nearest you by telephoning 1-800-222-1222. Specially trained nurses, pharmacists, and doctors answer the telephones at poison centers. The experts will ask some questions about the victim and the poison involved in the incident. For example, they will inquire when the possible poisoning happened, if the victim is showing any symptoms, and if he or she has any medical problems. The caller should be ready to provide the product's brand name and the amount involved.

The expert at the poison center will give the caller treatment advice immediately. Most of the time, the required treatment can be carried out on the spot, and the poison center will call back to check on the victim's condition. If the victim needs emergency medical care, the poison center will call for an ambulance, give advice to the ambulance personnel, and call the hospital emergency room.

ROSE ANN G. SOLOWAY
Associate Director, External Affairs
and Member Services
American Association of Poison Control Centers

See also FIRST AID.

**POITIER, SIDNEY.** See MOTION PICTURES (Profiles: Movie Stars).

# POLAND

The nation of Poland takes its name from the Slavic word *pole*, meaning "field." The name is fitting, for Poland covers part of a vast plain that extends across much of east central Europe. Poland lies between Germany in the west, the Czech Republic and Slovakia in the south, and Russia, Lithuania, Belarus, and Ukraine in the east. This location and a lack of natural barriers has greatly affected Polish history.

Poland was once one of the largest kingdoms in Europe. In later centuries, however, it was often conquered and occupied by other countries. Between the late 1700's and early 1900's, Poland disappeared from the map of Europe, its territory having been partitioned (divided) among its neighbors.

During this period, patriotism held the people of Poland together. Poland regained its independence in 1918, at the end of World War I. But it was invaded by German armies in 1939, at the outbreak of World War II. Much of Poland was destroyed during the fighting, and after the war's end in 1945, the Poles had to rebuild their country from ruins.

A Communist government was established in Poland following World War II, under the direction of the Soviet Union, backed by Soviet troops. The Communists held all power until 1989, when Poles, after the first free and open elections in more than fifty years, formed a government of their own choosing.

## ▶ THE PEOPLE

After World War II, Poland lost a large part of its eastern territory, which had an ethnically mixed population, to the Soviet Union. In return, Poland received part of defeated Germany. Poles, mostly from the eastern region of Poland taken over by the Soviet Union, settled in these former German lands, known as the Western Territories. The Germans, who were expelled from the region, were resettled in present-day Germany. Almost all of the population of Poland is now Polish.

**Language.** Polish is a Slavic (or Slavonic) language. It belongs to the Western Slavic group, which also includes Czech and Slovak. Polish is written in the Latin alphabet, which was introduced into Poland in the 900's and

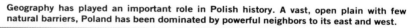

Geography has played an important role in Polish history. A vast, open plain with few natural barriers, Poland has been dominated by powerful neighbors to its east and west.

1000's by Christian missionaries from Western Europe.

**Education.** Polish children usually attend nursery school and kindergarten before beginning primary school at the age of 7. Eight years of primary education are compulsory, after which students may attend from two to four years of vocational school or general secondary school (high school). Secondary school graduates may go to a polytechnical (engineering) school or a university. Agricultural students spend some time working on farms. Industrial students work part-time in factories.

Most of Poland's colleges and universities are located in the large cities. The oldest, the Jagiellonian University in Cracow, was founded in 1364. All universities are state-controlled, except for the Catholic University in Lublin, which is operated by the Roman Catholic Church.

**Religion.** The great majority of the Polish people are Roman Catholic. Most Poles historically have associated their religious faith with their national identity. During the years of Communist rule, they strongly resisted any attempts by the government to discourage religious observance.

Poland's most famous religious shrine is at the monastery of Jasna Góra in Częstochowa. It is the site of the Black Madonna, an ancient painting of the Virgin Mary. The shrine celebrates an event in 1655, when the Virgin Mary is said to have appeared in the sky above the monastery, where monks and Polish soldiers withstood a siege by a powerful Swedish army. Each year in May hundreds of thousands of Polish Catholics make a pilgrimage to Jasna Góra.

The first Polish-born pope, John Paul II (the former Karol Cardinal Wojtyla), was elected in 1978. An article on Pope John Paul II appears in Volume J-K.

A small number of Poles belong to the Eastern Orthodox and Protestant churches. Only a few Jews remain of the more than 3 million who lived in Poland before World War II. Most Polish Jews were killed by the Germans during the war. Many of the remainder have emigrated to Israel and the United States.

▶ **THE LAND**

Most of Poland consists of a low, rolling plain dotted with many small lakes and forests. The land rises toward the south, reaching its greatest height in the Carpathian Mountains, along the border with Slovakia. The highest part of the Carpathian range is the Tatra Mountains. In the north, Poland borders on the Baltic Sea.

**Lakes and Forests.** The Masurian region in the northeast is an area of countless lakes and majestic forests. It is especially popular with tourists, who come here to enjoy water sports, hunting, and fishing. The Bialowieza Forest in eastern Poland is the site of a national park, where large herds of bison live in their natural state.

**Rivers.** Poland's longest river, the Vistula, flows north from its source in the Carpathians,

Poles long have linked their Roman Catholic faith with their nation's identity. John Paul II (*left*), the first Polish-born pope, received wide acclaim on his visits to Poland. The Black Madonna (*right*) is Poland's most venerated religious symbol.

past Cracow and Warsaw, Poland's capital, to Gdańsk on the Baltic Sea. West of the Vistula are the Oder and Neisse rivers, which mark Poland's border with Germany. In the east are the San and Bug rivers, both tributaries of the Vistula. The Bug forms part of the border with Belarus and Ukraine.

**Climate.** Winters in Poland are cold and frequently snowy. Summers are cool. The average January temperature near the German border is about 30°F (−1°C). In the east it is colder. The average annual precipitation (rain and snow) is 24 inches (600 millimeters).

**Natural Resources.** Poland has a variety of natural resources, including coal, copper, salt, lead, zinc, sulphur, and natural gas, as well as fertile soil. Its large deposits of coal have made Poland one of the world's leading producers of this fuel. The coal deposits are largely in western Poland, near the German-Polish border. The rich black soil of the Lublin plateau makes this one of Poland's most important agricultural regions.

▶ **THE ECONOMY**

**Agriculture.** Before World War II, Poland's economy was predominantly agricultural. Today less than one third of the work force is engaged in agriculture. Most Polish farms are small, 12.4 acres (5 hectares) or less in size.

POLAND

---

## FACTS AND FIGURES

**POLISH REPUBLIC** (Rzeczpospolita Polska) is the official name of the country.

**THE PEOPLE** are known as Poles.

**LOCATION:** East central Europe.

**AREA:** 120,725 sq mi (312,677 km²).

**POPULATION:** 38,000,000 (estimate).

**CAPITAL AND LARGEST CITY:** Warsaw.

**MAJOR LANGUAGE:** Polish.

**MAJOR RELIGION:** Roman Catholic.

**GOVERNMENT:** Republic. **Head of state**—president. **Head of government**—prime minister. **Legislature**—National Assembly (consisting of the Senate and the Sejm).

**CHIEF PRODUCTS: Agricultural**—rye, potatoes, wheat, sugar beets, oats, barley, livestock. **Manufactured**—iron and steel and other metal products, engineering equipment and machinery, chemicals, processed foods, textiles, ships, electrical and electronic appliances, transportation equipment, plastics, wood pulp, paper and paper products, leather goods, fertilizers. **Mineral**—coal, copper, salt, lead, zinc, sulphur, natural gas.

**MONETARY UNIT:** Zloty (1 zloty = 100 groszy).

**NATIONAL ANTHEM:** *Jeszcze Polska nie zginela* ("Poland is not yet lost").

---

The principal crops are rye, potatoes, wheat, sugar beets, oats, and barley. The raising of livestock, including pigs, sheep, and cattle, represents an important part of Polish agriculture. Meat products, particularly hams and sausages, are a leading export.

**Industry.** Industry is now the most important sector of the Polish economy. The chief industries involve the production of iron and steel and other metal products, engineering equipment and machinery, chemicals, processed foods, and textiles. Poland is also an important shipbuilding country, with shipyards located at Gdańsk and other port cities on the Baltic Sea.

Other manufactures include electrical and electronic appliances, transportation equipment, plastics, wood pulp, paper and paper products, leather goods, and fertilizers.

The mining industry is also of importance. Because Poland has almost no petroleum, it relies on coal and imported petroleum for most of its energy needs. Coal and other minerals, such as copper and sulfur, also are exported.

**Trade.** Before its breakup, the Soviet Union had been Poland's chief supplier of raw materials, including iron ore, cotton, and petroleum. For many years, Poland traded largely with the Soviet Union and other Communist nations of Eastern Europe. However, after Polish workers rioted in the 1970's over living conditions and high food prices, the government began to change its trade patterns. Grain was imported, and machinery was purchased from Western European countries and the United States in order to produce high-quality manufactured goods for export beyond the Soviet bloc. As a result, Poland's foreign debt grew enormously, and further imports were severely restricted. The government's economic policies led to shortages of consumer goods and higher prices, which brought about further worker protests in 1980. These protests eventually brought about the downfall of the old Communist regime in 1989.

Cracow, once the capital of the Polish kings, is an important cultural center. The Castle of Wawel, built between the 900's and 1300's, was the royal palace. Each day at noon from one of the towers of the church of the Virgin Mary, a trumpeter plays a tune that breaks off in the middle. This custom dates from the 1200's, when Cracow was threatened with an invasion by Tatar armies from the east. The guard in the tower had the task of warning the people of the enemy's approach by playing a certain melody on his trumpet. As the Tatars drew near, the guard began to play the warning notes, but he was killed by a Tatar arrow before he could finish.

Wroclaw (formerly Breslau), in the old German Western Territories, like many other cities that had once been part of Germany, was also largely destroyed during World War II and had to be rebuilt and resettled. In addition, the Poles had to construct new factories and

*Left:* Warsaw is Poland's capital and largest city and an important industrial center. Much of the city had to be rebuilt after the destruction caused by World War II. *Below:* The church of the Virgin Mary overlooks a square in the old city of Cracow. Once the capital of Polish kings, Cracow remains a center of Poland's cultural life.

▶ **CITIES**

Warsaw is the capital and the largest city of Poland and the center of its intellectual life. During World War II, about 75 percent of the city was destroyed. After the war, the Poles completely reconstructed the Old Town of Warsaw based on old plans and maps. Modern offices and apartment houses have been built in much of the rest of the city. See the article on Warsaw in Volume W-X-Y-Z.

shipyards in the Baltic port cities of Gdańsk, Gdynia, and Szczecin.

Other leading cities include Lódź, Poland's second largest city, Poznan, and Katowice.

## ▶ GOVERNMENT

From 1947 to 1989, Poland was a Communist state dominated by the Polish United Workers' Party, a Communist party. A few smaller political parties were allowed to function, but they supported the Communists. Amendments to the constitution in 1989 and 1990 paved the way for a return to representative government. An interim (temporary) constitution went into effect in 1992.

The parliament, or legislature, is the National Assembly, which is elected for four years. It is composed of two houses—the Senate, with 100 members, and the Sejm, with 460 members. The Sejm is the chief lawmaking body. The Senate reviews laws passed by the Sejm. A president, elected for five years, serves as head of state. The president appoints the Council of Ministers, led by a prime minister, who handles the day-to-day operations of the government. The appointment requires approval by the Sejm.

## ▶ HISTORY

**Early History.** Poland's recorded history dates from 966, when Prince Mieszko, leader of the united Polish tribes, was converted to Christianity. Mieszko claimed descent from Piast, the legendary founder of the first dynasty of Polish kings. By the 1000's, the kingdom of Poland had expanded to almost the borders of Poland today.

Over the next few centuries, however, Poland was a fragmented country, divided among petty princes. It was frequently at war with more powerful states and was devastated by invasions of the Tatars, descendants of conquerors from Asia. Casimir III (the Great), the last of the Piast kings, reunited Poland in the 1300's. He encouraged trade and industry, founded the University of Cracow (now the Jagiellonian University), and made Poland a center of learning.

**The Jagiellonian Era.** The marriage of Jadwiga of Poland to Grand Duke Jagiello of Lithuania in 1386 marked the beginning of the Jagiellonian dynasty, which lasted until 1572. Under King Jagiello and his successors, Poland, united with Lithuania, reached its greatest territorial expansion, extending deep into Russia.

The Jagiellonian era was a golden age of prosperity and culture for Poland. One of the famous people of the time was the Pole Nicolaus Copernicus, who is considered the founder of modern astronomy. (An article on Copernicus appears in Volume C.)

**Decline and Partition.** After the Jagiellonian dynasty, the Polish monarchy declined in power, while the Polish nobility became predominant. The nobles elected the kings of Poland, many of whom were foreigners. The last great Polish king was John III Sobieski. He is best remembered for leading the Polish army that in 1683 defeated the Turks at the siege of Vienna, the capital of Austria, thus halting Turkish expansion in Europe.

As rival nobles struggled for power, Poland grew weaker politically and became a prey for the territorial ambitions of its neighbors. Russia, Austria, and Prussia (now part of Germany) partitioned Poland among themselves three times—in 1772, 1793, and 1795. After the last partition Poland virtually ceased to exist as an independent state.

The Poles revolted against foreign rule a number of times. One of the heroes in the struggle for independence was Thaddeus Kościuszko, who had served with George Washington's army during the American Revolution. But after each uprising the Poles were defeated, and for many years the Polish nation existed only in the minds and hearts of its people.

**The Polish Republic.** In 1918, at the end of World War I, the victorious Allied powers, Britain, France, and the United States, restored the Polish state. The 1919 Treaty of Versailles with defeated Germany gave Poland a strip of land at the mouth of the Vistula River, in order to provide the country with access to the Baltic Sea at the port of Danzig (now Gdańsk). Polish territory separated East Prussia from the rest of Germany. Danzig was established as a free city under the supervision of the League of Nations, the forerunner of the United Nations. In 1920, Poland fought a short war with the Soviet Union over disputed territory in the east.

The famous pianist Ignace (Ignacy) Jan Paderewski served briefly as prime minister of Poland. The dominant figure of the time, however, was Marshal Józef Pilsudski, a military hero. Pilsudski became provisional president and commander of the army. He retired in 1922, but in 1926, following a period of instability, he overthrew the government and ruled as a dictator until his death in 1935.

**World War II.** On September 1, 1939, Germany suddenly invaded Poland, setting off World War II. On September 17, the Soviet Union also invaded Poland, occupying its eastern part. When Germany attacked the Soviet Union in 1941, all of Poland fell under German control. During the five years of occupation, some 6 million Poles, half of them Polish Jews, lost their lives. For more information, see the article HOLOCAUST in Volume H.

A Polish underground army rose up against the German troops in the capital, but the uprising was crushed and Warsaw was left in ruins. Soviet troops finally liberated the city in January 1945.

At the Yalta Conference in 1945, the Soviet Union, the United States, and Britain agreed that Poland would have free elections after the war. But only Communists and their allies were later allowed to run for office. Poland's Communist government became allied with the Soviet Union.

**Recent History.** The Polish people often were at odds with their government, and in 1980, led by Lech Walesa, they formed Solidarity, the first free labor union permitted in a Communist country. But when Solidarity leaders in 1981 called for a vote on whether the Communist party should continue to rule Poland, the government declared martial law (rule by the army). This was lifted in 1983, but Solidarity was banned.

Renewed labor unrest in the late 1980's eventually forced the government to compromise. An agreement in 1989 provided for legalized labor unions and democratic political reforms. In elections that followed, Solidarity's candidates won an overwhelming victory. Wojciech Jaruzelski, the former Communist party head, became president, and Tadeusz Mazowiecki, a Solidarity supporter, was named prime minister. In 1990, Lech Walesa was elected president by popular vote. For more information, see the biography of Walesa in Volume WXYZ.

In 1991, centrists won a majority of seats in parliament. But in 1993, the Democratic Left Alliance, the party that included former Communists, gained power, largely because

As head of the trade union organization Solidarity, Lech Walesa (center) led a revolt against Communist rule in Poland. He served as president from 1990 to 1995.

of Poland's difficult transition to a free-market economy. The former Communists solidified their victory in 1995 with the election of Aleksander Kwasniewski as president.

In 1999, Poland became one of three former Soviet-bloc nations to join the North Atlantic Treaty Organization (NATO). Kwasniewski was re-elected in 2000 on a campaign platform that emphasized seeking membership in the European Union (EU). Poland was also one of the few European nations to actively support the United States in the 2003 Iraq War and the postwar peacekeeping efforts. Poland joined the EU in 2004. In 2005, Lech Kaczynski, cofounder of the conservative Law and Justice Party, was elected president.

JAMES CHACE
Former managing editor, *East Europe*
Reviewed by M. K. DZIEWANOWSKI
Author, *Poland in the 20th Century*

**POLAR REGIONS.** See ANTARCTICA; ARCTIC.

# POLICE

Uniformed police officers are a visible part of every community. Popular television programs portray police officers using weapons to prevent crime and protect the public. However, while enforcing the law and protecting people's lives and property are the main responsibilities of police, only about 15 percent of their time is devoted to the kinds of activities shown on television. The remaining 85 percent is devoted to more routine services to the community, which over the years have become police duties. These include responding to emergencies, settling disputes, regulating traffic, taking care of sick and injured people, and responding to complaints. The police are on duty seven days a week, 24 hours a day, to provide these services.

## ▶POLICE IN MODERN SOCIETY

Police responsibilities are divided into three general areas: patrol operations, crime detection, and traffic control.

### Patrol

Uniformed patrol officers are assigned **beats** (areas or routes), which they patrol (survey), alone or with a partner, on foot, in squad cars, on motorcycles, and sometimes on horseback or by boat or helicopter.

Officers on patrol are responsible for preventing crime, apprehending criminals, and maintaining order. They keep alert for suspicious persons or circumstances, and they try to maintain peace on the beat assigned to them. Patrol officers keep in touch with one another and with their headquarters by means of walkie-talkies or two-way car radios. Sometimes they need to call for help to handle an accident, control a large crowd, or settle a family argument. Officers in patrol cars receive directions from headquarters telling them where to go and what to do next.

### Detection

When a community's police department becomes large enough to maintain special units, the first to be formed is usually a detective squad. A detective is a member of the uniformed force who has been selected to work out of uniform (usually in a business suit), and whose special assignment is solving and preventing crimes. These **plainclothes officers** re-

Police gather at their precinct for a daily briefing. The familiar blue uniforms will be a welcome sight to local citizens as the officers head out on their beats.

ceive special training for their jobs. They often work long hours because they must be prepared to devote whatever time is necessary to solve crimes as quickly as possible.

In many detective units in large cities, there are even more specialized units within the detective division to handle certain types of crimes. For example, members of the narcotics squad devote all their time and effort to eliminating drug traffic.

When certain crimes are committed so often that the entire community is concerned, the solution, as in the case of narcotics squads, is for the police to form a specialized detective unit. Many cities have squads trained to deal with such specific types of crime as burglary, robbery, vice (gambling and other activities considered to be "victimless" crimes), fraud, and homicide (murder). Many police departments also have special divisions to deal specifically with juvenile problems. An article on juvenile crime appears in Volume J.

1

2

6

## Traffic Control

In many towns and cities a special unit of uniformed officers is designated to control the flow of traffic, investigate traffic accidents, and issue traffic summonses to those who violate traffic laws.

Drunk driving is a major concern in the United States today. When a person is suspected of driving while intoxicated (under the influence of alcohol), it is the duty of the police to test the suspected driver and, if the driver fails the test or refuses to take it, to place the driver under arrest.

Accident investigation is another function of the traffic unit. Such investigations are particularly important in hit-and-run accidents, in which a driver who has hit another vehicle or even a person does not stop at the scene, as required by law. Skilled police investigators often can determine the color, make, and model of the car that left the scene.

Police officers often use radar guns to measure the speed of moving vehicles. They then relay a description of the speeding auto to another police car by radio so the speeder will be caught. This system is more accurate, and safer, for police officers than high-speed chases. Helicopters are also used to observe traffic conditions and to assist in emergencies.

## Special Forces

Other special units within a large community police department may include a search and rescue team, a bomb squad, a hostage

3

4

5

Uniformed officers protect and assist people (1)—but police personnel provide many other community services as well. They develop ways to prevent crime by sponsoring activities such as the recent program to fingerprint children (2). Police monitor and control traffic (3). They form special highly skilled teams, such as bomb squads, to deal with community emergencies (4). They work to solve crimes in a variety of ways—often working "under cover" (5). And, of course, they pursue and arrest criminals (6).

negotiating team, and a special weapons and tactics (SWAT) team.

Search and rescue teams look for people lost in remote areas. Bomb squads respond to bomb threats. They look for the bomb, and if there really is one they try to defuse it (prevent it from exploding) or to remove it in specially built trucks. Both search teams and bomb squads sometimes use specially trained police dogs, which can find both people and bombs by their acute sense of smell. Dogs can also be trained to "sniff out" drugs.

Hostage negotiating teams handle cases in which criminals hold innocent people captive. The negotiating unit tries to persuade the criminals to release the hostages unharmed. Special weapons units handle especially dangerous situations involving armed criminals. Members of these units are trained to carry out their missions without endangering innocent bystanders.

### Community Relations

Many police departments have special units to promote good relations between the police and the community. Officers assigned to such units have often had special training in psychology and community relations.

These units develop a variety of programs to encourage positive attitudes toward the police. One of the best known is the Police Athletic League (PAL). Open to boys and girls from ages 7 to 21, PAL programs emphasize sports as a way to prevent juvenile crime.

In the United States there are more than 40,000 independently operating national, state, metropolitan, and rural police departments.

### Federal Police Forces

The largest and best-known federal (national) law enforcement agency is the Federal Bureau of Investigation (FBI), which is a part of the U.S. Department of Justice. The FBI's crime laboratory, in Washington, D.C., is one of the most famous in the world. The FBI investigates federal crimes and handles robbery, kidnapping, hijacking, and other cases that may not remain confined to one state. Because FBI agents may operate across state lines, state and local police may call on them for assistance. An article on the FBI appears in Volume F.

Another federal agency within the Department of Justice is the U.S. Marshals Service. U.S. marshals have the same powers to enforce federal laws in their districts as sheriffs have to enforce state laws in their smaller districts.

Some of the many other federal law enforcement agencies include the Bureau of Alcohol, Tobacco, and Firearms; the Secret Service, which is responsible for protecting the president of the United States; the Border Patrol of the Immigration and Naturalization Service, which prevents people from entering the United States illegally; and the U.S. Customs Service, which is responsible for protecting U.S. points of entry against persons who try to bring illegal goods into the country.

### State and Local Police

Most states of the United States have their own police forces with full power to enforce state laws. By custom, state troopers (so called because in the past they were often on horseback) are mainly concerned with highway patrol and traffic regulation. But they may also assist local police in the investigation of major crimes. In some small towns, which may not have their own police force, the state police also serve as the local police department.

County police departments are usually called sheriff's departments. Sheriffs are generally elected to office and have the power to appoint individual officers (or deputies). A sheriff may perform such duties as running the county jail, delivering summonses, patrolling the county, and investigating accidents. The sheriff is usually the highest-ranking police officer in the county.

### Metropolitan Police

A metropolitan, or city, police department is responsible for enforcing state, criminal, and vehicular laws, as well as local laws, within the city. The department may have thousands of officers if the city is a large one, or only one or two if it is a small town. The department head may be known as the chief of police, commissioner, or superintendent and is appointed by the mayor or city manager.

Some large metropolitan police forces have special units to deal separately with housing, parks, transit, and youths.

### ▶CAREERS IN THE POLICE

Police work is an excellent way to serve the community. Police officers work long hours and sometimes face danger, but an officer's job is secure and seldom boring, and there are many opportunities for advancement.

Young men and women interested in careers as police officers should have at least a high school diploma. Some police departments require a college degree as well. Applicants must pass a Civil Service test and a rigorous physical examination.

Those who are accepted as new members of a police force generally attend police training schools, where they learn necessary skills. Many colleges offer degrees in law enforcement and criminal justice that may also lead to a career in the police.

### Police Careers for Civilians

In addition to sworn officers, there are other job opportunities for those who would like to be part of a police department.

**Laboratory Technicians.** Also called forensic scientists, these technicians examine evidence such as illegal drugs, blood, bullets, or guns to try to determine who committed a crime. These scientists may also appear in court as expert witnesses to explain their findings to the jury.

**Photographers.** Police photographers take pictures at accident and crime scenes, as well as pictures of suspects under surveillance (close observation). Often their photographs are used as evidence in court. Sometimes a review of such photographs will disclose evidence overlooked by visual inspection.

**Artists.** Police artists must be able to sketch profiles of suspects from the verbal descriptions of witnesses. These sketches are photocopied and distributed to patrol forces, often leading to the arrest of a suspect.

**Computer Programmers and Analysts.** The use of computers in police work is increasing. Computers are used to store records, compare fingerprints, keep track of the activities of suspects, and for a variety of other uses.

**Radio Dispatchers.** The radio dispatcher is often the citizen's first contact with police. How the dispatcher performs the job can make the difference between life and death, catching a criminal or not, or the success or failure of any police mission.

**Secretaries and Clerks.** Police departments of all sizes must have competent and efficient help with the record keeping that is an essential part of police organization.

▶ **POLICE AROUND THE WORLD**

The International Criminal Police Organization (INTERPOL) was established in 1923. Headquartered in Paris, Interpol keeps current files of information gathered from the police of its more than 125 member nations about criminals involved in international counterfeiting, kidnapping, smuggling, and drug cases. This information is given to any member nation requesting it.

The police systems of individual countries fall roughly into three types. In some countries the central government exercises almost complete control over all levels of the police department. In other countries the central government exercises a limited control only, and in still others the central government has very little control.

In countries where the police are tightly controlled by the central government, the police protect the government rather than the people. The people often fear the police instead of respecting them. The Gestapo in Nazi Germany was an extreme example of a police system tightly controlled by the central government.

The police system of Great Britain is an example of an organization that is partly government controlled. The London Metropolitan Police are under the authority of the Home

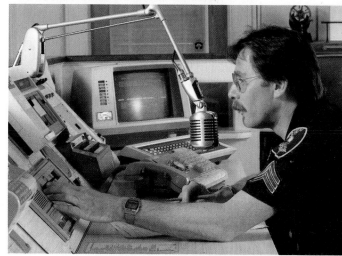

*Top:* Members of special police forces, such as this anti-terrorist squad, receive special training in handling weapons. *Middle:* The police radio dispatcher is often the first officer with whom a citizen comes in contact. *Bottom:* Forensic scientists work in crime labs examining evidence to determine who committed a crime.

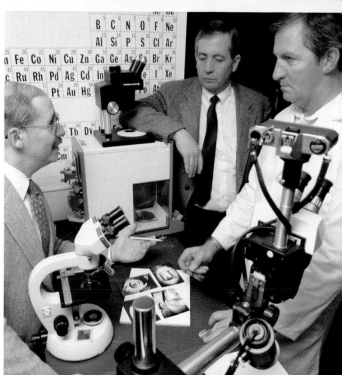

Office, a national government agency. Local police departments outside London are governed by a separate police authority, with the Home Office retaining the right to inspect local departments and make recommendations.

The police system of Canada is an example of an organization, much like that of the United States, that is run largely without central government control. The Royal Canadian Mounted Police is empowered to enforce all national laws, but the "Mounties" assist provincial police departments only at the request of the provinces. Individual provincial departments are not under the direct control of the national government.

In democratic societies people expect the police to help them in time of trouble. In the United States, for example, anyone who is sick, injured, lost, or the victim of a crime should know that the police are there to help.

Citizens in democratic societies also have the right to complain to the government—and to the press—about police abuse of authority, police brutality, and other misconduct.

▶ HISTORY OF POLICE ORGANIZATION

Little is known about the origins of police. Ancient armies had military police to control conquered nations. Imperial Rome, in the 1st century A.D., apparently had some civil police. But no evidence of an organized civil police force appears until many centuries later.

In 1754, Sir Henry Fielding, a well-known London lawyer and writer, and his brother, John Fielding, organized a private system of patrol in London. It was a voluntary system, paid for out of private funds and the money collected from fines. John Fielding believed that, along with men on foot patrol, there should be police officers able to rush to the scene of a crime. This group became known, therefore, as the Bow Street Runners. The Fielding system lasted 50 years, but as London grew, the Runners could no longer control crime.

In 1829, Sir Robert Peel organized the first modern police system. The London Metropolitan Police, with headquarters at Scotland Yard, began with 1,000 men spread over 17 districts. The officers were carefully selected and trained. From Sir Robert Peel's name come the familiar nicknames "bobby" and "peeler" for British police officers.

In the United States in the 19th century, large urban areas such as New York, Boston, and Philadelphia supported separate day and night "watches" (patrols). In 1845, New York combined its dual forces to form a single citywide police force modeled on the London Metropolitan Police. Other cities soon followed New York's lead.

Many of the new police first recruited in New York were Irish, and they refused to wear uniforms that reminded them of the political troubles they had left behind in Ireland. But after ten years, they accepted the idea of blue uniforms with copper buttons. It is said to be from those copper buttons that they got the nickname "coppers," which in modern times has been shortened to "cops."

Early police departments in the United States were often under the control of politicians. Police officers were poorly equipped and usually poorly paid. They often abused their authority. About 1900, commissions of investigation began recommending new procedures for choosing police officers. Gradually Civil Service examinations replaced political appointment as a method of choosing police officers.

Early police forces in the United States were made up only of men. Of the approximately 500,000 police officers in the United States today, about 3 percent are women. They are assigned interchangeably with male officers and perform the entire range of police duties.

▶ POLICING IN THE FUTURE

It is predicted that policing in the future will be much different than it is today. Advances in technology—particularly in computers, television, and communication—will assist the police in solving and preventing crimes. Advances in forensic science should make evidence more reliable and meaningful. All of these changes will be for the better if they help to improve the quality of police service.

LEO C. LOUGHREY
Chairman, Department of Law
and Police Science
John Jay College of Criminal Justice

See also CRIME AND CRIMINOLOGY; FEDERAL BUREAU OF INVESTIGATION; FINGERPRINTING; JUVENILE CRIME; LAW AND LAW ENFORCEMENT; LIE DETECTION.

**POLIO.** See DISEASES.

**POLISHING.** See GRINDING AND POLISHING.

# POLITICAL PARTIES

A political party is a group of voters organized to support certain public policies. The aim of a political party is to elect officials who will try to carry out the party's policies.

A political party offers candidates for public office. It sets out positions on issues that may range from war and taxes to how children should be educated. When people in a democracy disagree about what the government should do, voters express their opinions by voting for the candidates that most closely reflect their views. Political parties provide a way for voters to easily identify a candidate's positions.

Political parties may be large or small, national or local. Large political parties generally have millions of members and supporters. In democratic election campaigns, parties compete freely for votes. Such competition is one of the hallmarks of democracy.

▶ **HOW PARTIES BEGAN**

Political parties as we know them did not begin to develop until the late 1600's. The ancient Greeks, who were pioneers in developing democracy, had no organized political parties in the modern sense. The senate of the ancient Romans had two groups that represented people with different interests—the Patricians and the Plebeians. The Patricians represented noble families. The Plebeians represented the wealthy merchants and the middle class. Although these two groups often mingled, at times they voted as factions, or parties, on particular issues that were important to the groups they represented.

For many centuries after the fall of Rome (A.D. 476), the people of Europe had little voice in politics. Thus there were no true political parties—only factions that supported one noble family or another. Political parties developed as representative assemblies gained power. In England, this change began after what was called the Popish Plot of 1678.

**English Political Parties.** In 1678, a rumor spread through England that Roman Catholics were plotting to kill King Charles II and give the throne to Charles' brother, James, Duke of York (who was a Roman Catholic). There was no real Popish plot, but an alarmed Parliament barred all Roman Catholics from public office and tried to take away

Delegates at national conventions strive to elect public officials who will best carry out the policies of their political party.

the Duke of York's right to inherit the throne. But to King Charles II, Parliament seemed to be challenging royal authority, and he struck back by dissolving Parliament.

All over England people were either for or against the king's act. Those who urged the king to call a new Parliament were called Petitioners. Those who backed the king's deed were called Abhorrers because they abhorred any attempt to control the king's actions. Before long the two factions took on other names. Petitioners were called Whigs. "Whig" was an old term for Scottish Presbyterians who opposed the government. The king's supporters were called Tories. "Tory" was originally a name given to Irish Roman Catholics who had suffered under Protestant rule. These old names took on new meanings.

The basic difference between Whigs and Tories in the 1600's was their view of what

A poster shows the Democratic presidential ticket of 1856. The Democrats won the election, but disagreements over slavery soon divided the party.

government should do and how strong it should be. Tories wanted rule by a strong king. Whigs wanted ordinary people to have more rights and gain more control of their government. In time, as Parliament took greater control, the Whigs and Tories developed into organized parties.

### ▶ POLITICAL PARTIES IN THE UNITED STATES

The leaders of the American Revolution did not like the idea of parties and political battles between parties. Upon his retirement from public life in 1796, George Washington warned Americans against "faction" (parties). James Madison thought parties were probably necessary, although he did not entirely approve of them. Alexander Hamilton thought that faction was a vice to be guarded against at all times. Thomas Jefferson declared in 1789, "If I could not go to heaven but with a party, I would not go there at all."

Nevertheless, the men who held these views founded the first two great American political parties.

**Early U.S. Parties.** Hamilton and other leaders who wanted a strong central government banded together to put over their policies. In 1787 they began calling themselves the Federalists. This was the first United States political party. In 1796, anti-Federalists gathered around Jefferson. Members of Jefferson's group called themselves Democratic-Republicans. Northern businessmen, bankers, and merchants supported the Federalists. They believed in a strong national (or federal) government. Federalists held that capital and industry were the basis of a healthy republic and that the federal government should act to protect the country's infant industries. The Democratic-Republican Party drew its followers from planters, small farmers, and artisans. These people wanted government to leave them alone as much as possible. They wanted to limit the federal government's power and leave the most power in the hands of state and local governments. In foreign affairs the Federalists generally leaned toward England, while the Democratic-Republicans sympathized with Revolutionary France.

Early leaders such as John Adams, who succeeded George Washington as president, had Federalist sympathies. But the Federalists lost control of the government to Jefferson and his party in 1800. The Federalists lingered on as a minority party, especially in New England, for 20 years.

By 1820, American political life was being influenced by sharp differences of opinion between sections of the country. In time, these quarrels led to the Civil War. The slaveholding planters of the South, the frontier farmers of the West, and the manufacturing and banking industries based in the North each wanted the government to follow a different course of action.

In 1828, Andrew Jackson, a Democratic-Republican from Tennessee, was elected president. His party had great support in the South and West. Jackson changed the party's name to Democrats. People who had once been Federalists joined with anti-Jackson Democrats to form the National Republican, or Whig, Party. Between 1836 and 1852, Whigs gave Democrats strong opposition.

By 1854 the issue of slavery overshadowed all political debate. A related issue was states' rights. If a state government was in conflict with the national government, which government had the final authority? Debate over slavery and states' rights tore the parties apart. Northern Abolitionists—people who wanted to abolish slavery—left the Whig party. The Whigs also lost voters to the "Know-Nothing" Party, a new party that violently opposed Roman Catholics and foreigners. The Whig Party began to go to pieces.

At the same time, the issues of slavery and states' rights divided Democrats into Northern and Southern branches. Southern Democrats strongly favored slavery and states' rights. Extremists among them believed that a state had a right to secede (leave the Union) if the national government tried to interfere with slavery.

In 1854 antislavery forces and Free Soil forces (a group founded in Buffalo, New York) formed the Republican Party. The Republicans ran their first presidential candidate, John C. Frémont, in 1856. By 1860 the voters had a choice of four major parties—Northern Democrat, Southern Democrat, Republican, and the Constitutional-Union Party, which drew some ex-Whigs. Strong antislavery feeling helped Republicans capture the presidency for Abraham Lincoln. In 1861 the Southern states seceded and the Civil War began.

**Democrats and Republicans.** The defeat of the Southern Confederacy weakened the Democrats, who were associated in voters' minds with the Southern cause. For many years the Republicans were the major party. They favored business interests and high tariffs (taxes on imports). The Democrats supported free trade. They attracted farmers and the immigrants who poured into the country between the Civil War and the turn of the century.

The two major parties were not so deeply divided again until the 1930's. At that time the Great Depression struck the country. The presidential election of 1932 brought in Franklin D. Roosevelt and his New Deal programs. Roosevelt Democrats thought that the federal government must actively help people who had been hurt by the Depression. Under the New Deal the government passed economic relief measures, social security, laws helping unions, and other bills. Republicans thought the government was taking too much power and moving the country toward a welfare state. They fought against governmental interference with business.

Today both parties agree in general on social security, unemployment insurance, basic foreign policy, and civil rights. The issues on which they disagree often are not goals so much as means: how best to keep the economy growing, protect the environment, and maintain a strong national defense. In general, Republicans tend to oppose government programs as solutions to national problems. Democrats tend to believe that government can and should act for good. However, the parties' views on government's role often depend on the specific issue or program in question.

**U.S. Third Parties.** The United States has a two-party system. However, nothing in the Constitution requires two parties. The Democrats and Republicans have alternated in power since before the Civil War mainly because they have put forward candidates and policies that appeal to most Americans. But

A political cartoon from 1912 shows the presidential candidates riding the symbols of their parties—Woodrow Wilson on the Democratic donkey, William H. Taft on the Republican elephant, and Theodore Roosevelt on his own "Bull Moose."

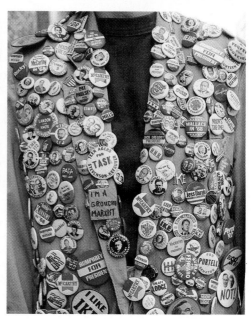

Party members show their support. *Above:* Patriotic accessories at a national convention. *Right:* Selected campaign buttons from past elections.

minor parties, or third parties, have often played a role in politics. Third parties focus attention on issues and ideas. Sometimes they draw enough support to affect the outcome of elections. Sometimes a third party gains part of its goals by supporting a major party that promises to act on the third party's views.

After the Civil War, Americans debated issues such as women's voting rights and labor reform. New political parties helped focus attention on these issues. In 1872, for example, Victoria Woodhull became the first woman to run for president. She shared the Equal Rights Party ticket with African American

leader Frederick Douglass. In the 1890's the People's Party of the U.S.A., or Populists, drew support from laborers and farmers.

In 1912 a disagreement among Republicans produced a splinter group called the Progressive, or "Bull Moose," Party. Theodore Roosevelt, the party's presidential candidate, outpolled the Republican candidate, William H. Taft. But the Republican split only helped the Democratic candidate, Woodrow Wilson, win the election. The Progressive Party's name was revived in the 1920's. The Progressives opposed big business monopolies and favored the interests of farmers and workers. The Socialist Party favored wider social welfare measures. It reached its greatest strength in the 1930's, during the Great Depression.

After World War II, Southern Democrats formed the States' Rights, or "Dixiecrat," Party to protest a growing movement to secure the civil rights of African Americans. The American Independent Party, led by Alabama governor George Wallace, also opposed racial integration. It was a factor in the presidential election of 1968. The Libertarian Party, formed in the 1970's, stressed individual rights. The 1990's saw the growth of the Reform Party, formed by Texas businessman H. Ross Perot. And the Green Party has formed as an outgrowth of the environmental movement. Like earlier third parties, these groups have helped focus attention on important social and political issues.

## WONDER QUESTION

### Why are some political parties called "left," and others "right"?

In 1789 the French Revolution overthrew the monarchy that had long ruled France. A new National Assembly took over the government. Several political parties were formed in the National Assembly, including the Jacobins, Cordeliers, Girondists, and others. The most radical reformers, the Jacobins, sat on the left side of the Assembly chamber, while the most conservative delegates sat on the right side. Some scholars think the terms "left" for radical and "right" for conservative began at this time.

**How U.S. Parties Work.** The major U.S. political parties are highly organized. The precinct is the smallest local division. The parties are run by county and state committees. Committee members may be elected at primaries, chosen at state conventions, or appointed by party officers. The two major parties also have national committees, made up of one man and one woman from each of the 50 states and U.S. territories. Every four years, parties hold national conventions. Delegates are chosen in primaries, by state conventions, or at gatherings called precinct caucuses. These delegates gather at the conventions to nominate a presidential and a vice-presidential candidate. Each party at its convention also drafts a platform. The platform is a statement of what the party stands for. If the party wins, the platform is supposed to guide the actions of the elected officials.

Parties today use computers to draw up lists of possible supporters and take public opinion polls to explore the views of voters on certain issues. They use advertising to mold public opinion and compete for favorable media coverage for their candidates. U.S. election campaigns are enormously costly, and fund-raising is a major part of the parties' work. Special-interest groups able to raise money and turn out voters for candidates they favor have grown in influence. State and federal laws control the ways political parties can raise and handle money.

▶ **POLITICAL PARTIES IN OTHER COUNTRIES**

Political parties are often a standard by which a country's political freedom can be measured. Some countries have only one political party. In China, for example, there is only one party, the Communist Party. Under such a system, people who do not agree with the party in power cannot express their objections by voting for another group. Often the ruling party holds power with the support of the army.

Democracies usually operate under either a two-party or a multiparty system. Like the United States, Britain has a two-party system. The major parties are the Labour Party and the Conservative Party, though there are active third parties. Canada also has two major parties, the Progressive Conservatives and the Liberals.

Multiparty systems are common in Europe and other parts of the world. In this system,

Members of Germany's pro-environment Green Party stage a protest march (*above*). Multiparty systems are common in democratic countries.

three or more parties each enjoy substantial support from voters. France, Germany, Israel, and South Africa are just a few examples. In these countries there may be many parties representing a wide range of political views. Because of the number of competing parties, it is sometimes difficult for any one party to get a clear majority of the votes. In such cases, leading parties that can agree on general policies form a coalition (a combination of parties) to run the country.

STEPHEN FLANDERS
Correspondent, Columbia Broadcasting System

See also ELECTIONS; GOVERNMENT, FORMS OF.

# JAMES K. POLK (1795-1849)

## 11th President of the United States

### FACTS ABOUT POLK

Birthplace: Mecklenburg County, North Carolina
Religion: Presbyterian
College Attended: University of North Carolina, Chapel Hill, North Carolina
Occupation: Lawyer
Married: Sarah Childress
Children: None
Political Party: Democratic
Offices Held Before Becoming President: U.S. congressman, governor of Tennessee
President Who Preceded Him: John Tyler
Age on Becoming President: 49
Years in the Presidency: 1845–1849
Vice President: George M. Dallas
President Who Succeeded Him: Zachary Taylor
Age at Death: 53
Burial Place: Polk Place, Nashville, Tennessee; remains moved (1893) to the state capitol grounds, Nashville

### DURING POLK'S PRESIDENCY

The U.S. Naval Academy was opened (1845) at Annapolis, Maryland. Texas was admitted to the Union (1845). *Left:* Elias Howe patented his sewing machine (1846). Mexican War was fought (1846–48). Treaty with Britain established the Oregon boundary at the 49th parallel (1846). Iowa was admitted to the Union (1846). *Below:* Gold discovered in California (1848) set off the great gold rush of 1849. Territory including present-day California, Nevada, Utah, and most of Arizona and New Mexico was acquired from Mexico by the Treaty of Guadalupe Hidalgo (1848). Wisconsin was admitted to the Union (1848). *Below left:* Department of the Interior was created (1849).

---

**POLK, JAMES KNOX.** James K. Polk became the first dark horse, or little-known candidate, to win the presidency when he unexpectedly defeated Henry Clay in the election of 1844. During his single term in office, Polk achieved all of the ambitious political goals he had set for himself. This included the addition to the United States of a vast area stretching from the Rocky Mountains to the Pacific Ocean. Opponents of his own day condemned him, for they believed that he desired only to extend the area of slavery. But most modern scholars reject this idea and generally rank Polk among the near-great U.S. presidents.

### ▶ EARLY YEARS

Polk was born in Mecklenburg County, North Carolina, on November 2, 1795, the eldest of ten children of Samuel and Jane Knox Polk. In 1806 the Polk family moved from North Carolina to Duck River, Tennessee, where Samuel Polk became a successful frontier farmer. James never developed the physi-

cal strength needed for farming. His parents therefore trained his mind, providing tutors for him and sending him to several preparatory schools. In 1815 he entered the University of North Carolina. He applied himself diligently to his studies, graduating first in his class in 1818, with honors in mathematics and the classics.

Polk then studied law and in 1820 was admitted to the bar. He began his practice in Columbia, Tennessee, and soon became a well-known lawyer. In 1823 he was elected to the Tennessee state legislature. As a young politician he became friendly with Tennessee's new U.S. senator, Andrew Jackson.

In 1824, Polk married Sarah Childress, the daughter of a prosperous family from Murfreesboro, Tennessee. She was a tall, handsome woman with a queenly bearing and considerable cultural refinement.

### ▶ CONGRESSMAN

In 1825, Polk was elected to the first of his seven terms in the U.S. House of Representatives. There he championed Andrew Jackson, who had just lost the contest for the presidency to John Quincy Adams. A courageous and able debater, Polk blunted the effect of the worst attacks by Jackson's enemies. When Jackson was elected president in 1828, Polk became one of his most trusted lieutenants. He was elected to the post of Speaker of the House in 1835 and re-elected in 1837.

During these years Polk had to preside over some of the stormiest sessions ever known in the House of Representatives. He was heckled unmercifully from the floor of the House and hounded by opponents, some of whom tried to goad him into a duel. Nevertheless, he served efficiently if unhappily.

President Polk's wife, Sarah, was educated and intelligent. Polk often discussed policy issues with her.

### ▶ GOVERNOR OF TENNESSEE

In 1839 the Tennessee Democrats, hoping to capture control of the state from the Whig Party, nominated Polk for the governorship. Although he would have preferred to remain in Congress, Polk consented to run for the good of the party. He was elected and served a 2-year term, from 1839 to 1841. His success proved more a personal than a party victory, for in the presidential election of 1840, most Tennesseans voted for the Whig candidate, William Henry Harrison. Polk ran for re-election as governor in 1841 and 1843 but suffered defeat each time. As the 1844 presidential election approached, however, he was mentioned as a possible candidate for the vice presidency.

### ▶ THE CONTROVERSY OVER TEXAS

In April 1844, President John Tyler (who had succeeded to office on the death of Harrison in 1841) submitted a treaty to the U.S. Senate to annex Texas to the United States. Formerly a part of Mexico, Texas had proclaimed its independence in 1836. The proposed treaty immediately started a national controversy. The entry of Texas into the Union, which was desired by most Texans, was popular in the South and Southwest. But many people, in the North and elsewhere, objected because it would add a new slave state to the United States. In addition, they felt that annexation would almost certainly lead to war with Mexico.

Two of the leading political figures of the day, Senator Henry Clay of Kentucky, a Whig, and former president Martin Van Buren, a Democrat, opposed the immediate annexation of Texas. Although Van Buren was expected to be the Democratic presidential candidate in 1844, his opposition to annexation ruined his chances for the nomination. Clay would win the Whig nomination, but his hold on the voters of the Southwest was greatly weakened. Andrew Jackson suggested Polk as a candidate who could lead the Democrats to victory.

### ▶ "WHO IS JAMES K. POLK?"

At the 1844 Democratic National Convention in Baltimore, Maryland, Polk was nominated on the ninth ballot. George M. Dallas of Pennsylvania was chosen as the vice-presidential candidate. Mocking the unknown candidate, the Whigs inquired, "Who is James K. Polk?"

The Democrats adopted a platform calling for the annexation of Texas and the acquisition of all of the Oregon Territory. This enormous territory included present-day Washington, Oregon, and Idaho; parts of Montana and Wyoming; and a large area of western Canada. It had been occupied by both the United States and Britain since 1818.

The Democratic platform emphasized Polk's devotion to Manifest Destiny—the concept that the United States must continue to expand

Polk was an advocate of America's territorial expansion. During the 1844 election, he called for the annexation of Texas and the acquisition of the Oregon Territory.

across the North American continent. President Tyler threw his support to Polk. In return, Polk promised to support the immediate annexation of Texas.

At his rainy inauguration, Polk said, "I regard the question of annexation [of Texas] as belonging exclusively to the United States and Texas."

### ▶ THE 1844 ELECTION

The 1844 election was one of the closest in U.S. history. Polk defeated Clay by an electoral vote of 170 to 105, but the difference in the popular vote was exceedingly narrow, with less than 40,000 votes separating the two candidates. James G. Birney of the Liberty Party, an antislavery party, received 62,300 votes. The vote for Birney's party in New York cost Clay the electors of that state and gave the victory to Polk.

On March 1, 1845, just before Polk's inauguration, President Tyler signed the resolution authorizing the annexation of Texas. Polk had thus redeemed half of his party's platform pledge three days before entering the White House.

### ▶ PRESIDENT

Polk was keenly aware that many leading Democrats doubted his qualifications for the presidency and expected to control his administration. He therefore felt a special compulsion to act firmly and with independence. His determination to exercise all his powers as president made him excessively suspicious of advice. Although he had early decided to

serve only one term, Polk asked all his cabinet members to pledge not to seek the presidential nomination in 1848. He hoped by this means to prevent conflicts of private ambition from interfering with public business.

**Political Goals.** At the beginning of his presidency, Polk boldly stated his political goals: "There are four great measures which are to be the measures of my administration: one, a reduction of the tariff; another, the independent treasury; a third, the settlement of the Oregon boundary question; and lastly, the acquisition of California."

Polk quickly accomplished the first two measures. In 1846 he signed into law the Walker-McKay Tariff, which greatly reduced import taxes. That same year he signed a measure restoring the independent treasury system. Under this system, the federal government kept its own funds instead of depositing them in state and private banks. The Independent Treasury Act remained in effect until 1913, when the Federal Reserve System was established.

It was foreign affairs, however, that would dominate Polk's administration.

**The Oregon Crisis.** The question of the Oregon boundary had been a continuing source of controversy between the United States and Britain. During the 1844 presidential campaign, the Democrats had demanded U.S. occupation of all of Oregon up to 54° 40′ north latitude. This included a large part of what is now the Canadian province of British Columbia. A favorite Democratic slogan was "Fifty-four forty or fight." Polk offered to compromise by setting the disputed boundary at the 49th parallel (its present boundary). But when the British minister curtly refused, the president withdrew the offer and declared his intention to press U.S. claims to the entire region. War over Oregon was avoided, however, and in 1846 the United States and Britain signed a treaty setting the boundary at the 49th parallel.

**War with Mexico.** Mexico had broken relations with the United States in 1845, in protest over the annexation of Texas. At this time two Mexican governments were struggling for control, and the distracted nation had failed to pay an installment on some $3 million claimed by U.S. citizens for loss of property. Polk tried to use these circumstances to persuade the government of President José Herrera to accept the Rio Grande as the southern boundary of Texas and to sell California to the United States.

When the effort failed, Polk dispatched U.S. troops to the Rio Grande border. After learning that they had been attacked in the disputed region by Mexican forces, he asked Congress for a declaration of war, stating that Mexico had shed "American blood on American soil." War was declared on May 13, 1846. The conflict caused great resentment in the North, where many people felt that it was unjustified and motivated chiefly by a Southern desire to expand the area of slavery.

The fighting lasted about a year and a half and resulted in Mexico's complete defeat. The Treaty of Guadalupe Hidalgo, which ended the war, was signed on February 2, 1848. By its terms the Rio Grande was established as Texas' southern boundary. The United States also acquired California and the New Mexico Territory (including what are now Nevada and Utah and most of Arizona and New Mexico). The United States paid Mexico $15 million and canceled the $3 million in U.S. claims. See the article on the Mexican War in Volume M.

On September 13, 1847, 16 months after Congress declared war on Mexico at Polk's request, U.S. troops took Chapultepec. The Mexican War ended the next day.

---

**IMPORTANT DATES IN THE LIFE OF JAMES K. POLK**

| | |
|---|---|
| **1795** | Born in Mecklenburg County, North Carolina, November 2. |
| **1818** | Graduated from the University of North Carolina. |
| **1820** | Admitted to the bar; began practicing law in Columbia, Tennessee. |
| **1823** | Elected to the Tennessee state legislature. |
| **1824** | Married Sarah Childress. |
| **1825–39** | Served in the U.S. House of Representatives. |
| **1839–41** | Served as governor of Tennessee. |
| **1845–49** | Served as eleventh president of the United States. |
| **1849** | Died in Nashville, Tennessee, June 15. |

---

**The Polk Doctrine.** In his first annual message to Congress in 1845, Polk set forth the Polk Doctrine, an extension of the Monroe Doctrine. (See the article on the Monroe Doctrine in Volume M.) Polk declared that the United States opposed "any European interference" in any country in the Americas. In addition, the United States would resist even the voluntary transfer of such a country or territory to a European power. Latin American nations, fearful of the United States, challenged the Polk Doctrine as an invasion of their sovereignty. Polk defended it on the ground that only a firm stand by the United States would prevent European control of weak American nations.

Polk's administration represents the point at which the United States began to regard itself as the equal of Europe. In his last annual message to Congress, Polk proudly announced that with the addition of the new territories, "the United States are now estimated to be nearly as large as the whole of Europe."

**Other Events.** Other important events occurred during Polk's administration. The Department of the Interior was established. Wisconsin and Iowa as well as Texas became states, while Minnesota and Oregon became federal territories. Congressman David Wilmot introduced the Wilmot Proviso to prohibit slavery in any territory acquired from Mexico. Although Wilmot's measure did not pass the Senate, it became the basis of the antislavery Free Soil Party and later of the Republican Party.

**Life in the White House.** In his character, Polk showed little imagination or humor. He organized his life methodically, seeking workable answers to practical problems. He labored harder and longer than perhaps any other president of the United States. During his four years in office, he spent only 37 days away from his desk. Typically, he arose at daybreak and applied himself to state business, usually until midnight. Before going to bed, he carefully recorded in a diary the details of the day's activities.

Sarah Polk greatly aided her husband. She maintained social life at the White House on a dignified and formal level, permitting no card playing, liquor, or dancing. She had political intelligence and social grace, and she was able to give her husband some protection from the constant pressure of office seekers. The Polks had no children.

▶ **DEATH**

Polk was succeeded as president in 1849 by General Zachary Taylor, a hero of the Mexican War. Worn out by his unceasing labor, Polk died at the age of 53 on June 15, 1849, scarcely three months after leaving office. He was buried at his home, Polk Place, in Nashville, Tennessee. In 1893 his body was moved to the state capitol grounds at Nashville. Sarah Polk, who died in 1891, is buried beside him.

PHILIP S. KLEIN
The Pennsylvania State University
Coauthor, *A History of the United States*

## POLLOCK, JACKSON (1912–1956)

The American painter Jackson Pollock was a key figure in the art movement known as abstract expressionism. His work contributed to the rise of the United States as an international center of artistic activity after World War II.

Pollock was born on January 28, 1912, on a farm near Cody, Wyoming. He first studied painting at the Manual Arts High School in Los Angeles. In 1929 he moved to New York City and became a pupil of Thomas Hart Benton (1889–1975), a well-known painter of

Jackson Pollock employed an unusual technique to create his dynamic, flowing works: He poured or dripped paint onto a canvas laid out on his studio floor.

scenes from the American Midwest. Following Benton's lead, Pollock traveled across the country during the 1930's, sketching American scenes. From 1938 until 1942 he worked on the Federal Art Project, a government-funded program.

Early in the 1940's, Pollock experimented with modern European styles. Gradually he began to create works that suggested feelings and moods but had no recognizable subject matter—a kind of painting that came to be called abstract expressionism. He developed a new style that was at first shocking and then greatly influential.

Pollock believed that an artist should be part of his paintings. He unrolled huge lengths of canvas on his studio floor. Walking all around and over the canvas, he dripped or poured paint on it. Sometimes he added sand or broken glass to the paint. The result was a work that showed the energy and emotion of the painter. The swirling mazes of color also had rhythms and orderly patterns. Within a few years, Pollock began to win worldwide recognition.

Pollock married the artist Lee Krasner in 1945. He died in a car accident near East Hampton, New York, on August 11, 1956.

Reviewed by HAROLD SPENCER
The University of Connecticut

**POLLUTION.** See AIR POLLUTION; WATER POLLUTION.

# POLO

Polo is a game played by two teams on horseback. The riders, using long-handled mallets, attempt to drive a ball down the field and through their opponents' goal.

Modern polo originated in India, where it had been played since 1862. British army officers took the game to England in 1869. Polo was introduced into the United States in 1876. Today polo is played in North and South America, Europe, Australia, New Zealand, India, and many other places.

Outdoors, polo is played by two teams made up of four players each. The field is 300 yards (274 meters) long and 160 yards (146 meters) wide. It is bounded on each side by sideboards 11 inches (28 centimeters) high. A white line extends across each end of the field. Goalposts are placed on these lines 24 feet (7.3 meters) apart and equal distances from the sideboards.

Indoor polo is played by two teams of three players each. The field is 100 yards (91.4 meters) long by 50 yards (45.7 meters) wide.

**Mounts.** The term "polo pony" stems from the early days of the game, when a height limit allowed only ponies to be used. There is no height limit today. Because of the demands of speed, polo ponies are sometimes Thoroughbreds. They are trained for the game, usually for at least a year.

**The Game.** Today the game consists of six or eight periods, called "chukkers," of seven minutes each. There are time-outs between chukkers during which the players change to fresh ponies.

Two mounted umpires are on the field, and one referee, unmounted, is on the sidelines. Rules to protect players from dangerous plays or unfair use of the mallet are enforced by the umpires. Violations of rules are called fouls and are penalized. The team that is fouled is given a free shot at its opponents' goal from a distance of 30, 40, or 60 yards (27, 37, or 55 meters) from the goal, depending on how severe the foul is.

The team that scores the most goals wins. If the score is tied at the end of the last period of play, extra periods are played until a goal is scored and the game is ended.

When the ball goes over the sideboards, it is returned to play by the umpire. It is thrown in between the players, who line up facing the umpire side by side where the ball went out of play. After a goal has been scored, the umpire throws the ball in from the center of the field. When the ball is knocked over the back line, it is returned to play by the defending team from the point where it went out of play.

The players play positions designated as No. 1, No. 2, No. 3, and No. 4. No. 1 spearheads the attack and stays at the front of the game, playing directly against defensive No. 4. No. 1 is the scoring position. The No. 2 position demands a player who rides hard and remains constantly on the attack. No. 3 is the key member of a team and usually the strongest player, whose work is divided between offense and defense. The No. 4 player, also known as the back, is almost entirely a defensive player.

Polo players are rated on a scale from 0 to 10, according to their individual experience and abilities. This rating is called a handicap. When a game is played on a handicap basis, the difference between the total handicaps of the teams is given in goals to the team of lesser total handicap.

CYRIL R. HARRISON
Official Polo Instructor
United States Polo Association

A polo player and his mount race to the attack. Polo is a fast, often dangerous sport that requires quick reflexes on the part of both riders and horses.

Marco Polo and his father and uncle traveled for 24 years on their 15,000-mile journey through Asia. A miniature from the 1300's shows them near the Yellow River in China.

# POLO, MARCO (1254–1324)

Marco Polo, the greatest of all travelers of the Middle Ages, was born in 1254 in Venice, then an independent city-state in northern Italy. His father and uncle, who were merchants, journeyed deep into Asia until they finally came to China and the court of Kublai Khan. This was the first contact in many centuries between Europe and China.

Kublai Khan, grandson of the conqueror Genghis Khan, was a man of intelligence and great energy. He was delighted with the Venetian gentlemen and eager to hear all they could tell him of far-off Christian Europe.

Marco was 15 when his father returned home. He was 17 when, in 1271, he left Venice to accompany his father and uncle on the long return journey across Asia to Cambaluc, the capital of China and the court of Kublai Khan. It was a very difficult journey and took three and a half years.

Because of his outspoken frankness and honesty, Marco at once became a favorite of the Khan, who often employed him as his special envoy to distant parts of his vast empire.

After an absence of 24 years, the Polos returned home to Venice. They brought with them a great fortune in jewels and other valuable things.

Some time after his return, Marco Polo commanded a Venetian war galley in a naval battle with Genoa. He was taken prisoner by the Genoese. While waiting to be ransomed by his family, Marco Polo dictated the story of his astonishing experiences to a fellow prisoner. This manuscript soon became the sensation of Europe. And after the invention of printing in the 1400's, the story of Marco Polo's travels appeared in many languages. Today the work is regarded as one of the greatest travel narratives in all literature.

Marco Polo was the first traveler to journey across the entire width of Asia, naming each kingdom along the route and describing the lands and their people. He described China under the rule of Kublai Khan: its great wealth; its trade, roads, long canals, and fast couriers; its government and postal system—and its paper money. But no one in Europe then would believe that paper could substitute for metal coins as money. Nor could they believe that China had black stones that burned, because coal was still unknown in Europe. And so, many of the wonders described by Marco Polo were considered lies.

In 1299, Marco Polo was released from prison. He returned to Venice, where he died in 1324. For many years afterward, he was regarded as Europe's greatest liar. Yet his work influenced the early map makers. Christopher Columbus possessed a Latin version of Marco Polo's travels, which inspired him to seek a westward sea route to Asia. It was on this voyage that Columbus reached America.

MANUEL KOMBROFF
Editor, *The Travels of Marco Polo*

**POLYGONS.** See GEOMETRY.

**POLYHEDRA.** See GEOMETRY.

# POMPEII

Pompeii was an ancient city on the southwestern coast of Italy, on the Bay of Naples. It was founded in the 7th century B.C. by a tribe called the Oscans. Later other peoples—Etruscans, Samnites, and Greeks—settled there. In the 1st century B.C., Pompeii was taken over by the Romans.

On August 24 in the year A.D. 79 the volcano Vesuvius, located about 5 miles (8 kilometers) north of Pompeii, suddenly came alive. Dark clouds, hot cinders and ash, and poisonous gases poured from its cone. The terrifying eruption buried Pompeii beneath 10 to 20 feet (3 to 6 meters) of cinders and volcanic ash. At least 2,000 of the city's 20,000 inhabitants were killed, and possibly many more. The layers of ash sealed up the people's homes with the furniture and other belongings inside. The nearby towns of Herculaneum and Stabiae were also destroyed in the eruption. In a matter of two days the once flourishing seaside city, where many wealthy Romans had their country homes, disappeared.

Most ancient cities either died gradually or were robbed and destroyed by conquerors. Pompeii was struck down in one swift blow by a natural disaster. It lay buried nearly 2,000 years.

In 1748, Charles III, King of Naples and Sicily, ordered the digging out of Pompeii to begin. He hoped that this excavation would uncover treasure to enrich his archaeological collection. Since then, almost all the city has come to light.

Today, when you go to Pompeii, you see not a heap of ruins but streets with paving stones worn by chariot wheels, well-preserved public buildings, wine shops, and restaurants. Some walls are scratched with Latin phrases praising or criticizing the wine and food or advertising fights between gladiators.

Many of the rich country homes and their gardens with ornamental pools can still be seen. The gateways were often guarded by dogs. One unfortunate beast was left tied to a gatepost by a master so anxious to escape that the dog was forgotten. In another house an unfinished meal was left on a table when guests fled for their lives. Citizens had little time to remove their valuables. In the crush near the city gates many inhabitants were choked to death by the poisonous gases. The imprint of their bodies remains in the hardened volcanic ash.

Most of the art treasures, cooking utensils, household furnishings, and implements from Pompeii and Herculaneum are now on view in the Naples National Museum. All these articles have been so well preserved that archaeologists are able to piece together in a remarkable way what everyday life was like in Roman times 2,000 years ago.

LEONARD COTTRELL
Author, *Lost Worlds*

The eruption of the volcano Vesuvius in A.D. 79 buried Pompeii under layers of cinders and ash. Centuries later, excavation revealed much about the life of an ancient city.

## PONCE DE LEÓN, JUAN (1460?–1521)

Juan Ponce de León discovered Florida while searching in vain for the legendary Fountain of Youth—a magic spring that would restore youth to the aged.

Ponce de León was born about 1460 to a noble family in Tierra de Campos, Spain. He was raised at the court of King Ferdinand II of Aragon and as a youth fought against the Moors in Granada. In 1493 he accompanied Christopher Columbus on his second voyage to the New World. There Ponce de León took part in the conquest of Hispaniola (now Haiti and the Dominican Republic). He established the first Spanish settlement in Puerto Rico and in 1509 became its governor.

While serving as governor, Ponce de León amassed a fortune in gold and slaves. At the same time, he learned of an island the Indians called Bimini, where the Fountain of Youth was supposedly to be found. Now in his 50's, Ponce de León was intrigued by the legend. In March, 1513, he set out to discover Bimini.

About 175 miles south of present-day St. Augustine, Ponce de León sighted a strange coastline and went ashore. Because of the many flowers he found there and because it was the Easter season, he named the new land Florida (from *Pascua florida*, Spanish for "flowery Easter"). He claimed it for Ferdinand (then king of Spain) but spent only a short time on land, most of it fighting the Indians.

Still searching for Bimini, he sailed past Miami Bay and the Florida Keys and back to Puerto Rico. He returned to Spain to report his discovery. The King commissioned him to settle the "island" of Florida (as it was then thought to be) and to continue the search for Bimini. In 1521 Ponce de León began his second voyage, with two ships and about 200 men as colonists. Soon after landing on the western coast of Florida, the expedition was attacked by Indians. Ponce de León was severely wounded and taken to Cuba, where he died a few days later. The rest of the expedition abandoned Florida.

SANFORD H. BEDERMAN
Georgia State College

---

## PONTIAC (1720?–1769)

Pontiac was a chief of the Ottawa. There are so many legends about him that it is difficult to separate fact from fiction. Some historians say he was a wise and courageous leader; others say he was really a cruel coward whose dream of uniting many Indian tribes never came about.

Pontiac was born about 1720, probably in Ohio. His father was an Ottawa chief. During his youth he saw increasing numbers of British colonists settle in Indian territory. Pontiac feared that the Indians would be forced to give up more of the land that belonged to them. During the last French and Indian War (1754–63) the Ottawa, under Pontiac, joined the French against the British. It is possible that Pontiac led his tribesmen in the defeat of General Edward Braddock (1695–1755) near Fort Duquesne in 1755.

According to the most widely accepted stories of Pontiac's life, he began to organize his Indian confederacy early in the 1760's. The union included tribes living in the Ohio Valley and Great Lakes regions. Pontiac believed that by banding together, the Indians would become strong enough to drive out the British settlers. He sent messengers to leaders of many tribes and told them of his plans. At a council near Fort Detroit in 1763, Pontiac addressed the chiefs. He spoke of the wrongs the British had inflicted on the Indians.

Pontiac planned to capture the British forts from Pennsylvania to Lake Superior. In May, 1763, the Indians attacked a dozen different forts and captured most of them. Pontiac led the attack on Fort Detroit. But he failed to capture the settlement and laid siege to it instead. The siege lasted several months and finally ended in failure. A peace treaty was signed at Detroit on August 17, 1765.

Pontiac died in 1769. According to some reports he was killed in a quarrel during a wild celebration. Other accounts say that the British bribed an Indian to murder him.

Reviewed by DANIEL JACOBSON
Montclair State College

A Pony Express rider leaves his weary horse at a relay station and makes a swift departure on a fresh mount in *Coming and Going of the Pony Express*, by Frederic Remington.

## PONY EXPRESS

The Pony Express, which carried mail between Missouri and California, is a famous chapter in the winning of the West. It operated for just 18 months—from April, 1860, to October, 1861—but it will never be forgotten.

When California became a state in 1850, about 3,200 kilometers (2,000 miles) of empty country separated it from the frontier states along the Missouri River. Stagecoaches carried passengers and mail over this great distance. It took them three weeks, traveling day and night, to make the journey. As the population grew in the 1850's, a faster mail service was needed.

In 1860, Senator William M. Gwin of California persuaded the freighting company of Russell, Majors, and Waddell to organize the Pony Express. They established a route of about 3,000 kilometers (1,900 miles) from St. Joseph, Missouri, to Sacramento, California. It was about 160 kilometers (100 miles) shorter than the stage route.

For most of the route, the Pony Express used the California Trail, which had been traveled by wagon trains since the 1840's. From St. Joseph this trail followed the Platte River over the Nebraska prairie. It passed famous posts and landmarks—Fort Kearny, Scott's Bluff, Fort Laramie, Independence Rock. It crossed the Rocky Mountains at South Pass, Wyoming. Beyond Fort Bridger the Pony Express route rounded the southern shore of the Great Salt Lake and crossed the vast desert of Utah Territory. At Carson City it climbed the Sierra Nevada and came down to Sacramento, California. From there the mail was hurried to San Francisco by steamboat on the Sacramento River.

Along the route, relay stations were established at intervals of about 24 kilometers (15 miles). Some stations were ranch houses or stagecoach depots; others were newly built for the Pony Express. Some were remote posts in hostile Indian country. Fast, wiry horses were kept at these stations. They galloped at full speed from one station to the next.

About 100 riders were hired for the express. They were young men—lean, hardy, and daring. One of the first riders was Buffalo Bill. All were expert riders who could break and train wild broncos. Riding day and night, they faced many dangers. Sandstorms and blizzards, wild animals, bandits, and hostile Indians all brought risk and adventure.

The Pony Express riders were paid $100 a month, a good salary at that time. They had to be trustworthy, loyal, and courageous. Every rider signed a pledge of good behavior.

In the first weeks of the service, each rider carried a Bible, a sheath knife, a horn, a cavalry rifle, and a pair of Colt revolvers. But the weight of these objects slowed the horses, and soon this equipment was reduced to a single revolver. The original postage charge was $5 for 14 grams (½ ounce); the fee was later reduced to $1. In his mochila a rider carried 9 kilograms (20 pounds) of mail.

The Pony Express crossed the plains and deserts at breakneck speed. Mark Twain in his book *Roughing It* gives an eyewitness account of a rider racing in from the trail. The rider "came crashing up to the station where stood two men holding a fresh, impatient steed [horse], the transfer of rider and mail-bag was made in the twinkling of an eye, and away flew the eager pair."

Each rider used five horses to cover a daily (or nightly) run of 120 kilometers (75 miles). If his replacement was not ready, he would dash on to the next relay station.

The Pony Express riders carried the mail about 3,200 kilometers in eight or nine days. This was less than half the time required by stagecoach. The Pony Express covered 400 kilometers (250 miles) a day—twice as far as a day's travel by stage.

While the express riders were racing across the West, workers were erecting poles and stringing wires from Missouri and eastward from California. When the two lines met, the East and West were linked by telegraph. On October 24, 1861, the Pony Express made its last run. Then the staccato chatter of telegraph keys replaced the clatter of horses' hooves, and the Pony Express became another frontier memory.

Reviewed by WALTER HAVIGHURST
Author, *First Book of the Oregon Trail*

---

**POPE.** See ROMAN CATHOLIC CHURCH; VATICAN CITY.

# POPE, ALEXANDER (1688–1744)

The English poet Alexander Pope was born into a Roman Catholic family in London on May 21, 1688. His father was a prosperous linen merchant. About 1700 the family moved to an estate at Binfield, in Windsor Forest.

As a boy, Alexander was bright and tiny. (He had a deformed spine and grew to only 4 feet 6 inches as an adult.) He liked to display his independence and was sometimes hard to get along with. His parents hired priests to tutor him in Latin and Greek. At 15, he insisted on going to London to master French and Italian. But he worked so hard that he became ill and soon returned home.

English laws prohibited Catholics from attending a university, and Pope learned to content himself at home. He rode in the forest, continued his studies, and wrote poetry imitating his favorite authors. His own poetry was almost all in couplets (two rhyming lines containing a complete thought). Some of Pope's lines—such as "to err is human, to forgive, divine"—are often quoted.

Several days a week, Pope rode with his neighbor, Sir William Trumball, a retired diplomat who encouraged Pope in his writing. By the time Pope was 21, some of his poetry had been published, and he was becoming known.

In his twenties, Pope began to write satirical verse. In *The Rape of the Lock* (1712; expanded, 1714), he made fun of a silly quarrel between two prominent families. In other poems he mocked established writers. But he made his living by serious writing. Pope's translation of Homer's *Iliad* (1715–20) brought him great success. He considered his *Essay on Man* (1733–34) his finest work.

In 1719, Pope and his mother moved into a villa on the Thames River at Twickenham. He enjoyed working in his garden and building an underground study. Occasionally he took a boat ride up to London. Jonathan Swift visited him in 1726 and brought along his manuscript of *Gulliver's Travels*. Pope dedicated his next major work to Swift. This was *The Dunciad*, a mock-heroic poem attacking writers whom Pope considered to be dull scribblers, or dunces. He kept revising this work and brought out an expanded *New Dunciad* in 1743. Pope died on May 30, 1744.

Reviewed by DAYTON HASKIN
Boston College

# POPULATION

Few things are more important to a country than to know how many people live there and whether the number is growing or declining. Information about population—the total number of people living in a country or region—is important in many ways.

How well a government serves its people depends partly on how many there are to be served and how large an area they live in. It is also important to know how many people are in each age group. Younger people will need schools, while health care and social security may be more important to older people. Business prospects, opportunities for jobs, and even crime rates are influenced by the size of the population.

Changes in population are caused by births, deaths, and the movement of people into and out of a country. The number of children born, called the fertility of a population, increases the size of the population. The number of deaths, called mortality, decreases the population. Migration—the number of people entering or leaving a country—can cause either an increase or a decrease. A natural increase in population of a country comes from a greater number of births than deaths.

The three factors that cause changes in population are talked about in terms of rates. Rates show how often an event happens, or how common it is. In the United States in 1990, for example, the number of births per 1,000 people (the birth rate) was 16.7. Scientists who study population changes and the results of these changes are called demographers. The study of population and population changes is called demography.

## ▶ WORLD POPULATION

Human beings have lived on earth for many thousands of years, and during most of that time their numbers were relatively small. Before agriculture was developed about 10,000 years ago, the death rate was high, partly because of a limited food supply. Probably no more than 8,000,000 people were alive at any one time. But after people began to grow crops and raise animals for food, the death rate fell. And the population of the world slowly grew.

At the beginning of the Christian era (the year A.D. 1), about 250,000,000 people inhab-

ited the earth. This number increased to about 800,000,000 by 1750. In the next century industrialization and scientific knowledge about the cause of disease began to spread quickly. There was a further increase in food supplies, as well as a decrease in deaths caused by diseases. The human population began to grow at an enormous rate. Although it had taken many thousands of years for the world to reach a population of 800,000,000, it has taken less than 250 years to reach its present number of over 6 billion.

**Population Density.** The population of the world is not spread evenly over the earth. The average number of people who live in an area is called the population density. The most densely populated continents are Asia and Europe. Cities, where people live in apartment houses or other crowded multiple-family dwellings, are more densely populated than rural areas, where most people live in single-family homes.

**Age Differences.** The countries of the world fall into two broad groups—those with young

---

### POPULATION OF THE WORLD BY REGION

| REGION | ESTIMATED POPULATION |
|---|---|
| Asia[1] | 3,737,000,000 |
| Africa | 823,000,000 |
| Europe[2] | 729,000,000 |
| North America | 486,000,000 |
| South America | 351,000,000 |
| Oceania, Australia and New Zealand | 31,000,000 |

[1]Including European Turkey.
[2]Including Asian Russia.

---

### THE TEN MOST POPULOUS COUNTRIES

| COUNTRY | ESTIMATED POPULATION |
|---|---|
| China, People's Republic of | 1,273,000,000 |
| India | 1,030,000,000 |
| United States | 281,400,000 |
| Indonesia | 204,300,000 |
| Brazil | 165,000,000 |
| Russia | 146,000,000 |
| Pakistan | 144,600,000 |
| Bangladesh | 129,200,000 |
| Japan | 123,500,000 |
| Nigeria | 123,000,000 |

populations and those with large numbers of older people. Countries where many babies are born and most of them survive have youthful populations. In Africa, Latin America, southern Asia, and the Middle East, about two persons in five are children under 15 years of age.

Countries where the birth rate has been low for several decades have not produced many children. This is the case in Western Europe, the United States, and Japan, where only about one person in five is under the age of 15. Because there are fewer children in countries with low birth rates, the proportion of older persons is high. In a number of European nations, including Sweden, Germany, and the United Kingdom among others, more than one in seven persons is over 64 years of age.

**Countries with the Largest Populations.** Over 60 percent of the world's people live in just ten countries. The country with the largest population is China. More than one fifth of the world's people live in China. However, the rate of growth of the Chinese population has slowed dramatically in recent years. The Chinese government has tried to get people to marry at a later age and to have only one child per family. In spite of great opposition to this plan at first, it seems to have had significant results.

Of the other nine countries, three—the United States, Russia, and Japan—are indus-

| COUNTRIES WITH HIGHEST AND LOWEST BIRTH RATES (NUMBER OF BIRTHS PER 1,000 PERSONS) | | | |
|---|---|---|---|
| HIGHEST | | LOWEST | |
| Kenya | 54 | Denmark | 10 |
| Rwanda | 53 | Germany | 10 |
| Malawi | 52 | Italy | 11 |
| Benin | 51 | Sweden | 11 |
| Niger | 51 | Switzerland | 11 |

trial nations with slow-growing populations. Six are developing countries with rapidly growing populations—India, Indonesia, Brazil, Bangladesh, Pakistan, and Nigeria. Of these six, three—India, Indonesia, and Brazil—have lowered their birth rates in recent years.

▶**POPULATION GROWTH**

Because of recent developments in medicine, many diseases from which people used to die can now be cured. This has brought a decrease in mortality rates. And babies who once might have died at birth, or shortly after, now live. As a result, the world's population has been growing rapidly. At its present rate of growth, the total population of the world will double in about 40 years.

**Growth Rates.** The most rapidly growing populations in the world are in Africa, which is doubling in population every 24 years. The

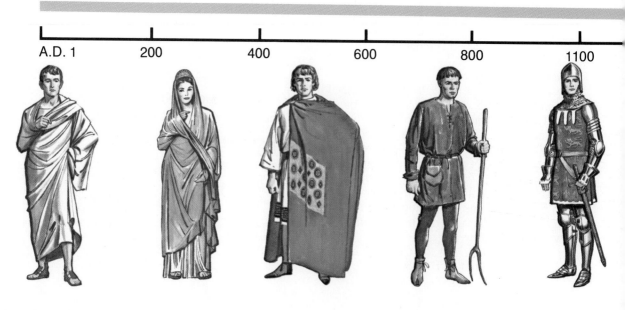

| A.D. 1 | 200 | 400 | 600 | 800 | 1100 |
|---|---|---|---|---|---|

## COUNTRIES WITH HIGHEST AND LOWEST INFANT MORTALITY RATES*

| HIGHEST | | LOWEST | |
|---|---|---|---|
| Afghanistan | 20.5 | Finland | 0.6 |
| Sierra Leone | 20.0 | Japan | 0.6 |
| Gambia | 19.3 | Sweden | 0.7 |
| Malawi | 16.5 | Iceland | 0.7 |
| Kampuchea | 16.0 | Switzerland | 0.8 |
| Guinea | 15.5 | Norway | 0.8 |
| Yemen (Sana) | 15.4 | Denmark | 0.8 |

\* Deaths of infants under one year of age per 100 live births.

continent with the slowest growth rate is Europe, where the population doubles only every 240 years.

Comparing projected figures of individual countries may be even more helpful. For example, the population of Nigeria, the most populous nation in Africa, is doubling every 22 years. At that rate, there would be about 156,000,000 Nigerians by the year 2000, and about 258,000,000 in 2020. In contrast, the present population of the United Kingdom, 56,000,000, will be about the same in the future if birth and death rates continue to equal. This would mean that by the year 2020, if population growth rates continue, Nigeria could have more than four times as many people as the United Kingdom.

The growth rate is affected by a country's mortality, or death, rate. For example, in some developing nations, about one in every five infants dies in its first year. This can be compared with about one or less in every hundred in industrialized nations. With improvements in medical care in developing nations, death rates, both in infants and adults, can be expected to drop. Therefore, if overpopulation is to be controlled, birth rates must drop even faster.

**Concern About Overpopulation.** The rapid population growth now taking place is sometimes called a population explosion. Many persons fear that population will grow faster than the resources—such as food, fuel, and housing—needed to support all the people. If this should happen, the first result would be lower standards of living. Then, as living standards fell below what was needed to keep the poorest people alive, the death rate would rise. If living standards were reduced to a point where dangerous diseases could not be controlled, death rates would rise among the wealthy as well as the poor.

Concern with overpopulation is not new. Almost two centuries ago, the English economist Thomas R. Malthus (1766–1834) argued that the growth of human population eventually takes away any gains made in living standards. He wrote at the beginning of the industrial age. He did not foresee the increase in material wealth that industry has produced or the safe, reliable ways to control fertility that have been developed.

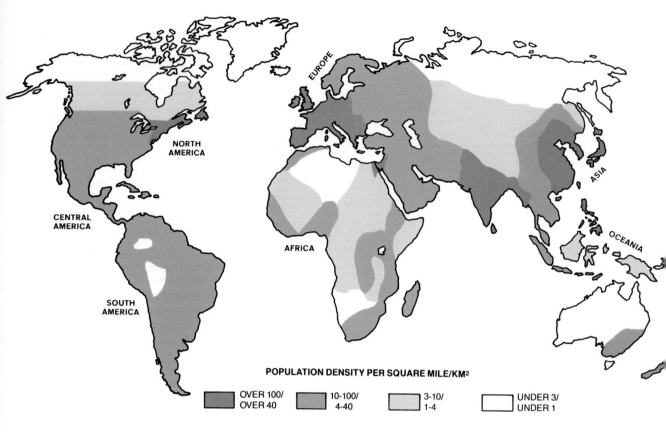

POPULATION DENSITY PER SQUARE MILE/KM²

| | | | |
|---|---|---|---|
| OVER 100/ OVER 40 | 10-100/ 4-40 | 3-10/ 1-4 | UNDER 3/ UNDER 1 |

**Will Population Growth Stop?** Is there truth in Malthus' view of the world as a place of limited resources? This remains an important question. If Malthus was right, then the growth of human population must stop sometime. The only questions are how and when. Will population growth be stopped by low birth rates or by a return to the high death rates of the pre-industrial past? Will this happen soon or not for several decades?

Answers to such questions can be given only for specific countries. In several countries of Western Europe, the population has already stopped growing, because of balanced birth and death rates. But these countries do not have all the resources they need. They must import metallic minerals, fuels, and food from other regions of the world. In fact, very few countries have the right combinations of resources to support their present populations— to say nothing of populations two or three times larger. In less developed regions of the world the situation is even more ominous.

**Future Trends.** In recent years famine and disease, particularly AIDS, have struck a number of African countries south of the Sahara desert. Death rates in several African nations were higher in the 1980's and 1990's than they had been previously. Nevertheless, Africa remains the continent with the most rapidly growing population. Even with major improvements in agricultural practices, several African countries may be unable to support their populations in the future. It remains to be seen whether, because of rising mortality or falling fertility, the population growth of Africa has slowed.

ROBERT E. KENNEDY, JR.
Author, *The Irish:*
*Emigration, Marriage, and Fertility*

See also CENSUS.

## COUNTRIES WITH HIGHEST AND LOWEST LIFE EXPECTANCIES (IN YEARS)

| HIGHEST | | LOWEST | |
|---|---|---|---|
| Iceland | 77 | Sierra Leone | 34 |
| Japan | 77 | Gambia | 35 |
| Netherlands | 76 | Afghanistan | 37 |
| Norway | 76 | Guinea | 40 |
| Sweden | 76 | Angola | 42 |
| Switzerland | 76 | Mali | 42 |

# PORCUPINES

Most people have never seen a real porcupine, but practically everyone knows about its long, needle-sharp quills. These quills are the porcupine's most distinguishing feature and provide this large rodent with a prickly and very effective form of self-defense.

The porcupine's short legs and heavy body make it a somewhat slow and clumsy animal. But its quills and spiny tail protect it from almost all predators. If threatened or attacked, the porcupine will turn its back and raise its back and neck quills—some of which measure up to 4 inches (10 centimeters) long.

If this threat does not deter an attack, the porcupine will swish its tail back and forth. This causes some quills, which are loosely attached to the porcupine's body, to shake out and stick to the face or body of the attacker. Each quill has a needle-sharp tip. Just below the end are tiny barbs, or hooks, that are directed backward. When a quill comes in contact with the skin of an animal, the barbs hold it in place.

Contrary to popular belief, a porcupine cannot shoot its quills. The quills just shake loose, but because they are light they may seem to fly through the air. Quills can also be lost as the porcupine walks or climbs through the woods. Like fingernails or hair, quills grow back after they are lost.

In addition to its stiff quills, the porcupine's 3-foot (1-meter) body is covered with brownish black hairs and a wooly underfur that keeps the animal warm in winter. (The porcupine does not hibernate but will seek shelter in holes or rock crevices.) It is also well equipped for climbing trees, with heavy claws on each foot. Long, orange-colored front teeth enable it to peel and eat the bark. Porcupines are especially fond of smooth-barked trees such as aspen and birch. They also eat tender buds, evergreen needles, fruits, and leaves.

The porcupine is well known for its habit of visiting cabins and lumber camps to find salt. Sweat-stained ax handles, tires that still have traces of road salt, door knobs, and old wooden chairs all attract porcupines.

Many porcupines, however, never come in contact with people. This is because they are usually nocturnal and live solitary lives in wilderness areas. The North American porcupine inhabits wooded regions from Alaska and

Long, needle-sharp quills distinguish the porcupine from all other rodents. These animals eat bark and will often spend several days in one tree.

Canada southward to the western United States and Texas. It is absent only from the southeastern United States. Other New World porcupines live in forest habitats in Mexico and Central and South America. Their Old World relatives live in Africa, southeastern Europe, and Asia.

Porcupines mate in the fall, and usually a single baby is born in May or June. A porcupine at birth weighs just over a pound (0.5 kilogram). It has a soft fur coat and half-inch (1-centimeter) quills. Six hours after birth it is able to waddle about and by the second day can already climb a tree. It continues to grow for about three years, up to a weight of about 30 pounds (14 kilograms).

The only predators that have learned to kill and eat porcupines are the mountain lion and the fisher, a weasel-like animal now absent from most of the porcupine's range. These animals flip the porcupine on its back to attack its soft belly. All other predators, however, know that a porcupine's sharp quills mean they must look elsewhere for a meal.

THOMAS D. FEGELY
Author, *Focus on Nature*

**PORPOISES.**  See DOLPHINS AND PORPOISES.
**PORTLAND (Maine).**  See MAINE (Cities).

## PORTLAND (OREGON)

The rugged beauty of northern Oregon provides a splendid setting for Portland, the state's largest city. Rich farmlands and forests surround the metropolitan area. The snowcapped peak of Mount Hood rises from the Cascade Range about 50 miles (80 kilometers) east of Portland. The city itself lies on the banks of the Willamette River, near its junction with the Columbia River.

Portland is known as a pleasant place to live. The climate is moderate. Nearly 530,000 people live in the city, which covers about 105 square miles (272 square kilometers). The metropolitan area has a population of more than 2 million.

The city is the economic center of Oregon and southern Washington. Oceangoing ships travel along the Willamette and Columbia rivers, making Portland a major Pacific port. Portland's manufactures include food products; paper, lumber, furniture, and other timber products; chemicals; and metal products. The 1980's brought the expansion of various high-technology and service industries.

Recreational and cultural opportunities abound. The Oregon Museum of Science and Industry is one of more than half a dozen museums in Portland. Portland's Forest Park is the nation's largest wilderness totally within a city's limits. Washington Park includes the Portland Zoological Gardens, the

The snowcapped peak of Mount Hood rises behind the Portland skyline. Oregon's largest city, Portland is also an economic and cultural center.

Japanese Gardens, the Western Forestry Center, and the International Rose Test Gardens. Because roses thrive in the moderate, moist climate, Portland is nicknamed the City of Roses. A week-long Rose Festival in June is a popular event.

The city is home to the Oregon Symphony Association, Portland Opera, and several theater and dance groups as well as the Portland Trail Blazers of the National Basketball Association. Portland State University, the Oregon Health Sciences University, Lewis and Clark College, the University of Portland, and Reed College are all in Portland. The Pacific Ocean is a one-hour drive to the west, and the mountains are a one-hour drive to the east.

The Portland area was settled by Indians long before white settlers arrived. In 1842 an Englishman built a cabin where South Portland now stands. Three years later two settlers, one from Boston and one from Portland, Maine, tossed a coin to see who should name the town. The Portland man won. By 1850, Portland had a sawmill, stores, churches, a school, and about 800 citizens.

Portland was a trading town from the beginning. Portlanders soon did a brisk business selling salmon. Then lumbering became the major industry. Later the city became a leading Pacific Coast livestock market and wheat port. During World War II, vast shipbuilding brought a boom.

In the 1970's and 1980's, a major redevelopment project helped to preserve and restore Portland's downtown area. Thanks to the Downtown Program, Portland today is a vital and modern city.

VANESSA E. BLAKE
Portland Chamber of Commerce
Reviewed by GORDON B. DODDS
Portland State University

**PORTSMOUTH.** See NEW HAMPSHIRE (Cities).

# PORTUGAL

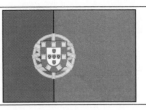

Portugal is the westernmost country on the European continent. It is situated on the Iberian Peninsula, at the southwestern edge of Europe, directly facing the Atlantic Ocean. From this location, Portuguese navigators, in the 1400's and 1500's, set sail to map the coasts of Africa, Asia, and South America and to open new trade routes with these continents. The discoveries of these bold explorers helped make Portugal the center of a vast and wealthy empire, many times greater than the country itself. Large areas of its former empire remained under Portuguese rule until recent times.

## ▶ THE PEOPLE

**Ethnicity, Language, and Religion.** The Portuguese are a mixture of the many different peoples who have occupied the Iberian Peninsula. These included the ancient Iberians, Celts, Phoenicians, Greeks, Carthaginians, Romans, Germanic tribes, and Moors from North Africa. In appearance, most Portuguese today are of medium height with dark hair and eyes, although some, particularly in the north, have the light hair and blue eyes inherited from their Germanic ancestors.

Portuguese belongs to the Romance group of languages, as do Spanish, Italian, and French. It is closely related to the Galician dialect of northern Spain. In religion, the people are mostly Roman Catholics.

**Way of Life.** Some aspects of Portuguese life vary from region to region, but there are many similarities throughout the country. Although Portugal has a number of cities of considerable size, the majority of the people live in rural areas or in small towns and villages, where life usually follows familiar patterns. Most rural Portuguese are farmers. Others make their living from the sea as fishermen. The average income is relatively small.

The high points of the year are the various religious festivals and pilgrimages that are celebrated in many of the towns and villages. Soccer is the favorite sport. In the larger towns, bullfights are also a major attraction,

With its long Atlantic Ocean coastline, Portugal historically has been a nation of seafarers, who once ruled a vast empire. These fishing boats lie beached at the town of Albufeira.

although in Portugal, unlike Spain, the bull is not killed. Dancing and folksinging are popular pastimes, and the sad, haunting melody of the fado, a traditional type of Portuguese song, often can be heard in cafés.

**Education.** Nine years of primary education is required by law for all children between the ages of 6 and 15. Secondary

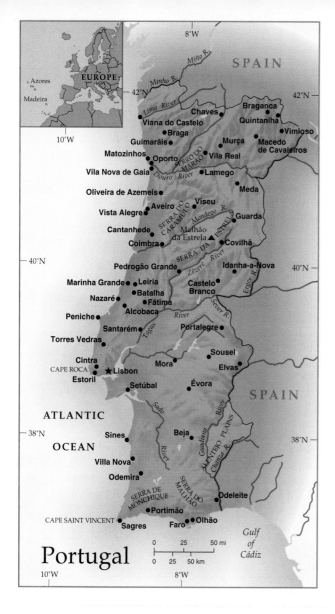

Portugal

The Tagus River divides Portugal into two quite different halves. To the north the country is mountainous. The major mountain range is the Serra da Estrela, whose highest peak, Malhão da Estrela, reaches 6,532 feet (1,991 meters). South of the river the land consists chiefly of rolling plains and plateaus. The majority of the people live in the region north of the Tagus, with the coastal areas and the valley of the Douro River the most densely populated areas.

**Climate.** Northern Portugal has a generally cooler climate than the south, with heavier rainfall. About 60 inches (1,500 millimeters) of rain falls in the northern mountains each year, compared to some 20 inches (500 millimeters) in the south. Temperatures are mild over most of Portugal during the winter, except in the mountains of the northern interior, where it is cold and snowy. Summers are warm in the northern valleys and coastal districts and hot in the dry plains of the south.

**Natural Resources.** Portugal has limited natural resources. Its soils are not especially fertile, except in the larger river valleys, and much of the land is suitable only for grazing

schooling, which is not compulsory, lasts for three years. In the final year, students take courses that will prepare them for either a university or for vocational training. Portugal's oldest university, the University of Coimbra, was founded in 1290.

▶ **THE LAND**

**Characteristics.** Portugal shares the Iberian Peninsula with its much larger neighbor, Spain. Several large rivers rise on the Spanish plateau and wind their way westward through Portugal to the sea. The largest and most important of these are the Douro, in the north, and the Tagus, which runs diagonally across the center of the country.

Northern Portugal has a hilly and often mountainous landscape, with high plateaus cut by deep valleys. Much of the land in the north is planted with vineyards.

livestock. Forests cover nearly one-third of the land. Of the varieties of trees found, the cork oak is the most valuable, economically. Tungsten ore, copper, tin, and coal are the most important minerals. The coastal waters are rich in a variety of fish, and the swift rivers of the north are an important source of hydroelectric power.

### ▶ MAJOR CITIES

**Lisbon** is Portugal's capital, largest city, chief port, and commercial center. The city is built on a series of hills rising from the Tagus River, near where it flows into the Atlantic Ocean. See the separate article on Lisbon in Volume L.

**Oporto (or Porto)** is Portugal's second largest city. Like Lisbon a city of hills, it is located in the northern part of the country, on the Douro River. It occupies the site of an ancient seaport known as Portus Cale, from which Portugal takes its name. Its most famed export is port wine, but it also produces textiles and clothing.

The only other Portuguese cities of any great size are Braga, Coimbra, and Setúbal. Braga, the most northerly of the major cities, is a historic religious center. Coimbra is famed for its ancient univer-sity, while Setúbal, situated to the south of Lisbon, is a fishing port as well as a shipbuilding center.

### ▶ MADEIRA AND THE AZORES

Madeira and the Azores are autonomous regions of Portugal, each with its own elected legislature. The Madeira Islands cover a land area of about 305 square miles (790 square kilometers) and are located in the Atlantic Ocean off the northwestern coast of Africa. Madeira, the largest island of the group, is a popular resort noted for its lush semitropical plant life and mild climate. Its best-known product is Madeira wine.

The Azores are a chain of nine small islands in the Atlantic Ocean, lying about 1,000 miles (1,600 kilometers) west of Lisbon and covering an area of about 893 square miles (2,313 square kilometers). For centuries the islands have served as stopping places for ships and airplanes crossing the Atlantic. Farming and fishing are the most important economic activities.

Fishing and wine making are traditional Portuguese industries. The man at left carries grapes for the country's famed port wine. The woman above processes sardines, one of its chief exports.

## THE ECONOMY

Agriculture and fishing were long the mainstay of the Portuguese economy. In recent years, however, the emphasis has been on industrial development. Agriculture, fishing, and forestry now employ less than 12 percent of the workforce; about 33 percent is engaged in manufacturing, mining, and construction; and the remainder in service industries and other occupations. Tourism has traditionally been an important source of income.

**Agriculture.** In spite of its declining percentage of the labor force, agriculture remains a vital economic activity. Wheat is grown extensively on large estates in the drier southern plains, while rice thrives in the moist northern lowlands. Grapes, corn, olives, potatoes, and tomatoes are other chief crops. The main livestock are cattle, grazed mainly in the north, and sheep, pigs, and goats, raised chiefly in the south.

**Fishing and Forestry.** Fishing remains an important industry. Portugal's offshore waters are a source of sardines, one of its major exports. Larger fishing vessels journey to the Grand Banks off Newfoundland to catch cod and other fish. Portugal's forests produce about half of the world's supply of cork. Other forestry products include resin and turpentine, which are also important exports, and paper, wood pulp, and timber.

**Manufacturing and Trade.** Textiles and clothing are the chief manufactured products, with clothing accounting for about 20 percent of Portugal's export earnings. Other manufactured goods include shoes,

**Prince Henry the Navigator (1394–1460) encouraged the explorations that led to Portugal's great age of discovery.**

electrical appliances, ceramics and glass, wood pulp, cork, and other forestry products. Lisbon and Oporto are the major manufacturing cities. Portugal's trade is primarily with other members of the European Union. Its chief imports are petroleum, iron and steel, motor vehicles, sugar, and cotton.

## GOVERNMENT

Portugal is a republic governed under a constitution adopted in 1976 and revised in 1982 and 1989. The head of state is the president, elected for five years, who appoints a prime minister to lead the government. The legislature is the Assembly of the Republic, whose members are elected for four years. There is, in addition, an advisory body, the Council of State, which is headed by the president. The judiciary consists of the Supreme Court, whose justices are appointed for life, and various other courts.

## HISTORY

**Early History.** The earliest inhabitants of what is now Portugal (and Spain) were the Iberians. Celtic peoples settled in the north around 1000 B.C., while Phoenicians, and later Greeks and Carthaginians, founded cities and colonies in the south. The Romans conquered the region in the 1st century A.D., after a long and stubborn resistance by a warlike people they called the *Lusitani*. With the collapse of the Roman Empire in the A.D. 400's, Visigoths and Suevi, two Germanic tribes, fought for control of the region. In the 700's, the Muslim Moors invaded the peninsula, conquering most of Spain and more than half of Portugal and adding a new element to the population.

The first independent Portuguese state came into being in 1143, when Afonso Henriques took the title of king as Afonso I. During the 1200's, his successors completed the reconquest of Portugal from the Moors.

**The Age of Discovery.** In 1385, John I founded the royal house of Avis, which ruled Portugal until 1580. His son Prince Henry, known as Henry the Navigator, encouraged the explorations that led to the great Portuguese age of discovery of the 1400's and 1500's. There were several famous Portuguese explorer-navigators of the period.

Bartholomeu Dias discovered the Cape of Good Hope at the southern tip of Africa, opening up a sea route to Asia. Vasco da Gama, following Dias, reached India and brought back spices and other evidence of its great wealth. Pedro Cabral discovered Brazil, claiming it for Portugal. Ferdinand Magellan's expedition, sponsored by the king of Spain, was the first to sail around the earth, although he did not live to complete the voyage. For more information, see the articles on Vasco da Gama in Volume G, Ferdinand Magellan in Volume M, and Exploration and Discovery in Volume E.

By the mid-1500's, Portuguese possessions stretched halfway around the world. But it was trade more than colonization that brought wealth to Portugal.

**Spanish Rule and Loss of Brazil.** In 1580, Portugal was annexed by Spain. The Portuguese successfully revolted against Spanish rule in 1640, when John IV, of the house of Bragança (Braganza), the last line of Portuguese kings, came to the throne. A period of renewed prosperity followed, but good fortune did not smile on Portugal for long.

In 1755 an earthquake almost destroyed Lisbon. During the Napoleonic Wars in the early 1800's, the country was a battleground for both British and French armies. The royal family fled to Brazil, where Rio de Janeiro temporarily became the capital of the Portuguese empire. In 1821, King John VI returned to Portugal, but his son Dom Pedro I remained in Brazil as its ruler. In 1822 he declared Brazil's independence.

**The Portuguese Republic.** During the 1800's, Portugal was torn by civil wars. In 1910 the last king, Manuel II, was overthrown and Portugal became a republic. The freely elected government did not last long, however. General António Óscar de Fragoso Carmona seized power in a military revolt in 1926. He was elected president in 1928 and held the office until his death in 1951. António de Oliveira Salazar, the minister of finance under Carmona, became prime minister in 1932. Over the years, Salazar's powers increased greatly, and he ruled Portugal virtually as a dictator until 1968.

**Colonial Affairs.** Portugal held on to its African territories—Portuguese Guinea (now Guinea-Bissau), São Tomé and Príncipe, Cape Verde, Angola, and Mozambique—longer than other colonial powers. The long and costly wars that Portugal fought to keep them divided the nation and resulted in a military coup, led by General António de Spínola, in 1974. The country's new leaders recognized the right of the territories to independence

Paraders in Lisbon commemorate the revolution of April 25, 1974, which overthrew the old authoritarian regime and brought democratic government to Portugal.

and promised to restore democratic government to Portugal.

Macao (or Macau), an overseas territory that was ruled by Portugal for 400 years, became the last remnant of Portugal's once-vast empire. Situated on the South China coast, it includes a portion of mainland area and two small islands. Under Portuguese administration, Macao's government was headed by a governor appointed by the president of Portugal with the approval of a territorial legislature. In 1999, after years of negotiations, Macao was returned to China as a special administrative and autonomous region.

**Recent History.** Although political conflicts threatened to lead to civil war, a stable, democratic government finally emerged. Portugal officially joined the European Community (now the European Union) in 1986. One of the country's leading political figures of this period was Mário Soares, who served as both prime minister and president, holding office as president until 1996, when he was succeeded by Jorge Sampaio. Sampaio was re-elected president in 2001.

VINCENT MALMSTROM
Dartmouth College

**POSEIDON.** See GREEK MYTHOLOGY (Profiles).

# POSTAL SERVICE

The postal service is the government agency that handles the mail. Its job is to deliver letters and packages to people and businesses all over the world. Its goal is to see that your mail gets to its destination as quickly as possible. People rely on the postal service to deliver important letters and even valuables, on time and to the right person.

Much of the world's business depends on the postal service. That is why most countries cooperate closely on postal matters. The mail always goes through. A flood in South America or an earthquake in Asia may cause a delay, but new routes are found and mail is delivered. A letter mailed from North America may travel to an African country by boat, plane, train, truck, and even horseback.

In a country as large as the United States, the operation of the postal service is big business. The United States Postal Service is responsible for delivering mail, printing stamps, and handling related duties. There are hundreds of thousands of postal workers, and the budget runs into billions of dollars a year. In many countries the post office also operates the telephone and telegraph systems.

A U.S. mail carrier delivers mail in a suburban community. Many carriers travel on foot, carrying mail in pouches or wheeling it in carts.

### ▶ HOW THE MAIL TRAVELS

Basically, mail is handled the same way in almost every country. A stamped letter is mailed at the post office or dropped in a mailbox. The mail is collected from mailboxes on a regular schedule. All letters, postcards, and small parcels are taken to a central post office, where many people work. The sacks of mail are emptied onto a long conveyor belt. As the belt moves along, mail handlers separate large envelopes, books, magazines, and parcels from letters and postcards. This is called **culling**.

The large pieces are postmarked (time and date stamped) and canceled (made non-reusable) by hand. Letters and postcards are turned in the same direction and placed in trays by hand or by machines. The machines also cancel the mail by printing lines and sometimes a slogan over the stamp. They postmark the envelopes by stamping the name of the city where the letter was mailed, the time of day (A.M. or P.M.), and the date. In small post offices, letters are postmarked by hand.

After the mail is postmarked, it is separated according to sections of the country. Modern post offices have machines, called optical character readers (OCR's), that separate letters according to their destinations. An OCR reads the typed address, then translates it into a code, which is sprayed onto the envelope with special ink. The OCR then reads the code and sends the letter into a bin, depending on its destination. At the destination post office, a machine reads the coded address and sorts the letter into another bin. The mail is then sent, usually by truck, to a local post office. There it is sorted again, this time for individual mail routes. All the mail for one route is given to the mail carrier, who delivers it to each mailbox.

Some countries have unique methods of postal delivery. Mail in London, England, speeds under the city in an automatic subway running across the center of the city. The cars run from a subway station to a post office, with stops along the way at several other post offices. The subway, which opened in 1923, is completely automated.

In Sweden the postal service uses skis in addition to the usual methods of delivering mail. Until 1963, dogsleds were used in Alaska. But the huskies have been replaced by airplanes.

### ▶ HISTORY OF MAIL SERVICE

The world's first known mail carriers hauled the inscribed clay tablets of Babylon more than 4,000 years ago. These young men must have been strong, since their burden was much heavier than the maximum of 35 pounds (16 kilograms) that can be carried today by a U.S. letter carrier.

In time the clay tablets were replaced by tablets of bronze, and messengers, or couriers, began traveling on horseback. In Persia in the 500's B.C., mail was carried by riders. Relay posts, where a courier either mounted a fresh horse or turned over the message to another courier, were used by the Chinese more than 2,000 years ago.

Postal services were an important means of communication during the time of Augustus, emperor of Rome, and of Charlemagne, emperor of the Roman Empire. In the Western Hemisphere, the Aztecs of Mexico and the Incas of Peru both used postal systems.

The word "post" comes from the French word *poste*, a station where couriers would stop. In France the postal service was started by Louis XI in the 1400's, but it was only for high court officials. The first public French postal service began in 1506. It was so expensive, however, only the rich used it.

England's first successful postal system, for the use of the royal family, was started in 1516. During the reign of Queen Elizabeth I (1558–1603), the warning phrase "Haste, Post, Haste, For Thy Lyfe, For Thy Lyfe, Haste" was often written on letters to remind postboys of their duty. The postboys carried the mail for about 200 years.

In 1639 the General Court of Massachusetts decreed that all mail arriving from abroad be delivered to Richard Fairbanks of Boston, who, for a penny, handled each letter. In 1672 a monthly post was begun between Boston and New York. Philadelphia's first post office was established in 1683. A postal route extending from Maine to Georgia was established over the routes that became the main highways of the eastern seaboard.

In 1692 the British Crown put Thomas Neale in charge of postal service in the American colonies. Neale appointed Andrew Hamilton, the governor of New Jersey, to organize and administer a colonial postal system. In 1737, Benjamin Franklin was appointed postmaster at Philadelphia. Franklin became joint deputy postmaster general for the northern British colonies in 1753. He served until 1774, when he was fired for being sympathetic to the cause of the colonists. Franklin was appointed head of the American postal system by the Continental Congress on July 26, 1775, at a salary of $1,000 a year. He served until November 7, 1776. The establishment of a dependable postal service in the United States was largely his work.

The organization now known as the U.S. Postal Service was one of the first government organizations established by the Second Continental Congress. After the U.S. Constitution was officially approved and the present form of government took shape, Samuel Osgood of Massachusetts was appointed postmaster general under President George Washington.

The postal service was an early user of the railroads (in the 1830's). Its support was partly responsible for the rapid growth of the railway system in the United States.

The U.S. Postal Service once used horse-drawn carriages to deliver mail. Today it operates a large fleet of cars and trucks.

A postal worker sorts incoming mail. After sorting, each piece of mail is postmarked with the date, the time of day, and the name of the city or town from which it was mailed.

The discovery of gold in California in 1849 hastened the rush westward, and the mails followed close behind. Mail from the East at first reached the West by ship. It was sent by steamer to Panama, where it was carried to the Pacific. The mail was then shipped to the Columbia River in the northwestern United States. In 1858 the first transcontinental overland mail was sent by stagecoach from St. Louis to San Francisco. The Pony Express began in 1860. This was a mail delivery service that used relays of men riding fast ponies or horses. For more information, see the article on the Pony Express in this volume.

Great dogsled teams traveled throughout northern Alaska to deliver mail in the late 1800's and early 1900's. The sleds could carry 700 pounds (300 kilograms) of mail. Sometimes two sleds were coupled together, and as many as 24 dogs were used. A typical dogsled route, over the bleak and dangerous trail between Kotzebue and Barrow, was 650 miles (1,040 kilometers) long.

Mail was carried by plane experimentally as early as 1911. Scheduled airmail service began in 1918. The first airmail pilots were postal employees. Among them was Charles A. Lindbergh, the "lone eagle." By demonstrating that airplanes could safely carry a payload, the Post Office Department played a vital role in the development of commercial passenger aviation.

▶ UNITED STATES POSTAL SERVICE

In 1970 the Postal Reorganization Act was adopted. It provided that within one year the Post Office would be converted into the U.S. Postal Service, an independent establishment in the executive branch of government. In 1971, the postmaster general left the president's cabinet.

The Postal Service is run by an eleven-member board of governors. Nine of the members are appointed by the president, with the approval of the Senate. These nine select a postmaster general, and this group of ten then chooses a deputy postmaster general. Postal rates are suggested by a Postal Rate Commission. The commission has five members, appointed by the president with the Senate's approval.

On an average day, more than 650 million pieces of mail move across the country—the equivalent of two letters a day for every man, woman, and child in the country. The United States Postal Service handles more mail than any other postal department in the world—more than 210 billion pieces a year.

There are about 38,000 post offices in the United States—one in almost every city and small town. Because of this, the Postal Service comes into close contact each day with more people than any other branch of the federal government.

The Postal Service owns and leases more than 215,000 cars and trucks, making it the nation's largest civilian fleet. Among these are specially designed vehicles that have the steering wheel on the right side, so that mail carriers do not have to get out to place mail in roadside mailboxes.

The department also uses thousands of vehicles for "star" routes, or highway contract routes. Star carriers are not Postal Service employees but are under contract to handle transportation and delivery in many areas. Usually star routes link a large post office to a post office in a rural section not served by airplanes, trains, or trucks. But many star routes serve cities. The longest one runs from Seattle, Washington, to Dallas, Texas.

Many mail carriers travel on foot, carrying the mail in pouches or wheeling it in carts.

They separate their mail into two or more pouches when the load for the full route is too heavy to carry all at once. When the mail from the first pouch is delivered, the carrier picks up the next pouch from one of the storage bins located on many street corners. These boxes are marked "Not for Deposit of Mail."

U.S. mail carriers wear bluish gray uniforms with the emblem of the Postal Service—a blue eagle poised for flight—on the sleeve. Letter carriers in other countries also wear distinctive uniforms to make them easily recognizable.

**Post Office Services.** The U.S. Postal Service offers many different services. Descriptions of some of them follow.

**Free delivery** of mail to homes and places of business is available to nearly every community of 2,500 or more people. In rural areas, service is provided by **rural free delivery**. Mail is usually delivered once a day, six days a week. In some business districts, commercial firms receive two deliveries a day.

There are four classes of mail, with different postage rates. **First-class mail** consists of letters, postcards, and similar items. **Second-class mail**, also known as periodical mail, is made up of magazines and newspapers. **Standard A mail**, formerly known as third-class mail, consists mostly of advertisements and catalogs. Books and other parcels are sent by **standard B**, formerly called fourth-class mail. Bulk rates are available for large commercial mailings.

Standard B provides for the mailing of packages. Fees depend on size, weight, and distance sent. **Special handling** is available for an additional fee, to provide special care and speedier service. **Insurance** for up to $5,000 can be obtained for Standard B as well as merchandise mailed at priority mail or first-class rates. Registered mail can be insured for up to $25,000.

Some mail cannot be delivered or returned to its sender because it is addressed incorrectly and does not have a return address. Such mail goes to the Mail Recovery Center. The mail is opened to try to determine the sender or addressee. If this is unsuccessful, the mail is destroyed, and any valuables are sold.

**Money orders** are like bank checks and are a safe way to send money by mail. They can

The U.S. Postal Service employs thousands and is one of the world's largest organizations. Its seal is an eagle poised for flight.

be bought and cashed at post offices and banks.

**Stamps** are sold in various denominations (values) for postal use and for collecting. Commemorative stamps are issued throughout the year. They usually honor important individuals or events and are often highly prized by collectors. **Semi-postal stamps** are those that help raise money (beyond the Postal Service's costs) for special causes. One example of this is the Breast Cancer Awareness stamp, which helped generate money for research. Postal cards, stamped envelopes, and stamp collecting kits and guides are also sold.

**Metered postage** is often used by businesses. Mail is stamped by a machine. A specific amount of postage is purchased from the post office, which sets the machine for that amount.

**Registered mail** offers postal customers extra safety for valuable mail at an additional fee. The post office insures such mail and keeps a careful record of it. The addressee must sign a receipt for it. **Certified mail** is similar but less expensive and does not provide insurance.

**Express mail** service guarantees quick delivery in most metropolitan areas. This service is available every day of the year including Sundays and holidays.

**Collect on delivery (C.O.D.)** allows a person to pay for something when it is delivered rather than in advance. The post office collects the money (plus postage) from the recipient and transmits it to the sender.

**Post office boxes** are locked mailboxes inside the post office. They are rented by people who find them more convenient or more private than regular service.

**General delivery** is a service for people without permanent addresses. Mail sent to a

## HOW A LETTER TRAVELS

Jenny mails a letter to her grandfather. She puts it into a mailbox.

The mail carrier, arriving by truck, empties the mailbox and puts Jenny's letter into a mailbag.

When the carrier returns to the post office, the mailbag with Jenny's letter is put with other mailbags onto a hand truck.

The hand truck moves the mailbags into the post office, where they are dumped on a moving belt to be sorted according to...

The mailbags of letters and packages going to grandfather's city are loaded into the plane on a moving belt.

Most mail flies at night so it can be delivered the next day.

When the plane arrives, the mailbags are unloaded into a mail truck again.

post office care of general delivery is picked up by the addressee.

A **mailgram**, a combination letter-telegram, can be sent by wire and delivered by a letter carrier. Mailgrams were first transmitted by satellite in 1974.

Some postal products and services are available on the Internet. Customers using the U.S. Postal Service web site can buy stamps, track and confirm package deliveries, calculate rates, get maps and directions to post offices, pay bills, download forms, obtain mailing and shipping information, change their addresses, and more.

**Other Services. Postal inspectors** also provide a service; they are the postal system's law enforcement and security arm. Postal inspectors investigate mail theft and consumer fraud and track down people who have forged money orders or used the mails to send bombs, poisons, illegal drugs, or extortion letters. They guard against sexual exploitation of children and the use of mail to preach the overthrow of the government by force.

Other duties of the U.S. Postal Service include the following: sale of U.S. savings bonds in places where banking facilities are not available; assisting the Bureau of the Census; helping obtain passports for individuals in places without State Department facilities; sale of migratory bird hunting stamps; distribution of federal income tax forms; and selective service registration.

The Postal Service cooperates with other federal agencies in obtaining statistical information. Rural letter carriers survey wildfowl populations, report forest fires, and distribute livestock and crop acreage survey cards. The department also locates relatives of deceased personnel for the armed forces.

**ZIP Codes and Abbreviations.** ZIP codes are five-number codes that appear at the end of addresses. They originated from the postal zone system that was first introduced in the 1940's (ZIP stands for "zone improvement plan"). For about 20 years the areas serviced by branch post offices in major cities had zone numbers. These numbers helped speed mail sorting.

The letters then go to a machine that cancels the postage stamps on the front of the letters.

Another machine, with many operators, sorts the mail according to ZIP codes.

At the back of this machine, clerks take the sorted letters out of special ZIP code marked bins and put them into trays for shipping to different cities and towns.

A truck takes Jenny's letter to the airport for its trip to grandfather's home in a distant city.

The truck takes the mailbags to a large post office, where they are sorted according to the towns to which they are going.

Jenny's letter is taken to the post office in grandfather's town.

There a postal worker puts Jenny's letter into a special case that has grandfather's address and the addresses of all his neighbors.

Grandfather is very happy when the carrier delivers Jenny's letter.

ZIP codes go a step further in helping direct the mail. The five-digit ZIP code was first introduced in 1963. The first three digits of this code represent a delivery area of the country; the last two, a post office within this delivery area.

In 1983 the Postal Service expanded the ZIP code to nine digits. The new code is called a ZIP + 4 code. The four new numbers help make automated machine-sorting of first-class mail easier. The first two new digits indicate a large delivery unit, such as a city block or group of blocks. The remaining two new digits indicate a small delivery unit, such as a building or group of post office boxes.

In addressing mail, many companies use mechanized systems. These systems allow only a limited amount of space for each line of an address. The Postal Service therefore devised special two-letter abbreviations for

## POSTAL SERVICE ABBREVIATIONS FOR STATES AND OTHER AREAS

| | | | | | | | |
|---|---|---|---|---|---|---|---|
| **AL** | Alabama | **ID** | Idaho | **MT** | Montana | **RI** | Rhode Island |
| **AK** | Alaska | **IL** | Illinois | **NE** | Nebraska | **SC** | South Carolina |
| **AZ** | Arizona | **IN** | Indiana | **NV** | Nevada | **SD** | South Dakota |
| **AR** | Arkansas | **IA** | Iowa | **NH** | New Hampshire | **TN** | Tennessee |
| **CA** | California | **KS** | Kansas | **NJ** | New Jersey | **TX** | Texas |
| **CZ** | Canal Zone | **KY** | Kentucky | **NM** | New Mexico | **UT** | Utah |
| **CO** | Colorado | **LA** | Louisiana | **NY** | New York | **VT** | Vermont |
| **CT** | Connecticut | **ME** | Maine | **NC** | North Carolina | **VA** | Virginia |
| **DE** | Delaware | **MD** | Maryland | **ND** | North Dakota | **VI** | Virgin Islands |
| **DC** | District of Columbia | **MA** | Massachusetts | **OH** | Ohio | **WA** | Washington |
| **FL** | Florida | **MI** | Michigan | **OK** | Oklahoma | **WV** | West Virginia |
| **GA** | Georgia | **MN** | Minnesota | **OR** | Oregon | **WI** | Wisconsin |
| **GU** | Guam | **MS** | Mississippi | **PA** | Pennsylvania | **WY** | Wyoming |
| **HI** | Hawaii | **MO** | Missouri | **PR** | Puerto Rico | | |

the states and some other areas. By using these abbreviations, mechanized systems can show city, state, and ZIP code all on one line. The public also uses these abbreviations, which are listed in the box in this article.

**New Technology.** In 1992 the Postal Service began using bar codes to speed the mail-sorting process. These codes make it easy to identify the delivery point of packages and letters. More recently, high-speed sorters were introduced that can process about 30,000 pieces of mail per hour.

The Postal Service also now offers an electronic postmark for e-mail, which is a time and date stamp for an electronic document or file.

Those who use it get the same legal protection for e-mail that exists for other (physical) mail. That is, it becomes a federal offense to open or tamper with such mail.

**New Challenges.** In 2001, the postal service began investigating the mailing of letters containing anthrax, a potentially fatal strain of bacteria. Letters containing this substance resulted in the death of two postal employees and three citizens. As public concern grew, postal inspectors also responded to thousands of suspicious mailings, hoaxes, and threats. At the same time, the U.S.P.S. began taking steps to make the mail more secure.

United States Postal Service

# POSTERS

Posters are signs, usually displayed in public, that inform people about events, products, or services. Billboards, safety campaign signs, advertisements on buses—all are posters. To be effective, a poster must deliver a clearly understandable message that can be grasped at a glance.

This poster urges people to use libraries. The most effective posters combine short written messages with attractive images.

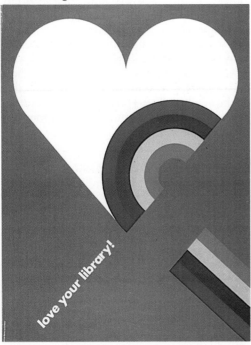

The history of posters is unclear. Leaflets, handbills, and posted notices informed and persuaded people wherever there was written language. From these the poster gradually developed. Posters as we know them were probably first used by theater companies to advertise their plays.

Modern posters—with the fewest possible words and greatest visual effect—came into widespread use late in the 1800's. The Industrial Revolution brought about an age in which competing companies began to advertise consumer products. These companies were able to make wide use of the poster because of the invention of color lithography, a method of printing. French artist Henri de Toulouse-Lautrec (1864–1901), in his beautiful posters for Paris cafés, demonstrated how effective printed posters could be.

Most commercial posters are printed in great quantity. Schools and clubs, however, display handmade posters to advertise plays, athletic events, or dances. Handmade posters are much more economical than printed ones and can be just as effective.

To make a poster, first decide on your text and how to match it with an effective and expressive picture. The colors and lettering should fit the purpose. Whatever design you use, remember that good posters must make people stop and look.

Reviewed by RAFAEL FERNANDEZ
Sterling and Francine Clark Art Institute

**POSTURE.** See PHYSICAL EDUCATION.

# POTATOES

Fried potatoes, whipped potatoes, baked potatoes—potatoes in their many forms are such a common food that they are taken for granted. Yet the white, or Irish, potato is the most important vegetable grown. It is a basic food for millions of people. Potatoes are grown in at least 80 countries.

## ▶ THE USES OF POTATOES

In European countries potatoes are used not only for food but also for livestock feed. Large quantities are manufactured into starch, flour, alcohol, and distilled liquors.

In the United States most of the potato crop is used for food. Only the extra potatoes and those too poor to use for food are turned into manufactured products. In Canada the crop is used mostly for food and for seed potatoes that are exported. Large quantities are also manufactured into starch, while still other potatoes are used for food for livestock.

Most potatoes used as food are sold fresh. But many potatoes are treated in some way before they are eaten. At least 53 different food products are made from potatoes. These include potato chips, frozen french fried potatoes, and dehydrated, pre-peeled, and canned potatoes.

**Food Value.** The potato has excellent food value. The main value of the potato is its starch (carbohydrate) content, which provides energy. It contains little protein and almost no fat. Potatoes also contain ascorbic acid (vitamin C) and some minerals, particularly potassium. One medium-sized, boiled, unpeeled potato provides 120 Calories.

The food value of potatoes differs in different varieties. It also varies with different conditions of soils, climate, fertilization, and temperature. The amount of vitamin C decreases as potatoes remain in storage. For the most nutrition, potatoes should be cooked with the skins on, as most of the vitamins and minerals are found in the skin.

The taste and texture of potatoes depend in part on the variety. People prefer mealy potatoes, which contain a high percentage of dry matter. Soggy potatoes are less desirable.

## ▶ THE POTATO PLANT

The potato plant is a member of the nightshade family. Other plants of the nightshade family are tomatoes and eggplant, as well as some narcotic-containing plants, such as tobacco, henbane, and belladonna.

The potato plant is an annual plant; that is, it goes through its entire life cycle within a year's time. It has a stout, erect stem that grows from 12 to 24 inches (30 to 60 centimeters) high. The flowers are white, rose, lilac, purple or blue. Under certain conditions, the plants may produce a smooth, round green or yellow berry (fruit). Each fruit may contain 100 to 200 seeds.

Soon after the potato stems appear above ground, slight growths develop on the underground portion of the stems. These growths lengthen for a time and then swell at their tips

The aboveground part of a potato plant has dark green leaves and small flowers. The edible parts are the thin-skinned tubers that grow underground. After being harvested by machine, the potatoes are sorted and graded.

to form tubers. The tuber, which is the part we call the potato, is a shortened, thickened stem.

The tubers differ according to the variety of potato. They may be oblong or oval, have a somewhat rough or a smooth skin, and have a light yellowish-brown or red skin color. With good growing conditions, certain varieties of potato plant will produce large tubers within 2½ or 3 months of planting.

▶ **GROWING AND HARVESTING POTATOES**

When new varieties are produced, potato plants are raised from seed. But in commercial potato growing, seeds are not used. The plants are grown from the potato itself. A whole small potato is planted, or a large potato is cut into pieces, each containing an **eye**. An eye is really the bud of an underground stem. Each piece, called a **seed piece**, has at least one eye and as much potato flesh as possible. The flesh around the eye provides the food for the new plant's first growth. Generally the seed pieces are planted in hills about 4 inches (10 centimeters) deep and 10 inches (25 centimeters) apart. The rows are about 34 inches (85 centimeters) apart.

Most garden soils are suitable for growing potatoes. Somewhat acid soil is preferable, as this prevents the potato from contracting a bacterial disease known as potato scab. Special fertilizers are used for potatoes. The fertilizer must be applied so that it does not touch the seed pieces. In addition, the growing plants must be thoroughly sprayed or dusted. No crop has been more troubled by diseases than the potato. Even the seed pieces are treated to prevent diseases. Potatoes can be badly affected by potato late blight, a fungus that infects the stems, leaves, and tubers of the plant. Potatoes also must be protected against the potato beetle, the blister beetle, and the potato leafhopper.

Potatoes are dug up in various stages of maturity. Varieties of potatoes that are grown early in the season may be left in the ground for a short while if the weather is not too warm and wet. In some warm locations it is safe to leave varieties of potatoes that are grown late in the season in the ground for 4 to 6 weeks after maturity.

Potato combines are used to harvest large potato crops. The digger of the combine brings potatoes out of the ground, shakes off the dirt and vines, and puts the potatoes into a truck. From here they are delivered to storage or to grading stations.

**Storage.** Potatoes should be stored in a cool, dry place. Too much light causes the skin of the potato to turn green. A bitter substance called solanin accumulates in green potatoes, making them unfit for eating.

▶ **POTATO PRODUCTION**

China is by far the world's leading potato-producing country, accounting for about 20 percent of the world's total production in 1998. Russia, with about 11 percent, is the second largest producer. Poland (with about 9 percent) and the United States (with about 7 percent) are next in importance. The chief U.S. potato-growing states, in order of production, are Idaho, Washington, Wisconsin, North Dakota, and Colorado.

▶ **HISTORY**

When the Spanish invaded South America in the middle of the 1500's, they found the white potato being grown by people of the Andes. Potatoes were brought back to Spain and by the end of the 1500's, they were common in Spain and Italy. The potato grew well in Europe and soon became important in Germany, Poland, and Russia.

There are legends that Sir Walter Raleigh or Sir Francis Drake introduced the potato into Britain at some time between 1585 and 1587. Soon afterward it was taken to Ireland, where it grew well and became the staple food of the country. In 1845 and 1846 there was a terrible potato blight in Ireland. The blight killed off practically all the potato crop. About 1.5 million people in Ireland died of starvation, and many others were forced to emigrate.

The potato was first grown in the United States in 1621, when it was brought to Virginia from Bermuda. In 1719, potatoes were brought from Ireland to New Hampshire. The potatoes that grew from those brought from Ireland were known as Irish potatoes.

The spread of the potato throughout the world is one of the miracles of agriculture. Today it is the world's second most important food crop, exceeded only by grains.

Reviewed by RODNEY W. DOW
State University of New York Agricultural and
Technical College at Farmingdale

# POTTER, HELEN BEATRIX (1866–1943)

Helen Beatrix Potter was born in London on July 28, 1866. Unlike her younger brother, who was sent off to school, Beatrix was educated at home by governesses. She had no playmates her own age, so she turned for friendship to the stuffed animals she played with in the nursery of her family's large house.

In the summer her parents took Beatrix and her brother to Scotland. These vacations opened her eyes to the wonders of the countryside. She made sketches of the animals, birds, and insects that she saw. Back in London she would entertain herself with her pet snails, mice, rabbits, and a hedgehog named Mrs. Tiggy-Winkle, which drank out of a doll's teacup.

As Beatrix grew older, she wrote many letters to her younger friends. These letters were filled with drawings and stories she made up to entertain them. One series of letters to the sick child of her former governess tells the original tale of the naughty Peter Rabbit. Her stories became so popular among her friends that, in 1900, she decided to publish *The Tale of Peter Rabbit* in a private edition. Her publisher was soon bringing out her stories as quickly as she could write and illustrate them.

The following years saw the publication of *The Tailor of Gloucester* (1902), *the Tale of Squirrel Nutkin* (1903), and *The Tale of Benjamin Bunny* (1904). Beatrix Potter believed that a small child's book should be small itself, so all of her tales appeared in little books, with only one or two sentences and a watercolor illustration on each page.

In 1905 she purchased Hill Top Farm in the village of Sawrey in northern England and began to raise sheep. Many of the scenes and animals in her most famous books were drawn from Hill Top Farm. The next eight years were Beatrix Potter's most creative period. She published her finest work, including the tales of Jeremy Fisher, Jemima Puddle-duck, Tom Kitten, the Flopsy Bunnies, Mrs. Tittlemouse, and Pigling Bland.

In 1913, Beatrix Potter married William Heelis, a lawyer. In her later years she dedicated herself to buying tracts of land in the Lake District in order to preserve the area from commercial development. In her will she turned over her vast holdings to the National Trust for future preservation.

**BEATRIX POTTER'S BEST LOVED CHARACTERS**

**PETER RABBIT,** who is naughty and careless and disobeys his mother, nearly gets put into a pie by Mr. McGregor when he steals into the farmer's garden to eat lettuce.

**THE TAILOR OF GLOUCESTER** works cross-legged on a table from morning till dark, making himself ill, so that his friends the mice must finish the Mayor's new coat.

**SQUIRREL NUTKIN,** his brother Twinkleberry, and their many cousins go to pick nuts on Old Brown's island, where naughty Nutkin teases the old owl once too often.

**BENJAMIN BUNNY,** Peter Rabbit's clever cousin, who has no opinion of cats, visits Flopsy, Mopsy, Cottontail, and Peter and rescues Peter's clothes from Mr. McGregor.

**JEREMY FISHER,** who likes getting his feet wet and never catches cold, goes out on his round green boat and has an adventure fishing in the middle of the pond.

**MRS. TITTLEMOUSE,** the wood mouse who lives in a barn, is terribly tidy but has a few too many uninvited visitors, including the very messy Mr. Jackson.

**MRS. TIGGY-WINKLE,** who is scrupulously clean, helps Lucie find her lost pocket handkerchief — all clean and starched and ironed — and gives her a friendly cup of tea.

Beatrix Potter died in Sawrey on December 22, 1943. Her home, now part of the National Trust, is open to the public.

RICHARD KELLY
University of Tennessee

An excerpt from Potter's *The Tale of Jemima Puddle-duck* appears on the following page.

### ►THE TALE OF JEMIMA PUDDLE-DUCK

Jemima Puddle-duck sets off to find a secret place to hatch her eggs. She meets an elegant gentleman with black ears and a long bushy tail, who offers her the use of his cozy wood-shed. But Jemima is such a foolish duck that she does not recognize her benefactor as—a fox!

He was so polite, that he seemed almost sorry to let Jemima go home for the night. He promised to take great care of her nest until she came back again the next day.

He said he loved eggs and ducklings; he should be proud to see a fine nestful in his wood-shed.

Jemima Puddle-duck came every afternoon; she laid nine eggs in the nest. They were greeny white and very large. The foxy gentleman admired them immensely. He used to turn them over and count them when Jemima was not there.

At last Jemima told him that she intended to begin to sit next day—"and I will bring a bag of corn with me, so that I need never leave my nest until the eggs are hatched. They might catch cold," said the conscientious Jemima.

"Madam, I beg you not to trouble yourself with a bag; I will provide oats. But before you commence your tedious sitting, I intend to give you a treat. Let us have a dinner-party all to ourselves!

"May I ask you to bring up some herbs from the farm-garden to make a savoury omelette? Sage and thyme, and mint and two onions, and some parsley. I will provide lard for the stuff—lard for the omelette," said the hospitable gentleman with sandy whiskers.

Jemima Puddle-duck was a simpleton: not even the mention of sage and onions made her suspicious.

She went round the farm-garden, nibbling off snippets of all the different sorts of herbs that are used for stuffing roast duck.

And she waddled into the kitchen, and got two onions out of the basket.

The collie-dog Kep met her coming out, "What are you doing with those onions? Where do you go every afternoon by yourself, Jemima Puddle-duck?"

Jemima was rather in awe of the collie; she told him the whole story.

The collie listened, with his wise head on one side; he grinned when she described the polite gentleman with sandy whiskers.

He asked several questions about the wood, and about the exact position of the house and shed.

Then he went out, and trotted down the village. He went to look for two fox-hound puppies who were out at walk with the butcher.

Jemima Puddle-duck went up the cart-road for the last time, on a sunny afternoon. She was rather burdened with bunches of herbs and two onions in a bag.

She flew over the wood, and alighted opposite the house of the bushy long-tailed gentleman.

He was sitting on a log; he sniffed the air, and kept glancing uneasily round the wood. When Jemima alighted he quite jumped.

"Come into the house as soon as you have looked at your eggs. Give me the herbs for the omelette. Be sharp!"

He was rather abrupt. Jemima Puddle-duck had never heard him speak like that.

She felt surprised, and uncomfortable.

While she was inside she heard pattering feet round the back of the shed. Some one with a black nose sniffed at the bottom of the door, and then locked it.

Jemima became much alarmed.

A moment afterwards there were most awful noises—barking, baying, growls and howls, squealing and groans.

And nothing more was ever seen of that foxy-whiskered gentleman.

Throughout history, a great variety of pottery has been produced by cultures around the world. These colorful pieces are the work of a contemporary British potter.

# POTTERY

Pottery consists of objects made from wet clay that are baked or fired so they will hold their shape. The term "pottery" usually refers to vessels, or containers, but can also include sculptures. (Another term, "ceramics," includes a wide range of materials and products, such as bricks, cement, and electrical insulators as well as pottery.)

People have made pottery for thousands of years. Pottery vessels have been used for cooking, storing, and serving food; as lamps; and even as burial containers. In some societies, women were responsible for making pottery; in others, the potters were mainly men. More recently, men and women have shared equally in the making of pottery.

## ▶ HOW POTTERY IS MADE

Pottery is traditionally made by hand. It must be formed into the desired shape, decorated, and then fired.

### Forming

In one of the simplest techniques, clay is rolled into coils, which are built up layer by layer into the desired shape and then smoothed with a scraper or paddle. In a similar method, clay is shaped into flat slabs that are then joined together while still wet.

Slabs of clay can also be formed by pressing them over a mold. In a process known as slipcasting, liquid clay, or "slip," can be poured into molds to form various shapes.

Another method of making pottery is known as throwing. In this method, wet clay is placed in the center of a round table called a potter's wheel. As the wheel spins, the potter shapes the clay with his or her hands.

### Decorating

Pottery can be decorated in a number of ways. Designs can be pressed into the wet clay or incised (scratched) onto the surface. Decorating with slip is also popular. In another technique, slip of one color is applied to a piece of pottery of a different color. Then designs are created by scratching away portions of the slip to expose the underlying color.

**Glazing.** One of the most common forms of pottery decoration is glazing. A glaze is a mixture of powdered minerals or glass and water that is applied to the surface of a piece

In one method of forming pottery, clay is "thrown" on a potter's wheel and shaped with the hands (*top*). After the pot has been fired in a kiln, it is usually decorated with glaze (*center*). The piece is fired again, turning the glaze into a shiny, waterproof covering (*bottom*).

of pottery. After application, the piece of pottery is fired again and the glaze becomes hard and glassy, waterproofing the piece and giving it a colorful, smooth surface. Among the many different kinds of glazes are celadon (a pale grayish green glaze), ash glaze (usually made of ground wood ash), and chun (a pale blue glaze used on stoneware).

Any kind of colored decoration applied to a piece of pottery before it is glazed is called an **underglaze**. An **overglaze**, or **enamel**, is any kind of colored decoration that is applied to a piece of pottery after it has been glazed and fired. After an overglaze is applied, the piece must be fired again.

### Firing

Pottery is fired in a special oven called a **kiln**. Firing changes the nature of the clay, making it hard and durable. Most glazed pottery is fired twice, first to harden the clay body and then again after glazing. Firing temperatures vary depending on the kind of clay and decoration used.

## ▶ KINDS OF POTTERY

There are three kinds of pottery: earthenware, stoneware, and porcelain. Some cultures have produced only earthenware, while other cultures have produced all three kinds at the same time.

### Earthenware

To make earthenware, clay is dug straight from the earth, formed while still wet, and then fired at a low temperature—below 2200°F (1200°C). Sometimes earthenware bricks are baked in the sun. The color of earthenware varies depending on the clay used to make it. Colors after firing range from reds and yellows to white, gray, or black. Because earthenware is porous (not watertight), it is often glazed. Earthenware sculpture is sometimes referred to as terra-cotta.

### Stoneware

Stoneware is made from special clays sometimes mixed with other materials, such as ground stone, and fired at a high temperature—about 2200°F (1200°C). As a result of this process, stoneware is made waterproof. The color of the clay after firing is usually gray or brown.

### Porcelain

Porcelain is made from a special white clay, called kaolin, that is mixed with a powdered rock and fired at a very high temperature—2400°F (1300°C). Porcelain is hard, white, and translucent (light can be seen through it).

# ▶ THE DEVELOPMENT OF POTTERY

Clay pots and other pottery pieces are among the oldest artifacts found at sites once occupied by ancient peoples. They provide archaeologists with a valuable record of daily life in these early cultures.

Earthenware was the first kind of pottery to be developed, emerging in various cultures worldwide between 5000 and 3000 B.C. But archaeological evidence indicates that the first pottery may have been created even earlier—some 30,000 years ago.

Several theories have been suggested to explain the origins of pottery. The basketweave pattern found on some early pieces has led to speculation that a layer of wet clay may have been pressed inside baskets to seal them. Then perhaps it was discovered that if the piece was placed in a fire, the basket would burn away and the clay would harden into a durable container. Another theory is that clay may have been used to line early fire pits, resulting in the formation of a simple pot that remained after the fire was put out.

Although exact dates are impossible to determine, it is thought that the first glazes were developed about 3500 B.C., probably in Egypt. And by 2500 B.C., the potter's wheel was being used in Egypt, Mesopotamia, and China.

## Asian Pottery

It is sometimes said that everything we know today about pottery was already known by the 1300's in China. Whether or not this is true, China has one of the oldest continuous ceramic traditions in the world. Not only were the Chinese among the earliest users of the potter's wheel, but they are also credited with the invention of porcelain. So great is the Chinese contribution to ceramics that "china" has become the common term for many types of pottery.

All of China's early pottery was made to serve a useful purpose, but it did not all look the same. Early Neolithic (New Stone Age) pottery ranged from hand-formed painted pieces (Yangshao culture, 5000–300 B.C.) that had geometric and figural patterns colored by

This early Neolithic (New Stone Age) era earthenware pot was made by China's Yangshao culture between 5000 and 300 B.C.

iron and manganese to eggshell-thin black pottery (Longshan culture, from about 2500–2000 B.C.) thrown on a fast-moving wheel. The Chinese Neolithic potters seemed to be ahead of their time, creating deep cups with handles around 2000 B.C. that look like modern-day coffee mugs. This type of pottery was self-glazing, and its exterior surface looked as if it had been polished by hand.

One of the most magnificent examples of early Chinese pottery is the thousands of life-size warriors and horses created to protect

A remarkable example of pottery sculpture is the army of life-size terra-cotta figures created to protect the tomb of a Chinese emperor.

This vase from the Ming dynasty (1368–1644) has the beautiful and delicate decoration characteristic of Chinese porcelain.

the tomb of Emperor Shi Huangdi against invaders in the afterlife. This terra-cotta pottery was created during the Qin dynasty (221–206 B.C.) and discovered in 1974. Each piece was originally decorated in vivid red, yellow, and blue pigments, but these colors have almost completely faded over time. The Chinese practice of placing pottery tomb figurines underground with the deceased reached its peak in the Tang dynasty (A.D. 618–906).

True porcelain had been created in China by the time of the Tang dynasty, and probably as early as the Sui dynasty (A.D. 581–618). The name "porcelain" is said to have come from Marco Polo, who compared the ceramics he found in China in the 1200's to a delicate seashell called *porcellana* in Italian. Some of the porcelain from the Yuan, Ming, and Qing dynasties (A.D. 1260–1912) was produced on assembly lines made up of dozens of craftspeople who assisted with each specialized portion of a piece. One person might have been the expert in painting floral designs, while another applied overglaze decoration. The porcelain from this period is famous for its beautiful decoration. Sometimes a deep cobalt blue or copper red underglaze was used, and other times brilliant-colored overglazes were applied. These traditions continue today in China.

Chinese potters also sought to duplicate the beauty of jade, a precious gemstone often carved into exquisite forms, in the glazes that covered their pottery. During the Five Dynasties period (A.D. 907–960), celadon glazes were developed and subsequently perfected during the Song dynasty (960–1279). To give the pottery the surface texture of jade, the glaze was applied up to five times and refired to create the desired richness.

The pottery traditions of Japan were influenced by those of China, but the Japanese also developed their own distinctive styles.

During Japan's Tumulus Period (A.D. 300–599), the Japanese placed hollow clay sculptures on the mounds that covered their royal tombs. These simple figures, known as *haniwa*, were made of unglazed earthenware that turned a warm buff color when fired. They were made in the shapes of cylinders, shields, warriors, animals, houses, and other objects. These figures tell us much of what daily life was like in Japan more than 1,500 years ago.

### Islamic Pottery

The Silk Road, an early trading route on which silk and other goods were transported, connected the Islamic world (the Middle East, northern Africa, Spain, and Central Asia) to the Far East. It stretched some 5,000 miles (8,000 kilometers) across deserts, mountains, and grasslands from western Iran to northwest China. The communication among potters in these two regions was constant. The Chinese probably obtained the first good source of cobalt, used for underglaze decoration, from

This plate's blue, white, and red colors and floral motifs are typical of the pottery made in Iznik, Turkey, during the 1500's.

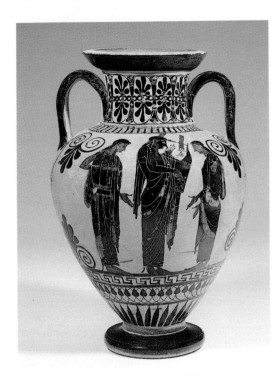

This Greek amphora (vase) from the 500's B.C. is an example of black-figure pottery.

the Islamic world and borrowed and adapted the shapes of many decorative objects crafted in metal into Chinese earthenware funerary forms. Both of these cultures used brilliant lead glazes during the A.D. 700's. One of the remarkable creations of Islamic potters was the use of luster as a decorative feature on their tin-glazed earthenwares beginning in the 800's in Iraq. (Tin glaze is a white, opaque glaze made with tin oxide.) These lusterwares were produced by painting special chemicals containing gold, silver, or copper onto the surfaces of the pottery. The pieces were baked in a fire with little oxygen to give the glazes a metallic sheen. Among the most breathtaking contributions of the Islamic world are the ceramics created in Iznik (Nicaea), an an-

cient city in Turkey, during the peak of the Ottoman Empire in the 1500's. A clear white body forms the background for bright blue, green, and red motifs that adorn dishes, mosque lamps, and tiles.

### Greek Pottery

The Greeks did not use glazes on their pottery. In the 500's and 400's B.C., they painted their polished pottery with figures and scenes using black slip on red earthenware (black-figure pottery). Later, they painted the background and some details with black slip, leaving the figures the color of the clay (red-figure pottery). This type of pottery is called Painted Attic (having characteristics common to ancient Athens). Typical designs include scenes from mythology, history, and daily life. The Greeks were among the earliest potters to sign their work, beginning around 530 to 330 B.C., and they often included inscriptions as part of the decoration. In Athens the potter owned and operated the kiln and employed several vase painters to decorate the pottery.

### African Pottery

Some of the finest pottery sculpture of all time originated in Africa. By about 500 B.C.,

The Nok culture (900 B.C.–A.D. 200) of Nigeria produced detailed terra-cotta sculptures of heads and figures.

sculptors in the area of northern Nigeria created terra-cotta figures that are considered the earliest preserved examples of sub-Saharan African sculpture known today. Terra-cotta heads and figures survive today from sites of the Nok culture, which lasted from 900 B.C. to A.D. 200. The pottery remains show human forms with elaborate hairstyles, facial features, and body ornaments. Ghana's Akan culture, whose potters were highly trained professional women, often depicted deceased royalty. Graceful terra-cotta figures were created between A.D. 1000 and 1200 in Djenné, located in present-day Mali, and provide some of the only documentation of these peoples' lives.

The life-size pottery sculptures known as "babies," created by the Olmec of Mexico, were hollow and typically made of white clay.

## Pottery in the Americas

The pottery of pre-Columbian America (America before the arrival of Columbus) is remarkable because the people never developed stoneware, porcelain, glazes, or the potter's wheel, and their kiln technology was limited. Created between 2000 B.C. and the A.D. 1500's by such cultures as the Remojadas, Olmec, Maya, and others, the earthenware, hand-formed, and slip-decorated pottery of this region is some of the most beautiful and imaginative in the world.

The most successful cultures were those of Mesoamerica (the land from central Mexico down to northwest Costa Rica) and Peru. Life-size figures, referred to as "babies," were made by the Olmec peoples of Mexico between the 1100's and 800's B.C. The figures were hollow, often constructed of white clay, and depicted entire human infant forms.

The earliest Native American pottery in North America dates from about 2,000 years ago. These fragile pieces, made by women for practical purposes, are decorated with fine line-drawings or matte-black designs on polished black backgrounds.

### European Pottery

Europeans greatly admired Chinese porcelain, which began appearing in the West through trade during the Middle Ages (A.D. 500–1500), but for centuries they did not know how to make it. Several different kinds of tin-glazed earthenwares were created that mimicked porcelain's white surface.

During the 1500's in Italy, potters created brightly decorated tin-glazed earthenware known as **majolica**. Their pottery style was referred to as *istoriato*, or narrative style, majolica. The pottery's white surface was used the way a painter uses a blank canvas. Pieces were decorated with portraits as well as images borrowed from sources such as the Bible and classical mythology. Works by famous artists such as Dürer and Raphael were also copied onto the pottery. The most important aspect of the piece was no longer its form but rather the images covering its form. At this time in Italy, pottery was considered nearly a fine art.

Other tin-glazed earthenwares created in Europe included France's **faience**, named after the Italian town of Faenza where the first examples came from; and the Netherlands' **delftware**, named for the town of Delft where much of it was made.

Attempts to create true porcelain in Europe during the late 1500's resulted in the discovery of what is referred to as soft-paste porcelain, which lacks the hardness of true porcelain due to its composition of clay and ground glass. The secret of true, or hard-paste, porcelain was fi-

The tin-glazed earthenware, or majolica, of the Italian Renaissance often featured biblical or mythological scenes.

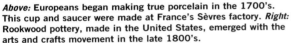

*Above:* Europeans began making true porcelain in the 1700's. This cup and saucer were made at France's Sèvres factory. *Right:* Rookwood pottery, made in the United States, emerged with the arts and crafts movement in the late 1800's.

nally discovered in Europe in 1709–10 by the alchemist Johann Friedrich Böttger (1682–1719) at Germany's Meissen factory, near Dresden. The famous factory of Sèvres, located just outside Paris, was among numerous soft-paste porcelain manufacturers in production until they began making true porcelain in 1768. **Bone china**, another kind of porcelain made by adding powdered animal bone to hard porcelain, was popularized about 1800 by Josiah Spode II (1754–1827).

In England during the mid-1700's, a highly successful company founded by Josiah Wedgwood (1730–95) produced a cream-colored earthenware covered with a transparent glaze. Designed after ancient Greek and Roman pottery, **Wedgwood** was cheap, strong, and easily mass-produced.

▶ **POTTERY TODAY**

Beginning in the mid-1700's in the United States and Europe, many objects—including pottery—that were once made by hand began to be mass produced. Many people felt that mass-production techniques had led to a decline in quality and craftsmanship. In response to this, the arts and crafts movement developed toward the end of the 1800's. This movement advocated a return to handcrafted products made in older styles, and it inspired individual artists—including potters—to reclaim art forms once almost lost.

Throughout the 1900's, handcrafted pottery displayed a revived sense of creativity and experimentation with materials and form. Schools established in the early 1900's taught the art and the science of pottery, and their students founded other schools or small shops that made pottery in the arts and crafts style.

Despite the renewed interest in handcrafted pieces, factories continue to mass-produce pottery, usually in the form of dinnerware (cups, plates, bowls, and the like). Some of this pottery, such as Lenox China, is of fine quality.

Today, more people are working with clay than ever before. They continue to create earthenware, stoneware, and porcelain pottery, and they strive to have their work viewed as fine art. In many poor countries, pottery-making remains an essential part of everyday life.

MARGARET CARNEY
Director, Schein-Joseph International
Museum of Ceramic Art

See also CERAMICS; DECORATIVE ARTS; GREECE, ART AND ARCHITECTURE OF.

**POUCHED MAMMALS.** See KANGAROOS; KOALAS; MARSUPIALS.

# POULTRY

Think about the foods you have eaten today. Perhaps you had eggs for breakfast and a bowl of noodle soup and a piece of cake at lunchtime. Chicken may be on the menu for dinner. All of these foods come from the products of the poultry industry.

Birds that are domesticated (tamed) to serve the purposes of people are called poultry. These birds are most often used to produce meat or eggs; but they may be bred as show stock or fighting cocks. Swans, guinea fowl, pea fowl, and ostriches may be listed as poultry. But the most important poultry in terms of numbers and commerce are chickens, ducks, turkeys, and geese.

▶**CHICKENS**

The chicken is the most widely raised kind of poultry. Chicken meat and eggs are enjoyed as food all over the world. Famous chicken recipes have come from many places: southern fried chicken from the United States; chicken in wine, or *coq au vin,* from France; barbecued chicken from China; chicken curry from India; and so on. Chicken eggs are nutritious and delicious when fried, boiled, poached, or scrambled. Eggs also are an important ingredient in many other foods, such as baked goods, noodles, and casseroles.

Female chickens are called "hens"; males are called "cocks" or "roosters." Young females—those less than one year of age—are known as "pullets."

The present domestic chicken breeds and varieties came from the jungle fowl found in Southeast Asia. Many small, brightly colored Red Jungle Fowl still run wild in the jungles of India. From this small, timid, but scrappy fowl, hundreds of breeds and varieties have been developed. In the past, chickens often were bred for their feather coloring, body shape or size, or ability to fight. Although this type of breeding is still practiced, most chickens are bred only for their ability to lay eggs or produce meat.

Many present breeds carry the name of the country or area in which they were domesticated and developed—for example, the Polish breed, from Poland; the Sussex, from the county of Sussex, England; the Rhode Island Red from the state of Rhode Island in the United States.

Chickens are developed with different characteristics for meat or for egg farming. Here a White Rock hen has been bred to produce an ideal broiler chick.

Many standard breeds and varieties have miniature look-alikes called bantams. They look just like the standard breed except for their smaller size. They are kept mainly for pleasure and hobby.

Chicken fanciers—people who raise chickens only for their appearance—get much pleasure and satisfaction from improving the recognized breeds and varieties for use in poultry shows. Chicken fanciers are interested only slightly in the chicken's ability to lay large numbers of eggs or to produce meat. The commercial chicken farmer, on the other hand, does not care what the chickens look like as long as they lay many dozens of premium eggs or produce many pounds of high-quality meat.

Commercial chicken farming is of two types—meat, or broiler, farming and egg farming. A breed that is good for one type of farming will not be satisfactory for the other. The broiler farmer wants a fast-growing, tender, meaty chicken that can be marketed at a young age. The egg farmer demands a small-bodied hen that lays many large, high-quality eggs and eats a minimum amount of feed. These two sets of traits have not yet been found in the same breed.

Chicken farms are always faced with the threat of a disease outbreak that can kill or make useless large numbers of chickens. Common chicken diseases are Marek's disease, infectious bronchitis, coccidiosis, Newcastle disease, and avian influenza. Constant attention is given to disease control programs designed to prevent outbreaks. When disease outbreaks do occur, proper diagnosis and treatment are essential.

## Broiler Farming

A broiler is a young chicken that is grown for its meat. Large specialized farms raise three or four flocks of broiler chicks each year, some flocks numbering 100,000 or more. The most popular size broiler weighs 4 to 5 pounds (1.8 to 2.3 kilograms) when 6 weeks of age. The size of the broiler may be varied by marketing a flock earlier or later, depending on what the market calls for. For example, a "roaster" weighing 6 or 7 pounds (2.7 to 3.2 kilograms) can be grown by keeping the broilers until they are 12 weeks of age; or a "squab broiler" weighing 2 pounds (0.9 kilogram) can be obtained at 4 weeks of age.

The broiler farmer may buy chicks from a hatchery specializing in hatching broiler chicks; buy scientifically mixed feeds from another company; and sell the live broilers to a company that prepares them for stores to sell. However, most broilers today are produced by companies that own farms, broiler houses, hatcheries, feed mills, and processing plants —integrating all the means necessary to market the ready-to-cook broiler. These "integrated" companies exist because they can produce broilers at less cost than can other types of farming.

Some companies specialize in the genetic improvement of broiler chicks. These companies breed male and female chickens that will produce chicks that grow faster on less feed. Crossbred chicks (chicks with parents from different breeds) grow faster and use less feed than purebred chicks (chicks with parents of the same breed). Most specialized breeding farms spend much of their time improving breeds that, when mated together, will make quality broilers.

The most popular broiler is crossbred from White Rock hens and white-feathered roosters, one of whose ancestors is the White Cornish male noted for its broad breast. This crossbred broiler carries the desirable traits of white feathers, yellow skin, fast growth, good feed conversion, and a broad breast.

Broiler chicks are fed a dry mash, scientifically formulated and nutritionally balanced, consisting mainly of ground corn, soybean meal, minerals, and vitamins. With 8 pounds (3.6 kilograms) of this feed, a broiler weighing 4 pounds (1.8 kilograms) can be grown in six weeks. No other animal is as efficient in converting feed into meat.

## Egg Farming

An egg is one of the marvels of nature. It is a nutritionally complete food providing all the carbohydrates, fats, proteins, vitamins, and minerals necessary for life.

Reproduction is nature's primary purpose in forming an egg. But humans recognized the egg as a good source of food and developed hens whose primary purpose is to lay large numbers of eggs for use as food.

*Above:* Broiler chicks are usually raised in large pens where they are fed a high-energy diet to make them grow rapidly. *Below:* Layers are most often raised in wire cages. Their eggs are collected on a belt that runs below the cages. On a well-automated egg farm, one worker can care for as many as 100,000 laying hens.

People's preference for smaller white turkeys led to the development of the 8- to 10-pound Beltsville Small White (*far left*). Geese are an important commercial species in Europe, but in North America they are usually raised only in small flocks on small farms (*left*). Chinese in origin, the Pekin duck is a popular breed because of its rapid growth. By 7 weeks of age, a Pekin may weigh 7 pounds and be ready for market (*below*).

A good egg-producing hen will lay 270 to 280 eggs per year. She weighs 4 pounds (1.8 kilograms) and uses 4 pounds of feed to produce a dozen large eggs. There are several crossbreeds that are good egg layers. The choice of which to use may depend on the color of the shell of the egg that it lays. A type of hen known as the White Leghorn strain cross hen lays a white-shelled egg and is very popular in some parts of the world.

Some people prefer a brown-shelled egg. A very popular brown-egg layer is the black pullet resulting from the mating of Barred Plymouth Rock hens with Rhode Island Red roosters. Brown eggs are not more nutritious than white ones. The color of the shell has nothing to do with the food value of the egg.

Egg farms are growing larger and more mechanized and automated each year. Layer houses are equipped with long rows of small wire cages, each cage housing several hens with their own water and feed. All the chores that the hired worker used to do are now mechanized—feeding, watering, ventilating, cooling, heating, manure handling, egg gathering, egg grading, and packaging.

The various stages in the egg-production cycle take place on different farms. A specialized farm handles the breeding improvement, another handles the hatching of chicks, another the growing of the pullets, another the manufacture of feed, and another the keeping of the egg layers. All the phases of the cycle often will be owned by one company.

## ▶TURKEYS

The strutting turkey with its tail feathers fanned out is a symbol of Thanksgiving. Traditionally from the time of the Pilgrims, turkey has graced the Thanksgiving table.

America is the native home of the turkey. Although they were found roaming wild over most of North America, the present domestic turkeys probably were developed from those originally found in Mexico.

Today, turkeys are an important source of meat in many parts of the world. Many of the turkeys produced in the United States are roasted as whole birds for holiday feasts. But turkey is also being eaten more in everyday diets as turkey steaks and ground turkey, as well as turkey bologna, turkey salami, turkey rolls, and other processed items.

One of the first varieties developed for commercial farming was the Broad-Breasted Bronze turkey. Tom (male) turkeys of this variety weigh 24 to 26 pounds (10.9 to 11.8 kilograms) at 22 weeks of age.

A dressed turkey is one that is ready for roasting. Cooks like dressed turkeys to be free of skin blemishes or marks. Many Broad-Breasted Bronze turkeys carried black marks under the skin left by immature feathers called pinfeathers. These marks made the finished turkey look unappetizing. Therefore the Broad-Breasted Large White turkey was developed, because white pinfeathers leave no marks. Today this variety is used almost exclusively in commercial production.

Turkey farming is big business. Flocks of 5,000 to 10,000 birds are common. Hens and toms are separated at hatching and raised separately. The hens, which mature at 16 to 18 weeks of age, are marketed earlier than the toms, which may be ready at 22 to 24 weeks of age. The trend is to produce turkeys during all seasons of the year. To do this, many turkey flocks are kept in enclosed sheds, where they can be protected from the weather.

## ▶GEESE

Goose traditionally was eaten in Europe during holiday celebrations. But it has never become very popular in North America.

The goose is valued for its size, flavor, feathers and down, and long productive life. A goose may reproduce for 25 years or more. Geese are sturdy, generally easygoing birds, but at times they may be quite disagreeable.

The goose is an excellent forager for food. It can live, and even grow fat, on green pasture. This is important in areas of the world where little grain is available to feed animals.

Nearly all domesticated geese in North America are kept in small flocks. Only a few farms specialize in raising geese. Geese are important on some farms as weeders of cotton, strawberries, or other cultivated crops.

Domestic geese are believed to have come from the greylag goose. The greylag goose can be found wild in Europe but once was scattered over the world. The names of some of the common domestic breeds—the Toulouse, Embden, African, Chinese, Canadian, and Egyptian—tell in which part of the world the breeds were domesticated.

## ▶DUCKS

The domestication of ducks began long ago. The ancient Chinese were known as duck raisers as far back as their records date. The modern Pekin breed is of Chinese origin.

Young Pekin ducklings grow very rapidly. As with other types of poultry used for meat, a white-feathered, fast-growing breed is used exclusively.

Until the 1970's, more ducks were grown on Long Island, New York, than in any other place in the United States, probably because of the closeness to the water and proximity to the duck market in New York City. But ducklings do not need to swim in a pond or river in order to thrive and grow. Now, many ducklings are grown in windowless, climate-controlled houses.

Ducks are also raised to lay eggs. In the United States, duck eggs are not popular, but in Europe and England they are considered a delicacy and are widely eaten.

Ducks, in general, are very good layers. Even the Pekin duck, bred principally for meat production, has been known to lay 100 eggs in 100 days. Average egg production in duck flocks often exceeds that for chicken hen flocks. Many egg-producing duck breeds have been developed, including the Khaki Campbell, Indian Runner, Aylesbury, Rouen, Cayuga, and Muscovy. Each is different in size, shape, carriage, and economic use.

JAMES R. CARSON
School of Agriculture, Purdue University
See also DUCKS, GEESE, AND SWANS; TURKEYS.

**POUND, EZRA.** See IDAHO (Famous People).

Poverty exists around the world. *Clockwise from top left:* Victims of war, such as this Albanian woman, are often forced to flee their homes and live in refugee camps. In poor African nations such as Rwanda, sick people may receive only minimal care. A Nicaraguan slum and a run-down U.S. neighborhood are examples of the unsafe housing in which many poor people must live.

# POVERTY

For many people, "poverty" is an abstract word. But it is very real for those who are poor. Poverty is being sick and not being able to see a doctor. Poverty is not being able to go to school and not knowing how to read. Poverty is not having enough clothes, not having a job, not being able to plan ahead, and fearing the future. Poverty is dying from an illness caused by unclean water or not being able to choose how or where you live.

Poverty means something different in different countries and regions, depending on the general standards of that country or region. Most commonly, a person is considered poor, or living beneath the **poverty line**, if he or she earns or consumes less than the amount considered necessary to meet minimum adequate levels of nutrition, shelter, and other necessities. This is also called **income poverty**.

In the United States, a person was considered poor in 2000 if he or she made less than about $8,800 per year. During the same period, a family of four was considered poor if its annual cash income was less than about $17,800. However, these income levels would be considered high in many developing nations. In some areas of sub-Saharan Africa, for example, a person was considered poor if, during the same period, he or she made less than $400 per year.

In general, even those who are considered poor in industrialized countries fare much better than those in developing nations, where poverty is far worse. In the United States, about 11 percent of the population was considered poor in 2000; in many African countries, despite much lower poverty lines, 50 percent or more of the population is poor.

In addition to most of Africa, other areas that have large percentages of poor people include South Asia and parts of Central and South America. In Eastern Europe and Central Asia, the number of very poor people is relatively low but has grown rapidly (from 7 million to 17 million) since the collapse of the Soviet Union in 1991.

Poverty not only varies from country to country but also according to where one lives within a country. In China, for instance, there are more poor people in rural and interior locations than in the cities. In other places it is just the opposite—poverty is concentrated in urban slums.

One's social group can determine economic status as well. In many U.S. cities, for example, nearly half of black or Hispanic single-mother households are considered poor compared with about 5 percent of white married couples living in the same area. In Latin America, people of Indian origin have much higher rates of income poverty than other groups.

Standards of poverty can also vary over time. Some things that are viewed as luxuries when they first appear—telephones and flush toilets in industrialized nations, for instance—are later seen as necessities. When this occurs, those who still do not have these things are considered poor.

## ▶ CAUSES OF POVERTY

People are poor for different reasons. Sometimes it is because they have no way to earn enough money. Their earning ability may be limited by inadequate education or poor health or by long-term economic change such as the decline of traditional oc-

Volunteers distribute grain to famine victims in Somalia. Short-term solutions to poverty often include food relief programs.

cupations (for example, textiles and steel in the United States and traditional farming in many developing countries).

Catastrophic events—either natural or caused by humans—frequently cause poverty. People who must grow their own food to survive may face poverty when drought, flooding, or other factors cause crops to fail. Throughout history, poverty has also been caused by war and other political conflict, as people are forced to flee from their homes, farms, or businesses. These events typically hurt those who are already poor the most, but they can drive formerly prosperous people into poverty as well.

Powerlessness, too, contributes to poverty. When people have no voice, they are unable to influence the decisions of those in power, including decisions that affect their economic status. In Nigeria, for instance, years of corrupt military rule have contributed to widespread poverty in a country that, given its oil wealth, might otherwise be rich.

## ▶ REDUCING POVERTY

Many countries have taken significant steps to reduce poverty. In richer countries, these include "safety net" programs designed to help specific groups. In the United States, for example, such programs include unemployment insurance and job training programs for people who are out of work. Social

Security and Medicare have reduced income poverty and increased access to health care among elderly people. Medicaid provides some groups of poor people with medical care. (For more information, see the article on Social Security in Volume S.) Other programs in wealthier countries are targeted at pockets of poverty in particular locales (such as inner cities) or among specific groups (such as poor children, the unemployed, or the homeless).

Reducing poverty in poorer countries has been more difficult, although some countries have succeeded. In very poor countries such as China, India, and Vietnam, income poverty decreased substantially during the 1990's due to rapid economic growth (the pace at which economic activity expands). This helped create more jobs and incomes for people and has provided government with more money to spend on services that poor people need, such as basic education and health care. Where growth has faltered, as in much of Africa, poverty levels have remained very high.

A father enrolls his son in a U.S. government-sponsored health insurance program. Poverty programs are often targeted to children or other specific groups.

But growth alone is not enough. It is also essential to enhance the opportunities open to poor people. Growth must generate good jobs and incomes for everyone, including low-skilled workers, owners of small farms or businesses, and self-employed poor people.

For poor people to get and keep good jobs, governments must also invest in basic education, for girls as well as boys. They must provide other goods and services to the poor, particularly clean water, decent sanitation, basic health care, and measures to address diseases such as AIDS and malaria. They must reduce environmental pollution, which typically hurts poor people the most.

In addition, countries must provide protective "safety nets" to give poor people security in times of crisis. Although the kinds of safety net programs found in rich countries are largely absent or ineffective in poor countries, there are some programs that can help. These include food-for-work and cash-for-work programs, as well as government support for small-scale businesses and food subsidies for the poor.

For any poverty reduction efforts to be effective in the long run, however, poor people must also have a voice. Democratic policies must be in place that allow them to express their views and participate in decision-making at the local level and to broaden their choices. In areas where this does not happen—when a government is not accountable to its citizens or officials are corrupt—poor people's choices are greatly reduced.

To aid poverty reduction efforts in developing countries, and to build the global partnership that is needed for these to succeed, the world community adopted the United Nations Millennium Declaration at the September 2000 Millennium Summit in New York City. The resulting Millennium Development Goals set ambitious targets for major improvements in income poverty, health, education, gender equality, and environmental protection for the year 2015. Meeting these goals is one of the most important global challenges of our century.

JOHN PAGE
Director, Poverty Reduction
The World Bank

**POWELL, ADAM CLAYTON, JR.** See UNITED STATES, CONGRESS OF THE (Profiles: House Representatives).

## POWELL, COLIN (1937– )

In 2001, Colin Luther Powell became U.S. secretary of state under President George W. Bush. He had previously served as assistant to the president for national security affairs (1987–89) and chairman of the Joint Chiefs of Staff (1989–93). He was the first African American to fill each post.

Powell was born to Jamaican parents on April 5, 1937, in the Bronx, New York. He entered the U.S. Army as a second lieutenant on his graduation from City College in 1958. In the early 1960's, Powell was one of the first American military advisers sent to Vietnam. On a second tour of duty (1968–69), his heroism earned him eleven medals, including a Purple Heart and two Bronze Stars. After Vietnam, Powell rose steadily in rank. In 1981 he was promoted to brigadier general. In 1987 he was named national security assistant by President Ronald Reagan, who also awarded Powell his fourth general's star.

In 1989, President George Bush selected Powell to head up the Joint Chiefs of Staff. Powell oversaw the 1989 invasion of Panama, which resulted in the surrender of its dictator

Manuel Noriega, and he was greatly responsible for the success of the 1991 Persian Gulf War against Iraq.

Powell retired in 1993 to devote time to a new career as a writer and public speaker. But in 1994 President Bill Clinton asked him to help negotiate the return to power of Haiti's exiled president, Jean Bertrand Aristide. His autobiography, *My American Journey*, was published in 1995.

After the September 11, 2001, terrorist attacks on the United States, U.S. secretary of state Powell gained the support of most world leaders in the war on terrorism. In early 2003 he warned the United Nations of the threat of aggression from Iraq. But he failed to win U.N. support for the use of force against Iraq's dictator, Saddam Hussein. After the United States and its allies ousted Hussein in April 2003, Powell tried to persuade the United Nations to send troops and money to help stabilize the country.

Powell resigned as secretary of state just before President Bush's second term began in 2005.

JIM HASKINS
Author, *Colin Powell*

---

# POWER PLANTS

There are many forms of energy—the energy of heat from the sun, moving air and water, burning fuels, and chemical reactions. Power plants convert these various forms of energy into electricity, which can then be used to provide lighting, heat, and power.

The two main types of power plants are hydroelectric and thermal. Hydroelectric plants use waterpower to produce electricity; thermal plants burn fuels, such as coal, oil, and natural gas. Hydroelectric power is the most important source of electricity in countries where waterpower is plentiful, such as Italy, Norway, Sweden, Switzerland, and Spain. Countries with abundant sources of fuel, such as the United States, Russia, Great Britain, Germany, France, and Japan, use thermal power to produce electricity.

▶ **HYDROELECTRIC POWER PLANTS**

In hydroelectric power plants, flowing water is used to turn turbines. These turbines run generators that produce electric power. The most convenient source of waterpower is a high waterfall. Since there are not enough natural waterfalls, artificial ones are created by building dams on rivers and lakes. Large dams can store water up to a height of several hundred feet (100 feet is equal to about 30 meters). Such dams, however, cannot be built on rivers in flat regions. A low-level dam on a river such as the Mississippi, for example, can provide a waterfall of only about 50 feet (15 meters). But the tremendous amount of water rushing down a river like the Mississippi can provide ample power to turn turbines that run electric generators.

Located in Foz do Iguazu, Brazil, the Itaipu hydroelectric power plant was completed in the early 1990's. It supplies 12,600 megawatts of electrical power to Brazil and Paraguay.

▶ **THERMAL POWER PLANTS**

In thermal power plants, a fuel such as coal or oil is burned to boil water and produce steam. The pressure of the steam turns the turbines that run the generators. These power plants generally use the most abundant fuel available in an area; power plants frequently are built near coal fields. It is easier to build power lines to transmit the electricity from the plants to the places where it is needed than it is to haul coal or other fuels over long distances to the power plants.

Heat for thermal power plants can also be obtained from solar energy and nuclear energy. In a solar thermal power plant, sunlight is converted to heat energy, which is then used to generate electricity. In a nuclear thermal power plant, heat is obtained from a nuclear reaction rather than from the burning of a fuel. For more information about thermal power plants, see SOLAR ENERGY in Volume S and NUCLEAR ENERGY in Volume N.

A problem with thermal power plants is that only about one-third of the energy used by the average plant is actually delivered as electricity. The rest is discharged as heat into the air or into cooling water. If the heat is discharged directly into a lake or river, the temperature of the water will rise, harming fish and other water life. This is known as **thermal (heat) pollution**. When fossil fuels such as coal and oil are burned, they can pollute the air unless special antipollution steps are taken. Another problem is that someday the supply of coal, oil, and natural gas will be depleted.

▶ **CONTROL AND AUTOMATION IN POWER PLANTS**

Controls are used in power plants in order to make equipment work efficiently and safely. In a hydroelectric plant, there are controls for opening and closing water valves, for regulating the speed of turbine generators, and for operating circuit breakers and switches that connect generators to transmission lines. In a thermal power plant, controls regulate the flow of fuel to boilers, the burning of fuel, and the speed of its turbine generators. Controls are important because the electricity generated by a power plant cannot be stored for later use. Each time electricity is needed, the plant must generate the added power necessary to produce it.

The accuracy required for controlling and operating complicated equipment in power plants created the need for automating the process, and computers and automatic regulators now coordinate the production of electric power in most large plants.

▶ **ALTERNATIVE METHODS OF ELECTRIC POWER GENERATION**

Alternative methods of generating electric power are being tested, and some of these methods have been used to generate electricity in space satellites and other spacecraft.

**Thermoelectric power generation** is based on a scientific principle called the Seebeck effect for its founder, Thomas Seebeck, a German physicist. In 1821, Seebeck found that if two different metals were joined at both of their ends and each junction was heated to a different temperature, an electric current would flow through the metals. Small thermoelectric generators have been used for limited jobs such as charging radio batteries.

A **thermionic generator**, which produces electricity from heat, consists of two electrodes inside a gas-filled chamber or a vacuum. If one of these electrodes, called the cathode, is heated to a higher temperature than the other electrode, called the anode, an electric current will flow between them.

A **fuel cell** converts the chemical energy of a fuel directly into electricity without going through the process of combustion. The first fuel cells were used to supply portable power for electronic equipment used by the military. The Consolidated Edison Company of New York constructed the first fuel-cell power plant for commercial purposes.

In a **magnetohydrodynamic (MHD) generator**, a very hot gas is forced through a magnetic field, and the energy in the hot moving gas is converted into electricity. In an MHD generator, however, the temperatures are extremely high—thousands of degrees Fahrenheit. New materials that can withstand this extreme heat must be developed, therefore, before MHD generators will be practical.

J. J. WILLIAM BROWN
General Electric Company
Reviewed by STANLEY W. ANGRIST
Author, *Direct Energy Conversion*

See also ELECTRIC GENERATORS; ELECTRICITY; NUCLEAR ENERGY; SOLAR ENERGY; WATERPOWER.

---

**POWERS, FRANCIS GARY.** See SPIES (Profiles).

# PRADO

The Museo del Prado in Madrid is the national museum of Spain. Although the building was not opened until November 19, 1819, the history of its collection goes back at least 400 years before that date.

The kings of Spain had always loved good art. Each monarch supported outstanding artists of his own time and collected the works of older masters. King Ferdinand and his wife, Queen Isabella, who sponsored the 1492 journey of Christopher Columbus, are usually credited with having founded the royal collection. Isabella was especially fond of the work of the painters of Flanders—*Flamencos*, as they are called in Spain.

Later rulers added works of Italian, French, Dutch, and German artists to the collection. Some of these foreign artists accepted invitations to live and paint at the Spanish court. Gifts

from foreign monarchs and careful purchases further enriched the collection. Some of the Prado's greatest treasures were bought from the estate of Charles I of England.

Although the Prado is a showplace of international art, it is best known for its Spanish collection. Every major Spanish artist from the Middle Ages to the 1800's is

The Prado Museum in Madrid, Spain, houses an important collection of international art. The building itself, designed by Juan de Villanueva, is an outstanding example of Spanish neoclassical architecture.

**Museum visitors view _Las Meninas_ (1656), a famous painting of members of the Spanish royal court by Diego Velázquez. The Prado has an especially fine collection of works by Spanish artists.**

represented. The collection includes 50 paintings by the court painter Diego Velázquez (1599–1660). An entire room is devoted to his most famous work, _Las Meninas_. The painting gives the impression that the artist was looking into a mirror and copying the scene in his studio. To make viewers feel as though they, too, were in the room, a real mirror has been placed on the wall opposite the painting. When visitors look into the mirror, they appear to be part of the activity in the studio.

Francisco Goya (1746–1828) also painted at court. He did many portraits of the family of Charles IV. Sometimes Goya's portraits show his scorn for the silly and cruel rulers who supported him. Today, 115 of his paintings and several hundred of his drawings are in the Prado.

As the collection grew, its fame spread throughout Europe. Finally, in 1816, Ferdinand VII and his Portuguese wife, Isabella de Braganza, decided to put many of the marvelous works on public display. They moved part of the collection from the royal palace to the abandoned Palace of Science. The Palace of Science had been designed by the well-known architect Juan de Villanueva (1739–1811). It was originally intended to house laboratories and exhibits of natural science. But foreign invasions and lack of funds stopped work on the project. During the French occupation of 1808, Napoleon's troops stabled their horses in the building. Ferdinand VII and Isabella used their own money to have the neglected science building converted into an art museum. When it opened, the museum already owned more than 2,000 works of art.

The building, located in a shady parklike area, or _prado_, is three stories high and has 97 rooms. It is considered one of the most important Spanish buildings in the neoclassic style. The dry air of Madrid has kept the paintings in beautiful condition, and there has been a minimum of handling and cleaning. The works are well hung, and the galleries are well lighted.

The Prado has been remodeled several times in a constant attempt to improve conditions for photographing and copying works and for study. The exhibition space has been enlarged, and the building has been fireproofed and made quieter. But even during remodeling, the museum has remained open every day without exception.

Ferdinand VII had wanted the Prado to serve teachers, students, artists, and those foreigners with a "proper curiosity." The museum was so popular in the early 1800's that it was difficult to keep a Sunday's crowd moving.

In the spirit of Velázquez—who advised the king on art and bought paintings for him—the Prado traditionally appoints working artists as directors. Under their expert supervision the museum has continued to be an important influence on artists who come to Madrid. Great masters and casual tourists alike cannot help but be inspired by the glorious treasures of the Prado.

Reviewed by DON FRANCISCO SÁNCHEZ CANTÓN
Director, Museo del Prado

# PRAGUE

Prague (Praha in Czech) is the capital and largest city of the Czech Republic, with a population of more than 1.2 million. It is the country's commercial, financial, and cultural center. It draws many art lovers, particularly to the historical center of the city, which dates from the Middle Ages.

**The City.** Prague is situated among low, scenic hills on both banks of the Vltava River. The two parts of the city are connected by a number of bridges. The oldest and best known of these is the Charles Bridge, built in the 1300's.

Most of the city is located on the river's east bank. Its most famous district is Staré Město (Old Town), in the heart of which lies Old Town Square. Old Town Square has two particularly striking buildings—Old Town Hall, with its astronomical clock from the 1400's, and Týn Church, a Gothic structure built in the 1300's. Part of Charles University is also located here. Founded in 1348, it is the oldest university in Central Europe. Nearby is the former Jewish ghetto, with its old synagogue and cemetery. Farther north, in the district of Nové Město (New Town), is Wenceslas Square, traditionally the site of celebrations and demonstrations.

Prague, capital and largest city of the Czech Republic, lies on the Vltava River. The Charles Bridge is the oldest of the bridges linking both parts of the city.

Prague's west bank includes the historic districts of Hradčany and Malá Strana. Hradčany Castle, once home to the kings of Bohemia, is now the official residence of the president. The most impressive of its many buildings is the medieval St. Vitus Cathedral. The palaces and mansions of the old nobility can be found along the winding cobblestoned streets of Malá Strana.

**Economic Activity.** Prague is an industrial city. Its manufactured goods range from electronic equipment, metal products, machinery, and chemicals to textiles, beer, and processed foods. Tourism and related services also provide a major source of income.

**History.** Prague was founded in the late 800's. It reached heights of prosperity in the late 1300's, when the Bohemian king Charles I was crowned Holy Roman emperor, as Charles IV, and made Prague the imperial capital. When the Austrian Habsburgs became Bohemia's rulers in 1526, however, the city's status began to deteriorate. An unsuccessful revolt against Habsburg rule erupted in Prague in 1618, setting off the Thirty Years' War. A second revolt, in 1848, also failed.

Prague became the capital of Czechoslovakia after its creation in 1918. It was occupied by Nazi Germany during World War II (1939–45) and later endured a harsh Communist regime. In 1968, in the brief period known as the "Prague Spring," reformers sought to liberalize the system, but they were crushed by the Soviet Union. Democracy was restored in 1989. But it was followed by the breakup of Czechoslovakia in 1993, with Prague becoming the capital of the new Czech Republic. In 2002, Prague suffered the worst floods in its recorded history. Damages were estimated in the billions of dollars.

EDWARD TABORSKY
University of Texas at Austin

# PRAIRIES

Prairies are broad expanses of grassland on the plains of the middle latitudes (between the polar and tropical regions). The name "prairie" (the French word for "meadow") is often given to any large area of flat land that has a natural grass cover.

True prairie grasses are fairly tall and have deep root systems. They grow in regions that have a subhumid climate—about 20 to 30 inches of rainfall annually. Drier (semiarid) plains with less than 20 inches of rain have shorter grasses and are known as steppes. "Steppe" comes from the Russian word for "treeless plain."

## Where Are the Prairies?

All of the continents except Antarctica have vast grassy plains in the middle latitudes. In North America the prairies lie in mid-continent and extend from Canada to Mexico. Before settlers plowed the eastern Great Plains and upper Mississippi Valley, the natural vegetation was tall grasses with strips of forest along the rivers. Small "wet" prairies are found in the states along the Gulf of Mexico. Short-grass steppes cover the higher plains between the Rocky Mountains and the tall-grass prairies.

The humid eastern Pampas of Argentina and the grasslands of nearby Uruguay form the major prairie lands of South America. There are also several small areas of steppe in the drier western Pampas and along the Andes in Patagonia.

A broad belt of grassland extends from Hungary in Europe to Manchuria in Asia. It is broken in places by mountain ranges and forests. The northern part of this grassy belt is tall-grass prairie. The drier southern portion includes the famous steppes of Russia. The grasslands of the High Veld in South Africa are similar to the prairies of the mid-western United States. *Veld* is a South African term for "open grassland." Australia's prairie lands lie in the Murray-Darling river basin, west of the Eastern Highlands. Large areas of steppe land, with shrubs as well as grasses, fringe the Australian deserts.

## Environment of the Prairies

The climates of the middle latitude grasslands vary from subhumid to semiarid. Rainfall averages 20 to 30 inches a year in most of the tall-grass prairies. More moisture is necessary for grass growth in hot climates than in cold. The prairie and steppe lands produce excellent crops when there is enough moisture. Where there is not enough rain to support tall prairie grasses, only short grasses or bunch grasses can grow. Under still drier conditions the vegetation is limited to scattered grasses and desert shrubs. Most of the precipitation in the middle latitude grasslands comes in summer. The amount varies greatly from year to year. Sometimes there are long periods of drought.

Winters are cold and summers are hot on the prairies and steppes. In the northern grasslands of Europe, Asia, and North America temperatures drop far below zero in winter, yet they climb above 100 degrees Fahrenheit in summer. There are storms with windblown snow in the Northern Hemisphere prairies in winter.

In summer there are thunderstorms. The Great Plains of the United States have frequent hailstorms, and tornadoes sometimes cause great damage. Winters in the Southern Hemisphere grasslands are not as cold as those in the Northern Hemisphere.

## Soil and Plant Life of the Prairies

The soils of the prairies and steppes are among the most fertile in the world. Because of the light rainfall, minerals that nourish plant life have not been leached (carried downward by water) from the topsoil. The dead stems and roots of the grasses provide organic matter. Many grassland soils also have a high lime content, which increases their fertility.

Although grasses are the main kind of vegetation in the prairies and steppes, there are many other kinds of plants. Strips of trees that are known as gallery forests grow along streams. In the United States cottonwoods and willows are common along the streams of the short-grass steppe. Sagebrush grows among the grasses of the drier high plains of North America.

In Texas grasses are mixed with thorny mesquite shrubs. The Pampas of Argentina has scattered scrub forests known as *monte*. Acacias and eucalypts are scrub trees of the Australian grasslands. The prairies also have many flowering plants.

Native animal life was abundant on the North American prairies before they were settled by farmers. Grazing animals such as the bison and antelope provided food for Native Americans on the Great Plains.

## Grazing on the Prairies

On the grassy plains, early human beings depended upon hunting wild animals and gathering berries and roots for food. When grazing animals were domesticated, the grasslands became vast pasturelands. People on the steppes of Russia and Central Asia have made their living for centuries by herding sheep, goats, and cattle. Many of these people are seminomads who move their animals frequently to better pastures.

Most of the grazing regions on the plains of North and South America, South Africa, and Australia were not settled until the 1800's. In North America the Native Americans were replaced by cattlemen, who developed huge ranches. On the Edwards Plateau of Texas, goats have become an important source of Angora wool. The grasslands of Argentina and Uruguay are the leading livestock regions of South America. Both nations export wool, and Argentina is one of the world's leading beef exporters. Sheep, goats, and cattle are grazed on the High Veld of South Africa.

Australia's grasslands are noted for Merino sheep, which produce fine wool. Australia leads the world in wool exports.

Grazing is an extensive form of land use. Some ranches have many thousands of acres of land and large numbers of sheep or cattle. In the drier grasslands several acres of land are needed to provide enough feed for one animal. For this reason, the population of grazing regions is usually sparse. The small towns and villages are widely scattered, and there are few large cities. Ranchers live many miles from their nearest neighbors.

## Farming on the Prairies

Before the invention of steel plows and heavy machinery, farmers could not cultivate the grasslands easily. It was easier to cut and burn forests to obtain farmland than to dig the thick, grassy sod with their simple tools. When it became possible to use more advanced implements, the prairies became the world's major grain-growing regions. The only grasslands developed for cultivation before the invention of the steel plow were the Russian steppes.

After the introduction of machinery, settlement spread rapidly into Siberia. Rye and wheat are the main crops of the Russian steppes today. Corn, flax, and hay are also grown. In southwestern Siberia irrigated

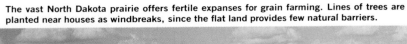

The vast North Dakota prairie offers fertile expanses for grain farming. Lines of trees are planted near houses as windbreaks, since the flat land provides few natural barriers.

farms produce cotton and fruits. The farmers of the steppes keep dairy cows and various meat animals.

On the wetter eastern prairies, North American farmers developed general farms for the production of grain crops, hay, and livestock. Corn, oats, soybeans, and hay are the main feeds for hogs and cattle.

The productive corn-hog belt of the upper Mississippi Valley extends westward into the prairies. Farther south, cotton is an important crop. During periods of high grain prices and favorable rainfall, farmers have cultivated land still farther west in the short-grass steppes. Spring wheat has been the leading crop of the Prairie Provinces of Canada and of the northern plains of the United States. In the central and southern plains states winter wheat is grown.

Because rainfall is not dependable in the drier grasslands, drought has often brought disaster to grain farms in the past. Many farmers left the Great Plains as a result of crop failures and dust storms in the 1930's. Modern farmers have learned how to overcome drought problems to some extent by better cultivation methods.

Grasses and forage crops have been planted to protect the soil against erosion and to help conserve moisture. Many thousands of acres of land have been returned to livestock grazing. In some places where water is available, irrigation projects have been developed. On irrigated land in the valleys of the Missouri River and its tributaries, farmers grow sugar beets, potatoes, alfalfa, and other kinds of vegetables.

The cultivated lands on Argentina's Pampas grow corn, wheat, flaxseed, and alfalfa—an important cattle feed. Like the rest of the world's cultivated grasslands, those in Australia have become important for wheat growing. Much of the wheat is grown on farms where sheep are also raised. The main wheat-sheep zone lies west of the Eastern Highlands. Drought has been a serious problem for Australian wheat farmers.

In South Africa the wetter parts of the High Veld have farms that grow corn and other grain crops for livestock feed. Beef cattle, dairy cows, and sheep are the principal farm animals. The farmsteads are widely spaced in the drier areas. Windmills are used to pump water from deep wells.

## Other Activities in the Prairie Lands

Mining has not been as important in the middle latitude grasslands as in mountainous regions. However, the North American Great Plains have huge deposits of lignite coal. Esterhazy, in Saskatchewan, has the world's largest deposit of potash. Oil fields have been widely developed in the Prairie Provinces of Canada and in North Dakota, Oklahoma, and Texas in the United States. Few minerals are known in the prairie regions of Uruguay and Argentina or in the tall grass region of Australia. Coal and oil are produced in the steppe regions of Russia. The High Veld of South Africa is noted for its gold and diamond mines. The Witwatersrand, in the vicinity of Johannesburg, is the world's leading gold mining area.

The prairies and steppes do not have many large manufacturing cities. Except in the few places where there is local coal or petroleum, power supplies are poor. Hydroelectric stations are also uncommon because the rivers flow too slowly over flat plains to generate enough waterpower.

The most important factories are those that process livestock products and various farm crops. These include meat-packing plants and flour mills. In irrigated regions there may be beet sugar refineries and vegetable canneries. Ore crushing plants or smelters are found in the mining areas. The major oil fields have oil refineries.

Because most of the world's grassy plains are located in the interiors of the continents, good transportation networks are needed to carry products to the ports. In North America the railway systems focus on cities at the eastern edge of the prairies, such as Chicago or Winnipeg. In the southern plains, products move to ports on the Gulf of Mexico. The Mississippi River is an important waterway for products like wheat and cotton.

The railway network of Argentina radiates from Buenos Aires and other ports on the Río de la Plata to farmlands on the Pampas. In Uruguay, Montevideo is the port that receives cattle and wool from the grazing lands. Both waterways and railroads serve the steppes in Russia, and the major ports for handling agricultural products are on the Black Sea. The High Veld of South Africa and the interior prairies of Australia are more isolated than the other major grassland

Steppes (treeless plains) in Russia.

regions, but railroads reach from these areas to seaports.

### The Future of the Prairies

Most of the world's grasslands were settled late in history. The humid prairies have become highly productive farmlands and are more densely populated than the steppes. Many parts of the semiarid steppes are still pioneer regions. In spite of the uncertainty of rainfall, farmers are finding better ways to manage pastures and cultivate croplands. Irrigation and soil conservation methods are helping to increase food production. As population increases in the wetter regions, more people will settle in the open spaces of the world's grassy plains to develop their agricultural and mineral resources.

HOWARD J. CRITCHFIELD
Western Washington State College

Oil refinery on the Canadian prairie.

Sheep ranch in Patagonia, Argentina.

# PRAYER

Prayer is the act of directing thoughts or words to God or another divine being. It is also the term for a specific set of words or rituals used in such an act.

People pray for many reasons: to give thanks, to ask for assistance, to request forgiveness, or to offer praise and adoration. In another form of prayer, sometimes called meditation, people seek inner peace, enlightenment, or a direct experience of the divine.

Prayer is part of every religious tradition, past and present. Each religion has its own prayers, although many are similar to one another. The most important prayers are usually found in a religion's sacred texts. For example, Judaism's Shema, "Hear, O Israel; the Lord our God, the Lord is One," is from the Torah. The Lord's Prayer, which is often recited by Christians, appears twice in the Bible's New Testament. It begins, "Our Father who art in Heaven, hallowed be thy name." A common prayer in Buddhism, from its Basket of Sutras, is the Sanskrit phrase "Om Mani Padme Hum." It is untranslatable, but refers to the joy and purity of fulfilled human life.

Each religion has its own festivals and holy days when the community prays together and remembers its essential teachings. Examples include the Jewish Yom Kippur and Passover, Christian Easter and Christmas, Muslim Ramadan and Id al-Adha (the Feast of Sacrifice), Buddhist New Year and Wesak (the Buddha's birthday), and Hindu Diwali (festival of lights) and Holi (spring festival).

Most religions have ritualized prayers for major life events, such as birth, marriage, and death. Many also have special prayers to mark new stages in the life of faith—for instance, baptism and confirmation among Christians and bar and bat mitzvah among Jews.

Prayer may be formal or informal, public or private. Informal, private prayer is accepted by all faiths. But some religions also require formal, public prayer in specific places at particular times (Sunday morning church services, for example). They may require that certain rituals be performed during prayer, such as burning incense or lighting candles. And they may specify that prayers should be said while standing, sitting, or kneeling, or with the hands clasped together.

Muslims, for example, must pray five times every day: at dawn, noon, mid-afternoon, sunset, and evening (at bedtime). During prayer—which usually consists of passages from the Koran—they must face the direction of Mecca (in Saudi Arabia), Islam's holiest city. They must also bow, kneel, and touch the forehead to the ground, to express submission to God.

## TYPES OF PRAYER

**The Calling Prayer**. A prayer that calls upon the divine is usually referred to as an invocation. Since the beginning of time, people have used some means of attracting divine attention. They shouted, rang a gong, or performed special gestures. Today people often begin calling prayers with a traditional phrase such as "O Lord, hear our prayer."

**The Prayer of Adoration**. In this prayer, a person expresses love and praise for the divine.

**The "Thank-You" Prayer**. This type of prayer gives thanks for blessings and favors received.

**The "I'm Sorry" Prayer**. People say "I'm sorry" when they have done something they know to be wrong. This type of prayer is also called a confession.

**The Prayer for Others**. A prayer that a person offers for others is called intercession.

**The Asking Prayer**. Asking prayers, in which people state their needs and ask for help, are called petitions.

**The Listening Prayer**. Sometimes prayer is silent. The person who is praying does not speak, but listens. This kind of prayer is called meditation or contemplation.

## A SELECTION OF PRAYERS

May all beings have happiness and the causes
of happiness;
May all be free from sorrow and the causes of
sorrow;
May all never be separated from the sacred
happiness which is sorrowless;
And may all live in equanimity, without too
much attachment and too much aversion,
And live believing in the equality of all that
lives.

Traditional Buddhist prayer

The Lord is my shepherd; I shall not want.
He maketh me to lie down in green pastures;
He leadeth me beside the still waters.
He restoreth my soul;
He guideth me in straight paths for His name's
sake.
Yea, though I walk through the valley of the
shadow of death,
I will fear no evil,
For Thou art with me;
Thy rod and Thy staff, they comfort me.
Thou preparest a table before me in the
presence of mine enemies;
Thou hast anointed my head with oil; my cup
runneth over.
Surely goodness and mercy shall follow me all
the days of my life;
And I shall dwell in the house of the Lord for
ever.

23rd Psalm, Old Testament

Glory to God in the highest, and on
earth peace, good will toward men.

New Testament

In the name of God, Most Gracious, Most
Merciful.
Praise be to God,
The Cherisher and Sustainer of the Worlds;
Most Gracious, Most Merciful;

Master of the Day of Judgment
Thee do we worship,
And Thine did we seek.
Show us the straight way,
The way of those on whom
Thou has bestowed thy Grace.
Those whose portion
Is not wrath,
And who go not astray.

Islamic prayer from the Koran

Our Father who art in heaven,
Hallowed be Thy name.
Thy kingdom come,
Thy will be done,
on earth as it is in heaven.
Give us this day our daily bread;
And forgive us our debts,
As we also have forgiven our debtors;
And lead us not into temptation,
But deliver us from evil. Amen.

The Lord's Prayer, Matthew 6:9–13 (Revised Standard<br>Version of the Bible)

(The phrase, "For Thine is the kingdom and the power<br>and the glory forever" is frequently added.)

You are the father of the world,
of animate and inanimate things;
its venerable teacher,
most worthy of worship
without equal.
Where in all three worlds
is another to match
your extraordinary power?
I bow to you,
I prostrate my body,
I beg you to be gracious worshipful Lord;
as a father to a son,
a friend to a friend,
a lover to a beloved,
O God, bear with me.

The Bhagavad Gita

Most other religions allow more variety in the forms of prayer that are recommended for their followers. Buddhists, for instance, may pray by chanting, meditating silently, setting out "prayer flags," performing ritual gestures, using prayer beads, or turning a prayer wheel.

Many prayers are collected into prayer books. Some of these are used for public worship, with specific prayers for certain days and occasions, while others are for personal use. But not all prayers are written in books. Some are spoken or thought informally and spontaneously in response to the need of the moment.

MARY FROHLICH<br>Catholic Theological Union

**PRECIOUS STONES.** See GEMS.

# PREHISTORIC ANIMALS

Animals first appeared on Earth about 700 million years ago. Since then they have changed, or evolved, into many different forms. Any animal that lived before the earliest known invention of writing—widely believed by scientists to have been about 5,500 years ago—is considered prehistoric.

Most of the animals that once lived on Earth no longer exist. They have become **extinct**. In fact, scientists estimate that 99.99

Fossils such as this *Tyrannosaurus rex* skeleton provide valuable information about prehistoric animals.

percent of all the animal life that has ever existed on Earth is now extinct.

Most of our information about prehistoric animals comes from **fossils**, which are the remains or evidence of ancient life. Fossils are often formed from bones or shells, but they also can be made from animal tracks, skin impressions, and burrows. Sometimes whole animals are preserved in frozen soil, tar pits, or hardened tree sap (called amber).

Scientists who study prehistoric life are called **paleontologists**. From fossil evidence, paleontologists have determined that prehistoric animals lived primarily during three distinct eras in Earth's history: the Paleozoic era (meaning "ancient life"), the Mesozoic era ("middle life"), and the Cenozoic era ("recent life"). Very different kinds of animals lived during each era. The eras ended with great changes in the Earth's surface and climate, causing widespread extinctions of many kinds of plants and animals.

## ▶ THE EARLIEST ANIMALS

Animals first appeared on Earth during the **Precambrian era**, a time period that began with the Earth's formation about 4.5 billion years ago. Scientists believe that the earliest animals were related to a group of single-celled organisms called choanoflagellates. These tiny organisms could form colonies of cells, which is a necessary feature found in the earliest true animals, the sponges.

Early animals lived in ancient seas. They had soft bodies, with no hard shells or bones that could form good fossils. For this reason, not much is known about them. We know of their existence from impressions made in ocean sediments that later hardened into rock.

## ▶ MOLLUSKS, FISH, AND AMPHIBIANS

Animals developed hard body parts (mostly shells) at the start of the **Paleozoic era**, about 600 million years ago. The rocks from that era contain an abundance of fossils and form the beginning of the fossil record.

The first part of the Paleozoic era is so important for animal life that it is called the **Cambrian explosion**. During a 35-million-year time span, almost all of the major animal groups appeared. These groups are based on 37 different body plans, into which all living and extinct animals can be classified.

Mollusks, such as snails, and arthropods, such as trilobites (a flat shellfish), were abundant during the early part of the Paleozoic era. So were other invertebrates (animals without backbones) such as corals, brachiopods, and bryozoa. These and all other animals lived in the sea. Millions of years later, primitive insects and spiders became the first animals to live on land.

*Archaeopteryx*, which lived about 150 million years ago, was one of the first feathered birds. Many of its skeletal features closely matched those of ancient reptiles.

During a part of the Paleozoic era known as the **Devonian period**, fish appeared and became the world's dominant vertebrates (animals with backbones). Amphibians, the first land vertebrates, also appeared, but they were very different from the frogs and salamanders we know today. These early forms were much larger, about the size of dogs.

An important development in the history of vertebrates took place about 360 million years ago: the amniote egg evolved. This egg has a protective outer covering, called an amnion. It allowed prehistoric animals to reproduce away from water and made possible the rise of a new group of animals: the reptiles.

The Paleozoic era ended about 240 million years ago, marked by the largest extinction in Earth's history. About 90 percent of all animal species on Earth died off.

### ▶ DINOSAURS AND BIRDS

Mollusks, corals, and bony fish dominated the seas at the start of the **Mesozoic era**, about 240 million years ago. On land, reptiles were the dominant animals, represented by about forty different groups.

Some 225 to 65 million years ago, reptiles dominated the land, sea, and air. Familiar forms included the sea-dwelling *Plesiosaurus*; the huge *Apatosaurus*; the winged *Pteranodon*; the small *Procompsognathus*; and the plated *Stegosaurus*. These animals (not drawn to scale) did not necessarily live together at the same time.

The most famous of these was the Archosauria, which included dinosaurs, pterosaurs (flying reptiles), and crocodiles.

Birds appeared from their dinosaur ancestors during a part of the Mesozoic era known as the **Jurassic period**. This period is sometimes called the Age of Giants because many animals in the sea and on land attained the largest sizes of any animals seen in the fossil record. In a sense, the end of the Mesozoic era marked the beginning of our modern world. At that time, many kinds of reptile, bird, and mammal groups appeared that still exist today. Bony fish dominated the seas, as they do today, and mollusks were abundant.

However, many kinds of animals also became extinct near the end of the Mesozoic era. The cause may have been a large meteor striking the Earth, which dramatically changed the world's climate, killing plants that were food for the dinosaurs. Without food, the dinosaurs died off. These extinctions then allowed mammals to take over as the dominant vertebrates on land.

### ▶ MAMMALS ON LAND AND IN THE SEAS

The first half of the **Cenozoic era**, which began 65 million years ago, is sometimes called the Age of Mammals. Mammals evolved into about forty different groups and eventually replaced reptiles and birds as the dominant vertebrates. Marsupial (pouched)

*Apatosaurus*

*Plesiosaurus*

*Pteranodon*

*Procompsognathus*

*Stegosaurus*

Coelodonta antiquitatus

Brontotherium

Mammuthus

Hyracotherium

Triconodon

Tritemnodon

Smilodon

Some prehistoric mammals that lived from 135 million to 100,000 years ago include the shrew-sized *Triconodon*; the fox-sized horse, *Hyracotherium*; the mammoth, or *Mammuthus*; the woolly rhinoceros, *Coelodonta antiquitatus*; the horned *Brontotherium*; the saber-toothed cat, *Smilodon*; and the slender *Tritemnodon*. These animals (not drawn to scale) did not necessarily live together at the same time.

mammals became common in the Southern Hemisphere. Placental mammals (those with a placenta, an organ in the mother's womb) dominated the Northern Hemisphere. For many millions of years, mammals were small land-dwelling creatures. Eventually, some mammals evolved to be very large and also to live in the seas, where animal life began. Whales, dolphins, and walruses appeared during this time. Coral reefs slowly built up in the seas and became increasingly important to marine life.

The second half of the Cenozoic era, known as the **Quaternary period**, began 2 million years ago and continues to this day. The appearance of glaciers—and the corresponding drop in sea level—had a great influence on animal life of this period. Many large mammal species became extinct. Exposed dry land allowed animals to migrate to other continents. Horses and camels, which originated in North America, spread to other parts of the globe. Humans migrated into the Americas for the first time.

▶ STUDYING ANIMALS OF THE PAST

Scientists who study the history of animal life look for trends that appear over time. They may observe the increasing complexity of the nervous system or the body's increased ability to use oxygen efficiently. By interpreting fossil evidence, they often try to understand how prehistoric animals moved about, what they ate, and how they reproduced.

An important trend in animal evolution is **niche specialization**, which describes how

well-suited an animal is to its niche, or habitat. Over time, animals have evolved to be more and more specialized in where they live and how they survive there.

One result of niche specialization is increased variety, or diversity, of animal species. Although some animal groups are extinct, others are as diverse and abundant today as they were millions of years ago. And many others have become far more diverse and abundant since their original appearance.

Another trend in the fossil record is the migration of animals from one continent to another. Paleontologists can see animals appear in one geographic area in the fossil record and then expand their ranges over time to other continents.

Many studies of prehistoric animals focus on which animals were predators and which animals were prey in each time period. For example, small reptiles were the top predators at the end of the Paleozoic era. Their prey were amphibians and other reptiles. By the Mesozoic era, the top predators—and their prey—were dinosaurs. Today the top predators and their prey are mammals.

A good way to study prehistoric animals is to view each time period as having a completely new cast of characters. But it also is challenging to understand how a few kinds of prehistoric animals lived through many time periods as the world changed dramatically around them.

MICHAEL BRETT-SURMAN
National Museum of Natural History
The Smithsonian Institution

See also DINOSAURS; EARTH, HISTORY OF; EVOLUTION; FOSSILS; ICE AGES; PREHISTORIC ART; PREHISTORIC PEOPLE.

# PREHISTORIC ART

Human beings have lived on Earth for many thousands of years. Early people lived very differently from the way we do today. Before the development of cattle herding and farming, people obtained food by gathering nuts, berries, and other plants. They hunted animals that they had learned were good to eat. There were no villages, shops, hospitals, or schools. Writing had not yet been invented. The word "prehistoric" is often used to refer to the time before people began to create written records of their history and world events.

Between 14,000 and 24,000 years ago, the entire Earth was as cold as the Arctic region is today. The world was passing through what is called the Ice Age. People of the Ice Age lived in the mouths of caves or under overhanging cliffs on the sunny sides of valleys. Life must have been fierce and hard. There were few of the comforts we expect today. It was a constant struggle to get enough to eat and to keep warm and safe.

People lived roughly, yet they also created art. They painted and engraved images on pieces of bone, antler, and stone. They sculpted animal and human figures from these same materials. And they made carvings, engravings, and paintings on rock surfaces. Artistic traditions varied greatly around the world. In what is today western Europe, much prehistoric rock art is found on the walls of deep caves. In Africa, Australia, Asia, and the Americas, images were frequently made on more exposed rocks.

### ▶ HOW DO WE KNOW ABOUT PREHISTORIC ART?

Much of what we know about prehistoric art has been found by digging up the home-sites of prehistoric people. Let us suppose that a family lived in the mouth of a cave. The ashes from the fire were never removed. Animals were cooked and eaten; the bones were thrown to one side. Broken tools were also discarded and left on the cave floor. Several generations of people lived at the same site, each leaving a layer of rubbish behind.

Archaeologists, scientists who study the remains of ancient cultures, have examined the layers of rubbish that accumulated at these sites. If nothing has disturbed the layers, they assume that the bones and tools of any lower level are older than the objects in the layers above. This is how they begin to date layers.

An Australian rock painting of a turtle is done in "X-ray style," in which the animal's internal organs are represented.

Next, archaeologists examine the objects themselves. They can determine that engravings and carvings must have been made with the very fine, specially pointed flint tools and knives found in the same layers. The way the engravings were made changed from time to time in the different levels. In this way the growth of art can be traced through long periods of time. They also find that objects sometimes differ according to different cultures.

### ▶ CAVE ART

The best-known examples of prehistoric rock art are the cave paintings of Altamira, Lascaux, Niaux, and other sites in northern Spain and southern France. But rock art is found in many different parts of the world, notably Australia and Africa, and new sites continue to be discovered. In 1994 a new site, the Chauvet cave, was discovered in southern France. The paintings on the walls of this cave were determined to have been made more than 30,000 years ago, making them the oldest known cave paintings. The skill with which these paintings were made sheds new light on the abilities of the earliest cave artists.

Caves are found in limestone areas. Today many caves are dry because the water that formed them has sunk to lower levels. Some caves are very long and have many complicated passages.

The opening of the Niaux cave, in the French Pyrenees, is halfway up a hillside, above a mountain stream. After several hundred feet, a series of red painted dots, dashes, and lines appears just where a narrow passage leads off to the right. At the end of a wide passageway, there are dozens of paintings of bison, ibex, and other creatures. These paintings have lasted so long because weather conditions never change in deep caves. Variations of dampness, temperature, and light quickly destroy paint.

The artists painted with natural lumps of **ocher**, a material easily found in the ground.

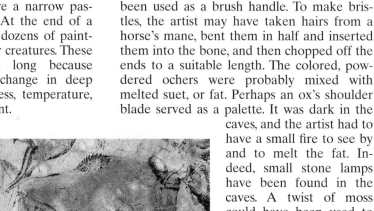

Crushed ochers give a red, orange, or yellow color. Charcoal black was also used. It has often survived despite the fact that it rubs off easily. The colors were put on the walls in various ways, sometimes with a brush. A small bone, snapped off at the end, may have been used as a brush handle. To make bristles, the artist may have taken hairs from a horse's mane, bent them in half and inserted them into the bone, and then chopped off the ends to a suitable length. The colored, powdered ochers were probably mixed with melted suet, or fat. Perhaps an ox's shoulder blade served as a palette. It was dark in the caves, and the artist had to have a small fire to see by and to melt the fat. Indeed, small stone lamps have been found in the caves. A twist of moss could have been used to make a wick.

Usually figures of animals were made. But there were also signs, patterns, and simplified drawings of natural things. Many of the animals that lived in the Ice Age no longer exist. But we know that they usually had long hair to help them keep warm. In the drawings we

The best-known examples of prehistoric rock art are the paintings found in caves in northern Spain and southern France. The reasons for the creation of such art by early people continue to be debated by scholars. *Above:* A painting of a bison from Altamira. *Below:* A grouping of horses and cattle from Lascaux.

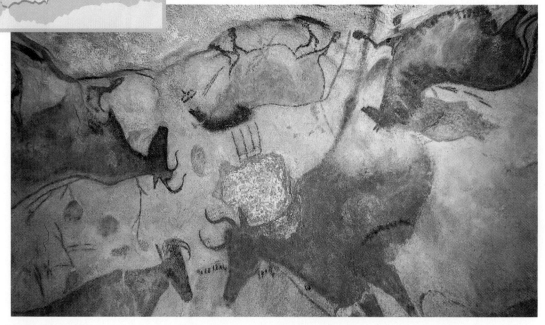

This 4½-inch-tall limestone figure, found in Willendorf, Austria, is one of many small statues of women made throughout Europe and Asia in prehistoric times.

can see the great woolly elephant, the woolly rhinoceros, the cave bear, and the cave lion. Some of the animals, such as the reindeer, still flourish. But today these animals are found in regions much colder than southern Europe, where the cave drawings were made.

The pictures of animals were often painted and engraved over each other. Like the layers of homesite rubbish, the figures underneath must be older than those that cover them. One can see, too, that not all the drawings and paintings were made in the same way.

## WHY WAS PREHISTORIC ART MADE?

Cave dwellers never lived in the pitch-dark depths of caves. For this reason, we know that cave paintings were not made simply for decorative purposes. Nor do they represent scenes of daily life. The pictures are mostly of animals—often animals, such as reindeer and bison, that were hunted by early people.

Scholars have debated the meaning of prehistoric cave art for many years. One explanation of why these pictures were made as they were is that the cave art was connected with the rituals and spiritual beliefs of prehistoric people. The caves, while not dwelling places, may have been important gathering places for rites or ceremonies. The animal images may have been made as a form of hunting magic—that is, they may have been created or used in rituals intended to ensure the success of a hunt. The paintings may depict the visions of a shaman—a person who was considered to have special magical powers. By studying the traditional beliefs

of more recent cultures, we know that shamans often enter trances as part of their rituals.

In the cave in France called Les Trois Frères (after the three brothers who found it), there is a large chamber with walls that are covered with engravings. At the end of this chamber is a small tunnel. Passing through and around this tunnel, we re-enter the main chamber at a higher level, standing on a sort of platform. This natural "pulpit"

Rock paintings from Tassili n'Ajjer, in Algeria, are outstanding examples of rock art from the Sahara region of Africa. *Above:* A cattle-herding scene painted on a flat rock surface. *Left:* A running figure from a cave fresco.

overlooks and dominates the area beneath it. Beside the platform is the painted image of a male figure with the face of an owl, the antlers of a reindeer, and the tail of a horse. It is easy to imagine a ritual ceremony taking place in this chamber thousands of years ago.

Because no written records exist to document the beliefs of prehistoric people, their reasons for creating their art will always be shrouded in mystery. But scientists and scholars continue to expand our understanding of the cultures and people who produced this incredible body of work.

MILES C. BURKITT
Author, *Our Early Ancestors*

# PREHISTORIC PEOPLE

The term "prehistoric" means "before written history." Written history has been developed by the world's peoples and their cultures at vastly different times. Scientists believe that the earliest known systems of writing came into use only about 5,000 years ago. This means that any people who lived before that time generally could be considered prehistoric, even though it would be imprecise to say that all prehistory dates back to that time. Since human beings are believed to have lived on Earth for more than 2.5 million years, it could be said that most of human history took place in prehistoric times.

For much of this long period, human beings lived in small family bands, or groups. These groups moved from place to place, hunting wild animals and gathering seeds, nuts, roots, and other plant foods.

The earliest humans lived only in tropical Africa, but eventually they spread to other parts of the world. By the end of the great Ice Age, about 15,000 years ago, people lived throughout the world. With the development of farming and civilization, the world's population grew rapidly.

## ▶ UNWRITTEN RECORDS OF THE PAST

Prehistoric people left no written records, but they left many clues about their ways of life. Archaeologists, scientists who study the remains of ancient cultures, have uncovered campsites and farming villages that contain food remnants, such as broken animal bones, edible seeds, and fish fragments. Artifacts such as stone tools, metal objects, and clay pots provide information about ancient technology. Archaeologists use these clues to reconstruct the lives of prehistoric people. They use the different artifact forms to distinguish one prehistoric society from another. (The vast majority of prehistoric societies lived during a technological stage called the Stone Age, a period when human societies had no metals. Instead, they used objects made of bone, stone, and wood for tools and weapons.)

To learn about the environment in which prehistoric people lived, scientists have studied evidence of climate change. They have determined that the global climate cooled significantly about 5 million years ago. In the past 750,000 years, at least six periods of worldwide cooling have taken place. Great sheets of ice, called glaciers, moved southward from the North Pole, covering parts of Europe, Asia, and North America. During this period of time, known as the great Ice Age, the weather south of these ice sheets was very cold. In response to changing climate conditions during the great Ice Age, prehistoric people developed increasingly elaborate tools to help them survive.

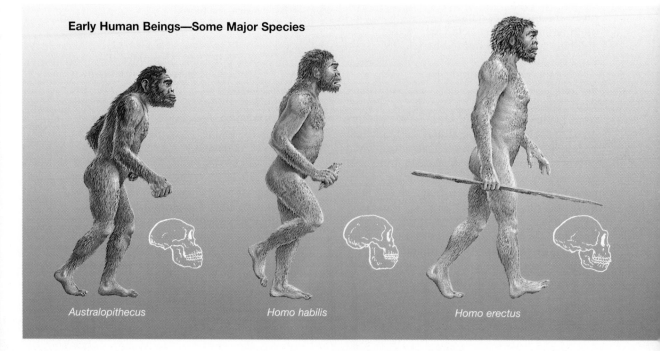

**Early Human Beings—Some Major Species**

*Australopithecus*　　　*Homo habilis*　　　*Homo erectus*

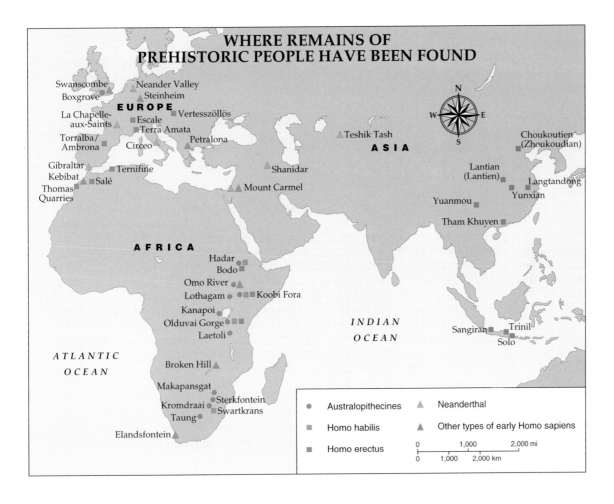

# WHERE REMAINS OF PREHISTORIC PEOPLE HAVE BEEN FOUND

**EUROPE**
Swanscombe
Boxgrove
Neander Valley
Steinheim
La Chapelle-aux-Saints
Escale
Vertesszöllös
Terra Amata
Torralba/Ambrona
Circeo
Petralona
Gibraltar
Kebibat
Ternifine
Salé
Thomas Quarries

**ASIA**
Teshik Tash
Shanidar
Mount Carmel
Choukoutien (Zhoukoudian)
Lantian (Lantien)
Langtandong
Yunxian
Yuanmou
Tham Khuyen

**AFRICA**
Hadar
Bodo
Omo River
Lothagam
Koobi Fora
Kanapoi
Olduvai Gorge
Laetoli
Broken Hill
Makapansgat
Kromdraai
Sterkfontein
Swartkrans
Taung
Elandsfontein

Sangiran
Trinil
Solo

*INDIAN OCEAN*

*ATLANTIC OCEAN*

Legend:
- ● Australopithecines
- ■ Homo habilis
- ■ Homo erectus
- ▲ Neanderthal
- ▲ Other types of early Homo sapiens

0   1,000   2,000 mi
0   1,000   2,000 km

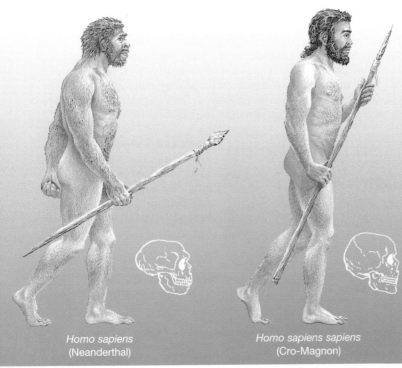

*Homo sapiens*
(Neanderthal)

*Homo sapiens sapiens*
(Cro-Magnon)

The story of prehistoric people, as we know it, comes from artifacts and fossil remains. One of our earliest known ancestors was the small, apelike *Australopithecus*. Still quite small, *Homo habilis* benefited from a larger brain and became the first early human to make tools. *Homo erectus*, whose posture, gait, and brain volume approached those of modern humans, fabricated a variety of tools and used fire. The Neanderthals, a type of early *Homo sapiens*, possessed well-developed tool-making and hunting techniques, and they were the first humans to bury their dead. Artifacts from Cro-Magnons reveal a sophisticated culture, advanced tool-making technology, and the adaptability to survive the Ice Age environment. Scientists believe that Cro-Magnons existed at the time of the Neanderthals and did not descend from them.

## ▶ THE EARLIEST HUMAN BEINGS

The term "hominid" refers to primates that walk on two legs. It includes modern humans as well as our earliest ancestors. The earliest known hominids lived in East Africa. One well-studied group is called *Australopithecus*, meaning "southern ape." Based on discoveries of fossilized bone and teeth, scientists have determined that these ancestors had apelike faces with small teeth resembling human teeth. Their brains were much smaller than those of modern humans but slightly larger than those of apes. In 2001, scientists reported that the fossilized skull of another type of early ancestor had been discovered. The evidence suggests that these hominids, named *Kenyanthropus platyops*, lived at the same time as *Australopithecus*.

Many different hominid forms flourished in Africa by 3 million years ago. By 2.5 million years ago, at least one form had developed a slightly larger brain and more skillful hands, enabling the fabrication of stone tools. This tool-making ability, combined with enhanced intelligence and communication ability, distinguished these individuals from other hominids. Known by scientists as *Homo habilis* ("handy person"), these are considered to be the first human beings.

The earliest stone tools, 2.5 million years old, come from Ethiopia in northeast Africa. Early humans at that time lived in open grassland areas, not in forests as their ancestors had done. Scattered stone flakes and broken animal bones have been found on the shores of Lake Turkana and Olduvai Gorge in East Africa, the earliest archaeological sites in the world. Artifacts have shown that our earliest ancestors lived on wild plant foods and meat scavenged from lion kills.

About 1.9 million years ago, a new human form appeared, called by scientists *Homo erectus* ("person who stands erect"). *Homo erectus* had more modern-looking bodies, with long, sturdy limbs. But they had sloping foreheads and brows that extended over their eyes. They had large teeth and receding chins.

*Homo erectus*, who appeared in Africa at a time when the climate was cooler, learned how to use fire. By 1.8 million years ago, these early humans had spread into southeast Asia. By 700,000 years ago, they were flourishing in northern China. They also settled in Europe by at least 600,000 years ago. By 250,000 years ago, many forms of *Homo erectus* lived throughout Africa, Asia, and Europe. They ate wild plant foods and animals they hunted with wooden spears. They wandered in small groups and used stone tools.

In 2004, on the Indonesian island of Flores, scientists found the bones of an early human that may have evolved from *Homo erectus*. This early human, called *Homo floresiensis*, stood about 3 feet (1 meter) tall and lived as recently as 13,000 years ago.

## ▶ THE NEANDERTHALS

Descending from *Homo erectus* at least 120,000 years ago were the Neanderthals, a type of early *Homo sapiens* ("wise person"). The Neanderthals lived in western Asia and parts of Europe. They were named after the Neander Valley in Germany, where the first Neanderthal skeleton was found.

Neanderthals displayed great physical variation. Those from western Asia were relatively tall, while later European Neanderthals were short and squat, with long heads, large brains, and jutting brows. They were the first humans to bury their dead.

About 100,000 years ago, the last glacial period brought bitterly cold conditions to Europe, lasting about 50,000 years. The Neanderthals adjusted by finding sheltered environments. They hunted large animals, such as the mammoth, with stone-tipped wooden spears, and they butchered their prey with stone knives. They also used stone scrapers to process animal skins for clothing.

## ▶ MODERN HUMANS

As the cold climate subsided, the first groups of modern humans appeared in southeastern Europe. They spread rapidly to the west.

**Neanderthal graves, such as the one containing this 60,000-year-old skeleton, provide evidence that the Neanderthals were the first humans to bury their dead.**

As prehistoric people advanced, so did the sophistication and complexity of their tools: (1) Crude pebble tools, about 1.7 million years old; (2) Stone hand ax, about 700,000 years old; (3) Stone hand ax, about 250,000 years old; (4) Bone harpoon, 10,000–17,000 years old.

Scientists believe that the newcomers replaced Neanderthal populations.

**Homo sapiens sapiens.** Scientists do not agree on the exact origins of modern human beings, known as *Homo sapiens sapiens*, a subspecies of *Homo sapiens*. Most evidence points to tropical Africa as the cradle of modern humanity, where it is believed the first people like ourselves appeared between 100,000 and 200,000 years ago, then spread rapidly elsewhere. A few scholars argue for the appearance of *Homo sapiens sapiens* in Africa, Asia, and Europe all about the same time. The earliest bones of modern-looking people appear in South Africa, dating from at least 110,000 years ago.

From tropical Africa, *Homo sapiens sapiens* spread across the Sahara and into western Asia by 90,000 years ago. About 50,000 years ago, modern people migrated into the rest of Asia and into Europe, replacing older human populations.

By 32,000 years ago, only modern human beings lived in Europe. By this time, modern people had also settled in central Asia and Siberia, China, and southeast Asia.

**The Cro-Magnons.** The earliest modern Europeans are known as the Cro-Magnons, named after a rock shelter in southwestern France where their skeletons were first found in 1868. They appeared about 35,000 years ago and survived as a distinct group until about 10,000 years ago.

The Cro-Magnons developed specialized tools for surviving extremely cold conditions. They were among the first humans to develop artistic traditions. Their cave paintings and engravings, which depict animals, are believed to have had deep spiritual meaning.

**The First Americans.** By 20,000 years ago, a few hunter-gatherer groups lived in northeastern Siberia. A land bridge created by low sea levels during an Ice Age linked Siberia to Alaska. People could walk from Asia to North America.

A few scientists believe the first Americans crossed into Alaska as early as 40,000 years ago. Most argue for a much later settlement, about 15,000 years ago.

Small groups of hunter-gatherers had spread as far south as Chile in South America by 12,500 years ago. These people, called Paleo-Indians, hunted large animals, such as bison, on the open plains. They also flourished in deserts and tropical forests, where they relied heavily on plant foods.

▶ **THE BEGINNINGS OF FARMING**

Global climatic conditions warmed up rapidly after 15,000 years ago. Glaciers retreated, sea levels rose to near-modern levels, and forests replaced arctic vegetation.

Human populations everywhere still lived in small groups. As the climate warmed, they developed more intensive, specialized methods of hunting and gathering. Many of the groups settled by lakes, rivers, and sea coasts, where they lived on fish and plant foods.

About 8000 B.C., the climate of southwestern Asia became drier, driving hunter-gatherer groups to well-watered locations. Some deliberately planted wild barley and wheat to supplement other wild foods. Within a few centuries, these hunter-gatherers had become farmers. They lived in small, permanent villages among their fields. The farmers grew wheat and barley and also tended herds of goats, sheep, and cattle.

Farming, or agriculture, spread rapidly throughout southwestern Asia and North Africa. Egyptians had become farmers by 7000 B.C. By 6000 B.C., cattle herders flourished in the heart of the Sahara, and agriculture had begun in Europe and southern Asia as well. By this time, northern Chinese villagers were cultivating millet and other crops along the Huang He River. Rice was domesticated and soon became a staple crop throughout southeast Asia. Tropical Africa was plentiful with game, so agriculture did not spread there until after 3000 B.C. The Sahara became drier, pushing farming people to the edge of the desert and later to the south.

Ancient Native Americans domesticated teosinte, a wild Central American grass that they developed into maize (corn) by 4000 B.C. This crop became one of the foundations of later Native American civilizations.

▶ **THE FIRST CIVILIZATIONS**

After about 8000 B.C., complex farming societies began to develop in several parts of the world. People living in one village came to depend on those living in other villages for essential goods. Long-distance trade networks soon linked communities together, especially in southwestern Asia. By 4000 B.C., some villages between the Tigris and Euphrates rivers in Mesopotamia (southern Iraq) had become small towns. Within a few centuries, these villages grew into cities with more than 5,000 inhabitants. The world's first civilizations developed here and along Egypt's Nile River.

We do not understand exactly how civilizations came into being. We do know that, among other factors, long-distance trade, metalworking, and the development of writing played important roles.

Trade routes extended into the Sahara and into the mountains surrounding Mesopotamia, bringing metals and other precious materials to the cities. Metalworking in copper and gold was well developed by about 3500 B.C. At first the metals were made into ornaments and later into weapons and agricultural tools.

Metalworkers in southwestern Asia learned to make bronze (a mixture of copper and tin) about 3500 B.C. The development of this metal—stronger and more durable than earlier materials—had a great impact on the way people lived. Unlike stone tools, tools made from bronze could be melted down and recast when they wore out. The period when bronze replaced stone as the most important material for tools and weapons is called the Bronze Age.

By about 3000 B.C., traders were using written scripts, such as Mesopotamian cuneiform and Egyptian hieroglyphs, to record commercial transactions. The development of writing, which allowed people to record their history, marked the end of the prehistoric period. However, many parts of the world remained without written histories for many centuries.

BRIAN FAGAN
University of California, Santa Barbara

See also ALPHABET; ANTHROPOLOGY; ARCHAEOLOGY; FIRE; FOSSILS; ICE AGES; PREHISTORIC ART; TOOLS.

**PRELUTSKY, JACK.** See CHILDREN'S LITERATURE (Profiles).

Some high school—age students attend private, independent secondary schools that are known as preparatory schools. Although these schools vary greatly in size, setting, and academic programs, all of them stress sound preparation for college.

## PREPARATORY SCHOOLS

Preparatory schools are independent secondary schools that prepare students for college. While the majority of today's secondary school students attend free public high schools, a smaller number attend nonpublic, or independent, schools. Because independent schools are not run by a city, county, state, or province, they are not supported by taxes and must charge fees, or tuition.

Independent schools are of many different types. In some independent schools, students live at home and commute to school each day. These schools are known as day schools. At other schools, called boarding schools, students live at the school and go home only on vacations. Some independent schools are run by religious groups, and others are organized as military academies. Some teach only boys, others only girls. The term "preparatory school," frequently shortened to "prep" school, generally refers to a particular type of independent school that developed in America shortly after the Civil War.

▶HISTORY

During much of early American history, few young people attended college. Those who did usually were prepared at home by private tutors or in schools known as grammar schools and academies. These schools charged small fees to teach subjects, such as Latin and Greek, that were required for admission to college.

Free public high schools, open to all, were not common until after the Civil War. The growth of industry and cities and the establishment of many new public colleges and universities led to the creation of more and more public high schools. By 1900 the public high school was the most common type of secondary school in America.

However, some parents, especially those from families who traditionally sent their children to college, felt that the public high schools tried to do too much. As a result, college preparation seemed neglected. For this and a number of other reasons, a type of secondary school new to America developed. These schools, because they were specially designed to prepare students for college, became known as preparatory schools.

Some preparatory schools were entirely new, while others were remodeled grammar schools or academies. They were greatly influenced by the famous British boarding schools, such as Eton, Harrow, and Rugby, and adopted many of their traditions.

While continuing to emphasize the subjects required for college admission, the new preparatory schools did more. Like the British schools, they provided dormitories in which students lived together under the supervision of a teacher who lived in the same building. They encouraged organized athletics as a way of teaching healthy competition, team work, school spirit, and sportsmanship. They sought to teach good manners, character, and proper behavior as well as academics. Most required attendance at frequent religious services, and many were run by the clergy.

Many of the new schools were located in the country or in small towns, because the growing cities were thought to be difficult places to raise children. Boys and girls almost always attended separate schools.

### ▶ PREPARATORY SCHOOLS TODAY

While traditional features remain, preparatory schools have changed over the years. Although in the United States the largest number are still located in the Northeast, where they originated, examples are now found throughout the country. Latin (and in some cases even Greek) is still taught, but students have a wider choice of subjects to study. Schools also actively seek students from a wide variety of backgrounds, and financial aid is available to qualified students. Student life in most schools is less formal than it once was, but perhaps the greatest change of all has been coeducation—the education of boys and girls in the same school.

Because preparatory schools educate a small percentage of high school-age children, they are not always well known or understood. Why do some students prefer to attend such a school? The main reason is sound preparation for college. Classes are usually smaller than in public school, and students receive a great deal of individual attention.

The programs offered by nearby schools do not always fit a student's personal or academic needs and interests. Students may wish to attend school in another part of the country or the world and meet people different from those they would meet at home.

While most preparatory schools have common features, they also differ in important ways. Some are quite small, while others enroll more than 1,000 students. Some offer religious instruction, which public schools are not allowed to teach. Preparatory schools also vary greatly in the levels of academic and athletic competition they provide. This variety makes it possible to find a school to fit a particular student.

### ▶ CHOOSING A SCHOOL

Local educators and professional counselors can help you find information on preparatory schools, and most public libraries contain directories of independent schools.

A general investigation should reveal several schools that seem appropriate. Write or telephone these schools for catalogs and other information and study this material carefully. At first, many schools may seem to be quite similar. Differences begin to appear when courses offered, graduation requirements, and special activities or athletics available are compared. The geographical distribution of students and the colleges and universities a school's graduates attend also provide important information about a school's reputation and the strength of its academic program.

After studying each school's materials, visits should be arranged in advance to those schools that seem best suited to the prospective student's needs. A visit will normally include at least one formal interview. Part of this interview will be with the student alone so the school can get an accurate sense of the student's personality. The student should come prepared to ask questions about financial aid, arts programs, and other concerns.

The more each side knows about the other, the better the "fit" between student and school. Try to meet the head of the school and talk with faculty members or a coach if a particular sport is of interest. Visit a class and a dormitory and, if possible, attend an athletic or extracurricular event. Ask for copies of the school newspaper and other publications. Make it a point to talk with students.

If a campus visit leads to positive impressions, a formal application for admission should be submitted. Most applications require the prospective student to write at least one essay and to submit test scores from a national examination. Applications should be made to schools of differing degrees of competitiveness. If a candidate is accepted at several schools, a second visit to some or all may be necessary to obtain more information.

The Editors of Bunting and Lyon, Inc. Publishers, *Private Independent Schools* Directory
See also EDUCATION.

**PREPOSITION.** See PARTS OF SPEECH.

**PRESERVATION OF FOOD.** See FOOD PRESERVATION.

George
Washington
1789-97

John
Adams
1797-1801

Thomas
Jefferson
1801-09

James
Madison
1809-17

James
Monroe
1817-25

John
Quincy
Adams
1825-29

# PRESIDENCY OF
# THE UNITED STATES

Every four years, on the first Tuesday after the first Monday of November, millions of Americans go to the polls to choose a new leader in a free and open election. The candidates, nominated during the preceding summer at the conventions of their respective political parties, have waged vigorous campaigns. Through the media of radio, television, newspapers, and magazines, they have made known their views on both national and international affairs and have become familiar faces to the people of the nation.

On Inauguration Day, January 20, the successful candidate for the high office of president of the United States takes this oath of office:

> "I do solemnly swear (or affirm) that I will faithfully execute the Office of President of the United States, and will to the best of my Ability, preserve, protect and defend the Constitution of the United States."

This is the same oath that has been taken by every American president since George Washington. And yet, in the two centuries since the first president was inaugurated, the obligations and duties implied in the oath have changed. The key to the changes lies in the words, "the Office of the President." Exactly what is the office of the president? What was it originally intended to be? And what has it become?

▶ **THE GROWTH OF THE PRESIDENCY**

The men who wrote the Constitution of the United States were opposed to the idea of an all-powerful head of state. America's Founding Fathers thought of the presidency as an office of great honor and dignity, but one with little real power. The American colonists in general favored the parliamentary system of government but did not believe that all governmental powers should rest within any one body. So, in framing the Constitution, they provided for three separate branches—legislaive, executive, and judicial.

Article I of the Constitution deals with the functions of the House of Representatives and the Senate. Not until Article II is any mention made of the president. This article states

Andrew Jackson
1829-37

Martin Van Buren
1837-41

William Henry Harrison
1841

John Tyler
1841-45

James K. Polk
1845-49

Zachary Taylor
1849-50

that the president shall be the head of the executive branch of the government. But to limit and restrict the office, the Constitution provides Congress with checks against any president who may try to assume too much authority.

The framers of the Constitution believed that in the presidency they had created an office of prestige but little power. They would be astounded if they knew the changes that have occurred. The powers and responsibilities of the president have grown enormously. The president has become the leader of his country in fact as well as in name. His words and deeds affect the course of history not only in the United States but in every country throughout the world.

The men who were presidents early in the history of the republic were able to carry on the duties of their office with little assistance. When George Washington served as first president of the United States, his staff consisted of a secretary, one or two clerks, and household servants who acted as messengers. But with the enormous growth in presidential power and responsibilities, the office of the presidency now must be run by a large staff.

Today the president of the United States requires the assistance of over 1,500 people.

The employees assigned to jobs directly relating to the office of the presidency are staff members of the Executive Office of the President. The Executive Office was created by Congress, but it can be reorganized by the president through executive orders.

### The Cabinet

The president's cabinet is one of the most important parts of the executive branch of the government. The cabinet was not provided for by the Constitution, nor was it created by an act of Congress. It developed through necessity. The cabinet traces its beginnings to George Washington's assembling his department heads in 1793 to discuss U.S. neutrality in the French Revolutionary wars.

The cabinet is made up of the heads of the 15 executive departments of the government. Its function is to advise the president on matters of the greatest importance. One of the first tasks of a new president is to select a cabinet. You can read more about this presidential advisory group in the CABINET OF THE UNITED STATES article in Volume C.

Millard
Fillmore
1850-53

Franklin
Pierce
1853-57

James
Buchanan
1857-61

Abraham
Lincoln
1861-65

Andrew
Johnson
1865-69

Ulysses
S. Grant
1869-77

The first executive posts, which became the president's cabinet, were created in 1789. They were the following:

Secretary of Foreign Affairs (State)
Secretary of War
Secretary of the Treasury
Attorney General

The present-day cabinet includes the following heads of executive departments:

Secretary of State
Secretary of the Treasury
Secretary of Defense
Attorney General (Justice Department)
Secretary of the Interior
Secretary of Agriculture
Secretary of Commerce
Secretary of Labor
Secretary of Health and Human Services
Secretary of Education
Secretary of Housing and Urban Development
Secretary of Transportation
Secretary of Energy
Secretary of Veterans Affairs
Secretary of Homeland Security

The president may also choose other members of government to serve in the cabinet; the vice president, the White House chief of staff, and the director of the Office of Management and Budget may all join the cabinet at the president's discretion.

▶ PRESIDENTIAL LEADERSHIP

The vast and complicated structure needed to run today's government has brought many changes to the office of the presidency. With each new president, the machinery of government becomes more complex.

The rise of presidential power did not come about all at once. Nor did the growth of leadership follow a fixed and steady course. Some presidents have strongly exercised the power of leadership. Others have been relatively weak leaders.

Since the time of George Washington many presidents have contributed to changing the powers of the office. People often have different views as to whether a president has acted wisely and exercised his power for the general good of the entire nation. Leadership takes many forms, and all leaders cannot appeal to all people. The leadership qualities of a few presidents, however, will serve to show how some have used the power of their office.

Thomas Jefferson was the nation's third president. Even though he served so early in the history of the office, he understood that in order to gain the results he desired, he would have to exercise a great deal of political power. Jefferson skillfully organized his sympathizers in Congress into a strong political group. These men worked together so well that they often were able to defeat their opponents in many important matters. This plan of Jefferson's was the start of the system of political parties as we know it today.

Andrew Jackson, seventh president of the United States, was another strong leader. Jackson was the first man of the people to be elected to the presidency. Many of the men in the government were not friendly to the new president or to his views. But Jackson was determined to overcome his opponents. In critical issues he relied on the support of the people and removed cabinet members who disagreed with his policies. By the skillful use of his leadership qualities, he was able to carry out many of his programs.

The strongest desire of President Abraham Lincoln was to preserve the Union. At the outbreak of the Civil War, Lincoln did not have the power to call up troops or to take certain other actions. But he knew that in order to protect the Union he would have to assume wartime powers. Many people disapproved of his actions. But Lincoln seized the power he felt he must have. By exercising leadership in a time of crisis, he succeeded in preserving the Union.

Woodrow Wilson, during whose term the bitter battles of World War I were fought, had one great dream. The dream was for the creation of a League of Nations that would help to prevent future wars. The League of Nations finally was established at the close of the war. But in spite of Wilson's strength, his own country refused to join. Wilson died a disappointed man. But under his leadership the office of the presidency outgrew the bounds of the United States and became an office with international responsibilities.

In another period of serious trouble for the United States, Franklin D. Roosevelt served as president. During the Depression of the 1930's Roosevelt sought tremendous powers. He recommended to Congress legislation that would create jobs for those who could find no work, in order to get the country back on its

## FACTS ABOUT THE PRESIDENCY

**Qualifications:** (1) Natural-born citizen of the United States. (2) At least 35 years old. (3) At least 14 years a resident of the United States.

**Nomination:** Candidates are usually nominated at national party conventions held in the summer of the election year. Although only men have served as president, women are eligible to hold the office.

**Election:** By a majority vote of the Electoral College.

**Term:** 4 years. A president may not serve more than 2 terms (plus 2 years of an unexpired term).

**Salary:** (1) $400,000 plus additional allowances for expenses, travel, and official entertainment. (2) Provided with White House, household help, transportation, health care. (3) Lifetime pension.

**Removal:** May be impeached (accused of serious wrongdoing) by a majority of the House of Representatives; must then be tried by the Senate and convicted by a two-thirds vote.

**Succession:** If the president dies or is disabled in office, the line of succession is as follows:

1. Vice President of the United States
2. Speaker of the House
3. President Pro Tempore of the Senate
4. Secretary of State
5. Secretary of the Treasury
6. Secretary of Defense
7. Attorney General
8. Secretary of Homeland Security
9. Secretary of the Interior
10. Secretary of Agriculture
11. Secretary of Commerce
12. Secretary of Labor
13. Secretary of Health and Human Services
14. Secretary of Housing and Urban Development
15. Secretary of Transportation
16. Secretary of Energy
17. Secretary of Education
18. Secretary of Veterans Affairs

## ASSASSINATIONS AND ATTEMPTS

**1835** January 30: Andrew Jackson escaped assassination by Richard Lawrence in Washington, D.C.

**1865** April 14: Abraham Lincoln shot by John Wilkes Booth in Washington, D.C. Died April 15.

**1881** July 2: James A. Garfield shot by Charles J. Guiteau in Washington, D.C. Died September 19.

**1901** September 6: William McKinley shot by Leon Czolgosz in Buffalo, New York. Died September 14.

**1933** February 15: Franklin D. Roosevelt escaped assassination by Giuseppe Zangara in Miami, Florida.

**1950** November 1: Harry S. Truman escaped assassination by two Puerto Rican nationalists in Washington, D.C.

**1963** November 22: John F. Kennedy shot and killed in Dallas, Texas.

**1975** September 5 and 22: President Gerald R. Ford twice escaped assassination in California.

**1981** March 30: Ronald W. Reagan was wounded in an assassination attempt in Washington, D.C.

# INTERESTING FACTS ABOUT PRESIDENTS

**JOHN QUINCY ADAMS** and **ANDREW JOHNSON** were the only men to serve in Congress after being president.

**MARTIN VAN BUREN** was the first president born after the signing of the Declaration of Independence.

**WILLIAM HENRY HARRISON** was president for the shortest time. He died of pneumonia 31 days after his inauguration.

**JAMES BUCHANAN** was the only president who never married.

**ABRAHAM LINCOLN** at 6 feet 4 inches, was the tallest president.

**THEODORE ROOSEVELT** was the youngest person to become president (at age 42, following the assassination of McKinley) and the first to win the Nobel Peace Prize.

**WILLIAM HOWARD TAFT** was the only president who also served as Chief Justice of the Supreme Court.

**HERBERT HOOVER** was the first president born west of the Mississippi River.

**FRANKLIN D. ROOSEVELT** was the only president to be elected to more than two terms.

**JOHN F. KENNEDY** was the first Roman Catholic president and the youngest person to be *elected* president (at age 43; compare with T. Roosevelt).

**RICHARD M. NIXON** was the only president to resign from office.

**GERALD R. FORD** was the first president who had not been elected to the presidency or vice presidency.

**RONALD REAGAN** was the oldest person (69) to be elected president and the first ever to be divorced.

**Eight vice presidents became president when their predecessors died. They were:**

**JOHN TYLER** (succeeded William Henry Harrison)

**MILLARD FILLMORE** (succeeded Zachary Taylor)

**ANDREW JOHNSON** (succeeded Abraham Lincoln)

**CHESTER ARTHUR** (succeeded James A. Garfield)

**THEODORE ROOSEVELT** (succeeded William McKinley)

**CALVIN COOLIDGE** (succeeded Warren G. Harding)

**HARRY S. TRUMAN** (succeeded Franklin D. Roosevelt)

**LYNDON B. JOHNSON** (succeeded John F. Kennedy)

**Seven presidents won fame as soldier-heroes. They were:**

**GEORGE WASHINGTON** in the American Revolutionary War

**ANDREW JACKSON** in the War of 1812

**WILLIAM HENRY HARRISON** in the War of 1812

**ZACHARY TAYLOR** in the Mexican War

**ULYSSES S. GRANT** in the Civil War

**THEODORE ROOSEVELT** in the Spanish-American War

**DWIGHT D. EISENHOWER** in World War II

**Some presidents were related to other presidents. They were:**

**JOHN ADAMS** and **JOHN QUINCY ADAMS** (father and son)

**THEODORE ROOSEVELT** and **FRANKLIN D. ROOSEVELT** (distant cousins)

**WILLIAM HENRY HARRISON** and **BENJAMIN HARRISON** (grandfather and grandson)

**GEORGE BUSH** and **GEORGE W. BUSH** (father and son)

feet. He even attempted to change the structure of the Supreme Court by increasing the number of justices. During World War II he extended United States influence in the field of international relations.

Even though the president of the United States is today one of the most important individuals in the world, he is not all-powerful. There is an authority that is higher than that of the president. It is the will of the people of the United States, who have reserved to themselves the final authority that is called sovereignty.

▶ **DUTIES AND POWERS OF THE PRESIDENT**

"The executive Power shall be vested in a President of the United States of America. He shall hold his Office during the Term of four Years …."

These words form the opening of Article II of the Constitution, outlining the powers and duties of the president. The four sections of the article also state how the president shall be elected and paid, and who shall succeed him if he is unable to serve out his term. This Article, written in a careful and straightforward manner, suggests that the document's framers were on their guard against the possibility of a too ambitious president. It gives little hint, however, that they had any idea of how enormous and important the office of the presidency would one day become.

To the average citizen it often seems that the power of the president is unlimited. But that is far from the truth. What acts is the president permitted to perform without restrictions of any kind? What is he prohibited from doing? The answers to these questions give some idea of the powers of the president and of the system of checks and balances provided by the Constitution.

Article II states that the president shall be commander in chief of the Army and the Navy. He shall have the power to make treaties—provided two-thirds of the Senate agrees. He shall appoint ambassadors, Supreme Court justices, and other officials—"by and with the Advice and Consent of the Senate." Section 3 of the Article provides that he shall address Congress on the state of the Union, see that laws are carefully carried out, and receive foreign ambassadors and ministers. Basically, all these provisions of the Constitution are still in force today.

Rutherford
B. Hayes
1877-81

James A.
Garfield
1881

Chester
Alan
Arthur
1881-85

Grover
Cleveland
1885-89
1893-97

Benjamin
Harrison
1889-93

William
McKinley
1897-1901

Even within the framework of the Constitution the duties and powers of the president have become highly complex. The best way to understand them is to examine the various branches of the government and see how the president functions in each.

### Executive and Administrative Powers

The president stands at the head of the executive branch of the government. He is elected by the entire nation and is responsible for carrying out and administering the laws approved by the legislative branch—Congress. The Constitution outlined these powers only in the most general terms. Most presidential authority, therefore, has been granted by acts of Congress.

**Power of Appointment and Removal.** The president has the power to appoint important officials. The list of these officials includes ambassadors, members of the cabinet and their assistants, federal judges, military and naval officers, heads of agencies, and United States attorneys and marshals. In almost all cases Senate approval is assured. The president does, therefore, exercise a great deal of power in the choice of the people named for

key government posts. In 1926 the Supreme Court ruled that since the president has the power to appoint officers, the president also should have the power to remove them.

**Executive Ordinances.** Administration of policies outlined by Congress usually is left to the executive branch. The president (or subordinates acting for him) spells out the details in the form of executive orders that have the force of law.

### Legislative Powers

The president is given certain legislative powers that make it possible for him to exert considerable influence over Congress.

**Power to Recommend Legislation.** At the beginning of each session of Congress the president delivers his "State of the Union" message. In his address he recommends a legislative program. This is followed by a proposed budget and economic report. The president also may submit special messages from time to time on particular subjects. In this way he makes known to Congress the laws he considers necessary.

**Veto Power.** Every bill or joint resolution passed by Congress must be sent to the presi-

Theodore
Roosevelt
1901-09

William
Howard
Taft
1909-13

Woodrow
Wilson
1913-21

Warren G.
Harding
1921-23

Calvin
Coolidge
1923-29

Herbert
Hoover
1929-33

## THE EXECUTIVE OFFICE OF THE PRESIDENT

Council of Economic Advisers
Council on Environmental Quality
Domestic Policy Council
National Economic Council
National Security Council
Office of Administration
Office of Faith-Based and Community Initiatives
Office of Global Communications
Office of Management and Budget
Office of National AIDS Policy
Office of National Drug Control Policy
Office of Science and Technology Policy
Office of the United States Trade Representative
President's Foreign Intelligence Advisory Board
USA Freedom Corps
White House Military Office

dent for action. If he signs it, it becomes law. If he vetoes it, he must send it back with the reasons for his veto. The veto power enables the president to act as a check on Congress.

### Judicial Powers

The chief executive can exercise judicial power in several ways. He recommends to the Senate his choices for attorney general (to head the Department of Justice) and Supreme Court justices. In every district of the country he appoints federal court judges and the U.S. district attorneys.

**Pardoning Power.** The president has the power to pardon a citizen of an offense. He may also grant a reprieve, or postponement of punishment. He cannot exercise this power in impeachment cases, where a pardon can never be granted.

### Powers in Foreign Affairs

The president has enormous powers in the field of foreign affairs. He is the nation's chief diplomat. He receives diplomatic representatives, ambassadors, and ministers from foreign countries, and sometimes attends special international conferences.

Franklin D.
Roosevelt
1933-45

Harry S.
Truman
1945-53

Dwight D.
Eisenhower
1953-61

John F.
Kennedy
1961-63

Lyndon
Baines
Johnson
1963-69

Richard M.
Nixon
1969-74

**Power of Recognition.** The president has the power of recognition—the formal approval of the government of a foreign country. Without recognition, normal trade and diplomatic relations cannot exist between two countries.

**Treaty Power.** If the United States wants to enter into commercial pacts, define its boundaries, make peace, or enter into any other international agreement, the president may negotiate a treaty with the country or countries concerned. The president shares this power with the Senate. Two-thirds of that body must ratify, or approve, a treaty before it goes into effect.

**Executive Agreements.** Agreements between the president and the chief executive (rather than the official government) of a foreign country are not subject to Senate approval.

### Military Powers

As stated in the Constitution, the president is commander in chief of the armed forces. This position guarantees that the people always shall control the Army through their elected civilian leaders. Here, too, the president's powers are shared with Congress. Congress makes rules for the armed forces, sets

### PRESIDENTIAL DISABILITY

The Constitution made no clear provisions for what would happen if a president became disabled in office. In 1965, Congress approved a projected 25th constitutional amendment that deals with this problem. The amendment became part of the Constitution in 1967, when it received the approval of three-fourths of the states.

The main provisions of the amendment are:

1. If the president is disabled, he informs the vice president and the congressional officers—the president pro tempore of the Senate and the Speaker of the House of Representatives. The vice president then takes over as acting president.

2. If the disabled president fails to inform the congressional officers, then the vice president, with the written approval of a majority of the cabinet "or of such other body as Congress may by law provide," so informs the congressional officers. The vice president then takes over as acting president.

3. When the president has recovered, he informs the congressional officers. However, if the vice president and a majority of the cabinet or of the "other body" do not agree that the president has recovered, it is up to Congress to decide. A two-thirds vote of both houses would be needed to continue the vice president as acting president.

Gerald R.
Ford
1974-77

James Earl
Carter, Jr.
1977-81

Ronald W.
Reagan
1981-89

George H.W.
Bush
1989–93

William J.B.
Clinton
1993–2001

George W.
Bush
2001-

apart funds for defense, and has the power to declare war. Appointments or commissions of military officers must be confirmed by the Senate. But in many emergencies the president can act without the consent of either house of Congress. He may use armed forces in combat abroad without a formal declaration of war. He may send troops to protect the mails and interstate commerce. At the request of a governor or state legislature, he may send troops into a state in case of domestic violence which is beyond the control of state and local police.

## Political Party Leader

The president is the leader of his party. In this role he influences party policy in national and international affairs. He makes wide use of his patronage power—the power to appoint members of his own party to government posts. He also has the power to grant favors of many kinds to officials of either party.

## The Presidency Today

The United States and its position in the world have changed greatly since the president's duties were outlined in the Constitution. The role of the president has grown from that of a largely honorary officer to a powerful leader in national and international affairs. He is the single, unifying force in a political system in which power is highly dispersed. Probably no other person exercises as much influence in today's world as the president of the United States.

But no matter how popular or powerful a president may be, his term of office is limited. At the end of four years he must submit his record to the people. If they do not re-elect him, he must surrender his power. The 22nd Amendment to the Constitution provides that no president can be elected more than twice. As long as these safeguards exist, complete sovereignty will remain subject to the will of the people.

GERALD W. JOHNSON
Author, *The Presidency*
Reviewed by DAVID C. WHITNEY
Author, *The American Presidents*

See also CABINET OF THE UNITED STATES; ELECTORAL COLLEGE; IMPEACHMENT; VICE PRESIDENCY OF THE UNITED STATES.

**PRESIDENTS' WIVES.** See FIRST LADIES.
**PRESLEY, ELVIS.** See ROCK MUSIC (Profiles).

# PRIESTLEY, JOSEPH (1733–1804)

Joseph Priestley, a great scientist, was also a minister and a schoolteacher. He spoke out fearlessly in defense of liberty and of his religious, social, political, and scientific ideas. He wrote and preached tirelessly on many subjects, but he is best known for his scientific discoveries.

Priestley discovered a number of gases, then known as "airs." They include oxygen, nitrous oxide (laughing gas), sulfur dioxide, ammonia, and carbon monoxide. He also invented reliable ways of testing and making each gas.

Priestley was born in Birstal Fieldhead near Leeds in England on March 13, 1733. His family was poor, so at a young age Joseph was sent to live with an aunt. His education was directed toward the ministry though he often had to interrupt his studies in order to earn money. In 1761 he became a teacher at a religious academy. There he taught science by encouraging his pupils to do experiments. This was unusual because laboratory teaching was almost unknown in England at that time.

Priestley, who was deeply committed to his religious beliefs, became a minister in 1762. He was also married the same year. Though his duties as a minister took up much of his time, he continued with his scientific studies. In 1767 he wrote the still-famous book, *History of Electricity*, with the help of Benjamin Franklin, who loaned him books and supported his studies.

In 1773, Priestley became librarian to the Earl of Shelburne. He still found time for laboratory work and wrote five of his six great books on gases as well as several books on religion.

Priestley's greatest scientific triumph came in 1774. In that year he heated a red powder —mercury oxide—and noticed that it produced an "air" that differed in many ways from ordinary air. The French scientist Antoine Lavoisier later combined two Greek words to give this "air" the name it is known by today—oxygen, meaning "acid producer."

Although he was respected as a scientist, Priestley was often unpopular as a minister. He wrote and spoke frequently on religious and political matters and stated views that made him many enemies. For example, he openly sided with the Americans in their

The discovery of oxygen is just one of Joseph Priestley's many accomplishments. In addition to being a scientist, he was also a minister, a schoolteacher, and an author.

grievances against the British, and he sympathized with the French revolutionaries. These views were extremely unpopular in England at the time.

In 1791, Priestley's opposition to the Church of England along with his other ideas made him so unpopular that a mob burned his house and chapel in Birmingham. The fire destroyed his scientific apparatus, laboratory notebooks, and other important papers. In 1794, Priestley and his wife left England for the United States, settling permanently in Northumberland, Pennsylvania, where their two sons lived.

Joseph Priestley died on February 6, 1804, in Northumberland. He was honored then as he is today as one of the most accomplished scientists of his time. To the very last, Priestley continued his writing and preaching and experimenting. And in a tribute to this devoted scientist, Thomas Jefferson, who knew him well, said that his life was "one of the few lives precious to mankind."

LOUIS I. KUSLAN
Southern Connecticut State University

**PRIMARY SCHOOLS.** See EDUCATION; SCHOOLS.

# PRIMATES

More than 70 million years ago, in the shadow of *Tyrannosaurus rex*, lived tiny mammals, probably smaller than squirrels. Their world, ruled by the fearsome dinosaurs, was a dangerous place. But these hardy creatures survived and evolved into a group of animals known as primates, the order of mammals that includes monkeys, apes, and humans.

There are 233 species, or kinds, of primates. Typically scientists separate primates into two major groups: **anthropoids**, which include human beings, apes, and monkeys, and **prosimians**,

which include aye-ayes, galagos, lemurs, lorises, pottos, and tarsiers. Most primates live in the tropics and subtropics of Africa, Asia, and the Americas, although a few, such as the Japanese macaque, live in temperate areas. Human beings are the only primates that populate almost every environment throughout the world.

## ▶ CHARACTERISTICS OF PRIMATES

As a group, primates have many traits in common, although not every primate has every trait. When you pick up an object with your hand, you demonstrate one of the most important characteristics of primates: Almost all primates have five digits on each limb. Primates have fingers and, in some cases, toes that can grasp and lock on to objects of many different shapes. Scientists believe that the early primates survived by living in the trees, away from large animals, where the ability to grasp branches is an important advantage. Most primates have flat nails on their fingers

and toes, rather than long claws, which get in the way of grasping.

All primates are able to climb trees, and most of them still spend most of their lives above the ground. Those that dwell primarily

on the ground include some of the larger monkeys, such as baboons and macaques, the gorilla, and, of course, humans. The anthropoids are diurnal, or active in the day, while most prosimians are nocturnal, or active at night.

Primates have a keen sense of vision, the most important of their five senses. Unlike many mammals, most primates have large eyes set in the head so that they look straight forward.

Primates have developed from a common ancestor into a wide array of animals, such as the mandrill (*below*), human beings (*far left*), and ring-tailed lemurs (*left*), each with its own distinct features.

The anthropoids can focus both eyes on the same object. This ability helps them judge how far away an object is. The placement of the eyes also enables primates to see in three dimensions, while many other mammals see things as flat. For animals that must jump from branch to branch and judge distances in a split second, seeing in three dimensions is a big advantage. The primates with the best

lemur species and monkeys will eat insects, while pottos will kill young birds. For most primates, plants are the main food source. Humans are the primates most likely to eat meat. Baboons and chimpanzees also include the meat of larger animals, such as gazelles and monkeys, in their diets.

▶ **THE LIFE OF PRIMATES**

The vast majority of primates are social animals; that is, they live in groups and interact regularly with one another. Among the exceptions are the weasel lemurs and the aye-ayes of Madagascar, which live mostly solitary lives. Prosimians tend to form much smaller groups than those of the higher primates, the largest groups of which are the baboons and macaques. These social groups, which often consist of several hundred individuals, can have complicated structures and relationships among their members.

Chimpanzees live in loose groups called **communities** and share a particular area of a habitat. All members of the community do not gather or travel together at the same time within this territory, but they remain neighbors and communicate with one another. The chimpanzees in a community keep a stern watch over their territory, guarding its boundaries from other neighboring groups and attacking those that invade it. Sometimes wars occur between two communities. The wars can be so fierce that one of the communities is completely destroyed.

Not all primate communities have large populations or defend their territories. Squirrel monkeys form groups with a few dozen members and do not seem to defend their territories. Each group of squirrel monkeys is made up of smaller groups—pregnant females form their own group, as do females with young, and adult males. Some primates, including indri lemurs, marmosets, and tamarins, form small family units consisting of adult pairs and their offspring.

The reproductive cycles of primates vary. Most primates, except for lemurs and lorises, have no definite times of the year that they mate. While most males are capable of breed-

Long, powerful upper limbs allow the gibbon (*above*) to swing quickly and gracefully from branch to branch. With its large staring eyes, the tarsier (*inset*) is well adapted to its nocturnal way of life.

eyesight also see colors. Anthropoids have color vision. Most prosimians do not, but colors are not very visible at night, so they are not at a disadvantage. Moreover, prosimian eyes are very large and can gather whatever light is available from the moon and stars.

Most primates have large, well-developed brains and are among the most intelligent of mammals. Certain parts of their brains are particularly well developed. Among these are the parts used in seeing and in controlling movement. However, primates do not depend much on their sense of smell, and that part of the brain is smaller than in many mammals.

A wide variety of foods are consumed by primates, including fruits, buds, roots, leaves, and small animals, such as lizards. Some

Both of these marmosets benefit from a friendly act of grooming (*right*). Many primates, such as the orangutan (*far right*), are attentive parents.

ing at any time, most females have a reproductive cycle that allows them to breed only at specific times. Fewer offspring are born to primates than most other mammals. A mother bears only one or two young at a time. Another difference between primates and other mammals is that the young stay with the mother for a longer period. The long time that primate offspring stay with their mothers allows for learning. In many other mammal groups, the young strike out on their own early in life, and so their behavior is based mostly on instinct. Young primates have instincts, too, but they also learn behavior patterns from their mothers and from the group they live in. Generally, the father primate does not care for the young, although he will protect them and defend them from enemies.

▶ PRIMATES AND THEIR ENVIRONMENT

What separates primates from all other animals is that one of them, the human species, is causing worldwide environmental change that endangers some primates and many other creatures as well. Several primates are threatened with extinction, including some of the smallest, such as the golden lion tamarin, and the largest, the mountain gorilla.

The greatest threat to primates is the destruction of their habitats, particularly the great tropical rain forests. Primate habitats are disappearing because of human activities, such as the clearing of land for agriculture and development and the unrestricted cutting of trees

The golden lion tamarin stands at the brink of extinction due to disappearing habitat and its capture for use as a pet and in zoo exhibits.

for timber. Some primates, especially baboons, are killed as pests because they sometimes raid farmers' crops. In some parts of the world, such as West Africa and South America, monkeys are considered a human food source. Hunting endangered few primate populations in the past, but today, because their numbers are dwindling, it is an ever-increasing threat.

Another threat to the primate population exists because some primates are very similar to human beings. Vast numbers of monkeys and apes have been removed from the wild for use in medical research and testing. Although this practice has helped create surgical techniques and medicines that have saved countless human lives, it is the subject of heated debate. Some people believe it is wrong to use primates—or any other animal—in research. Others believe such research is necessary but that it should be more tightly controlled.

The breeding of rare primates such as gorillas and cotton-topped tamarins in zoos is increasing. It is being done not so that they can be used in research but to keep their species from becoming extinct. However, unless habitat is conserved, many primates will not survive in the wild.

EDWARD R. RICCIUTI
Coauthor, *The Audubon Society Book of Wild Animals*
See also MAMMALS.

# PRIME MINISTER

In many countries of the world the head of government is called a prime minister or premier. Both "prime" and "premier" mean "first." The prime minister or premier, therefore, is literally the first, or chief, minister of the government.

**Appointment and Function.** The prime minister usually is appointed by a country's official head of state—who may be a king or queen in a monarchy or a president in a republic. (In the United States and a number of other countries a president serves as both head of state and head of government.) Generally, the head of state appoints as prime minister the leader of the political party that wins a majority (more than half) of the seats in the legislature in an election. If no party wins a majority, the prime minister may be the leader of a coalition government—one based on a combination of political parties. The prime minister chooses a number of other ministers to serve as heads of the various departments of the government. These ministers form an advisory group, usually known as the cabinet.

In many countries, such as Great Britain, where the office of prime minister originated, the prime minister is an especially powerful figure. With the help of the cabinet, the prime minister has the major responsibility for government policy. In fact, the prime minister and cabinet are known as the government. The prime minister and cabinet in turn are responsible to the legislature, of which they must be members. In Great Britain the legislature is called the Parliament, and the prime minister and cabinet are members of its elected chamber, the House of Commons. The cabinet system is sometimes called the parliamentary system of government.

**Limits on the Prime Minister's Power.** The election system works to prevent a prime minister from misusing the powers of office. If the legislature defeats one of the government's important measures, this is called a "vote of no confidence." After such a vote, an election must be held. If the prime minister's party loses the election, the party with the most votes forms a new government. And the leader of that party becomes prime minister.

The prime minister may also call for elections at other times, to find out whether the voters support the government's policies. In any case, an election must be held after a certain number of years—usually about five.

The power of the prime minister varies from country to country. A prime minister's actual power depends partly on the country's constitution and the powers it gives the head of state. In many countries the role of the head of state, whether monarch or president, is mostly ceremonial. The prime minister is usually the real executive head of the government. There are exceptions, however. The constitution of France, for example, gives more power to the president than to the premier. This is true also in some other countries, where the prime minister may handle the day-to-day operations of the government under the leadership of the president.

The terms "prime minister" and "president" were sometimes used when referring to the governments of Communist countries. But this was often misleading, since real political power rested with Communist party leaders. Most of the former Communist countries of Eastern Europe now have governments that are truly led by presidents or prime ministers who govern at the will of the people.

**Origin of the Prime Minister's Office.** The office of prime minister evolved from the British cabinet and parliamentary system of government. Sir Robert Walpole (1676–1745) is usually regarded as Great Britain's first prime minister. The development of the modern office of prime minister, however, is generally considered to date from the 1800's, and the title of prime minister itself was not formally adopted in Great Britain until the early 1900's. The British system of parliamentary government spread around the world as lands that once had been part of the British empire gained independence and adopted the British system.

Parliamentary forms of government, headed by prime ministers, developed as well in other European countries. (In Germany the head of government is called the chancellor.) These countries also brought their systems of government to territories that once were their colonies but are now independent nations. As a result, many of the world's people today are governed under parliamentary systems of one kind or another headed by prime ministers.

JOHN S. MOIR
University of Toronto

See also PARLIAMENTS.

William Pitt, the Younger
(1759–1806), Great Britain

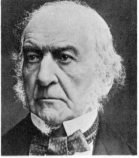

William Ewart Gladstone
(1809–98), Great Britain

Winston Churchill
(1874–1965), Great Britain

Georges Clemenceau,
(1841–1929), France

Otto von Bismarck
(1815–98), Germany

Jawaharlal Nehru
(1889–1964), India

Indira Gandhi
(1917–84), India

Eamon de Valera
(1882–1975), Ireland

David Ben-Gurion
(1886–1973), Israel

John A. Macdonald
(1815–91), Canada

Wilfrid Laurier
(1841–1919), Canada

William Lyon Mackenzie King
(1874–1950), Canada

Margaret Thatcher
(1925–    ), Great Britain

Golda Meir
(1898–1978), Israel

Biographies of the following prime ministers can be found
in *The New Book of Knowledge*:

Asquith, Herbert Henry
Attlee, Clement
Balfour, Arthur James
Begin, Menachem
Ben-Gurion, David
Bhutto, Benazir
Bhutto, Zulfikar Ali
Bismarck, Otto von
Blair, Tony
Brown, George
Campbell, Kim
Chamberlain, Neville
Chrétien, Jean
Churchill, Sir Winston
Clark, Charles Joseph
Clemenceau, Georges
Diefenbaker, John George
Disraeli, Benjamin
Gandhi, Indira
Gandhi, Rajiv
Gladstone, William Ewart

King, William Lyon Mackenzie
Laurier, Sir Wilfrid
Lloyd George, David
Macdonald, Sir John A.
Macmillan, Harold
Major, John
Meir, Golda
Mulroney, Martin Brian
Nehru, Jawaharlal
Pearson, Lester
Peel, Sir Robert
Pitt, William, Earl of Chatham
Pitt, William, the Younger
Schmidt, Helmut
Schröder, Gerhard
Thatcher, Margaret
Trudeau, Pierre Elliott
Turner, John Napier
Walpole, Sir Robert
Wellington, Duke of

# PRINCE EDWARD ISLAND

*Prince Edward Island's flag (above) and coat of arms (opposite page) recall its historical ties with England. The three oak saplings, representing the province's three counties, grow near the large oak, which stands for England. The British lion tops the design. P.E.I.'s provincial bird is the blue jay (right); its flower, the lady's slipper (opposite page).*

Prince Edward Island is one of the four Atlantic Provinces of Canada. The other three are Nova Scotia, New Brunswick, and Newfoundland and Labrador. Because of its location in the Gulf of St. Lawrence, its fertile soil, favorable climate, and many farms, Prince Edward Island is often called the Garden of the Gulf. It is the smallest of the Canadian provinces and the only island province. (Newfoundland is an island, but Labrador is part of the mainland.)

The original inhabitants of Prince Edward Island, the Micmac Indians, called it *Abegweit,* which means "home cradled on the waves." The first European settlers, the French, named it Ile Saint Jean (Saint John's Island). In 1799 the province was named for Prince Edward, Duke of Kent, the fourth son of King George III of Great Britain. Today Prince Edward Island is usually referred to simply by its initials—P.E.I.

## ▶ THE LAND

Prince Edward Island is shaped roughly like a crescent, or a half-moon. It is nearly 120 miles (190 kilometers) long but varies greatly in width because of the many inlets of the sea. In some places, the island is as little as 3 miles (5 kilometers) wide. In others, it is almost 40 miles (65 kilometers) wide.

To the north of the province lies the Gulf of St. Lawrence; to the south, the Northumberland Strait. The neighboring provinces of Nova Scotia and New Brunswick lie only a few miles away, across the Northumberland Strait. The town of Borden in Prince Edward

Island is only 9 miles (14 kilometers) from Cape Tormentine in New Brunswick. The eastern end of Prince Edward Island is only 14 miles (23 kilometers) from Nova Scotia.

The soft sandstone of Prince Edward Island has been worn down over the centuries by erosion, and the island now has a gentle, rolling landscape. There are a few hilly areas, and the highest point, which lies in the southeastern part of the island, is only 465 feet (142 meters) above sea level. The province has only one lake and a few real rivers. Most of the valleys are formed by tidal inlets of the sea.

The coastline of Prince Edward Island is very irregular, with many bays and inlets that jut far inland. On the north coast of the province, sandbars run across the mouths of the bays. Long stretches of beautiful, sandy beaches line this coast. The coastal waters are shallow, and the island has few good ports. To keep some of the ports open, channels have to be dredged, or cleared of sediment.

### Climate

Prince Edward Island has the most favorable climate of all the Atlantic Provinces. It is free of fog in winter, and in summer it benefits from the warm waters of the Gulf of St. Lawrence. In summer, the weather is usually warm and sunny. The average July temperature is over 67°F (19°C). For this reason, the province is a popular summer resort area.

In winter the climate is not much different from that of the neighboring coastal areas. Cold air masses from inland Canada sometimes bring temperatures of 0°F (–18°C).

## FACTS AND FIGURES

**Location:** Eastern Canada. **Latitude**—45°58′ N to 47°04′ N. **Longitude**—61°59′ W to 64°27′ W.

**Joined Canadian Confederation:** July 1, 1873, as the 7th province.

**Population:** 135,294 (2001 census). **Rank among provinces**—10th.

**Capital and Largest City:** Charlottetown, pop. 32,245 (2001 census).

**Physical Features: Area**—2,185 sq mi (5,660 km²). **Rank among provinces**—10th. **Rivers**—Hillsborough, Yorke. **Bays**—Egmont, Bedeque, Malpeque, Orwell, Hillsborough, Cascumpeque, Tracadie. **Highest point**—465 ft (142 m), in southeast P.E.I.

**Industries and Products:** Potatoes, dairy products, turnips, fruits, grains, poultry, eggs, beef; cod, herring, lobster, oyster, and halibut fishing; construction; mink and fox furs; food products; shipbuilding; wood products; lumber; tourism.

**Government:** Self-governing province. **Titular head of government**—lieutenant governor, appointed by the governor-general in council. **Actual head of government**—premier, leader of the majority in the legislature. **Provincial representation in federal parliament**—4 appointed senators; 4 elected member(s) of the House of Commons. **Voting age for provincial elections**—18.

**Provincial Bird:** Blue jay.

**Provincial Flower:** Lady's slipper.

**Provincial Motto:** *Parva sub ingenti* (The small under the protection of the great).

But the average January temperature is 19°F (–7°C). This is warmer than inland New Brunswick but colder than southern Nova Scotia. The Gulf of St. Lawrence and the Northumberland Strait are covered with ice in the winter. Winds blowing across the ice to Prince Edward Island also keep temperatures low.

### Natural Resources

The island's rich red soil, or loam, is one of Prince Edward Island's most valuable natural resources. This loam is usually quite fertile. The many streams and coastal waters are filled with different fish and shellfish. The most valuable mineral resource is sand and gravel. Other important resources include a sparkling shoreline and a countryside of unusual natural beauty.

The forests of Prince Edward Island were once important for shipbuilding and lumbering. But most of the forests have been cleared for farming. The remaining forests are a mixture of deciduous and coniferous trees. The chief deciduous trees found on the island are maple, birch, beech, ash, elm, and oak. The coniferous trees include red and black spruce, fir, pine, hemlock, and cedar.

### ▶ THE PEOPLE AND THEIR WORK

Prince Edward Island is the most densely populated of all the Canadian provinces, and the population is fairly evenly distributed throughout the island.

Farming long has been the main occupation. Improved transportation systems and mechanization in the 20th century made modern farming possible. But modern methods required fewer people. The same was true of the fishing industry. A number of small industries have recently located on the island. But it is still necessary for many islanders to seek employment outside the province.

Most of the people are of British, Scottish, or Irish origin. About one-fifth of the people are of French descent, and French is still spoken in some areas. There are also some islanders of Dutch, Lebanese, and German stock and a few hundred members of the Micmac tribe. Nearly half the people are Catholics. The rest belong mainly to the United Church and to the Presbyterian, Anglican, and Baptist churches.

### Industries and Products

Although farming is the basic activity, fishing, logging, manufacturing, and the tourist industry add to the economy of the province.

**Agriculture.** More than half of the land is farmed. Because of the fertile soil, the gently rolling land, and the favorable summer climate, a variety of crops can be grown successfully. The province is famous for potatoes—its principal crop. Very large quantities are marketed each year in Canada, the United States, and other parts of the world. Many of the potatoes are sold as seed potatoes.

Dairy farming and cattle raising are also important. Prince Edward Island exports large amounts of cheese, butter, and other dairy products. Other farm products include turnips, grains, fruits, beef, poultry, and eggs. There

are also some fox and mink ranches, where the animals are bred for their pelts.

**Fishing.** Cod, herring, halibut, and other fish are found in various parts of the Gulf of St. Lawrence. The lack of convenient harbors for large ships limits this type of fishing, and it is not as important here as in the other Atlantic Provinces. But the lobster and oyster fisheries are very valuable. The island has a large annual lobster catch, and it is noted for its excellent oysters. Mussels are also a valuable industry.

**Forest Industries.** Logging is of some importance on the island. The trees provide wood for fuel, railway ties, and lumber and for export as wood pulp.

**Manufacturing.** Small plants throughout the island process farm products and fish. Other manufacturing industries include printing and publishing and the building of ships and boats. But manufacturing is limited by problems of transportation and lack of raw materials and by the high cost of power. Since there are few rivers, hydroelectric power cannot be produced, and electricity must be generated by a more costly means—diesel engines.

**Tourism.** The tourist industry is one of the major sources of revenue for the province. Each summer large numbers of visitors come to Prince Edward Island to enjoy the sunshine, the sandy beaches, golfing, swimming, and other sports and, most of all, the beautiful countryside and shoreline. In addition to hotels and motels, many farms take in guests during the tourist season.

**Transportation and Communication**

A railway system connects many of the communities in Prince Edward Island. The island has many good paved roads. The main road, which runs the length of the island, is considered part of the Trans-Canada Highway. Air service is provided by Air Canada, Canadian Pacific Air, and Atlantic Air.

Ferry service between Borden and Cape Tormentine was discontinued when the Confederation Bridge opened in 1997. The bridge, spanning 8 miles (13 kilometers), connects Borden to mainland New Brunswick. During the ice-free season, ferries operate between Wood Islands and Caribou in Nova Scotia.

The province has three daily newspapers—the *Guardian* and the *Patriot,* published in Charlottetown, and the *Journal-Pioneer,* published in Summerside. A weekly journal, *The Eastern Graphic,* enjoys a large circulation. It is published in Montague. Several radio and television stations serve the island.

*Opposite page:* The distinctive red soil of Prince Edward Island is very fertile, and more than half of the land is farmed. *Right:* Potatoes are the principal crop of the province. *Below:* Fishing also contributes to the island's economy, and lobster traps and fishing boats are a common sight in the small coastal villages. *Bottom:* A third important industry is tourism. Sandy beaches such as this one at Cavendish draw large numbers of visitors.

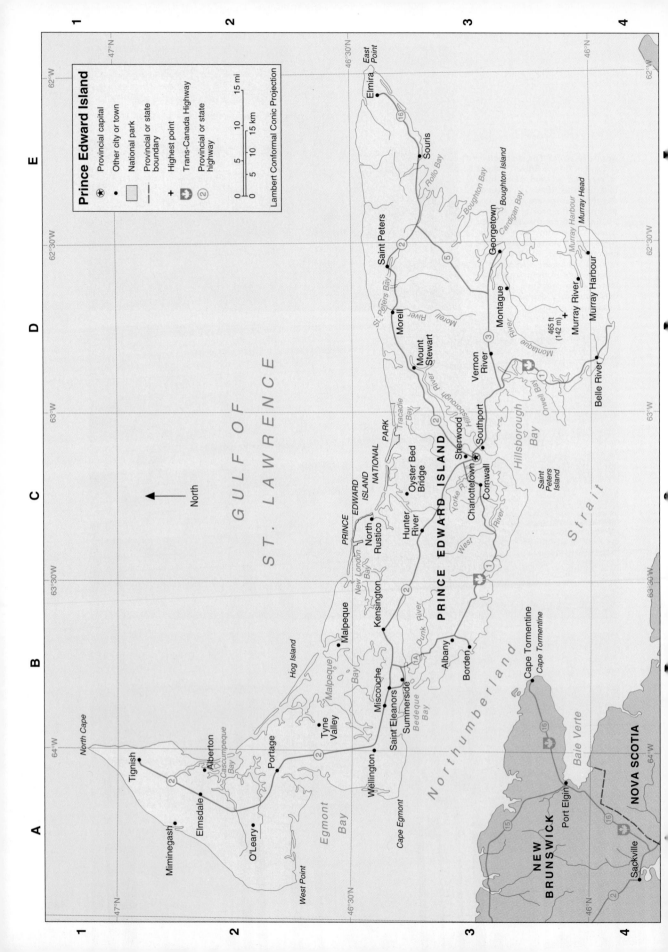

# Prince Edward Island

- ⊛ Provincial capital
- • Other city or town
- ▢ National park
- —¦— Provincial or state boundary
- + Highest point
- ⯈ Trans-Canada Highway
- ② Provincial or state highway

Lambert Conformal Conic Projection

0   5   10   15 mi
0   5  10  15 km

North

GULF OF ST. LAWRENCE

East Point
Elmira
Souris
Rollo Bay
Saint Peters
Boughton Bay
Boughton Island
Georgetown
Cardigan Bay
Montague
Murray Harbour
Murray Head
Murray River
465 ft (142 m)
Murray Harbour
Belle River
Morell River
Morell
Mount Stewart
Vernon River
Southport
Sherwood
Charlottetown
Cornwall
Saint Peters Island
Orwell Bay
Hillsborough Bay
Hillsborough River
Tracadie Bay
St. Peters Bay
PRINCE EDWARD ISLAND NATIONAL PARK
Oyster Bed Bridge
Hunter River
North Rustico
New London Bay
Yorke R.
West River
PRINCE EDWARD ISLAND
Kensington
Dunk River
Malpeque
Hog Island
Malpeque Bay
Miscouche
Summerside
Saint Eleanors
Bedeque Bay
Wellington
Albany
Borden
Cape Egmont
Cape Tormentine
Northumberland Strait
Egmont Bay
West Point
North Cape
Tignish
Miminegash
Elmsdale
Alberton
O'Leary
Portage
Tyne Valley
Cascumpeque Bay
Baie Verte
Port Elgin
Sackville
NEW BRUNSWICK
NOVA SCOTIA

62°W  62°30'W  63°W  63°30'W  64°W

47°N  46°30'N  46°N

## INDEX TO PRINCE EDWARD ISLAND MAP

## ▶ EDUCATION

Primary education is free, and school attendance is compulsory for all children up to age 15. The school system is paid for by the provincial government and by local school boards. The province has one university, the University of Prince Edward Island at Charlottetown. In addition, vocational schools are located in Charlottetown and Summerside.

**Libraries.** The main public library of Prince Edward Island is located in Charlottetown. Many branch libraries are located throughout the province.

## ▶ PLACES OF INTEREST

The island abounds in places for recreation, as well as historic and scenic places.

**Confederation Centre of the Arts**, in Charlottetown, is Canada's national memorial to the Founders of the Confederation. It is the major center of cultural activity on Prince Edward Island. Built in 1964, the center houses a memorial hall, a library, an art gallery, a museum, and a theater.

**Confederation Chamber**, in the Provincial Building at Charlottetown, is known as the Cradle of Confederation and the Birthplace of Canada. In this room, in 1864, the Founders of Confederation met and planned the Confederation of Canada.

**EPTEK Centre**, in Summerside, houses the Prince Edward Island Sports Hall of Fame and various cultural exhibitions.

**Fort Amherst National Historic Park**, near Charlottetown, is the site of an old British fort and an earlier French settlement. The park has a visitors' center that includes a small theater.

**Garden of the Gulf Museum**, at Montague, displays historical objects from pioneer days.

**Prince Edward Island National Park**, between Cavendish and Tracadie on the north coast, is a favorite seashore resort. In the park near Cavendish is the farmhouse that served as the setting for the novel *Anne of Green Gables*, by Lucy Maud Montgomery.

Green Gables, in Prince Edward Island National Park, is a popular tourist attraction. It was the setting for *Anne of Green Gables*, a well-loved novel by the Canadian writer Lucy Maud Montgomery.

**Robert Harris Memorial Art Gallery**, in Charlottetown, has exhibits of paintings and sculpture.

**St. Peter's Anglican Church**, in Charlottetown, is famous for its murals, painted by the Canadian artist Robert Harris.

**Souris, Malpeque**, and **Murray Harbor** are fishing villages. Souris is noted for its deep-sea fishing and Malpeque for its oysters.

**Strathgartney Park**, between Borden and Charlottetown, is a recreation area on the island's south shore.

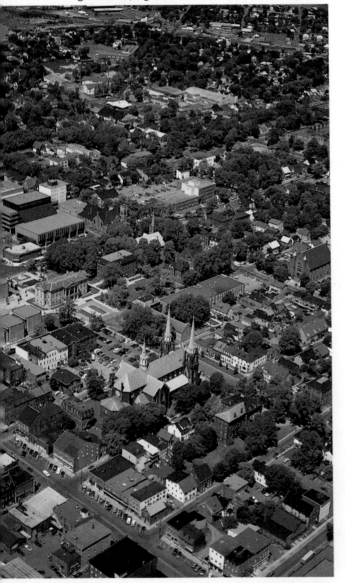

Charlottetown, the provincial capital, is a center of government, higher education, and cultural activity.

▶ **CITIES**

Charlottetown, the capital, is the only city and the largest settlement on the island. With a population of about 32,000, it is situated on the south shore of a long estuary, or inlet, that nearly cuts the island in two. The town of Summerside has a population of about 15,000. It is located farther west, in the best farmlands on the island. Summerside is also situated on Bedeque Bay, which is noted for its oysters. Other important towns are Montague, Souris, and Kensington.

▶ **GOVERNMENT**

The government of Prince Edward Island is composed of the lieutenant governor, the Executive Council, and the Legislative Assembly. There is also a judiciary made up of the Supreme Court and the Provincial Court. The lieutenant governor, who is appointed by the governor-general of Canada on the advice of the prime minister, serves as the honorary head of the province. The real head of government is the premier. The premier is the leader of the majority party in the Legislative Assembly and chairman of the Executive Council, which acts as the premier's Cabinet. The Legislative Assembly makes the laws of the province. It is composed of 27 members who are elected for terms of up to five years. Elections must be held every five years, although they may be held more often.

▶ **HISTORY**

The first European to sight Prince Edward Island was the French explorer Jacques Cartier. He landed on the island in 1534. Samuel de Champlain claimed the territory, which he called Ile Saint Jean, for France in 1603. But European colonization of the island did not begin until more than 100 years later. The first permanent settlement, Port La Joie, was established in 1719.

French settlement progressed very slowly and was followed by a struggle with Britain for control of the region. The British took the island in 1745, after capturing the fortress of Louisbourg on nearby Cape Breton Island. The French regained Prince Edward Island in 1748 but lost it for good in 1763 under the Treaty of Paris, which ended the Seven Years' War. Under the British, the island became part of the colony of Nova Scotia. Charlottetown was established as the new capital.

## IMPORTANT DATES

**1534** Jacques Cartier discovered the island on his first voyage of exploration to North America.

**1603** Island claimed for France by Samuel de Champlain and named Ile Saint Jean.

**1719** The French established the first settlement on the island at Port La Joie (later Charlottetown).

**1745** The British took possession of the island.

**1748** Island restored to France.

**1763** Treaty of Paris, ending the Seven Years' War, ceded territory to Great Britain; Saint John's Island (the British name for the island) became part of Nova Scotia.

**1767** Grants of land on the island were given to landlords in England.

**1769** Saint John's Island was detached from Nova Scotia and established as a separate colony.

**1799** Colony renamed Prince Edward Island.

**1851** Responsible government (self-government) granted by Great Britain.

**1864** Fathers of Confederation met at Charlottetown and discussed plans for a confederation of Canada.

**1873** Prince Edward Island became part of the Confederation of Canada.

**1874** Island railway system began operation.

**1875** Land Purchase Act provided funds to buy land back from absentee landlords.

**1964** Confederation Centre of the Arts opened in Charlottetown.

**1973** P.E.I. celebrated the centennial of its entry into the Canadian Confederation.

**1997** Confederation Bridge opened, linking Borden with mainland Canada.

Province House, in Charlottetown, was the site of the 1864 conference that led to the Confederation of Canada.

Saint John's Island—as the British called it —was divided into 67 lots. The lots were given to people in England who were supposed to colonize and develop the land. But few people did this, and the problem of ownership of the land by absentee landlords caused bitter disputes for many years.

In 1769 the island was separated from Nova Scotia and became a colony on its own. In 1799 it was renamed Prince Edward Island. Responsible government (self-government) was granted by Britain in 1851.

The first part of the 19th century was a period of prosperity for Prince Edward Island. Shipbuilding was a thriving industry. It remained so until the middle of the century, when steamships began to replace the old wooden sailing ships.

In 1864, delegates from Prince Edward Island, Nova Scotia, and New Brunswick met at Charlottetown to discuss a union of the three provinces. Representatives from what are now Ontario and Quebec joined them and suggested a union of all the provinces. This led to the Confederation of Canada in 1867. Prince Edward Island, however, did not join the other provinces in 1867 but waited until 1873 before becoming part of Canada.

In 1875, under the Land Purchase Act, money was provided to buy out the absentee British landlords who had held back the economic growth of the province. The islanders were thus able to purchase their own land and clear it for farming.

Today Prince Edward Island, like all the other Canadian provinces, receives a considerable amount of assistance from the federal government. Tourism has also been on the increase, as millions of Canadian and American vacationers come to enjoy the quiet pleasures of this friendly, rural island.

FRANCIS W. P. BOLGER
University of Prince Edward Island

# PRINTING

Printing is the art and technology of rapidly reproducing multiple copies of images, such as words and pictures, on paper, cloth, or other surfaces. Every day billions of printed items are produced, including books, magazines, newspapers, posters, food packages, stamps, wallpapers, and fabrics. Because printed materials can quickly communicate ideas and information to millions of people, printing is considered one of the most important and influential inventions in history.

From the mid-1400's until the beginning of the 1900's, printing was the only form of mass communication. Education depended on the availability of reading materials. Even after the inventions of radio, television, and motion pictures, printed materials remained the world's primary source of information. Today, printing is an important industry in every advanced country in the world.

▶ THE PRINTING PROCESS

Before a printed product is ready for market or display, it must go through a series of steps that include typesetting, artwork preparation, image assembly, platemaking, printing, and finishing operations.

### Typesetting

Every character printed is created from **type.** Each type character represents one letter, number, or punctuation mark. Setting the type (typesetting) is the first step in the printing process. It is the method by which words (called copy) are converted into a style suitable for printing.

Today, most type is set by computers. Modern typesetting is called **phototypesetting** or computer composition. Computers have revolutionized the typesetting industry. Whereas newspaper printers once had to set each character by hand with individual pieces of type,

*Left:* Film negatives are stripped into flats for platemaking. *Below left:* Computerized systems make color corrections and remove blemishes from photographs. *Below right:* Automatic platemaking machines use photographic negatives to make image-carrying plates. *Opposite page:* A fully equipped press room contains machinery for all printing stages, including finishing and binding operations. *Inset:* As it passes through the yellow printing unit of a web offset press, paper picks up images from a lithographic plate.

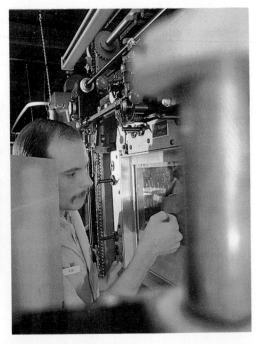

## THE PRINTING PROCESS

All printed products must go through a series of procedures before they are ready for market. These steps include:

(1) typesetting text material, or putting words (called text copy) into type;

(2) preparing artwork (such as illustrations and photographs) for reproduction;

(3) assembling images (or designing layouts) by combining and arranging the typeset copy and artwork;

(4) preparing an image-carrying surface (called a plate) that, when mounted on a press, will transfer the image of the typeset copy and artwork onto the paper or other material;

(5) printing the image on a printing press, which inks the plate and brings it into contact with the paper or other material;

(6) and, in the case of most printed items, finishing the product by cutting, folding, binding, or other means.

today a reporter can type a story on a computer keyboard and send it electronically to an automatic typesetting machine. These machines are capable of setting type at rates of more than 10,000 characters per second.

In phototypesetting, each typeset character is created from a master image of that character. Master images are stored either photographically or as digital information in a computer. (You can read more about this in the article TYPE in Volume T.)

### Image Assembly

Once type has been set, it is combined with illustrations and put into position on the page. This process is called **layout.** Film of the type is combined with film of the illustrations in a process called **stripping.** This final combined film of each page is used for platemaking.

One printing plate usually carries the images of many different pages. The final films of all the pages are positioned on the plate so that the pages will be in the correct sequence after a sheet is printed and folded. This process is called **imposition stripping.**

### Platemaking

After all the films of typeset copy and artwork have been assembled into layouts, **proofs** are made to make sure all of the pieces and colors are in the proper place. "Pulling" a proof gives the customer a chance to check the work for errors and to see what the printed job will look like.

The final, corrected layouts (or flats) are used to make the **plate,** from which the images will be printed. Plates are made of hard substances, such as metals, rubber, or plastics. The images to be printed are transferred to the plate in one of a number of different ways. Images are printed when an inked plate is pressed against paper or other material. (Since each printing method has different requirements for platemaking, platemaking procedures are covered in the sections on Letterpress Printing, Lithography, and Gravure Printing in this article.)

### Printing Presses

Once the printing plates are made, they are mounted on machines called **presses** to be used to print on paper or other materials. Presses perform a number of automatic functions: They apply ink to the plates; feed the

paper or other material to the plates; print the images by transferring the ink from the plate to the paper or other material; and stack the printed pieces. Some presses, called **perfecting presses,** can print both sides of the paper at the same time.

Presses are either **sheet-fed** (using one sheet at a time) or **web-fed** (using a continuous roll, or web, of paper or other material.) They can print one color or a number of colors. On a multicolor press, each color requires a separate printing unit, each with its own plate and ink.

There are many different kinds of presses, but each kind falls into one of three basic categories: platen (or flat-bed) presses; cylinder

---

▶**PREPARING ARTWORK FOR PRINTING**

Modern typesetting machines produce copy that is easily prepared for printing. However, artwork must be specially photographed before it can be reproduced. Photography for printing is called **process photography.** Special cameras, lights, lenses, high-contrast films, and developing systems are used to produce films from which printing plates are made.

There are two basic categories of artwork in terms of preparation for printing: line illustrations and continuous tone illustrations. **Line illustrations** are the simplest to prepare for printing. They are usually printed in one color (black is used most often). Shading can be accomplished with heavy concentrations of lines or dots, for example. However, line illustrations contain no gray tones. Examples include pen-and-ink drawings and etchings.

The process of preparing line illustrations for printing begins with photographically enlarging or reducing the illustration to the desired size. A photographic negative is made and used to create the image on the plate.

**Continuous tone illustrations** are black-and-white or color illustrations that have a range of gray tones between black and white or that have varying shades of color. Examples include black-and-white or color photographs and artwork.

### Halftone Photography

Continuous tone illustrations are prepared for printing using a process called halftone

presses; and rotary presses. Of the three categories the rotary press is the kind used most often today. Each kind of press is more fully discussed in the section on Letterpress Presses in this article.

## Finishing and Binding

After materials are printed, they must usually undergo final operations to become finished products. Some singly printed sheets, such as posters or stationery, can be shipped without further processing. However, most products are printed on large sheets containing a number of separate images. After these sheets are printed and folded, they are called **signatures.** Signatures are assembled into the proper sequence, bound, and trimmed. The work required to fold and cut signatures, or to make a variety of special packaging and advertising materials, is called **finishing.** The procedure of sewing, stapling, or gluing pages together along a spine (to create materials such as books, magazines, and catalogs) is called **binding.**

There are many different printing methods, but there are three kinds most commonly used. Their differences lie for the most part in the type of plates, or printing surfaces, they use: **letterpress** printing is done from a raised printing surface; **lithography** is done from a flat printing surface; and **gravure** is done from a sunken printing surface.

photography. The continuous tone illustration is photographed with a **process camera** using a **halftone screen.** The screen, which consists of a grid of dots, is in contact with the film during exposure.

The halftone screen breaks down the continuous tone illustration into a pattern of dots. At a normal reading distance of 10 to 12 inches (25 to 30 centimeters), for example, two dots separated by ½₂₅₀ inch (.01 centimeter) look like one dot. A screen that produces more than 125 dots per inch (50 dots per centimeter) produces an illustration that looks like continuous tone because the eye cannot distinguish the individual dots. Therefore, a halftone is really an optical illusion. Because the dots generally cannot be seen without the aid of a magnifying glass, the human eye interprets them as continuous tone.

The number of lines of dots in a halftone screen determines the quality of the reproduction. Screens range from 60 lines per inch (24 lines per centimeter) in low quality printing, such as newspaper printing, to 150 lines per

Simple line illustrations, such as the pen-and-ink drawing on the left, contain no gray tones. Shading is accomplished with a pattern of lines or dots. Gray tones in continuous-tone illustrations, such as in the photographs on the right, are created by dots of varying size that are produced by a halftone screen.

Fine halftone reproductions are made with halftone screens containing more than 100 lines per inch (40 lines per centimeter). The photograph on the left was made with a screen containing 133 lines per inch (53 lines per centimeter); the coarser reproduction below was made with a screen containing only 63 lines per inch (25 lines per centimeter).

▶**LETTERPRESS PRINTING**

Letterpress, or relief, printing is the oldest printing method. A simple example of the letterpress principle is a rubber stamp. The image to be printed is carved out of a flat piece of rubber, leaving the images raised above the surface. When ink is applied to this raised surface, then pressed against paper or some other material, the image is printed.

The Chinese used the relief method when they created the *Diamond Sutra* (A.D. 868), which was possibly the first book ever printed. It was made by carving Chinese word characters in relief out of wood blocks. Ink was applied to the raised characters, which were then pressed by hand against mulberry-bark paper.

Most historians credit Johann Gutenberg of Mainz, Germany, with the invention of letterpress printing as we know it today. Gutenberg did not use the hand and block method. About 1440, he invented a hand-held mold to make individual pieces of type out of molten (melted) lead, tin, and other metals. This mold could make many identical copies of the same character, and all characters could be made from molds in the same size, which allowed them to line up and fit together accurately. Because these pieces of metal type could be re-used and moved around, the invention was called **movable type.** This method of printing was called letterpress because it printed individual letters on a press.

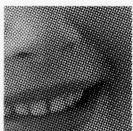

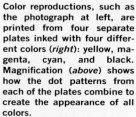

Color reproductions, such as the photograph at left, are printed from four separate plates inked with four different colors (*right*): yellow, magenta, cyan, and black. Magnification (*above*) shows how the dot patterns from each of the plates combine to create the appearance of all colors.

inch (60 lines per centimeter) in high quality printing. Therefore, the highest quality halftone reproductions contain the most dots.

Once line illustrations and halftones have been photographed, plates are made from the resulting films. The process of preparing plates of artwork for letterpress printing is called **photoengraving;** the process for lithography is called **photolithography;** and the process for gravure is called **gravure-photoengraving.**

## Color Reproduction

All continuous tone artwork must be converted to halftones. Black-and-white artwork

is photographed once, and only one plate—which prints with black ink—needs to be made. Color artwork, however, requires four separate plates for printing.

Before a color illustration can be reproduced, its colors must be separated into the three primary colors—red, green, and blue. This process is called **color separation.** Traditionally, separation negatives have been created by photographing the artwork three times, each time through a different primary-colored filter. Each of the separation negatives is used to create a plate for printing: The separation negative made with the red filter is used to create the plate that will print the blue and

## Letterpress Plates

Most of the plates used for letterpress printing are actually **duplicate plates,** or copies of an original plate. Original plates are made from flat sheets of zinc, magnesium, or copper that have been coated with light-sensitive chemicals. After being exposed to light through a film negative, chemicals eat away at the unexposed non-image areas, leaving the images to be printed raised above the surface. These original plates, called **engravings,** are used to make the duplicate plates.

There are four types of duplicate plates most commonly used for letterpress printing. They are electrotypes, stereotypes, plastic plates, and rubber plates.

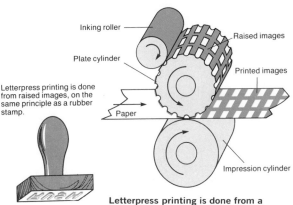

Letterpress printing is done from raised images, on the same principle as a rubber stamp.

Letterpress printing is done from a raised surface. On a rotary press, printing occurs when a sheet of paper passes between the inked plate, which is mounted on a rotating plate cylinder, and the impression cylinder.

green images in the artwork. This plate is printed in **cyan** (bluish green)-colored ink. The separation negative made with the green filter is used to create the plate that will print the blue and red images in the artwork. This plate is printed in **magenta** (bluish red)-colored ink. The separation negative made with the blue filter is used to create the plate that will print the red and green images in the artwork. This plate is printed in **yellow** ink. (For more information on how colors combine to create other colors, see the article COLOR in Volume C.)

A fourth separation negative is also made to create a plate that will print in **black** ink. This negative is made by exposing film through all three primary-colored filters or through a special filter. The addition of black extends the range, or contrast, of the artwork. Black also combines with other colors to produce neutral shades of gray.

Each separation negative must then be screened to create the dot patterns that will give the appearance of continuous tone. The screen is placed at a slightly different angle when photographing each of the four colors so that, when the artwork is reproduced, the different color dots will print next to or overlap each other. The combined use of cyan, magenta, yellow, and black inks to produce color prints is called **four-color process printing.**

Today, most color separations are made on electronic scanners that can read colors and produce screened separation negatives without using photographic equipment.

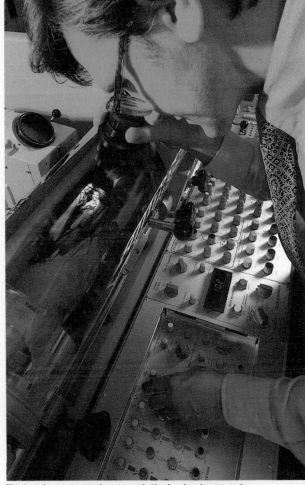

Electronic scanners have revolutionized color reproduction. They automatically read, separate, and correct colors and create separation negatives for platemaking.

Until the 1800's, all printing was done manually. Typesetters would create separate lines of text by arranging individual pieces of type. Early printing was done on screw presses, similar to those built to crush grapes for making wine.

The Gutenberg Bible, published in 1455, was the first book printed on a press using movable type. It is also known as the 42-line Bible because each column contains 42 lines. Each page was set by hand using approximately 2,500 individual pieces of type. Fewer than 50 copies are still in existence.

### Letterpress Presses

Gutenberg used what is called a **platen press** to print his famous Bible. A platen press has two flat surfaces; one is called the **bed** and the other is called the **platen.** The bed holds the printing plate; the platen holds the paper. The plate is inked by inking rollers. Paper or other materials are sheet fed manually or automatically to the platen. The platen and the bed open and close like a clam shell.

A **cylinder press** also has a flat bed that holds the printing plate. However, a rotating cylinder provides the pressure for printing. Paper or other material is picked up by the cylinder and held by steel clamps called grippers. The plate on the flat bed moves in sideways to meet the cylinder. The paper is passed over the inked plate. The cylinder completes its rotation and delivers the printed piece as the flat bed moves back to its original position. The manufacture of flat-bed cylinder presses was discontinued in the United States in 1962 when the more productive rotary press came into widespread use.

Today, most letterpress printing is done on web-fed rotary presses. A rotary press has no flat beds. Instead it uses a plate cylinder and an impression cylinder. The plate is curved to fit the plate cylinder; the impression cylinder provides the pressure. The paper or other material is printed as it passes between the rotating plate cylinder and impression cylinder.

When phototypesetting was invented in the late 1940's, the use of cast-metal type and letterpress printing began to decline. Today, letterpress has been replaced in popularity by flexography (relief printing using rubber or plastic plates), lithography, and gravure.

### ▶ LITHOGRAPHY (OFFSET PRINTING)

In lithography, images are printed from a flat, rather than a raised, surface. The process is based on the principle that oil (grease) and water do not mix. When lithography was discovered in 1798 by Aloys Senefelder in Munich, Germany, it was the first significant printing development in more than 350 years. Today more items are printed by lithography than by any other method.

The term lithography comes from two Greek words, *lithos* and *graphos,* which together mean "writing on stone." Senefelder used a greasy crayon or liquid to draw an illustration on a flat stone. Then he dampened the entire stone with water. The greasy illustration (the image) repelled the water (the water would not cling to the grease). However, the rest of the stone, containing the non-image areas, accepted the water and remained wet. When Senefelder put oil-based ink on the stone, it stuck to the greasy drawing, but not to any wet areas. When he pressed a piece of paper against the stone, Senefelder printed the first lithograph.

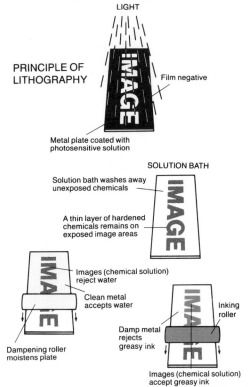

PRINCIPLE OF LITHOGRAPHY

LIGHT

Film negative

Metal plate coated with photosensitive solution

SOLUTION BATH

Solution bath washes away unexposed chemicals

A thin layer of hardened chemicals remains on exposed image areas

Images (chemical solution) reject water

Clean metal accepts water

Dampening roller moistens plate

Damp metal rejects greasy ink

Inking roller

Images (chemical solution) accept greasy ink

Lithographic plates are coated with light-sensitive solutions. Image areas are on the same plane, or level, as non-image areas. Coated plates are exposed to light through film negatives, making just the image areas receptive to ink.

## Lithographic Plates

Today, practically all lithographic plates are made with finely grained sheets of aluminum, most of which have been specially treated to make the non-image areas more receptive to water. Then the plates are coated with a photosensitive (light-sensitive) solution.

A photographic negative of the image areas (the laid-out typeset copy and artwork) is used to make a lithographic plate. A strong light is passed through the negative, exposing the image areas on the plate. When the exposed plate is developed, the photosensitive solution hardens only on the exposed image areas. These are the only areas to which ink will cling; the unexposed non-image areas, when dampened, will repel ink.

## Lithographic Presses

Throughout the 1800's, all lithographic printing was done on flat-bed presses, using stone plates. About 1900, a rotary press for lithographic printing was invented. Stone plates could not be mounted on the cylinders, so metal plates were substituted.

The most important improvement in lithographic printing was the invention of the **offset**

Most lithographic printing is done on offset presses. Instead of printing directly from the plate onto the paper or other material, inked images are first transferred, or "offset," onto a rubber blanket. The images are printed when a rotating impression cylinder presses the paper against the rotating blanket. *Inset:* The yellow printing unit of a web offset press prints only yellow images and is used for four-color process printing. Inking rollers transfer yellow ink to the lithographic plate. (Only the image areas on the plate will accept the ink.) The images are then offset from the plate onto the blanket, and finally, onto the paper (*bottom*).

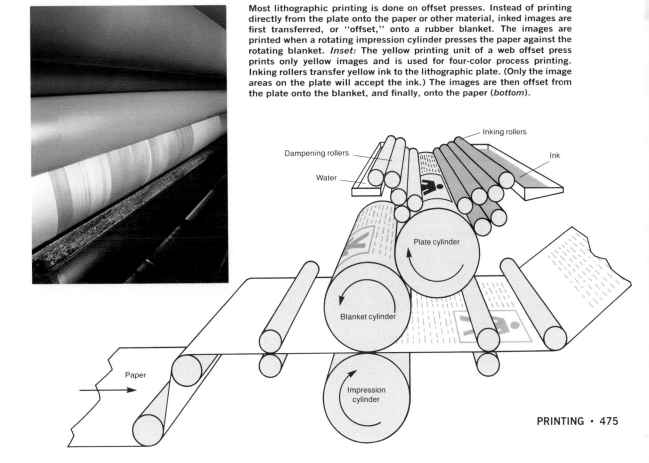

Inking rollers

Dampening rollers

Ink

Water

Plate cylinder

Blanket cylinder

Paper

Impression cylinder

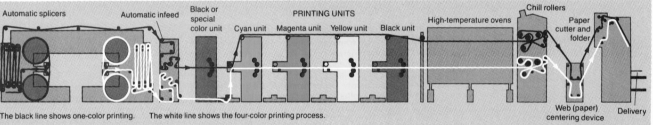

| Automatic splicers | Automatic infeed | Black or special color unit | PRINTING UNITS | | | | High-temperature ovens | Chill rollers | Paper cutter and folder |
|---|---|---|---|---|---|---|---|---|---|
| | | | Cyan unit | Magenta unit | Yellow unit | Black unit | | | |

The black line shows one-color printing.    The white line shows the four-color printing process.

Web (paper) centering device    Delivery

**The web offset press prints from enormous rolls of paper. This side-view diagram shows the press operations: Splicers join the end of one roll of paper to the beginning of another; the infeed adjusts the paper flow to each of the color printing units; ovens drive solvents from the ink; chill rollers set and dry the ink; and special devices cut or fold the paper into sheets or signatures.**

**press** in 1906. On an offset press, the images are not printed directly from the plate to the paper or other material. Instead, the images are transferred from the plate cylinder to a rotating rubber blanket cylinder. (The images are "offset" onto a rubber blanket.) When the impression cylinder, carrying the paper or other material, presses against the rubber blanket cylinder, the images are printed.

Another type of offset printing press commonly used today is the **perfecting blanket-to-blanket press.** This type does not use impression cylinders. Instead it uses two rubber blanket cylinders. A perfecting press prints both sides of the paper on one pass through the press. Each side's rubber blanket cylinder serves as the impression cylinder for the other side. The paper is printed on both sides, or perfected, as it passes between the two rubber blanket cylinders.

The offset principle gives lithography several advantages over letterpress printing. Offsetting gives lithography the ability to print on rough surfaces, which the letterpress method cannot do well. And because lithographic plates only come into contact with soft rubber blankets, plate life is lengthened considerably.

### ▶GRAVURE PRINTING

Gravure is an intaglio process. The word *intaglio* comes from the Italian, meaning to carve or engrave. In gravure printing, images are printed from a sunken, rather than a flat or raised, surface. Gravure evolved from the art of engraving, a method of printing illustrations that was invented in Germany about 1476.

An engraving is made by hand carving images into a flat metal plate, using sharp instruments. The plate is covered with ink. When the engraver wipes the surface of the plate clean, the ink remains trapped in the sunken images. Then paper is forced against the plate and picks up the ink remaining beneath the surface of the plate, thus printing the images.

Gravure printing works on the principle of engraving; however, the plates are made photomechanically, rather than carved by hand. The process was developed in 1878 by Karl Klič, a Czech artist who used the process to make multiple high-quality reproductions of works of art.

#### Gravure Plates and Cylinders

Gravure plates and cylinders used to be made from continuous-tone film positives of page layouts exposed onto specially coated paper called carbon tissue. After exposure and processing, the tissue was transferred to a copper-plated cylinder, and the image was etched into the copper with chemicals. This was a long and tiresome process that required considerable time and extremely skilled operators. This process is still used for some short and specialized print runs; however, in most cases, it has been replaced by halftone gravure.

Although most rotogravure cylinders today are engraved by electromechanical machines, highly skilled workers are still required to make touch-ups and corrections.

Halftone gravure uses halftone positives and electromechanical engraving machines. These machines "read" the image electronically. Computer-controlled engraving heads carve about 4,000 "cells" per second on the cylinder. Lasers are also now being used to engrave plastic coatings on gravure cylinders.

#### Gravure Presses

Although some gravure printing is done on sheet-fed presses that use gravure plates, most is done on rotary web-fed presses that use gravure cylinders. This method is called **rotogravure.** A printing unit on a rotogravure press consists of a gravure cylinder, an impression cylinder, an inking system, a sharp scraper called a doctor blade, and an ink dryer. There are as many units on the press as colors to be printed. As the gravure cylinder rotates, it is inked by rollers or by spray, filling the sunken images with ink. Then a doctor blade scrapes the excess ink from the surface of the gravure cylinder. The impression cylinder squeezes the paper or other material against the gravure cylinder, thus printing the images.

In rotogravure printing, images are engraved into the printing plate. As the plate cylinder rotates, it is inked. The plate's surface is then scraped clean, but ink remains trapped in the sunken cells. Images are printed when the rotating impression cylinder presses the paper against the cells in the rotating plate cylinder.

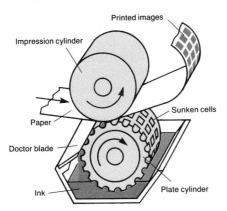

## OTHER PRINTING METHODS

Letterpress, lithography, and gravure traditionally have been the most commonly used printing methods. However, advanced technology and equipment have recently popularized several other methods, including screen printing, flexography, heat transfer printing, and photocopying.

### Screen Printing

Also called **silk screening** or **serigraphy,** screen printing is done with a fine screen, usually made of wire or nylon, that is mounted on a frame. A stencil is produced on the screen to cover up the non-image areas. (The images to be printed are cut out of or exposed onto the stencil.) Ink is squeezed through the stencil and screen onto fabric, paper, or other material.

Because more ink is used in screen printing than in other printing methods, screen prints usually must be passed through an ink dryer before they are stacked. The process is often used to make art prints, decal stickers, greeting cards, clothing, and many other products.

### Flexography

Flexography is a form of letterpress printing done on a web-fed rotary press. The process uses flexible rubber or plastic plates and inks that do not smear easily. Flexography is one of the simplest methods of printing and is being used increasingly for newspaper printing. Eventually it is expected to completely replace letterpress in newspaper printing.

### Heat Transfer Printing

In heat transfer printing, images are first printed on paper with special inks. The inked images are then transferred to fabric or some other surface by heat and pressure (usually an iron is used). T-shirts are frequently printed by the heat transfer method.

### Photocopying

Photocopying is also known as **xerography.** It is a fast and economical printing method used in businesses for quick copies of letters and office memorandums.

Photocopying works on static electricity. A rotating cylinder, coated with selenium (a nonmetallic element) and charged with static electricity, serves as the printing plate. Selenium discharges in non-image areas when exposed to light. Images, light-projected through a lens onto the cylinder, retain the charge. Negatively charged black powder is attracted to the positively charged image areas on the cylinder. When paper is passed over the cylinder, it picks up the black-powdered images. Then the powdered paper is slightly heated to make the powder stick to the paper.

## HISTORY

The history of recorded information dates from the cave drawings of more than 30,000 years ago. By 2500 B.C., Egyptians were carving hieroglyphics in stone. But printing as we know it today was not invented until relatively recently—little more than 500 years ago.

The Chinese made many discoveries. They invented paper in the 1st century and movable type made out of clay by the 11th century. The Koreans first made movable type out of bronze in the mid-13th century. But there is no known connection between these early Asian inventions and the discovery of printing in Europe in the 15th century.

In Europe, before printing was invented, all recorded information was hand written. Books were carefully copied by **scribes** who would often take years to complete a single volume. This method was slow and expensive, and few people had the opportunity, or the ability, to read the finished works.

Johann Gutenberg's inventions in the 1440's—movable type and the printing press—played a significant role in bringing Europe out of the ''dark ages.'' Printing made books and other reading materials available to the general public. People learned to read. As they became educated, they started exchanging ideas and information that led to new discoveries and inventions. Europe entered into a period of growth and exploration, known as the Renaissance.

There were few developments in printing between 1440 and the start of the Industrial Revolution about 1800. However, in the 1800's tremendous advancements were made in printing methods and machinery. Industrialization made possible the inventions of the steam-powered cylinder press, the rotary press, paper-making machines, and automated typesetting machines. Machines reduced the cost of printed materials and made them more readily accessible. In addition, photography, photoengraving, and coal-tar dyes to make colored inks also were discovered.

## IMPORTANT DATES IN THE HISTORY OF PRINTING

| | |
|---|---|
| **105** | Paper invented by Ts'ai Lun in China. |
| **868** | Oldest known book created from wood blocks, the *Diamond Sutra,* printed in China. |
| **1045?** | Movable type made from hardened clay invented by Pi Sheng in China. |
| **1250?** | Movable type made from bronze invented in Korea. |
| **1440** | Movable metal type and first wooden printing press invented in Europe by Johann Gutenberg in Germany. |
| **1455** | Gutenberg Bible, the first book printed on a press using movable type, published in Germany. |
| **1460?** | Woodcuts first used to illustrate books in Europe. |
| **1475** | *The Recuyell of the Histories of Troy,* the first book printed in the English language, published by William Caxton in England. |
| **1476** | Copperplate engravings for reproducing illustrations introduced in Germany. |
| **1487** | Printing presses began operating in Rome, Venice, Paris, and other European cities. |
| **1539** | First printing press in North America began operating in Mexico City. |
| **1638** | First printing press in the American colonies began operating at Harvard College in Cambridge, Massachusetts. |
| **1798** | Lithography invented by Aloys Senefelder in Germany. |
| **1811** | First steam-powered cylinder press invented by Friedrich König in Germany. |
| **1814** | Steam-powered press first used to print a newspaper, the *Times* of London. |
| **1826** | Photographic process invented by Joseph Nicéphore Niépce in France. |
| **1829** | Wet mat process using papier mâché for duplicate platemaking patented by Claude Gennoux in France. |
| **1837** | Photographic process perfected by Louis Daguerre in France. |
| **1846** | First rotary press using two cylinders invented by Richard Hoe in the United States. |
| **1849** | Curved stereotype plates invented by Jacob Warms in France. |
| **1852** | Photoengraving process patented by William Fox Talbot in England. |
| **1855** | Photolithography invented by Alphonse Louis Poitevin in France. |
| **1865** | First perfecting web-fed rotary press invented by William Bullock in the United States. |
| **1872** | Photoengraving process for making letterpress plates first used by Charles Gillot in France. |
| **1878** | First illustrations printed using gravure method invented by Karl Klič in Austria. |
| **1884** | First typesetting machine, the Linotype, invented by Ottmar Merganthaler in the United States. |
| **1885** | Halftone screen for photography perfected by Frederick Ives in the United States. |
| **1887** | Monotype typesetting machine patented by Tolbert Lanston in the United States. |
| **1893** | Color photoengraving process for making letterpress plates introduced in the United States. |
| **1905** | Offset printing accidentally discovered by Ira Rubel in the United States. |
| **1907** | Screen process for printing developed by Samuel Simon in England. |
| **1920's** | Teletypesetter (TTS) automated typesetting, using perforated tape, invented. |
| **1947** | First phototypesetting machine, the Fotosetter, invented. |
| **1948** | Reprography (photocopying) invented. |
| **1950** | Electronic scanners for color printing invented. |
| **1954** | First practical phototypesetting machine, the Photon, invented. |
| **1969** | Introduction of electronic magnification in scanners. |
| **1970's** | Computers simplified pre-press operations and made cast-metal type almost obsolete. |
| **1972** | Introduction of electronic dot generation (EDG) in scanners. |
| **1979** | First electronic color pre-press system, the Scitex, invented. |
| **1980** | Introduction of automatic toning systems (ATM) for off-press color proofing. |
| **1987** | Digital Data Exchange Specification (DDES) adopted, allowing interfacing of scanners and pre-press systems. |
| **1990's** | Computer-controlled ink-jet and laserjet printers widely used, rivaling the quality of traditional color printing. |

## Modern Printing Developments

At the end of the 1900's, advanced technology and electronics continued to change the printing industry. Letterpress became less important, used only in a few large daily newspapers and for some label and packaging printing, business forms, and job printing.

Flexography will eventually replace letterpress in newspaper printing. It will continue to grow in commercial packaging and book publishing. In addition, reprography is becoming more and more available, and the widespread use of word processors and electronic scanners are reducing printing costs.

Recently developed methods of gravure, using electromechanical and laser engraving of plastic-coated cylinders as well as electron-beam etching and photosensitive plates, are lowering the costs of cylinder making. New electronic systems have made it possible to make printing cylinders directly from original copy without films or manual operations. The future development of satisfactory water-based inks will further limit costs and pollution problems. This will assure gravure an even larger share of the printing market.

The rate of technological progress will continue to accelerate. Now that the world is in the midst of an information explosion, the printing industry will also progress and continue to record and distribute that information well into the new century.

MICHAEL H. BRUNO
Editor, *Pocket Pal: A Graphic Arts Production Handbook*

See also BOOKS; COLOR; GRAPHIC ARTS; GUTENBERG, JOHANN; PHOTOGRAPHY; TYPE.

Prisons are designed to isolate criminals from society. Maximum-security prisons (*left*) hold dangerous criminals and are secured by thick walls and barbed-wire fences. Minimum-security prisons (*right*) hold minor offenders and are less closely guarded.

# PRISONS

A prison is a place of confinement. People who commit crimes are removed from society and placed in prisons as punishment for their offenses. There are many different types of institutions that hold people accused of a crime: jails, detention centers, work camps, police lockups, and federal and state prisons. But only convicted criminals who have been sentenced to a year or more are imprisoned.

In the United States today there are more than half a million adults and children under the age of 18 serving time in prison. Most prisoners are male high-school dropouts between the ages of 18 and 29. Most of them have committed violent crimes against other people (such as murder or assault with a deadly weapon), property crimes (such as theft or burglary), or "white collar" crimes (such as tax evasion or embezzlement). Less than 5 percent of the convicted criminals in the United States are women.

## ▶TYPES OF PRISONS

There are many different types of prisons, or correctional facilities, in the United States. The facility chosen for confinement usually depends on the offender's age and the crime.

**Jails.** Municipal and county jails and detention centers are institutions maintained to hold people who have been accused of a crime and are awaiting a court trial. People are also sent to jails as punishment for a minor offense, such as disorderly conduct. These facilities are meant to serve as temporary places of confinement. However, if an accused offender is sentenced by the court to serve one year or longer, then he or she will be sent to a federal or state prison.

**Federal Prisons.** Criminals convicted of federal crimes, such as smuggling drugs across state lines or not paying income taxes, are sent to federal prisons. Federal prisons in the United States are administered by the Bureau of Prisons, a division of the Justice Department. Perhaps the best-known federal prison in operation today is the United States Penitentiary in Leavenworth, Kansas.

**State Prisons.** Each state has its own prison system to punish criminals convicted of crimes committed in that state. Some famous state prisons include San Quentin, a maximum-security prison in California; Sing-Sing (Ossining Correctional Facility) in New York; and the Michigan state prison in Jackson, which is the largest walled prison in the United States, having approximately 4,000 inmates.

While prisons can be quite different from one another, the life of a prisoner tends to be the same: Prisoners lose their freedom to come and go as they please; all of their activities are supervised; and they live in a small cell with little more than a bed, a wash basin, and a toilet.

A typical day in prison begins early in the morning. Prison guards unlock each prisoner's cell to take a head count. When all of the prisoners have been accounted for, they file into the dining room for breakfast. After breakfast, they take part in various activities: Some have chores; others go to school; and still others go to prison workshops to make products for sale, such as license plates. Many others simply go back to their cell areas to read or watch television. After lunch, another head count is taken, followed by recreational activities. Dinner is usually served around 5 P.M. By 9 P.M., the prisoners are locked up in their cells for the night.

When prisoners misbehave, special measures are taken to punish them. Their recreation time may be suspended, or days may be added to their sentence. However, the most common form of punishment is placing a prisoner in isolation. He or she is kept apart from others and is unable to receive visitors.

### Rehabilitation Programs

Many prisons provide rehabilitation programs to prepare prisoners for their return to society. Programs are available to help those with drug and alcohol problems. Educational programs enable prisoners to earn a high-school or even a college degree. Other programs teach job skills to prepare prisoners for work after they are released. Some minimum-security facilities even permit some prisoners to work outside the prison, although they must return for the night. However, this is a privilege granted only to model prisoners who are well behaved and close to completing their sentence.

### Parole and Probation

Prisons are very expensive to build and maintain and are severely overcrowded. This situation has led to the increased use of parole and probation to handle the criminal population. Parole means releasing a prisoner before the whole sentence is served. The person, however, remains under the supervision of a parole officer until the sentence is completed. Probation means attempting to reform convicted criminals outside prison walls. Supervised by trained probation officers, criminals on probation are able to escape the harsh effects of prison life and the disgrace of having served a prison sentence.

▶HISTORY

Until the 1500's, when the first workhouses, or houses of correction, were built in England and the Netherlands, criminals were not punished by being put in prison. The only persons punished in this way were those who could not pay their debts or who were out of favor for political or religious reasons. Persons accused of a crime usually were imprisoned only while they were waiting to be tried. If found guilty, they were generally punished by various forms of corporal punishment (inflicting pain on the body of the offender). Some were executed or sent into exile. During the 1500's European countries began transporting criminals in work gangs to their colonies in the New World. England sent thousands out to its American colonies before the beginning of the Revolutionary War. Between 1787 and 1875 thousands more were sent to the British penal colonies in Australia. France exiled its criminals to colonies in Africa, New Caledonia, and French Guiana for many years. Labor camps in Siberia received prisoners transported by both the czarist and Soviet governments.

England's American colonies inherited the methods of punishment of the mother country. In Pennsylvania the Quakers, or members of the Society of Friends, were determined to do away with corporal punishment. After the American Revolution the criminal code of Pennsylvania was changed. Imprisonment became the chief form of punishment. By 1826 the other states had followed this example.

The first prisons did not have separate cells for convicts. Men and women waiting to be tried, as well as those already convicted, were herded together into large rooms. However, Quakers and other prison reformers were greatly influenced by the ideas set forth in 1777 by an Englishman, John Howard in his book, *The State of the Prisons*. Howard had been extremely impressed by his visits to the Hospice of San Michele in Rome and to the workhouse in Ghent, Belgium. Both institutions provided for the separation of different classes of inmates, medical care, the housing of inmates in individual cells, and their employment at useful labor.

Authorities at the Hospice of San Michele believed that prisoners could be made to feel penitent (sorry) for their crimes if they were confined and treated well. This idea appealed to Howard, and from it developed the penitentiary system. In England the Penitentiary Act was passed by Parliament in 1779, but construction of the first English penitentiary did not begin until about 1812.

In 1790 a section of separate cells for the worst criminals was provided in the Walnut Street Jail in Philadelphia, as a result of reforms urged by Pennsylvania Quakers. It thus became America's first penitentiary.

### The Auburn and Pennsylvania Systems

The first prison to be built entirely with separate cells was opened in Auburn, New York, in 1819. In the Auburn system of punishment, convicts were allowed to leave their cells, eat in the prison dining room, and work in silence in the prison shops. This came to be known as the **silent** or **congregate system**.

The first separate-cell prison in Pennsylvania, the Western Penitentiary, was built in Pittsburgh in 1826. In the Pennsylvania system, each convict had a cell in which to eat, sleep, and work when ordered to do so. Attached to each cell was a small exercise yard. Inmates were not allowed to speak to anyone other than prison officials, nor could they leave their cells. This came to be known as the **separate system**.

The Auburn system was cheaper to run and easier to administer than the Pennsylvania system and became the model for state prisons in the United States. Most of the prisons built in Europe during the 1800's, however, were of the Pennsylvania type.

### The Development of Reformatories

Programs geared to reforming prisoners to make them fit to return to society were first introduced in Ireland in the late 1850's by Sir Walter Crofton, one of the greatest of all prison reformers. He provided work and education for prisoners and encouraged them to reform by allowing them to gain early release through good behavior and hard work.

Crofton's Irish system attracted the attention of American reformers, who used the system to set up prisons for young offenders. These came to be known as reformatories. The first reformatory was opened in Elmira, New York, in 1876. In the United States the Irish system became known as the **Elmira system**.

Reform programs for adult prisoners were not introduced until the 1930's. Reformers tried to change the prisoner's ways of thinking and acting. Experts provided better prison schools and workshops where the prisoners could learn a trade. But in spite of these advances, few prisons even today are able to successfully reform many prisoners. This has led to the greater use of parole, probation, and other alternatives.

### Punishment of Women and Children

In London during the 1800's, Elizabeth Fry organized the Association for the Improvement of Female Prisoners in Newgate Prison. Among the reforms she advocated was the separation of women and men prisoners.

In the United States, women were kept in the same prisons as men, although in different sections. In 1873 Indiana built a separate prison just for women, and today most states have separate institutions for women prisoners.

For many years young people convicted of crimes were put in prison with adult convicts. The first prison for children in the United States opened in New York City in 1825.

In the 1800's, reformers in Europe began to build small cottages for young convicts in order to give them more homelike surroundings. The first cottage system in the United States was for girls. It was opened in Lancaster, Massachusetts, in 1856. The following year one was opened for boys in Lancaster, Ohio. These institutions were later called **reform schools**. Today they are called training schools and are administered by the states. Aftercare programs also have been established to help young offenders return to society once their sentences are over.

HARRY ELMER BARNES
Coauthor, *New Horizons in Criminology*
Updated by ANNA KOSOF
Author, *Prison Life in America*

See also COURTS; CRIME AND CRIMINOLOGY; LAW AND LAW ENFORCEMENT.

**PROBABILITY.** See MATHEMATICS; MATHEMATICS, HISTORY OF.

# PROGRAMMED INSTRUCTION

Programmed instruction, also referred to as programmed learning, is a way of individualizing instruction. Programmed teaching materials or programs are self-instructional and are made up of many small units, or steps, arranged so that each one leads logically to the next. Students work independently and advance in their units of study at their own pace.

Each program has a set of goals for a particular unit of study. These goals are called **behavioral objectives**. A behavioral objective is a statement of what skills and abilities students are expected to acquire as a result of their exposure to the program. For example, a behavioral objective for a mathematics program may be the following: "The student will be able to add decimal numbers." The program also contains instructional materials considered essential to achieving each stated objective.

Students usually work through the objectives in a program by following these steps:

1. Students are given information to read or a visual image to look at. They are asked questions about what they read or observe. They respond by writing an answer or drawing a picture or a diagram.
2. Students get immediate feedback by checking their answer against the correct answer.
3. If their answer is incorrect, students are guided to additional instructional material. When they are able to demonstrate that they have learned the objective, they proceed to the next one.
4. At regular intervals, students are tested to determine if they remember and understand what they are being taught.

In the early days of programmed instruction, students used programmed textbooks or worked on special machines called teaching machines that combined instruction and testing. Programmed instruction today is most often presented on a computer or on an interactive multimedia system that uses a computer linked to a videodisc or to a CD-ROM device.

Reviewed by IBRAHIM M. HEFZALLAH
Fairfield University

See also EDUCATION.

# PROHIBITION

The term prohibition refers to laws that prohibit, or forbid, the manufacture, sale, and transportation of alcoholic beverages. It is most commonly used in reference to an era in American history (1920–33) when all alcoholic beverages, including beer and wine, were illegal under the terms of the 18th Amendment to the Constitution. The federal ban on alcohol was lifted in 1933 with the passage of the 21st Amendment, which repealed (canceled) the 18th Amendment.

### The Temperance and Prohibition Movements

The passage of the 18th Amendment was the result of a century-long reform movement to restrain people from drinking alcohol. The movement was joined by people who recognized that alcoholic beverages can be a dangerous drug when drunk too often or in large quantities.

During the prohibition years, federal agents seized and disposed of illegal alcoholic beverages under the authority of the Volstead Act.

## Profiles

**Judith Ellen Horton Foster** (1840–1910), born in Lowell, Mass., was an attorney who wrote the constitution of the Woman's Christian Temperance Union (WCTU). A close associate of Frances Willard

Carry Nation

(*see right*), Foster eventually came to disagree with Willard's plan for the WCTU. Foster believed that the WCTU should concentrate exclusively on the issue of prohibition and do so by influencing the Democratic and Republican political parties, not through a separate prohibition party. She continued her efforts toward temperance reform by establishing a nonpartisan branch of the WCTU. Foster later helped formulate the strategy of the Anti-Saloon League.

**Carry Amelia Moore Nation** (1846–1911), born Garrard County, Ky., became notorious for her destructive campaigns against illegal saloons. Nation, a former teacher, settled in Kansas with her second husband in 1889. Prohibition was enacted in Kansas in 1880, but the law was widely violated. Nation, whose first husband died an alcoholic, took it upon herself to attack saloons that openly violated the law, and her actions were dramatic. She used a hatchet to destroy whiskey bottles and beer barrels, and she threw rocks. Her violent actions, which she said were justified because her victims were criminals, gained her an international reputation as a fanatic supporter of prohibition. The WCTU rejected what were known as her "hatchetation" campaigns. Nation's actions helped promote public support in Kansas for enforcement of the prohibition law. Her notoriety on the lecture circuit also earned her large sums of money, which she donated to charity.

**Wayne Bidwell Wheeler** (1869–1927), born near Brookfield, Ohio, spent his entire career working for the Anti-Saloon League. He became active in the league while attending Oberlin College in Ohio, where the Anti-Saloon League was founded in 1893. After receiving a law degree (1898) from Western Reserve University, Wheeler became an attorney for the league in Washington, D.C., serving as its superintendent (1904–15) and general counsel (1915–27). Wheeler was known as a dedicated politician capable of engineering successful campaigns against the league's opponents. Although he was not the organization's most important leader, Wheeler sought publicity and became the best-known advocate of prohibition in the United States. He played a key role in the adoption of the 18th Amendment and advocated a policy of strict enforcement of the law.

**Frances Elizabeth Caroline Willard** (1839–98), born in Churchville, N.Y., was an educator and leading organizer of the temperance movement in the United States. Well educated for a woman of her day, she worked as a teacher and later served as dean of the Woman's College of Northwestern University in Evanston, Ill. Willard was a popular speaker who expressed a vision of a better world. She focused her energies on several causes, including women's rights. In 1879, the Woman's Christian Temperance Union (WCTU) elected her president, and she served in that position until her death. In 1883, Willard founded a world temperance union. Thereafter she was considered the best-known woman in the English-speaking world after Queen Victoria.

---

The roots of the prohibition movement were found in religion, especially in the Protestant churches. In the 1800's, many Protestants believed that after slavery, drunkenness was the nation's greatest evil. At first the reformers tried to persuade people to stop drinking on their own—or at least to drink less, or be "temperate." Organizations such as the American Temperance Society, founded in 1826, tried to get people to pledge to stop drinking. But many eventually decided that the only way to help people resist the temptation to drink was to outlaw the businesses that made and sold alcohol. To achieve this end, the prohibition movement had to become a political as well as a social movement, and in 1869 the Prohibition Party was established.

Prohibition was one of the first large political movements in the United States in which women played an important role. The Woman's Christian Temperance Union (WCTU), founded in 1874, was especially influential in the fight against alcohol abuse, but the organization focused on other causes as well, notably obtaining for women the right to vote. The prohibition movement gained momentum after 1893, when the Anti-Saloon League was founded. Unlike the WCTU, the league focused only on the issue of prohibition and supported candidates of any political party who would vote for prohibition laws.

Several state and local governments passed prohibition laws, especially where Protestant voters were numerous. By 1916 prohibition reformers were so successful in the U.S. congressional elections that they were confident of achieving national prohibition. Congress proposed the 18th Amendment to the Constitution the following year, and it was ratified by two thirds of the states on January 16, 1919. Before the 18th Amendment went into effect in January 1920, Congress passed the Volstead Act to make provisions for the government to enforce prohibition. This act was named for the U.S. representative who proposed it—Andrew J. Volstead of Minnesota.

### The Dry Years (1920–33)

In the 1920's, many Americans stopped drinking, and alcohol-related diseases and accidents declined. However, many people continued to crave alcohol and were willing to obtain it illegally. This demand gave rise to a huge black-market business controlled primarily by gangsters, such as the notorious Al Capone. Those who smuggled liquor into the United States from other countries or made illegal alcohol for sale were called bootleggers; the saloons where people went to drink in secret were called speakeasies.

As time wore on, prohibition became increasingly unpopular. Leading the opposition were wealthy men and women who believed they could relieve their tax burden if the government would legalize alcohol and tax alcohol-related businesses. In addition, many Americans objected to the bootleggers and gangsters, who seemed to be the main beneficiaries of prohibition.

### The End of Prohibition

When the Great Depression began in 1929, prohibition lost many supporters. Those in favor of repealing the 18th Amendment argued that legalizing alcoholic beverages would create badly needed jobs in related businesses. In addition, the taxes imposed on the manufacture and sale of alcoholic beverages would raise money for the benefit of local, state, and federal governments.

In 1933 the opponents of prohibition were successful in persuading two thirds of the states to ratify the 21st Amendment, and prohibition was repealed. The Amendment went into effect on December 6, 1933, and the making and selling of alcoholic beverages once again became legal in the United States, although some state and local laws continue to restrict their use.

K. AUSTIN KERR
Author, *Organized for Reform: A New History of the Anti-Saloon League*

---

**PROJECTS, SCIENCE.** See EXPERIMENTS AND OTHER SCIENCE ACTIVITIES.

## PROKOFIEV, SERGEI (1891–1953)

Sergei Prokofiev, an outstanding Russian composer of the 20th century, was born in Sontzovka, Ukraine, on April 23, 1891. His mother, an amateur pianist, gave him his first music lessons. He showed unusual talent in both piano and composition, and by the age of 9 he had written a complete opera.

When he was 13, Sergei was sent to the conservatory in St. Petersburg, where he studied piano and composition with the finest teachers of the day, including Nikolai Rimsky-Korsakov (1844–1908). On his graduation in 1914, he was awarded the Anton Rubinstein prize for his performance of his First Piano Concerto. Three years later he wrote one of his most popular orchestral works, the *Classical Symphony*.

In 1918, Prokofiev left Russia on a concert tour of the world. He traveled first through Siberia and Japan and then to the United States. In 1921 his opera *Love for Three Oranges* was produced in Chicago. The following year he settled in Paris. Here he renewed his acquaintance with the director of the famous Russian Ballet, Sergei Diaghilev (1872–1929), who produced several of Prokofiev's ballets.

In 1934, Prokofiev returned to the Soviet Union, where he wrote some of his most famous works. These include the *Lieutenant Kijé* suite (1933), the ballet *Romeo and Juliet* (1935–36), the cantata *Alexander Nevsky* (1938), and the opera *War and Peace* (1941–43). Prokofiev's Fifth Symphony (1944) is considered by many people to be one of the greatest works of his generation. His piano music is also popular.

Beginning in 1948, Prokofiev was severely criticized by the Soviet government for allegedly composing music that was inappropriate for the Soviet people. The government later changed its position, and he was returned to favor.

Except for this short period, Prokofiev enjoyed success in the Soviet Union, and in 1951 he was awarded the Stalin prize. When he died in Moscow on March 5, 1953, his works had become familiar to audiences around the world. Perhaps the most beloved is *Peter and the Wolf* (1936), a fairy tale told in both words and music.

Reviewed by RONALD L. BYRNSIDE
Author, *Music: Sound and Sense*

**PRONOUN.** See PARTS OF SPEECH.

# PRONUNCIATION

Where there is a language there is pronunciation. Pronunciation is language being spoken.

**Pronouncing by Ear.** As children grow up they learn to understand and speak, just by living with other people. They copy the pronunciation of those about them. The Australians pronounce the word "late" so that most Americans would hear "light." In England, London cockneys drop the *h* at the beginning of words, so that "he" becomes " 'e." In all countries people of certain regions have special oddities of pronunciation.

**Pronouncing Written Words.** We sometimes see new words for the first time in print. The pronunciation of such new words may be difficult because one letter may stand for different sounds in different words. The letter *o,* for example, stands for completely different sounds in t*o*p, s*o,* d*o,* c*o*rn, m*o*ther, and w*o*men. O is one of the five vowel letters in the Roman alphabet, used for writing English. The other vowel letters are *a, e, i,* and *u.* The remaining 21 letters of the alphabet are all consonants, although *y* is sometimes used as a vowel. Most of the consonant letters have the same pronunciation every time they are used.

Some dictionaries, encyclopedias, and other reference books have pronunciation keys, or guides. Pronunciation guides differ. The following list shows one way of writing the consonant sounds of English, with one or more of the common ways to spell each sound:

| | | | |
|---|---|---|---|
| **b** | as in *b*ill | **r** | as in *r*ow |
| **ch** | as in *ch*ill, wa*tch* | **s** | as in *s*o, *c*ent |
| **f** | as in *ph*one, *f*an, laug*h* | **sh** | as in ma*ch*ine, na*ti*on, so*ci*al, *sh*one, tis*s*ue |
| **g** | as in *g*et, *gh*ost | **t** | as in coo*k*ed, *Th*omas, *t*ill |
| **h** | as in *h*and, *wh*o | | |
| **j** | as in *J*ill, ju*dg*e, *G*eorge | **th** | as in *th*in |
| | | **th** | as in *th*an |
| **k** | as in *k*ill, *c*at, si*ck*, a*ch*e, *q*uick | **v** | as in *v*an, o*f* |
| | | **w** | as in *w*e, q*u*ick |
| **l** | as in *l*ow | **y** | as in *y*es, on*i*on |
| **m** | as in ra*m* | **z** | as in *z*one, ea*s*y |
| **n** | as in ra*n* | **zh** | as in plea*s*ure, a*z*ure, divi*s*ion |
| **ng** | as in ra*ng*, i*n*k | | |
| **p** | as in *p*ill | | |

The letters *c, q,* and *x* are not listed. C sounds are represented by **k** as in *c*at and **s** as in *c*ent. The **k** also stands for *q,* as in *q*uick, and **ks** supplies the *x* sound found in ta*x*i.

Some written words contain consonant letters that are silent. Pronunciation guides omit these silent letters when spelling out words to show how they are pronounced: **det** (de*b*t), **lim** (lim*b*), **not** (*k*not), **rist** (*w*rist).

Vowel sounds are harder to show than consonant sounds because five vowel letters (and sometimes *y*) have to show 14 basic sounds. So we use some double letters and special marks. There are two kinds of vowels: simple vowels and diphthongs. The simple vowels that most Americans use are **a** as in b*a*t; **e** as in b*e*t; **i** as in b*i*t; **o** as in c*o*t; **ô** as in c*au*ght; **oo** as in p*u*t, g*oo*d; **u** as in b*u*t.

The most common unaccented vowel sound in English is called a **schwa,** for which the symbol is an upside-down *e,* that is: ə. A pronunciation guide might use the schwa in words like stanza (stanzə), sister (sistər), and so on. It is almost the same sound that is stressed in b*u*t, and sometimes the schwa is used instead of *u:* bət.

The diphthongs are really two vowels pronounced together. The pronunciation slides from one to the other. The diphthongs most used by Americans are:

| | | | |
|---|---|---|---|
| **ā** | as in f*a*te, b*ai*t, *eigh*t, pl*ay* | **ō** | as in v*o*te, b*oa*t, sh*ow*, th*ough* |
| **ē** | as in *e*ve, f*ee*t, b*ea*t, k*ey*, w*e*, ma*chi*ne | **oi** | as in b*oy*, s*oi*l |
| **ī** | as in b*i*te, fl*y,* f*igh*t | **ōo** | as in fl*u*te, b*oo*t, thr*ough* |
| | | **ou** | as in b*ou*t, f*ow*l |

**Syllables and Accents.** Words are made up of one or more syllables. A syllable is a speech sound or group of speech sounds pronounced as a unit. It may be a whole word or part of a word. "Go" is a syllable and a whole word. In "going" it is the first of two syllables. In words of more than one syllable, one syllable is stressed. To show which syllable is stressed, a mark called an accent is placed after the syllable (go'ing) or over the vowel (góing).

**Diacritical Marks.** Other aids in pronunciation are the diacritical marks put on letters, such as the lines over *ô* and *ē.* Standard dictionaries list these marks and illustrate how they are used.

J. DONALD BOWEN
University of California at Los Angeles

See also ALPHABET; LANGUAGES; articles on individual letters of the alphabet.

# PROOFREADING

The word "manuscript" originally meant "written by hand." Today manuscripts (material for articles, newspapers, magazines, books) are typed before being sent to the printer. In the printshop the typesetter sets this material into lines of type. Since this is done with great speed, errors are sometimes made. For this reason proofs are made. Proof reproduces the type exactly as it has been set by the printer. By reading proof, a proofreader discovers the errors.

**Galleys.** First proofs, called galleys, are long sheets that contain print for about three pages of a regular-size book. The margins are wide so that the proofreader can make his corrections in them. When the proofs are returned to the printer he does not read all of the print. He merely makes the corrections indicated in the margin. This is why all corrections should be clearly and carefully indicated—so that the final printed pages will be perfect. In most instances the author also reads proof and indicates changes.

**Page Proof.** Because the typesetter has the type for each galley proof in a heavy metal tray (called a galley), making corrections is a slow, hard task. It often means moving the lines of type about. The printer makes all the corrections indicated on the returned galleys. Then he divides the type into pages and submits page proof to the proofreader. This is the last proof before the presses roll. It is important to have "clean" typewritten copy in the beginning in order to avoid errors and added expense at this stage. Every writer—the professional author and the student alike—should proofread his own written work before handing it in to a publisher or a teacher.

**Proofreaders' Marks.** So that all printers can understand the changes or corrections made in the copy they are printing from, a code of proofreaders' marks has been devised. These marks cover corrections in spelling, capitalization, punctuation, kind of type to be used, spacing, paragraphing, and so on. Corrections must be neatly made. It is best to draw a light line from the correction indicated in the margin to the precise spot for the correction.

**Proofreading Schoolwork.** Although few stu-

## PROOFREADERS' MARKS

| | |
|---|---|
| ∧ | Insert a word or phrase. |
| ∧ | Insert comma. |
| ∨ | Insert apostrophe. |
| ∨∨ | Insert quotation marks. |
| ;/ | Insert semicolon. |
| :/ | Insert colon. |
| ⊙ | Insert period. |
| ?/ | Insert question mark. |
| -/ | Insert hyphen. |
| ℒ | Delete. |
| ¶ | Begin a new paragraph. |
| No ¶ | Do not begin a new paragraph. |
| Tr | Transpose. |
| Sp | Spell out. |
| Cap | Use CAPITAL. |
| ⌢ | Close up. |
| # | Space. |
| [ | Move to left. |
| ] | Move to right. |
| x | Broken letter. |
| stet | Restore word crossed out (place dots under word to be kept). |
| bf | Set in **boldface**, type that has thick, heavy lines and is used for headings and emphasis. |
| ital | Set in *italic* type, a style in which letters usually slant to the right. |

dents see their work in print, every student prepares some written material. In language and literature classes, particularly, the teacher often corrects student-written paragraphs and compositions and indicates in the margin where errors have been made. To avoid writing an individual note to each student about his mistakes, the teacher frequently uses proofreaders' marks.

Some proofreaders' marks are boxed on this page. The first 14—through "Sp"—are marks commonly used in correction of both written and typewritten work. The marks following "Sp" are more technical marks used in correcting material prepared for printing. All the marks listed above are necessary, of course, in correcting proof for final printing.

Most dictionaries give a complete list of proofreaders' marks.

MARY C. FOLEY
Author, *Language for Daily Use*

# PROPAGANDA

Propaganda is any effort to spread an idea. It can take many forms. It may be talk between people or words on the printed page. It may be films flashed on a screen or sounds transmitted over the air. It may be pictures at an exhibition or songs in a show.

The word "propaganda" comes from the Latin verb *propagare,* "to propagate." Originally "propagate" meant "to reproduce" or "to spread." It came to mean also "to transmit" and "to spread from person to person."

In the classic sense, propaganda is the art of communicating a message. But it goes beyond communicating. It reaches the point of persuading others. In the international sense, it means the attempt to persuade others of the rightness of one's cause.

Because propaganda at times has helped stir people to violent action, it is often thought to be bad. But propaganda can be good or bad, depending on its aims.

### History

Ever since people began to live together, they have tried to influence one another. In some cultures, witch doctors performed tricks and wove spells to show they were in touch with the gods. Their magic helped them control the people. In early Babylonian, Egyptian, and Roman times, priests played on popular superstitions to keep themselves in power. They used auguries (omens) and sacrifices to hold people's attention. Later, military leaders advertised their might by taking part in magnificent processions, in which they showed off the slaves and treasure they had captured.

The word "propaganda" may well have been first used in its present meaning when Pope Gregory XV set up the Sacred Congregation of Propaganda in 1622. This was a committee appointed to study ways of spreading the Christian faith through the world.

Before the American Revolutionary War, Samuel Adams wrote pamphlets against the British to spur the revolt of the colonies. Patrick Henry made his famous "Give me liberty or give me death" speech. Benjamin Franklin and George Washington both expressed views that stirred the already seething settlers. Every effort was made to play on long-standing resentments.

By this time, propaganda was no longer only

Forms of propaganda were used by both sides in World War II. Left: This poster urged people of the Allied countries to unite to win the war. Right: Adolf Hitler used his powers as a speaker to win support in Germany.

a matter of the spoken word. Organizations produced pamphlets to air their views. Newspapers and periodicals published editorials.

By the 1900's, hundreds of organizations of all types had begun to spread their own doctrines. Some were political, some economic. Some were frankly commercial, advertising products for the public to buy.

Beginning about 1915, motion pictures became a forceful means of influencing people. Radio reached its full development in the 1920's, and television followed on its heels. Each offered propagandists a wider platform.

## Methods

There are many means of propaganda. The oldest, and still one of the most effective, is person-to-person. In this regard, most governments are aware that their citizens overseas can play a critical role as messengers of goodwill. Information may be provided in many other ways, but a personal link may prove vital in making any message meaningful.

Printing is perhaps the most popular way to reach large numbers of people. Any person or group can print pamphlets, write articles, or place advertisements in newspapers to express a political view, promote a cause, or sell a product. Every daily newspaper has an editorial page, where the publisher's views and comments on the news appear.

The arts can also be used for purposes of propaganda. Playwrights present their views on stage, screen, and television. In both fiction and nonfiction, authors may plead for a special cause. Artists paint pictures and posters to arouse the public. With just a few strokes of the pen, cartoonists can ridicule people and events.

Press agents and public relations firms try to build prestige and increase business for their clients. Advertising agencies influence people to buy certain products. They conduct market research studies to find out which method of propaganda brings the best results for their clients.

## Governments

Propaganda is most often thought of as a tool of governments. It is a key weapon in dictatorships, which seek to direct the will of the people. Dictatorships control all media (means) of communication. They thereby control what people see, hear, read, and learn. Pro-

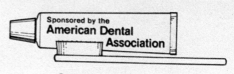

© 1979 American Dental Association

Propaganda can be good or bad, depending on its aims. This poster performs a public service by promoting better dental care for children.

paganda surrounds the people in their homes, their schools, and their communities.

Democracies use, but do not monopolize, the various media of communication. They try to offer a choice of viewpoints. They encourage debate. More than one political party vies for public favor. As times change, the parties in power change. When this happens, the official propaganda of the government may change as well.

In the collision of political beliefs among nations, propaganda has taken on new dimensions. Opposing governments use many of the same words but mean different things. Each government tries to express itself in ways that will make people think well of it. In so doing, it may have to deal with contrary ideas spread by hostile forces.

Today most governments make use of propaganda. The United States government engages in propaganda to try to win support for its foreign policies and national interests abroad. This is done through the United States Information Agency (USIA). The agency is best known through its broadcast division, the Voice of America (VOA).

CARL T. ROWAN
Former Director
U.S. Information Agency

Martin Luther (on left) helped launch the Protestant Reformation by challenging certain beliefs and practices of the Roman Catholic Church.

## PROTESTANTISM

Protestantism, one of the three main branches of Christianity, is the religious practice and tradition that resulted from the Reformation in Europe in the Middle Ages. It is the world's second largest Christian religion, with approximately 400 million followers. Protestantism is found in nearly every nation on Earth and is the dominant religion of northwest Europe, North America, Australia, and New Zealand. Although there are more than a thousand Protestant denominations, or sects, and a wide range of religious views, all Protestants share certain beliefs.

### ▶ BELIEFS

Like other Christians (Roman Catholic and Eastern Orthodox), most Protestants believe in one God who is represented as a trinity, or single deity with three persons: the Father, the Son, and the Holy Spirit. They believe that Jesus Christ, the Son, was born of woman, preached, was crucified, and died. They also believe that he rose from the dead and ascended into heaven, and that by doing so he saved people from sin.

Beyond this, Protestantism is often defined by what its followers do not believe. This is why this religion is called Protestantism. It was originally a protest against certain doctrines and practices of the medieval Roman Catholic Church.

The key doctrines of Protestantism reflect these origins. They include what is called "justification by grace through faith," a universal "priesthood of believers," and the authority of the Bible.

Justification by grace through faith means that people are saved from their sin and its punishment through God's grace by faith in Jesus Christ. While the Roman Catholic Church emphasizes salvation through grace as well, it teaches that salvation must also be earned by good works. The first Protestants rejected this teaching because they felt that good works should be performed out of concern for another person or group, and not to save one's soul.

The concept of a priesthood of believers means that all Protestants are equal. That is, all have the same connection to God, whether they are clergy or not, and can be saved without the intervention of a priest, saint, or other religious authority.

Protestantism also emphasizes the authority of the Bible—Christianity's most sacred book. According to Protestant doctrine, every person, or individual church, may read and interpret the Bible as desired. This doctrine was a reaction to the medieval Roman Catholic Church's claim that it was the only legitimate authority for teaching matters of faith. Protestants not only disagreed with this, but also felt that the Catholic Church did not place enough importance on the Bible.

In connection with these beliefs, particularly the priesthood of believers, Protestants also reject the idea of a central religious authority such as the Roman Catholic pope. Although there are numerous Protestant sects that are organized in different ways, many churches have a minimal connection with a larger organization and are led by pastors or ministers hired by individual congregations. Some congregations also determine church policies and theology. In some instances, individual church members may lead worship services, organize church activities, or perform other tasks sometimes reserved for the clergy.

There are a few exceptions, however. One is the Anglican Church, also known as the Episcopal Church or Church of England. This sect does have a hierarchy (organizational structure) that is similar to that of the Roman Catholic Church, with ranks of bishops and priests. It is headed by the Archbishop of Canterbury and England's king or queen.

Because views among Protestant sects can vary considerably, the core beliefs of Protestantism have had many different interpretations. These differences can be significant, particularly regarding the Bible. For example, some sects believe that the Bible should be interpreted literally, while others regard it as symbolism. Still others believe that although the Bible is the divinely inspired word of God, it is also symbolic.

In many instances, a sect's view of the Bible also influences other beliefs, such as creationism and evolution. That is, Protestants who interpret the Bible literally may believe in creationism (that God created the Earth in six days), while others believe that this biblical account symbolizes the process of evolution.

Among Protestants, baptism represents one's entry into the community of Christians. Both infants and adults can be baptized, individually or in groups.

Another key issue that varies according to biblical interpretation is the concept of salvation. Although some Protestants believe that only Christians can attain salvation, others maintain that it is available to all.

▶ **PRACTICES**

Protestants worship in many different ways. Some services are highly liturgical (primarily Anglican and Lutheran), which means they follow a specific sequence of prayers, rituals, hymns, and scriptural readings. Priests and ministers may wear vestments that are similar to those worn during Roman Catholic and Eastern Orthodox services. In other Protestant churches, services are less structured. These typically revolve around a sermon and may include music and prayers.

Protestant worship services can also feature the Eucharist, known to some as Holy Communion. The Eucharist, a rite practiced by all Christians, is the ritual consumption of bread and wine, which are believed to represent Christ's body and blood.

Baptism, another Protestant rite, often takes place as part of a worship service as well. Baptism represents one's entry into the community of Christians and, to some, the washing away of sin. During baptism, the body is immersed in water, or water is sprinkled on the head. Both children and adults can be baptized.

Like other Christians, Protestants observe Easter and Christmas, the two main religious holidays. Christmas celebrates the birth of Christ, and Easter is the day on which he is believed to have risen from the dead. Anglican Protestants also celebrate saints' days and holidays such as Ascension Day (forty days after Easter, when Jesus was supposed to have ascended into heaven).

▶ HISTORY

Protestantism began in Western Europe in the 1500's as a result of the Protestant Reformation. The leaders behind the Reformation felt that the Roman Catholic Church had become too powerful, wealthy, and rigid. Others felt that the beliefs of the church were out of touch with the simple teachings of Jesus Christ in the Bible's New Testament.

This desire for change and renewal within the church was recognized at least a century before the Reformation began, as the church spent large sums of money on art, buildings, and luxuries for its leaders. This spending was widely resented because the money came from taxes people paid on crops and land, and from the sale of indulgences. Indulgences were payments made to the church that people believed would release them from punishment for their sins.

Another factor that contributed to increasing dissatisfaction with the church was a

John Calvin (*left*) and John Knox (*below*) were among the key figures of the Protestant Reformation. Both believed in the concept of predestination.

growing spirit of nationalism (interest in one's own country). People were less willing to support the church in Rome than they had been in the past.

The date for the birth of the Protestant Reformation is usually given as October 31, 1517. That was when Martin Luther (1483–1546), a German monk and theology professor, first spoke out officially against the Roman Catholic Church. He posted 95 propositions in Wittenberg, Germany, inviting theological debate on the sale of indulgences.

Luther did not want to leave the Roman Catholic Church or to begin a new church. His protest was so strong, however, that he was excommunicated (deprived of the sacraments and church membership) from the Catholic Church and became the recognized leader of Protestantism. Luther was followed by other leaders of Protestant reform in Europe: John Calvin (1509–64) in Geneva, Huldreich Zwingli (1484–1531) in Zurich, John Knox (1513?–72) in Scotland, and later, in England and the colonies of the New World, John Wesley (1703–91).

Because Protestants believed that Roman Catholics did not make the Bible central enough to their teachings, they began to study it more. One of Luther's first tasks was to translate the Bible from Greek and Hebrew into German, the common language of his people. As a result, many more people could study the scriptures themselves, without priestly interpreters.

**Major Groups**

Three major types of Protestantism emerged from the Reformation. The first type consisted of Lutheran and Calvinistic (sometimes called Reformed or Presbyterian) churches, which spread through Germany, the Netherlands, the Scandinavian countries, and

Britain, and later to North America. There were differences between Lutherans and Calvinists, mostly on interpretation and how the church should be governed. But they formed the main movement of Protestantism in Europe and America. As the name suggests, the various branches of the Lutheran Church adopted the views of Martin Luther. Calvinists (Reformed and Presbyterians) see John Calvin as their spiritual ancestor.

The second type of Protestantism emerged in England, under Henry VIII (1491–1547). This is often called the Anglican or Episcopal Church, or the Church of England. Because the English Reformation was fueled more by politics than religion, it was not as critical of Roman Catholic doctrine and worship as the Lutheran or Calvinistic churches. The Church of England combines elements of both Catholicism and Protestantism.

A third group of churches, mostly in Switzerland, Germany, and the Netherlands, tried to carry church reforms much further than either Luther or Calvin had. These smaller and usually unorganized churches became known as the Radical Reformation or left-wing Protestantism. They were highly independent on matters of church government, interpretation of the scriptures, and beliefs. This type of Protestantism was never very strong in Europe or England. In America, however, it grew rapidly into many different kinds of churches, including Baptist.

**Growth and Variety**

The chief forms of early Protestantism spread quickly as explorers discovered new lands and as the German, Dutch, English, Swedish, and others established colonies in North America. Before the Revolutionary War, Anglicans (or Episcopalians) had settled into communities in New England and the South. Reformed (Calvinistic) churches were founded by

During the 1800's, Protestant churches such as this one were prominent in many rural American communities.

the Dutch in New York and New Jersey. Puritans came from England, Presbyterians from Scotland, Lutherans from Germany and Scandinavia, and Mennonites and Moravians from Germany.

In the 1700's, Protestantism in Europe and America was also influenced by the Enlightenment, or Age of Reason. This intellectual and social movement stressed science and rationalism over traditional (and unproven) views. It led people to question the historical accuracy of the Bible and the practices of some sects and marked the beginning of a more liberal Protestant tradition.

During the 1800's, Protestantism in the United States was further transformed. As the country expanded, the number of churches multiplied and many more sects emerged. And the American tradition of free expression encouraged differences of opinion in religious matters. The slavery issue and the Civil War led to further division, and virtually all U.S. Protestant churches were divided into Northern and Southern branches (which were later reunified).

Two well-known and uniquely American denominations arose during this period: the Church of Jesus Christ of Latter-day Saints (Mormon) and the Church of Christ, Scientist (Christian Scientist). The Mormons combine biblical concepts with a more modern interpretation—*The Book of Mormon* (1830), by Joseph Smith (1805–44). Their most famous leader was Brigham Young (1801–77), who settled Salt Lake City, which became the Mormon headquarters. Christian Science is

## PROTESTANT CHURCHES

The official or accepted names of the major Protestant denominations are given here. In many instances there are several kinds of church bodies using the same name in some form.*

Adventist

Baptist

Brethren

Christian Churches
(Disciples of Christ)

Church of Christ, Scientist
(Christian Scientists)

Church of England
(Anglican)

Church of God

Church of the Nazarene

Friends, Society of
(Quakers)

Jehovah's Witnesses

Latter-Day Saints
(Mormons)

Lutheran

Mennonite

Methodist

Moravian

Pentecostal

Presbyterian

Protestant Episcopal

Reformed

Unitarian-Universalist

United Church of Canada

United Church of Christ

*Source: *Yearbook of American and Canadian Churches*, edited by Eileen W. Lindner, National Council of the Churches of Christ in the U.S.A., 475 Riverside Drive, New York, N.Y. 10115, and published by Abingdon Press.

based on a combination of beliefs from the Bible and from the book *Science and Health, with Key to the Scriptures* (1875), by Mary Baker Eddy (1821–1910). Christian Scientists believe that bodily ills can be cured through faith.

Protestantism in the United States has always been more varied (and less organized) than in Europe, and by the first half of the 1900's there were more than 200 American Protestant denominations. Most were based on the Lutheran, Calvinistic, Anglican, and "radical" traditions. In each case there were divisions and regroupings according to language, custom, or belief, which often created conflict inside and outside church circles.

But with variety there has also been growth. In the United States in 1850, only 16 percent of the people were members of Protestant churches. One hundred years later the figure was nearly 60 percent—almost twice the rate of growth for the total population. Today, this figure remains approximately the same.

### Renewal and Reunion

Much of the competition among the various Protestant churches in the 1800's gave way after World War II to the ecumenical movement, which gained momentum when the World Council of Churches was established in 1948. The ecumenical movement sought to overcome the differences that had divided Christians. Many reunions and mergers of Protestant churches took place, notably in the Presbyterian, Methodist, and Congregationalist traditions. For example, in 1957, four originally separate churches (Evangelical Synod, Reformed Church, Congregational Church, and Christian Church) came together to form the United Church of Christ.

The ecumenical movement also led to greater unity between Protestants and Roman Catholics. Vatican II, a Catholic ecumenical gathering held from 1962 to 1965, helped overcome many of the differences that had separated Catholics and Protestants since the Reformation.

More recent developments have included shifts in church membership. Some denominations now have fewer members (Episcopal, Presbyterian, Methodist, and United Church of Christ), while others have more. Churches in this second category include Baptist, Missouri Synod Lutherans, Seventh-Day Adventists, and the Church of the Nazarene.

Other trends include continued political activism. Protestants (Quakers and Mennonites)—among the first to speak out against slavery in the American colonies—were also at the forefront of the civil rights movement 300 years later. A key figure in this movement (the struggle for equal rights for African Americans) was a Baptist minister, Dr. Martin Luther King, Jr.

One denomination, the Episcopal Church in the United States, has taken steps to grant gays and lesbians full religious equality. In August 2003, it made history when it confirmed the election of an openly gay bishop and recognized the blessing of same-sex unions.

At the same time, there has been a greater emphasis on fundamentalist Protestantism, not only in the United States, but in Central and South America. These Protestants reject ecumenism, the theory of evolution, homosexuality, and the scientific view of creation. In the United States, they have also been active in the right wing of the Republican Party.

THE REV. MARTHA M. CRUZ
American Baptist Churches
United Church of Christ

# PROTOZOANS

Protozoans are one-celled organisms with animal-like characteristics. The tens of thousands of species, or kinds, of protozoans have survived for millions of years. By slowly evolving and changing, they have adapted to many different environments. They are found wherever there is water or moisture—in hot springs, in the ice of the Arctic, in deserts, in air, even inside the bodies of animals.

These adaptable creatures have fascinated humans from the time they were first seen in the 1600's. It was then that Dutch scientist Anton van Leeuwenhoek examined a drop of pond water using simple microscopes he had built. The water teemed with activity! Creatures of all different shapes and sizes moved through the water, feeding and multiplying. He called these tiny organisms "animalcules."

Based on their characteristics, the water creatures were originally classified as animals and placed in the animal kingdom within the phylum, or group, Protozoa. However, as the microscopic organisms were studied, some were seen to resemble animals, while others were seen to more closely resemble plants. Today, some scientists suggest that protozoans are neither animals nor plants, so they should be classified with other simple organisms in the kingdom Protista.

## ▶CHARACTERISTICS OF PROTOZOANS

Protozoans have many features that are common to multicellular organisms, such as human beings. But all of these complex features are designed so that the protozoan can live independently with just one cell.

**Size and Shape.** There is considerable variety in the size and shape of protozoans. A few are large enough to see with the naked eye, but most protozoans can be seen only with a microscope. In fact, they are so small they are measured in micrometers. A micrometer is about 1/25,000 inch. Protozoans range from 1 micrometer to 2,000 micrometers in length, with most protozoans measuring about 600 micrometers.

The bodies of some types of protozoans, like the amoeba, are formless. They gently flow from one shape into another as they

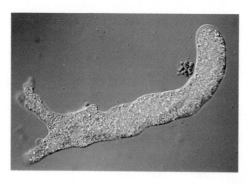

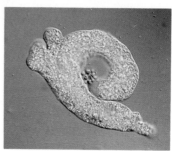

A sarcodine, such as the amoeba (*left*), uses flowing cell extensions to capture food. It slowly reaches out and surrounds the food, then takes it into the cell to digest it (*below*).

move. Other kinds have bodies shaped like barrels, cups, and radiating suns.

**Structure.** While protozoans can appear quite different, they all have similar basic structures. Like other kinds of cells, protozoans have a thin outer covering called a cell membrane. Inside their cells, protozoans have specialized structures surrounded by membranes called organelles, or little organs. Essential functions take place within the organelles that help protozoans move, feed, and reproduce.

The nucleus is an organelle that contains the cell's genes—the basic units of heredity. Genes, which are made of a chemical called DNA (*d*eoxyribo*n*ucleic *a*cid), ensure that every new generation of cells will have characteristics similar to its parents. Because the cell of a protozoan has a distinct nucleus that is separated from other cell parts, protozoans are considered to be more sophisticated organisms than other one-celled creatures, such as bacteria. In fact, **protozoologists**, scientists who study protozoans, have found that the protozoan cell has the same main features as the cells of higher, more advanced animals.

Along with the nucleus, protozoans have a variety of organelles called vacuoles. Vacuoles may help digest food or hold extra water. For example, a specialized water vacuole, called a contractile vacuole, helps some protozoans get rid of extra water. When too much water collects in the cell, the vacuole moves to the outer surface of the cell and squeezes out the water. This helps keep the cell from swelling up and bursting.

**Feeding Habits.** Protozoans hunt, digest, and store food. Most are heterotrophs, that is, they feed on others to get the organic sub-

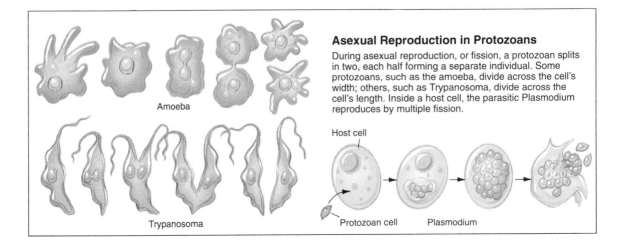

## Asexual Reproduction in Protozoans

During asexual reproduction, or fission, a protozoan splits in two, each half forming a separate individual. Some protozoans, such as the amoeba, divide across the cell's width; others, such as Trypanosoma, divide across the cell's length. Inside a host cell, the parasitic Plasmodium reproduces by multiple fission.

Amoeba

Trypanosoma

Host cell

Protozoan cell

Plasmodium

stances, such as nitrogen and carbon, they need to live. Protozoans actively seek out bacteria and other living creatures as food. They also can control the amounts of water, wastes, and gases in their cell that result from the digestive process.

**Reproduction.** The ability to rapidly multiply and form new cells has played a major role in the long survival of protozoans. They can grow and reproduce using both sexual and asexual reproduction. All protozoans multiply by simple asexual reproduction, or fission. During fission, one cell splits into two similar daughter cells. Some divide across the length of the cell, while others divide across the width. Certain parasitic protozoans—those that live and reproduce only within the cells of other organisms—form many new cells by multiple fission, or division, within the host.

Sexual reproduction also occurs during the life of some protozoans. Sometimes two protozoan cells, each carrying half their normal genetic material, fuse to form a new cell. Other protozoans can exchange some of their genes during mating. The exchange and mixing of genetic material help protozoans evolve and adapt to new conditions.

### ▶TYPES OF PROTOZOANS

As the methods used to study protozoans have improved, many more species have been identified. Today, about 40,000 species are known. The addition of newly discovered kinds of protozoans has altered how they are grouped,

The paramecium is a ciliate.

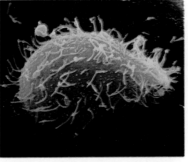

or classified. Some protozoologists have classified them according to how they reproduce or the stages of their life cycles. However, the most common method is to group them according to how they move. Based on locomotion, there are four groups: sarcodines, ciliates, flagellates, and sporozoans.

### Sarcodines

Sarcodines have constantly changing shapes. They move by sending out fingerlike extensions of their cell membranes called pseudopods, or "false feet." These organisms use their pseudopods to find, trap, and eat food. Pseudopods slowly reach out, surround the food, and form a food vacuole around it. Once the food is inside the cell, it is digested.

The amoeba, whose name comes from the Greek word for "change," is an example of a sarcodine. Most amoebas are found in fresh or salt water. Some ocean-living amoebas can make a hard external shell. Through holes in their shells, they send out long, thin pseudopods to trap their food. Shells from these protozoans accumulate on the ocean floor forming chalk deposits. A few types of amoebas produce disease in humans; for example, the protozoan Entamoeba causes intestinal illness and diarrhea.

### Ciliates

Some of the most beautiful and interesting protozoans to watch in pond water are those that are covered with many short hairs, called **cilia**. Some of these protozoans, or ciliates, have clumps of cilia, while others are completely covered with thousands of cilia. The motion of the cilia helps the protozoans move about and capture food.

The paramecium is a well-known member of the ciliates. It is also called the "slipper animal" because of its long, footlike shape.

A colony of flagellates (*Leishmania tropica*).

Cilia cover the paramecium's body. They move like waves beating down and across its body. The short hairs move the paramecium by turning, rotating, and propelling the cell forward. The cilia also sweep food and water into a funnel-like mouth. A membrane at the end of the groove surrounds the food to form a vacuole. The food is digested and waste material is released from a small opening at the end of the cell.

This group of protozoans can also have different sizes of nuclei. The large nucleus is called a macronucleus and the many smaller ones are called micronuclei. Some protozoans exchange their micronuclei during sexual mating. Helpful genetic variations can occur because of this exchange.

Most ciliates can change into tough-walled forms called cysts. They can hide inside these shells when food is scarce or when it is too cold, hot, or dry. These cysts awaken and become active when conditions become better.

## Flagellates

A third group of protozoans move by using long, thin structures called **flagella**. Flagella are like flexible whips that can bend in many directions. Most of these protozoans, known as flagellates, have one or two flagella sticking out of one end of the cell. But some have several.

Although there are flagellates that live free in water, most live in the bodies of plants and animals. They get nutrients by eating other organisms or by absorbing food molecules through their cell membrane. Some flagellates help the organisms they invade. For example, those found in the gut of termites help to digest the wood that the termites eat. Other flagellates may harm the host. Several human diseases, including African sleeping sickness, are caused by parasitic flagellates.

## Sporozoans

Most of these protozoans cannot move. They do not have any specialized structures for movement. A few, which have flagella or pseudopods, are able to move.

All sporozoans are parasites. This small-celled protozoan has special organelles that allow it to invade a host cell. Some sporozoans have to live in two or more hosts to survive and multiply. They reproduce sexually in one host and then reproduce asexually in a second host. The parasite can damage the cells of the host during reproduction. Plasmodium, the organism that causes malaria, is an example. It needs both a human or other vertebrate and a mosquito to complete its life cycle.

## ▶ IMPORTANCE OF PROTOZOANS

While we have concern for the diseases that protozoans can cause, we must remember that most protozoans are harmless and some are helpful. Protozoans contribute to the natural balance that exists in our world.

Enormous numbers of protozoans are important as a source of food for larger animals. Protozoans also help in the exploration for oil. Scientists look-

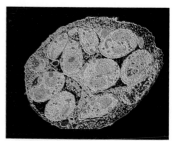
Sporozoans (*Toxoplasma gondii*) infecting a cell.

ing for oil deposits search for certain kinds of protozoan fossils, knowing that oil will be found nearby.

Characteristics that make protozoans deadly make them useful, too. They reproduce rapidly and are easily maintained in the laboratory. Because they reproduce asexually, a large pool of cells with the same genetic makeup can be developed and studied over time. Researchers can use this pool of genetically constant cells to study the hereditary mechanisms of living organisms.

CYNTHIA V. SOMMER
University of Wisconsin at Milwaukee

See also CELLS; DISEASES; MICROBIOLOGY.

# PROVERBS

A proverb is a traditional saying that sums up a situation, passes judgment on a past matter, or recommends a course of action for the future. Some proverbs state a fact, such as "Honesty is the best policy." But most proverbs are metaphorical. When people say, "Don't cry over spilled milk," they are not referring to milk. They are using a metaphor to tell another person not to worry about something that cannot be undone.

Proverbs consist of at least one topic and one comment about that topic. They can have as few as two words: "Money talks"; "Know thyself"; "Time flies." Many proverbs fall into one of several traditional patterns. They may present an alternative ("Sink or swim"; "Do or die"; "Now or never") or an equation ("Seeing is believing"; "Knowledge is power"; "Enough is enough"). Proverbs often make use of contrast: "A good beginning makes a good ending"; "Soon ripe, soon rotten"; "One man's meat is another man's poison." Sometimes the contrast is emphasized by parallel structure: "Out of sight, out of mind"; "Waste not, want not"; "In for a penny, in for a pound." Still another characteristic is the use of rhyme: "An apple a day keeps the doctor away"; "April showers bring May flowers"; "Haste makes waste."

Proverbs are one of the oldest forms of folklore. The earliest writings of ancient civilizations all contain numerous examples. An entire book of the Old Testament is devoted to proverbs. Many proverbs in common use can be traced back to the Bible: "Money is the root of all evil"; "Pride goeth before a fall"; "Physician, heal thyself." Other proverbs can be traced to ancient Latin and Greek literature: "Love is blind"; "Rome was not built in a day"; "Two heads are better than one." Sometimes poets borrow from folklore. Shakespeare used a proverb as the title for one of his plays: "All's well that ends well." Sometimes a poet's proverb is borrowed by the folk. An example is Alexander Pope's "A little learning is a dangerous thing."

Proverbs are found among most of the peoples of the world, but very few have been reported from among the Indians of North and South America. Nowhere is the proverb more common than among the peoples of Africa. Most Africans use proverbs in their everyday conversation. In almost every kind of situation—even in a court of law—an appropriate proverb may be cited for the traditional wisdom and universal truth it contains.

It is often supposed that proverbs are always full of wisdom. In fact, a proverb has been defined as "the wisdom of many and the wit of one." However, a proverb may be found to support almost any view. "Look before you leap" urges caution, but "He who hesitates is lost" urges immediate action. Proverbs fit certain situations; they are not true in all cases.

Many proverbs, like certain folktales, folk songs, and legends, are truly international. The American proverb "A bird in the hand is worth two in the bush" has parallels in most European countries. Typical examples are the Romanian "Better a bird in the hand than a thousand in the garden" and the Portuguese "Better a sparrow in the hand than two flying."

Proverbs often come from stories. "Don't count your chickens before they hatch" is from a folktale in which a girl, daydreaming about what she will do with the money from selling soon-to-be-hatched chickens, drops her basket and breaks all the eggs. Someone who does not know the story behind a proverb may fail to understand the proverb. It is impossible to guess the meaning of the Burmese proverb "I am not angry, but the buffalo's tail is shorter" without knowing its story. The story is about a farmer plowing his field with a water buffalo. At noon he is hungry, but his wife fails to appear with his lunch. After a few more hours he is so hungry that he cuts the tail off the buffalo, cooks it, and eats it. Finally his wife comes with his lunch. She asks him whether he is angry with her. His reply is the proverb.

Proverbs are often used to educate the young. In school, proverbs may be the subjects of themes and essays. They also appear on standard aptitude tests. The student must be able to explain their meaning.

ALAN DUNDES
University of California

**PROVIDENCE.**  See RHODE ISLAND (Cities).

**PROXMIRE, EDWARD WILLIAM.**  See UNITED STATES, CONGRESS OF THE (Profiles: Senators).

**PSORIASIS.**  See DISEASES (Descriptions of Some Diseases).

**PSYCHIATRY.**  See MENTAL ILLNESS.

## PSYCHOLOGY

Do you ever wonder what it means to be smart, to be mentally ill, or to love someone? Do you sometimes wish you could be more successful in school, or at least more interested in what school has to teach you? If you answered yes to any of these questions, you may be interested in psychology.

▶ **WHAT IS PSYCHOLOGY?**

Psychology is the study of the mind (the means by which people learn, think, and feel) and behavior (what people do). Scientists who study psychology are called **psychologists**. Psychologists generally focus on the individual person, either alone or in relation to other people and to the environment. Psychologists are not the only scientists who study people. Two other kinds of scientists who study people are sociologists and cul-

**Psychology examines the mind and studies behavior to better understand such things as what we think and feel; how we learn and change; and why we act the way we do.**

tural anthropologists. They study people in ways that are somewhat different from those of psychologists, however.

**Sociologists** study human relationships and how those relationships are affected by people working and living together. For example, sociologists might be interested in comparing the family lives of people who have jobs with the family lives of people who are unemployed. **Cultural anthropologists** seek insights into various cultures. For example, they might be interested in comparing the customs of people in Mexico City, Mexico, to the customs of people in Tokyo, Japan. What distinguishes psychologists from sociologists and anthropologists, then, is that psychologists focus on individuals, whether by themselves or in relation to the world. All three kinds of scientists have common goals, however.

### ▶ GOALS OF PSYCHOLOGISTS

In their work, psychologists generally have four goals: description, explanation, prediction, and modification (change) of behavior. Psychologists typically begin their work by describing behavior.

**Description** involves observing what, when, and how people think, feel, or act in various kinds of situations. To create accurate descriptions, psychologists must make observations and gather **data** (observable facts).

For example, psychologists might try to describe the kinds of behavior that distinguish children who succeed in school from those who do not. The data the psychologists would seek might then be the observed behavior of the children who are succeeding and of those who are not succeeding. The psychologist would be most interested in the kinds of behavior the successful students show that the unsuccessful ones do not show, as well as the behavior the unsuccessful students show that the successful students do not show. The psychologist would also be interested in explaining why the two groups of students show these different behaviors.

**Explanation** concerns why people think, feel, or act as they do. To explain various data, psychologists propose **theories**, which are organized sets of general ideas or principles that explain a phenomenon. Theories give rise to possible **hypotheses**, which are specific ideas about how to interpret and explain the particular data that are observed.

For example, suppose psychologists observe that successful students pay more attention to their teachers in the classroom than do unsuccessful students. How might the psychologists explain the behavior they have described? One theory might be that the difference between students who pay attention and those who do not is interest in schoolwork. A hypothesis following from this theory would be that the successful students will describe themselves as more interested in schoolwork than will unsuccessful students.

Other theories could also explain the data. Here, as is usually the case in psychology, more than one theory can be used to explain data; the psychologist must figure out which theory is correct. For example, it may be that the successful students pay more attention not because they are interested in what the teacher says, but because they want to get good grades in school. A hypothesis following from this theory would be that the successful students would tell a psychologist that grades matter a lot to them, while unsuccessful students would tell the psychologists that grades do not matter so much. If this hypothesis is correct, one could predict that the successful students are likely to want to get high grades in the future as well.

**Prediction** refers to educated guesses about what will happen in the future. Part of the job of a psychologist is to predict future behavior from past behavior.

For example, one task of psychologists is to try to predict future success in school. Of course, one basis for their predictions is past success: Students who get higher grades in their early school years tend to get higher grades in their later school years. But psychologists can also use other measures to predict future success in school. Often the goal of such prediction is to know when psychological techniques might be used to modify behavior in order to help people obtain greater future success than is currently predicted for them.

**Modification** refers to change. Psychologists help people modify, or change, their behavior when that behavior results in

Psychologists generally try to describe, explain, predict, and modify (change) behavior. For example, to explain why some students do well in school, a psychologist might theorize that such students are more interested, pay closer attention, or want better grades than less successful students.

Tests provide a way of measuring certain characteristics. Achievement tests are used to measure the skills and knowledge a person has acquired through education.

unsatisfactory life outcomes for those people.

For example, a psychologist might work with students to help them achieve higher grades in school or simply to help them pay more attention in class. Psychologists therefore not only assess people but also help them to change so that they can be happier and more successful in their lives. In order to help people change, however, psychologists use a variety of methods in order to figure out exactly what problems the people face.

## ▶ METHODS IN PSYCHOLOGICAL RESEARCH

As scientists, psychologists use a variety of methods to study behavior and the thoughts and feelings that lie behind it. They choose the methods that best fit the problem they wish to study. Five of the main methods they use are tests, surveys, case studies, naturalistic observation, and experiments.

A **test** is a procedure for measuring a characteristic at a particular time and in a particular place. Tests can measure many different kinds of characteristics.

For example, an **ability test** might measure how well you are able to do something, such as remembering people's names or faces. An **achievement test** might measure your knowledge of a school subject, such as mathematics or biology. Ability and achievement tests typically have "right" and "wrong" answers, or at least "better" and "worse" answers, but not all tests do. A **personality test** might measure what you are like as a person—for example, how much you like to be with other people versus how much you prefer to be alone. There are no right or wrong, or better or worse, answers on personality tests, only answers that show a person to be one way or another.

Another method that assesses what people are like is a **survey**. This is a measure of beliefs or opinions. Surveys never have right or wrong answers—they only assess what people think or believe. For example, a psychologist might conduct a survey of people's preferences in political candidates, such as conservative versus liberal candidates, or a survey looking at people's preferences in foods, for example, meat versus fish.

Surveys usually provide a relatively small amount of information about a lot of people. Sometimes, though, psychologists want more detailed information about fewer people. In such instances, a **case study** may be more appropriate. This involves very intensive investigation of just a few individuals, or even of only one individual. Usually, psychologists will investigate a few individuals very intensively in order to be able to draw general conclusions about how these individuals think or feel. Some sources of information psychologists might use as data include autobiographies (first-hand accounts of people's lives), notebooks, and products the people have created. If the people being studied are alive, their activities can also be observed. The psychologists may then apply the conclusions to other people as well. A potential problem with case studies is that because only a small number of individuals are studied, the conclusions may not always apply to other people.

Surveys gather information on people's beliefs or opinions through the use of questionnaires and interviews.

## What is personality?

The word "personality" means the behavioral characteristics of a person. These characteristics include ways of perceiving, thinking, feeling, and acting. When people say that someone has "a lot of personality," they may mean that he or she does things in an outgoing, warm, or charming manner. One person does not actually have more personality than another, but different people do have different personality traits. These traits include shyness, sociability, generosity, hostility, aggressiveness, and a sense of humor.

Some psychologists describe people's behavior in terms of personality types. For example, the Swiss psychologist Carl Jung (1875–1961) defined **extroverts** as people whose interests are directed toward the world around them and toward other people and **introverts** as people who are directed toward their

When taking a Rorschach test, a person describes what he or she "sees" in a series of inkblots. These interpretations are used to assess various aspects of the individual's personality.

own thoughts and feelings. An extrovert might prefer to spend the day meeting new people, while an introvert might prefer to spend the day reading, writing, or listening to music. No one, however, is completely one personality type or the other.

For example, a psychologist interested in what qualities make a composer great might do an intensive case study of Wolfgang Amadeus Mozart, the great classical composer. In doing this case study, the psychologist's goal would be to figure out what it was about Mozart that enabled him to be such a wonderful composer. Another psychologist interested in leadership might study Winston Churchill, the great British prime minister, or perhaps Martin Luther King, Jr., the great American civil rights leader.

Another way to find out what makes a great composer or leader is through **naturalistic observation**. Also known as **field study**, this involves watching and listening to people and recording what they do as they go about their everyday, normal activities. A psychologist interested in leadership might decide to study what makes great leaders by actually observing them at work. For example, the psychologist might carefully observe the day-to-day activities of a general in the military or of a spiritual leader of a religion. The goal of the psychologist would be to understand what it is the leaders do, and how it is they feel and think, that enables

them to succeed as leaders. Such observations, though, are typically only of a small number of individuals; moreover, it is sometimes difficult for psychologists not to let their prior beliefs influence the conclusions they draw.

Another method, that of the **experiment**, remedies these problems. Strictly speaking, an experiment is an investigation in which the experimenter makes a careful and controlled study of cause and effect. For example, an experimenter may study a type of behavior under one set of conditions. The experimenter would then explore how a change in those conditions affects the behavior being studied. The experimenter is able to determine such cause-and-effect relationships by controlling **variables**, which are characteristics that vary across people or situations. An experiment requires that the psychologist be able to control certain variables.

For example, suppose the experimenter has a theory that success in school is a result of student interest. The experimenter hypothesizes that students will learn a lesson better if it is presented in an interesting way than if it is presented in a boring way. In order to study whether student interest causes greater or lesser success in learning, the experimenter needs to be able to control the variable of student interest. The variable that the experimenter controls is called the **independent variable**. How might the experimenter control the independent variable of student interest?

The experimenter might present exactly the same lesson in two different ways. Under one set of conditions, the lesson might be presented in a way that makes it very interesting to students (for example, by showing how the lesson is relevant to the students' lives). Under a second set of conditions, the exact same lesson content might be presented in a way that makes it very boring to students (by showing that the lesson has nothing at all to do with the students' lives). In both sets of conditions, students are tested at the end of the lesson on the material they learned. The test scores are referred to as the **dependent variable**, because their values depend on the values of the independent variable (in this case, student interest).

If the experimenter is correct, then students with interesting presentation of material should learn better than students with boring presentation of material. If the students in the first condition do learn better, the experimenter's hypothesis is confirmed: Levels of student interest (the independent variable) determine students' demonstrated levels of learning (the dependent variable).

Some investigations resemble experiments but are not truly experiments. One example is a **correlational study**, where levels of performance on one variable are related to levels of performance on another variable. No independent variable is controlled, however. For example, suppose a psychologist asks a large group of students how interested each of them is in school and creates a measure of

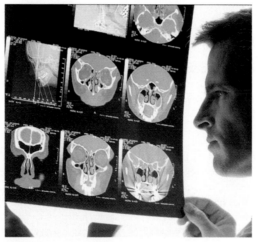

Biological psychologists study biological structures (such as the brain) and processes to understand why a person thinks, feels, and behaves in certain ways.

the students' interest. The experimenter is not varying student interest through an experimental manipulation but is simply recording levels of student interest in an existing course of study. The psychologist also finds out how well the students are doing in school. Suppose that the students who are more interested in school are also doing better in school. Can we conclude that being more interested in school led to better grades?

The answer is no. Why? In this correlational study the experimenter did not have control of the variable of student interest, as in the true experiment described earlier. In this study, it is possible that greater interest led to better grades—but there are also two other sensible interpretations of the data.

A second interpretation is that better grades led to greater interest—that receiving high grades resulted in students being more interested in their schoolwork. A third interpretation is that both interest and school grades were dependent on something else, such as the amount of time students spent on their work. It is possible that students willing to put more time into their schoolwork became more interested in this work and also received higher grades.

When the investigator does not have control of the variable being studied (in this case, student interest), the investigator cannot draw firm conclusions about what caused what. The extent to which an investigator can gain control depends in part upon the specific field of psychology in which he or she works, because in some fields it is easier to gain control than in others.

## ▶ FIELDS OF PSYCHOLOGY

Although psychology can be seen as a single science, it is often divided into various fields of specialization. Many psychologists

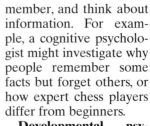

A clinical psychologist helps her patient deal with his fear of heights by working with him on the rooftop of a tall building. If not treated, fears like this can make it difficult for a person to function effectively in everyday situations.

identify themselves as specializing in one (or more) of these fields. Six fields of specialization are biological psychology, clinical psychology, cognitive psychology, developmental psychology, personality psychology, and social psychology. These fields represent only a small number of the many different possibilities for specialization.

**Biological psychology** (also called **psychobiology**) deals with the biological structures and processes that give rise to thoughts, feelings, and behavior. For example, a biological psychologist might study the parts of the brain that are involved in anger or in fear.

**Clinical psychology** deals with the understanding and treatment of abnormal behavior. For example, a clinical psychologist might investigate why some people are afraid of being in very high places, such as at the top of a high building looking down, even if the people are inside the building and thus safe from falling.

**Cognitive psychology** deals with how people perceive (that is, see and hear), learn, re-

member, and think about information. For example, a cognitive psychologist might investigate why people remember some facts but forget others, or how expert chess players differ from beginners.

**Developmental psychology** is the study of how people change, but also remain the same, over time. For example, a developmental psychologist might study how children's use of language changes as the children grow older.

**Personality psychology** focuses on the relatively permanent personal qualities that lead people to behave as they do. For example, a personality psychologist might study why some people are tense and nervous, even in apparently safe settings, while other people are relaxed and hardly ever feel or act nervous.

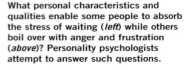

What personal characteristics and qualities enable some people to absorb the stress of waiting (*left*) while others boil over with anger and frustration (*above*)? Personality psychologists attempt to answer such questions.

**Social psychology** is concerned with how people interact with each other, both as individuals and in groups. For example, a social psychologist might study why people are sometimes generous and helpful, while at other times they are not. The social psychologist focuses more on the situations that lead a given person to behave in a particular way, while the personality psychologist focuses more on people who behave in one way or another, regardless of situation.

▶ **HISTORY OF PSYCHOLOGY**

The various fields of specialization within psychology have evolved over time, as has psychology as a whole. Just how has thinking in psychology evolved?

**Origins in Philosophy**

The history of psychological thinking has its origins some two thousand years ago in the work of ancient philosophers (and may go back even farther than that to times for which we do not have written records). Two of the most important philosophers of ancient times were Plato and Aristotle.

Plato (427?–347 B.C.), a philosopher who lived in ancient Greece, believed that the mind resides in the brain. He also believed that much of what we know we are actually born knowing—but we are unaware that we know it. According to Plato, for example, you were born knowing much of the mathematics you learn in school. What schooling helps you do is to become aware of what you already know!

Aristotle (384–322 B.C.), a student of Plato, believed that the mind resides in the heart. Unlike Plato, Aristotle believed that most knowledge is acquired from the environment.

The roots of psychology can be traced back many centuries to several important philosophers (*counterclockwise from left*): René Descartes of France; Plato and his student Aristotle of ancient Greece; Immanuel Kant of Germany; and John Locke of England. The philosophers of ancient Greece were the first to propose ideas on how the mind works.

Structuralists focused on the mind's more immediate experiences. For example, a structuralist would want to know exactly what you see when you look at this picture—tall, multishaped objects rising into the air. The concept of a city would be of no interest.

For example, you are not born knowing mathematics—you learn it in school or at home.

Centuries later, René Descartes (1596–1650), a French philosopher, agreed with Plato that many of the ideas we have (such as about mathematics) are inborn. The English philosopher John Locke (1632–1704), in contrast, agreed with Aristotle that what we learn we learn from the environment. Immanuel Kant (1724–1804), a German philosopher, tried to bring together the two positions, arguing that some categories of knowledge are inborn, but other categories are learned from the environment.

### Schools of Psychology

By the late 1800's, psychology had separated itself from philosophy. People had begun to realize that psychology had its own contribution to make toward our understanding of people, independent of the contribution of philosophy. Psychologists began to invent and then follow different **schools of thought**, or ways of thinking, about psychological phenomena.

The first of these schools was called **structuralism**. Its goal was to understand the structure (relations of elements) of the mind by discovering its basic components or contents. An early structuralist was Wilhelm Wundt (1832–1920), a German psychologist who believed that psychology should focus on immediate and direct experience. For example, suppose you look at a green, grassy lawn. To Wundt, the concepts of lawn and grass would be of no interest. Wundt would want to know

exactly what you see—your basic sensations—for example, narrow, pointed, vertical green objects sticking out of the ground.

Many psychologists came to believe that structuralism had little to do with how people really thought about things in their lives or in the world. For example, when you see a lawn, you think about the grass on it and how nice it looks, not about narrow, pointed, vertical green objects sticking out of the ground.

William James (1842–1910), an American philosopher and psychologist, helped found a school of thought called **functionalism**, which dealt with what people do and why they do it. For example, the functionalist might be concerned with why people plant and maintain lawns in the first place, rather than with exactly what people see when they look at a lawn.

An outgrowth of functionalism was a school of thought called **pragmatism**, whose followers believed that knowledge is important only to the extent that it is useful. For example, John Dewey (1859–1952), an American philosopher, educator, and psychologist, studied how psychology can be applied to improving education for children. Dewey suggested, for example, that children will learn best if they are genuinely interested in what they learn. He believed, therefore, that schools should make what they teach interesting to their students.

American psychologist Edwin Guthrie (1886–1959), like John Dewey, was interested in learning. Guthrie was a believer in **associationism**, which held that learning occurs when two observed events become associated in people's minds because the events occur closely together in time. For example, if every time you wear a certain hat people compliment you, eventually you will learn that wearing that hat leads to compliments—you have associated that particular hat with the compliments.

*Far left:* Cognitivists try to understand human behavior by studying how people think. For example, does the mind of a stock trader—typically bombarded by thousands of rapid-fire pieces of information—process this information a piece at a time? Or are many pieces of information processed all at once?

*Left:* The work of American psychologist B. F. Skinner greatly influenced the school of thought known as behaviorism.

behaviorist, John Watson (1878–1958), believed that he could take any baby and turn the baby into whatever he wanted—such as a lawyer, a doctor, a dancer, or even a thief— just by controlling the child's environment throughout the child's development. Later, American psychologist B. F. Skinner (1904– 90) proposed what he called the experimental analysis of behavior. He suggested that all of our learning and thinking could be understood in terms of how we respond to the rewards and punishments of the environment in which we live.

Today many psychologists interested in learning and thinking have rejected behaviorism in favor of **cognitivism**, which is the belief that much of human behavior can be understood in terms of how people think. Cognitivists such as American social scientist Herbert Simon (1916–    ) and English psychologist Donald Broadbent (1926–88) suggested that in some ways people function much like computers, processing one piece of information after another, more flexibly but not nearly as fast as does a computer. Other cognitivists, such as American psychologist David Rumelhart (1942–    ), have suggested that people process a lot of information all at once, rather than one piece after another.

At the same time that some psychologists have focused on the cognitive and rational side of the human mind, others have focused more on the emo-

Not everyone agreed with Guthrie. Edward Lee Thorndike (1874–1949), an American psychologist, suggested that learning occurs not as a result of two things occurring closely together in time but, rather, as a result of reward. According to Thorndike, you learn to associate the hat with compliments not because the compliments occur right after you put on the hat but because you feel rewarded when you receive the compliments.

Some psychologists carried the basic ideas of associationism to an extreme. A school of thought that grew out of associationism, known as **behaviorism**, suggested that psychologists should focus only on observable behavior. Mental activities such as thinking or feeling were not viewed as relevant to psychology because they could not be observed.

Behaviorists were (and continue to be) very interested in how the environment could be controlled in order to produce certain kinds of behavior. For example, an early American

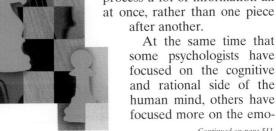

*Continued on page 511*

## CONTEMPORARY THEORY AND RESEARCH IN PSYCHOLOGY

At the beginning of this article, a number of questions were raised—exactly the types of questions that psychologists seek to answer. These questions provided just a sample of the whole range of questions psychologists consider. Let us return to those questions at the beginning of the article and look at some of the work psychologists are doing today to answer them.

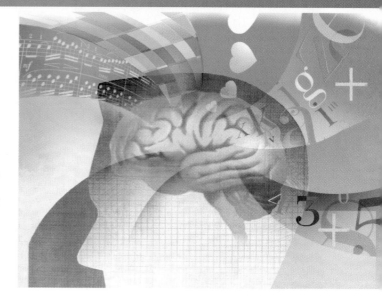

### What Does It Mean to Be Smart?

Intelligence is usually defined as the ability to adapt to the environment and to changes in it. But what, exactly, is intelligence, and how can it be measured?

At the beginning of the 1900's, French psychologist Alfred Binet was asked to create a test of intelligence that would distinguish between those children who were unsuccessful in school because they were genuinely very low in intelligence and those children who were unsuccessful because they showed problems in their social behavior. Binet and his collaborator, psychologist Theodore Simon, devised such a test, which measured children's word knowledge, their ability to perform basic arithmetical operations, and their ability to see similarities and differences between words and pictures. Binet and Simon's test came to be referred to as an **intelligence test**.

Theories of intelligence from the early 1900's, and from more recent times as well, emphasize the kinds of abilities Binet and Simon tested as central to intelligence. For example, Charles Spearman, an English psychologist, viewed the ability to see the relations (similarities and differences) between words and pictures as one important aspect of intelligence. American psychologist Louis Thurstone believed that a wider range of abilities, including word knowledge, number skills, memory, and the ability to imagine objects rotating in one's head, was also important to intelligence.

Today psychologists are suggesting even wider ranges of abilities as important to intelligence. For example, Howard Gardner, an American psychologist and neurologist, has suggested

*Above:* Some psychologists believe that artistic and creative abilities (such as musical skills), along with practical abilities, are important to intelligence.

*Right:* Severe depression—marked by feelings of overwhelming sadness, helplessness, hopelessness, and a lack of enthusiasm—is an example of mental illness.

Severely depressed people may be treated with psychotherapy. Some psychotherapy techniques use discussion to help people recover from their problems.

the importance of bodily movement abilities such as those shown by athletes or dancers and of musical abilities such as those shown by orchestra musicians as important to intelligence. Robert Sternberg, an American psychologist and educator, has suggested that creative abilities (the abilities involved in producing new and useful ideas) as well as practical abilities (the abilities involved in getting along with other people and in getting one's work done) are important to intelligence. Moreover, he and his colleagues have shown that when students are taught in school in a way that fits well with their abilities, they learn more than when they are taught in a way that does not fit well. Current work in psychology, therefore, is making progress in helping teachers solve the problem of how best to support children's learning in school settings.

### What Does It Mean to Be Mentally Ill?

People who are mentally ill are unable to function effectively in their daily lives. In the past, there was little we could do for such people. Today, as psychologists come to understand mental illness more completely, they are better able to recognize and treat it.

An example of a mental illness is **major depression**. All of us are depressed from time to time. But people suffering from major depression are severely depressed much or even all of the time. They tend to think little of themselves, have trouble going to sleep or getting up in the morning, and expect things to go badly for them. Often, they lose interest in eating as well as in other activities that form important parts of almost everyone's day.

There are different theories of depression. These theories are not necessarily in conflict—depression may well have multiple causes. For example, some psychodynamic psychologists suggest that depression can start with our feeling as though we have lost the love of someone important to us, perhaps because the person died or perhaps because the person has simply ceased to love us. Some behaviorist psychologists believe that depressed people do not get enough rewards in their lives or get too many punishments. And some cognitively oriented psychologists suggest that depressed people tend to think in distorted ways—for example, they exaggerate their faults and fail to recognize their strengths.

Can anything be done to help people who are depressed? **Psychotherapy**—interventions that use the principles of psychology to help people feel better—has been shown to be effective in aiding people with depression. For example, a psychotherapist might help people to overcome the sense of loss of love, or to find ways of producing more rewards in their lives, or to recognize their strengths as well as their failings. Moreover, drug therapy, especially when it is used in addition to psycho-therapy, has been found to be effective in treating people who are depressed. In short, psychotherapists today can help people over-come depression and

other mental illnesses that once might have ruined years of these people's lives.

### What Does It Mean to Love Someone?

Psychology helps us understand not only things that make people unhappy but also

Love may be difficult to define with words, but it is easy to recognize the intimate connection, even after many years, between two people in love.

things that make people happy. One such thing is love. Some recent work is providing us with a new understanding of what love is.

For example, Robert Sternberg has proposed that three major components of love are intimacy—how close we feel to someone, how well we communicate with the person, how comfortable we are with the person, and how much we trust the person; passion—how excited we feel about a person; and commitment—the extent to which we view our love for a person as something that will last forever. Different kinds of love arise from different combinations of these components.

Another theory of love suggests that there are three different ways of loving, in particular, and that which way we love will depend on experiences we have as infants. Psychologists Phillip Shaver and Cynthia Hazan have argued that some people, when they love, tend generally to feel happy and secure in the love they give and receive. Other people tend to be avoidant—they always seem to be trying to create distance, or a sense of separation, between themselves and the people

they love. Still other people never feel as though they receive enough love—they are always afraid the love they receive will not be enough, or even that they will lose the person they love.

According to Shaver and Hazan, these different patterns of loving start in infancy, when, according to Mary Ainsworth, a well-known American developmental psychologist, infants attach to their mothers in one of these three ways. In other words, Shaver and Hazan have evidence to suggest that the kind of relationship the infant forms with the mother will determine the kind of loving relationship the person later forms as an adult.

### What Makes Students Interested in Schoolwork?

What should parents and teachers do if they would like to help children become interested in their schoolwork? There have been a variety of answers to this question. For example, behaviorally oriented psychologists who emphasize the role of reward might suggest the importance of grades or of various kinds of prizes to keep students interested and performing well. Or parents might give their children gifts to reward the children's good performance.

Research by psychologists, including Americans Mark Lepper and Edward Deci, however, suggests that concrete rewards such as grades, prizes, and gifts may actually decrease children's interest in their schoolwork. The result of such rewards may be that children focus on their work not for its own sake but merely for the sake of the rewards. No one is suggesting that rewards never be used. But Lepper and Deci, like John Dewey many years before them, have realized that the best way to interest children in anything is to make it exciting.

*Left:* Sigmund Freud founded the school of psychoanalysis. He suggested that early childhood experiences have a great influence on how well-adjusted and happy people are as adults.

*Right:* According to humanistic psychology, people can achieve personal excellence and reach their full potential if they set their minds to it.

tional and sometimes less rational side. For example, the **psychodynamic** school of thought, formulated by Sigmund Freud (1856–1939), an Austrian physician and the founder of psychoanalysis, suggested that very early childhood experiences, over which people have almost no control, contribute greatly to people's happiness and adjustment later in their lives. Freud suggested a series of stages children go through early in their development that later lead them either to be better or more poorly adjusted in their lives. Freud also suggested that much of the thinking we do is **unconscious**—below our level of awareness. He further believed that

## SOME FIELDS OF PSYCHOLOGY

**Academic psychologist**—works in a college or university teaching and doing research.

**Clinical psychologist**—diagnoses and treats patients for psychological problems.

**Consumer psychologist**—helps determine consumer preferences in products and services.

**Human-factors psychologist**—works in organizations to design machines that are convenient and comfortable for people to use.

**Industrial/organizational psychologist**—works in business or industry to help in hiring and placement and in creating a good work environment.

**Military psychologist**—works in the armed forces to help in selection, placement, and counseling.

**School psychologist**—works in schools to help diagnose and correct students' problems.

we use this unconscious thinking to defend ourselves against unwanted thoughts. Freud actually proposed a specific list of mechanisms we use to defend ourselves against such thoughts. For example, **repression** is a defense mechanism whereby we hold troubling thoughts at an unconscious level, preventing them from becoming conscious so that we will not be troubled by them.

Some psychologists believed that Freud placed too much emphasis on unconscious thinking and also the extent to which we lack control of our own lives. According to the **humanistic** school of psychology, represented by psychologists such as Americans Carl Rogers (1902–87) and Abraham Maslow (1908–70), most thinking is conscious. Humanistic psychologists emphasize mental well-being and believe that people can take control of their lives and reach their full potential if only they set their minds to it.

All of these different schools of thought have led to the discipline of psychology as it exists today.

ROBERT J. STERNBERG
IBM Professor of Psychology and Education
Yale University

See also ARISTOTLE; BODY, HUMAN; BRAIN; CHILD DEVELOPMENT; DESCARTES, RENÉ; DEWEY, JOHN; FREUD, SIGMUND; INTELLIGENCE; JUNG, CARL; KANT, IMMANUEL; LEARNING; PLATO; TESTS AND TEST TAKING.

# PUBLIC HEALTH

Public health is the measurement, improvement, and maintenance of a community's health by people who use specialized scientific methods, skills, and beliefs to control and prevent disease. Public health programs are usually funded and administered by government agencies. These agencies develop special programs for people at high risk for disease, such as the elderly, persons with chronic disease, disability, or addiction, and those living in poverty.

In a manner similar to how a medical doctor diagnoses and treats a patient, a public health agency also diagnoses and treats a community. First, an agency performs an assessment by asking careful questions of and about those people possibly affected by a particular disease. After deciding which people or groups may be at risk, the agency makes estimates of how much actual risk of disease or disability there is. The agency uses this information to design and implement preventive solutions tailored to each unique community. For example, during an infectious disease outbreak, a public health agency responds by investigating its cause and the likelihood of further spread of disease. It then develops and coordinates a program to treat all infected people as well as protect those not infected. After the emergency is over, the agency formulates a plan to prevent future outbreaks.

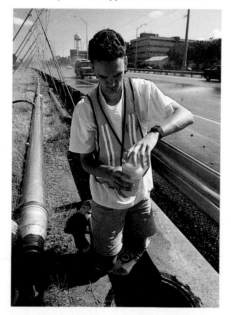

Testing runoff for pollutants is one of the ways a local health department makes sure a community's water supplies remain clean.

▶ THE HISTORY OF PUBLIC HEALTH

Early in civilization, people began to realize that some members of the community who lived in less crowded spaces with clean air, clean water, and clean food were often healthier than others less fortunate. These observations motivated many societies to develop ways to improve their people's health. Examples of this include the Jewish laws of hygiene, the Greek belief in the link between human disease and the character of the air, water, and dwelling, and the Romans' construction of sewage systems and aqueducts.

These lessons were forgotten, though, during the Middle Ages. Many people lived with their cattle and other livestock crowded into walled cities. These conditions resulted in water polluted with animal and human excrement and streets teeming with rats and other vermin. Many diseases, like the plague, spread freely among the people who lived there.

During the 1800's, scientific studies called attention to the relationship between an unclean environment and disease and led to new ideas about public health. In 1798, an English doctor named Edward Jenner used careful observation and analysis to develop and test an effective vaccine to prevent smallpox. In the mid-1800's, another British doctor, John Snow, scientifically studied epidemics of diseases to understand a deadly outbreak of disease in London and was able to identify its cause. Using meticulous observation, Dr. Snow linked the cholera outbreaks with certain community water pumps and reported his findings to the city's leaders.

It was not long before governments began to take on the responsibility of protecting the public's health. The rapidly growing population in the United States began to cause serious problems in cities. Citizen pressure caused many city governments to begin to improve health conditions of their inhabitants. The first city to establish a board of health was New York City in 1866.

▶ THE FUNCTIONS OF PUBLIC HEALTH

The basic functions of public health are the study, surveillance, control, and prevention of diseases. These functions are carried out by public health care workers and agencies when they are dealing with a variety of problems. For example, when dealing with a communicable disease such as AIDS, the result of their work includes understanding how the AIDS virus makes people ill, developing systems to report when a person is diagnosed with AIDS, creating consensus among doctors about the most effective way to treat patients infected with the AIDS virus, and inspecting the national supply of donated blood to ensure that it is not contaminated. Other types of public health issues for which these functions are used include chronic illnesses, special high risk populations, behavioral public health issues, and environmental concerns.

The public health system has a special function during an outbreak of disease that affects a large number of people, also called an epidemic. The public health system works to protect the community by ensuring that nurses, doctors, and public health officials report all cases of certain diseases to the health department, including whooping cough, diphtheria, hepatitis, measles, poliomyelitis, tetanus, and AIDS. Rapid reporting helps identify new outbreaks of disease in the community. All local cases are reported to the state and eventually to the United States Public Health Service (PHS). During an epidemic, the local health department can ask the state and in turn the PHS for extra help with the problem.

▶ **THE UNITED STATES PUBLIC HEALTH SERVICE (PHS)**

The PHS supervises all federal public health programs and collaborates with state and local public health departments, voluntary agencies, and private health foundations. In addition to helping coordinate various services, the PHS also promotes research, provides aid to medical education programs, and controls the spread of communicable diseases on a national level. The PHS pays for scientists to perform research in their laboratories and at medical schools, universities, and pharmaceutical companies. The PHS coordinates

The prevention of communicable diseases is one of the major concerns of public health agencies. Organized efforts to combat contagious diseases include vaccinating people at risk (*left*) and publishing educational materials (*below*).

research efforts. For example, one of its divisions, the Food and Drug Administration, sponsors a nationwide program to improve communication and cooperation among scientists and physicians who test new cancer drugs. PHS makes the education of physicians, dentists, nurses, and other health workers possible by supplying schools and colleges with grants to build laboratories and classrooms and improve training. Loans to help students pay for their education also come from PHS. PHS studies the country's future

Scientists at the U.S. Centers for Disease Control work as "disease detectives" to identify the dangerous viruses that cause deadly outbreaks around the world.

# The United States Public Health Service

The United States Public Health Service (PHS) was first established as the Marine Hospital Service in 1798. PHS is a division of the Department of Health and Human Services and has eight divisions and eleven service program offices.

| PHS DIVISIONS | FUNCTIONS |
|---|---|
| Agency for Health Care Policy and Research (AHCPR) | Produces and distributes information on the quality of health care, its effectiveness, and cost. |
| Agency for Toxic Substances and Disease Registry (ATSDR) | Reduces or eliminates illness, disability, and death from toxic substances. |
| Centers for Disease Control and Prevention (CDC) | Prevents disease, disability, and premature death, while promoting healthy lifestyles. |
| Food and Drug Administration (FDA) | Studies, regulates, and monitors products such as foods, drugs, cosmetics, and medical devices and the industries that produce them. |
| Health Resources and Services Administration (HRSA) | Guides health services; acts as a resource to improve access, distribution, quality, and cost of care. |
| Indian Health Service (IHS) | Provides health services for Native Americans, including the Inuit (Eskimos) of Alaska. |
| National Institutes of Health (NIH) | Performs biomedical research. |
| Substance Abuse and Mental Health Services Administration (SAMHSA) | Reduces the occurrence of mental health disorders and substance addictions; improves treatment methods for them. |

| SERVICE PROGRAM OFFICES | FUNCTIONS |
|---|---|
| Commissioned Corps of the Public Health Service | Acts as a mobile health corps. |
| Disease Prevention, Health Promotion, Health Planning and Evaluation | Improves disease prevention and health promotion efforts. |
| Emergency Preparedness | Coordinates emergency preparedness, response to emergencies, and recovery activities. |
| HIV/AIDS Policy | Assists the HIV/AIDS policy planning process. |
| International and Refugee Health | Creates and administers the health policy for refugee and alien health care. |
| Minority Health | Supplies technical assistance to minority health projects; improves public awareness of them. |
| Population Affairs | Acts as a resource on population and reproductive health issues; supplies policy advice on issues. |
| President's Council on Physical Fitness and Sports | Promotes exercise and sports to improve physical fitness and health. |
| Research Integrity | Investigates and resolves allegations of research misconduct in PHS-funded research programs. |
| Surgeon General | Manages the PHS Commissioned Corps. |
| Women's Health | Strives to improve the health of women. |

needs for health care workers so that resources for institutions and individuals can be made available.

The PHS prevents many diseases from entering the country by checking for animals or people infected with diseases such as smallpox, yellow fever, cholera, and plague. Quarantine officers do this by examining potential visitors before arrival in the United States as well as at all United States ports of entry.

## THE METHODS AND TECHNIQUES OF PUBLIC HEALTH

Public health workers use many different methods and techniques to identify, monitor, understand, treat, and prevent health problems. To provide public health care, health workers use such sciences as biostatistics, epidemiology, and nutrition. Public health care also includes the use of policy and management methods to improve the system of health care delivery and to decrease public health risks. All of these methods are used to develop areas of service such as nutrition, which helps the community as a whole, and maternal and child health, which helps a particular part of the population. Below are some methods and techniques and areas of service with descriptions of how they are used to provide public health care to a community.

**Biostatistics**—an essential tool that scientists and public health workers use to understand subtle relationships between the causes and outcomes of health problems.

**Environmental Health**—works to detect and prevent adverse health effects from chemical and physical factors in work and community settings.

**Epidemiology**—studies the frequency and distribution of disease to understand what causes it.

**Maternal and Child Health**—concentrates on ways to improve the health of mothers and children.

**Molecular and Cellular Toxicology**—examines the effects of environmental chemicals on the health of human beings.

**Nutrition**—works to improve nutrition and therefore health by understanding the influence of diet on health and works to educate researchers, practitioners, and the public.

**Population and International Health**—develops methods to help poor countries improve the health of their people despite few resources.

**Social and Behavioral Sciences**—attempts to understand challenges to the health of populations and to develop programs to improve health and quality of life.

**Tropical Public Health**—performs research on the biological aspects of diseases caused by tuberculosis and parasites such as protozoans and helminths (worms). It also works to develop vaccines and improve tools for diagnosis and disease control.

Doctors and inspectors check all travelers for proof of proper vaccination and signs of communicable disease. They inspect imported animals and animal products and have the authority to quarantine any person, animal, or product considered infected.

### ▶ THE WORLD HEALTH ORGANIZATION (WHO)

The international relief effort initiated after World War II ultimately led to the formation of the World Health Organization (WHO) of the United Nations in 1948. Today, the WHO is the largest coordinating international health agency and continues to work on health problems common to many countries. For example, the WHO regularly sets up large-scale campaigns to eradicate the mosquitoes in tropical areas that carry diseases such as malaria, yellow fever, and yaws. The global eradication of smallpox, the last case of which was diagnosed in Somalia in 1977, is the greatest success of the international programs of this sort.

Insecticides are sprayed on nesting sites to rid tropical areas of disease-carrying mosquitoes.

The WHO continues to monitor new epidemics by warning all the world's governments about outbreaks of serious diseases such as plague, cholera, typhus, influenza, poliomyelitis, Ebola, and the human immuno-deficiency virus (HIV). Lastly, the WHO also conducts health care worker education and research programs and helps many countries solve sanitation, nutritional, and other health problems in their communities.

### ▶ PUBLIC HEALTH IS PREVENTION

Many people do not realize the importance and scope of public health services because the outcomes are often hidden. Public health services prevent major disasters: epidemics, polluted waters, and unsafe food, to name a few. Ignoring the importance of good health is costly. The AIDS epidemic emerged as a major public health threat to all people in the

1980's, as did the re-emergence of syphilis and tuberculosis.

Good health is not just the responsibility of the public health system, a network of hardworking and dedicated professionals including physicians, dentists, nurses, and public health workers. Good health is the responsibility of all individuals. By keeping public health recommendations in mind, now more than ever, people can protect their health and the health of others in their community.

CHRISTOPHER W. SHANAHAN M.D., M.P.H.
Assistant Professor of Medicine
School of Medicine, Boston University

**PUBLICITY.** See PUBLIC RELATIONS.

# PUBLIC LANDS

In 1780 the Second Continental Congress recommended that certain states give up their western lands to the national government. Massachusetts, Connecticut, New York, North and South Carolina, Virginia, and Georgia all claimed vast stretches of land between the Appalachian Mountains and the Mississippi River. Most of them required, as a condition for giving up their claims, that the lands be sold to pay off the Revolutionary War debt.

In this way, between 1781 and 1802, the "public domain" was created. It originally included nearly four-fifths of the nation's area. These public lands were added to as the years went by. Some were added by treaties of purchase or by treaties ending wars, others by annexation or territorial division. Finally, they reached to the Pacific Coast and Alaska. Today the federal government owns about 771 million acres (312 million hectares) of public lands, including those that have been set aside for national parks and forests, for recreation, and for other special purposes.

### Early Methods of Sale and Survey

The western lands were needed to produce revenue. Also, many veterans of the Revolutionary War looked to these lands for settlement. To meet these pressures, the national government passed the Ordinance of 1785. This ordinance established a system of rectangular survey that later was used in Canada and in many other countries. Townships 6 miles square were divided into 36 sections, each 1 mile square, or 640 acres, in area.

The ordinance required that all Native American claims to the lands be settled before they were surveyed. Lands were sold chiefly by auction to the highest bidder. This type of sale tended to attract speculators with ready cash, who hoped to make a profit by reselling small tracts of land. But this type of public land sale was not very successful.

Not until the passage of the Harrison Act in 1800 were actual settlers favored. By this act, local land offices were set up, purchases could be made on liberal credit payments, and half-sections (320 acres) were to be surveyed and sold. However, by an act of 1820 the credit system was abolished. From this time on, lands were to be surveyed in parcels as small as half-quarter sections (80 acres). These "eighties" sold at the minimum price of $1.25 per acre.

### Cheap Land for Settlers

In the 1830's President Andrew Jackson's administration ushered in an even cheaper land program. At last settlers were given a preference (or pre-emption) in buying a quarter-section before the auction and at the minimum price. This system was made permanent in 1841 and was a decided victory for settlers. In 1832 Congress agreed to survey and sell parcels as small as 40 acres. These were known as "forties" or "quarter-quarters." Swamplands, lands in distant territories, lands that had been on the market for some time, and other special lands were sold for even less than the minimum price. Some lands were even given to settlers who agreed to settle and improve them.

### Free Land and Land Grants

Not until the Homestead Act of 1862 was the system of free land realized. Under its terms any settler was given title to the land who agreed to live on a tract not larger than a quarter-section and to improve it for a period of five years. This act has been called one of history's great democratic measures. Nevertheless, settlers had a difficult time establishing homesteads on the Great Plains.

The government aided the building of western communities in many other ways. The Ordinance of 1785 established the system of giving land grants for aiding public schools and universities. Section 16 of every township was set aside for public schools. In 1848 this amount was doubled. Beginning in 1850 many western railroads were given land grants. The railroads then resold this land to settlers. Under the Morrill Act of 1862 public lands for the founding of agricultural and mechanical arts colleges (known as land-grant colleges) were given to each state according to its population.

### Exploitation

After the Civil War the public lands were actually thrown wide open to exploitation. The Mining Act of 1866 opened all of the mining country to development, subject only to the local mining laws and regulations. In much the same way, Texas cattlemen were allowed to drive their herds northward and graze the lands of the Great Plains. This brought about a clash with the homesteaders who were trying to settle that region. Elsewhere, on the public domain of Wisconsin, Minnesota, and the Far West, lumber companies were cutting down valuable timber.

Gradually public opinion became aroused. In 1891 Congress passed the General Revision Act. It did away with the sale of lands by auction and with the pre-emption laws. Only the Homestead Act remained as the means of obtaining public lands.

### Conservation and a Permanent Public Domain

From 1891 to the present day a national program of conserving the public lands has been developed. Many millions of acres of lands have actually been bought back by the government for the purpose of saving the nation's valuable forests and park lands, for developing electric power, for flood control, and for recreation.

Finally, in 1934 and 1935, the remaining public lands (except in Alaska) were closed to homesteading by executive order of President Franklin D. Roosevelt. They remained open to the staking of mining claims and for public hunting, fishing, camping, and other recreation. These lands are known as the national land reserve.

The United States has been singularly generous in encouraging the private enterprise of its citizens by grants of cheap or free lands. In the public domain as well, there still exists a rich heritage for the future.

ROY M. ROBBINS
Municipal University of Omaha

See also TERRITORIAL EXPANSION OF THE UNITED STATES; WESTWARD MOVEMENT.

---

**PUBLIC OPINION POLLS.** See OPINION POLLS.

# PUBLIC RELATIONS

When the founders of the United States wrote the Declaration of Independence, they said that a "decent respect" for the opinion of people everywhere required the American colonies to tell the world why they were freeing themselves of British rule. The American leaders believed that their cause could not win unless they had the confidence of the people of other countries.

Public relations, too, tries to win the confidence and goodwill of people. No company, government agency, school, hospital, or other institution can flourish if it pays no attention to what the people think of it. Public relations is the activity of giving a business or other organization information about how its actions might affect public opinion—or how public opinion might affect its actions. It is also the job of the public relations officer to tell the public about a company's activities, plans, or ideas. This is necessary because people are likely to have more confidence in a company if they know something about it.

There is not just one big public whose opinion a company has to worry about if it is to survive and grow. Only a few organizations, such as a national government, are so

---

**What is the difference between public relations and advertising?**

Advertising tries to gain public confidence and goodwill so that people will buy a company's products or services. Public relations aims at getting the public to understand and approve of a company and its actions. In a sense, public relations may be thought of as a type of advertising—institutional advertising—which tries to make an important point about a company rather than about a product.

large that all the public has some opinion about their actions. Most companies and organizations have to think about the opinions of smaller groups—their customers, for instance, or their workers or their shareholders. A company must also have the trust and goodwill of its neighbors in the places where it has factories and offices. The company must be on good terms with the government, because every business can be seriously affected by government laws or regulations.

Gaining the confidence of others requires, first of all, thoughtfulness about other people's beliefs, interests, and feelings. Public relations begins by planning one's actions so as to respect the rights and beliefs of other people. Unless a public relations program takes these things into account, it can do little to help a company. Not all the money in the world, nor the most skillful writers or speakers, can make a company look as if it cares about other people if the company really does not care. Most companies, therefore, consider how any action, such as moving to a new location or buying another business, will affect public opinion. Having made a decision, the company wants everyone to understand the decision and the reasons it was made.

Most large companies have a public relations department, which tells the public about the company's plans and activities. The department is made up of writers, editors, photographic and picture experts, and researchers.

There are many ways to reveal a company's activities and character. A very effective one is through speeches by officials of the company before organizations such as the local chamber of commerce and various clubs. The speeches are usually reported in the newspapers and are often reprinted for distribution to government officials, educators, journalists, and others who might be interested in the company's views. Printed pamphlets and booklets, including the company magazine and the annual report of the management to the shareholders, also help inform the public about a company. Motion-picture films are often used to show people something about a company. A company may also, as a public service, undertake projects not directly connected with its business, to help make society better.

Besides using their own public relations staffs, many companies hire independent public relations firms, which work for several clients at once. Specially trained outsiders often see trends or problems that people inside a company might miss because they are too close to the situation.

Anyone who plans to do public relations work should get as broad an education as possible. In addition to a college education, work in some area of the communications field—on a newspaper or with a broadcasting station—is useful for the future public relations officer.

ARTHUR B. TOURTELLOT
Formerly, Earl Newsom & Company
See also ADVERTISING.

---

**PUBLIC SCHOOLS.** See SCHOOLS; EDUCATION.

## PUBLIC SPEAKING

The term "public speaking" defines itself. It is the act of making a speech in public. The purpose of good public speaking is to add to the information and knowledge of listeners or to lead them to think or do as the speaker advises. Speechmaking is vital to the work of such people as the clergy, lawyers, and public officials. Public speaking also is important for many others. Business people, club members, schoolteachers, and boys and girls—these are but a few of those who use public speaking more and more each year.

Public speaking used to be called oratory.

Oratory, which dates back to ancient Greece and Rome, is one of the oldest regular studies in Western civilization. Since those early times almost every generation of civilized people has given time to the study of the rules, methods, and practice of public speaking. For many centuries in Europe and then in the United States, pupils learned to make speeches in Latin. It was thought that if they could make good speeches in Latin, they certainly could do so in their native tongue.

Through the ages, teachers and writers of books on speaking have agreed that to be a good speaker, a person needs natural ability, teaching, and practice. Some people are naturally better speakers than others. But most people can become fairly good speakers. They can improve their ability by studying and practicing the principles of good speechmaking and by intelligently following the example of good speakers.

People who make public speeches believe that they have a message. They have something worth saying, and there is a group of people who ought to hear the message and take the advice. That means that public speakers must know three basic things: (1) They must know (better than most people do) the subject on which they will speak. (2) They must know, as nearly as possible, their audience's needs, habits, wishes, and ways of thinking. (3) They must know how to build their speeches so that the speeches will have the greatest effect on the audience.

Public speakers will not think of themselves, therefore, as putting on shows of which they are authors, heroes, and leading actors. They should think of themselves, instead, as bringing people and valuable ideas together so that the people will grasp useful ideas correctly.

## ▶ PREPARING A SPEECH

In building their speeches, good speakers keep three very important matters in mind. First, they make their ideas as easy as possible for the audience to understand. Second, they make themselves seem like persons whose advice can be trusted. Third, they make their listeners want to understand, believe, or do what they propose.

If the ideas are going to be clear and understandable, a speech must be orderly. To make the speech orderly, a speaker usually sees that it has a real beginning, middle, and end. More formally, the parts of a speech are the **introduction, body,** and **conclusion.**

A lively, friendly introduction gets the attention and interest of listeners and leads to the **main idea.** The body of a speech gives the main ideas in good, clear, declarative sentences. Each idea is filled out with various kinds of **explaining and supporting material.** The most useful kinds of material with which to explain or support ideas are (1) facts and information, (2) examples, (3) comparisons and contrasts, and (4) opinions of authorities. The conclusion restates the main ideas and urges listeners to follow a certain line of action or thought.

To keep the plans of speeches clearly in mind, speakers find it useful to sketch out the body of each speech in a kind of outline. This usually consists of writing the main idea out in a declarative sentence and then noting the explaining and supporting material under the main idea. Here is an example of a plan:

**Main idea:** The gymnasium in our school is too small.

**Facts:** It was intended for 50 students per period.
Each class now has almost 100.
At basketball games only half the fans can get seats.

**Example:** In my class yesterday half of us had to sit doing nothing while the others tumbled on the mats.

**Comparison and Contrast:** It is like buses at rush hour—standing room only.
East Junior High has fewer students than our school but twice as much gymnasium space.

**Opinion of authority:** Our physical training teacher says that in our gymnasium he cannot give us the work we ought to have.

If speeches are to be clear, they must be orderly. And the ideas must be expressed in language that is familiar to the listeners and is full of meaning for them. Speakers choose definite words instead of vague words, lively words instead of weak words. They make their sentences simple and straightforward, not fancy. They pay attention to their listeners' needs, not to their own performance.

## ▶ DELIVERING A SPEECH

Giving a speech aloud before an audience is called delivery. Good speakers are easy to hear. Their pronunciation is sharp and correct. Their voices are pleasant and lively.

Speakers can prepare for one of three main kinds of delivery: (1) In speaking from memory, speakers may have learned their speeches by heart. This kind of delivery can be good for formal occasions, but it often sounds mechanical. (2) Many speakers read their speeches from typewritten copy or from a teleprompter. Reading is preferred by many government officials, television performers, and business people without time to prepare carefully for delivery. (3) The best all-round method of delivery is called **extemporaneous**. This means that speakers have prepared their material well, planned and outlined their speeches, and possibly practiced out loud. They have the plan firmly in mind but use the words as the words come to them. This kind of speaking seems more natural than speeches read or memorized.

A fourth kind of delivery is called **impromptu**. The speaker makes no preparation but speaks on the spur of the moment.

▶ PUBLIC SPEAKING TODAY

Public speaking has always taken many forms. Fashions and means of communication constantly change. Public speaking today is usually less formal and more conversational than it once was. One possible reason for the change is that it is no longer the fashion—as it was in ancient Greece and later in Europe and America—to think of public speaking as a fine art, a means of creating beauty. Today it is thought of, for the most part, as a very practical kind of public communication. Speakers wish to appear as natural as possible to live audiences and to audiences that see them on television or hear them on radio. Modern life has become less formal—in clothes, social customs, language, and the like. Public speaking also has become informal.

DONALD C. BRYANT
Coauthor, *Fundamentals of Public Speaking*
See also DEBATES AND DISCUSSIONS; ORATORY.

# PUBLIC UTILITIES

A public utility is an industry or commercial enterprise that supplies services or products that people need for health and convenience. Water, electricity, gas, telephone, and telegraph companies are public utilities.

Generally, a public utility (or public service) company is the only one in an area that supplies a certain product or service. A company is said to hold a monopoly when it is the only one that supplies and sells a product. Businesses that are best run as monopolies are called natural monopolies.

Economists believe that public utilities are run most successfully as natural monopolies for these two reasons: First, one public utility company in an area is usually more practical than several companies that would have to compete for room under city streets—or on poles—for different sets of gas or water pipes and power lines. Second, one large plant can provide a public service, such as electricity or telephone service, more cheaply than can several small plants that are competing with one another.

But when any product is made and sold as a monopoly, the users, or consumers, of the product face a problem. Often they must have the product or service, and they cannot go elsewhere for it. They must pay the price the company sets and accept the quality given.

In the case of public utilities, consumers are protected in one of two ways. Either the national or local government operates the public utility or the government regulates the companies that operate utilities owned by private investors.

In the United States a public utility company owned by individuals must receive a special franchise from the community in which it operates. The franchise gives the company the right to install equipment under or along the city streets. Federal, state, and local commissions regulate the activities of public utility companies to make sure they give good service and charge fair and reasonable prices.

In other countries, private companies may be licensed by the government or supervised by a particular government bureau. In still other countries, public utilities are run by the state.

Elsewhere, the amount of ownership by governments varies from country to country. In Britain, the telephone system and electric power and gas utilities are all government-owned. But most of the water companies are privately owned. In general, throughout the world there is a combination of government and private ownership of public utilities.

In the United States most gas and electric utilities are run by private (investor-owned) companies. More water companies are owned and operated by the local government than by private companies. Government-owned electric plants produce about 20 percent of the country's electric power.

### ▶ FOUR MAJOR PUBLIC UTILITIES

Electric power, gas, waterworks, and the telephone all contribute to the industrial development of nations and to the health and comfort of individuals.

Public rail, bus, and air transportation systems are also public utilities in a broad sense because they provide service to the public. But people pay for these services on the basis of individual use, and they are provided outside the home.

For these reasons, transportation services are generally not considered public utilities. Cable television is not regulated by public utility commissions. But it is under the control of the Federal Communications Commission. It does offer a service to the public and may therefore be considered a public utility in the broad sense.

### Electric Power

Electricity is a form of energy. It supplies light, heat, and power. But it cannot be stored in large amounts for use as it is needed. It must constantly be produced or generated so that it is available whenever anyone flips on a light switch or plugs in an appliance.

Electricity is produced in a generating plant or power plant, which may be far from the place in which electricity is needed. From the power plant, electric current is sent with nearly the speed of light through wires that lead into homes, schools, and other places.

Most of the world's electricity is produced in plants that are run by steam. These are called steam, or thermal, power stations. In conventional thermal power stations, the heat that creates the steam is produced by burning a fuel such as coal or oil.

Nuclear power plants may also be considered thermal stations. They run on steam that is produced by nuclear fuels. The first nuclear power station in the United States was built in 1957. More and more electricity has been generated by nuclear power plants. But the possibility of accidents has caused public opposition to nuclear power, and in some areas the number of future nuclear power plants may be restricted.

The force of flowing water is used to run another type of power plant, the hydroelectric plant. In Sweden, there is not enough fuel to run steam plants. But there is a great deal of waterpower, and hydroelectric plants produce a large share of the electricity. The United States and Canada also have many hydroelectric plants.

The first electric generating plant in the United States was started by Thomas Edison in 1882. It transmitted, or sent, power only about 5,000 feet (1,500 meters) in distance, and it served only 59 customers. Today the power system of the United States is the largest in the world. China has the second largest power system.

In many countries today, large power companies connect their lines, forming a network of power systems. In this way the power com-

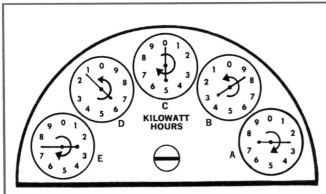

### ELECTRIC METER

The size of your electric bill varies with the amount of electricity you use. This amount is measured in units called **kilowatt-hours** (KWH)

by a device called a **kilowatt-hour meter.** For example, a small electric oven may use 1,000 watts, or one kilowatt, in one hour. Ten light bulbs of 100 watts each would also use one kilowatt in one hour.

In the meter, a small motor turns the pointer of dial A. The more electricity you use, the faster the pointer turns. When the pointer has gone a whole space (for example, from 2 to 3), one KWH has been used.

Each pointer is connected by gears (toothed wheels) with the next pointer. As pointer A makes a full *turn* clockwise, showing that 10 KWH have been used, it turns pointer B one *space* counterclockwise (for example, from 8 to 9). Thus, pointer A measures single KWH's, B measures tens, C measures hundreds.

The reading that is shown here is 71,082 kilowatt-hours.

pany for a certain area can draw on other companies to help meet the demand in times of trouble.

### Gas

Gas is used to cook food, dry clothes, heat water, burn refuse, and heat and cool homes, factories, and public buildings. Gas that is used for these purposes is called fuel gas.

There are two kinds of fuel gas—natural and manufactured. The most important fuel gas today is natural gas. Natural gas is found in many parts of the world. Large natural gas fields exist in the United States, Canada, Mexico, and Russia.

Wells must be drilled to find natural gas in the pores, or small spaces, of certain kinds of rock. The wells may be as little as a thousand feet or as much as 5 miles (8 kilometers) deep. From the wells the gas is piped great distances to the cities in which it is to be used.

When gas from the pipeline reaches a city, it is measured, or metered, so that the company that piped the gas will know how much has been sold to the gas company in a particular city.

The gas is then delivered through the pipes, or mains, of the city's gas company to smaller pipes that lead into people's houses and other buildings. In these buildings the gas again passes through a meter that measures the amount of gas used. At regular times, a gas company employee checks the meter, which tells how much gas has been used. The company then sends the user a bill.

Most of the gas used in the 1800's was manufactured from coal, coke, or oil. Today manufactured gas is still in use where natural gas is not available through the large pipelines that cross the United States. Limited supplies of natural fuels have led researchers to improve or develop ways of producing synthetic natural gas, gasoline, and fuel oil from coal.

### Water Supply

Water is one of the necessities of life. People cannot live more than a few days without liquids. At one time people got water by carrying it from wells or streams or by storing rainwater in cisterns (underground tanks). In the developing countries people still use these methods to obtain water.

Where industry developed and cities grew up, supplying people with water became a community problem. In cities, potable (drinkable) water must be distributed to factories, schools, stores, office buildings, individual homes, and apartment buildings. Water is needed for fighting fires and other public uses.

A city's water usually comes from a central source. It may be either an underground or surface source. An underground source is called an aquifer. This is usually a large area of material such as sandstone or gravel that is porous enough to contain water.

Often surface water is stored in a reservoir formed by damming a river. If the source of a city's water is far from the city, the water is sent in closed pipes or in canals from the source to the city.

In a modern community a water treatment plant takes water from the central source and treats it, if necessary, to make it safe for people to drink. The plant stores enough for periods of great demand and distributes the rest.

Most water obtained from surface sources must be purified. First, the water is treated in tanks with chemicals, to help remove harmful bacteria, fine particles of matter that are suspended in it, and undesirable tastes, odors, and color. The chemicals used include chlorine, aluminum sulfate (alum), and powdered activated carbon.

Next, the water is filtered through beds of sand to remove the last traces of bacteria and suspended matter. Then it is disinfected again. Water from underground wells usually requires no treatment except a small amount of disinfectant, usually chlorine.

After treatment the water is ready for distribution. In many cities water is pumped from the treatment plant into elevated storage tanks to ensure that there is always water on hand to meet periods of great demand. From the storage tanks the water is delivered into the city's water mains and then into smaller pipes to each point of use. In most cities the water is metered in homes, and the customer is billed for the amount used.

### The Telephone

Each day millions of people use the telephone for business and social purposes. In emergencies, it is used to call the police, the fire department, or a doctor.

Wires from each telephone lead to a central office. From there, local, long-distance, and overseas telephone connections are made. These connections are made by automatic equipment or by operators.

Most calls are transmitted through wires. The wires may be strung on poles. Or a protected bundle of wires, called a cable, may be buried under city streets or under a lake or river. Cables on the ocean floor are used in making calls from continent to continent. Some intercontinental calls are carried by radio waves and may be relayed by communications satellites. New methods of transmission include light waves, sent through microscopic glass fibers, and microwaves.

In the United States, most telephone systems are privately owned. In other countries, telephone systems are government-owned. In the United States the Bell system (American Telephone and Telegraph) was by far the largest phone company. But in 1983, Bell was broken up into a number of smaller independent companies to increase competition.

In Canada a very large percentage of the telephones are operated by Bell Canada, a private company, and by a number of small, independent companies. The remainder of the telephones are operated by the provinces.

The government has controlling interest in the telephone system in Denmark. But three private companies are licensed by the government. Several co-operative telephone companies are operating in the Danish islands.

When a telephone is installed in the United States, a fee is charged for installation. After that a monthly bill is sent to the user of the telephone. In some countries people receive their telephone bills every six months.

In Japan, where the government owns the telephones, a person must buy a government bond before the telephone is installed. Then regular bills for service are sent.

Today, telephones are found almost everywhere. People can make calls from their homes and from telephone booths in stores and railroad stations, on city streets, and along busy highways.

Reviewed by GEORGE E. SYMONS
Engineering Editor/Consultant

See also ELECTRICITY; NATURAL GAS; POWER PLANTS; TELEPHONE; WATER.

# PUBLISHING

Publishing is the business of bringing the printed word to the public in books, magazines, and newspapers. Thousands of men and women work in publishing. Some are writers, some are editors, who adapt the writers' works, and others are in charge of putting the publication together. Still others handle the publicity and advertising that bring the publication to the attention of the reading public.

Books, magazines, and newspapers are the three basic fields of publishing. These three fields operate in different ways, although they have some characteristics in common.

In book publishing an author submits his manuscript to a publishing house. Some publishing houses, particularly those that publish encyclopedias, have their own teams of staff writers who are assigned articles on different subjects. Newspapers are almost completely staff written by writers and reporters who are experts in different areas of the news. Newspapers have their own printing presses so that they can print the news almost as soon as it happens.

Magazine publishing has some of the characteristics of both book and newspaper publishing. Weekly news magazines are published in much the same way as newspapers, although they are printed by an outside printing press. The monthly or biweekly magazines assign articles in advance, just as publishers of encyclopedias and other reference works do.

Over the past few years publishing firms with different specialties have begun to join together. Many magazine publishing companies now put out books and even encyclopedias. Newspaper publishing still remains, for the most part, completely separate.

▶ KINDS OF PUBLISHING

Book publishing is divided into several categories. **Trade book publishing** includes fiction, biography, history, poetry, and **juveniles** (children's books). To find out what a publisher is going to put out, booksellers consult the publisher's list. The list is an announcement of all the books the publisher is offering. Lists of new books can be found in advertisements in literary magazines and special booklets sent out by the publishers. Publishers issue their lists in the spring and the fall. Some publishers also send out a summer list.

**Textbook publishing** covers the many fields studied in schools. Textbook publishers work with experts in education to make sure their textbooks meet educational standards. Many textbooks are written at the suggestion of teachers who feel a present textbook is not adequate. Folders describing textbooks are sent out to teachers to keep them informed about new publications.

**Scientific and technical publishing** provides information on the many new developments in these fields and is generally aimed at people with a scientific or technical background. **Medical, law, and religious publishing** also have their special audiences. Many of their publications are sold mainly by advertising leaflets mailed out to buyers the publishers think would be interested.

Reference books, dictionaries, and atlases are usually put out by companies that specialize in compiling information. Other specialized areas of publishing produce **art books, music,** and **maps.**

**Subscription book publishing** produces encyclopedias, sets of classics, and similar books that are sold by salesmen directly to buyers.

A **university press** is a publishing house attached to a university. University presses publish scholarly works, textbooks for the university, and trade books they feel have special merit. The first university presses were officially established at the English universities of Oxford and Cambridge in the 16th century.

When a person publishes with a **vanity press**, he pays for the publishing himself instead of being paid by the publisher. He is said to be publishing out of vanity because commercial publishers do not think his book would have a wide enough market for them to publish it. Vanity presses are very useful for volumes of poetry and collections of family letters. Usually a limited number of copies are printed.

Governments publish a large number of pamphlets and books every year. These pub-lications provide information on farming, various trades, new technical developments, and many other areas.

**Paperbacks.** A very important development in American book publishing is the rise of paperbacks. Although paperbacks have been published in the United States since the 1830's, their real success did not come until a hundred years later. At first, paperbacks were limited to detective stories, westerns, and other tales of adventure. Today almost all the classics and works of major poets, playwrights, historians, scientists, philosophers, and recent novelists are being reprinted in paperback. Usually, as soon as a new hard-cover book proves itself successful, it is issued as a paperback. Some titles appear originally as paperbacks.

Books reach their readers in various ways—through bookstores, libraries, mail order, house-to-house salesmen, and book clubs. Book club members agree to buy a certain number of books a year. Each month a folder describing the books chosen for that month is mailed to every member. The books are selected by specialists in various fields.

Authors' and publishers' profits depend on the number of books sold on the market. For each book that is sold, the author receives part of the book price. This is a fixed sum and is known as a **royalty**. The publisher uses the rest of the sales price to cover his operating costs and make his own profit. When a publisher accepts a book, he decides how many copies he should have printed. The number depends on the kind of book and the demand for it. Sometimes as many as 250,000 copies of a school textbook are printed, while a book of Renaissance drawings might be limited to 2,000 copies. For a trade book to pay its own way, it must sell between 7,500 and 10,000 copies. Publishers also sometimes sell different kinds of **rights** to help make a trade book profitable. These rights include the right to use the book as a book club selection, publish it in paperback, or adapt it for the screen or for television. These rights are called **subsidiary rights**, and the money made by their sale is shared with the author.

Many publishing firms employ a special person to handle these subsidiary rights, which have become an important source of revenue for both publisher and author. Literary agents represents authors frequently in such business arrangements, usually on a commission basis of 10 percent of the sum received. Some agents also act for publishers in arranging paperback reprint rights.

The book publishing industry is not one of the giant industries, but its importance and influence greatly outweigh its size in dollars. It is very difficult to compare book production in different countries because not all countries count their books in the same way. In the United States and many European countries, books are counted as **titles.** The United States publishes over 40,000 titles each year.

When a U.S. publishing company announces it has 50 titles, it means it has 50 different books. A best-seller, for instance, counts as one title even though thousands of copies of it are made and it may represent a major share of the publisher's profit for the year. To qualify as a title in the United States, a book must have at least 49 pages. Government publications are not counted.

Every year, publishers from all over the world attend the Frankfurt Book Fair in Germany. During the Middle Ages, Frankfurt was the center for another kind of fair, a merchant's fair. But instead of filling stalls with cloth or spices, the publishers bring their own special wares, books. These exhibits fill over five enormous buildings.

The fair is a busy place for publishers. Not only do they want to see what books each country is putting out, but they get together to plan for future books. Many books that come out simultaneously in different countries were first planned at the Frankfurt Fair. The publishers also arrange for translations or the use of illustrations by artists from different countries. A book may come out today that was written by an author of one country, translated by a writer of a second country, illustrated by an artist of a third, and finally published in yet another country.

ANNE J. RICHTER
R. R. Bowker Company

See also BOOKS; JOURNALISM; MAGAZINES; NEWSPAPERS; PRINTING.

## PUCCINI, GIACOMO (1858–1924)

Giacomo Puccini, a famous opera composer, was born in Lucca, Italy, on December 22, 1858. For generations the Puccini family had produced talented musicians. As a boy, Giacomo showed no great talent or liking for music. But his mother insisted that he go to music school. There he learned to love music, and he soon became a church organist and choirmaster.

When he was 17, Puccini attended a performance of Verdi's opera *Aïda*. He was so excited by this opera that he decided to become an opera composer. With the help of a scholarship, he studied for three years at the Milan Conservatory (1880–83).

Puccini's first operas, written after he left the conservatory, were only moderately successful. His first triumph, *Manon Lescaut*, was produced in 1893. Three years later came *La Bohème*, a sad love story of Bohemian life in Paris. These operas made Puccini world-famous. They were followed in 1900 by another great success, *Tosca*.

Puccini married Elvira Gemignani in January 1904. A month later his new opera *Madama Butterfly* was first performed at La Scala opera house in Milan. The audience did not like this Japanese love story and hissed at the performance. After making minor changes in the work, he produced it a few months later in Brescia, with great success.

In 1907, Puccini went to New York City for the first performance at the Metropolitan Opera of *Madama Butterfly*. While he was there he wrote an opera on an American subject, *The Girl of the Golden West*, which was first performed in December 1910. Puccini's next major work, after he had returned to Europe, was *Il Trittico* ("The Triptych"), a group of three one-act operas—*Il Tabarro* ("The Cloak"), *Gianni Schicchi*, and *Suor Angelica* ("Sister Angelica").

Puccini was at work on the last act of his opera *Turandot* when he died on November 29, 1924, in Brussels. At its first performance in 1926, the conductor Arturo Toscanini stopped with the last notes Puccini wrote.

Reviewed by WILLIAM ASHBROOK
Philadelphia College of the Performing Arts

**PUEBLO.** See COLORADO (Cities).

# PUERTO RICO

Puerto Rico has long been known as one of the most beautiful islands in the Caribbean. Its rugged mountains, colorful tropical plant life, and scenic coastlines have impressed visitors since the explorer Christopher Columbus first visited the island in 1493.

Puerto Rico, a commonwealth associated with the United States, lies about 1,000 miles (1,600 kilometers) southeast of Florida. Once chiefly a farming area, Puerto Rico is now crisscrossed by modern highways, with factories, shopping centers, and fine hotels. Although Puerto Rico means "rich port" in Spanish, the island has many poor people. But great social and economic progress has been made in the past century, and Puerto Rico now has one of the highest standards of living in the Caribbean and in Latin America.

▶ **PEOPLE**

Two-thirds of Puerto Rico is mountainous or dry, and most of the population is densely concentrated in the remaining third of the island. Almost half the people live in the greater San Juan metropolitan district on the northern coast.

The original inhabitants of Puerto Rico were Taínos, a branch of the Arawak Indian civilization. Perhaps as many as 40,000 Taínos were living on the island when Spanish explorers and settlers first reached the island about 500 years ago. Most Taínos soon died of disease or from slave conditions imposed by the Spanish settlers. For centuries, there have been no pure-blooded Taínos on the island, but many Puerto Ricans have some Taíno ancestors.

*Above:* Many of these young Puerto Ricans have African, Taíno, and European ancestors. *Left:* The Spanish-constructed El Morro is a landmark of Old San Juan, which occupies a small island near the modern city. Once a defensive structure, the old fortress is now part of a national historical site.

From the 1500's through the 1700's, African slaves were brought to Puerto Rico to work on sugar and, later, coffee plantations. In the 1800's, revolutions in Haiti, in Latin America, and even in Europe caused many displaced French and Spanish people from those countries to immigrate to Puerto Rico. Since the Spanish-American War of 1898, when Puerto Rico was ceded to the United States, Americans have also become part of the island's melting pot. But regardless of national or racial backgrounds, the language and traditions of Puerto Ricans are mainly Spanish.

**Language.** Spanish remains the traditional language of the island. English, however, is taught in the schools and many Puerto Ricans speak it.

**Religion.** Puerto Rico's constitution guarantees religious freedom for all faiths, although Roman Catholicism, brought by the Spanish colonists, remains the dominant religion. During the 1900's, Protestant groups gained many converts. Today Jewish synagogues, Muslim mosques, and other houses of worship can also be found on the island.

**Education.** Children are required to attend school between the ages of 6 and 16. Most students attend Spanish-language public schools, but there are also many parochial and private schools, some of which conduct classes in English.

Established in 1903, the University of Puerto Rico, with campuses in San Juan and throughout the island, is the commonwealth's oldest and largest university system. There are also several private colleges and universities, the best known of which is InterAmerican University. Schools in Puerto Rico are held to the same official standards as schools in the United States.

**Sports.** Puerto Ricans enjoy a wide variety of sports and games, including baseball, basketball, boxing, horse racing, and cockfighting. Baseball is particularly enjoyed, and Puerto Ricans have helped to popularize the game throughout the Caribbean. Many Puerto Ricans have played in the major leagues, including Roberto Clemente, the first Puerto Rican to be elected to the Baseball Hall of Fame.

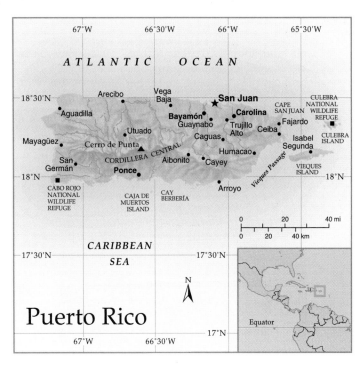

Puerto Rico

**Food and Drink.** Traditional food in Puerto Rico is a mix of Spanish, African, Taíno Indian, and creole influences. From the Taínos came local ingredients—fruits such as pineap-

## FACTS and figures

**COMMONWEALTH OF PUERTO RICO** is the official name of the island.

**LOCATION:** Greater Antilles, Caribbean Sea.

**AREA:** 3,435 sq mi (8,897 km²).

**POPULATION:** 3,808,610 (2000 U.S. census).

**CAPITAL AND LARGEST CITY:** San Juan.

**MAJOR LANGUAGE:** Spanish, English (both official).

**MAJOR RELIGIOUS GROUP:** Roman Catholic.

**GOVERNMENT:** Home-rule commonwealth, associated with the United States. **Head of state and government**—governor. **Legislature**—senate and house of representatives.

**CHIEF PRODUCTS: Agricultural**—dairy products, livestock, chicken, sugarcane, coffee, bananas, plantains, pineapples, citrus fruits, melons. **Manufactured**—processed foods, textiles and apparel, electronic equipment, pharmaceuticals, petrochemicals, metal products, stone, marble, clay and glass products, rum, sugar. **Mineral**—limestone, clay, sand and gravel, gold, silver, copper, iron ore, platinum.

**MONETARY UNIT:** U.S. dollar (1 dollar = 100 cents).

ple and soursop, tubers such as yucca and sweet potatoes, and corn. Spanish settlers brought pigs, chickens, and other livestock as well as rice, olive oil, and various spices. The ships that brought slaves to Puerto Rico also brought African foods—plantains (a starchy banana-like fruit), bananas, coconuts, and pigeon peas. Islanders also enjoy many other ethnic foods, including Mexican, Italian, and American.

## ▶LAND

Puerto Rico is the smallest island in a group of Caribbean islands called the Greater Antilles. It is about 100 miles (160 kilometers) long and 35 miles (56 kilometers) wide. The interior of the island is mountainous, and its tallest peak, Cerro de Punta, stands 4,389 feet (1,338 meters) above sea level. The central mountain range is bounded on the north and south by flat coastal plains, which have been irrigated to become Puerto Rico's best farmlands.

**Rivers and Coastal Waters.** Puerto Rico has more than 2,000 rivers and streams. The longest, Río de la Plata, is 46 miles (74 kilometers) in length. Along the coast, saltwater lagoons provide a rich shelter for young sea animals and coastal bird communities. The Atlantic Ocean rolls into Puerto Rico along the northern coast, resulting in rougher waters, especially during winter months. Calmer Caribbean waters are found along the remaining coastlines.

**Climate.** Puerto Rico lies in the tropics, where the climate is warm all year. Average temperatures along the coast range between 79 and 84°F (26 and 29°C). The climate is cooler in the mountains.

The island is located in the belt of the northeast trade winds, which bring heavy rains to the mountains and northern coast. Especially in summer, sudden, brief showers

*Left:* Plantations such as Hacienda San Pedro grow coffee beans in the rugged highlands. *Below:* Puerto Rico's sunny beaches, such as this one on Culebra Island, draw local and international vacationers.

The manufacture of pharmaceuticals is an important industry in Puerto Rico. Many prescription drugs are exported to the United States.

are common. The southern coastal plain is dry, for the high mountains block rain clouds.

Like other islands in the Caribbean, Puerto Rico is subject to hurricanes during the late summer and early fall. These destructive storms can occasionally cause great damage to crops and buildings. In 1928 the San Felipe hurricane destroyed most of the island's coffee plantations and citrus groves. Another violent storm, Hurricane Georges, did serious damage in 1998.

**Natural Resources.** Puerto Rico's climate, beaches, lush vegetation, and farmlands are among its greatest natural assets. The chief minerals include limestone, marble, clay, and sand and gravel. There are copper deposits that have not been mined, and small amounts of gold, silver, platinum, and iron ore.

▶ **ECONOMY**

Until the 1940's, Puerto Rico's economy was based largely on farming. Then the island government took an active role in modernization and industrialization. Public utilities were expanded to supply water, electricity, sanitation, and transportation. Under a program called Operation Bootstrap, the government of Puerto Rico encouraged investors from the United States and other countries to provide jobs for people by opening factories on the island.

But the island's economy has not been able to generate enough jobs for its people. Since the 1950's many Puerto Ricans have migrated to the United States, especially New York, New Jersey, Pennsylvania, Illinois, and New England. There are now about 2.7 million Puerto Ricans in the United States, half of whom were born there. In recent years, however, some Puerto Ricans have returned to the island, seeking economic opportunities.

**Services.** One of the most important developments in the island's economy since the 1950's has been the increase in tourism. The tropical climate, sandy beaches, and sparkling sea attract year-round visitors. Other attractions include historic monuments and the colorful local culture.

**Manufacturing.** Manufacturing is now the largest contributor to Puerto Rico's economy, accounting for about 40 percent of all goods and services produced. Some of the most important products manufactured in Puerto Rico include pharmaceuticals, clothing, shoes, processed foods, electronic equipment, plastics, chemicals, and petrochemicals.

A number of Puerto Rican industries are based on the processing of agricultural products. Some sugar is made into rum, which is a very profitable export. Locally grown tobacco is used to make cigars. There is also a small tropical juice industry.

**Agriculture.** Until the 1940's, sugarcane was the main crop. It accounted for over half the value of all agricultural products. More than half the people were employed in harvesting sugarcane or in processing and shipping the crop. Sugarcane plantations were modernized mainly with money from the United States. The sugar industry thrived because Puerto Rico was included within the United States tariff (import tax) system. Tobacco and coffee were the second and third leading crops.

In recent years, animal food products, such as meat, dairy products, and poultry, have replaced sugarcane, tobacco, and coffee as the most important agricultural products. Sugarcane is grown on the flat lands, which are irrigated in some areas. Coffee is grown in the central and western highlands. Pineapples are grown and canned on the island. Efforts have been made to produce larger amounts of melons, citrus fruits, mangoes, avocados, vegetables, green peppers, and cherries. Bananas and plantains remain important crops.

**Energy.** The burning of fossil fuels such as oil supplies most of the power for industry and electricity for homes, although hydroelectric power sites have also been developed. New thermal plants based on natural hot springs have been built in an attempt to meet growing demands for electricity.

**Trade.** Puerto Rico's chief exports are pharmaceuticals, electronics, clothing, canned tuna, rum, coffee, beverage concentrates, and medical and high-technology equipment. Major imports include chemicals, foodstuffs, machinery and automobiles, clothing and footwear, and fuel and petroleum products.

**Transportation.** More than 8,000 miles (12,880 kilometers) of roads crisscross Puerto Rico. Most Puerto Rican families own at least one car, and cars are the major form of transportation. There are also buses and vans known as públicos that transport people around the cities and between towns. Puerto Rico's position as a gateway to the Caribbean also supports an active shipping industry.

**Communication.** Three major daily newspapers, including *The San Juan Star*, which is published in both English and Spanish, reach readers across the island. News and other information is also broadcast on dozens of local Spanish-language radio stations and several television stations. Many homes have cable television, which enables Puerto Ricans to tune in to broadcasts from the United States. In recent years, Puerto Rico has invested billions of dollars in high-tech communications, including telephone, fax, cellular phone, and computer systems.

▶ **MAJOR CITIES**

In the large cities, new jobs in industry and business have created a way of life similar to that in the cities of the United States. Many smaller cities and towns throughout the island serve as resorts and marketplaces, where people bring farm products and fish and in turn buy their food, clothes, and other goods.

**San Juan** is the capital and largest city of Puerto Rico. It was the site of some of the first Spanish fortresses built in the New World. Most of the old city still stands, including El Morro, a fortress. The tomb of the Spanish explorer and first colonial governor, Juan Ponce de León, is in the Cathedral of San Juan Bautista (the patron saint of the island). La Fortaleza has been the residence of the governors since colonial times. In the old part of the city, there are narrow cobblestone streets and fine old Spanish buildings. Modern stores and many new housing developments are found in the newer parts of the city. The modern airport near San Juan is the busiest terminal in the Caribbean.

**Bayamón**, the second largest city, is located within the San Juan metropolitan area. San Juan and its suburbs serve as the cultural, political, and educational center of the island.

**Ponce** is Puerto Rico's third largest city. It was named after Juan Ponce de León and is one of the oldest European settlements in the Western Hemisphere. The city still preserves its old Spanish atmosphere. It is a busy industrial center and an important port. Its tourist attractions include one of the finest museums in the Caribbean, an Indian ceremonial cen-

---

## PUERTO RICO AND THE UNITED STATES

Puerto Rico is a self-governing commonwealth associated with the United States. The Spanish name for Puerto Rico's government is *estado libre asociado*, meaning "free associated state."

The United States and Puerto Rico share a common defense, economic market, currency, and postal service. As U.S. citizens, Puerto Ricans travel easily back and forth between the island and the mainland. Products are also shipped easily back and forth, without tariffs or import taxes. However, Puerto Rico is allowed to impose a special tax on imported coffee. Puerto Ricans do not vote in U.S. elections, and are represented in the U.S. Congress solely by a resident commissioner. The commissioner has a voice but no vote in the House of Representatives.

Puerto Ricans do not pay most federal taxes, except those, such as social security taxes, that are imposed by the consent of both governments. Federal excise taxes on shipments of alcoholic beverages (mainly rum) and tobacco products between Puerto Rico and the United States are collected. The money, however, is then returned to the commonwealth treasury. American social welfare programs such as food stamps, Medicare, Medicaid, aid to dependent children, welfare, and unemployment insurance are extended to Puerto Rico. But in some cases the payments are lower than in the United States.

Puerto Ricans are also subject to service in the U.S. Armed Forces, and have fought in all American wars since World War I.

*Right:* Shoppers in Ponce stroll past stalls along the plaza outside the Fox Delicias Mall. This modern-day complex was built to resemble the historical colonial style. *Below:* Genuine historic buildings, such as those along Blue Stone Street in Old San Juan, represent some of the oldest European architecture in the Americas.

ter, a restored coffee plantation, and the mansion of a local rum-producing family.

**Caguas,** the island's leading inland city, is located about 22 miles (35 kilometers) southeast of San Juan. Once a rich farming region, Caguas today is a center of manufacturing, particularly for sugar milling and refining.

**Mayagüez,** on the western coast, serves as the port for the coffee-producing region. It also has a number of fish-processing plants, which process and can much of the tuna fish consumed in the United States. The Mayagüez campus of the University of Puerto Rico contains the Institute of Tropical Agriculture's large collection of tropical plants and Puerto Rico's only major zoo.

▶ **CULTURAL HERITAGE**

Puerto Rico's diverse cultural influences—Taíno Indian, Spanish, African, Caribbean, European, and American—have mingled to produce a dynamic cultural life, rich in folk music and rhythmic dances. Since 1898, the United States has greatly influenced the island's popular culture. Nevertheless, ties to Spanish traditions remain strong.

Puerto Ricans appreciate music, whether it be the classical music of operas and orchestras, the folk music highlighted during holiday seasons, or the contemporary music of pop idols. The dance music known as salsa, which combines Afro-Caribbean rhythms with big-band melodies, has long been the music of choice in Puerto Rican nightclubs.

▶ **GOVERNMENT**

Puerto Rico is administered by a governor, who, since 1948, has been elected directly by the Puerto Rican people to a 4-year term. The governor appoints all members of his cabinet and all judges of the island's supreme court. The legislature, composed of a senate and a house of representatives, is also elected directly by the people for 4-year terms.

Luis Muñoz Marín, founder of the Popular Democratic Party, was the first popularly elected governor of Puerto Rico.

# ▶ HISTORY

**Early History.** Early inhabitants of Puerto Rico descended from a branch of the Arawak culture from northern South America. Those who settled on the island, which they called Boriquén, developed a distinct culture known as Taíno.

**Spanish Colonial Period.** Christopher Columbus discovered Puerto Rico in 1493 on his second voyage to the New World. In 1508 a Spanish settlement was established by Juan Ponce de León. The Spanish colonists were not kind to the Taíno natives, many of whom died of disease or were forced into slavery. For centuries, Puerto Rico was an important

Supporters of Puerto Rican independence cheer enthusiastically at a political rally in San Juan.

military post, linking Spain with its colonies in Central and South America.

In the 1800's, most of Spain's colonies in the Americas became independent republics. A brief revolt for Puerto Rican indepen-dence in 1868 was crushed by the Spanish military. In 1897, Puerto Rico was granted autonomy, or local self-government, but it was still controlled by Spain.

**U.S. Territory.** In 1898, Puerto Rico became a part of the United States as a result of a war with Spain. For more information, see the article SPANISH-AMERICAN WAR in Volume S. Since then, the United States Congress has granted Puerto Rico an increasing degree of self-government. Puerto Ricans were granted American citizenship in 1917. In 1948 they elected their first governor, Luis Muñoz Marín (1898–1980), founder of the Popular Democratic Party. In 1952, under Muñoz Marín's leadership, Puerto Rico became a self-governing commonwealth "freely associated" with the United States.

**Political Status.** Since 1967, a series of referendums (popular votes) have been held to determine the political future the Puerto Rican people desire for their commonwealth. While the Popular Democratic Party seeks to maintain commonwealth status, the New Progressive Party favors statehood for Puerto Rico. Two smaller parties seek complete independence. In 1998, Governor Pedro Rosselló of the New Progressive Party authorized the most recent referendum on Puerto Rico's status. Although many people voted against remaining a commonwealth, neither statehood nor independence won a majority of the votes. This indecisive outcome indicates that the future relationship between Puerto Rico and the United States remains uncertain.

JOHN F. LOUNSBURY
Arizona State University
Reviewed by GONZALO F. CÓRDOVA
Department of History, University of Puerto Rico

# PULITZER PRIZES

The Pulitzer Prizes are annual awards for excellence in American journalism, literature, and music. First awarded in 1917, the prizes are given each spring by the trustees of Columbia University on the recommendation of an advisory board. The board acts on the reports of juries appointed by the university in each of the categories. Each prize is $10,000.

The journalism prizes are awarded for work that appears in U.S. newspapers during the previous year. The categories are public service (winners receive a gold medal, but no cash), breaking news reporting, investigative reporting, explanatory reporting, national reporting, beat reporting, international reporting, feature writing, commentary, criticism, editorial writing, editorial cartooning, breaking news photography, and feature photography.

Six awards in literature and one in music are given. The literature awards are for fiction, history, biography, drama, poetry, and general nonfiction.

The prizes were established by Joseph Pulitzer, an American newspaper publisher.

Joseph Pulitzer, an American newspaper publisher, founded the Pulitzer Prizes, awarded annually for excellence in American journalism, literature, and music.

He was born on April 10, 1847, in Mako, Hungary. When he was 17, he went to the United States and fought in the Union Army during the U.S. Civil War. He became a U.S. citizen in 1867.

The following year, Pulitzer began reporting for the *Westliche Post*, a German-language newspaper in St. Louis, Missouri. In 1878 he bought the *St. Louis Dispatch*. He joined the *Dispatch* with another paper, the *Evening Post*, to form the *St. Louis Post-Dispatch*. Pulitzer's crusades in the public interest made the *Post-Dispatch* one of the most influential papers in the United States. He later bought the *New York World*, repeating his success of the *Post-Dispatch*.

Pulitzer believed in encouraging excellence in the arts and journalism. In his will, he gave $2 million to Columbia University. Part of it was to found the Columbia School of Journalism, which opened in 1912, and part was to create the Pulitzer Prizes. Pulitzer died on October 29, 1911.

The following lists give the winners of the Pulitzer Prizes for fiction, history, biography, drama, poetry, and general nonfiction. No awards were given in the years not listed.

---

## FICTION

For distinguished fiction in book form by an American author, preferably dealing with American life.

**1918**  Ernest Poole, *His Family.*
**1919**  Booth Tarkington, *The Magnificent Ambersons.*
**1921**  Edith Wharton, *The Age of Innocence.*
**1922**  Booth Tarkington, *Alice Adams.*
**1923**  Willa Cather, *One of Ours.*
**1924**  Margaret Wilson, *The Able McLaughlins.*
**1925**  Edna Ferber, *So Big.*
**1926**  Sinclair Lewis, *Arrowsmith.*

**1927**  Louis Bromfield, *Early Autumn.*
**1928**  Thornton Wilder, *The Bridge of San Luis Rey.*
**1929**  Julia M. Peterkin, *Scarlet Sister Mary.*
**1930**  Oliver La Farge, *Laughing Boy.*
**1931**  Margaret Ayer Barnes, *Years of Grace.*
**1932**  Pearl S. Buck, *The Good Earth.*
**1933**  T. S. Stribling, *The Store.*
**1934**  Caroline Miller, *Lamb in His Bosom.*
**1935**  Josephine W. Johnson, *Now in November.*
**1936**  Harold L. Davis, *Honey in the Horn.*
**1937**  Margaret Mitchell, *Gone With the Wind.*
**1938**  John P. Marquand, *The Late George Apley.*
**1939**  Marjorie Kinnan Rawlings, *The Yearling.*
**1940**  John Steinbeck, *The Grapes of Wrath.*
**1942**  Ellen Glasgow, *In This Our Life.*

| 1943 | Upton Sinclair, *Dragon's Teeth.* |
| 1944 | Martin Flavin, *Journey in the Dark.* |
| 1945 | John Hersey, *A Bell for Adano.* |
| 1947 | Robert Penn Warren, *All the King's Men.* |
| 1948 | James A. Michener, *Tales of the South Pacific.* |
| 1949 | James Gould Cozzens, *Guard of Honor.* |
| 1950 | A. B. Guthrie, Jr., *The Way West.* |
| 1951 | Conrad Richter, *The Town.* |
| 1952 | Herman Wouk, *The Caine Mutiny.* |
| 1953 | Ernest Hemingway, *The Old Man and the Sea.* |
| 1955 | William Faulkner, *A Fable.* |
| 1956 | MacKinlay Kantor, *Andersonville.* |
| 1958 | James Agee, *A Death in the Family.* |
| 1959 | Robert Lewis Taylor, *The Travels of Jaimie McPheeters.* |
| 1960 | Allen Drury, *Advise and Consent.* |
| 1961 | Harper Lee, *To Kill a Mockingbird.* |
| 1962 | Edwin O'Connor, *The Edge of Sadness.* |
| 1963 | William Faulkner, *The Reivers.* |
| 1965 | Shirley Ann Grau, *The Keepers of the House.* |
| 1966 | Katherine Anne Porter, *Collected Stories of Katherine Anne Porter.* |
| 1967 | Bernard Malamud, *The Fixer.* |
| 1968 | William Styron, *The Confessions of Nat Turner.* |
| 1969 | N. Scott Momaday, *House Made of Dawn.* |
| 1970 | Jean Stafford, *Collected Stories.* |
| 1972 | Wallace Stegner, *Angle of Repose.* |
| 1973 | Eudora Welty, *The Optimist's Daughter.* |
| 1975 | Michael Shaara, *The Killer Angels.* |
| 1976 | Saul Bellow, *Humboldt's Gift.* |
| 1978 | James Alan McPherson, *Elbow Room.* |
| 1979 | John Cheever, *The Stories of John Cheever.* |
| 1980 | Norman Mailer, *The Executioner's Song.* |
| 1981 | John Kennedy Toole, *A Confederacy of Dunces.* |
| 1982 | John Updike, *Rabbit Is Rich.* |
| 1983 | Alice Walker, *The Color Purple.* |
| 1984 | William Kennedy, *Ironweed.* |
| 1985 | Alison Lurie, *Foreign Affairs.* |
| 1986 | Larry McMurtry, *Lonesome Dove.* |
| 1987 | Peter Taylor, *A Summons to Memphis.* |
| 1988 | Toni Morrison, *Beloved.* |
| 1989 | Anne Tyler, *Breathing Lessons.* |
| 1990 | Oscar Hijuelos, *The Mambo Kings Play Songs of Love.* |
| 1991 | John Updike, *Rabbit at Rest.* |
| 1992 | Jane Smiley, *A Thousand Acres.* |
| 1993 | Robert Olen Butler, *A Good Scent From a Strange Mountain.* |
| 1994 | E. Annie Proulx, *The Shipping News.* |
| 1995 | Carol Shields, *The Stone Diaries.* |
| 1996 | Richard Ford, *Independence Day.* |
| 1997 | Steven Millhauser, *Martin Dressler: The Tale of an American Dreamer.* |
| 1998 | Philip Roth, *American Pastoral.* |
| 1999 | Michael Cunningham, *The Hours.* |
| 2000 | Jhumpa Lahiri, *Interpreter of Maladies.* |
| 2001 | Michael Chabon, *The Amazing Adventures of Kavalier & Clay.* |
| 2002 | Richard Russo, *Empire Falls.* |
| 2003 | Jeffrey Eugenides, *Middlesex.* |
| 2004 | Edward P. Jones, *The Known World.* |
| 2005 | Marilynne Robinson, *Gilead.* |

## HISTORY

For a distinguished book on the history of the United States.

| 1917 | J. J. Jusserand, *With Americans of Past and Present Days.* |
| 1918 | James Ford Rhodes, *History of the Civil War.* |
| 1920 | Justin H. Smith, *The War with Mexico.* |
| 1921 | William Sowden Sims, *The Victory at Sea.* |
| 1922 | James Truslow Adams, *The Founding of New England.* |
| 1923 | Charles Warren, *The Supreme Court in United States History.* |
| 1924 | Charles Howard McIlwain, *The American Revolution: A Constitutional Interpretation.* |
| 1925 | Frederick L. Paxton, *A History of the American Frontier.* |
| 1926 | Edward Channing, *History of the United States,* Vol. VI. |
| 1927 | Samuel Flagg Bemis, *Pinckney's Treaty.* |
| 1928 | Vernon Louis Parrington, *Main Currents in American Thought.* |
| 1929 | Fred A. Shannon, *The Organization and Administration of the Union Army, 1861–65.* |
| 1930 | Claude H. Van Tyne, *The War of Independence.* |
| 1931 | Bernadotte E. Schmitt, *The Coming of the War, 1914.* |
| 1932 | Gen. John J. Pershing, *My Experiences in the World War.* |
| 1933 | Frederick J. Turner, *The Significance of Sections in American History.* |
| 1934 | Herbert Agar, *The People's Choice.* |
| 1935 | Charles McLean Andrews, *The Colonial Period of American History.* |
| 1936 | Andrew C. McLaughlin, *A Constitutional History of the United States.* |
| 1937 | Van Wyck Brooks, *The Flowering of New England.* |
| 1938 | Paul Herman Buck, *The Road of Reunion.* |
| 1939 | Frank Luther Mott, *A History of American Magazines.* |
| 1940 | Carl Sandburg, *Abraham Lincoln: The War Years.* |
| 1941 | Marcus Lee Hansen, *The Atlantic Migration.* |
| 1942 | Margaret Leech, *Reveille in Washington.* |
| 1943 | Esther Forbes, *Paul Revere and the World He Lived In.* |
| 1944 | Merle Curti, *The Growth of American Thought.* |
| 1945 | Stephen Bonsal, *Unfinished Business.* |
| 1946 | Arthur M. Schlesinger, Jr., *The Age of Jackson.* |
| 1947 | Dr. James Phinney Baxter, III, *Scientists Against Time.* |
| 1948 | Bernard De Voto, *Across the Wide Missouri.* |
| 1949 | Roy F. Nichols, *The Disruption of American Democracy.* |
| 1950 | O. W. Larkin, *Art and Life in America.* |
| 1951 | R. Carlyle Buley, *The Old Northwest: Pioneer Period, 1815–1840.* |
| 1952 | Oscar Handlin, *The Uprooted.* |
| 1953 | George Dangerfield, *The Era of Good Feelings.* |
| 1954 | Bruce Catton, *A Stillness at Appomattox.* |
| 1955 | Paul Horgan, *Great River: The Rio Grande in North American History.* |

**1956** Richard Hofstadter, *The Age of Reform.*
**1957** George F. Kennan, *Russia Leaves the War.*
**1958** Bray Hammond, *Banks and Politics in America —From the Revolution to the Civil War.*
**1959** Leonard D. White and Jean Schneider, *The Republican Era: 1869–1901.*
**1960** Margaret Leech, *In the Days of McKinley.*
**1961** Herbert Feis, *Between War and Peace: The Potsdam Conference.*
**1962** Lawrence H. Gipson, *The Triumphant Empire, Thunder Clouds Gather in the West.*
**1963** Constance McLaughlin Green, *Washington, Village and Capital, 1800–1878.*
**1964** Sumner Chilton Powell, *Puritan Village: The Formation of a New England Town.*
**1965** Irwin Unger, *The Greenback Era.*
**1966** Perry Miller, *The Life of the Mind in America: From the Revolution to the Civil War.*
**1967** William H. Goetzmann, *Exploration and Empire: The Explorer and Scientist in the Winning of the American West.*
**1968** Bernard Bailyn, *The Ideological Origins of the American Revolution.*
**1969** Leonard Levy, *Origins of the Fifth Amendment.*
**1970** Dean Acheson, *Present at the Creation: My Years in the State Department.*
**1971** James MacGregor Burns, *Roosevelt: The Soldier of Freedom.*
**1972** Carl N. Degler, *Neither Black Nor White.*
**1973** Michael Kammen, *People of Paradox: An Inquiry Concerning the Origins of American Civilization.*
**1974** Daniel J. Boorstin, *The Americans: The Democratic Experience*, Vol. III.
**1975** Dumas Malone, *Jefferson and His Time*, Vols. I-V.
**1976** Paul Horgan, *Lamy of Santa Fe.*
**1977** David M. Potter, *The Impending Crisis.*
**1978** Alfred D. Chandler, Jr., *The Visible Hand: The Managerial Revolution in American Business.*
**1979** Don E. Fehrenbacher, *The Dred Scott Case.*
**1980** Leon F. Litwack, *Been in the Storm So Long: The Aftermath of Slavery.*
**1981** Lawrence A. Cremin, *American Education: The National Experience 1783–1876.*
**1982** C. Vann Woodward (editor), *Mary Chesnut's Civil War.*
**1983** L. Isaac Rhys, *The Transformation of Virginia, 1740–1790.*
**1985** Thomas K. McCraw, *The Prophets of Regulation.*
**1986** Walter A. McDougall, *… the Heavens and the Earth: A Political History of the Space Age.*
**1987** Bernard Bailyn, *Voyagers to the West: A Passage in the Peopling of America on the Eve of the Revolution.*
**1988** Robert V. Bruce, *The Launching of Modern American Science, 1846–1876.*
**1989** Taylor Branch, *Parting the Waters.* James M. McPherson, *Battle Cry of Freedom.*
**1990** Stanley Karnow, *In Our Image: America's Empire in the Philippines.*
**1991** Laurel Thatcher Ulrich, *A Midwife's Tale: The Life of Martha Ballard, Based on Her Diary, 1785–1812.*
**1992** Mark E. Neely, Jr., *The Fate of Liberty: Abraham Lincoln and Civil Liberties.*
**1993** Gordon S. Wood, *The Radicalism of the American Revolution.*
**1995** Doris Kearns Goodwin, *No Ordinary Time: Franklin and Eleanor Roosevelt: The Home Front in World War II.*

**1996** Alan Taylor, *William Cooper's Town: Power and Persuasion on the Frontier of the Early American Republic.*
**1997** Jack N. Rakove, *Original Meanings: Politics and Ideas in the Making of the Constitution.*
**1998** Edward J. Larson, *Summer for the Gods: The Scopes Trial and America's Continuing Debate over Science and Religion.*
**1999** Edwin G. Burrows and Mike Wallace, *Gotham: A History of New York City to 1898.*
**2000** David M. Kennedy, *Freedom from Fear: The American People in Depression and War, 1929–1945.*
**2001** Joseph J. Ellis, *Founding Brothers: The Revolutionary Generation.*
**2002** Louis Menand, *The Metaphysical Club: A Story of Ideas in America.*
**2003** Rick Atkinson, *An Army at Dawn: The War in North Africa, 1942–1943.*
**2004** Steven Hahn, *A Nation Under Our Feet.*
**2005** David Hackett Fischer, *Washington's Crossing.*

## BIOGRAPHY OR AUTOBIOGRAPHY

For a distinguished biography or autobiography by an American author.

**1917** Laura E. Richards and Maude Howe Elliott, assisted by Florence Howe Hall, *Julia Ward Howe.*
**1918** William Cabell Bruce, *Benjamin Franklin, Self-Revealed.*
**1919** Henry Adams, *The Education of Henry Adams.*
**1920** Albert J. Beveridge, *The Life of John Marshall.*
**1921** Edward Bok, *The Americanization of Edward Bok.*
**1922** Hamlin Garland, *A Daughter of the Middle Border.*
**1923** Burton J. Hendrick, *The Life and Letters of Walter H. Page.*
**1924** Michael Pupin, *From Immigrant to Inventor.*
**1925** M. A. DeWolfe Howe, *Barrett Wendell and His Letters.*
**1926** Harvey Cushing, *Life of Sir William Osler.*
**1927** Emory Holloway, *Whitman, An Interpretation in Narrative.*
**1928** Charles Edward Russell, *The American Orchestra and Theodore Thomas.*
**1929** Burton J. Hendrick, *The Training of an American: The Earlier Life and Letters of Walter H. Page.*
**1930** Marquis James, *The Raven* (Sam Houston).
**1931** Henry James, *Charles W. Eliot.*
**1932** Henry F. Pringle, *Theodore Roosevelt.*
**1933** Allan Nevins, *Grover Cleveland.*
**1934** Tyler Dennett, *John Hay.*
**1935** Douglas Southall Freeman, *R. E. Lee.*
**1936** Ralph Barton Perry, *The Thought and Character of William James.*
**1937** Allan Nevins, *Hamilton Fish, the Inner History of the Grant Administration.*
**1938** Odell Shepard, *Pedlar's Progress* (Bronson Alcott). Marquis James, *Andrew Jackson.*
**1939** Carl Van Doren, *Benjamin Franklin.*
**1940** Ray Stannard Baker, *Woodrow Wilson, Life and Letters.*

1941 Ola Elizabeth Winslow, *Jonathan Edwards.*
1942 Forrest Wilson, *Crusader in Crinoline* (Harriet Beecher Stowe).
1943 Samuel Eliot Morison, *Admiral of the Ocean Sea* (Columbus).
1944 Carleton Mabee, *The American Leonardo: The Life of Samuel F. B. Morse.*
1945 Russel Blaine Nye, *George Bancroft: Brahmin Rebel.*
1946 Linnie Marsh Wolfe, *Son of the Wilderness* (John Muir).
1947 William Allen White, *The Autobiography of William Allen White.*
1948 Margaret Clapp, *Forgotten First Citizen: John Bigelow.*
1949 Robert E. Sherwood, *Roosevelt and Hopkins.*
1950 Samuel Flagg Bemis, *John Quincy Adams and the Foundations of American Foreign Policy.*
1951 Margaret Louise Coit, *John C. Calhoun: American Portrait.*
1952 Merlo J. Pusey, *Charles Evans Hughes.*
1953 David J. Mays, *Edmund Pendleton, 1721–1803.*
1954 Charles A. Lindbergh, *The Spirit of St. Louis.*
1955 William S. White, *The Taft Story.*
1956 Talbot F. Hamlin, *Benjamin Henry Latrobe.*
1957 John F. Kennedy, *Profiles in Courage.*
1958 Douglas Southall Freeman, *George Washington,* Vols. I-VI; John Alexander Carroll and Mary Wells Ashworth, Vol. VII.
1959 Arthur Walworth, *Woodrow Wilson, American Prophet.*
1960 Samuel Eliot Morison, *John Paul Jones.*
1961 David Herbert Donald, *Charles Sumner and the Coming of the Civil War.*
1963 Leon Edel, *Henry James:* Vol. II, *The Conquest of London, 1870–1881;* Vol. III, *The Middle Years, 1881–1895.*
1964 Walter Jackson Bate, *John Keats.*
1965 Ernest Samuels, *Henry Adams.*
1966 Arthur M. Schlesinger, Jr., *A Thousand Days.*
1967 Justin Kaplan, *Mr. Clemens and Mark Twain.*
1968 George F. Kennan, *Memoirs (1925–1950).*
1969 Benjamin Lawrence Reid, *The Man from New York: John Quinn and His Friends.*
1970 T. Harry Williams, *Huey Long.*
1971 Lawrence R. Thompson, *Robert Frost: The Years of Triumph, 1915–1938.*
1972 Joseph P. Lash, *Eleanor and Franklin.*
1973 William A. Swanberg, *Luce and His Empire.*
1974 Louis Sheaffer, *O'Neill, Son and Artist,* Vol. II (Eugene O'Neill).
1975 Robert A. Caro, *The Power Broker: Robert Moses and the Fall of New York.*
1976 Richard W. B. Lewis, *Edith Wharton.*
1977 John E. Mack, *A Prince of Our Disorder* (T. E. Lawrence).
1978 Walter Jackson Bate, *Samuel Johnson.*
1979 Leonard Baker, *Days of Sorrow and Pain: Leo Baeck and the Berlin Jews.*
1980 Edmund Morris, *The Rise of Theodore Roosevelt.*
1981 Robert K. Massie, *Peter the Great.*
1982 William S. McFeely, *Grant: A Biography.*
1983 Russell Baker, *Growing Up.*

1984 Louis R. Harlan, *Booker T. Washington: The Wizard of Tuskegee, 1901–1915.*
1985 Kenneth Silverman, *The Life and Times of Cotton Mather.*
1986 Elizabeth Frank, *Louise Bogan: A Portrait.*
1987 David Garrow, *Bearing the Cross: Martin Luther King Jr. and the Southern Christian Leadership Conference.*
1988 David Herbert Donald, *Look Homeward: A Life of Thomas Wolfe.*
1989 Richard Ellmann, *Oscar Wilde.*
1990 Sebastian de Grazia, *Machiavelli in Hell.*
1991 Steven Naifeh and Gregory White Smith, *Jackson Pollock: An American Saga.*
1992 Lewis B. Puller, Jr., *Fortunate Son: The Healing of a Vietnam Vet.*
1993 David McCullough, *Truman.*
1994 David L. Lewis, *W.E.B. Du Bois: Biography of a Race, 1868–1919.*
1995 Joan D. Hedrick, *Harriet Beecher Stowe: A Life.*
1996 Jack Miles, *God: A Biography.*
1997 Frank McCourt, *Angela's Ashes: A Memoir.*
1998 Katharine Graham, *Personal History.*
1999 A. Scott Berg, *Lindbergh.*
2000 Stacy Schiff, *Vera (Mrs. Vladimir Nabokov).*
2001 David L. Lewis, *W.E.B. Du Bois: The Fight for Equality and the American Century, 1919–1963.*
2002 David McCullough, *John Adams.*
2003 Robert A. Caro, *Master of the Senate.*
2004 William Taubman, *Khrushchev: The Man and His Era.*
2005 Mark Stevens and Annalyn Swan, *de Kooning: An American Master.*

## DRAMA

For a distinguished play by an American author, preferably original in its source and dealing with American life.

1918 Jesse Lynch Williams, *Why Marry?*
1920 Eugene O'Neill, *Beyond the Horizon.*
1921 Zona Gale, *Miss Lulu Bett.*
1922 Eugene O'Neill, *Anna Christie.*
1923 Owen Davis, *Icebound.*
1924 Hatcher Hughes, *Hell-Bent fer Heaven.*
1925 Sidney Howard, *They Knew What They Wanted.*
1926 George Kelly, *Craig's Wife.*
1927 Paul Green, *In Abraham's Bosom.*
1928 Eugene O'Neill, *Strange Interlude.*
1929 Elmer Rice, *Street Scene.*
1930 Marc Connelly, *The Green Pastures.*
1931 Susan Glaspell, *Alison's House.*
1932 George S. Kaufman, Morrie Ryskind, and Ira Gershwin, *Of Thee I Sing.*
1933 Maxwell Anderson, *Both Your Houses.*
1934 Sidney Kingsley, *Men in White.*
1935 Zoë Akins, *The Old Maid.*
1936 Robert E. Sherwood, *Idiot's Delight.*
1937 George S. Kaufman and Moss Hart, *You Can't Take It with You.*
1938 Thornton Wilder, *Our Town.*

1939 Robert E. Sherwood, *Abe Lincoln in Illinois.*
1940 William Saroyan, *The Time of Your Life.*
1941 Robert E. Sherwood, *There Shall Be No Night.*
1943 Thornton Wilder, *The Skin of Our Teeth.*
1945 Mary Chase, *Harvey.*
1946 Russel Crouse and Howard Lindsay, *State of the Union.*
1948 Tennessee Williams, *A Streetcar Named Desire.*
1949 Arthur Miller, *Death of a Salesman.*
1950 Richard Rodgers, Oscar Hammerstein II, and Joshua Logan, *South Pacific,* based on James A. Michener's 1948 prize-winning book, *Tales of the South Pacific.*
1952 Joseph Kramm, *The Shrike.*
1953 William Inge, *Picnic.*
1954 John Patrick, *Teahouse of the August Moon.*
1955 Tennessee Williams, *Cat on a Hot Tin Roof.*
1956 Frances Goodrich and Albert Hackett, *The Diary of Anne Frank.*
1957 Eugene O'Neill, *Long Day's Journey into Night.*
1958 Ketti Frings, *Look Homeward, Angel.*
1959 Archibald MacLeish, *J. B.*
1960 George Abbott, Jerome Weidman, Sheldon Harnick, and Jerry Bock, *Fiorello!*
1961 Tad Mosel, *All the Way Home,* based on James Agee's 1958 prize-winning book, *A Death in the Family.*
1962 Frank Loesser and Abe Burrows, *How to Succeed in Business Without Really Trying.*
1965 Frank D. Gilroy, *The Subject Was Roses.*
1967 Edward Albee, *A Delicate Balance.*
1969 Howard Sackler, *The Great White Hope.*
1970 Charles Gordone, *No Place to Be Somebody.*
1971 Paul Zindel, *The Effect of Gamma Rays on Man-in-the-Moon Marigolds.*
1973 Jason Miller, *That Championship Season.*
1975 Edward Albee, *Seascape.*
1976 Michael Bennett, James Kirkwood, Nicholas Dante, Marvin Hamlisch, and Edward Kleban, *A Chorus Line.*
1977 Michael Cristofer, *The Shadow Box.*
1978 Donald L. Coburn, *The Gin Game.*
1979 Sam Shepard, *Buried Child.*
1980 Lanford Wilson, *Talley's Folly.*
1981 Beth Henley, *Crimes of the Heart.*
1982 Charles Fuller, *A Soldier's Play.*
1983 Marsha Norman, *'night, Mother.*
1984 David Mamet, *Glengarry Glen Ross.*
1985 Stephen Sondheim and James Lapine, *Sunday in the Park with George.*
1987 August Wilson, *Fences.*
1988 Alfred Uhry, *Driving Miss Daisy.*
1989 Wendy Wasserstein, *The Heidi Chronicles.*
1990 August Wilson, *The Piano Lesson.*
1991 Neil Simon, *Lost in Yonkers.*
1992 Robert Schenkkan, *The Kentucky Cycle.*
1993 Tony Kushner, *Angels in America: Millennium Approaches.*
1994 Edward Albee, *Three Tall Women.*
1995 Horton Foote, *The Young Man from Atlanta.*
1996 Jonathan Larson, *Rent.*
1998 Paula Vogel, *How I Learned to Drive.*
1999 Margaret Edson, *Wit.*
2000 Donald Margulies, *Dinner with Friends.*
2001 David Auburn, *Proof.*

2002 Suzan-Lori Parks, *Topdog/Underdog.*
2003 Nilo Cruz, *Anna in the Tropics.*
2004 Doug Wright, *I Am My Own Wife.*
2005 John Patrick Shanley, *Doubt, a parable.*

## POETRY

For a distinguished volume of verse by an American author. Before this prize was established in 1922, awards were provided by the Poetry Society. Prize-winning works were *Love Songs* by Sara Teasdale (1918) and *Old Road to Paradise* by Margaret Widdemer and *Corn Huskers* by Carl Sandburg (1919).

1922 Edwin Arlington Robinson, *Collected Poems.*
1923 Edna St. Vincent Millay, *The Ballad of the Harp-Weaver; A Few Figs from Thistles; Eight Sonnets in American Poetry, 1922; A Miscellany.*
1924 Robert Frost, *New Hampshire: A Poem with Notes and Grace Notes.*
1925 Edwin Arlington Robinson, *The Man Who Died Twice.*
1926 Amy Lowell, *What's O'Clock.*
1927 Leonora Speyer, *Fiddler's Farewell.*
1928 Edwin Arlington Robinson, *Tristram.*
1929 Stephen Vincent Benét, *John Brown's Body.*
1930 Conrad Aiken, *Selected Poems.*
1931 Robert Frost, *Collected Poems.*
1932 George Dillon, *The Flowering Stone.*
1933 Archibald MacLeish, *Conquistador.*
1934 Robert Hillyer, *Collected Verse.*
1935 Audrey Wurdemann, *Bright Ambush.*
1936 Robert P. Tristram Coffin, *Strange Holiness.*
1937 Robert Frost, *A Further Range.*
1938 Marya Zaturenska, *Cold Morning Sky.*
1939 John Gould Fletcher, *Selected Poems.*
1940 Mark Van Doren, *Collected Poems.*
1941 Leonard Bacon, *Sunderland Capture.*
1942 William Rose Benét, *The Dust Which Is God.*
1943 Robert Frost, *A Witness Tree.*
1944 Stephen Vincent Benét, *Western Star.*
1945 Karl Shapiro, *V-Letter and Other Poems.*
1947 Robert Lowell, *Lord Weary's Castle.*
1948 W. H. Auden, *The Age of Anxiety.*
1949 Peter Viereck, *Terror and Decorum.*
1950 Gwendolyn Brooks, *Annie Allen.*
1951 Carl Sandburg, *Complete Poems.*
1952 Marianne Moore, *Collected Poems.*
1953 Archibald MacLeish, *Collected Poems.*
1954 Theodore Roethke, *The Waking.*
1955 Wallace Stevens, *Collected Poems.*
1956 Elizabeth Bishop, *Poems, North and South.*
1957 Richard Wilbur, *Things of This World.*
1958 Robert Penn Warren, *Promises: Poems 1954–1956.*
1959 Stanley Kunitz, *Selected Poems 1928–1958.*
1960 W. D. Snodgrass, *Heart's Needle.*
1961 Phyllis McGinley, *Times Three: Selected Verse from Three Decades.*
1962 Alan Dugan, *Poems.*
1963 William Carlos Williams, *Pictures from Brueghel.*

**1964** Louis Simpson, *At the End of the Open Road.*
**1965** John Berryman, *77 Dream Songs.*
**1966** Richard Eberhart, *Selected Poems (1930–1965).*
**1967** Anne Sexton, *Live or Die.*
**1968** Anthony Hecht, *The Hard Hours.*
**1969** George Oppen, *Of Being Numerous.*
**1970** Richard Howard, *Untitled Subjects.*
**1971** William S. Merwin, *The Carrier of Ladders.*
**1972** James Wright, *Collected Poems.*
**1973** Maxine Winokur Kumin, *Up Country.*
**1974** Robert Lowell, *The Dolphin.*
**1975** Gary Snyder, *Turtle Island.*
**1976** John Ashbery, *Self-Portrait in a Convex Mirror.*
**1977** James Merrill, *Divine Comedies.*
**1978** Howard Nemerov, *Collected Poems.*
**1979** Robert Penn Warren, *Now and Then.*
**1980** Donald R. Justice, *Selected Poems.*
**1981** James Schuyler, *The Morning of the Poem.*
**1982** Sylvia Plath, *The Collected Poems.*
**1983** Galway Kinnel, *Selected Poems.*
**1984** Mary Oliver, *American Primitive.*
**1985** Carolyn Kizer, *Yin.*
**1986** Henry Taylor, *The Flying Change.*
**1987** Rita Dove, *Thomas and Beulah.*
**1988** William Meredith, *Partial Accounts: New and Selected Poems.*
**1989** Richard Wilbur, *New and Collected Poems.*
**1990** Charles Simic, *The World Doesn't End.*
**1991** Mona Van Duyn, *Near Changes.*
**1992** James Tate, *Selected Poems.*
**1993** Louise Gluck, *The Wild Iris.*
**1994** Yusef Komunyakaa, *Neon Vernacular.*
**1995** Philip Levine, *The Simple Truth.*
**1996** Jorie Graham, *The Dream of the Unified Field.*
**1997** Lisel Mueller, *Alive Together: New and Selected Poems.*
**1998** Charles Wright, *Black Zodiac.*
**1999** Mark Strand, *Blizzard of One.*
**2000** C. K. Williams, *Repair.*
**2001** Stephen Dunn, *Different Hours.*
**2002** Carl Dennis, *Practical Gods.*
**2003** Paul Muldoon, *Moy Sand and Gravel.*
**2004** Franz Wright, *Walking to Martha's Vineyard.*
**2005** Ted Kooser, *Delights & Shadows.*

## GENERAL NONFICTION

For a distinguished book not eligible for consideration in any other existing category.

**1962** Theodore H. White, *The Making of the President, 1960.*
**1963** Barbara W. Tuchman, *The Guns of August.*
**1964** Richard Hofstadter, *Anti-intellectualism in American Life.*
**1965** Howard M. Jones, *O Strange New World.*
**1966** Edwin Way Teale, *Wandering Through Winter.*
**1967** David Brion Davis, *The Problem of Slavery in Western Culture.*
**1968** Will and Ariel Durant, *Rousseau and Revolution.*
**1969** Norman Mailer, *Armies of the Night.* René Jules Dubos, *So Human an Animal.*
**1970** Eric Erikson, *Gandhi's Truth.*
**1971** John Toland, *The Rising Sun.*
**1972** Barbara W. Tuchman, *Stillwell and the American Experience in China.*

**1973** Frances FitzGerald, *Fire in the Lake.* Robert M. Coles, *Children of Crisis,* Vols. II and III.
**1974** Ernest Becker, *The Denial of Death.*
**1975** Annie Dillard, *Pilgrim at Tinker Creek.*
**1976** Robert N. Butler, *Why Survive? Being Old in America.*
**1977** William W. Warner, *Beautiful Swimmers: Watermen, Crabs and the Chesapeake Bay.*
**1978** Carl Sagan, *The Dragons of Eden.*
**1979** Edward O. Wilson, *On Human Nature.*
**1980** Douglas R. Hofstadter, *Gödel, Escher, Bach: An Eternal Golden Braid.*
**1981** Carl E. Schorske, *Fin-de-Siècle Vienna: Politics and Culture.*
**1982** Tracy Kidder, *The Soul of a New Machine.*
**1983** Susan Sheehan, *Is There No Place on Earth for Me?*
**1984** Paul Starr, *The Social Transformation of American Medicine.*
**1985** Studs Terkel, *The Good War: An Oral History of World War II.*
**1986** Joseph Lelyveld, *Move Your Shadow: South Africa, Black and White.* J. Anthony Lukas, *Common Ground: A Turbulent Decade in the Lives of Three American Families.*
**1987** David Shipler, *Arab and Jew: Wounded Spirits in a Promised Land.*
**1988** Richard Rhodes, *The Making of the Atomic Bomb.*
**1989** Neil Sheehan, *A Bright Shining Lie.*
**1990** Dale Maharidge and Michael Williamson, *And Their Children After Them.*
**1991** Bert Holldobler and Edward O. Wilson, *The Ants.*
**1992** Daniel Yergin, *The Prize: The Epic Quest for Oil, Money and Power.*
**1993** Garry Wills, *Lincoln at Gettysburg: The Words That Remade America.*
**1994** David Remnick, *Lenin's Tomb: The Last Days of the Soviet Empire.*
**1995** Jonathan Weiner, *The Beak of the Finch: A Story of Evolution in Our Time.*
**1996** Tina Rosenberg, *The Haunted Land: Facing Europe's Ghosts After Communism.*
**1997** Richard Kluger, *Ashes to Ashes: America's Hundred-Year Cigarette War, the Public Health, and the Unabashed Triumph of Philip Morris.*
**1998** Jared Diamond, *Guns, Germs and Steel: The Fates of Human Societies.*
**1999** John McPhee, *Annals of the Former World.*
**2000** John W. Dower, *Embracing Defeat: Japan in the Wake of World War II.*
**2001** Herbert P. Bix, *Hirohito and the Making of Modern Japan.*
**2002** Diane McWhorter, *Carry Me Home: Birmingham, Alabama, the Climactic Battle of the Civil Rights Revolution.*
**2003** Samantha Power, *"A Problem From Hell": America and the Age of Genocide.*
**2004** Anne Applebaum, *Gulag: A History.*
**2005** Steve Coll, *Ghost Wars.*

JOHN HOHENBERG
Author, *The Pulitzer Prizes*

**PULLMAN, GEORGE MORTIMER.** See RAIL-ROADS (Profiles).

The Crab Nebula

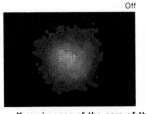

Off    On

X-ray images of the core of the Crab Nebula reveal the pulsar that appears to blink on and off (*above*) as its constant short bursts of radiation reach observers on Earth.

## PULSARS

In 1967, radio astronomers at Cambridge, England, were astounded to find strange radio signals coming from certain places in space. The signals came in short rapid bursts, or pulses, each lasting only a few hundredths of a second but repeated with extraordinary regularity. Scientists realized these radio signals were coming from objects sending streams of radiation into space. From Earth, this radiation is seen as short bursts, or pulses, and these objects became known as **pulsars**.

The pulses that astronomers receive from these objects are very sharp, so they conclude that pulsars are very tiny and have a radius of only about 10 miles (16 kilometers). When an object emits a burst of radio-wave radiation, the waves from different parts of the object arrive at the Earth at different times. This causes the original burst of radiation to become blurred. The smaller the object, however, the sharper the burst, or pulse.

Only one other object in the universe—a **neutron star**—is known to have such a small size yet is able to emit such bursts of radiation. Neutron stars mark the final stage in the life of many giant stars. When a giant star has used up most of its fuel and its nuclear reactions begin to lessen, the star collapses. As it collapses, gases and other materials are compressed. Then, the hot, compressed gases explode, creating what is known as a **supernova**. The remaining materials in the dying star continue collapsing inward, producing enormous pressures that crush the nuclei of atoms together, forming particles called neutrons. The resulting ball of neutrons, called a neu-tron star, is very small and dense. The density of matter in a neutron star is about one billion tons per cubic inch.

A pulsar is a neutron star that spins rapidly and has a strong magnetic field because of its great density. It acts like a radio transmitter, beaming a narrow radio wave into space. As a pulsar spins, this radio wave sweeps through space like the light from a revolving lighthouse beacon. Astronomers on Earth can only detect the radio wave when it is pointed directly at our planet, appearing to blink on and off as it arrives as a series of short pulses. As neutron stars age, they tend to rotate more slowly and no longer act as pulsars. In fact, most neutron stars in the universe are not pulsars.

Astronomers tried to link neutron stars and pulsars by studying the Crab Nebula—a cloud of gas produced by a supernova that occurred in A.D. 1054. They reasoned that if neutron stars are the remains of supernova explosions and pulsars are neutron stars, then they should find a pulsar in the remains of a supernova explosion. In 1968, astronomers found a pulsar at the center of the Crab Nebula, precisely where the neutron star from the supernova should be located.

Since then, more than 1,000 pulsars have been found. Many emit not just radio energy, but energy across the spectrum, including X-rays and visible light. In 2003, the first two-pulsar binary was found. (Binaries are systems in which two stars orbit each other.) Pulsars are so dense they can exert extreme gravitational forces on their binary companions. Scientists study the effects of these forces to test theories about gravity.

ROBERT JASTROW
Mount Wilson Institute

See also ASTRONOMY; RADIO ASTRONOMY; STARS; TELESCOPES; UNIVERSE.

**PUMICE.** See ROCKS (Igneous Rock).

# PUMPS

A pump is a machine that moves liquids and sometimes solids from one level to another and from one place to another. Pumps are very useful. They help bring water to homes and other buildings; they help provide water for irrigating crops; they make it easy to move oil, gasoline, chemicals, and waste out of industrial plants.

Pumps are among the oldest and most commonly used machines, and were used long ago by people in ancient Egypt, China, India, Greece, and Rome. Today pumps are the second most commonly used kind of industrial equipment. Electric motors rank first.

### How Do Pumps Work?

Pumps move liquids by pressure or by suction, and sometimes by both methods, in the same way that you do when you sip a drink through a straw. As you suck through a straw, you pull some of the air out of it, which reduces the air pressure in the straw. This makes a space of lower pressure in the straw. The higher pressure on the surface of the drink pushes the liquid up into the straw to equalize the pressure, and the liquid flows into your mouth.

Air pressure is sometimes called **atmospheric pressure**. In 1643 the Italian scientist Evangelista Torricelli proved that air has weight. At sea level this weight is 14.7 pounds per square inch (1.036 kilograms per square centimeter).

A simple lift pump, like the old-fashioned suction pump, moves liquid with the help of this atmospheric pressure. The machinery of the pump is designed so that it can create a vacuum inside. Atmospheric pressure on the liquid outside pushes the liquid into the pump. Once the liquid is inside the pump and is in contact with the pumping machinery, the machinery pushes the liquid to higher levels.

Atmospheric pressure can hold water up to 34 feet (10 meters) high in a vertical pipe when the bottom of the pipe is in water and the top of the pipe is closed. Often, however, there is some leakage out of the pipe, and the vacuum created is not perfect. For this reason, suction pumps are not expected to lift a liquid more than about 25 feet (7.5 meters) high at sea level. If the liquid has to be lifted any higher, a pressure pump must be used.

Once in a while, air gets into the interior of a pump and can air-bind it, which prevents it from moving. It then needs to be **primed**—that is, the air in the pump needs to be removed. This is done by adding liquid to the pump or by using special priming machines. Some pumps are made in such a way that they are self-priming.

### Kinds of Pumps

Pumps may be divided into several types, according to the ways in which liquids are moved by them. Positive displacement pumps move liquids by the action of a mechanical device in a tightly enclosed space. The device may move up and down, as in a piston pump, or by rotating, as in a gear pump. Turbomachinery pumps use rapidly rotating elements in a casing to set fluids in motion. Centrifugal and propeller pumps are also in this class.

**How A Suction Pump Works**

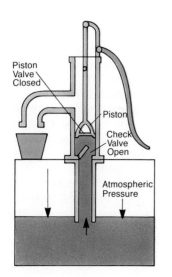
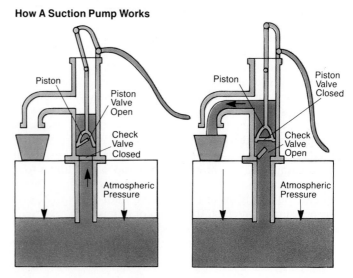

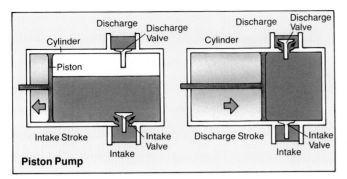

Piston Pump

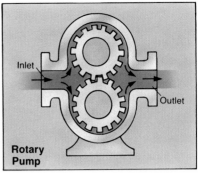

Rotary Pump

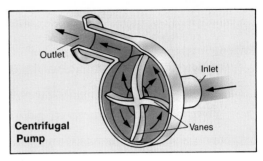

Centrifugal Pump

**Piston Pumps.** Piston pumps work by the up-and-down movement of a tightly fitting piston in a cylinder. When the piston moves one way, it sucks liquid into the cylinder through an opening called an intake port. On the return stroke it forces the liquid out through another opening called a discharge port. Valves control the flow of liquid into and out of the cylinder. A simple pump of this type is the hand-operated lift pump, which uses atmospheric pressure to move liquids. Fluids may also be moved in a piston pump by pressure applied to the piston. Fluid is discharged only on the return stroke, unless the pump is a double-acting one.

**Rotary Pumps.** In these pumps, rotating parts inside a close-fitting case cause a liquid to move because of the differences in pressure within the case. The parts may be two gears meshing together. As the gears unmesh, a partial vacuum is formed and liquid is drawn into the pump. On the side where the gears mesh, pressure forces the liquid out. In vane pumps the rotating part is located off center in the case. Liquids are forced out as the space between the vanes becomes smaller at the outlet side. Rotary pumps do not need valves, and they deliver a constant flow of liquid.

**Centrifugal Pumps.** Centrifugal force causes a rotating body to move away from the center of rotation. In a centrifugal pump, rapidly rotating elements such as vanes cause the fluid in the case to rotate. Centrifugal force pushes the fluid out of the discharge line. A vacuum is created inside the case as a result, and atmospheric pressure forces more fluid into the case. Centrifugal pumps are particularly useful for moving large flows of water against relatively low pressure.

Reviewed by Igor J. Karassik
Consulting Engineer

# PUNCTUATION

Ancient writers used few marks of punctuation. The words carved on ancient monuments are usually run together, and it is almost impossible to figure out their meaning. After the printing press was invented in the 1400's, type was set in sentences and paragraphs. Punctuation marks were used to help the reader understand the thoughts of the writer. Today punctuation marks are a necessary part of written communication.

▶**RULES FOR PUNCTUATION**
We must know the rules of punctuation and use them in our writing so that our meaning will be clear to the reader.

**Period (.).** The period is used after
(1) Sentences that are declarative (make a statement) or imperative (make a command).

The plane landed just before midnight.
Open the door, please.

**(2)** Many abbreviations.

| | | |
|---|---|---|
| Mr. | M.D. | Feb. |
| Rev. | A.M. | Ltd. |
| Jr. | vol. | Co. |

(Many other examples are given in the article ABBREVIATIONS in Volume A.)

**Question Mark (?).** The question mark is used after an interrogative sentence.

Are you coming?

**Exclamation Point (!).** The exclamation point is used after a word, phrase, or sentence that expresses a sudden or strong emotion.

Oh! How dare you!

**Comma (,).** The comma is used to set off

**(1)** Nouns in direct address (the name of a person you are speaking to directly).

Dick, you are wanted on the telephone.

**(2)** An appositive (a word or phrase that identifies a noun or pronoun).

Mrs. Newman, the school principal, told me.

**(3)** Disconnected words, phrases, or clauses.

Yes, I'll do it for you.
Well, what do you think?
The news, to say the least, was a surprise.
He will, I believe, recover completely.

**(4)** Nonrestrictive phrases or clauses (information not essential to the meaning of the sentence).

Jimmy, who was making a last try, passed the other contestants.
The flag, as it floated in the breeze, was a sign of victory.

**(5)** Items in addresses and dates.

Edmonton, Alberta
October 12, 1980
Savannah, Georgia

**(6)** The salutation in a friendly letter and the complimentary close in all letters.

Dear Joan,
Sincerely yours,
Respectfully yours,

**(7)** Items in a series.

The three R's are reading, writing, and arithmetic.

**(8)** Adjectives that modify a noun individually. If the conjunction "and" can be put between the adjectives, a comma is used.

He was a brave, honest man.
(He was a brave and honest man.)

**(9)** Two independent clauses (clauses each containing a subject and a verb) joined by a co-ordinating conjunction (*and, but, or*).

I think he is wrong, but I cannot prove it.

**(10)** Adverbial clauses (clauses that modify the verb) at the beginning of a sentence.

If he can come next Thursday, he will.

**(11)** A direct quotation, to separate the speaker from what is said.

"That isn't possible," he declared.

A comma is used to clarify the meaning of a sentence that might be misread.

Soon after, the officer left.
To Mary, Jane was always right.

**Semicolon (;).** The semicolon is used

**(1)** To set off parts of a sentence that already contain commas.

They traveled all over the country, from Bangor, Maine, to Miami, Florida; from Chicago, Illinois, to Houston, Texas.

**(2)** To separate independent clauses in a compound sentence when they are not joined by a conjunction.

He did not go to the baseball game; he went swimming.

**Colon (:).** The colon is used

**(1)** After the salutation of a business letter.

Dear Dr. Brown:

**(2)** To introduce a list (three or more items).

He spoke four languages: French, German, Russian, and Chinese.

**(3)** To separate hour and minute figures in writing time.

The Boston train leaves at 10:35 P.M.

**Dash (—).** The dash is used

**(1)** To indicate a break in thought.

I'll help you—if you want help.

**(2)** Before a summary statement.

Food, clothing, shelter—these are the basic necessities.

**Parentheses ( ).** Parentheses are used to enclose an aside or an explanation.

She was just 18 (the legal age for voting).
He was (and still is) my friend.

**Hyphen (-).** The hyphen is used

**(1)** To separate the syllables of a word that falls at the end of a line of writing and must be continued on the following line.

If you have any doubt, consult the schedule about the time of the train.

**(2)** To divide the parts of a compound word.

forty-five
brother-in-law

**Apostrophe (').** The apostrophe is used

**(1)** To denote the possessive (ownership) case of nouns and indefinite pronouns.

The boy's coat was lost.
Boys' overcoats are on sale.
Everybody's business is nobody's business.

**(2)** To indicate that figures or letters have been left out.

The class of '64 held its reunion.
It isn't fair to the group.
I'll come with you.

**(3)** To form the plural of letters and figures.

Dot your *i*'s and cross your *t*'s.
Your 3's look like 8's.

**Quotation Marks (" ").** Quotation marks are used

**(1)** To enclose a direct quotation (the exact words of a speaker).

"Are you ready?" she called.
"It will take less time," Tom's father said, "if you will help me."

A quotation within a quotation is enclosed in single quotation marks.

"Then," he continued, "we heard the cry 'Breakers ahead!' "

If a direct quotation consists of more than one paragraph, put quotation marks at the beginning of each paragraph and at the end of the last paragraph only.

**(2)** To enclose the title of a poem, a short story, a song, or an article if the title appears in a sentence.

Canada's national anthem is "O Canada."

**Italics or Underlining.** Italics in printed matter are the same as underlining in writing or typescript. They are used

**(1)** To indicate the title of a book, play, motion picture, newspaper, or magazine if the title appears in a sentence.

The girl's favorite novel is *The Yearling*.

**(2)** To show the name of a ship or an airplane if the name appears in a sentence.

The *Queen Elizabeth 2* was one of the largest ocean liners.
Charles Lindbergh crossed the Atlantic Ocean in the *Spirit of St. Louis*.

**(3)** To indicate foreign words or phrases.

The Latin words *id est* means "that is."

**Capitals.** Capitalize the following:

**(1)** The first word of every sentence.

The meeting began promptly.

**(2)** In many poems, the first word of a line.

It is an ancient Mariner,
And he stoppeth one of three.

**(3)** The first word of a direct quotation (unless the quotation is used as a part of your own sentence).

Patrick Henry cried, "Give me liberty, or give me death!"
The candidate called for a "new look in government."

**(4)** Proper nouns (names of particular persons, places, or things) and most adjectives derived from proper nouns.

| | |
|---|---|
| Massachusetts | Sunday |
| Fourth of July | Fifth Avenue |
| Atlantic Ocean | June |
| Middle Ages | Red Cross |
| World War II | Protestant |
| House of Commons | Catholic |
| Council of Trent | Magna Carta |
| Supreme Court | European |
| King George V | Spanish |

**(5)** Nouns and pronouns referring to the Deity (God) and sacred writings.

| | |
|---|---|
| God | Bible |
| Allah | Old Testament |
| Torah | Great Spirit |
| Koran | Yahweh |

**(6)** Titles used with proper names or in place of proper names.

Captain Jones          Her Majesty

**(7)** In literary titles, the first and last words and all other words except articles, coordinating conjunctions, and short prepositions.

*The Wind in the Willows*
*A Child's Garden of Verses*

**(8)** The words *North*, *South*, *East*, and *West* when they denote a recognized area.

The West is noted for its beautiful scenery and climate.

**(9)** Words denoting family relationship when used instead of the person's name or when used with the name (but not when a possessive pronoun is used).

Mother                          my cousin
Uncle John                      her father

**(10)** The pronoun I.

If you wait, I will get the book.

**(11)** The first word and all nouns in the salutation of a letter; the first word only in the complimentary close.

Dear Jack,                      Very truly yours,
Dear Madam or Sir:              Sincerely,

**(12)** The first word of main topics and subtopics in an outline.

I. Means of promoting health
  A. Balanced diet
  B. Proper exercise
  C. Adequate rest

Do not capitalize the following:

**(1)** Names of seasons—winter, spring, fall, summer—when used in a sentence.

It was a hot summer.

**(2)** Subjects of study, except languages, when used in a sentence.

I chose algebra and French.

**(3)** *North, south, east,* or *west* when referring to direction.

The plane was flying north.

Any writer, from a student doing homework to a country's president preparing a speech, must organize ideas and state them strongly and clearly. Punctuation is important. We should know how to use punctuation to help make our meaning clear.

MARY C. FOLEY
Author, *Language for Daily Use*

---

# PUNIC WARS

Ancient Rome and Carthage, a city-state in North Africa, fought three wars with each other. They are known as the Punic Wars, from the Latin word for Phoenicians, an early people who founded Carthage. The conflicts resulted from competition between the two states for control of the island of Sicily and the western Mediterranean Sea. Rome was victorious in all three wars, the last of which resulted in the destruction of Carthage.

The First Punic War (264–241 B.C.) was fought mainly in Sicily. It was especially noteworthy because it saw the development of the Roman Navy. Neither side was able to win until the Romans succeeded in forcing the Carthaginians to the western part of Sicily and then defeated the Carthaginian fleet in a great naval battle. As a result of its defeat, Carthage was forced to give up the island and pay an enormous war tax.

The Second Punic War (218–201 B.C.) stemmed from Roman fears that Carthage, involved in the conquest of Spain, would use Spanish resources and soldiers to start a new war. Rome demanded that Carthage give up some of its Spanish territory. War broke out when Hannibal, the Carthaginian general in Spain, refused Rome's demands and crossed the Alps to invade Italy. For the next 16 years, Hannibal ravaged Roman territory and defeated the Romans in four major battles.

Rome, however, refused to surrender. In 202 B.C., Hannibal was forced to return to Africa to face a Roman army threatening Carthage. The Romans defeated Hannibal at Zama, west of the city, ending the war.

To keep Carthage in check, Rome deprived the city of its navy and its Spanish possessions. It also established a rival North African state called Numidia. The Third Punic War (149–146 B.C.) broke out when Carthage, angered over Numidian raids against its territory, attacked Rome's ally. The Romans followed the advice of a senator named Cato, who ended every speech with the words, "Carthage must be destroyed." They declared war on Carthage, which immediately surrendered. But the Carthaginians rebelled when they learned that Rome intended to force them from their city into a new one. After a difficult siege lasting three years, the Romans captured Carthage and destroyed it. It marked the end of Rome's most feared enemy.

Some 30 years later the Romans established their own colony on the site in what is now Tunisia. It eventually became the Roman city of Carthage, the leading city, after Rome itself, in the western half of the Roman Empire.

R. BRUCE HITCHNER
University of Virginia

See also HANNIBAL.

# PUPPETS AND MARIONETTES

A puppet is any animated figure that is operated directly by a person. A marionette is a type of puppet that is controlled from above by strings attached to its body. Puppets may be made from any number of materials. A person who operates a puppet is called a puppeteer.

## ▶ KINDS OF PUPPETS

There are four basic kinds of puppets.

**Hand Puppets.** The hand puppet, also known as the fist puppet, glove puppet, or *guignol*, is worn over the hand like a glove or mitten. The index finger is inserted in the neck and the thumb and middle finger in the arms.

**Rod Puppets.** The rod puppet, sometimes called the stick puppet, is supported from below by a rod held in one hand. The puppeteer's other hand operates rods attached to the puppet's hands. Rod puppets are particularly popular in Asia. Japanese *Bunraku*, or puppet theater, is a highly developed form of theater that uses puppets about 4 feet (a little over 1 meter) tall. The puppeteers are dressed in black and work in full view of the audience, using their skilled fingers to operate the figures.

**Shadow Puppets.** The shadow puppet is a form of rod puppet. As its name suggests, its shadow is cast on a cloth screen by a strong light from behind. In elaborate shows, the figures are made of colored material, such as plastic or parchment, that is translucent (that is, it allows light to pass through). So both color and shape are shown on the screen. Through special design and clever joining of body parts, delightful animation is worked by the attached rods. Shadow puppets are always worked from below or behind the figure.

**Marionettes.** The marionette, or string-operated puppet, is the most complicated of all types. It is the only kind of puppet that can be moved freely around the total stage area. Great skill and experience are necessary to make and operate the kind of marionette you may have seen professional puppeteers use. This kind sometimes requires 30 or more strings. There is a simpler marionette, however, which requires only nine strings.

**Other Puppets.** Several other kinds of puppets fit no particular category and are not considered true puppets. One is the dummy used in ventriloquist performances. It is usually about one-half adult size. Seated on the ventriloquist's knee, it is supported and animated by one hand through its back. The act consists of action and conversation between the dummy and the ventriloquist, who makes the dummy seem to talk. For more informa-

Marionettes are controlled by strings. The puppeteers, hidden from audience view, operate them from above the stage.

tion, see the article VENTRILOQUISM in Volume U-V.

The finger puppet gets its name from the use of the puppeteer's index and middle fingers as the puppet's legs. Shoes fit over the ends of these fingers, and the body is held in position by an elastic strap over the puppeteer's hand. For the stage, the puppeteer's arms may be disguised by long black sleeves.

The humanette is a puppet body that incorporates the exposed head and hands of the performer, the rest of whom is hidden behind a partition. This type of puppet is used mainly for short novelty acts.

## ▶ HISTORY

The origin of the puppet is something of a mystery. Some historians think puppets were

*Continued on page 548*

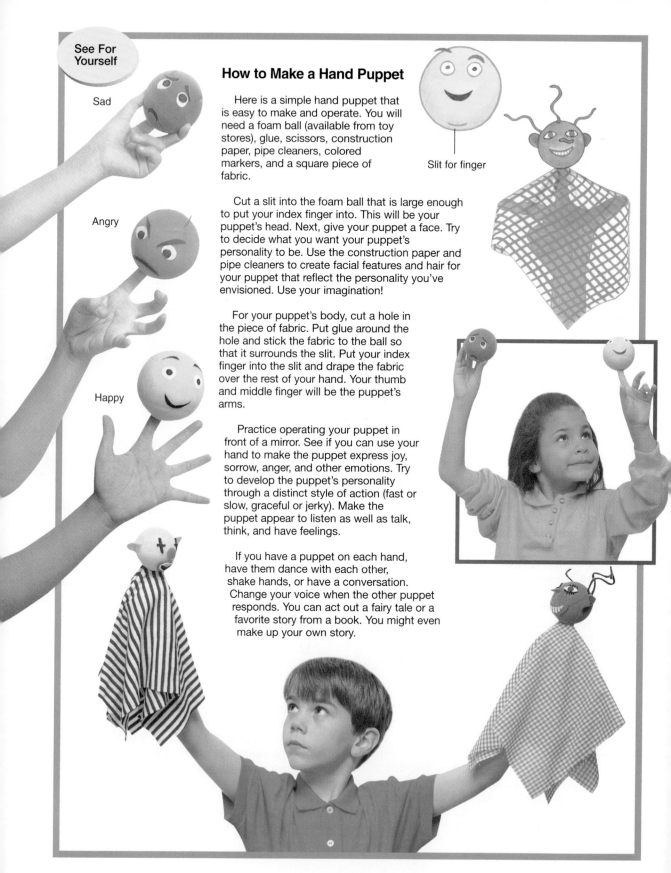

Sad

Angry

Happy

# How to Make a Hand Puppet

Here is a simple hand puppet that is easy to make and operate. You will need a foam ball (available from toy stores), glue, scissors, construction paper, pipe cleaners, colored markers, and a square piece of fabric.

Slit for finger

Cut a slit into the foam ball that is large enough to put your index finger into. This will be your puppet's head. Next, give your puppet a face. Try to decide what you want your puppet's personality to be. Use the construction paper and pipe cleaners to create facial features and hair for your puppet that reflect the personality you've envisioned. Use your imagination!

For your puppet's body, cut a hole in the piece of fabric. Put glue around the hole and stick the fabric to the ball so that it surrounds the slit. Put your index finger into the slit and drape the fabric over the rest of your hand. Your thumb and middle finger will be the puppet's arms.

Practice operating your puppet in front of a mirror. See if you can use your hand to make the puppet express joy, sorrow, anger, and other emotions. Try to develop the puppet's personality through a distinct style of action (fast or slow, graceful or jerky). Make the puppet appear to listen as well as talk, think, and have feelings.

If you have a puppet on each hand, have them dance with each other, shake hands, or have a conversation. Change your voice when the other puppet responds. You can act out a fairy tale or a favorite story from a book. You might even make up your own story.

## How to Make a Simple Stage

You can make a simple stage in a doorway by hanging a blanket on a rod just high enough to hide yourself from the audience. Or you can make a stage by cutting and decorating a large cardboard box.

After your stage is all set up, you may wish to rehearse what your puppets are going to say and do. Practice a few times, and before you know it, you will be ready to give your show!

## How to Make a Marionette

To make this ghostly fellow, a simplified version of a marionette, you will need an elasticized fabric, cotton balls, rope, a needle and thread, muslin, glue, two wooden dowels, six screw eyes, string, paint, and buttons.

Sew or glue a length of fabric to make a tube. Stuff it with cotton balls to create three sausage shapes. Leave another section unstuffed for a neck. Sew up the ends of each section.

Give the face features by stitching or gluing the fabric. Use buttons for eyes and enhance the features with paint.

Cut two lengths of rope for arms. Shape and sew two pieces of fabric into hands and attach them to the ropes. Then sew or glue the other ends of the ropes to the shoulders.

Cut two ragged squares of muslin. Sew or glue one to the upper body and arms and the other to the lower body.

Tape the dowels together. Ask an adult to attach the screw eyes, then loop on the strings as shown. Knot the ends of the string. Sew the knots to the hands, head, and the two back sections of the body.

To fly the ghost, hold the dowels horizontally and sweep him through the air so that his robe flaps behind him.

*Bunraku* is a popular type of puppetry in Japan. The puppeteers are dressed in black and work in full view of the audience while operating the figures.

first made along the banks of the Ganges River in India. Others claim that the Egyptians were the first to invent puppets and marionettes. Well-preserved marionettes have been discovered among the relics of ancient Egyptian tombs and dug up from under the pyramids.

Chinese puppets, usually shadow figures, are a very old tradition. Japan and other Asian countries also have long-standing puppet traditions. The Greeks, too, according to the earliest accounts that have come down to us, had puppet theaters. Later, the Romans borrowed puppetry from the Greeks, as they did other art forms. Both Greek and Roman puppet shows were given in private homes as well as in public places in the cities. Traveling shows gave performances on the road.

This Indonesian shadow puppet is controlled behind a screen. Only the puppet's shadow can be seen, cast by a strong light.

Every country in Europe, Asia, and Africa has had marionettes and puppets of one kind or another. Of them all, Italy is perhaps best known for its puppetry. In the Middle Ages, Italian showmen carried their *castelli dei burattini* (portable puppet theaters) to England, Germany, Spain, and France. These countries then adapted the shows to their own tastes. At first the plays presented by the puppet theaters consisted of sacred scenes from the Bible and stories of saints and martyrs. Then fables and comic characters and everyday situations were introduced.

One of the most famous Italian puppets was a character called **Pulcinella**, a rogue and a merrymaker. When the Italian puppeteers took to traveling the highways and visiting the villages of France with their merry puppet shows, Pulcinella had his name changed to the French form, Polichinelle. In 1662 Polichinelle was brought to London. There his name was changed to Punch, and he was given a wife named Joan, later, due to mispronunciation, changed to Judy. Punch is a real fighter and triumphs over everybody, including the devil. Generations of audiences have delightedly watched bad old Punch whacking his way through life with his slapstick. Punch first appeared in America in the mid-1700's, much to the amusement of audiences in Philadelphia and New York.

Puppetry has been developed to a high art in the theater. Some puppet theaters are world famous. Throughout Germany and Austria, Hanswurst and Kasperl, traditional puppet characters, continue to perform on many toy stages. Slavic countries also enjoy their share of this art form.

Television has made puppets very popular in the United States. Howdy Doody, Kukla and Ollie, and the marionettes of Bil and Cora Baird and ventriloquism puppets of Shari Lewis delighted a generation of children. Later, the popular television program *Sesame Street* introduced the Muppets, puppet characters created by Jim Henson. They are popular, too, on film.

RUFUS ROSE
Rufus Rose Marionettes
Reviewed and revised by ROD YOUNG
The Rod Young Puppets

# PURIM

The festival of Purim is the most joyous of all Jewish holidays. It is a time of feasting, merrymaking, and thanksgiving, for it celebrates the rescue of the Jews of Persia many centuries ago from a plot to destroy them. Purim is observed on the 14th day of the Hebrew month Adar, which usually falls in late February or early March. During Jewish leap years it is celebrated later in March. Purim, also called the Feast of Lots, is so named because the day chosen for the killing of the Jews was decided by chance, or lots. The Hebrew word for "lot" is *pur*. The events of the Purim story, as told in the Bible's Book of Esther, took place in Susa, the capital city of Persia, during the reign of King Ahasuerus (known to history as Xerxes) in the 400's B.C. Haman, prime minister to the king, is the villain. Queen Esther, the king's Jewish wife, is the heroine, and Mordecai, her cousin, is the hero.

Haman hated the Jews because Mordecai, one of their leaders, refused to bow down to him. He decided to punish Mordecai by destroying not only him, but all the Jews in the kingdom. Haman made the king angry at the Jews by telling him they did not keep the king's laws. (King Ahasuerus did not know that his wife, Esther, was Jewish or that she was related to Mordecai.) Haman asked that the Jews be destroyed. The king consented.

Mordecai learned of the plan and asked Esther to plead with her husband for the lives of her people. Esther decided to have a party where both Haman and the king were present, then tell her husband about Haman's plot to kill the Jews. The night before the party, the king could not sleep and had the court records read to him. From them he learned how Mordecai had once saved his life. The king sent for Haman and asked how a man who pleased his king should be honored. Haman believed he was the man the king was thinking of. He advised that the man should be dressed in the king's robes and crown and should ride through the town on the king's horse. So the king directed that this be done with Mordecai that very night.

During the Jewish holiday of Purim, children dress up as characters from the Bible's Book of Esther and participate in plays and carnivals.

The next day at the party, Esther told the king about Haman's evil plot. She revealed to the king that she, too, was Jewish and begged him to save her people. The king directed that Haman be hanged on the gallows that Haman had prepared for Mordecai. The threatened massacre of the Jews turned into a victory.

Purim is celebrated in many ways. At the morning and evening services, the Book of Esther, called the *Megillah*, is read in the synagogue. Whenever the name of Haman is mentioned, a wave of noise sweeps over the congregation. The children are encouraged to take part in the uproar. They sound noisemakers called groggers. Everyone enjoys the noisy change from the usual quiet behavior that marks the Jewish religious service.

In synagogues and homes people present plays and hold masquerade parties as part of the Purim celebration. The most popular costumes are those of Haman, Mordecai, and Queen Esther. Prizes are given for the best costumes. People exchange gifts of food and give charity to the poor. Purim banquets are held in homes, to which friends and neighbors are invited. Special pastries called *hamantaschen* are served. These are three-cornered cakes filled with poppy seeds or fruit. Their triangular shape is supposed to be that of the three-cornered hat Haman wore when he was prime minister to Ahasuerus.

RABBI MORTIMER J. COHEN
Author, *Pathways Through the Bible*
Reviewed by LAWRENCE GROSSMAN
Coeditor, *The American Jewish Year Book*

# PURITANS

The Puritans were Protestant reformers who originated in England and later spread to the New England colonies. Because their goal was to "purify" religion and politics of all corruption, these Protestants were at first called Puritans by their enemies. Eventually they adopted the name for themselves as a badge of honor.

### ▶ THE PURITANS IN ENGLAND

The Puritan movement began as a part of the Protestant Reformation in England in the early 1500's, when King Henry VIII broke ties with the Pope and the Roman Catholic Church. Henry's daughter, Queen Elizabeth I, continued to move the country toward Protestantism. However, some reformers felt that Elizabeth was not extreme enough in her measures to rid the country of Catholic influences. These people came to be known as the Puritans.

The Puritans emphasized the importance of an individual's personal relationship to God and to the Bible. They wanted to eliminate all frivolity and decoration from the church, such as organ music, stained-glass windows, incense, and fancy religious robes—anything that drew attention away from one's inner spirituality. The Puritans also wished to improve the quality of the ministry. They encouraged ministers to write their own original and inspiring sermons, rather than simply quoting from *The Book of Common Prayer*.

Due to their criticism of England's established church, the Puritans were severely persecuted by the English king Charles I and his archbishop, William Laud. Numerous Puritans went into hiding in England, while others fled into exile throughout Europe. Others escaped to the New World. Eventually, the Puritans who remained in England engaged in a civil war against the king. Under the Puritan leadership of Oliver Cromwell, King Charles I was executed, and Cromwell briefly took control of England (1649–60).

### ▶ MIGRATION TO THE NEW WORLD

In 1630, sailing on a ship called the *Arbella*, John Winthrop (1588–1649) led the first group of English Puritans to Massachusetts Bay in New England. Although they were among the first immigrants to come to America in search of a better life, they were not the "poor, huddled masses" known to later generations. Most were well-educated ministers, lawyers, merchants, and farmers, who enjoyed connections to religious and political leaders back in England.

The Puritans thought of New England as a place to experiment with new structures of church and state governments that could later serve as models for reform in England and other parts of the world. Winthrop, a founder and four-term governor of the Massachusetts Bay Colony, believed in **theocracy**—a form of government that combines the laws of church and state and emphasizes the greater good of the community over personal gain. Winthrop envisioned "a city upon a hill" that could serve as "a model of Christian charity." Other early Puritan leaders who embraced these beliefs included the ministers John Cotton (1584–1652); John Harvard (1607–38), founder of Harvard College (1638); Richard Mather (1596–1669); Richard's son Increase Mather (1639–1723); and Increase's son Cotton Mather (1663–1728). They and their followers established

Puritans in England became increasingly critical of Catholic influences on the Church of England, which brought them into conflict with the king.

churches in Boston and Newtown (present-day Cambridge), in Massachusetts; Hartford and New Haven, in Connecticut; and other towns in New England.

## ▶ RELIGIOUS BELIEFS

The Puritans borrowed many of their religious doctrines from the writings of the Protestant reformer John Calvin (1509–64), as did the Huguenots, a group of French Protestants whose beliefs were similar to those of the Puritans. Calvin believed in predestination, meaning that God had long since decided who would and who would not go to heaven. Good Puritans had to have faith that they

Many Puritans immigrated to New England, where they hoped to build a new life free from religious intolerance.

would achieve salvation and had to examine their daily lives for signs of God's disfavor. For example, when the poet Anne Bradstreet's house burned down, she took it as a message from God to be stronger in her faith.

To help them develop their faith, the Puritans relied on three books: *The New England Primer*, which taught them the alphabet as well as moral lessons; *The Bay Psalm Book*, which offered English translations of the Psalms to be sung at church services; and the Bible. To help them understand and decode the Bible, the Puritans listened to hundreds of hours of sermons. At least twice each week, ministers would explain how scripture should be used both as a guide to daily living and as a way to predict future events.

The Puritans believed that the simple way was the quicker and better way to God. Ministers wrote their sermons in what is called the **plain style**, a way of writing and speaking without complicated words, distracting references to unknown books, or quotations in foreign languages. They also favored plain, black garments over the fancy, colorful robes of the Catholic Church and held services in small white chapels instead of in elaborately decorated churches.

## ▶ CONTROVERSY AND DISSENT

The Puritans of New England experienced many conflicts almost from the moment they arrived in the New World. Several notable Puritan dissenters, including Roger Williams and Anne Hutchinson, were ordered out of the Massachusetts Bay Colony because they would not conform to the strict codes of the Puritan leaders. Certain others who failed to follow the rules of religion and society were put on trial as witches and sometimes executed, the most notable incident being the Salem Witch Trials of 1692. In addition, the Puritans warred almost continuously with Native Americans. It is one of the great curiosities of history that the Puritans—who had fled persecution in England—would themselves establish a rigid and intolerant society in New England.

## ▶ PURITAN LEGACIES

Although strict Puritanism died out in the mid-1700's, many of the ways and beliefs of the Puritans became a permanent part of the American culture. For example, the Puritans' resistance to centralized authority in favor of locally ruled towns and churches was a forerunner to American democratic principles. Today's immigrants still share the Puritan dream that life will be better for those who come to America. In addition, the Puritan work ethic continues to teach that hard work and discipline will earn both spiritual and material rewards.

MICHAEL KAUFMANN
Temple University

See also AMERICAN LITERATURE (The Colonial Experience); CALVIN, JOHN; COLONIAL LIFE IN AMERICA (Life in the New England Colonies); ENGLAND, HISTORY OF (Charles I Clashes with the Puritans); HUGUENOTS; HUTCHINSON, ANNE; MASSACHUSETTS (History; Famous People); PLYMOUTH COLONY (The Puritans); THIRTEEN AMERICAN COLONIES (Massachusetts Bay Colony); WILLIAMS, ROGER.

## PUSAN

Pusan is the second largest city of the Republic of Korea (South Korea) and one of Asia's chief seaports. Situated on the southeastern tip of the Korean Peninsula, Pusan covers 167 square miles (432 square kilometers) and has a population of about 4 million. It has special city (provincial) status, and its mayor, who is appointed by the president, has the rank of a government cabinet member.

Pusan is a major industrial center as well as the nation's chief port. Its chief economic activities include shipbuilding and the manufacture of automobiles, textiles, shoes, machinery, chemicals, and a wide range of electronic goods. The city also serves as a base for the industry and commerce of surrounding South Kyŏngsang Province.

Pusan's recreational and cultural attractions include Haeundae Beach, the most popular of several beach resorts, and the Buddhist temples that dot the nearby mountainsides. The city is home to Pusan National University and Dong-A University. It is also the site of a United Nations cemetery, con-

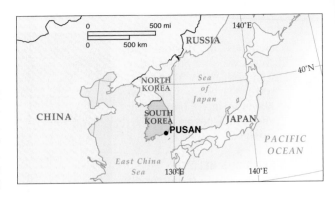

taining the remains of many U.S. and allied soldiers killed in the Korean War (1950–53).

Pusan first appeared under its present name in 1368 as a port for rice shipments to Japan. It was opened to general foreign trade in 1876. Pusan's beginnings as a major industrial city date from the period of Japanese colonial rule (1910–45). During the Korean War, it served as the temporary capital and was the chief supply base for United Nations and South Korean forces fighting the Communist invasion from the north.

DAVID I. STEINBERG
Author, *Korea: Nexus of East Asia*

## PUTIN, VLADIMIR (1952– )

Vladimir Vladimirovich Putin was elected president of the Russian Federation on March 26, 2000, the second man to hold that position. He had been serving as acting president since the resignation of the former president, Boris Yeltsin, on December 31, 1999.

Putin was born in Leningrad (now St. Petersburg) on October 7, 1952. After graduating from Leningrad University's law school in 1975, he joined the KGB, the Soviet Union's foremost intelligence organization.

Inspired by the political reforms of Mikhail Gorbachev, the last leader of the Soviet Union, Putin turned to politics, becoming deputy mayor of St. Petersburg in 1994. In 1996, however, he moved to Moscow to work for the government of Boris Yeltsin, who had become the first president of Russia following the collapse of the Soviet Union in 1991.

Putin's rise in government was rapid. Beginning in 1997, he served as director of the presidential staff, coordinator of government relations with Russia's provincial governments, and head of Russia's Federal Security

Service, the successor to the KGB. In August 1999, Yeltsin named Putin prime minister. In this position, he directed the war against the rebels in the Russian republic of Chechnya. Public opinion supported the war, and as the Russian army made gains against the rebels, Putin's popularity soared. He received strong support during Russia's parliamentary elections in the fall. He became acting president when Yeltsin resigned in December.

After his inauguration in May 2000, Putin set about re-establishing his government's control over rebellious provinces. In foreign affairs, he signed a friendship treaty with China and supported the American war against terrorism that began in Afghanistan in 2001. But in 2003 he opposed the U.S.-led war against Iraq. In his annual address to parliament, he called for continued economic reforms and promised to strengthen the Russian military. He was easily re-elected to a second term in 2004.

Reviewed by ILYA PRIZEL
University of Pittsburgh

# PUZZLES

A puzzle is a problem or device created to challenge your mind. People have always enjoyed solving puzzles. Oral riddles, the earliest known form of puzzles, are thought to have begun long ago with the development of language.

There are three broad classes of puzzles: riddles and word puzzles (see CROSSWORD PUZZLES and CHARADES in Volume C); mathematical puzzles (see NUMBER PUZZLES AND GAMES in Volume N); and mechanical puzzles, which are described below. Historical evidence tells us that all three classes of puzzles were present in the Middle East as far back as three to four thousand years ago.

### Put-Together Puzzles

Put-together puzzles are solved by assembling or fitting the pieces together. The **jigsaw puzzle**, the most popular put-together puzzle, was invented around 1760 by the London mapmaker John Spilsbury as a way to teach geography to children. Another puzzle, the Chinese **Tangram**, has been popular since the 1800's. It uses seven pieces, called tans, that can be assembled in various ways to form silhouettes of people, animals, and objects.

Sam Loyd, America's greatest puzzle maker, designed thousands of puzzles in the late 1800's and the early 1900's. One of his best is the **Trick Mules** Puzzle, which has three rectangular pieces showing two riders and two mules. To solve the puzzle, a person must arrange the pieces (without bending or folding them) so that the two riders are riding at a fast pace. It sounds simple, but it is very difficult.

### Take-Apart Puzzles

In a take-apart puzzle, the goal is to open the object, take the object apart, or find a secret compartment. Among the many take-apart puzzles are wooden balls with secret compartments, locks with hidden keyholes, and puzzle boxes with sliding panels. The object of the **Three Ring Puzzle** is to remove the rings without bending the bar running through them. Many kinds of products and events were advertised on this type of puzzle in the 1890's.

### Interlocking Puzzles

Interlocking puzzles, which can be simple cubes or complex geometric shapes, are meant to be taken apart and then put back together. The three-dimensional wooden cross-shaped interlocking puzzles are called "burrs" because they resemble the seed burs of plants. In 1890, William Altekruse invented an interlocking burr puzzle that used twelve identical pieces. Stewart Coffin, a modern designer of interlocking puzzles, created a

---

## PUZZLES TO MAKE AND SOLVE

### Tangram:

Copy the seven tans shown below on a 5-by-8-inch index card. Cut them out and use them to form the five figures on the left.

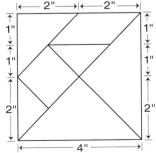

### 14-15 Puzzle:

Cut a $3\frac{1}{8}$ - by $3\frac{1}{8}$ -inch square hole in a piece of thick cardboard. Glue this piece onto another piece of cardboard that is the same size but without a hole. Write the numbers 1 through 15 on small pieces of paper and glue these to 15 pennies. Within the square hole, put the first 13 pennies in numerical order. Then place numbers 14 and 15 in reverse order, as shown. Now try to put all the pennies in numerical order by sliding them around within the square.

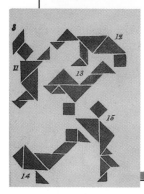

## SOLUTIONS

### Tangram:

The correct arrangements of tans for the five figures are shown in the drawings to the left. Remember, the seven tans are used to make each figure.

### 14-15 Puzzle:

The original 14-15 puzzle cannot be solved. However, your coin version can be solved. While you are sliding the pennies around, the numbers 6 and 9 must be rotated 180 degrees and exchanged so that the 6 becomes 9 and vice versa.

| 1 | 2 | 3 | 4 |
| 5 | 6 | 7 | 8 |
| 9 | 10 | 11 | 12 |
| 13 | 14 | 15 | |

---

similar burr puzzle with 14 identical pieces in the 1970's.

### Disentanglement Puzzles

The object of disentanglement puzzles is to remove parts such as rings or loops of string that are trapped within them. In the late 1800's, Sam Loyd used a loop of string fastened to a 6-inch-long stick to create the **Buttonhole Puzzle**. The object of this puzzle was to remove the string loop, which was fastened through the buttonhole, without cutting the string. One of Loyd's most successful puzzles, it was used as a promotional item for the New York Life Insurance Company.

### Sequential Movement Puzzles

In sequential movement puzzles, pieces are moved around according to rules in order to reach a certain goal. The **Fifteen Puzzle**, a sliding block puzzle with 15 numbered blocks, appeared in 1880 and is still popular. In one version, the 14-15 Puzzle, the 15 blocks were placed in numerical order except for the last two, which were reversed. The challenge was to rearrange the blocks into the correct numerical order by sliding them around within a confined space.

Another famous, and very difficult, sequential movement puzzle is **Rubik's Cube**. In the 1980's, this cube became one of the most popular puzzles of all time. The cube initially has a different solid color on each of its six sides. The colors can be scrambled by twisting the cube in different directions. The object of the puzzle is to restore the colors as they appeared initially on each of the sides.

### Dexterity Puzzles

Dexterity puzzles are solved through eye-hand coordination, and sometimes through logical thinking. **Cup and Ball** dexterity puzzles, in which a wooden ball is tossed in the air and caught in a cup or on the pointed end of a stick, have been popular for at least 400 years. A rolling-ball dexterity puzzle called **Pigs in Clover** was a huge success when it was introduced in 1889, and a modern version is still popular today. Anyone with enough patience and dexterity can solve it by rolling four marbles into the "pen" in the center of the circular maze.

### Puzzle Jugs

Puzzle jugs were popular in Europe 400 years ago. The object of a **puzzle jug** is to drink from the container without spilling the contents through numerous holes. The secret is to find and use the hidden built-in tubes to suck the liquid as you would with a straw.

JERRY SLOCUM
Author, *The Puzzle Arcade*

See also CHARADES; CROSSWORD PUZZLES; NUMBER PUZZLES AND GAMES; WORD GAMES.

**PYGMALION.** See GREEK MYTHOLOGY (Profiles).
**PYLE, ERNIE.** See JOURNALISM (Profiles).
**PYLE, HOWARD.** See DELAWARE (Famous People).

# P'YŎNGYANG

P'yŏngyang is the capital and largest city of the Democratic People's Republic of Korea (North Korea), one of the world's few remaining Communist countries. The city is located in west central North Korea, on the banks of the Taedong River, some 30 miles (48 kilometers) upstream from the Yellow Sea. It covers an area of 77 square miles (199 square kilometers) and has a population of 2.7 million. North Korean citizens can live in P'yŏngyang only by permit. Apart from the personnel of the embassies and consulates of countries that have diplomatic relations with North Korea, few foreigners live there.

**The City.** P'yŏngyang has modern hotels, pleasant parks, museums, theaters, several circuses, and many sports facilities. The city has two subway lines that meet in the center of town. Its stations are lavishly decorated with mosaic murals and crystal chandeliers. Places of interest include the Korean Revolution Museum, with its massive statue of Kim Il Sung, North Korea's leader from 1945 to 1994; the mausoleum of Kim Il Sung; the

The Yu Kyong Hotel rises above a picturesque park in the modern city of P'yŏngyang, the capital and largest city of North Korea.

Tower of the Juche Idea, topped with a sculpted flame; the Arch of Triumph, near Peony Hill; and Mangyongdae, the ancestral village of Kim Il Sung, just west of the city center. Kaeson Youth Park, Peony Hill Park, and the park along the Potong River are all pleasant summer destinations. Mansu Hill Art Theater and P'yŏngyang Grand Theater both have musical shows and productions. Kim Il Sung University and Kim Chaek University of Technology are two of the best-known universities.

**Economic Activity.** P'yŏngyang is a transportation center for roads and railways and a distribution center for goods. In and around the city are chemical, textile, electronics, and machine-tool manufacturers, as well as iron and steel mills and chemical plants. Its most important function, however, is to serve as the nation's administrative, educational, and cultural center.

**History.** Formerly known as Wanggom Song, in the 100's B.C. the city became the capital of the Old Chosŏn kingdom. In 427, King Changsu of the Koguryo kingdom named it P'yŏngyang and made it his capital. In 668, the kingdom of Silla defeated Koguryo and formed the kingdom of Paekche. P'yŏngyang was incorporated into the new state. Although it was no longer the capital, P'yŏngyang remained an important regional city.

Along with the rest of Korea, P'yŏngyang was controlled from 1910 to 1945 by Japan, which made it into a major industrial center. After World War II (1939–45), Korea was divided into two states—North Korea and South Korea. P'yŏngyang became the capital of North Korea in 1948.

CLARK W. SORENSEN
Korea Regional Studies Program
University of Washington

# PYRAMIDS

In architecture the term "pyramid" refers to a monument that resembles the geometric figure of a pyramid. Such monuments were built in ancient times in both the Old World, in Egypt and Sudan, and the New World, in areas of Mexico and Central America. But pyramids from the two regions differed in form and function.

### ▶ EGYPTIAN PYRAMIDS

The Egyptian pyramid is square at the base, with four triangular sides that meet in a point at the top. Pyramids served as tombs for kings and their families. For almost a thousand years, during the periods known as the Old and Middle kingdoms (about 2650–1640 B.C.), the pyramid was the standard type of royal burial monument in Egypt.

About fifty of these royal pyramids have survived. They were built at the edge of the desert, on the west bank of the Nile River. The earliest is the Step Pyramid of King Zoser at Saqqara. It consisted of a series of terraces, each one smaller than the one beneath it, resulting in stepped sides. Later pyramids, such as the Great Pyramid of Cheops (Khufu) at Giza, are smooth sided. This pyramid covers more than 13 acres (5.2 hectares) and was built of some 2.3 million stone blocks weighing several tons each.

Most of the surviving Egyptian pyramids are much smaller than the Great Pyramid and less well preserved. While the earlier pyramids were made of solid stone blocks, mined from nearby quarries, the later pyramids had rubble or mud brick cores with outer casings of stone. All the pyramids were robbed in ancient times. Thieves stole the gold and other valuables left in the burial chambers.

The Egyptian pyramid was just one part of a larger complex of structures. On its eastern side stood the pyramid temple. From this temple a walled causeway led down to a val-

The ancient pyramids at Giza dominate the desert landscape. Egyptian pyramids were built as tombs for royalty.

A cutaway of the Great Pyramid at Giza shows its internal plan. The entrance (1) led to a corridor (2) that descended to an abandoned underground chamber (3). An ascending corridor (4) gave access to the Queen's Chamber (5) and opened into the Grand Gallery (6), which led to the King's Chamber (7). Air shafts (8) ventilated this chamber, which was capped by stone beams (9).

ley temple with access to the Nile. Also included within the pyramid complex were smaller pyramids for the queens and princesses. The walls of the mortuary temple, causeway, and valley temple were decorated with relief sculpture, and statues of the king filled the courtyards and rooms. The burial chambers within the pyramid itself were at first plain and unadorned, but beginning about 2300 B.C. they were decorated with hieroglyphic inscriptions. The inscriptions spelled out formulas intended to ensure the king's successful rebirth in the afterlife.

The pyramid fields are known today by the Arabic names of the nearest Egyptian towns. Thus we have the pyramids of Giza, Saqqara, and Dahshur, to name only the most famous. In antiquity, each pyramid had its own name, which was combined with the name of the king buried inside the pyramid. The Great Pyramid of Cheops, for example, was known

The Step Pyramid of King Zoser at Saqqara is the oldest Egyptian pyramid and probably the first large stone building in history.

in ancient times as Akhet-Khufu, "the horizon of Cheops."

No more pyramids were built in Egypt after 1640 B.C. The custom was revived many hundreds of years later by the kings of Sudan (750 B.C.–A.D. 350), who adopted ancient Egyptian funerary practices. The Sudanese pyramids are smaller than the ancient Egyptian ones and built at a more acute angle. The major pyramid fields in Sudan are those of Nuri, Gebel Barkal, and Meroë.

▶ **AMERICAN PYRAMIDS**

Long before the arrival of Europeans, native peoples of Mexico and Central America had developed advanced civilizations. In studying their architecture, the term "pyramid" is used loosely, to refer to a wide variety of mound forms, usually with flat summits that support altars, shrines, or temples. Most of these pyramids are rectangular in plan and rise in successively smaller stages to the summit. Some, however, have circular plans, while a famous pyramid built by the Olmec people at La Venta, in Tabasco, Mexico, may have had the form of a fluted cone. Most of the pyramids have a staircase in the center of one side that rises to the summit. Others have staircases located in the centers of all four sides.

The pyramids generally have earth or rubble cores, often faced with stone and plaster. The surfaces were sometimes decorated with sculpture. In addition to having altars or temples on their summits, many of the pyramids enclose tombs of important individuals. Usu-

The construction of the Great Pyramid at Giza was an amazing feat of engineering. Huge stone blocks cut from nearby quarries were loaded on sledges, dragged up ramps, and set in place on the pyramid. It took thousands of workers about 20 years to complete the job.

The Pyramid of the Sun is the oldest monument at Teotihuacán, in central Mexico. The mountainlike structure was built over a natural cave.

built about A.D. 150–200. Its core was made of stones and mud, while the exterior was constructed of carved stone and covered with painted stucco. This west-facing pyramid rises in several levels, or platforms. Each level consists of a vertical panel above a sloping base. Both vertical and sloping surfaces are decorated with carved stonework, including curving feathered serpents and monstrous faces that might represent headdresses. Feathered serpents also adorn the ramplike elements flanking the staircase. Some 200 sacrificial victims were buried beneath and around the base of the pyramid. Many of the individuals were dressed as warriors and had their wrists tied behind their backs. Presumably a mass human sacrifice was carried out to dedicate the structure.

ally the body was entombed in a pit or chamber at or below ground level, and the pyramid was built over it. Thus the tomb could not be entered later. Sometimes the tomb was dug into an existing structure, which was then covered by a larger pyramid. Many temples were remodeled and enlarged over time.

Several of the largest and most important pyramids in Mexico and Central America are located at Teotihuacán in central Mexico, north of present-day Mexico City. The immense Pyramid of the Sun, made of layers of clay faced with stone, resembles a mountain in form. Built about A.D. 1–150, this pyramid is the oldest monumental stone structure at Teotihuacán. The pyramid, which faces west, was constructed over a natural underground cave consisting of a long passage that ends in chambers shaped like a clover leaf near the center of the pyramid's base. In native mythology, the first humans were said to have emerged from a cave. The Pyramid of the Sun may have been built to sanctify the cave beneath it as humankind's place of origin.

A later structure at Teotihuacán is the Pyramid of the Feathered Serpent,

A beautiful and unusual pyramid was built by the Maya at Palenque, in Chiapas, Mexico. Known as the Temple of the Inscriptions, the north-facing pyramid rises in nine stages. Atop its summit is a vaulted temple, decorated with carved stone and modeled stucco sculpture. The pyramid was built to house the tomb of a Palenque ruler named Pacal, who died in A.D. 683. His body lay within an elaborately carved stone sarcophagus, in a vaulted chamber located inside the pyramid's base. A vaulted staircase led down to the tomb chamber from the temple above. After the ruler's body was buried, the tomb chamber was sealed, the bodies of human sacrificial victims were deposited, and the staircase was closed by filling it with rubble.

LAWRENCE M. BERMAN
MARGARET YOUNG-
SÁNCHEZ
The Cleveland
Museum of Art

The Temple of the Inscriptions, in Chiapas, Mexico. Like many such structures built in the Americas, it has a temple atop its flat summit.

## PYRRHUS (319?–272 B.C.)

Pyrrhus was a king of ancient Epirus, a mountainous region in what is now northwestern Greece and southern Albania. He was born about 319 B.C. and came to the throne at the age of 12. He was deposed some four years later but regained his throne in 297 B.C. An ambitious monarch, he fought to expand his own territory and free Epirus from domination by the kingdom of Macedonia to the east. He had limited success, winning control of parts of Macedonia and other lands but losing them soon after.

Pyrrhus is most famous, however, for his expedition into southern Italy and his military campaigns to assist the Greek cities there against the growing power of the Romans. In 280 B.C. he defeated a Roman army at the Battle of Heraclea, and the following year he defeated the Romans

again at the Battle of Ausculum. But he was unable to follow up his victories because of the extensive casualties in his own army. In accepting congratulations on his second victory, he is reported to have said, "If we win one more battle against the Romans, we shall be utterly ruined," thereby giving rise to the expression Pyrrhic victory, or a victory in which the losses outweigh the gains.

Frustrated, Pyrrhus turned to military adventures on the nearby island of Sicily. These

proved unsuccessful and he returned to the Italian mainland, where he suffered heavy losses in yet a third battle against the Romans, at Beneventum in 275 B.C. Retiring from Italy with less than one-third of his original force, Pyrrhus resumed his wars at home against the Macedonians. He died in 272 B.C., while campaigning in southern Greece.

EUGENE N. BORZA
Author, *In the Shadow of Olympus*

## PYTHAGORAS (560?–480? B.C.)

Pythagoras was an early Greek philosopher and mathematician. He was born about 560 B.C. on Samos, an island in the Aegean Sea. He was introduced to the mathematics of ancient Egypt and Babylonia during his travels as a young man. At about the age of 30, he moved to a Greek colony in southern Italy. There he founded a secret society known as the Pythagoreans.

Pythagoras taught his followers that everything in the universe can be explained with numbers, specifically with whole numbers. He perhaps came to this belief as a result of his discovery that musical harmony can be explained with numbers. For example, he learned that doubling the length of a plucked string produces a note one octave lower.

Many important concepts of mathematics have been credited to the Pythagoreans. They proved that certain measures, such as the diagonal of a square, cannot be expressed as a ratio of two whole numbers. This discovery was difficult for them to accept because it contradicted their own philosophy; for a time they tried to keep it secret. Such numbers

were later classified as irrational numbers. The idea most associated with Pythagoras, the **Pythagorean theorem**, was known to ancient civilizations, but he may have demonstrated its first proof. The theorem states that in a right triangle the square of the length of the hypotenuse is equal to the sum of the squares of the lengths of the other two sides.

It is also thought that the Pythagoreans recognized that Earth is a sphere, that Venus is both the morning and the evening star, and that the planets are at different distances from Earth. They also held other beliefs that had little to do with science or mathematics. They believed that a soul can pass from a human to an animal or the reverse. They were vegetarians, but they considered beans sacred and would not eat them.

It is not known exactly how or when Pythagoras died. One legend has it that he was killed when enemies burned down the society's meeting place.

BRYAN H. BUNCH
Coauthor, *The Timetables of Science*

See also GEOMETRY; MATHEMATICS, HISTORY OF.

# Index

**HOW TO USE THE DICTIONARY INDEX**

See the beginning of the blue pages in Volume 1.

Page, William Tyler (American author)  U:161
Pageants  E:270; P:12 see also the annual events section of
        state articles
Page proof (in printing)  B:330; P:487
Pagers, electronic  C:468; T:47, 56
    electronics in business and industry  E:162
    office machines  O:58
    radio, uses of  R:51
    picture(s)  T:55
Pages (apprentice knights)  K:276
Pagination (computer designing of newspapers)  N:202
Pagliacci, I (opera by Leoncavallo)  O:160
Pagodas (Buddhist shrines)  A:366
    Myanmar's cultural heritage  M:557, 560
    Shwe Dagon Pagoda (Yangon, Myanmar)  M:560
    picture(s)
        Shwe Dagon Pagoda  M:557
Pago Pago (American Samoa)  U:84
Pahang River (Malaysia)  M:56
Pahari school (in Indian art)  I:137
Pahlavi, Mohammed Reza (shah of Iran) see Mohammed Reza
        Pahlavi
Pahlavi, Reza Shah (shah of Iran) see Reza Shah Pahlavi
Pahlavi dynasty (of Iran)  I:309
Pahoehoe (lava)  V:382
Paige, Satchel (Leroy Robert Paige) (American baseball player)
        B:90 profile
    picture(s)  B:90
Pain
    anesthesia  A:254–57; S:513
    hypnotism as an anesthetic  H:327, 328
    medical management of  M:208h
    narcotics as painkillers  N:15
    reflex actions respond to pain  N:116, 118
    tooth nerves  T:43
    what to do if you feel pain after exercising  P:227
    Why doesn't it hurt to cut your hair?  H:5
Paine, Lewis (American abolitionist)  U:17
Paine, Lewis (American conspirator in Lincoln's assassination,
        1844–1865)  B:335
Paine, Thomas (English-born American writer)  P:12–13
    American literature  A:205
    founder of the United States  F:392
    how Declaration of Independence was adopted  D:59
    magazine publishing  M:19
    Revolutionary War pamphlets  R:202
    picture(s)  W:268
Painkillers (drugs)  D:332, 334; N:15; O:116
Paint see Paints and pigments
Painted Attic (Greek pottery style)  P:411
Painted Desert (Arizona)  A:394, 400
Painted-lady butterfly  B:478
    picture(s)  B:481
Painted turtles  T:355–56
Painters (cats) see Mountain lions
Painters Eleven (Canadian artists)  C:73
Painting  P:14–32 see also the names of individual artists,
        such as Rembrandt, and art of specific countries, as
        Italy, art and architecture of
    Africa, art of  A:75
    art of the artist  A:432–33
    Audubon's birds  A:491
    Australian aboriginal painters  A:501
    baroque art  B:63–68
    Byzantine  B:493, 494
    Canada  C:72, 73
    Dutch and Flemish art  D:357–70
    Egyptian art in royal tombs  E:116
    finger painting  F:130–32
    folk art  F:292–94
    French art  F:424–32
    German art  G:167–72
    Gothic art  G:270
    Greek art  G:347–48, 350–51, 352

    Islamic art  I:357–58
    modern art  M:386–96b
    Renaissance art  R:163–71
    Romanesque art  R:295
    romanticism in art  R:302–3
    Rome, art of  R:319
    Spanish painting  S:382, 383, 384, 385
    United States  U:127
    watercolor  W:54–57
    picture(s)
        American folk art  F:292, 293
        rock paintings  P:435, 436, 437
Painting, industrial  P:33–34
Painting, religious see Religious art
Painting with White Border (painting by Wassily Kandinsky)
    picture(s)  G:172
Paints and pigments  P:30, 32–34 see also Lacquers;
        Varnishes
    colors  C:425–26
    effect on art of manufactured paints  P:24, 27
    face and body painting  D:25, 30
    ink  I:229
    lead  L:94
    oil paints  P:30
    pigments of prehistoric paintings  P:15
    plastics  P:322, 324
    soybean oil used in  S:337
    textiles  T:143
    watercolor paints  W:54
Pairing Off (card game)  C:108
Paiute (Indians of North America)  I:182, 183, 186; N:128,
        134
Pakistan  P:35–40a
    Afghanistan, relations with  A:44
    ancient Harappan civilization  A:240
    Bangladesh  B:50–51
    Bhutto, Benazir  B:155b
    Bhutto, Zulfikar Ali  B:155b
    earthquake (2005)  E:41
    ethnic groups in the United Kingdom  U:47, 48
    India  I:133, 134
    Jinnah, Mohammed Ali  J:109
    Karachi  K:193
    Kashmir dispute  A:457; K:198
    mass migrations of Hindus from  H:142
    refugees  R:136
    terrorism, war on  T:116
    picture(s)
        flag  F:237
        Hindu Kush  P:38
        Id al-Fitr celebration  R:155
        Islamabad  P:39
        Karachi  K:193; P:39
        Mohenjo-Daro  P:40
        people  P:35
        sugarcane field  P:38
        vegetation  C:363
        village  P:36
Paksas, Rolandas (president of Lithuania)  L:263
Palace Ladies Tuning the Lute (painting by Zhou Fang)
    picture(s)  C:274
Palace of the Governors (Santa Fe, New Mexico)  N:188
Palaces
    Babylonian palaces  A:365
    Brunei sultan's is largest in the world  S:333
    Iolani Palace (Honolulu)  H:52
    Islamic architecture  I:357, 358
    Minoan architecture  A:236
    Versailles  A:372; B:66; P:72
    picture(s)
        Iolani Palace  H:52
        Schönbrunn Palace (Vienna)  V:332j
        Versailles  B:66
Palacio González, Alfredo (president of Ecuador)  E:69
Palamas, Costis (Greek poet)  G:359

Palau (island nation, Pacific Ocean)   P:40b; T:113; W:313
  *picture(s)*
    flag   F:237
    Kayangel atoll   P:2
Palawai (mountain, Hawaii)   H:51
Palawan (island, Philippines)
  *picture(s)*   P:183; S:329
Palazzo Vecchio (palace in Florence, Italy)   F:258
Palenque (Mexico)   A:243; M:184; P:558
Paleoanthropology   A:301, 350
Paleocene epoch (in geology)   E:29
Paleoecology (ecological study of extinct species)   E:53
Pale of Settlement (Russian territory restricting Jews)   J:106
Paleo-Indians (early inhabitants of the Americas)
                I:164–65; P:441; U:252
Paleolithic period *see* Old Stone Age
Paleontology (scientific study of fossils)   F:380, 382, 383,
                387, 388–89 *see also* Fossils
  careers in biology   B:199, 200
  earth science   E:8
  Earth's history   E:24
  mass extinctions   E:425–26
  prehistoric animals   P:432, 434
Paleozoic era (in geology)   E:27–28; F:385–87
  prehistoric animals   P:432–33
  *table(s)*   E:25; F:384
Palestine (the Holy Land)   P:40c–43
  Arab-Israeli War (1967)   J:132
  Arabs   A:343, 346–47
  Arafat, Yasir   A:349
  Ben-Gurion, David   B:142
  Herodian dynasty   H:123
  Holocaust rescue efforts   H:174
  Israel, history of   C:369; I:369, 375
  Jerusalem   J:80–84
  Jesus Christ   J:85–89
  Jewish immigration   J:107
  Jordan   J:132
  map at the time of Jesus Christ   J:86
  Syria   S:552
  World War I   W:285
  Zionism   Z:386
Palestine Liberation Organization (PLO)   P:42, 43
  Arafat, Yasir   A:349
  Israel and   A:456–57; M:305
  Israel's invasion of Lebanon   I:376
  Jordan   H:307; J:132
  Lebanon   L:122
Palestinian Arab refugees   I:375; P:42; R:136
  Jordan   H:307; J:129
  Lebanon   L:122, 123
Palestinian Arabs *see also* Palestinian Arab refugees
  culture   I:374
  Jerusalem   J:84
  Kuwait   K:308
  self-rule issue   I:376; M:305
  *picture(s)*   I:370; J:83
Palestinian National Authority (Arab governing body in Palestine)
                A:349; P:42, 43
Palestrina, Giovanni Pierluigi da (Italian composer)   M:538;
                P:43
  choral music   C:283
  hymns   H:322
  Renaissance music   R:173–74
  vocal polyphony   I:410
Pali (language)   I:141
Palikir (capital of Federated States of Micronesia)   M:280
Palindromes (word games)   W:236
Palisades (fences of pointed stakes)   F:378
Palisades (on the Hudson River)   N:166
Palk Strait (Sri Lanka)   S:415
Palladianism (revival of classical architecture)   A:372; E:259
Palladio, Andrea (Italian architect)   A:372; R:161 *profile*,
                170
Palladium (element)   E:175; J:96

Pallas Athena *see* Athena
Pallets (devices in timepieces)   C:370
Pallium (Greek garment)   C:375
Palm (part of the hand)   F:79
Palma, Ricardo (Peruvian author)   L:68
Palmate compound leaves   L:113
  *picture(s)*   L:113
Palmate veins (of trees)   T:308
Palm Beach (Florida)   F:270
Palm civets (Toddy cats) (animals)   M:419
Palme, Olof (Swedish prime minister)   S:529
Palmer, Arnold (American golfer)   G:257, 258 *profile*
  *picture(s)*   G:258
Palmer, Nathaniel (American sea captain)   A:295
Palmer, William J. (American railroad builder)   C:439
Palmer House (hotel, Chicago, Illinois)   H:259
Palmerston North (New Zealand)   N:236
Palmetto (tree)
  *picture(s)*   F:261; S:297
Palmetto State (nickname for South Carolina)   S:296, 297
Palm Sunday (religious holiday)   E:43; R:154
Palmtop computers   C:480; O:55
  *picture(s)*   C:481
Palm trees
  books made from leaves   B:320
  carnauba   B:377
  coconut palm   C:392
  dates   D:41
  jungles   J:157
  wax obtained from   W:78
  *picture(s)*
    coconut palm   T:302
Palmyra (Syria)
  *picture(s)*   A:453
Palo Alto, Battle of (1846)   T:32
Palo Duro Canyon (Texas)   T:126, 132
Palomar, Mount (California) *see* Mount Palomar Observatory
Palomino horses   H:237
  *picture(s)*   H:238
Palouse Hills (Washington)   W:16
Paloverde (tree)
  *picture(s)*   A:393
Palsy, cerebral *see* Cerebral palsy
*Pamela: or Virtue Rewarded* (novel by Richardson)   E:279
Pamir (Pamirs) (mountains of central Asia)   T:11
  *picture(s)*   T:10
Pampas (plains of South America)   S:277, 283, 290
  Argentina   A:382, 384, 385, 386, 386a, 386b–386c
  prairies   P:426, 427, 428
  soil   S:282
  *picture(s)*   A:386; G:314
    prairies   P:429
Pampas ostriches *see* Rheas
Pamunkey (Indians of North America)   I:178
Pan (in Greek mythology)   G:363
Panama   C:172, 173, 174; P:44–49
  American military burial ground   N:29
  Balboa named it Darien   B:20
  Cuna Indians   I:195
  Latin America   L:49, 59
  United States, relations with   J:122
  *map(s)*   P:46
  *picture(s)*
    flag   F:237
    Kuna Indians   C:172; N:294; P:45
    Panama City   P:47
    Panama Railroad   P:45
    sidewalk vendors   P:44
    U.S. troops   P:48
Panama, Isthmus of   P:44, 45, 49, 50
Panama Canal   P:48, 49–51
  Army Corps of Engineers   U:106
  canal construction   C:90
  Caribbean Sea made a major waterway   C:112

Eiffel, Alexandre-Gustave **E:**118
Lesseps, Ferdinand de **L:**157
territorial expansion of the United States **T:**112
*map(s)* **P:**49
*picture(s)*
locks **P:**50
**Panama Canal Area** **P:**51
**Panama Canal Zone** **P:**51; **R:**331; **T:**112
**Panama City** (capital of Panama) **P:**47
*picture(s)* **P:**47
**Panama hats** **E:**68–69
**Panama-Pacific International Exposition** (San Francisco,
California, 1915) **F:**16
**Pan American Day** **H:**167
**Pan-American Exhibition** (Buffalo, 1901) **F:**16
**Pan-American Highway** **C:**253
**Pan American Union** **H:**39
**Pan Am flight 103** (airplane destroyed by bomb, 1988)
**L:**190; **Q:**2; **T:**114
**Panchatantra** (fables from India) **F:**3
**Panch'en Lama** (Tibetan Buddhist religious leader) **T:**189,
190, 191
**Pancreas** (gland) **B:**292; **G:**227, 228
Banting's findings on insulin extract **B:**59
cystic fibrosis **D:**191
diabetes **D:**145
digestive system **B:**281; **D:**164
insulin production **H:**227, 228
mumps may cause swelling of **D:**197
**Pandas** (animals) **A:**442; **M:**73; **P:**52; **Z:**392
China **C:**263
giant pandas are related to bears **B:**104–5, 107
*picture(s)* **C:**263; **E:**211; **P:**52; **Z:**391
**Panday, Basdeo** (prime minister of Trinidad and Tobago)
**T:**315
**Pandemic diseases**
influenza (1918–19) **I:**228
**Pandora** (in Greek mythology) **G:**364, 367
*picture(s)* **G:**367
**Pandora** (moon of Saturn) **S:**58
**Panel cartoons** **C:**127, 129
**Panel discussions** *see* Discussions
**Panel paintings** **S:**382
**Panfish, baits for** **F:**213
**Pangea (Pangaea)** (prehistoric continent) **G:**111, 113; **O:**16
*picture(s)* **G:**110
**Pangnirtung** (Nunavut) **N:**412
**Pangolins** (mammals) **A:**283; **M:**74
*picture(s)* **M:**73
**Panhandle State** (nickname for West Virginia) **W:**126
**Panhard-Levassor** (automobile) **A:**540
**Panhellenic festivals** (in ancient Greece) **G:**343
**Paniagua, Valentin** (interim president of Peru) **P:**165
**Panic attack** (anxiety disorder) **M:**222
**Panic disorder** (anxiety disorder) **M:**222
**Panics and depressions** *see* Depressions and recessions
**Pankhurst, Christabel** (British suffragist) **W:**215
**Pankhurst, Emmeline Goulden** (British suffragist) **W:**215
*profile*
*picture(s)* **W:**215
**Pankhurst, Sylvia** (British suffragist) **W:**215
**Panmunjom** (South Korea) **K:**306
**Panniers** (side bags for bicycles) **C:**48
**Panniers** (skirt hoops) **C:**377
**Panning** (for gold) **G:**251; **M:**233
**Panning** (in candy making) **C:**98
**Panoan** (Native American language family) **I:**197
**Panoramas** (curved pictures) **D:**2
**Panpipes** (ancient musical instruments) **O:**219
**Pansy** (flower)
*picture(s)* **G:**44
**Pantaloon** (clown) **C:**386
**Pantheon** (temple in Rome, Italy) **A:**369; **R:**306
**Panthéon** (Paris) **P:**73

**Panthers** (animals) **F:**265; **L:**155
*picture(s)* **E:**210; **L:**155
**Pantomimes** (dramatic action without words) *see also* Charades
charades **C:**186–87
clowns **C:**386
**Pantothenic acid** (a B-complex vitamin) **V:**370c–370d
*table(s)* **V:**372
**Panzer (Armored) divisions** (in World War II) **W:**296
**Papacy** *see also* Popes
emperors *versus* popes in Italy **I:**388
history of Roman Catholic Church **R:**288–89
**Papadopoulos, George** (Greek president) **G:**338
**Papadopoulos, Tassos** (president of Cyprus) **C:**617
**Papago** (North American Indians) *see* O'odham
**Papain** (substance from papaya plant) **T:**317
**Papal Inquisition** **R:**290
**Papal Line of Demarcation** *see* Line of Demarcation
**Papal Schism** *see* Great Western Schism
**Papal States** (in central Italy) **I:**388, 389
Renaissance, growth of city states during **R:**157
Roman Catholic Church, history of the **R:**288, 294;
**V:**282
**Papandreou, Andreas** (Greek political leader) **G:**338
*picture(s)* **G:**338
**Papandreou, George** (Greek prime minister) **C:**527; **G:**338
**Papaya** (tropical fruit) **T:**317
*picture(s)* **T:**317
**Papeete** (capital of French Polynesia) **P:**9
**Paper** **P:**53–58
bamboo used for making **G:**318
buttons made of paper **B:**484
Chinese invention of **B:**320; **I:**280
communication, history of **C:**464
drawing, history of **D:**315, 316
drawing materials **D:**308, 311, 312, 313
gift wrapping **G:**206–7
How is paper recycled? **P:**57
illustration tradition **I:**79
Japanese houses, room dividers in **H:**193–94
materials from plants **P:**298
New Hampshire, industry in **N:**156
origami **O:**228–30
paper money **M:**413–14
papier-mâché **P:**58b–58c
photo printing paper **P:**217
Quebec production **Q:**10b
recycling **R:**125
rubbings **R:**348b–349
watercolor paper **W:**54
wax paper, invention of **W:**78
Wisconsin a leader in paper products **W:**196
**Paperback books** **P:**58a
children's literature **C:**237
history of **B:**322
illustration and illustrators **I:**82
publishing **P:**524
**Paper birch trees**
*picture(s)* **T:**304
**Paperboard** **P:**57
**Paper chromatography** **E:**393
*Paper Crane, The* (book by Molly Bang)
*picture(s)* **C:**236
**Paper mills** **A:**529; **P:**54
*picture(s)* **N:**138c; **P:**298
**Paper money** **M:**413–14
bank notes **B:**53, 54
dollar bills **D:**261, 263
Engraving and Printing, Bureau of **T:**294
**Paper wasps**
*picture(s)*
nest **I:**246
**Paper work** *see* Papier-mâché
**Papier-mâché** **D:**267; **P:**58b–58c
*picture(s)* **P:**58b, 58c
**Papillae** (structures on the tongue) **B:**290

**Papillons** (dogs)
*picture(s)* **D:**246

**Papineau, Louis-Joseph** (Canadian lawyer and politician) **Q:**15

**Papoulias, Karolos** (president of Greece) **G:**338

**Paprika** (spice) **H:**121, 295
*picture(s)* **H:**121

**Papua** (formerly **Irian Jaya**) (Indonesia) **I:**206, 208, 209, 212; **N:**148
New Guinea **N:**149
*picture(s)* **N:**148

**Papua New Guinea** **N:**148, 149; **P:**58d–59
Admiralty Islands **I:**361; **P:**8
Bismarck Archipelago **P:**8
Bougainville **P:**8
Buka **P:**8
New Britain **P:**9
New Ireland **P:**10
*picture(s)*
flag **F:**237
Melanesian boys **P:**9
open-pit copper mine **P:**4

**Papyrus** (plant)
early writing material **P:**57
inventions **I:**280
paper: origin of name **P:**53
"paper" rolls for books **B:**318–19
*picture(s)*
libraries of ancient Egypt **L:**171

**Par** (in golf) **G:**254

**Parables** (teachings of Jesus) **J:**87, 89

**Parabola** (curved plane figure) **G:**123 *see also* Conic sections

**Parabolic mirrors** **T:**58

**Paracelsus, Philippus A.** (Swiss doctor) **C:**207; **R:**162; **Z:**385

**Parachutes** **P:**60
Garnerin parachutes from balloon **B:**35
skydiving **S:**190
spacecraft module lowered **S:**340j
United States Air Force Pararescuers **U:**113
*picture(s)*
Leonardo da Vinci's design **L:**154
Navy paratroopers **U:**115
smoke jumpers fighting forest fires **F:**153

**Parades** **P:**61
circus acts **C:**307
Easter parade, origin of the **E:**44
*picture(s)*
Brazil's Carnival **H:**163
Lisbon (Portugal) **P:**395
New York City's Chinatown **N:**283
New York City's Puerto Rican Day **H:**148
Rhode Island **R:**216
Soviet celebrations **U:**35, 40
Toronto's Caribana parade **T:**244

**Paradise** (religious belief) **K:**292

*Paradise* (woodcarving)
*picture(s)* **F:**298

**Paradisefish** **F:**204

**"Paradise Lost"** (poem by John Milton) **M:**312; **P:**353

**Paradise Tree** (forerunner of the Christmas tree) **C:**297

**Paradox** (statement that seems to contradict itself)
humor **H:**291
twin paradox in relativity theory **T:**204

**Paraffin**
candles **C:**96
petroleum waxes **W:**78

**Parafoil** (type of kite) **K:**266b

**Paraguay** **L:**49; **P:**62–66
languages **S:**288
War of the Triple Alliance **S:**295
*map(s)* **P:**63
*picture(s)*
Asunción **P:**65
flag **F:**237
gaucho **P:**62

Gran Chaco **P:**62
Itaipú Dam **P:**64
traditional dance **P:**62
worker burning rain forest **R:**100

**Paraguay River** (South America) **P:**63; **R:**244; **S:**280
*picture(s)* **P:**62

**Parakeets** (birds) **B:**249; **P:**178–79
*picture(s)* **B:**250; **P:**86

**Parallax** (apparent change in position of a celestial body measurement in astronomy) **A:**476; **S:**428

**Parallel bars** (in gymnastics) **G:**432
*picture(s)* **G:**432, 433

**Parallel connection** (of batteries) **B:**103a

**Parallel lines** (in geometry) **G:**121
*picture(s)*
Euclidean and non-Euclidean geometries **M:**169

**Parallelograms** (geometric forms) **G:**121

**Parallel postulate** (assumption of Euclidean geometry) **G:**128

**Parallel racing** (skiing competition) **S:**184f

**Parallels** (of latitude) **L:**77

**Paralympic Games** (international athletic competition for people with physical disabilities) **O:**115
*picture(s)* **D:**178

**Paralysis**
muscular system disorders **M:**521
polio called "infantile paralysis" **D:**200
spinal cord damage **N:**118

**Paramaribo** (capital of Suriname) **S:**517
*picture(s)* **S:**517

**Paramecium** (micro-organism) **K:**258; **M:**276; **P:**497
*picture(s)* **C:**159; **K:**258; **L:**198; **P:**496
reproduction **L:**198

**Paramedics** (medical experts who care for victims on the way to the hospital) **A:**199; **F:**162

**Paraná River** (South America) **R:**244; **S:**280
Argentina **A:**385
Itaipu Dam **L:**27
Paraguay's rivers **P:**63, 64

**Paranoid personality disorder** **M:**224

**Parapsychology** (study of extrasensory perception) **E:**427–28

**Pararescuers** (special forces of the United States Air Forces) **U:**113

**Parasites** **L:**206
arachnids **A:**348
cattle-raising, problems of **C:**154
endangered species **E:**209
flatworms **W:**322
fungi **F:**498, 499
hookworms **W:**321–22
leeches **W:**321
mollusks are hosts to **M:**406
parasitic diseases **D:**187, 189
parasitic plants **P:**288, 314
pinworms **D:**199
protozoans **P:**496, 497
tapeworms **D:**206
ticks **T:**192
vectors carry parasites **V:**284
viruses **M:**277
viruses grow only inside cells **V:**361

**Parasitic diseases** (caused by protozoa and worms) **D:**187, 189
malaria **M:**51–52
pinworm infection **D:**199
tapeworms **D:**206
trichinosis **D:**207

**Parasympathetic nerves** **N:**117

**Parathyroid glands** **B:**292; **G:**228

**Parboiling** (soaking and steaming of rice) **R:**229

**Parcel post** (mail service) *see* Standard B mail

**Parcheesi** (game) *see* Game of India

**Parchment** (writing material) **P:**57
books' earliest codex forms **B:**319–20
illustrated parchment books **I:**79
invention of **I:**280

Parmigianino (Parmigiano), Il (Italian painter)   I:399
   picture(s)
      Madonna with the Long Neck (painting)   I:399
      Saint Thais (engraving)   E:294
Paro (Bhutan)   B:155a
Parochial schools   E:76, 87
   church-controlled colleges   U:223
Parody (form of humor)   H:291
   Beerbohm, Sir Max   E:288
   folk music   F:326
Parole   P:481
   aliens   A:189
Parole boards and parole officers   L:92
Parotid glands (found in front of the ear)   D:197; G:226–27
Parr, Catherine (sixth wife of Henry VIII of England)   H:114
Parrakeets see Parakeets
Parrot fever (disease)   B:249; P:178–79
Parrotfish   A:277; F:199
   picture(s)   F:201
Parrots   P:85–86
   endangered species   B:248; E:209
   flightless birds   O:242
   pet birds   B:249–50; P:178–79
   picture(s)   P:85, 86
      Amazon parrot   P:178
      gray parrot   B:234
Parry (blocking movement in fencing)   F:87
Parsifal (opera by Richard Wagner)   H:175; O:160
Parsis (Parsees) (Indian followers of Zoroastrianism)   F:495; Z:394
Parsley (herb)   F:281
Parsnips (vegetable)   V:290
Parsons, Charles A. (English inventor)   T:342
Partch, Harry (American composer)   U:210
Parthenogenesis (development of unfertilized egg)   E:97
Parthenon (temple in Athens, Greece)   A:238, 368, 476c
   Doric style of Greek architecture   G:348
   Elgin Marbles   G:350
   Nashville (Tennessee) has a full-size reproduction   N:16; T:79
   Pericles   P:152
   relief sculptures   G:350
   picture(s)   A:476c; E:340; G:339, 348
Parthians (ruling people of Persia)   I:308; P:155, 156
Participles (verb forms)   P:93
Particle accelerators (atom-smashing machines)   S:70; V:264
Particleboard   F:515; W:227
Particles, subatomic see Subatomic particles
Particle theory of light   L:212–13, 222–23; R:46–47
Particulates (air pollutants)   A:122, 123
Parties   P:87–91 see also Games
   etiquette   E:339
   Halloween party   H:14
   magic tricks   M:23–25
Parties, political see Political parties
Parti Québécois (Canadian political party)   C:85; Q:15, 17
Partisans (guerrilla forces)   S:126; Y:368
Partita (musical form) see Suite
Partnership (type of business)   B:470–71
Parton, Dolly (American singer and songwriter)   C:573; T:86
   profile
   picture(s)   C:572; T:86
Partridges (birds)   Q:4a
Parts of speech   G:289–90; P:92–94
Parvanov, Georgi (Bulgarian president)   B:446
Parzival (romance by Wolfram von Eschenbach)   G:176
Pascal, Blaise (French mathematician and philosopher)
   computers, history of   C:490
   discovered the principle of hydraulic systems   H:311
   France, literature of   F:438
   invented an adding machine   O:60
   number patterns   N:381
   probability theory   M:166–67
   vacuum experiments   V:265
Pascal III (antipope)   R:292

Pascal I, Saint (pope)   R:292
Pascal II (pope)   H:112; R:292
Pascal's Law (of liquid pressure)   H:311
Pascal's triangle (mathematical lattice)   N:381–83
Paschal (antipope)   R:292
Pascoli, Giovanni (Italian poet)   I:408
Pas de deux (in ballet)   B:29
Pashto (language)   A:43
Pashtuns (Pathans; Pushtuns) (a people of Afghanistan)   A:42, 43, 44
   Pakistan   K:193; P:35
   picture(s)   A:42; P:35
Pasillo (Latin American music)   L:72
Pasolini, Pier Paolo (Italian film director and author)   I:409
Pasqueflower
   picture(s)   S:313
Passaic River (New Jersey)   N:167
Passamaquoddy Indians (of Maine)   I:177; M:41, 50
Passau (Germany)   D:35
Passchendaele, Battle of (1917)   W:288
   picture(s)   W:281
Passed ball (in baseball)   B:83
Passenger pigeons (extinct birds)   D:290; E:209, 426
Passenger ships   O:30–33; S:153, 159
   picture(s)   S:159
Passenger trains   L:288; R:81–82, 90
Passing (in football)   F:355–56
   picture(s)   F:355
Passion (musical form)   B:70; C:283; M:540
Passion flower (state wildflower of Tennessee)   T:78
Passion fruit (tropical fruit)   T:317
   picture(s)   T:317
Passion plays, medieval   G:152; P:12; S:319
Passive immunity   A:313; I:95
Passive smoking (inhalation of tobacco smoke by nonsmokers)   S:207
Passive solar heating systems   H:97
Passos, John Dos (American novelist) see Dos Passos, John
Passover (Jewish holiday)   P:95–96; R:153
   Cup of Elijah   E:189
   dietary precautions   J:146b
   Easter   E:43, 44
   Jews' Exodus from Egypt   J:102, 146a
   picture(s)
      Seder   J:146a; P:95; R:153
Passports   F:371; P:96
   picture(s)
      cover of U.S. passport   P:96
Pastas (dried dough)   G:281
   food of Italy   I:382
   food shopping   F:348–49
Paste (type of adhesive)   G:243
   collage making   C:402
Pasteboard (used for printing playing cards)   C:111
Pastels (artists' material)   D:312; P:30
   picture(s)   D:310
Pasternak, Boris Leonidovich (Russian novelist)   N:363; R:384
   picture(s)   R:383
Paste-up artists (people who prepare artwork for printing)   C:458
Pasteur, Louis (French chemist)   P:97–98
   biochemistry, history of   B:186
   fermentation of wine   F:90–91
   immune system   I:98
   medicine, contributions to   M:207, 208b, 208c; S:513
   microbes, study of   M:277–78
   science, milestones in   S:72
   vaccination, history of   M:205
   picture(s)   B:186; M:207, 278; P:97; S:72
Pasteurization (to kill micro-organisms)   M:278; P:98
   food preservation   F:342
   germ theory of disease   M:207
   milk, processing of   D:7–8
   picture(s)   D:8; F:342
Pastoral novels   S:388

**Pastoral poetry** (about country life)   E:272; G:358
**Pastrana Arango, Andrés** (Colombian president)   C:408
  *picture(s)*   C:408
**"Pasture, The"** (poem by Robert Frost)   F:480
**Pasture grasses**   G:317
**Pastures**
  feeding the dairy herd   D:5
  grazing lands in national forests   N:34
  pasture grasses   G:317
  prairies   P:427
**Patagonia** (plateau region of South America)   A:385–86, 386a; S:277, 280
  *picture(s)*   A:385; P:429
**Patan** (Nepal)   N:109
**Patasse, Ange-Felix** (president of Central African Republic)   C:171
**Patch logging** (of timber)   L:340
**Patchwork quilting**   N:101
**Patella (Kneecap)** (bone of the leg)   S:184
  *diagram(s)*   F:79
**Patent and Trademark Office, United States (PTO)**   C:455; P:99
**Patent Co-operation Treaty** (1978)   P:99
**Patent leather**   L:111
**Patents**   P:99
  Edison's record number of   E:70
  inventions   I:277
  pharmaceutical industry   D:336
**Patents Act** (Great Britain, 1949)   P:99
**Pater, Walter** (English writer)   E:284
**Pater Noster** *see* Lord's Prayer
*Paterson* (epic poem by William Carlos Williams)   W:176
**Paterson** (New Jersey)   N:175, 178; T:146
**Paterson, Andrew Barton (Banjo)** (Australian bush balladist)   A:500, 501
**Paterson, Katherine** (American author)   C:235 *profile*, 238
  *picture(s)*
    illustration by Donna Diamond for *Bridge to Terabithia*   C:238
**Paterson, William** (American public official)   N:179 *profile*
**Pathans** (a people of Afghanistan) *see* Pashtuns
**Pathetic fallacy** (figure of speech)   F:122–23
**Pathet Lao** (rebel group of Laos)   L:43
**Pathfinder** (American explorer) *see* Frémont, John Charles
*Pathfinder* (spacecraft) *see* Mars Pathfinder
*Pathfinder, The* (novel by James Fenimore Cooper)   C:549
**Pathfinders** (Canadian Girl Guides)   G:217
**Path integration** (method of navigation) *see* Dead reckoning
**Pathogens** (disease-producing organisms)   D:187; S:33; V:282–83, 285
**Pathology** (study of the nature of diseases)   B:199; H:249
**Pathum Thani** (Thailand)   T:151
*Patience* (operetta by Gilbert and Sullivan)   G:209
**Patios** (central courtyards in Spanish homes)   L:52
*Pato* (game)   A:384
**Paton, Alan Stewart** (South African author, educator, and politician)   A:76d
**Patos, Lagoa dos** (lake, Brazil)   S:281
**Pátrai (Patras)** (Greece)   G:336
**Patriarchal family**   F:42
**Patriarchs** (original rulers of a tribe or family)
  Eastern Orthodox churches   E:45
**Patriarchy** *see* Patriarchal family
**Patricians** (Roman social class)   P:369; R:311, 313
**Patrick, Saint** (patron saint of Ireland)   P:100
  converted the nation of Ireland   R:287
  Fenian Cycle tales   I:325
  Ireland, history of   I:323
  Saint Patrick's Day   H:165
  slavery   S:196 *profile*
  *picture(s)*   P:100
**Patriot Act** (United States, 2001)   H:182; T:117
**Patriote, Le** (Canadian theater group)   C:69
**Patriotic holidays**   H:167–69
**Patriotic songs** *see* National anthems and patriotic songs

**Patriotism**
  American Legion   A:199
  veterans' organizations   U:121
**Patriot missile**   M:349; U:106
  *picture(s)*   M:344, 346
**Patriots** (colonists critical of British rule)   R:198
**Patriot's Day**   D:59; M:141
**Patroclus** (in Greek mythology)   I:61
**Patrol dogs** (used by the armed forces) *see* Scout dogs
**Patrol officers** (police)   P:363
**Patrol ships and craft**   U:115
**Patron** (in Roman society)   R:311
**Patronage, political** *see also* Spoils system
  power of the United States president over appointments and removals   P:450, 453
  Renaissance city-states   R:157
**Patronymic method** (of name giving)   N:5
**Patroons** (Dutch landowners in American colonies)   T:175
**Patterned glass**   G:231
**Patterns** (for sewing)   C:380, 381; S:130
**Patterns** (in interior design)   I:259
**Patterns** (learning tool)   L:100
**Patterns** (of numbers) *see* Number patterns
**Patterson, Carly** (American gymnast)   O:120
**Patterson, Floyd** (American boxer)   B:351, 352, 353 *profile*
**Patterson, Martha Johnson** (acting first lady in Andrew Johnson's administration)   F:172
**Patterson, Percival** (prime minister of Jamaica)   J:19
**Pattie, James** (American trailblazer)   O:275
**Patton, George S.** (U.S. Army general)   P:100; W:312
  *picture(s)*   W:308
**Patwin** (Indians of North America)   I:187
**Patzcuaro, Lake** (Mexico)
  *picture(s)*   N:287
**Paul** (acting ruler of Yugoslavia)   Y:368
**Paul, Alice** (American reformer)   P:101; W:212b, 213
  *picture(s)*   P:101
**Paul, Les** (American guitar designer)   G:412
**Paul, Saint** (apostle of Jesus Christ)   A:329; P:101
  Christianity, history of   C:288, 292
  Pauline Epistles   B:166–67
  Roman Catholic Church   R:284, 285
  *picture(s)*   C:289; P:101
**Paul, William Louis, Sr.** (Native American politician and lawyer)   A:157 *profile*
**Paul I, Saint** (pope)   R:292
**Paul II** (pope)   R:293
**Paul III** (pope)   R:293
**Paul IV** (pope)   R:293
**Paul V** (pope)   R:293
**Paul VI** (pope)   P:102; R:293
**Pauli, Wolfgang** (Austrian physicist)   P:238
**Pauline Epistles** (in the New Testament)   B:166–67; P:101
**Pauling, Linus** (American chemist)   B:187; P:102
  *picture(s)*   P:102
**Paulo Afonso Falls** (Brazil)   S:280; W:58, 59
*Paul Revere* (painting by Copley)   U:127
  *picture(s)*   U:127
**"Paul Revere's Ride"** (poem by Longfellow)
  excerpt from   P:350; R:192
**Pauly, Samuel** (Swiss inventor)   G:419
**Pavane** (dance)   D:26; R:173
**Pavarotti, Luciano** (Italian opera singer)   O:140–41 *profile*
  *picture(s)*   O:141
**Pavers** (machines for mixing concrete)   R:250
**Pavese, Cesare** (Italian novelist)   I:409
**Pavia** (Italy)   I:388
**Pavlov, Ivan** (Russian biologist)   L:98; P:103
**Pavlova, Anna** (Russian ballet dancer)   B:29, 32
**Pawcatuck River** (Rhode Island–Connecticut)   R:214
**Pawnee** (Indians of North America)   I:180; K:186
  Kansas museum   K:184
**Pawtucket** (Rhode Island)   R:217, 220, 221
  textile industry   I:221; R:226
**Pawtuxet River** (Rhode Island)   R:214

**Pax House** (London, center for World Association of Girl Guides and Girl Scouts)  **G:**219
**Pax Romana (Roman Peace)** (in Roman history)  **R:**316, 317
**Payload** (objects carried by a rocket)  **R:**257, 259
   warheads of missiles  **M:**347–48
**Payne, Cecilia** (British-American astronomer)  **A:**473
**Payne-Aldrich Act** (United States, 1909)  **T:**4–5
**Payne's Landing, Treaty of** (1832)  **O:**237
**Paysandú** (Uruguay)  **U:**238, 240
**Payton, Walter** (American football player)  **F:**363 *profile*
   *picture(s)*  **F:**363
**Paz, Alonso de la** (Guatemalan sculptor)  **L:**62
**Paz, Juan Carlos** (Argentine composer)  **L:**73
**Paz, Octavio** (Mexican writer)  **L:**69, 70; **M:**247
   *picture(s)*  **L:**69
**Paz Estenssoro, Victor** (Bolivian political leader)  **B:**310
**Paz Zamora, Jaime** (president of Bolivia)  **B:**310
**PBI (Polybenzimidazole)** (manufactured fiber)  **F:**111
**PBX's** *see* Private Branch Exchanges
**PCB's** *see* Polychlorinated biphenyls
**PCP** (drug)  **D:**331
**PCs (Personal computers)** *see* Personal computers
*Peace: Burial at Sea* (painting by Turner)
   *picture(s)*  **T:**354
**Peace Conference** (Washington, D.C., 1861)  **T:**368
**Peace Corps**  **K:**209; **P:**104
**Peace for our time** (Chamberlain's announcement of Munich Pact, 1938)  **W:**295
**Peace Garden State** (nickname for North Dakota)  **N:**322, 323
**Peacekeeper missile**
   *picture(s)*  **U:**110
**Peacemaker** (revolver) *see* Single Action Army Colt
**Peace movements**  **P:**105–6 *see also* Disarmament
   Addams, Jane  **A:**21
   international relations  **I:**270
   Isaiah's call for peace  **I:**345
   League of Nations  **L:**95
   Nobel prizes  **N:**266–68
   United Nations  **U:**63–71
   Vietnam negotiations  **V:**338
   What is a conscientious objector?  **P:**106
**Peace of God**  **F:**103
**Peace River district** (British Columbia)  **A:**166; **B:**402, 405
**Peach**  **P:**107–8, 109 *see also* Plum
   *diagram(s)*  **P:**107
   *picture(s)*
     flower  **D:**89
     growing in Georgia  **G:**133
     sun drying of peaches  **F:**339
**Peach Festival** (Japan) *see* Girls' Day
**Peach State** (nickname for Delaware)  **D:**102
**Peach State** (nickname for Georgia)  **G:**132, 133
**Peachtree Street** (Atlanta, Georgia)  **A:**477; **G:**132
   *picture(s)*
     during Sherman's capture of Atlanta  **C:**342
**Peacock butterfly**
   *picture(s)*  **I:**230
**Peacocks** (birds)
   *picture(s)*  **B:**219; **C:**426
**Pea crabs** (crustaceans)  **C:**581; **M:**406
**Peak flow meter** (for self monitoring by people with asthma)  **A:**463
**Peale, Anna Claypoole** (American painter)  **P:**110
**Peale, Charles Willson** (American painter)  **M:**133 *profile;* **P:**110; **U:**127
   *picture(s)*
     *The Artist in His Museum* (painting)  **P:**110
**Peale, James** (American painter)  **P:**110
**Peale, Margaretta Angelica** (American painter)  **P:**110
**Peale, Norman Vincent** (American clergyman)  **O:**77 *profile*
**Peale, Raphaelle** (American painter)  **P:**110
   *picture(s)*
     *After the Bath* (painting)  **P:**110
**Peale, Rembrandt** (American painter)  **P:**110
**Peale, Rubens** (American painter)  **P:**110

**Peale, Sarah Miriam** (American painter)  **P:**110
**Peale, Titian Ramsay** (American painter)  **P:**110
**Peale family** (of American artists)  **P:**110
**Peanut butter**  **A:**191; **P:**112
**Peanut oil**  **O:**79; **P:**112
*Peanuts* (comic strip)  **C:**128; **M:**339
   *picture(s)*  **C:**129
**Peanuts and peanut products**  **P:**111–12; **V:**290
   allergies  **A:**191
   Carver's work at Tuskegee Institute  **C:**130
   peanut butter, how to make  **P:**112
   peanut oil  **O:**79
   South American crop carried to Africa  **A:**99
   *picture(s)*  **A:**93
**Pear**  **P:**113
*Pearblossom Hwy., 11-18th April 1986* (photocollage by Hockney)  **H:**159a
**Pea Ridge, Battle of** (1862, Civil War)  **A:**416, 418
**Pea Ridge National Military Park** (Arkansas)  **A:**414
**Pearl danio** (fish)  **P:**204
**Pearl Harbor** (United States naval base near Honolulu, Hawaii)  **H:**50, 52, 62, 215
   aviation  **A:**566
   Japan  **J:**46
   World War II  **U:**196; **W:**302–3
   *picture(s)*
     *Arizona,* USS, Memorial  **H:**52
     World War II  **H:**62; **U:**195; **W:**293, 302
**Pearl Jam** (American rock band)  **R:**263 *profile*
**Pearl Mosque** (Delhi, India)
   *picture(s)*  **I:**139
**Pearl of the Orient** (nickname for Sri Lanka and Manila)  **M:**79; **S:**413
**Pearl River** (Louisiana–Mississippi)  **L:**316
**Pearls**  **G:**74; **P:**114–16
   amulets  **G:**72
   How are artificial pearls made?  **P:**116
   Japan's cultured pearl industry  **J:**39
   jewelry  **J:**95
   organic gems  **G:**75
   oysters  **O:**291
   *picture(s)*  **G:**74, 75
     Japanese divers  **G:**75
**Pearl S. Buck Foundation**  **B:**422
**Pearly nautiluses** (mollusks) *see* Chambered nautiluses
**Pearse, Pádhraic** (Irish patriot)  **I:**324
**Pearson, Hesketh** (English biographer)  **E:**288
**Pearson, Karl** (English mathematician)  **S:**443
**Pearson, Lester B.** (prime minister of Canada)  **C:**85; **P:**116
**Peary, Robert E.** (American explorer)  **P:**117
   Arctic exploration  **A:**380; **E:**414
   Henson, Matthew  **H:**115
   *picture(s)*  **P:**117
**Peas** (vegetable)  **V:**286, 289, 290, 292
   Mendel crossbred to prove genetic theories  **G:**90
   *picture(s)*
     leaves  **P:**305
     Mendel crossbred  **P:**299
**Peasants** (farm workers on feudal manors)  **F:**102 *see also* Serfs
   famine a cause of medieval uprisings  **F:**45
   Middle Ages, social classes of the  **M:**292
   Russia  **R:**357, 369, 370, 372; **U:**35, 39, 40
   *picture(s)*  **F:**101, 103
**Peasants' Revolt** (1381, in England)  **E:**241
*Peasant Wedding Feast* (painting by Pieter Bruegel the Elder)
   *picture(s)*  **W:**264
**Peat**  **W:**147
   coal formation  **C:**388
   fuel  **F:**488, 489
   peat mosses  **G:**42; **M:**472, 473
   raw materials from plants  **P:**298
   *picture(s)*
     cutting turf  **P:**298

Pecan (tree)   N:434
  *picture(s)*   T:125
Peccaries (piglike mammals)   H:220; P:248
  *picture(s)*   H:217
Pechstein, Claudia (German athlete)   O:118
Peck (measure of volume)   C:541
Pecking orders (among birds)   B:226
Pecos (Indians of North America)   I:183
Pecos Bill (American folk hero story)   G:202
Pecos River (New Mexico–Texas)   N:182–83; R:234; T:126
Pécs (Hungary)   H:297
Pectoral fins (of fish)   F:188
Pectoral muscle (in birds)   B:222
Pectorals (chest pieces)
  *picture(s)*   J:98
Peculiar galaxies   U:214
Pedals (of a piano)   P:240–41
Pediatrics (medical specialty)
  baby   B:3–4
  hospitals   H:247
  nurses, specializations of   N:417
  Taussig, Helen Brooke, and pediatric cardiology   T:24
Pedicabs (vehicles)
  *picture(s)*   B:50
Pedicel (part of ant's abdomen)   A:319
Pedigree (list of ancestors)
  dairy cattle breed associations   D:4
  mapping the genome   G:87
Pediments (in architecture)   A:368
Pedipalps (appendages of spiders)   S:402, 403, 406
Pedodontist (in dentistry)   D:115
Pedrarias Dávila (Pedro Arias de Avila) (Spanish colonial
  governor)   B:20; D:138
Pedrell, Carlos (Uruguayan composer)   L:73
Pedrell, Felipe (Spanish composer)   S:392b
Pedro I, Dom (emperor of Brazil)   B:383–84; P:395
Pedro II, Dom (emperor of Brazil)   B:384
Pee Dee River (South Carolina)   S:298
Peekaboo Gulch (Utah)
  *picture(s)*   U:244
Peel, Sir Robert (British prime minister)   P:118, 368
Peelites (political followers of Sir Robert Peel)   G:225
Peer group (social group composed of members of equal
  standing)   F:39; J:168–69
*Peer Gynt* (play by Henrik Ibsen)   G:381; I:2
Peer mediation programs (in schools)   E:88
Peer review (of journal articles)   S:67
Pegasus (constellation)   C:532
Peg dolls   D:266
Peggy's Cove (Nova Scotia)   N:355
  *picture(s)*   C:57; N:352
Pegmatite dikes (rock masses)   G:71
Pegu (Myanmar)   M:560
P. E. I. *see* Prince Edward Island
Pei, I. M. (Chinese-American architect)   P:118; U:136
  East Building of the National Gallery of Art   N:38
  Louvre's new entrance   A:376; L:333
  *picture(s)*   I:93
    Louvre's new entrance   L:331
Peiping (China) *see* Beijing
Peipus, Lake (Estonia–Russia)   E:324; L:33
Peirsol, Aaron (American swimmer)   O:119
Pekin ducks   P:417
  *picture(s)*   P:416
Peking (China) *see* Beijing
Peláez, Amelia (Cuban painter)   C:609
Pelagic (Water) environment (of the ocean)   O:23, 25
Pelagius I (pope)   R:292
Pelagius II (pope)   R:292
Pele (Hawaiian volcano goddess)   G:74; H:48
Pelé (Brazilian soccer player)   P:119
Peléean eruption (kind of volcanic eruption)   V:381
Peleliu Island (Pacific Ocean)   W:313
Pelham Bay Park (New York City)   N:231
Pelias (in Greek mythology)   G:367

Pelicans (birds)   B:236; P:119–20
  Louisiana   L:314
  "The Reason for the Pelican" (poem by Ciardi)   N:275
  *picture(s)*   B:227; F:264; L:315
Pelican State (nickname for Louisiana)   L:314, 315
Péligot, Eugène (French chemist)   U:230
Pella (Iowa)
  *picture(s)*
    19th-century lithograph of   C:318
Pellagra (disease)   V:370c
Pellan, Alfred (Canadian artist)
  *picture(s)*
    *Végétaux Marins* (painting)   C:73
*Pelléas et Mélisande* (opera by Claude Debussy)   O:160–61
Pellegra (nutrition-deficiency disease)   M:208c; N:429
Pelletier, David (Canadian athlete)   O:117
  *picture(s)*   O:117
Pellicle (seed coat of a nut kernel)   N:431
Peloponnese (peninsula of Greece)   G:333
Peloponnesian War (431–404 B.C.)   A:238, 476d; G:343–44;
  P:120a
  Pericles   P:152
  Thucydides' history of   G:357
  *picture(s)*
    red-figured pottery   W:260
Pelops (in Greek mythology)   G:367
Pelota (jai alai ball)   J:12
Pelton wheel (type of water turbine)   T:341
Pelts (skins of fur-bearing animals)   F:501, 502–4
Pelvic fins (of fish)   F:188
Pelvis (hipbone)   S:184
Pemba (island, Tanzania)   T:17
Pemberton, John (American Civil War general)   C:341
Pembina (North Dakota)   N:334
PEMEX (Mexican petroleum agency)   M:245
Pemmican (dried food)   I:190
Penal colonies (of exiled criminals)   P:481
  Australia   A:515
  French Guiana   F:466
  Siberia was formerly a Russian penal colony   S:170
Penal Laws (imposed on Ireland)   I:323
Penance (sacrament of Roman Catholic Church)   C:287;
  R:285
Penang (now Pinang) (Malaysia)   M:58, 59
Pencil and paper games   G:17
Pencils   P:143–44
  drawing, history of   D:318
  drawing materials   D:308, 311
  What is the "lead" in a lead pencil?   L:94
  *picture(s)*   D:310
Pendants (jeweled ornaments)   J:94, 99
Pendentives (in architecture)   A:370, 371; B:490
Penderecki, Krzysztof (Polish composer)   M:544
Pendergast, Thomas J. (American politician)   T:324
Pendleton Civil Service Act (United States, 1883)   A:437;
  C:331; U:188–89
Pendulum   C:369–70, 372
  Galileo discovers laws governing   G:5
  seismometer, used in a   E:37
Penelope (in Greek mythology)   G:369; O:53, 54
Penetrating rays   R:45–46
Peneus (Greek god)   G:366
Penfield, Wilder (American-Canadian neurosurgeon)   B:369
Penguins   P:120b–124
  Antarctica   A:293
  emperor penguin   B:244
  flightless birds   O:242
  *picture(s)*   A:292
    emperor penguin   B:236
    king penguin   B:235
Pénicaud, Nardon (French artist)   E:205
Penicillin (antibiotic)   A:306, 307, 308, 310
  artificial production made possible by X-ray diffraction
    X:350

**Pepperboxes** (pistols with several barrels)   **G:**421
  *picture(s)*   **G:**421
**Pepperell, Sir William** (American merchant)   **M:**49 *profile*
**Peppermint lobster**
  *picture(s)*   **O:**25
**Peppers**   **V:**290, 291
  microscope, some things to see with   **M:**283
  *picture(s)*
    farm workers picking peppers   **A:**79b
**Pepsin** (digestive enzyme)   **B:**281; **D:**164; **S:**461
**Peptic ulcers** (disease of the stomach)   **D:**198–99; **S:**461
  *picture(s)*   **D:**198
**Pepys, Samuel** (English diarist)   **D:**149; **E:**276; **S:**408 *profile*
  *picture(s)*   **D:**149
**Pequots** (Indians of North America)   **I:**177
  Connecticut   **C:**512, 520
  Indian wars   **I:**177, 202
  Rhode Island   **R:**224
  *picture(s)*
    Foxwoods Casino   **C:**516
**Perak River** (Thailand–Malaysia)   **M:**56
**Peralta, Pedro de** (Spanish colonial governor)   **N:**192
**Percentage**   **F:**400–402; **I:**255; **P:144–46**
**Percentile** (value on a scale of 100)   **P:**145
**Percentile rank score** (in test taking)   **T:**119
**Percé Rock** (Gaspé Peninsula, Quebec)
  *picture(s)*   **Q:**10b
*Perceval* (poem by Chrétien de Troyes)   **H:**175
**Perch** (fish)   **F:**213
  *picture(s)*   **F:**185, 187, 190, 213
**Percheron horses**   **H:**241
**Perchloroethylene** (solvent used in dry cleaning)   **D:**341
**Percier, Charles** (French architect)   **L:**333
**Percival** (knight of King Arthur's court)   **A:**438
**Percolator** (coffeepot)   **C:**397
**Percussion caps** (for guns)   **G:**417–18, 419
  *picture(s)*   **G:**416
**Percussion instruments**   **M:**546, 551; **P:147–49**
  Africa, music of   **A:**78
  bands and band music   **B:**42–45
  bells and carillons   **B:**141–42
  dance accompaniment   **D:**24–25
  drum   **D:**337–40
  nontraditional instruments   **M:**551
  orchestra   **O:**194–95, 196
  orchestra seating plan   **O:**196
  sound classified as music   **S:**263
  *picture(s)*
    African instruments   **A:**77; **M:**545
**Percy, Sir Henry** (English nobleman)   **H:**109
**Percy, Walker** (American novelist)   **A:**218–19
**Perdido River** (Alabama–Florida)   **F:**263
**Pereda, José María de** (Spanish writer)   **S:**390
**Pere David's deer**   **D:**82
**Peregrine falcons** (birds)   **F:**32; **R:**215
  *picture(s)*   **A:**279; **B:**232; **C:**525; **F:**33
**Père-Lachaise** (cemetery, Paris, France)   **P:**73
**Perennials** (plants)   **F:**287; **P:**311
  gardens and gardening   **G:**29–30, 40
  grasses   **G:**317
**Père Noël** (French Santa Claus)   **C:**297, 300
**Peres, Shimon** (Israeli political leader)   **I:**376
*Perestroika* (restructuring of Soviet society and economy)   **G:**263; **U:**44
**Peretz, Isaac Leibush** (Yiddish author)   **Y:**361
**Pérez, Carlos Andrés** (Venezuelan president)   **V:**299
**Pérez, Juan** (Spanish voyager)   **B:**407
**Pérez Balladares, Ernesto** (president of Panama)   **P:**49
**Pérez de Cuéllar, Javier** (secretary-general of the United Nations)   **U:**70 *profile*
**Pérez Galdós, Benito** (Spanish writer)   **S:**390
  *picture(s)*   **S:**390
**Pérez Jiménez, Marcos** (dictator of Venezuela)   **V:**299
**Perfect binding** (of books)   **B:**333

**Perfect flowers** (those with both pollen and seed producing parts)   **F:**283; **P:**307, 308; **T:**310
  *picture(s)*   **P:**306, 309
**Perfecting presses** (for printing)   **P:**470, 476
**Perfect numbers**   **N:**386
**Perforation numbers** (of stamps)   **S:**423
**Performance pieces** (type of drama)   **D:**307
**Performance tests** (to demonstrate skills)   **T:**118
**Performing arts** *see* Ballet; Clowns; Dance; Motion pictures; Television programs; Theater
**Perfumes**   **P:150–51**
  ambergris   **W:**150, 154
  civet musk used in perfume   **M:**419
  flowers used for   **F:**280
  What are toilet water and cologne?   **P:**150
**Pergamum (Pergamon)** (Asia Minor)   **G:**351–52; **L:**172
  *picture(s)*   **G:**352
**Pergolesi, Giovanni Battista** (Italian operatic composer)   **I:**412
**Peri, Jacopo** (Italian composer)   **B:**70; **O:**139
**Pericarditis** (heart disease)   **H:**84
**Pericardium** (fluid-filled sac around the heart)   **H:**80
**Pericles** (Greek statesman)   **H:**123; **O:**190; **P:**120a, **152**
  *picture(s)*
    statue   **G:**343
*Pericles* (play by Shakespeare)   **S:**138
**Peridots** (gems) *see* Olivines
**Perigee** (point of a satellite's orbit nearest Earth)   **M:**446; **S:**53
**Perihelion** (point of a planet's orbit closest to the sun)
  Mars   **M:**105
  Mercury   **R:**143
  solar system   **S:**242
  *picture(s)*
    Mercury   **R:**144
**Periodicals** *see* Magazines
**Periodic table** (of chemical elements)   **C:**202, 204, 209–10; **E:**167–70; **S:**73
**Periodontal disease**   **D:**199
**Periodontist** (in dentistry)   **D:**115
**Periods** (in geologic time scales)   **F:**383; **G:**110
**Periods** (punctuation marks)   **P:**541–42
**Periods, menstrual** *see* Menstruation
**Periosteum** (membrane around bone)   **B:**278
**Periostracum** (outer layer of a mollusk's shell)   **S:**149
**Peripatetics** (followers of Aristotle's philosophy)   **A:**387
**Peripheral nervous system** (of the body)   **B:**364; **N:**116–17, 118
**Peripherals** (input and output units of a computer)   **C:**481, 491
**Periscopes** (optical instruments)   **O:**181
**Perissodactyla** (order of odd-toed hoofed mammals)   **H:**217–18
  *picture(s)*
    black rhinoceros as example   **M:**73
**Peristalsis** (muscle contractions in digestion)   **D:**163; **S:**461
**Periwinkle** (plant)   **F:**281
**Perjury** (lying under oath)   **C:**368
**Perkin, William Henry** (English chemist)   **D:**378
**Perkins, Jacob** (American inventor)   **R:**135
**Perkins, W. H.** (English inventor)   **T:**142
**Perlman, Itzhak** (Israeli violinist)   **I:**373
**Permafrost** (permanently frozen subsoil)   **A:**146, 378–79; **B:**210; **T:**331 ; **Y:**370
**Permanent Commission on Human Rights** (United Nations) *see* United Nations Commission on Human Rights
**Permanent Court of Justice** (The Hague) *see* International Court of Justice
**Permanent magnets**   **M:**32
**Permanent residents** (immigrants living permanently in the United States)   **N:**61
**Permanent waves** (in hairstyling)   **H:**8
**Permeability** (of membranes)   **O:**240

**Petroglyphs** (carved drawings on canyon walls) *see* Rock art
**Petrograd** (Russia) *see* Saint Petersburg
**Petrol** (fuel) *see* Gasoline
**Petroleum and petroleum refining**  P:167–76
   Africa's resources  A:49
   Alabama  A:136
   Alaska  A:144, 149, 151, 152, 158
   Arctic petroleum transported south by pipelines  A:380
   Asia's resources  A:442
   Australia  A:510
   automobiles' lubrication systems  A:548
   Azerbaijan  A:574
   Bahrain  B:18
   Brunei  B:415
   Canada's oil deposits and production  C:61–62; N:341
   carbon  C:106
   Colorado  C:437
   desert development  D:130
   distillation process  D:219
   Ecuador's leading industry  E:67, 68
   energy supply  E:219, 220–21
   engineering  E:226
   Europe, oil resources of  E:360
   fertilizers  F:98
   gasoline a product of  G:62
   geologists work for oil companies  G:119
   global warming  G:239
   hydrocarbon products in the home can be poisonous  P:355
   Iran  I:306
   Iraq's oil resources  I:313
   Kansas  K:178, 180, 183, 185
   kerosene derived from  K:235
   Kuwait's oil reserves  K:309, 311
   Libya  L:189
   liquid fuels  F:487, 490
   Louisiana  L:318
   lubricants  L:335
   Mexico  M:243, 244, 245
   Middle East  M:303–4
   Montana  M:435
   natural resources, distribution of  N:66
   Nigeria  N:255, 256, 258
   North American mineral resources  N:292
   North Sea deposits of oil and natural gas  U:53, 57
   Norway  N:346, 349
   ocean pollutant  E:302–3; W:65–66
   oil-well brine a source of iodine  I:287
   Oklahoma  O:82, 85, 88, 91
   Oklahoma City  O:97
   Oman  O:121
   Organization of Petroleum Exporting Countries  O:222
   Persian Gulf War  P:158
   plastics  P:326
   protozoans help in exploration  P:497
   Qatar  Q:3, 4
   Russia  R:363
   Saudi Arabia  S:58a, 58c, 58d
   Scotland  S:87
   seismic prospecting with explosives  E:423
   Singapore  S:181
   Sudan  S:479
   tankers  S:155
   Texas  T:124, 128, 140
   transportation industry  T:291
   Tulsa (Oklahoma)  T:330
   tundra  T:331
   United Arab Emirates  U:45
   United States production  U:91, 93–94
   Venezuela  V:297, 299
   waxes made from  C:96; W:78
   White, Israel Charles  W:139
   world production  O:222
   Wyoming  W:338, 340, 347
   Yemen  Y:359

   *diagram(s)*
     fractionating tower  P:173
     rotary rig  P:170
   *picture(s)*
     Alberta oil sands recovery plant  A:169
     Basra (Iraq)  B:314
     Canadian refinery  P:429
     Ecuadorian workers  E:68
     Iranian workers  I:306
     Libyan oil fields  A:64; L:189
     Libyan refinery  S:7
     North Sea  E:360
     oil pumps  N:303
     oil refineries  A:452; M:303; P:173, 174
     oil rigs  A:149; E:221; L:321; M:57; N:346; O:88; P:167; S:333; T:125; W:340
     oil tanker in Nigeria  N:256
     Oklahoma worker  O:83
     Red Sea drilling  A:347
     Saudi Arabian refinery  D:131; S:58d
     tanker unloading crude oil  F:486
     Titusville (Pennsylvania) oil well  P:140
     Venezuelan oil rigs  V:297
     worker adjusting pipeline  M:247
**Petroleum engineers**  E:226
**Petroleum jelly**  W:78
**Petronas Towers** (Kuala Lumpur, Malaysia)  E:187; M:58; S:334
   *picture(s)*  M:54; S:334
**Petronius** (Roman writer)  L:76
**Petrosyan, Tigran** (Armenian chess champion)  A:421
**Pets**  P:177–79
   birds  B:249–50a
   cats  C:137–40
   dogs  D:257–60
   farm birds as pets  B:250a
   fish as pets  F:203–5
   gerbils  G:410
   guinea pigs  G:409
   hamsters  G:409–10
   lizards  L:275
   nature, study of  N:68
   parrots  P:86
   rabbits  R:25
   ticks, how to remove  T:192
   turtles no longer popular pets  T:357
**PET scanning** *see* Positron emission tomography
**Pet therapy** (animals' visits to health-care facilities)  D:257
   *picture(s)*  D:257
**Petticoat breeches** (garments)  C:377
**Pettit, Bob** (American basketball player)  B:95j *profile*
   *picture(s)*  B:95j
**Pettoruti, Emilio** (Argentine artist)  L:63, 64
**Petunia** (plant)
   *picture(s)*  G:28, 38, 48
**Peul** (a people of Africa) *see* Fulani
**Pevsner, Antoine** (Russian sculptor)  M:392; S:104
   *picture(s)*
     *Developable Column*  M:393
**Pewter** (metal)  A:316b; K:285; M:57; T:209
**Peyo (Pierrot Culliford)** (Belgian cartoonist)  B:134
**Peyote cactus**  C:5
*Pfiesteria* (toxin-producing dinoflagellate)  A:181
**PGA** *see* Professional Golfers' Association
**Phagocytes** (body cells)  I:96
**Phainopepla** (desert bird)
   *picture(s)*  B:241
**Phalangers** (marsupials)  M:113
**Phalanges** (bones of the hands and feet)  S:183, 184
   *diagram(s)*  F:79, 80
**Phalangist Party** (Lebanese)  L:122–23
**Phalanx Close-in Weapons System**  U:118
*Phantom of the Opera* (musical by Lloyd Webber)  M:555
**Pharaoh hounds** (dogs)
   *picture(s)*  D:248

Pharaohs (rulers of ancient Egypt)   A:235, 237; E:106, 108;
     P:95
Pharisees (strict sect of Judaism)   H:123
Pharmaceuticals see Drugs
Pharmacogenomics (science combining pharmacology and
     genetics)   B:190
Pharmacology (science of preparation, uses, and effects of
     drugs)   B:188, 190; D:334
Pharmacy (practice of preparing and selling medicines)
     D:335; H:249; M:205
     picture(s)   D:207
Pharos (lighthouse of Alexandria, Egypt)   L:227; W:219–20
Pharynx (of the body)   B:282; D:163; L:343
Phase contrast microscopes   M:284
Phases (grains in alloys)   A:193
Phases (of celestial bodies)
     Mercury   M:230
     moon   M:447
     observing Mercury and Venus   P:278
     picture(s)
          moon   M:448–49
Pheasant (game bird)   S:312, 316
     picture(s)   B:235; S:313
Pheasant Capital of the World (nickname for South Dakota)
     S:312
Phèdre (play by Jean Racine)   D:301
Pheidippides (champion Athenian runner)   O:106
Phelps, Michael (American swimmer)   O:113, 119
     picture(s)   O:119
Phenol (organic chemical)   C:391
Phenol-formaldehyde (plastic)   P:328
Phenotypes (in genetics)   G:79, 80
Phenylalanine (amino acid)   B:187; D:199
Phenylketonuria (PKU) (disease)   B:187; D:193, 199; R:190,
     191
Pheromones (chemicals secreted by animals)   A:318; F:194;
     I:235
Phi Beta Kappa (honor society)   V:351
Phidias (Greek sculptor)   G:349; O:104; W:218
Philadelphia (Pennsylvania)   P:126, 133, 135, 138, 139,
     180–81
     colonial life in America   C:419
     colonial sites you can visit today   C:422
     cultural center   P:131
     fire fighting, history of   F:145
     Franklin and the Library Company   L:175
     Franklin's activities   F:454–55
     Independence Hall   I:113
     Liberty Bell   L:170
     Revolutionary War   R:203, 204
     signing of Declaration of Independence   D:57
     United States mint established   M:340
     world's fairs   F:16–17
     picture(s)   P:127
          Bank of the United States (building)   B:52
          City Hall   P:130, 180
          Elfreth's Alley   P:181
          Independence Hall   I:113; P:131
          Liberty Bell   P:127, 181
Philadelphia Athletics (baseball team)   B:91
Philadelphia Orchestra   P:131
     diagram(s)
          orchestra seating plan   O:196
Philately see Stamps and stamp collecting
Philbrook Museum of Art (Tulsa, Oklahoma)   O:88
Philemon (book of the New Testament)   B:166, 167
Philharmonic Hall (Lincoln Center for the Performing Arts) see
     Avery Fisher Hall
Philip (antipope)   R:292
Philip (Metacomet) (Native American chief)   I:177, 202;
     M:149; R:225
Philip (prince of the United Kingdom of Great Britain and
     Northern Ireland, duke of Edinburgh)   E:192, 254–55
     picture(s)   E:254; S:88; U:60
Philip II (Philip Augustus) (king of France)   M:290–91; P:182

Philip IV (Philip the Fair) (king of France)   M:291; P:182
Philip VI (king of France)   F:413; H:292
Philip II (king of Macedonia)   A:177, 238; P:182
Philip I (king of Spain)   N:120d
Philip II (king of Spain)   E:191; H:2; P:182; S:377
     England and Elizabeth I   E:243–44
     Netherlands, history of   N:120d
     Spanish Armada   S:393
     picture(s)   S:377
Philip IV (king of Spain)   S:377; V:294
Philip V (king of Spain)   C:81; P:182; S:377–78
Philip Augustus (king of France)   L:332
Philip of Anjou see Philip V (king of Spain)
Philip of Bethsaida, Saint (one of the Apostles)   A:328, 329
Philippe de Vitry (French composer)   F:444
Philippi, Battle of (42 B.C.)   A:495
Philippians (book of the New Testament)   B:166
Philippics (forceful speeches)   O:190
Philippine mahogany see Lauan
Philippines   P:183–88
     American occupation   T:111
     Aquino, Corazon C.   A:338
     dance   F:300, 303
     economy   S:332, 333
     MacArthur, Douglas   M:2
     Manila   M:79
     McKinley accepts for the United States   M:193
     Pershing, John J.   P:153
     problem of lack of common language   E:75
     Quezon, Manuel   Q:20
     Spanish-American War   S:392c, 392d
     Taft, William Howard, was governor   T:4
     terrorism, war on   T:117
     World War II   W:303–4, 305, 313, 314
     map(s)   P:184
     picture(s)
          flag   F:237
          Manila   M:79; P:187
          Palawan   P:183; S:329
          people   A:445; P:183
          rice fields   N:62; P:186
          stilt houses   J:158
          World War II   W:312
Philippine Sea   O:46
Philipse Manor (farm, New York)
     picture(s)   C:416
Philip the Good (Duke of Burgundy)   D:371
Philistines (ancient people who established themselves in
     Canaan)   D:42; J:102; P:40c
Phillip, Arthur (British colonizer of Australia)   A:515; E:411
Phillips, Wendell (American abolitionist)   W:212a
Phillips Exeter Academy (New Hampshire)   N:155
Phillips-head screws   N:2; T:229
     picture(s)   N:3
Philodendron (plant)
     picture(s)   L:115
Philology (study of ancient texts)   H:284
Philosopher's stone (mythical substance sought by alchemists)
     C:207
Philosophes (French writers)   E:295–98; F:415, 467
Philosophy   P:189–92
     Aquinas, Saint Thomas   A:338
     Aristotle   A:386d–387
     atheism   A:476b
     Confucius   C:498
     Descartes, René   D:124
     Dewey, John   D:144
     ethics   E:328–29
     Greek literature   G:343, 357, 359
     humanism   H:284
     Hume, David   H:288
     James, William   J:21
     Kant, Immanuel   K:191
     Leibniz, Gottfried Wilhelm von   L:138

**Philosophy** (cont.)
 Locke's empiricism **L:**281
 logic **L:**289–90
 Mill's utilitarian view of human rights **C:**325
 Plato **P:**330
 Socrates **S:**232
 Spinoza, Baruch **S:**410
**Phineus** (in Greek mythology) **G:**364
**Phipps, James** (British boy, first to be vaccinated against
 smallpox) **M:**205
**Phloem** (plant tissue) **F:**93; **L:**114, 116; **P:**304
**Phlogiston, theory of** **C:**208–9; **L:**83
**Phlox** (flowers) **G:**46
 *picture(s)* **G:**28, 50
**Phnom Penh** (capital of Cambodia) **C:**37, 38; **S:**334
**Phobia** (very strong, irrational fear) **H:**329; **M:**222
**Phobos** (moon of Mars) **M:**109; **P:**278–79; **S:**52, 247
**Phoebe** (moon of Saturn) **S:**58
**Phoebes** (birds) *see* Flycatchers
**Phoebus Apollo** *see* Apollo
**Phoenicians** (early people of the eastern Mediterranean coast)
 **I:**88
 alphabet **A:**194a; **C:**463; **I:**280
 earliest known people in Lebanon **L:**121
 exploration by ancient civilizations **E:**399–400
 Mediterranean Sea **M:**212
 origin of the trade fair **F:**17
 sailors and traders **S:**156; **T:**283
 settlements in Africa **A:**65, 187
 Spain, history of **S:**370, 375
 *picture(s)*
  alphabet **A:**194b
**Phoenix** (Arizona) **A:**397, 399, 401, 404, 405; **P:**192–93
 urban growth **U:**96
 water use **W:**75
 *picture(s)* **P:**193; **U:**98
  business district **A:**401
  state capitol building **A:**401
**Phoenix** (missile) **M:**349; **U:**115
**Phoenix Islands** (Pacific Ocean) **K:**265
**Pholidota** (order of mammals)
 *picture(s)*
  long-tailed pangolin as example **M:**73
**Phonemes** (speech sounds) **A:**194; **R:**109
**Phonics** (study of the relationships between written letters and
 speech sounds) **P:**194, 486; **R:**109
**Phonograms** (symbols that stand for sounds) **H:**130
**Phonograph** **P:**194–95
 communication, history of **C:**467
 Edison invented **E:**72; **I:**284
 high-fidelity systems **H:**132
 recording industry **R:**122
 sound recording **S:**267b
 talking books for the blind **B:**258
 *picture(s)*
  early advertising poster **C:**467
  Edison invented **E:**71
  gramophone **R:**122
  "His Master's Voice" **P:**195
**Phony War** (1939–1940) **W:**296
**Phosphate rock**
 Banaba **K:**265–66
 Florida **F:**265, 268
 Morocco **M:**460
 Nauru **N:**71
 North American mineral resources **N:**292
**Phosphates** (chemical compounds)
 detergents, environmental problems of **D:**141; **E:**301
 fertilizers **F:**97
 minerals in the ocean **O:**28
 ocean water, presence in **O:**17
 Tunisia is a leading producer **T:**335
**Phosphazene** (synthetic rubber) **R:**346
**Phospholipids** **L:**268
**Phosphor bronze** (alloy) **B:**409

**Phosphorescent paints** **P:**34
**Phosphoric acid** **O:**289
**Phosphors** (materials that exhibit phosphorescence) **C:**429;
 **E:**150; **L:**236; **T:**63
**Phosphorus** (element) **B:**295; **E:**175; **F:**97; **T:**274–75; **V:**371
 *table(s)*
  food sources and DRI's **V:**372
**Photic (Lighted) habitat** (of the ocean) **O:**23, 26
**Photocells** *see* Photoelectric cells
**Photochemical smog** **A:**123; **E:**303
**Photocollages** (in art) **H:**159a
**Photoconductive cells** **P:**196, 197
**Photocopying** **C:**464; **O:**59; **P:**478
**Photodetectors** (sound recording and playback devices)
 **S:**267a; **V:**332f
**Photodiode** (type of photoconductive cell) **P:**197
**Photoelectric cells (Photocells)** **B:**103c; **P:**196–97
**Photoelectricity (Photoelectric effect)** **L:**223; **P:**196–97, 231,
 237; **S:**240
**Photoelectric theory** **R:**47
**Photoelectric tubes** *see* Phototubes
**Photoengraving** **I:**80–81; **M:**27; **P:**472
**Photogrammetry** (science of measuring by photography)
 **O:**183–84
**Photography** **P:**198–218
 animation **A:**288–89, 290
 atmosphere, images of **A:**481
 blueprint **B:**263
 Brady, Mathew B. **N:**224
 communication, history of **C:**466–67
 cosmic rays recorded by **C:**563
 Daguerre, Louis **D:**2
 Eastman, George **E:**48
 electronic *see* Electronic photography
 filming motion pictures **M:**478–79, 481, 483
 magazine publishing **M:**17
 modeling, fashion **M:**384
 newspapers, important part of **N:**201–2, 204
 observatories, use in **O:**10, 12
 photogrammetry **O:**183–84
 police work, use in **P:**366–67
 preparing artwork for printing **P:**470–73
 separations of color for book illustrations **B:**331–32
 silver compounds **S:**178
 space probes **S:**357–60
 special uses of **P:**208–9
 telescopes **T:**58
 video recording **V:**332h
 *picture(s)*
  first successful photograph **P:**211
  types of shots used in motion pictures **M:**482
**Photojournalism** **P:**211, 214
**Photolithography** **I:**80–81; **P:**472; **T:**278
**Photometers** (tools used in observatories) **A:**476; **O:**12; **S:**428
**Photomicrography** (photography of microscopic objects)
 **P:**209
 *picture(s)* **P:**198, 209
**Photons** (subatomic particles) **A:**489
 forces **F:**366b
 lasers **L:**46b
 light **L:**213, 223, 224, 226
 quantum theory **P:**237
 radiant energy **L:**46a
 radiation **R:**43, 47, 65
 X-rays **X:**349
**Photo paper (Photographic printing paper)** **P:**217
**Photoperiodism** *see* Day and night
**Photophores** (light-producing organs of sea organisms)
 **B:**205; **O:**27; **S:**167; **U:**25
**Photorealism** (in art) **R:**115; **U:**135
**Photoreceptors** (light-sensitive cells in the eye) **E:**430
**Photoresist** (light-sensitive material) **T:**278
**Photosphere** (of the sun) **S:**492

**Piano** (cont.)
    *diagram(s)*
        cross section of a grand piano  **P:**241
    *picture(s)*  **K:**238; **M:**548; **P:**240, 242
***Piano Lesson, The*** (play by August Wilson)
    *picture(s)*  **D:**307
**Piazza di Venezia** (city square, Rome, Italy)  **R:**306
**Piazza Navona** (city square, Rome, Italy)  **F:**393–94
**Piazzi, Giuseppe** (Italian astonomer)  **S:**244
**Pica** (size of type)  **T:**370
**Picadors** (in bullfighting)  **B:**451
**Picaresque (Rogue) novels**  **E:**279–80; **S:**388
**Picasso, Pablo** (Spanish-born painter of the French school)
    **P:**243–44
    art of the artist  **A:**433
    Braque, Georges  **B:**371
    collage  **C:**402
    cubism  **C:**612
    drawing, history of  **D:**318
    modern art  **M:**390
    modern French art  **F:**431–32
    modern Spanish art  **S:**385
    painting in the 20th century  **P:**29–30
    Picasso museum (Barcelona, Spain)  **M:**525
    Picasso museum (Paris, France)  **P:**70
    sculpture  **S:**103–4
    *picture(s)*
        *Child with a Dove* (painting)  **P:**243
        *Demoiselles d'Avignon, Les* (painting)  **M:**390
        drawing of Manuel de Falla  **S:**392b
        *Girl Before a Mirror*  **A:**433
        *Girl with a Mandolin* (painting)  **D:**136
        *Green Still Life* (painting)  **P:**31
        *Guernica* (mural)  **S:**385
        *Head of a Woman* (sculpture)  **S:**104
        ink drawing of two pigeons  **D:**318
        portrait of Gertrude Stein  **S:**446
        *Three Musicians* (painting)  **P:**243
        *Woman with a Mandolin*  **C:**612
**Piccadilly Circus** (London, England)  **L:**294
    *picture(s)*  **L:**294
**Piccard, Auguste** (Swiss scientist, inventor, and explorer)
    **B:**36; **E:**416; **P:**244; **U:**27
**Piccard, Bertrand** (Swiss balloonist)  **B:**36
**Piccard, Jacques** (Swiss scientist)  **P:**244
**Piccolo** (musical instrument)  **M:**549; **O:**193; **W:**185
    *picture(s)*  **M:**549
**Pick** (used in playing a guitar)  **G:**411
**Pickering, Edward** (American astronomer)  **A:**472
**Picketing** (labor union tactic)  **L:**8, 10
    *picture(s)*  **L:**10
**Pickett, Tydia** (American athlete)  **O:**112
**Pickford, Mary** (American actress and producer)  **M:**489, 491
    *profile*
**Pickling** (in steel production)  **I:**336
**Pickling** (of food)  **F:**344; **O:**101
**Pickup baler** (farm machine)  **F:**58
**Pick-up-sticks** (game)  **G:**18
**Pickup trucks**
    *picture(s)*  **T:**320
**Pickup tubes** (in television cameras)  **T:**62
***Pickwick Papers*** (book by Charles Dickens)  **D:**151
**Picnics**  **O:**262
**Pictographs (Pictograms)** (early form of writing) *see* Picture
    writing
**Pictographs (Picture graphs)** (style of graph)  **G:**310
**Picts** (early people of Scotland)  **E:**236; **S:**88
**Picture books**  **C:**228, 237
    Caldecott, Randolph  **C:**10
    Caldecott Medal  **C:**11–12
    children's book awards  **C:**240
    list of  **C:**242–43
**Picture editors** (of magazines)  **M:**17
**Picture-in-picture** (television feature)  **T:**67
**Picturephone** *see* Video telephone

**Pictures** (works of art) *see* Cartoons; Engraving; Illustration and
    illustrators; Painting; Photography; Posters
**Picture tubes** (of television sets) *see* Cathode-ray tubes
**Picture writing**  **C:**463; **H:**22 *see also* individual letters of the
    alphabet
    alphabet  **A:**194a
    Chinese pictograms  **B:**320
    cuneiform, development of  **C:**613
    development of languages  **L:**38
    hieroglyphic writing systems  **H:**129–31
**Pidgin** (simplified form of English)  **S:**252
**Pieces of eight** (term derived from Spanish money)  **D:**261
**Pie charts** (circle graphs)  **G:**310–11; **S:**441–42
**Pied coats** (of dogs)  **D:**242
**Piedmont glaciers**  **A:**132; **G:**223
**Piedmont Region** (eastern United States)  **N:**166, 285; **P:**128;
    **U:**78
    Maryland  **M:**122, 124
    North Carolina  **N:**310
    South Carolina  **S:**298, 299, 300, 303, 306
    Virginia  **V:**348, 349, 350, 352
**"Pied Piper of Hamelin, The"** (poem by Robert Browning)
    excerpt from  **B:**413
**Pieh, Sengbe** (Mende leader of the Amistad Rebellion) *see*
    Cinque, Joseph
**Pierce, Franklin** (14th president of the United States)  **H:**65;
    **N:**158, 162; **P:**245–47
    *picture(s)*  **N:**162; **P:**245, 247, 447
**Pierce, Jane Means Appleton** (wife of Franklin Pierce)  **F:**170;
    **P:**246, 247
    *picture(s)*  **F:**170; **P:**246
**Pierce, John Davis** (American educator)  **M:**264
**Pierce, Webb** (American singer)  **C:**572
**Piérola, Nicolás de** (president of Peru)  **P:**165
**Pierpont Morgan Library** (New York City)  **M:**456
**Pierre** (capital of South Dakota)  **S:**312, 318–19, 322, 326
    *picture(s)*  **S:**324
**Pierrot** (character in French pantomime)  **C:**386
**Piers** (in construction) *see* Caissons
***Piers Plowman*** (English poem)  **E:**269
**Pies** (baked goods)  **B:**387
***Pietà*** (sculpture by Michelangelo)  **M:**257; **V:**280
    *picture(s)*  **M:**257
**Pietri, Dorando** (Italian runner)  **O:**114
**Piezoelectricity** (of quartz crystals)  **C:**614; **F:**365; **Q:**7
**Pig** (number game)  **N:**394
**Pigalle, Jean Baptiste** (French sculptor)  **S:**101
**Pigeons** (birds) *see* Doves and pigeons
**Pig frogs**  **F:**477
**Piggyback** (freight hauling method)  **R:**83, 84; **T:**289
**Piggy banks**  **P:**58c
**Pig iron**  **I:**218, 332; **O:**217
**Pig Latin** (secret language)  **C:**395
**Pigments** *see* Paints and pigments
**Pigmies** *see* Pygmies
**Pignotti, Lorenzo** (Italian fabulist)  **F:**4
**Pigpen cipher**  **C:**394–95
**Pigs**  **P:**248
    biotechnology, risks of  **B:**214
    Chinese agriculture  **C:**264
    hoofed mammals  **H:**219–20
    livestock  **L:**271–72
    pigskin leather  **L:**109
    raising pigs for market  **M:**195–96
    *picture(s)*  **M:**67, 374
        cloned  **M:**209
        embryo development  **E:**374
        hind foot  **H:**218
**Pigs, Bay of** (Cuba)  **C:**610; **K:**209
**Pigs in Clover** (puzzle)  **P:**554
**Pigskin leather**  **L:**109
**Pigweed**  **W:**106
**Pikas** (animals of rabbit family)  **R:**24
**Pike** (diving position)  **D:**225
    *picture(s)*  **D:**224

**Pike** (fish)
*picture(s)* **F:**211
**Pike, Zebulon Montgomery** (American soldier) **C:**442; **M:**338; **N:**91; **O:**272
**Pikes Peak** (Colorado) **H:**91; **N:**23
*picture(s)* **C:**439
**Pilasters** (in architecture) **B:**494
**Pilate, Pontius** (Roman governor of Judea) **J:**88
**Pilâtre de Rozier, Jean François** (French balloonist) **B:**34
**Pilcomayo River** (South America) **B:**307
**Pile** (of rugs and carpets) **R:**353, 354–55
**Pileated woodpeckers** (birds)
*picture(s)*
feet **B:**220
**Pile drivers** **B:**400
*picture(s)* **B:**437
**Pile fabrics** **T:**142
**Pile foundation** (in construction) **B:**437
**Pileus** (ancient Roman hat) **H:**45
**Pilgrimages**
Buddhism **B:**426; **H:**138
Chaucer's *Canterbury Tales* **C:**191; **E:**270
Crusades **C:**598–600
holy places of Hindus **H:**140–41
Muslims to Mecca **I:**349; **M:**199; **R:**148; **S:**58b
*romerías* of Dominican Republic **D:**280
*picture(s)*
holy places of Hindus **H:**140
Muslims to Mecca **A:**344; **R:**145
**Pilgrim Pope** (nickname for Paul VI) **P:**102
**Pilgrims** (Separatists from the Church of England) **C:**409; **D:**37; **M:**188; **P:**344–47; **T:**153–54, 170–72
*picture(s)* **M:**146; **T:**153, 167
*Pilgrim's Progress* (book by John Bunyan) **C:**229; **E:**276
**Pili** (bacterial structures) **B:**11
**Pilipino** (national language of the Philippines) **P:**184; **S:**329
**Pilkington, Alastair** (English glassmaker) **G:**234
**Pill** (contraceptive) **B:**250b
**Pillar cranes** (machines) **H:**159b–159c
**Pillars** (in architecture) *see* Columns
**Pillars of Hercules** **G:**204
**Pillboxes** (fortifications) **F:**379
*Pillow Book, The* (book by Sei Shonagon) **J:**41
**Pillow lava** **V:**382
**Pilon, Germain** (French sculptor) **F:**424
*Pilot, The* (novel by James Fenimore Cooper) **C:**549
**Pilotage** (airplane navigation method) **A:**118
**Piloting** (navigational system) **P:**201; **N:**72–74
**Pilotis** (thin columns in architecture) **A:**374, 375
**Pilots, airplane** **A:**569, 570–71
**Pilot snakes** *see* Copperheads
**Pilot whales (Blackfish; Potheads)** **W:**149, 150
*picture(s)* **D:**275; **W:**150
**Pilsen** (Czech Republic) *see* Plzeň
**Pilsudski, Józef** (Polish statesman) **P:**361–62
**Pima** (Native Americans) *see* O'odham
**Pima cotton** **C:**568
**Pina** (plant fiber) **F:**109
*Pinafore* (operetta by Gilbert and Sullivan) *see H.M.S. Pinafore*
**Pinang** *see* Penang
**Piñata** (Latin-American Christmas custom) **C:**301; **L:**56; **M:**242
**Pinatubo, Mount** (volcano, Philippines) **E:**15; **P:**185
*picture(s)* **E:**15
**Pinchback, Pinckney Benton Stewart** (American politician) **A:**79c
**Pinch hitters** (in baseball) **B:**80
**Pinchincha, Battle of** (1822) **E:**69
**Pinchot, Gifford** (American conservationist) **C:**526; **F:**377; **N:**30–31; **R:**331; **T:**5
**Pinckney, Charles** (American statesman, 1757–1824) **S:**309, 311 *profile*
**Pinckney, Charles Cotesworth** (American statesman, 1746–1825) **S:**310–11 *profile*

**Pinckney, Elizabeth Lucas** (West Indies-born American who initiated indigo culture) **S:**310 *profile*
**Pinckney, Thomas** (American statesman) **S:**311 *profile*
**Pinckney's Treaty** (1795) **W:**44
**Pincushion cacti** **C:**5
**Pindar** (Greek poet) **G:**356; **O:**52, 104
**Pindus** (mountain range in Greece) **G:**333
**Pineal gland** **G:**228
**Pineapple** **F:**109; **H:**48, 56; **N:**98; **P:**249
*diagram(s)* **P:**249
*picture(s)* **H:**55, 207; **P:**296
**Pine Barrens** (New Jersey) **N:**164, 166, 167, 172
**Pine Bluff** (Arkansas) **A:**415
**Pine Creek Gorge** (Pennsylvania) **P:**134
**Piñeda, Alonso de** (Spanish explorer) **T:**137
**Pine grosbeaks** (birds) **A:**277
**Pine-knot torches** **L:**231
**Pinel, Philippe** (French doctor) **M:**208f
**Pinelands National Reserve** (New Jersey) **N:**164, 172
**Piñera, Virgilio** (Cuban novelist) **C:**609
**Pine snakes** **S:**212
**Pine squirrels** *see* Red squirrels
**Pine trees**
Arizona has world's largest stand of ponderosa pines **A:**394
bristlecone pine is oldest living thing **T:**300
western white pine is state tree of Idaho **I:**49
white pine was the most useful tree in the United States **L:**338
*picture(s)* **N:**307
eastern white pine **M:**37, 259
loblolly pines **A:**133
Mississippi's Piney Woods **M:**352
Montana forest attacked by pine beetles **P:**286
piñon pine **N:**123, 181
ponderosa pine **M:**429
red pine **M:**327
Scotch pine **P:**305
seed **P:**307
shortleaf **A:**407
southern pine **A:**131
sugar pine **T:**301
uses of the wood (white and yellow) and its grain **W:**224
western white pine **I:**47
white pine **T:**301
**Pine-tree shillings** (coins) **M:**340
**Pine Tree State** (nickname for Maine) **M:**36, 37
**Piney Woods** (Mississippi) **M:**352, 353, 354
*picture(s)* **M:**352
**Pinfeathers** (immature feathers) **P:**417
**Ping-Pong** *see* Table tennis
**Pings** (sound pulses sent out by sonar sets) **R:**40
**Pinhole camera** **E:**388; **L:**217
**Pinion** (smaller of a pair of gears) **G:**65
**Pinkerton, Allan** (Scottish-American detective) **C:**221 *profile*
**Pinkney, Jerry** (American illustrator) **C:**235 *profile*
*picture(s)* **C:**234
**Pinna** (part of the outer ear) **E:**4
*picture(s)* **E:**5
**Pinnate compound leaves** **L:**112
*picture(s)* **L:**113
**Pinnate veins** (of trees) **T:**308
**Pinnipeds** (fin-footed mammals)
fur seals **F:**518
sea lions **S:**106
seals **S:**107–8
walruses **W:**6–7
*picture(s)*
hooded seal as example **M:**71
*Pinocchio* (animated cartoon) **M:**493
**Pinochet Ugarte, Augusto** (Chilean military and political leader) **C:**255
*picture(s)* **C:**255
**Pinocytosis** (of animal cells) **C:**161

**Piñon** (pine tree)
    *picture(s)*    **N:**123, 181
**Pins** (jewelry)    **J:**95
    *picture(s)*    **J:**95, 96, 100
**Pinski, David** (Yiddish playwright)    **Y:**361
**Pint** (measure of volume)    **C:**540–41; **W:**113, 115
*Pinta* (ship of Christopher Columbus)    **C:**446; **E:**404
**Pinter, Harold** (British playwright)    **D:**305; **E:**290
**Pinto** (horse marking)    **H:**237
    *picture(s)*    **H:**238
**Pinto da Costa, Manuel** (president of São Tomé and Príncipe)
        **S:**41
**Pin tumbler cylinder locks**    **L:**282–83, 284
    *diagram(s)*    **L:**283
**Pinturicchio** (Italian artist)
    *picture(s)*
        court life    **R:**157
        fresco of Virgin Mary and Christ Child    **M:**119
**Pinworms**    **D:**199
**Pinyin** (system for representing Chinese in the Roman
        alphabet)    **C:**258
**Pinyon** (pine tree) *see* Piñon
**Pinzón, Vicente Yáñez** (Spanish explorer)    **H:**208
*Pioneer* (space probes)    **S:**340c, 359, 360
    Jupiter    **J:**159; **P:**279
    observatories in space    **O:**10
    search for life on other planets    **L:**211
    Venus    **V:**303a
**Pioneer Day** (Utah state holiday)    **S:**24
**Pioneer life**    **C:**421; **P:250–61**
    in American literature    **A:**214; **R:**304
    Boone, Daniel    **B:**334
    Bowie knife, origin of    **B:**347
    Buffalo Bill    **B:**431
    Campus Martius Museum (Ohio)    **O:**70
    cosmetics made at home    **C:**561
    Crockett, Davy    **C:**592
    folklore, American    **F:**316
    fur trade in North America    **F:**519–24
    gold discoveries    **G:**250–52
    guns and ammunition    **G:**418
    guns used for signal communication    **C:**465–66
    Montana    **M:**439
    Oklahoma "Sooners"    **O:**82
    overland trails    **O:**268–82
    Pony Express    **P:**383–84
    Turner's theory of the frontier in American history    **W:**207
    westward movement    **W:**140–44
    Wilder, Laura Ingalls    **W:**170–71
    *picture(s)*
        Fort Sisseton Historical Festival (South Dakota)
            **S:**317
        Laura Ingalls Wilder Festival (South Dakota)    **S:**313
**Pioneers** (Soviet youth organization)    **U:**36
*Pioneers, The* (novel by James Fenimore Cooper)    **C:**549
**"Pioneer" trees** (new growth after forest fire)    **F:**376
**Pipelines**    **T:**289
    across Panama to relieve congestion in the canal    **P:**50
    Israel's water supply    **M:**302
    natural gas    **N:**59
    Trans-Alaska Pipeline    **A:**152, 158
    transporting petroleum products    **P:**172
    *picture(s)*    **M:**301; **N:**60
**Pipe organ**    **K:**236–37; **M:**551; **O:**218–19
    *picture(s)*    **K:**237
**Piper Cub** (airplane)    **A:**110, 111
**Pipes** (for conducting liquids, gases, or semisolids)    **I:**337;
        **P:**339–40; **V:**269–70
**Pipes** (for smoking)
    *picture(s)*    **I:**180
**Pipes** (vertical lava mass in which diamonds are usually found)
        **G:**70
**Pipes of Pan** *see* Panpipes
**Pipestone National Monument** (Minnesota)    **M:**334
**Pipe welding**    **P:**340

**Pipil** (Indians of Central America)    **E:**198
*Pippi Longstocking* (book by Astrid Lindgren)    **C:**239
**Pippin, Horace** (American artist)
    *picture(s)*
        *Mr. Prejudice*    **A:**79m
**Pippin, Scottie** (American basketball player)
    *picture(s)*    **B:**95f
**Piracy** (unauthorized copying of commerical recordings)
        **R:**124
**Piraeus** (Greece)    **A:**476c; **G:**335, 336
**Pirandello, Luigi** (Italian novelist and dramatist)    **D:**305;
        **I:**387, 409
**Piranha** (fish)    **F:**199; **S:**283
**Pirarucú** (fish)    **B:**378
**Pirates**    **P:262–64** *see also* Vikings
    Caribbean Sea and islands    **C:**115
    Kidd, Captain William    **K:**241
    Laffite, Jean    **L:**23
    Ottoman corsairs    **O:**259–60
    *picture(s)*
        buccaneers    **P:**263
*Pirates of Penzance, The* (operetta by Gilbert and Sullivan)
        **G:**208–9; **M:**553
**Pisa** (Italy)
    *picture(s)*
        cathedral and leaning tower of    **C:**134; **I:**391
**Pisano, Giovanni** (Italian sculptor and architect)    **I:**393
**Pisano, Nicola (Niccolo)** (Italian sculptor and architect)
        **I:**393; **S:**98, 100
    *picture(s)*
        Baptistery of Pisa Cathedral pulpit    **I:**393
*Pisanosaurus* (dinosaur)    **D:**174
**Piscataqua River** (Maine–New Hampshire)    **N:**152
**Pisces** (constellation)    **C:**529; **Z:**386
**Pi Shing** (Chinese inventor)    **C:**464
**Pissarro, Camille** (French painter)    **F:**430; **I:**103; **M:**387
**Pistachio nuts**    **N:**434–35
**Pistils** (of flowers)    **F:**282; **P:**307
**Pistols** (small guns)    **D:**350; **G:**415, 421, 423
    *picture(s)*    **G:**418, 421, 423
**Piston engines** *see* Reciprocating engines
**Piston rings** (of the internal-combustion engine)    **I:**262
**Pistons** (mechanical devices)
    airplane engines    **A:**115
    automobile engines    **A:**547
    brakes    **A:**551
    hydraulic machines    **H:**311–12, 313
    internal-combustion engines    **E:**230; **I:**262, 263
    jet engines compared to piston engines    **J:**92
    piston engines    **E:**229
    pneumatic tools    **H:**314
    pumps    **P:**541
    steam engines    **S:**443
**Pita** (Greek bread)    **B:**385
**Pitcairn, John** (British commander)    **R:**198
**Pitcairn Island** (Pacific Ocean)    **B:**255; **P:**10
**Pitch** (in music)    **A:**79; **J:**57; **M:**533–35, 537; **V:**377
**Pitch** (of sound)    **S:**258, 396, 398
    detecting hearing loss    **D:**49
**Pitch** (sticky substance exuded from certain trees)    **R:**184
**Pitchblende** (ore)    **C:**614; **U:**230
**Pitcher** (in baseball)    **B:**79–80
**Pitcher, Molly** (American heroine of Revolutionary War)    **R:**207
**Pitcher plants**    **P:**314
    *picture(s)*    **N:**141; **W:**146
**Pitching** (movement of an airplane)    **A:**113, 114
**Pitch Lake** (Trinidad and Tobago)    **T:**315
**Pith** (of a woody stem)    **W:**222
**Piton de la Rivière Noire** (highest point in Mauritius)    **M:**181
**Pitons** (used in mountain climbing)    **M:**500
**Pitot-static tube** (of an airspeed indicator)    **A:**118
**Pit quarry**    **Q:**6
**Pitt, William, Earl of Chatham** (British statesman)    **F:**464;
        **O:**191; **P:**265

**Pitt, William, the Younger** (British statesman)  **E:**252; **O:**191; **P:**265
*picture(s)*  **P:**459
**Pitti Gallery** (Florence, Italy)  **M:**525
**Pittsburgh** (Pennsylvania)  **P:**126, 133, 135, **266–67**
  air pollution control  **F:**291
  cultural center  **P:**131
  overland trails  **O:**270
  *picture(s)*  **P:**135, 266
    bridges  **B:**395
    Carnegie Museum of Natural History  **P:**134
**Pittsburgh, University of**  **P:**266
**Pituitary gland**  **B:**292; **G:**227, 228
  growth hormone  **H:**227
  hormonal diseases  **D:**194
  relation to the brain  **B:**365
**Pit vipers** (poisonous snakes)  **S:**211, 213, 215, 216, 217
  *picture(s)*
    skull and teeth  **S:**212
**Piura** (Peru)  **P:**162
**Pius I, Saint** (pope)  **R:**292
**Pius II** (pope)  **R:**293
**Pius III** (pope)  **R:**293
**Pius IV** (pope)  **R:**293
**Pius V, Saint** (pope)  **O:**260; **R:**293
**Pius VI** (pope)  **R:**293
**Pius VII** (pope)  **N:**10; **R:**293
**Pius VIII** (pope)  **R:**293
**Pius IX** (pope)  **R:**293, 294
**Pius X, Saint** (pope)  **H:**324; **R:**293; **S:**18d *profile*
**Pius XI** (pope)  **R:**293
**Pius XII** (pope)  **P:268**; **R:**293
**Pivot joints** (in the skeleton)  **S:**184b
**Pixels** (digital picture elements)  **A:**290, 298; **P:**199, 205; **T:**62
**Pixies** (fairies)  **F:**9
**Pixii, Hippolyte** (French instrument maker)  **E:**154
**Pizan, Christine de** (French writer)  **F:**436
**Pizarro, Francisco** (Spanish conqueror of Peru)  **P:**164, **268**
  conquest of the Incas  **A:**245; **I:**110, 173; **S:**293
  De Soto, Hernando  **D:**138
  Ecuador  **E:**69
  exploration of the New World  **E:**409
  married Huayna Capac's daughter  **I:**195
  *picture(s)*  **A:**235; **S:**292
**Pizza** (Italian food)  **M:**277
  *picture(s)*  **F:**335
**Pizzicato** (plucking the string of a musical instrument)  **V:**345
**PKU** *see* Phenylketonuria
**Place, Etta** (American outlaw)  **U:**254
**Place de la Concorde** *see* Concorde, Place de la
**Place des Arts** (Montreal)  **C:**68
**Placekicking** (in football)
  *picture(s)*  **F:**356
**Place names**
  personal names derived from places  **N:**4
**Placenta** (organ attached to uterus)  **B:**2; **R:**179
**Placental mammals**  **M:**69, 114
**Placentia** (Newfoundland and Labrador)  **N:**145
**Placer mining**  **G:**251; **M:**323
**Place Royale** (Quebec City)  **Q:**13
**Placers** (alluvial deposits containing minerals)  **G:**248–49; **O:**217
**Place settings** *see* Table settings
**Places of interest** *see* the places of interest section of country, province, and state articles
**Place value** (in numeration systems)  **A:**389; **D:**56; **F:**400; **N:**405
**Placid, Lake** (New York) *see* Lake Placid
**Plague** (disease)  **D:**212; **L:**298; **V:**284 *see also* Bubonic plague
**Plain-breasted ground doves**  **D:**289
**Plainchant** *see* Plainsong
*Plain City* (book by Virginia Hamilton)
  *picture(s)*  **C:**246

**Plainclothes officers** (in community police)  **P:**363
**Plains** (stretches of flat land)  **E:**344; **P:**426–29 *see also* Great Plains; Tundra
**Plains bison**  **B:**430
**Plains Indians of North America**  **I:**179–82; **U:**188
  Bird Dance  **D:**25
  Indian Wars  **I:**205
  moveable homes  **H:**189
  museum in Browning (Montana)  **M:**433
  music  **M:**545
  White Buffalo Woman myth  **M:**577
  *picture(s)*  **I:**175
**Plains of Abraham** *see* Abraham, Plains of
**Plainsong (Chant; Plainchant)** (musical form)  **M:**538 *see also* Gregorian chants
  choral music  **C:**282–83
  English music  **E:**291
  Germany, music of  **G:**183
  hymns  **H:**324
  Italy, music of  **I:**410
  Middle Ages, music of the  **M:**296
  musical notation, development of  **M:**535
**Plain style** (of writing sermons)  **P:**551
**Plains zebras**  **H:**243; **Z:**379
**Plaintiff** (in law)  **C:**574; **L:**90
**Plamondon, Antoine Sébastien** (Canadian artist)
  *picture(s)*
    *Portrait of Soeur Saint-Alphonse* (painting)  **N:**40
**Planar defects** (in crystals)  **M:**153
**Planarians** (worms)  **W:**322
**Plan Barbarossa** (German invasion of Soviet Union in World War II)  **W:**300
**Planck, Max** (German physicist)  **L:**222–23; **P:**231, 236, 237 *profile*; **R:**47; **S:**73
  *picture(s)*  **P:**237
**Planck's constant**  **L:**224
**Plane geometry**  **G:**120–21; **M:**157
**Plane mirrors**  **L:**214
**Plane projections** (of maps)  **M:**97
**Planers** (tools)  **F:**515; **L:**342; **T:**232
**Planes** (flat surfaces in design)  **D:**136
**Planes** (tools)  **T:**228–29, 234
**Planes, inclined** (simple machines) *see* Inclined planes
**Planetariums**  **M:**523–24; **P:269–73**
  *picture(s)*  **P:**269
**Planetary gears**  **T:**280
**Planetary nebulas** (in astronomy)  **N:**96; **S:**431
**Planetesimal theory** (of origin of solar system)  **E:**23; **S:**249; **U:**231
  *picture(s)*  **E:**22
**Planetoids** *see* Asteroids
**Plane trigonometry**  **T:**312–13
**Planets**  **P:**275–82 *see also* Earth; the names of planets
  astronomy, history of  **A:**469–71
  discoveries of planets  **A:**470–71
  Do planets exist beyond our solar system?  **P:**282
  dust-cloud hypothesis of formation  **E:**22–23
  experiments and other science activities  **E:**389–90
  formation  **S:**431
  geology in the solar system  **G:**118–19
  planetariums  **P:**269–73
  planetoids (asteroids)  **S:**241, 244
  planets as seen from Earth  **S:**244, 246–47
  radio astronomy studies  **R:**69
  satellites  **S:**52
  spacecraft tracking  **S:**340L
  space probes  **S:**357–60
  theories about the sun and planets  **S:**248–49
  What is the outermost planet in the solar system?  **N:**113
  Would you weigh the same if you lived on a planet other than Earth?  **P:**277
  *picture(s)*
    relative sizes  **P:**276–77
**Planet X hypothesis** (of dinosaur extinction)  **D:**177

**Plankton** (drifting mass of small organisms)  **A:**181; **P:283–85**
  bivalves feed on  **O:**290
  crustaceans  **C:**601
  ocean life  **O:**23–24
  oceanographic studies  **O:**35, 40
**Planned Parenthood Federation of America**  **B:**251
*Planned Parenthood* v. *Casey* (1992)  **W:**213
**Planographic printing**  **G:**302
**Plan Overlord** (invasion of France, World War II)  **W:**310
**Plan position indicator (PPI)** (of radar systems)  **R:**38–39
**Plantagenet family** (rulers of England)  **E:**244
**Plantain** (bananalike fruit)  **L:**53; **T:**317
  *picture(s)*  **T:**317
**Plantain** (broad-leafed weed)
  *picture(s)*  **W:**105
**Plantations**
  African American history  **A:**79e–79f
  colonial America  **C:**414, 416
  rubber  **R:**344, 348a
  sugarcane and pineapple plantations in Hawaii  **H:**48, 54, 56, 62
  *picture(s)*
    colonial America  **C:**420
    slaves working in field  **U:**184
    tea plantation in Sri Lanka  **S:**414
**Plant breeding** *see* Breeding, plant
**Plant defenses**  **P:**316–17; **R:**99–100; **W:**104, 106
**Plant diseases**  **P:**288–89 *see also* the names of individual plants, as Corn
  endangered species  **E:**209
  fungi  **F:**498, 499
  vectors of disease  **V:**282
  viruses in plants  **V:**367, 370a
**Plant enemies** *see* Plant diseases; Plant pests
**Planters** (machines for sowing seed)  **F:**55, 60
  *picture(s)*  **F:**56
**Planting** (of crops)  **F:**49, 55–56
  gardens and gardening  **G:**30, 39–41
  houseplants  **H:**265–69
  vegetables  **V:**286–88
  *table(s)*
    when, how and where to plant  **G:**49
**Plant kingdom**  **K:**253, 256; **L:**208, 209; **P:**299
**Plant pests** (insects harmful to plants)  **P:286–91**
  boll weevils  **C:**568–69
  corn, enemies of  **C:**558
  famine  **F:**44
  vectors of disease  **V:**282
  weeds  **W:**104–6
**Plant propagation**  **P:**310
  apple trees  **A:**333
  gardens and gardening  **G:**40, 51
  grapes and berries  **G:**298
  grasses  **G:**316–17
  houseplants  **H:**267
**Plants**  **P:292–321** *see also* Botany; Vegetation; the names of plants, such as Corn; the natural resources section of continent, country, province, and state articles
  acid rain's effects  **A:**10
  Arctic region  **A:**378, 379
  atmosphere, formation of  **E:**23
  biological clocks  **L:**203–4, 207
  bioluminescence  **B:**205
  biomes  **B:**206, 207, 208, 210, 212
  bogs  **W:**146–47
  botanical gardens  **B:**342–43
  botany  **B:**343
  breeding *see* Breeding, plant
  cactus  **C:**4–5
  capillary action draws water through plant  **W:**50
  cave life  **C:**158
  cell structure  **C:**160–61
  climate and vegetation regions  **C:**362
  coloration  **C:**427–28

defenses *see* Plant defenses
desert plants  **D:**128–29
diseases *see* Plant diseases
Do growing plants break up rocks?  **S:**235
dyes, sources of  **D:**376–77
Earth, history of  **E:**24–29
Earth's geology affected by  **G:**117
ecology  **E:**53–55
ecosphere  **N:**63
endangered species  **E:**208–10
enemies *see* Plant diseases; Plant pests
evolution of  **E:**372–79; **F:**386–87
experiments in life sciences  **E:**381, 395–96, 397
extinction  **E:**425–26
ferns  **F:**93–95
fertilizer elements, hunger signs for  **F:**96
first plants had no flowers  **F:**280
flowers  **F:**280–87
food chain producers  **L:**205
food plants *see* Plants, food
fossils  **F:**380–89
gardens and gardening  **G:**26–52
genetics  **G:**77–91
glands  **G:**226
grasses  **G:**314–19
hormones  **H:**228
houseplants  **H:**265–69
How big can a plant grow?  **P:**302
Humboldt's geographic findings on  **G:**105
hydrologic cycle  **W:**52
jungle  **J:**157–58
kingdoms of living things  **K:**253, 256
leaves  **L:**112–18
mechanisms for seed dispersal  **F:**286–87; **T:**310; **W:**106
medicinal plants *see* Plants, medicinal
Mendel, work of  **G:**90; **M:**218
mosses  **M:**472–73
nature, study of  **N:**67–70
ocean life  **O:**23–24, 26, 28
osmosis  **O:**241
pests *see* Plant pests
photosynthesis  **P:**219–21
poisonous plants *see* Plants, poisonous
prairies  **P:**426
propagation *see* Plant propagation
reproduction, types of  **R:**175–76
seeds, dispersal of  **F:**286–87
smallest known flowering plant  **D:**91
taxonomy  **T:**27–29
terrariums  **T:**102
trees  **T:**300–311
tundra  **T:**331
weeds  **W:**104–6
Which plant has the biggest seed?  **P:**307
Why do leaves change color in the autumn?  **P:**306
  *picture(s)*
    perfume oils from natural materials  **P:**151
  *table(s)*
    Earth, history of  **E:**25
**Plants, food**  **F:**329–30
  grain and grain products  **G:**280–87
  grasses  **G:**314–19
  herbs and spices  **H:**119–21
  oils and fats  **O:**80
  vegetables  **V:**286–92
**Plants, medicinal**
  drug industry  **D:**334
  herbs and spices  **H:**119, 120, 121
  sphagnum moss  **M:**472
**Plants, poisonous**  **A:**191; **H:**269; **L:**117; **P:**316
**Plant viruses**  **V:**367
**Planula** (coral larva)  **C:**555
**Plaque** (bacteria killed by viruses)  **V:**368
**Plaque** (cholesterol buildup in the arteries)  **H:**82; **N:**430
**Plaque** (film of bacteria that sticks to the teeth)  **D:**199

**Plasma** (fourth state of matter)   **I:**289; **M:**178; **N:**368; **R:**262; **S:**430

**Plasma, blood**   **B:**259, 284; **D:**325; **O:**241; **T:**273

**Plasma monitor** (television display)   **T:**64

**Plasmids** (of bacteria)   **G:**78

**Plasmodium** (protozoan)   **M:**51; **P:**497; **V:**283

**Plassey, Battle of** (1757)   **I:**132

**Plastic explosives**   **E:**423

**Plastic flow** (of glaciers)   **G:**221

**Plasticine** *see* Modeling clay

**Plasticity**   **S:**250

**Plasticizers** (ingredients used in plastics)   **P:**324

**Plastic (Acrylic) paint**   **P:**30

**Plastics** (artificial materials)   **P:322–29**
   airplane models   **A:**104, 107
   automobile model kits   **A:**534
   balloons   **B:**37
   biodegradable   **B:**214
   contact lenses   **C:**535
   dies and molds   **D:**158, 159
   furniture   **F:**517
   industrial design   **I:**214
   jewelry   **J:**97
   manufacturing   **M:**89
   natural gas, industrial uses of   **N:**58
   nonbiodegradable materials   **W:**62
   nylon and other synthetic fibers   **N:**436–40
   pollution by synthetic chemicals   **E:**303
   recycling   **R:**125
   resins used in   **R:**185
   science, milestones in   **S:**74
   shoes made of   **S:**160
   Tupper, Earl   **I:**283
   *picture(s)*
      manufacturing   **P:**325
      recycling   **P:**324, 327

**Plastid** (plant cell structure)   **P:**294

**Plastron** (lower part of turtle's shell)   **T:**355, 356

**Plata, Río de la** (estuary of the Paraná, Uruguay, and Paraguay rivers, South America)   **A:**386a; **R:**245; **S:**280; **U:**238, 240
   Buenos Aires   **B:**428
   *picture(s)*   **U:**239

**Plataea, Battle of** (479 B.C.)   **G:**343

**Plateaus** (elevated land areas)   **A:**47

**Platelets** (blood cells)   **B:**260, 261, 262, 284; **O:**238
   *picture(s)*   **B:**259, 260

**Platen presses** (for printing)   **P:**470, 474, 475

*Plateosaurus* (dinosaur)   **D:**172
   *picture(s)*   **D:**166

**Plateresque style** (of architecture)   **L:**60–61; **S:**383

**Plates** (in printing)   **P:**470, 472–73, 475, 477
   *picture(s)*   **P:**468

**Plates** (of Earth's crust)   **E:**11–13
   earthquakes, theory of   **E:**36
   geology   **G:**113–15
   mountain building   **E:**13
   oceanography   **O:**35
   oceans, origin of the   **O:**16
   volcanoes   **E:**15
   *diagram(s)*   **E:**13

**Plate tectonics** (geological concept)   **E:**11, 36; **G:**113–15; **S:**71
   Earth, history of   **E:**24
   mountain formation   **M:**501, 504, 505
   volcanoes   **V:**385–86

**Platforms, political**   **P:**373

**Platform tennis** (sport)   **R:**37
   *picture(s)*   **R:**37

**Plath, Sylvia** (American poet)   **A:**218; **H:**276; **M:**149 *profile*

**Plating, electric** *see* Electroplating

**Platinum** (element)   **E:**170, 175; **J:**96; **M:**236; **T:**164
   *table(s)*   **M:**235

**Platinum record** (in the recording industry)   **R:**264

**Plato** (Greek philosopher)   **P:**189–90, **330**
   Aristotle was a pupil of   **A:**386d
   communist society   **C:**472
   education, history of   **E:**78
   Greece, language of   **G:**353
   Greek literature   **G:**357
   physics, history of   **P:**233
   psychology, history of   **P:**505
   science, milestones in   **S:**68
   *picture(s)*   **G:**357; **P:**505; **S:**68

**Platonic solids** (in geometry)   *see* Regular polyhedra

**Platoons** (army troop unit)   **U:**104

**Platt Amendment** (Cuba–United States pact)   **C:**609

**Platte River** (United States)   **R:**244
   along the Oregon Trail   **O:**277
   Colorado   **C:**432
   Nebraska   **N:**82, 84, 86, 89
   *picture(s)*
      sandhill cranes on banks   **N:**85

**Platypuses** (duckbills)   **A:**506; **B:**366; **E:**96; **M:**68; **P:331–32**
   *picture(s)*   **A:**277; **M:**68, 75; **P:**331, 332

**Plautus, Titus Maccius** (Roman playwright)   **D:**299; **L:**74, 75; **Q:**22

**Play**   **P:333–34** *see also* Games; Hobbies; Sports; Toys
   activities of kindergartens and nursery schools   **K:**246–48, 249
   child development   **C:**225, 226
   dogs need to play   **D:**260
   dolphins' play   **D:**278
   folklore, American   **F:**315–16
   playgrounds   **P:**80
   toys   **T:**247–51

**Playa lakes** (shallow lakes of brackish water)   **O:**205

**Playboats** (small kayaks)   **K:**199

*Playboy of the Western World, The* (play by John Millington Synge)   **I:**327

**Play dough** (modeling material)   **C:**354

**Player, Gary** (South African golfer)   **G:**259 *profile*
   *picture(s)*   **G:**259

**Playgrounds**   **K:**248; **P:**80

**Playing cards** *see* Card games

**Play of color** (in gems)   **G:**70

**Play-party games**   **F:**326

**Plays** (stories performed in front of audiences)   **P:335–38;** **T:**156–58 *see also* Drama
   how to make a stage for puppets   **P:**547
   Where did the terms "downstage" and "upstage" come from?   **P:**337

**Playwrights (Dramatists)** (writers of plays)   **T:**157

**Plaza** (public square in a city)   **L:**52

**Plaza de toros** (bullfighting arena)   **B:**451

**Plea bargaining** (in criminal law)   **L:**90

**Pleadings** (in law)   **C:**574

**Plebeians** (social class in ancient Rome)   **P:**369; **R:**311, 313

**Plebiscite**   **G:**276

**Plectrum** (used in playing a guitar)   *see* Pick

**Pledge of Allegiance** (to the flag of the United States)   **F:**246

**Pléiade** (French poets)   **F:**437

**Pleiades** (star cluster)   **N:**96

**Pleiku** (South Vietnam)   **V:**337

**Pleistocene epoch** (in geology)   **E:**29; **I:**10, 164–65

**Plenty Coups** (Crow Indian chief)   **M:**441 *profile*

**Plenzdorf, Ulrich** (German writer)   **G:**182

*Plesiosaurus* (dinosaur)
   *picture(s)*   **P:**433

*Plessy* v. *Ferguson* (Supreme Court ruling on separate-but-equal facilities)   **A:**79i; **C:**328; **J:**109; **S:**114

**Pleura** (membrane around the lung)   **L:**343

**Plexuses** (networks of spinal nerves)   **N:**116, 117

**Pliers** (tools)   **T:**230
   *picture(s)*   **T:**230

**Plies** (of a tire)   **T:**211, 212

**Plimoth Plantation** (Massachusetts)   **M:**144

**Plimouth Colony** (Massachusetts)   *see* Plymouth Colony

**Plinian eruption** (kind of volcanic eruption)   **V:**381

Pliny the Elder (Roman historian)    E:207; G:108, 232; L:76;
    M:286
Pliny the Younger (Roman orator and writer)    G:199; L:76
Pliocene epoch (in geology)    E:29
Plique-à-jour (enameling technique)    E:205
PLO see Palestine Liberation Organization
Ploeşti oil fields (Romania)    R:297
    picture(s)    R:298
Plotinus (Greek philosopher)    G:359
    picture(s)    G:358
Plots (in fiction)    C:478; N:358
Plotts (dogs)    D:249
Plough and the Stars, The (play by O'Casey)    I:327
Plovdiv (Bulgaria)    B:444
Plow-plant (Once-over tillage) method (for planting seeds)
    F:55–56
Plows    F:54
    agriculture, history of    A:97, 98, 99, 100
    Deere, John    I:222; V:318
    inventions    I:279
    prairies developed by cultivation    P:427–28
    preparing the soil for planting    F:48–49
    picture(s)    C:413
        plowing field with cattle    L:51
Plowshare (blade of a moldboard plow)    F:54
Plucked stringed instruments (in music)    M:547
Plugs (lures for fishing)    F:211
Plum    P:108, 109
Plumage (feather coats of birds)    B:218
Plumb bob (tool)    T:234
Plumbing (piping system in a building)    P:339–40
    origin of the word    L:93; P:340
    picture(s)
        installing water pipes    B:435
Plurality (method of deciding an election)    E:126
Plush (fabric) see Cut-pile fabric
Plutarch (Greek biographer)    G:358
Pluto (planet)    P:282, 341–44
    astronomy, history of    A:471
    ice    W:51
    Is Pluto really a planet?    P:341
    not always the outermost planet    N:113; S:241
    observing Pluto    P:281
Pluto (Roman god) see Hades
Plutonium (element)    E:176; U:230
    breeder reactors    N:370
    fission    F:223
    nuclear weapons    N:374
    radioactive wastes    N:373
Plutonium dioxide    S:362
Plying (of yarn)    T:141
Plymouth (Massachusetts)    C:422; M:144; P:346, 347
Plymouth Colony (in Massachusetts)    P:344–47
    American colonies    M:146; T:171–72
    colonial life in America    C:409, 415
    King Philip's War    I:202
    Mayflower    M:188
    Samoset    S:25
    Thanksgiving Day    T:153–54
    United States, history of the    U:174
Plymouth Company (business company to colonize America)
    T:168, 170
Plymouth Rock (landing spot of Pilgrims)    P:346
Plywood    F:515; W:226–27, 230
Plzen (Czech Republic)    C:621
PMS see Premenstrual syndrome
Pneumatic systems    H:314
Pneumatic tires    A:552; T:210, 211
Pneumatic trailers (for trucks)    T:321
Pneumococcus (bacterium)    D:200
Pneumocystic carinii pneumonia    D:200
Pneumonia (infection of lungs)    D:188, 200, 203; L:345;
    P:355
    picture(s)    D:200
P-n junctions see Diodes

Po, Fernão do (Portuguese explorer who discovered Cameroon)
    C:41
Poaching (illegal hunting)    E:209
Pobeda Peak (highest point in Kyrgyzstan)    K:313
Pocahontas (Native American princess)    I:177 profile; J:22,
    23; V:356, 358
    Smith, John    S:205
    picture(s)    I:177
Pocatello (Idaho)    I:51, 55
Pocket billiards see Pool
Pocket gophers (rodents)    R:276
Pocket mice    R:276
Pocket veto see Veto
Pocket watches
    picture(s)    W:45
Pocono Mountains (Pennsylvania)    P:129
Podgorica (Serbia and Montenegro)    S:125
Pods (groups of whales)    W:149
Pods (of plants)    V:292
Podzolic soils    S:237
Poe, Edgar Allan (American writer)    P:348
    Eldorado (poem)    P:348
    fiction, types of    F:115
    mystery and detective stories    M:563, 566
    place in American literature    A:209
    short story, definition of    S:161–62
    The Tell-Tale Heart, excerpt from    S:163–64
Poems on Various Occasions (by Phillis Wheatley)    A:206
Poetic Edda (Icelandic book of songs and legends, basis of
    Norse mythology)    N:277, 279, 281
Poet laureate (of Great Britain)
    Hughes, Ted    H:276
    Jonson, Ben, was first officially appointed    E:273
    Tennyson, Alfred, Lord    T:100
Poet laureate (of the United States)
    Dove, Rita Frances    O:77
    Warren, Robert Penn    W:12
Poetry    P:349–54 see also the literature of each country; the
    names of poems and poets
    African poetry    A:76b
    Arabic literature    A:341, 342
    Arcadian poetry    I:408
    ballads    B:24
    Bible    B:159
    blues form    J:58
    book reports on    B:316
    children's literature    C:236–37, 240
    children's literature, list of    C:247–48
    Chinese art combined painting and poetry    C:275
    early Greek literature    G:354–56
    figures of speech    F:122–24
    heroic couplet    E:276
    Hindu poetry    H:142
    how to write poetry    P:354
    Latin America, literature of    L:67, 68
    limericks    N:274–75, 276
    nonsense rhymes    N:273–76
    nursery rhymes    N:414–16
    odes    O:52
    Pulitzer Prizes    P:537–38
    romanticism in literature    R:303
    Scandinavian literature    S:58h, 58i
    Spenserian stanza    S:401
    types of literature    L:259
    World War I    W:288
Poetry (magazine)    A:214b
Poets' Corner (Westminster Abbey, London)    C:191
Poets of the Confederation (Canadian poets)    C:86
Pogonia (plant)
    picture(s)    E:210
Pogrom (organized massacre)    H:174; J:106
Pohamba, Hifikepunye (president of Namibia)    N:9
Pohnpei (Pacific island)    M:280; P:10
Poindexter, John (American public official)    I:310
Poinsett, Joel R. (American botanist and legislator)    C:298

Poinsettia (plant)   C:298
  picture(s)   L:112
Point-and-shoot cameras   P:202, 203, 207, 212, 213, 218
Point Año Nuevo (California)
  picture(s)   C:21
*Point Counter Point* (book by Huxley)   H:309
Point defects (in crystals)   M:152, 153, 155
Point du Sable, Jean Baptiste (American pioneer) *see* Du Sable, Jean Baptiste Point
Pointe-Noire (Congo)   C:506
  picture(s)   C:506
Pointers (dogs)   D:246, 252; H:300
Point Four Program (foreign aid)   T:326
Pointillism (impressionist method of painting)   F:431; I:106; M:387
Pointing (by dogs)   D:246
Pointing (in sculpture)   S:92
Point-of-sale (POS) devices (office machines)   O:56
Point Pleasant, Battle of (1774)   V:359
Point system (of type measurements)   T:370
Point zero (explosion point of a nuclear weapon)   N:375
Poiret, Paul (French fashion designer)   C:379
Poirot, Hercule (fictional character)   M:564
Poison centers   P:355, 356
Poison dart frog   A:271, 283
  picture(s)   A:273; F:477
Poisoning *see* Poisons
Poison ivy   A:191; D:123; L:117; P:316–17
  picture(s)   F:161
Poison oak   A:191; L:117; P:316–17
  picture(s)   L:117
Poisonous animals *see* Animals, poisonous
Poisonous plants *see* Plants, poisonous
Poisons   P:355–56
  alcohols   A:172
  algae   A:181
  amulets to warn against poison   G:72
  control of plant pests   P:291
  first aid   F:161
  hazardous wastes   H:72–73
  lead   L:94
  liver removes from blood   L:269
  mushrooms   F:499, 500; M:529
  occupational health   O:13
  plumbing made of lead   P:340
  poisonous plants   P:316–17
  preventive measures   S:4
  rat control   H:264
  snake venom   S:211, 213, 215, 216
  stingrays   S:145
  Toxic Substances and Disease Registry, Agency for   H:79
  toxins produced by germs   D:186, 187, 188, 204
  vaccination and inoculation   D:211
  venom of some fish   F:201
  water pollution   W:64–65
Poison sumac   P:316–17
Poitier, Sidney (American actor)   A:79c; M:491 *profile,* 495
Poitiers, Battle of (732) *see* Tours, Battle of
Poitiers, Battle of (1356)   H:293
Pokémon
  picture(s)   V:332c
Poland   P:357–62
  Belarus, history of   B:129
  Brezhnev's role in 1970 riots   B:389
  food   F:331
  Holocaust   H:173–74
  invasion by Hitler   W:296
  Jewish community   J:105
  John III (John Sobieski)   J:112
  Lithuania, history of   L:263
  opera   O:146–47
  Roman Catholic Church fought Communism   C:295
  Ukraine, history of   U:11, 12
  Walesa, Lech   W:4

Warsaw   W:13
World War I   W:290, 291
World War II   W:315
  picture(s)
    Cracow   P:360
    farmers and hay wagon   E:341
    farmland   P:357
    flag   F:238
    Warsaw   P:360; W:13
Polar bears   A:272, 275; B:104, 106
  picture(s)   A:272; B:105; C:60; M:70
    mother and cub   N:283
Polar easterlies (winds)   W:189
Polar exploration   E:414–15
  Amundsen, Roald   A:226
  Antarctica   A:295
  Arctic   A:380–81
  Byrd, Richard   B:485
  Hudson, Henry   H:273
  Peary, Robert E.   P:117
*Polar Express, The* (motion picture, 2004)
  picture(s)   A:290
Polar front jet stream   J:93
Polaris (Nunavut)   N:412
Polaris (star) *see* North Star
Polaris missile   M:349
Polarity   S:493–94, 496
Polarization (of light)   A:319; H:202; L:22
Polarizing filters (in photography)   P:207–8
Polar molecules   W:48
Polar night jet stream   J:93
Polaroid Land Cameras   P:215
Polar orbit (of artificial satellites)   S:54
Polar regions *see also* Polar exploration
  Antarctica   A:292–95
  Arctic   A:378–81
  climate   C:362
  deserts   D:125, 127, 128
  glaciers   G:221–25
  high-pressure areas   W:82
  latitudes of North and South poles   L:77
  longitudes of North and South poles   L:78
  Mars, polar caps of   M:108
  measuring depth of ice and snow   I:6–7
  North America, climate of   N:290
  picture(s)
    birds   B:244
Polders (low land reclaimed from a body of water, in the Netherlands)   N:120a
Polecats (related to weasels)   O:255
Polenta (corn meal dish of Italy)   I:382
Poles (for fishing)   F:209
Poles, magnetic (in physics)   E:140, 152; M:28–29, 30
Poles, magnetic (of Earth)   E:11; G:437; R:48–49
Poles, telephone   W:226
Pole vault (field event)   T:257
  world record   T:261
  picture(s)   T:252, 256
Police   P:363–68
  bulletproof clothing   P:329
  careers in law enforcement   L:87, 92
  courts   C:574–75
  crime and criminology   C:585–86
  crystallography used to identify poisons   C:605
  electronics   E:162
  forensic science   F:372–73
  local departments helped by FBI   F:76
  motorcycles, use of   M:498
  Peel, Sir Robert   P:118
  radar used to catch speeding automobiles   R:39
  Royal Canadian Mounted Police   C:78; P:368; R:342–43
  scuba diving squads   S:187
  Soviet secret police   U:41, 42
  ultraviolet radiation, uses of   L:221

Police (cont.)
  violence and society   **V:**344
  *picture(s)*   **M:**514
    British "bobby"   **E:**353
    handcuffing crime suspects   **C:**584
    handgun training   **G:**414
    Royal Canadian Mounted Police   **N:**295; **R:**343
    Washington, D.C.   **C:**585
**Police** (English rock group)   **R:**264
**Police Athletic League (PAL)**   **P:**365
**Police dogs**   **D:**255–56; **P:**365
  *picture(s)*   **D:**241
**Police procedural novel** (type of fiction)   **M:**567
**Polichinelle** (Italian puppet character) *see* Pulcinella
**Policy debates** (form of debating)   **D:**52
**Poliomyelitis (Infantile paralysis)** (virus disease)   **D:**200–201, 211
  Kenny, Elizabeth   **M:**339
  Roosevelt, Franklin D., believed to have been victim of   **R:**322–23
  vaccination   **S:**75; **V:**260
  *picture(s)*
    polio virus   **D:**201; **V:**362
**Polis** (city-state) *see* City-states
**Polisario** (Saharan independence group)   **M:**461; **W:**124
**Polish Corridor** (created by Treaty of Versailles, after World War I)   **G:**162; **P:**361; **W:**296
**Polished rice**   **R:**228
**Polishing** *see* Grinding and polishing
**Polish language**   **P:**357–58
  tongue twister used to catch German spies   **T:**225–26
**Polish Partitions** (1772, 1793, 1795)   **P:**361; **U:**11
*Polish Rider, The* (painting by Rembrandt van Rijn)
  *picture(s)*   **P:**25
**Polish United Workers' Party**   **P:**361
**Politburo** (governing body of Soviet Communist Party)   **U:**37
**Political action groups**   **P:**494; **R:**294
**Political cartoons** *see* Cartoons, political
**Political conventions** *see* Conventions, political
**Political economy** *see* Economics
**Political geography**   **G:**103
**Political parties**   **P:**369–73 *see also* the government section of country articles; the names of parties
  beginnings of party system in England   **E:**249, 253
  cartoon symbols   **C:**127
  democratic right to choose   **D:**106
  elections   **E:**128
  Electoral College   **E:**131, 132
  government systems determined by   **G:**274
  national nominating convention originated in Jackson's administration   **J:**6
  organization in Congress   **U:**168, 169
  parliaments   **P:**83
  prime minister   **P:**458
  Progressive (Bull Moose) formed by Theodore Roosevelt   **R:**332
  state legislatures do business on party basis   **S:**438
  United States, history of the   **U:**178
  United States president is his party's leader   **P:**453
  vice presidency of the United States   **V:**326
  What was the Know-Nothing Party?   **F:**128
  Why are some political parties called "left," and others "right"?   **P:**372
**Political platforms** *see* Platforms, political
**Political science** (study of government and political organization)   **I:**269–70
**Political writing** (United States)   **A:**204–5
**Polity** (government by the many)   **G:**273
**Poliziano** (Italian poet)   **I:**406
**Polk, James Knox** (11th president of the United States)   **M:**239b, 427; **P:**374–78
  *picture(s)*   **P:**374, 375, 376, 446
**Polk, Sarah Childress** (wife of James K. Polk)   **F:**169; **P:**374, 378
  *picture(s)*   **F:**169; **P:**375

**Polka** (dance)   **D:**26–27
**Polk Doctrine** (American foreign policy)   **P:**377
**Pollack** (fish)   **F:**217
**Pollaiuolo, Antonio** (Italian painter)   **I:**396
**Polled Hereford** (breed of beef cattle)   **C:**151
**Pollen and pollination**   **F:**282, 284–86
  air pollution   **A:**122
  allergies   **A:**190
  bees   **B:**117
  corn   **C:**558
  flowers and seeds of plants   **P:**308
  fossil pollen from Ice Ages   **I:**14–15
  fruitgrowing   **F:**483
  hummingbirds   **H:**289
  nutritional supplement   **H:**212
  reproduction   **P:**310; **R:**177
  trees   **T:**309–10
**Pollio, Vitruvius** (Roman author)   **E:**228
**Polliwogs** *see* Tadpoles
**Pollock, Jackson** (American painter)   **P:**378
  action painting in modern art   **M:**396b
  American painting in the 20th century   **P:**31; **U:**134
  drawing, history of   **D:**318
  surrealism's influence on   **S:**518
  watercolor painting   **W:**57
  *picture(s)*   **P:**378
    *Number I* (painting)   **M:**396
    *Number 3* (painting)   **D:**133; **U:**134
**Polls** (survey of people's opinions) *see* Opinion polls
**Poll tax** (fixed amount of money levied on citizens of a community)   **A:**79i; **C:**330; **U:**160
**Pollution and pollutants** *see also* Air pollution; Water pollution
  air pollution   **A:**122–25; **E:**303–5
  chemical industry   **C:**197
  chemical poisoning of the environment endangers species   **E:**209, 426
  cities, problems of   **C:**319–20
  detergents   **D:**141; **E:**301
  energy sources, environmental problems of   **E:**219–20
  environment, quality of   **E:**301–6
  experiments and other science activities   **E:**391–92
  fertilizers   **E:**301
  food chain affected by   **B:**248
  hazardous wastes   **H:**72–73
  insecticides   **E:**303
  national parks, challenges to   **N:**56
  natural resources, how people affect   **N:**63, 66
  noise   **N:**271
  petroleum, environmental problems of   **P:**175–76
  poverty, effects on   **P:**420
  sanitation, sewage, and refuse (solid waste) disposal   **E:**301–2, 305–6; **S:**33
  *Silent Spring* (book by Carson)   **S:**75
  steel industry   **I:**338
  technology, effects of   **T:**41
  water pollution   **E:**301–3; **W:**62–67
**Pollux** (star in Gemini constellation)   **C:**531
**Polo** (sport)   **P:**379
  *picture(s)*   **H:**241
**Polo, Marco** (Venetian traveler)   **P:**380
  brought back ice cream recipes   **I:**22
  China   **C:**269
  described Oriental cities   **C:**315
  discovered source of spices   **H:**120
  porcelain, origin of the word   **P:**410
  predecessor of the age of exploration   **E:**401–2
  Venice, history of   **V:**300, 301
  *picture(s)*
    miniature painting   **P:**380
**Polochic River** (Guatemala)   **G:**396
**Polonium** (element)   **C:**614; **E:**176
**Polo ponies**   **P:**379
**Poltava, Battle of** (1709)   **S:**529
**Poltergeist** (type of ghost)   **G:**200
**Polyakov, Valery** (Russian cosmonaut)   **S:**349

Polyandry (form of marriage)   F:43
Polybenzimidazole (manufactured fiber) *see* PBI
Polybius (Greek historian)   G:358; H:150
Polycarbonate (plastic)   P:328
Polychaetes *see* Bristle worms
Polychlorinated biphenyls (PCB's) (toxic chemicals)   H:73;
   T:272
Polyclitus (sculptor)   G:349
Polyconic projections (of maps)   M:97
Polydectes (in Greek mythology)   G:365
Polyester (class of synthetic fibers)   F:111–12; N:437
   *picture(s)*
      micrograph of fibers   F:110
Polyethylene (plastic)   I:283; P:323–24, 327
Polyethylene terephthalate (PET) (plastic)   P:328
Polygamy (form of marriage)   F:43
Polygenes (interacting genes)   G:80
Polygonal numbers   N:386–88
Polygons (in geometry)   G:64, 121
Polygraph (lie detector)   L:193
Polygyny (form of marriage)   F:42; L:166; U:255
Polyhedral viruses   V:362
Polyhedrons (in geometry)   G:123
Polymerase chain reaction (PCR)   B:187, 189–90; G:91
   *diagram(s)*   B:190
Polymers and polymerization   P:323–24, 329
   adhesives   G:243
   chemical term defined   C:204
   chemistry, history of   C:211
   contact lenses   C:535
   fibers   F:110, 111; N:440
   how to make polymer "slime"   E:391
   leather finishing   L:111
   Ohio industry   O:69, 72
   petroleum refining   P:172
   synthetic rubber   R:346
Polynesia (Pacific islands)   P:3–4
Polynesian art
   *picture(s)*
      beaten barkcloth   T:141
Polynesians (Pacific islanders)   P:4–5
   Hawaii   H:54, 60
   Heyerdahl, Thor, studied origins of   H:125
   Maoris of New Zealand   N:235
   Micronesia, Federated States of   M:280
   Tonga   T:224
   Western Samoa   W:124
   *picture(s)*   P:8, 10
Polyolefins (artificial fibers)   F:111
Polyphemus (in Greek mythology) *see* Cyclops
Polyphony (in music)   I:410; M:537, 538
   Africa, music of   A:79
   baroque music   B:69
   choral music   C:283
   hymns   H:322
   Leonin and Perotin (French composers)   F:444
   Middle Ages   M:296–97
   religious music   G:183
Polyplacophorans (mollusks)   M:407
Polypody (fern)   F:94
Polypropylene (plastic)   P:324; R:334
Polyps (form of jellyfish and other coelenterates)   C:555–56;
   J:73, 74, 75, 76–77
Polystyrene (plastic)   P:324
Polytheism (belief in several gods)   E:107, 109; R:146
Polytonality (in music)   M:398
Polyunsaturated fats   N:425; O:80
Polyurethane (synthetic rubber)   L:111; R:346–47; S:182;
   U:228
Polyvinylchloride (PVC)   F:214; P:324
Pomade (perfumed ointment)   P:151
Pomaks (Bulgarian-speaking Muslims)   B:442
Pomanders (bags or boxes containing fragrant substances)
   P:150
Pome fruits   P:113

Pomegranate (fruit)
   Byzantine mosaics used designs of pomegranates
      B:489–90
Pommel horse (in gymnastics)   G:432
   *picture(s)*   G:431
Pomo (Indians of North America)   I:186
Pomona College (Claremont, California)   O:231
Pompadour, Marquise de (French noblewoman)   L:311
*Pomp and Circumstance* marches (by Elgar)   E:188, 293
Pompeii (Italy)   D:76; G:352; P:17, 381; R:319
Pompey the Great (Roman statesman)   C:6; R:315–16
Pompidou, Georges Jean Raymond (French political leader)
   F:420
Pompidou Center (Paris, France)   P:70
   *picture(s)*   F:432
Pompion (colonial American name for pumpkin)   C:411
Ponape (Pacific island) *see* Pohnpei
Ponca (Indians of North America)   I:179
Ponca City (Oklahoma)   O:89
Ponce (Puerto Rico)   P:530–31
   *picture(s)*   P:531
Ponce, Manuel M. (Mexican composer)   L:73
Ponce de León, Juan (Spanish explorer)   P:382
   exploration of the new world   E:407
   Florida   F:260, 271
   Puerto Rico   P:532
   tomb in Cathedral of San Juan Bautista (Puerto Rico)
      P:530
   *picture(s)*   A:87
Poncho (cloak or shawl worn in South America)   C:404
Pond, Peter (American fur trader)   A:171
Ponderosa pine trees   A:394
   *picture(s)*   M:429
Ponds (small bodies of water)   I:3–4; M:283; W:49, 63
Pong (early video game)   V:332b
Pongal (holiday in India)   H:161
   *picture(s)*   H:161
Ponies (small horses)   H:241; P:379; V:354
   *picture(s)*   H:241; N:55; V:348
Ponor, Catalina (Romanian gymnast)   O:120
Pons (part of the brain stem)   B:365
Pontchartrain, Lake (Louisiana)   L:33; N:195, 196
Pontchartrain Causeway (Louisiana)   L:33
Pont du Gard (Roman aqueduct near Nîmes, France)
   *picture(s)*   E:228; R:318
Ponte Milvio (bridge, Rome, Italy)   R:305
Ponte Vecchio (bridge, Florence, Italy)   F:258
   *picture(s)*   F:258
Pontiac (chief of the Ottawa Indians)   I:179 *profile*, 203–4;
   O:74; P:382
Pontiac's Rebellion (1763–1766)   I:203–4; P:382
   *picture(s)*   W:141
Pontian, Saint (pope)   R:292
Pontic Mountains *see* Northern Anatolian Mountains
Pontil (rod used in shaping glass)   A:316
Pontius Pilate *see* Pilate, Pontius
Pont Neuf (bridge, Paris, France)   F:425
Pontoons (landing gear of seaplanes)   A:114
Pontoppidan, Henrik (Danish author)   S:58i
Pony (small horse) *see* Ponies
Pony clubs   H:229
Pony Express (mail service)   C:465; P:383–84, 398
   *picture(s)*
      stamp   S:421
Pony of the Americas (POA) (horse breed)   H:241
Poodles (dogs)   D:242
Pooh (character in A. A. Milne's stories)
   *picture(s)*   M:311
Pookas (fairies)   F:9
Pool (pocket billiards)   B:179
Pool, Thomas (American circus promoter)   C:310
Pool checkers (game)   C:193
Poole, Elijah *see* Muhammad, Elijah
Poole, William Frederick (American librarian)   L:180

**Pool of Water Lilies** (painting by Monet)
  *picture(s)*  **F:**430
**Poopó, Lake** (Bolivia)  **B:**307; **S:**281
**Poor** *see* Poverty
**Poor, John** (American lawyer and railroad executive)  **M:**49
  *profile*
**Poor Henry** (romance by Hartmann von Aue)  **G:**176
**Poor People's March (Campaign)** (on Washington, D.C.)  **A:**142
**Poor Richard's Almanack** (by Benjamin Franklin)  **A:**204;
  **F:**454
  *picture(s)*  **C:**418
**Poorwills** (birds)  **H:**127
**Pop** (beverage) *see* Soft drinks
**Pop art**  **M:**396b; **P:**31–32; **U:**134
  Hockney, David  **H:**159a
  Johns, Jasper  **J:**114
  Warhol, Andy  **W:**7
**Popcorn**  **C:**558
**Popé** (Native American leader)  **I:**183; **N:**192, 193 *profile*
**Pope, Albert** (American bicycle maker)  **B:**177
**Pope, Alexander** (English poet)  **E:**277–78, 321; **P:**384; **Q:**22
**Pope, Dick, Jr.** (American waterskier)  **W:**71
**Pope, John** (American Union general)  **C:**339
**Pope, John Russell** (American architect)  **N:**38; **W:**32
**Popes** (of Roman Catholic Church)  **R:**283, 284, 286, 287,
  290, 292–93
  forms of address  **A:**22
  Gregory VII, Saint  **G:**377
  Gregory XIII  **G:**377
  Holy Roman Empire  **H:**175–79
  infallibility  **R:**294
  John XXIII  **J:**113
  John Paul II  **J:**114
  Leo III  **L:**151
  Leo XIII  **L:**152
  Paul VI  **P:**102
  Peter, Saint  **P:**166
  Pius XII  **P:**268
  power grows in Middle Ages  **M:**294
  Vatican City  **V:**280–82
**Popeye** (comic strip)  **C:**128
**Popham colony** (in Maine history)  **M:**49
**Popish Plot** (1678)  **E:**246; **P:**369
**Poplar trees**
  *picture(s)*
  uses of the wood and its grain  **W:**224
**Popocatepetl ("Smoking Mountain")** (volcano, Mexico)
  *picture(s)*  **M:**243
**Popol Vuh** (collection of Mayan myths)  **G:**397; **L:**66; **M:**187,
  571
**Poppen, Sherman** (American inventor of the snowboard)
  **S:**218
**Poppy** (flowering plant)  **F:**281; **N:**15; **W:**288
  *picture(s)*  **C:**19; **E:**344; **G:**46; **P:**318
**Pop-rivets** (fasteners)  **N:**3
**Popular Front** (in France)  **F:**418
**Popular Front** (in Spain)  **S:**393
**Popular music**  **M:**541; **R:**262a
  compared to folk music  **F:**321
  country music  **C:**571–73
  rock music  **R:**262a–264
  United States, music of the  **U:**210
**Popular sovereignty** (in a democracy)  **D:**106
**Popular (Squatter) sovereignty** (in United States history)
  **D:**288; **K:**191; **L:**243, 244
**Popular vote** (for electors of the Electoral College)  **E:**131
**Population**  **P:**385–88 *see also* the facts and figures sections
  of continent, country, province, state, and city articles
  Africa  **A:**54–55
  Asia  **A:**444–45
  birth control  **B:**250b
  census  **C:**167
  continents' populations compared  **C:**538
  density *see* Population density

environment and population  **E:**300–301
food supply  **F:**45, 350
genetic distribution  **G:**86
How is the U.S. population census taken?  **C:**167
human beings and their environment  **H:**283
immigration  **I:**87–94
natural resources, demands on  **C:**523, 526; **N:**65
North America  **N:**294–95, 298
old age  **O:**98–100
population geography  **G:**102–3
races, human  **R:**30–33
rapid growth is world problem  **W:**254
South America  **S:**284–85, 288–89
United States, increases in  **U:**73–74
*picture(s)*
  chart of food production increase and  **F:**351
  chart of growth in world population  **F:**350
**Population** (in biology)  **B:**198; **E:**53; **L:**204
**Population cycles** (in animals)  **A:**286
**Population density** (number of people who live in an area)
  **C:**311–12; **P:**385
  cities  **C:**311–12
  Europe  **E:**351–52
  *diagram(s)*  **P:**388
  *map(s)*
    Africa  **A:**58
    Asia  **A:**446
    Australia  **A:**509
    Canada  **C:**54
    China  **C:**259
    India  **I:**120
    North America  **N:**296
    Russia  **R:**359
    South America  **S:**286
    United States  **U:**74
**Population ecology**  **E:**53, 55
**Population explosion**  **E:**300–301; **G:**103; **M:**251; **P:**387
**Population geography**  **G:**102–3
**Populist Party** (in the United States)  **H:**40; **P:**372; **U:**188
**Pop-up ads** (on the Internet)  **A:**31
**Pop-up books**  **B:**322
**Pop Warner League Football** (for children)  **F:**361
**Poquelin, Jean Baptiste** (French actor-manager and dramatist)
  *see* Molière
**Porcelain**  **D:**74–75; **P:**408, 409, 410
  antiques  **A:**316a
  ceramics  **C:**176, 177
  coated steels  **I:**337
  Danish industry  **D:**110, 111
  dolls made of  **D:**267–68
  Japanese art and architecture  **J:**51
  Korean celadon  **K:**297
  *picture(s)*  **P:**413
    Chinese incense burner  **D:**75
    Chinese vases  **P:**410
    Korean celadon  **K:**297
**Porch of the Maidens** (Erechtheum, Athens, Greece)  **G:**348
  *picture(s)*  **G:**349
**Porcupines** (rodents)  **M:**74; **P:**389; **R:**277–78
  *picture(s)*  **P:**389; **R:**274
**Porgera** (Papua New Guinea)  **N:**149
**Porgy and Bess** (folk opera by George Gershwin)  **G:**190;
  **M:**554; **O:**148, 149, 161
  *picture(s)*  **M:**552; **O:**149
**Po River** (Italy)  **A:**194d; **I:**382, 383, 384; **R:**245
**Pork** (meat of hogs)  **D:**207; **M:**196
  *picture(s)*
  cuts of pork  **M:**197
**Pork-barrel bills** (laws to win votes for politicians)  **A:**437
**Porphyry** (rock)  **R:**266
**Porpoises** (small whales) *see* Dolphins and porpoises
**Por que fue sensible** (aquatint by Goya)  **G:**307
**Port** (left side of a boat or ship)  **S:**11, 154
**Porta, Giambattista della** (Italian scientist)  **C:**395
**Portable life-support systems** (for astronauts)  **S:**340h, 343

**Positron emission tomography (PET)** (medical technique)
B:369; I:86; M:208d
*picture(s)*
    brain of person with obsessive-compulsive disorder
    M:224
**Positrons** (subatomic particles) A:489; C:563
*Possessed, The* (novel by Dostoevski) D:287
**Possums** (American marsupials) *see* Opossums
**Possums** (Australian marsupials) M:115
**Postage stamps** *see* Stamps and stamp collecting
**Postal inspectors** (detectives of the United States Postal
    Service) P:400
**Postal Rate Commission** (United States) P:398
**Postal Reorganization Act** (United States, 1970) P:398
**Postal service** P:396–402
    automation A:532–33
    canceled stamps in a collection S:420
    communication, history of C:464–65
    mail cars are post offices on wheels R:82
    mail order M:34–35
    Persia, ancient P:155
    Pony Express P:383–84
    Universal Postal Union (UPU) U:69
    *picture(s)*
        how a letter travels P:400–401
        sorting mail P:398
**Postal Service, United States** P:396, 398–402; U:96
    *picture(s)*
        eagle emblem P:399
        horse-drawn carriages P:397
        mail carrier P:396
**Post and lintel construction** (in architecture) A:367–68
**Postboys** (early English mail carriers) P:397
**Posters** A:30; P:402; S:78; T:246
    *picture(s)*
        early phonograph C:467
        Gaiety shows M:553
        Harry Potter book advertisement A:33
        promotion of dental care P:489
        railroad posters encouraging pioneers P:259
        Soviet propaganda U:34
        World War I propaganda W:277
        World War I recruiting poster W:283
        World War II medical poster A:306
        World War II propaganda P:488
**Post-hypnotic suggestion** H:329
**Postimpressionism** (in art) F:430–31; I:106; M:388; P:29
    *see also* the artists by name, as Cézanne, Paul
**Postmarks** (on mail) P:396, 402
**Postmaster general** (of the United States) P:398
**Postmaster's Provisionals** (stamps) S:420
**Postmodernism**
    architecture A:376; J:123; U:136
    dance D:33
    furniture F:517
**Post office boxes** P:399
**Post-production sound mixers** (for motion pictures) M:486
**Postsecondary Education, Office of** (United States) E:89
**Post-traumatic stress disorder (PTSD)** E:204; M:222, 224–25
**Potable (Drinkable) water** W:73
**Potala** (former seat of the Dalai Lama, Tibet) T:190
    *picture(s)* T:191
**Potash** (potassium fertilizer) F:97
    Canada's natural resources C:61, 64
    Esterhazy (Saskatchewan) P:428
    glass G:229
    Saskatchewan's deposits may be the world's largest S:48
**Potassium** (element) E:176; F:97; V:372–73
    *table(s)*
        food sources and DRI's V:372
**Potassium-40** (radioactive element) R:75
**Potassium argon dating** (in archaeology) A:357; R:75
**Potassium hydroxide** O:81
**Potassium nitrate** (chemical compound) E:420

**Potatoes** P:403–4; V:290
    agriculture, history of A:99
    Burbank variety B:452
    fungus blight and famine in Ireland F:44, 500; I:323;
        P:286
    how to look at starch grains through a microscope M:283
    Idaho is nation's leading producer I:53
    Incas' use of freeze-drying F:336
    New World crops brought to Europe and Ireland A:99
    Peru P:161
    Prince Edward Island P:461
    propagation experiment P:310
    starch, source of S:425
    tubers P:305
    vegetable growing V:287
    *picture(s)*
        Idaho is nation's leading producer I:52
        Idaho potato farmer N:294
        irradiated to prevent sprouting F:344
        Maine agriculture M:43
        Peru P:162
        Prince Edward Island P:463
**Potato famine** (Ireland, 1845–49) I:391; P:317
**Potawatomi** (Indians of North America) C:220; I:179; M:269
**Potemkin, Grigori Aleksandrovich** (Russian political figure)
    E:298
**Potential difference** (in positive and negative electrical charges)
    B:363
**Potential energy** E:212; H:89; W:246
**Potential infinity** (in mathematics) N:400
**Poti** (Republic of Georgia) G:148
**Potiphar** (character in the Bible) J:133
**Potlatch** (Indian custom of lavish giving) I:189–90
**Potomac, Army of the** (Civil War) C:337–43
    *picture(s)* C:337
**Potomac River** (United States) M:122–23; R:245; V:348;
    W:29, 128
**Potosí** (Bolivia) B:308
**Potsdam Conference** (1945)
    *picture(s)*
        Attlee, Truman, and Stalin S:419
**Pott, Percival** (English surgeon) O:13
**Pottawatomie Creek massacre** (Kansas) C:335
**Potter, Harry** (fictional character) C:235; R:342
**Potter, Helen Beatrix** (English artist and writer) P:405–6
    illustration I:82
    *The Tale of Jemima Puddle-duck,* excerpt from P:406
    *The Tale of Peter Rabbit* C:239
    *picture(s)*
        illustration I:81
**Potter's clay** (modeling material) C:354
**Potter's wheel** C:266; P:407, 409; W:159
    *picture(s)* P:408
**Potter wasps** (insects) I:247
    *picture(s)* I:230
    nest I:246
**Pottery** P:407–13 *see also* Vases
    Africa, art of A:75
    ancient Greek art form G:345
    antique A:316–16a
    archaeological sites A:354, 355, 356
    ceramics C:176–77
    fired pottery discovered by early people F:142
    Greek vase painting P:16–17
    Indians, American I:166, 170
    Japanese Jomon vessels J:51
    Korean art K:297
    *picture(s)*
        African woman making pottery A:60
        ancient Peruvian jug C:176
        contemporary British pottery P:407
        Guatemala L:51
        Indians, American I:172
        Japanese Jomon vessels J:50

Kentucky craft **K:**216
Korean art **K:**297
New Mexico crafts **N:**181
Zapotec pottery **W:**261
**Potting** (of plants) **H:**265–66
**Pottos** (primates) **P:**456
**Pouched mammals** see Marsupials
**Pouchless marsupials** **M:**114
**Poulenc, Francis** (French composer) **F:**448; **O:**148
**Poultry** **P:**414–17
Arkansas is leading producer **A:**406, 412
bantam chickens as pets **P:**178
cooking, methods of **C:**543
Delaware's Sussex County **D:**88, 95, 102
farm birds as pets **B:**250a
food regulations and laws **F:**345
food shopping **F:**349
livestock **L:**272
safety of refrigerated foods **F:**343
turkeys **T:**350
*picture(s)*
food inspection **F:**335
**Poults** (young turkeys) **T:**350
**Pound** (measure of weight) **W:**114, 115
**Pound, Ezra** (American poet) **A:**214a–214b; **I:**59 *profile*
**Pound nets** (for fishing) **F:**220
**Pourbus, Frans, the Younger** (Flemish artist) **F:**426
**Poussin, Nicolas** (French painter) **B:**66; **F:**426
*picture(s)*
*The Judgment of Solomon* (painting) **S:**251
*Moses Saved from the Waters* (painting) **F:**425
**Poverty** **P:**418–20 *see also* Unemployment; Welfare, public
Brazil **B:**376
developing countries **D:**143
disasters a major cause of **D:**183, 184
famine **F:**44–45
food supply **F:**351
homelessness **H:**183
Inuit **I:**276
malaria and **M:**52
Mexico **M:**244
older people **O:**99, 100
United States, remains a problem in the **U:**99
**Poverty Point** (archaeological site in Mississippi) **I:**167
**Powdered eggs** **F:**340
**Powdered milk** **F:**340
**Powderly, Terence V.** (American labor leader) **L:**13–14
**Powder metallurgy** **M:**236
**Powder puff trees**
*picture(s)* **H:**53
**Powders** (cosmetics) **C:**560
**Powdery mildew** (plant disease) **P:**288–89
**Powell, Adam Clayton, Jr.** (American politician) **U:**142 *profile*
**Powell, Anthony** (English novelist) **E:**290
**Powell, Colin** (American army officer and government official) **A:**79c; **P:**421; **T:**116
*picture(s)* **A:**80; **P:**421
**Powell, John Wesley** (American geologist and explorer) **G:**105, 290
**Powell, Lake** (Arizona–Utah) **A:**395; **L:**33; **U:**244, 245, 250
**Powell, Mike** (American athlete) **T:**263
*picture(s)* **T:**253
**Power** (in mechanics) **W:**251–52
energy **E:**212–17
experiment examining power **W:**252
gears for passing along motion and power **G:**65–66
hydraulic and pneumatic systems **H:**311–14
internal-combustion engines **I:**262–65
new sources for the Industrial Revolution **I:**217, 218
rocket power **R:**258
sources for manufacturing **M:**87–88
transmissions change power to speed and torque **T:**279
waterpower **W:**69–70
*diagram(s)*
diesel engines' power cycle **D:**161

**Power** (in optical instruments) **O:**179
**Power** (of government) **G:**272
**Power, electric** see Electric power
**Powerboats and powerboat racing** **B:**266–69; **H:**315
**Power conditioners** (electronic devices) **E:**154
*Power of Positive Thinking, The* (book by Peale) **O:**77
*Power of Sympathy, The* (novel by William Hill Brown) **A:**208
**Power plants** **P:**421–23
acid rain **A:**9
air pollution **E:**304
Canadian waterpower **C:**62
coal-burning **C:**391
dams **D:**16
electric generators **E:**133–34
how people use water **W:**53
public utilities **P:**521
steam from hot springs **G:**193
thermal pollution **E:**305
transformers **T:**271
*picture(s)*
coal-fired **U:**249
dams **D:**18
solar power plant **S:**240
**Power politics** see Balance of power
**Power resources** see individual continent, country, and state articles
**Powers, Francis Gary** (American pilot) **S:**409 *profile*
**Powers, Ross** (American athlete) **O:**118
**Power shovels** **E:**30–31
**Powers of numbers** (in mathematics) **A:**183; **N:**382, 403
**Power steering** (of automobiles) **A:**550
**Power take-offs** (from farm tractors) **F:**53
**Power tools** **T:**230, 235; **W:**230, 231
**Powhatan** (Native American chief) **I:**177, 178
Jamestown colony **J:**22; **V:**355, 356, 358
**Powwow** (Native American gathering)
*picture(s)* **N:**129
**Poynton, Dorothy** (American diver) **D:**229
**PPI** see Plan position indicator
**Practical nurses** see Licensed practical nurses
**Prado** (museum, Madrid, Spain) **M:**15, 528; **P:**423–24
*picture(s)* **P:**423
**Praetorian Guard** (in ancient Rome) **R:**316
*picture(s)*
relief carving **R:**316
**Praetorius, Michael** (German composer) **C:**118; **G:**184
**Pragmatic Sanction** (decree of Austria's Charles VI) **A:**524; **H:**3
**Pragmatism** (school of philosophy) **D:**144; **J:**21; **P:**506
**Prague (Praha)** (capital of Czech Republic) **C:**621, 622; **P:**425
*picture(s)* **C:**618, 619; **P:**425
**Prague Spring** (in Czechoslovakian history) **C:**624
**Praia** (capital of Cape Verde) **C:**102
*Prairie, The* (novel by James Fenimore Cooper) **C:**549
**Prairie crocus** (flower)
*picture(s)* **M:**81
**Prairie dogs** (rodents) **R:**276
**Prairie Hills** (South Dakota) **S:**314
*Prairie Home Companion, A* (radio program) **M:**339
**Prairie lily** (flower)
*picture(s)* **S:**43
**Prairie Provinces** (Canadian provinces of Alberta, Manitoba, Saskatchewan) **A:**164–72; **C:**55; **M:**80–86; **S:**42–51; **W:**190b
**Prairies** **P:**426–29
in American literature **A:**214
Drift Prairie region of North Dakota **N:**322, 324
grassland biomes **B:**207
Indiana's protected prairie lands **I:**147
Mississippi **M:**350
North American soils **N:**291
**Prairie State** (nickname for Illinois) **I:**62, 63
**Prairie States Forestry Project** **D:**356
**Prairie style** (of Frank Lloyd Wright) **A:**374; **W:**326

Prairie wolves *see* Coyotes
*Praising Angels* (tapestry) *see* Angeli Laudantes
Prajadhipok (king of Thailand)   T:152
Prandtauer, Jacob (Austrian architect)   G:171
Prang, Louis (German-born American lithographer and
    engraver)   C:298; G:376
Praseodymium (element)   E:176
Praslin (island, Seychelles)   S:131
Prather, Victor A., Jr. (American military balloonist)   B:36
Pratolini, Vasco (Italian novelist)   I:409
Pratt, Daniel (American manufacturer)   A:142
*Pravda* (Russian newspaper)   N:199
Praxiteles (Greek sculptor)   G:350
   *picture(s)*
    *Hermes and the Infant Dionysus*   G:349
Prayer   P:430–31
   *Engel* v. *Vitale* and school prayer   S:509
   hymns   H:320–26
   Islam   I:348; K:293; R:148
   Judaism   J:143, 146, 147, 148
   litanies (ritual prayers)   E:46
   public schools   F:163
   saints   S:18c
Prayer, Book of Common   E:243, 245; R:132
Prayer, The Lord's   *see* Lord's Prayer
Prayer of Manasseh (apocryphal book of the Bible)   B:164
Praying mantis (insect)   *see* Mantis
Praying towns (of Massachusetts)   M:148–49
Preakness Stakes (horse race)   H:234
Precambrian time (in geology)   E:26; F:383, 385; P:432
   *table(s)*   E:25; F:384
Precedent (in law)   C:574
Precession (wobbling motion)   G:436–37; P:271; Z:387
Precincts (voting districts)   P:373; V:392
Precious metals   E:167
Precious stones   A:194f; G:69–75; J:95
Precipitation (rain, snow, sleet, and hail)   R:93–97 *see also*
    the climate section of continent, country, province, and
    state articles
   acid rain   A:9–10
   Arctic region   A:379
   Australia   A:505–6
   climate   C:361–64
   clouds   C:382–85
   desert environments   D:127
   drought   D:328, 329
   Dust Bowl restoration   D:356
   fog   F:290–91
   hydrologic cycle   W:73
   Nebraska's extreme conditions   N:85
   river flow   R:237–38
   weather, creation of   W:84, 85, 86
   *map(s)*
    Africa   A:50
    Asia   A:438h
    Australia   A:503
    Canada   C:58
    China   C:262
    India   I:122
    South America   S:278
    United States   U:82
Precocial birds   B:233
Precognition (kind of extrasensory perception)   E:428
Pre-Columbian art (of Middle and South American Indian
    civilizations)
   architecture   A:367
   decorative arts   D:75
   Peru   P:164; T:143
   pottery   P:412
   *picture(s)*
    Chimu woven tunic   T:141
    embroidered Peruvian cloak   N:100
    gold ornament of Colombia   C:407
    Mayan sculpture   H:208; I:170
    Moche funeral sculpture   I:170

Predators   C:141–50; D:82; L:205–6; O:26 *see also* Birds of
   prey
Predestination (in Calvinism)   C:34; P:551; R:131
Pre-diabetes (medical condition)   D:145
Predicate adjectives   P:93
Prediction (in psychology)   P:500
Predictions (in scientific research)   S:64
Pre-emption laws (for settlers of public lands)   P:516, 517
Preening (of waterfowl)   D:345
Prefabricated buildings   B:440
   *picture(s)*   B:440
Preferred stocks (those with priority in payment of dividends)
   S:454
Prefixes (additions at front of root parts of words)   W:239
Pregnancy   M:69
   abortion   A:8
   AIDS can be passed to fetus   A:100b
   baby   B:2–3
   birth control (prevention of pregnancy)   B:250a–251
   child development   C:223–24
   folic acid   V:370c
   gestational diabetes   D:145
   menstruation   M:219, 220
   nutrition   N:427
   smoking, dangers of   H:75
Prehensile tails
   lizards   L:277
   monkeys   M:421
   opossums   M:115
Prehistoric animals   P:432–34
   cats   C:142
   dinosaurs   D:166–77
   elephants   E:183
   evolution   E:373–74
   fossils   F:380–89
   marsupials   M:113
Prehistoric art   P:435–37
   art as a record   A:428–29
   decorative arts   D:72–73
   painting   P:14–15
   sculpture   S:92–93
   watercolor painting in caves   W:55
   *picture(s)*
    bison carving   A:428
Prehistoric people   P:438–42 *see also* Stone Age
   Africa   A:65
   agriculture, history of   A:97
   archaeologists' study of   A:302, 351, 359; W:258
   biological anthropology   A:301
   caves   C:157
   cereal grains   G:286–87
   chemistry, history of   C:206
   clothing of   C:372
   communication, history of   C:463
   dairying, history of   D:10
   domestication of the horse   H:243–44
   etiquette, history of   E:337
   Europe   E:363
   family, history of the   F:37
   fire and early people   F:141–42
   funeral customs   F:495
   grass and civilization   G:314
   hunters and gatherers of food   F:335–36
   Ice Age   I:12–13
   Indonesia   I:212
   leather through the ages   L:111
   magic used for curing disease   M:206
   metallurgy, history of   M:236
   numeration systems   N:403
   obsidian used by   G:232
   oldest known fossils of modern humans   E:334
   poetry in the dance   P:354
   pottery   F:142; P:407, 409
   radiocarbon dating   R:76

religions **R:**145, 146, 147
Southeast Asia, remains in **S:**334
Stonehenge **S:**462
technology, beginnings of **T:**40
tools **T:**232–33
toys **T:**250
tunnel building **T:**339
*picture(s)*
    fossil skull **A:**46
    Stone Age lighting **L:**231
**Prehistory** (before writing was invented) **A:**351, 359
**Preindustrial civilizations** *see* Ancient civilizations
**Prejudice**
dwarfism **D:**375
Hispanic Americans **H:**148, 149
overcome by understanding diversity **A:**300
racism **R:**34b–34c
segregation **S:**113
**Prelude** (musical form) **M:**542
**Prelutsky, Jack** (American poet) **C:**235 *profile*
"Jellyfish Stew" **N:**274
**Premadasa, Ranasinghe** (Sri Lankan president) **S:**416
**Premature baby** **B:**2, 3; **L:**345; **V:**370d
**Premenstrual syndrome (PMS)** (group of symptoms related to a
    woman's menstrual cycle) **M:**220
**Premier** *see* Prime minister
**Premises** (in logic) **L:**289, 290
**Premiums** (insurance payments) **I:**251
**Premolars** *see* Bicuspids
**Přemysl dynasty** (Bohemia) **C:**622
**Prenatal gene testing** **G:**87
**Prendergast, Maurice** (American painter) **W:**57
**Preparators** (in museums) **M:**527
**Preparatory drawings** (in art) **D:**315, 317
**Preparatory schools** **C:**512; **P:443–44**
**Prepositional phrases** (in sentences) **P:**94
**Prepositions** (words that relate a noun or pronoun to other
    words in sentences) **G:**289; **P:**94
**Pre-Raphaelite Brotherhood** (group of 19th-century painters and
    poets) **E:**263, 285; **R:**338
**Presbycusis** (deterioration of hearing with age) **D:**49
**Presbyopia** (focusing disorder of the eye) **E:**431
**Presbyterian Church** **P:**492, 493, 494; **R:**131
Church of Scotland **U:**48
Knox, John **K:**289
**Presbyters** (of the church) **C:**289; **R:**285
**Preschool** *see* Nursery schools
**Prescott** (Arizona) **A:**404
**Prescott, Samuel** (American patriot) **R:**193
**Prescott, William** (American soldier) **R:**200
**Prescott, William Hickling** (American historian) **A:**210; **H:**152
**Prescription drugs** **D:**331–32, 333–34
**Preservation Hall Jazz Band**
*picture(s)* **L:**318
**Preservation of American Antiquities, Act for** (1906) **N:**45
**Preservation of archaeological sites** **A:**301, 350
**Preservation of food** *see* Food preservation
**Presidency of the United States** **P:445–53** *see also* the names
    of presidents
autographs of presidents **A:**527
Cabinet officers advise the president **C:**2
candidate qualifications **E:**128
Cleveland: one man, two presidents **C:**357
commander in chief of armed forces **U:**100
Congress and the Presidency **U:**144
disability, provisions for **P:**452
election of 2000 **U:**205
elections, frequency of **E:**130
Electoral College **E:**131–32
executive branch of the government **U:**169–70
first ladies **F:**164–80b
first to die in office was William Henry Harrison **H:**43
forms of address **A:**22
how many were lawyers **L:**92

impeachment **I:**99
libraries *see* Presidential libraries
naturalized citizens may not become president **C:**324;
    **N:**61
New Hampshire primary election **N:**150
Ohio was home of many presidents **O:**62
presidential consideration of Congressional bills **U:**166
Presidential Succession Act (1947) **V:**328
Roosevelt re-elected for fourth term **R:**326
three-time runners: Bryan **B:**416
three-time runners: Clay **C:**353
Twenty-fifth Amendment **U:**160
Twenty-second Amendment **U:**159
vice presidency of the United States **V:**324–31
Washington may not have been first president **C:**536
Washington's influence as first president **W:**43–44
White House **W:**164–66
**Presidential governments** **G:**276
**Presidential libraries**
Dwight D. Eisenhower Library **K:**181, 184
Franklin D. Roosevelt Library **N:**214, 217
Gerald R. Ford Library **M:**264
Harry S. Truman Library-Museum **M:**370, 373
Herbert Hoover Presidential Library **I:**298
Jimmy Carter Presidential Library **G:**137
John Fitzgerald Kennedy Library **M:**141, 144
Lyndon B. Johnson Library **T:**130
National Archives administers some **N:**24
Rutherford B. Hayes Library **O:**67
**Presidential Medal of Freedom** **D:**71
**Presidential Range** (New Hampshire) **N:**152
**Presidential Succession Act** (United States, 1947) **V:**328
**Presidential Unit Citation** (American award)
*picture(s)* **D:**70
**President pro tempore** (of the Senate) **U:**169; **V:**325
**President's Commission on the Status of Women** **W:**212b
**Presidents' Day** (in the United States) **H:**164, 165
**President's Foreign Intelligence Advisory Board** (of the United
    States) **P:**451
**President's Own, The** (Marine Corps band) **U:**122
**Presidents' wives** *see* First ladies
**Presley, Elvis** (American entertainer) **R:**263 *profile*
birthplace **M:**358
Graceland **T:**82
Memphis was his home **M:**217
rock music **R:**262c
*picture(s)* **M:**520; **R:**262b
    birthplace **M:**358
**Press, freedom of the** *see* Freedom of the press
**Press agents** *see* Public relations
**Press and blow method** (of making glass containers) **G:**231
**Press associations** *see* News services
**Pressburg** (Slovakia) *see* Bratislava
**Pressed glass** **G:**233–34
*picture(s)* **G:**234
**Presses, hydraulic** **H:**313; **M:**234
**Presses, printing** **N:**202; **P:**470–71, 474, 475–76, 477
*picture(s)* **E:**81; **P:**469
**Press forging** (of metals) **M:**234
**Pressing** (extracting fats and oils from plant seeds or pulp)
    **O:**80
**Press release** (document delivering information to a
    newspaper) **N:**201
**Pressure** (in mechanics)
gases **G:**56–59
hydraulic systems **H:**311–13
ice melted by skates' pressure **I:**4
pneumatic systems **H:**314
**Pressure, air** (atmospheric) *see* Air pressure
**Pressure cookers** (for cooking food) **C:**542; **H:**91
**Pressure gradient force** (in meteorology) **W:**186
**Pressure points** (for control of bleeding) **F:**159
*picture(s)* **F:**159
**Pressure-treated wood** **W:**230
**Pressure waves** *see* Sound waves

Pressurized space suits *see* Space suits
Presto (musical term)  M:537
Prestressed concrete  C:166
Pretend play (of children)  P:333–34
Pretoria (administrative capital of South Africa)  S:271, 272
Pretzels (food)  B:388b
Prevailing winds (climatic control)  C:361, 363
Préval, René Garcia (Haitian president)  H:12
Prevention of disease *see* Disease, prevention of
Prévost, Antoine (Abbé Prévost) (French novelist)  F:440
Prez, Josquin des (Flemish composer) *see* Josquin des Prez
PRI (Mexican political party) *see* Institutional Revolutionary
    Party
Pribilof Islands (Alaska)  F:518; I:367; O:44
Price, Leontyne (American soprano)  O:141 *profile*
    *picture(s)*  O:141
Price, Mark (American basketball player)
    *picture(s)*  B:95h
Price, Ray (American singer)  C:572
Prices  E:56–57, 61
    Consumer Price Index  C:533
    farm prices  A:91, 92; F:61–62
    food shopping  F:348
    globalization's effect on  G:239
    inflation and deflation of  I:226–27
    Nixon's wage-price freeze  N:262e
    retail pricing  S:21
    stock prices in depressions and recessions  D:122
    Universal Price Code  S:498
Price supports (for farm crops)  F:61
Prickly pear (cactus)  C:5; M:241; P:290
    *picture(s)*  L:112
Pride, Charlie (American singer)  C:573
Prides (of lions)  C:144
Priesthood of believers (Protestant doctrine)  P:490–91
Priestley, Joseph (English scientist)  L:83; O:288; P:454; S:72
    *picture(s)*  P:454
Priests (in ancient Egypt)  E:106, 107
Priests (of the Roman Catholic Church)  M:294; R:284, 291
Primary batteries  B:103a–103b
    *diagram(s)*  B:103b
Primary colors  C:424–25; D:378
Primary elections  E:129, 131; N:150
Primary motor cortex (part of the cerebrum)  B:367
Primary products (raw materials)  I:270–71
Primary State (nickname for New Hampshire)  N:151
Primates (order of mammals)  P:455–57
    apes  A:325–27
    hands  F:83–84
    human beings  H:281–83
    monkeys  M:420–22
    *picture(s)*
        chimpanzee as example  M:69
Primaticcio, Francesco (Italian artist)  F:424; R:171
Primatology (anthropological study of primates)  A:301
*Primavera* (*Spring*) (painting by Botticelli)  P:20; U:3
    *picture(s)*  B:345
Prime (grade of meat)  F:349
Prime meridian (Greenwich meridian)  G:374b; I:266; L:78;
    M:96; T:203
Prime minister (Premier)  P:458–59
    Canada  C:75
    Canada: forms of address  A:22
    Canada, list of  C:74
    Canada: profiles of  C:76–77
    England, history of  E:249, 252
    England, list of  E:247
    Gladstone's career  G:225
    parliaments  P:83–84
    Sri Lanka had first woman prime minister  S:416
    United Kingdom  U:60
    Walpole considered Britain's first prime minister  W:5
Prime mover (energy source)  E:133
Prime numbers  C:494; N:385
Primer (explosive charge)  E:421

Prime rate (lowest interest rate on loans)  B:57
Primers (textbooks)  E:82, 337
    *picture(s)*  E:82
Prime time (on television)  T:68
Priming (of pumps)  P:540
Priming powder (for guns)  G:416
Primitive art
    folk art  F:292–98
    Metropolitan Museum of Art collection  M:239a
    as a record  A:428–29
    sculpture  S:92
Primitive people
    art as a record  A:428–29
    dance celebrations  D:25–26
    North American Indian beginnings  I:164–65
    superstition  S:503
Primitive religion *see* Religion, primitive
Primo de Rivera, Miguel (Spanish political leader)  S:378
Primroses (flowers)
    *picture(s)*  N:127
Primus, Pearl (American choreographer)  D:31, 32
*Prince, The* (political work) *see* Principe, II
Prince Albert (Saskatchewan)  S:49
Prince Albert National Park (Saskatchewan)  S:47
Prince Edward Island (Canada)  C:54, 64; P:460–67
    *map(s)*  P:464
    *picture(s)*
        beach at Cavendish  P:463
        Charlottetown  P:466, 467
        farm with red soil  P:462
        fishing industry  P:463
        Green Gables  P:465
        potato farming  P:463
Prince Edward Island National Park (Prince Edward Island)
    P:465
Prince George (British Columbia)  B:406c
    *picture(s)*  B:405
*Prince of Wales* (British warship)  W:304
Prince of Wales (eldest son of the British monarch)  W:4
Prince of Wales National Heritage Centre (Yellowknife,
    Northwest Territories)  N:343
*Prince Phillip Prosper of Spain* (painting by Diego Velázquez)
    P:24
    *picture(s)*  P:22
*Princesse X* (sculpture by Constantin Brancusi)
    *picture(s)*  A:427
*Princess Ida* (operetta by Gilbert and Sullivan)  G:209
*Princess Mary* (early commercial airliner)
    *picture(s)*  I:284
"Princess on the Pea, The" (story by Hans Christian Andersen)
    F:26
Princeton, Battle of (1777)  R:202–3
Princeton University (Princeton, New Jersey)  N:169
    Wilson, Woodrow: university president  W:179–80
    *picture(s)*  N:169; U:221
Princip, Gavrilo (Serbian assassin of Archduke Francis
    Ferdinand)  T:114; W:276
Principal (amount of money borrowed)  I:255
Principal focus (of a lens)  L:144–45
*Principe see* São Tomé and Príncipe
*Principe, II* (political work by Machiavelli)  I:407
*Principia* (book by Isaac Newton)  S:71
Pring, Martin (English explorer)  N:160
Printers (for computer output)  C:481; O:55–56; P:217
    *picture(s)*  C:482
Printing  P:468–79
    advertising  A:34
    air conditioning affects  A:102
    Bible editions, production of  B:158
    book design  B:327, 329
    books  B:332
    cartoons, history of  C:127
    change in education produced by  E:81
    colonial America  C:418

Program music   G:187; M:543; R:304
Programs, radio see Radio programs
Programs, television see Television programs
Program Support Center (United States)   H:78
Progressive Conservative Party (in Canada) see Conservative
     Party (in Canada)
Progressive education   K:249–50
Progressive Era (in United States history)   U:190
Progressive movement (in United States history)   W:206
Progressive Muslims   I:353
Progressive Party (Bull Moose Party) (in the United States)
     P:372; R:332; T:6, 326; W:180–81
     picture(s)
          cartoon   P:371
Prohibition (laws against alcoholic beverages)   P:483–85
     Coolidge's administration   C:547–48
     Eighteenth Amendment   U:158
     Maryland's opposition   M:134
     organized crime   O:223–24
     outlaws   O:263
     Twenty-first Amendment   U:159
Prohibition Party (American history)   P:484
Project Head Start see Head Start programs
Projections (of maps)   M:97
Projection TV's   T:64
Projectors   M:479, 487; P:270–72, 273
Project Phoenix (to search for intelligent extraterrestrial life)
     R:70
Projects see also Experiments and other science activities;
     How to; Indoor activities
     4-H club projects   F:395–96
Prokaryotes (single-celled organisms without nuclei)   F:383;
     L:209
     picture(s)
          antibiotics' effects on   A:309
Prokofiev, Sergei (Russian composer)   O:148; P:485; R:386
Promessi sposi, I (The Betrothed) (novel by Alessandro Manzoni)
     I:408
Prometheus (in Greek mythology)   G:363–64, 365; M:572
Prometheus (moon of Saturn)   S:58
Promethium (element)   E:167, 176
Prominences (flames extending from the sun)   S:495
     picture(s)   S:492
Promised Land (Canaan)   M:469
Promontory (Utah)   R:89; U:250, 255
Pronghorn (hoofed mammal)   H:219
     picture(s)   B:208; H:217; I:47
          hind foot   H:218
Pronouns (words that take the place of nouns)   P:92–93
Pronunciation   P:486 see also individual letters of the
     alphabet
     English language   E:267
     French compared to English   F:435
     German language   G:175
     Latin language   L:74
     phonics   P:194
     pronunciation guide to this encyclopedia   A:590–91
     slang imitates sounds   S:191
     some Hawaiian words   H:55
     speech   S:395, 396
     speech disorders   S:397
     vocabulary building, use in   V:374
Proof (amount of alcohol in a beverage)   W:161
Proof (in engraving and etching)   E:294, 326
Proof (in printing)   L:251; P:470
Proof coins (struck for collectors)   C:399
Proofing (of yeast)   B:388
Proofreaders' marks   P:487
Proofreading   B:326, 330; P:487; R:183; S:400
Propaganda   P:488–89
     genocide   G:96
     Nazi success in 1930's Germany   N:79
     Un-American Activities Committee, House   U:13
Propagation (of plants) see Plant propagation

Propane (gas, used as fuel)   B:38; F:488
     picture(s)
          tanks   F:488
Propellants (rocket fuels and oxidizers)   M:344, 345; R:258,
     259–60
Propellers
     airplanes   A:39, 115, 116–17
     screw propellers of ships   S:159
     turboprop engines   J:91
Proper factors (of numbers)   N:386
Proper fractions   F:397
Proper nouns   P:92
Properties (articles used in plays) see Props
Properties (chemical)   C:199; E:167
Properties (of materials)   M:151, 153–54
     metals   A:192; M:233
Properties (of numbers)   N:398–99
Propertius, Sextus (Roman writer)   L:76
Property
     census   C:167
     Communism, origins of   C:472
     crimes against property   C:584; J:167
     personal property disposed of by a testament (will)
          W:177
     real property   R:112d–113
Property insurance see Insurance, property
Property management (of real estate)   R:113
Property rights (of property owners)   R:112d
Prophet Daniel, The (statue by Aleijadinho)
     picture(s)   L:62
Prophets (books of the Old Testament)   B:159–62
Prophets (in Islam)   I:346; K:292; R:148
Prophets, Hebrew
     Elijah   E:189
     Isaiah   I:345
     Jeremiah   J:79
     Moses   M:469
Propodeum (part of ant's abdomen)   A:319
Propolis (sticky material that bees use as cement)   H:212
Proportion (in art)   A:371; D:134
Proportion (in mathematics)   R:107
Proportional representation (electoral system)   E:130
Proprietary drugs see Over-the-counter drugs
Proprietary hospitals   H:252
Proprietor (of a business)   B:470
Prop roots (of plants)   P:303
Props (used in plays)   D:298; P:336, 338; T:157
Propulsion, jet see Jet propulsion
Propulsion system (in missiles)   M:344–45; R:257–62
Propylene (monomer)   P:324
Pro Rodeo Hall of Champions (Colorado Springs, Colorado)
     C:438
     picture(s)   C:438
Proscenium stage   T:156
     picture(s)   T:156
Prose (nonpoetic literature)   G:357, 358–59
Prosecutors (in law)   C:575; J:163; L:87, 91
Prose Edda (book by Snorri Sturluson)   N:277, 278, 279
Proserpina (Roman goddess) see Persephone
Pro set (formation in football)   F:359
Prosimians (group of primates)   P:455, 456
Prospecting (hunting for minerals)   M:319–20, 324
     gold   G:251
     for uranium with Geiger counters   G:67
"Prosperity is just around the corner" (slogan)   H:225
Prostaglandins (hormones)   M:208g
Prosthetic limbs see Artificial limbs
Prosthodontist (in dentistry)   D:115
Prostitution   J:168
Protactinium (element)   E:176
Protection (of disaster victims)   D:185
Protection competitions (for dogs)   D:253
     picture(s)   D:253
Protectionism (in trade)   G:76d; I:271

**Protective coloration**   A:283
  amphibians   A:222; F:477
  birds   B:227
  butterflies and moths   B:478
  cephalopods   O:50
  fish   F:200
  insects use for protection   I:243
  molting of birds   B:218
  optical illusion helps animals to survive   O:175
  shrimps   S:167
  tigers   T:198
  *picture(s)*
     butterflies and moths   B:479
**Protective devices** (of animals and plants)   A:282–83
  aardwolf   H:319
  amphibians   A:222–23
  arachnids   A:348
  birds   B:226–27
  butterflies and moths   B:478
  cats, wild   C:149
  eel's body mucus   E:93
  frogs and toads   F:477
  hedgehogs' spines   H:101, 102
  hibernating animals' choice of safe places   H:126
  insects   I:243
  leaves, special functions of   L:117
  lizards   L:276
  mammals' weapons for attack   M:74
  mollusks   M:407
  mustelids spray foul-smelling liquid   O:254
  olingos discharge foul-smelling secretion   R:29
  opossums play dead   O:171
  porcupines' quills   P:389; R:278
  skunks' chemical defense   O:253; S:189
  snakes   S:217–18
  spiders   S:405
  turtles' shells   T:356
  *picture(s)*
     insects   I:242
**Protective tariff**   T:23
**Protein drugs**   B:213
**Proteins**
  biochemistry, studies in   B:185–86
  biological classification determined by   L:209
  blood   B:259, 261
  body chemistry   B:273, 295, 296–97, 298, 299; L:199
  bread is a source of   B:385
  chromatography, separation by   B:188
  cotton meal is a source of   C:569
  digestion of   B:281; D:163, 164–65
  enzymes   E:307
  evidence of evolution   E:374–75
  fibers   F:108
  gene splicing of bacteria   G:83
  genetics   G:78, 79, 80, 88, 89, 90
  grain and grain products   G:281, 282, 284
  green tobacco leaves are a source of   T:215
  hormones   H:228
  liver produces   L:269
  making of proteins   B:299
  milk has two kinds   M:307
  muscle cells contain special proteins   B:279; M:521
  nutrition   F:330; N:423
  proteomics   B:190
  soybeans   S:337
  sulfur as a component   S:486
  vegetarian diet   V:293
  viruses   V:363, 364, 366
  *picture(s)*
     chromatography, separation by   B:189
**Proteomics** (biochemical study of proteins)   B:190
**Proterozoic Eon** (in geology)   E:26
  *table(s)*   F:384
**Protestant Episcopal Church** *see* Anglican Church

**Protestantism**   P:490–94
  Amish   A:220
  baroque art, influence on   B:64
  Bible, versions of the   B:158
  Calvin, John   C:34
  Christianity   C:287, 291–95
  education, history of   E:81
  English church under Henry VIII and Elizabeth I   E:191, 242–43
  forms of address for the clergy   A:22
  fundamentalism   F:492
  Huguenots   H:279
  Hus, Jan   H:306
  hymns   H:322–24
  Latin America   L:51
  Luther, Martin, led Reformation   L:346
  major denominations   P:494
  marriage rites   W:101–2
  Northern Ireland   N:336, 337
  prohibition   P:484
  Puritans   P:550–51
  Quakers   Q:4a–5
  Reformation   R:130–32
  Reformation spread standard form of German language   G:175
  reforms in the Roman Catholic Church   R:291
  Thirty Years' War   T:179
  *picture(s)*
     Evangelical Protestants in Brazil   B:373
**Protest literature**   A:216
**Protests** *see* Demonstrations and protests
**Protist kingdom** (group of one-celled organisms)   K:253, 258; L:208, 209; T:27
  algae, classification of   A:180
  protozoans, classification of   P:495
  separating animals from plants   A:264
**Protoceratops** (dinosaur)   D:176
**Protocol** (kind of etiquette)   E:337; T:296
  computers' networking protocol   C:487
**Protons** (atomic particles)   A:485, 488; C:201, 202, 204
  cosmic rays   C:562, 563
  elements   E:166
  ions and ionization   I:287–89
  nuclear energy   N:366, 367
  positive charges of electricity   E:135
  radiation   R:43
  radioactive elements   R:64
**Proto-oncogene** (genetic material)   C:92, 93; V:369–70
**Protoplasm** (living matter)   C:160; O:241
**Proto-science** (term used for mythology)   M:575
**Protostars**   A:473
**Prototypes** (in automobile design)   A:553
**Protozoans** (one-celled organisms)   D:189; K:258; M:276; P:495–97
  *picture(s)*   A:265
**Protozoologists** (scientists who study protozoans)   P:495
**Protractor** (mechanical drawing tool)   G:121; M:200
**Proudhon, Jean-Pierre** (French writer)   A:226
**Proust, Marcel** (French novelist)   F:115, 442; N:361
**Proved reserves** (of natural gas)   N:60
**Provenance** (history of a piece of jewelry)   J:94
**Provençal** (French dialect)   F:433
**Provensen, Alice and Martin** (American writers and illustrators)   C:240
  *picture(s)*
     illustration from *The Glorious Flight*   C:247
**Proverbs** (book of the Old Testament)   B:163
**Proverbs** (traditional sayings)   P:498 *see also* Quotations
  Africa, literature of   A:76a, 76b
  folklore   F:311
  *Poor Richard's Almanack*   F:454, 455
**Providence** (capital of Rhode Island)   R:215, 217, 219, 220, 221, 224, 225; U:174
  founded by Roger Williams   T:174; W:175

**Public Health Service, United States** P:513–15
Health and Human Services, United States Department of
H:78–79
National Institutes of Health N:43
smoking, efforts against S:207
**Public houses (Pubs)** (taverns) U:50
*picture(s)* I:318; U:50
**Public housing** N:230
**Publicity** (programs of public relations) B:333; P:518
**Public lands** N:30–34; P:260–61, **516–17**
**Public law** (of the United States) L:87
**Public libraries** *see* Libraries
**Public opinion** I:268; O:169; P:488–89, 517–18
**Public radio** A:29; R:56, 57
**Public records** (used in genealogical research) G:76b–76c
**Public relations** P:**517–18**
propaganda P:488–89
public opinion polls O:169
What is the difference between public relations and
advertising? P:517
**Public schools** (in England) U:48
**Public schools** (in the United States) E:75, 76; S:61
battle for tax supported schools E:83–84
*Engel* v. *Vitale* and school prayer S:509
Michigan had first public school system M:264
school prayer F:163
uniforms E:88
**Public service advertising** A:35; C:456
*picture(s)* A:35
**Public services** *see* Public utilities
**Public speaking** P:**518–20** *see also* Oratory
ancient schools of rhetoric E:78
debates and discussions D:52
formal speech S:395
oral book reports B:317
outlines O:265–67
**Public transportation** *see* Transportation
**Public utilities** B:473; P:**520–23** *see also* Water supply
**Public welfare** *see* Welfare, public
**Public works**
ancient civilizations A:228–29
**Public Works Administration (PWA)** N:138h
**Publishing** P:**523–25** *see also* Book fairs; Copyright; Printing
bookbinding B:332–33
books: from author to reader B:323–33
comic books C:453–54
commercial art C:457, 458
communication, advances in C:464
copyright C:555
encyclopedias E:206–7
freedom of the press F:163
journalism J:135–41
librarians' publishers L:181
magazines M:16–20
mass communication C:471
Newbery, John N:137
newspapers N:197–205
New York City N:218
Pulitzer, Joseph, and Pulitzer Prizes P:533–38
**Pubs** *see* Public houses
**Pucas** (fairies) *see* Pookas
**Puccini, Giacomo** (Italian composer) P:**525**
*Bohème, La* (opera) O:151
*Madama Butterfly* (opera) O:156
opera I:412; O:147–48
*Tosca* (opera) O:164
*Turandot* (opera) O:165
**Pucelle, Jean** (French painter) F:423
**Puck** (fairy) F:9
**Puck** (used in ice hockey) I:23, 24–25, 27
**Pudus** (deer) D:80
*picture(s)* D:81
**Puebla** (city, Mexico) M:247
**Puebla** (state, Mexico) M:241
**Pueblo** (Colorado) C:439

**Pueblo Indians** (of Arizona and New Mexico) I:172, 183–84;
N:184, 190
adobe houses H:186
Anasazi A:227
conflicts with Europeans I:202, 203; N:192, 193
*picture(s)* N:294
kachina doll A:428
Wupatki National Monument N:51
**Pueblos** (Native American settlements) A:227; I:172; N:188,
190
**Puerto Barrios** (Guatemala) G:397
**Puerto Limón** (Costa Rica) C:564, 566
**Puerto Rican Defense** (organization) C:326
**Puerto Rico** P:**526–32**
Caribbean Sea and islands C:113, 114, 115
holidays H:169
immigration to the mainland United States H:144, 146,
148–49
Latin America L:49
Ponce de León P:382
Spanish-American War S:392d
territorial expansion of the United States T:111–12
*map(s)* P:527
*picture(s)*
coastline N:282
coffee plantation P:528
Culebra Island beach P:528
people P:526
pharmaceutical industry P:529
Ponce P:531
radio observatory at Arecibo R:67
rum bottling C:114
San Juan P:526, 531; U:84
**Puerto Rico Trench** (Atlantic Ocean) A:478
**Puerto San José** (Guatemala) G:397
**Pueyrredón, Prilidiano** (Argentine artist) L:63
*picture(s)*
*A Stop in the Country* (painting) L:63
**Puffballs** (mushrooms) M:529
*picture(s)* K:257
**Puffed cereals** G:284; W:156
**Pufferfish** F:199, 200
**Puffin** (seabird)
*picture(s)* N:140, 145
**Pugachev, Emelian** (Russian rebel leader) C:136
**Puget Sound** (Washington) W:16, 21, 26
**Pugilism** (boxing) B:351
**Pugin, Augustus Welby** (English architect) E:262
**Pugs** (dogs) D:241, 242
*picture(s)* D:246
**Puja** (Hindu ritual devotion) H:140
**Pulaski, Casimir** (Polish general) R:203
**Pulci, Luigi** (Italian poet) I:406
**Pulcinella (Polichinelle)** (Italian puppet character) C:386;
P:548
**Pulis** (dogs)
*picture(s)* D:249
**Pulitzer, Joseph** (Hungarian-born American newspaper
publisher) C:127; J:138 *profile;* N:204; P:533
*picture(s)* I:92; P:533
**Pulitzer Prizes** P:**533–38**
**Pullets** (young female chickens) P:414
**Pulleys** (simple machines) E:185, 188; W:249–50
**Pullman, George Mortimer** (American industrialist) R:88
*profile*
*picture(s)* R:88
**Pullman strike** (1894) C:221; D:53; L:14; R:88
**Pulmonary artery** (of the circulatory system) H:81
**Pulmonary circulation** (of the body) C:306
**Pulmonary veins** (of the circulatory system) H:81
**Pulp, dental** *see* Dental pulp
**Pulp, wood** *see* Wood pulp
**Pulp magazines** M:567; S:80–81
**Pulque** (alcoholic drink made from maguey) M:241
**Pulsars** (radio wave sources) A:474; P:**539;** R:69–70; S:433

**Pulsating variable stars** see Variable stars
**Pulse** (contractions of the heart and arteries)   **C:**305; **H:**85
   counting your pulse during aerobic exercise   **P:**225, 226
   experiments and other science activities   **E:**397
   *picture(s)*
      medical technique of taking the pulse rate   **F:**157
**Pulse dialing** (of telephones)   **T:**53–54
**Pulses** (of radio signals)   **R:**39, 40
**Pulsimeter** (type of chronograph)   **W:**46
**Pumas** see Mountain lions
**Pumice** (lava rock)   **G:**392; **R:**266; **V:**383
**Pummelo** (citrus fruit)   **O:**189
**Pumpernickel bread**   **R:**390
*Pumping Iron* (motion picture, 1977)   **B:**294
**Pumpkin**   **C:**411; **H:**13, 14; **V:**290
   *picture(s)*   **W:**197
**Pump-oxygenators** see Heart-lung machines
**Pumps**   **P:**540–41
   air pressure experiments of Robert Boyle   **B:**354
   fountains   **F:**394
   heart works as a pump   **H:**81
   heat pumps   **H:**96
   hydraulic systems   **H:**311, 313
   steam engines   **S:**444
   vacuum, formation of   **V:**263
**Puna** (plateau in Argentina)   **A:**385
**Puncak Jaya** (highest point on New Guinea)   **N:**148
**Punch and Judy** (puppet characters)   **P:**548
**Punchbowl** (national cemetery, Hawaii) see National Memorial
   Cemetery of the Pacific
**Punched card systems** (for computers)   **A:**533; **C:**490, 492
**Punctuated equilibrium** (in evolution)   **E:**378
**Punctuation**   **P:**541–44
**Punic Wars** (264–146 B.C.)   **H:**26; **P:**544; **R:**314
**Punishment**
   amnesty allows people to avoid   **A:**221
   colonial America   **C:**417
   crime and criminology   **C:**584, 586
   juvenile crime   **J:**167–70
   law enforcement   **L:**90
   prisons   **P:**480–82
   reformatories   **P:**482
**Punjab** (state of India)   **I:**125, 128, 134
**Punjabis** (people of Asia)   **P:**35
   *picture(s)*   **P:**35
**Punk rock music**   **R:**264
**Puns** (plays on words)   **H:**203, 290; **J:**126
**Punt** (ancient civilization)   **E:**398–99
**Punt** (in football)   **F:**355–56
   *picture(s)*   **F:**356
**Punta, Cerro de** (mountain, Puerto Rico)   **P:**528
**Puntarenas** (Costa Rica)   **C:**566
**Pup, The** (companion star to Sirius)   **S:**429–30
**Pupa** (resting stage of insect cycles)   **I:**232–33
   ants   **A:**321
   bees   **B:**119
   beetles   **B:**127
   butterflies and moths   **B:**476
   metamorphosis   **M:**238
   protection of   **I:**249
   *picture(s)*
      butterflies and moths   **B:**477
**Pupil** (of the eye)   **B:**279; **E:**430; **L:**149
   *picture(s)*   **M:**520
**Puppets and marionettes**   **P:**545–48
   Indonesian puppet plays   **I:**211
   Japanese *Bunraku*   **J:**32–33, 53
   Malay shadow plays   **M:**58
   motion picture special effects   **M:**484
   theater of China and Japan   **T:**162
   three-dimensional animation   **A:**289
   *picture(s)*
      hand puppets   **P:**546
      Indonesian shadow puppet   **P:**548

   Japanese *Bunraku*   **P:**548
   marionettes   **P:**545, 547
   mental-health treatment of children   **M:**225
**Puppies**   **D:**251, 254, 258, 259, 260
   *picture(s)*   **D:**251
*Puranas* (Sanskrit literature)   **H:**142; **I:**140
**Purcell, Henry** (English composer)   **B:**70; **C:**184; **E:**292
**Purdue University** (Indiana)
   *picture(s)*   **I:**148
**Purebred animals and plants**
   cats   **C:**137, 138, 139
   cattle   **D:**4
   dog breeds   **D:**245, 258
   genetic engineering   **G:**82
**Pure car truck carriers** (ships)   **S:**154–55
**Pure Food and Drug Act** (United States, 1906) see Food and
   Drug Act, Federal
**Purgatory** (Roman Catholic belief)   **R:**283, 291
**Purges** (in the Soviet Union under Stalin)   **C:**473–74; **R:**372;
   **U:**42
**Purification of the Virgin Mary** see Candlemas Day
**Purim (Feast of Lots)** (Jewish festival)   **J:**146a; **P:549**
**Puritan Revolution** see Civil War, English
**Puritans** (in English and American colonial history)   **P:**550–51
   American literature   **A:**201–3
   Calvin's teachings   **C:**34
   Charles I clashes with the Puritans   **E:**245
   Christianity, history of   **C:**294
   Christmas carols outlawed by   **C:**299
   colonial life in New England   **C:**409, 417–18
   Connecticut settled by   **C:**520
   Cromwell, Oliver   **C:**595
   diaries written by   **D:**149
   England, history of   **E:**243
   Hawthorne, Nathaniel, works of   **H:**65, 66
   Hutchinson, Anne   **H:**308
   Massachusetts Bay Colony   **T:**172–73
   Protestantism in colonial America   **P:**493
   Reformation   **R:**132
   relations with Plymouth Colony   **P:**344–45, 347
   tax-supported schools   **E:**82
**Purl stitch** (in knitting)   **K:**279
**Purple** (color)   **C:**429
**Purple City** see Forbidden City
**Purple finches** (birds)
   *picture(s)*   **B:**242; **N:**151
**Purple fireweed** (flower)
   *picture(s)*   **Y:**371
**Purple Heart** (medal for bravery)   **D:**69
   *picture(s)*   **D:**70
*Purple Sea* (Finnish tapestry by Oili Maki)
   *picture(s)*   **T:**22
**Purple tube sponge**
   *picture(s)*   **S:**411
**Purse seines** (fishing nets)   **F:**218
   *picture(s)*   **F:**219
**Purseweb spiders**   **S:**403
**Pursuivants** (assistants to heralds)   **H:**116
**Purusha** (Hindu cosmic being)   **H:**139
**Purvis, Robert** (American abolitionist)   **A:**6a *profile*
**Pus** (fluid in infected sores)   **D:**205
**Pusan** (South Korea)   **K:**302, 305; **P:**552
   *picture(s)*   **K:**302
**PUSH, Operation** see Operation PUSH
**Pusher prop** (airplane engine)   **A:**117
**Pushkin** (Russia)
   *picture(s)*   **R:**377
**Pushkin, Aleksander** (Russian writer)   **D:**302; **N:**360; **R:**381
**Pushtuns** (a people of Afghanistan) see Pashtuns
**Push-ups** (exercise)   **P:**225
   *picture(s)*   **P:**225
**Push waves** (of earthquakes) see P-waves
**Pussy willows**   **T:**309–10
**Putin, Vladimir** (president of Russia)   **P:552; R:**373
   *picture(s)*   **R:**373

## PHOTO CREDITS

The following list credits the sources of photos used in THE NEW BOOK OF KNOWLEDGE.
Credits are listed, by page, photo by photo—left to right, top to bottom. Wherever appropriate, the
name of the photographer has been listed with the source, the two being separated by a dash. When
two or more photos by different photographers appear on one page, their credits are separated by
semicolons.

### P

Cover © David Mendelsohn—Masterfile
2   © R. Stuart Cummings—Southern Stock/Index
    Stock; © Douglas Faulkner—Photo Research-
    ers; © Lee Boltin.
3   © Photo Network; © Lee Boltin.
4   © Jack Fields—Photo Researchers; © David
    Austen—Woodfin Camp & Associates.
5   © Lee Boltin
7   The Granger Collection (all photos on page).
8   © Jack Stein Grove—Tom Stack & Associ-

9   ates; © Jeffrey Aaronson—Network Aspen.
    © Ian Steele—International Stock; © Jeffrey
    Aaronson—Network Aspen.
10  © Timothy O'Keefe—Southern Stock/Index
    Stock; © Kal Muller—Woodfin Camp & Asso-
    ciates.
14  Art Reference Bureau
16  Art Reference Bureau
19  Vatican Library, Rome—Art Reference Bureau;
    Photographie Giraudon—Louvre, Paris; Art
    Reference Bureau.
20  Art Reference Bureau
21  Louvre, Paris—Art Reference Bureau

22  The Metropolitan Museum of Art; Art Refer-
    ence Bureau; Kunsthistorisches Museum,
    Vienna—Art Reference Bureau.
25  Frick Collection—New York; Pinacothek,
    Munich—Art Reference Bureau; Louvre,
    Paris—Art Reference Bureau.
26  National Gallery, London—Art Reference
    Bureau; Louvre, Paris—Art Reference Bureau.
27  Real Academia de Belles Artes de San
    Fernando, Madrid—Art Reference Bureau; Art
    Reference Bureau.
28  The National Gallery, London—Art Refer-

ence Bureau; Louvre, Paris—Art Reference Bureau.

31 The Museum of Modern Art, New York; The Museum of Modern Art, New York photo—Marlborough-Gerson Gallery, New York; Whitney Museum of American Art, New York.

33 The Sherwin-Williams Co.

35 © Arvind Garg—Liaison Agency; © Fabry/Sipa—Leo de Wys; © Arvind Garg; © Arvind Garg—Liaison Agency.

36 © Fabry/Sipa—Leo de Wys; © Bill Kaufman—Leo de Wys.

38 © Emil Muench—Photo Researchers; © Josef Polleross—The Stock Market.

39 © Photo Researchers; © John Giordano—SABA.

40 The Bettmann Archive; © Paolo Koch—Photo Researchers.

40a © Keystone—Hulton/Archive by Getty Images

40d © Raymond Dabolli—Corbis-Sygma; © Maxim Clermont—Woodfin Camp & Associates; © Richard Nowitz.

41 UPI/Bettmann

43 © Jacques Langevin—Corbis-Sygma

47 © Harvey Lloyd—The Stock Market; © Robert Frerck—Woodfin Camp & Associates.

48 © Timothy Ross—Picture Group

50 © Robert Frerck—The Stock Market; © Harvey Lloyd—The Stock Market.

51 The Granger Collection

52 © Robert C. Simpson—Tom Stack & Associates

53 © J. Allan Cash Ltd.

54 © Joseph Sohm—The Stock Market; © Ulrich Zillmann/Okapia—Photo Researchers.

55 © Tommaso Guicciardini/Science Photo Library—Photo Researchers

56 © Ted Horowitz—The Stock Market

57 © Stephanie Maze—Woodfin Camp & Associates

58a © Robert W. Ginn—Unicorn Stock Photos

58b © Two-Can Publishing Ltd.

58c © Lorenz Books, Anness Publishing Inc. (all photos on page).

58d © Alpha

60 United States Parachute Association

61 © William E. Shapiro

62 © Joe Viesti—The Viesti Collection, Inc.; © Maya Pejic—Lineair Zichzending/Peter Arnold, Inc.; © Joe Viesti—The Viesti Collection, Inc.

64 © Carlos Sanuvo—Bruce Coleman Inc.

65 © IFA/eStock Photo

68– © Jeremy Woodhouse—Photodisc Green/Getty
69 Images

69 © Stefano Amantini—Bruce Coleman Inc.; SIME s.a.s./eStock Photo

70 © David Barnes—Danita Delimont, Agent

72 © Jeremy Woodhouse—Masterfile; © Peter Bowater—Photo Researchers.

73 © Steve Vidler—eStock Photo; © Stuart Westmorland—Danita Delomont, Agent.

75 © Dagli Orti—Musee de Cluny, Paris/The Art Archive; © Dave G. Houser—Houserstock.

76 © Bettmann/Corbis

77 © Kevin Schafer—Peter Arnold, Inc.; © Alan Schein Photography—Corbis; © Peter Pearson—Stone/Getty Images.

78 © Chad Slattery—Stone; © Robin Smith—Stone.

79 © The Walt Disney Company—Corbis-Sygma

80 © Bonnie Kamin—PhotoEdit; © Jean Higgins—Unicorn Stock Photos.

84 Keystone

85 © William S. Peckover—Peter Arnold, Inc.; © Jean-Michel Labat—Jacana/Photo Researchers; © Tom McHugh—Photo Researchers.

86 © Tom McHugh—Photo Researchers; © Gunter Ziesler—Peter Arnold, Inc.; © Steve Littlewood—Oxford Scientific Films/Animals Animals.

95 © ASAP Ltd./Flash Focus/Index Stock

96 © C. Sherburne/PhotoLink/PhotoDisc

97 The Granger Collection

100 The Granger Collection

101 UPI/Bettmann Archive; The Granger Collection.

102 AP/Wide World Photos

103 The Granger Collection

104 C. Redenios—Peace Corps

105 © Jean-Pierre Laffont—Corbis-Sygma

107 Ministry of Agriculture, Paris

108– © Grant Heilman Photography
109

110 Courtesy of the Pennsylvania Academy of the Fine Arts, Philadelphia. Gift of Mrs. Sarah Harrison (The Joseph Harrison, Jr. Collection); The Nelson-Atkins Museum of Art, Kansas City,

114 Missouri (Purchase: Nelson Trust).

114 Cultured Pearl Associations of Japan and America; © Michel Roudnitska—Liaison Agency.

115 © James Pozarik—Liaison Agency; © Claus Meyer—Black Star; © Christophe Loviny—Liaison Agency.

117 UPI/Bettmann Newsphotos

118 © Bernard Bisson—Corbis-Sygma

119 Syndication International

120 John Foster—U.S. Fish and Wildlife Service

120b © Philip Smith—National Audubon Society—Photo Researchers

122 © L. G. Richards—Black Star

123 © David Linton; © David Linton; U.S. Navy.

125 © John Warham (all photos on page)

127 © Ed Wheeler—The Stock Market; © Kunio Owaki—The Stock Market; © J. Patton—H. Armstrong Roberts.

128 © H. Mark Weidman; © Isaac Geib—Grant Heilman Photography.

130 © J. Nettis—H. Armstrong Roberts; © Terry Wild Studio.

131 © James Blank—Root Resources

132 © Larry Lefever—Grant Heilman Photography

133 US STEEL; © Larry Lefever—Grant Heilman Photography.

134 © H. Mark Weidman; © H. Mark Weidman; © John A. Wee; © H. Mark Weidman.

135 © H. Mark Weidman

136 © Terry Wild Studio

138 Courtesy of the Pennsylvania Dutch Convention & Visitors Bureau, Lancaster, PA

139 The Granger Collection

140 The Granger Collection; The Bettmann Archive.

141 The Bettmann Archive

146 © Jon Levy—Liaison Agency

147 © Peter Arnold, Inc.

148 © Ed Bock—The Stock Market

149 The Metropolitan Museum of Art, The Crosby Brown Collection of Musical Instruments, 1889.

154 © SuperStock

155 Art Resource

156 © Bevilacqua—Salmer

157 The Bettmann Archive; The Granger Collection.

158 © Patrick Durand—Corbis-Sygma

159 © Miréille Vautier—Woodfin Camp & Associates; © Wolfgang Kaehler—Corbis; © Miréille Vautier—Woodfin Camp & Associates; © Miréille Vautier—Woodfin Camp & Associates.

161 © Robert Frerck—Woodfin Camp & Associates

162 © Lineair—Peter Arnold, Inc.; © Miréille Vautier—Woodfin Camp & Associates.

163 © Bill Bachmann—The Image Works

164 © Keren Su—Corbis

165 © Janis Burger—Bruce Coleman Inc.

167 © Keith Wood—Stone

169 © Joe Whyte—Photo Network

173 © Inga Spence—Tom Stack & Associates

174 Photo courtesy of Phillips Petroleum Company

175 © Michelle Barnes—Liaison Agency

176 © Vanessa Vick—Photo Researchers; © Greg Vaughn—Tom Stack & Associates.

177 © Spectrum Colour Library; © Hans Reinhard—Bruce Coleman Inc.

178 © Picturepoint

179 © Chapius—Atlas Photo

180 © Mark E. Gibson—The Image Finders

181 © Andre Jenny—Unicorn Stock Photos; © Leif Skoogfors—Woodfin Camp & Associates.

182 The Granger Collection

183 © Melvyn Calderon—Liaison Agency; © Jerry Alexander—Stone.

186 © Paul Steel—The Stock Market

187 © Melvyn Calderon—Liaison Agency; © Victor Englebert.

188 © James Cachero—Corbis-Sygma

193 © Andre Jenny—Unicorn Stock Photos

195 "Nipper" is a trademark of RCA Corp.

196 © Dewitt Jones—Woodfin Camp & Associates

197 © World View/Bert Blokhuis—Science Photo Library—Photo Researchers

198 © Jeff Hester and Paul Scowen, Arizona State University/NASA; © Andreas Feininger—Time Life Pictures/Getty Images; © Alfred Pasieka—Science Photo Library/Photo Researchers.

199 © Chip Simons; © Adrian Myers—Taxi/Getty Images.

201 Hulton/Archive by Getty Images

203 © The Museum of Modern Art/Licensed by Scala/Art Resource, NY

205 © Beth Kaiser—AP/Wide World Photos; Stapleton Collection/The Bridgeman Art Library.

206 © White Light (all photos on page).

207 © 1990 Amon Carter Museum, Fort Worth, Texas, Bequest of the artist

208 © David Young-Wolff/PhotoEdit; © Justin D. Pyle—U.S. Army/Getty Images.

209 NASA/Science Photo Library/Photo Researchers; © Manfred P. Kage—OKAPIA/Oxford Scientific Films, Ltd.

210 Department of the Interior, National Park Service/National Archives at College Park

211 Gernsheim Collection/The Harry Ransom Humanities Research Center/The University of Texas at Austin; AP/Wide World Photos.

212 © White Light (all photos on page).

213 © White Light (all photos on page).

214 © Henri Cartier-Bresson—Magnum Photos

215 © Arnold Newman—Getty Images; © Elliott Erwitt—Magnum Photos.

216 © White Light

217 CBS Photo Archive/Hulton/Archive by Getty Images; © Max Nash—AP/Wide World Photos.

218 © Frans Lanting—Minden Pictures

219 © John R. MacGregor—Peter Arnold, Inc.

220 © Claude Nuridsany

222 © Brian Brake—Photo Researchers

223 © Glyn Cloyd

224 © David Young-Wolff—Stone/Getty Images; © Pictor International/Pictor International, Ltd./PictureQuest

225 © Bob Daemmrich—The Image Works

227 © Tony Freeman—PhotoEdit

228 © CERN/P. Loiez/Science Photo Library—Photo Researchers

229 © Stone; © Leonard Lessin—Peter Arnold, Inc.

230 © Peter Pearson—Stone

232 © C. R. O'Dell—Rice University/NASA/Space Telescope Science Institute (all photos on page).

233 The Granger Collection

234 The Granger Collection

236 © Floyd Clark—Globe Photos; © Louise Parker—Courtesy, AIP Emilio Segre Visual Archives/American Institute.

237 © Science Photo Library—Photo Researchers; © AIP Emilio Segre Visual Archives—W. F. Meggers Collection/American Institute of Physics; © Paul Ehrenfast—AIP Niels Bohr Library—Jay M. Pasachoff.

238 © AIP Emilio Segre Visual Archives—Francis Simon Collection/American Institute of Physics; The Granger Collection; © Stanford University.

239 © 1984 Royal Observatory, Edinburgh—Jay M. Pasachoff

240 © Andy Sacks—Stone/Getty Images

242 © Colouriser AL—Lebrecht Music; Photodisc Blue/Getty Images; Photodisc Blue/Getty Images.

243 Philadelphia Museum of Art, Gallatin Collection; © SPADEM Paris 1975, Courtesy of Lady Aberconway, Michael Holford Picture Library.

245 National Portrait Gallery, Smithsonian Institution/Art Resource; The Granger Collection; The Granger Collection; The Granger Collection.

246 The Pierce Brigade

247 The Granger Collection

248 Comet Photo

250 Kansas State Historical Society

252 Oregon Historical Society

253 Kansas State Historical Society

254 Western History Collections, University of Oklahoma Libraries; Kansas State Historical Society.

255 Kansas State Historical Society

257 Kansas State Historical Society; Culver Pictures.

258 Western History Collections, University of Oklahoma Libraries

259 Missouri Historical Society; DeGolyer Library, Southern Methodist University.

260 Archives and Manuscripts, Division of the Oklahoma Historical Society

261 Mark O. Thiessen—© National Geographic Society

262 The Granger Collection (all photos on page).

263 Mary Evans Picture Library; Peter Newark's Historical Pictures; Mary Evans Picture Library.

264 Mary Evans Picture Library

266 © John A. Wee

269 Courtesy of the Reuben H. Fleet Space Theater; The Granger Collection.

270 Courtesy of Carl Zeiss, Inc.; © Hayden Planetarium.

271 Courtesy of Carl Zeiss, Inc.; Published with permission of Evans and Sutherland Computer Corporation.

272 © Mark E. Gibson; © Brian Sullivan—The American Museum of Natural History/Hayden Planetarium.

273 © Jim Schwabel—New England Stock Photo

274 Courtesy of the Discovery Place, Chapel Hill, North Carolina

275 DigitalStock; JPL/NASA

278 © Tom Pantages (all photos on page).

278– Cornell—JPL/NASA
279

280 JPL/NASA

281 © Tom Pantages

285 © Douglas P. Wilson

286 © Mickey Gibson—Animals Animals

287 © Patti Murray—Earth Scenes

288 © E. R. Degginger—Animals Animals

289 © Gilbert Grant—Photo Researchers

290 © Garry D. McMichael—Photo Researchers; © Holt Studios—Earth Scenes

292 © David Muench

293 © Ray Coleman—Photo Researchers; © Willard Clay; © David Muench.

294 © Myrleen Cate—Photo Network

295 © Martha Cooper—Peter Arnold, Inc.; The Granger Collection; © Robin Jane Solvang—Bruce Coleman Inc.

296 © David R. Frazier; © Ulrike Welsch—Photo Researchers; © Thomas Kitchin—Tom Stack & Associates.

297 © Alon Reininger—Photo Network; © Hans Reinhard—Bruce Coleman Inc.

298 © Adrian Baker—Leo de Wys; © Charles West—The Stock Market; © Lee L. Waldman—The Stock Market.

299 © Leslie Holzer—Science Source—Photo Researchers; © Diego Goldberg—Corbis-Sygma; © Hans Pfletschinger—Peter Arnold, Inc.

300 © Kenneth W. Fink—Photo Researchers

302 © Stephen J. Krasemann—Peter Arnold, Inc.; © John Mead—Science Photo Library—Photo Researchers.

306 © S. N. Nielsen—Bruce Coleman Inc.

307 © D. Cavagnaro—Peter Arnold, Inc.

308 © Peter Arnold—Peter Arnold, Inc.; © Jeremy Burgess/Science Photo Library—Photo Researchers.

310 © David R. Frazier

312 © Jack W. Dykinga—Bruce Coleman Inc.; © E. R. Degginger—Bruce Coleman Inc.

313 © Stephen Collins—Photo Researchers; © Lee Rentz—Bruce Coleman Inc.

314 © Ed Reschke—Peter Arnold, Inc.

315 © Ed Reschke—Peter Arnold, Inc.; © Ed Reschke—Peter Arnold, Inc.; © Nuridsany et Perennou—Photo Researchers.

316 © Matt Meadows—Peter Arnold, Inc.; © Willard Clay.

317 © Michael J. Balick—Peter Arnold, Inc.

318 © Stephen J. Krasemann—Peter Arnold, Inc.

320 © Willard Clay; © Willard Clay; © Wendell Metzen—Bruce Coleman Inc.

321 © Jim Nilsen—Tom Stack & Associates; © Willard Clay; © Willard Clay; © Willard Clay.

322 © John Welzenbach—The Stock Market; Courtesy, Chrysler Corporation; Courtesy, Bayer Corporation.

324 © Bob Schatz—Liaison Agency

325 © Ed Lello—Liaison Agency; © David Pollack—The Stock Market.

326 © Peter Steiner—The Stock Market

327 © Phil Degginger—Bruce Coleman Inc.; © Peter Beck—The Stock Market.

328 © Ed Horowitz—The Stock Market

329 © John Marmaras—Woodfin Camp & Associates; Courtesy, DuPont Kevlar.

330 Art Reference Bureau

331 New York Zoological Society

332 New York Zoological Society

333 © Philip & Karen Smith—Stone; © Elie Bernager—Stone; © David J. Sams—Stone.

334 © Jeff Greenberg—Leo de Wys; © Stan Osolinski—Oxford Scientific Films.

335 © Rosanne Olson—Stone

338 © Lawrence Migdale

341 Courtesy of the Lowell Observatory

343 NASA—ESA

345 Courtesy of The New York Historical Society, New York City

348 Courtesy of The New York Historical Society, New York City

350 Robert Frost Library, Amherst College

351 © Nathan Benn—Woodfin Camp & Associates

352 © Sovfoto/Eastfoto/PictureQuest

353 © Scala/Art Resource, NY

357 © Chris Niedenthal—Black Star

358 © Liaison Agency; © Polska Agencja Interpress.

360 © Adam Tanner—Comstock; © Steve Leonard—Black Star.

362 © Adam Tanner—Comstock

363 © Bonnie Rauch—The Image Bank

364 © Richard Hutchings—Photo Researchers; © Mick Hicks—Liaison Agency; © Paul Katz—The Image Bank.

365 © Walter Bibikow—The Image Bank; © John V. A. F. Neal—Photo Researchers; © Yvonne Hemsey—Liaison Agency.

367 © Randy Taylor—Corbis-Sygma; © Richard Wood—Taurus Photos; © Alvis Upitis—The Image Bank.

369 © Joe Traver—Liaison Agency

370 © Blank Archives—Archive Photos

371 The Granger Collection

372 © Gilles Mingasson—Liaison Agency; © Blank Archives—Archive Photos.

373 © Regis Bossu—Corbis-Sygma

374 The Granger Collection; Brown Brothers; U.S. Department of the Interior; The Granger Collection.

375 Collection of the James K. Polk Memorial Association; The Granger Collection.

376 The Granger Collection

377 The Granger Collection

378 © Rudolph Burckhardt

379 © Jerry Cooke—Photo Researchers

380 The Granger Collection

381 © Ray Pfortner—Peter Arnold, Inc.

383 The Thomas Gilcrease Institute, Tulsa, Oklahoma

389 © John Cancalosi—Tom Stack & Associates

390 © Jeff Gnass—The Stock Market

391 © Paul Thompson—Photo Network

393 © Catherine Karnow—Woodfin Camp & Associates; © Gilles Bassignac—Liaison Agency; © Snowdon/Hoyer/Focus—Woodfin Camp & Associates.

394 The Granger Collection

395 © Tony Arruza—Stone

396 Courtesy, United States Postal Service

397 Courtesy, United States Postal Service

398 Courtesy, United States Postal Service

403 © Alvis Upitis—SuperStock

406 © Frederick Warne & Co.—Penguin Books

407 © The Bridgeman Art Library

408 © Abe Rezny—The Image Works (all photos on page).

409 © Victoria and Albert Museum, London/Art Resource, NY; © Jerry Alexander—Stone/Getty Images.

410 © Silvio Fiore—SuperStock; Christie's Images.

411 Christie's Images; © Werner Forman—Art Resource, NY.

412 The Granger Collection; © Nimatallah—Art Resource, NY.

413 © M. Beck-Coppola—Réunion des Musées Nationaux/Art Resource, NY; Christie's Images.

414 Courtesy of James R. Carson

415 © Grant Heilman Photography; © John Colwell—Grant Heilman Photography.

416 © Grant Heilman Photography; © Grant Heilman Photography; © John Colwell—Grant Heilman Photography.

418 © Hidajet Delic—AP/Wide World Photos; © Betty Press—Woodfin Camp & Associates; © Blair Seitz—Photo Researchers.

419 © Jacob Holdt; © Betty Press—Woodfin Camp & Associates.

420 © Jon C. Hancock—AP/Wide World Photos

421 © Brad Markel—Liaison Agency

422 © Manfred Gottschalk—Tom Stack & Associates

423 © John Lamb—Stone

424 © Jeffrey Aaronson—Network Aspen

425 © Jon Bradley—Stone

427 © Grant Heilman Photography

429 © Bert Glinn—Magnum Photos; © G. R. Roberts; © Photo Researchers.

430 © David Sanger—Danita Delimont, Agent

432 © Mark Newman—Photo Network

435 © David Austen—Stone

436 © Robert Frerck—Stone; © Explorer/SuperStock.

437 © Erich Lessing—Art Resource; © George Holton—Photo Researchers; © Algeria/Holton Collection/SuperStock.

440 The Natural History Museum, London

441 The Natural History Museum, London; © John Reader/Science Photo Library—Photo Researchers; The Natural History Museum, London; Giraudon/Art Resource.

443 Greens Farms Academy, Greens Farms, CT

445– © James Cooper
447

450 © James Cooper

451 © James Cooper; The White House.

452– © James Cooper
453

454 The Granger Collection

455 © David Austen—Stone; © John Giustina—The Wildlife Collection; © John Giustina—The Wildlife Collection.

456 © Gerry Ellis Nature Photography; © BIOS/A. Compost—Peter Arnold, Inc.

457 © Kenneth W. Fink—Photo Researchers; © BIOS/Compost/Visage—Peter Arnold, Inc.; © Gerard Lacz—Peter Arnold, Inc.

459 The Bridgeman Art Library/Art Resource; The Bettmann Archive; The Bettmann Archive; The Granger Collection; Culver Pictures; Culver Pictures; © Karsh—Rapho Guillumette; © Jean Louis Atlan—Corbis-Sygma; Culver Pictures; © Karsh—Rapho Guillumette; Culver Pictures; The Bettmann Archive; © Georges DeKeerle—Liaison Agency; © Christian Simonpietri—Corbis-Sygma.

462 © Joseph R. Pearce—Valan Photos

463 © G. Zimbel—Monkmeyer; © R. Vroom—Miller Services; © O. Fitzgerald—Miller Services.

465 © Leo de Wys

466 © Barrett & MacKay—Masterfile

467 © G. Zimbel—Monkmeyer

468 Arcata Graphics Book Group; Ron May for W. A. Krueger Co., printers; Ron May for W. A. Krueger Co., printers.

469 Ron May for W. A. Krueger Co., printers; S. D. Warren Company.

471 © John Colwell—Grant Heilman Photography

472 © Thomas Bruckbauer—Index Stock

473 Ron May for W. A. Krueger Co., printers

474 The Bettmann Archive (all photos on page).

475 Ron May for W. A. Krueger Co., printers

476 S. D. Warren Company

480 © Jean-Pierre Laffont—Corbis-Sygma; © Bob Daemmrich—The Image Works.

483 The Bettmann Archive

484 © Stock Montage, Inc.

488 The Bettmann Archive; © H. Roger-Viollet.

489 American Dental Association

490 © SuperStock

491 © A. Ramey—PhotoEdit; © SuperStock.

492 © Stock Montage/SuperStock (all photos on page).

493 The Granger Collection

495 © Michael Abbey/Science Source—Photo Researchers; © Michael Abbey/Science Source—Photo Researchers.

496 © David M. Phillips—Visuals Unlimited

497 © CNRI/Science Photo Library/Photo Researchers; © CNRI/Science Photo Library/Photo Researchers.

500 © Jim Argo

501 © Jose L. Pelaez—The Stock Market; © Dick Young—Unicorn Stock Photos.

502 © Will & Deni McIntyre—Photo Researchers

503 © Paul Steel—The Stock Market

504 © Jacques Chenet—Woodfin Camp & Associates; © Deneve Feigh Bunde—Unicorn Stock Photos; © Chuck Savage—The Stock Market.

505 © David M. Grossman—Photo Researchers; The Granger Collection; The Granger Collection; The Granger Collection; The Granger Collection.

506 © Chad Slattery—Stone

507 © Jon Riley—Stone; Corbis-Bettmann.

508 © Tom Stewart—The Stock Market; © K. S. Berndt—Unicorn Stock Photos.

509 © B. W. Hoffmann—Unicorn Stock Photos

510 © Myrleen Ferguson Cate—Photo Network

511 The Granger Collection; © Mike Timo—Stone.

512 © Bob Daemmrich—Stock, Boston

513 © Russell D. Curtis—Photo Researchers; © Sam C. Pierson, Jr.—Photo Researchers; © Corbis-Sygma.

515 © Armando Waak—Pan American Health Organization

526 © Bob Krist—Corbis; © Tom Bean—Corbis.

528 © Tony Arruza—Corbis; © Bob Krist—Corbis.

529 © David R. Frazier Photolibrary

531 © Macduff Everton—Corbis; © Ken Hawkins—Stock South/PictureQuest.